INDIAN ECONOMY

FOR CIVIL SERVICES EXAMINATION

ABOUT THE AUTHOR

Ramesh Singh, a Delhi School of Economics alumnus is an **Educational Consultant** with over two and half decades of experience in providing guidance to aspirants for an array of competitive and professional examinations. He has authored books in Hindi and English with **McGraw Hill Education, India,** the popular ones being *Indian Economy, Bharatiya Arthavyavastha, Bharat ka Bhugol, Bhaugolik Models, Objective Indian Economy and Social Development, 1000 Plus Questions on General Science* and *Contemporary Essays.* He is a popular columnist of the reputed Government journals *YOJANA* and *KURUKSHETRA*. Mr Singh lives in Delhi with his wife and two daughters and remains busy in reading, writing and mentoring the civil services aspirants.

INDIAN ECONOMY

FOR CIVIL SERVICES EXAMINATION

Ramesh Singh

McGraw Hill Education (India) Private Limited

Published by McGraw Hill Education (India) Private Limited

Indian Economy, 9e

Copyright © 2017 by McGraw Hill Education (India) Private Limited

No Part of this publication may be reproduced or distributed in any form or by any means, electronic, mechanical, photocopying, recording, or otherwise or stored in a database or retrieval system without the prior written permission of the publishers. The program listings (if any) may be entered, stored and executed in a computer system, but they may not be reproduced for publication.

McGraw Hill Education (India) Private Limited

McGraw Hill Education (India) Private Limited
CHENNAI

McGraw Hill Education Offices
Chennai New York St Louis San Francisco Auckland Bogotá Caracas
Kuala Lumpur Lisbon London Madrid Mexico City Milan Montreal
San Juan Santiago Singapore Sydney Tokyo Toronto

McGraw Hill Education (India) Private Limited

Published by McGraw Hill Education (India) Private Limited,
444/1, Sri Ekambara Naicker Industrial Estate, Alapakkam, Porur,
Chennai - 600 116, Tamil Nadu, India

Indian Economy, 9e

ISBN (13) : 978-93-5260-614-6
ISBN (10) : 93-5260-614-0

Typeset at Kaushik Laser Point & Printers, Tis Hazari Court, Delhi-110053 and printed at

Magic International Pvt. Ltd., Plot No. 26E, Sector-31 (INDUSTRIAL), Site-IV, Greater Noida - 201306

Cover printed at: Magic International

Cover Design: Rajesh Pandey

DAQDCRZMDRXXR

Visit us at: www.mheducation.co.in

To my parents for whom
educated children are better
than hefty bank deposits—they really are
visionaries in human
resource management and
applied economics

PREFACE TO THE NINTH EDITION

It feels great to present the 9th edition of the book *Indian Economy* to its readers. With increasing popularity, its revision work has become increasingly intense—to remain among the list of *best-sellers* is quite challenging a task, I can feel it.

The past few years have been quite eventful for Indian economy. With every passing year, we have seen the government's urge to change the very landscape of economic policy. Some moves of economic reforms were so fundamental that they have been called 'transformative' in nature. For example, the government's willingness to set up the *bad bank* for solving the burden of the non-performing assets of the public sector banks; the *PARA* (public sector asset rehabilitation agency) for addressing the *twin balance sheet* problem; *universal basic income* and the critical move of *demonetising* the high value currency notes—have been some of the most revolutionary initiatives of the recent times.

The revision process of this edition has been quite aware and sensitive to the changing contours of the economy and policy making. Accordingly, this edition has been fully *restructured, revamped* and *streamlined* to the emerging times and needs of the aspirants.

What is new in this edition?

- The new edition has been thoroughly 'revised' as per the changing times and requirements—duly including the inputs from *India 2017; Economic Survey 2016-17; Union Budget 2017-18* and the latest volume of *India Development Report 2015.*

- Updated information of *National Income*; highlights of the new *World Happiness Report-2017*; changing dimensions of *Planning* and *Economic Reforms* together with the transformational reforms have been duly included.

- Farmers' suicides; safeguarding agri-trade and doubling farm income are some of the new topics added in the chapter *Agriculture and Food Management.*

- Current disinvestment policy; apparel and footwear industries; ease of doing business, private sector and urbanisation; PPP models are new topics added in the chapter *Industry and Infrastructure.*

- *Services Sector* has been fully updated with the latest inputs together with the anomalies of formality and informality of the sector.

- The section on the *Financial Market* has been fully revised added with several new topics such as—cooperative banks; rising NPAs and the resolution—5/25 refinancing, ARCs, AQR, S4A; the PARA; high power money being the major ones.

- *External Sector* and *International Economic Organisation* chapters have been revised and updated together with addition of several new entries such as—the latest data of forex reserves and composition of external debt; new write-up on SEZ; global FDI; India's external scenario; need of exchange rate monitoring; need of shift in trade policy; trans-pacific partnership and trans-atlantic trade and investment partnerships; deglobalisation & India and OECD.

- *Tax* and *Government Budgeting* chapters have been thoroughly revised and updated with addition of new topics such as—implementation process of the GST; direct tax reforms; income and consumption anomaly; latest situation of FRBM review; macro-economic policy stance of the Government and the Fiscal Outlook for 2017-18.

- Emerging challenges in implementing the INDCs of India; National Tariff Policy; Global Emissions; COP 22 and climate change topics have been revamped in the chapter *Sustainability and Climate Change*.

- A new chapter, *Burning Socio-Economic Issues*, is being added in this edition with ten new topics—Bad Bank; Demographic Dividend; Twin Balance Sheet Crises; Universal Healthcare; Aftereffects of Demonetisation; Addressing Inequality; Universal Basic Income; Legitimacy in State and Socio-economic Transformation; Farm Indebtedness and Agri-policy and Deglobalisation—the Aftereffects.

- The chapter, *Human Development in India*, has been fully revised, and appended with several new topics—Privacy of Women; Accessible India Campaign and the latest Employment and Education Scenario.

- The chapter on *Economic Concepts and Terminologies* has been updated and added with new entries such as—Bad Bank; Countervailing Duty; Net Income; Purchase Tax; etc.

- The *Multiple Choice Questions* have been fully revised and several old questions have been replaced by new questions which are based on the recent developments such as—Bad Bank; NPAs; Disinvestment Policy; Human Resource Reforms for Results; Coach Mitra; Countervailing Duty; Net Income; Purchase Tax; Official Development Assistance; European Investment Bank; composition of the External Debt; Current and Capital Accounts; Inflation and Disinflation; Government's Schemes and Programmes; Hybrid Annuity Model (HAM) of the PPP in road sector; new System of National Accounts; economics for Agriculture; Swiss Challenge; Marginal Cost of funds based Lending Rate (MCLR); Price Deficiency Payment; Direct Benefit Transfer; Limited Liability Partnership (LLP) firm; NITI Aayog and NDC; restructuring of the CSSs; Product & Production taxes and deglobalisation.

- The chapter on *Model Answers* for the written examinations (i.e., Main Exam) has been fully updated and several new model questions and their answers have been added on the issues such as—need of monitoring exchange rate of rupee; need of policy shift in India's trade policy; government's stand on the review of the FRBM Act; disinvestment of the public sector companies; income and consumption pattern of India; transformational reforms; women's fundamental right to privacy; and institutional lending and farmers' suicide.

- As in the previous editions of the book, separate chapters have been given based on the *Economic Survey 2016-17* and the *Union Budget 2017-18*.

Hereby, I present this new edition to the readers, with the hope that it serves their purpose in the right way. Constructive suggestions from the readers are always welcome.

Wishing the readers all the very best for their upcoming examinations!

 www.facebook.com/IndianEconomyMHE

Ramesh Singh
dr.rmsh@gmail.com

PREFACE TO THE FIRST EDITION

I felt my first serious inclination towards writing when my first article was published in the journal *Mainstream* way back in 1988 while pursuing my post graduation studies at the Delhi School of Economics. My interaction with students inside and outside the classroom in 1990–91, when India faced a serious financial crisis, made me realise that there was an immediate need of a book on Indian economy, which could educate the students about the various aspects and challenges of the Indian economy in a simple and lucid manner. It took nearly two decades to fulfil this dream of mine.

The book has been designed to cater to the requirements of the General Studies paper for various Civil Services Examinations (Union as well as the States), and the optional Economics. It would also be useful for graduate and postgraduate courses in Economics of various universities. Adequate and required notes and references have been given after consulting and referring to an array of sources. I have taken care of both the objective as well as the subjective aspects based on my classroom experience of interacting with the students.

I am grateful to Prof. Majid Husain for the inspiration and motivation I got from him to complete this work. I have especially learnt the art and importance of work, punctuality and honesty in a very practical way from him.

Thanks are also due to Mr. Rajesh Kumar Baghel, Mr. Rakesh Kumar, Md. Ishtiaq, and Mr Vikash. I am indebted to my wife, Mrs Ila Singh, for her full support and my two little daughters, Medha and Smiti, for providing the sparkle in an otherwise monotonous work.

Finally, my special thanks to the team from McGraw-Hill, who took great pains to finalise the project and complete it in a record time with all the possible expertise. I welcome from the readers constructive advice, and comments, which could guide me in further revision of this book.

RAMESH SINGH

ABOUT THE CIVIL SERVICES EXAMINATION

The Civil Services Examination comprises of two successive stages:

(i) Civil Services (Preliminary) Examination (Objective Type) for the selection of candidates for Main Examination; and

(ii) Civil Services (Main) Examination (Written and Interview) for the selection of candidates for the various services and posts.

Scheme and subjects for the Preliminary and Main Examination.

A. PRELIMINARY EXAMINATION

The Examination shall comprise of two compulsory Papers of 200 marks each.

Note :

(i) Both the question papers will be of the objective type (multiple choice questions).

(ii) The question papers will be set both in Hindi and English. However, questions relating to English Language Comprehension skills of Class X level will be tested through passages from English language only without providing Hindi translation thereof in the question paper.

B. MAIN EXAMINATION

The written examination will consist of the following papers:

Qualifying Papers:

Paper A: (One of the Indian Language to be selected by the candidate from the Languages included in the Eighth Schedule to the Constitution).   **300 Marks**

Paper B : English   **300 Marks**

The papers on Indian Languages and English (Paper A and Paper B) will be of Matriculation or equivalent standard and will be of qualifying nature. The marks obtained in these papers will not be counted for ranking.

Papers to be counted for merit

Paper I: Essay   **250 Marks**

Paper II: General Studies–I   **250Marks**
(Indian Heritage and Culture, History and Geography of the World and Society)

Paper III: General Studies –II   **250 Marks**
(Governance, Constitution, Polity, Social Justice and International relations)

Paper IV: General Studies –III   **250 Marks**
(Technology, Economic Development, Bio-diversity, Environment, Security and Disaster Management)

Paper V: General Studies –IV   **250 Marks**
(Ethics, Integrity and Aptitude)

Paper VI: Optional Subject – Paper 1   **250 Marks**

Paper VII: Optional Subject – Paper 2   **250 Marks**

Sub Total (Written test)   **1750 Marks**

Personality Test   **275 Marks**

Grand Total   **2025 Marks**

Candidates may choose any one of the optional subjects from amongst the list of subjects given below:

List of Optional Subjects for Main Examination:

(i)   Agriculture

(ii)   Animal Husbandry and Veterinary Science

(iii) Anthropology

(iv) Botany

(v)   Chemistry

(vi) Civil Engineering

(vii) Commerce and Accountancy

(viii) Economics

(ix) Electrical Engineering

(x)   Geography

(xi) Geology

(xii) History

(xiii) Law

(xiv) Management

(xv) Mathematics

(xvi) Mechanical Engineering

(xvii) Medical Science

(xviii) Philosophy

(xix) Physics

(xx) Political Science and International Relations

(xxi) Psychology

(xxii) Public Administration

(xxiii) Sociology

(xxiv) Statistics

(xxv) Zoology

(xxvi) Literature of any one of the following

Assamese, Bengali , Bodo, Dogri, Gujarati, Hindi, Kannada, Kashmiri, Konkani, Maithili, Malayalam, Manipuri, Marathi, Nepali, Oriya, Punjabi, Sanskrit, Santhali, Sindhi, Tamil, Telugu, Urdu and English.

TABLE OF CONTENTS

INTRODUCTION

Economics is the study of how goods and services are produced, distributed and consumed. As resources are always in short supply, the British economist Lionel Robbins in 1935 described the discipline as 'the science of scarcity'. *

* David Orrel and Borin Van Loon, **Introducing Economics: A Graphic Guide**, *Faber & Faber, London, 2011, p. 3*

ECONOMICS: THE DISCIPLINE

The study of every discipline starts with the process of defining it. Economics is no exception to this. But the challenge of articulating an over arching definition of any discipline has never been an easy task, and at the end one has to be satisfied with a partial definition. Different economists have seen the discipline with differing perspectives and have been coming up with differing definitions— at times, a large number of such definitions became either narrow or incomprehensible. But it is necessary to have a working definition of the subject if one intends to study it.

Before arriving at our own working definition of the subject, we may cite here two highly acclaimed and internationally established attempts in this direction:

1. Economics is the study of how societies use scarce resources to produce valuable commodities and distribute them among different people.[1]

As per the definition, there are two key ideas in economics—that goods are scarce and that society must use its resources efficiently. Indeed, economics is an important subject because of the fact of scarcity and the need for efficient use of the resources.

Over the last half a century, the study of economics has included such varied topics that the subject serves different purposes to different students of economics. Some study it to make money (basically, most of its students in the developed world study economics to earn more money. But the same is not correct in the case of the developing world. The truth is that in the developing world economics has only been read and taught, not applied—if we do a sweeping generalisation). Others study economics to know about poverty, unemployment, human development, shares and debentures, banking norms, prices and their movements, e-commerce, etc. Still others might be studying the discipline to enhance their knowledge of economics.

2. Economics studies how individuals, firms, governments, and other organisations within our society make choices and how these choices determine a society's use of its resources.[2]

Human life depends on the consumption of various materials which are made up of the resources available on earth. As there is no limit to human wants, we need infinite resources to gratify our needs. But the resources are limited! Now it is upto the individual and humanity at large as to how they try to satisfy their competing needs to get fulfilled by the limited resources. It means we need to make some choices before we utilise the scarce resources by prioritising some of our needs. In this process, some needs might never get fulfilled. At the same time, there might be some needs which may be fulfilled again and again with the available resources.

Economics is the discipline which studies how individual, society and the government make their prioritised choices in the process of using the scarce resources to gratify the various needs and wants of life. Making such choices is an art as well as a science. As times change, the choices change. As space changes human needs change and so modify the choices. After studying and surveying the various choices made by humanity at large in different time and space, there evolved the discipline of economics. As economics is an exercise in the *space-time continuum* and it deals with living human beings, it is a very dynamic subject and should only be read in this perspective to have the real feel.

A Working Definition

It is essential to feel the subject one intends to study. The fundamental way of doing this is

---

1. Samuelson, P.A. and Nordhaus, W.D., *Economics,* Tata McGraw-Hill Pub. Company Ltd., N. Delhi, 2005, p.4.

2. Stiglitz, J.E. and Walsh, C.E., *Economics,* W.W. Norton & Company, New York, 2006, p.6.

starting with the definition of the subject. But the definition, at times, or even most of the times, becomes very abstract, jargon-laden and technical. Such a definition might not give a proper feel and understanding of the subject to a person who does not belong to economics. Most of the students of economics face difficulty in understanding the complete meaning of the definition. That is why a very *general* and *layman's* definition is needed.

Human beings in their day-to-day lives are busy doing so many things. There are different activities we are involved in throughout our lives. These activities fall under different categories.

Economics studies the economic activities of mankind. Similarly, political, social and administrative activities of mankind are studied under Political Science, Sociology and Public Administration, respectively. That is why these disciplines are broadly categorised as **humanities** as all of them study human activities. There are many more specialised human activities which are studied under many more disciplines.

Which activities of mankind are *economic activities*? The activities which involve profit, loss, livelihood, occupation, wage, employment, etc., are economic activities. Economics studies all these activities. Today, economics has many branches and studies highly diverse subject matters, right at the global, macro and micro levels.

Why do some people go for fuel-efficient cars while others go for fuel-guzzling sports cars? Why the poor are poor? Is capitalism doomed to intensify economic inequality? Will the process of globalisation be able to bridge the poor–rich divide and have a universal homogenising impact on the world? Such varied and many more questions fall under the domain of economics. These days we also can see information technology giving a typically new dimension to economics.

Economics and The Economy

The relation between economics and the economy, simply saying, is that of theory and practice. While the former is a discipline studying economic behaviour of human beings, the latter is a still-frame picture of it. Economics will come out with theories of market, employment, etc., and an economy is the real picture of the things which emerges after the application of those theories.

Economy is economics at play in a certain region. This region is best defined today as a country, a nation—the Indian Economy, the Russian Economy, the French Economy, etc. Economy as such means nothing. It gets meaning once it is preceded by the name of a country, a region, a block, etc. When we say developed economies, we mean economies of developed countries.

Countries of the world might be facing some common economic challenges. At the same time, they might be facing some highly specific challenges. Economists, during the period of evolution of economics, have suggested some fixed number of theories and methods of solving those economic challenges. Now it depends upon the choice of the countries as to which set of principles and theories they select for solving their economic challenges. Further, many countries selecting the same remedy and tools to fight the same problems might have similar or dissimilar results during a given period. At the same time, two economies selecting different tools to solve the same economic problems might experience the same results or completely different results. Why is this so?

Basically, economic theories are expectations of human behaviour about their economic activities and as human behaviour depends greatly on many internal and external factors, the results are likely to have diversities. The level and quality of natural resources, the quantity and quality of human resources, the socio-political milieu, the historical background, the psychic make of the human resource, etc., are some of the factors which individually as well as collectively impact an economy while carrying out economic activities. These things make it highly difficult for economists to forecast the kind of impact a particular economic policy will have on a particular economic setting. Ultimately, implementation and delivery systems also play a highly vital role in solving economic challenges in a country, which economists started studying after the 1960s. Therefore, it is correct to say that economics has less diversity than the economies. There will not be any exaggeration if we say that no two economies of the world are exactly the same, though we might classify them into broader categories like developed and developing, agrarian and industrial, etc.

This diversity makes economics a highly interesting discipline. It is through these diverse facts of the economies that economists have been able to modify and remodify their ideas on the subject of economics. The evolutionary history of economics is nothing but modifications in the past theories on the basis of contemporary results and experiences of the economies. It will be correct to say that economics has developed out of real life practices and especially from the evolution of practice into theory. As practices will be having newer dimensions, the theories of economics will also have newer and more imaginative dimensions.

The Focus of Economics

What is the real purpose of studying economics? What have economists ultimately been trying to articulate? And what has been the focus of economics and the economists since the birth of the discipline?

Though economics today studies a wide range of issues and topics, if we take an overall picture, its essence has been very simple—the betterment of human life on earth. Improving living conditions of the humanity at large has been the real and ultimate goal of the discipline. In this process, economists have been articulating a number of theories and propositions as to how an economy may maximise its economic potential and worth. The first and the most famous work

in this direction was by the Scottish philosopher-economist, Adam Smith in *The Wealth of Nations* (1776). One can trace the origin of the classical school of economics to this work. Similarly, in the following years and centuries, many outstanding works were produced by many great economists who were trying to improvise better ways of maximising the fruits of economic activity. Economics and the economists have a common goal, i.e., searching for possible alternatives for the betterment of human life.

Challenges of the Economies

The main challenge of any economy is to fulfil the needs of its population. Every population needs to be supplied with some **goods** and **services** for its survival and well-being. These goods might include basic needs such as food, shelter, garments, etc., while it might also consist of refrigerators, air conditioners, cars, medicines, computers, etc. Similarly, the services people need may range from healthcare, drinking water supply, education to advanced and highly sophisticated services like banking, insurance, airways, telephones, internet, etc. As an economy moves up the ladder of development, the process of fulfilling the needs of the population becomes a never-ending phenomenon. As an economy achieves success in supplying one set of goods and services to its population, the population starts demanding another set of goods and services, which are of a higher order. And thus goes on the struggle of the economy—solving one challenge and focusing on another. The standard of living of one set of population varies from another depending upon the attempts and the successes of the concerned economies as to which extent they have been able to fulfil the needs of their population.

There are two aspects of the challenge that economies face. First, the availability of the goods and services required by the population and second, the presence of the supply network. Every economy has to, at first, guarantee the required level of goods and services out of its production process. For this, proper level of production capacity should be built which requires a particular level of capital formation or investment. From where the investible funds will be managed is altogether a separate question. Whether the investment will come from the government, the domestic private sector or the foreigners? Once these details are cleared and selected as per the socio-economic condition of the economy, a proper distribution network for goods and services produced is assured.

Distribution Network Models

In the arena of *distribution network*, we have three historically existing models—**state**, **market** and **state-market mix**. In the first type of distribution system, the state (i.e., the government) takes the sole responsibility of supplying goods and services required by the population with no payments being done by the consumer—the former Soviet Union and Communist China being the best examples. In the second category comes the market mode of distribution which functions on the basis of price mechanism. In this system, goods and services are made available in the market and on the basis of their demand and supply, their prices are determined in the open market and finally they get distributed to the population. This was the distribution system of the capitalist economies—the whole of Euro-America. The third and the most prevalent mode of distribution, the state-market mix, developed out of the experiences of the former two systems. This distribution system has certain goods and services which might be made available to the population freely or at the subsidised prices by the state and some might be supplied by the market for which consumers need to pay. Almost all economies of the world today follow one or the other kind of distribution system. As the socio-economic composition of the population of an economy changes, the mixture of the goods and services to be supplied by the state

and the market get redefined in the economies from time to time.

ORGANISING AN ECONOMY

One issue which has affected the civilised history of mankind the most and has been a point of contentious is how the production process in an economy should be organised. Should production should be the sole responsibility of the state/ government or should it be left altogether to the private sector? Again, will it be better to carry on production with a joint effort—a mixture of state and private enterprises?

Depending upon the dominant view of the time in a particular country, different forms of production patterns evolved and different economic systems finally came up, providing alternative ways of organising an economy. The three models of economic system which evolved in the course of human history are basically the different stages in the evolutionary process of the experiments to define a better way of organising an economy. We must have a concise overview of this evolutionary process:

1 Capitalistic Economy

The capitalistic form of economy has its origin in the famous work of Adam Smith—*Wealth of Nations* (1776). Adam Smith (1723–1790), the Scottish philosopher-economist professor at the University of Glasgow, whose writings formed the basis of classical economics, had stressed certain fine ideas which were to take fancy among some of the western countries and finally capitalism took birth. He raised his voice against the heavy-handed government regulation of commerce and industry of the time which did not allow the economy to tap its full economic worth and reach the level of well-being. Stressing 'division of labour' and an environment of 'laissez faire' (non-interference by the government), he proposed that the 'invisible hand' of 'market forces' (price mechanism) will bring a state of equilibrium in the economy and a general well-being for the countrymen. For such an economy to function for public well-being, he acknowledged the need of *competition* in the *market*.

Once the USA attained independence, the ideas of Adam Smith were made part of its public policy—just one year after the *Wealth of Nations* was published. From here, the idea spread to other parts of Euro-America—by 1800 the economic system called 'capitalism' was established which was later known by different names—Private Enterprise System, Free Enterprise System or Market Economy.

The decisions of what to produce, how much to produce and at what price to sell are taken by the market, by the private enterprises in this system, with the state having no economic role.

2. State Economy

Rooted in the ideas of historical change proposed by the German philosopher Karl Marx (1818–1883), more specifically, this kind of economic system first came up in the erstwhile USSR after the Bolshevik Revolution (1917) and got its ideal shape in the People's Republic of China (1949). This form of economic system also spread to other countries in Eastern Europe. Here we see two versions of the state economy—in erstwhile USSR known as the *socialist economy* and in pre-1985 China as the *communist economy*. While a socialistic economy emphasised collective ownership of the means of production (property and assets), it also ascribed a large role to the state in running the economy, while communist economy, on the other hand, advocated state ownership of all properties including labour with absolute power to state in running the economy. Though for Marx, Socialism was a transitional stage to communism, it never did happen in reality.

Basically, this form of economy came in reaction to the prevalent popular economic system of capitalism and proposed just the opposite. The decisions related to production, supply and prices were all suggested to be taken solely by the state only. Such economies were also known as Centralised Economy, Centrally Planned Economy or Non-market Economy.

The socialist and communist economies used to criticise capitalistic economics of being based on exploitation. In response, the capitalist economies called them the practioners of 'state capitalism', where the state was the sole exploitator. The communist and anti-communist propagandas resulted in serious intellectual discussions almost upto the mid-1980s.

3. Mixed Economy

The belief in the self-correcting quality of the market and the 'invisible hand' of Adam Smith got a major setback in early 20th century during the Great Depression (1929). The impact of the depression spread from the USA to other economies of Western Europe escalating large scale unemployment, downfall in demand and economic activities and lockouts in industrial enterprises. The prevailing Smithonian macro ideas failed to check the crisis. A new approach was needed which came in the famous work, *The General Theory of Employment, Interest and Money* (1936) by the English economist at Cambridge University, John Maynard Keynes (1883–1946).

Keynes questioned the very principles of 'laissez-faire' and the nature of the 'invisible hand'. He even opined that the invisible hand brings equilibirium to the economy but by 'strangulating the poor'. He suggested that prices and wages are not flexible enough to provide employment to all. It means there will be some people unemployed when the economy will be at its full potential. Ultimately, a fall in demand will be imminent resulting in recession and if unchecked, in depression which happened in 1929. Questioning the limitations of the market mechanism, Keynes suggested *strong government intervention* in the economy. To get the economy out of the depression, he suggested an increase in government expenditures, discretionary fiscal policy (fiscal deficit, lower interest rates, cheap money supply, etc.) to boost the demand of goods and services as this was the reason behind the depression. As Keynesian policies were followed, the concerned economies were successfully pulled out of the Great Depression.

While Keynes was inquiring into the causes and cures of the Great Depression he questioned the capitalist economic system being practised throughout Euro-America. He suggested the capitalistic order to assimilate the goals of the socialistic economy (economic ideals of the socialists, i.e., the ex-USSR). In the capitalist economies of the time, all the basic goods and services were part of the market mechanism, i.e., being produced and supplied by the private sector. It meant that almost everything the people required was supplied by the private enterprises via the market which was ultimately an undimensional movement of money and wealth (from the mass of people to the few who controlled the production and supply chain) and the masses were going through the process of pauperisation every day, thereby weakening their purchasing power. In the end, it affected overall demand and culminated in the Great Depression.

As a follow up to the Keynesian advices, many trendsetting economic policies were initiated throughout the capitalist economies. One very important initiative which came out was the government's active role in the economy. The governments of the time started producing and supplying some basic goods and services which are known as 'public goods'. These goods basically intended to guarantee minimum level of nutrition to all, healthcare, sanitation, education, social security, etc. The expenditure on public goods were incurred on the public exchequer even if it

required deficit financing. Starting from 1930s upto 1950s, almost 50 per cent of the GDP in the Euro-America was spent by the governments on public goods which also become popular as the *social sector.* The essential goods and services which were till date being purchased by the people as 'private goods', were soon made available by the state 'free-of-costs', giving people more spare money to create demand for the goods and services which were part of the market.

The above instance has been cited here just to show the process as to how capitalism redefined itself by including some useful traits of the non-market economy, i.e., the state economy. The *mixed economy* arrived in this way and the classical capitalistic economy was challenged by it.

On the margins of these developments, it is interesting to note the developments that occured in the state economies of the time. It was **Oscar Lange (1904–65),** the Polish philosopher, who in 1950s suggested the same things for the socialist economy as Keynes had suggested for the capitalist economy. Lange praised the state economy for many of its good things, but also suggested inclusion of some of the good things of the capitalistic economy.[3] He advised the *state economies* to adopt 'market socialism' (the term was coined by him). His suggestions were outrightly rejected by the state economies as such compromises in the socialistic economic order were blasphemous at that time (this was taken as a suggestion towards democracy from dictatorship).

As Keynes has suggested that the capitalist economy should move few steps towards socialistic economy, Lange was suggesting just the same in the case of the state economies. Democracies are flexible thus they were able to go for an experiment which paid them in coming times. But as the socialist and communist political systems had

---

3. Galbraith, J.K., *A History of Economics*, Penguin Books, London, 1991, pp. 188–89.

been stubborn by nature, they did not go for any experiment and thus started moving towards their economic decay.

It was in communist China, under the leadership of Mao Tse-tung, from where the first opinion came against the total state economic control. The ultimate example of the state economy (i.e., China) started its preparation towards a limited market economy under the political design of dictatorship. In 1985, China announced its 'open door policy', the first experiment in 'market socialism'—Lange had the last laugh. Other state economies, though caught unprepared, followed the Chinese experiment towards market socialism. However, the switch over to market socialism has not been smooth for most of the state economies. The efforts towards market socialism in the Soviet Union, fuelled by the lofty ideas of 'glasnost' (openness) and 'perestroika' (restructuring), resulted in the very *disintegration* of the nation-state. The experts consider it 'a political fallout of an economic mismanagement'. The other state economies experienced major economic breakdowns in their transition phases to market socialism. Basically, for smooth transition to market socialism some prerequisites were required to be put in place aforehand. China was well ahead doing this homework since Mao's time (specially since 1975 onwards) which emerged as a real winner—the ideal type example of state economy getting smoothly metamorphosed into a giant market economy.

These two events spanning many decades were nothing but timely and rational selections of economic traits from each other's economic systems and experiences. The world by the late 1980s was having neither a pure example of capitalistic economy nor of a state economy.

There were many states of the world that opted for a mixed economy in the post-Second World War period after coming out of the colonial rule, such as India, Malaysia, Indonesia, etc., to name a few. The leadership of these countries could be considered visionaries which was to be proved by the mid-1990.

Though at a practical level, the world looked flat for the mixed economy model, a formal opinion on the goodness, immediacy and the ultimate viability of the mixed economic system was yet to emerge. The first such authoritative opinion, in this direction, came from the World Bank (WB) which accepted the goodness and the need of 'state intervention' in the economy.[4] This was a turning point in the world economic thinking as the World Bank and the International Monetary Fund (IMF) were ardent votaries of virtues of the free market economy.

The concluding consensus emerged with the publication of the World Development Report (1999) titled *Entering the 21st Century* in which the WB said, "Governments play a vital role in development, but there is no simple set of rules that tells them what to do." The WB went on to suggest that every country should determine the **areas** and the **extent** of the market and the state intervention, depending upon its own stage of economic development, socio-political and other historical factors.

The last WB document had basically rejected both the historically existing economic orders, namely the free-market economy, and the state economy—which meant Adam Smith and Karl Marx were cancelled and rejected outrightly, that too on the basis of the historical experiences of both the worlds. Rather, the document advocates for a 'mixture' of both the economic orders, i.e., the mixed economy. The long-standing ideological dilemma as to whether the market economy or the state economy was the better or the best way of organising the economy was solved for all times to come. The document pin-pointed good things of both the systems and concluded that they don't have the relationship of dichotomy, but that of complimentarity. The real issue is not whether to

---

4. *The East Asian Miracle*, W.B. Study, 1993.

have market or the state but having both of them together makes more sense. Market economy might suit one economy, while it might not suit another due to the different socio-economic conditions of the economies in reference. Similarly, the state economy model might serve one economy, but might not serve the other.

The real answer seems going for neither the market nor the state but a judicious mix of both. As the state-market mix depends upon the socio-economic and political conditions of an economy, there can never be a mechanical prototype of the mixed economy, which could be applied upon every economy universally. Every economy needs to explore its own mixture of market and state. Again, the same state might need to redefine composition of the state-market mix in the coming times according to its changed socio-eco-political scenario.

The process of economic reforms in India started in 1991. It was, in fact, the search for a new 'state-market mix', while India had been a mixed economy since Independence.

After Independence, India opted for a mixed economy when the state-market dilemma was at its peak globally . In the process of organising the economy, some basic and important infrastructural economic responsibilities were taken up by the state/governments (centre and state) and rest of the economic activities were left to private enterprises, i.e., the market. The kind of state-market mix for which India went was thought to be fit for the socio-economic and political conditions of the time. Once the country started the process of economic reforms in early 1990s, the prevailing state-market mix was redefined and a new form of mixed economy began to be practised. As the socio-economic conditions had changed, the state-market mix also changed. The redefined mixed economy for India had a declared favour for the market economy. Many economic roles which were under complete government monopolies were now opened for participation by the private

sector. Examples are many—telecommunication, power, roads, oil and natural gas, etc. At the same time, the responsibilities which were till date being shouldered by the state alone and which could be taken up by the state only were given extra emphasis. In this category comes the whole social sector—education, healthcare, drinking water, sanitation, nutrition, social security, etc.

The economic system of India was a mixed economy in the pre-1991 years as it is in the post-1991 years, but the composition of state-market mix has gone for a change. In future, as the socio-economic and political factors will be changing, India will be redefining its mixed economy, accordingly.

The emergence and evolution of the mixed economy was thus able to settle the long-standing debate as to what was the best way to organise an economy. Starting in 1776 with the *Wealth of Nations* of Adam Smith, it continued till we had the *World Development Report* of 1999 by WB.[5] The dilemma continued for almost two and a quarter centuries (1776–2000). Today, once the World Trade Organization (WTO) has taken over the world economy, the brand of the mixed economy it advocates, is more inclined towards the free market economy. However, it does not propagate to make the state an economic non-entity, i.e., it leaves scope for greater state intervention in required areas if needed.

ROLE OF THE STATE IN AN ECONOMY

The dilemma of searching the ideal way of organising an economy, as it evolved, was also going to solve another riddle. This riddle was the role of the state in an economy.[6] If we look back

---

5. World Bank, World Development Report, 1999.
6. A highly concise and to-the-point idea on the issue comes from Joseph. E. Stiglits, **'The Role of Government in Economic Development'**, the keynote address at the Annual World Bank Conference on Development Economics, 1996.

into the economic history of the world, we see *three* possible roles for the state/government in an economy:

(i) As a **regulator** of the economic system (where the state takes important economic decisions, announces the required kind of economic policies, takes the sole responsibility to get them implemented, and controlling and punishing those who don't oblige to those economic decisions).

(ii) As a producer and/or supplier of **'private goods and services'** (these include all those goods and services which constitute the part of market and which will be distributed among the needy according to the principles of market mechanism. Here the state earns profit as a private enterprise).

(iii) As a producer and/or supplier of **'public goods'** or **'social goods'** (these include goods and services which look essential from the perspective of social justice and well-being for the people. Education, healthcare, sanitation, drinking water, nutrition, caring for the differently abled and old, etc., come under this category. These goods which are generally distributed free of cost at times, might reach the beneficiaries at subsidised prices. The loss incurred by the state in this way is paid out of the public exchequer which means that the whole economy pays for the cause of a few people).

As different economies select different roles for the state according to their socio-political ideologies, the world had differing ways of organising the economy and had resulted in the establishment of different economic systems in the past.

On the issue of regulating the economy there has been no debate, as we see all economic systems being regulated by the state only. But the selection of other two functions of the state in an economy made the real difference. The economy which selected both the roles (ii and iii) for the state under monopoly we called them the state economies. This category of economy had two variants in the socialist economy at least the labour was not owned and exploited by the state unlike the other—the communist economy where labour used to be under complete state control. These economies had almost no market.

The economic system which left both the roles (ii and iii) as the sole responsibilities of the private sector was called the capitalistic economic system. Here the state had almost no economic role but played a passive role as the regulator.

Mixed economies had at least kept one economic role fixed for the state (i.e., iii), of supplying public goods to the needy people. In some of the mixed economies the state went on to take some of the roles of supplying the private goods (i.e., ii) even by carrying a heavy burden of subsidies.

The WB document—the *World Development Report*, 1999—was a judgement on the possible and suitable role of the state in the economy, which suggested a timely shuffling of state's role in the economy as per the socio-economic and political needs of the economy. We may understand the moot question via Keynes for whom the political problem of mankind is to combine three things:

(i) economic efficiency,

(ii) social justice, and

(iii) individual liberty

In the process of realising the above-mentioned objectives, an economy cannot go for either allowing only state's role in the economy or only the market's role in the economy. These challenges could only be faced properly once the state and the market both are given a balanced role in an economy—the balance to be defined by its present condition and the direction of future goal of the economy. Striking the right balance between the role of the state and the market in the economies came to be known as the process of economic reform in the post-WTO world.

If we analyse the need of an economy, we see some compulsory roles for the state in it:

(i) If the regulation and control of an economy is left to private individuals or groups (i.e., firms) they will be using the regulatory powers to maximise their profits and returns at the cost of others. That is why this role must rest with the state. It looks more logical in the democratic political set-up, wherein the interest of the largest numbers is being represented in the regulatory provisions.

(ii) The responsibility of producing and distributing private goods to the people could be well handled by the private sector as this is a profit-fetching area. The state should not burden itself with this responsibility as this could be well taken up by the private sector. But in the absence of the proper presence of the private sector in an economy, many countries in the world gave this responsibility also to the state; India being one among them. But as the private sector became capable, in some countries this responsibility was given up by the state in favour of the private sector and better development has been possible in those economies. In this sense, India delayed this process while in Indonesia, Malaysia, Thailand and South Korea allowed entry of the private sector much earlier.

(iii) The responsibility of producing and supplying the social/public goods to the needy cannot be left to the private sector as this is a loss-making exercise. It means, the state will have to take the sole responsibility or may need to expand its role in such areas—as we see it in post-reform India.

As the private sector becomes capable of playing the proper role in producing and supplying the private goods, state saves its important human and economic resources which is transferred to take care of the production and distribution of public goods.

Basically, the WB study, the *East Asian Miracle* (1993), recognises the above-given shift of one kind of mixed economy to another kind of mixed economy—in the cases of the Malaysian, Thai and South Korean economies—taking place since the mid-1960s. Experts believe that this shift could not take place in time in India. And once it started (1991–92) it was too late and this choice was not voluntary but obligatory. The East Asian economies had gone for the same kind of reform process but by their choice.

WASHINGTON CONSENSUS

The term 'Washington Consensus' was coined by the US economist John Williamson[7] (in 1989) under which he had suggested *a set of policy reforms* which most of the official in Washington (i.e., International Monetary Fund and World Bank) thought would be good for the crisis-driven Latin American countries of the time. The policy reforms included **ten** propositions:

(i) Fiscal discipline

(ii) A redirection of public expenditure priorities toward fields offering both high economic returns and the potential to improve income distribution, such as primary health care, primary education, and infrastructure.

(iii) Tax reform (to lower marginal rates and broaden the tax base)

---

7. John Williamson, **'What Washington Means by Policy Reform'**, Chapter 2 in John Williamson (ed.), *Latin American Adjustment: How Much Has Happened?*, 1990; Institute for International Economics and John Williamson, **'What Should the Bank Think About the Washington Consensus'**, Background Paper to the World Bank's *World Development Report 2000*, Washington DC, July 1999.

(iv) Interest rate liberalisation

(v) A competitive exchange rate

(vi) Trade liberalisation

(vii) Liberalisation of FDI inflows

(viii) Privatisation

(ix) Deregulation (in the sense of abolishing barriers to entry and exit)

(x) Secure property rights

However, in coming times, the term became synonymous to *neo-liberalism* (in Latin America), *market fundamentalism* (as George Soros told in 1998) and even *globalisation* across the world. It has often been used to describe an extreme and dogmatic commitment to the belief that **markets can handle everything**.

But the reality has been different—the *set of polices* was already being recommended by the IMF (International Monetary Fund) and the WB (World Bank) together with the US Treasury, especially during the period of the eighties and early nineties.[8] The prescription was originally intended to address the real problems occurring in Latin America at the time, and their use later to handle a wide array of other situations has been criticised even by original proponents of the policies. The name of the Washington Consensus has often been mentioned as being somewhat unfortunate, especially by its creator. John Williamson[9], says that audiences the world over seem to believe that this signifies a set of neo-liberal policies that have been imposed on hapless countries by the Washington-based international financial institutions and have led them to crisis and misery—there are people who cannot utter the term without foaming at the mouth. He further adds that many people feel that it gives the impression that the points outlined represent a set of rules imposed on developing nations by the United States. Instead, Williamson always felt that the prescription represented a consensus precisely because they were so universal. Many proponents of the plan do not feel that it represents the hard-line *neo-liberal* agenda that anti-free-trade activists say it does. They instead present it as a relatively conservative assessment of what policies can help bring a country to economic stability.

But the policy prescription led to processes which are known as Liberalisation, Privatisation, Globalisation, thus cutting down the role of the State in the economy—more so in the nations which got developmental funding from the WB or went to the IMF in times of the Balance of Payment crises (as in the case of India which commenced its reform process in 1991 under the 'conditions' of the IMF). It was as if the Adam Smith's prescription of 'free market' (liberalism) has taken its rebirth (in neo-liberalism).

Many scholars believe today that the recent financial crises of the US and the European nations are somehow born out of the ideas rooted in the Consensus. In the aftermath of the Great Recession (after the 'US sub-prime' crisis) in the Western economies, it is believed that dependence on market to correct the growth and development may not sustain any longer—and the world might agree in favour of a *development state,* as in the case of the East Asian nations which never went for the Consensus for their robust growth. The Keynesian idea of 'interventionist state' seems the ultimate alternative in the present times, as is suggested by the US Nobel economist Paul Krugman and being followed by the Japanese Prime Minister, Shinzo Abe (the *Three Arrows of Abenomics*).

8. Stiglitz, J. E., **Initiative for Policy Dialogue**, a paper presented at the conference *From the Washington Consensus towards a new Global Governance*, Barcelona, September 2004. The conference was sponsored by the Ford Foundation, the MacArthur Foundation, and the Mott Foundation.

9. Williamson, J., ***Did the Washington Consensus Fail?***, Institute for International Economics, Washington DC, 2002.

SECTORS OF AN ECONOMY

Every economy tries to maximise the returns of economic activities in which it is involved. Whatever be the organising principles of an economy, the economic activities are broadly classified into three broad categories, which are known as the three sectors[10] of the economy.

1. Primary Sector

This sector includes all those economic activities where there is the direct use of natural resources as agriculture, forestry, fishing, fuels, metals, minerals, etc. In some of the economies, mining activities are considered as part of the secondary sector, though we see direct use of natural resources here. Broadly, such economies term their agricultural sector as the primary sector. This is the case in India.

2. Secondary Sector

This sector is rightly called the manufacturing sector, which uses the produce of the primary sector as its raw materials. Since manufacturing is done by the industries, this sector is also called the industrial sector—examples are production of bread and biscuits, cakes, automobiles, textiles, etc.

3. Tertiary Sector

This sector includes all economic activities where different 'services' are produced such as education, banking, insurance, transportation, tourism, etc. This sector is also known as the services sector.

TYPES OF ECONOMIES

Depending upon the shares of the particular sectors in the total production of an economy and the ratio of the dependent population on them for their livelihood, economies are categorised as:

1. Agrarian Economy

An economy is called agrarian if its share of the primary sector is 50 per cent or more in the total output (the GDP) of the economy. At the time of Independence, India was such an economy. But now it shows the symptom of a service economy with the primary sector's contribution falling to almost 18 per cent of its total produce, while almost 49 per cent of the population depends on the primary sector for their livelihood. Thus, in *monetary terms* India is no more an agrarian economy, however the dependency ratio makes it so—India being the first such example in the economic history of the world.

2. Industrial Economy

If the secondary sector contributes 50 per cent or more to the total produce value of an economy, it is an industrial economy. Higher the contribution, higher is the level of industrialisation. The western economies which went for early industrialisation earning faster income and developing early are known as developed economies. Most of these economies have crossed this phase once the process of industrialisation saturated.

3. Service Economy

An economy where 50 per cent or more of the produced value comes from the tertiary sector is known as the service economy. First lot of such economies in the world were the early industrialised economies. The tertiary sector provides livelihood to the largest number of people in such economies. In the last decade (2003–04 to 2012–13), growth has increasingly come from the services sector,[11] in which contribution to overall growth of the economy has been 65 per cent, while that of the

---

10. Michael P. Todaro and Stephen C. Smith, *Economic Development*, Pearson Education, 8th Ed., N. Delhi, p. 440.

11. Ministry of Finance, *Economic Survey 2012–13*, Government of India, New Delhi, 2013, p. 30

industrial and agricultural sectors have been 27 per cent and 8 per cent, respectively.

By the end of the 19th century, it was a well-established fact, at least in the western world, that industrial activities were a faster way to earn income in comparison to agrarian activities. The Second World War had established the fact for the whole world—and almost every country started their preparation for the process of industrialisation. As country after country successfully industrialised, a pattern of population shift occured from one to another sector of the economy, which was known as the *stages of growth* of an economy.[12] With the intensification of industrialisation, dependency on the primary sector for livelihood decreased and dependency on the secondary sector increased consistently. Similarly, such economies saw a population shift from the secondary to the tertiary sector—and these were known as the 'post-industrial' societies or the services societies. Almost the whole Euro-America falls under this category—these economies are having over 50 per cent of their total produce value being contributed by the tertiary sector and over half of the population depends on this sector for their livelihood. Many other countries which started the process of industrialisation in the post-war period did show abberations in this shift of the population and the income—India being one among them.

THE IDEA OF NATIONAL INCOME

Income is probably the most frequently used term in economics, used by experts and lay men. Income level is the most commonly used tool to determine the well-being and happiness of nations and their citizens. This remains true even today, Even if we know that 'income' is not an exhaustive idea to know about the well-being

of the society. There has been some reason for such a perception about the concept of income. Basically, when the idea of 'human development' came into being in the early 1990s, the concept of the 'human development index' ultimately was heavily dependent on the level of 'income' of an individual in a country. Education and life expectancy can only be enhanced once the required amount of 'investment' (expenditure on them) could be mobilised. Thus, somehow, income came to be established as the 'focal point' of 'development/human dvelopment'.

As income of a single person can be measured, it can be measured for a nation and the whole world, although the method of calculation (accounting) may be a little bit complex in the latter's case. In due course, *four ideas/ways* to calculate the income of a nation[13] developed, which are the subject matter of the 'national income accounting'. These four ways to calculate the 'income' of an economy, although different from each other in some ways, are the concepts of GDP, NDP, GNP and NNP. All are a form of the national income, but are different from one another. They all present a different story about the income of a nation in their own specific way. Here, we will objectively discuss each one of them.

GDP

Gross Domestic Product (GDP) is the value of the all *final* goods and services produced within the boundary of a nation during one year period. For India, this calendar year is from 1st April to 31st March.

---

12. Walt W. Rostow, *The Stages of Economic Growth: A Non-Communist Manifesto*, Cambridge University Press, London, 1960, pp. 1–5.

13. The discussion on National Income Accounting is based on several textbooks of economics and the documents released by the **International Monetary Fund (IMF)** and the **World Bank (WB)** in the areas of **Comparative Economics** and **International Economics.** It was **Simon Kuznets,** a Nobel Prize winning economist from the USA who first conceived the idea of GDP in 1934.

It is also calculated by adding national private consumption, gross investment, government spending and trade balance (exports-minus-imports). The use of the exports-minus-imports factor removes expenditures on imports not produced in the nation, and adds expenditures of goods and service produced which are exported, but not sold within the country.

It will be better to understand the terms used in the concept, *'gross'*, which means same thing in Economics and Commerce as 'total' means in Mathematics; *'domestic'* means all economic activities done whithin the boundary of a nation/country and by its own capital; *'product'* is used to define 'goods and services' together; and *'final'* means the stage of a product after which there is no known chance of value addition in it.

The ***different uses*** of the concept of GDP are as given below:

(i) Per annum percentage change in it is the 'growth rate' of an economy. For example, if a country has a GDP of Rs. 107 which is 7 rupees higher than the last year, it has a growth rate of 7 per cent. When we use the term 'a growing' economy, it means that the economy is adding up its income, i.e., in quantitative terms.

(ii) It is a 'quantitative' concept and its volume/size indicates the 'internal' strength of the economy. But it does not say anything about the 'qualitative' aspects of the goods and services produced.

(iii) It is used by the IMF/WB in the comaparative analyses of its member nations.

NDP

Net Domestic Product (NDP) is the GDP calculated after adjusting the weight of the value of 'depreciation'. This is, basically, *net form* of the GDP, i.e., GDP minus the total value of the 'wear and tear' (depreciation) that happened in the assets while the goods and services were being produced. Every asset (except human beings) go for depreciation in the process of their uses, which means they 'wear and tear'. The governments of the economies decide and announce the rates by which assets depreciate (done in India by the Ministry of Commerce and Industry) and a list is published, which is used by different sections of the economy to determine the real levels of depreciations in different assets. For example, a residential house in India has a rate of 1 per cent per annum depreciation, an electric fan has 10 per cent per annum, etc., which is calculated in terms of the asset's price. This is ***one way*** how depreciation is used in economics. The ***other way*** it is used in the external sector while the domestic currency floats freely as against the foreign currencies. If the value of the domestic currency falls following market mechanism in comparison to a foreign currency, it is a situation of 'depreciation' in the domestic currency, calculated in terms of loss in value of the domestic currency.

Thus, *NDP = GDP – Depreciation.*

This way, NDP of an economy has to be always lower than its GDP for the same year, since there is no way to cut the depreciation to zero. But mankind has achieved too much in this area through developments, such as 'ball-bearing', 'lubricants', etc., all innovated to minimise the levels of depreciation.

The ***different uses*** of the concept of NDP are as given below:

(a) For domestic use only: to understand the historical situation of the loss due to depreciation to the economy. Also used to understand and analyse the sectoral situation of depreciation in industry and trade in comparative periods.

(b) To show the achievements of the economy in the area of research and development, which have tried cutting the levels of depreciation in a historical time period.

However, NDP is not used in comparative economics, i.e., to compare the economies of the world. Why this is so? This is due to different rates of depreciation which is set by the different economies of the world. Rates of depreciation may be based on logic (as it is in the case of houses in India—the cement, bricks, sand and iron rods which are used to build houses in India can sustain it for the coming 100 years, thus the rate of depreciation is fixed at 1 per cent per annum). But it may not be based on logic all the time, for example, upto February 2000 the rate of depreciation for heavy vehicles (vehicles with 6-wheels and above) was 20 per cent while it was raised to 40 per cent afterwards—to boost the sales of heavy vehicles in the country. There was no logic in doubling the rate. Basically, depreciation and its rates are also used by modern governments as a tool of economic policymaking, which is the ***third way*** how depreciation is used in economics.

GNP

Gross National Product (GNP) is the GDP of a country added with its 'income from abroad'. Here, the trans-boundary economic activities of an economy is also taken into account. The items which are counted in the segment 'Income from Abroad' are:

(i) *Private Remittances:* the net outcome of the money which inflows and outflows on account of the 'private transfers' by Indian nationals working outside of India (to India) and the foreign nationals working in India (to their home countries). On this front India has always been a gainer- till the early 1990s from the Gulf region (which fell down afterwards in the wake of the heavy country-bound movements of Indians working there due to the Gulf War) and afterwards from the USA and other European nations.

Today, India is the highest recipient of private remittances in the world—as per the World Bank projected at $72 billion in 2015 (in 2013 it was $70 billion, the year's highest). China falls second ($ 64 billion) in 2015.

(ii) *Interest on External Loans:* the net outcome on the front of the interest payments, i.e., balance of inflow (on the money lend out by the economy) and outflow (on the money borrowed by the economy) of external interests. In India's case it has always been negative as the economy has been a 'net borrower' from the world economies.

(iii) *External Grants:* the net outcome of the external grants i.e., the balance of such grants which flow to and from India. Today, India offers more such grants than it receives. India receives grants (grants or loan-grant mix) from few countries as well as UN bodies (like the UNDP) and offers several developmental and humanitarian grants to foreign nations. In the wake of globlisation, grant outflows from India has increased as its economic diplomacy aims at the playing bigger role at international level.

Ultimately, the balance of all the three components of the 'Income from Abroad' segment may turn out to be positive or negative. In India's case it has always been negative (due to heavy outflows on account of trade deficits and interest payments on foreign loans). It means, the 'Income from Abroad' is subtracted from India's GDP to calculate its GNP.

The normal formula is *GNP = GDP + Income from Abroad.* But it becomes GNP = GDP + (– Income from Abroad), i.e., GDP – Income from Abroad, in the case of India. This means that India's GNP is always lower than its GDP.

The **different uses** of the concept GNP are as given below:

(i) This is the 'national income' according to which the IMF ranks the nations of the world in terms of the volumes—at purchasing power parity (PPP). For a detailed discussion on PPP please see *Chapter 24*. India is ranked as the *3rd largest economy* of the world (after China and the USA), while as per the nominal/prevailing exchange rate of rupee, India is the *7th largest economy* (IMF, April 2016). Now such comparisons are done using the GDP, too.

(ii) It is the more exhaustive concept of national income than the GDP as it indicates towards the *'quantitative'* as well as the *'qualitative'* aspects of the economy, i.e., the *'internal'* as well as the *'external'* strength of the economy.

(iii) It enables us to learn several facts about the production behaviour and pattern of an economy, such as, how much the outside world is dependent on its product and how much it depends on the world for the same (numerically shown by the size and net flow of its 'balance of trade'); what is the standard of its human resource in international parlance (shown by the size and the net flow of its 'private remittances'); what position it holds regarding financial support from and to the world economies (shown by the net flow of 'interests' on external lending/borrowing).

NNP

Net National Product (NNP) of an economy is the GNP after deducting the loss due to 'depreciation'. The formula to derive it may be written like:

NNP = GNP – Depreciation

or,

NNP = GDP + Income from Abroad – Depreciation.

The **different uses** of the concept of NNP are as given below:

(i) This is the **'National Income' (NI)** of an economy. Though, the GDP, NDP and GNP, all are 'national income' they are not written with capitalised 'N' and 'I'.

(ii) This is the *purest form* of the income of a nation.

(iii) When we divide NNP by the total population of a nation we get the *'per capita income'* (PCI) of that nation, i.e., 'income per head per year'. A very basic point should be noted here that this is the point where the rates of dipreciation followed by different nations make a difference. Higher the rates of depreciation lower the PCI of the nation (whatever be the reason for it logical or artificial as in the case of depreciation being used as a tool of policymaking). Though, economies are free to fix any rate of depreciation for different assets, the rates fixed by them make difference when the NI of the nations are compared by the international financial institutions like the IMF, WB, ADB, etc.

The 'Base Year' together with the 'Methodology' for calculating the National Accounts were revised by the Central Statistics Office (CSO) in January 2015, which is given in the forthcoming pages.

Cost and Price of National Income

While calculating national income the issues related to 'cost' and 'price' also needs to be decided. Basically, there are two sets of costs and prices; and an economy needs to choose at which of the two costs and two prices it will calculate its national income. Let us understand the confusion and the relevance of this confusion.[14]

(i) *Cost:* Income of an economy, i.e., value of its total produced goods and services may be calculated at either the 'factor cost' or the 'market cost'. What is the difference between them? Basically, *'factor cost'* is the 'input cost' the producer has to incur in the process of producing something (such as cost of capital, i.e., interest on loans, raw materials, labour, rent, power, etc.). This is also termed as *'factory price'* or 'production cost/price'. This is nothing but 'price' of the commodity from the producer's side. While the *'market cost'* is derived after adding the indirect taxes to the factor cost of the product, it means the cost at which the goods reach the market, i.e., showrooms (these are the cenvat/central excise and the CST which are paid by the producers to the central government in India). This is also known as *'ex-factory price'*. The weight of the state taxes are then added to it, to finally derive the 'market cost'. In general, they are also called *'factor price'* and *'market price'*.

India officially used to calculate its national income at *factor cost* (though the data at *market cost* was also released which were used for other purposes by the governments, commerce and industry). Since January 2015, the CSO has switched over to calculating it at *market price* (i.e., *market cost*). The market price

is calculated by adding the *product taxes* (generally taken as the *indirect taxes* of the Centre and the States) to the factor cost. This way India has not switched over the popular international practice. Once the proposed GST gets implemented it will be easier for India to calculate its national income at market price.

(ii) *Price:* Income can be derived at two prices, constant and current. The difference in the constant and current prices is only that of the *impact of inflation*. Inflation is considered stand still at a year of the past (this year of the past is also known as the *'base year'*) in the case of the constant price, while in the current price, present day inflation is added. Current price is, basically, the maximum retail price (MRP) which we see printed on the goods selling in the market.

As per the new guidelines the *base year* in India has been revised from 2004–05 to 2011–12 (January 2015). *India calculates its national income at constant prices*—so is the situation among other developing economies, while the developed nations calculate it at the current prices. Though, for statistical purposes the CSO also releases the national income data at current prices. Why? Basically, inflation has been a challenging aspect of policymaking in India because of its level (i.e., range in which it dwindles) and stability (how stable it has been). In such situations growth in the income levels of the population living below the poverty level (BPL) can never be measured accurately (due to higher inflation the section will show higher income) and the government will never be able to measure the *real* impact of its poverty alleviation programmes.

Here, one important aspect of income needs to be understood. Income of a person has three forms—the first form is **nominal income** (the wage someone gets in hand per day or per

14. The information on issues like 'cost', 'price', 'taxes' and 'subsidies' are based on the different **Discussion Papers** released by the **Central Statistical Organisation** (GoI) from time to time.

month), the second form is *real income* (this is nominal income minus the present day rate of inflation—adjusted in percentage form), and the last one is the *disposable income* (the net part of wage one is free to use which is derived after deducting the direct taxes from the real/nominal income, depending upon the need of data). What happens in practice is that while the nominal income might have increased by only 5 per cent, it looks 15 per cent if the inflation is at the 10 per cent level. Unlike India, among the developed nations, inflation has been around 2 per cent for many decades (it means it has been at lower levels and stable, too. This is why the difference between the incomes at constant and current prices among them are narrow and they calculate their national income at current prices. They get more reliable and realistic data of their income).

Taxes & National Income

While accounting/calculating national income the taxes, direct and indirect, collected by the government, needs to be considered. In the case of India, to the extent the **direct taxes** (individual income tax, corpoarate income tax, i.e., the corporate tax, divident tax, interest tax, etc.) are concerned, there is no need of adjustment whether the national income is accounted at factor cost or market cost. This is so because at both the 'costs' they have to be the same; besides these taxes are collected at the income of source of the concerned person or group.

But the amount of **indirect taxes** (cenvat, customs, central sales tax, sales tax/vat, state excise, etc.) needs to be taken into account if the national income is accounted at 'factor cost' (which is the case with India). If the national income is calculated at factor cost then the corpus of the total indirect taxes needs to be deducted from it. This is because, indirect taxes have been added twice: once at the point of the people/group who pay these taxes from their disposable income while purchasing things from the market, and again at the point of the governments (as their income receipts). Collection/source of indirect taxes are the 'disposable income' (which individuals and companies have with them after paying their direct taxes—from which they do any purchasing and finally, the indirect taxes reach the government). Thus, if the national income is calculated at factor cost, the formula to seek it will be:

National Income at Factor Cost = NNP at Market Cost – Indirect Taxes

However, if the national income is being derived at 'market cost', the indirect taxes do not need to be deducted from it. In this case, the government do not have to add their income accruing from indirect taxes to the national income. It means, that the confusion in the case of national income accounting at factor cost is only related to indirect taxes.

Subsidies & National Income

Similar to the indirect taxes, the various subsidies which are forwarded by the governments need to be adjusted while calculating national income. They are added to the national income at market cost, in the case of India. Subsidies are added in the national income at market cost to derive the national income at factor cost. This is because the price at which subsidised goods and services are made available by the government are not their real factor costs (subsidies are forwarded on the factor costs of the goods and services) otherwise we will have a distorted value (which will be less than its real value). Thus, the formula will be:

National Income at Factor Cost = NNP at Market Cost + Subsidies

If the national income is derived at the market cost and governments forward no subsidies there is no need of adjustments for the subsidies, but after all there is not a single economy in the world today which does not forward subsidies in one or the other form.

Putting 'indirect taxes' and 'subsidies' together, India's National Income will thus be derived with the following formula (as India does it at factor cost):

National Income at Factor Cost = NNP at Market Cost – Indirect Taxes + Subsidies

REVISION IN THE BASE YEAR AND METHOD OF NATIONAL INCOME ACCOUNTING

The Central Statistics Office (CSO), in January 2015, released the **new** and **revised** data of National Accounts, effecting two changes:

1. The *Base Year* was revised from 2004–05 to 2011–12. This was done in accordance with the recommendation of the National Statistical Commission (NSC), which had advised to revise the base year of all economic indices every five years.

2. This time, the *methodology* of calculating the National Accounts has also been revised in line with the requirements of the System of National Accounts (SNA)-2008, an internationally accepted standard.

The **major changes** incorporated in this revision are as given below:

(i) **Headline growth rate** will now be measured by *GDP at constant market prices*, which will henceforth be referred to as 'GDP' (as is the practice internationally). Earlier, growth was measured in terms of growth rate in *GDP at factor cost and at constant prices*.

(ii) Sector-wise estimates of Gross Value Added (GVA)[15] will now be given at **basic prices**[16] instead of factor cost. The relationship between GVA at factor cost, GVA at basic prices, and GDP (at market prices) is given below:

GVA at basic prices = CE + OS/MI + CFC + production taxes less production subsidies.

GVA at factor cost = GVA at basic prices – production taxes less production subsidies.

GDP = GVA at basic prices + product taxes – product subsidies.

[Where, **CE**: compensation of employees; **OS**: operating surplus; **MI**: mixed income; and **CFC**: consumption of fixed capital (i.e., deprication). **Production taxes** or **production subsidies** are paid or received with relation to production and are independent of the volume of actual production. Some examples of **production taxes** are *land revenues, stamps and registration fees* and *tax on profession*.

---

15. GVA, which measures the difference in value between the final good and the cost of ingredients used in its production, widens the scope of capturing more economic activity than the earlier 'factor cost' approach—a sum of the total cost of all factors used to produce a good or service, net of taxes and subsidies.

16. The **basic price** is the amount receivable by the producer from the purchaser for a unit of a good or service produced as output minus any tax payable (such as sales tax or VAT the buyer pays), and plus any subsidy receivable, on that unit as a consequence of its production or sale; it excludes any transport charges invoiced separately by the producer. In other words, the basic price is what the seller collects for the sale, as opposed to what the buyer pays.

Some **production subsidies** are subsidies to Railways, input subsidies to farmers, subsidies to village and small industries, administrative subsidies to corporations or cooperatives, etc. **Product taxes** or **subsidies** are paid or received on per unit of the product. Some examples of product taxes are excise tax, sales tax, service tax and import and export duties. **Product subsidies** include food, petroleum and fertilizer subsidies, interest subsidies given to farmers, households, etc., through banks, and subsidies for providing insurance to households at lower rates].

(iii) Comprehensive coverage of the *corporate sector* both in manufacturing and services by incorporation of annual accounts of companies as filed with the Ministry of Corporate Affairs (MCA) under their e-governance initiative, MCA21. Use of MCA21 database for manufacturing companies has helped in accounting for activities other than manufacturing undertaken by these companies.

(iv) Comprehensive coverage of the *financial sector* by inclusion of information from the accounts of stock brokers, stock exchanges, asset management companies, mutual funds and pension funds, and the regulatory bodies including the Securities and Exchange Board of India (SEBI), Pension Fund Regulatory and Development Authority (PFRDA) and Insurance Regulatory and Development Authority (IRDA).

(v) Improved coverage of activities of *local bodies* and *autonomous institutions*, covering around 60 per cent of the grants/transfers provided to these institutions.

INCOME ESTIMATES FOR 2016-17

The latest data (1st Advance Estimates) of India's national income for the fiscal 2016-17 were released by the CSO (Central Statistics Office) on **January 6th, 2017**—major highlights are given below (*Economic Survey 2016-17* and the *Union Budget 2017-18* are based on the same data estimates):

(i) **GDP** (gross domestic product) at *constant prices* (2011-12) is likely to be Rs. 121.55 lakh crore with a growth rate of 7.1 per cent (down from 7.6 per cent of 2015-16). GDP at *current prices* is estimated to be Rs. 151.93 lakh crore showing a growth rate of 11.9 per cent.

(ii) **GVA** (gross value added) at basic *constant prices* (2011-12) is anticipated to be Rs. 111.53 lakh crore with a growth rate of 7.0 per cent (down from 7.2 per cent of 2015-16).

(iii) **PCI** (per capita income) at *constant prices* (2011-12) is estimated to be Rs. 81,805 with a growth rate of 5.6 per cent (down from 6.2 per cent of 2015-16). At *current prices* the PCI is estimated to be Rs. 1,03,007 with a growth rate of 10.4 per cent (up from 7.4 per cent of 2015-16).

2

GROWTH, DEVELOPMENT AND HAPPINESS

Since 1971, Bhutan has rejected GDP as the only way to measure progress—in its place, it has championed a new approach to development, which measures prosperity through formal principles of gross national happiness (GNH) and the spiritual, physical, social and environmental health of its citizens and natural environment. For decades, this belief that wellbeing should take preference over material growth has remained a global oddity. Now, in a world beset by collapsing financial systems, gross inequity and wide-scale environmental destruction, this tiny Buddhist state's approach is attracting a lot of interest. In 2011, the UN adopted Bhutan's call for a holistic approach to development, a move endorsed by 68 countries. A UN panel is now considering ways that Bhutan's GNH model can be replicated across the globe. *

* As Annie Kelly writes in The Guardian, Washington, DC, 1st December. 2012.

INTRODUCTION

Similar to seers and philosophers, economists, were also party to human's quest for a better tomorrow. We have been a witness to a number of notions coming in from the literature of Economics in this area—starting with a very humble and layman's word like 'progress' to technical terms like 'growth', 'development' and 'human development'. With greater dependence on the idea of the 'economic man', the world created immense wealth in the post-War decades. It was in the 1980s that social scientists started finer studies in the area of mankind's actions, finally challenging the very idea of the 'economic man' ('rational man'). Thus starts mankind's urge to introspect the lives of humanity on the planet earth. Meanwhile, humanity was faced with an unique riddle of climate change. By now, courtesy the UNO, the world has the World Happiness Report.

PROGRESS

Progress is a general term frequently used by experts to denote betterment or improvement in anything. In economics, the term was used for a long time to show the positive movement in the lives of people and in an economy. It had both quantitative and qualitative aspects to it. After a point of time, some economists started using all the three terms—progress, growth and development—interchangeably to mean almost the same thing. But it was only during the 1960s, 1970s and 1980s that a clear meanings of these terms really evolved.[1] The term 'progress' became a general term with no specific meaning in economics or denoting both growth and development. But growth and development were allotted their clear-cut meanings.

ECONOMIC GROWTH

A term coming from the life sciences, 'growth' in economics means economic growth. An increase in economic variables over a period of time is economic growth. The term can be used in an individual case or in the case of an economy or for the whole world. The most important aspect of growth is its *quantifiability*, i.e., one can measure it in absolute terms.[2] All the units of measurement may be applied, depending upon the economic variable, where growth is being studied. We have a few examples:

(i) An economy might have been able to see growth in food production during a decade which could be measured in tonnes.

(ii) The growth of road network in an economy might be measured for a decade or any period in miles or kilometres.

(iii) Similarly, the value of the total production of an economy might be measured in currency terms which means the economy is growing.

(iv) Per capita income for an economy might be measured in monetary terms over a period.

We may say that *economic growth is a quantitative progress.*

To calculate the *growth rate* of an economic variable the difference between the concerned period is converted into percentage form. For example, if a dairy farm owner produced 100 litres of milk last month and 105 litres in the following month, his dairy has a growth rate of 5 per cent over a period of two months. Similarly, we may calculate the growth rate of an economy for any given successive periods. Growth rate is

1. Based on the analyses in Michael P. Todaro and Stephen C. Smith, *Economic Development,* Pearson Education, 8th Ed., New Delhi, 2004, pp. 9–11.

2. As the IMF and the WB considered this yardstick of development as quoted in Gerald M. Meier and James E. Rauch, *Leading Issues in Economic Development,* Oxford University Press, New Delhi, 2006, pp. 12–14.

an *annual concept* which may be used otherwise with the clear reference to the period for which it is used.

Though growth is a value neutral term, i.e., it might be positive or negative for an economy for a specific period, we generally use it in the positive sense. If economists say an economy is growing it means the economy is having a positive growth otherwise they use the term '*negative growth*'.

Economic growth is a widely used term in economics which is useful in not only national level economic analyses and policymaking, but also highly useful in the study of comparative economics. International level financial and commercial institutions go for policymaking and future financial planning on the basis of the growth rate data available for the economies of the world.

ECONOMIC DEVELOPMENT

For a comparatively longer period of time after the birth of economics, economists remained focused on aspects of expanding the quantity of production and income of a country's economy. The main issue economists discussed was—how to increase the quantity of production and income of a country or a nation-state. It was believed that once an economy is able to increase its production, its income will also increase and there will be an automatic betterment (quality increase) in the lives of the people of the economy. There was no conscious discussion over the issue of quality expansion in the lives of the people. Economic growth was considered as a cause and effect for the betterment of the lives of the people. This was the reason why economists, till the 1950s, failed to distinguish between growth and development, though they knew the difference between these terms.

It was during the 1960s and in the later decades that economists came across many countries where the growth was comparatively higher, but the quality of life was comparatively low. The time had come to define economic development differently from what the world meant by economic growth. For economists, development indicates the quality of life in the economy, which might be seen in accordance with the availability of many variables such as:

(i) The level of nutrition

(ii) The expansion and reach of healthcare facilities—hospitals, medicines, safe drinking water, vaccination, sanitation, etc.

(iii) The level of education

(iv) Other variables on which the quality of life depends

Here, one basic thing must be kept in mind that if the masses are to be guaranteed with a basic minimum level of quality-enhancing inputs (above-given variables such as food, health, education, etc.) in their life, a minimum level of income has to be guaranteed for them. Income is generated from productive activities. It means that before assuring development we need to assure growth. Higher economic development requires higher economic growth. But it does not mean that a higher economic growth automatically brings in higher economic development—a confusion the early economists failed to clarify. We may cite an example here to understand the confusion: two families having same levels of income, but spending differing amounts of money on developmental aspects. One might be giving little attention to health, education and going for saving, and the other might not be saving but taking possible care of the issues of health and education. Here the latter necessarily will have higher development in comparison to the former. Thus, we may have some diverse cases of growth and development:

(i) Higher growth and higher development

(ii) Higher growth but lower development

(iii) Lower growth but higher development

The above-given combinations, though comparative in nature, make one thing clear, that, just as for higher income and growth we need conscious efforts, same is true about economic development and higher economic development.

Without a conscious public policy, development has not been possible anywhere in the world. Similarly, we can say, that without growth there cannot be development either.

The first such instance of growth without development, which the economists saw, was in the Gulf countries. These economies, though they had far higher levels of income and growth, the levels of development were not of comparable levels. Here started the branch of economics which came to be be known as *'development economics'*. After the arrival of the WB and IMF, conscious economic policies were framed and prescribed for the growth and development of less developed economies.

We can say that *economic development is quantitative as well as qualitative progress* in an economy.[3] It means, when we use the term growth we mean quantitative progress and when we use the term development we mean quantitative as well as qualitative progress. If economic growth is suitably used for development, it comes back to accelerate the growth and ultimately greater and greater population brought under the arena of development. Similarly, high growth with low development and ill-cared development finally results in fall in growth. Thus, there is a circular relationship between growth and development. This circular relationship broke down when the Great Depression occurred. Once the concept of the *'welfare state'* got established, development became a matter of high concern for the governments of the world, policymakers and economists alike. A whole new branch of economics—*welfare economics* has its origin in the concept of welfare state and the immediacy of development.

Measuring Development

Although economists were able to articulate the differences between growth and development (Mahbub ul Haq, a leading Pakistani economist had done it by the early 1970s), it took some more time when the right method of measuring development could be developed. It was an established fact that the goal of progress goes beyond the mere 'increase in income'. International bodies such as the UNO, IMF and WB were concerned about the development of the comparatively underdeveloped regions of the world. But any attempt in this direction was only possible once there was a tool to know and measure the level of development in an economy and the determinants which could be considered as the traits of development. The idea of developing a formula/method to measure the development was basically facing two kinds of difficulties:

(i) At one level it was difficult to define as to what constitutes development. Factors which could show development might be many, such as levels of income/consumption, quality of consumption, healthcare, nutrition, safe drinking water, literacy and education, social security, peaceful community life, availability of social prestige, entertainment, pollution-free environment, etc. It has been a realty difficult task to achieve consensus among the experts on these determinants of development.

(ii) At the second level it looked highly difficult to quantify a concept as development constitutes quantitative as well as qualitative aspects. It is easy to compare qualitative aspects such as beauty, taste, etc., but to measure them we don't have any measuring scale.

---

3. *World Bank,* **World Development Report 1991,** Oxford University Press, New York, 1991, p. 4.

Human Development Index

The dilemma of measuring the developmental level of economies was solved once the United Nations Development Programme (UNDP) published its first Human Development Report (HDR) in 1990. The report had a human development index (HDI) which was the first attempt to define and measure the level of development of economies. The 'index' was a product of select team of leading scholars, development practioners and members of the Human Development Report office of the UNDP. The first such team which developed the HDI was led by **Mahbub ul Haq** and **Inge Kaul.** The term 'human development' is a corollary of 'development' in the index.

The HDR measures development by combining three indicators—*Health, Education* and *Standard of Living*—converted into a composite human development index, the HDI. The creation of a single statistic in HDI was a real breakthrough which was to serve as a frame of reference for both 'social' and 'economic' development. The HDI sets a minimum and a maximum for each dimension, called *goalposts,* and then shows where each country stands in relation to these goalposts, expressed as a value between 0 and 1 (i.e., the index is prepared on the *scale of one*). The *three* indicators[4] used to develop the composite index are as given below:

The **Education** component of the HDI is *now* (since HDR-2010) measured by two other indicators—

(i) **Mean of years of schooling (for adults aged 25 years):** This is estimated based on educational attainment data from censuses and surveys available in the UNESCO Institute for Statistics database and *Barro and Lee* (2010) methodology.

(ii) **Expected years of schooling (for children of school entering age):** These estimates are based on enrolment by age at all levels of education and population of official school age for each level of education. Expected years of schooling is capped at 18 years.

These indicators are normalised using a minimum value of zero and maximum values are set to the actual observed maximum value of mean years of schooling from the countries in the time series, 1980–2012, that is 13.3 years estimated for the United States in 2010. The *education index* is the geometric mean of two indices.

The **Health** component is measured by the *life expectancy* at birth component of the HDI and is calculated using a minimum value of 20 years and maximum value of 83.57 years. This is the observed maximum value of the indicators from the countries in the time series, 1980–2012. Thus, the longevity component for a country where life expectancy birth is 55 years would be 0.551.

The **Standard of Living** component is measured by *GNI* (Gross National Income/ Product) per capita at 'Purchasing Power Parity in US Dollars' (PPP $) instead of GDP per capita (PPP $) of past. The *goalpost* taken for minimum income is $100 (PPP) and the maximum is US $87,478 (PPP), estimated for Qatar in 2012. The HDI uses the logarithm of income, to reflect the diminishing importance of income with increasing GNI.

The scores for the three HDI dimension indices are then aggregated into a composite index using geometric mean. The HDI facilitates instructive comparisons of the experiences within and between different countries.

The UNDP ranked[5] the economies in accordance of their achievements on the above-given three parameters on the scale of one (i.e.,

4. UNDP, *Human Development Report, 2013* and *Human Development Report, 2010,* United Nations Development Programme, New York, USA, 2013 and 2010.

5. Todaro and Smith, *Economic Development*, p. 58.

0.000–1.000). As per their achievements the countries were broadly classified into three categories with a range of points on the index:

(i) High Human Development Countries: 0.800–1.000 points on the index.

(ii) Medium Human Development Countries: 0.500–0.799 points on the index.

(iii) Low Human Development Countries: 0.000–0.499 points on the index.

The *Human Development Report 2015* is discussed in Chapter 21 together with India's relative position in the world.

The Debate Continues

Though the UNDP commissioned team had evolved a consensus as to what constitutes development, academicians and experts around the world have been debating this issue. By 1995, economies around the world had officially accepted the concept of human development propounded by the UNDP. Basically, the UNDP designed HDR was used by the World Bank since the 1990s to quantify the developmental efforts of the member countries and cheap developmental funds were allocated in accordance. Naturally, the member countries started emphasising on the parameters of income, education and life expectancy in their policymaking and in this way the idea of HDI got obligatory or voluntary acceptance around the world.

For many years, experts and scholars came up with their own versions of defining development. They gave unequal weightage to the determinants defining development, as well as selected some completely different parameters which could also denote development in a more suitable way. Since quality is a matter of value judgement and a normative concept, there was scope for this representation. Most of such attempts were not prescriptions for an alternative development index, but they were basically trying to show the incompleteness of the HDI, via intellectual satires. One such attempt was made by economists and scholars of the London School of Economics in 1999 which concluded that, Bangladesh was the most developed country in the world with the USA, Norway, Sweden getting the lowest ranks in the index.

Basically, it is very much possible to come out with such an index. As for example, we may say that peace of mind is a necessary element of development and betterment in human life which depends heavily on the fact as to how much sleep we get everyday. House theft and burglary are major determinants of a good night's sleep which in turn depends on the fact as how assured we go to sleep in our homes at night from burglars and thieves. It means we may try to know a good sleep by the data of thefts and burglaries in homes. Since minor house thefts and burglaries are under-reported in police stations, the surveyor, suppose tried to know such cases with data as how many 'locks' were sold in a country in a particular year. In this way a country where people hardly have anything to be stolen or no risk of being burgled might be considered having the best sleep in night, thus the best peace of mind and that is why this will be the most developed country.

Basically, the HDI could be considered as one possible way of measuring development which was evolved by the concerned group of experts with the maximum degree of consensus. But the index which calculates the development of economies on certain parameters might be overlooking many other important factors, which affect the development of an economy and standard of living. As per experts, such other determinants affecting our living conditions might be:

(i) cultural aspects of the economy,

(ii) outlook towards aesthetics and purity of the environment,

(iii) aspects related to the rule and administration in the economy,

(iv) people's idea of happiness and prestige,

(v) ethical dimension of human life, etc.

Introspecting Development [6]

Confusion about the real meaning of development started only after the World Bank and the International Monetary Fund came into being. As experts were studying the development process of the developing world, they were also surveying the performance reports of the developed world. As the western world came to be regarded as developed, having top twenty ranks on the HDI, social scientists started evaluating the conditions of life in these economies. Most of such studies concluded that life in the developed world is anything but happy. Crime, corruption, burglaries, extortion, drug trafficking, flesh trade, rape, homicide, moral degradation, sexual perversion, etc.—all kinds of the so-called vices—were thriving in the developed world. It means development had failed to deliver them happiness, peace of mind, a general well-being and a feeling of being in good state. Scholars started questioning the very efforts being made for development around the world. Most of them have suggested a need of redefining development which could deliver happiness to mankind.

Why has development not delivered happiness to the developed world? The answer to this question does not lie in any one objective fact, but touches so many areas of human life. First, whenever economists from the outset talked about progress they meant overall happiness of human life. Social scientists, somehow have been using terms such as progress, growth, development,

---

6. There were diverse opinions about the real meaning of 'development'—by mid-1940s upto almost the whole 1950s it meant 5–7 per cent growth rate in an economy—even by the IMF and WB. By the late 1960s *new views* of development started emerging. **Arthur Lewis** had seen development in the sense of *human freedom* in 1963 itself when he concluded that "the advantage of economic growth is not that wealth increases happiness, but that it increases the range of human choice." For him development means a freedom from 'servitude'—mankind could be free to have choices to lead a life full of material goods or in spiritual contemplation (W. Arthur Lewis, *The Theory of Economic Growth,* Allen & Unwin, London, 1963, p. 420).

For **Dudley Seers** development meant more employment and equality besides a falling poverty ('The Meaning of Development', a paper presented at the 11th World Conference of the Society for International Development, New Delhi, 1969, p. 3). Dudley Seers was later supported by many other economists such as **Denis Goulet (***The Cruel Choice: A New Concept in the Theory of Development,* Atheneum, New York, 1971, p. 23), Richard Brinkman (1995), P. Jegadish Gandhi (1996) and many others.

The **International Labour Organization** (ILO) had also articulated by the mid-1970s that economic development must be able to deliver the economic ability that people can meet their basic needs (the concept of 'sustenance') besides the elimination of absolute poverty, creating more employment and lessening income inequalities (*Employment, Growth and Basic Needs,* ILO, Geneva, 1976). **Amartya Sen** articulated a similar view via his ideas of 'capabilities' and 'entitlements' ("Development: Which Way Now?", *Economic Journal 93,* December 1983, pp. 754–57).

By 1994, the United Nations looked to including the element of 'capabilities' in its idea of development when it concludes that 'human beings are born with certain potential capabilities and the purpose of development is to create an environment in which all people can expand their capabilities in present times and in future. Wealth is important for human life. But to concentrate exclusively on it is wrong for two reasons. First, accumulating wealth is not necessary for the fulfillment of some important human choices.... Second, human choices extend far beyond economic well-being' *(UNDP, Human Development Report 1994,* Oxford University Press, New York, 1994, pp. 13–15).

The **World Bank** by 1991 had also changed its views about development and had concluded that for improving the *quality of life* we should included education, health, nutrition, less proverty, cleaner environment, equality, greater freedom and richer cultural life as the goals of development.

Amartya Sen, a leading thinker on the meaning of development attracted attention for articulating human goals of development. He opined that enhancing the lives and the freedoms we enjoy, should be the concerns of development known as the 'capabilities' approach to development (see his *Commodities and Capabilities*, North Holland, Amsterdam, 1985 and *Development as Freedom*, Alfred Knopf, New York, 1999).

well-being, welfare as synonyms of *'happiness'*. Happiness is a normative concept as well as a state of mind. Therefore, its idea might vary from one economy to the other.

Second, the period in which development was defined, it was considered that with the supply of some selected material resources human life can be improved. These resources were pin-pointed as, a better level of income, proper level of nutrition, healthcare facilities, proper levels of literacy and education, etc.

Happiness is a broader thing than development. The so-called 'development' for which the world has been striving hard for the last many decades is capable of delivering material happiness to mankind. Happiness has its non-material side also. It means, while the world has been trying to maximise its prospects of development, i.e., material happiness, it could not attend the non-material part of happiness. The non-material part of our life is rooted in ethics, religion, spiritualism and cultural values. As development or human development was defined in material terms, it could only deliver us material happiness which is visibly available in the developed world. Due to partial definition of development, the developed world has been able to achieve development, i.e., happiness, but only of material kind. For the non-material part of happiness, we need to redefine our 'ideas' of development.

Somehow a very small kingdom had been able to define development in its own way, which included material as well as non-material aspects of life and named it the Gross National Happiness (GNH). This country is Bhutan.

Gross National Happiness: Bhutan, a small Himalayan kingdom and an economic non-entity, developed a new concept of assessing development in the early 1970s—the Gross National Happiness (GNH). Without rejecting the idea of human development propounded by UNDP, the kingdom has been officially following the targets set by the GNH. Bhutan has been following the GNH since 1972 which has the following parameters to attain happiness/development:

(i) Higher real per capita income

(ii) Good governance

(iii) Environmental protection

(iv) Cultural promotion (i.e., inculcation of *ethical* and *spiritual* values in life without which, it says, progress may become a curse rather than a blessing)

At the level of real per capita income, the GNH and the HDI are the same. Though the HDI is silent on the issue of 'good governance', today it should be considered as being promoted around the world once the World Bank came with its report on it in 1995 and enforced it upon the member states. On the issue of protecting environment, though the HDI didn't say anything directly, the World Bank and the UNO had already accepted the immediacy of sustainable development by then and by early 1990s there was a seperate UN Convention on the matter (follow up on this convention has been really very low till date which is a different issue).

It means the basic difference between the GNH and the HDI looks at the level of assimilating the ethical and spiritual aspects into our (UNDP's) idea of development.

An impartial analysis sufficiently suggests that material achievements are unable to deliver us happiness devoid of some ethics at its base. And ethics are rooted in the religious and spiritual texts. But the new world is guided by its own scientific and secular interpretation of life and the world has always been suspicious about recognising the spiritual factor in human life. Rather the western idea of secularism was defined after rejecting the very existence of anything like God and also rejecting the whole traditional hypothesis of spiritualism as instances of ignorance and orthodoxy. And there should not be any doubt in accepting it that the western ideology in the name of development has ultimately, dominated the modern world and its way of life. The idea of development which was followed by a large part of the world has been cent per cent 'this-worldly'. And anybody can assess today what kind of happiness the world has been able to achieve in the end.

A recent study by a senior economist from the UNDP on the Bhutanese development experience under the GNH has vindicated the idea of 'gross happiness' which development must result into. As per the study, the period 1984–98 has been spectacular in terms of development with life expectancy increasing by a hopping 19 years, gross school enrolment reaching 72 per cent and literacy touching 47.5 per cent (from just 17 per cent).[7]

After the terror attack on the World Trade Centre in the USA the whole world has gone for a psychic metamorphosis and at least the euphoria of development from this world to that world has been shaken from its very base. The world which is in the process of globalisation at one hand has started introspecting whether multicultural co-existence is possible. The Human Development Report of 2004 was titled as *Cultural Liberty in Today's Diverse World*. We may conclude that mankind is passing through a phase of serious introspection and transition where the dominant view in the world may metamorphose into redefining the very idea of development by including ethical values and spiritualism as important parts. But till now the proponents of development look a bit shy in believing and accepting whole-heartedly that there exists a non-material part of life, which needs to be realised to make our development result into happiness.

---

7. **Stefan Priesner**, a senior economist with the UNDP conducted the study for the John Hopkins University, USA, in 2005.

HAPPINESS

The *World Happiness Report 2017* (WHR 2017) was released on 20th March 2017 (the International Day of Happiness) by the Sustainable Development Solution Network (an UN body). The report is a 155-nation survey, fifth of its kind (the first being in 2012)—is the outcome of coalition of researchers.[8] The report measures happiness and well-being of the nations to help guide public policy on the basis of the following six parameters:

1. GDP per capita (at PPP)
2. Social support (someone to count on)
3. Healthy life expectancy at birth
4. Freedom to make life choices
5. Generosity
6. Perception of corruption

Major highlights of the WHR 2017 are as given below:

- Norway is the happiest nation in the list followed by Denmark, Iceland, Switzerland, Finland, Netherlands, Canada, New Zealand, Australia, Sweden (top ten nations). Top ten countries remained the same as WHR 2016 with minor shuffling.

- Some of the important rankings are— Israel (11th), Costa Rica (12th), Austria

---

8. The WHRs have three editors: **1. John F. Helliwell**, Vancouver School of Economics, University of British Columbia, and the Canadian Institute for Advanced Research (CIFAR); **2. Richard Layard**, Director, Well-Being Programme, Centre for Economic Performance, London School of Economics; **3. Jeffrey D. Sachs**, Director, The Earth Institute, Columbia University. [The reports were written by a group of independent experts acting in their personal capacities—any views expressed in these reports do not necessarily reflect the views of any organisation, agency or programme of the United Nations

(13th), United States (14th), Ireland (15th), Germany (16th), UK (19th) and Brazil (22nd).

- Central African Republic is the last in the list (155th) preceded by Burundi, Tanzania, Syria, Rwanda and Togo.

- India ranks at 122nd (118th)—China 79th (83rd), Bhutan 97th (84th), Pakistan 80th (92nd), Nepal 99th (107th), Bangladesh 110th (110th) and Sri Lanka 120th (117th). Rankings of WHR 2016 are given in the brackets.

- Despite recent declines in oil prices, oil-rich Norway still moved into the top spot (from 4th to 1st rank), illustrating once more that high happiness depends on much more than income.

- In rich countries, the biggest single cause of misery is mental illness.

- The falling American happiness (in the last decade) has been primarily due to social rather than to economic causes.

- This year, the report gave special attention to the social foundations of happiness, including happiness at workplace. Happiness is a result of creating strong social foundations, the report adds for which it is time to build 'social trust' and 'healthy lives', not guns or walls.

- Happiness differs considerably across employment status, job type, and industry sectors. People in well paid roles are happier, but money is only one predictive measure of happiness. work-life balance, job variety and the level of autonomy are other significant drivers.

The efforts of the 'sub-national governments' (for example, by the Madhya Pradesh government in India) in this direction have been praised by the report, as experimentation at local levels are more fruitful—such efforts are being supported by the organizations like *Happiness Research Institute* (Copenhagen) and the *Action for Happiness* (London)—designed to foster and transmit locally-inspired and delivered innovations in the direction. The report suggests the world governments to restructure their public policies to promote 'human well-being'—the foundation of happiness.

The Meaning of Happiness

The word 'happiness' is quite complex and is not used lightly. Happiness is an aspiration of every human being, and can also be a measure of social progress. Yet, are the citizens of different countries, happy? If they are not, what, if anything, can be done about it? The key to proper measurement must begin with the meaning of the word 'happiness'. As per the WHR 2013, the problem, of course, is that happiness is used in at least **two** ways :

(i) As an emotion ['Were you happy yesterday?'], and

(ii) As an evaluation ['Are you happy with your life as a whole?'].

If individuals were to routinely mix up their responses to these very different questions, then measures of happiness might tell us very little. Changes in reported happiness used to track social progress would perhaps reflect little more than transient changes in emotion. Or impoverished persons who express happiness in terms of emotion might inadvertently diminish society's will to fight poverty. Fortunately, respondents to the happiness surveys do not tend to make such confusing mistakes. Both the WHRs did show that the respondents of the surveys clearly recognise the difference between *happiness as an emotion* and *happiness in the sense of life satisfaction*. The responses of individuals to these different questions are highly distinct. A very poor person might report himself to be happy emotionally at a specific time, while also reporting a much lower sense of happiness with life as a whole; and indeed, people living in extreme poverty do express low levels of happiness with life as a whole. Such answers should spur our societies to work harder to end extreme poverty.

The **WHR** is based on the primary measures of subjective well-being;[9] life evaluations;[10] life satisfaction;[11] and happiness with life as a whole.[12] Thus, happiness, appears twice, once as an emotional report, and once as part of a life evaluation, giving considerable evidence about the nature and causes of happiness in both its major senses.

Trends in Happiness

The report presents data for the world showing the levels, explanations, changes and equality of happiness. The world has become a *slightly happier* and *more generous* place over the past five years, despite the obvious detrimental happiness impacts of the financial crisis (2007–08), as per the report. Because of continuing improvements in most supports for better lives in

Sub-Saharan Africa, and of continued convergence in the quality of the social fabric within greater Europe, there has also been some progress toward equality in the distribution of well-being among global regions. There have been important continental crosscurrents within this broader picture. Improvements in quality of life have been particularly notable in Latin America and the Caribbean, while reductions have been the norm in the regions most affected by the financial crisis, Western Europe and other western industrial countries; or by some combination of the financial crisis, and political and social instability, as in the Middle East and North Africa.

The HDR Linkage

The *WHR 2013* investigated the conceptual and empirical relationships between 'human development' (the UNDP idea used in the *Human Development Report*) and 'life evaluation' approaches to understanding human progress. It argues that both approaches were, at least in part, motivated by a desire to consider progress and development in ways that went beyond the mere comparison of GDPs, and to put people at the centre. And while 'human development' is at heart a conceptual approach, and 'life evaluation' an empirical one, there is considerable overlap in practice—many aspects of human development are frequently used as key variables to explain subjective well-being. The two approaches provide complementary lenses which enrich our ability to assess whether life is getting better.

Conclusion

At the end, it may be concluded that there is now a rising worldwide demand that policy be more closely aligned with *what really matters to people* as they themselves characterise their lives. In past few years, more and more world leaders (such as the German Chancellor Angela Merkel, South Korean President Park Geun-hye and British Prime Minister David Cameron) have been

---

9. *Guidelines on Measuring Subjective Well-being*, OECD, Paris, 2013.

10. Used in the *World Values Survey*, the *European Social Survey* and many other national and international surveys. It is the core 'life evaluation' question recommended by the OECD (2013), and used since the first *World Happiness Report*.

11. The *Gallup World Poll (GWP)* – the GWP includes the 'life satisfaction' question on a 0 to 10 scale on an experimental basis, giving a sample sufficiently large to show that when used with consistent samples the two questions provide mutually supportive information on the size and relative importance of the correlates.

12. The *European Social Survey* contains questions about 'happiness with life as a whole', and about life satisfaction, both on the same 0 to 10 numerical scale. The responses provide the scientific base to support the WHR findings that answers to the two questions give consistent (and mutually supportive) information about the correlates of a good life.

talking about the importance of well-being as a guide for their nations and the world. The *World Happiness Report* was published in support of these efforts to bring the study of happiness into public awareness and public policy. This report offers rich evidence that the systematic measurement and analysis of happiness can teach us much about ways to improve the world's well-being and sustainable development. Now it depends on the nations as how they use the findings of the *WHR*.

The Background

In July 2011 the UN General Assembly passed a historic resolution.[13] It invited member countries to measure the happiness of their people and to use this to help guide their public policies. This was followed in April 2012 by the **first** UN high-level meeting on happiness and well-being, chaired by the Prime Minister of Bhutan. At the same time the **first** *World Happiness Report* was published,[14] followed some months later by the OECD Guidelines setting an international standard for the measurement of well-being.[15]

Re-imagining the Idea of Happiness

Search for a 'happier' life for humanity has been the ultimate aim of not only saints, seers and philosophers, but of economists too. The whole gamut of economics literature on progress, growth and development is ultimately aimed at bringing more 'happiness' into the lives of human beings. Over the time, diverse ideological currents impressed upon the humanity to take variety

of 'meanings' out of the highly subjective term 'happiness'—and finally, the humanity is where it is today.

A time also came when many scholars and world leaders raised the ultimate question—are we happier today? And in the wake of this increased 'scrutiny' around the world, there came the UN resolution of 2011 which invited member countries to measure the happiness of their people and to use this to help guide their public policies. The *WHR 2012* itself provides a very interesting and eye-opening inquiry into the state of human happiness in the world. To understand the 'shift' which is expected to take place among policymakers around the world in coming years, it will be better to *lift some ideas* from the **first WHR**:[16]

(i) This is an age of stark contradictions. While at the one hand the world enjoys technologies of unimaginable sophistication, at the other hand, at least one billion people are living without enough to eat. The world economy is propelled to soaring new heights of productivity through ongoing technological and organisational advances; yet it is relentlessly destroying the natural environment in the process. Countries achieve great progress in economic development as conventionally measured; yet along the way countries succumb to new crises of obesity, smoking, diabetes, depression, and other ills of modern life. These contradictions would not come as a shock to the greatest sages of humanity, including **Aristotle** and the **Buddha**, who taught humanity, time and again, that material gain alone will

13. UN General Assembly, *Happiness: Towards a Holistic Approach to Development,* United Nations 19 July 2011.

14. J. F. Helliwell, R. Layard & J. Sachs (eds.), *World Happiness Report 2012,* Earth Institute, New York, USA, 2012.

15. OECD; **Guidelines on Measuring Subjective Well-being,** Organisation for Economic Co-operation and Development, Paris, 2013.

16. J. F. Helliwell, R. Layard and J. Sachs (eds.), *World Happiness Report 2012,* Earth Institute, New York, USA, 2012.

not fulfil our deepest needs. Material life must be harnessed to meet these human needs, most importantly to promote the end of suffering, social justice and the attainment of happiness.

(ii) The *WHR 2012* took key examples from the USA—the world's economic superpower—which has achieved striking economic and technological progress over the past half century without gains in the self-reported happiness of the citizenry with the following serious 'concerns' of today:

(a) uncertainties and anxieties are high,

(b) social and economic inequalities have widened considerably,

(c) social trust is in decline, and

(d) confidence in government is at an all-time low.

Perhaps for these reasons, life satisfaction in the USA has remained nearly constant during the decades of rising Gross National Product (GNP) per capita.

(iii) The realities of poverty, anxiety, environmental degradation, and unhappiness in the midst of great plenty should not be regarded as mere curiosities. They require our urgent attention, and especially so at this juncture in human history. For we have entered a new phase of the world, termed the *Anthropocene*[17] by the world's Earth system scientists. The Anthropocene will necessarily reshape our societies. If we continue mindlessly along the current economic trajectory, we risk undermining the Earth's life support systems—food supplies, clean water and stable climate—necessary for human health and even survival in some places. In years or decades, conditions of life may become dire in several fragile regions of the world. We are already experiencing deterioration of life support systems in the dry lands of the Horn of Africa and parts of Central Asia.

On the other hand, if we act wisely, we can protect the Earth while raising quality of life broadly around the world. We can do this by adopting *lifestyles* and *technologies* that improve **happiness** (or life satisfaction) and reduce human damage to the environment. Sustainable Development is the term given to the combination of human well-being, social inclusion and environmental sustainability. There is no doubt in concluding that the 'quest for happiness' is intimately linked to the 'quest for sustainable development'.

(iv) In an impoverished society, the urge for material gain typically makes a lot of sense. Higher household income (or higher per capita GNP) generally signifies an improvement in the life conditions of the poor. The poor suffer from dire deprivations of various kinds: lack of adequate food supplies, remunerative jobs, access to health care, safe homes, safe water and sanitation, and educational opportunities. As incomes rise from very low levels, human well-being improves. Not surprisingly, the poor report a rising satisfaction with their lives as their meager incomes increase.

---

17. The Anthropocene is a newly invented term that combines two Greek words: 'anthropo' for human; and 'cene' for new, as in a new geological epoch. The Anthropocene is the new epoch in which humanity, through its technological prowess and population of 7 billion, has become the major driver of changes of Earth's physical systems, including the climate, carbon cycle, water cycle, nitrogen cycle and biodiversity.

On the opposite end of the income spectrum, for most individuals in the high-income world, the basic deprivations have been vanquished. There is enough food, shelter, basic amenities (such as clean water and sanitation), and clothing to meet their daily needs. In fact, there is a huge surfeit of amenities above basic needs. Poor people would swap with rich people in a heartbeat. Yet all is not well. *The conditions of affluence have created their own set of traps.*

Most importantly, the lifestyles of the rich imperil the survival of the poor. Human-induced climate change is already hitting the poorest regions and claiming lives and livelihoods. It is telling that in much of the rich world, affluent populations are so separated from the poor that there is little recognition, practical or moral, of the adverse spillovers (or 'externalities') from their own behaviour.

(v) **Affluence** has also created its own set of afflictions and addictions (problems)—obesity, adult-onset diabetes, tobacco-related illnesses, eating disorders such as anorexia and bulimia, psychosocial disorders, and addictions to shopping, TV and gambling, are all examples of disorders of development. So too is the loss of community, the decline of social trust and the rising anxiety levels associated with the vagaries of the modern globalised economy, including the threats of unemployment or episodes of illness not covered by health insurance in the United States (and many other countries).

(vi) Higher average incomes do not necessarily improve average well-being, the US being a clear case in point, as noted famously by Professor Richard Easterlin[18]—where GNP per capita has risen by a factor of three since 1960, while measures of average happiness have remained essentially unchanged over the half-century. The increased US output has caused massive environmental damages, notably through greenhouse gas concentrations and human-induced climate change, without doing much at all to raise the well-being even of Americans. Thus, we don't have a trade off between short-run gains to well-being versus long-run costs to the environment; we have a pure loss to the environment without offsetting short-term gains.

The *paradox* that Easterlin noted in the US was that at any particular time richer individuals are happier than poorer ones, but over time the society did not become happier as it became richer. This is due to *four* reasons:

(a) Individuals compare themselves to others. They are happier when they are higher on the social (or income) ladder. Yet when everybody rises together, relative status remains unchanged.

(b) The gains have not been evenly shared, but have gone disproportionately to those at the top of the income and education distribution.

(c) The other societal factors—insecurity, loss of social trust, declining confidence in government—have

---

18. Among the foremost contributors to the *Happiness Economics*, Easterlin is particularly known for his 1974 article '**Does Economic Growth Improve the Human Lot? Some Empirical Evidence**' (his ideas are today known as the ***Easterlin Paradox,*** was proposed by him in this article). Here he concluded that contrary to expectation, happiness at a national level does not increase with wealth once basic needs are fulfilled.

counteracted any benefits felt from higher incomes.

(d) Individuals may experience an initial jump in happiness when their income rises, but then at least partly return to earlier levels as they *adapt* to their new higher income.

(vii) These phenomena put a clear limit on the extent to which rich countries can become happier through the simple device of *economic growth*. In fact, there are still other general reasons to doubt the formula of ever rising GNP per person as the route to happiness. While higher income may raise happiness to some extent, the *quest* for higher income may actually reduce one's happiness. In other words, it may be nice to have more money, but not so nice to crave for it. **Psychologists** have found repeatedly that individuals who put a high premium on higher incomes generally are less happy and more vulnerable to other psychological ills than individuals who do not crave higher incomes. Aristotle and the Buddha advised humanity to follow a middle path between asceticism on the one side and craving material goods on the other.

(viii) Another problem is the creation of new material '**wants**' through the incessant *advertising* of products using powerful imagery and other means of persuasion. Since the imagery is ubiquitous on all of our digital devices, the stream of advertising is more relentless than ever before. Advertising is now a business of around US $500 billion per year. Its goal is to overcome satiety by *creating wants and longings* where none previously existed. Advertisers and marketers do this in part by preying on psychological weaknesses and unconscious urges.

Cigarettes, caffeine, sugar, and trans-fats, all cause cravings if not outright addictions. Fashions are sold through increasingly explicit sexual imagery. Product lines are generally sold by associating the products with high social status rather than with real needs.

(ix) The thinking of becoming happier by becoming richer is challenged by the law of *diminishing marginal utility of income*[19]—after a certain point, the gains are very small. This means that poor people benefit far more than rich people from an added dollar of income. This is a good reason why tax-and-transfer systems among high-income OECD countries on balance take in net revenues from high-income households and make net transfers to low-income households. Put another way, the inequality of household income is systematically lower with net of taxes and transfers than before taxes and transfers.[20]

(x) The **western economist's** logic of ever higher GNP is built on a vision of humanity completely at variance with the wisdom of the sages, the research of psychologists, and the practices of advertisers. Economists assume that individuals are '**rational decision-**

---

19. Suppose that a poor household at Rs. 1,000 income requires an extra Rs. 100 to raise its life satisfaction level (or happiness) by one notch. A rich household at Rs. 1,000,000 income (one thousand times as much as the poor household) would need one thousand times more money, or Rs. 100,000, to raise its well-being by the same one notch. Gains in income have to be of equal proportions to household income to have the same benefit in units of life satisfaction.

20. On an average across, the OECD countries, cash transfers and income taxes reduce inequality by one third. Poverty is around 60 per cent lower than it would be without taxes and benefits. Even among the working-age population, government redistribution reduces poverty by about 50 per cent (*OECD, 2008*).

makers' who know what they want and how to get it, or to get as close to it as possible, given their budget. Individuals care largely about themselves and derive pleasure mainly through their consumption. The individual's preferences as consumers are a given or change in ways actually anticipated in advance by the individuals themselves. Some economists even say that drug addicts have acted 'rationally', consciously trading off the early benefits of drug use with the later high toll of addiction.

(xi) We understand that we need a very different model of humanity, one in which we experienced complicated interplay of emotions and rational thought, unconscious and conscious decision-making, **fast** and **slow** thinking. Many of our decisions are led by emotions and instincts, and only later rationalised by conscious thought. Our decisions are easily 'primed' by associations, imagery, social context and advertising. We are inconsistent or 'irrational' in sequential choices, failing to meet basic standards of rational consistency. And we are largely unaware of our own mental apparatus, so we easily fall into *traps* and *mistakes*. Addicts do not anticipate their future pain; we spend now and suffer the consequences of bankruptcy later; we break our diets now because we aren't thinking clearly about the consequences. We also understand (again!) that we are **social animals** through and through. We learn through imitation, and gain our happiness through meeting *social norms* and having a sense of *belonging to the community*.

(xii) Human beings feel the pain of others, and react viscerally when others are sad or injured. We even have a set of 'mirror neurons' that enable us to feel things from the point of view of others. All of this gives us a remarkable capacity to **cooperate** even with strangers, and even when there is little chance of reward or reciprocity, and to punish 'non-cooperators', even when imposing punishment on others is costly or puts us at risk.

Of course there are limits to such cooperation and fellow feeling. We also cheat, bluff, deceive, break our word, and kill members of an out-group. We engage in identity politics, acting as cruel to outsiders as we are loving to our own group. All these lessons of human nature matter more than ever, more even than when the Buddha taught humanity about the illusions of transient pleasures, and the Greeks warned us against the tempting Siren songs that could pull us off our life's course. For today we have more choices than ever before. In the ancient world, the choice facing most of humanity most of the time was little choice indeed—to work hard to secure enough to eat, and even then to face the risk of famine and death from bad weather or bad luck.

(xiii) Today, we face a set of real choices. Should the world pursue GNP to the point of environmental ruin, even when incremental gains in GNP are not increasing much (or at all) the happiness of affluent societies? Should we crave for higher personal income at the cost of the community and social trust? Should our governments spend even a tiny fraction of the $500 billion spent on advertising each year to help individuals and families to understand better their own motivations, wants and needs as consumers? Should we consider some parts of our society to be "off bounds" to the profit motive, so that we can foster the **spirit of cooperation**, trust and **community**? A recent analyst[21] of Finland's school system, for example, writes that Finland's excellence (ranking near the top of international comparisons in student performance) has been achieved by fostering a spirit of community and equality in the schools. This is in **sharp contrast** to the education reform strategy at work in the US, where the emphasis is to put on *testing, measurement,* and *teacher pay* according to student test performance.

At the End

The introspecting observations of the *WHR 2012* simply concluded that there are enough reasons to believe that we need to **re-think** the economic sources of well-being, more so even in the rich countries than in the poor ones. High-income countries have largely ended the scources of poverty, hunger and disease. Poor countries rightly yearn to do so. But after the end of poverty, what comes next? What are the pathways to well-being when basic economic needs are no longer the main drivers of social change? What will guide humanity in the Anthropocene: advertising, sustainability, community or something else? What is the path to happiness?

Most people agree that societies should foster happiness of their citizens. The founding fathers of the US recognised the inalienable right to the pursuit of happiness. British philosophers talked about the greatest good for the greatest number. Bhutan has famously adopted the goal of Gross National Happiness (GNH) rather than Gross National Product. China champions a harmonious society. Yet most people probably believe that happiness is in the eye of the beholder,

an individual's choice, something to be pursued individually rather than as a matter of national policy. Happiness seems far too subjective, too vague, to serve as a touchstone for a nation's goals, much less its policy content. That indeed has been the traditional view. Yet the evidence is rapidly changing this view.

A generation of **studies** by psychologists, economists, pollsters, sociologists and others have shown that happiness, though indeed a subjective experience, can be objectively measured, assessed, correlated with observable brain functions, and to the characteristics of an individual and the society. Asking people whether they are happy or satisfied with their lives, offers important information about the society. It can signal underlying crises or hidden strengths. It can suggest the need for change. Such is the idea of the emerging scientific study of happiness, whether of individuals and the choices they make, or of societies and the reports of the citizenry regarding life satisfaction—the *WHR 2012* summarises the fascinating and emerging story of these studies on **two** broad measurements of happiness:

(i) the ups and downs of daily emotions and

(ii) an individual's overall evaluation of life

The former is sometimes called 'affective happiness,' and the latter 'evaluative happiness'.

This is important to know that both kinds of happiness have predictable causes that reflect various facets of our human nature and our social life. *Affective happiness* captures the day-to-day joy of friendship, time with family and sex, or the downsides of long work commutes and sessions with one's boss. *Evaluative happiness* measures very different dimensions of life, those that lead to overall satisfaction or frustration with one's place in society. Higher income, better health of mind and body, and a high degree of trust in one's community ('social capital') all contribute to high life satisfaction; poverty, ill health and deep divisions in the community all contribute to low life satisfaction.

21. Pasi Sahlberg, 'Education Policies for Raising Student Learning: The Finnish Approach; *Journal of Education Policy, 22*(2), March 2007, World Bank, Washington DC, pp. 147–171.

Happiness differs systematically across societies and over time, for reasons that are identifiable, and even alterable through the ways in which public policies are designed and delivered. It makes sense, in other words, to pursue policies to raise the public's happiness as much as it does to raise the public's national income. **Bhutan** is on to something path breaking and deeply insightful. And the world is increasingly taking notice. A household's income counts for life satisfaction, but only in a limited way—other things matter more:

(i) community trust,

(ii) mental and physical health, and

(iii) the quality of governance and rule of law.

Raising income can raise happiness, especially in poor societies, but fostering cooperation and community can do even more, especially in rich societies that have a low marginal utility of income. It is no accident that the happiest countries in the world tend to be high-income countries that also have a high degree of social equality, trust and quality of governance. In recent years, Denmark has been topping the list. And it's no accident that the US has not experienced *rise of life satisfaction for half a century, a period in which inequality has soared, social trust has declined, and the citizens have lost faith in its government.*

It is, of course, one thing to identify the correlates of happiness, and quite another to use **public policies** to bring about a society-wide rise in happiness (or life satisfaction). That is the goal of Bhutan's GNH, and the motivation of an increasing number of governments dedicated to measuring happiness and life satisfaction in a reliable and systematic way over time. The most basic goal is that by measuring happiness across a society over time, countries can avoid '*happiness traps*' such as in the USA in recent decades, where GNP may rise relentlessly while life satisfaction stagnates or even declines.

The idea of GNH in Bhutan tells a story of exploration and progress since its King declared (1972) the goal of happiness over the goal of wealth. For Bhutan happiness became much more than a guidepost or inspiration; it became an organising principle for governance and policymaking as well. The 'GNH Index' is the **first** of its kind in the world, a serious, thoughtful and sustained attempt to measure happiness, and use those measurements to chart the course of public policy. It is believed that in coming years many more countries in the world will be taking clues from Bhutan and the recently published two World Happiness Reports.

INSIGHTS INTO HUMAN BEHAVIOUR

The World Bank in its latest report (*World Development Report 2015: Mind, Society, and Behaviour*) said that development policies become more effective when combined with insights into human behaviour. It further adds that policy decisions informed by **behavioural economics** can deliver impressive improvements in promoting development and well-being in society. It sites some examples from India in the areas of healthcare and education:

- Open defecation dropped 11 per cent from very high levels after a Community-Led Total Sanitation (CLTS) programme was combined in some chosen villages with the standard approach of subsidies for toilet construction and information on the transmission of diseases.

- The likelihood of default on loans became three times less with a simple change in the periodicity of meetings between microfinance clients and their repayment groups to weekly rather than monthly.

- Research showed that boys from backward classes were just as good at solving puzzles as boys from the upper castes when caste identity was not revealed. However, in mixed-caste groups, revealing the boys' castes before puzzle-solving sessions created a significant "caste gap" in achievement with the boys from backward classes underperforming by 23 per cent (making caste salient to the test takers invoked identities, which in turn affected performance, as per the report).

The *Report* has recommended that the presence of a stereotype can contribute to measured ability differences, which in turn reinforce the stereotype and serve as a basis for exclusion, in a vicious cycle—finding ways to break this cycle could increase the well-being of marginalised individuals enormously.

Social Norms, Culture and Development

Economic development is not only dependent on fiscal policy, monetary policy and taxation, but is also rooted in human psychology, sociology, culture and norms. In economics, there has been a bit of resistance in emphasising other aspects of development, because it is thought of giving ground to the neighbouring disciplines.[22] The recent *World Development Report (WDR)* of 2015 focuses on the behavioural and social foundations of development, and has been very well received.

Government documents (generally, hard-nosed), usually, make no mention of the role of social norms and culture in promoting development and economic efficiency. However, there is now a growing body of literature that demonstrates how certain social norms and cultural practices are vital ingredients for economic efficiency and growth. Groups and societies that are known to be honest and trustworthy tend to do better than societies that do not have this reputation. There have been broad cross-country studies and also laboratory experiments that illustrate this. More generally, what is being argued is that a nation's success depends of course on its resources, human capital and economic policies, for instance fiscal and monetary policies, but also on the cultural and social norms that permeate the society. Societies that are endowed with personal integrity and trustworthiness have the natural advantage, in that no third party is required to enforce contracts. For outsiders the mere knowledge that a particular society is trustworthy is reason to do more business and trade with it. One reason why these 'social' causes of development do not get enough recognition in the literature on economic policy is that the science of *how* these economics-friendly social qualities are acquired is not yet fully understood. Fortunately, the new discipline of **behavioural economics** is beginning to give us some insights into the formation of customs and behaviour:[23]

- It is, for instance, known that buildings and office spaces which are cleaner and aesthetically better maintained result in individuals being more honest and desisting corrupt activity. It is almost as if we have a mental inclination not to defile a good ambience through acts of corruption.

- New York city's notorious high crime was controlled, among other things, by cleaning up the city and removing graffiti from the walls. New York's police department took a decision to deter

---

22. Kaushik Basu, Chief Economist, World Bank, *Livemint*, N. Delhi, 3 February, 2015.

23. Ministry of Finance, *Economic Survey 2009–10*, Government of India, N Delhi, pp. 34–35.

vandalism and graffiti that scar public spaces. This act of making the cityscape more aesthetic somehow made potential criminals less prone to crime.

- One sees casual evidence of this in the behaviour of Delhites using the metro. It has been widely noted that people behave better when they travel on Delhi's well-maintained metro (postponing their bad behaviour to when they come up to the surface again, some would add).

All this is in keeping with the influential *broken windows* theory in sociology, which maintains that, if we control low level, anti-social behaviour and take small steps to improve the environment, this will have a natural deterrent effect on larger criminal behaviour and acts of corruption. Also, the sheer recognition and awareness that some collective qualities of citizens, such as honesty and trustworthiness, enable the entire society to do well, prompts individuals to adopt those qualities and overcome the ubiquitous free-rider problem.

There is a growing literature[24] in economics arguing that **pro-social behaviour**, which includes *altruism* and *trustworthiness*, is innate to human beings and, moreover, forms an essential ingredient for the efficient functioning of economies. In other words, human beings have a natural ability to forego personal gains for the sake of other people or because that is what is required because of a promise the person had made. This trait may well have evolutionary roots, but its existence is now well demonstrated in laboratory tests by recent studies.

Values and Economics

There is research[25] in psychology and evolutionary biology which shows that **morality**, **altruism**, and other-regarding **values** are an innate part of the human mind, even though the social setting in which a person lives can nurture or stunt these traits. However, the recognition that these human and moral qualities can have a large impact on economic development came relatively late to economics. Hence, the literature on this is relatively recent and brief. In fact, recent research shows that having a few 'good' human beings in society can give rise to dynamics through which we end up with an overall better society. There is also evidence that social norms and habits that at first sight seem ingrained in a society can change over short periods of time. By this argument it is possible for a country to nurture and develop the kinds of social norms that enable a more vibrant economy.

In talking about a nation's economic progress, all attention, including both praise and criticism, is usually focused on the government. It is, however, important to recognise that much also depends on civil society, the firms, the farmers and ordinary citizens. The social norms and collective beliefs that shape the behaviour of these agents play an important role in how a nation performs.

---

24. Over half a dozen contemporary works have been cited as references by the Ministry of Finance, *Economic Survey 2010–11,* Government of India, N Delhi, p. 40.

25. Several recent literature have been quoted by the *Economic Survey 2011-12*, Ministry of Finance, GoI, N Delhi, p. 44:

 (i) F. Fukuyama, *Trust: The Social Virtues and the Creation of Prosperity*, Free Press, New York, 1996.

 (ii) A. S. Guha, and B. Guha, 'The Persistence of Goodness', *Journal of Institutional and Theoretical Economics,* 2012.

 (iii) M. D. Hauser, *Moral Minds*, Harper Collins, New York, 2012.

 (iv) T. Hashimoto, 'Japanese Clocks and the History of Punctuality in Modern Japan', *East Asian Science, Technology, and Society 2*, 2008.

Honesty, punctuality, the propensity to keep promises, the attitude towards corruption are matters shaped in great part by norms, and social beliefs and the behaviour patterns can become habitual. Moreover, in a democracy like India, what can be done by government depends in great measure on how ordinary people think and what people believe in. That is what electoral politics is all about. An important reason why this got so little attention in the past is because so much of traditional economics was written as if these non-economic facets of life did not matter. But we now know that a market economy cannot function if people are totally self serving. While self-interest is a major driver of economic growth, it is important to recognise that honesty, integrity and trustworthiness constitute the cement that binds society. At times economists treated these social norms, preferences and customs as unalterable. If that were so, there would not be much point in analysing their effect. But we do know that these qualities in a people can change. Honesty and integrity can be nurtured and aversion to corruption can be shored up.

If these traits are absent or inadequate in a nation, it is likely that that nation will stagnate and remain in a chaotic poverty trap. Take for instance, **contracts** which enable markets to develop and form the basis of economic life. If the contractual system in a nation is so weak that when a bank gives a 20-year mortgage to a person for buying a house, there is high risk of default, the implication of this is not that banks in that country will make large losses. The implication is that banks will not give loans; and the housing market will remain severely underdeveloped and the total number of houses will be few and far between.

Enforcing complicated or large contracts, especially ones protracted over a long period of time, is the responsibility of the state. The state provides the laws and enforcement to enable people to sign contracts. However, economic life is full of everyday 'contracts' (for example, you let me ride in your taxi, and I will pay you at the end of it; I pay you money now and you paint my house over the next two days; or you paint my house over the next two days and I will pay you after that). In these everyday situations it is too cumbersome to bring in the state or the law courts. Here the main guarantor has to be the people's personal **integrity** and **trustworthiness**. Societies that have successfully nurtured these qualities have done well; societies that have done poorly on these fronts, tend to do poorly in terms of economic progress.

It is not known precisely how these values can be inculcated in society. But, hopefully, writing about their importance will catalyse change, as ordinary people realise that for *economic* advancement these *social* qualities are as important as policies that concern directly with the economy—like operating the stock market or setting the rules of market competition.

Further, basic literacy and better education are helpful since people can then, on their own, reason and reach these conclusions. Literacy has the added value that it implies ordinary people will demand policies which are truly better, rather than those that merely look good on the surface. In a democratic setting like India, this will incentivise politicians to adopt better policies. Finally, if political leaders and policymakers act as *role models* in terms of these qualities of honesty, integrity and trustworthiness, that can set the ball rolling. Inclusion of the behavioural dimension of human existence in policymaking has potential to play a huge role in promoting well-being.

3

EVOLUTION OF
THE INDIAN ECONOMY

After 1757, when the East India Company took over the governance of Bengal, the British relationship with India became exploitative, as exports to Britain and opium exports to China were financed out of the tax revenue from Bengal. There is not much evidence of significant transfer of European technology to Asia. To understand why, it is useful to scrutinise the experience of China and India, as they accounted for three-quarters of the Asian population and GDP in 1500 AD.*

- ❑ The Background
- ❑ Prime Moving Force: Agriculture vs. Industry
- ❑ Planned and Mixed Economy
- ❑ Emphasis on the Public Sector

* *Angus Maddison,* **Growth and Interaction in the World Economy: The Roots of Modernity,** *The AEI Press, Washington DC, 2005, p. 60.*

THE BACKGROUND

The economic profile of India was in complete distress at the time of Independence. Being a typical case of colonial economy, India was serving a purpose of development not for herself but for a foreign land—the United kingdom. Both agriculture and industry were having structural distortions while the state was playing not even a marginal role. During the half century before India became independent, the world was having accelerated development and expansion in its agriculture and industry on the shoulders of the active role being played by the states, with the same happening in the UK itself.[1]

There was not only the unilateral transfer of investible capital to Britain by the colonial state (the 'drain of wealth'), but the unequal exchange was day by day crippling India's commerce, trade and the thriving handloom industry, too. The colonial state practiced policies which were great impediments in the process of development in the country. Throughout the colonial rule, the economic vision that the state had was to increase India's capacity to export primary products, and increase the purchase/import of the British manufactured goods and raise revenues to meet the drain of capital as well as meet the revenue requirements of the imperial defence.[2]

The social sector was a neglected area for the British rulers which had a negative impact on the production and productivity of the economy. India remained a continent of illiterate peasants under British rule. At the time of Independence, its literacy was only 17 per cent with 32.5 years of life expectancy at birth.[3]

Industrialisation of India was also neglected by the colonisers—the infrastructure was not built to industrialise India but to exploit its raw materials. Indian capitalists who did emerge were highly dependent on British commercial capital and many sectors of the industry were dominated by British firms, e.g., shipping, banking, insurance, coal, plantation crops and jute.[4]

The pre-independence period was altogether a period of near stagnation showing almost no change in the structure of production or in the levels of productivity—the aggregate real output during the first half of the 20th century estimated at less than 2 per cent a year or less.[5]

The overall economic performance of India under the British rule was very low. According to economic statistician Angus Maddison, there was no per capita growth in India from 1600 to 1870—per capita growth was a meagre 0.2 per cent from 1870 to 1947, compared with 1 per cent in the UK.[6] The per capita incomes of Rs. 18 for 1899 and Rs. 39.5 for 1895 in current prices say the true story of the abject poverty Indian masses were faced with.[7] The repeated famines and disease

1. Bipan Chandra, Mridula Mukherjee and Aditya Mukherjee, *India After Independence,* Penguin Books, New Delhi, p. 341.

2. Bipan Chandra, 'The Colonial Legacy' in Bimal Jalan (ed.) *The Indian Economy: Problems and Prospects*, Penguin Books, New Delhi, Revised Edition, 2004, p. 5.

3. B. R. Tomlinson, *The Economy of Modern India 1860–1970,* Cambridge University Press, Cambridge, 1993, p. 7.

4. Angus Maddison, *The World Economy: A Millennial Perspective,* OECD, Paris, 2001, p. 116.

5. A. Vaidyanathan, 'The Indian Economy Since Independence (1947–90)', in Dharma Kumar (ed.), *The Cambridge Economic History of India,* Vol.II, Cambridge University Press, Cambridge, England, Expanded Edition, 2005, p. 947.

6. Angus Maddison, **The World Economy**, p. 116.

7. The respective data of Digby and Atkinson have been quoted by Sumit Sarkar, *Modern India 1885–1947,* Macmillan, New Delhi, 1983, p. 42.

epidemics during the second half of the nineteenth century and the first half of the twentieth century show the greatest socio-economic irresponsibility and neglect of the British government in India at one hand and the wretchedness of the masses at the other.[8]

The political leaders and the industrialists both were very much aware and conscious about the economic inheritance once India became independent. Somehow, these dominant lot of people who were going to lay down the foundation stones of the independent Indian economy were almost having consensual[9] view, even before the Independence, on many major strategic issues:

(i) State/governments should be given a direct responsibility for development.

(ii) An ambitious and vital role to be assigned to the public sector.

(iii) Necessity for the development of heavy industries.

(iv) Discouragement to foreign investment.

(v) The need for economic planning.

Once India became independent, it was a real challenge for the government of the time to go for a systematic organisation of the economy. This was a task full of every kind of challenges and hurdles as the economy had hardly anything optimistic. The need of delivering growth and development was in huge demand in front of the political leadership as the country was riding on the promises and vibes of the nationalist fervour.

---

8. Recounted vividly by Mike Davis in his *Late Victorian Holocaust: El Nino Famines and the Making of the Third World* (Verso, London & New York, 2001, p. 162), where he links the monsoon failures in India to El Nino—Southern Oscillation (ENSO) climate fluctuations in the western Pacific. The monsoon failure leading to drought and hunger one year and then to a severe malaria epidemic the next when the rains reappeared and a burst of mosquito abundance afflicted a weakened population.

9. Bipan Chandra et. al., *India's Struggle for Independence,* p. 15.

It was not a simple task.

Now the decisions which were to be taken by the political leadership of the time were going to shape the very future of India. Many important and strategic decisions were taken only by 1956 which shaped Indian economic journey till date—undoubtedly they heavily dominated the pre-reform period, but the post-reform period is also not completely free of their impact. To understand the nature and scope of the Indian economy in current times it is not only useful but essential to go through the facts, reasons and the delicacies which made the economy evolve and unfold the way it evolved and unfolded. A brief overview follows.

PRIME MOVING FORCE: AGRICULTURE VS. INDUSTRY

A topical issue of the debate regarding India has been the choice for the sector which will lead the process of development. The government of the time opted for industry to be India's prime moving force of the economy. Whether India should have gone for agriculture as its prime moving force for better prospects of development, is a highly debatable issue even today among experts.

Every economy has to go for its development through exploitation of its natural and human resources. There are priorities of objectives set by the economy which is attempted to be realised in a proper time frame. The availability and non-availability of resources (natural as well as human) are not the only issues which make an economy decide whether to opts for agriculture or industry as its prime moving force. There are many more socio-political compulsions and objectives which play their roles in such decision making.

The political leadership selected industry as the leading force of the economy after Independence—this was already decided by the dominant group of the nationalist leaders way back in the mid-1930s when they felt the need for economic planning in India before setting up the National Planning Committee in 1938. Given the available resource base it seems an illogical decision as India lacked all those pre-requisites which could suggest the declaration of industry as its prime mover:

(i) Almost no presence of infrastructure sector, i.e., power, transportation and communication.

(ii) Negligible presence of the infrastructure industries, i.e., iron and steel, cement, coal, crude oil, oil refining and electricity.

(iii) Lack of investible capital—either by the government or the private sector.

(iv) Absence of required technology to support the process of industrialisation and no research and development.

(v) Lack of skilled manpower.

(vi) Absence of entrepreneurship among the people.

(vii) Absence of a market for industrial goods.

(viii) Many other socio-psychological factors which acted as negative forces for the proper industrialisation of the economy.

The obvious choice for India would have been the agriculture sector as the prime moving force of the economy because:

(i) The country was having the natural resource of fertile land which was fit for cultivation.

(ii) Human capital did not require any kind of higher training.

By only organising our land ownership, irrigation and other inputs to agriculture, India could have gone for better prospects of development. Once there was no crises of food, shelter, basic healthcare, etc., to the masses, one goal of development could have been realised—a general welfare of the people. Once the masses were able to achieve a level of purchasing capacity, India could have gone for the expansion

of industries. India was capable of generating as much surplus income for its masses as was required by the emerging industries for a market success. The People's Republic of China did the same in 1949—taking a realistic evaluation of its resources, it declared agriculture as its prime moving force for the economy. The surplus generated out of agriculture was suitably invested to develop the pre-requisites for industrialisation and the country went for it in the 1970s.

The emergence of industrial China was so vibrant that its impact was felt in the so-called highly developed and industrialised economies of the world—the industrial homework of China catapulted it into a giant.

Was the political leadership of independent India not able to analyse the realities as we did above and conclude that agriculture should have been the moving force of the economy in place of industry? Is it possible that Pandit Nehru in command could have missed the rational analysis of the Indian realities, a giant among the Asian visionaries of the time (Mao was still to emerge on the international scene)? How India could have not opted for agriculture as its prime moving force whose leadership had fought the nationalist movement on the Gandhian fervour of villages, agriculture and rural development. Even if Gandhi was not in the government there were many devout Gandhians in it and no one should doubt that the main internal force which vibrated throughout the governmental decisions were nothing but 'Gandhian Socialism'. There were many decisions which were taken under the influence of the main political force of the times, still some very vital ones were influenced by the visionary hunches of the political leadership mainly being J. L. Nehru. This is why the economic thinking of independent India is considered and said to be nurtured by Nehruvian Economics even today. If we go through the major literatures on the Indian economic history, views of the critiques of the time and the contemporary experts, we may be able to feel the answer as to why India went for industry as its prime moving force in place of an obvious and logical choice of agriculture (we should not be happy to know that even today this is a highly debatable issue among experts):

(i) Looking at the resources available, agriculture would have been the obvious choice as the prime moving force (PMF) of the economy (i.e., cultivable land and the humanpower). But as Indian agriculture was using traditional tools and technology its modernisation as well as future mechanisation (later to some extent) would have been blocked due to the lack of indigenous industrial support. If India would have gone for import this would have required enough foreign reserves and a natural dependence on foreign countries. By choosing industry as the prime moving force, India opted to industrialise the economy as well as modernise the traditional mode of farming.

(ii) The dominant ideology around the world as well as in the WB and the IMF was in favour of industrialisation as a means to faster growth, which could be translated into faster development. These international bodies were supporting the member countries from every point of view to industrialise. Same was the case with the developed economies. It was possible not only to industrialise faster on these supports of the organisations but there was a hope for emerging as an industrial exporter in the future. The same kind of support was not offered to an economy that opted for agriculture as the prime moving force. Basically, going for the agriculture sector was considered a symbol of 'backwardness' at that time. The political leadership wanted to carry India ahead, and not in the backward direction. It was only in the 1990s that the world and the WB/IMF changed its opinion regarding the agriculture sector. After the 1990s emphasis on this sector by an economy was no more considered a sign of backwardness.

(iii) The second World War has proved the supremacy of defence power. For defence a country needs not only the support of science and technology, but also an industrial base. India also required a powerful defence base for herself as a deterrent force. By opting for industries as the prime moving force of the economy India tried to solve many challenges simultaneously—first, industry will give faster growth, second, agriculture will be modernised in time and third the economy will be able to develop its own defence against external threats . Since the economy had also opted for scientific and technological preparedness, its achievements were to sustain the pace of modernisation.

(iv) Even before Independence, there was a socio-economic consensus among social scientists along with the nationalist leaders, that India needed a boost towards social change as the country lagged behind in the areas of modernisation. A break from the traditional and outmoded way of life and cultivation of a scientific outlook was a must for the country. Such feelings also made the political leadership of the time go in favour of wholehearted industrialisation.

(v) By the time India got her independence the might of industrialisation was already proven and there were no doubts regarding its efficacy.

Given above are some of the important reasons that worked to make Indian political leadership go in favour of industry as the economy's prime moving force. Probably, the resource related and temperamental realities of India got marginalised in the hope and wish of a future industrialised and developed India. It is yet impossible to conclude whether the economy has completely failed to do so. Experts have divided opinions on this issue.

The last decade of the 20th century (i.e., the decade of the 1990s) saw major changes taking place in the world economic idea about the agriculture sector. It was no more a symbol of backwardness for an economy that emphasises on the agriculture sector as the engine of growth and development. China had proved to the world how agriculture could be made the prime moving force of an economy and generate internal as well as external strength to emerge as an industrial economy. In the wake of the ongoing reform process, India was introspecting almost all economic policies it followed since Independence. It was time for the agriculture sector to have the prime attention. A major shift[10] took place in the Indian economic thinking when the government announced in 2002 that from now onwards, in place of industry, **agriculture will be the prime moving force** of the economy. This was a policy shift of historic importance which was announced by the highest economic think tank of the country—the Planning commission—as the economy commenced the Tenth Plan (2002–07). As per the Planning Commission[11] such a policy shift will solve the three major challenges faced by the economy:

(i) Economy will be able to achieve food security with the increase in agricultural production. Besides, the agricultural surplus will generate exports in the globalising world economy benefiting out of the WTO regime.

(ii) The challenge of poverty alleviation will be solved to a great extent as the emphasis will make agriculture a higher income-generating occupation and induce growth in the rural economy by generating more gainful employment.

(iii) The situation of India as an example of 'market failure' will cease.[12]

Though the world's perception regarding agriculture had changed by the mid-1990s, India recognises the sector as the prime moving force of the economy a bit late, i.e., by 2002. Now, there is a consensus among experts and policymakers regarding the role of agriculture in the Indian economy. Agriculture and allied activities remained the major source of livelihood for nearly half of the Indian population—its share in employment being **48.7** per cent, with **17.4** per cent contribution in the GDP.[13]

Once India started the process of economic reforms, it commenced in the industrial sector—as the economy had got its structure through the

---

10. The Government of India had shown such an intention in two regular Union Budgets (i.e., the fiscals 2000–01 and 2001–02) but has not announced the shift officially.

11. Planning Commission, *Tenth Five Year Plan (2002–07)*, Government of India, New Delhi, 2002.

12. It has been argued by economists time and again that India is a typical example of 'market failure'. Market failure is a situation when there are goods and services in an economy and its requirement too, but due to lack of purchasing power the requirements of the people are not translated into demand. Whatever industrial goods and services India had been able to produce they had stagnated or stunted sales in the market as the largest section of the consumers earned their livelihood from the agriculture sector, which is unable to create a purchasing power to the levels required by the market. As agricultural activities will become more gainful and profitable, the masses depending on it will have the level of purchasing capacity to purchase the industrial goods and services from the market. Thus, the Indian market won't fail. The view has been articulated by Amartya Sen and Jean Dreze in their monograph titled *India: Economic Development and Social Opportunity*, United Nations University, 1996.

13. Ministry of Finance, **Economic Survey 2015–16**, Government of India, Vol. 2, p. 98.

successive industrial policies, it looks a normal thing. To the extent the agriculture sector is concerned reforms were initiated a bit late—better say by early 2000s. Three *major reasons* may be cited for this delay:

(i) Agriculture being always open for the private sector, it was now difficult to go for further privatisation for encouraging investments. The need was for 'corporate' and 'contract' farming under the leadership of the *corporate world*.

(ii) Lack of awareness about the contours of the economic reforms among the farm community.

(iii) The heavy dependency of population on agriculture for livelihood could not permit the government to go for the right kind of agricultural reforms at the right time—first, the industrial sector (via manufacturing) needed expansion to lessen the population dependency on the agriculture sector.

Any one sector in which the governments at the Centre and states have been facing the biggest hurdles has been the farm sector. The major reform needs and the hurdles being faced may be summed up in the following points:

(i) A *national agri-market* is the need of the hour, but there lacks a political will among the majority of states to put in place a right kind of Agricultural Produce Market Committees.

(ii) The need of promoting *corporate investment* in the farm sector is hurdled by the lack of an effective and transparent land acquisition law.

(iii) *Labour reforms* needs fine-tuning to promote industrial farming, which is hurdled by a long tradition of complex kind of labour laws of the country.

(iv) *Farm mechanisation* is hindered by the lack of investment in industries.

(vi) *Research and development* needs huge investment from the private sector, but there lacks a conducive atmosphere for it.

(vii) Right kind of *'downstream and upstream requirements'* together with a proper kind of *'supply chain management'* is bsent in the area of agri-goods.

(viii) Expansion of the right kind of *commodity trading* in—agri commodities.

(ix) Strengthening the farm sector to face the competition posed by the agricultural sector of the developed world, with regard subsidies and prices, in wake of the globalising world economy.

(x) Making farming *remunerative* to check farm crisis of contemporary times.

Experts believe that for taking the right policy steps in the sector there needs a high degree of federal maturity in the country. Increased awareness among farmers together with the right government support to prevent farm distress will serve the purpose in a great way.

PLANNED AND MIXED ECONOMY

Independent India was declared to be a planned and a mixed economy. India needed national planning, which was decided by the political leadership almost a decade before Independence.[14] India was not only facing regional disparities at the level of resources, but inter-regional disparities were also prevalent, since centuries. Mass poverty could

---

14. **National Planning Committee,** GoI, N. Delhi, 1949.

only be remedied once the government started the process of economic planning. Economic planning was thus considered an established tool of doing away with such disparities.

Basically, it was the abject poverty of the masses which made the government go for planning so that it could play an active role in the allocation of resources and mobilise them for equitable growth and development. Though India was constitutionally declared a federation of states, in the process of planning, the authority of regulation, directing and undertaking economic activities got more and more centralised in the Union government.[15]

India's decision for a planned economy was also moulded by some contemporary experiences in the world.[16] *firstly,* the Great Depression of 1929 and the reconstruction challenges after the second world War had made experts to conclude in favour of a state intervention in the economy (opposite to the contemporary idea of 'non-interference' as proposed by Adam Smith). *Secondly,* it was the same time that the command economies (i.e., state economies) of the soviet Union and the East European countries started making news about their faster economic growth. In the 1950s and 1960s, the dominant view among policymakers around the world was in favour of an active role of the state in the economy. *Thirdly,* a dominant role for the state in the economy to neutralise market failure situations (as happened during the period of the Great Depression when demand fell down to the lowest levels) was gaining ground around the world. For many newly independent developing nations, economic planning was therefore an obvious choice. Economic planning was considered to help states to mobilise resources to realise the prioritised objectives in a well-defined time frame.

Once the political leadership had decided in favour of a planned economy for India and a major role for the state in the economy, they needed to clarify about the organisational nature of the economy—whether it was to be a state economy or a mixed economy—because planning was not possible in a free market economy (i.e., capitalistic economy). The idea of planning in India was inspired from the soviet planning which was a command economy and did not suit the requirements of democratic India, which was till now a privately owned economy.[17] The dominant force behind planning in India, at least after Independence, was Nehru himself who had strong socialist leanings. He thought it important to define the role of the state in the economy, which was going to be at times similar to the state in the soviet Union and at times completely dissimilar to it. Though there was an example of a capitalistic-democratic system going for planning, France by that time (1947), it had little experience to offer the Indian policymakers (France had gone for a mixed economy by 1944–45). With the basic urge to accelerate the process of economic growth, the planners went to define the respective roles of the state and the market, in the very first Plan itself. The following lines look refreshingly ahead of the times and crystal-clear about the scope of the government's role in the economy vis-á-vis the private sector.

"This brings us to the problem of the techniques of planning. A possible approach to the problem is, as mentioned earlier, through a more or less complete nationalisation of the means of production and extensive system of government controls on the

15. Bimal Jalan, *India's Economic Policy,* Penguin Books, New Delhi, 1993, p. 2.

16. C. Rangarajan, *Perspectives on Indian Economy,* UBSPD, New Delhi, 2004, p. 96.

17. Rakesh Mohan, 'Industrial Policy and Control' in Bimal Jalan (ed.), *The Indian Economy: Problems and Prospects,* p. 101.

allocation of resources and on the distribution of the national product. Judged purely as a technique of planning, this may appear a promising line of action. But, viewed against the background of the objectives outlined above, and in the light of practical considerations, such an expansion of the public sector is, at the present stage, neither necessary nor desirable. Planning in a democratic set-up implies the minimum use of compulsion or coercion for bringing about a realignment of productive forces. The resources available to the public sector have, at this stage, to be utilised for investment along new lines rather than in acquisition of existing productive capacity. Public ownership of the means of production may be necessary in certain cases; public regulation and control in certain others. The private sector has, however, to continue to play an important part in production as well as in distribution. Planning under recent conditions thus means, in practice, an economy guided and directed by the state and operated partly through direct state action and partly through private initiative and effort."[18] the above-quoted lines are imaginatively ahead of the times. It will be suitable to note here that as 1950s and 1960s made the world experts favour state intervention in the economy, the *East Asian Miracle*[19] of the coming three decades was going to define the very limits of such an intervention. The East Asian economies were able to sustain a high growth rate over three decades and had revived again the discussions regarding the respective roles of the state and the market as well as the nature of the state's role in the economy. The kind of conclusions drawn were very similar to the view presented in India's First Plan itself which was presented by the World Bank in 1993.

The real nature of the Indian brand of mixed economy, though beautifully outlined in 1951

itself, went through a process of detailed evolution in the decade of the 1950s.[20] By the end of the 1950s, the concept of the mixed economy was almost buried and rose from hibernation only by mid-1980s and finally early in 1990s, in the wake of the process of economic reforms.

We see the government modifying the process of planning and functions of the Planning Commission in wake of the reform process—an attempt to redefine the roles of government and private sector in the economy. In a sense, India was increasingly getting more dependent on the latter for the promotion of growth and development.

By early 2015, we saw some major changes taking place in the area of planning in India. The Government replaced the existing body, *Planning Commission,* with the *NITI Aayog* (a new economic 'Think Tank'), with the aim of 'overhauling' the very process and method of planning in the country. This move is believed to originate out of India's experiences of development planning spanning over six decades. Co-operative federalism, bottom-up approach, holistic and inclusive development with the need of an Indian model of development are some of the hallmarks of the new design. The move is also seen in light of the changed needs of the economy.

EMPHASIS ON THE PUBLIC SECTOR

The state was to be given an active and dominant role in the economy, it was very much decided by the time India became independent. There were no doubts about it in the minds of the people who formed the dominant political force at the time. Naturally, there was going to be a giant structure of the government-controlled enterprises to be known as the public sector undertakings (PSUs). Criticism aside, there were at that time, a strong logic behind the glorification of PSUs. Some of the

18. Planning Commission, *The First Five Year Plan: A Draft Outline,* GoI, New Delhi, 1951.

19. *The East Asian Miracle,* World Bank, Washington D.C, 1993.

20. We see the process of evolution specially in the industrial policies, India pursued since 1948 to 1956.

reasons for heavy investments in the PSUs were purely natural while others were consequential in nature. There were certain highly commendable objectives set for them, some other goals would go on to serve the very soul of the mixed economy. We must go for an impartial and rational analysis of the matter, in the midst of all the criticism of PSUs and the contemporary moves of privatising them, to understand their roles in the Indian economy. We may understand the reasons behind the ambitious expansion of the PSUs in the face of the following major requirements.

1. Infrastructural Needs

Every economy whether it is agrarian, industrial or post-industrial, needs suitable levels of infrastructure such as power, transportation and communication. Without their healthy presence and expansion, no economy can grow and develop.

At the eve of Independence, India was having almost no presence of these three basic requirements. There was just a beginning in the area of railways, and post and telegraph. Power was restricted to selective homes of government and the princely states. [It means, even if India had opted for agriculture as its prime moving force, it had to develop the infrastructure sector.]

These sectors require too much capital investment as well as heavy enginering and technological support for their development. Expansion of the infrastructure sector was considered not possible by the private sector of the time as they could possibly not manage the following components:

(i) heavy investment (in domestic as well as foreign currencies),

(ii) technology,

(iii) skilled manpower, and

(iv) entrepreneurship.

Even if these inputs were available to the private sector, it was not feasible for them as there was no market for such infrastructure. These infrastructures were essential for the economy, but they needed either subsidised or almost free supply as the masses lacked the market-determined purchasing capacity. Under these typical condition, it was only the government which could have shouldered the responsibility. The government could have managed not only the inputs required for the development of the sector, but could also supply and distribute them to the needy areas and the consumers for the proper growth of the economy. There were no alternatives and that is why the infrastructure sector in India has such a dominant state presence that many areas have obvious government monopolies—as in power, railways, aviation, telecommnication, etc.

2. Industrial Needs

India had opted for the industrial sector as its prime moving force, as we saw in the earlier pages. Now there were some areas of industries which the government had to invest in, due to several compulsive reasons. For industrialisation and its success, every economy needs the healthy presence of some 'basic industries', which are also known as the 'infrastructure industries'.[21] There are six basic industries which every industrialising economy requires, namely—

(i) Iron and Steel

(ii) Cement

(iii) Coal

(iv) Crude oil

(v) Oil refining and

(vi) Electricity

[Note: At present, there are eight Core Industries in India (with the Base: 2004–05=100), six existing 'basic/infrastructure industries' with two new additions, i.e., Natural Gas and Fertilizer. Core industries together have a combined weight

---

21. 'Infrastructure sector' and 'infrastructure industries' are quite different things.

of 37.90 per cent in the Index of Industrial Production (IIP). Individual percentages of them are: Coal (weight: 4.38 per cent); Crude Oil (weight: 5.22 per cent); Natural Gas (weight: 1.71 per cent); Petroleum refinery (weight: 5.94 per cent); Fertilizer (weight: 1.25 per cent); Steel (weight: 6.68 per cent); Cement (weight: 2.41 per cent); and Electricity (weight: 10.32 per cent).]

Similar to the infrastructure sector, these basic industries also require high level of capital, technology, skilled manpower and articulation in entrepreneurship which was again considered not feasible for the private sector of the time to manage. Even if the private sector supplied goods from the 'basic industries', they might not be able to sell their products in the market due to the lower purchasing power of the consumers. Perhaps, that is why again the responsibility of developing the basic industries was taken up by the government.

Out of the six basic industries, the cement industry had some strength in the private sector, while in the iron and steel industry a lone private company was present. The coal industry was controlled by the private sector and crude oil and refining was just a beginning by then. The level of demands of an industrialising India was never to be met by the existing strength of the basic industries. Neither the required level of expansion in them was possible by the existing number of private players. With no choice left, the government decided to play the main role in industrialising the country. In many of them we as a result, see a natural monopoly for the PSUs, again.

3. Employment Generation

The PSUs were also seen as an important part of the employment generation strategy. A government in a democratic set up cannot think only economics, but it has to realise the socio-political dimensions of the nation too. The country was faced with the serious problem of poverty and the workforce was increasing at a fast rate. Giving employment to

the poor people is a time-tested tool of poverty alleviation. The PSUs were thought to create enough jobs for the employable workforce of the economy.

There was also felt an immediacy for a social change in the country. The poverty of a greater section of the country was somehow connected to the age-old caste system which propitiated the stronghold of the upper castes on the ownership of land, which was the only means of income and livelihood for almost above 80 per cent of the population. Along with the ambitious policy of land reforms, the government decided to provide reservations to the weaker sections of the society in government jobs. The upcoming PSUs were supposed to put such jobs at the disposal of the goverment which could have been distributed along the decided reservation policy—such reservations were considered an economic tool for social change.

In the highly capital-intensive sectors in which the government companies were going to enter, managing investible funds to set them up was not going to be an easy task. The government did manage the funds with sources like taxation, internal and external borrowing and even taking last refuge in the printing of fresh currencies. The government went to justify the high taxation and heavy public indebtness in supplying employment to the Indian employable population.

The PSUs were considered by the government as the focus of the 'trickle-down effect'. The government did everything to set up and run the PSUs as the benefits were supposed to percolate to the masses, finally reinforcing growth and development in the country. Employment in the PSUs was seen as the effort of the trickle down theory, simply said. At a point of time, Nehru even mentioned the PSUs as the 'temples of modern India'. The government went to commit even a job in every household via the PSUs—without calculating the dimensions of the future labour force in the country and the required resources to create jobs at such a high scale. But the government went on creating new PSUs without analysing the fiscal repercussions—moreover believing them to be the real engine of equitable growth. The employment generation responsibility of the PSUs was extended to such an extent by the government that most of them had over-supply of the labour force which started draining its profits on account of salaries, wages, pensions and provident funds (the latter two had late financial impact).

4. Profit and Development of the Social Sector

The investment to be made by the government in PSUs was in the nature of asset creation and these entities were to be involved in production activities. It was natural for the government to gain control over the profits and dividends accruing from them. The goods and services the PSUs produced and sold provided disposable income to the government. The government had a conscious policy of spending the income generated by the PSUs. They were to be used in the supply of the 'social goods' or what is called the 'public goods'. And thus, India was to have a developed social sector. by social goods the government meant the universal supply of certain goods and services to the citizen. These included education, healthcare, nutrition, drinking water, social security, etc., in India. It means that the PSUs were also visioned as the revenue generators for the development of the social sector. Due to many reasons the PSUs would not be able to generate as much profit as was required for the healthy development of the social sector. This eventually hampered the availability of public goods in the country. In place of giving profits back to the government, a large number of the PSUs started incurring huge losses and required budgetary support at regularly.

5. Rise of the Private Sector

As the PSUs took the responsibility of supplying the infrastructure and the basic industries to the economy, a base for the rise of private sector industries was slowly established. With the rise of private sector industries in the country, the process of industrialisation was thought to be completed. Out of the many roles the PSUs were supposed to play, this was the most far-sighted. What happened to the different roles the PSUs were assigned is a totally different matter, to which we will return while discussing the industrial scenario of the country. Here we have analysed why the government of India after Independence went for such an ambitious plan of expansion of the public sector.

Besides, the PSUs were aimed at many other connected areas of developmental concerns, such as, self-sufficiency in production, balanced regional development, spread of small and ancillary industries, low and stable prices, and long-term equilibrium in balance of payment. Over time the PSUs have played a critical role in promoting the growth and development of the country.[22]

By the mid-1980s, there emerged a kind of consensus across the world (including the IMF & World Bank) regarding the inefficiency and under-performance of the PSUs (in the wake of the idea of the Washington Consensus which is said to promote 'neo-liberal' economic policies across the world). In the wake of it, there commenced a process of privatisation and disinvestment of the PSUs among majority of

22. Sumit Bose and Sharat Kumar, 'Public-sector Enterprises', in Kaushik Basu and Annemie Maertens (eds.), *The New Oxford Companion to Economics in India,* Vol. II, Oxford University Press, New Delhi, 2012, p. 578–83.

the economies in the world—India being no exception to it. By late 1990s, new studies proved that under-performance and inefficiency could be there in the private sector companies, too. By mid-2000s (in the wake of the US *sub-prime crisis*) a new consensus emerged among the international organisations that state/government need not exit the economy and a kind of slow down towards privatisation moves of the PSUs across the world (the world in a sense is pushing the 'pause' button on neo-liberalism) is under process.

India pursued a less ambitious disinvestment policy from 2003–04 to 2015–16 (the government has decided to own controlling shares among the divested PSUs). Since 2016–17 financial year, the government has decided to restart the process of 'strategic disinvestment' (in which the ownership of the PSUs may also be transferred to the private sector). Such a policy of disinvestment was launched by the government in 2000 which was paused by the UPA-I in 2003–04). The government has also decided in favour of selling increased shares of the PSUs to the foreign institutions, at par with the domestic financial institutions. Such policy moves of the recent times should be seen in the light of certain important contemporary realities—need of promoting investment in the economy; need of the government to quit undesirable areas of economic activities and expanding in the areas of need and where private sector will not enter (welfare actions); revenue generation by stake sale and enhanced profit from the PSUs (by selling majority stakes in the PSUs at one hand the government will de-burden itself from the owner's responsibility, while on the other hand its share of revenue from the divested PSUs will increase as the new owner will run the enterprise on market principles); etc.

4

ECONOMIC PLANNING

The idea of planning and a planned society is accepted now in varying degrees by almost everyone. But planning by itself has little meaning and need not necessarily lead to good results. Everything depends on the objectives of the plan and on the controlling authority, as well as, of course, the government behind it.*

* New Jawaharlal Nehru, **The Discovery of India**, *Oxford University Press, 6th Impression (1st Edition 1946, Oxford, London), N. Delhi, 1994, p. 501.*

INTRODUCTION

In order not to limit the discussion on economic planning to just an academic exercise, we need to discuss it taking real life examples from different economies. Without a historical background to planning, we would not be able to understand the meaning and role of planning in India. This small chapter intends to introduce the reader to all the **whats, hows** and **whys** of the concept of economic planning with due recourse to the experiments by different countries from time to time, including India. It could also be considered a theoretical backgrounder for the next chapter, *Planning in India.*

DEFINITION

A number of definitions have been forwarded by different economists from time to time since the term 'planning' entered the domain of economics. To make us develop a clear understanding of planning, we need to see only a few of them which will enable us to draw out a working definition that fits contemporary time.

A large number of economists and experts have agreed that perhaps the best definition is given by H. D. Dickinson, according to whom, economic planning is, "the making of major economic decisions—what and how much is to be produced and to whom it is to be allocated by the conscious decision of a determinate authority, on the basis of a comprehensive survey of the economic system as a whole."

It was the National Planning Committee, set up in 1938 by the Indian National Congress which, for the first time, tried to define planning (in 1940, though, its final report was published in 1949) in India. It could be considered the broadest possible definition of planning: "Planning, under a democratic system, may be defined as the technical coordination, by disinterested experts of consumption, production, investment, trade, and income distribution, in accordance with social objectives set by bodies representative of the nation. Such planning is not only to be considered from the point of view of economics, and raising of the standard of living, but must include cultural and spiritual values, and the human side of life."[1]

By the late 1930s, there was an almost political consensus that independent India will be a planned economy. As India commenced economic planning by the early 1950s, the planning commission of India also went on to define planning. According to the Planning Commission, "Planning involves the acceptance of a clearly defined system of objectives in terms of which to frame overall policies. It also involves the formation of a strategy for promoting the realisation of ends defined. Planning is essentially an attempt at working out a rational solution of problems, an attempt to coordinate means and ends; it is thus different from the traditional hit-and-miss methods by which reforms and reconstruction are often undertaken".[2]

In the post-War period, a large number of the newly independent countries were attracted towards planning. Many new forces of change kept refining the very idea of planning due to the compulsive necessities of industrialisation or the issue of sustainability of the development process. But to carry forward our discussion, we need a working as well as a contemporary definition of planning. We may define it as *a process of realising well-defined goals by optimum utilisation of the available resources.*[3] While doing economic planning the government sets developmental

---

1. S. R. Maheshwari, *A Dictionary of Public Administration,* Orient Longman, New Delhi, 2002, p. 371.

2. Planning Commission, *First Five Year Plan (1951–56),* Government of India, New Delhi, 1991, p. 7.

3. After the emergence of the concept of **Sustainable Development** (1987) experts across the world started using the term 'optimum' in place of the hitherto used term 'maximum'.

objectives and attempts to deliberately coordinate the economic decision making over a longer period to influence, direct and in some cases even to control the level and growth of a nation's main economic variables (i.e., income, consumption, employment, saving, investment, exports, imports, etc.).[4]

An economic plan is simply a set of specific economic targets to be achieved in a given period of time with a stated strategy. Economic plans may be either comprehensive or partial. A **comprehensive plan** sets targets to cover all major aspects of the economy, while a **partial plan** may go for setting such targets for a part of the economy (i.e., agriculture, industry, public sector, etc.). Taken broadly, the planning process itself can be described as an exercise in which a government first chooses social objectives, then sets various targets (i.e., economic targets), and finally organises a framework for implementing, coordinating and monitoring the development plan.[5]

One very important thing which should be clear to all is that the idea of planning first emerged in its applied form and after studying and surveying the experiences of different countries which followed it, experts started theorising about planning. Thus, in the case of planning, the direction has been from practice to theory. This is why the form and the nature of planning kept changing from country to country and from time to time. As we will see in the following pages, the types of planning itself evolved through time as different countries experimented with it.

As per our working definition, we may say the following things about planning:

(i) **Planning is a process.** It means planning is a process of doing something. Till we have some goals and objectives left regarding our lives, the process might continue. With the changing nature of our needs, the nature and scope of the planning process might undergo several changes. Planning is not an end in itself. As processes accelerate and decelerate, change direction and course, so also does planning.

(ii) **Planning must have well-defined goals.** After the Second World War, several countries went for development planning. As these nations had enormous socio-economic hurdles, they first set some goals and objectives and then started their process of realising them via planning. In due course of time, there emerged a consensus that planning must have some goals and those goals should be well-defined (not vaguely defined)—so that the government's discretionary intervention in the economic organisation could be democratically transparent and justified. Even in the non-democratic nations (i.e., erstwhile USSR, Poland, China, etc.) the goals of planning were clearly defined.[6]

(iii) **Optimum utilisation of the available resources.** Here we see two catch concepts. *First,* is the way of utilising the resources. Till the idea of sustainability emerged (1987) experts tried to 'maximise' the resource exploitation. But once experts around the world introspected the untenability of such a method of resource utilisation, the sustainable approach was included into planning and here in entered the idea of utilising resources at its 'possible best', so that environmental

4. Michael P. Todaro, **Development Planning: Models and Methods.** Oxford University Press, Nairobi, 1971.

5. United Nations Department of Economic Affairs, **Measures for Economic Development of Underdeveloped Countries,** UNO, DEA, New York, 1951, p. 63.

6. The Gosplan, **First Five Year Plan (1928–33),** USSR, 1928.

degradation could be at its minimum and the future generations could also be able to continue with their progress. *Second* is the idea of the natural resources which are available. Resources (i.e., natural as well as human) could be of indigenous origin or exogenous. Most of the countries doing planning tried to utilise their indigenous resources, yet some tried to tap the exogenous resources too, taking leverage of their diplomatic acumen. For example, the first country going for national planning, i.e., Soviet Union, leveraged resources available in the East European countries. India also used exogenous resources for her development planning wherever it was necessary and possible to tap.[7]

By the 1950s, planning had emerged as a method or tool of utilising resources to achieve any kind of goals for policymakers, around the world:

(i) Trying to achieve a particular size of family for different countries came to be known as *family planning*.

(ii) The process of providing suitable physical and social infrastructure for the erstwhile or the upcoming urban areas came to be known as *town/urban planning*.

(iii) A country trying to optimise the use of its revenues for different categories of expenditures came to be known as *financial planning*. Financial planning is more popularly known as *budgeting*. Every budget, be it of the government or of the private sector is nothing but an excercises in financial planning.

(iv) Similarly, at the macro and micro levels, there might be any number of planning processes—agricultural planning, industrial planning, irrigation planning, road planning, house planning, etc.

Simply said, the art of achieving any kind of goal by the use of the resources we have is the process of planning. We may cite a very general example—students of a class are able to join the class at the right time coming from different places of their stay. How they are able to do so? All of them must be planning their time in such a way that they are able to join the class at the same time though their places of residence are not at an equal distance from the class. All might be having their own ways of time planning—some might be having bed-tea, some might not, some might be having breakfast at their place, yet others might think to take their breakfast in the college canteen, etc.

It means that even if we are not consciously planning or have not announced it as yet, we are always planning our days. Same is correct in the case of countries. Many countries announced that they will be planned economies, yet some others didn't go for any such policy announcements. The soviet Union, Poland, China, France, India are examples of the former category while the USA, Canada, Mexico fall in the latter category.[8] But here we are concerned with the conscious process of planning. There will be some methods, some tools and types of planning emerging through time as different countries will start their processes of planning.

ORIGIN AND EXPANSION OF PLANNING

Planning as a method of achieving faster economic progress. It has been tried by different countries at

---

7. Many of the PSUs in the 1950s and the early 1960s were not only set up with natural resources (capital as well as machines) from USSR, Germany, etc., but even the human resource was also tapped from there for few years.

8. Though the USA was the first to go for planning, but at the regional level (Tennessee Valley Authority, 1916)—it never announced its intention for national planning.

different times and at different levels. We may see them as under:

1. Regional Planning

It was at the regional level that planning was used as a part of development policy by any country for the *first time*. It was the USA which started the first regional planning after the Tennessee Valley Authority (TVA) was set up in 1916—for a large-scale rehabilitation in south-eastern USA covering parts of seven states. With the primary aim of flood control, soil conservation and providing electricity, the TVA/the regional plan was also involved in many related activities such as industrial development, forestry, wildlife conservation, town planning, construction of road and rail, encouraging sound agricultural practices and malaria control in the defined region.[9] The US experience of regional planning became such a success in realising its well-defined goals that it emerged as a role model and an object of inspiration for many countries around the world in the coming decades—the Damodar Valley Corporation (DVC) in India (1948), the Volta River Project in Ghana (1966), etc.

2. National Planning

The official experiment in the area of national planning is rooted in the Bolshevik Revolution of Russia (1917)—the Soviet Union. Dissatisfied with the pace of industrialisation, it was in 1928 that Joseph Stalin announced its policy of central planning for the Soviet Union. The collectivisation of agriculture and forced-draft industrialisation were other radical new policy initiatives announced by Stalin besides economic planning in 1928.[10] The Soviet Union went for its first five year plan for the period 1928–33 and the world was to have its *first* experience of *national planning*. The famous Soviet slogan "great leap forward" was initiated for rapid industrialisation through the introduction of economic planning at the national level. The nature and scope of Soviet planning (called **the Gosplan**) will have its direct or indirect bearings on all those countries which went for economic planning, be state or capitalist or mixed economies. India was to have direct influence of Soviet planning on its planning process. In the first Soviet Plan, heavy industries was favoured over light industry, and consumer goods were the residual sector after all the other priorities had been met. We see the same emphasis in the Indian planning process.[11] The Soviet model of economic planning spread to the East European countries, especially after World War II and found its purest form of such planning in the People's Republic of China (1949). During the early 1940s, the concept of national planning was borrowed by France and the world saw national planning being initiated by a hitherto capitalist economy as well as by a non-centralised political system (i.e., democratic system). France started economic planning at the national level after announcing itself as a mixed economy.

TYPES OF PLANNING

After the first national planning was started by the Soviet Union, many more countries followed it, but with variations in their methods and practices. Though there are many variants of planning the

9. Leong, G.C. and Morgan, G.C., *Human and Economic Geography*, Oxford University Press, Oxford, 1982, p. 145.

10. Alec Nove, *An Economic History of the USSR*, 3rd ed., Penguin Books, Baltimore, USA, 1990, p. 139.

11. Rakesh Mohan 'Industrial Policy and Controls' in the Bimal Jalan (eds), *The Indian Economy: Problems and Prospects*, Penguin Books, New Delhi, 2004., p. 101. Also see Bipan Chandra et. al., *India After Independence*, Penguin Books, New Delhi, 2000, pp. 341–42, as well as A. Vaidyanathan, 'The Indian Economy Since Independence (1947–70)' in Dharma kumar (ed.), *The Cambridge Economic History of India*, Vol. II, Cambridge University Press, Cambridge, 1983, pp. 949–50.

most important one is on the basis of the type of economic organisation (i.e., state economy, mixed economy). During the course of evolution, planning has been classified into two types, based upon the type of economic system prevalent in the country.

1. Imperative Planning

The planning process followed by the state economies (i.e., the socialist or communist) is known as the imperative planning. Such planning is also called as *directive* or *target planning.* Such planning had two main variants. In the socialist system, all economic decisions were centralised in the hands of the state with collective ownership of resources (except labour). In the communist system (i.e., China of the past) all resources were to be owned and utilised by the state (including labour). Thus, communist China was the purest example of such planning. In the case of the Soviet Union a little bit of 'market' did exist—even after the collectivisation of agriculture was enacted by Stalin in 1928 only 94 per cent of Soviet peasants could be included in the process.[12] Basic features of such planning are as under:

(i) *Numerical (i.e., quantitative) targets* of growth and development are set by the plan. As for example, five lakh tonnes of steel, two lakh tonnes of cement, 10,000 kms of national highways, 5,000 primary schools, etc., will be produced/built in the coming 5 or 6 years.

(ii) As the *state* controls the ownership rights over the resources, it is very much possible to realise the above-cited planned targets.

(iii) almost *no role for the market*, no price mechanism with all economic decisions to be taken in the centralised way by the state/government.

(iv) no private participation in the economy, only the state plays the economic role.

The *Command Economies* followed this kind of planning. That is why such economies are also known as the *Centrally Planned Economies*—the USSR, Poland, Hungary, Austria, Romania, etc., and finally China. Basically, it was the migration of some of the great economists from the Soviet Bloc countries to Britain and the USA that a proper study and discussion started on the very nature and purpose of planning in the command economies. Many of these economists went back to their countries of origin after the Second World War to serve and in some measure, suffer the revolution there.[13] It was their articulate and contemporary economic thinking which formed the basis for the idea of mixed economy in the post-War world. One among them was Oskar Lange, the famous Polish economist, who after returning home to serve as the Chairman of the Polish State Economic Council (as India has the Planning Commission) suggested and coined the concept of *'market socialism'* in the 1950s. His ideas of market socialism were cancelled by not only Poland but also by other state economies of the time.[14]

---

12. Samuelson, P. A. and Nordhaus, W. D, *Economics,* McGraw-Hill Companies Inc., N. York, 2005., p. 591.

13. From Poland two great economists Oskar Lange (1904–65) and Michal Kalecki (1899–1970); from Hungary, William J. Fellner (1905–83), Nicholas Kaldor (1908–86), Thomas Balogh (1905–85) and Eric Roll (1907–95); from post-war Austria Ludwig von Mises (1880–1973), Friedrich A. von Hayek (1899–1992), Fritz Machlup (1902–83), Gottfried Haberler (1900–96) and Joseph A. Schumpeter (1883–1950) [J.K. Galbraith, *A History of Economics,* Penguin Books, London, 1987, pp. 187–90].

14. It was blasphemous to preach in favour of market in the socialist world at that time—he was not put behind the bars was a great mercy on him. Oskar Lange towards the end of his life told Paul M. Sweezy, the most noted American Marxist scholar, that during this period he did not retire for the night without speculating as to whether he might be arrested before the dawn (J.K. Galbraith, *A History of Economics,* p. 189).

The peak of this type of planning was reached in China after the Cultural Revolution (1966–69), which led to an economic slowdown in the country, which had adopted a soviet-style central planning system after 1949. Under Deng Xiaoping (1977–97), China decentralised a great deal of economic power with its announcement of the open door policy in 1985 to save the economy. The Chinese **open door policy** was an initiative in the direction of 'market socialism' under the communist political design (a popular student demand for political reform in favour of democracy was ruthlessly repressed in Tiananmen Square in 1989). Similarly, the Soviet Union under the leadership of Mikhail Gorbachev began a process of political and economic reforms, called **prestroika** (i.e., restructuring) and **glasnost** (i.e., openness) in 1985 to save the failed economic experiments in the state economy. Other East European economies followed similar economic reforms from 1989 onwards. Thus, the whole world of the state economies had moved towards market economy by the late 1980s. Since then none of the countries have followed imperative planning.

2. Indicative Planning

In the following two decades after the soviet planning commenced, the idea of planning got attention from the democratic world. A time came when some such economies started national planning. As they were neither state economies nor communist/socialist political systems, the nature of their planning was different from the command economies. Such planning has been termed as indicative planning by economists and experts. The identifying features of indicative planning may be summed up as under:

(i) every economy following the indicative planning were mixed economies.

(ii) unlike a centrally planned economy (countries following imperative planning) indicative planning works through the market (price system) rather than replaces it.[15]

(iii) side by side setting numerical/quantitative targets (similar to the practice in the imperative planning) a set of economic policies of indicative nature is also announced by the economies to realise the plan targets.

(iv) the indicative nature of economic policies, which are announced in such planning, basically encourage or discourage the private sector in its process of economic decision making.

After converting to a mixed economy by the mid-1940s, France commenced its first six year plan in 1947, which got popularity as the **Monnet Plan** (he was the first chairman of the General Planning Commission and the then Cabinet Minister for planning in France).[16] Later, Monnet Plan became synonymous with indicative planning. This plan is also sometimes described as the *basic sector planning* as the government had selected eight basic industries as the core of development in which the nature of planning was almost *imperative*, i.e., under state monopoly (these sectors were owned by the private sector till 1944 when France went for their nationalisation).[17] Other economic activities were open for private participation for which indicative kind of policy-planning was essential. France as well as Japan have followed indicative planning with great success. It was in 1965 that the UK commenced such a planning with the National

15. **Collins Internet-linked Dictionary of Economics**, Glasgow, 2006.
16. George Albert Steiner, **Government's Role in Economic Life,** McGraw-Hill, New York, 1953, p. 152.
17. India had a French influence on its development planning when it followed almost state monopoly in the six infrastructure industries also known as the **core** or the **basic** industries, i.e., cement, iron and steel, coal, crude oil, oil refinery and electricity.

Plan and abandoned in 1966 after being overtaken by events (a balance of payment crisis resulting in a deflationary package of measures). Since then the UK never went for planning.[18]

Though the first use of economic planning as an instrument of economic progress was done by the USA (with the Tennessee Valley Authority in 1916 at the regional level), it never went for a *formal* national planning. In the 1940s, some economists had suggested in favour of the use of national planning. We may have a reflex of indicative planning in the USA if we look at the *Presidential Reports* which come after regular intervals. These reports are just 'benchmarks' in the area of resource utilisation and governmental announcements of its objectives—basically trying to motivate the private sector towards the area of public objectives. The indicative planning as it is practised by the mixed economy, any growth target could only be achieved once the public and the private enterprises worked in tandem. This is why besides the plan targets, the governments need to announce some set of indicative policies to encourage and motivate the private sector to accelerate their economic activities in the direction of the plan targets.

After the Second World War, almost all the newly independent countries adopted the route of planned development. Though they followed an overall model of the indicative planning, many of them had serious inclination towards imperative planning. As in the case of India, the heavy bias towards imperative planning could only be reformed once the process of economic reforms was started in 1991.

Today, as there are mostly only mixed economies around the world, any country's

development planning has to be only of the indicative type. After the revival of the role and the need of market in promoting growth and development via the Washington Consensus (1985), the World Trade Organisation (1995) and the Santiago/New Consensus (1998) only indicative planning has remained possible with the state playing only a marginal role in the economy, especially in the areas of social importance (i.e., nutrition, healthcare, drinking water, education, social security, etc.).

There are still many **other types** of planning depending upon the point of view we are looking at. For example, from the territorial point of view, planning could be *regional* or *national.* From the political point of view planning could be *central, state* or *local.* Similarly, from the participatory point of view, planning has been categorised into *centralised* and *decentralised.* Again, from the temporal point of view planning could be *long-term* or *short-term* (in relative sense). Finally, from the value point of view planning could be *economic* or *developmental.*

A major classification of planning is done on the basis of societal emphasis. The type of planning which gives less emphasis upon the social and institutional dimensions is known as *systems planning.* In such planning, the planners just search for the best possible results in relation to the established goals giving less importance to issues like caste, creed, religion, region, language, marriage, family, etc. Opposed to it, the *normative planning* gives due importance to the socio-institutional factors. This is a planning from social-technical point of view, but only suitable for a country which has lesser degree of social diversities (naturally, not fit for the Indian conditions). But in the coming years there was a shift in the very thinking of policymakers. The *Economic Survey 2010–11* is probably the first document of the Government of India which advocates the need for a *normative approach* to planning in India. It is believed that until a

18. Though the planning agencies the National Economic Development Council (NEDC) and the Economic Development Committees (EDCs) continued functioning, it was in 1992 that the NEDC was abolished (*Collins Dictionary of Economics,* 2006).

programme/scheme run by the governments are not able to connect with the customs, traditions and ethos of the population, their acceptability will not be of the desired level among the target population. Establishing an empathic relationship between the programmes/schemes and target population is now considered an important aspect of planning and policymaking. Such a change in the thinking is based on the experiences of India and other countries of the world.

In January 2015, the Government of India replaced the erstwhile body, Planning Commission, by the *NYTI Aayog* (a policy *think tank*). If we look into the functions and guiding principles of the new body we come to know that India has officially moved towards **normative planning**— the new body has to follow a *development model* which is 'all round, all pervasive, all inclusive and holistic'. In this process the NITI Aayog has been further asked to enable the country to draw on the vitality and energy of the bedrock of our *ethos, culture* and *sustenance*.

The ***Economic Survey 2015–16*** points out how the government has come to recognise the importance of influencing *social norms* in a wide variety of sectors, such as:

(i) persuading the rich to give up subsidies they do not need,

(ii) reducing social prejudices against girls,

(iii) educating people about the health externalities of open defecation, and

(v) encouraging citizens to keep public spaces clean.

Today, governments all over the world have embarked on systematic ways of studying how to promote *behavioural change*. The importance and need of behavioural change were highlighted by the *World Development Report 2015* (World Bank), too. All such policy interventions are examples of **normative** policymaking.

Economic planning is classified into more types—***sectoral*** and ***spatial.*** In sectoral planning, the planners emphasise the specific sector of the economy, i.e., agriculture, industry or the services. In spatial planning development is seen in the spatial framework. The spatial dimensions of development might be defined by the pressure and requirements of national economic development. Indian planning has been essentially —single level economic planning with a greater reliance on the sectoral approach though the multi-level regional and normative dimensions are being increasingly emphasised since the early 1990s.

CHAPTER 5

PLANNING IN INDIA

> *For the first eight Plans the emphasis was on a growing public sector with massive investments in basic and heavy industries, but since the launch of the Ninth Plan in 1997, the emphasis on the public sector has become less pronounced and the current thinking on planning in the country, in general, is that it should increasingly be of an indicative nature.**

* Montek S. Ahluwalia addressing the inaugurating of the Seminar on 'India's Economic Reforms' at Merton College, Oxford University, London, June 1993.

INTRODUCTION

It was the Soviet Union which explored and adopted *national planning* for the first time in the world. After a prolonged period of debate and discussion, the First Soviet Plan commenced in 1928 for a period of five years. But the world outside was not fully aware of the modus operandi of development planning till the 1930s. It was the exodus[1] of the east European economists to Britain and the United States in the 1920s and 1930s that made the world aware as to what economic/national planning was all about. The whole lot of colonial world and the democracies of the time were fascinated by the idea of planning as an instrument of economic progress. The nationalist leaders with socialistic inclination of the erstwhile British colonies were more influenced by the idea of economic planning. The whole decade of the 1930s is the period in the Indian history when we see nationalists, capitalists, socialists, democrats and academicians advocating for the need of economic planning in India at one point or the other.[2]

Independent India was thus destined to be a planned economy. The economic history of India is nothing but the history of planning.[3] Even if the so-called economic reforms started in 1991–92, all the humble suggestions regarding the contours of reforms were very much outlined by the Planning Commission by then.[4] Once the reforms commenced, the think tank started outlining the major future direction for further plans.[5] Going through the history of planning in India is a highly educational trip in itself—for though the Planning Commission has been a political body, it never hesitated in pointing out good economics time and again. Let us therefore look into the unfolding of the planning process in India.

BACKGROUND

By the decade of the 1930s, the idea of planning had already entered the domain of intellectual and political discussion in India. Many fresh proposals suggesting immediacy of planning in India were put forward, though the erstwhile British government remained almost immune to them. But these humble proposals of planning served their purpose once India became independent and decided to adopt a planned economy.

The Visvesvaraya Plan

The credit of proposing the first blueprint of Indian planning is given to the popular civil engineer and the ex-Dewan of the Mysore state, M. Visvesvaraya. In his book *The Planned Economy of India*, published in 1934, he outlined the broad confours of his plan proposal.[6] His ideas of state planning were an exercise in democratic capitalism (similar to the USA) with emphasis on industrialisation—a shift of labour from agricultural to industries, targeting to double the national income in one decade. Though there was

1. J.K. Galbraith, *A History of Economics,* (London: Penguin Books 199), p. 187.

2. Bipan Chandra, 'The Colonial Legacy', in Bimal Jalan (ed.), *The Indian Economy: Problems and Prospects,* (New Delhi: Penguin books, 2004).

3. Arjun Sengupta, 'The planning Regime since 1951' in N.N. Vohra and Sabyasachi Bhattacharya (eds), *Looking Back: India in the Twentieth Century* (New Delhi: National Book Trust, 2001), p. 121.

4. Planning Commission, *Seventh Five Year Plan (1985–90),* (New Delhi: Government of India), 1985.

5. Planning Commission, *The 8th, 9th, 10th and 11th Plans,* New Delhi: Government of India.

6. Sumit Sarkar, *Modern India: 1855–1947,* (New Delhi: Macmillan, 1983), pp. 360–361.

no follow up by the British government on this plan, it aroused an urge for national planning among the educated citizens of the country.

The FICCI Proposal

In 1934, a serious need of national planning was recommended by the Federation of Indian Chambers of Commerce and Industry (FICCI), the leading organisation of Indian capitalists. Its President N.R. Sarkar proclaimed that the days of undiluted laissez-faire were gone forever and for a backward country like India, a comprehensive plan for economic development covering the whole gamut of economic activities was a necessity. Voicing the views of the capitalist class, he further called for a high powered 'National Planning Commission' to coordinate the whole process of planning so that the country could make a structural break with the past and achieve its full growth potential.[7]

By the late nineteenth century, the economic thinking of the nationalists (such as M.G. Ranade and Dadabhai Naroji) was in favour of a dominant role of the state in the economy and doubted the prudence of the 'market mechanism'. This thinking was further reinforced by the Keynesian ideas in the wake of the Great Depression, the *New Deal* in the USA and the Soviet experiment in national planning. Thus, the Indian capitalist class were also influenced by these events which were voiced in the FICCI articulation for planning.

The Congress Plan

Though the Gandhians and some of the business and propertied representatives were opposed to commit the party to centralised state planning (including Mahatma Gandhi),[8] it was on the

initiative[9] of the INC president Subhash C. Bose that the National Planning Committee (NPC) was set up in October 1938 under the chairmanship of J. L. Nehru to work out concrete programmes for development encompassing all major areas of the economy. Basically, the NPC was set up in a conference of the Ministers of Industries of the Congress-ruled States (though other states were also invited to participate) where M. Visvesvaraya, J.R.D. Tata, G.D. Birla and Lala Sri Ram and many others including academicians, technocrats, provincial civil servants, trade unionists, socialists and communists, etc., were also invited. The 15-member NPC with 29 sub-committees and a total of 350 members produced 29 volumes of recommendations.[10] The work of the committee was interrupted when the Second World War broke out and in the wake of the Quit India Movement many of its members including the chairman were arrested, and between 1940 and 1945 the Committee had only a nominal existence. Though the final report of the NPC could only be published in 1949, many developments related to planning took place during the Interim Government upto 1946.

"A series of valuable reports were published which brought together the constructive thinking done by the committee and the sub-committees and the materials collected in the course of their work. The importance of the NPC lies not so much in these reports as in the wide interest it created throughout the country for co-ordinated planning as the only means of bringing about a rapid increase in the standards of living and its emphasis on the need for bringing fundamental changes in the social and economic structure."[11]

Some of the important developments after the NPC was set up which prepared a foundation for

---

7. Bipan Chandra etal., *India After Independence, 1947–2000,* (New Delhi: Penguin Books, 2000), p. 341.

8. A. Vaidyanathan. 'The Indian Economy Since Independence (1947–70)', in Dharma Kumar (ed), *The Cambridge Economic History of India,* Vol.II, (Cambridge: Cambridge University Press, 1983), p. 949.

9. Sumit Sarkar, *Modern India,* p. 360.

10. Publications Division, *The Gazetteer of India,* Vol.3, (New Delhi: Government of India, 1975), p. 2.

11. *Ibid.,* pp. 2–3.

coordinated planning in Independent India are given below:

(i) ***Post War Reconstruction Committee:*** Early in June 1941, the Government of India formed (on popular demand) a Post-War Reconstruction Committee which was to consider various plans for the reconstruction of the economy.[12]

(ii) ***Consultative Committee of Economists:*** A consultative committee of economists under the chairmanship of Ramaswamy Mudaliar was set up in 1941 as a 'think tank' to advise the four Post-War Reconstruction Committees for executing national plan for the country.

Though the committee suggested many plans for different areas of the economy, they had negligible practical significance as these suggestions were imbued with academic biases.

(iii) ***Planning and Development Department:*** After all possible delays, it was in 1944 that the government created a Planning and Development Department under a separate member of the Viceroy's Executive Council for organising and co-ordinating economic planning in the country. Ardeshir Dalal (the controller of the Bombay Plan) was appointed as one of its acting members. More than 20 panels of experts were set up. The central departments and the governments of the Provinces and Indian states were invited to prepare detailed plans for industrialisation.[12] This Department was abolished in 1946.

(iv) ***Advisory Planning Board:*** In October 1946, the Government of India appointed a committee called the 'Advisory Planning Board'[13] to review the planning that had already been done by the British government, the work of the National Planning Committee, and other plans and proposals for planning and to make recommendations regarding the future machinery of planning and also in regard to objectives and priorities. The Board strongly recommended the creation of "a single, compact authoritative organisation ... responsible directly to the Cabinet ... which should devote its attention continuously to the whole field of development."[14] This was an emphatic advice for the creation of a National Planning Commission, similar to FICCI's view of 1934, which will have autonomy and authoritative say on the process of development planning, working in tandem with the Union Cabinet and also influencing the developmental decisions of the states. This happened in 1950 with the setting up of the Planning Commission.

The Board, in its Report of January 1947, emphatically expressed the opinion that the "proper development of large-scale industries can only take place if political units, whether in the provinces or states, agree to work in accordance with a common plan."[15] This suggestion worked as a great influence on the planning process of Independent India as it always tried to give

---

12. There was a popular view in favour of rapid industrialisation among the important nationalists, economists and the business class of that time.

13. The Board was set up by the Interim Government formed in 1946.

14. Dharma Kumar (ed.), *The Cambridge Economic History of India,* Vol.II, p. 950.

15. Kalikinkar Datta, *An Advanced History of India,* 4th Edition (New Delhi: Macmillan, 2006), pp. 955–56.

unifying nature to development planning. But, this process also induced a serious tendency of centralisation in the Indian planning to which a number of states were to pose objections and straining the centre-state relations, time and again.[16] However, the political leadership, right from the 1920s, was very conscious of the need for decentralised planning in the country.[17]

The Bombay Plan

The Bombay Plan was the popular title of 'A Plan of Economic Development for India', which was prepared by a cross-section of India's leading capitalists. The eight capitalists involved in this plan were Purshotamdas Thakurdas, J.R.D. Tata, G.D. Birla, Lala Sri Ram, Kasturbhai Lalbhai, A.D. Shroff, Avdeshir Dalal and John Mathai.[18] The Plan was published in 1944–45. Out of these eight industrialists, Purshotamdas Thakurdas was one among the 15 members of the National Planning Committee (1938);[19] J.R.D. Tata, G.D. Birla and Lala Sri Ram, were members of the sub-committees (29 in total) of the National Planning Committee.[20]

The popular sentiments regarding the need of planning and criss-cross of memberships between the NPC and the Bombay Plan club made possible some clear-cut agreements between these two major plans, which ultimately went to mould the very shape of the Indian economy after

Independence. We may have a look at some of the very important agreements:[21]

(i) A basic agreement on the issue of the *agrarian restructuring*—abolition of all intermediaries (i.e., zamindari abolition), minimum wages, guarantee of minimum or fair prices for agricultural products, cooperatives, credit and marketing supports.

(ii) Agreement on *rapid industrialisation* for which both the plans agreed upon an emphasis on heavy capital goods and basic industries (the Bombay Plan had allocated 35 per cent of its total plan outlay on basic industries).

(iii) Taking clues from the Soviet Planning, the NPC and the Bombay Plan both were in favour of a simultaneous *development of the essential consumer goods* industries, but as a low-key affair.

(iv) Both the plans agreed upon the importance of promoting the *medium-scale, small-scale* and *cottage industries* as they could provide greater employment and require lesser capital and lower order of plants and machineries.

(v) Both the plans wanted the *state to play an active role* in the economy through planning, controlling and overseeing the different areas of the economy, i.e., trade, industry and banking, through state ownership (public sector) or through direct and extensive control over them.

(vi) Large-scale measures for *social welfare* were favoured by both the plans, which suggested to be based on issues like, right to work and full employment, the guarantee of a minimum wage, greater state expenditure on housing, water

16. S.N. Jha and P.C. Mathur (eds), *Decentralisation and Local Politics,* (New Delhi: Sage Publications, 2002), pp. 28–30.

17. A. H. Hanson, *The Process of Planning: A Study of India's Five-Year Plans, 1950–1964* (london: Oxford University Press, 1966), pp. 152–55.

18. Bipan Chandra, 'The Colonial Legacy', p. 23.

19. Partha Chatterjee, 'Development Planning and the Indian Planning', in Partha Chatterjee (ed.), *State and Politics in India* (New Delhi: Oxford University Press, 1997), p. 273.

20. Rakesh Mohan, 'Industrial Policy and Contorls', in Bimal Jalan (ed.), *Indian Economy: Problems and Prospects* (New Delhi: Penguin Books, 1994).

21. Bipan Chandra, 'The Colonial Legacy', pp. 23–31.

and sanitation, free education, social insurance to cover unemployment and sickness and provision of utility services such as electricity and transportation at a low cost through state subsidies.

(vii) Both the plans agreed upon a planning which could do away with gross *inequalities.* Through measures like progressive taxation and prevention of concentration of wealth. Inequality was considered undesirable as it tended to restrict the domestic market.

The Gandhian Plan

Espousing the spirit of the Gandhian economic thinking, Sriman Narayan Agarwal formulated The Gaudhian Plan in 1944. The plan laid more emphasis on agriculture. Even if he referred to industrialisation, it was to the level of promoting cottage and village-level industries, unlike the NPC and the Bombay Plan which supported a leading role for the heavy and large industries. The plan articulated a 'decentralised economic structure' for India with 'self-contained villages'.

It needs to be noted here that the Gandhians did not agree with the views of the NPC or the Bombay Plan, particularly on issues like centralised planning, dominant role of the state in the economy and the emphasis on industrialisation being the major ones.[22] For Gandhi, the machinery, commercialisation and centralised state power were the curses of modern civilisation, thrust upon the Indian people by European colonialism. It was industrialism itself, Gandhi argued, rather than the inability to industrialise, which was the root cause of Indian poverty. This was until the 1940s that the Congress supported the above-given view of Gandhi to mobilise a mass movement against the colonial rule. But

it was in the NPC that the Congress tried to articulate a different view on these issues, almost taking a break from Gandhi's ideas. The very first session of the NPC was brought to an impasse by J.C. Kumarappa (the lone Gandhian on the 15-member NPC) by questioning the authority of the NPC to discuss plans for industrialisation. He said on the occassion that the national priority as adopted by the Congress was to restrict and eliminate modern industrialism. The impasse was normalised after Nehru intervened and declared that most members of the NPC felt that large-scale industry ought to be promoted as long as it did not 'come into conflict with the cottage industries'.[23] This was a long-drawn ideological impasse which made it necessary to articulate the Gandhian view of planning via this plan.

The People's Plan

In 1945, yet another plan was formulated by the radical humanist leader M.N. Roy, Chairman of the Post-War Reconstruction Committee of Indian Trade Union. The plan was based on Marxist socialism and advocated the need of providing the people with the 'basic necessities of life'.[24] Agricultural and industrial sectors, both were equally highlighted by the plan. Many economists have attributed the socialist leanings in Indian planning to this plan. The common minimum programmes of the United Front Government of the mid-nineties (20th century) and that of the United Progressive Alliance of 2004 may also be thought to have been inspired from the same plan. 'Economic reforms with the human face', the slogan with which the economic reforms started in the early 1990s also has the resonance of the People's Plan.

---

22. Dharma Kumar, ***The Cambridge Economic History of India***, p. 949.

23. Partha Chatterjee, 'Development Planning and the Indian Planning', p. 275.

24. S.K. Ray, ***Indian Economy*** (New Delhi: Prentice Hall, 1987), p. 369.

The Sarvodaya Plan

After the reports of the NPC were published and the government was set to go for the five-year plans, a lone blueprint for the planned development of India was formulated by the famous socialist leader Jayaprakash Narayan—the Sarvodaya Plan published in January 1950. The plan drew its major inspirations from the Gandhian techniques of constructive works by the community and trusteeship as well as the Sarvodaya concept of Acharya Vinoba Bave, the eminent Gandhian constructive worker. Major ideas of the plan were highly similar to the Gandhian Plan like emphasis on agriculture, agri-based small and cottage industries, self-reliance and almost no dependence on foreign capital and technology, land reforms, self-dependent villages and decentralised participatory form of planning and economic progress, to name the major ones.[25] Some of the acceptable ideas of the plan got their due importance when the Government of India promoted five year plans.

By the early 1960s, Jayaprakash Narayan had become highly critical of the Indian planning process, especially of its increasing centralising nature and dilution of people's participation in it. Basically, the very idea of democratic decentralisation was disliked by the established power structure, namely, the MLAs/MPs, the bureaucracy and the state-level politicians.[26] This led the Jayaprakash Narayan Committee (1961) to decide against the centralising nature of Indian planning. The committee pointed out that after having accepted Panchayati Raj as the agency responsible for planning and execution of plans, there is "no longer any valid reason for continuing

the individual allocations subjectwise even to serve as a guide."[27]

Disregarding the humble advice of the committee, central schemes like small farmers development agency (SFDA), drought-prone area programme (DPAP), intensive tribal development programme (ITDP), intensive agricultural district programme (IADP), etc., were introduced by the government and were put totally outside the purview of the Panchayats.

It was only after the 73rd and 74th Amendments effected to the Constitution (1992) that the role of local bodies and their importance in the process of planned development was accepted and the views of Jayprakash got vindicated.

Some Area-wise Reports

The idea for the need of a planned development of India became more and more popular by the decade of the 1940s. It was under this popular pressure that the Government of India started taking some planned actions in this direction. In the 1940s, we see several area-specific reports being published:[28]

(i) Gadgil Report on Rural Credit

(ii) Kheragat Report on Agricultural Development

(iii) Krishnamachari Report on Agricultural Prices

(iv) Saraiya Report on Cooperatives

(v) A series of reports on Irrigation (ground water, canal, etc.)

All these reports, though prepared with great care and due scholarship, the government had hardly any zeal to implement the plans on their findings. But independent India was greatly benefited when the planning started covering all these areas of concern.

25. A.H. Hanson, *The Process of Planning*, p. 175.

26. George Mathew, ***Power to the People,*** in M.K. Santhanam (ed.), ***50 Years of Indian Republic*** (New Delhi: Publications Division, Government of India, 200), p. 32.

27. L.C. Jain, et al., ***Grass Without Roots*** (New Delhi: Sage Publications, 1985).

28. A. H. Hanson, ***The Process of Planning,*** p. 180.

There is no doubt in drawing the conclusion that prior to Independence, there was thus a significant measure of agreement in India between the Government of India under the Secretary of State, the Indian National Congress, prominent industrialists and the others on the following principles:[29]

(i) There should be central planning, in which the state should play an active part, for social and economic development to bring about a rapid rise in the standard of living;

(ii) There should be controls and licencing in order, among other things, to direct investments into the desired channels and ensure equitable distribution;

(iii) While there should be balanced development in all sectors of the economy, the establishment of basic industries was specially important. In this, state-owned and state-managed enterprises have an important role to play. There were, however, differences of approach with regard to the specific fields to be allocated to the public and private sectors.

It is highly interesting and important to note that all the above agreements and opinions were reached through an evolutionary manner in the last two-decades before Independence in the deliberations and excercises regarding the need for economic planning in the country.

"The plans prepared by the Governmnt of India, the Bombay Plan and other above-discussed plans (except the NPC and the Sarvodaya Plan) suffered from serious limitations. When they were prepared, it was known that transfer of power was to take place quite soon; but the exact form of the future government was not known, the plans consisted largely of proposals of experts, which were not effectively co-ordinated. They had no social philosophy behind them. With the advent of Independence, they became inadequate, though the thinking that had taken place on planning generally and its techniques proved useful for the future."[30]

MAJOR OBJECTIVES OF PLANNING

Planning for India was an instrument to realise the aspirations and dreams of the future. We know that the foundations of future India were not laid in one day. The cherished dream about future India had evolved through a long-drawn process of the entire period of the freedom struggle. These aspirations and goals got their proper places and due importance in the reports of the National Planning Committee (NPC), in the deliberations of the Constituent Assembly and finally in the Constitution of India. From the margins of the ripening nationalist movement, as well as taking clues from the Soviet and the French styles of planning, the NPC articulated the objectives of planning in India. The process of planning in India tried to include all the aspirations of the nationalist movement as well as of the future generations. But this will be a highly general comment upon the objectives of planning in India. We need to delve into the specific and objective goals of planning in India to further our discussions. Some of the historic deliberations regarding planning will serve our purpose:

(i) Reviewing the entire situation, in the light of the social philosophy evolved over decades, the Constituent Assembly came to the conclusion that to guide this 'revolution of rising expectations' into constructive channels, India should make determined efforts through carefully planned large-scale social and economic development and the application of modern scientific and technological improvements, to bring about a rapid and

29. Publications Division, *The Gazatteir of India,* p. 5.

30. Ibid., p. 5.

appreciable rise in the standard of living of the people, with the maximum measure of social justice attainable. On the whole it was a call for India becoming a welfare state.[31] This important deliberation does not only call for the necessity of planning for the country, but it also outlines the broader objectives of planning.

(ii) There are three important features included in the constitutional provisions, which pertain to the objectives of planning in the country:[32]

(a) 'Economic and social planning' is a concurrent subject. Also, while framing the 'Union', 'State' and 'Concurrent' lists, allocating subjects and other provisions, the Constitution vests power in the Union to ensure co-ordinated development in essential fields of activity, while preserving the initiative and authority of the states in the spheres allotted to them.

(b) The Constitution includes provisions for promoting cooperation on a voluntary basis between the Union and the states and among states and groups of states in investigation of matters of common interest, in legislative procedures and in administration, thus avoiding the rigidities inherent in federal constitutions (Articles 249, 252, 257, 258, 258-A, and 312). In other words, the objective is cooperative federalism.

(c) The Constitution also sets out in broad outline the pattern of the welfare state envisaged and the fundamental principles on which it should rest.

These are the major cornerstones of planning and its objectives enshrined in the Constitution that will breed enough Union–State tussle in coming decades and make it compulsive for the government to resort to 'reforms with a human face' rhetoric. We can see the methodology of planning taking a U-turn in the era of the economic reforms since the early 1990s.

(iii) The government resolution announcing the setting up of the Planning Commission (March 1950) started with a reference to the constitutional provisions bearing on the socio-economic objectives of the Constitution. The Fundamental Rights and the Directive Principles of the Constitution assure every citizen, among other things, adequate means of livelihood, opportunities for employment and a socio-economic order based on justice and equality. Thus, the basic objectives[33] of planning were already given in the provisions of the Constitution of India. These were emphatically stated in the First Five Year Plan (1951–56) itself, in the following words:

"The urge to economic and social change under present conditions comes from the facts of poverty and of inequalities in income, wealth and opportunity. The elimination of poverty cannot obviously, be achieved merely by redistributing existing wealth. Nor can a programme aiming only at raising production remove existing inequalities. These two have to be considered together...."

(iv) The above objectives of planning were time and again emphasised in one form or the other in the coming times. As the Second Five Year Plan (1956–61) said:

---

31. Ibid.
32. Ibid., pp. 7–10
33. Ibid.

"The Plan has to carry forward the process initiated in the First Plan period. It must provide for a larger increase in production, in investment and in employment. Simultaneously, it must accelerate the institutional changes needed to make the economy more dynamic and more progressive in terms no less of social than of economic ends."

(v) The same objectives were repeated by the Sixth Five Year Plan (1980–85) in the following words:

"The basic task of economic planning in India is to bring about a structural transformation of the economy so as to achieve a high and sustained rate of growth, a progressive improvement in the standard of living of the masses leading to eradication of poverty and unemployment and providing a material base for a self-reliant economy."

(vi) It will be highly needful to enquire about the objectives of planning in the era of the economic reforms initiated in the fiscal 1991–92 as this new economic policy (NEP) made the experts and economists to conclude many questionable things about the objectives of planning in the country:

(a) The need to shift dependence from wage to self-employment.

(b) The state is rolling back and the economy is becoming pro-private and sector-wise the social purpose of the planning will be lacking.

(c) The objectives of planning nearly outlined hitherto have been blurred.

(d) The promotion of foreign investment will induce the economy into the perils of neo-imperialism, etc.

But all the above-given doubts were cleared by the forthcoming plans in straightforward words. We may quote from the following plans:

• "For the future economic development, the economy will be more dependent upon private participation and the nature of planning will become more indicative with the major objectives of planning remaining the same". This was announced by the government while launching the economic reforms (July 23, 1991) and commencing the Eighth Five Year Plan (1992–97). "There was no change in the basic objectives of planning even though there was change in instruments of policy"—this was announced by the government while announcing the new economic policy (1991).

• While the Ninth Plan (1997–2002) was being launched, it was announced that "The goals of planning in India, which were set by Panditji have not changed. The Ninth Plan does not attempt to reinvent the wheel. At the same time, the goals and targets this Plan attempts to achieve are based on the lessons of experience including the Eighth Plan. They address today's problems and challenges and try to prepare the nation for tomorrow as well."[34]

---

34. Deputy Chairman, Planning Commission, May 1999. It is interesting to note here that the composition of the polity in the Centre was dominated by the BJP, while the Deputy Chairman, Planning Commission was K.C. Pant (an old congress man)—continuity in the basic ideas and objectives of planning being maintained.

Finally, a broad consensus looks evolving through the process of planning and crystallising on the six major objectives of planning[35] in India which are as follows:

(i) **Economic Growth:** Sustained increase in the levels of production in the economy is among the foremost objectives of planning in India, which continues till date and will be so in future, without any iota of doubt in it.

(ii) **Poverty Alleviation:** Poverty alleviation was the most important issue which polarised the members of the NPC as well as the Constituent Assembly that a highly emphatic decision in favour of a planned economy evolved even before Independence. Several programmes have been launched in India directing the cause of poverty alleviation by all the governments till date and the process continues even today with more seriousness (we see the National Rural Employment Guarantee Programme—NREGP—being launched by the UPA Government in 2006 by passing an Act in the Parliament—the matter has started attracting such high political concern).

(iii) **Employment Generation:** Providing employment to the poor has been the best tool of economics to alleviate poverty. Thus, this objective of planning in India comes naturally once it commits itself to alleviate poverty. Employment generation in India has been, therefore, part and parcel of the objective of poverty alleviation in India. General programmes and schemes have been launched by the governments from time to time in this direction, some based on the wage employments still, others based on self-employment.

(iv) **Controlling Economic Inequality:** There were visible economic inequalities in India at the inter-personal as well as at the intra-personal levels. Economic planning as a tool of checking all kinds of economic disparities and inequalities was an accepted idea by the time India started planning.[36] To fulfil this objective of planning the governments have enacted highly innovative economic policies at times even inviting a tussle with regard to the Fundamental Rights enshinned in the Constitution.

Though Indian Planning has socio-economic objectives to fulfil, only economic planning was made a part of the planning process (technically speaking) and social planning (better called social engineering) was left to the political process. That is why reservation in government jobs and admissions in premier academic institutions, land reforms, promoting inter-caste marriages, etc., do not fall under the purview of the Planning Commission.

(v) **Self-reliance:** During the 1930s and 1940s, there was an ardent desire among the nationalists, capitalists and the NPC for making the economy self-reliant in all economic sphere. Self-reliance was defined not as autarchy, but as an effort to strike against a subordinate position in the world economy. As Jawaharlal Nehru asserted: self-reliance, "does not exclude international trade, which should be encouraged but with a view to avoid economic imperialism."[37] India still strives for self-reliance in every field of the economy, as well as serving

---

35. Publications Division, *India* (New Delhi: Government of India, various years).

36. Duely discussed by the NPC as well as the Constituent Assembly.

37. *National Planning Committee Report;* Also Nehru in *The Discovery of India.*

the realities of higher interdependence in the globalising world post-World Trade Organisation (WTO).

(vi) **Modernisation:** Modernising the traditional economy was set as a foremost objective of planning. Specially, the agriculture sector of the economy needed an immediate inclusion of modern methods and techniques of farming dairying, etc. Similarly, in education too, India needs to go for inclusion of modern education system.

India did not miss the chance of accepting the importance of modern science and technology. As the economy had selected industry as its prime moving force (PMF), it was essential to adopt the changing dimensions of science and technology.

The major objectives of planning in India are not only broad but open-ended. That is why it hardly needed any change and modification with changing times. It means, after the completion of one plan the objectives for the new plan are automatically set. Coming to the composition of the objectives, we may confidently conclude that all the aspirations of the Preamble,[38] the Directive Principles of the State Policy,[39] the Fundamental Duties and the Fundamental Rights have got their due place and weightage. All the aspirations of the nationalists and the freedom fighters look resonating in the very soul of the Indian planning system.

The above-given objectives of planning got abolished with the Planning Commission. Under the new body—NITI Aayog—a *holistic and federal* objectives of planning have been set by the GoI (they have been discussed under the sub-title, NITI Aayog at the end of this Chapter).

PLANNING COMMISSION

Once the National Planning Committee published its Report (1949), there was a firm inclusion of the need for 'Economic and Social Planning'[40] in the Constitution, the stage was set for the formal launching of planning in the country. Though the economy was run on the principles of planning very much after the Independence itself[31] it was in a piecemeal manner only. For formal planning to begin, for the whole economy at the national level, there was a need for a permanent expert body which could take over the responsibility of the whole gamut of planning, i.e., plan formation, resource aspects, implementation and review—as planning is a technical[42] matter. Thus, in March 1950[43] the Planning Commission (PC) was set up by the government by a Cabinet Resolution (without resorting to legislation). Important details regarding the composition, legal status, etc., of the PC were as under:

---

38. The Preamble was declared by the Supreme Court as an *integral part of the Constitution* and any amendments amounting to a change in its meaning and spirit amounted to the violation of the 'basic feature' of the Constitution (Keshvanand Barti, 1973 and S.R. Bommai, 1994 cases). This further magnified the objectives and role of Planning in India.

39. As the different Articles of the Directive Principles got interpreted as being complementary parts of the Fundamental Rights, their enforcement became obligatory for the Government in coming times, still broadening the objectives of planning in the country.

40. Distribution of Legislative Power, List-III, Entry 20.

41. Though formal planning commenced in the fiscal 1951–52, planning has already commenced with the Industrial Policy Resolution, 1948. More so, the Prime Minister of India who headed the NPC had already taken firm decision that India would be a planned economy by August 1937 (Congress Working Committee, Wardha). Thus, the economy takes its first wink in the planned era!

42. Alan W. evans, 'Economic and Planning', in Jean Forbes (ed.), *Studies in Social Science and Planning* (Edinburgh: Scottish Academy Press, 972), p. 121.

43. I.   Publications Division, *The Gazetter of India*, p. 10.

    II. S.R. Maheshwari (Indian Administration New Delhi: Orient Longman, 2002, p. 121).

    III. ('The Indian Economy Since Independence', p. 949).

(i) An ***extra-constitutional*** (i.e., non-constitutional) and ***non-statutory*** body (though planning originates from the Constitution there is no reference to the PC in it).

(ii) An ***advisory body*** to the Government of India on an array of issues of economic development.

(iii) A 'think tank' on economic development with the Prime Minister as its ex-officio Chairman and with the provision or a Deputy Chairman.[44] The main function of the Deputy Chairman was to ***co-ordinate*** the work of the Commission.[45]

(iv) Had an open provision for the number of its membership (as many area experts are required by the particular proposed period of planning) other than six Union Cabinet Ministers as its ***ex-officio members***[46] and a Member Secretary. The Minister of Planning is already an ex-officio member of the PC.[47]

(v) An ***autonomous body*** entitled to form its own views on important issues and place them before the governments. It worked closely with the Union and State cabinets and had full knowledge of their policies.

(vi) Was invariably ***consulted*** on changes proposed in social and economic policies. To ensure free and full exchange of ideas, the PC had established a ***convention*** that it will not give publicity to differences of views between the Commission and the Union and State governments.

(vii) ***Linked*** with the Union Cabinet at the secretariat level. The PC was part of the Cabinet organisation and the 'demand for grants' for it was included in the budget demand for the Cabinet Secretariat.

(viii) Seated at the 'Yojana Bhavan', the Commission had a staff of secretaries and advisers and also a research organisation.[48]

(ix) The PC was a ***technical body*** with experts and professionals coming from an array of specific areas as per the need of planning of the concerned period (see footmote 42).

(x) The Commission had ***executive powers.***[49]

Functions of the PC

Though the PC was set up with a definite purpose of planning, nobody knew that it would extend its functions over the entire spectrum of administration in the country. It was described as the 'economic Cabinet of the country as a whole' even encroaching upon the constitutional body like the Finance Commission[50] and not being

---

44. The post of Deputy Chairman was later given a Cabinet rank in the Union Council of Minister.

45. Publications Division, *Gazetteer of India,* p. 11.

46. Publications Division, *India 2008* (New Delhi: Ministry of Information and Broadcasting, Govrnment of India, 2009), p. 676.

47. There was a provision of only *three* Cabinet Ministers as its ***ex-officio*** members namely the Finance, Human Resource Development and Defence upto July 2004 when the United Progressive Alliance Government increased it to include the other *three* Cabinet Ministers, viz., the Railways, Agriculture and Information Technology. It has been only once in the history of the PC that it had *six* Cabinet Ministers as its ex-officio members, i.e., in the final years of the Rajiv Gandhi regime (*The Economic Times,* 16 July 2004, N. Delhi Edition).

---

48. Publications Division, *Gazetteer of India,* p. 11.

49. Prima facie a body should have been either constitutional or statutory to wield the executive powers, but as a number of Cabinet Ministers as well as the PM himself were directly involved with the PC, it used to weild executive powers for all practical purposes.

50. Rajamannar was the Chairman of the Fourth Finance Commission. See Ministry of Finance Report of the Fourth Finance Commission (New Delhi: Government of India, 1965) pp. 88–90.

accountable to the Parliament.[51] Through time it built up a heavy bureaucratic organisation[52] which led even Nehru himself to observe—"The Commission which was a small body of serious thinkers has turned into a government department complete with a crowd of secretaries, directors and of course a big building."[53]

Though the functions of the PC were extended to include timely changes in the planning needs (in the reforms era), its functions were announced by the same government order which did set up the Planning Commission. The order[54] says:

"The Planning Commission will—

(i) Make an assessment of the material, capital and human resources of the country, including technical personnel, and investigate the possibilities of augmenting such of those resources as are found to be deficient in relation to the nation's requirements;

(ii) Formulate a plan for the most effective and balanced utilisation of the country's resources;

(iii) On a determination of priorities, define the stages in which the plan should be carried out and propose the allocation of resources for the due completion of each stage;

(iv) Indicate the factors which are tending to retard economic development, and determine the conditions which, in view of the current social and political situation, should be established for the successful execution of the plan;

(v) Determine the nature of the machinery which will be necessary for securing the successful implementation of each stage of the plan in all its aspects;

(vi) Appraise from time to time the progress achieved in the execution of each stage of the Plan and recommend the adjustments of policy and measures that such appraisal may show to be necessary; and

(vii) Make such interim or ancillary recommendations as appear to be appropriate either for facilitating the discharge of the duties assigned to it; or on a consideration of the prevailing economic conditions, current policies, measures and development programmes; or on an examination of such specific problems as may be referred to it for advice by Central or State governments."

With the commencement of the Tenth Plan (2002–07), the government handed over **two new functions** to the Planning Commission in 2002, namely:

(i) To monitor the plan implementation with special reference to the process of 'economic reforms' with the help of the steering committees.

It should be noted here that once the process of economic reforms was

51. By the 1950s it was a general criticism of the PC which looked highly logical. But through the entire period of planning the Government never did think to convert the PC into a constitutional body. Practically enough, the Union Cabinet and the whole Government is accountable to the Parliament for the functions of the PC as it has complete mandate and support of the governments of the time.

52. Appleby, *Public Administration in India: Report of A Survey,* Ford Foundation, 1953, p. 22.

53. As quoted in D.D. Basu, *An Introduction to the Constitution of India* (New Delhi: Wadhwa & Company, 1999), p. 330.

54. Publication Division, *The Gazetteer of India, Vol. 3,* op.cit., pp.10–11.

initiated in the country (early 1990s) there was a diminishing role proposed for the state in the economy in some areas and increased role for the state in some other areas. The re-definition of the state's role in the economy (though it was the contemporary thinking world wide) made most of the experts and the business community to conclude as if there will be no role for planning in the economy. The New Economic Policy (NEP) of 1991–92 was a prima-facie proposal for the expansion of the market economy in the country. But it was not the case altogether. Planning has not become irrelevant though it needed to search for a new orientation. And it was highly essential that the process of planning keeps its relevance to the bigger and the broader process of economic reforms. This particular new function of the PC must be seen in this light.

(ii) To monitor the progress of various Central Ministries. It should be noted here that for the first time, the PC went to set the 'monitorable targets' for 10 areas indicating development. The Central Ministries have been linked to these monitorable targets. The timely performances of the Ministries are now monitored by the PC as per its new function.

With the inclusion of the above-mentioned two functions in the existing functions (which were already very broad), the PC had emerged as a real 'supercabinet'. Since it was basically the Deputy-Chairman who officiated the general meetings of the Commission, he

had a high-level say[55] in articulating the direction and the nature of the economic policies. Through the first new function it articulated, the future dimensions of the economic reforms and through the second new function, it influenced the works of the various ministries—ultimately it seems as if the PC had been able to emerge as the real think-tank of development in the country.[56]

The PC had also been able to influence the economic policies of the states since 2002 in a great way. Though the PC did not make the state plans[57] it was able to influence the overall economic policies of the states. It had been possible due to the setting of 'monitorable targets' for states for the same development indicators/areas as was been set for the Centre.[58] The states were liable for being monitored by the PC concerning their performances

---

55. It is not without that the Government decides to call in Montek Singh Ahluwalia, an economist of international repute to officiate as the Deputy Chairman of the PC. Every idea and opinion of Mr. Ahluwalia was understood by the coalition partners of the UPA Government as a thing the Government is necessarily going to implement in future. One can imagine the increased role of the office of the PC. There is always a hue and cry every time the Deputy Chairman articulates an idea or opinion. Though the PC is chaired by the PM, it seems that the Deputy Chairman has started availing enough autonomy to speak his mind.

56. Ibid.

57. As per the original mandate, the PC was supposed to formulate the state plans also. By 1960s, with the decision to follow the multi-level planning (MLP) in the country the states started having their own state planning boards (SPBs).

58. In setting these targets the concerned states were consulted approach of planning was followed.

regarding these monitorable targets. This way the Central Government had started having its say over the state governments via the new functions of the PC.

We may conclude that the PC had been able to unify not only the various economic policies of the Centre, but also those of the states with the help of these two new functions. Earlier, there had always been a lack of congruence among the policies of the various central ministries and the ideas articulated by the PC.

An Epitaph to the PC

On January 1, 2015, the government formally abolished the PC by replacing it with the newly created body—the NITI Aayog. With this there ended an era in the economic history of independent India. Whether it was better to revive the PC or abolish it has been a matter of much debate among the discipline experts, politicians and the media. The debate, at times, had emotional tones, too. But the government has its own wisdom behind the action (a detailed discussion on it has been included as the last *sub-topic* of this Chapter titled **'NITI Aayog'**).

As an 'epitaph' to the PC (may be an 'ode'), it will be quite relevant to have an eye on the report of the Independent Evaluation Office (IEO) on the former which was submitted to the Prime Minister Office by late June 2014. As per it, the PC was created in response to the unique challenges faced by a nascent democracy and a fledgling economy—it conceived a 'top-down approach' to planning that envisaged a dynamic Central government building up the economic and social order of weak states. The report called the PC in its current form and function a hindrance and not a help to India's development. It further added that it is not easy to reform such a large *ossified body* and it would be better to replace it with a new body

that is needed to assist states in ideas, to provide long-term thinking and to help cross-cutting reforms. Some of the **major** recommendations of IEO on the PC are as follows:

(i) The PC be scrapped and replaced with the *Reform and Solutions Commission* (RSC), which should be staffed with experts with domain knowledge and kept free from any ministerial administrative structure. The new body should have full-time representation of major trade and industry organisations, civil society representatives, academics, etc., so as to capture their concerns and benefit from their expertise in formulating long–term strategy.

(ii) The RSC will perform *three* main functions:

(a) Serve as a solutions exchange and repository of ideas that have been successful in different aspects of development in various states and districts, and in other parts of the world;

(b) Provide ideas for integrated systems reform; and

(c) Identify new and emerging challenges and provide solutions to preempt them.

(iii) The current functions of the PC be taken over by other bodies, 'which are better designed to perform those functions'.

(iv) Since the state governments have better information about local requirements and resources than the central government and central institutions, they should be allowed to identify priorities and implement reforms at the state level, independent of mandatory diktats from the central institutions.

(v) The task of long-term economic thinking and coordination can be performed by a new body established to act solely as a 'think tank' within the government.

(vi) The Finance Commission be made a *permanent body* responsible for the allocation of centrally collected revenue to the states and the finance ministry be tasked with the division of funds among the various central ministries.

The recommendations of the IEO (a brainchild of the PC itself) on the PC were quite surprising, even shocking to few. Whether the new body replacing the PC will be a betterment over the latter and will be able to carve out its desired aims is a matter to be evaluated and analysed in future. Meanwhile, we can visibly find some of the recommendations of the IEO resonating in the newly created body, the NITI Aayog, the replacement for the PC.

[**Note:** While a detailed literature has been included on the 'NITI Aayog' in this edition (as the last *sub-topic*), the literature on the PC has been left unchanged for ease of understanding and comparative purpose.]

NATIONAL DEVELOPMENT COUNCIL

The National Development Council (NDC) was set up on August 6, 1952 by a Resolution[59] issued from the Cabinet Secretariat. The first Plan recommended its formation with a very concise and suitable observation:

"In a country of the size of India where the states have under the constitution full autonomy within their own sphere of duties, it is necessary to have a forum such as a National Development Council at which, from time to time, the Prime Minister of India and the Chief Ministers of the states can review the working of the plan and of its various aspects."[60]

There were some strong reasons why the NDC was set up, which may be seen as follows:

(i) The Central Plans were to be launched in the states and the UTs with the participation of the state-level personnel. The Planning Commission was not provided with its own implementation staff (though the PC was given the responsibility of plan implementation) for this purpose. Therefore, the consent and co-operation of these federal units was a must.

(ii) Economic planning as a concept had its origin in the centralised system (i.e., Soviet Union). For India, to democratise/decentralise the very process of planning was not a lesser task/challenge than promoting development itself. Indian planning is rightly said to be a process of trial and error in striking a balance between liberty and progress, central control and private initiative and national planning with local authority.[61]

The setting up of the NDC can be considered as a step towards decentralised planning.

(iii) In the constitutional design of the federal rigidities it was necessary to provide the whole planning process a unified outlook. The NDC serves the purpose of diluting the autonomous and rigid federal units of the Union of India.[62]

59. Cabinet Secretariat, *Resolution No. 62/CF/50* (06.08.1952) Government of India, New Delhi.

60. Planning Commission, First Five year Plan: A Draft Outline (New Delhi: Government of India, 1957), p. 253.

61. Publications Divisions, *The Gazetteer of India*, p. 10.

62. The Advisory Planning Board (1946) set up by the Interim Government had suggested for such a consultative body with the representatives from the provinces, the princely states and some other interests to advise the Planning Commission for the success of planning in India.

The NDC initially comprised the Prime Minister of India (de facto Chairman), the Chief Ministers of all States and the Members of the Planning Commission. In the first meeting of the NDC held on November 8–9, 1952, Jawaharlal Nehru stated that NDC is "essentially a forum for intimate cooperation between the State Governments and the Central Government for all the tasks of national development". In the *words* of Nehru, setting up of the NDC may be regarded as one of the most significant steps taken for promoting understanding and consultation between the Union and the State Governments on planning and common economic policies.

Considering the recommendations of the 'Administrative Reforms Commission', the NDC was reconstituted and its functions redefined by a Cabinet Resolution on October 7, 1967. The reconstituted NDC comprises the Prime Minister, all Union Cabinet Ministers, Chief Ministers of all States and Union Territories and the Members of the Planning Commission. Delhi Administration is represented in the Council by the Lt. Governor and the Chief Executive Councillor, and the remaining Union Territories by their respective Administrators. Other Union Ministers and State Ministers may also be invited to participate in the deliberations of the council. In the reconstituted Council, the Secretary of the Planning Commission acts as Secretary to the NDC and the Planning Commission is expected to furnish such administrative or other assistance for the work of the Council as may be needed. The baisc nature, origin and legal status of the Council are similar to the Planning Commission. The **revised functions**[63] of the NDC are:

(i) to consider the proposals formulated for Plans at all important stages and accept them;

(ii) to review the working of the Plans from time to time;

(iii) to consider the important questions of social and economic policy affecting national development; and

(iv) to recommend measures for the achievement of the aims and targets set out in the national plan, including measures to secure the *active participation* and cooperation of the people, improve the efficiency of the administrative services, ensure the fullest development of the less advanced regions and backward sections of the community and through sacrifices borne equally by all citizens, build up resources for national development.[64]

Though the first Plan of India was launched before the arrival of the NDC, the body had many meetings before the terminal year of the plan and useful deliberations (almost all) after due consideration were included by the government into the planning process. But after the death of Jawaharlal Nehru—the greatest champion of democratic decentralisation in the country[65] the NDC had become a small gathering of only those who had the same vested interests with only the

---

63. Other than the *Cabinet Resolution,* it is also quoted is The *Gazetteer of India* (Publications Divsion, The Gazetteer of India, p. 15).

64. The *italicised* words are here highlighting the level of the Government's consciousness about the concerned issues of decentralised planning, regional and individual inequalities to which the planning was to be specially attentive.

65. George Mathew, undoubtedly among the legendary commentator on the Panchayat Raj/democratic decentralisation calls Nehru as "its most eminent champion at the national level". Similarly, the reputed historians Bipan Chandra and others call Nehru as "the greatest champion of planned economic development". For Nehru the process of planning in the country was to be democratic about which seems very clear, as his writings support.

Congress CMs participating in its meetings. The CMs belonging to other political parties usually did not come to its meetings; the government hardly gave any importance to their advice. A phase of tussle between the Centre and the states started worsening from here onward with a degradation in principles of the **co-operative federalism,** with every five-year plans which followed. It was only by the mid-1990s that we see the revival of the lost glory of NDC as well as that of the spirit of decentralised planning. This has been possible due to three major reasons:

(i) In the era of economic reforms, with greater dependence on the private capital made it necessary to allow states greater autonomy in economic matters. Once the WTO regime started it became an economic compulsion.

(ii) The enactment of the Constitutional Amendments 73rd and the 74th had made local level planning a constitutional compulsion.

(iii) And lastly it was the compulsion of coalition politics in the formation of the Union Government which made the Centre to favour the states.

As per the major experts on the issue of decentralised planning, the last of the above given three reasons has played the most important role. By 2002, in the area of development planning we find an enhanced level of federal maturity and we see the last three five years plans (10th, 11th and 12th) adopted by a consensual support of the NDC members.

The NDC had its last meeting held in December 2015 (57th meeting). It is believed that in coming times the NDC will be merged with the *Governing Council* of the NITI Aayog. The Governing Council is a better equipped body than the NDC to establish a better Union-State co-ordination.

CENTRAL PLANNING

The Plans which are formulated by the Central Government and financed by it for the implementation at the national level are known as Central Plans. Over the years, the Centre has launched three such plans and the governments have maintained continuity in their implementation. The three central plans are:

A. Five-Year Plans,

B. Twenty-Point Programme, and

C. Member of Parliament Local Area Development Scheme.

An introductory description of these plans is given as follows:

A. The Five-Year Plans

This is the most important among the central plans and is being continuously implemented one after the other since planning commenced in India. As planning has been a purely political excercise in India, the five-year plans of the country have seen many unstable and critical moments till date. Several new developments related to planning also took place during the years. Given below is a concise summary of the plans as we see their different periods of implementation:

First Plan

The period for this plan was 1951–56. As the economy was facing the problem of large-scale foodgrains import (1951) and the pressure of price rise, the plan accorded the highest priority to agriculture including irrigation and power projects. About 44.6 per cent of the plan outlay went in favour of the public sector undertakings (PSUs).

The Plan was launched with all the lofty ideas of socio-economic development, which had frustrating outcomes in the following years.

Second Plan

The plan period was 1956–61. The strategy of growth laid emphasis on rapid industrialisation with a focus on heavy industries and capital goods.[66] The plan was developed by Professor Mahalanobis. Due to the assumption of a closed economy, shortages of food and capital were felt during this Plan.

Third Plan

The Plan period was 1961–65. The Plan specifically incorporated the development of agriculture[67] as one of the objectives of planning in India besides, for the first times, considering the aim of balanced, regional development.

Enough misfortunes awaited this plan—two wars, one with China in 1961–62 and the other with Pakistan in 1965–66 along the Gujarat border and a severe drought-led famine in 1965–66 had to be faced. Due to heavy drain and diversion of funds, this plan utterly failed to meet its targets.

Three Annual Plans

The period of the three consecutive Annual Plans was 1966–69. Though the Fourth Plan was ready for implementation in 1966, the weak financial situation as well as the low morale after the defeat by China, the government decided to go for an Anuual Plan for 1966–67. Due to the same reasons the government went for another two such plans in the forthcoming years. The broader objectives of these Annual Plans were inside the design of the Fourth Plan which would have been implemented for the period 1966–71 had the financial conditions not worsened by then.

Some economists as well as the opposition in the Parliament called this period as a discontinuity in the planning process, as the Plans were supposed to be for a period of five years. They named it a period of "Plan Holiday", i.e., the planning was on a holiday.[68]

Fourth Plan

The Plan period was 1969–74. The Plan was based on the Gadgil strategy with special focus to the ideas of growth with stability and progress towards self-reliance. Droughts and the Indo-Pak War of 1971–72 led the economy to capital diversions creating financial crunch for the Plan.

The politicisation of planning started from this plan, which took serious 'populist' design in the coming plans. Frequent double-digit inflations, unreigned increase in the fiscal deficits, subsidy-induced higher non-plan expenditures and the first move in the direction of 'nationalisation' and greater control and regulation of the economy were some of the salient features of this plan, which continued unchanged till the early 1990s. The search for political stability at the Centre converted planning into a tool of real politics with greater and greater 'centralisation' ensuing plan after plan.

Fifth Plan

The Plan (1974–79) has its focus on poverty alleviation and self-reliance.[69] The popular rhetoric of poverty alleviation was sensationalised

---

66. Sukhomoy Chakravarti, *Development Planning: The Indian Experience* (New Hork: Oxford University Press, 1989), pp. 9–11.

67. C. Rangarajan, *Indian Economy: Essays on Money and Finance* (New Delhi: UPSBD, 1998), p. 272.

68. It should be noted here that as per the official version of the Government of India, the planning has been a *continuous process* in the country and there is no term like 'Plan Holiday' in Its official documents. The term was given by the critics and popularised by the contemporary media.

69. Experts believe this Plan to be somewhat based on the ideas of D.P. Dhar, the Minister for Planning at that time.

by the government to the extent of launching a fresh plan, i.e., the Twenty-point Programme (1975) with a marginal importance being given to the objective of 'growth with stability' (one of the major objectives of the Fourth Plan).

The planning process got more politicised. The havocs of hyper-inflation led the government to hand over a new function to the Reserve Bank of India to stabilise the inflation (the function which the RBI carries forward even today). A judicious price wage policy was started to check the menace of inflation on the wage-earners. This Plan saw an increase in the socio-economic and regional disparities despite the many institutional, financial and other measures which were initiated by the government to attend to them. The nationalisation policy continued. There was an overall decay in the quality of 'governance'. A nexus of the 'criminal-politician-bureaucrat' seems to emerge for the first time to hijack the political system.[70]

The plan period was badly disturbed by the draconian emergency and a change of the government at the Centre. The Janata Party came to power with a thumping victory in 1977. As the government of the time had then complete say in the central planning in India, how could the new government continue with the Fifth Plan of the last government which had still more than one year to reach its completion. The dramatic events related to Indian planning may be seen objectively as given below:

(i) The Janata Government did cut-short the Fifth Plan by a year ahead of its terminal year, i.e., by the fiscal 1977–78, in place of the decided 1978–79.

(ii) A fresh Plan, the Sixth Plan for the period 1978–83 was launched by the new government which called it the **'Rolling Plan'**.[71]

(iii) In 1980, there was again a change of government at the Centre with the return of the Congress which abandoned the Sixth Plan of the Janata Government in the year 1980 itself.

(iv) The new government launched a fresh new **Sixth Plan** for the period 1980–85. But by that time, two financial years of the Janata Government's Sixth Plan had already been completed. These two years of the Plan were adjusted by the Congress Government in a highly interesting way:

(a) The first year, i.e., 1978–79 was added to the fifth plan which was cut-short by the Janata Government to four years. And thus the Fifth Plan officially became of 5 years again (1974–79).

---

70. **N.N. Vohra Committee Report,** Government of India, N. Delhi, 1993.

71 It should be noted here that there is nothing like the 'Rolling Plan' in the official documents of planning in India. Basically, the origin of the concept of the 'Rolling Plan' goes back to the period when India went for the Annual Plans (1966–69) for the first time and the critics noted it as a *discontinuity* in the planning process, calling it a period of the 'plan holiday'. The basic trait of the 'Rolling Plan' was its *continuity*, while the Congress commenced its Sixth Plan (1980–85) the idea of the 'Rolling Plan' was cancelled, as for the new Government the element of 'rolling' (continuity) was already in the Indian Planning—India was following the approach of the 'perspective planning'. A separate Division of Perspective Planning was already functioning in the Yojana Bhavan since the mid-1970s. The two elements which make a plan a 'perspective plan' are, firstly, the 'continuity' and secondly, 'evaluation-based' planning. For the Congress Government, logically, the planning in India was not only 'rolling' but more than that it was evaluation-based, too.

(b) Now what to do with the second year, i.e., 1979–80. The Congress Government announced this year to be a year of one Annual Plan. This Annual Plan (1979–80) may be considered the lone independent remnant of the 'Rolling Plan' of the Janata Government.

The Sixth Plan (1978–83) which could not become an official plan of India had emphasis on some of the highly new economic ideas and ideals with almost a complete no to foreign investment; new thrust on price control; rejuvenation of the Public Distribution System (PDS); emphasis on small-scale and cottage industries; new lease of life to Panchayati Raj Institutions (PRIs) (i.e., the 2nd Phase of the revival of the PRIs); agriculture and the subject of rural development getting the due; etc., being the major ones.

Sixth Plan

This Plan (1980–85) was launched with the slogan of '*Garibi Hatao*' (alleviate poverty).[72] Already, a programme (the TPP) was tested and tried by the same government in the Fifth Plan which tried to improve the standard of living of the poor masses with the 'direct approach' (the idea of poverty alleviation, but such a slogan of '*Garibi Hatao*' was not given to the programme).

Some of the major issues addressed by the Plan were—emphasis on socio-economic infrastructure in rural areas; eliminating rural poverty and reducing regional disparities through the IRDP (1979); 'target group'[73] approach

initiated; a number of national level programmes and schemes were launched during the plan, which tried to attend to the specific areas and the specific concerns of socio-economic development (this is the 'target group' approach):[74]

(i) National Rural Employment Programme (NREP)—1980

(ii) Restructured Twenty-Point Programme–1982

(iii) Biogas Programme—1982

(iv) Development of Women and Children in Rural Areas (DWERA)—1983

(v) Rural Landless Employment Guarantee Programme (RLEGP)—1983

(vi) Self-Employment to Educated Unemployed Youth Programme (SEEUP)—1983

(vii) Dairy Development Programme (DDP)—1983

(viii) Village and Small Industries Development Programme (VSIDP)—1983

(ix) Tribal Development Agency (TDA)—1983

(x) Village and Small Industries Development Programme (VSIDP)—1983

(xi) National Seeds Programme (NSP)—1983

(xii) Intensive Pulses Development Programme (IPDP)—1983

(xiii) Intensive Cotton Development Programme (ICDP)—1983

(xiv) Khadi and Village Industries Programme (KVIP)—1983

(xv) Programme for Depressed Areas (PDA)—1983

(xvi) Special Programme for Women and Children (SPWC)—1983

---

72. Some experts see this Plan as a symbol of the planning being converted to a complete politics—with utter populism entering into the planning process of India. The circle of the politicisation of planning gets completed with this Plan.

73. 'Target group' approach of planning is selecting the group of people where a particular problem is and attacking the problem directly. The TPP was the first such programme in India.

74. Publications Division, *India 1980–1983* (New Delhi: Government of India).

Seventh Plan

The Plan (1985–90) emphasised on rapid foodgrain production, increased employment creation and productivity in general. The basic tenets of planning, i.e., **growth, modernisation, self-reliance** and **social justice** remained as the guiding principles.[75] The *Jawahar Rojgar Yojana* (JRY) was launched in 1989 with the motive to create wage-employment for the rural poors. Some of the already existing programmes, such as the IRDP, CADP, DPAP and the DDP were re-oriented.

Till date, the government has been evaluating the achievements of all the developmental programmes, courtesy the youngest PM of India. Somehow, democracy and development got connected with a major change in the thinking of the political elite, which decided to go in for democratic decentralisation to promote development. It laid strong foundations for itself as the constitutional amendments—the 73rd and 74th were possible by the early 1990s.

Though the economy had better growth rates throughout the 1980s, specially in the latter half, yet it was at the cost of bitter fiscal imbalances. By the end of the Plan, India had a highly unfavourable balance of payments situation. Heavy foreign loans on which the governmental expenditures depended heavily during the period, the economy failed to service.[76] The Plan was not laid with a strong financial strategy, which put the economy into a crisis of unsustainable balance of payments and fiscal deficits.[77] India basically tried to attend its growth prospects by commercial and other external borrowings on hard terms, which the economy failed to sustain. In the process of liberalisation, an expansion of internal demand for the home market was permitted without generating equitable levels of exports and ultimately Indian imports were financed by the costly external borrowings. Such an 'inward looking' fiscal policy proved to be a mistake when the external aid environment for the economy was deteriorating.[78]

Two Annual Plans

The Eighth Plan (whose term would have been 1990–95) could not take off due to the 'fast-changing political situation at the Centre'.[79] The pathbreaking and restructuring-oriented suggestions of the Eighth Plan, the sweeping economic reforms ensuing around the world, as well as the fiscal imbalances of the late 1980s were the other important reasons for the delay in the launch of the Eighth Plan. The new government, which assumed power at the centre in June 1991, decided to commence the Eighth Plan for the period 1992–97 and that the fiscals 1990–91 and 1991–92 should be treated as two separate Annual Plans. The two consecutive Annual Plans (1990–92) were formulated within the framework of the approach to the Eighth Plan (1990–95) with the basic thrust on maximisation of employment and social transformation.

Eighth Plan

The Eighth Plan (1992–97) was launched in a typically new economic environment. The economic reforms were already started (in July 1991) with the initiation of the structural adjustment and macro-stabilisation policies

75. Planning Commission, **Seventh Five Year Plan (1980–85)** (New Delhi: Government of India, 1980).

76. Similar financial strategy to promote growth and development had led the Soviet Union to economic collapse via the balance of payment crisis during Gorbachev's regime by 1991, as is pointed out by Jeffrey Sachs in **The End of Poverty** ((London: Penguin Books, 2005), pp. 131–34).

77. C. Rangarajan, **Indian Economy**, p. 274.

78. **Bimal Jalan** in Bimal Jalan (ed.), 1992, pp. 190–191, op.cit.

79. This is the official version for the delay (Publications Division, **India 2007** (New Delhi: Government of India, 2007), p. 680.

necessitated by the worsening balance of payments, higher fiscal deficit and unsustainable rate of inflation.

This was the first plan which went on for an introspection of the macro-economic policies which the country had been pursuing for many decades. The major concerns and pathbreaking suggestions[80] which this Plan articulated may be summarised as follows:

(i) an immediate re-definition of the state's role in the economy was suggested;

(ii) 'market-based' development advised in areas which could afford it, i.e., a greater role for the private sector in the economy;[81]

(iii) more investment in the infrastructure sector, especially in the laggard states as the ongoing emphasis on greater private sector investment could not be attracted towards these states;

(iv) rising non-plan expenditure and fiscal deficits need to be checked;

(v) subsidies need restructuring and refocussing;

(vi) planning immediately needs to be 'decentralised';

(vii) special emphasis on 'co-operative federalism' suggested;

(viii) greater focus on 'agriculture' and other 'rural activities' was suggested for which the Plan cited empirical evidences as they encourage the economy to achieve

enhanced standard of living for its people and to promote the cause of balanced growth—a shift in the mindset of planning.

As the economy moved towards liberalisation, criticism came from every quarter against the move. The process of planning was also criticised on the following counts:

(i) As economy moves towards the market economy, the planning becomes 'irrelevant';

(ii) When the state is 'rolling back', planning makes no sense;

(iii) The planning process should be 're-structured' in the era of liberalisation; and

(iv) There should be increased thrust on the 'social sector' (i.e., education, healthcare, etc.)

Ninth Plan

The Ninth Plan (1997–2002) was launched when there was an all round 'slowdown' in the economy led by the South East Asian Financial Crisis (1996–97). Though the liberalisation process was still criticised, the economy was very much out of the fiscal imbroglio of the early 1990s. With a general nature of 'indicative planning', the Plan not only did target an ambitious high growth rate (7 per cent), but also tried to direct itself towards time-bound 'social' objectives. There was an emphasis on the seven identified Basic Minimum Services (BMS) with additional Central Assistance for these services with a view to obtaining complete coverage of the population in a time-bound manner. The BMS[82] included:

(i) Safe drinking water;

(ii) Primary health service;

80. It should be noted here that the kind of economic reforms India started in 1991–92 were *almost ditto suggested* by the Eighth Plan. The suggestions were based on India's own experience and the experiences of the world economies after the Second World War. The Sixth and the Seventh Plans had suggested almost on the similar lines which made the Governments of the time go for the so-called 'liberalisation' moves in the mid-1980s

81. C. Rangarajan, *Indian Economy*, p. 275–276.

82. Publications Division, *India 2007*, pp. 682–83.

(iii)   Universalisation of primary education;

(iv)   Public housing assistance to the shelter-less poor families;

(v)   Nutritional support to children;

(vi)   Connectivity of all villages and habitations; and

(vii)   Streamlining of the public distribution system.

The issue of fiscal consolidation became a top priority of the governments for the first time, which had its focus on the following[83] related issues:

(i)   Sharp reduction in the revenue deficit of the government, including centre, states and the PSUs through a combination of improved revenue collections and control of in-essential expenditures;

(ii)   Cutting down subsidies, collection of user charges on economic services (i.e., electricity, transportation, etc.), cutting down interest, wages, pension, PF, etc;

(iii)   Decentralisation of planning and implementation through greater reliance on states and the PRIs.

Tenth Plan

The Plan (2002–07) commenced with the objectives of greater participation of the NDC in their formulation. Some highly important steps were taken during the plan, which undoubtedly points out a change in the planning policy mindset of the government, major ones being:[84]

(i)   Doubling per capita income in 10 years;

(ii)   Accepting that the higher growth rates

are not the only objective—it should be translated into improving the quality of life of the people;

(iii)   For the first time the Plan went to set the 'monitorable tragets' for eleven select indicators of development for the Centre as well as for the states;

(iv)   'Governance' was considered a factor of development;

(v)   States' role in planning to be increased with the greater involvement of the PRIs;

(vi)   Policy and institutional reforms in each sector, i.e., reforms in the PSUs, legal reforms, administrative reforms, labour reforms, etc;

(vii)   Agriculture sector declared as the prime moving force (PMF) of the economy;

(viii)   Increased emphasis on the social sector (i.e., education, health, etc.);

(ix)   Relevance between the processes of economic reforms and planning emphasised; etc.

The Mid-term Appraisal of the Plan was approved by the NDC in June 2005. The assessment gives a mixed picture regarding its performance. As per the appraisal, the country performed well in many areas and these gains needed to be consolidated, but there were some important weaknesses also, which, if not corrected, can undermine even the current performance level.[85]

Eleventh Plan

The Plan targets a growth rate of 10 per cent and emphasises the idea of 'inclusive growth'. In the approach paper, the Planning Commission shows its concerns regarding realising the growth targets

83.   Ministry of Finance, *Economic Survey* (1998–200) (New Delhi: Government of India, Various Years); Publications Division, *India 2007,* p. 683.

84.   Planning Commission, *Tenth Five year Plan (2002–07),* (New Delhi: Government of India).

85.   Planning Commission, *Mid-Term Appraisal of the Tenth Plan* (New Delhi: Government of India).

on account of the compulsions towards the Fiscal Responsibility and Budget Management Act. In recent times some aberrations in the economy have started to increase the government's concerns in meeting the Plan target of 10 per cent growth. The major concerns are:

(i) A higher inflation (above 6 per cent) led to the tightening of the credit policy forcing lower investment in the economy (which will lower production);

(ii) A stronger rupee is making export earnings shrink fast;

(iii) Costlier foodgrains and other primary articles playing havoc for the poor masses;

(iv) Costlier oil prices becoming a burden for the national exchequer; etc.

Not only the government but the Confederation of Indian Industry (CII) as well as the World Bank expressed doubts in the Eleventh Plan realising the ambitious 10 per cent growth.

Eleventh Plan: Performance

The Planning Commission (PC) had attempted the mid-term appraisal of the Plan, which was considered and approved by the National Development Council in July 2010. The appraisal document reviewed the developments and provided a comprehensive assessment of the performance of the economy during the Eleventh Plan period so far, in different sectors, together with suggested mid-course corrections. It has drawn attention to the problems in some selected areas and identified constraints that would be of relevance for the balance period of the Eleventh Plan and also for the Twelfth Plan. These include inter-alia:

(i) Restoring dynamism in agriculture,

(ii) Managing India's water resources,

(iii) Problems in achieving power generation targets,

(iv) Issues pertaining to urbanisation, and

(v) Special problems of tribal development.

In respect of *agriculture,* the mid-term appraisal notes that though performance of agriculture and the rate of growth in the Eleventh Plan is likely to be better than that in the Tenth Plan, it may, however, not reach the target of 4 per cent per year. The need to focus on agriculture and other critical issues mentioned above would require *concerted action* by the Centre and the states.

The Review by the PC regarding the **Poverty Estimates** is also important when the issue has become a matter of debate in the country. The Planning Commission is the nodal agency for estimating poverty in the country, both at the national level and across the states. It estimates poverty on the basis of poverty line defined in terms of monthly per capita consumption expenditure. The Commission has been estimating poverty line and poverty ratio since 1997 on the basis of the methodology contained in the report of the Expert Group on 'Estimation of Number and Proportion of Poor' (known as *Lakdawala Committee Report*). The Head-count poverty ratio has been estimated by using the above mentioned poverty lines from a large size sample survey of household consumption expenditure carried out by the National Sample Survey Office (NSSO) with an interval of 5 years approximately.

The Planning Commission constituted an Expert Group in December 2005 under the chairmanship of Prof. Suresh D. Tendulkar to review the methodology for estimation of poverty. The Expert Group submitted its report in December 2009. While acknowledging the multi-dimensional nature of poverty, the Expert Group recommended moving away from anchoring the poverty lines to the calorie intake norm, adopting the Mixed Reference Period (MRP) based estimates of consumption expenditure as the basis for future poverty lines, adopting MRP equivalent of urban Poverty Line Basket (PLB) corresponding to 25.7 per cent urban headcount ratio as the new reference PLB for rural areas. On the basis of the above methodology, the all-India rural poverty headcount ratio for 2004–05 was estimated at 41.8 per cent, urban poverty headcount ratio at 25.7 per cent and all India level at 37.2 per cent. It may however be mentioned that the Tendulkar Committee's estimates are not strictly comparable to the present official poverty estimates because of different methodologies. As has been indicated in the Mid-Term Appraisal of the Eleventh Five Year Plan, the revised poverty lines and poverty ratios for 2004–05 as recommended by the Tendulkar Committee have been accepted by the Planning Commission. The Tendulkar Committee has specifically pointed out that the upward revision in the percentage of rural poverty in 2004–05, resulting from the application of a new rural poverty line, should not be interpreted as implying that the extent of poverty has increased over time. These estimates, as reported by the Committee, clearly show that whether we use the old method or the new, the percentage of the population below poverty line has declined by about the same magnitude.

The performance on the **Fiscal Scenario**, according to the Planning Commission, the expansionary fiscal measures taken by the government in order to counter the effects of the global slowdown were continued in 2009–10, and this led to further increase in the key deficit indicators. The fiscal deficit of the Centre, which was 2.5 per cent in 2007–08 increased substantially to 6.0 per cent in 2008–09 and further to 6.4 per cent in 2009–10, but it declined to 5.1 per cent in 2010–11 (RE) and the Budget Estimates for 2011–12 put the fiscal deficit at 4.6 per cent of the GDP. Similarly, the revenue deficit of the Centre increased from 1.1 per cent in 2007–08 to 4.5 per cent in 2008–09 and further to 5.2 per cent in 2009–10 and declined to 3.4 per cent for 2010–11 (RE). As per 2011–12 (BE), the revenue deficit is projected at the same level of 3.4 per cent of the GDP. The increase in the deficit levels of the Centre owes to revenue foregone on account of reduction in indirect tax rates and enhanced public expenditure in order to boost demand in the economy amidst global meltdown.

The issue of **Price Stability** remained resonating for more than half of the Plan period. To ward off the crisis of rising prices, the government needed to announce several tax concessions at one hand, while it could not pass the burden of the costlier imported oil prices on the masses. That would have resulted in ultimately putting the exchequer in a fund-crunch mode, at the end, creating a short-supply of investible funds in government's hand, hence, causing the Eleventh Plan to perform at the levels below its target.

Twelfth Plan

The 'Draft Approach Paper' of the Twelfth Plan (2012–17) was prepared by the Planning Commission after widest consultation till date—recognising the fact that citizens are now better informed and also keen to engage. Over 950 civil society organisations across the country provided inputs; business associations, including those representing small enterprises have been consulted; modern electronic and 'social media' (Google Hangout) were used to enable citizens to give suggestions. All state governments, as well as local representative institutions and unions, have been consulted through five regional consultations. Though the Approach Paper for the Plan was approved by the NDC by mid-2011, the Plan Document was finalised much later after the launch of the plan (like the Tenth and Eleventh Plans).

The Draft Approach Paper lays down the major targets of the Plan, the key challenges in meeting them, and the broad approach that must be followed to achieve the stated objectives which are summed-up as follows:

(i) Growth rate of 9 per cent is targeted for the Plan. However, in view of the uncertainties in the global economy and the challenges in the domestic economy, the Approach Paper indicates that it could be achieved only if some **difficult decisions** are taken.

(ii) It emphasizes the need to intensify efforts to have 4 per cent average growth in **the agriculture** sector during the Plan period; with foodgrains growing at about 2 per cent per year and non-food grains (notably, horticulture, livestock, dairying, poultry and fisheries) growing at 5 to 6 per cent.

(iii) The higher growth in agriculture would not only provide broad based income benefits to the rural population but also help restrain **inflationary pressure**, which could arise if high levels of growth are attempted without corresponding growth in domestic food production capabilities.

(iv) It proposes that the major **flagship programmes** which were instrumental for promoting inclusiveness in the Eleventh Plan should continue in the Twelfth Plan—there is a need to focus on issues of implementation and governance to improve their effectiveness.

(v) The Plan indicates that the **energy** needs of rapid growth will pose a major challenge since these requirements have to be met in an environment where domestic energy prices are constrained and world energy prices are high and likely to rise further.

(vi) For the GDP to grow at 9 per cent, commercial energy supplies will have to grow at a rate between 6.5 and 7 per cent per year. Since India's domestic energy supplies are limited, dependence upon imports will increase. Import dependence in the case of petroleum has always been high and is projected to be **80** per cent in the Twelfth Plan.

(vii) Even in the case of **coal**, import dependence is projected to increase as the growth of thermal generation will require coal supplies, which cannot be fully met from domestic mines.

(viii) It suggests the need to take steps to reduce energy intensity of production processes, increase domestic energy supply as quickly as possible and ensure rational energy pricing that will help achieve both objectives, viz., reduced energy intensity of production process and enhance domestic energy supply, even though it may seem difficult to attempt.

(ix) It draws attention to evolving a holistic **water** management policy aiming at more efficient conservation of water and also in water use efficiency, particularly in the field of agriculture.

(x) It argues that a new legislation for **land acquisition** is necessary, which strikes an appropriate balance between the need for fair compensation to those whose land is acquired and whose livelihood is disrupted, and the need to ensure that land acquisition does not become an impossible impediment to meeting our needs for infrastructure development, industrial expansion and urbanisation.

(xi) It maintains that **health, education** and **skill development** will continue to be the focus areas in the Twelfth Plan, and that there is a need to ensure adequate resources to these sectors—*'universal healthcare'* proposed by it, emphatically.

Simultaneously, it also points to the need to ensure maximum efficiency in terms of outcomes for the resources allocated to these sectors. The need to harness *private investment* in these sectors has also been emphasised by the approach.

(xii) It takes cognizance of the fact that achieving 9 per cent growth will require large **investments** in infrastructure sector development—notes greater momentum to public investment and Public Private Partnerships (PPPs) in infrastructure sector needs to be imparted so that present infrastructure shortages can be addressed early.

(xiii) It has emphasised the importance of the process of **fiscal correction**. However, the paper cautions that fiscal consolidation would imply that total resources available for the Plan in the short run will be limited. Resource limitations imply the need to prioritise carefully and that some *priority areas*, e.g., health, education and infrastructure will have to be funded more than others.

(xiv) It also emphasizes the need for focusing more on **efficient use** of available resources in view of the resource constraints. The Paper makes several suggestions in this regard, including giving implementing agencies greater amount of freedom, flexibility, promoting convergence between resources from different Plan schemes and the need for much greater attention to capacity building, monitoring and accountability.

B. Twenty-Point Programme

The Twenty Point Programme (TPP) is the second Central Plan which was launched in July 1975. The programme was conceived for coordinated and intensive monitoring of a number of schemes implemented by the Central and the state governments. The basic *objective* was of improving the quality of life of the people, especially of those living below the poverty line. Under this, a thrust was given to schemes relating to poverty alleviation, employment generation in rural areas, housing, education, family welfare and health, protection of environment and many other schemes having a bearing on the quality of life in rural areas.

The programme was restructured in 1982 and 1986. The programme, known as the *'TPP-86'* has 119 items grouped into 20 points which are related to the improvement in the quality of life in rural areas. Among the total items, 54 are monitored on the basis of evaluatory criteria, 65 against pre-set physical targets and rest of the 20 important items on monthly basis. The targets are fixed by the Ministries at the Centre in consultation with the states and the UTs. The allocation for the programme is done under the various Five Year Plans.

The 'TPP-86' was restructured and named 'TPP-2006' keeping in view the challenges of the 21st century with particular reference to the process of economic reforms. This was in harmony with the National Common Minimum Programme (NCMP) of the UPA Government.

This was the first programme which had 'direct attack' aproach on rural poverty. The forthcoming five year plan (i.e., the 6th Plan, 1980–85), launched with the slogan "Garibi Hatao", was based on the experiences of the TPP—a right mix of economics and real politic. Over the years, the programme has been implemented uninterrupted by all political parties which came to power at the Centre.

By **mid-2015,** the Ministry of Statistics and Programme Implementation (MOSPI), which monitors the programme, in a report to the Prime Minister's Office, had advised to wrap it up as it has outlived its utility. While the PMO decided to 'restructure' it on the recommendations of the Inter-Ministerial Group, which is presently working on it. It should be noted that the Government has restructured the existing 50 Centrally Sponsored Schemes (CSSs) into 30 under the active participation of the Governing Council of the NITI Aayog.

C. MPLADS

The Member of Parliament Local Area Development Scheme (MPLADS) is the last of the Central Plans and latest to have been launched, too. The scheme was launched on December 23, 1993 with only Rs. 5 lakh given to each MPs which was increased to Rs. 1 crore in the year 1994–95. When the MPs did put a demand to increase the sum to Rs. 5 crore in 1997–98, finally the government enhanced it to Rs. 2 crore since 1998–99. In April 2011 the corpus was enhanced to Rs. 5 crore while announcing the new guidelines for the scheme.

Basically, in the early 1990s there came a demand from the MPs cutting across party lines for such a scheme so that the fruits of development could directly reach the masses via their representatives. The government of the time decided to go in for such a scheme and the MPLADS came.

Under this scheme the Members of Parliament[86] recommend some works (i.e., creation of fixed community assets, based on locally felt developmental needs) to the concerned District Magistrate. The scheme is governed by a set of guidelines, which have been comprehensively revised and issued in November 2005. Its performance has improved due to pro-active policy initiatives, focus monitoring and review.[87]

In recent years, many criticisms of the scheme came to the public notice, which concerned either misappropriation of the funds or non-use of the funds, especially from the backward states. The people's representative at the PRI level have been demanding scrapping of the scheme as it infringes the idea of decentralised planning. In it's place, they want the funds to be given to the local bodies directly for the same kind of works specified by the MPLADS.[88]

In May 2014, MOSPI issued the **revised guidelines** for the scheme which is simple, clear and understandable to all concerned. The fine points of the guidelines are as given below:

- It provides not only the list of prohibited items under the scheme, but also that of permissible items.

- In order to encourage *trusts* and *societies* to work for the betterment of tribal people, the ceiling of Rs. 50 lakh, stipulated for building assets by trusts and societies in areas occupied by tribals, has been enhanced to Rs. 75 lakh.

- Further, to promote cooperative movement and rural development, the Cooperative Societies have also been made eligible under the MPLAD Scheme.

- The abandoned or suspended MPLAD work to be completed by the states.

- Natural and man-made calamities can also be allocated funds under it.

---

86. For development works the MP, Lower House (the Lok Sabha) may select one or more districts of his/her constituency; the MP, Upper House (the Rajya Sabha) may select any one or more districts from his/her constituency (i.e., a state or an UT); and the nominated MPs may select any one or more districts from their constituency (i.e., the whole country).

87. As the Government reports in Publications Division, *India 2007,* pp. 711–12.

88. We may especially quote the '21 Point Memorandum' handed over by the *All India Panchayat Adhyakshas Meet,* mid-2002, N. Delhi to the President and the Central Government of the time.

- Now the funds can be allocated by a MP outside of Constituency/State/UTs, too.
- It can converge with the other approved Central (like MGNAREGA) and State Government schemes.
- Funds from local bodies can be pooled with MPLADS works.
- Public and community contribution is made permissible in the scheme.
- 'One MP–One Idea', an annual competition for best innovation in solving local problems.
- A proper mechanism for its implementation and auditing have also been put in place.

To provide MPs a greater choice under the scheme, the list of indicative and illustrative shelf of projects has been expanded touching the fields of infrastructure development, drinking water, education, roads, health, sanitation, natural calamity, etc. The scheme has been given more dynamism and flexibility.

MULTI-LEVEL PLANNING

It was by the late 1950s and early 1960s that the states demanded the right to plan at the state level. By the mid-1960s, the states were given the power to plan by the Centre, advising them that they should promote planning at the lower levels of the administrative strata, too, i.e., at the district level planning—via the municipalities and corporations in the urban areas and via block level through panchayats and the tribal boards. By the early 1980s, India was a country of multi-level planning (MLP) with the structure and strata of planning as follows:

First Strata: Centre-Level Planning

At this level three types of Central Plans had evolved over the years—the Five Year Plans, the Twenty-Point Programme and the MPLADS.

Second Strata: State-Level Planning

By the 1960s, the states were planning at the state level with their respective planning bodies, the state Planning Boards with the respective CMs being their de-facto Chairman. The plans of the states were for a term of five years and parallel to the concerned Five Year Plans of the Centre.

Third Strata: District-Level Planning

By the late 1960s all the districts of the states were having their own plans with their respective District Planning Boards[89] with the respective District Magistrate being the de-facto chairman. The district-level plans are implemented now via municipalities or corporations in the urban areas and the panchayats via the blocks in the rural areas.

Fourth Strata: Block-Level Planning

As a part of the district-level planning the block level planning came up which had the District Planning Boards as their nodal body. Below the blocks, India developed the planning at the local level, too.

Fifth Strata: Local Level Planning

By the early 1980s, plans were being implemented at the local level via the blocks and had the District Planning Boards (DPBs) as the nodal agency. Due to socio-economic differentiations among the population, local-level planning in India developed with its three variants,[90] namely:

---

89. After the implementation of the 74th Constitutional Amendments they have become the District Planning Committees (DPCs).

90. While people in some areas have socio-cultural similarities (as in the hill areas with no tribal population and the people living in the plains, i.e., villages) they lack economic similarities. Similarly, while people living in the tribal areas and the hill areas have economic similarities they lack socio-cultural similarities. That is why all these three habitations had three sets of planning patterns.

(i) Village-Level Planning

(ii) Hill Area Planning

(iii) Tribal Area Planning

Basically, the MLP was started to promote the process of decentralised planning in the country. It was the Indian version of democratic planning which ultimately sought to guarantee the people's participation in the process of planning. But it failed to do so due to many reasons. The reasons have been discussed below:

(i) It could not promote people's participation in the formation of the various plans. The basic idea of the MLP model was that once the local-level plans will be handed over to the blocks, the blocks will make their plans and once the blocks hand over their plans to the districts, the district-level plans will be formulated. Similarly, the state plans and finally the Five Year Plan if the Centre will formulate one. By doing so, every idea of planning will have the representation of everybody in the country at the time of plan formation—a special kind of plan empathy would have developed out of this process. But this was not the reality. Every strata made their own plans—lacking the empathy factor.

(ii) Only Central Plans were implemented as the states lacked the required level of finance to support the plans. They ultimately had to be satisfied by implementing the Central Plans which failed to include the states' empathy.

(iii) As the local bodies in India were not having any constitutional mandate, they just played the complementary roles to the state planning process. As they had no financial independence, their plans, even if they were formulated, remained only on paper.

(iv) The MLP, thus, failed to include the people's participation in planning, badly betraying the local aspirations.[91]

But at least the failure of MLP made the government to think in the direction of decentralised planning afresh leading to the enactment of the two important Constitutional Amendments—the 73rd and 74th.

WAY TO DECENTRALISED PLANNING

Economic planning was basically an element of the centralised kind of political system (i.e., the socialist and the communist). When India decided in favour of a planned economy it was to face double challenges:

(i) The first challenge was to realise the objectives of planning in a time-bound frame, and

(ii) Making economic planning a suitable instrument of development in the democratic set up—to democratise and decentralise the process of planning itself.

The government tried to decentralise the planning process by setting up the NDC and promoting the MLP, but without being able to achieve the desired results. By the late 1980s, a direct link was established[92] between development

---

91. G.V.K. Rao Committee (CAARD), 1985; L.M. Singhvi Committee (CCPPRI), 1986 and Sarkaria Commission, 1988 all discussed this inter-connection (Suresh Mishra, *Legislative Status of Panchayat Raj in India* (New Delhi: Indian Institute of Public Administration, 1997).

92. Governments' failure in including the local aspirations in the process of planned development has been considered by major experts as the foremost reason behind the success of the regional political parties, which has led to the governments of the 'compromises', i.e., coalition governments, at the Centre and in the states via the 'hung parliaments' and the 'hung assemblies', respectively.

and democracy. And it was established that the above-given challenges were basically complementary—without solving the second challenge (i.e., decentralisation) the first challenge (i.e., development) cannot be solved. Finally, once the PRIs were given the constitutional status, first time planning became a constitutional excercise at any level, i.e., at the panchayat level.

Though the planning at the central and the state levels are still extra-constitutional activities, it has become constitutional at the level of local bodies. Kerala has shown some pathbreaking good works via local body planning.[93] But still there are many hurdles to be solved before the local bodies are really able to plan for their proper development. These hurdles as per the experts are as under:

(i) The financial status of the PRIs is still not stabilised.

(ii) Which taxes the PRIs can impose are still not clear.

(iii) The state assemblies have been procrastinating in delegating timely and needful powers to the PRIs.

(iv) Low level of awareness among the local people regarding their Right to Information and the right functioning of the PRIs

(v) Use of money and muscle power in the PRI elections in some states

By mid-2002, there took place an all India Panchayat Adhyaksha Sammelan in New Delhi. At the end of the conference , the Panchayat Adhyakshas handed over a '21 Point Memorandum' to the government which specially dealt with the financial status of the PRIs. In July 2002, while the then PM was addressing the

93. Jose George, 'Panchayats and Participatory Planning in Kerala', *The Indian Journal of Public Administration,* Vol. XLIII, No.1, January–March 1997.

annual meet of the District Rural Development Agency (DRDA), he announced that the PRIs will be given 'financial autonomy' very soon. He further added that once there is a political consensus, the government might go in for further constitutional amendment. Unfortunately, the same coalition (i.e., the NDA) did not come to power in the forthcoming general elections. But the UPA Government did not look less serious on the issue of participatory development. By mid-2006, the Planning Commission wrote letters to every Chief Minister of each state that before the Eleventh Plan commences it wants that all the PRIs are duly delegated their functional powers of planning from the concerned states. Otherwise, the funds kept for local development would not flow to the states. This shows the seriousness of the Central Government.

Meanwhile, the Central government is aimed at **redrawing** the contours of decentralised planning in the country. The new development 'think tank'—*NITI Aayog*—has a completely new orientation towards decentralised planning:

- The body has to design the development policies keeping in mind the needs of *nation, states* and the *PRIs*. This will be one of its kind—a fully 'integrated' planning process.

- It has to use the '*bottom-up*' approach unlike the one-size-fits-all ('Top-down') approach of the past.

- To the extent the finalisation of plans and required funds are concerned, all stakeholders will be having their says (through the Governing Council which is composed of the CMs of states and the Chiefs of UTs).

- Promoting the idea of '*Team India*' which will be working on a common 'National Agenda'.

- It has to promote the idea of *co-operative federalism,* which is in itself a highly decentralised style of promoting development planning.

By early 2015, we saw a change in the Central government's outlook towards the fund requirements by the states, viz.,

(i) States now get *42 per cent* share in the pool of taxes of the Centre (recommendation of the Fourteenth Finance Commission accepted).

(ii) States are getting *liberal funding* (loan plus grants) from the Centre to implement the State Plans.

(iii) One of the aims behind implementing the proposed GST is to the enhance the internal financial capacity of the states as the new tax will increase the gross tax collections of the states.

(iv) States are now free to go for higher *market borrowings* without any permission from the Centre (but such a move has to come from the Centre). The UDAY (Ujwal Discom Assurance Yojana), launched in 2015–16 is one of such approvals of the Central government under which states are allowed to issue 'UDAY Bonds' up to 75 per cent of the dues of the electricity distribution companies (Discom) of the states (by mid-2016, the total discom debt in the country amounted to Rs. 4.3 lakh crore).

THE PLANNING COMMISSION & THE FINANCE COMMISSION

Federal political systems provide independent financial control to the central as well as the state governments so that they are able to perform their exclusive functions.[94] For the same objective, the Constitution of India has made elaborate provisions,[95] i.e., setting up of a Finance Commission to recommend to the President certain measures relating to the distribution of financial resources between the Union and the states. But the powers given to the Finance Commission by the Parliament limited its functions to the extent of finding out revenue gap of the states, besides recommending for the 'grant-in-aids to the states from the Centre. The finance commission cannot determine the capital-related issues of the states (though the Constitution does not classify between the capital or revenue related roles of the commission while determining the Centre's assistance to the states).

In the meantime, to promote the process of planning, an extra-constitutional body, i.e., the Planning Commission was set up even before the First Finance Commission was set up. The Planning Commission played a very vital role in the process of determining Central assistance to the states as all development plans, programmes and projects are within its purview. All grants or loans given by the Centre to the states for developmental works are practically dependent on the recommendations of the Planning Commission. And that is why the role of the Planning Commission was said to 'confine'[96] the role of the Finance Commission, i.e., a non-constitutional body eclipsing a constitutional body. P.J. Rajamannar who headed the Finance Commission (1966–69) suggested to clearly define the relative scope and functions of the two commissions by amending the Constitution, and the Planning Commission was advised to be made a statutory body independent of the government. But no such follow ups came from the successive governments at the Centre. But one thing was important, most of the finance commissions

94. As *K.C. Wheare* writes about the classical federal constitutions in *Federal Government* (New Delhi: Oxford University Press, 1956), p. 97.

95. Articles 270, 273, 275 and 280 of the *Constitution of India.*

96. Ministry of Finance, *Report of the Fourth Finance Commission,* p. 88.

devoluted some extra shares in the central taxes (i.e., the income tax and the central excise) and grants-in-aid.

Since the decade of the 1990s, certain events made the Central Government change its mindset regarding the role of the states in the process of development. Major events may be counted as under:

(i) The process of economic reforms started in 1991–92 required active economic participation from the states.

(ii) The constitutional requirement of 'participatory planning' mandated by the 73rd and 74th Constitutional Amendments was enacted in 1993.

(iii) The arrival of coalition era at the Centre when over a dozen political parties, having regional affiliations came together to form the government.

(iv) The recommendations of the Tenth Finance Commission followed by a Constitutional Amendment making Alternative Method of Devolution a law in 1995.

(v) Various new needs of the time, such as, tax reforms, agricultural development, industrial expansion, etc.

The year 2002 could be considered a watershed in the area of promoting the states' need for financial resources in promoting their developmental requirements. In July 2002, while the government was setting up the Twelfth Finance Commission (2005–10) the then Minister of Finance announced that in future the Planning Commission will be *playing more or less a role of collaborator to the Finance Commission*. In the same announcement, the government made one member of the Planning Commission, a member of the Finance Commission too (a symbol of physical and ideological connection between the

two bodies).[97] It was as if the government had accepted the suggestions of the Fourth Finance Commission to a great extent. Though the critics took it as an infringement of a constitutional body by a non-constitutional one, the government clarified by calling it a symbol for promoting the contemporary needs of the economy and fiscal federalism.

Another milestone was created in the enactment of the Fiscal Responsibility and Budget Management (FRBM) Act in 2003, which empowers the state governments to go for market borrowings to fulfil their plan expenditure without prior permission from the Central Government (provided they have enacted their respective Fiscal Responsibility Acts).[98] This has boosted the participatory planning in the country by guaranteeing greater autonomous plan participation from the states.

If we look at the tax reforms process, we see a general tendency of enabling the states to collect more and more taxes, the Value Added Tax (VAT) being a glaring example by which almost all states have been able to increase their gross tax revenue receipts. The cause will be served more once the economy goes for the proposed enactment of the Goods and Services Tax (GST).

In January 2015, the NITI Aayog replaced the Planning Commission, thus the comparison between the latter and the Finance Commission no more exits, but it will always have its *academic*

---

97. In the 10th Plan, **Som Pal** was that common member in both the Commissions (who resigned from the PC once the UPA-I came to power). But this arrangement has been followed by the government in all new Commissions since then—with **B. K. Chaturvedi** and **Prof. Abhijit Sen** (Members, PC) being the *Additional Members* of the *13th* and *14th Finance Commissions*.

98. This should be considered a great fiscal freedom to the states (which even the constitution could not forsee) and also making them behave with more responsibility in fiscal matters. More than 20 states have passed their Fiscal Responsibility Acts (FRAs) by now and are borrowing from the market for their planned needs.

importance in the area of development planning in the country. Such experiences of the past will function as a directives for the policy makers in the future.

Meanwhile, the new body, the NITI, is totally different in its approach towards fund allocations to the states to promote the cause of development planning. Basically, the states now sit in the NITI itself, in a very strong position. The NITI has been termed by the Central Government as the *'bestfriend of states in the Centre'*.

THE CHANGING NATURE AND THE ROLE OF PLANNING

Led by various inter-connected and experience-based factors, a great many **new elements** have been included in the Indian planning process in recent years. Some of the new elements are too path breaking to reverse the very established thinking of planning in the country. Still some of them could be seen as the government's attempt to address some of the long-standing and overdue criticisms of planning in India. The inclusion of the new **methods** and **strategies** of planning has gone to change the very **nature**, **role** and **scope** of planning in the country. It was the Tenth Plan which is credited in doing this. Many 'first time' initiatives were taken up by the Plan. Usually, the plan projections in India did talk about development in the recognised sectors, but here the Tenth Plan imaginatively forges ahead towards new goals—it was undoubtedly a historic moment. The new measures initiated by the Plan[99], which led to changes in planning may be seen as under:

---

99. Planning Commission, *Tenth Five Year Plan* (New Delhi: Government of India, 2002).

1. The Role of the State in Planned Development

It was for the first time that the Planning Commission not only went for a detailed talk on the states' concerns but also emphasised and recognised their role in the process of development planning (in Vol. III, Tenth Plan). The Plan accepts that unless the states achieve their targets, a nation cannot achieve its targets. This is an open acceptance of the state's role in planning and a clear pointer to the need for decentralised planning. The meeting of the Planning Commission which passed the Tenth Plan advised two important ideas in this regard:

(i) to make the Tenth Plan a *'People's Plan'*, and

(ii) to make development a *'People's Movement.'*

The Deputy Chairman, Planning Commission articulated on the ocassion that 'people's say in Plan is a must'. The Chairman, Planning Commission emphasised that only economic growth should not be our objective but improvement in the quality of life of the masses should be the real goal of planned development. He further added that people's participation in the planning process is a must to make development a mass movement and helpful to all. This idea continued in the Eleventh Plan and proposes the Twelfth Plan (2012–17).

2. Agricultural Sector Accepted as the Driving Force of the Economy

There had been a bias against the agricultural sector around the world after the Second World War—emphasis on agrarian economy was considered a symbol of backwardness. This mindset, ultimately, changed by the early 1990s to which the World Bank also agreed. Though the Union Budgets of 2000–01 and 2001–02 clearly referred to the proposition, it was the Tenth Plan which clearly accepted the 'agriculture sector' as the Prime Moving Force (PMF) of the economy. The Nobel Laureate Amartya Sen has also suggested on the same lines.[100]

The Plan further adds that by prioritising agriculture (in place of industry) the economy will be able to solve three major problems which have been ailing the economy:

(i) With the increase in agricultural production, the economy will have food security,

(ii) Emphasis on agriculture will give a great thrust to employment generation (92 per cent of the employment is today generated by the unorganised sector with agriculture being the biggest), and

(iii) Purchasing power of the masses will increase, which will reverse the long-standing situation of 'market failure' in the economy (that is why India sells lesser industrial goods and the industries lack the market for their products. It means by emphasising upon the agriculture sector, the economy will be able to boost its income from the industries).

Accepting agriculture as the 'core element' of the economy, the Plan suggested key reforms which are at their various stages of implementations:

(i) Elimination of inter-state barriers to trade and commerce;

(ii) Encouraging contract farming and permitting leasing in and leasing out of agriculture lands;

(iii) Need to amend the Essential Commodities Act;

(iv) Liberalising agri-industry, agri-trade and exports;

(v) Replacement of various Acts concerning food by one comprehensive 'Food Act';

(vi) Permitting 'future trading' in all commodities;

(vii) Removal of restrictions on financing of stocking and trading.

3. Governance Recognised the Most Important Factor of Development

It was for the first time that the economic think tank, the Planning Commission went to comment upon the issue of governance (which has been only of political concern till date and the Planning Commission never thought to ponder upon such issues). In its first comment upon it, the Planning Commission recognised governance among the most important factors to realise the planned goals (a full chapter devoted to it in Vol. I of the Tenth Plan). The government also did set up an empowered committee on the matter which advised a list of reforms:

(i) Improved people's participation through PRIs;

(ii) Increased involvement of civil society and NGOs;

(iii) Civil service reforms for improving transparency, accountability and efficiency; security of tenure for the civil servants with more equitable system of rewards and punishments;

(iv) Right sizing both the size and role of the government;

(v) Revenue and judicial reforms; and

(vi) Use of Information Technology for 'good governance'

After the World Bank report on 'Good Governance' in the mid-1990s, the government has been trying to sensitise the issue. Finally, it was the Tenth Plan which accepted the immediate need for good governance.

---

100. While he was in India to receive the 'Bharat Ratna' award in 2001.

4. New Steps for Economic Reforms to be Taken by the State

In a major decision it was articulated that from now onwards all the new steps of economic reforms will be taken by the states with the Centre playing a supportive role. It was the time when the government initiated the Second Generation of Economic Reforms. Till date the states had been playing a secondary role in the process of economic reforms. That is why the economy had not been able to tap the expected benefits from it. Now the method and strategy from the reforms process have gone in for a change.

5. Monitorable Targets of Development Set for the First Time

There used to be planned targets in the past, but this time an innovative way of setting these targets was initiated. The Plan did set, for the first time, a national-level monitorable targets in 11 broad areas.

The monitorable targets have importance as the concerned central ministries are parties to its realisation. The ministries hand over an undertaking to the Planning Commission about their strategies of realising the targets, and performance reports are submitted by them, which become the bases for monitoring by the Planning Commission.

6. Differential Development Strategies Adopted

The Tenth Plan accepts that national targets do not necessarily translate into balanced regional development. It further adds that the potential and constraints of each state differ from the other. That is why the Plan goes on to adopt a differential development strategy. Under this strategy, separate state-wise growth and other monitorable targets were worked out by the Planning Commission for the states with their consultation so that the states can focus on their

development plans. The states are getting central plan support according to their development requirement, as against the past pattern of plan allocations. The developmental funds to the states and the central loans to them now accrue subject to their performance concerning the monitorable targets set for the states (to which they agreed).

7. Monitoring the Progress of Various Central Ministries

With the Tenth Plan the government has started a process under which the progress of different central ministries was monitored by the Planning Commission This is how the policy initiatives of the various ministries and the Planning Commission's idea of development have been streamlined. The Planning Commission did really emerged as a 'super cabinet' in this way.

8. Relevance of Planning to Economic Reforms

After the two five-year plans (the eighth and the ninth) were already implemented, the government took up the cause of establishing a relevance between the process of planning and the broader process of economic reforms. Different steering committees have been set up which look after the plan implementation of the different sectors according to the idea of economic reforms. This step should be seen as the government's answer to the critics who opined that planning has become irrelevant in the era of economic reforms.

9. Reforming the Planning Process

The government called this Plan a 'reform plan' rather than a 'resource plan'. There has been a long-standing criticism about Indian plans that they are mere excercises in resource mobilisation. Probably, the Planning Commission has tried to do away with this criticism. The above given points visibly prove that the Tenth Plan was not merely a 'resource plan'. Basically, the Plan initiates many pathbreaking changes in the planning process—its methods, strategies and ideas—all at the same time. Rightly, it has been called a 'reform plan' by the Planning Commission. Second, this was the first plan in the era of economic reforms which accepts to go for establishing relevance to the process of economic reforms. From this perspective, too, this Plan is a 'reform plan'.

The inclusion of the above-given new elements into the Indian planning process has gone to really change the nature, role and scope of planning in the country. All these new elements are today carried forward by the Eleventh Plan with an emphasis wherever it is required. The planning process is more established today in India as the changes in the political arrangements at the Centre do not seem to be affecting it unlike the past.

MONITORABLE TARGETS SET BY THE TWELFTH PLAN

To focus the energies of the government and other stakeholders in development, it is desirable to identify monitorable indicators, which can be used to track the progress of our efforts. Given the complexity of the country and the development process, there are very large number of targets that can and should be used. However, there is a **core set of indicators** which could form the objectives towards which all development partners can work, which includes not only the Central and state governments, but also local governments, CSOs (Civil Society Organisations) and international agencies. The **Twelfth Plan (2012–17)** has set *twenty-five monitorable targets* in *seven broad areas* reflecting its (India's) *'vision of rapid, sustainable* and more *inclusive growth'*: [101]

---

101. Planning Commission, *Twelfth Five Year Plan (2012–2017),* Vol. I – Inclusive and Sustainable Growth (New Delhi: Government of India, 2012), pp. 34–36.

Economic Growth

(i) Real GDP growth rate of 8 per cent.

(ii) Agriculture growth rate of 4.0 per cent.

(iii) Manufacturing growth rate of 10.0 per cent.

(iv) Every state must have an average growth rate in the Twelfth Plan preferably higher than that achieved in the Eleventh Plan.

Poverty and Employment

(v) Head-count ratio of consumption poverty to be reduced by 10 percentage points over the preceding estimates by the end of Twelfth Five Year Plan.

(vi) Generate 50 million new work opportunities in the non-farm sector and provide skill certification to equivalent numbers during the Twelfth Five Year Plan.

Education

(vii) Mean Years of Schooling to increase to seven years by the end of the Twelfth Five Year Plan.

(viii) Enhance access to higher education by creating two million additional seats for each age cohort aligned to the skill needs of the economy.

(ix) Eliminate gender and social gap in school enrolment (i.e., between girls and boys, and between SCs, STs, Muslims and the rest of the population) by the end of the Twelfth Five Year Plan.

Health

(x) Reduce IMR to 25 and MMR to 1 per 1,000 live births, and improve Child Sex Ratio (0–6 years) to 950 by the end of the Twelfth Five Year Plan.

(xi) Reduce Total Fertility Rate to 2.1 by the end of the Twelfth Five Year Plan.

(xii) Reduce under-nutrition among children aged 0–3 years to half of the NFHS-3 levels by the end of the Twelfth Five Year Plan.

Infrastructure, Including Rural Infrastructure

(xiii) Increase investment in infrastructure as a percentage of GDP to 9 per cent by the end of the Twelfth Five Year Plan.

(xiv) Increase the Gross Irrigated Area from 90 million hectare to 103 million hectare by the end of the Twelfth Five Year Plan.

(xv) Provide electricity to all villages and reduce AT&C losses to 20 per cent by the end of the Twelfth Five Year Plan.

(xvi) Connect all villages with all-weather roads by the end of the Twelfth Five Year Plan.

(xvii) Upgrade national and state highways to the minimum two-lane standard by the end of the Twelfth Five Year Plan.

(xviii) Complete Eastern and Western Dedicated Freight Corridors by the end of the Twelfth Five Year Plan.

(xix) Increase rural tele-density to 70 per cent by the end of the Twelfth Five Year Plan.

(xx) Ensure that 50 per cent of the rural population have access to 40 lpcd piped drinking water supply, and 50 per cent gram panchayats achieve Nirmal Gram Status by the end of the Twelfth Five Year Plan.

Environment and Sustainability

(xxi) Increase green cover (as measured by satellite imagery) by 1 million hectare every year during the Twelfth Five Year Plan.

(xxii) Add 30,000 MW of renewable energy capacity in the Twelfth Plan.

(xxiii) Reduce emission intensity of GDP in line with the target of 20 per cent to 25 per cent reduction over 2005 levels by 2020.

Service Delivery

(xiv) Provide access to banking services to 90 per cent Indian households by the end of the Twelfth Five Year Plan.

(xxv) Major subsidies and welfare related beneficiary payments to be shifted to a direct cash transfer by the end of the Twelfth Plan, using the Aadhar platform with linked bank accounts.

States are encouraged to set *state-specific targets* corresponding to the above, taking account of what is the reasonable degree of progress given the initial position. Sector-wise monitorable growth targets set by the states have also been given by the Plan.

A CRITICAL EVALUATION

Planning has been subject to a number of criticisms right since its inception in the country. With the passage of time, not only the number of criticism increased, but more importantly the shortcomings of planning were pointed out. Although after considerable delay, the governments took note of the shortcomings besides taking some major steps. The criticisms stand even today, but with one difference that the government is not only conscious of them but also trying to do away with them. We may briefly discuss the major criticisms of planning in India as well as the follow ups from the government to do away with them as under:

1. Lack of 'Perspective' in Planning

According to experts, if a nation is going for economic planning it must have 'perspective' element in it. To have perspective in planning, two basic elements need to be fulfilled, namely—

(i) Planning should be evaluation-based, and

(ii) 'Long-term' goals should be followed up besides the 'short-term' goals.

In the Indian content, the succeeding plans have been always commenced without the full evaluation of the preceding Plan. This was mainly due to the following reasons:

(a) Lack of a nodal body responsible for data collection at the national level;

(b) Federal nature of polity made data collection full of delays and also due to higher dependence on the states; and

(c) Speedier data delivery was not possible.

After the recommendations of the National Statistical Commission (Chaired by C. Rangarajan), 2000, the government discussed to set up a nodal body for data collection at the pan-India level, cutting across federal hurdles. Computerisation is already being done for speedier data delivery. For the time being the Plans are launched on the basis of projected data (provisional, latest, etc.), which is almost near the real data. But once the above discussed arrangements are in place, Indian planning will be based on evaluation, undoubtedly. In the meantime, the 'Quarterly Review' and the 'Performance Budgeting' of the Union Budgets have brought in the evaluation element to a greater degree.

The First Plan had set long-term goals (for the coming 20 years) besides the short-term goals (for five years). But over the time, falling confidence in mobilising required resources and political uncertainties at the Centre made it a convention to set only short-term targets of planning. This shortcoming seems to be done away with after the commencement of the Tenth Plan. The Plan did not go for setting long-term goals only, but even did set monitorable targets for the Eleventh Plan, too.

Point should be noted here that the government had been conscious about the need for perspective planning as a separate division with the same name, which has been functioning in the Yojana Bhavan since the mid-1970s.

2. Failure in Promoting a Balanced Growth and Development

Indian planning is blamed for failing the objective of a regionally balanced growth and development. Though the Second Plan itself had noticed this fact, the measures taken were not sufficient or were short-sighted. Economic planning at the national level has proved to be a highly effective tool of promoting balanced growth. But in the Indian case it turned out to be the opposite.

To take care of the issue of balanced growth, the planning process has been using the right tools, i.e., allocating plan funds on a sectoral (primary, secondary and federal reasons) basis. But due to political reasons, enough discrepancies cropped up in the method of allocating funds to the states. At the theoretical level, the governments knew the remedies, but at the practical levels politics dominated the planning process. Democratic immaturity and politicisation of the planning process is to be blamed for this.

Now things have changed for the better. The government is following a two-pronged strategy to achieve the objective of a balanced growth and development in the country:

(i) Backward regions today are prioritised in directing the Central Government investment (very much the same since the 1950s), but a new beginning in the 'differential development strategy' has been made by the Centre with the Tenth Plan. Under this strategy, the developmental constraints of different states are to be tackled with a differentiation in the strategy. The more needy states get more funds and assistance from the Centre for their planned development, cutting across the political party lines (it is seen today as a symbol of political maturity on the issue of economic development, at least).

(ii) There is also a complementary strategy of the planning to address the matter of regional imbalance in the country. After the country started the process of economic reforms, the nature of planning was to incline more and more towards indicative planning. The economy was to be more and more dependent on private sector investment for its future development. And the private sector will be, naturally, more interested in investing in the regions, which have better infrastructure support. Since the developed regions have better infrastructure they will attract the highest level of private investment, which will again accelerate the process of imbalanced growth. To tackle this problem, the Centre is promoting the states with lower, infrastructure so that they can overcome the disadvantage. The process is slower, but at least the government is addressing the issue, which is not less satisfying and there is no criticism to this strategy. Still balanced growth and development is going to be a great challenge for planning in India.

3. Highly Centralised Nature of Planning

Decentralising the process of planning has been a major goal of the governments since the 1950s. But after Nehru, with every Plan we see greater tendency of centralisation in the planning process. Setting up of the NDC and promoting multi-level planning (MLP) did not serve much purpose in this direction. It has been among the criticised areas of planning in India as the National Planning Committee as well as the First Plan itself had called for 'democratic planning' in the country.

By the mid-1980s, the mindset of the Centre went for a change and the need for decentralised

planning got proper attention. Finally, by early 1990s two constitutional amendments (i.e., the 73rd and the 74th) promoted the cause of decentralised planning by delegating constitutional powers to the local bodies. With this, a new era of planning began, but still the planning of local bodies is in a nascent stage due to lack of proper financial provisions for them. Once the financial provisions for local bodies are evolved to the adequate level or the local bodies are given financial autonomy, the process of decentralised planning will surely get a new direction and meaning, as the experts believe.

In the meantime, the Tenth Plan emphasised greater role for the states in the planning process. The Plan started a concerted effort to include the states' participation in the national planning process. The Centre is today more concerned about the developmental constraints of the states and is trying to adequately support the State Plans to the extent possible. In return, the Centre wants greater and transparent fiscal compliance from the states. This approach continued during the Eleventh Plan and so has been committed for the Twelfth Plan, too. After some time we may hope that this criticism of Indian planning will lose it's ground.

It is high time now that the planning process of the nation tries including the mass participation. The *Economic Survey 2011–12* rightly devotes a section to dwell into contracts and how the **civil society** and citizens play a key role in fostering economic growth. *"Honesty, punctuality, the propensity to keep promises, the attitude towards corruption are matters shaped in great part by norms and social beliefs and the behaviour patterns can become habitual. Moreover, in a democracy like India, what can be done by government depends in great measure on how ordinary people think and what people believe in,"* it says. The Survey further adds that the **civil society** has been campaigning to put in place new institutions, such as the Lokpal Act, to ensure the quality of service and bring about transparency through steps such as auction of natural resources while the government has either been slow or resisted several changes.[102]

4. Lop-sided Employment Strategy

Planning in India has been tilted heavily in favour of 'capital intensive' industries, especially from the Second Plan onwards. Such industries in the public sector could not generate enough employment. In place of it India should have gone in for 'labour-intensive' industries. In the era of economic reforms, the attitude changed and the planning process is promoting the agriculture sector with an emphasis on agri-industries and agro-exports to create more gainful and quality employment opportunities. The earlier emphasis on 'wage-employment' has shifted towards 'self-employment' to do away with the lop-sided employment strategy of the past.

5. Excessive Emphasis on PSUs

Indian planning emphasised on public sector undertakings (PSUs) for the right reasons, but in the wrong way and for a considerably longer period of time. The state's monopolies in certain areas continued over such a long period that too in losses that there came a demand-supply gap in the major goods and services produced by the PSUs. Though very conducive policy changes were effected after the country started the reform processes, the hangover of the past is still looming large. Several reforms in the PSUs as well as a more liberal approach towards the private sector with market reforms are needed to phase out the discrepancies created by the over emphasis on PSUs.

6. Agriculture Overshadowed by the Industry

Promoting the cause of faster industrialisation over time became so dear to the planning process that the agriculture sector got badly over-shadowed. Though the Plans were highlighting or prioritising agriculture, the industrial sector and the PSUs were glorified in such a way that time and resources both were scarce for the agriculture sector. Such a policy always created a situation of food insecurity (even today) for the country and the masses who depended upon agriculture for their livelihood and income (still it is 58.2 per cent)[103] could never increase their purchasing power to a level that the economy could reverse the situation of 'market failure'. In India, even today, industrial growth is badly dependent on agricultural growth.

The Tenth Plan recognises agriculture as the 'core element' of development. This is a welcome ideological change in the strategy of planning. Now the industries can sustain themselves, but the laggard agriculture sector needs some special care and promotion from the government, so that the masses who earn their livelihood from agriculture can benefit out of the WTO-promoted globalisation. The agriculture sector is in urgent need of attention, otherwise, the process of globalisation is going to be ineffective in benefitting the masses.

7. Faulty Industrial Location Policy

There are time-tested theories of 'industrial location' considering the nearness of raw materials, market, cheaper labour, better transportation and communication, etc. But the Plans always prioritised setting up of new industrial units (i.e., the PSUs) in the backward regions of the country, which falsify the theories of industrial location. The government needs to develop all industrial infrastructures besides setting up certain PSUs. As the PSUs require skilled labour force, the regions failed to gain any employment from the PSUs too. The government still continues with the same

---

102. Ministry of Finance, *Economic Survey 2011–12* (New Delhi: Government of India, 2012), p. 30.

103. Ministry of Finance, Economic Survey 2012–13 (New Delhi: Government of India, 2013), p. 173.

policy of setting up industries, but now the new PSUs are hardly set up in traditional areas.

8. Wrong Financial Strategy

Mobilising resources to support the highly capital-intensive Plans (courtsey the PSUs) has always been a challenge for the government. To support the Plans, no stones were left unturned namely, going for a highly complex and liberal tax structure, nationalising the banks, etc. Ultimately, tax evasion, the menace of parallel economy and lesser and lesser capital for the private sector were the bane of India. Expansion of subsidies, salaries and the interest burden every year gave an upward push to the non-plan expenditure leading to scarcity of funds to support the plan expenditure (i.e., the developmental expenses).

In the era of reforms, the government has started giving attention to the financial strategy of supporting the Plans in the right way. Besides tax reforms, the financial reforms, as well as fiscal consolidation have been given proper care in recent years.

9. Politicisation of the Planning Process

In a democratic political system, almost every issue of socio-political importance is influenced by politics. It is more correct in the case of lesser matured democracies. The same stands true for the process of planning in our country. Greater and greater politicisation of the planning process culminated in such a design that at times economic planning served the opposite purpose. For example, we know that planning is a tool for promoting regionally balanced growth, but in India in the process of serving vested political interests of the Centre, it resulted into promoting an imbalanced growth.

In recent years, the government has tried to address the major criticism of planning in India. More such constructive steps with better results are expected in future. More aware and better informed citizens will lead to better and better planning in future.

There has been a general anger among the sections of society regarding coalition politics, scams, etc., in recent years. The *Economic Survey 2014–15* rightly *blames coalition politics* and the *federal structure* for tardy decision making in several areas—from oil subsidy to tax reforms, FDI in retail and free movement of foodgrains. Almost everyone outside the government blamed it for *policy paralysis*. The Survey notes it as an area of concern. The Survey notes that *politicians* and *policymakers* can set the ball rolling by acting as *role models,* but it also cited the poor record on enforcement of contract to argue that people's attitude needs to change. *"In these everyday situations (such as hiring a cab or a painter) it is cumbersome to bring in the state and the law courts. Here the main guarantor has to be people's personal integrity and trustworthiness"*, it says. The statement comes from a government that has been battling a spate of *corruption scandals*—ranging from those in the telecom sector to Commonwealth Games and criticism over poor governance standards and inability to push through critical decisions.[104]

The *Economic Survey 2012–13* suggested a new objective for the Planning Commission—the global economic and financial crisis which has persisted for the last five years has not only exposed the vulnerability of almost all the countries over the globe to external shocks, but also has lessons for the *planning process*, viz., countries need to have inbuilt social safety nets for facing such eventualities, which affect the weak and vulnerable the most, and wipe out the fruits of growth for years. India with its focus on inclusive development and timely interventions has, however, been able to weather the crisis better than many other countries.[105]

---

104. *Economic Survey 2011-12,* MoF, GoI, N. Delhi, p. 30.
105. Ministry of Finance, *Economic Survey 2012–13,* p. 269.

INCLUSIVE GROWTH

Inclusive growth is a growth process which yields broad-based benefits and ensures equality of opportunity for all (*UNDP* and the *11th Plan*). Fundamentally, the ideas of growth and development already include the element of 'inclusiveness' in them, but at times, due to certain reasons, the processes might occur in non-inclusive manner.

It was in 2000–01 that the Government of India came to think clearly about 'inclusiveness' in the economy, while reviewing the performance of the economic reforms. It was found that the reform process enabled economy towards faster and higher 'wealth creation', but all could not be part of it. Only the people with resources (physical or human) were able to get benefits out of the reforming economy. It was assessed that the fruits of reforms could not percolate to the *disadvantaged* and *marginalised* sections of the society. It means, the growth process during reforms was not able to include a big segment of the Indian population. In this backdrop, we see the government adopting a conscious policy towards 'inclusive growth'. Even before reforms commenced in the country, this element was lacking. But during reforms it became more glaring due to the higher pace of growth which the economy attained during this period. Though the government started attending to this issue since 2000–01 itself, it was given real attention in the *11th Plan* (2007–12), where we see a clear policy evolving towards the idea of inclusive growth in the country—'including the disadvantaged and marginalised sections of the society, specially, SCs, STs, OBCs, Minorities and Women' in the processes of growth and development. By the *12th Plan* (2012–17), the focus increased when we see the issue of inclusiveness entering into the very slogan of the Plan—'Faster, Sustainable and More Inclusive Growth'. During the course of time, we see the government evolving a clear *short-term* and *long-term* policy towards the cause of inclusive growth.

Short-term policy

This policy is aimed at supplying those goods and services to the disadvantaged and marginalised sections of society which are bare minimum and are essential in nature. Several Central Sector Schemes and Centrally Sponsored Schemes are run by the governments for this purpose. This policy touches the areas like:

- Food and nutirition (Annapurna, Antodaya, Mid-Day Meal, and the last being National Food Security Act, etc.);
- Healthcare and sanitation (National Health Mission, Total Sanitation Campaign, ASHA, Mission Indradhanush, and the last being Swachh Bharat Abhiyan, etc.);
- Housing (Indira Aawas Yojana, Rajiv Aawas Yojana, etc.);
- Drinking water (National Rural Drinking Water Programme, etc.);
- Education (Sarva Shiksha Abhiyan, Rashtriya Madhyamik Shiksha Abhiyan, Model School Scheme, etc.).

The short-term policy has two drawbacks-*Firstly*, the schemes in it are subsidy-based, which incurr heavy drain on the national exchequer (it means it will not be fiscally sustainable in the long run). *Secondly*, the schemes fail to make the target population self-dependent. This is why the government has also evolved a long-term policy in this regard.

Long-term policy

This policy is aimed at bringing in self-dependence in the target population. This policy contains in itself the sustainabilty element, too. The attempts by the governments may be classified as given below:

- All the schemes which aim at poverty alleviation and employment generation;
- All the programmes which promote education at any level;
- Vocationalisation of education (one such old idea has been the Industrial Training Institutes); and
- Skill Development (a recent idea).

In recent time, we see increased emphasis on imparting right 'skill' among the population. Towards this, the government decided in 2008–09 to launch a skill development programme in the country through the National Skill Development Corporation (a joint venture not-for-profit company under the Ministry of Finance. There is an overall target of skilling/upskilling 500 million people in India by 2022, mainly by fostering private sector initiatives in skill development programmes and provide funding. The new government at Centre has also given the same call in the *'Skill India'*.

This way, we can see a initiative fool proof policy towards inclusive growth getting evolved by the GoI which is sustainable, too. The Planning Commission *(11th Plan)* says that inclusive growth can only be ensured if there is a degree of empowerment that creates a true feeling of participation so necessary in a democratic polity. Empowerment of disadvantaged and hitherto marginalised groups is therefore an essential part of any vision of inclusive growth. India's democratic polity, with the establishment of the third layer of democracy at the PRIs level, provides opportunities for empowerment and participation of all groups with reservations for SCs, STs and women. These institutions should be made more effective through greater delegation of power and responsibility.

The strategy for inclusive growth in the *11th* and *12th Plans* is not just a conventional strategy for growth to which some elements aimed at inclusion have been added. On the contrary, it is a strategy which aims at achieving a particular type of growth process, which will meet the objectives of *inclusiveness* and *sustainability*. A key feature of the inclusive growth strategy is that growth of "GDP should not be treated as an end in itself, but only as a means to an end". This is best done by adopting *monitorable targets*, which would reflect the multi-dimensional **economic** and **social** objectives of inclusive growth. Furthermore, to ensure efficient and timely implementation of the accompanying projects and programmes, these targets need to be disaggregated at the level of the states which implement many of the programmes.

RESOURCE MOBILISATION

Resource mobilisation is a broad term which includes raising and directing the resources (physical and human) of the economy to realise the desired socio-economic objectives. It involves all the economic policies activated by the governments—we can percieve it to be the very essence and the end result of the 'fiscal policies' of both the Centre and the states.

For Indian economy to move on the path of desired growth and development, the Government of India (GoI) needs to take care of the issue of resource mobilisation for various agents in the economy, namely –

1. GoI,
2. State governments,
3. Private sector, and
4. General public

In India, the responsibility of mobilising resources for the *planned* development of the country was given to the Planning Commission (PC). The commission used to take care of the fund requirements of the centre and the state governments. Practically, it was the PC which has to put in place the means by which the required funds for the *planned targets* of the economy were moblised. These plan targets are set by the GoI through the PC itself. The plan targets set by the states are also duly taken care of the PC in due course of this process. Though the effective responsibilities to moblise resources ultimately rests with the Ministry of Finance in which the various departments and divisions of the ministry play their diverse and highly focused roles.

1. **GoI:** To the extent GoI is concerned it needs funds to realise two categories of the **planned targets**, namely:

    (i) *Infrastructural targets* (which chiefly include power, transportation and communication; in coming years so many other sectors got attached with it, for example, technology parks, urban infrastructure, etc.); and

    (ii) *Social sector targets* (which includes education, health, social security, etc.—known as the Human Development related targets since 2010–11). These funds get mobilised through the *Plan Finance-II Division* of the Ministry of Finance.

2. **State Governments:** Other than the fund requirements of the GoI, the states also need funds for their developmental requirements (similar to the GoI)—they get the funds mobilised through three sources: *firstly,* through their own sources of income and market borrowings (after the recommendations of the 13th Finance Commission states are allowed to finance 25 per cent of their Plan Expenditure through market borrowing for which they do not need any permission from the GoI, provided they have effected their Fiscal Responsibility Acts); *secondly,* through the loans they get from the GoI on the advice of the PC (Ministry of Finance, GoI, shows these expenditures in the *Plan Finance-I Division*); and *thirdly,* through the GoI Central Sector

Schemes, Centrally Sponsored Schemes and Additional Central Allocations (this includes the fund transfer to the states under 'Special Category States').

3. **Private Sector:** Other than the government, a large amount of fund is required by the private sector to meet their short-term (working capital) and long-term (capital market) requirements. The GoI needs to take care of this issue also—the financial system is managed in such a way that other than the government the private sector is also able to mobilise resources for its various requirements. This becomes even more important in a mixed economy, which is reforming and favours increased participation in the economy from the private sector.

    This needs focused reform in the financial system as it was structured to channelise more funds and resources towards government needs before the reforms commenced. The main idea here is to prevent the governments from 'crowding out' the funds and let it flow smoothly towards the private sector—the process of reforms in the financial sector, tax structure, fiscal policies of the Centre and states, etc., come under it.

4. **General Public:** Other than the government and the private sector, common people of an economy also need funds for their *general spending* and *investment*. The government needs to put in place such a fiscal policy which enables them (too) to have their access to funds. The savings common people do is used as investment provided they are able to save. Other than savings people, must get incentive and enough funds which they might directly invest in the primary or secondary security markets or in financial instruments (shares, bonds, mutual funds,

pension funds, insurance, etc.). Common people are the main drivers of 'demand' in an economy. In the periods of reforms, the government sets *twin targets*—at the one hand promoting private sector so that 'supply' can be optimised in the economy (through *'structural reforms'*) and at the other it tries to create adequate 'demand' in the economy (by the process of *'macroeconomic stabilisation'*).

The government used different 'means' to mobilise resources since Independence, in order to realise the desired and required kind of developmental goals. A part of resources are mobilised for investment purposes (i.e., the creation of productive assets) for which different *'investment models'* have been tried by now.

INVESTMENT MODELS

Investment is a process of putting money in productive activities to earn income. It can be done *directly* (in different activities in the primary, secondary or tertiary sectors) or *indirectly* (as in financial securities, such as shares, debentures, bonds, mutual funds, etc.). In the case of India, 'Investment Models' are the *means and tools* by which the GoI has tried to mobilise required funds (resources) to promote the different goals of planned development. Since India started the planning process (1951), we see differing **models** being tried by the governments to mobilise resources—it has been a kind of 'evolutionary' process. We may understand them in the following 'phases'.

Phase-I (1951—69)

This was the phase of 'state-led' development in which we see the GoI utilising every internal and external means to mobilise required resources. The main areas of resource allocations were for infrastructure and social sector. The famous Mahalanobis Plan gets implemented during this

period. In this period, we see the whole financial system, tax system and fiscal policy of the country getting regulated to drive in maximum funds for the government to meet its planning related financial responsibilities.

This phase was marred by visible mismatches between the need and availability of investible fund—there always prevailed a lag between the requirement of funds and their mobilisation. Thus, investment targets of the government got derailed many times (war with China and a limited war with Pakistan also eroded and diverted the resource allocation mechanism). But overall, the government was able to start the process of industrialisation almost from nothing by mobilising heavy funds in favour of the infrastructure sector and infrastructure industries (the core sector)—education, health care also got funds but in a subdued manner as the GoI remained greatly preoccupied with 'glorification of the public sector'. This was the age when GoI used to consider the PSUs as the 'temples of modern India'.

Phase-II (1970—73)

With the enactment of the Industrial Policy of 1970 we see GoI deciding infavour of including 'private capital' in the process of planned development—but not in a big and open way. The idea of 'Joint Sector' comes under which a combination of partners—Centre, state and private sector—could enter the industrial sector. This was done basically, to make private sector come up in areas which were open for them, but due to certain technical and financial reasons they were not able to take part. In due course of time the government did quit such ventures and such industrial settlements came under complete private control.

This is for the first time we see the government inclining on private funding for planned development, but we do not see any private entry in the GoI's monopoly areas of industrial activities (which takes place only after the reform process begins in 1991).

Phase-III (1974–90)

With the enactment of the FERA in 1974 we see the government, for the first time, proposing to take the help of 'foreign capital' in the process of planned development—but not via cash foreign investment—only through the 'technology transfer' route that too up to only 26 per cent of the total project value proposed by the private sector. Basically, under FERA government tightened the flow of foreign currency inflow into the Indian private sector, which started hampering the technological upgradation process and initiation of the state-of-the-art technologies from the world—the technology transfer route was put in place to fill this gap. It means that even if GoI tried to include foreign investment in the developmental process its entry remained restricted in two ways:

(i) It was not either 'direct' (as we see FDI during the reform process) or 'indirect' (as the PIS), but via technology transfer.

(ii) Foreign entities could enter only those industrial areas which were open for the Indian private sector (under Schedule B of the Industrial Policy Resolution, 1956). The 'monopoly' industries under GoI (some of the most attractive industries for the private sector) remained closed for entry.

It also means, that India failed to articulate an *investment model* which could tap the better elements of the foreign capital—state-of-the-art technologies, better work culture and most importantly, scarce investible capital. Experts believe it as a missed opportunity for India. By 1965–66, the South East Asian economies like Malaysia, Indonesia, Thailand and South Korea had opened up their economies for both forms of foreign investments—direct as well as indirect—

and the governments there 'decontrolled' the industrial sectors, which were earlier fully under government controls (it should be noted here that these economies had started exactly the same way as India had started after Independence). This gave those economies a chance to tap not only scarce investible fund into their economies, but the state-of-the-art technologies from the world and world class work culture and entrepreneurship, too. Soon these economies came to be known as the Asian Tigers.

The period after 1985 saw dynamism in the area of resource moblisation—two consecutive Planning Commissions suggested for opening up of the economy and inclusion of the Indian and foreign private capital in industrial areas which were hitherto reserved for the government. It suggested that GoI to withdraw from areas where the private sector was capable and fit to function (for example, infrastructure sector) and concentrate on areas where private sector would not be interested to operate (for example, the social sector). In a sense, during this time, we see an ideological shift in the government towards giving an 'active' or 'central' role to the private sector in the process of economic development. This was an advice for a completely different kind of *investment model*. But due to lack of political will, the governments of the time could not go in for the same. Though, we find the govenrment going for a kind of limited degree of economic reforms through the Industrial Policies of 1985 and 1986 (this should not be taken as Economic Reforms in India which officially starts in 1991 only).

As a **summary** of the investment models up to 1990, we can highlight the following points.

(i) Government remains the main investor in the economy and experts believe that India did undue delay in putting in place an *investment model* by which the potential of the private sector could be channelised into the process of developmental investment.

(ii) Emphasis on the public sector continued together with nationalisation drives also by late 1960s and early 1980s (the PSUs, to a large extent, were privatised by the South East Asian economies by now, making these socially-oriented and loss-making units to catapult into hubs of profit and real drivers of growth and development).

(iii) Tax system was structured to raise maximum tax revenue (which led to tax evasion and excessive tax burdens on the citizens).

(iv) GoI continued cutting its non-plan expenditures so that resources could be allocated for the purpose of planned development (which led to expenditure cuts even in essential areas like education, health care, etc.).

(v) Excessive government dependence on the financial system continued 'crowding out' funds, and as a result, the private sector could not mobilise suitable levels of funds for their requirements.

(vi) Technological upgradation and initiation of new technologies into the economy got hampered due to non-availability of foreign currency to the private sector (GoI, by late 1970, started facing the difficulty of paying its external liabilities, which were mainly created due to the expansion of the PSUs).

(vii) Main sources of fund in this model were, government's tax revenue, internal borrowings, external borrowings and the freshly printed currencies.

There always prevailed a lag between the requirement of funds and their mobilisation resulting into government investment targets getting derailed most of the times. In the meanwhile, the biggest crisis was building-up in the areas of infrastructure shortcomings. By early 1960s itself the Indian private sector was eager to enter this sector so that adequate levels of infrastructure could be developed. But due to several reasons we see the GoI continuing as the monopoliser in these sectors.

Phase-IV (1991 onward)

Due to prolonged follow-up of weak fundamentals of economics and immediated after Gulf War-I, India headed for a severe Balance of Payment crisis by late 1980s, which made India go to the IMF for financial help. It comes up but at some 'conditions'—the design of the 'conditions' made India to go for a 'restructuring' of the economy under the process of economic reforms commencing in 1991.

Reform era shifted India towards including the 'private sector' (domestic as well as foreign) for the future development of the economy—and here comes a different *investment model*. Main elements of this investment model are as given below.

1. The hitherto monopoly sectors of the industry were opened up for private investment—barring Nuclear Research, Nuclear power and Railways (latter two areas are partially opened)—in all of them direct foreign investments have also been allowed (between 26 to 100 per cent). We see the 'investment model' for *'infrastructure sector'* shifting from 'government-led' to 'private-led'.

2. In coming times, GoI articulated the idea of the Public Private Partnership (PPP) model of investment for this sector, to provide confidence and space to the private sector to enter the sectors (as the private sector was not much interested to participate due to some inter-related problems in the sector, for example lack

of 'market reforms'). By the 10th Plan we see private sector putting in around 21 per cent of funds required for the infrastructure projects in the PPP mode which increased up to 32 per cent by the 11th Plan. On the basis of past two plans the PC projected that private sector will put in around 50 per cent (48 per cent, to be precise) of the funds required for infrastructure development during the 12th Plan (which could not be achieved due to several internal and external reasons till 2015). Here, one point should not be missed that in future the infrastructure sector is to be fully handled by the private sector—as per the idea of the reform process.

3. In 2002, the government, articulated the idea of PPP (Public-Private-People-Partnership) through the 10th Plan (2002–07). The idea has its use at the local level where the resources are to be mobilised for the creation of physical and social infrastructure. It was launched in watershed management successfully. Gujarat had shown highly successful model of this investment in its 'Pani Panchayat'.

4. To support the private sector to mobilise their share of fund in the infrastructure PPP, the government has set up the Infrastructure Development Fund, which also has provision for the Viability Gap Funding (VGF).

5. Inside the general idea of PPP, the government has also put in place some other options of investment models, such as BOT (Build-Opetare-Transfer); BOO (Build-Own-Operate); BOOT (Build-Own-Operate-Transfer); BLT (Build-Lease-Transfer); BOLT (Build Operate-Lease-Transfer); DBFO (Design-Build-Finance-Operate); DBOT (DesignBuild-Operate-Transfer); DCMF (Design-Construct-Manage-Finance); etc.

6. In the area of mobilising resources for the expansion of the **Social Sector**, we see an increased focus coming from the governments. But the government still thinks inadequacy of funds for the proper and timely development of the sector. Thus, by 2012, the GoI proposed plans to include the participation of private sector in the sector, mainly, education and health care through the PPP mode, which is still to be formally launched. Meanwhile, the provision regarding corporate social responsibilty (CSR) via the Companies Act, 2013, some additional funds have started flowing to the fund-starved social sector. By early 2015, the government has asked the PSUs to flow their part of the CSR expenditures to the GoI for the newly launched sanitation drive, the Swachch Bharat Abhiyan.

7. So that the *corporate sector* is able to mobilise enough resources for its investment needs in the economy, the governments started to restructure the whole gamut of the tax structure, financial structure and its fiscal policy. Now, as the economy will depend more on private participation for its developmental requirements, the government avoid crowding out the fund from the economy—a process of fiscal consolidation starts in. An increased emphasis comes on the fronts of 'targeting' the subsidies, their better delivery, pension reforms, etc., so that the government could de-burden the financial system from its fund requirements and enough finance flows in the system for the private sector.

8. To take care of the spending and investment requirements of the *general public*, the government is committed to put in place a cheap interest rate regime, right kind of financial environment, an stable inflation and exchange rate besides other instruments. Bringing in 'inclusiveness' in the growth process is now the declared policy stance of the government.

9. Once the new government came to power by mid-2014, we find a renewed synergy in creating conducive environment for the private sector so that the economy could be able to attract enough investible fund to further the process of development. The government looks committed to the cause of improving the *'ease of doing business'* in the country. Aimed to this we find the government busy in putting in place the 'right' kind of land acquisition law, labour law, companies law, tax laws, digitalisation of government processes, etc.

Overall, the current investment model of the economy is **private-led** and for this the GoI proposes to put in place the right kind of financial system, legal framework, labour laws, etc. The main idea of this model is to 'unshackle' the hidden potential of the private sector. To the extent the role of the government is concerned, it will be limited to being a regulator with an increased tone of a "facilitator" and a caretaker of the well being of the disadvantaged and marginalised sections of the society, so that the face of the economic reform remains 'humane'. In wake of the financial crisis in the western economies, the challenge of mobilising resourecs has become tougher and it will be really good that the government is able to devise out a working investment model.

CENTRAL SECTOR SCHEMES AND CENTRALLY SPONSORED SCHEMES

The exercise of planned development in India has evolved two type of schemes over the time, viz.,— **Central Sector Scheme** and **Centrally Sponsored Scheme**. The names are derived from the pattern of funding and the modality for implementation.

The *Central Sector Schemes* are 100 per cent funded by the Union Government and implemented by the Central Government machinery. These schemes are mainly formulated on subjects from the *Union List*. In addition, the Central ministries also implement some schemes directly in the states/UTs, which are called Central Sector Schemes, but resources under these schemes are not generally transferred to states.

As per the **Union Budget 2016–17**, the existing 1,500 such schemes have been restructured into 300 by the GoI. This will prevent overlapping of expenditure and help in better monitoring and evaluation.

Under the *Centrally Sponsored Schemes (CSSs)* a certain percentage of the funding is borne by the Centre and the states in the ratio of 50:50, 70:30, 75:25 or 90:10 and the implementation is done by the state governments. CSSs are formulated in subjects from the *State List* to encourage states to prioritise in areas that require more attention. Funds are routed either through the Consolidated Fund of the states and or are transferred directly to state/district level autonomous bodies/implementing agencies. As per the *Baijal Committee Report* (1987), CSSs have been defined as the schemes which are funded directly by Central ministries/departments and implemented by the states or their agencies, irrespective of their pattern of financing, unless they fall under the Centre's sphere of responsibility, i.e., the Union List.

Conceptually, both CSS and Additional Central Assistance (ACA) schemes have been passed by the Central Government to the state governments. The difference between the two has arisen because of the *historical evolution* and the way these are being budgeted and controlled and release of funds takes place. In case of CSSs, the budgets are allocated under concerned ministries themselves which look after the entire process of the release of funds, too.

Central Plan Assistance

Financial assistance provided by the GoI to support State's Five Year Plans is called Central Plan Assistance (CPA) or Central Assistance (CA), which primarily comprises the following:

(i) **Normal Central Assistance (NCA):** The distribution of the NCA is formula based (Gadgil-Mukherjee Formula) and is untied. Gadgil Formula of determining the Central Assistance to the State is being adopted from the Fourth Plan and revised subsequently—allocation is made by the Planning Commission.

(ii) **Additional Central Assistance (ACA):** This is provided for implementation of externally aided projects (EAPs), and for which presently there is no ceiling. Unlike NCA, this is scheme based. The details of such schemes are given in the Statement 16 of the Expenditure Budget Vol. I. There can be one time ACA and advance ACA. **One time ACA** are assistance given by the Planning Commission to particular states for undertaking important state specific programmes and schemes. These are one time assistance and thus not recurring. These assistances are discretionary in nature. **Advance ACA** are advances given to *Special Category States* in times of financial stress and recoverable in 10 years.

(iii) **Special Central Assistance (SCA):** This is provided for special projects and programmes, e.g., Western Ghats Development Programme, Border Areas Development Programme, etc. (in exceptional situations, ACA, may also be provided). This special plan assistance is given only to *Special Category States* to bridge the gap between their Planning needs and resources. In other words, SPAs are ACA for the special category states.

CPA is provided, as per scheme of financing applicable for specific purposes, approved by the Planning Commission. It is released in the form of *grants* and/or *loans* in varying combinations, as per terms and conditions defined by the Ministry of Finance, Department of Expenditure. Central assistance in the form of ACA is provided also for various Centrally Sponsored Schemes, viz., Accelerated Irrigation Benefits Programme, Rashtriya Krishi Vikas Yojana, etc., and SCA is extended to states and UTs as additive to Special Component Plan (renamed Scheduled Castes Sub Plan) and Tribal Sub Plan. Funds provided to the states under Member of Parliament Local Area Development Scheme (MPLADS), i.e., Rs.5 crore per annum per MP also count as CA central assistance.

CSSs Restructured

For the 12th Plan period (2012–17) the existing 137 CSSs were restructured into 66 schemes, including the 17 *flagship programmes*. The government had set up an expert Committee Chaired by B. K. Chaturvedi, member of the erstwhile Planning Commission) for the purpose which submitted its report by late-2011.

The *14th FC* recommended that sector-specific transfers from the Union to the states/UTs should be confined to sectors like education, health, drinking water and sanitation. However, in view of the preponderance of CSSs being interventions in key sectors of national importance, the GoI kept **50** of the **66** ongoing CSSs in the *Union Budget 2015-16*. The balance were in the process of being either taken into the Central Sector, or reformulated as new Umbrella Schemes or were transferred to the states. The CSSs funds are released as central assistance to state plans which are routed through the states' budgets (new method as per the *Union Budget 2014–15*). This provides greater autonomy, authority and responsibility to the states in implementation of the schemes.

In **March 2015**, to rationalise the CSSs, a Sub-Group of Chief Ministers was set up in pursuance of the decision taken by the *Governing Council* of the NITI Aayog. The *guiding principles* of the sub-group was defined as—the Union and the states/UTs to work as Team India in the spirit of 'Cooperative Federalism' towards realisation of the goals of VISION 2022 when India will celebrate the 75th year of Independence. The broad objectives of the VISION are:

(i) Providing basic amenities to all citizens in an equitable and just manner for ensuring a life with self-respect and dignity, and

(ii) Providing appropriate opportunities to every citizen to realize her potential.

Accordingly, as per the **Union Budget 2016–17,** the existing **50** CSSs have been rationalised and restructured into **30** schemes. This will avoid overlapping of expenditure, provide visibility and impact. The **major features** of the restructuring are as given below:

- The CSSs have been divided into — *Core* and *Optional* schemes.
- The new expenditure sharing pattern for the *Core Schemes* is—for 8 North Eastern (NE) states and 3 Himalayan states 90:10; for other States 60:40 (Centre:States) and for UTs 100 per cent to be borne by the Centre.

- For *Optional Schemes* the expenditure sharing pattern is—for 8 NE and 3 Himalayan states 80:20; for other states 50:50 (Centre:States) and for the UTs 100 per cent to be borne by the Centre.

- Amongst the Core Schemes, those for social protection and social inclusion should form the *Core of the Core* and be the first charge on available funds for the National, Development Agenda.

- Funds for *Optional Schemes* would be allocated to the states by the Ministry of Finance as a **lump sum,** and states would be *free* to choose which Optional Schemes they wish to implement. In such schemes, states have been given the *flexibility* of *portability* of funds to any other CSSs.

- Henceforth, the CSSs will come up only in key identified sectors which comprise the *National Development Agenda* (to be decided by the NITI Aayog, in co-ordination with its Governing Council).

- NITI Aayog to have concurrent jurisdiction in *monitoring* of the schemes in the states and Central ministries.

- Third-party *evaluation* by NITI Aayog.

This way, with the commencement of the new fiscal 2016–17, the long-drawn process of restructuring the CSSs seems to have reach a logical end.

INDEPENDENT EVALUATION OFFICE

An Independent Evaluation Office (IEO) has been created by the GoI in February 2014, at an arm's distance from the government with the objective of strengthening public accountability of some of the important social sector programmes, which account huge resource mobilisation such as the flagship programmes. Conceived on the lines of Independent Evaluation Office (IEO) of the IMF,[106] the body has been created on the basis of international experiences, in cooperation with the *World Bank* and the British *DFID* (Department for International Development)—It is modelled on the lines of Mexico's National Council for the Evaluation of Social Development Policy.

The IEO will be an independent office attached to the Planning Commission under a Governing Board chaired by the Deputy Chairman of the Planning Commission. The IEO is to be funded by the Planning Commission and will have, as its head, a full-time Director General (Ajay Chhibber) in the rank and status of Member of the Planning Commission / Union Minister of State. The DG has a tenure of 3 years extendable to 5 years. Its staff will be selected by the DG without any interference and will have its independent budget.

It is felt that the government programmes can benefit enormously from concurrent independent evaluation. Presently concurrent evaluation is done by the concerned ministries as an on-going parallel process. Expert evaluation of programmes that have been in operation is done by the Programme Evaluation Organisation (PEO) of the Planning Commission—the IEO is expected to strengthen this evaluation process. **Main aims** of the office is:

---

106. An Independent Evaluation Office (IEO) functions in the International Monetary Fund (IMF) since 2001, which conducts independent and objective *evaluations* of Fund's policies and activities. Under its Terms of Reference, it is fully independent from the Management of the IMF and operates at arm's length from the Board of Executive Directors with the following *three* missions—(i) Enhancing the learning culture within the Fund, (ii) Strengthening the Fund's external credibility, and (iii) Supporting institutional governance and oversight *(Source: Independent Evaluation Office, IMF, Washington DC, 2014).*

(i) To help improve the effectiveness of government policies and programmes by assessing their impact and outcomes.

(ii) To set guidelines and methodology for all evaluations done by various departments, and agencies and encourage a culture of openness and learning in government systems.

(iii) To connect India to the best international evaluated evidence in development practice and knowledge to learn from others success and mistakes.

Main features about the functioning of the office may be summed-up as given below:

(i) It will conduct independent evaluations of plan programmes—especially flagship programmes—and assess their effectiveness, relevance and impact. Besides, it has the freedom to conduct independent evaluations on any programme which has access to public funding or implicit or explicit guarantees from the government.

(ii) The work programme of the IEO will be prepared through an open process of consultations, including feedback from **civil society** and will be made public.

(iii) The IEO will prepare the *Terms of Reference* for all independent evaluations, which will be conducted by selected institutes and researchers, selected on competitive basis.

(iv) IEO will provide guidance to any agency or department of the government to improve the quality of it's self evaluation and monitoring system. Such support is intended to bring all evaluations under a common internationally accepted methodology, help achieve better development outcomes and encourage a *culture of learning* in the government.

(v) Besides making available on it's website and other public avenues, its reports will be submitted to the Parliament and the Prime Minister's Office.

(vi) It will also make internationally available findings from independently and professionally evaluated Indian programmes in the spirit of South-South learning and cooperation.

(vii) IEO will **represent** India as it's independent evaluation authority at international forums on development and effectiveness and will endeavour to improve India's evaluation systems in line with international best practices.

The evaluations in areas such as the public distribution system and health issues were among the first to be undertaken by the IEO with MGNREGA and JNNURM were to follow later.

Meanwhile, early September 2014, the DG of the IEO was relieved from his services by the government, leaving the institution in a state of limbo (with little clarity, *as on date,* over its future role). The debate on the IEO has been going on in the PMO questioning the creation of the new institution in the light of a similar body called the *Programme Evaluation Organisation (PEO)*, which already exists in the Planning Commission. The Committee of Secretaries set up for the purpose has decided to strengthen the PEO, leaving the option of either absorbing the IEO under the PEO or shutting down the institution.

PROGRAMME EVALUATION ORGANISATION

The Programme Evaluation Organisation (PEO) was established in October 1952, as an independent organisation, under the general guidance and direction of the Planning Commission (PC) with a specific task of evaluating the community development programmes and other Intensive Area Development Schemes. The evaluation set up was further strengthened by the development of methods and techniques of evaluation in the 1st Plan and setting up of evaluation machineries in the States during the 3rd (1961–66) and 4th (1969–74) Plans. Gradually, with the extension of the programmes/schemes in a variety of sectors, viz., agricultural cooperation, rural industries, fisheries, health, family welfare, rural development, rural electrification, public distribution, tribal development, social forestry, etc., the evaluation work undertaken by the PEO was extended to other important CSSs.

The broad **functions** of the PEO include undertaking evaluation of selected programmes/schemes under implementation, as per the requirement of the various Divisions of the PC, Central Ministries and Departments of the Government of India. The evaluation studies are designed to *assess* –

(i) the performance,

(ii) the process of implementation,

(iii) the effectiveness of the delivery systems, and

(iv) the impact of programmes.

The **objectives** of the PEO:

(i) Objective assessment of process and impact of the development programmes,

(ii) Identifying the areas of success and failures at different stages of administration and execution, and analysis of reasons for success or failure,

(iii) Examining extension methods and people's reactions thereto and deriving lessons for future improvement in the formulation and implementation of the new programmes/schemes.

Organisational Structure

The PEO is primarily a *field level* organisation under the overall charge of the Deputy Chairman, PC. It has a **three-tier** structure:

First Tier: At the apex is the Headquarters at the PC, which is responsible for evolving suitable methodologies, including statistical designs for various type of evaluation studies, organising execution and monitoring of sample surveys, data processing, statistical analysis and interpretation of qualitative and quantitative data generated by the field units and also for bringing out the Evaluation Reports. The organisation is headed by the Adviser (Evaluation).

Second Tier: The middle link of the PEO represents Regional Evaluation Offices, which are 7 in number located at Chandigarh, Chennai, Hyderabad, Jaipur, Kolkata, Lucknow and Mumbai.

Tird Tier: The Field Units, known as Project Evaluation Offices constitute the third tier of PEO. These are located in the capital cities of 8 major states of the country, viz., Guwahati, Bhubaneshwar, Shimla, Bangalore, Bhopal, Patna, Thrivananthapuram and Ahmedabad.

Evaluation as Plan Scheme

The 10th Plan document pointed out that one of the most common reasons for the failure of programmes and schemes was the faulty and incomplete design of the programme/projects/scheme. Care and attention must be taken to formulate programmes, projects and schemes in a more systematic and professional manner. It is essential to strengthen the existing mechanisms for *monitoring* and *evaluation*, in order to make sure that plans are being implemented as envisaged and the impact is also as planned. The strategy proposed above would definitely contribute to efficiency in resource use and improved performances of plan programmes. But the evaluation capacity within and outside the government is limited. To make evaluation, an effective tool for this, capabilities of evaluation organisations will have to be enhanced. The *'Working Group for Strengthening Monitoring and Evaluation System'* set up (late 2012) by the PC

recommended to enhance the evaluation capacity and incorporate evaluation in the Plan Scheme.

The PEO also encourages State Evaluation Organisations (SEOs) to send the evaluation reports to the PC so that these reports can also be put on the Internet (now, it may be sent to the **NITI Aayog**—a decision yet to be taken by the government). By late 2014, the government decided to strengthen the PEO—further actions in this direction is awaited.

NITI AAYOG

By mid-2014, India did show a quite strong mandate and a very stable government came at the Centre. We find the new government showing a renewed vigour and zeal in several areas. One such area has been its attempts at 'redefining' the federal polity of the country for the purpose of promoting growth and development. We see a pronounced policy shift in the direction of 'empowering and keeping state in front' by giving them more financial space and responsiblities.[107] Keeping its promises in the direction, the government abolished the Planning Commission (PC) and replaced it by a new body—the NITI Aayog. The acronym **NITI** stands for **National Institution for Transforming India**. We see the government aspiring for the emergence of the 'Team India' in the new body. It will be premature to be conclusive on this shift from "Planning to NITI"

107. Such a stance in the process of planning we find in the document of the 10th Plan (2002–07) for the first time when the government of the time (the NDA-led) made the call : **'if states are developed, the nation is developed'**. We find a pronounced shift towards 'decentralised planning' (the Plan was nicknamed as the 'People's Plan'). The new idea of 'monitorable targets' also commenced in this plan giving states more say and accountibility in the process of planned development (these targets were continued within the forthcoming Plans). Several other steps were also taken in this Plan aimed at bringing the states in the mainstream of the developmental process, viz., by giving them increased role and accountibility.

(as the government calls). Even an academic comparison between the old and the new bodies will also not serve enough purpose as it needs some time when the outcome of the change will be available. Judegemnts on this shift will be only good once it is done after some period of time. In the meantime, India remains a planned economy. The discussion given here is mainly based on the documents and releases which came out from the GoI before and after the NITI Aayog was set up (January 1, 2015). In these documents, the government has not only provided the reasons as why does India need to go in for a new body, but charts out a very encouraging and out of tradition role/function for the new body. An attempt has been made to closely follow the 'government line' of thinking so that the 'spirit' of it is lost.

Transforming India

The government aims at 'transforming the development agenda of India' with the help of the NITI Aayog and has given a slogan, 'from planning to NITI'. India has undergone a paradigm shift over the past six decades—politically, economically, socially, technologically as well as demographically. The role of the government in national development has seen a parallel evolution. Keeping with these changing times, the government decided to set up the **NITI Aayog** as a means to better serve the needs and aspirations of the people of India. The government thinks the new institution to function as a catalyst to the developmental process—nurturing an overall enabling environment, through a *holistic approach* to development going beyond the limited sphere of the public sector and the GoI, which will be built on the foundations of:

(i) An empowered role of states as equal partners in national development; operationalising the principle of *Cooperative Federalism*.

(ii) A knowledge hub of internal as well as external resources, serving as a repository of good governance best practices, and a *Think Tank* offering domain knowledge as well as strategic expertise to all levels of the government.

(iii) A collaborative platform facilitating *Implementation*; by monitoring progress, plugging gaps and bringing together the various ministries at the Centre and in states, in the *joint pursuit* of developmental goals.

Changing Contours of India

The government agrees that the Planning Commission has served India well. However, India has changed dramatically over the past 65 years at *multiple levels* and across *varied scales*. These transformatory forces have changed the very contours of India—highlighted by the government document in the five areas:

1. **Demographic shift:** India's population has increased over three-fold to reach 121 crores. This includes an addition of over 30 crore people to Urban India. As well as an increase of 55 crore youth (below the age of 35), which is more than one and a half times the total population of the country then. With increasing levels of development, literacy and communication, the aspirations of the people have soared, moving from *scarcity and survival* to *safety and surplus*. Today, we are looking at a completely different India, and country's governance systems need to be transformed to keep up with the changing India.

2. **Economic shift:** India's economy has undergone a paradigm shift. It has expanded by over a hundred times, going from a GDP of Rs. 10,000 crore to Rs. 100 lakh crore at current prices, to emerge as one of the world's largest economics. Agriculture's share in the GDP has seen a dramatic drop, from more than 50 per

cent to less than 15 per cent. The plan size of Rs. 43 lakh crore of the 12th Plan dwarfs the plan size of Rs. 2,400 crore of the 1st Plan. Priorities, strategies and structures dating back to the time of the birth of the Planning Commission, must thus be *revisited*. To align with this shift and sheer scale, India needs to *overhaul* the very *nature* of the planning processes, the government says.

3. **Shift in the private sector:** The nature of the Indian economy, and the role of the government in it, has undergone a paradigm shift. Driven by an increasingly open and liberalised structure, India's private sector has matured into a vibrant and dynamic force. The sector is not operating just at the international cutting edge, but also with a global scale and reach. This changed economic landscape requires a new *administrative paradigm* in which the role of the government must evolve from simply allocating resources in a command and control eco system, to a far more nuanced one of directing, calibrating, supporting and regulating a *market eco system*. National development must be seen beyond the limited sphere of the 'Public Sector'. Government must, thus, transition from being a 'provider of first and last resort' and 'major player' in the economy, to being a 'catalyst' nurturing an 'enabling environment', where the entrepreneurial spirits of all, from small self-employed entrepreneurs to large corporations, can flourish. This importantly, frees up the government to focus its precious resources on public *welfare* domains such as essential entitlements of food, nutrition, health, education and livelihood of vulnerable and marginalised groups of the society.

4. **Forces of globalisation:** In recent decades, the world at large has also evolved. We live today in a 'global village', connected by modern transport, communications and media, and networked international markets and institutions. In this milieu, India's economic actions 'contribute' to the global dynamics, while our economy also get influenced by the happenings far away from us. The framework of *policy making* together with the *functioning of governments* need to incorporate the realities of our continuing integration with the global economic system.

5. **Role of the states:** Indian states have evolved from being mere appendages of the Centre, to being the actual drivers of national development. The development of states must thus become the national goal, as the nation's progress lies in the progress of states. As a consequence, the *one-size-fits-all approach*, often inherent in centralised planning, is no longer practical or efficient. States need to be heard and given the flexibility required for effective implementation. The government quotes Dr. B. R. Ambedkar to bring the point home: "it is unreasonable to centralise powers where central control and uniformity is not clearly essential or is impracticable". Thus, while emanating from global experiences and national synergy, India's strategies need to be calibrated and customised to *local needs* and opportunities.

6. **Technology paradigm:** Technology advancements and information access have unleashed the creative energy of India. They have integrated our varied regions and ecosystems in an interlinked national economy and society, opening

up newer avenues of coordination and cooperation. Technology is also playing a substantial role in enhancing transparency as well as efficiency, holding the government more accountable. Thus, India needs to make it central to systems of policy and governance.

Change must come

The above-given changes have been recognised by the experts for years now. With changing contours of the economy, the institutions guiding the economy should also change. The government quotes several such *instances* when appropriate changes were advised in the Planning Commission by the experts, committees, even the PC, among others:

(i) The *8th Plan* (1992–97) document (the very first after the reform process commenced in 1991) categorically stated that, as the role of the government was reviewed and restructured, the role and functions of the PC too needed to be rethought. The PC also needed to be reformed to keep up with changing trends, relieving itself of the old practices and beliefs, which had lost relevance, and adopting new ones based on past experiences of India as well as other nations. Specifically, the PC needed to be in tune with the process of economic reforms.

(ii) The *Standing Committee on Finance* of the 15th Lok Sabha observed in its 35th Report on Demand for Grants (2011–12) that the "PC has to come to grips with the emerging social realities to re-invent itself to make itself more relevant and effective for aligning the planning process with economic reforms and its consequences, particularly for the poor". This was the need of making the planning process relevant to the process of economic reforms.

(iii) The former Prime Minister, Dr. Manmohan Singh, in his farewell address to the PC (April 2014), also urged reflection on 'what the role of the PC needs to be in this new world. Are we still using tools and approaches which were designed for a different era? What additional roles should the Planning Commission play and what capacities does it need to build to ensure that it continues to be relevant to the growth process?" This observation has quite high relevance, as Dr. Singh is himself a "noted" economist.

Taking the clues for a change, the government quotes Mahatma Gandhi before going for the change: "Constant development is the law of life, and a man who always tries to maintain his dogmas in order to appear consistent drives himself into a false position". The government adds further, keeping true to this principle our institutions of governance and policy must evolve with the changing dynamics of the new India, while remaining true to the founding principles of the Constitution of India, and rooted in our *Bharatiyata* or wisdom of our *civilizational history* and *ethos*. It was, in every sense, a kind of pledge to devise India's own means, methods, tools and approaches to promote development.

For the government, the NITI Aayog is to be the *institution* to give life to these aspirations (discussed above). The Aayog is being formed based on extensive consultation across a spectrum of stakeholders, including inter alia state governments, relevant institutions, domain experts and the people at large.

Functions of NITI Aayog

With the process of maturity and deepening in Indian nationhood, the country has embraced a greater measure of pluralism and decentralisation. This necessitates a *paradigm shift* in Central government's approaches to the governments in the state, as well as at the local levels. The *states governments* and the *local bodies* must be made equal partners in the development process through the following changes:

(i) understanding and supporitng their developmental needs and aspirations,

(ii) incorporating varied local realities into national policies and programmes with the required flexibility.

This way the new body, NITI Aayog, is designed to live up to the principle of 'Team India' with its following **officially demarcated functions:**

1. *Cooperative and Competitive Federalism:* It will be the 'primary platform' for operationalising cooperative federalism, enabling states to have active participation in the formulation of national policy, as well as achieving time-bound implementation of quantitative and qualitative targets through the combined authority of the Prime Minister and the Chief Ministers. This will be by means of systematic and structured interactions between the Union and state governments, to better understand developmental issues, as well as forge a consensus on strategies and implementation mechanisms. The above would mark the replacement of the *one-way* flow of policy from centre-to-state, with a genuine and continuing *Centre-State partnership.* The Aayog is supposed to further this cooperation with the enhanced vibrancy of *Competitive Federalism;* the Centre competing with the states and vice versa, and the states competing with each other, in the joint pursuit of national development.

2. *Shared National Agenda:* It will 'evolve' a shared vision of national development priorities and strategies, with the active involvement of the states. This will provide the framework 'national agenda' for the Prime Minister and Chief Ministers to implement.

3. *State's Best Friend at the Centre:* It will support states in addressing their own challenges, as well as building on strengths and comparative advantages. This will be through various means, such as *coordinating* with ministries, championing their ideas at the Centre, providing 'consultancy' support and 'building capacity'.

4. *Decentralised Planning:* The new body is to 'restructure' the planning process into a 'bottom-up model', empowering states, and guiding them to further empower local governments in developing mechanisms to formulate credible plans at the village level, which are progressively aggregated up the higher levels of the government. The maturing of India's governmental institutions has enabled increasing the specialisation of their functions. There is, thus, a need to separate as well as energise the distinct 'strategy' element of governance from the usual 'process' and 'implementation' element. As a dedicated 'Think Tank' of the government, NITI Aayog will carry out this 'directional' role, strategically charting the future of the nation. It will provide specialised inputs—strategic, functional and technical—to the Prime Minister and the government (Centre as well as the state), on matters critical to the fulfillment of the national development agenda. It means, the new body is to function like a 'think tank'.

5. *Vision & Scenario Planning:* To 'design' medium and long-term strategic frameworks of the big picture vision of India's future—across schemes, sectors, regions and time; factoring in all possible alternative assumptions and counterfactuals. These would be the 'drivers of the national reforms agenda', especially focussed on identifying critical gaps and harnessing untapped potentialities. The same would need to be intrinsically dynamic with their progress and efficacy constantly monitored for necessary mid-course recalibration; and the overall environment (domestic and global) continuously scanned for incorporating evolving trends and addressing emerging challenges. This would mean a fundamental transition from merely planning for where the nation's money goes, to planning where we want the nation to go. And given its unique position as the aggregator and integrator of all developmental initiatives of the Government of India and the states, the new body would be ideally suited for the same.

6. *Domain Strategies:* To 'build' a repository of specialised domain expertise, both sectoral and cross-sectoral; to assist ministries of the Central and state governments in their respective development planning, as well as problem solving needs. This will especially enable the imbibing of good governance best practices, both national as well as international, especially with regards to structural reforms in the country.

7. *Sounding Board:* To be an 'in-house sounding board' whetting and refining government positions, through objective criticisms and comprehensive counter-views in the economy.

8. *Network of Expertise:* To 'mainstream' external ideas and expertise into government policies and programmes through a collaborative community of national and international experts, practitioners and other partners. This would entail being government's link to the outside world, roping in academia (universities, think tanks and research institutions), private sector expertise, and the people at large, for close involvement in the policymaking process. To bring the point home, the document quotes the Rigveda – 'let us welcome noble thoughts flowing in from all directions'.

9. *Knowledge and Innovation Hub:* The body to be an 'accumulator' as well as 'disseminator' of research and best practices on good governance, through a state-of-the-art Resource Centre which identifies, analyses, shares and facilitates replication of the same. The document further adds, an increasingly mature Indian population has steadily increased the focus on, and demand for, actual delivery and results. To keep up with such enhanced aspirations, the new body will have the mandate to go beyond mere planning and strategising, to facilitating *implementation* of the development agenda as well. This would involve making implementation central to the planning process, through an emphasis on tangible outcomes, realistic targets, strict time lines and robust monitoring and evaluation—a transition from the isolated conceptualisation of merely 'planning', to 'planning for implementation'. It will also act as a 'catalyst' to the government machinery at large—filling gaps, enhancing capabilities and de-clogging bottlenecks, as and where required.

10. *Harmonisation:* To 'facilitate harmonisation' of actions across different layers of the government, especially when involving cross-cutting and overlapping issues across multiple sectors through: communication, coordination, collaboration and convergence among all stakeholders. The emphasis will be on bringing all together on an integrated and holistic approach to development.

11. *Conflict Resolution:* To provide a 'platform' for mutual resolution of inter-sectoral, inter-departmental, inter-state as well as centre-state issues; facilitating consensus acceptable and beneficial to all, to bring about clarity and speed in execution.

12. *Coordinating interface with the World:* It will be the 'nodal point' for strategically harnessing global expertise and resources in India's developmental process—coming in from across nations, multilateral institutions and other international organisations.

13. *Internal Consultancy:* It will offer an internal 'consultancy' function to Central and state governments on policy and programme design—providing frameworks adhering to basic design principles such as decentralisation, flexibility and a focus on results. This would include specialised skills such as structuring and executing PPPs.

14. *Capacity Building:* To enable 'capacity building' and 'technology up-gradation' across governments, benchmarking with latest global trends and providing managerial and technical knowhow.

15. *Monitoring and Evaluation:* It will 'monitor' the implementation of policies and programmes, and 'evaluate' their impact; through rigorous tracking of performance metrics and comprehensive programme evaluations. This will not only help identify weaknesses and bottlenecks for necessary course-correction, but also enable data-driven policymaking; encouraging greater efficiency as well as effectiveness.

The Guiding Principle

The government document has categorically pointed out the very 'purpose' of the new body—in the process of carrying out its functions, the Aayog will be guided by an overall vision of development which is inclusive, equitable and sustainable. The instituion is to follow a strategy of empowerment built on human dignity and national self-respect—the document quote Swami Vivekanada to emphasise this: "to encourage everyone in his struggle to live up to his own highest idea". The new body to follow a development model which is *all round, all pervasive, all inclusive* and *holistic.*

Antyodaya: To prioritise service and upliftment of the poor, marginalised and downtrodden, (the document quotes the idea of 'Antodaya' as articulted by Pandit Deendayal Upadhyay). Development is incomplete and meaningless, if it does not reach the farthest individual. "Nothing is more dreadfully painful than poverty" (the centuries old sage-poet Tiruvallur has been quoted).

Inclusion: To empower vulnerable and marginalised sections, redressing identity-based inequalities of all kinds—gender, region, religion, caste or class—the document quoted from Sankar Dev—"to see every being as equivalent to one's own soul is the supreme means (of attaining deliverance)". Weaker sections must be enabled to be masters of their own fate, having equal influence over the choices the nation makes.

Village: To integrate our villages into the development process, to draw on the vitality and energy of the bedrock of our *ethos, culture* and *sustenance*.

Demographic Dividend: To harness our greatest asset, the people of India, by focussing on their development, through *education* and *skilling,* and their *empowerment,* through productive livelihood opportunities.

People's Participation: To transform the developmental process into a *people-driven* one, making an awakened and participative citizenry— the driver of good governance. This includes our extended Indian family of the non-resident Indian community spread across the world, whose significant geo-economic and geo-political strength must be harnessed.

Governance: To nurture an open, transparent, accountable, pro-active and purposeful style of governance, transitioning focus from *Outlay to Output to Outcome.*

Sustainability: Maintain sustainability at the core of our planning and developmental process, building on our ancient tradition of respect for the environment.

Structure of the NITI

The Aayog will be a lean organisation, modelled as a network of expertise, focusing on functionality, flexibility and domain knowledge, with the following 'structure' and 'mechnaism':

(i) *Chairman:* the Prime Minister of India (de-facto).

(ii) *Governing Council:* will comprise the Chief Ministers of all states and Lt. Governors of union territories.

(iii) *Regional Councils:* will be formed to address specific issues and contingencies impacting more than one state or region. Strategy and planning in the Aayog will be anchored from state-level; with regional councils convened by the Prime Minister for identified priority domains, put under the joint leadership of related sub-groups of states (grouped around commonalities which could be geographic, economic, social or otherwise) and central ministries. The regional councils will have the following features:

(a) Will have specified tenures, with the mandate to evolve strategy and oversee implementation.

(b) Will be jointly headed by one of the group Chief Ministers (on a rotational basis or otherwise) and a corresponding Central Minister.

(c) Will include the sectoral central ministers and secretaries concerned, as well as state ministers and secretaries.

(d) Will be linked with corresponding domain experts and academic institutions.

(e) Will have a dedicated support cell in the Aayog's secretariat.

(iv) *Special Invitees:* It will have experts, specialists and practitioners with relevant domain knowledge as special invitees nominated by the Prime Minister.

(v) *Full-time Organisational Framework:* In addition to PM as its Chairman it will comprise:

(a) Vice-Chairperson—to be appointed by the PM.

(b) Members: all as full-time.

(c) Part-time Members: maximum of 2, from leading universities, research organisations and other relevant institutions in an *ex-officio* capacity. Part time members will be on a rotational basis.

(d) Ex-Officio Members: maximum of 4 members of the Union Council of Ministers to be nominated by the PM.

(e) Chief Executive Officer: to be appointed by the PM for a fixed tenure, in the rank of Secretary to the Government of India.

(f) Secretariat: as deemed necessary.

Specialised Wings in the NITI Aayog

The Aayog will house a number of specialised 'Wings', as per the government document:

(i) **Research Wing:** It will develop in-house sectoral expertise as a dedicated think tank of top notch domain experts, specialists and scholars.

(ii) **Consultancy Wing:** It will provide a market-place of whetted panels of expertise and funding, for Central and state governments to tap into; matching their requirements with solution providers, public and private, national and international. By playing match-maker instead of providing the entire service itself, NITI Aayog will be able to focus its resources on priority matters, providing guidance and an overall quality check to the rest.

(iii) **Team India Wing:** It will comprise representatives from every state and ministry and will serve as a permanent platform for national collaboration. Each representative in this Wing will:

(a) Ensure every state/ministry has a continuous voice and stake in the Aayog.

(b) Establish a direct communication channel between the state/ministry and the Aayog for all development related matters, as the dedicated liaison interface.

A national "Hub-Spoke" institutional model will be developed, with each state and ministry encouraged to build dedicated *mirror institutions*, serving as the interface of interaction. These institutions, in turn, will nurture their own networks of expertise at the state and ministry level. NITI Aayog will function in close cooperation, consultation and coordination with the ministries of the Central government, and state governments. While it will make recommendations to the Central and state governments, the responsibility for taking and implementing decisions will rest with them.

Vehicle of Good Governance

The Aayog will seek to facilitate and empower the critical requirement of good governance, which is people-centric, participative, collaborative, transparent and policy-driven. It will provide critical directional and strategic input to the development process, focussing on deliverables and outcomes. This, along with being as incubator and disseminator of fresh thought and ideas for development, will be the core mission of NITI Aayog. The document, at the end, quotes from Chanakya to emphasise the importance and need of good governance – "good governance is at the root of a nation's wealth, comfort and happines".

This way, the idea of the NITI Aayog looks not only 'innovative' in its approach but contemporary, too—imaginatively forging into the emerging idea and need of 'happiness' (as being sponsored by the UNO in the *World Happiness Report*). It gives a call for inclusion of *ethos* and *cultural elements* of India in the development model, delicately linking the issue of growth and development to the 'behavioural' dimensions of the people of India (rightly in sync with the recent proposition of the World Bank in its *World Development Report 2015*). We find several such shining 'stars' in the newly set up body, which will be surely analysed and discussed again and again by analysts, experts, scholars. At the end, we can wisely conclude that the erstwhile PC was aimed at serving some purposes which was suitable for the old time, while the current times require us to carry on the legacy to a new level where we can build India, which can combine and integrate the energy and potential of all who belong to the nation being all open to the world (agreeing categorically to the idea of globalisation).

RECENT DEVELOPMENTS

Since the NITI was set up, replacing the erstwhile Planning Commission, these have been much **confusion** regarding several aspects of development planning in the country. Some of them have been analysed here in the pursuit of searching a settled position:

(i) *About the fate of planning:* A state of confusion has been there whether the GoI will stop launching the Five Year Plans? The earliest official word regarding it came from the Finance Minister himself when he was enquired about it by media while he was going to attend the 1st meeting of the Governing Council of the NITI Aayog on **February 8, 2015**. He gave inconclusive answers to media—it was yet undecided whether India will be involved in planning in future.

(ii) *What in place of Plans?:* Some hints regarding it came from the Vice Chairman (Arvind Panagariya) of the NITI Aayog itself in his interaction with the media (by early **March 2016**). According to him, the Government may not be going for the five year plans after the 12th Plan— it may be **replaced** by a *medium-term fiscal framework* that will project revenue and expenditure allocations for the next three years beginning 2017–18. In this process the last two years of the 12th Plan (2012–17) will be used as transition. He further added that to introduce medium term fiscal framework may entail some sense of prediction what the next two or three years, what the revenues are likely to be, how the resulting expenditure will be allocated across different ministries. In his opinion, if the funds are allocated to a ministry then there should be some sense of responsibility to deliver. At the end of the year there will be an assessment. Under the current Five Year Plan system, the review of implementation is done mid-way through the plan and sometimes targets are revised.

It should be noted that the Union Budget 2016–17 has already announced about doing away with the classification of *Plan* and *Non-Plan* expenditures in the backdrop of 2016–17 being terminal year of the 12th Plan period (2012–17). In future, the expenditures of the GoI will be classified as *Revenue* and *Capital*— it has been already used by the 14th Finance Commission (*Development* and *Non-development* classification was used by India till 1986-87). Meanwhile, the 15-year 'Vision Document' (in place of the 13th plan) is supposed to be released by the NITI Aayog any time till end-March so that it could get effective from April 2017.

(iii) *Actual role of the NITI Aayog:* Much confusion remains whether the body is an 'institution', a 'think tank' or an 'organisation'. On this, the NITI Aayog Vice Chairman said that if Plans are replaced by *medium-term fiscal framework* then the Aayog will be *an agency to mediate* this. He further added—the Finance Ministry will deal with finances and other ministry will deal with the action, but besides both of these somebody must do planning of expenditure— most importantly ex-post assessment of delivery. As per him, the Aayog will provide policy support and monitor.

(iv) *Fund allocation:* The Planning Commission used to have the highest say in the area of fund allocation (to the Central Plans, Central Sector Schemes, Centrally Sponsored Schemes, Additional Support to States, etc.). Will this role be played by the NITI Aayog? With passing times the experts have come to believe that the ultimate power to allocate funds will rest with the Finance Ministry, but the amount of funds, funding patterns, etc., will be decided by the Governing Council of the Aayog following the guiding principle of 'co-operative federalism'. In a sense, states and UTs will be sitting in the capacity of decision makers as how much funds they should be given! Suppose it works as per the design, it will really lead India towards setting the new examples of *federal co-operation* and the emergence of *Team India.*

(v) *About the state plans:* Together with the Centre, it is believed that the states will also stop launching their five year plans and will replace them by the similar medium-term fiscal framework. It will be necessary for the purpose of integrating the developmental actions by both the governments.

(vi) *The Unique Identification Authority of India (UIDAI):* In September 2015, the body, which issues **Aadhaar** (a 12-digit individual identification number), was shifted to the Ministry of Communication and Information Technology from NITI Aayog. It used to be an attached body of the erstwhile Planning Commission. The decision has been taken keeping in mind the government's ambitious 'Digital India' programme as the Aadhaar numbers are being linked with several services.

The issuance of Aadhaar cards, started by the then UPA government, has come under the scrutiny of the Supreme Court, which held (mid-2015) that the card would not be mandatory for availing benefits of government's welfare schemes. In wake this, the **Union Budget 2016–17** announced to support the Aadhar by an Act of the Parliament. Accordingly, the *Aadhaar (Targeted Delivery of Financial and other Subsidies, Benefits and Services) Act, 2016* has been enacted which provides the Aadhaar a statutory backing and make it the mainstay of the government's direct benefit transfer (DBT) programme for the disbursal of the various subsidies.

Meanwhile, certain other related issues are still there to be settled - the National Development Council (NDC); the Independent Evaluation Office (IEO); the Programme Evaluation Organisation (PEO). The possible ways to settle them have been discussed in this chapter itself at relevant places.

CHAPTER 6

ECONOMIC REFORMS

An important feature of India's reform programme, when compared with reforms underway in many other countries, is that it has emphasised gradualism and evolutionary transition rather than rapid restructuring or 'shock therapy'. This gradualism has often been the subject of unfavourable comment by the more impatient advocates of reform, both inside and outside the country. *

* Montek S. Ahluwalia Addressing at the inaugural session of the Seminar on 'India's Economic Reforms', Merton College, Oxford University, London, June 1993.

INTRODUCTION

The economic reforms initiated in 1991 is now into the 26th year. In this period there was hardly a day that some news, news analysis, write-up or article did not appear in the newspapers regarding the reform process. Several highly acclaimed books have been authored on India's economic reforms by some of the best experts of economics from India and abroad. Still students, especially coming from non-economics background, are generally at a loss on the 'pros' and 'cons' of the reform process.

ECONOMIC REFORMS

Popularly, economic reforms denote the process in which a government prescribes declining role for the state and expanding role for the private sector in an economy. So let's unravel the reform process based on the author's classroom interactions with students. It is safer to see economic reform as a policy shift in an economy from one to another or *'alternative development strategies'*. Economists attribute the differences in the performance of economies to the differences in the 'strategies' they follow. The different strategies of development evolved through a long period of trial and error by different countries under the influence of different sets of ideologies. But the process has been like an educational trip. To understand the term 'economic reform' and more so to clarify the confusion concerning it in the Indian context, we must see the different 'alternative development strategies' which evolved through time. A brief description is given below:

1. Planning Model

Till the rise of the Soviet Union, the prevalent development strategy in the Euro-American countries was the capitalist system of economy, which promoted the principles of laissez-faire and dominant role for private capital in the economy. Once the Soviet Union went for the planning model (Later the East European countries and finally China in 1949) most of the developing countries after their independence were influenced by socialism and the governments there took a central role in planned development. As these economies were dominated by foreign colonisers, they worried that opening the economy to foreign investment would lead to a new form of domination, the domination by large multinationals. That is why most of these countries went for 'protectionist' economic policy with *import substitution* as one method, side by side. But by the 1970s, the world was having convincing proofs that the socialist as well as the planned economies[1] were inclined to follow their kind of development strategies—either because they had very slow and lower growth rates or were stagnating. The experiences of these economies gave rise to a new ideology which became popular as the *'Washington Consensus'*.

2. Washington Consensus

By the early 1980s, a new development strategy emerged. Though it was not new, it was like the old idea getting vindicated after failure of a comparatively newer idea. After the world recognised the limits of a state-dominated economy, arguments in favour of the market, i.e., the private sector, was promoted emphatically. Many countries shifted their economic policy just to the other extreme arguing for a minimal role of the government in the economy. Governments of the socialist or the planned economies were urged/suggested to privatise and liberalise, to sell off state-owned companies and eliminate government

---

1. There were many developing non-socialist countries which also accepted the economic planning as their development strategy (France should not be counted among them as it was a developed economy by then). These countries were following the 'mixed economy' model, but their form was closer to the command economies, i.e., the state economy or the socialist economy.

interventions in the economy. These governments were also suggested to take measures which could boost the aggregate demand in the economy (*i.e.,* **macroeconomic stability measures**). The broad outlines of such a development strategy were regarded as being inspired by the **Washington Consensus.**[2]

This consensus is broadly termed as the popular meaning of the 'economic reform' followed by almost all the socialist, communist and planned developing economies during the 1980s in one form or the other[3]—the term economic reform got currency around the world during this period. The term was usually seen as a corollary for promoting 'naked capitalism', openness in the economy and an open attitude towards foreign investments, etc. The governments of the developing economies were criticised by the political parties in the opposition and the critiques for being soft to the dictates of the IMF and the WB, and becoming a party to promote 'neo-imperialism'.

But these policies, in many cases proved little better than the previous policies in promoting economic growth over an extended period of time. But somehow a mood in favour of the market economy had gained ground. The United Kindom under Mrs. Thatcher had gone for politically most vocal privatisation moves without any political debates (the only such example of privatisation moves among the democracies, till date).[4] It should be noted here that after the Great Depression of 1929 a 'strong state intervention' was suggested (by J. M. Keynes) and such a policy did really help the Euro-American countries to mitigate the crisis. The favour for the state intervention in the economy was being reversed by the Washington Consensus. But soon this consensus was also to be replaced by another development strategy. More detailed discusstion on the Washington Concensus is given in *Chapter 1*.

3. Mixed Economy

By the mid-1990s, it had become increasingly clear that neither of the extremes—the Washington Consensus or the state-led planned economy—were the ultimate strategies of development.[5] The success achieved by the East Asian economies even if we take into account their setback due to the financial crisis of 1997–98, stands out in marked contrast to the experiences of other economies of the time who were following the Washington Concensus.[6] The East Asian economies have not only been able to propel higher growth rates, but they have been greatly successful in reducing poverty, promoting education and healthcare, etc.

The East Asian economies had promoted a development strategy, which had its most distinctive feature as the balance they were able to strike between the role of the state/government and the market/the private sector in their economies. This was really a new kind of mixed economy, which was never permanently inclined towards either state intervention or the free market, but always a balanced mix of the state and the market according to the requirement of the socio-economic situation of the economy. The East Asian countries had pursued market-oriented policies that encouraged development

2. As the strategy was advocated by the IMF, the WB and the US Treasury (i.e., US Ministry of Finance) all located in Washington, it properly came to be known as Washington Consensus.

3. Without changing the broad contours of economic policy, the Government in India had also come, under the influence of this consensus, followed a great many *liberal* policies (during Rajiv Gandhi's regime) in the 1980s.

4. *Collins Dictionary of Economics,* Glasgow, 2006, pp. 417–18.

5. World Bank, *The East Asian Miracle: Economic Growth and Public Policy.* (Washington DC: Oxford University Press, 1993).

6. *Ibid.*

of the private sector—augmenting and governing the market, not replacing it.[7]

Technically speaking, shifting of economic policy of a country from one to the other above-given three 'alternative development strategies' is economic reform. But in the history of world economy, it was inclination of the economies towards the market economy, which have been referred as economic reforms. In the Indian case, economic reform has always been used in this sense. Here, one should note that when India started the programme of economic reforms in the early 1990s, the world view was in favour of privatisation, liberalisation, de-nationalisation, etc., as the main plank of economic reforms. But by the mid-1990s, not only the world view has polarised in favour of a mixed economy', but one another change was about to sweep the world economies, i.e., the favour for globalisation sponsored by the World Trade Organisation (WTO). Now, the developing economies (mixed economies with planning as their development strategy) as well as the transition economies (Russia and the whole Eastern Europe, and China)—who were already promoting the market-oriented reform process were faced with a dilemma. To prosper and compete in the globalising environment while they needed immediate liberation from their state-dominated mode of economies at one hand, they also needed to strike a balance between the state and the market on the other. Each one of them tried to strike the balance in their own way with mixed results. In India, the governments have not been able to convince the masses that the economy needs reforms and the attempted reforms will benefit all. In every election since the reforms of 1991, the voters have not supported a pro-reform government. Though the process of economic reforms started in India with the slogan *'reforms with human face'*—the slogan has utterly failed

to garner the empathy of the masses. We may hope that in coming times the masses will start connecting with the reforms and will able to get the message clear, i.e., reforms are to benefit all.

ECONOMIC REFORMS IN INDIA

On July 23, 1991, India launched a process of economic reforms in response to a fiscal and balance-of-payment (BoP) crisis. The reforms were historic and were going to change the very face and the nature of the economy in the coming times. The reforms and the related programmes are still going on with changing emphasis and dimensions, but they are criticised as being slow ever since the UPA Government came to power in May 2004. Back in the mid-1980s, the governments had taken its first steps to economic reforms. While the reforms of the 1980s witnessed rather limited deregulation and 'partial liberalisation of only a few aspects of the existing control regime, the reforms started in early 1990s in the fields of industries, trade, investment and later to include agriculture, were much 'wider and deeper'.[8] Though liberal policies were announced by the governments during the reforms of the 1980s itself, with the slogan of 'economic reforms', it was only launched with full conviction in the early 1990s. But the reforms of the 1980s, which were under the influence of the famous *'Washington Consensus'* ideology had a crippling impact on the economy. The whole Seventh Plan (1985–90) promoted further relaxation of market regulations with heavy external borrowings to increase exports (as the thrust of the policy reform). Though the thrust increased the growth rate led by higher industrial growth (riding on costly imports supported by foreign borrowings, which the industries would not be able to pay back and service), it also led to a substantial increase in foreign indebtedness that

---

7. As is concluded by Stiglitz and Walsh, p. 800, op. cit.

8. Jeffrey D. Sachs, Ashutosh Varshney and Nirupan Bajpai, *India in the Era of Economic Reforms,* (New Delhi: Oxford University Press, 199), p. 1.

played a major role in the BoP crisis of 1991.[9] The crisis was immediated by the First Gulf War (1991) which had two-pronged negative impact on the Indian foreign exchange (forex) reserves. First, the war led the oil prices to go upward forcing India to use its forex reserves in comparatively shorter period and second, the private remittances from Indians working in the Gulf region fell down fast (due to their emergency evacuation)—both the crises were induced by a single cause, i.e., the Gulf War. But the balance of payments crisis also reflected deeper problems of rising foreign debt, a fiscal deficit of over 8 per cent of the GDP and a hyper-inflation (over 13 per cent) situation.[10]

The minority government of the time had taken a highly bold and controversial step in the form of economic reforms criticised throughout the 1990s by one and all—right from the opposition in the Parliament, to the communist parties, to the industrial houses, the business houses, media, experts and by the masses also. By now as the benefits of the reforms have accrued to many, the criticism has somewhat calmed down, but still the reform process is considered as 'anti-poor' and 'pro-rich' by at least the masses—the people who decide the political mandate for the country to rule. At least one belief is followed by everybody, i.e., the benefits of reforms are not tickling to the masses (the *'aam aadami'*) with the desirable pace.[11] The need of the hour is to go for 'distributive growth', though the reform has led the economy to a higher growth path.

Obligatory Reform

Similar reform process started by some other economies since the 1980s were voluntary decisions of the concerned countries. But in the case of India it was an involuntary decision taken by the government of the time in the wake of the BoP crisis. Under the Extended Fund Facility (EFF) programme of the IMF, countries get external currency support from the fund to mitigate their BoP crisis, but such supports have some obligatory conditionalities put on the economy to be fulfilled. There are no set rules of such conditions already available with the IMF, though they are devised and prescribed to the BoP-crisis-ridden economy at the time of need. A point needs to be referred here is that the conditionalities put upon India were of the nature which required all the economic measures to be formulated by them. It means that the reforms India carried or is carrying out at present were neither formulated by India nor mandated by the public. Yes, there was a large section of experts inside and outside the government who believed in similar economic measures to bring the economy on the right path. Some of them were arguing the same since the 1970s, while many other experts believed in them since the mid-1980s.[12] But why after all was the Rao-Manmohan Government credited to start the reform process in India? It is because they thought it suitable to follow and make it politically possible in India. Imagine, a government proposing to sell the state-owned companies to the private sector or closing them down in a country which has been convinced that these companies will be the 'temples of modern India'. The masses were

9. J. Barkley Rosser, Jr. and Marina V. Rosser, *Comparative Economics in a Transforming World Economy,* 2nd Edition (New Delhi: Prentice Hall of India, 2005), p. 469.

10. Vijay Joshi and I. M. D. Little, *India's Economic Reforms, 1991–2001,* (Oxford: Clarendon Press, 1996), p. 17.

11. The feeling is even shared by the government of the present time. One may refer to the similar open acceptance by India's Minister of Commerce at the Davos Summit of the World Economic Forum (2007). In an interview to the *CNN-IBN* programme, the Cabinet Minister for Panchayat Raj, and the North East (Mani Shankar Aiyar) on 20 May 2007 opined that benefits of higher growth are going to the selected 'classes' and not to the 'masses'.

12. The Seventh and the Eight Plans have many such suggestions to give to the governments of the time, especially the latter Plan called for the same nature of the reform process, very clearly.

convinced that the government has bowed down to the dictats of the IMF, the imperialist forces, the multinationals, etc. Even today such feelings are there in several quarters of the economy. The politics of economic reforms damaged India more than the reform has benefitted the country. It would not be an exaggeration if we conclude that economic reforms had no political consensus. Political parties in India are divided on the issue of reforms—the parties together with the masses lack the level of political maturity required for the success of the reform programme. It is right, democratic maturity comes to a multi-party political system, but it takes time. It takes even more time where masses are unaware and ignorant. The emotional issues of religion, caste, etc., play their own roles in such situations.

The **IMF conditions** put forth for India were as under:

(i) Devaluation of the rupee by 22 per cent (which was effected in two phases and the Indian rupee fell down from Rs. 21 to Rs. 27 per US Dollar).

(ii) Drastic reduction in the peak import tariff from the prevailing level of 130 per cent to 30 per cent (India completed it by 2000–01 itself and now it is voluntarily cut to the level of 15 per cent).

(iii) Excise duties (i.e., CENVAT now) to be hiked by 20 per cent to neutralise the revenue short falls due to the custom cut (a major tax reform programme was launched to streamline, simplify and modernise the Indian tax structure which is still going on).

(iv) All government expenditure to be cut down by 10 per cent, annually (i.e., cutting the cost of running the government and denotes, interests, pays, pension PF and subsidies. A pressure on the government

to consolidate the fiscal deficit and go for fiscal prudence).

Though India was able to pay back its IMF dues in time, the structural reform of the economy was launched to fulfil the above-given conditions of the IMF. The ultimate goal of the IMF was to help India bring about equilibirium in its BoP situation in the short-term and go for macroeconomic and structural adjustments so that in future the economy faces no such crisis.

There was enough scope for the critics to criticise India's economic reforms as prescribed and dictated by the IMF. The process of economic reforms in India had to face severe criticism from almost every quarter of the economy concerned, although the reforms were aimed to boost growth and deliver competitiveness to the economy.[13]

Reform Measures

The economic reform programme, that India launched, consisted of *two* categories of measures:

1.Macroeconomic Stabilisation Measures

It includes all those economic policies which intend to boost the aggregate *demand* in the economy—be it domestic or external. For the enhanced domestic demand, the focus has to be on increasing the purchasing power of the masses, which entails an emphasis on the creation of gainful and quality employment opportunities.

2.Structural Reform Measures

It includes all the policy reforms which have been initiated by the government to boost the aggregate supply of goods and services in the economy. It naturally entails unshackling the economy so that it may search for its own potential of enhanced

---

13. Ministry of Finance, *Economic Survey 1991–92: Part II Sectoral Developments & New Industrial Policy, 1991,* GoI, New Delhi.

productivity. For the purchasing capacity of the people to be increased, the economy needs increased income, which comes from increased levels of activities. Income so increased is later distributed among the people whose purchasing power has to be increased—this will take place by properly initiating a suitable set of macroeconomic policies. For the income to get distributed among the target population, it takes time, but the efforts a government initiates to increase the supply, i.e., increasing production becomes visible soon. As production is done by the producers (i.e., the capitalists), *prima facie* the structural reform measures look 'pro-rich' and 'pro-industrialist' or 'pro-capitalist', known with different names. Ignorant people easily get swayed by the logic that everything which is 'pro-rich' has to be necessarily 'anti-poor'. But it was not the case with the process of economic reforms. Unless the economy is able to achieve higher growth (i.e., income) wherefrom the purchasing power of the masses will be enhanced? And increased income takes time to reach everybody. If the economy lacks political stability, this process takes even more time due to short-term goals set by the unstable and frequently changing governments—the exact case is with India.

The LPG

The process of reforms in India has to be completed via three other processes namely, liberalisation, privatisation and globalisation, known popularly by their short-form, the LPG. These three processes specify the characteristics of the reform process India initiated. Precisely seen, liberalisation shows the *direction* of reform, privatisation shows the *path* of reform and globalisation shows the ultimate *goal* of the reform. However, it would be useful to see the real meanings of these terms and the exact sense in which they are being used worldwide and particularly in India.

LIBERALISATION

The term liberalisation has its origin in the political ideology 'liberalism', which took its form by early nineteenth century (it developed basically in the previous three centuries). The term is sometimes protrayed as a *meta-ideology* capable of embracing a broad range of rival values and beliefs. The ideology was the product of the breakdown of feudalism and the growth of a *market* or *capitalist* society[14] in its place, which became popular in economics via the writings of Adam Smith (its founding father in the USA) and got identified as a principle of *laissez-faire.*[15]

The term liberalisation has the same connotation in economics as its root word liberalism. Pro-market or pro-capitalistic inclination in the economic policies of an economy is the process of liberalisation. We see it taking place in the whole Euro-America in the 1970s and particularly in the 1980s.[16] The most suitable example of this process could be China of the mid-1980s when it announced its *'open door policy'*. Though China lacks (even today) some trademark traits of liberalism, as for example, individualism, liberty, democratic system, etc., still China was called a liberalising economy.

We may take an example from the history of the world economy—putting the USA of the early 20th century and the communist China on the two poles of the scale—thus representing the best historical example of the liberal economy and China being the best example of the 'illiberal' economy. With the USA on the south pole and China on the north any policy movement towards

---

14. Andrew Heywood, *Politics*, (New York: Palgrave, 2002), p. 43.

15. Robert Nisbet, *Prejudices: A Philosophical Dictionary*, (Massachusetts: Harvard University Press, 1982), p. 211.

16. *'Economics: Making Sense of the Modern Economy' The Economist,* London, 1999, pp. 225–26.

'the south' is 'liberalisation'. The movement from the south to the north will be known as 'illiberalisation'.

It means that the process of decreasing traits of a state economy and increasing traits of a market economy is liberalisation. Similarly, the opposite will be the process of illiberalisation. Technically speaking, both the processes will be known as the processes of economic reforms, since 'reform' as a term does not say anything about the 'direction'. All the economic reforms in the world have been from the 'north to the south'. Similar is the case with the process of liberalisation.

It means, in the Indian case the term liberalisation is used to show the direction of the economic reforms—with decreasing influence of the state or the planned or the command economy and increasing influence of free market or the capitalistic economy. It is a move towards capitalism. India is attempting to strike its own balance of the 'state-market mix'. It means, even if the economic reforms have the direction towards market economy it can never be branded a blind-run to capitalism. Since the economy was more like the state economy in the former years, it has to go for a greater degree of mix of the market. But in the long run, Liberalism curtails the powers of the Parliament.[17]

PRIVATISATION

The decades of the 1980s and 1990s witnessed a 'rolling back' of the state by the governments, especially in the USA and UK under the inspiration of the New Right priorities and beliefs.[18] The policies through which the 'roll back' of the state was done included deregulation, **privatisation** and introduction of market reforms in public services. Privatisation at that time was used as a process under which the state assets were transferred to the private sector.[19] The root of the term privatisation goes to this period which got more and more currency around the world once the East European nations and later the developing democratic nations went for it. But during the period several connotations and meanings of the term 'privatisation' have developed. We may see them as follows:

(i) Privatisation in its purest sense and lexically means **de-nationalisation**,[20] i.e., transfer of the state ownership of the assets to the private sector to the tune of 100 per cent. Such bold moves took place only once anywhere in the world without any political fallouts—in the early 1980s of the UK under the Thatcher regime. This route of privatisation has been avoided by almost all democratic systems. In the mid-1990s some West European nations—Italy, Spain and France—besides the USA went for such moves.[21] India never ventured into any such privatisation move.

(ii) The sense in which privatisation has been used is the process of **disinvestment** all over the world. This process includes selling of the shares of the state-owned enterprises to the private sector. Disinvestment is de-nationalisation of less than 100 per cent ownership transfer from the state to the private sector. If an asset has been sold out by the government to the tune of only 49 per cent the ownership remains with the state though it is considered privatisation. If the sale of shares of the state-owned assets has been to the tune of 51 per cent, the ownership

17. J.K. Galbraith, *A History of Economics,* (London: Penguin Books,), p. 123, 1780.

18. Andrew Heywood, *Politics,* p. 100.

19. Stiglitz and Walsh, *Economics,* pp. 802–3.

20. Collins, Oxford, Penguin, *Dictionary of Economics,* relevent pages.

21. Samuelson and Nordhaus, *Economics,* p. 199.

is really transferred to the private sector even then it is termed as privatisation.

(iii) The third and the last sense in which the term privatisation has been used around the world, is very wide. Basically, all the economic policies which directly or indirectly seem to promote the expansion of the private sector or the market (economy) have been termed by experts and the governments as the process of privatisation. We may cite few examples from India—de-licencing and de-reservation of the industries, even cuts in the subsidies, permission to foreign investment, etc.[22]

Here we may connect liberalisation to privatisation in India. Liberalisation shows the direction of economic reforms in India, i.e., inclination towards the dominance of market. But how will it be achieved? Basically, privatisation will be *the path* to reform. It means, everything which includes promotion of the 'market' will be the path of the reform process in India.

GLOBALISATION

The process of Globalisation has always been used in economic terms though it has always taken the political and cultural dimensions. Once economic changes occur it has several socio-political manifestations.[23] Globalisation is generally termed as 'an increase in economic integration among nations'.[24] Even before several nation-states were not even born, the countries around the world had gone for globalisation, i.e., 'a closer integration of their economies'.[25] This globalisation lasted from 1800 to almost 1930, interrupted by the Great Depression and the two Wars which led to retrenchment and several trade barriers were erected since early 1930s.[26]

The concept was popularised by the Organisation of Economic Cooperation and Development (OECD) in the mid-1980s again after the Wars. In its earlier deliberatization, the organisation had defined globalisation in a very narrow and business-like sense—'*any cross-border investment by an OECD company outside its country of origin for its benefit is globalisation'.* After this summit of the OECD, proposals for replacing the GATT by the WTO were pushed by the developed economies of the world, better known as the starting of the Uruguay Round of GATT deliberations which ends in Marrakesh (1994) with the birth of WTO. In the meantime, the OECD had defined globalisation officially, (1995) too— "a shift from a world of distinct national economies to a global economy in which production is internationalised and financial capital flows freely and instantly between countries."[27]

The official meaning of globalisation for the WTO is movement of the economies of the world towards *"unrestricted cross border movements of goods and services, capital and the labour force"*. It simply means that the economies who are signatories to the process of globalisation (i.e., signatories to the WTO) for them there will be nothing like foreign or indigenous goods and services, capital and labour. The world becoming a flat and level-playing field emerging in the due process of time.[28]

For many political scientists (which is today a very dominant force in the world), globalisation is the emergence of a situation when our lives are

22. New Industrial Policy, 1991 & several documents of GoI since then.
23. Talcott Parsons, *The Structure of Social Action*, (New York: McGraw Hill, 1937).
24. Samuelson and Nordhaus, *Economics,* p. 32.
25. Stiglitz and Walsh, *Economics,* p. 804.
26. Thomas L. Friedman, *The World is Flat,* (London: Penguin Books, 2006), 9. Stiglitz & Walsh, *Economics,* p. 804.
27. As quoted in Andrew Heywood, *Politics,* p. 139.
28. As Friedman shows in his best-seller, *The World is Flat,* p. 9.

increasingly shaped by the events that occur at a great distance from us about which the decisions are not taken by our conscious self. One section of experts believe that globalisation subordinates the state, while the other section argues that the local, national and global events constantly interact under it without any subordination of one by the other. Rather, globalisation highlights the deepening as well as broadening of the political process in this sense.[29]

India became one of the founding members of the WTO and was obliged to promote the process of globalisation, though its economic reforms started with no such obligations. It is a different thing that India started the process of globalisation right after the reforms 1991.[30]

Now we may connect the three simultaneous processes—the LPG with which India launched its reform programme. The process of liberalisation shows movement of the economy towards the market economy, privatisation is the path/route through which it will travel to realise the ultimate 'goal', i.e., globalisation.

It should be noted here that the Indian idea of globalisation is deeply and frequently inclined towards the concept of welfare state, which keeps coming in the day to day public policy as an emphatic reference. The world, including the IMF, the WB and the developed nations have now increasingly shown their recognition to the fact that the official goal of globalisation of the world economies would not take place without giving the poor of the world a better standard of living. Even if globalisation is complete without including almost one-fifth of the world population, i.e. the poor, will it be called development of the world?

GENERATIONS OF ECONOMIC REFORMS

Though there were no such announcements or proposals while India launched its reforms in 1991, in the coming times, many 'generations' of reforms were announced by the governments.[31]A total of *three* generations of reforms have been announced till date, while experts have gone to suggest the *fourth* generation, too. We may substantiate the components of the various generations of reforms to properly understand the very characteristics and nature of the reform process in India.

First Generation Reforms (1991–2000)[32]

It was in the year 2000–01 that the government, for the first time, announced the need for the Second Generation of economic reforms and it was launched in the same year. The ones which had been initiated by then (i.e., from 1991 to 2000) were called by the government as the reforms of the First Generation. The broad coordinates of the First Generation of reforms may be seen as under:

(i) Promotion to Private Sector

This included various important and liberalising policy decisions, i.e., 'de-reservation' and

---

29. As put by the *Oxford's Dictionary of Politics*, N. Delhi, 24 pp. 222–25; Andrew Heywood, *Politics*, p.138.

30. It should be noted here that the whole Euro-America has already started promoting globalisation by the mid-1980s as the WTO deliberations at Uruguay started. The formation of the WTO only gave globalisation an official mandate in 1995, once it started its functions. It means, for India, globalisation was a reality by 1991 itself—one has to move as the dominant forces move.

31. It should be noted here that many economists regard the economic reforms of the mid-1980s as the First Generation reforms. However, the governments of the time have not said anything like that. It was only in the year 2000–01 that India officially talks about the generations of reform for the first time.

32. Based on the *New Industrial Policy, 1991* & several *Economic Surveys* as well as many announcements by the governments.

'de-licencing' of the industries, abolition of the MRTP limit, abolition of the compulsion of the phased-production and conversion of loans into shares, simplifying environmental laws for the establishment of industries, etc.

(ii) Public Sector Reforms

The steps taken to make the public sector undertakings profitable and efficient, their disinvestment (*token*), their corporatisation, etc., were the major parts of it.

(iii) External Sector Reforms

They consisted of policies like, abolishing quantitative restrictions on import, switching to the floating exchange rate, full current account convertibility, reforms in the capital account, permission to foreign investment (direct as well as indirect), promulgation of a liberal Foreign Exchange Management Act (the FEMA replacing the FERA), etc.

(iv) Financial Sector Reforms

Several reform initiatives were taken up in areas such as banking, capital market, insurance, mutual funds, etc.

(v) Tax Reforms

This consisted of all the policy initiatives directed towards simplifying, broadbasing, modernising, checking evasion, etc.

A major re-direction was ensued by this generation of reforms in the economy—the 'command' type of the economy moved strongly towards a market-driven economy, private sector (domestic as well as foreign) to have greater participation in the future.

Second Generation Reforms (2000–01 onwards)[33]

The government launched the second generation of reforms in 2000-01. Basically, the reforms India launched in the early 1990s were not taking place as desired and a need for another set of reforms was felt by the government, which were initiated with the title of the Second Generation of economic reforms. These reforms were not only deeper and delicate, but required a higher political will power from the governments. The major components of the reform are as given below:

(i) Factor Market Reforms

Considered as the 'backbone' for the success of the reform process in India, it consists of dismantling of the Administered Price Mechanism (APM). There were many products in the economy whose prices were fixed/regulated by the government, viz., petroleum, sugar, fertilizers, drugs, etc. Though a major section of the products under the APM were produced by the private sector, they were not sold on market principles which hindered the profitability of the manufacturers as well as the sellers and ultimately the expansion of the concerned industries leading to a demand-supply gap. Under market reforms these products were to be brought into the market fold.

In the petroleum segment now only kerosene oil and LPG remained under the APM, while petrol, diesel (by March 2014), lubricants have been phased out. Similarly, the income tax paying

---

33. Based on the Ministry of Finance, *Economic Survey 2000–01 (New Delhi: Government of India, 2001)*; and *Union Budget, 2001–02* especially besides other official announcements by the GoI in the coming years.

families don't get sugar from the TPS on subsidies; only urea, among the fertilizers, remain under APM, while many drugs have also been phased out of the mechanism. Opening the petroleum sector for private investment, cutting down the burden of levy on sugar (levy obligation was abolished by mid-2013), etc., are now giving dividends to the economy. But we cannot say that the Factor Market Reforms (FMRs) are complete in India. It is still going on. Cutting down subsidies on essential goods is a socio-political question in India. Till market-based purchasing power is not delivered to all the consumers, it would not be possible to complete the FMRs.

(ii) Public Sector Reforms

The second generation of reforms in the public sector especially emphasises on areas like greater functional autonomy, freer leverage to the capital market, international tie-ups and greenfield ventures, disinvestment[34] (*strategic*), etc.

(iii) Reforms in Government and Public Institutions

This involves all those moves which really go to convert the role of the government from the 'controller' to the 'facilitator' or the administrative reform, as it may be called.

(iv) Legal Sector Reforms

Though reforms in the legal sector were started in the first generation itself, now it was to be deepened and newer areas were to be included, such as, abolishing outdated and contradictory laws, reforms in the Indian Penal Code (IPC) and Code of Criminal Procedure (CrPC), Labour Laws, Company Laws and enacting suitable legal provisions for new areas like Cyber Law, etc.

(v) Reforms in Critical Areas

The second generation reforms also commit to suitable reforms in the infrastructure sector (i.e., power, roads, especially as the telecom sector has been encouraging), agriculture, agricultural extension, education and healthcare, etc. These areas have been called by the government as *'critical areas'*.[35]

These reforms have two segments. The first segment is similar to the FRMs, while the second segment provides a broader dimension to the reforms, viz., corporate farming, research and development in the agriculture sector (which was till now basically taken care of by the government and needs active participation of the private sector), irrigation, inclusive education and healthcare.

Other than the above-given focus of this generation of reforms, some other important areas were also emphasised:

(a) **State's Role in the Reform:** For the first time, an important role to the state was designed, in the process of economic reforms. All new steps of the reforms were now to be started by the state with the centre playing a supportive role.

(b) **Fiscal Consolidation:** The area of fiscal consolidation, though it was a major co-ordinate of reform in India since 1991 itself, gets a constitutional commitment and responsibility. The FRBM Act is passed by the Centre and the Fiscal Responsibility Act (FRAs) is followed by the states as an era of new commitments to the fiscal prudence starts in the country.

---

34. Basically 'disinvestment' started in India in its 'token' form, which is selling of government's minority shares in PSUs. While in the Second Generation, the government went for 'strategic' kind of disinvestment, which basically involved the transfer of ownership of the PSUs from the state to the private sector—MFI2, BALCO, etc., being the firsts of such disinvestments. Once the UPA Government came to power in May 2004, the latter form of disinvestment was put on hold. We will discuss it in detail in the chapter on *Indian Industry.*

35. Ministry of Finance, *Economic Survey 2000–01.*

(c) **Greater Tax Devolution to the States:** Though there was such a political tendency[36] by the mid-1990s itself, after the second generation reforms started, we see a visible change in the central policies favouring greater fiscal leverage to the states. Even the process of tax reforms takes the same dimension. Similarly, the Finance Commissions as well as the Planning Commission start taking greater fiscal care of the states. And for the first time the states had a net revenue surplus collections in the fiscal 2007–08.[37]

(d) **Focussing on the Social Sector:** The social sector (especially healthcare and education) gets increased attention by the government with manifold increases, in the budgetary allocation, as well as show of a greater compliance to the performance of the development programmes.

We see mixed results of the second generation reforms though the reforms still continue.

Third Generation Reforms

Announcement of the third generation of reforms were made on the margins of the launching of the Tenth Plan (2002–07). This generation of reforms commits to the cause of a fully functional Panchayati Raj Institution (PRIs), so that the benefits of economic reforms, in general, can reach to the grassroots.

Though the constitutional arrangements for a decentralised developmental process was already effected in the early 1990s, it was in the early 2000s that the government gets convinced of the need of 'inclusive growth and development'. Till the masses are not involved in the process of development, the development will lack the 'inclusion' factor, it was concluded by the government of the time. The Eleventh Plan goes on to ratify the same sentiments (though the political combination at the centre has changed) and views regarding the need for the third generation of reforms in India.

Fourth Generation Reforms

This is not an official 'generation' of reform in India. Basically, in early 2002, some experts coined this generation of reforms which entail a fully 'information technology-enabled' India. They hypothesised a 'two-way' connection between the economic reforms and the information technology (IT), with each one reinforcing the other.

THE REFORM APPROACH

The process of economic reforms commenced in the world by mid-1980s (in Western Europe and Northern America). Once the idea of the Washington Consensus gained ground, we find similar reforms being followed by different countries cutting across continents. Over the time, experts together with the IMF/WB, started classifying such countries into two categories, viz., one which went for the 'Gradualist Approach' and the other which went for the 'Stop-and-Go Approach'.

India's reform process which commenced in 1991 has been termed by experts as **gradualist** (also called incremental)[38] in nature with traits of occasional reversals, and without any big

---

36. We see it, especially, when the Coalition Government (i.e., the UF Government) goes to amend the constitution so that the Alternative Method of Devolution (AMD) of the tax suggested by the Tenth Finance Commission becomes a law before the recommendations of the Eleventh Finance Commission. It should be noted that the AMD has increased the gross tax devolution to the states by a hefty 5 per cent.

37. The Comptroller and Auditor General, *Provisional Report*, May 2007.

38. **Isher J. Ahluwalia,** *Industry* in Kaushik Basu & Annemie Maertens edited *The New Oxford Companion to Economics in India*, Oxford University Press, N. Delhi, India, 2012, Vol. 2, pp. 371-375.

ideological U-turns - coalitions of various political parties at the Centre and different political parties ruling the states lacked a general sense of consensus on reforms. It reflects the compulsions of India's highly pluralist and participative democratic policy-making process.[39] Though such an approach helped the country to avoid socio-political upheavals/instability, it did not allow the desired economic outcome could have accrue from the reforms. The first generation of economic reforms could not bring the expected results due to lack of some other set of reforms for which India goes after almost over a decade—the second generation of economic reforms. Similarly, the economic benefits (whatever accrued) remained non-inclusive, in absence of an active public policy aimed at inclusion (commencing via the third generation of economic reforms). This created a kind of disillusionment about the prospects of reforms and failed the governments to muster enough public support in favour of reforms.

Unlike India, several other countries (such as Brazil, Argentina, South Africa, etc.) also went for the **stop-and-go** kind of reforms. In such reforms, the governments first decide the sector where reform is needed—then they pinpointed the prerequisites (which will create a conducive atmosphere for reforms to take place), and finally both set of the reforms are activated simultaneously. In their cases, economic results from reforms were on the expected lines. Though these nations took high risks on the socio-political front, in their case, in medium-term itself, the governments were able to mobilise enough public support in favour of reforms (which encouraged the governments to go for further reforms). Such reforms do not look possible in the case of India— this is why the latest *Economic Survey 2016–17* expects an **incremental approach** to reforms.

Presently, we see the Government of India pushing for *'transformational reforms'* (as the *Union Budget 2017-18* described it). Some of such reforms have been:

(a) Inflation targeting and setting up the Monetary Policy Committee by amending the RBI Act, 1934;

(b) Restarting of the 'strategic disinvestment' of the PSUs;

(c) Demonetisation of the high denomination currency notes (aimed at checking corruption, black money, tax evasion, fake currency and terrorism);

(d) Enactment of the new Benami Law (aimed at checking black money);

(e) Bankruptcy Law (aimed at promoting the 'ease of doing business'); and

(f) Enactment of the Aadhar Act (aimed at rationalising and weeding out corruption in the present subsidy regime); etc.

The latest *Economic Survey 2016-17* rightly remarked, "economic reforms are not, or not just, about overcoming vested interests, they are increasingly about shared narratives and vision on problems and solutions". Naturally enough, the actual course of the reform process will be ultimately decided by the socio-economic space available to the government of the time.

---

39. **Montek S. Ahluwalia,** *Planning* in Kaushik Basu & Annemie Maertens edited *The New Oxford Companion to Economics in India*, Oxford University Press, N. Delhi, India, 2012, Vol. 2, pp. 530-536.

CHAPTER 7

INFLATION AND
BUSINESS CYCLE

Fluctuations in the level of economic activity, alternating between periods of depression and boom, led by one prominent factor, i.e., the expectations of the future demand—intertwined with the inflation—has always been a fascinating topic for economists.*

* See Joseph E. Stiglitz and Carl E. Walsh, Economics, 4th Edition (New York: W.W. Norton, 2005), 494–496; Collins internet-linked Dictionary of Economics, (Glasgow, Scotland: Harper Collins, 2006), pp. 48–49.

SECTION-A

INTRODUCTION

For a layman, inflation is just price rise. It becomes a matter of everyday discussion if the prices of daily or weekly items start rising. Whatever impact it might be having on other areas of economy, inflation might take an ugly turn and lead to a political crisis—at least in the developing economies. India has seen governments thrown out of power in elections due to price rise in daily-use items. This is not the case in the developed economies, but inflation takes its political toll there, too. In the developed economies, more aware and informed voters get carried away by the greater impact of higher or lower inflations in the elections. In this chapter, we will try to examine the concept of inflation from all possible dimensions to have an overall understanding.

DEFINITION

A rise in the general level of prices;[1] a sustained rise in the general level of prices;[2] persistent increases in the general level of prices;[3] an increase in the general level of prices in an economy that is sustained over time;[4] rising prices across the board[5]—is inflation. These are some of the most common academic definitions of inflation. If the price of one good has gone up, it is not inflation; it is inflation only if the prices of *most* goods have gone up.[6]

1. Samuelson, Paul A. and Nardhaus, William D., *Economics*, Tata McGraw-Hill, N. Delhi, 2006, p. 439.

2. Mc Cormick, B.J. et.al, *Introducing Economics*, Penguin Education, Great Britain, 1974, p.609.

3. *Penguin Dictionary of Economics*, Penguin Books, London, 7th Ed., 2003.

4. *Collins internet-linked Dictionary of Economics*, Harper-Collins Publishers., Glasgow, 2006.

5. Mathew Bishop, *Pocket Economist*, *The Economist,* London, 2007, p. 121.

6. Stiglitz, Joseph E. and Walsh, Carl E., *Economics*, W.W. Norton & Company, New York, 2005, p. 509.

When the general level of prices is falling over a period of time this is *deflation*, the opposite situation of inflation. It is also known as *disinflation*. But in contemporary economics, deflation or disinflation not used to indicate fall in prices. Instead, a price rise is termed a 'rise in inflation' and a price fall is termed a 'fall in inflation'. The terms deflation or disinflation have become part of the macroeconomic policy of modern governments. In policy terms, deflation or disinflation means a reduction in the level of national income and output, usually accompanied by a fall in the general price level. Such a policy is often deliberately brought about by the governments with the objective of reducing inflation and improving the balance of payments (BoP) by reducing import demand. As instruments of deflation, the policy includes fiscal measures (as for example, tax increase) or monetary measures (as for example, increase in interest rate).

The rate of inflation is measured on the basis of price indices which are of two kinds—Wholesale Price Index (WPI) and Consumer Price Index (CPI). A price index is a measure of the average level of prices, which means that it does not show the exact price rise or fall of a single good. The rate of inflation is the rate of change of general price level which is measured as follows:

Rate of inflation (year x) = Price level (year x) –Price level (year x-1) / Price level (year x-1)×100

This rate shows up in percentage form (%), though inflation is also shown in *numbers,* i.e., *digits*. A price index is a weighted average of the prices of a number of goods and services. In the index the total weight is taken as 100 at a particular year of the past (the *base year*), this when compared to the current year shows a rise or fall in the prices of current year, there is a rise or fall in the '100' in comparison to the base year—and this inflation is measured in digits.

Inflation is measured '*point-to-point*'. It means that the reference dates for the annual inflation is January 1 to January 1 of two consecutive years (not for January 1 to December 31 of the concerned year). Similarly, the weekly rate of inflation is the change in one week reference being the two consecutive last days of the week (i.e., 5 p.m. of two Fridays in India).

WHY INFLATION OCCURS

Economists have been giving different explanations throughout the 19th and 20th centuries for the occurrence of inflation—the debate still goes on. But the debate has certainly given us a clearer picture of inflation. We shall see the reasons responsible for inflation in two parts—

1. Pre-1970s

Till the rise of the monetarist school, economists used to agree upon two reasons behind inflation:

(a) Demand-Pull Inflation

A mis-match between demand and supply pulls up prices. Either the demand increases over the same level of supply, or the supply decreases with the same level of demand and thus the situation of demand-pull inflation arise. This was a Keynesian idea. The Keynesian School suggests cuts in spending as the way of tackling excess demand mainly by increasing taxes and reducing government expenditure.

In practice, the governments keep tracking the demand-supply matrix to check such inflation. Depending upon the situation, the goods in short supply are imported, interest on loans increased and wages revised.

(b) Cost-Push Inflation

An increase in factor input costs (i.e., wages and raw materials) pushes up prices. The price rise which is the result of increase in the production cost is cost-push inflation. The Keynesian school

suggested controls on prices and incomes as direct ways of checking such an inflation and, 'moral suasions' and measures to reduce the monopoly power of trade unions as indirect measures (basically, cost-push inflations chiefly used to happen due to higher wage demanded by the trade unions during the era).

Today, the governments of the world use many tools to check such inflations—reducing excise and custom duties on raw materials, wage revisions, etc.

2. Post-1970s

After the rise of Monetaristic School of Economics in the early 1970s (monetarism developed in opposition to post-1945 Keynesian idea of demand management), the school provided monetarist explanation for inflation, the so-called 'demand-pull' or the 'cost-push' which is excessive creation of money in the economy.

(a) Demand-Pull Inflation

For the monetarists, a demand-pull inflation is creation of extra purchasing power to the consumer over the same level of production (which happens due to wage revisions at the micro level and deficit financing at the macro level). This is the typical case of creating extra money (either by printing or public borrowing) without equivalent creation in production/supply, i.e., 'too much money chasing too little output'—the ultimate source of demand-pull inflation.

(b) Cost-Push Inflation

Similarly, for the monetarists, 'cost-push' is not a truly independent theory of inflation—it has to be financed by some extra money (which is created by the government via wage revision, public borrowing, printing of currency, etc.). A price rise does not get automatically reciprocated by consumers' purchasing. Basically, people must have got some extra purchasing power created that's why they start purchasing at higher prices also. If this has not been the reason, people would have cut-down their consumption (i.e., overall demand) to the level of their purchasing capacity and the aggregate demand of goods would have gone down. But this does not happen. It means every cost-push inflation is a result of excessive creation of money—increasing money flow or money supply.

For the monetarists, a particular level of money supply for a particular level of production is healthy for an economy. Extra creation of money over the same level of production causes inflation. They suggested proper monetary policy (money supply, interest rates, printing of currencies, public borrowing etc.), to check situations of inflationary pressure on the economy. Monetarists rejected the Keynesian theory of inflation.

3. Measures to Check Inflation

From the above-given reasons for inflation and the measures to control it, which of the measure the governments of the world should apply in their policymaking? In practice, governments around the world distance themselves from this debate and have been taking recourse to all possible options while controlling inflation. The governments resort to the following options to check rising inflation:

(i) As a **supply side measure**, the government may go for import of goods which are in short-supply—as a short-term measure (as happened in India in the case of 'onion'[7] and meeting the buffer stock norm of wheat). As a long-term measure, governments go on to increase the production to matching the level of demand. Storage, transportation, distribution, hoarding are the other

aspects of price management of this category.

(ii) As a **cost side measure,** governments may try to cool down the price by cutting down the production cost of goods showing price rise with the help of tax breaks—cuts in the excise and custom duties (as happened in June 2003 in India in the case of crude oil and steel[8]). This helps as a short-term measure. In the long-term, better production process, technological innovations etc., are helpful. Increasing income of the people is the monetary measure to avoid the heat of such inflation.

(iii) The governments may take recourse to tighter monetary policy to cool down either the demand-pull or the cost-push inflations. This is basically intended to cut down the money supply in the economy by siphoning out the extra money (as RBI increases the Cash Reserve Ratio of banks in India)[9] from the economy and by making money costlier (as RBI increases the Bank Rate or Repo Rate in India)[10]. This is a short-term measure. In the long-run, the best way is to increase production with the help of the best production practices.

Again, this measure does not work if the price rise is taking place in items of everyday use such as salt, onion, wheat, etc. (because nobody purchases such goods by borrowing from the banks). This measure helps if the prices are rising due to extra demand of cement, iron and steel, etc.

---

7. As per the *Economic Survey, 1997–98,* Ministry of Finance, GoI, N. Delhi, p. 89.

8. As per the *Economic Survey, 2003–04*, p. 90.

9. As the CRR for banks was revised upward to 6.5 per cent by the RBI in its **Credit and Monetary Policy** for April 2007 onwards and again increased to 7 per cent in the **Review**, July 31, 2007.

10. As the RBI increased the Repo Rate to 7.75 per cent in its *Credit & Monetary Policy* announced on March 31, 2007.

The governments might utilise any of the above or all the three measures to check and manage inflation in their day to day price management policy.

TYPES OF INFLATION

Depending upon the range of increase, and its severity, inflation may be classified into three broad categories.

1. Low Inflation

Such inflation is slow and on predictable[11] lines, which might be called small or gradual[12]. This is a comparative term which puts it opposite to the faster, bigger and unpredictable inflations. Low inflation takes place in a longer period and the range of increase is usually in 'single digit'. Such inflation has also been called as '*creeping inflation*'.[13] We may take an example of the monthly inflation rate of a country for six months being 2.3 per cent, 2.6 per cent, 2.7 per cent, 2.9 per cent, 3.1 per cent and 3.4 per cent. Here the range of change is of 1.1 per cent and over a period of six months.

2. Galloping Inflation

This is a '*very high inflation*' running in the range of double-digit or triple digit (i.e., 20 per cent, 100 per cent or 200 per cent in a year).[14] In the decades of 1970s and 1980s, many Latin American countries such as Argentina, Chile and Brazil had such rates of inflation—in the range of 50 to 700 per cent. The Russian economy did show such inflation after the disintegration of the ex-USSR in the late 1980s.

Contemporary journalism has given some other names to this inflation—*hopping inflation,* *jumping inflation* and *running or runaway inflation*.[15]

3. Hyperinflation

This form of inflation is '*large and accelerating*'[16] which might have the annual rates in million or even trillion.[17] In such inflation not only the range of increase is very large, but the increase takes place in a very short span of time, prices shoot up overnight.

The best example of hyperinflation that economists cite is of Germany after the First World War—in early 1920s. At the end of 1923, prices were 36 billion times higher than two years earlier.[18] This inflation was so severe that paper German currencies (the Deutsche Mark) were more valuable as stove fuel than as actual money.[19] Some recent examples of hyperinflation had been the Bolivian inflation of mid-1985 (24,000 per cent per annum) and the Yugoslavian inflation of 1993 (20 per cent per day).[20]

Such an inflation quickly leads to a complete loss of confidence in the domestic currency and people start opting for other forms of money, as for example physical assets, gold and foreign currency (also known as 'inflation proof' assets) and people might switch to barter exchange.[21]

11. Samuelson and Nordhaus, *Economics*, p. 671.
12. *Collins Dictionary of Economics*, p. 251.
13. Ibid.
14. Samuelson and Nordhaus, *Economics*, p. 671
15. As popularised by *The Economist, The Wall Street Journal, The Economic Times* (India), etc.
16. *Collins Dictionary of Economics*, p. 251
17. Samuelson and Nordhaus, *Economics*, p. 671.
18. Thomas Sargent, 'The Ends of Four Big Inflations', in R. Hall, *Inflations, Causes and Effects* (as quoted by Stiglitz and Walsh, *Economics,* p. 513).
19. Stiglitz & Walsh, *Economics*, p. 512.
20. Sachs, Jeffery, *The End of Poverty*, Penguin Books, London, 2005, pp. 92–108
21. Hyperinflation erodes the value of money very fast and that too at a very high scale. We may put it with an example, suppose the annual rate of inflation is 100 per cent, money loses half its value every year. It means that a note of Rs. 100 will have a value of just Rs. 3 after five years.

OTHER VARIANTS OF INFLATION

Other than the three broad categories we analysed above, some other variants of inflation are also considered by governments in their policymaking:

I. Bottleneck Inflation

This inflation takes place when the supply falls drastically and the demand remains at the same level. Such situations arise due to supply-side accidents, hazards or mismanagement which is also known as 'structural inflation'. This could be put in the 'demand-pull inflation' category.

II. Core Inflation

This nomenclature is based on the inclusion or exclusion of the goods and services while calculating inflation. Popular in western economies, core inflation shows price rise in all goods and services excluding *energy* and *food articles*. In India, it was first time used in the financial year 2000–01 when the government expressed that it was under control—it means the prices of manufactured goods were under control.[22] This was criticised by experts on account of excluding food articles and energy out of the inflation and feeling satisfied on the inflation front. Basically, in the western economies, food and energy are not the problems for the masses, while in India these two segments are of most vital importance for the common people.

OTHER IMPORTANT TERMS

Inflationary Gap

The excess of total government spending above the national income (i.e., fiscal deficit) is known as inflationary gap. This is intended to increase the production level, which ultimately pushes the prices up due to extra-creation of money during the process.

Deflationary Gap

The shortfall in total spending of the government (i.e., fiscal surplus) over the national income creates deflationary gaps in the economy. This is a situation of producing more than the demand and the economy usually heads for a general slowdown in the level of demand. This is also known as the *output gap*.

Inflation Tax

Inflation erodes the value of money and the people who hold currency suffer in this process. As the governments have authority of printing currency and circulating it into the economy (as they do in the case of deficit financing), this act functions as an income to the governments. This is a situation of sustaining government expenditure at the cost of people's income. This looks as if inflation is working as a tax.[23] That is how the term inflation tax is also known as *seigniorage*. It means, inflation is always the level to which the government may go for deficit financing—level of deficit financing is directly reflected by the rate of inflation.

It could also be used by the governments in the form of prices and incomes policy under which the companies pay inflation tax on the salary increases above the set level prescribed by the government.[24]

Inflation Spiral

An inflationary situation in an economy which results out of a process of wage and price interaction *'when wages press prices up and prices pull wages up'*[25] is known as the inflationary spiral. It

---

22. Ministry of Finance, *Economic Survey, 2000–01*, (New Delhi: Government of India, 2001).

23. Stiglitz and Walsh, *Economics*, p. 511.
24. *Penguin Dictionary of Economics*.
25. Ibid.

is also known as the ***wage-price spiral***. This wage-price interaction was seen as a plausible cause of inflation in the year 1935 in the US economy, for the first time.[26]

Inflation Accounting

A term popular in the area of corporate profit accounting. Basically, due to inflation the profit of firms/companies gets overstated. When a firm calculates its profits after adjusting the effects of current level of inflation, this process is known as inflation accounting. Such profits are the real profit of the firm which could be compared to a historic rate of inflation (inflation of the base year), too.

Inflation Premium

The bonus brought by inflation to the borrowers is known as the inflation premium. The interest banks charge on their lending is known as the ***nominal*** interest rate, which might not be the real cost of borrowing paid by the borrower to the banks. To calculate the real cost a borrower is paying on its loan, the nominal rate of interest is adjusted with the effect of inflation and thus the interest rate we get is known as the real interest rate. Real interest is always lower than the nominal interest rate, if the inflation is taking place—the difference is the inflation premium.

Rising inflation premium shows depleting profits of the lending institutions. At times, to neutralise the effects of inflation premium, the lender takes the recourse to increase the nominal rate of interest.[27] In recent times, it was done by the Indian banks in July 2003 to ward off their depleting profits when inflation had crossed the 7 per cent level—the level of inflation was

threatening to deplete even the capital base of the banks. Since then the RBI has been following a tighter credit policy as inflation was going beyond the upper limit of its healthy range (i.e., 4–5 per cent in the Indian case).

Phillips Curve

It is a graphic curve which advocates a relationship between inflation and unemployment in an economy. As per the curve there is a 'trade off' between inflation and unemployment, i.e., an inverse relationship between them. The curve suggests that lower the inflation, higher the unemployment and higher the inflation, lower the unemployment.[28] During the 1960s, this idea was among the most important theories of the modern economists. This concept is known after the economists who developed it—Alban William Housego Phillips (1914–75). Bill Phillips (popular name) was an electrical engineer from New Zealand and was an economist at the London School of Economics when propounded the idea. In 'The Relation between Unemployment and the Rate of Change of Money Wage Rates in the United Kingdom, 1861–1957' (published in *Economica* in 1958), he provided empirical evidence to support his ideas.[29]

By the early 1960s, an economic wisdom emerged around the world that by following a certain kind of monetary policy, unemployment could be checked forever and at the cost of a slightly higher inflation, unemployment could be reduced permanently. The central banks of the developed world started framing the required kind of monetary policies mixing the trade-off between inflation and unemployment. The idea became popular among the developing economies too by the late 1960s, though they were a bit confused, as most of them

26. J.K. Galbraith, *A History of Economics*, (London: Penguin Books, 1991), p. 205, pp. 267–70.

27. Patrick Lane, *Economics* (London: The Economist, 199), p. 270.

28. Stiglitz and Walsh, *Economics*, pp. 821–22.

29. *Penguin Dictionary of Economics*, pp. 297–98.

were fighting the menace of higher inflations (double digit) along with high level of unemployment.[30]

By the early 1970s, two American economists, Milton Friedman (Nobel Laureate, 1976) and Edmund Phelps challenged the idea of the Phillips Curve. According to them the trade-off between inflation and unemployment was only short-term, because once people came to expect higher inflation they started demanding higher wages and thus unemployment will rise back to its '*natural rate*' (the unemployment rate that occurs at full employment when the economy is producing at potential output, it is usually called the natural rate of unemployment).[31] They advocated that there was no long-term trade-off between inflation and unemployment. In the long run, monetary policy can influence inflation. They suggested that if monetary policy tried to hold unemployment below its natural rate, inflation will be rising to higher level, which is also known as the **non-accelerating inflation rate of unemployment (NAIRU)**.[32] The NAIRU is that rate of unemployment which is consistent with a constant rate of inflation. It means at NAIRU, the upward and downward forces on price (inflation) and wage (unemployment) neutralise each other and there is no tendency of change in the rate of inflation. We may say that the NAIRU is the lowest unemployment rate that an economy can sustain without any upward pressure on inflation rate.

Reflation

Reflation is a situation often deliberately brought by the government to reduce unemployment and increase demand by going for higher levels of economic growth.[33] Governments go for higher public expenditures, tax cuts, interest rate cuts, etc. Fiscal deficit rises, extra money is generally printed at higher level of growth, wages increase and there is almost no improvement in unemployment.

Reflation can also be understood from a different angle—when the economy is crossing a cycle of recession (low inflation, high unemployment, low demand, etc.) and government takes some economic policy decisions to revive the economy from recession, certain goods see sudden and temporary increase in their prices, such price rise is also known as reflation.

Stagflation

Stagflation is a situation in an economy when inflation and unemployment both are at higher levels, contrary to conventional belief. Such a situation first arose in the 1970s in the US economy (average unemployment rate above 6 per cent and the average rate of inflation above 7 per cent)[34] and in many Euro-American economies. This took place as a result of oil price increases of 1973 and 1979 and anticipation of higher inflation. The stagflationary situation continued till the early 1980s. Conventional thinking that a trade-off existed between inflation and unemployment (i.e., Phillips Curve) was falsified and several economies switched over to alternative ways of economic policies, such as monetaristic and supply-side economics.

When the economy is passing through the cycle of stagnation (i.e., long period of low aggregate demand in relation to its productive capacity) and the government shuffles with the economic policy, a sudden and temporary price rise is seen in some of the goods—such inflation is also known as stagflation. Stagflation is basically a combination of high inflation and low growth.[35]

30. Gerald M. Meier and James E. Ranch, **Leading Issues in Economic Development** (New Delhi: Oxford University Press, 2006), pp. 37–39.

31. Stiglitz and Walsh, *Economics*, p. 822.

32. Samuelson and Nordhaus, *Economics*, pp. 680–87.

33. *Collins Dictionary of Economics*, p. 446.

34. Stiglitz and Walsh, *Economics*, p. 478.

35. C. Rangarajan, *Indian Economy: Essays on Money and Finance*, (New Delhi; UBSPD, 1998), p. 58.

INFLATION TARGETING

The announcement of an official target range for inflation is known as inflation targeting. It is done by the Central Bank in an economy as a part of their monetary policy to realise the objective of a **stable** rate of inflation[36] (the Government of India asked the RBI to perform this function in the early 1970s).

India commenced inflation targeting 'formally' in *February 2015* when an agreement between the GoI and the RBI was signed related to it—the **Agreement on Monetary Policy Framework.** The agreement provides the aim of inflation targeting in this way—'it is essential to have a modern monetary framework to meet the challenge of an increasingly complex economy. Whereas the objective of monetary policy is to primarily maintain *price stability*, while keeping in mind the objective of *growth*.' The highlights of the agreement is as given below:

1. The RBI will aim to bring CPI-C Inflation below 6 per cent by January 2016. The target for financial year 2016–17 and all subsequent years shall be 4 per cent with a band of +/- 2 per cent (it means the *'healthy range of inflation'* to be 2–6 per cent).

2. RBI to publish the *Operating Target(s)* and establish an *Operating Procedure* of monetary policy to achieve the target. Any change in the operating target(s) and operating procedure in response to evolving macro-financial conditions shall also be published.

3. Every six months, the RBI to publish a document explaining:

(a) Source of inflation;

(b) Forecasts of inflation for the period between six to eighteen months from the date of the publication of the document; and

4. The RBI shall be seen to have failed to meet the target if inflation is:

(a) More than 6 per cent for three consecutive quarters for the financial year 2015–16 and all subsequent years.

(b) Less than 2 per cent for three consecutive quarters in 2016–17 and all subsequent years.

5. If the RBI fails to meet the target it shall set out in a report to the GoI:

(a) the reasons for its failure to achieve the target under set in this agreement;

(b) remedial actions proposed to be taken by the RBI; and

(c) an estimate of the time-period within which the target would be achieved pursuant to timely implementation of proposed remedial actions.

6. Any dispute regarding the interpretation or implementation of the agreement to be resolved between the Governor, RBI and the GoI.

It should be noted that the *Urjit Patel Committee* set by the RBI on monetary policy gave similar advices by early 2014—the move is seen as a follow up to this. This way India joined the club of inflation targeting countries such as USA, UK, European Union, Japan, South Korea, China, Indonesia and Brazil. It was New Zealand which went for inflation targeting in 1989 for the first time in the world.[37]

---

36. Samuelson and Nordhaus, *Economics*, p. 723.

37. New Zealand passed a law to do this with a target of 0 to 2 per cent inflation with a provision that the Governor of the Reserve Bank of New Zealand could be fired if inflation crosses the 2 per cent upper limit—now this target range has been revised to 1 to 3 per cent (Stiglitz and Walsh, *Economics*, p. 849).

Skewflation

Economists usually distinguish between inflation and a relative price increase. 'Inflation' refers to a sustained, across-the-board price increase, whereas 'a relative price increase' is a reference to an episodic price rise pertaining to one or a small group of commodities. This leaves a *third phenomenon*, namely one in which there is a price rise of one or a small group of commodities over a sustained period of time, without a traditional designation. '**Skewflation**' is a relatively new term to describe this third category of price rise.

In India, food prices rose steadily during the last months of 2009 and the early months of 2010, even though the prices of non-food items continued to be relatively stable. As this somewhat unusual phenomenon stubbornly persisted, policymakers conferred on how to bring it to an end. The term 'skewflation' made an appearance in internal documents of the Government of India, and then appeared in print in the *Economic Survey 2009–10* GoI, MoF.

The **skewedness** of inflation in India in the early months of 2010 was obvious from the fact that food price inflation crossed the 20 per cent mark in multiple months, whereas wholesale price index (WPI) inflation never once crossed 11 per cent. It may be pointed out that the skewflation has gradually given way to a lower-grade generalised inflation (with the economy in the middle of 2011 inflating at around 9 per cent with food and non-food price increases roughly at the same level).

Given that other nations have faced similar problems, the use of this term picked up quickly, with the *Economist* magazine (*January 24, 2011*), in an article entitled *'Price Rises in China: Inflated Fears',* wondering if China was beginning to suffer from an Indian-style skewflation.

GDP Deflator

This is the ratio between GDP at *Current Prices* and GDP at *Constant Prices.* If GDP at Current Prices is equal to the GDP at Constant Prices, GDP deflator will be 1, implying no change in price level. If GDP deflator is found to be 2, it implies rise in price level by a factor of 2, and if GDP deflator is found to be 4 , it implies a rise in price level by a factor of 4. GDP deflator is acclaimed as a *better measure* of price behaviour because it covers all goods and services produced in the country (because the weight of services has not been equitably accounted in the Indian 'headline inflation', i.e., inflation at WPI).

BASE EFFECT

It refers to the impact of the rise in price level (i.e., last year's inflation) in the previous year over the corresponding rise in price levels in the current year (i.e., current inflation). If the price index had risen at a high rate in the corresponding period of the previous year, leading to a high inflation rate, some of the potential rise is already factored in, therefore, a similar absolute increase in the Price index in the current year will lead to a relatively lower inflation rates. On the other hand, if the inflation rate was too low in the corresponding period of the previous year, even a relatively smaller rise in the Price Index will arithmetically give a high rate of current inflation. For example:

	Price Index				Inflation		
	2007	2008	2009	2010	2008	2009	2010
Jan	100	120	140	160	20	16.67	14.29

The index has increased by 20 points in all the three years, viz., 2008, 2009 and 2010. However, the inflation rate (calculated on 'year-on-year' basis) tends to decline over the three years from 20 per cent in 2008 to 14.29 per cent in 2010. This is because the absolute increase of 20 points in the price index in each year increases the *base year price index* by an equivalent amount, while the absolute increase in price index remains the same. The 'year-on-year' inflation is calculated by the formula :

Current Inflation Rate = [(Current Price Index – Last year's Price Index)] ÷ Last year's Price Index] x 100

EFFECTS OF INFLATION

There are multi-dimensional effects of inflation on an economy both at the micro and macro levels. It redistributes income, distorts relative prices, destabilises employment, tax, saving and investment policies, and finally it may bring in recession and depression in an economy. A brief and objective overview of the effects of inflation is given below:

1. On Creditors and Debtors

Inflation redistributes wealth from creditors to debtors, i.e., lenders suffer and borrowers benefit out of inflation. The opposite effect takes place when inflation falls (i.e., deflation).

2. On lending

With the rise in inflation, lending institutions feel the pressure of higher lending. Institutions don't revise the nominal rate of interest as the 'real cost of borrowing' (i.e., nominal rate of interest minus inflation) falls by the same percentage with which inflation rises.

3. On Aggregate Demand

Rising inflation indicates rising aggregate demand and indicates comparatively lower supply and higher purchasing capacity among the consumers. Usually, higher inflation suggests the producers to increase their production level as it is generally considered as an indication of higher demand in the economy.

4. On Investment

Investment in the economy is boosted by the inflation (in the short-run) because of two reasons:

    (i) Higher inflation indicates higher demand and suggests enterpreneurs to expand their production level, and

    (ii) Higher the inflation, lower the cost of loan (as shown above in no. 2)

5. On Income

Inflation affects the income of individual and firms alike. An increase in inflation, increases the 'nominal' value of income, while the 'real' value of income remains the same. Increased price levels erode the puchasing power of the money in the short-run, but in the long-run the income levels also increase (making the nominal value of income going upward). It means, in a given period of time income may go up due to two reasons, viz., inflationary siituation and increased earning. The concept 'GDP Deflator' (GDP at current prices divided by GDP at constant prices) gives the idea of 'inflation effect' on income over a given period.

6. On Saving

Holding money does not remain an intelligent economic decision (because money loses value with every increase in inflation) that is why people visit banks more frequently and try to hold least money with themselves and put maximum with the banks in their saving accounts. This is also known as the ***shoe leather cost***[38] of inflation (as it consumes the precious time of the people visiting the bank frequently tagging their shoe). It

---

38. Samuelson and Nordhaus, **Economics,** p. 674.

means that saving rate increases. But this happens as a short-term effect of inflation. In the long-run, higher inflation depletes the saving rate in an economy. Just the opposite situation arises when inflation falls or shows falling traits with decreasing saving, in the short-run and increasing saving in the long-run, respectively.

7. On Expenditure

Inflation affects both the forms of expenditures —consumption as well as investment. Increased prices make our consumption levels fall as goods and services we buy get costlier. We see a tendency among the people to cut their consumption levels aimed at neutralising the impact of price rise—making consumption expenditure fall. Exact opposite happens once prices head downward.

On the other hand inflations makes 'investment' expenditure increase as a result of decreased cost of money/finance (inflation brings benefit to borrower—known as 'inflation premium'). In times of price fall just opposite happens.

8. On Tax

On tax structure of the economy, inflation creates two distortions:

(i)   Tax-payers suffer while paying their direct and indirect taxes. As indirect taxes are imposed ad valorem (**on value**), increased prices of goods make tax-payers to pay increased indirect taxes (like cenvat, vat, etc., in India).

Similarly, due to inflation, direct tax (income tax, interest tax, etc.) burden of the tax-payers also increases as tax-payer's gross income moves to the upward **slabs** of official tax brackets (but the real value of money does not increase due to inflation; in fact, it falls). This problem is also known as **bracket creep**—i.e.,

inflation-induced tax increases.[39] Some economies (as in the US and many European countries) have **indexed** their tax provisions to neutralise this distortion on the direct tax payers.

(ii)   The extent to which tax collections of the government are concerned, inflation increases the nominal value of the gross tax revenue, while real value of the tax collection does not compare with the current pace of inflation as there is a lag (**delay**) in the tax collection in all economies.

But governments get an advantage on their interest burden, on their borrowings as inflation benefits borrowers. This benefit, however, depends upon the contemporary levels of fiscal deficit and the total national debt.

In the case of a government incurring high fiscal deficit (increased borrowing, printing currency), inflation functions as a tax, i.e., **inflation tax** via which the government fulfils its expenditure by cutting down the expenditure and consumption of the people.

9. On Exchange Rate

With every inflation the currency of the economy **depreciates** (loses its exchange value in front of a foreign currency) provided it follows the flexible currency regime. Though it is a comparative matter, there might be inflationary pressure on the foreign currency against which the exchange rate is compared.

10. On Export

With inflation, exportable items of an economy gain competitive prices in the world market. Due to this, the volume of export increases (keep in

---

39.   Samuelson and Nordhaus, **Economics,** p. 674.

mind that the value of export decreases here) and thus export income increases in the economy. It means export segment of the economy benefits due to inflation. Importing partners of the economy exert pressure for a stable exchange rate as their imports start increasing and exports start decreasing (see the next point).

11. On Import

Inflation gives an economy the advantage of lower imports and import-substitution as foreign goods become costlier. But in the case of compulsory imports (i.e., oil, technology, drugs, etc.) the economy does not get this benefit and loses more foreign currency instead of saving it.

12. On Trade Balance

In the case of a developed economy, inflation makes trade balance favourable, while for the developing economies inflation is unfavourable for their balance of trade. This is because of composition of their foreign trade. The benefit to export which inflation brings in to a developing economy is usually lower than the loss it incur due to its compulsory imports which become costlier due to inflation.

13. On Employment

Inflation increases employment in the short-run, but becomes neutral or even negative in the long run (see the Phillips Curve and the NAIRU in the earlier sections).

14. On Wages

Inflation increases the nominal (face) value of wages, while their real value falls. That is why there is a negative impact of inflation on the purchasing power and living standard of wage employees. To neutralise this negative impact the Indian government provides *dearness allowance* to its employees twice a year.

15. On the Self-employed

Inflation has a neutralising impact on the self-employed people in the short-run. But in the long-run they also get affected as the economy as a whole gets affected.

16. On the Economy

All the segments discussed above belong to an economy, but we must know the overall short-term and long-term impacts of inflation on an economy.

Experiences of the world economies in the late 1980s show that a particular level of inflation is healthy for an economy. This specific level of inflation was called as the 'range' of inflation and every economy needs to calculate its own range. Inflation beyond both the limits of the range is never healthy for any economy. In the case of India, it is considered 2 to 6 per cent at CPI(C), which is also known as the 'comfort zone' of inflation in India since 2015. Similarly for Australia, New Zealand, the USA, Canada and the European Union, the healthy range today is 1 to 3 per cent. This is why every economy today utilises *inflation targeting* as part of its monetary policy.

Inflation beyond the limits of the decided/prescribed range brings in recession to depressions. (We will see them in Section B of this Chapter, 'Business Cycle.)

INFLATION IN INDIA

Every economy calculates its inflation for efficient financial administration as the multi-dimensional effects of inflation make it necessary. India calculates its inflation on two price indices, i.e., the wholesale price index (WPI) and the consumer price index (CPI). While the WPI-inflation is used at the macro-level policymaking, the CPI-inflation is used for micro-level analyses. The inflation at the WPI is the inflation of the economy. Both the indices follow the 'point-to-point' method and may be shown in *points* (i.e., digit) as well as in *percentage* relative to a particular *base year*.

Wholesale Price Index

The first index number of wholesale prices commenced in India for the week January 10, 1942. It was having the base week ending August 19, 1939 = 100, which was published by the office of the Economic Adviser to the Government of India (Ministry of Industry).[40] Independent India followed the same series with more number of commodities included in the index. Several changes regarding inclusion of commodities, assigning them the logical weights took place in the coming times including revisions in the *base years* for the WPI. The WPI base year has been revised five times till date. The base years are as given below:

   (i)   1952–53 Base Year (112 Commodities) issued from June 1952.

   (ii)   1961–62 Base Year (139 Commodities) issued from July 1969.

   (iii)   1970–71 Base Year (360 Commodities) issued from January 1977.

   (iv)   1981–82 Base Year (447 Commodities) issued from January 1989.

   (v)   1993–94 Base Year (435 Commodities) issued from July, 1999.

   (vi)   2004–05 Base Year (676 Commodities) released in September 2011.

New Series of WPI

With the purpose of making inflation data in India more transparent, updated and similar to the practices among most of the economies, a *Working Group for Revision of WPI Number* was set up under the Chairmanship of the Planning Commission member, Prof. Abhijit Sen.

---

40.   Ministry of Finance, **Economic Survey 2006–07** (New Delhi: Government of India, 2007), p. 85.

In light of the recommendations the government recently announced the *New Series of Wholesale Price Index*.

Headline inflation in India is measured in terms of Wholesale Price Index (WPI) and the Office of the Economic Adviser, Department of Industrial Policy & Promotion is entrusted with the task of releasing this index. WPI is an important statistical indicator, as various policy decisions of the government, like inflation management, monitoring of prices of essential commodities, etc., are based on it.

It is one of the key variables for monetary policy changes by the Reserve Bank of India. In addition to its role as a policy variable, WPI is also used by various departments for arriving at the escalation costs of various contracts.

Considering the importance of WPI as a tool for various policy decisions, it is necessary to disseminate the most comprehensive, credible and accurate information, reflecting the realities of the present economic situation of the country. In order to capture the structural changes happening in the economy, the base year of WPI needs to be updated.

The Office of the Economic Adviser undertook the work relating to revision of the existing series of WPI (base 1993–94=100), which not only addressed the issue of change in the base year, but also revised the entire commodity basket and the weighting diagram so as to better reflect the price trends in economy. The revised series of WPI was officially launched on **September 14, 2010** by the Ministry of Commerce & Industry.

Features of the Revised Series of WPI

A representative commodity basket comprising **676 items** has been selected in the new series (base 2004–05=100) as against 435 in the old series (base 1993–94=100) and weighting diagram has been derived for the new series consistent with the structure of the economy. There has been a substantial increase in the number of quotations selected for collecting price data for the above items. The number of price quotations for the new series is **5482** whereas in the old series, it was 1918.

The selection of the base year and the commodity basket was made on the basis of the recommendations of the Working Group set up specifically for this purpose. The Working Group was headed by Professor Abhijit Sen, Member, Planning Commission and included as its members all stakeholders covering the users of the price data and the providers of the prices. The working group in its Technical Reports gave detailed recommendations with regard to the choice of the base year, the method of selection of items, preparation of weighting diagram and the collection of prices. The new index along with the base year and the commodity basket was also examined by the Technical Advisory Committee (TAC) on Prices and Cost of Living based in Central Statistical Organisation. Before the launch of the new index, inter-departmental consultations were held and opinions obtained from the Economic Advisory Council of the Prime Minister.

A comparative statement of weights, number of items and number of quotations between the **old series** and **new series** at Group level is given below:

Major Group / Group	Weight		No. of items		No. of Quotations	
	2004–05	1993–94	2004–05	1993–94	2004–05	1993–94
All Commodities	100.00	100.00	676	435	5482	1918
Primary Articles	20.12	22.02	102	98	579	455
Fuel & Power	14.91	14.23	19	19	72	72
Manufactured Products	64.97	63.75	555	318	4831	1391

Many new items have been included in the new series basket such as flowers, lemon and crude petroleum in **Primary Articles** and ice cream, canned meat, palm oil, readymade/instant food powder, mineral water, computer stationary, leather products, scooter / motorcycle tyre, polymers, petrochemical intermediates, granites, marbles, gold and silver, construction machinery, refrigerators, computers, dish antenna, transformer, microwave oven, communication equipments (telephone instruments), TV sets, VCD, washing machine and auto parts in **Manufactured Products**.

Revised Series: New Initiatives

There has been a substantial increase, both in terms of the number of commodities and its geographical coverage, in the revised series of WPI (base 2004–05=100), as compared to the earlier revisions undertaken so far.[41] This would, undoubtedly, disseminate the more realistic and reliable data, facilitating better decision making and policy intervention.

The revised series of WPI (base 2004–05=100) has also addressed the issue of flow of regular data. The NIC unit of the Office of the Economic Adviser has developed an online data transmission mechanism, whereby, the manufacturing units can supply price data through the internet. Also, an arrangement has been made with the National Sample Survey Office (Field Operations Division)

---

41. The three major classifications of the items in the WPI were followed for the first time when India went for the third revision of the prices with 1970–71 as the base year which was introduced in January 1977. The same classification is followed till date with changes in the assignments of weights to the items (Ministry of Finance, Economic Survey 2006–07, p. 85).

to get price data on regular basis. These measures have improved the flow of price data.

The new series of the WPI with the base year 2012 (i.e., 2011–12), which could be compatible to the base year of the new series of the CPI (released February 2015), was to be released by mid-2015. But it is still awaited (*Economic Survey 2016–17*).

Since **November 2009** the WPI data are already being released in the following way:

(i) the first set of data of WPI (for the '*Manufactured Products*') are released on monthly basis.

(ii) the second set of data of WPI (for the '*Primary Articles*' and '*Energy and Fuel Group*') are released on weekly basis.

Consumer Price Index

Other than the WPI, India also calculates inflation at the consumer level, similar to all the economies of the world. As consumers in India show wide differentiation of their choice of consumption, purchasing powers. etc., a single consumer price index (CPI) has not been possible yet which can encompass all the Indian consumers.[42]

Depending upon the socio-economic differentiations among consumers, India has four differing sets of CPI with some differentials in the basket of commodities allotted to them. Though these four types of CPIs is proposed to be withdrawn in coming times, data for them are still released. A brief account of the four CPIs are as under:

---

42. The economies of the Euro-American region have a single CPI as the majority of consumers show the same consumer behaviour (see J.B. Rosser and M.V. Rosser, *Comparative Economics in a Transforming World Economy* (Cambridge USA: Prentice Hall, MIT Press, 2004)).

1. CPI-IW

The Consumer Price Index for the industrial workers (CPI-IW) has 260 items (plus the services) in its basket with 2001 as the base year[43] (the first base year was 1958–59). The data is collected at 76 centres with one month's frequency and the index has a time lag of one month.

Basically, this index specifies the government employees (other than banks' and embassies' personnel). The wages/salaries of the central government employees are revised on the basis of the changes occurring in this index, the dearness allowance (DA) is announced *twice* a year. When the Pay Commission recommends pay revisions, the base is the CPI (IW).

2. CPI-UNME

The Consumer Price Index for the Urban Non-Manual Employees (CPI-UNME) has 1984–85 (first base year was 1958–59) as the base year and 146–365 commodities in the basket for which data is collected at 59 centres in the country—data collection frequency is monthly with two weeks time lag.[44]

This price index has limited use and it is basically used for determining dearness allowances (DAs) of employees of some foreign companies operating in India (i.e., airlines, communications, banking, insurance, embassies and other financial services). It is also used under the Income Tax Act to determine *capital gains* and by the CSO (Central Statistical Organisation) for deflating selected services sector's contribution to the GDP at factor cost and current prices to calculate the corresponding figure at constant prices.

---

43. Ministry of Finance, *Economic Survey 2006–07*, p. 90.
44. Ministry of Finance, *Economic Survey 2001–02*, p. 90.

On the advice of its governing council the NSSO (National Sample Survey Organisation) is at present conducting a Family Living Survey (FLS) to obtain the profile of the present consumption pattern of urban non-manual employees so that the CPI (UNME) could be shifted to the present base year.

Presently, the CSO is also examining the possibility of constructing a consumer price index for the urban employees (a new index which might be like CPI–UE).

3. CPI-AL

The Consumer Price Index for Agricultural Labourers (CPI-AL) has 1986–87 as its base year with 260 commodities in its basket. The data is collected in 600 villages with a monthly frequency and has three weeks time lag.

This index is used for revising minimum wages for agricultural labourers in different states. As the consumption pattern of agricultural labourers has changed since 1986–87 (its base year), the Labour Bureau proposes to revise the existing base year of this index. For the revision, the consumer expenditure data collected by the NSSO during its 61st NSS Round (2004–05) is proposed to be used.

The governments at the Centre and states remain vigilant regarding the changes in this index as it shows the price impact on the most vulnerable segment of the society, this segment spends almost 75 per cent of its total income on the purchase of food articles. Governments' failure to stabilise the index in the long range can make them politically volatile and be translated into political debacles. That is why the FCI is always kept ready to supply cheaper foodgrains in the situations of any price rise.

4. CPI-RL

There is yet another Consumer Price Index for the Rural Labourers (CPI-RL) with 1983 as the base

year, data is collected at 600 villages on monthly frequency with three weeks time lag, its basket contains 260 commodities.

The agricultural and rural labourers in India create an overlap, i.e., the same labourers work as the rural labourers once the farm sector has either low or no employment scope. Probably, due to this reason this index was dropped by the government in 2001–02.[45] But after the government change at the Centre the index was revived again.[46]

Revision in the CPI

It was in 2011 that the government announced a new Consumer Price Index (CPI) – CPI (Rural); CPI (Urban) and by combining them into a 'national' CPI-C (where 'C' stands for 'Combined'). Menawhile, the data for the existing four CPIs were also being published by the CSO. The base year was also revised from the existing 2004–05 to 2010–11.

In **February 2015,** the CPI was *again* revised by the CSO. Together with changing the base year, in this revision, many *methodological changes* have been incorporated, in order to make the indices more robust. The major changes introduced in the revised series are as given below:

1. The base year has been changed from 2010=100 to 2012=100.

2. The basket of items and their weighing diagrams have been prepared using the Modified Mixed Reference Period (MMRP) data of Consumer Expenditure Survey (CES), 2011–12, of the *68th Round* of National Sample Survey (NSS). This has been done to make it consistent with the *international practice* of shorter reference period for most of the food items and longer reference period for the items of infrequent consumption. The

45. Ministry of Finance, *Economic Survey 2001–02,* p. 91.

46. Ministry of Finance, *Economic Survey 2006–07,* p. 90.

weighing diagrams of old series of CPI were based on the Uniform Reference Period (URP) data of CES, 2004–05, of the 61st Round of NSS.

With this change in the weighing diagrams, the gap between Weight Reference Year and Price Reference Year (Base Year), which was *six years* in the old series, has now been reduced to *six months* only. Due to change in the *consumption pattern* from 2004–05 to 2011–12, the weighing diagrams (share of expenditure to total expenditure) have changed. A comparison of weighing diagrams of the old and revised series is given below:

Comparison of weighing diagrams of the existing and revised series of CPI

Group Description	Old Series of CPI (Weights computed on the basis CES 2004–05)			Revised Series of CPI (Weights computed on the basis CES 2011–12)		
	Rural	Urban	Combd.	Rural	Urban	Combd.
Food and beverages	56.39	35.81	47.58	34.18	36.29	45.86
Pan, tobacco and intoxicants	2.72	1.34	2.13	3.26	1.36	2.35
Clothing and Foodwear	5.36	3.91	4.73.	7.36	5.57	6.53
Housing	–	22.54	9.77	–	21.67	10.07
Fuel and Light	10.42	8.40	9.49	7.94	5.50	6.84
Miscellaneous	24.91	28.00	26.31	27.26	29.53	28.32
Total	**100.00**	**100.00**	**100.00**	**100.00**	**100.00**	**100.00**

Source: CSO, February 2015. Here, 'Combd.' stands for Combined while '-' stands for 'not available'.

3. The number of *Groups,* which was five in the old series, has now been increased to **six**. 'Pan, tobacco and intoxicants', which was a Sub-group under the group 'Food, beverages and tobacco', has now been made as a separate group. Accordingly, the group 'Food, beverages and tobacco' has been changed to 'Food and beverages'.

4. Egg, which was part of the sub-group 'Egg, fish and meat' in the old series, has now been made as a separate sub-group. Accordingly, the earlier sub-group has been modified as 'Meat and fish'.

5. The elementary/item indices are now being computed using Geometric Mean (GM) of the Price Relatives of Current Prices with respect to Base Prices of different markets in consonance with the international practice. In the old series, Arithmetic Mean (AM) was used for that purpose. The advantage of using GM is that it moderates the volatility of the indices as GM is less affected by extreme values.

6. Prices of PDS items under Antyodaya Anna Yojana (AAY) have also been included for compilation of indices of PDS items, in addition to Above Poverty Line (APL) and Below Poverty Line (BPL) prices being taken in the old series.

7. Sample size for collection of house rent data for compilation of *House Rent Index,* which was 6,684 rented dwellings in the old series, has now been doubled to 13,368 rented dwellings in the revised series.

8. Apart from All-India CPIs (Rural, Urban, Combined) for sub-group, group and general index (all-groups), which were

released for the old series, all India Item CPIs (Combined) will also be available.

9. The Consumer Food Price Indices (Rural, Urban, Combined) will be compiled as weighted average of the indices of following sub-groups, as practiced earlier in the old series (only the weights have been revised):

All India Weights of different Sub-groups within Consumer Food Price Index

Sub-Group Code	Sub-group Description	Rural	Urban	Combined
(1)	(2)	(3)	(4)	(5)
1.1.01	Cereals and products	26.14	22.24	24.77
1.1.02	Meat and fish	9.26	9.23	9.25
1.1.03	Egg	1.05	1.21	1.10
1.1.04	Milk and products	16.34	17.98	16.92
1.1.05	Oils and fats	8.90	9.49	9.11
1.1.06	Fruits	6.10	9.80	7.40
1.1.07	Vegetables	15.78	14.88	15.46
1.1.08	Pulses and products	6.25	5.84	6.11
1.1.09	Sugar and confectionery	3.61	3.28	3.49
1.1.10	Spices	6.57	6.05	6.39
	All Sub-groups of CFPI	100.00	100.00	100.00

Source: CSO, February 2015. Here, CPFI stands for Consumer Food Price Index.

Trends in Inflation

Inflation has been a highly sensitive issue in India right since Independence and it has been so during the ongoing reforms process period, too. It has an incessant tendency of resulting into 'double digits', taking politically explosive proportions like governments falling at the Centre and state levels due to price rise of the commodities such as edible oil, onion, potato, etc. In such situations the government in general has been taking recourse to tighter money supply to contain the state level disturbances due to price rise of the commodities such as edible oil, onion, potato, etc., although it has contained inflation, but at the cost of higher growth. Price rise got rooted in India's political psyche in such a way that the government did check frequent famines quickly at the cost of long-term endemic hunger and sustained malnutrition.[47]

Decadal inflation in India looks comparatively normal with reference to many developing economies.[48] But it has sporadic incidences of double-digit tendencies mainly due to supply-side shortfalls caused by droughts (monsoon failures), price rise of crude oil in the international market or fund diversions due to

---

47. Pranab Bardhan agrees to Amartya Sen (How is India Doing?', **New York Review of Books,** December 1982) in: 'A Political Economy Perspective on Development' in Bimal Jalan ed. **Indian Economy Problems and Prospects,** (New Delhi: Penguin Books, 1992), p. 369.

48. Rosser and Rosser, **Comparative Economics in a Transforming World Economy.**

wars (the Chinese war of 1962 and the Pakistan wars of 1965–66 and 1971). The decadal inflation in India has been as given below:[49]

(i) *During 1950s:* remained at 1.7 per cent.

(ii) *During 1960s:* remained at 6.4 per cent.

(iii) *During 1970s:* remained at 9.0 per cent.

(iv) *During 1980s:* remained at 8.0 per cent.

(v) *During 1990s:* remained at 9.5 per cent (though it reached 0.5 per cent by the fourth quarter of the fiscal 1998–99)

(vi) *During 2000s:* Inflation was at lower levels between 2000–08 (from 3 to 5 per cent). But from 2009 onwards it started moving upward with 'sttuborn' tendencies.[50] Between 2009–13, the headline inflation remained stuck at uncomfortable levels, primarily due to 'food articles' *(food inflation)* led by protein-rich items *(protein inflation)* in the consequence of shift in dietary habit, income effect (via MGNREGA kind of schemes), increased wages, increase in prices of commodities in the global market (especially, food articles), costlier fodder, costlier energy and fuel, etc. By late 2010, India had the phenomenon of *'skewflation'* with inflation being in the range of 9–10 per cent.

(vii) *During 2010s:* From 2010–11 to 2013–14 inflation remained higher—the average inflation at WPI and CPI was 8 per cent and 9.7 per cent, respectively. Food inflation, led by protein items, breached into double digit[51]. Since mid-2014 inflation started moderating—WPI inflation remained in negative (-5.1 per cent by August 2015) and CPI inflation

positive of 4.9 per cent end-December 2016)—showing a 'wedge' of 10 per cent. During **2016-17**, inflation has been characterized by the following features, as per the *Economic Survey 2016-17*:

(a) *CPI inflation* moderated to 3.4 per cent by December 2016 (due to good kharif crops led by pulses).

(b) *WPI inflation* reversed from negative to a positive of 3.4 per cent by December 2016 (due to rising international oil prices).

(c) The *wedge* between CPI and WPI inflation, seen in 2015-16 has narrowed down to zero.

(d) *Core inflation* has been more stable—hovering between 4.5 to 5.0 per cent.

(e) The outlook for the *headline inflation* (i.e., CPI-C) for 2016-17 is below the RBI's target of 5 per cent (a trend likely to be assisted by 'demonetisation').

An analysis of inflationary trends in India does not pin-point any one reason behind it. Economists have pointed out all possible reasons (the so-called **'good'** and **'bad'**) behind the inflationary pressures in the economy of which we may have a brief review:

1. Structural Inflation

With few exceptional years, India has been facing the typical problem of bottleneck inflation (**i.e., structural inflation**) which arises out of shortfalls in the supply of goods, a general crisis of a developing economy, rising demand but lack of investible capital to produce the required level of goods.[52] Whenever the government managed

49. Based on Rangarajan, **Indian Economy,** p. 63; Jalan,

50. Ministry of Finance, **Economic Survey 2013–14** (New Delhi: Government of India, 2014), pp. 75–77.

51. Ministry of Finance, **Economic Survey 2014–15** (New Delhi: Government of India, 2015), Vol. 2, pp. 69–75.

52. Desai, Meghnad, 'Development Perspectives' in I. J. Ahluwalia and I.M.D. Little, (eds), **India's Economic Reforms and Development,** (New Delhi: Oxford University Press, 1998), p. 41.

to go for higher growths by managing higher investible capital it had inflationary pressures on the economy (seen during 1970s and 1980s, especially) and growth was sacrificed at the altar of lower inflation (which was politically more justified).[53] Thus, the supply-side mismatch remained a long-drawn problem in India for higher inflation. After some time even if the government managed higher expenditure, most of it went to the non-developmental areas, which did show low growth with higher inflation—signs of a stagnating economy.

2. Cost-Push Inflation

Due to 'inflation tax' the price of goods and services in India have been rising as the government took alternative recourse to increase its revenue receipts.[54] We see it taking place due to higher **import duties** on raw materials also.[55] The **non-value-added** tax (non-VAT) structure of India in the past was also having cascading effect on the prices of commodities in the country.[56] The government needed higher revenues to finance its planned development, thus the above given factors looked inescapable.

3. Fiscal Policy

To finance the developmental requirements of the economy, the governments became trapped in the cyclical process of over-money supply. At first it was done by external borrowings, but by the late 1960s onwards (once **deficit financing** got acceptance around the world) the government started taking recourse to heavy internal borrowings as well as printing of fresh currency too. A major part of the government's internal borrowing is contributed by the Reserve Bank of India (RBI) which leads to price rise.[57] For any government deficit if the Central Bank (RBI) is purchasing primary issues of the Government securities or creating fresh advances to the government, the combined effect has to be higher inflation, lower savings rates and lower economic growth[58]—the vices of unsound fiscal policy. The higher fiscal deficit tends to bring about higher interest rates as demand for funds rise, excess demand raises expected inflation and expected depreciation of the currency.[59] Once the foreign exchange (Forex) reserves started increasing with a faster pace by the early 2000–01 fiscal, its cost of maintenance has been translated into higher prices, as the RBI purchases the foreign currencies it supplies into equivalent rupees into the economy, which creates extra demand and the prices go up.[60]

The higher revenue deficits (driven by high interest payments, subsidies, salaries and pensions, basically) and fiscal deficits make the government supply more money which push the inflation in the upward direction. Once the Fiscal and Budget Management Act came into force in 2003, the scenario improved in the coming times. Though the period from 1999 to 2003 did show high growth with low inflation and the lowest interest rates in India.

---

53. Jalan Bimal, *India's Economic Policy,* (New Delhi: Penguin Books, 1992), pp. 52–58.

54. C. Rangarajan, 'Development, Inflation and Monetary Policy', in I.J. Ahluwalia and I.M.D. Little (eds), *India's Economic Reforms and Development*, (New Delhi: Oxford University Press, 1998), pp. 56–57.

55. Jalan, *India's Economic Policy,* pp. 191–203.

56. *Chelliah Committee Report,* 1993.

57. V.M. Dandekar, 'Forty Years After Independence', (New Delhi: Penguin Books, 1992), pp. 81–88. in the Bimal Jalan (ed.), *Indian Economy: Problems and Prospects.*

58. Y.V. Reddy, *Lectures on Economic and Financial Sector Reforms in India* (New Delhi: Oxford University Press, 2002), pp. 176–77.

59. Ashima Goya, 'Puzzles in India Performance: Deficits without Diaster' in Kirit S. Parikh and R. Radhakrishna (eds), *India Development Report, 2004–05* (New Delhi: IGIDR and Oxford University Press, 2005), pp. 191–208.

60. Kaushik Basu, *India Emerging Economy: Performance and Prospects in the 1990's and Beyond* (New Delhi: Oxford University Press, 2004), pp. 89–103.

Healthy Range of Inflation

Higher inflation and higher growth as a trade-off was questioned in the late-1980s by the developed economies as the economic and social costs of higher inflation also needed policy attention—a costly 'trade-off'.[61] In coming times, most of the world economies went in favour of a stable inflation (i.e., *inflation targeting*) though the idea has been *protested*.[62] India also started inflation stabilisation (informed targeting at WPI) by the early 1970s. It was in 1973 that inflation crossed the 20 per cent mark on account of the international oil price rise and the government (the Indira Gandhi Government) devised a severe anti-inflation package which included directly restricting the disposable incomes of the people (this measure was used for the *first* time in India[63]). The package had an impact and by March 1975 the inflation calmed down to 5.7 per cent. This was the time when the RBI was given a new function 'inflation stabilisation' and India entered the era of monetary controls for inflation. With inflation targeting there started a debate concerning the healthy range of inflation for the Indian economy, i.e., by mid-1970s. We may have some official and non-official versions of the suitable range of inflation pointed out from time to time:

(i) The *Chakravarty Committee (1985)* treated 4 per cent inflation as acceptable for the economy in its report on the monetary system. He also added that this level of price rise will facilitate the purpose of attracting investment for the desired level of growth.

(ii) The *Government of India* accepted a range of 4 to 6 per cent inflation as acceptable for the economy citing the world average of 0 to 3 per cent at the time (1997–98).[64]

(iii) The RBI Governor *C. Rangarajan* advocated that inflation rate must come down initially to 6 to 7 per cent and eventually to 5 to 6 per cent on an average over the years.[65]

(iv) The *Tarapore Committee* on Capital Account Convertibility recommended an acceptable range of 3 to 5 per cent inflation for the three year period (1997–98 to 1999–2000).[66]

In the recent times (June 2003 onwards) the government/the RBI has maintained a general policy of keeping inflation below 5 per cent mark—at any cost—as if fixing 4 to 5 per cent as the healthy range of inflation for the economy.[67]

The medium-term objective (i.e., target) of the government is to keep inflation in the 4–4.5 per cent range.[68] One thing should be kept in mind that inflation has always been a political matter in the country. Every time the RBI tried to check the rising inflation via monetary measures a majority of experts objected to it by calling it a move to sacrifice growth for lower price levels.

61. S. Fisher, 'Modern Central Banking', in F. Capie etal., The Future of Central Banking, The Tercentenary Symposium of the Bank of England (Cambridge: Cambridge University Press, 1994) pp. 262–308.

62. Paul Krugman, 'Stable Prices and Fast Growth: Just Say No., **Economist** 31 (1996): pp. 15–18.

63. Ahluwalia and Little, *India Economic Reforms and Development*, p. 2.

64. Ministry of Finance, **Economic Survey 1997–98** (New Delhi: Goverment of India, 1998), p. 92.

65. Rangarajan, 'Development, Inflation and Monetary Policy, pp. 61–63.

66. We may refer to almost all the credit and monetary policies announced by the RBI during this period.

67. As the RBI put it in its Credit and Monetary Policy Review of July 31, 2007.

68. It should be noted here that the level of inflation was below 5 per cent till the new Government came to power and the outgoing Government was blamed to freeze the inflation data to a more politically digestable level (i.e., below 5 per cent). The new Government in the process of preparing a producer price index (PPI) has also committed to make the inflation data automated like the share indices.

A tighter monetary policy decelerates investment and growth, hampers the growth prospects of the middle class in general and the entrepreneurs in particular while the wage-earners as well as the poor segment of society feels relieved (at least in short term).

In **February 2015**, India formally commenced the process of 'inflation targeting'. Now, the new monthly CPI (C), is taken as the measure of **headline inflation** and is tracked by the RBI to **anchor** its monetary policy and the healthy annual range for it is between 2 to 6 per cent.

Producer Price Index

A working group was set up in mid-2003–04 under the chairmanship of Prof. Abhijit Sen, Member, Planning Commission to fulfil the twin tasks of:

(i)   revising the current series of WPI (i.e., base 1993–94) and

(ii) recommending a producer price index (PPI) for India which could replace the WPI.

As follow-up to its advices, the new series (*base year*) for the WPI has been revised to 2004–05.

The proposal of switching over to the PPI (from the WPI) came up from the government by mid-2003 and the working group has been getting inputs from the IMF regarding it. The PPI measures price changes from the perspective of the producer while the consumer price index (CPI) measures it from the consumers' perspective. Wholesellers charge higher prices to retailers, in turn retailers charge higher prices to consumers and the price increase is translated into the higher consumer prices—thus the PPI is useful in having an idea of the consumer prices in the future.[69] In PPI, only basic prices are used while taxes, trade margins and transport costs are excluded. This index is considered a better measure of inflation as price changes at primary and intermediate stages can be tracked before it gets built into the finished goods stage.[70] Due to its better use many economies have switched over to the PPI—the oldest such series is maintained by the Bureau of Labor Statistics (BLS) for the US economy—the index is capable of measuring prices at the wholesaler or the producer stage—widely used by private business houses in their price targetting.[71]

Once India shifts from the WPI to the upcoming PPI, the economy is supposed to have a better idea about the trends of inflation.

Housing Price Index

India's official Housing Price Index (HPI) was launched in July 2007 in Mumbai. Basically developed by the Indian home loans regulator, the National Housing Bank (NHB) the index is named **NHB Residex**. Presently, the index has been introduced as a pilot project for five cities—Bangalore, Bhopal, Delhi, Kolkata and Mumbai, —till now it has been updated up to the quarter ended March 2016.

There are various concepts of housing price indices, and many sources and ways for compilling price data—both private and public. The methodology of constructing such indices varies from country to country depending upon the use and purpose as well as the data availability. A Technical Advisory Group (TAG) was set up under the chairmanship of an adviser from the Ministry of Finance in 2006–07 which had members and experts from public and private bodies of the concerned field, i.e., NHB, CSO, RBI, HDFC, HUDCD, LIC Housing Finance Ltd., Labour Bureau, Dewan Housing Finance Corporation Ltd., and the Society for Development Studies (SDS). After reviewing international best practices and the methodology, sampling techniques, collection of price data for

69.   Stiglitz and Walsh, **Economics**, p. 517.

70.   Ministry of Finance, *Economic Survey 2006–07,* p. 92.

71.   Samuelson and Nordhaus, **Economics,** p. 441.

construction of real estate price indices in the USA (index developed by the office of Federal Housing Enterprise Dversight), Canada (New Housing Price Index) and the UK (Halifax Index), the TAG suggested a proper methodology for India.

The TAG decided to take 2001 as the *base year* for the index which was consistent with the base period of the other indices, i.e., 2001 for the revised CPI (IW), 2000–01 for the revised WPI and 1999–2000 for the revised GDP series. The base year was revised to 2007 in March 2014.

With an overall objective of bringing transparency in the Indian real estate market, the index is expected to serve some highly important and timely purposes:

(i) Whether a broker is quoting too high a price for houses in the cities.

(ii) Banks/housing finance bodies will be able to estimate only if the loan applications are realistic for the properties.

(iii) This will also show the level of non-performing assets in the housing sector.

(iv) And most importantly it will serve as a realistic price index for the buyers. (At present a buyer has no means, to judge whether a rise in property price was in the offing with the general level of inflation (i.e., at WPI) in the country, or has been scaled up disproportionately. Other than quotes from brokers, there are no means at present to evaluate the changes in price in this sector. At present the only index that gave some idea of housing price changes was the CPI (IW) which being a national index did not show *regional variations*.)

By early 2017, index was being developed only for residential housing sector. However, at a later stage, the scope of the index is to be expanded to develop separate indices for commercial property and land. This is to be combined to arrive at the real estate price index. The aim is to develop a residential property price index for select cities and subsequently an **all India composite index** by combining the city level indices to capture the relative temporal change in the prices of houses at different levels.

Service Price Index

The contribution of the tertiary sector in India's GDP has been strengthening for the past 10 years and today it stands above 60 per cent. The need for a service price index (SPI) in India is warranted by the growing dominance of the sector in the economy.[72] There is no index, so far, to measure the price changes in the services sector. The present inflation (at the WPI) only shows the price movements of the commodity-producing sector, i.e., it includes only the primary and the secondary sectors—the tertiary sector is not represented by it.

The need for such an index was recommended by the working group (under the Chairmanship of Prof. Abhijit Sen, Member, Planning Commission) set up to revise the WPI (1993–94) series which was reiterated by the National Statistical Commission (headed by C. Rangarajan). The office of the Economic Adviser, Ministry of Commerce and Industry has been making an effort to develop sector-specific service price index for the country with the technical assistance being received under the World Bank Assisted Economic Reforms Projects (WBAERPs). At present, efforts are being made to develop service price indices for selected services initially on an experimental basis (covering road transport, railways, airways, business, trade, port, postal telecommunications, banking and insurance services only).

---

72. Ministry of Finance, *Economic Survey 2006–07,* p. 94.

The basic studies of index construction are complete. Before formal launching of the index, the complete study is supposed to be discussed with academicians, practitioners and the users of the services. The need to construct a service price index for the economy was felt more after the *OECD-Eurosat Report of 2005* on the subject.[73]

7th PAY COMMISSION IMPACT

There has been a concern about the impact of the 7th Pay Commission (PC) recommendations on inflation. As per the ***Economic Survey 2015–16,*** the historical evidence suggests that the 6th PC award hardly had any such impact (between September 2008 to September 2009) even if it gave huge arrears. The Survey adds that the 7th PC is unlikely to have any big impact on inflation even if fully implemented (including railways) – wage bill of the GoI will go up around 52 per cent (it went up by 70 per cent in case of the 6th PC). The Survey provides **three factors** in favour—

(i) Inflation reflects the degree to which aggregate demand exceeds aggregate supply. Wages determine only one small part of aggregate demand—in fact, they do not even determine government demand (which depends on the overall fiscal deficit). Fiscal deficit is the difference between how much the state is injecting into the economy through overall spending and how much it is taking away through taxes. Since the government remains committed to *reducing the fiscal deficit* (from 3.9 per cent of 2015–16 to 3.5 per cent in 2016–17), the pressure on prices will diminish, even if wages go up.

(ii) A sharp increase in public sector wages could affect inflation if it spilled over into private sector wages (and hence private sector demand). But currently this channel is *muted*, since there is considerable slack in the private sector labour market, as evident in the softness of rural wages. And even if private sector wage increases nonetheless do quicken somewhat, the existence of *substantial capacity underutilisation* suggests that firms might find it difficult to pass the cost increase onto consumer prices.

(iii) Lastly, there will be some mechanical impact of the increase in the house rent allowance (HRA) on the housing component of the CPI. But this effect is likely to be modest between 0.15 and 0.3 percentage points (the weight of rented government housing—centre and state—in the CPI is 0.35 per cent). And even then it will merely have a one-off effect on the level of the CPI, rather than the rate of inflation going forward, which is the real target of the RBI.

This way, the Survey concludes that there will not be any big and long-term impact on inflation even if the Government decides to implement the 7th PC award.

---

73. 'The number of National Statistical Agencies collecting service producer prices data, though growing, is still small', points out the **OECD-Eurosat, 2005 Inquiry on National Collection of Services Producer Prices Preliminary Report,** giving information on 45 such countries. The report further adds that while some such agencies have focused exclusively on the price of services provided to enterprises, others have approached the subject more broadly through the development of services producer price indices with varying approaches and coverage. As per the report, at present, 30 countries collect services producer prices while prelimilary works have started in other countries, particularly the European countries under the auspices of the Eurosat. Other than the developed Euro-American economies some other countries which worked as inspiration for India which have such an index are China, Hong Kong, Czech Republic, Slovak Republic, Poland, Lithuania, Israel and Vietnam.

BUSINESS CYCLE

INTRODUCTION

The discussion on growth and development has shown their internal interdependence. If the quality of life in an economy is to be enhanced, there is a need of conscious public policy which can spend and invest in areas like food, nutrition, health, education, shelter, social security, etc. But for such expenditures and investments, the economy needs equitable level of income, too. The income enhancement in any economy takes place via increasing the level of production in the economy, i.e., real gross national product (GNP). It means, development requires higher growth, i.e., higher levels of economic activities. With the help of suitable kind of economic policies, the government of an economy keeps trying to maintain a higher level of economic activity. But, at times, economy keeps failing in this objective. And, thus economies fluctuate between the best and the worst levels of economic activities which is known in economics as **boom** and **depression**, respectively. They can be called different phases of the economic activities of the economies. In between boom and depression, there might be many other situations of the economic activities, such as—**stagnation**, **slowdown**, **recession** and **recovery**. The fluctuations in the level of economic activity between the depressions and booms has been called by the economists as **business cycle** or **trade cycle** with recession and recovery as the main intermediate stages.[74] Stagnation[75] and slowdown may be considered as other intermediate stages of

the business cycle. We intend here to understand the actual meanings of each of the stages. Economists have pointed out that the business cycle is characterised by **four** phases or **stages** in which economies alternate:

   (i) Depression

   (ii) Recovery

   (iii) Boom

   (iv) Recession

DEPRESSION

Though depression has visited the world economy only once in 1929, economists have pin-pointed enough number of traits to recognise it. The **major** traits of depression could be as given below:

   (i) an extremely low aggregate demand in the economy causes activities to decelerate;

   (ii) the inflation being comparatively lower;

   (iii) the employment avenues start shrinking forcing unemployment rate to grow fast;

   (iv) to keep the business going, production houses go for **forced labour-cuts** or **retrenchment (to cut down production cost and be competitive in the market,)** etc.

The economic situations become so chaotic in the phase of depression that governments have almost no control over the economy. The Great Depression of 1929[76] gave rise to the ideas of **strong**

---

74. *Collins internet-linked Dictionary of Economics,* Glasgow, 2006 & *Oxford Business Dictionary,* N. Delhi, 2004.

75. Simon Cox (ed.), **Economics** (London: The Economists, 2007), p. 60.

76. A very lively description of the Great Depression has been presented by **Lee Iacocca** in his autobiography. This is known as the Great Depression due to its length and depth—the economies could recover fully out of it only by the mid-1940s (Stiglitz and Walsh, p. 495).

government intervention[77] in the economy, such as deficit financing, monetary management, etc.

What the governments may do if depression visits the economy? The simple answer the world has been able to find is to repeat the policy measures of 1929. The best way to avoid depression is not to let it visit. This is why every modern economy keeps extra-vigil on the major symptoms of its economy so that the prevention-measures can be taken in time and depression is avoided.

RECOVERY

An economy tries to come out of the low production phase to survive. The low production phase might be depression, recession or slowdown with the former being the worst and rare, governments take many new fiscal and monetary measures to boost demand and production and ultimately a recovery in an economy is managed. The business cycle of recovery may show the following *major* economy traits:

(i) an upturn in aggregate (total) demand which has to be accompanied by increase in the level of production;

(ii) production process expands and new investments become attractive;

(iii) as demand goes upward, inflation also moves upward making borrowing cheaper for investors;

(iv) with an upturn in production, new employment avenues are created and unemployment rate starts declining; etc.

With the above symptoms, people's income go for a certain increase which creates new demand and a cycle of demand and production (supply) starts playing hand-in-hand to recover the economy. To recover an economy, governments usually go for tax-breaks, interest cuts, an increase in salaries of its employees, etc. Assimilation of innovations by the entrepreneurs and search for new frontiers of enterprise do play a very vital role in the process of recovery provided these activities are at first incentives by the governments.

The Euro-American economies recovered out of the Great Depression with the help of the measures cited above. Such recoveries have been seen many times around the world when economies recovered from slowdown or the recessionary phases. The best example of recent times could be cited from India of 1997 to 2002 when the economy suffered severe bouts of slowdown and recession.[78]

BOOM

A strong upward fluctuation in the economic activities is called boom.[79] As economies try to recover out of the phases of slowdown, recession and depression at times the measures taken by the governments as well as the private sector might put economic activities as such which the economic systems fail to digest. This is the phase of the *boom.* The *major* economic traits of boom may be listed as given below:

(i) an accelerated and prolonged increase in the demand;

(ii) demand peaks up to such a high level that it exceeds sustainable output/production levels;

(iii) the economy heats up and a demand-supply lag is visible;

(iv) the market forces mismatch (*i.e., demand and supply disequilibirium*) and tend to create a situation where inflation start going upward;

(e) the economy might face structural problems like shortage of investible

---

77. Suggested by John Meynard Keynes in his seminal work *The General Theory of Employment, Interest and Money* (New York: Harcourt, 1935).

78. *Economic Surveys, 1996–97 to 2002–03,* MoF, GoI, N. Delhi.

79. Stiglitz & Walsh, op. cit., p. 945.

capital, lower savings, falling standard of living, creation of a sellers' market.

The phase of recovery is considered good for the economy and it reaches the stage of boom which is considered better. But the boom has its negative side also. Boom is usually followed by price rise.[80] As a boom is a strong upward fluctuation in an economy, the supply-side pattern of the economy starts lagging behind the pace of the accelerated aggregate demand.[81] But the dilemma of recovery puts every economy on the path to boom—this has been the experience in the developed world during the 1990s, especially in the US economy. The same scenario developed in India after the economy recovered from the recessionary period of 1996–97 by the year 2002–03 when the rate of inflation peaked to almost 8 per cent for a few months. Majority of the experts felt that Indian economy at that time was passing through a phase of boom and we have seen how the government has been facing difficulty in containing inflation around the 5 per cent mark. Even the government accepted that the economy was over-heating by mid-2007. *The symptoms of overheating are as follows:*

(i) There is a downturn in the aggregate demand on overall fall in the demand;

(ii) as demand falls, the level of production (output) in the economy also falls;

(iii) as producers cut down their production levels, new employment opportunities are not created—thus employment growth rate falls;

(iv) as demand keeps on falling, usually producers start cutting down their labour force to adjust their overhead expenditure and the cost of production (labour-cut is not 'forced' here but, 'voluntary')—

resulting in increase in the unemployment rate;

(v) if the government fails to rescue the economy from the phase of recession, the dangerous stage of *depression* remains the logical follow up;

(vi) the rate of inflation always remains at lower levels—discouraging new investments and lending.

RECESSION

This is somewhat similar to the phase of 'depression' — we may call it a *mild form* of depression — fatal for economies as this may lead to depression if not handled with care and in time. The financial crises which followed the US 'sub-prime crisis' in almost the whole Euro-American economies has basically brought in 'severe recessionary' trends there. Major traits of recession, to a great extent, are similar to that of 'depression' [except the point (iv) of the Depression, discussed earlier]—may be summed up as follows:

(i) there is a general fall in demand as economic activities takes a downturn;

(ii) inflation remains lower or/and shows further signs of falling down;

(iii) emloyment rate falls/unemployment rate grows;

(iv) Industries resort to 'price cuts' to sustain their business.

In the financial year 1996–97, the Indian economy was taken up by the cycle of recession—basically due to a general downturn in domestic as well as foreign demands, initiated by the South East Asian Currency Crisis of mid-1990s.[82] The whole plan of economic reforms in India was derailed and it was only by the end of 2001–02 that the economy was able to recover. What may a government do to

80.   Samuelson and Nordhaus, op.cit. pp. 680–84.

81.   Stiglitz and Walsh, op.cit. pp. 495–796.

82.   *Economic Survey, 1996–97*, MoF, GoI, N. Delhi.

rescue the economy from the phase of recession? The usual remedies are given below:

(i) Direct and indirect taxes should be cut down, so that the consumers have higher disposable incomes (income after paying direct tax, i.e., income tax) on the one hand and the goods should become cheaper on the other hand, thus there is hope that the demand might pick up.

(ii) The burden of direct taxes, especially the income tax, divdend tax, interest tax are slashed to enhance the disposable income (*i.e, income after direct tax payment*)—

(iii) Salaries and wages should be revised by the government to encourage general spending by the consumers (as the Government of India implemented the recommendations of the fifth pay commission without much deliberation in 1996–97).

(iv) Indirect taxes such as custom duty, excise duty (cenvat), sales tax, etc., should be cut down so that produced goods reach the market at cheaper prices.

(v) The government usually goes on to follow a cheap money supply policy by slashing down interest rates across the board and the lending procedure is also liberalised.

(vi) Tax breaks are announced for new investments in the productive areas, etc.

All the above-given measures were taken up by the United Front Government in 1996–97 to pull the economy out of the menace of the recession.[83] The forthcoming government took several other such measures by the end of 1998–99 onwards (the NDA Government). Ultimately, the measures taken up by the governments acompanied by a general recovery in the world economy, the Indian economy started recovering from the bout of recession. Many experts had already predicted

a possibility of depression with a zero per cent rate of inflation.[84] Although this did not happen.[85]

GROWTH RECESSION

An expression coined by economists to describe an economy that is growing at such a slow pace that more jobs are being lost than are being added. The lack of job creation makes it "feel" as if the economy is in a recession, even though the economy is still advancing. Many economists believe that between 2002 and 2003, the United States' economy was in a growth recession. In fact, at several points over the past 25 years the U.S. economy is said to have experienced a growth recession. That is, in spite of gains in real GDP, job growth was either non-existent or was being destroyed at a faster rate than new jobs were being added.

Experts have revived this term in the wake of the ongoing financial crises in the Euro-American economies since 2010. The situation is better described by the term *'double-dip recession'*.

DOUBLE-DIP RECESSION

The concept of 'recession' in the USA and Euro Zone is quite precise and technical—'*two consecutive quarters of falling* GDP'—is how it is defined in these economies. And the idea of the 'double-dip recession' is an extension of it.

83. *Economic Survey, 1996–97*, MoF, GoI, N. Delhi.

84. It should be noted here that as an impact of recession the rate of inflation (at WPI) had been falling down throughout the mid 1998–99 fiscal finally to the level of 0.5 per cent for a fortnight (*Economic Survey, 1998–99,* GoI, N. Delhi).

85. The literature of Economics and the empirical world experiences suggest that the phase of recession has all the symptoms of depression except one. Every thing being the same till producers are cutting the labour by force 'involuntarily (*i.e. forced labour cut*) it is the starting of depression—to be competitive in the market every producer starts 'forced labour cuts'—ultimately putting the economy into the grip of a full grown depression.

A double-dip recession refers to a recession followed by a short-lived recovery, followed by another recession—the GDP growth sliding back to negative after a quarter or two of positive growth. The causes for such a recession vary but often include a slowdown in the demand for goods and services because of layoffs and spending cutbacks done in the previous downturn. A double-dip (which may be even 'triple-dip') is a worst-case scenario—fear/speculation of it moves the economy into a deeper and longer recession and recovery becomes too difficult. As the world saw in the case of the Euro Zone crisis—there was a fear of such a recession by first quarter of 2013.

(For discussion on '**Retrocession**' see *Chapter 22*).

ABENOMICS

This new term has been in news for some time now. The term originates from the name of the Japanese Prime Minister **Shinzo Abe** and indicates the 'set of economic measures' he took to rejuvenate the sluggish Japanese economy from the spells of recession-like situation—after his December 2012 re-election to the post he last held in 2007. This is also known as the '*Three Arrows of Abenomics*'—the three economic measures under it are:

(i) **Fiscal Stimulus:** The government has initiated a massive fiscal stimulus to encourage public and private investments in the desired areas of the economy—investment in public works/infrastructure (which are by now 50 years old and need heavy investments), fiscal, concessions to private sector companies which invest in research & development, create jobs, increase salary, etc.

(ii) **Quantitative Easing:** The Bank of Japan (its Central bank) has been maintaining the official interest rate (like India's Repo Rate) near sub-zero to encourage lending by the banks. The aim is to double the amount of money in circulation by 2014 and reach the annual inflation target of 2 per cent. This makes the Japanese currency (Yen) to depreciate, too. Thus, this measure is intended to boost both domestic and external demands to propel the growth prospects of the economy. This measure, while at one hand increase the government expenditures, at the other it cuts the government's tax revenue, too – leading to higher fiscal deficit. This measure revolves around the current strength of the economy to 'absorb' higher levels of inflation (which plays a major role in the growth process).

(iii) **Structural Reforms:** Under this measure the government has promised a variety of deregulations in the economy, mainly aimed at increasing 'competitiveness' of the economy and attaining a sustained growth path. This arrow still remains least concrete. By now, the government has set up a *Group of Experts* (mainly formed of CEOs of large, medium and small companies) that is supposed to propose suitable measures to the government in the next three years regarding required set of 'structural' reforms needed by the economy. This measure also includes Japanese plan to 'join' TPP (Trans Pacific Partnership) and to go for a new FTA (Free Trade Agreement) between the countries in the Asis-Pacific region aimed at increasing its export potential.

The *Three Arrows of Abenomics* are a suite of economic measures which any economy may try in situations of any of the bad stages in the 'Economic Cycle'. Such economic measures were suggested by J. M. Keynes for the first time (in wake of the Great Depression of 1929). Today, its most famous exponent is the Nobel Economist Paul Krugman. Meanwhile, experts have mixed opinions on the success possibilities of the Abenomics.

CONCLUSION

Business cycles are basically fluctuations in the production levels of economies above and below the trend of the equilibirium levels.[86] But why do economies fluctuate? There are many factors which are said to be responsible for it, as per the experts:

(i) Economic instability and uncertainty (due to logical or illogical expectations)

may discourage investments thereby reducing growth in the long-term.

(ii) A lack of the creative destruction (i.e. innovation) may put the economy in a slump or slowdown in its overall production.

(iii) Anti-inflationary government policies (especially when general elections are nearing) may direct the attraction of investors in the economy.

(iv) Unforseen disasters may cause economies to fluctuate.

---

86.   Cox, Simon, op. cit., p. 58.

8

AGRICULTURE AND FOOD MANAGEMENT

Between 2000 and 2010, the contribution of cereals and pulses in the overall per capita food expenditure reduced from 40 per cent to 28 per cent, while that of animal-based products and fruits and vegetables rose from 36 per cent to 42 per cent—this change in consumption pattern has improved productivity of Indian farmers as well and studies show agricultural output per worker increased two times between 2000 and 2010. Barring this small tract, however, India's agriculture presents a dismal scenario with stagnating yield and low farmers income. *

* See **Third Food and Agriculture Integrated Development Action Report** titled 'India as an Agriculture and High-value Food Powerhouse: A New Vision for 2030', prepared jointly by CII and McKinsey & Company, N. Delhi, Released on 12th April 2013.

INTRODUCTION

Agriculture remains the most important sector of the Indian economy, whether it be the pre-independence or the post-independence periods. This fact is emphatically proved by the large number of people who depend on it for their livelihood. Before starting any discussion on Indian agriculture, we must look into its *special features*:

(i) From the monetary point of view the share of the agriculture sector in the economy remains at *17.5 per cent of the GDP.*[1] In the fiscal 1950–51 agriculture accounted for 55.4 per cent of the GDP.

(ii) The share of agriculture has been falling in the country's gross income, while industrial and services sectors' shares have been on a rise constantly. But from the livelihood point of view still *49 per cent* of the people of India depend on the agriculture[2] sector. This makes it a more important sector than the industry and the services (for Nepal and Tanzania the dependency for livelihood on agriculture is still higher at 93 per cent and 81 per cent, respectively). It means that 49 per cent of the population lives with only 17.5 per cent of the total income of the Indian economy—this fact clearly substantiates the reason why the people who depend on agriculture are poor. In the developed economies such as the USA, France, Norway, the UK and Japan, agriculture contributes only 2 per cent of their GDP with only 2 per cent of the people dependent on this sector for their livelihood.

(iii) Agriculture is not only the biggest sector of the economy, but also the biggest private sector too. It is the only profession which still carries no burden of individual income tax.

(iv) This is the biggest *unorganised sector* of the economy accounting for more than 90 per cent share in the total unorganised labour-force (93.4 per cent of the total labour force of the economy, i.e., 39.8 crores is employed in the unorganised sector).[3]

(v) India has emerged as a significant agri-exporter in few crops, namely—cotton, rice, meat, oil meals, spice, guar gum meal and sugar. As per[4] the *WTO's Trade Statistics*, the share of India's agricultural exports and imports in the world trade in **2015** were 2.40 per cent and 1.40 per cent, respectively. Agricultural exports as a percentage of agricultural GDP increased from 7.95 per cent in 2009–10 to 12.3 per cent in 2015–16. During the same period, agricultural imports as a percentage of agricultural GDP also increased from 4.90 per cent to 5.9 per cent.

(vi) According to the export figures, agriculture is deeply related to industrial growth and the national income in India—1 per cent increase in the agricultural growth leads to 0.5 per cent increase in industrial output (growth) and 0.7 per cent increase in the national income of India.[5]

(vii) The industrial sector was selected as the *'prime moving force'* of the economy in

---

1. *Ministry of Agriculture*, GoI, N. Delhi, February 2017.
2. *Ministry of Finance*, GoI, N. Delhi, February 2017.
3. *Labour Bureau*, Ministry of Labour and Employment, Government of India, N. Delhi, February 2017.
4. *Trade Statistics*, WTO, Geneva, Switzerland, February 2017.
5. This corelation has been pointed out by many great economists in India since 1960s, for example, by *Raj Krishna (1976)*, *S. Chakravarty (1974–79)* and *C. Rangarajan (1982)* to quote some of the most important names.

the late 1940s. But due to market failure the sector failed to lead the economy after independence. Without increasing the income of the people who depend on agriculture for their livelihood, the market was not going to support the industries. As a result, the Government of India announced agriculture as the prime moving force of the economy only in 2002.[6]

(viii) With 1 per cent increase in the share of agricultue in India's total exports, the money which flows into agriculture is calculated to be Rs. 8,500 crores.[7]

(ix) In 2016-17 foodgrains production is estimated to be a record 270.1 million tonnes of which is around 7 per cent higher than the total production of 2015-16 (252.23 MT)[8].

(x) **Productivity** of major crops are lower in case of India in comparison to the world's best practice. Though it has been improving with a slow pace, the productivity of rice, wheat and pulses improved from 2,202 kg, 2,802 kg and 625 kg per hectare of 2007–08 to 2,390 kg, 2,872 kg (falling from 3,026 kg of 2011-13) and 744 kg per hectare in 2014-15.[9]

(xi) A total of 66.1 per cent of the cropped area in the economy still depends on the uncertainties of **monsoon** for their irrigational requirements.[10]

KHARIF & RABI

There are certain special terms used to understand the cropping seasons of India. The agricultural crop year in India is from *July to June.* The Indian cropping season is classified into two main seasons- (i) kharif and (ii) rabi based on the monsoon. The kharif cropping season is from *July to October* during the South-West/Summer Monsoon and the rabi cropping season is from *October to March* (North-East/Returning/Winter Monsoon). The crops grown between March and June are summer crops, known as *jayads.*

Pakistan and Bangladesh are two other countries that are using the term 'kharif' and 'rabi' to describe their cropping patterns. The terms 'kharif and 'rabi' originate from Arabic language where kharif means *autumn* and rabi means *spring.*

The kharif crops include rice, maize, sorghum, pearl millet/bajra, finger millet/ragi (cereals), arhar (pulses), soyabean, groundnut (oilseeds), cotton, etc. The rabi crops include wheat, barley, oats (cereals), chickpea/gram (pulses), linseed, mustard (oilseeds) etc.

FOOD PHILOSOPHY OF INDIA

Indian food philosophy[11] is generally seen divided into three phases with their own objectives and challenges:

The First Phase

This phase continued for the first three decades after Independence. The main aim and the struggle

6. Planning Commission, *Approach Paper to the Tenth Five Year Plan* (New Delhi: Government of India, 2002).

7. This was the general opinion of the experts throughout the 1990s, but the official document which accepted this contention was the *Foreign Trade Policy 2002-07,* of the Ministry of Commerce. This View continued with the govenment in all its forthcoming trade policies till about four decades.

8. *Ministry of Agriculture*, GoI, N. Delhi, February 2017.

9. *Ministry of Agriculture*, GoI, N. Delhi and *Economic Survey 2016-17*, Vol. 1, Ministry of Finance, GoI, N. Delhi.

10. Ministry of Finance, *Economic Survey 2015-16,* Vol. 2, p. 103.

11. *Indian Council of Agricultural Research (ICAR),* N. Delhi, 1998.

of this phase was producing as much foodgrains as required by the Indian population, i.e., achieving *physical access* to food.

The idea of the Green Revolution at the end of this phase at least gave India the confidence of realising the objective. At the end of the 1980s, India was a self-sufficient country with regard to food.

The Second Phase

Meanwhile India was celebrating its success of the first phase, a new challenge confronted the country—achieving *economic access* to food. The situation went on worsening and by early 2000 there was a paradoxical situation in the country when it was having more than three times buffer stocks of foodgrains in the central pool, but in several states people were dying due to lack of food—a complete mockery of the logic behind maintaining buffer stock, success of green revolution and the concept of India being a welfare state.[12] The Supreme Court intervened after a PIL was filed by the People's Union for Civil Liberties (PUCL) and a national level Food for Work Programme came up (to be merged with the National Rural Employment Guarantee Scheme). The courts took the governments on task if foodgrains rot either in godowns or destroyed in oceans to manage market price for the foodgrains, or if the Centre had to go for exporting wheat at very low price. In this process India emerged as the *seventh largest* exporter of wheat (2002). Basically, we were exporting the share of wheat which was not consumed by many Indians due to lack of economic reach to food.

As the inputs of the Green Revolution were costlier, its output naturally were to be costlier. To fight the situation there should have been a time-bound and target-oriented macro-economic policy support, which could deliver comparative increase in the purchasing capacity of the masses to make food affordable for them. India badly failed in it. The crisis was managed by throwing higher and higher subsidies ultimately affecting government expenditure on the infrastructural shortcomings in the agriculture sector. Even after providing higher food subsidies, some people failed to purchase food and they were left with no option but to die of hunger.

India is still in this phase and trying to solve the crisis through twin approach, firstly, by creating maximum number of gainful employment, and secondly, by cutting cost of foodgrains (via the second green revolution based on biotechnology).

It must be kept in mind that the food self-sufficiency happiness was a temporary thing for India. By the mid 1990s, India realised that its foodgrain production was lagging behind its population increase. It means India is still fighting to achieve physical reach to the required level of food.

The Third Phase

By the end of the 1980s, world experts started questioning the very way world was carrying on with different modes of production. Agricultural activity was one among them which had become hugely based on industries (chemical fertilizers, pesticides, tractors, etc.). All developed economies had declared their agriculture to be an industry.[13]

It was time to look back and introspect. By the early 1990s, several countries started going for ecologically friendly methods and techniques

---

12. Publication Division, **India 2000** (New Delhi: Government of India, 2001); Ministry of Finance, *Economic Survey 2000–01*, (New Delhi: Government of India, 2001).

13. *Brundtland Report* on Sustainable Development after the deliberations at the summit *"Our Common future"*, 1987.

of industrial, agricultural and services sectors development. The much-hyped Green Revolution was declared ecologically untenable and the world headed for organic farming, green farming, etc.

It meant that achieving physical and economic reach to food was not the only challenge India was facing, but such aims should not be realised at the cost of the precious ecology and biodiversity—a new challenge. India needed a new kind of green revolution which could deliver it the physical, economic as well as *ecological access* to food—the Second Green Revolution—an all-in-one approach towards the agriculture sector.

LAND REFORMS

The official stance and emphasis on land reforms in India have been changing over the time in wake of the emerging issues, which may be seen in the following two phases.

Phase-I

This phase commences just after Independence.

All economies were agrarian before they were industrialised, only their periods vary. Once democratic systems developed, the first thing the developed countries of today did was to complete the agrarian reforms in a time-bound way. As land remains the means of livelihood for the larger section of society in an agrarian economy, the successful completion of agrarian reforms benefitted the maximum number of people thereby improving their economic conditions. At the time of Independence, India was a typical agrarian economy and had inherited a very inequitable agrarian system. Land reforms will be a major plank of independent India and as part of the agrarian reforms it was made clear by the pledge of the Indian National Congress in 1935 itself. Land reforms in India had three objectives similar to the other economies which opted for it in the past:

(i) Removing *institutional discrepancies* of the agrarian structure inherited from the past which obstructed increasing agricultural production, such as, the size of agricultural holding, land ownership, land inheritance, tenancy reforms, abolition of intermediaries, introduction of modern institutional factors to agriculture, etc.

(ii) The other objective of the land reforms in India was related to the issue of *socio-economic inequality* in the country. The high inequality in land ownership not only had a its negative economic impact on the economy; but it was badly intertwined with the caste system in India and the allocation of social prestige and status by the society at large.[14] More than 80 per cent of the population from its livelihood inherited the agrarian system which had inequitable ownership of the asset, i.e., land to earn income. The government wanted to go for a restructuring of land ownership in the economy on logical grounds and with public welfare approach. This objective of land reforms got enough socio-political attention as it tried to dismantle the age-old agrarian structure in the country. It became such a hot issue that land reforms in India got a 'bad-name', synonymous to land-grabbing by the government and allotting them to the landless masses.

(iii) The third objective of land reforms in India was highly contemporary in nature, which did not get enough socio-political attention—it was the objective of *increasing agricultural production*

---

14. L.I. Rudolph and S.H. Rudolph, *In Pursuit of Lakshmi: The Political Economy of the Indian State* (Bombay: Orient Longman, 1987), pp. 45–50.

for solving the inter-related problems of poverty, malnutrition and food insecurity.

To realise the objectives of land reforms, the government took three main steps which had many internal sub-steps:

1. Abolition of Intermediaries

Under this step, the age-old exploitative land tenure systems of the Zamindari, Mahalwari and Ryotwari were fully abolished.

2. Tenancy Reforms

Under this broader step, three inter-related reforms protecting the land-tenants were effected:

(i) *Regulation of rent* so that a fixed and rational rate of rent could be paid by the share-croppers to the land owners;

(ii) *Security of tenure* so that a share-cropper could feel secure about his future income and his economic security; and

(iii) *Ownership rights to tenants* so that the landless masses (i.e., the tenants, the share-croppers) could get the final rights for the land they plough—*"land to the tillers"*.

3. Reorganisation of Agriculture

This step again has many inter-related and highly logical provisions in the direction of rational agrarian reforms:

(i) *Redistribution of land* among the landless poor masses after promulgating timely **ceiling laws**—the move failed badly with few exceptions, such as West Bengal, Kerala and partially in Andhra Pradesh.

(ii) *Consolidation of land* could only succeed in the regions of the Green Revolution (i.e., Haryana, Punjab and western Uttar Pradesh) and remained marred with many loopholes and corruption.

(iii) *Cooperative farming,* which has a high socio-economic moral base, was only used by the big farmers to save their lands from the draconian ceiling laws.

The whole attempt of land reforms in India is considered a big failure by majority of experts. Many consider the issue of land reforms in India as the most complex socio-economic problem of human history.[15] Data regarding the numerical achievements of land reforms have been highly discouraging.[16]

(i) Tenancy reforms provided tenants with rights, but only on 4 per cent of the total operated areas in the country (14.4 million hectares of operated area by 11 million tenants by 1992).

(ii) Redistribution of ownership rights of land took place, but only upto 2 per cent of the total operated area in the country (less than 2 million hectares among the 4.76 million people by 1992).

(iii) Taken together, the whole process of land reforms could benefit only 6 per cent of the operated area of the country with a negligible socio-economic positive impact.

It was the failure of land reforms which made the government easily attracted towards the new policy of the Green Revolution in the coming times—land reforms had failed to increase agricultural production, thus the government opted for the route of increasing, productivity to reach the same goal, i.e., initiation of new techniques of agriculture.

---

15. This was the view of the majority of experts around the world by the late 1960s.

16. P.S. Appu, *Land Reforms in India: A Survey of Policy, Legislation and Implementation,* (Mussouri: Land Reforms Unit, Lal Bahadur Shastri National Academy of Administration, 1995), pp. 232–33.

Reasons for Failure of Land Reforms

Out of the many reasons forwarded by the experts responsible for the failure of the land reforms in India, the following three could be considered the most important ones:

(i) Land in India is considered a symbol of social prestige, status and identity unlike the other economies which succeeded in their land reform programmes, where it is seen as just an economic asset for income-earning.

(ii) Lack of political will which was required to affect land reforms and make it a successful programme.

(iii) Rampant corruption in public life, political hypocrisy and leadership failure in the Indian democratic system.

Land Reforms & Green Revolution

Once the government launched the Green Revolution, the issue of land reforms almost got marginalised due to the following reasons:

(i) There is an inherent diabolic relationship between the Green Revolution and the land reforms as the former suits bigger and economic land holdings, while the latter intended to fragment the land among a large number of the masses.

(ii) The land reforms were socially opposed by the land-owning caste lobbies, while there was no such opposition to the Green Revolution.

(iii) The level of legislative attempts taken by the governments regarding the land reforms till date had almost no positive socio-economic impact on the country, while the Green Revolution was having all potential of proving higher yields of foodgrains.

(iv) The subsidised supplies of foodgrains under PL 480 were hampering India from carving out its independent diplomacy, as well as there has always remained a doubt about the regular supplies of wheat.

(v) International pressure as well as the suggestions from the World Bank besides the success stories of the Green Revolution from the countries where it had increased the yield of wheat.

Phase-II

The second phase of land reforms can be traced in the process of economic reforms. Economic reforms exposed the economy to the new and emerging realities, such as, land acquisition and leasing, food-related issues and the agricultural provisions of the World Trade Organization (WTO). We see a shift (Economic Survey 2012–13) in the thinking of the Government of India towards the issue of land reforms—a clear three step policy looks emerging:

(i) Mapping land carefully and assigning conclusive title,

(ii) Devising a fair but speedy process of land acquisition, and

(iii) Putting in place a transparent and effective land leasing policy.

Land is probably the single most valuable asset in the country today. Not only could greater liquidity for land allow more resources to be redeployed efficiently in agriculture, it could ease the way for land-utilising businesses to set up. Perhaps, as important, it could allow land to serve as collateral for credit.

The **National Land Records Modernisation Programme** (NLRMP), started in 2008, aims at updating and digitising land records by the end of the Twelfth Plan. Eventually, the intent is to move from *presumptive title* (where registration of a title does not imply the owner's title is legally valid) to *conclusive title* (where it does). Important points related to this process may be summarised as follows:

(i) Digitisation will help enormously in lowering the costs of land transactions, while conclusive title will eliminate legal uncertainty and the need to use the government as an intermediary for acquiring land so as to 'cleanse' title.

(ii) Given the importance of this programme, its rollout in various states needs to be accelerated—easier and quicker land transactions will especially help small and medium enterprises that do not have the legal support or the management capacity that large enterprises have.

(iii) Prohibitory *land leasing norms* raises the cost to rural-urban migration, as villagers are unable to lease their land, and often have to leave the land untilled or leave a family member behind to work on the land. Lifting these restrictions can help the landless (or more efficient landowners) get land from those who migrate, even while it will allow landowners with education and skills to move to industry or services.

(iv) Compulsory registration of leaseholds and of the owner's title would provide tenants and landowners protection. For such a leasing market to take off, owners should be confident that long-term tenancy would not lead to their losing ownership. With a vibrant leasing market, and clear title, there should be little reason for not strengthening ownership rights.

(v) For large projects with a public purpose, such as the National Industrial and Manufacturing Zones, which will facilitate the setting up of small and medium enterprises, large-scale land acquisition may be necessary.

(vi) Given that the people currently living on the identified land will suffer significant costs including the loss of property and

livelihoods, a balance has to be drawn between the need for economic growth and the costs imposed on the *displaced*.

Moving onwards, the Government of India passed the *Land Acquisition Bill, 2013*. The bill, besides proposing to amend the *Land Acquisition, Rehabilitation and Resettlement Act, 2011* proposed to put in place a transparent, effective and speedy laws reagrding the need of land reforms related to leasing and acquisition. By 2015, the new government at the Centre proposed a new land bill *(Right to Fair Compensation and Transparency in Land Acquisition, Rehabilitation and Resettlement Bill, 2015)*, which aimed at removing the inadequacies of the Land Act of 2013. The Bill is being opposed by the political parties belonging to the opposition (it is still to be passed by the Parliament, though the government has done around ten amendments to it). The country cannot afford to compromise the economic security of land owners (farmers) in the process of evolving a speedier process of land acquisition—the law dealing with it should be transparent, justified, effective and speedier, too.

Finer points of this *PHASE* can be summed up in the following way:[17]

(i) Leasing seems a better choice in face of farmer's opposition seen in recent times in different states toward attempts at land acquisition. Again, if the country needs to attract investment from the organised private sector (domestic or foreign) land leasing seems a better option than land acquisition.

(ii) Corporate farming has not taken place in the country in a big scale, especially in the areas of foodgrains production, which

17. The discussion is based on several volumes of the **Economic Survey** and **India** published by the Government of India between the period 2010 to 2017 and the **12th Plan**.

India needs to ensure food security and compete in the global grain market, in particular, and the agri-market in general. This has become even more important in the wake of the Right to Food given to a large segment of the population.

(iii) Giving primacy to 'leasing' will solve several problems:

(a) It will keep land ownership in the hands of the existing farmers;

(b) It will prevent mass landlessness and unemployment among the farmers;

(c) Farmers will get a permanent source of income (in the meantime, they might be imparted skills and provide better employment in industries); and

(d) It will make land easily available for use of public and private purposes.

Meanwhile, the Model Land Leasing Law proposed by the NITI Aayog in 2016 is giving encouraging results in the states.

(iv) In the wake of the process of globalisation, if the country intends to bring in benefits to agriculture sector it needs to enhance its agriculture production to surplus levels—and for this India needs to garner in the investment potential of the private sector. This cannot happen till the country is able to bring out effective land leasing and acquisition policies.

(v) The recent emphasis on the promotion of the 'manufacturing sector' and 'smart cities' are hugely dependent on smoother and speedier process of land acquisition. Without expanding the industrial sector to its optimum levels, the agriculture sector can emerge a remunerative profession—the country needs to migrate the extra labour force of the agriculture sector to industry, smoothly.

(vi) The issue of land acquisition is to establish a logical equation with 'environmental issue', in order to make the process of development sustainable (NITI Aayog gives a right call for it).

It should be noted that while the Government of India has changed its orientation towards the issue of land reforms, the states in India are still trying to accelerate and continue the process of land reforms of *PHASE I* (but due to enough resistance from the land-owning section in the country, the process does not seem happening, politically).

Agriculture Holdings

The average size of land holding in India is continuously decreasing due to rapid and high population growth. The continuous division and fragmentation of holdings has increased the number of holdings, obviously of smaller size. As per the latest (9th) Agriculture Census 2010–11:

(i) The total number of operational holdings in the country has increased from 129 million in 2005–06 to 138 million 2010–11 (an increase of 6.61 per cent).

(ii) There is a marginal increase in the operated area from 158.32 million hectare (ha) in 2005–06 to 159.18 million ha in 2010-11 (an increase of 0.54 per cent). The operated area has primarily increased because the State of Jharkhand participated for the *first time* in the Agriculture Census 2010–11 (since the state came into being in the year 2000).

(iii) The *average size* of operational holding has declined to 1.16 ha in 2010–11 as compared to 1.23 in 2005–06.

(iv) The percentage share of *female* operational holders has increased from 11.70 in 2005–06 to 12.79 in 2010–11, with the corresponding operated area of 9.33 and 10.36.

(v) The *small* and *marginal* holdings taken together (below 2.00 ha) constitute **84.97** per cent in 2010–11, as against 83.29 in 2005–06, with a share of 44.31 per cent in the operated area in the current Census, as against the corresponding figure of 41.14 per cent in 2005–06.

(vi) The *large* holdings (10.00 ha & above) were 0.73 per cent of the total number of holdings in 2010–11 with a share of 10.92 per cent in the total operated area, as against 0.85 per cent and 11.82 per cent respectively for 2005–06 Census.

(vii) Share of different *social groups* in operational holdings stands as: 12.40 per cent for **SCs**, 8.71 per cent for **STs**, 0.18 per cent for institutional and 78.72 per cent for others.

(viii) In a total of **137.76** million *operational holdings* in the country, the highest number belonged to Uttar Pradesh (22.93 million) followed by Bihar (16.19 million) and Maharashtra (13.70 million).

(ix) Out of a total of **159.18** million hectares of the *operated area* in the country, the highest contribution was made by Rajasthan (21.14 million ha) followed by Maharashtra (19.84 million ha) and Uttar Pradesh (17.09 million ha).

Agricultural holdings have been classified into *three* categories:

1. Economic Holding

It is that holding which ensures a minimum satisfactory standard of living in a family. In other words, economic holding is a minimum essential area for profitable agriculture.

2. Family Holding

Family holding is that holding which gives work to an average size family having one plough under the traditional farming system. In other words, family holding is a *'plough unit'* which is neither less nor more for an average size family to cultivate it properly.

3. Optimum Holding

Maximum size of the holding which must be possessed and owned by a family is called optimum holding.

GREEN REVOLUTION

It is the introduction of new techniques of agriculture, which became popular by the name of Green Revolution (GR) in early 1960s—at first for **wheat** and by the next decade for **rice**, too. It revolutionised the very traditional idea of food production by giving a boost by more than 250 per cent to the productivity level.[18] The Green Revolution was centred around the use of the High Yielding Variety (HYV) of seeds developed by the US agro-scientist Norman Borlaug doing research on a British Rockfellor Foundation Scholarship in Mexico by the early 1960s. The new wheat seeds which he developed *in vivo* claimed to increase its productivity by more than 200 per cent. By 1965, the seeds were successfully tested and were being used by farmers in food deficient countries such as Mexico, Taiwan.

Components of the Green Revolution

The Green Revolution was based on the timely and adequate supply of many inputs/components.

18. ***Consultative Group on International Agricultural Research*** (CGIAR), World Bank, Washington DC, 1971.

A brief review on the Green Revolution is given below:

1. The HYV Seeds

These seeds were popularly called the '*dwarf* variety of seeds. With the help of repeated mutations, Mr. Borlaug had been able to develop a seed which was raised in its nature of nutrients supplied to the different parts of the wheat plant—against the leaves, stem and in favour of the grain. This made the plant dwarf and the grain heavier—resulting in high yield.[19]

These seeds were non-photosynthetic, hence non-dependent on sun rays for targeted yields.

2. The Chemical Fertilizers

The seeds were to increase productivity provided they got sufficient level of nutrients from the land. The level of nutrients they required could not be supplied with the traditional compostes because they have low concentration of nutrients content and required bigger area while sowing—it meant it will be shared by more than one seed. That is why a high concentration fertilisers, were required, which could be given to the trageted seed only—the only option was the chemical fertilisers—urea (N), phosphate (P) and potash (K).[20]

3. The Irrigation

For controlled growth of crops and adequate dilution of fertilizers, a controlled means of water supply was required. It made two important compulsions—firstly, the area of such crops should be at least free of flooding and secondly, artificial water supply should be developed.[21]

4. Chemical Pesticides and Germicides

As the new seeds were new and non-acclimatised to local pests, germs and diseases than the established indigenous varieties, use of pesticides and germicides became compulsory for result-oriented and secured yields.

5. Chemical Herbicides and Weedicides

To prevent costlier inputs of fertilisers not being consumed by the herbs and the weeds in the farmlands, herbicides and weedicides were used while sowing the HYV seeds.

6. Credit, Storage, Marketing/Distribution

For farmers to be capable of using the new and the costlier inputs of the Green Revolution, availability of easy and cheaper credit was a must. As the farmlands suitable for this new kind of farming was region-specific (as it was only Haryana, Punjab and western Uttar Pradesh in India) storage of the harvested crops was to be done in the region itself till they were distributed throughout the country. Again, the countries which went for the Green Revolution were food-deficient and needed the new yield to be distributed throughout the country and a proper chain of marketing, distribution and transport connectivity was necessary. All these peripheral infrastructure were developed by the countries going for the Green Revolution with softer loans coming from the World Bank—India being the biggest beneficiary.[22]

---

19. *International Maize and Wheat Improvement Centre* (CIMMYT), Mexico, 1971.

20. This made it compulsory to use highly concentrate chemical fertilizers, pushing the traditional organic fertilizers (i.e., composte) out of fashion.

21. This was the reason why the GR was implemented firstly in the rainfall deficient regions of India, i.e., Haryana, Punjab and western Uttar Pradesh.

22. Publication Division, India 2002 (New Delhi; Government of India, 2013).

Impact of the Green Revolution

The Green Revolution had its positive as well as negative socio-economic and ecological impacts on the countries around the world, we will specially study India here.

1. Socio-economic Impact

Food production increased in such a way (wheat in 1960s and rice, by 1970s) that many countries became self-sufficient (self sufficiency of food must not be confused with the idea of food security) and some even emerged as food exporting countries.

But the discrepancy in farmers' income, it brought with itself increased the inter-personal as well as inter-regional disparities/inequalities in India.[23] Rise in the incidence of malaria due to water-logging, a swing in the balanced cropping patterns in favour of wheat and rice putting pulses, oilseeds, maize, barley on the margins, etc., were negative impacts.

2. Ecological Impact

The most devastating negative impact of the Green Revolution was ecological. When the issues related with it were raised by the media, scholars, experts and environmentalists, neither the governments nor the masses (what to say of the farmers of the GR region— they were not educated enough to understand the side effects of the inputs of the GR) were convinced. But a time came when the government and other government agencies started doing studies and surveys focused around the ecological and environmental issues. The major ones among them may be glanced in their chronological order:

(i) **Critical Ecological Crisis:** On the basis of on-field studies[24] it was found that critical ecological crises in the GR region are showing up—

(a) *Soil fertility being degraded:* Due to the repetitive kind of cropping pattern being followed by the farmers as well as the excessive exploitation of the land; lack of a suitable crop combination and the crop intensity, etc.

(b) *Water table falling down:* As the new HYV seeds required comparatively very high amount of water for irrigation—5 tonnes of water needed to produce 1 kg of rice.

(c) *Environmental degradation:* Due to excessive and uncontrolled use of chemical fertilizers, pesticides and herbicides have degraded the environment by increasing pollution levels in land, water and air. In India it is more due to *deforestation* and extension of cultivation in ecologically fragile areas. At the same time, there is an excessive pressure of animals on forests—mainly by goats and sheeps.

(ii) **Toxic Level in Food Chain:** Toxic level in the food chain of India has increased to such a high level that nothing produced in India is fit for human consumption. Basically, unbridled use of chemical pesticides and weedicides and their industrial production combined together had polluted the land, water and air to such an alarmingly high level that the

---

23. See Various volumes of the *Economic Surveys,* specially 1985–86 to 1994–86 to 1994–95, published by the Government of India.

24. Based on various empirical studies in the 1990s conducted separately by *Vandana Shiva, C.H. Hanumantha Rao, ICAR, Planning Commission,* etc.

whole food chain had been a prey of high toxicity.

Conclusion

The above studies and the reports were eye-openers in the area of ecologically non-sustainable kind of agriculture as well as a big question mark on it. This was the time when agro-scientists suggested for a really 'green' (eco-friendly) revolution, which is today known among the experts with many more names—the *evergreen revolution,* the *second;* green revolution and *green farming.*

CROPPING PATTERNS

The set and combination of crops which farmers opt for in a particular region, in their farm practices, is cropping pattern of the region. Multiplicity of cropping systems has been one of main features of Indian agriculture and it is attributed to rainfed agriculture and prevailing socio-economic situations of the farming community.

The cropping pattern in India has undergone significant changes over time. As the cultivated area remains more or less constant, the increased demand for food, because of increase in population and urbanisation, puts agricultural land under stress, resulting in *crop intensification* and *crop substitution* of food crops with commercial crops.

Cropping systems of a region are decided, by and large, by a number of soil and climatic parameters, which determine the overall agro-ecological setting for nourishment and appropriateness of a crop or set of crops for cultivation. Nevertheless, at farmers' level, potential productivity and monetary benefits act as guiding principles, while opting for a particular crop or a cropping system. These decisions with respect to choice of crops and cropping systems are further narrowed down under influence of several other forces related to infrastructure facilities, socio-economic and technological factors, all operating interactively at the micro-level. These factors are:

(i) Goegraphical factors: Soil, landforms, precipitation, moisture, altitude, etc.

(ii) Socio-cultural factors: Food habits, festivals, tradition, etc.

(iii) Infrastructure factors: Irrigation, transport, storage, trade and marketing, post-harvest handling and processing, etc.

(iv) Economic factors: Financial resource base, land ownership, size and type of land holding, household needs of food, fodder, fuel, fibre and finance, labour availability, etc.

(v) Technological factors: Improved varieties of seeds and plants, mechanisation, plant protection, access to information, etc.

Prevalent Cropping Systems

Multiplicity of cropping systems has been one of the main features of Indian agriculture. This may be attributed to the following two major factors:

(i) Rainfed agriculture still accounts for over 92.8 million hectare or 65 per cent of the cropped area. A large diversity of cropping systems exists under rainfed and dryland areas with an over-riding practice of intercropping, due to greater risks involved in cultivating larger area under a particular crop.

(ii) Due to prevailing socio-economic situations, such as, dependency of large population on agriculture, small land-holding size, very high population pressure on land resource, etc.

Improving household food security has been an issue of supreme importance to many million farmers of India, with the following farm holdings—

(a) 56.15 million marginal (<1.0 ha),

(b) 17.92 million small (1.0–2.0 ha), and

(c) 13.25 million semi-medium (2.0–4.0 ha).

They together are 90 per cent of the 97.15 million operational holdings. An important consequence of this has been that crop production in India remained to be considered, by and large, a *subsistence* rather than *commercial* activity. One of the typical characteristics of subsistence farming is that most of the farmers resort to grow a number of crops on their farm holdings, primarily to fulfil their household needs and follow the practice of rotating a particular crop combination over a period of 3–4 year, interchangeably on different farm fields.

Under the influence of all the above factors, te cropping systems remain dynamic in time and space, making it difficult to precisely determine their spread using conventional methods, over a large territory. However, it has been estimated that more than **250** double cropping systems are followed throughout the country. Based on the rationale of spread of crops in each district in the country, *30 important cropping systems* have been identified— rice-wheat, rice-rice, rice-gram, rice-mustard, rice-groundnut, rice-sorghum, pearlmillet-gram, pearl millet-mustard, pearl millet-sorghum, cotton-wheat, cotton-gram, cotton-sorghum, cotton-safflower, cotton-groundnut, maize-wheat, maize-gram, sugarcane-wheat, soybean-wheat, sorghum-sorghum, groundnut-wheat, sorghum-groundnut, groundnut-rice, sorghum-wheat, sorghum-gram, pigeonpea-sorghum, groundnut, sorghum-rice, groundnut-sorghum and soybean-gram.

Changes in the Cropping Patterns

Due to various reasons, the cropping pattern of Indian farmers have undergone changes over the time—we can see them in following three phases.

Pre-Green Revolution Period: In this phase we see Indian farmers going in for a cropping system (generally), which was primarily decided by the socio-cultural and economic factors—more or less they were closer to being *sustainable* as they had developed through the long process of trial and error of their forefathers. A combination of crops we see being grown by farmers across the country with judicious mixture of crops till the Green Revolution. This was a period of subsistence farming with high dependency of population for livelihood on it. The nature of the cropping pattern was too stubborn to change by incentives.

Green Revolution Period: Under the spell of the New Agricultural Strategy (NAS), more popularly as the Green Revolution, since 1965 onwards, we see a *major shift* in the cropping pattern of Indian farmers. The main forces of change were economic, infrastructural and technological. Initiation of high yeilding varieties of seeds, financial supports of chemical and other inputs together with the provisions of minimum support price (MSP) gave major shift to the farmers' choices of crops. In the GR regions we see a highly repetitive kind of cropping pattern with the 'wheat-rice' having predominance. In coming times, the Government of India started announcing MSPs for many other crops, which had its own impact on the farmers' choices of crops in their cropping systems.

This period was primarily guided by the singular objective of attaining self-sufficiency in food, which may lead the nation to attain food security. By the late 1980s, India was able to manage self-sufficiecy in foodgrains. We see the emergence of big farmers in the GR regions for whom at least farming did not remain subsistence —*commercial dimension* enters the Indian farm practices, for the first time.

This is the period when the traditional cropping pattern of India got exposed to new inputs of farming and geographical dimensions of crop selection were undermined. Soon (by

1996–97), the government came to know that the GR farm practices were ecologically damaging and unsustainable. The Government of India officially adopts the idea of *sustainable* agriculture by 1997.

Reform Period: Another wave of change in the cropping pattern comes with the process of economic reforms commencing in 1991, which brings in new opprotunities together with the challenges in the area of farm sector:

- The issue of food security continued to give pressure on policymakers as foodgrains production was not able to keep pace with the population growth rate. The situation becomes even more serious with Food Rights (NFSA) given to a large population of the country recently.

- Globalisation brought in new opportunities of farm exports together with the challenge of cheap production (need of farm mechanisation and commercial farming so that Indian farm products can compete in the global market) in wake of the agricultural provisions of the World Trade Organisation. It made India think of mobilising huge investments in the sector. India accepts agriculture as an industry (2000) giving green signal to *corporate* and *contract* farmings.

- Ecologically sustainable farming becomes the need of the hour due to ensuing danger of climate change and environment related constraints.

- The Government of India proposes for the Second Green Revolution in 2002 with inclusion of the genetically modified foods (GMFs).

In wake of the above-cited factors, experts and the governments expect a major change coming in the cropping patterns of the country. Now, the issue is, how to face up the emerging challenges together with making farm practices and cropping patterns sustainable. Experts suggested the following steps

(by late 1990s), which were discussed and almost accepted by the Planning Commission together with the Ministry of Agriculture:

(i) Putting in place the right kind of agricultural policy with the provisions of prize and punishment, inclining farmers to go for the right kind of cropping pattern.

(ii) Evolving the right trade policy, which can protect Indian farm products from the negative affects of global competition and enable Indian agriculture to expand exports.

(iii) Bringing in proper labour laws, and land leasing and acquisition policies to encourage the entry of Indian and foreign private sector in agriculture.

(iv) Keep pressurising the WTO so that a neutral and judicious regime of agricultural provisions are evolved by it accepting the realities of India's subsistence farming and issues related with the high agriculture subsidies, which developed countries forward to their farm sector.

(v) Evolving the right environmental policy framework for the initiation of GMFs in the farm sector and promotion to the non-GMF related reasearch and development in the country, through corporate participation.

(vi) Factoring in the issue of environment and climate change in the domain of agricultural policy framework.

(vii) Emphasising the need of farmers' awareness and education for the changing times. For this the PRIs involvement will be crucial.

(viii) Attending to issues like plant protection, checking farm wastage, pest management, commercial production and commercial availability of green inputs.

(ix) Evolving the right kind of credit and insurance policies for the farm sector at the macro and micro levels.

(x) Immediate inclusion of other factor in the farm sector like, a national market for agricultural products, upstream and downstream requirements, proper supply chain management, logistics, agro-processing industries, storage, etc.

ANIMAL REARING

The economics of animal rearing plays a very vital role in the country. The agriculture sector in India is predominantly a mixed crop-livestock (animals, birds and fishes) farming system. Animal rearing has always remained an integral part of it. Animal rearing (which includes rearing of cows, camels, buffaloes, goats, pigs, ships, etc.), besides directly contributing to the national income and socio-economic development, plays the following **vital functions** in the country:

(i) Supplements family income and generates gainful employment in the rural sector;

(ii) Particularly helps the landless labourers, small and marginal farmers and women (economic empowerment of women);

(iii) Provides cheap nutrititional food;

(iv) Functions as the best insurance against drought, famine and other natural calamities;

(v) It is more *inclusive* in nature; and

(vi) Promotes the cause of *sustainable* agriculture.

The **significance** of this sector can be seen by the following facts:

(i) The livestock sector as a whole achieved an average growth rate of 4.8 per cent during the *11th Plan* which is *higher* than the farm sector growth (3.5 per cent) and the foodgrains growth (around 1 per cent).

(ii) The livestock population of India is around 530 million. It accounts for about 26 per cent of the total agricultural, fishing and forestry sectors.

(iii) Meat production has a growth rate of 5.7 per cent with a total production of 4.8 million tonne (still this sector has huge demand-supply gap and there is enormous scope of expansion.

Dairy Sector: India ranks first in the world in milk production with a production of around 146.3 million tonne and the per capita availability (pca) of 322 grams (world pca is 294 grams) by the end of 2014–15.

Some of the important GoI programmes/schemes for meeting the growing demand of milk:

- Intensive Dairy Development Programme.
- Strengthening Infrastructure for Quality and Clean Milk Production, Assistance to Cooperatives.
- Dairy Entrepreneurship Development Scheme.
- National Project for Cattle and Buffalo Breeding.

A new scheme, the *National Dairy Plan*, Phase I, has been launched in March 2012 with the following objectives:

(i) Improving productivity of milch animals,

(ii) Strengthening and expanding village-level infrastructure for milk procurement, and

(iii) Providing producers greater access to the market in the dairy sector.

Pig Rearing Scheme: This scheme is aimed to assist farmers/landless labourers/co-operatives and the tribals particularly in the North-Eastern states by raering pigs under stall fed condition for quality pork production and organised pork marketing in rural areas and semi-urban areas. The main objectives of the shceme are:

(i) Encourage commercial rearing by adopting scientific methods and infrastructure creation;

(ii) Production and supply of improved germ plasm;

(iii) Organise stakeholders to popularise scientific practices;

(iv) Create supply chain for the meat industry;

(v) Encourage value addition for better income.

Adequate availability of *feed and fodder* for livestock is vital for increasing milk production and sustaining the ongoing genetic improvement programme. Green fodder shortage in the country is estimated at about 34 per cent. The central government has put in place a modified Centrally Sponsored Fodder and Feed Development Scheme since 2010 to supplement the efforts of the states to improve fodder production. Besides, the Accelerated Fodder Development Programme was launched as a component of the Rashtriya Krishi Vikas Yojana in 2011–12 to promote production of fodder.

Animal Health: With the improvement in the quality of livestock through launching of extensive cross-breeding programmes, the susceptibility to various diseases, including exotic diseases has increased. In order to reduce morbidity and mortality, efforts are being made by the state/UT governments to provide better health care through polyclinics/veterinary hospitals/dispensaries/ first-aid centres including mobile veterinary dispensaries. For the prevention of various diseases, 27 veterinary vaccine production units are working with dominance of the public sector (20 are in the public sector and rest in the private sector). The 'Livestock Health & Disease Control' is being run as a centrally sponsored scheme to assist the attempts of the states and UTs in the area.

Suggestions for further development of the sector.

(i) Developing progeny tested semen for artificial insemination.

(ii) Expansion of fodder availability through innovative means.

(iii) Facilities of animal health centres need to be upgraded and the disease control systems made more effective on the veterinary side.

(iv) In the drylands and mountain ecosystems, livestock contribute anywhere between 50 to 75 per cent of the total household income of the rural population. Support to these massive and highly diverse livestock populations in these regions is lacking.

(v) Raising the capability of the rural poor to conserve and manage their livestock resources, and enables them to derive sustainable incomes from these resources.

(vi) Decentralisation and convergence of policy support for these options is crucial for diversification of livelihoods in small-holder farming.

FOOD MANAGEMENT

Managing enough food in the domestic market has been the prime focus of the governement since Independence. Meeting the physical target of food together with the challenge of enabling Indians to procure food for their consumption was also there. Over the year, we see the government devising various ways and means to handle the twin challenges. Once, the country joined the WTO, a new need was felt for producing surplus and competing with the world, so that the benefits of globalisation could also be reaped by the agriculture sector. This section discusses the challenges to management of food in the country.

Minimum Support Price

Minimum Support Price (MSP) is a form of market intervention by the Government of India to insure agricultural producers against any sharp fall in farm prices —a guarantee price to save farmers from distress sale. The MSPs are announced at the beginning of the sowing season for certain crops on the basis of the recommendations of the Commission for Agricultural Costs and Prices (CACP, 1985). The major objectives are to support the farmers from distress sales and to procure food grains for public distribution. In case the market price for the commodity falls below the announced minimum price due to bumper production and glut in the market, government agencies purchase the entire quantity offered by the farmers at the announced minimum price.

Commencing with 'wheat' for the 1966–67, currently the MSPs are announced for **24** commodities including seven cereals (paddy, wheat, barley, jowar, bajra, maize and ragi); five pulses (gram, arhar/tur, moong, urad and lentil); eight oilseeds (groundnut, rapeseed/mustard, toria, soyabean, sunflower seed, sesamum, safflower seed and nigerseed); copra, raw cotton, raw jute and virginia flu cured (VFC) tobacco. The MSPs are fixed at *incentive level*, to fulfil the following purposes:

(i)   to induce more investment by farmers in the farm sector,

(ii) to motivate farmers to adopt improved crop production technologies, and

(iii) to enhance production and thereby farmers, income.

In the absence of such a guaranteed price, there is a concern that farmers may shift to other crops causing shortage in these commodities. The agricultural price policy in India emerged in the backdrop of *food scarcity* and *price fluctuations* provoked by *drought, floods* and *international prices* for exports and imports.[25]

Market Intervention Scheme

The Market Intervention Scheme (MIS) is similar to MSP, which is implemented on the request of state governments for procurement of perishable and horticultural commodities in the event of fall in market prices. The scheme is implemented when there is at least 10 per cent increase in production or 10 per cent decrease in the ruling rates over the previous normal year. Proposal of MIS is approved on the specific request of the state/UT governments, if the states/UTs are ready to bear 50 per cent loss (25 per cent in case of North-Eastern states) incurred on its implementation.

Procurement Prices

In 1966–67, the Government of India announced a 'procurement price' for wheat, a bit higher than its MSP (the purpose being security of food procurement for requirement of the PDS). The MSP was announced before sowing, while the procurement price was announced before harvesting—the purpose was to encourage farmers to sell a bit more and get encouraged to produce more. But this increased price hardly served the purpose as a suitable incentive to farmers. It would have been better had it been announced before sowing and not after harvesting. That is why since the fiscal 1968–69 the government announced only the MSP, which is also considered the effective procurement price.[26]

---

25. **New Agricultural Strategy, 1965**; Reports of the **CACP** and **Ministry of Agriculture**, GoI, N. Delhi.

26. **New Agricultural Strategy, 1965**; the **CACP, 1967** and **Ministry of Agriculture**, GoI, N. Delhi.

Issue Price

The price at which the government allows offtake of foodgrains from the FCI (the price at which the FCI sells its foodgrains). The FCI has been fetching huge losses in the form of food subsidies.[27] The foodgrains procured are transported to the godowns of the FCI located across the country (counted in the buffer stock). From here they head to the sale counters—to the TPDS or Open Market Sale. The transportaion, godowning, the cost of maintaining the FCI, carriage losses, etc., make the foodgrains costlier (the additional expenses other than the MSP is known as the 'economic cost of foodgrains'). To make the foodgrains affordable to the consumers, the issue prices for foodgrains are set lower than the total cost of procurement and distribution—the gap converts into the 'food subsidy'.

BUFFER STOCK

India has a policy of maintaing a minimum reserve of foodgrains (only for wheat and rice) so that food is available throughout the country at affordable prices round the year. The main supply from here goes to the TPDS (the PDS was restructured as the Targeted PDS in 1997) and at times goes for Open Market Sale to check the rising prices, if needed.

The Buffer Stocking norms (of 2005) was revised[28] by the government (by mid-2014) in the backdrop of increased requirement of foodgrains to run the TPDS in the last few years and with the coming into force of the National Food Security Act (NFSA). The new norms are as given in the table below:

Revised Buffer Stock

As on	Existing since April, 2005 (in million tonnes)	Revised
1st April	21.2	21.04
1st July	31.9	41.12
1st Oct	21.2	30.77
1st Jan	25.0	21.41

As income levels of the BPL segment grows, in future, the buffer norms for the foodgrains are supposed to be revised downward. But the logic of maintaining such stocks will remain for the purpose of market intervention by the government.

Decentralised Procurement Scheme

The decentralised procurement (DCP) scheme was operationalised by the government in 1997 (together with the Centre and some of the states also procure foodgrains from the farmers, locally). Under this scheme, the designated states procure, store and also issue foodgrains under the TPDS. The difference between the economic cost of the states and the central issue price (CIP) is passed on to the states by the Government of India as subsidy. The decentralised system of procurement, helps to cover more farmers under the MSP operations, improves efficiency of the PDS, provides varieties of foodgrains more suited to local taste, and reduces the transportation costs of the FCI.[29]

The Government of India urged *all states* to adopt the DCP scheme so that costs of distribution can be saved and outreach of price support mechanism to the farmers in hitherto weaker areas can be improved. To overcome the problem of gaps in the flow of information about procurement operations on day-to-day basis, an *Online Procurement Monitoring System (OPMS)* has been evolved for reporting and monitoring on a daily basis, procurement operations for wheat, paddy and coarse grains in the country.

---

27. **New Agricultural Strategy, 1965**; Reports of the **CACP** and **Ministry of Agriculture**, GoI, N. Delhi.

28. Ministry of Finance, *Economic Survey 2014–15,* Vol. 2 (New Delhi: Government of India, 2015), p. 85.

29. Ministry of Finance, *Economic Survey 2011–12,* (New Delhi: Government of India, 2012).

Two decisions[30] of the Government of India that will impact procurement and stocks of rice and wheat from are:

(i) To limit procurement from states that are declaring bonus over and above the MSP to the extent of targeted TPDS and other welfare schemes (OWS) requirements. In the case of non-DCP states declaring bonus, the FCI will not take part in MSP operations in those states.

(ii) To cap the percentage of levy on rice at 25 per cent.

STORAGE

The total capacity available for storage of foodgrains as by 2014 was 727 lakh MT, comprising covered godowns of 567 lakh MT capacity and cover and plinth (CAP) facilities of 160 lakh MT capacity. The existing warehousing facility is limited not only in terms of capacity, but also to certain crops. The stockholding capacity has not kept pace with the increase in production and demand for a long time. The challenges of storage have been outlined by the *Economic Survey 2014–15* in the following way:

(i) The CAP of 160 lakh MT capacity cannot be treated as scientific storage.

(b) Public agencies do not have warehouses for proper storage of even half of the wheat and rice procured by them.

(c) In the wake of persistent seasonal inflation in perishables like fruits and vegetables, there was no effective strategy to control inflation on a sustainable basis.

(iv) Cold storage capacity for all type of food items is just 29 MT *(Planning Commission 2012)*. The production of potato alone is about 35 MT.

(v) Cold storage facility is available for only 10 per cent of fruits and vegetables produced in India *(Planning Commission 2011)*.

To bridge the gap between the requirement and availability of scientific storage capacity is the immediate need of the hour. For this, it is advisable to promote the policies by which private sector investment can be attracted to it.

Economic Cost of Foodgrains

The economic cost of foodgrains consists of three components, namely the MSP including central bonus (the price paid to farmers), procurement incidentals, and the cost of distribution. The economic cost for both wheat and rice witnessed significant increase during the last few years due to increase in MSPs and proportionate increase in incidentals as well as other costs. As per the Government, the economic costs of wheat and rice in 2016–17 are estimated to be over Rs. 30 and Rs. 22 per kg, respectively (they were around Rs. 20 and Rs 15 in 2010–11).

High economic cost necessitated a detailed review of the open-ended procurement policy, especially in states that offer high bonus on top of MSP and those that impose high taxes and statutory levies, as well as stocking and distribution policies. In this regard, the government set up a *High Level Committee (HLC)* in August 2014 (Shanta Kumar as its Chairman) to suggest inter-alia *restructuring* or *unbundling* of the FCI with a view to improve its operational efficiency and financial management.

Open Market Sale Scheme

The FCI has been undertaking sale of wheat at pre-determined prices (reserve prices) in the open market from time to time, known as the Open Market Sale Scheme (OMSS). This is aimed at serving the following *objectives:*

---

30. Ministry of Finance, *Economic Survey 2014–15*, p. 84.

(i) to enhance market supply of foodgrains;

(ii) to exercise a moderating influence on open market prices; and

(iii) to offload surplus stocks.

Under the Open Market Sale Scheme (Domestic), the government now adopts a policy of differential prices to encourage sale of older stock first—sticking to the following policy stance:

(i) Keeping the reserve price above MSP, but reasonably below the acquisition cost or economic cost of wheat, so that the buyers remain attracted to purchase of wheat from the *mandis* during the harvest season and the market remains competitive.

(ii) Maintaining that the market price during the lean season does not increase much and inflation remains under check.

Price Stabilisation Fund

The Government of India, by late *March 2015,* launched the Price Stabilisation Fund (PSF) as a Central Sector Scheme to support market interventions for price control of perishable agri-horticultural commodities. The cost to be borne between the centre and the states in equal ratio (in case of the North Eastern-states, the respective share will be 75:25). The scheme will commence with only two crops, viz., onion and potato.

FARM SUBSIDIES

Farm subsidies form an integral part of the government's budget. In the case of developed countries, the agricultural or farm subsidies compose nearly 40 per cent of the total budgetary outlay, while in India's case it is much lower (around 7.8 per cent of GDP) and of different nature.

Direct farm subsidies: These are the kinds of subsidies in which direct cash incentives are paid to the farmers in order to make their products more competitive in the global markets. The developed countries (USA and Europe) spend huge amounts of their annual budgets on the agriculture, farm and fisheries subsidies. Direct farm subsidies are helpful as they provide the right levels of purchasing power to the farmer and can significantly help in raising the standards of living of the rural poor. They also help in checking the misuse of public funds as they help in the proper identification of the beneficiaries.

Indirect farm subsidies: These are the farm subsidies which are provided in the form of cheaper credit facilities, farm loan waivers, reduction in irrigation and electricity bills, fertilizers, seeds and pesticides subsidy as well as the investments in agricultural research, environmental assistance, farmer training, etc. These subsidies are also provided to make farm products more competitive in the global market.

The subsidies provided on the fertilizers as 'input' subsidies are in the form of *indirect* subsidies. But if the government does not incentivize the farmer by an effective cost reduction in prices of the fertilizers, but provides direct cash incentives after the produce, is known as a *direct* subsidy.

The World Trade Organization (WTO) has put some ceilings on the amount of direct and indirect subsidies being provided by the various developing and developed nations due to the fact that these subsidies *distort the free market forces* which have their own implications.

First thoughts are encouraging. A panel headed by Montek Singh Ahluwalia (the then Deputy Chairman, *Planning Commission*) recommended that the power ministry, instead of paying power-distribution companies, hand out electricity subsidies **directly** to farmers through a smart card linked to the unique identity number.

India spends about Rs. 1,60,000 crore every year or roughly 2 per cent of its GDP on subsidies, **all indirectly**. For example, in fertilizers, which accounts for two-thirds of total subsidies, the government fixes a low selling price and compensates the producers by paying the difference between the selling price and the actual production costs (plus a pre-decided profit margin) as subsidy. *Important issues* related to farm subsidies are as given below:

(i) The indirect subsidy has been blamed for benefiting big farmers more than the small and medium farmers, for whom the subsidy is intended. This is because the bulk of the subsidised fertilizers is picked up by the rich farmers, because the small and marginal farmers account for just 37 per cent of the farm land.

(ii) Indirect subsidy has also discouraged improvements in production processes since manufacturers have no incentive to increase efficiency. This will also play a big part in bringing down India's overall subsidy bill. For instance, according to industry estimates, the money spent on poor farmers could potentially come down to Rs. 37,000 crore from the current Rs. 100,000 crore.

(iii) Another advantage of cash subsidies is that it will free up the distribution system and allow the people who receive the subsidy to choose where they buy their goods from. The complexity is not so much in the transfer of funds, as it is in the identification of the beneficiaries.

Other Countries: The idea of disbursing subsidies directly to the beneficiaries is becoming popular among the development thinkers and policymakers. It's already a part of policy in many parts of the world—predominantly, in Latin America where 16 countries have this practice, and also in other countries such as Jamaica, Philippines, Turkey and Indonesia.

The biggest and most cited of such programmes is Brazil's *Bolsa Familia*. It started in 2001, with a programme aimed at education. It expanded in 2003 to include a range of services like food and fuel, and now covers 2.6 million families in that country. The government *transfers cash* straight to a family, subject to conditions such as school attendance, nutritional monitoring, pre-natal and post-natal tests. By many measures, the programme is a success. Brazil's poverty levels dropped by 15 percentage points between 2003 and 2009, at least a sixth, thanks to Bolsa Familia (economic growth played a big part, too.) Millenium Development Goals initiative, which in 2000 sought to halve poverty by 2015, doesn't even mention cash transfers. But, Brazil achieved the goals 10 years ahead of the deadline. And the cost of these transfers has been 0.4 per cent of GDP.

The big question is not whether a direct cash transfer is the perfect solution, but whether it's an improvement over the existing systems. The evidence—its success in other parts of the world—and the poor performance of indirect subsidies so far would suggest so. Looking at it, the GoI has already started a pan-India scheme to disburse all forms of subsidies directly, through the *Direct Benefit Transfer (DBT)* since 2015–16 onwards.

FOOD SECURITY

India attained self-sufficiency in food by late 1980s, though food security still evades the country. Food security means making food available at affordable prices at all times, to all, without interruptions. Though India's GDP growth has been impressive and the agricultural production has also increased over the past few decades, hunger and starvation still persist among the poorer sections of the population.

Lack of food security hampers the nutritional profile of the vulnerable section of the population. Calorie and protein intake of a large number of people in India, specially in rural areas, are lower than normal.[31] As per the *State of Food Insecurity in the World, 2015 (FAO)*, India has the second highest number of undernourished people at 194.6 million which is around 15.2 per cent of the world's total undernourished population.

Two important things need attention regarding India's food security –

(i) Around 27 per cent of India's population is BPL and a greater portion (one conservative estimate puts it at 75 per cent) of their household income is spent on food.

(ii) There is a strong correlation between stability in agricultural production and food security. Volatility in agricultural production impacts food supplies and can result in spikes in food prices, which adversely affect the lowest income groups of the population.

Therefore, along with provision of food subsidy, stability in agricultural commodity prices is essential for making the poorer sections food secure. It means, in the direction of assuring food security, India needs to tackle mainly two hurdles–

(i) *Enhancing its food production*: If food (i.e., foodgrains) is to be supplied to all today India will face deficit of around 30 million tonnes of foodgrains. This shows the food insecurity dimension of India.

(ii) *Strengthening supply chain:* Managing the issues like storage, transportation, proper retailing and integrating the segmented agri-markets into a national agrimarket.

Due to high level of undernourishment and volatility in agricultural prices, India has one of the largest number of food schemes in the World to ensure food security –

(i) There is entitlement feeding programmes like the Integrated Child Development Scheme (ICDS – covers all Children under six, pregnant and lactating mothers)

(ii) Mid Day Meal Schemes(MDMS),

(iii) Food subsidy programmes like the Targeted Public Distribution System (through which the National Food Security Act is being implemented)

(iv) Annapurna (10 kgs of free food grain for destitute poor) and the

(v) Employment Programmes like Mahatma Gandhi National Rural Employment Guarantee Scheme (100 days of employment at minimum wages) to ensure food security.

Till the vulnerable population is not enabled with the market-linked purchasing capacity, these programmes will be relevant in case ensuring food security in the country. There is a need to run these schemes with utmost focus of the beneficiaries.

PDS & FOOD SUBSIDY

The Public Distribution System (PDS was changed to Targeted PDS in 1997) strives to ensure food security through timely and affordable distribution of foodgrains to the BPL population as this section can not afford to pay market prices for their food. This involves procurement of foodgrain at MSP by the Government, building up and maintenance of food stocks, their storage, and timely distribution, making foodgrains accessible at reasonable prices to the vulnerable sections of the population.

However, the system of PDS has many weaknesses leading to leakages and targeted beneficiaries being left out of the system. The PDS incurs high costs for procurement, storage and distribution of foodgrains. There is scope to increase efficiency of the PDS operations and reduce costs. Only a small proportion of the

---

31. 66th Round (2009-10) and 68th Round (2011-12) of the **NSSO**, as quoted by the **Economic Survey 2015-16**, op. cit., Vol. 2, p.117.

public expenditure/subsidy on PDS reaches the beneficiary. There is a case for introducing **DBT** (Direct Benefit Transfer) for consumers of food and kerosene as is under way in *Andhra Pradesh*. Though, there are challenges in implementing DBT.

As per the **Economic Survey 2016-17,** despite increased procurement of foodgains offtakes from PDS have been declining in past few years. This suggests that despite enhanced availability in the PDS and high inflation in foodgrains, dependence on the PDS is reducing – this could be only due to two reasons –

(i) Foodgrains are not made available timely by the PDS, and/or

(ii) Quality of the PDS foodgrains are inferior in comparison to their counterparts in the open market.

There are certain anomalies in India's food management under the PDS which need immediate attention –

(i) The percentage distribution of the economic cost of wheat and rice has been rising fast. The pooled cost of foodgrains *(MSP plus the Bonus which are offered by the individual states)* accounts for *two-thirds* of the economic cost of wheat and rice. This has made the economic cost of foodgrains to the Food Corporation of India (FCI) increase over the years.

(ii) Increasing costs of labour, fertilizers, pesticides and other inputs have made production of crops costlier over the time. This forced the government to keep on increasing the MSPs of the crops, too.

(iii) The increase in the food subsidy bill is determined by the rate at which the MSPs for wheat and rice increase and the *economic cost* of handling grains (their procurement, stocking and distribution to the targeted households). This has been the major factor for ballooning

food subsidy bill. Food subsidy bill has increased to over **15** per cent of agri-GDP by 2016-17 from 5 per cent of 2005-06 (as per the *Commission for Agricultural Costs and Prices-CACP*).

(iv) The procurement incidentals of wheat and rice consist of costs related to mandi charges and taxes, cost of gunny bags, *arhatiya* commission, *mandi* labour, forwarding charges, internal movement, storage charges, interest, administrative charges and others. Out of these costs, *mandi* charges and taxes constitute more than **40** per cent of the total costs.

Opportunity cost of running the PDS have been very high. This is particularly due to increased levels of fund diversion for food subsidy, the government could not support adequate amount of investment in the agricultural sector. This prevented capacity building in the sector.

Over the time, several discrepancies seeped into the PDS, such as,

(i) high operation costs,

(ii) high levels of leakages,

(iii) high administrative costs,

(iv) corruption, and

(v) mismanagement.

Subsidies created some other problems, too. *Firstly,* subsidies brought distortions in the market, which hamper the domestic as well as the external interests and *secondly,* caused a heavy drain on the government exchequer. PDS poses even higher challenge when domestic or international prices are on the rise and the government is forced to raise the MSPs of crops.

AGRICULTURE MARKETING

India's agrimarket is presently regulated by the Agricultural Produce Market Committee (APMC) Act enacted by the state governments. There are about 2,477 principal regulated agrimarkets and 4,843 sub-market yards regulated by the respective APMCs in India. Thus, India has not one, not 29 (number of states) but thousands of agricultural markets. This Act notifies agricultural commodities produced in the region such as cereals, pulses, edible oilseed, fruits and vegetables and even chicken, goat, sheep, sugar, fish, etc., and provides that first sale in these commodities can be conducted only under the aegis of the APMC through the commission agents licensed by the APMCs set up under the Act.

The typical *amenities* available in or around the APMCs are: auction halls, weigh bridges, godowns, shops for retailers, canteens, roads, lights, drinking water, police station, post-office, bore-wells, warehouse, farmers amenity center, tanks, water treatment plant, soil-testing laboratory, toilet blocks, etc. Various taxes, fees/charges and cess levied on the trades conducted in the *mandis* are also notified under the Act.

As per the *Economic Survey 2014–15,* the APMCs of the states levy multiples fees of substantial magnitude which are non-transparent and hence work as a source of political power. The functioning of the APMCs have always been a matter of debate among experts and policymakers alike—**major issues** being the following:

- They charge a market fee from buyers, and they also charge a licensing fee from the commissioning agents who mediate between buyers and farmers.

- They also charge small licensing fees from a whole range of functionaries (warehousing agents, loading agents, etc.).

- In addition, commissioning agents charge commission fees on transactions between buyers and farmers.

- The levies and other market charges vary widely in the states. Statutory levies/mandi tax, VAT, etc., are a major source of market distortions.

- Such high taxes at the first level of trading have significant cascading effects on commodity prices, as the commodities passes through the supply chain. For rice, these charges can be as high as 14.5 per cent in Andhra Pradesh (excluding the state VAT) and close to 10 per cent in Odisha and Punjab.

- Even the model APMC Act (described below) treats the APMC as an arm of the state, and, the market fee, as the tax levied by the state, rather than fee charged for providing services. This is a crucial provision which acts as *a major impediment to creating national common market* in agricultural commodities. Removal of this provision will pave the way for creating competition and a national common market for agricultural commodities.

- Moreover, though the market fee is collected just like a tax, the revenue earned by the APMCs does not go to the state exchequer and hence does not require the approval of the state legislature to utilise the funds thus collected. Thus, APMC operations are independent of scrutiny.

- The rate of commission charged by the licensed commission agents is exorbitant, because, unlike direct taxes, which are levied on net income, the commission is charged on the entire value of the produce sold. The license fee charged from various market licensed operators is nominal, but the small number of licences granted creates a premium, which is believed to be paid in cash.

- There is a perception that the positions in the market committee (at the state level) and the market board (which supervises the market committee) are occupied by politically influential persons. They enjoy a cosy relationship with the licensed commission agents who wield power by exercising monopoly power within the notified area, at times by forming cartels. The resistance to *reforming* APMCs is perceived to be emanating from these factors.

The scope of the *Essential Commodities Act, 1955* (EC Act) is much broader than the APMC Act. It empowers the central and state governments concurrently to control production, supply and distribution of certain commodities, including pricing, stock-holding and the period for which the stocks can be kept and to impose duties. The APMC Act on the other hand, controls only the first sale of the agricultural produce. Apart from food-stuffs which are covered under the APMC Act, the commodities covered under the EC Act generally are: drugs, fertilisers, textiles and coal.

Model APMC Act

Since the State APMC Acts created fragment markets for agricultural commodities and curtailed the freedom of farmers to sell their produce other than through the commission agents and other functionaries licensed by the APMCs, the Ministry of Agriculture (GoI) developed a *Model APMC Act, 2003* and has been pursuing the state governments to modify their respective Acts along its line. The Model APMC Act provides the following new things:

(i) Direct sale of farm produce by the farmer to contract farming sponsors;

(ii) Setting up 'special markets' for 'specified agricultural commodities'— mostly perishables;

(iii) Permits private persons, farmers and consumers to establish new markets for agricultural produce in any area;

(iv) A single levy of market fee on the sale of notified agricultural commodities in any market area;

(v) Replaces licensing with registrations of market functionaries, which would allow them to operate in one or more different market areas;

(vi) Establishment of consumers' and farmers' markets to facilitate direct sale of agricultural produce to consumers;

(vii) Creation of marketing infrastructure from the revenue earned by the APMCs;

(viii) Provides some freedom to the farmers to sell their produce directly to the contract-sponsors or in the market set up by private individuals, consumers or producers;

(ix) Increases the competitiveness of the market of agri-produce by allowing common registration of market intermediaries.

Many of the states have partially adopted the provisions of the model APMC Act and amended their respective APMC Acts. Some of the states have not framed rules to implement the amended provisions, which indicate *hesitancy* on the part of the state governments to liberalise the statutory compulsion on farmers to sell their produce through the APMCs. Some states (such as Karnataka)[32] have however adopted changes to create greater competition within the state— popularly known as the ***Karnataka Model***.

The central government is closely working with state governments to re-orient states' APMC Acts in order to provide for establishment of

---

32. Other states like Maharashtra, Tamil nadu and Andhra Pradesh did also for reforms in their APMC's taking clues from the Modekl APMC Act—making these states also to have some synergy coming into their agriculture market.

private market yards/private markets. As per the **Union Budget 2017–18** and **Economic Survey 2016-17** some of the **recent initiatives** taken in this regard are as follows:

(i) A comprehensive advisory issued to the states to go beyond the provisions of the Model Act and declare the entire state a *single market* with one licence valid across the entire state and removing all restrictions on movement of agricultural produce within the state.

(ii) The **NAM** (National Agriculture Market) through an Agri-Tech Infrastructure Fund (ATIF) has been established by Government of India in July 2015, which will be implemented up to 2017–18. NAM will provide a common *e-market platform* of regulated wholesale markets in states/UTs (those states /UTs that are desirous to joint he platform). The SFAC (Small Farmers Agribusiness Consortium) will implement this e-platform and will cover 250, 200 and 135 **mandis** during 2015–16, 2016017 and 2017–18 respectively.

The DAC & FW (Department of Agriculture, Cooperation Farmers Welfare) will meet expenses on software and its customisation for the regulated mandis of the states/UTs **free of cost.** To Integrate with the NAM, the APMCs of the states/UTs will need to meet certain pre-requisites, which are given below:

(a) a single license to be valid across the states,

(b) single point levy of market fee, and

(c) provision for electronic auction as a mode for price discovery.

Majority of the states and all of the UTs have shown their interest to join the e-platform.

(iii) On the request of the central government, a number of state governments have exempted the marketing of fruits and vegetables from the purview of the APMC Act. The NCT of Delhi has put fruits and vegetables outside its APMC. The Small Farmers Agribusiness Consortium (SFAC) has taken the initiative for developing a *Kisan Mandi* in Delhi with a view to providing a platform to FPOs for direct sale of their produce to prospective buyers, totally obviating or reducing unnecessary layers of intermediation in the process. The SFAC plan to scale its activities in other states based on the outcome of the experience of the Delhi kisan mandi.

SAFEGUARDING AGRITRADE

In recent times, India has become more conscious towards protecting its agricultural trade interests at the international platforms. At the *10th Ministerial Conference* of the WTO (Nairobi, December 2015), the Government of India adopted the following approach towards agritrade policy:

(i) A Special Safeguard Mechanism (SSM) for developing countries.

(ii) Public stockholding food for security purposes,

(iii) A commitment to abolish export subsidies for farm exports, and

(iv) Measures related to cotton.

Decisions were also taken regarding preferential treatment to LDCs in the area of services and the criteria for determining whether exports from LDCs may benefit from trade preferences.

Policy stability: The changes in the agritrade policy hampers the concept of a market and needs to be discontinued with, due to the following reasons[33]:

(i) Frequent changes in the policy parameters (goal posts) of trade in agricultural products in the form of changes in import duties and minimum export prices, etc., create instability of policy for any investment in the *agro-processing* industry.

(ii) The changes in policy parameters have limited impact on the price the consumer pays, because of the time taken to arrive at the decision and the same translating into additional/reduced supplies.

(iii) It certainly does not impact the farmer who has received his remuneration based on the price prevailing at the time the produce leaves the farm gate.

(iv) High prices of commodities in a particular year do not translate into benefits to the farmer in the same year, but create expectations, possibly not rational, of the same in the next year, enhancing cropped area in the next year/cropping season, leading to oversupply and reduction in prices and consequently of incomes.

COMMODITY FUTURES MARKET

By the early 2017, out of the 113 commodities notified for futures trading, 43 were actively traded in 4 national exchanges and 6 commodity-specific exchanges. Share of agricultural commodities in the total turnover was over 20 per cent in 2015–16, with food items (refined soya oil, soyabean, chana, coriander and rapeseed/mustard seed) contributing over 50 per cent of it. The remaining (80 per cent) turnover was contributed by bullion, metals and energy contracts.

A *Committee* set up by the Ministry of Finance, which submitted its report in April 2014, and has observed that hedging efficiency of the commodity futures markets is low. In order to ensure that forward markets in commodities are well regulated and the Indian commodity futures market is compliant with international regulatory requirements, the regulatory framework for the commodity futures market needs to be strengthened at the earliest. The Government of India decided to merge the commodity market regulator, the Forward Market Commission (FMC) with the Security & Exchange Board of India (SEBI) in **2015–16** with enhanced and effective regulatory power given to it.

UPSTREAM & DOWNSTREAM REQUIREMENTS

'Upstream' and 'downstream' are business terms applicable to the production processes that exist within several industries. Upstream, downstream and midstream make up the stages of the production process for different industries.

Upstream: The upstream stage of the production process involves searching for and extracting raw materials—it does not do anything with the material itself, such as processing the materials. In upstream, firms simply find and extract the raw material. Thus, any industry that relies on the extraction of raw materials commonly has an *upstream stage* in its production process. In a more general sense, upstream can also refer to any part of the production process relating to the extraction stages.

Downstream: The downstream stage in the production process involves processing the materials collected during the upstream stage into a finished product. It further includes the actual sale. End users will vary depending on the finished

33. Ministry of Finance, *Economic Survey 2015–16,* Vol. 2, p. 122.

product. Regardless of the industry involved, the downstream process has direct contact with customers through the finished product.

Midstream: Several points in between the two points (the place where raw is extracted and till it reaches the final consumer as finished product) are taken as the midstream. It depends on the reference point as how many or which stage is considered as the midstream by an industry.

Whether an activity is upstream or downstream depends on the point of analysis in a supply chain. A manufacturer considers suppliers as upstream and customers as downstream. Within a manufacturer, control over activities in the supply chain is subject to a company's management. Even so, a manufacturing activity that occurs prior to another is considered an upstream activity. Control over activities outside the company is subject to inter-company negotiations, cooperation and technology. The firms involved in the chain of upstream and downstream processes keep their eyes on several other dimensions, such as *strategies, integration* and *improvement.*

(i) It is important to understand the *strategies* of supply chain partners. A supplier may have a strategy to grow and begin to perform manufacturing functions infringing on other supply chain member's markets. Understanding the incentives of suppliers, as well as customers, helps to plan for these types of changes. In order to remain a powerful player in a supply chain, a company can no longer afford to focus on its own business or those of its competitors, it must understand supply chain members business as if they were their own.

(ii) *Integration* of business processes throughout a supply chain depends on cooperation of members. For example, a manufacturer who decides to sole-source a component with one supplier can control and integrate with the supplier to streamline business processes. Technology can be implemented to make business processes between companies easier to perform. For example, a supplier can change from requiring a purchase order for every delivery to having an open purchase order that simply keeps track of shipments based on material requirements plans from the manufacturing resource planning software of a manufacturer. This type of integration becomes less likely when suppliers serve many manufacturers.

(iii) Manufacturers in a supply chain make 'make-or-buy' decisions that affect the chain. They do this based on cost and scheduling *improvements* available. Manufacturers may also begin using distributors to capture additional markets or decide to concentrate on larger customers whom they can serve directly. All of these types of potential improvements depend on understanding the motivations and incentives of the companies in a supply chain.

Industries, to have a smooth and uniterrupted fuctioning, depend heavily on the upstream and downstream requirements. In the case of *India*, we find several bottlenecks in both the processes:

(i) In the case of the private sector, the downstream process seems better. But it is not so. Upto the level of 'wholesale' it is somewhat organised, but the retail trading is quite fragmented. India's *retail business* remains least organised. Organised retail is yet to evolve in the country, thus, the levels of uncertainities, potential of market access, monitoring and regulation of retail market are too weak.

(ii) Upstream processes are also not up-to-the-mark. From the stage where the wholesale comes into picture, things look better. But outsourcing the raw from the local producers is an uphill task in the country. Due to this the upstream segment of the economy has remained too weak and frgamented.

(iii) The industrial and manufactured sectors have been managing their upstream and downstream requirements, but their heavy depenence on the unorganised sector is a challenging issue in front of India.

(iv) In the case of agricultural products, the situation is even worse. Agrimarkets of regulations by the APMCs did not allowed India to establish a common and single market. This has hampered not only the growth and business prospects, but it has also crippled the agricultural sector in a very serious way. It has taken the heaviest toll on the agriculture sector which still remains a non-remunerative profession.

(v) As India is to compete in the global market, it immediately needs to stregthen it upstream and downstream process. For this, India is advised to pick the best practices from around the world and integrate itself with the developed world with the better ways and the state-of-the-art tools and means.

SUPPLY CHAIN MANAGEMENT

A *supply chain* is a network of facilities and distribution options that performs the functions of procurement of materials, transformation of these materials into intermediate and finished products, and the distribution of these finished products to customers. Supply chains exist in both services, and manufacturing organisations, although the complexity of the chain may vary greatly from industry to industry and firm to firm.

Traditionally, marketing, distribution, planning, manufacturing, and the purchasing organisations along the supply chain operated independently. These organisations have their own objectives and these are often conflicting. Marketing's objective of high customer service and maximum sales conflict with manufacturing and distribution goals. Many manufacturing operations are designed to maximise output and lower costs with little consideration for the impact on inventory levels and distribution capabilities. Purchasing contracts are often negotiated with very little information beyond historical buying patterns. The result of these factors is that there is not a single, integrated plan for the organisation—there were as many plans as businesses. Clearly, there is a need for a mechanism through which these different functions could be integrated. Supply chain management is a strategy through which such an integration can be achieved.

Supply chain management is typically viewed to lie between fully vertically integrated firms, where the entire material flow is owned by a *single firm*, and those where each channel member operates independently. Therefore, coordination between the various players in the chain is key in its effective management. Supply chain management can be compared to a well-balanced and well-practiced 'relay team'—such a team is more competitive when each player knows how to be positioned for the hand-off. The relationships are the strongest between players who directly pass the baton, but the entire team needs to make a coordinated effort to win the race.

Supply chain management, then, is the active management of supply chain activities to maximise customer value and achieve a sustainable competitive advantage. It represents a conscious effort by the supply chain firms to develop and run supply chains in the most effective and efficient ways possible. Supply chain activities cover everything, such as:

(i) Product development,

(ii) Sourcing,

(iii) Production,

(iv) Logistics, and

(v) Information systems (for proper coordination).

The organisations that make up the supply chain are 'linked' together through *physical* flows and *information* flows. Physical flows involve the transformation, movement, and storage of goods and materials. They are the most visible piece of the supply chain. But just as important are information flows—information flows allow the various supply chain partners to coordinate their long-term plans, and to control the day-to-day flow of goods and material up and down the supply chain.

FDI IN UPSTREAM, DOWNSTREAM AND SUPPLY CHAIN MANAGEMENT

This segment of India has seen least organised development, even in the reforms period. Due to lack of proper 'market reforms' in the area of agricultural products (as APMCs of different states have failed to develop) which hampered so many aspects of it—storage, grading, packaging, etc. It is believed that this field needs huge investments from the corporate sector. The corporate sector has not been much attracted to this sector. Main factors for the unwillingness among the private sector to put in their money in it are, scarcity of capital, logistics, experience and non-conducive policy framework in the agriculture market. This is the reason why the Government of India has allowed more freedom to FDI in retail chain development. It is expected that the willing foreign firms will not only bringing the needed fund to the sector, but alongwith them India will get international experience and best practices.

To compete in the globalising world markets and to gain economic benefits out of globalisation,

India needs the following features in its supply chain management:

(i) An organised retain sector

(ii) Proper levels of logistics

(iii) Fully updated data of raw materials, production, cropping pattern, etc.

(iv) International class packaging, care to wards phyto-sanitary aspects

It is felt that the above-cited features will be easier to manage for the top global players as they have fund, experience and a willingness to expand their businesses in the growing regions of the world.

To strengthen and broad base of the market, the Forward Markets Commission (FMC), which is *the regulator* for commodity futures trading under the provisions of the Forward Contracts (Regulation) Act 1952, has taken many initiatives such as:[34]

(i) Conducted awareness programmes in 2011, such as a media campaign under the *Jago Grahak Jago Programme* about the Dos and Don'ts of trading in the commodity futures market;

(ii) Police training programmes in the states of Madhya Pradesh, Chhattisgarh, Tamil Nadu and Delhi with regard to dabba trading / illegal trading;

(iii) A massive awareness and capacity-building programme for various stakeholders, with primary focus on farmers.

(iv) On the regulatory front, the FMC undertook measures for the development of the commodity futures market, which include ensuring more effective inspection of members of the exchanges on regular basis and in a comprehensive manner covering all aspects of the regulatory regime.

---

34. Ministry of Finance, *Economic Survey 2011–12*, p. 199.

(v) Bringing out a guidance manual for improving audit practices, prescribing penalty structure for client code modification and for executing trade.

(vi) Granting exemptions for short hedge for soyabean/oil futures, issuing directives for segregation of client accounts.

FARM WASTE DEBATE

A recent study,[35] undertaken by the Central Institute of Post-Harvest Engineering and Technology (CIPHET), a government-run institute, has estimated the value of farm waste in India at Rs. 92,651 crore (at the prices of 2014), that is around 9 per cent of the total produce, which is much lower than the oft-stated 40 per cent level. Although cereals, such as wheat and rice, pulses and oil seeds accounted for around two-thirds of the wastage, the loss in case of fruits and vegetables was the highest at up to 18 per cent of the total produce.

Attending the causes of storage and processing facilities, something the Government of India is emphasising, this level could come down significantly and can serve great purpose in helping the economy to fight the repeated price shocks of the past two years in case of fruits, vegetables and foodgrains to a great extent.

The losses take place in almost all stages of farming, but *the study* looked at harvesting, collection, grading, cleaning, packaging, transportation and storage. If cultivation was also included the loss figure would be much higher. The government has said that adoption of better technology has brought about a reduction in losses.

IRRIGATION

The Planning Commission[36] classified irrigation projects/schemes in India on the following lines :

(i) *Major Irrigation Schemes*—those with cultivable command areas (CCA) of more than 10,000 hectares.

(ii) *Medium Irrigation Schemes*—those with cultivable command areas (CCA) between 2,000 and 10,000 hectares.

(iii) *Minor Irrigation Schemes*—those with cultivable command area (CCA) upto 2,000 hectares. Expansion of irrigation facilities, along with consolidation of the existing systems, has been the main part of the strategy for increasing production of foodgrains.

With a view to ensuring early completion of projects for providing irrigation benefits to the farmers, Rural Infrastructure Development Fund (RIDF) has been in operation since 1995–96. The government launched the Accelerated Irrigation Benefits Programme (AIBP) in 1996–97 to give loan assistance to the states to help them complete some of the incomplete major/medium irrigation projects, which were in an advanced stage of completion.

There is **need** to expand the acreage under irrigation along with adoption of appropriate technologies for efficient utilisation of water through suitable pricing to raise agricultural productivity in India. This could be done through– (i) Adoption of irrigation technologies which improve efficiency in the use of water is imperative in a scenario where flood irrigation has resulted in wastage of water. (ii) Focus on efficient irrigation technologies is important with

35. *Central Institute of Post-Harvest Engineering and Technology (CIPHET),* ICAR, Ministry of Agriculture, GoI, Ludhiana, Study released in September, 2016.

36. *Planning Commission*, GoI, N. Delhi, 1961.

increasing water shortages owing to climate change and indiscriminate wastage of water in agriculture and other uses.

Having *'more crop per drop'* through efficient irrigation technologies should be the motto to improve productivity in agriculture which can ensure food and water security in the future.

Irrigation Potential & Use

As per the latest available data[37] on irrigation, the all India percentage distribution of net irrigated area to total cropped area during 2012–13 was 33.9 per cent. There is regional disparity in irrigated farming, with net irrigated area to total cropped area at more than 50 per cent in the states of Punjab, Tamil Nadu and Uttar Pradesh, while it is at less than 50 per cent in the remaining states. There is need and scope for increasing the coverage of irrigated area across the country to increase productivity in agriculture. The total UIP (Ultimate Irrigation Potential) of India is about **140** million hectares (Mha). There is substantial gap between IPC (Irrigation Potential Created) and IPU (Irrigation Potential Utilized). There is perceptible decline in the ratio of IPU to IPC mainly due to:

(i) lack of proper operation and maintenance,

(ii) incomplete distribution system,

(iii) non-completion of command area development,

(iv) changes in cropping pattern, and

(v) diversion of irrigated land for other purposes.

There is need to arrest the declining trend in efficient utilization of irrigation potential and also reverse it. A larger share of funds available under the Mahatma Gandhi National Rural Employment Guarantee Scheme (MGNREGS) and other employment generating schemes need to be deployed for promotion of irrigation—*for creation and maintenance of community assets, de-silting and repair of tanks and other water bodies.*

Irrigation Efficiency

Agricultural productivity can be boosted in a big way by enhancing irrigation efficiency in the use of irrigation systems. Over the time, the conventional systems of irrigation have become non-viable in many parts of India[38] due to:

(i) increasing shortages of water,

(ii) wastage of water through over irrigation, and

(iii) concerns of salination of soil.

Economically and technically efficient irrigation technologies like – **drip** and **sprinkler** irrigation – can improve water use efficiency, reduce costs of production by reducing labour costs and power consumption. [One of the objectives of the *PMKSY* (Prime Minister's Krishi Sinchai Yojana) is to enhance on-farm WUE (Water-Use-Efficiency) spatially and temporally to reduce wastage by promoting precision irrigation like sprinkler, drip etc.] There good instances of MI (Micro Irrigation) technology in enhancing irrigation efficiency and cutting costs[39] –

(a) The adoption of *sprinkler irrigation* resulted in 35 to 40 per cent savings of irrigation water in the cultivation of groundnut and cotton in Gujarat, Karnataka and Andhra Pradesh.

(b) The adoption of *drip irrigation* resulted in 40 to 65 per cent savings in water for horticulture crops and 30 to 47 per cent for vegetables. Such examples need to be emulated by other areas/crops in

---

37. Ministry of Finance, **Economic Survey 2015–16**, Vol. 2, P. 103.

38. NITI Aayog, *Task Force on Agriculture*, 2015, as quoted Ministry of Finance, **Economic Survey 2015–16**, Vol. 2, p. 104.

39. *National Committee on Plasticulture Applications in Horticulture* study has been quoted by Ministry of Finance, **Economic Survey 2015–16**, p. 104

these states and in other states for a larger basket of crops.

Water Productivity

Water productivity in India is very low. The overall irrigation efficiency of the major and medium irrigation projects in India is estimated at around 38 per cent. As per the **NITI Aayog**, efficiency of the *surface irrigation* system can be improved from about 35-40 per cent to around 60 per cent and that of *groundwater* from about 65-70 per cent to 75 per cent. Water productivity needs to be enhanced by the following methods –

(i) tapping, harvesting and recycling water,

(ii) efficient on-farm water management practices,

(iii) micro irrigation,

(iv) use of waste water, and

(v) resource conservation technologies.

In order to promote judicious use of water ensuring *'more crop per drop'* of water in agriculture for drought proofing, the GoI recently launched the PMKSY aiming at providing water to every field of agriculture

FARM MECHANISATION

India needs to introduce better equipment for each farming operation in order to reduce drudgery, to improve efficiency by saving on time and labour, improve productivity, minimize wastage and reduce labour costs for each operation. Agricultural mechanisation in case of India is increasingly needed as:

(i) Due to shortage of labour for agricultural operations owing to rural-urban migration, shift from agriculture to services and rise in demand for labour in non-farm activities, there is need to use labour for agricultural operations

judiciously, which makes a strong case for mechanisation of farming.

(ii) Indian agriculture has a high proportion of female workforce in both the cultivation and processing stages of farming. Therefore, ergonomically designed tools and equipment for reducing drudgery, enhancing safety and comfort and also to suit the needs of women workers would help in better adoption of technologies in agriculture.

Some *important facts* regarding mechanisation of the farm sector in India:

(i) Although India is one of the top countries in agricultural production, the current level of farm mechanisation, which varies across states, averages below 50 per cent as against more than 90 per cent in developed countries *(Economic Survey 2015–16)*.

(ii) The farm mechanization in India has been growing at a rate of less than 5 per cent in last two decades*(Economic Survey 2014–15)*.

(iii) Tractor penetration in the country is 38 per cent for large farmers (with more than 20 acres), 18 per cent for medium farmers (5–20 acres) and just around 1 per cent for marginal farmers.[40]

(iv) The economic benefit of adoption of improved implements is about Rs. 83,000 crore per annum, which is only a small fraction of the potential *(NITI Aayog, 2016)*.

(iv) Farm mechanisation has resulted in generating employment to rural youth and artisans for the production, operation,

---

40. *Agricultural Machinery and Manufacturers Association in India (AMMAI)* was quoted in the **Economic Survey 2015-16**, op. cit., Vol. 2, p. 105.

and maintenance of machines (*Economic Survey 2013-14.*

Two important and contemporary policy **suggestions**[41] may be given in this regard:

(i) Due to increased fragmentation of landholdings and low rates of tractor penetration among small farmers, there is need for a market in *tractor rentals*, akin to cars and road construction equipment, driven by private participation.

(ii) Appropriate farm equipment which are durable, light weight and low cost, region, crop and operation specific using indigenous/adapted technologies need to be made available for small and marginal farmers to improve productivity.

SEED DEVELOPMENT

Seed is the basic input for increasing productivity in agriculture. It is estimated that the quality of seed accounts for 20 to 25 per cent of productivity.[42] Thus, the adoption of quality seeds needs promotion in India. There are multiple challenges to the development and adoption of quality seeds in the form of –

(i) Inadequate research inputs for development of new seeds especially,

(ii) Early ripening and resistant (to pest, moisture variations, etc.) varieties,

(iii) High cost of seeds for small and marginal farmers,

(iv) Shortage of supply of quality seeds,

(v) Non-resolution of issues related to adoption of Genetically Modified Seeds, and

(vi) Inadequate number of players restricting competition.

The **issues**[43] that require immediate attention are:

(i) *Affordability:* Open pollinated varieties of seeds can be developed by farmers from their own harvested crops. However, for high-yielding hybrid varieties, the farmer has to depend on the market for each crop which gets very costly for the small and marginal farmers.

(ii) *Availability:* Quality seeds have shortage in supply. While there is a demand for banning non-certified seeds, certification *per-se* does not ensure quality seeds. Presence of more players (both public and private) and competition in the market for seeds would improve this situation.

(iii) *Research and Development of Seeds and Seed technology:* The first Green Revolution was driven by indigenously developed High Yielding Varieties (HYVs) of seeds for paddy and wheat. Inadequate research and genetic engineering has been a constraint in the development of seeds and seed technologies in major crops during the past few decades in India. There is need to encourage development of seed technologies in both private and public sectors to initiate another round of Green Revolution. This development should cover all agricultural segments.

(iv) *GM crops and seeds:* Concerns about its affordability, environmental and ethical issues, risks to the food chain, disease spread and cross pollination have resulted in their non-introduction.

---

41. Ministry of Finance, **Economic Survey 2015–16**, p. 105.

42. As per the *DAC&FW (Department of Agriculture, Cooperation & Farmers Welfare)* – as quoted by the **Economic Survey 2015-16**, Vol. 2, p. 105.

43. Ministry of Finance, **Economic Survey 2015–16**, pp. 105-107.

FERTILISERS

In improving agricultural output, fertiliser is a critical and expensive input. Since the Green Revolution (mid-1960s), there has been a sharp increase in the use of fertilizers in India. To facilitate and promote the use of fertilizers, the Government has been providing fertilizer subsidy to farmers. Today, the fertiliser subsidies stand at around **10** per cent of the total agricultural GDP.[44]

However, the use of fertilisers has not resulted in commensurate growth in agricultural productivity. The declining response ratio or marginal productivity of fertilisers since the 1970s is a pointer to their inefficient use in Indian agriculture. The yield of grain per kilogram use of NPK fertilizer has declined from 13.4 kg grain per ha in 1970 to 3.7 kg grain per ha in irrigated areas by 2005.

In the post Green Revolution agriculture scenario, there have been **imbalances** in the use of fertilizers such as –

(i) Excessive dependence on urea owing to low/distorted prices of fertilisers, especially urea and regional imbalance in the use,

(ii) Neglect/low use of compost, manure and other forms of natural nutrient providers,

(iii) Discontinuing practices of inter and rotational cropping.

(iv) Diversion of the subsidised fertilisers to non-agricultural use.

(v) Indiscriminate use of fertilisers has not proportionally improved the yield of crops, but has resulted in the depletion of soil fertility and salination of soil in many areas.

There is need to rationalise fertiliser subsidy in an *input, crop and region neutral format* and minimise diversions. The disbursal of subsidy on fertilisers should shift to DBT (the GoI has already started the process as announced in the Union Budget 2016–17), the benefits of which will be maximised, if all controls (including imports) on the fertiliser industry/outputs are lifted, simultaneously. In the case of P (phosphate) and K (potash) fertilizer subsidy, with the Nutrient Based Subsidy (NBS) scheme, a fixed amount of subsidy will be given on each grade based on their content. Certain *improvements in fertilisation* needed in the Indian farm sector may be summed up as follows:

(i) *Crop-responsive & balanced use of fertilisers:* There is need to facilitate the optimal use of fertilisers depending on the soil health and fertility status. Linking the *soil health card* to provide profile of the soil and fertilizer on the basis of the same profile utilizing fertilizer, (even if not subsidised) can improve the yield of crops.

(ii) *Micro nutrients & organic fertilisers:* Indian soils show deficiency of micro nutrients (like boron, zinc, copper and iron) in most parts of the country which limiting crop yields and productivity. Fertilisers which supplement micro nutrients can provide an additional yield in cereals in the range of 0.3 to 0.6 ton per hectare.[45] This deficiency can be overcome if there by expansion in the use of organic fertiliser. Besides, being cheaper to use organic composting and manure it can help improve and retain soil fertility, too., There is great scope for enhancing

---

44. Ministry of Finance, **Economic Survey 2015–16**, p. 107.

45. As per the conducted by the *Indian Council of Agricultural Research (ICAR)* – quoted by the **Economic Survey 2015-16**, Vol. 2, p.108.

the use of organic fertilisers as around 67 per cent of Indian soil is characterised by low organic carbon.

(iii) *Nutrient Management:* To maintain soil health and productivity, judicious use of chemical fertilisers, bio-fertilisers and locally available organic manures like farmyard manure, compost, vermi-compost and green manure based on soil testing is necessary.

With over 12 crore farm holdings in India, it is a big challenge to provide soil-testing facilities for overcoming the multi-nutrient deficiencies in soils so as to improve agricultural output. Use of information technology and providing soil fertility maps to farmers can go a long way in efficient nutrient management.

(iv) *Regional disparity in fertilizer consumption:* India has wide regional disparities in the consumption of fertilizers. This may be attributed to the availability of irrigation facilities in the high consuming states (since irrigation is a requirement for proper absorption of fertilizers). It is necessary to reduce the disparities through appropriate soil-testing facilities and other policy measures.

PESTICIDES

Due to the presence of weeds, pests, diseases and rodents, the crop yield losses range from 15 to 25 per cent in India. Even though pesticides are essential for improving crop yields, per hectare pesticide use is much lower in India in comparison with other countries. Presently, India uses a low amount of 0.5 kg per ha pesticide compared to 7.0 kg per ha in the USA, 2.5 kg per ha in Europe, 12 kg per ha in Japan and 6.6 kg per ha in Korea. Besides, there are certain concerns regarding pesticides use in the country –

(i) Use of pesticides without following proper guidelines,

(ii) Use of sub standard pesticides, and

(iii) Lack of awareness about pesticide use.

These practices have given rise to *pesticide residues* being found in food products in India, posing major threats to the environment and human beings. Some **policy steps** which may be suggested in this regard are:

(i) Farmers need to be educated about the classification of insecticides on the basis of their toxicity and their suitability for aerial application.

(ii) The CIBRC (Central Insecticide Board and Registration Committee) has issued guidelines for the application of pesticides, their dosage, minimum intervals to be maintained, and the levels of toxicity. This information needs to be widely disseminated among farmers.

(iii) Greater focus on IPM (Integrated Pest Management) which will encompass a judicious mix of pest control methods by leveraging the cultural, mechanical, biological methods and need-based use of chemical pesticides. It gives preference to the use of bio-pesticides and bio-control agents, too.

(iv) Being environment friendly, nontoxic and cost effective, bio-pesticides need to be promoted among small farmers to improve productivity in agriculture.

AGRI-CREDIT & FARMER'S SUICIDES

Agricredit is an important mediating input for agriculture to improve productivity. Access to institutional credit enables the farmer to enhance productivity by investing in machinery and purchase of variable inputs like fertilizers, quality seeds, and manure and providing funds till the farmer receives payment from sale of produce, which is at times delayed and staggered. Input use by farmers is sensitive to credit flows to the agriculture sector. Some of the concerns regarding agri-credit are as given below.

(i) Predominance of *informal sources* of credit: farmers still avail as much as 40 per cent of the funds from informal sources – 26 per cent of the total agricultural credit flow from the local money lenders (highly exploitative lenders).[46] In respect of high interest rates, **DBT** may be considered to replace subvention of interest rates. The intermediation and refinance model to promote agricultural credit needs to be revisited and replaced with DBT that shall subsidise the interest paid by the farmer, instead of subsidising refinance to financial institutions.

(ii) The ratio of agricultural credit to agricultural GDP has increased from 10 per cent in 1999–2000 to around 40 per cent by 2015–16. However, the share of long-term credit (for more than 5 years) in agriculture or investment credit has declined from 55 per cent in 2006–07 to 37 per cent in 2015–16. The decline in the share of long-term credit in agriculture needs to be arrested and reversed.

(iii) There is regional disparity in the distribution of agricultural credit. The coverage is very low in the north-eastern and eastern regions of the country.

(iv) Crop Loans being short-term (for less than 15 months) in nature are meant to meet the current expenditure till the crop is harvested fail to promote major investments in agriculture. Farm loans upto Rs. 3 lakh are disbursed at an interest rate of 7 per cent per annum (effective interest rate becomes 4 per cent after 3 per cent interest subvention). For the fiscal 2017-18, farm credit has been increased by the **Union Budget 2017-18** to Rs. 10 lakh crore (which was Rs. 9 lakh crore for the year 2016-17, as per the *Economic Survey 2016-17*).

Farmer's Suicide

Bankruptcy and indebtedness have been cited as a major cause for farmer's suicides (around 37 per cent of all suicides by the farmers) in the country in which local money-lenders were usually portrayed as the villain. But as per the latest NCRB (National Crime Records Bureau) data, 80 per cent of the farmers who committed suicides in 2015 due to 'bankruptcy or debts' had borrowed money from institutional sources (banks and registered microfinance institutions). Besides, the country has seen a threefold increase in the famers' suicide due to bankruptcy and indebtedness (from 1163 of 2014 to 3097 in 2015). In 2015, a total of 8007 farmers committed suicides due to various reasons. It was for the *first time* that the NCRB categorised farmers' suicides due to debt or bankruptcy based on the source of loans.

Looking at the current scenario only the size of fund allocated by the government for agriculture credit does not look sufficient. India needs to strengthen other support systems also related to enhancing the farm income together with expanding the agriculture insurance in a speedy manner.

AGRICULTURE EXTENSION SERVICES

Another key input to farm sector is 'agriculture extension services (AES)'. These services can improve productivity by providing timely advisory services to farmers to adopt best practices, technology, meet with contingencies, market information etc. The AES (also called

46. **NSSO**, 70th Round data quoted by the **Economic Survey 2015-16**, Vol. 2, p. 110.

'rural advisory services') has been defined[47] as "consisting of all the different activities that provide the information and services needed and demanded by farmers and other actors in rural settings to assist them in developing their own technical, organisational and management skills and practices so as to improve their livelihoods and well-being".

Though there are multiple agencies in India offering agricultural advisory services the system is not efficient enough due to the following reasons:[48]

(i) Lack of functional autonomy,

(ii) Rigid hierarchical structures leading to lack of innovative methods of providing extension services, and

(iii) Coordination failures at multiple levels.

For the improvement of the AES in the country the suggested policy steps are:[49]

(i) Implementing a new scheme or additional outlays in existing schemes.

(ii) Need of 'one-stop-shop' that offers both hardware and software solutions to raise the incomes of farmers, especially small and marginal farmers.

(iii) Need of an approach which is 'neutral to input, crop and region'.

(iv) Minimizing wastage in inputs as well as produce, till it leaves the farm gate.

(v) Efforts to enhance post harvest processing/value added activities at the farm.

(vi) Need to share with the farmer, information on weather, in order to improve yield, and minimize damage to crops.

(vi) Promoting inter and rotational cropping and efficient utilization of the inputs.

(vii) Need to shift to demand-driven agricultural advisory services.

(viii) Need of a virtual connect, using IT (mobile and internet) and integration of agricultural extension services.

Over the time, the GoI has taken variety of initiatives[50] to strengthen the AES in the country, major ones being – *Kisan TV* set up; broadcasting of agri-information by AIR; *Agri-Clinic & Agri-Business* (by agriculture graduates); Extension education institutes set up; model training courses for horticulture, animal husbandry, etc started; National Centre for Management of Agricultural Extension (acronym for which is *MANAGE*) set up as an apex institute to train middle and senior level officers of the states/UTs.

PMFBY

The Government of India launched a new agricultural insurance scheme in January 2016. The new scheme[51]—Pradhan Mantri Fasal Bima Yojana (PMFBY)—has been termed as a *path breaking scheme for farmers' welfare*. The highlights of this scheme are as given below:

• There will be a uniform premium of only 2 per cent to be paid by farmers for all kharif crops and 1.5 per cent for all rabi crops.

• In case of annual commercial and horticultural crops, the premium to be paid by farmers will be only 5 per cent.

• The premium rates to be paid by farmers are very low and balance premium will be paid by the government to provide full insured amount to the farmers against crop loss on account of natural calamities.

47. *GFRAS (Global Forum for Rural Advisory Services)*, 2010 – quoted by the **Economic Survey 2015-16**, Vol. 2, p. 111.

48. NITI Aayog, **Task Force on Agriculture**, 2015.

49. Ministry of Finance, **Economic Survey 2015–16**, p. 112.

50. Ministry of Finance, **Economic Survey 2015–16**, Pulbication Division, **India 2016;** Ministry of Finance, **Economic Survey 2014–15**.

51. **Government of India**, N. Delhi, January 13th, 2016.

- There is no upper limit on Government subsidy. Even if balance premium is 90 per cent, it will be borne by the Government.

- 25 per cent of the likely claim will be settled directly on farmers account and there will be one insurance company for the entire state as well as farm level assessment of loss for localised risks and post harvest loss.

- Earlier, there was a provision of *capping* the premium rate which resulted in low claims being paid to farmers. This capping was done to limit Government outgo on the premium subsidy. This capping has now been removed and farmers will get claim against full sum insured without any reduction.

- The use of technology will be encouraged to a great extent. Smartphones will be used to capture and upload data of crop cutting to reduce the delays in claim payment to farmers. Remote sensing will be used to reduce the number of crop cutting experiments.

The PMFBY replaced the existing[52] *NAIS (National Agricultural Insurance Scheme)* of 1999 and *Modified NAIS* of 2010–11. The scheme is being implemented by the private sector as well as the public sector (AICIL) agriculture insurance companies. The scheme is estimated to cover 50 per cent of the cropped area by 2018-19 (which was 30 per cent by 2016-17), as per the **Union Budget 2017-18**. Looking at the frequent droughts and floods, this scheme is seen as an important initiative from the government.

NATIONAL MISSION FOR SUSTAINABLE AGRICULTURE (NMSA)

The NMSA, launched in 2011–12, **aims** at enhancing food security and protection of resources such as land, water, biodiversity and genetic resources by developing strategies to make Indian agriculture more resilient to climate change.[53] The *Economic Survey 2011–12* discusses the *Impacts of Climate Change on Indian Agriculture* in the following points:

(i) Indian agriculture, with two-third rainfed area remains vulnerable to various vagaries of monsoon, besides facing occurrence of drought and flood in many parts of the country. Natural calamities such as drought and flood occur frequently in many parts of the country.

(ii) Climate change will aggravate these risks and may considerably affect food security through direct and indirect effects on crops, soils, livestock, fisheries and pests. Building climate resilience, therefore, is critical.

(a) Potential adaptation **strategies** to deal with the adverse impacts of climate change are :

(b) Developing cultivars tolerant to heat, moisture and salinity stresses;

(c) Modifying crop management practices; improving water management;

(d) Adopting new farm practices such as resource-conserving technologies;

(e) Crop diversification; improving pest management;

---

52. Ministry of Finance, **Economic Survey 1990–2000** (New Delhi: Government of India, 2000); Ministry of Finance, **Economic Survey 2010-11** (New Delhi: Government of India, 2011).

53. *Prime Minister's Council on Climate Change (PMCCC)* approved the Mission in September 2010 and the Ministry of Agriculture initiated activities under the Mission in 2011–12.

(f) Making available timely weather-based advisories;

(g) Crop insurance; and harnessing the indigenous technical knowledge of farmers.

The Indian Council of Agricultural Research has initiated a scheme on *National Initiative on Climate Resilient Agriculture (NICRA)*. The initiative has been planned as a multi-disciplinary, multi-institutional effort covering crops, livestock and fisheries, and focusing mainly on adaptation and mitigation of climate change in agriculture. It also has a component for demonstration of climate-coping technologies on farmers' fields in 100 most vulnerable districts. State-of-the-art infrastructure is being set up at key research institutes to undertake frontier research on climate change adaptation and mitigation.

WTO AND THE INDIAN AGRICULTURE: PROSPECTS AND CHALLENGES

With the operationalisation of the provisions of the World Trade Organization (WTO), the process of globalisation commenced in the major parts of the world—the non-member countries, in the coming few years, also started negotiating for entry into the club. There has always been an air of confusion among the members and the non-members of the WTO in assessing the pros and cons of globalisation on the health of their economies. The sector which has created the highest number of deliberations in the WTO as well as views and counterviews has been agriculture—an area of utmost concern for the developed and the developing worlds alike. India is no exception to it, better say it has been among the few countries in the world spear-heading the campaign against the biased provisions of the WTO concerning agriculture.

India was skeptical about the issue even before joining the organisation, but once it became a part of it, it started assessing the situation objectively and moved towards crisis mitigation. Globalisation as such opened unlimited prospects for the economies, but at the same time brought several challenges too. Yes, the challenges were different in nature for the developed and the developing countries. We need to enquire the prospects and the challenges brought by the WTO for Indian agriculture.

Had the agriculture of the leading and politically vocal developing economies not be of subsistence level, the course of the world would have been completely different. It is the biggest hurdle in the process of globalisation and the success of the World Trade Organization. Yes, the process of converting the sector into an industry has already started in most of the leading developing economies amidst tough resistance from the farmers, political parties and the NGOs alike.

The Prospects

The oldest and the first document regarding the impact of the implementation of the provisions of the WTO, Uruguay Round (1995–2005) was prepared jointly by the World Bank, the GATT[54] and the OECD[55]. According to the joint document, the WTO provisions were supposed to have the following positive impacts on the world trade:

(i) By 2005 there will be an addition of $745 billion in the world merchandise trade.[56]

---

54. General Agreement on Trade and Tariff (GATT) was a multi-lateral arrangement (not an *organisation* like WTO whose deliberations are binding on the member countries) promoting multi-lateral world trade. Now the GATT has been replaced by the WTO (*since January. 1995*).

55. *Organisation for Economic Cooperation and Development* (OECD) was set up as a world body of the developed economies from the Euro-American region, which today includes countries from Asia, too (such as Japan and South Korea). The first idea of 'globalisation' was proposed by the OECD in the early 1980s at one of its Annual Meet (*at Brussels*).

56. Merchandise trade does not include services.

(ii) The *GATT Secretariat* provided a full break-up of the above-projected trade increase in the following way:

    (a) The clothing sector to have a share of 60 per cent.

    (b) The agricultural, forestry and fisheries products to have a share of 20 per cent.

    (c) The processed food, beverages and drinks to have a share of 19 per cent.

It means that due to the implementation of the WTO provisions, there will be only *one per cent* increase in the trade of all other goods excluding the above-cited sectors. It was a highly inflated view and became a matter of debate around the world. But the areas which were projected to have very high increase in their trade were not mere projections either. Member countries went home and started going for their own studies, estimations and projections—India being no exception. We must see the assessment of India:

(i) The products which were projected to have the maximum increase in their trade, India had a traditional great export potential in them. It means the WTO has a great prospect for agriculture in store as maximum goods fell in the agriculture sector. Assuming that India's share in the world exports improves from 0.5 per cent to 1.0 per cent, and India is able to take advantage of the opportunities that are created, the trade gains may conservatively be placed at $2.7 billion extra exports per year. A more generous estimate will range from $3.5 to $7 billion worth extra exports.[57]

(ii) The NCAER (National Council for Applied Economic Research) survey of the WTO on the Indian economy is cited as the best document in this area. The survey[58] had all important things to say on this issue:

(a) The exports of agricultural products will be boosted by the WTO accepted regime.

(b) Only the foodgrains trade that too of wheat and rice were projected to be around $270 billion.

(c) The survey also pointed out that almsot 80–90 per cent of the increased supply of foodgrains to the world is going to originate from only two countries China and India as they are having the scope for increasing production.

(d) But the survey painted a very wretched picture about the preparedness of Indian agriculture sector to exploit the opportunities. It concluded China to be far better than India is this matter.

(e) It suggested almost every form of preparedness for the agriculture sector (at a glance we may have been on the Second Green Revolution in India— basically the revolution is modelled on the findings and suggestions of the survey).

(f) Lastly, the survey ended at a high note of caution and concern that if India fails in its preparations to make agriculture come out as a winner in the WTO regime the economy will emerge as the biggest importer of agricultural products. At the same time the cheaper agri-imports might devastate Indian agricultural structure and the import-dependence

---

57. Ministry of Finance, *Economic Survey 1994–95* (New Delhi: Government of India, 1995).

58. *NCAER Survey* headed by its chairman Rakesh Mohan, GoI, 1994.

may ruin the prospects of a better life for millions of poor Indians.

(g) Even if India does not want to tap the opportunities of the globalising world it has to gear up in the agriculture sector since the world market will hardly be able to fulfil the agri-goods demands of India by 2025. It means, it is only India which can meet its own agri-goods demand in the future.

There is no doubt that the WTO has brought problably **the last opportunity** to make our masses have better income and standard of living via better income coming from agriculture. But provided we go for the right kind of preparation at the right time. There are enough prospects, undoubtedly.

The Challenges[59]

If the WTO brings high prospects for Indian agriculture, it also brings in some hard-boiled challenges in front of it. These could be seen as individual challenges of the similar economies as well as joint challenges of such economies. The **first** category of challenges pertains to the area of relevent preparations, investment and restructuring of agriculture. And the **second** category of challenges are nothing less than a revision in the very agricultural provisions of the WTO itself (around which today revolves the success and faliure of the organisation itself). We may take a look at the challenges before the Indian agriculture:

(i) *Self-sufficiency of Food:* Due to inflow of cheaper foodgrains from the world it would not remain economically viable in

India to produce them and farmers might incline in favour of the profitable agri-products. This will make India heavily dependent upon the world market for its food supplies, marring its achievement of food self-sufficiency. This will have serious political and ethical outcomes for India.[60]

(ii) *Price Stability:* Dependence on the world market for the supply of agricultural products and specially for foodgrains will never be safe for India. As the international market for the products is highly speculative and full of variations (due to natural factors) the price stability will be always in danger—fluctuations hamper the producers and consumers of agri-goods in India. It would be very tough to fight *dumping* of surplus agri-goods from other countries.

(iii) *Cropping Pattern:* The cropping pattern of agriculture might take a very imbalanced shape, which will be highly detrimental to the ecology at large[61] as the farmers will always be in favour of going for the crops and commodities which have comparative price advantage.

(iv) *Weaker Sections:* The benefits of globalisation may not be neutral to areas, crops and the people. There will never prevail a certainty as to which area/region or crops or the people are going to benefit

---

59. The challenges and their possible remedies discussed in this sub-topic are based on some of the finest and timely debates and articles which appeared in many renowned journals and newspapers between the period 1994 and 2007. For better understanding of the readers only the consensual as well as the less-complex parts have been provided here.

60. Almost 50 per cent of the Indian population spends 75 per cent of its total income on the purchase of foodgrains—this is why their standard of life and nutrition depends on the indigenously grown food in a great way. Once the self-sufficiency is lost their lives will depend upon the **diplomatic uncertainties** of its regular supply. It will have serious political outcomes for the political scenario of India. Similarly, irregular supply of the foodgrains will create a high ethical dilemma, too.

61. Farmers might go for highly repetitive kind of cropping pattern creating problems for soil fertility, water crisis, etc. This will have highly adverse effects on the agriculture insurance companies, too.

from globalisation in which year. At the same time globalisation is a process where profits can be made, but it is a market-based concept. Those who are unable to produce due to lack of capital, investment and entrepreneurship will have no gains from it. They will be net consumers or buyers. Since India has a vast population of the weaker sections (as other third world countries have) this population will neither be able to increase its income nor be able to purchase the agri-goods having no price stability.

It means that the weaker sections of India might miss this chance of growth and development. We need to make the benefits of globalisation reach these people, too. This could be done by a timely and society-oriented public policy which is a big challenge.[62]

(v) *WTO Commitments:* There are certain time-bound obligatory commitments of India towards the provisions of the WTO in the area of agriculture, which are highly detrimental to the people and the economy. We may see this challenge from two angles—

(a) According to the agricultural provisions, the total subsidies forwarded by the government to the sector must not cross 10 per cent of the total agricultural outputs. At the same time, exemptions to farmers are to be withdrawn—hampering the public distribution system badly. India's subsidies are still far below this limit, but commitments pose a threat to the sovereign decision making.

(b) The subsidies (with different names) to agriculture, which are forwarded by the developed countries are highly detrimental to Indian agriculture and they are very high, too.[63]

None of the above-given challenges are easy to fight. These are not to be fought by India alone, but almost all developing countries are to face it. Once the WTO comes into operation, many experts from India and abroad have provided ways to fight these challenges, which may be summed up in the following way—

(i) To fight the challenges related to self-sufficiency in food, the price stability and the cropping pattern a judicious mix of suitable kind of agricultural and trade policies will be the need of the hour. To the extent agricultural policy is concerned, India has a limited level of freedom. But the WTO regime does not allow the member countries to impose higher tarrif or tarrif itself to ward off cheaper agri-goods from entering the economy—this is the main reason behind the above challenges. It means it is essential to modify, change or revise the provisions of the WTO.

Similarly, the issue of agricultural subsidies (*the Boxes*) need to be equitably defined so that they do not look biased. Here also the provisions of the WTO need revision.

---

62. The primary examples of corporate and contract farming have given enough hints that economically weaker sections of society have meagre chances of benefitting from the globalisation of agriculture—with major profits going to the corporate houses. Naturally, the governments (centre and states) will need to come up with highly effective policies which could take care of the economic interests of the masses.

The policies may focus on areas such as *healthcare, education, insurance, housing, social security,* etc. Already the governments have started emphasising the delivery and performance of the *social sector* but in the future, more focused and accountable programmes in the sector will be required.

63. Some of the developed economies are still forwarding subsidies to the agricultural areas to the tune of 180–220 per cent! Again, the justification for such high subsidies have been provided by defining agriculture subsidies according to their ease—highly blurring and confusing.

To fight out this typical challenge, experts suggested that the **WTO is not God-given**. Its provisions may go in for change if concerted efforts are made by the member countries in this direction. Like-minded nations who face the same kind of crises should come together and go for a joint effort, from inside the WTO, for the revisions or relaxations in its provisions. Morality related and ethical issues might be used as eye-openers and a handy tool to have the attention of the developed nations and the WTO alike.

Prima facie this suggestion looked as a preach easier said than done. Post-1995 saw a polarisation of like-minded countries inside the WTO that finally culminated into failure of the **Seatle Round** of the WTO deliberations. The most powerful country in the world failed to convene a meeting that too in its most distant region (the Alaska)—a moral triumph of the poor over the rich. This incidence while indicating a possible failure of the WTO itself, boosted the morale of the developing countries to go for stronger groupings and even sub-groupings under the WTO.

After the Doha Round the USA had hinted to forget multilateralism and indicated its intentions towards bilateralism. The European Union had the same intentions, but it did not show it as openly as the USA. The year 2002 came as a watershed period for the WTO when the EU in its new diplomatic move announced to hear the agriculture-related issues of the developing nations. The USA announced the intentions few days after the EU announcement—just few days before the **Cancun Meet** of the WTO. The Hongkong deliberation of the WTO, though it did not give anything concrete to the develolping world, provided enough hope, there is no doubt in it. The real picture emerges in the next meet for which the different pressure groups had serious deliberations on alternatives of bargaining power.

The second level suggestion to India was in the area of preparedness for the WTO regime. India was required to set new and internationally best standards in the area of production by boosting areas such as—research and development, biotechnology, information technology, health and phytosanitary matters. This will make Indian goods and services compete in the international market.[64]

WTO AND AGRICULTURAL SUBSIDIES[65] AMS

The subsidies provided by the government to the agricultural sector (i.e., domestic support) is termed by the WTO as Aggregate Measure of Support (AMS).[66] It is calculated in terms of *product* and *input* subsidies. The WTO argues that the product subsidies like minimum support prices and input subsidies (non-product) like credit, fertilizers, irrigation and power will cut production cost of farming and will give undue advantage to such countries in their access to the world market—such subsidies are called to cause *'distortions'* to the world trade. Such subsidies are not permitted in one sense as they have a minimum permissible limit *de minimis* under the provisions which is 5 per cent and 10 per cent of their total agricultural output in the case of developed and developing countries, respectively.

The Boxes

The agricultural subsidies, in the WTO terminology have in general been identified by 'boxes' which have been given the colours of the

---

64. Because even the agriculture related provisions are modified the global market will always run after the agri-products which are the best—pricewise, qualitywise, etc.

65. A simplified and 'easy-to-understand' analysis done on the basis of the documents of the **Information and Media Relations Division** of the World Trade Organisation Secretariat, Geneva, Switzerland, October, 2007.

66. Defined in **Article 1** and **Annexures 3 & 4,** Agreement on Agriculture (AoA), WTO, 1994.

traffic lights—*green* (means permitted), *amber* (means slow down, i.e., to be reduced) and *red* (means forbidden).

In the agriculture sector, as usual, things are more complicated. The WTO provisions on agriculture has nothing like *red box* subsidies, although subsidies exceeding the reduction commitment levels is prohibited in the *'amber box'*. The *'blue box'* subsidies are tied to programmes that limit the level of production. There is also a provision of some exemptions for the developing countries sometimes called the 'S & D box'.[67]

We may see them individually though they are very much connected in their applied form. The objective meaning of each one of them becomes clear, once one has gone through all of them.

Amber Box

All subsidies which are supposed to distort production and trade fall into the amber box, i.e., all agricultural subsidies except those which fall into the blue and green boxes.[68] These include government policies of **minimum support prices** (as MSP in India) for agricultural products or any help directly related to production quantities (as power, fertilizers, pesticides, irrigation, etc).

Under the WTO provisions, these subsidies are subject to reduction commitment to their minimum level—to 5 per cent and 10 per cent for the developed and the developing countries, respectively, of their total value of agricultural outputs, per annum accordingly. It means, the subsidies **directly related** to production promotion above the allowed level (which fall in either the blue or green box) must be reduced by the countries to the prescribed levels.

In the current negotiations, various proposals deal with issues like deciding the amount by which such subsidies should be reduced further, and whether to set product-specific subsidies or to continue with the present practice of the *'aggregate'* method.

Blue Box

This is the *amber box with conditions.* The conditions are designed to reduce distortions. Any subsidy that would normally be in the amber box, is placed in the blue box if it requires farmers to go for a certain production level.[69] These subsidies are nothing but certain direct payments (i.e., direct set-aside payments) made to farmers by the government in the form of assistance programmes to encourage agriculture, rural development, etc.

At present there are no limits on spending on subsidies in the blue box. In the current negotiations, some countries want to keep blue box as is because they see it as a crucial means of moving away from distorting the amber box subsidies without causing too much hardship. Others want to set limits or reduction commitments on it while some advocate moving these subsidies into the amber box.

Green Box

The agricultural subsidies which cause minimal or no distortions to trade are put under the green box.[70] They must not involve price support.

This box basically includes all forms of government expenses, which are not targeted at a particular product, and all direct income support programmes to farmers, which are not related to current levels of production or prices. This is a **very wide box** and includes all government subsidies like—public storage for food security, pest and disease control, research and extension, and some direct payments to farmers that do not stimulate

---

67. WTO, **Article 6.2, AoA**, 1994.
68. WTO, **Article 6, AoA**, 1994.

69. WTO, **Article 6, Para 5** AoA, 1994.
70. WTO, **Annexure 2, AoA**, and **Para 1** AoA, 1994.

production like restructuring of agriculture, environmental protection, regional development, crop and income insurance, etc.

The green box subsidies are allowed without limits provided they comply with the policy-specific criteria.[71] It means, this box is exempt from the calculation under subsidies under the WTO provisions because the subsidies under it are not meant to promote production thus do not distort trade. That is why this box is called *'production-neutral box'*. But the facts tell a different story.[72]

In the current negotiations, some countries argue that some of the subsidies forwarded under this box (by the developed economies) do seriously distort trade (opposed to the view of minimal distortion as used by Annexure 2)— it is the view of the developing countries. These countries have raised their fingers on the direct payments[73] given by the developed countries to their farmers via programmes like income insurance and income-safety schemes,[74] environmental protection, etc. Some other countries take the opposite view and argue that the current criteria are adequate, and advocate to make it more flexible (so that it could be increased) to take better care of non-trade concerns such as environmental protection and animal welfare.

---

71. WTO, *Annexure 2, AoA*, AoA, 1994.
72. Basically, a large part of this box is used by the farmers in the USA and the European Union as basic investments in agriculture. India as well as other like-minded countries have this view and want this box to be brought under the AMS i.e. under the reduction commitments. The USA at the Hongkong Ministerial meet (December 2005) announced to abolish such subsidies in the next 12 year commencing 2008. The EU also proposed to reduce its 'trade distorting subsidies' by 70 per cent. None of them used the name green box which shows some internal vagueness.
73. WTO, *Para 5, Green Box, AoA,* 1994.
74. WTO, *Para 7, Green Box, AoA,* 1994.

S&D Box

Other than the above-discussed highly controversial boxes of agricultural subsidies, the WTO provisions have defined yet another box, i.e., the Social and Development Box (S & D Box)[75] allows the developing countries for some subsidies to the agriculture sector under certain conditions. These conditions revolve around *human development issues* such as poverty, minimum social welfare, health support, etc., specially for the segment of population living below the poverty line. Developing countries can forward such subsidies to the extent of less than 5 per cent of their total agricultural output.[76]

Export Subsidies

For export subsidy the WTO has provisions in two categories:

(i) Reduction in the total budgetary support on export subsidies, and

(ii) Reduction in the total quantity of exports covered by the subsidy.

Higher reduction commitment for the developed countries and lower for the developing countries are the provisions. But the developed nations forward such an inflated support to their agricultural exports that even after the committed reductions it will be highly price distorting against the agri-exports of the developing countries. It is therefore opposed by the developing countries.

Sanitary and Phytosanitary Measures

The provisions of the WTO allow member countries to set their own health and safety standards provided they are justified on scientific grounds and do not result in arbitrary or unjustified barrier to trade. The provisions encourage use of

---

75. WTO, *Para 8*, *Green Box, AoA,* 1994.
76. WTO, *Article 6.2, AoA,* 1994.

international standards and also include certain special and differential treatment in favour of developing countries.[77]

Though this provision has realised the scope of unjustified kind of health and phytosanitory measures on the developing countries, the developed nations have been beautifully able to do so by validating their health and related rules on scientific grounds. Such instances have distorted trade in favour of these countries and the developing countries' agriculture has been the real loser. The developing countries accuse such measures as the non-tarrif barriers used by the developed nations to block goods from the developing nations.

NAMA

The Non-Agricultural Products Market Access (NAMA) is a part of the WTO provisions which deals with the idea of encouraging market reach to the non-agricultural goods of the member countries.[78] But the encouragement was objected/opposed by the developing countries, especially pointing to the non-tariff barriers enforced by the developed countries. At the Doha Ministerial Conference (November 2001), ministers agreed to start negotiations to further liberalise trade of non-agricultural products. By early 2002, a Negotiating Group on NAMA was created. The members at the meet decided to go for tariff reductions on non-agricultural products adopting the **Swiss Formula.**

One major concern that the members took note was of the small and vulnerable economies for whom a flexibility was committed while going for tariff reductions. For India, market access is not

an issue of tariffs alone, but it means elimination of tariff peaks and tariff escalation in the markets of the developed countries. It will also end the abuse of anti-dumping laws and remove non-tariff barriers (NTBs) used to block goods from developing countries.

Swiss Formula

A variety of alternative methods are possible in the process of tariff reductions—some are more common than others. Some are based on *formulas*. But one thing should be kept in mind that whatever formula be agreed upon it does not have value unless it is properly implemented. Even after a formula or combination of formulas has been agreed upon, the final outcome of tariff reductions may depend on the bargaining capacity between countries.

The **Swiss Formula**[79] belongs to the classification of formulas known as having harmonising impact. Since such a formula prescribes a higher/steeper cut on higher tariffs and lower cuts on lower tariffs it is seen to harmonise the rates by bringing the final rates becoming closer and bridging the gap.

The formula was proposed by Switzerland in the Tokyo round negotiations of GATT (1973–79). But Switzerland opposes using this method in the current agriculture negotiations—it prefers the **Uruguay Round formula.**

The Uruguay Round (1986–94) negotiations in agriculture produced an agreement for developed countries to cut tariffs on agricultural products by an average of 36 per cent over six years (6 per cent per year) with a minimum tariff cut of 15 per cent on each product for the period. It was a version of *flat rate* method of tariff reductions.[80]

77. WTO, *Article 14, AoA,* 1994.

78. As per the provisions of the WTO *fishes, fisheries products* and *forest products* don't fall under agriculture and have been classified as the non-agricultural products.

79. WTO, *"Formula Approaches to Tariff Negotiations"* (Revised), Oct. 2007.

80. *Uruguay Round of GATT,* 1994.

NATIONAL FOOD SECURITY ACT

The National Food Security Act was enacted by the Ministry of Consumer Affairs, Food and Public Distribution by end-December 2013. India's most ambitious and world's largest social welfare programme provides legal right to about 82 crore people for subsidised foodgrains—a historic initiative towards ensuring food and nutritional security. Major highlights of the programme are as given below:

(i) It will cover upto 75 per cent rural and 50 per cent urban population (around two thirds of the total popultion) with uniform entitlement of 5 kg foodgrains per month at highly subsidised prices of Rs. 3, Rs. 2 and Rs. 1 per kg for rice, wheat and coarse grains, respectively. The *poorest of poor* households continue to receive 35 kg foodgrains per household per month under the *Antyodaya Anna Yojna* at the same subsidised prices.

(ii) It provisions for special focus on nutritional support to women and children—*pregnant* women and *lactating* mothers, besides being entitled to nutritious meals as per the prescribed nutritional norms will also receive maternity benefit of at least of Rs. 6,000. *Children* in the age group of 6 months to 14 years will be entitled to take home ration or hot cooked food as per prescribed nutritional norms.

(iii) Eldest woman of eighteen years of age or above will be head of the household for issue of ration card, and if not available, the eldest male member is to be the head of the household.

(iv) For effective implementation, the Act also contains provisions for **reforms** in PDS through *doorstep delivery* of foodgrains, application of information and communication technology (ICT) including end-to-end computerisation,

leveraging *'Aadhaar'* for identification of beneficiaries, diversification of commodities under TPDS, etc.

(v) The Act provisions state and district level **redressal mechanism** with designated officers. The states will be allowed to use the existing machinery for District Grievance Redressal Officer (DGRO), State Food Commission, if they so desire, to save expenditure on establishment of new redressal set up. It also provides for **penalty** on public servants or authority, if found guilty of failing to comply with the relief recommended by the DGRO.

(vi) Provisions have also been made for disclosure of records relating to PDS, **social audits** and setting up of Vigilance Committees in order to ensure transparency and accountability.

The work of identification of eligible households is left to the states/UTs, which may frame their own criteria or use Social Economic and Caste Census (SECC) data, if they so desire. The central government will provide funds to states/UTs in case of *short supply* of food grains from the central pool. In case of non-supply of food grains or meals to entitled persons, the concerned state/UT governments will be required to provide such food security allowance as may be prescribed by the central government to the beneficiaries. In order to address the concern of the states regarding additional financial burden, The central government will provide assistance to the states towards cost of intra-state transportation, handling of foodgrains and FPS dealers' margin, for which norms will be developed. This will ensure timely transportation and efficient handling of foodgrains.

While enacting the Act, the Ministry estimated an annual foodgrains requirement of 61.23 MT, which will accrue estimated food subsidy of Rs.1,24,724 crore. Meanwhile, a High Level Committee (headed by Shanta Kumar), by early 2015, suggested the Government of India to revise the covergare population under the Act from 67 to 40 per cent. The recommendation was severely criticised by the experts and the political parties in the country. The government is yet to take the final call on the issue.

FOOD PROCESSING

Indian food processing industry (FPI)[81] has not grown with the pace which we see in the developed countries—there has been certain reasons for it:

(i) India has a lower urban population (around 30 per cent of the population).

(ii) Whatever urban population India has it does not have the *typical* urban food habits. As majority of it is second or third generation in the urban areas they still continue with the non-urban/rural food habits detrimental to the consumption of the agro-precessed items.

(iii) In recent times, there has come enough awareness among the population across the country regarding the chemicals which are used in the agro-processing industries—creating a general tendency to avoid such food articles (much damage has been done to the industry by the 'fast foods', adulteration in food items such as sweets, milk, etc.).

(iv) A wave across the world towards comsuming more 'which comes on plants' than 'what is produced in plants'. A similar wave of 'slow food' has gained popularity across Europe and other parts of the world originating from France.

Moreover, India's agro-processing policy today guided by the following **drivers**:

(i) As urban population rises and urban food habits evolve, there will be increased demand for processed foods as it happened across the urbanising developed world. The economy has already started having an informed and increased demand in such food items as 'dietary habits' are in the process of shift (NSSO, 2014).

(ii) External dimension to it was also accepted by the government by mid-1990s. As per a joint GATT-OECD study, processed food are supposed to account for around 19 per cent of the increased trade after the provisions of the WTO are implemented.

(iii) A very high percentage of food items which have short shelf life get wasted in India. It does not look good for a country which is crippled by the short-supply of food and high rate of hunger.

Importance

While increased productivity is an essential component of a vibrant agricultural sector, improved post-harvest handling and processing is essential to ensure value addition, reduction in wastage and to make good quality products reach the markets. Too often, even when the yields are high, producers lose income due to poor post-harvest practices.

Aim: Food processing aims to make food more *digestible*, *nutritious* and *extend the shelf life*. Due to the seasonal variations high levels of wastage or shortages can arise if adequate measures are not taken to preserve and store the food. Food processing covers all the processes that food items go through from the *farm to the consumers' plate*. It includes basic cleaning, grading and packaging as in case of fruits and vegetables and also alteration of the raw material to a stage just before the final preparation. Value addition processes to make 'ready-to eat' food like bakery products, instant

---

81. The analyses are based on several volumes of *Economic Survey, India* and the relevant documents of the Government of India between the period 2005 and 2015.

foods, flavored and health drinks, etc., are also included in this *definition*.

Food processing *offers* an opportunity for the creation of sustainable livelihoods and economic development for the rural communities. Food processing has come a long way in the last few decades. The everchanging lifestyles, food habits and tastes of customers globally have altered the dynamics of the industry. Food processing benefits all the sections of the society:

(i) *Farmers* get better returns, higher yield, and lower the risks drastically;

(ii) *Consumers* get access to a greater variety, better prices and new products;

(iii) *Economy* gets benefit via creation of new business opportunities, while the workforce gets employment.

With a huge production base, India can easily become one of the leading food suppliers to the world while at the same time serving the vast growing domestic market of over a billion people. India's large market size with growing incomes and changing life styles also creates incredible market opportunities for food producers, food processors, machinery makers, food technologists and service providers in this sector.

Growth in the food processing sector is also expected to open up a lot of opportunities for players having strong linkages in the agri-value chain. Significant investment opportunities are yet to be tapped in the areas of *supply chain management, cold storages, financing, retailing* and *exports*.

Historically, agriculture and FPI have been plagued by factors such as:

(i) Low public investment,

(ii) Poor infrastructure,

(iii) Inadequate credit availability, and

(iv) High levels of fragmentation.

Rules and Regulations

Rules and regulations regarding the industry is as given below:

(i) Most food processing enterprises have been exempted from industrial licensing under the Industries (Development and Regulation) Act, 1951 with the exception of beer and alcoholic drinks, and items reserved for the small scale sector.

(ii) For foreign investment, automatic approval is given even up to 100 per cent equity for a majority of processed foods.

(iii) For manufacture of items reserved for MSEs, FDI is permissible under automatic route up to 24 per cent.

Attractive **packaging** makes the product more appealing to consumers who are therefore willing to pay more if the product offered is of good quality and easy to use. The policy initiatives of the government also include assistance for opening up of mega food park, cold chain and development of agri-export zones, skill development and R&D activities. Apart from the various schemes from the central government, various state governments are implementing their own food processing promotion policies and schemes.

Contributions

The sector contributes around 10 per cent of GDP in agriculture and manufacturing sector. During the last 5 years, FPI sector has been growing at an average annual growth rate (AAGR) of around 6 per cent as compared to around 4 per cent in agriculture and 7 per cent in manufacturing.

Infrastructure Development

The Ministry of Food Processing Industries (MoFPI) has been implementing a scheme for the creation of modern enabling infrastructure which includes mega food parks scheme, scheme for cold chain, value addition and preservation infrastructure and the scheme for construction and modernisation of abattoirs.

Mega Food Parks Scheme (MFPS)

The Mega Food Parks Scheme *aims* to accelerate the growth of the food processing industry in the country by facilitating establishment of strong food processing infrastructure backed by an efficient supply chain. Under this scheme, capital grant of 50 per cent of the project cost is provided in general areas and 75 per cent in difficult and ITDP (Integrated Tribal Development Programme) notified areas (with a ceiling of Rs 50 crore). Each Mega Food Park takes about 30–36 months to be completed.

Cold Chain, Value Addition and Preservation

The Scheme for Cold Chain, Value Addition, and Preservation Infrastructure was approved in 2008 with an *objective* to provide integrated and complete cold chain, value addition and preservation infrastructure facilities without any break, for perishables from the farm gate to the consumer. The assistance under the scheme includes financial assistance (grant-in-aid) of 50 per cent of the total cost of plant and machinery and technical civil works in general areas and 75 per cent for the North Eastern region and difficult areas (subject to a maximum of Rs. 10 crore).

Modernisation of Abattoirs

The Ministry has approved 10 projects in first phase which are at various stages of progress. Two projects have been completed. A proposal for up-scaling the scheme is under consideration.

Technology Upgradation

Under the Scheme for Technology Upgradation, Establishment, Modernisation of FPIs, financial assistance is provided in the form of 'grants-in-aid' for the setting up of new food processing units as well as technological upgradation and expansion of existing units in the country. The GoI extends financial assistance in the form of grant-in-aid to entrepreneurs at 25 per cent of the cost of Plant & Machinery and Technical Civil Works subject to a maximum of Rs. 50 lakhs in general areas or 33.33 per cent subject to a maximum of Rs. 75 lakhs in difficult terrains. The Scheme has now been transferred to the states with the launching of the National Mission on Food Processing (NMFP) in the 12th Plan.

Quality Assurance, Codex Standards, R & D and Promotional Activities

In the global market today, quality and food safety gives a competitive edge which is an important factor for the enterprises producing processed foods and providing services. Apart from domestic standards for food products, processes and management practices, Codex prescribes international standards for safety and quality of food as well as codes of good manufacturing practices, which are accepted worldwide. Further, equal emphasis is required to be accorded to R&D activities for the development of innovative products, cost effective processes and efficient technologies for the food processing sector. The scheme for Food Safety Codex and R&D has been successful in making a dent in this area in the country.

Human Resource Development

The human resource development is very critical for sustained growth in the sector. Extensive training and entrepreneurship development is given top priority:

(i) Creation of infrastructural facilities for running degree/diploma courses in food processing

(ii) Entrepreneurship Development Programmes (EDP)

(iii) Setting up of Food Processing Training Centres (FPTC)

(iv) Training at recognised national/state-level institutes, etc., sponsored by MoFPI or other training programme

Indian Institute of Crop Processing Technology (IICPT)

Indian Institute of Crop Processing Technology (IICPT) formerly known as Paddy Processing Research Centre (PPRC), Thanjavur is an autonomous organisation under the administrative control of MoFPI. It has been in existence for the last three decades. As other commodities such as millets, pulses and oil seeds are gaining importance, it was decided in 2001 to expand the mandate of this Institute to include the above commodities also. The institute is being upgraded into a national level institute now.

National Meat and Poultry Processing Board (NMPPB)

The GoI established the National Meat and Poultry Processing Board 2009. The Board is an autonomous body and was initially funded by the GoI for 2 years and is be managed by the industry itself. This industry-driven institution has been launched to work as a *National Hub* for addressing all key issues related to the meat and poultry processing sector for its systematic and proper development. The Board serves as a *single window* service provider for producers, manufacturers and exporters of meat and meat products, for promoting the meat industry as a whole.

Indian Grape Processing Board

The GoI, in 2009, gave its approval for the establishment of the Indian Grape Processing Board (IGPB) at Pune, Maharashtra which is close to the principal grape growing and processing areas in the country. The functions and objectives of the IGPB are:

(i) To focus on R&D, extension, quality upgradation, market research, information, domestic and international promotion of *Indian wine*.

(ii) To foster sustainable development of Indian wine industry.

(iii) To formulate a vision and action plan for the growth of Indian wine sector including R&D for quality upgradation in new technologies.

During three years of its existence, the Board has focused on the promotion of *Wines of India* in the domestic as well as international market by participating in important and relevant exhibitions, fairs, consumer awareness and training programmes, undertaking advocacy work with the various state governments/central ministries on various issues related to taxes/levies and promotion aspects. The Board is going to implement a traceability programme "wine-net" for standards and quality in wine sector.

National Institute of Food Technology, Entrepreneurship & Management (NIFTEM)

For developing a vibrant food processing sector, India needs not only world-class food technologists to undertake R&D in frontier areas, develop new products, processes, technologies and machineries, set food standards and protocol testing, but also business leaders and managers well versed with the requisite mix of technologies, management and entrepreneurship who can exploit major opportunities in the expanding global food trade.

In the emerging global scenario, there is a need for setting up of an institution of global excellence, which could cater to the needs of the booming food processing sector, various stakeholders such as entrepreneurs, industry, exporters, policymakers, government and other research institutions. NIFTEM was conceived by MoFPI to create an international *Center of Excellence* in the field of Food Sciences & Food Technology. NIFTEM will grow into an apex world class institute to promote cooperation and networking among existing institutions both within the country and various international bodies. The institute will offer high quality educational, research and management programme specific to the food industry, provide referral advise on food standards, disseminate knowledge on the food sector and provide business incubation facility. It is situated (2006) at Kundli, Sonipat (Haryana).

National Mission on Food Processing (NMFP)

India enjoys a 'competitive advantage' in food processing sector given its huge production base of a number of agricultural, dairy, fishing and horticultural items. To ensure that this sector gets the stimulus it deserves, the MoFPI has been implementing a number of schemes for infrastructure development, technology upgradation and modernisation, human resources development and R&D in this sector. In the context of the *12th Plan*, it is felt that there is a need to decentralise the implementation of schemes through involvement of the states/UTs for better outreach, supervision, monitoring and ensuring job creation. Accordingly, National Mission on Food Processing (NMFP) was launched as a centrally sponsored scheme in 2012. The NMFP contemplates establishment of a National Mission as well as corresponding Missions at the state and district levels.

Challenges

The most important challenges among others in the sector include avoidance of the significant 'wastage' at every level and in value addition. High food inflation, high post-harvest wastage particularly in fruits and vegetables, low level of processing, etc., are the main challenges in the food processing sector. Addressing these core concerns by reducing wastage of food, increasing

shelf life and enhancing value of agricultural produce are some of the objectives of the food processing industry. In terms of employment, the contribution of the sector is significant. Presently, the total number of *persons employed* in the food processing sector is about 17 lakh. The National Manufacturing Policy, 2011 seeks to give special attention to food processing industries to ensure job creation. To promote industrial growth along with the objective of inclusive growth the food processing sector will get higher attention from the government.

Outlook for the Future

So that the FPI expands as per the expectations emphasis is needed on the following fronts:

(i) Given the need for *wastage reduction*, *value addition* and the *high employment* potential of the sector, there is a need to substantially step up the allocations given the importance of the sector in terms of its contribution to the economy.

(ii) There is also a need for greater *involvement of state* governments for better outreach, supervision and monitoring (keeping this in view, government has already launched centrally sponsored National Mission on Food Processing).

(iii) There is a need for greater emphasis on creation of infrastructure with full participation of state governments and *private sector*. The main infrastructure schemes for setting up food parks and cold chains are at present 'closed ended'. This should be 'open ended' permitting the Ministry to fund all the viable projects proposals received under these schemes rather than limiting the number of projects.

(iv) The credit dimension of the sector is also a vital issue.

With the idea of 'Team India' under the NITI Aayog, it is believed that a new synergy will come to the food processing industry. The nature of industry requires active participation from not only the concerned states, but the loacal bodies, too. Experts believe that the emerging emphasis by the government on the issue of 'ease of doing business' will be of great help to the sector.

DOUBLING FARM INCOME

Remunerative farming is not a precondition for enriching farm community only but it is considered the biggest incentive to enhance the agricultural output, too. This is why enhancing farm income has emerged among the most immediate policy concerns for the government in recent times. Recently, a shift has been seen in the Government's strategy towards the agriculture sector—from increasing farm output to increasing farm income. Aimed at *doubling the farmers' income by 2022*, the Government of India has announced a 'seven-point strategy'. The details of the strategy are as given below:

(i) Focus on irrigation with bigger budgets aimed at 'per drop, more crop'.

(ii) Provision of quality seeds and nutrients based on soil health.

(iii) Strengthening warehousing and cold chains to prevent post-harvest crop losses.

(iv) Promoting value addition through food processing.

(v) Creation of a national farm market, removing distortions and e-platform.

(vi) Mitigating risks at affordable cost through suitable kind of farm insurance.

(vii) Promoting ancillary activities like poultry, beekeeping and fisheries.

Agri-experts together with the foremost Indian agriculture scientist M.S. Swaminathan have appreciated this initiative of the Government. The challenge of doubling farmers' income within the prescribed time frame is very much possible supported by a good strategy, well-designed

programmes, adequate resources and good governance.

THE WAY AHEAD

Agriculture sector is estimated to achieve a growth rate of 4.1 per cent during 2016-17, as per the CSO *(1st Advance estimates, January 2017)* on the back of good monsoon (the growth rate was 1.2 per cent in the previous year). The ***Union Budget 2017-18*** has given high priority to the agriculture sector (like the previous Budget) and through it the Government has repeated its commitment towards doubling the farmers' income by 2022. We may have a look on the broad outline of suggested policy steps to strengthen the farm sector of the country in the following points[82]:

(i) Need to increase agricultural output through *productivity* increases by investing in *water-efficient irrigation* to achieve 'more crop per drop', along with effective use of other inputs like fertilizers, quality seeds and pesticides.

(ii) Increasing availability of agricultural produce by reducing wastages.

(iii) Need to increase the share of *processing* by increasing reliance on markets, rationalizing and targeting subsidy, as well as disbursing it through DBT.

(iv) Need of rationalising *fertiliser subsidy* (in an input, crop and region neutral format) and to minimise diversions. The disbursal of subsidy on fertilisers should shift to DBT (direct benefit transfer), benefits of which will be maximized, if all controls (including on imports) on the fertiliser industry/outputs are lifted simultaneously.

---

82. Based on the documents – Ministry of Finance, *Economic Survey 2016-17;* Union Budget 2017-18; — *Economic Survey 2015-16;* NITI Aayog, **Task Force on Agriculture,** 2015 and **Indian Council of Agricultural Research (ICAR).**

(v) *Credit availability* needs attention on several fronts. In respect of high interest rates, the system of DBT may be considered to replace subvention of interest rates.

(vi) *Refinance* model to promote agricultural credit needs to be revisited and replaced with DBT that shall subsidise the interest paid by the farmer (in place of the existing system which subsidises the financial institutions).

(vii) Need of *emulating* (imitating) the success of the dairy industry by other farm produce and producers. The *major* factors behind the success of the dairy industry have been:

(a) integrated co-operative system of milk collection,

(b) transportation,

(c) processing and distribution,

(d) conversion to value added products,

(e) minimising seasonal impact on suppliers and buyers,

(f) retail distribution of milk and milk products, and

(g) sharing of profits with the farmer, which are ploughed back to enhance productivity.

(viii) Need to replace the present system of MSP-based PDS with DBT and *freeing the market* of all controls on domestic movement and import. This vitiates the concept of a market and needs to be discontinued to enhance productivity in agriculture.

(ix) Need to make farming a remunerative profession so that right amount of investment and talent can be attracted to the sector.

The latest **Economic Survey 2016-17** has summarised the situation of the agricultural sector in the following words—"The agriculture sector is entwined in regulation, a living legacy of the era of socialism. While progress has been made in the last two years, producers in many states are still required by the Agricultural Produce Marketing Act to sell only to specified middlemen in authorized markets *(mandis)*. And when this system nonetheless generates price increases deemed to be excessive, the Essential Commodities Act is invoked to impose stock limits and controls on trade that are typically pro-cyclical, thereby exacerbating the problem" (quoted from the *Subramanian Committee Report, 2016* on incentivising pulses production).

CHAPTER 9

INDUSTRY AND INFRASTRUCTURE

*In China I was greatly attracted to the Industrial Co-operatives—
the Indusco movement—and it seems to me that some such movement is
peculiarly suited to India. It would fit in with the Indian background, give
a democratic basis to small industry, and develop the co-operative habit.
It could be made to complement big industry. It must be remembered that,
however rapid might be the development of heavy industry in India, a vast
field will remain open to small and cottage industries. Even in the Soviet
Russia owner-producer co-operatives have played an important part in
industrial growth.**

* As Jawaharlal Nehru writes in **The Discovery of India**, Oxford University Press, 6th Impression (1st Edition 1946, Oxford, London),
N. Delhi, 1994, p. 406.

INTRODUCTION

Many of the western economies have already written their success stories of industrialisation leading to accelerated growth and development by the time India became an independent economy. Independent India needed to rejuvenate its economy from a completely dilapidated state. The country had many tasks in front of it—the abject mass poverty, shortage of foodgrains, healthcare, etc., calling for immediate attention. The other areas of attention included industry, infrastructure, science and technology and higher education, to name a few. All these areas of development required heavy capital investment as they had been severly avoided by the colonial ruler for the last 150 years or so. Increasing the growth of the economy and that too with a faster pace was the urgent need of the economy. Looking at the pros and cons of the available options, India decided that the industrial sector should be the 'prime moving force' (PMF) of the economy—the logical choice for faster growth (a fully established idea at that time, the world over). The secondary sector will lead the economy, was well-decided in the 1930s itself by the dominant political forces among the freedom fighters.

As the government of the time had decided upon an active role for the governments in the economy, naturally, the industrial sector was to have a dominant state role—the expansion of the government-owned companies (i.e., the PSUs) to glorious heights. In many ways the development of the Indian economy has been the development of the government sector. Once this idea of state's role in the economy went for a radical change in the early 1990s with the process of economic reforms, the hangover or the drag of it is still visible on the economy. The industrial policies which the governments announced from time to time basically moulded the very nature and structure of the economy. Any discussion on the Indian economy must start with a survey of the industrial policies of the country. Here we have a brief review of the various industrial policies of India till date.

REVIEW OF INDUSTRIAL POLICIES UPTO 1986

For a better understanding of the Indian economy, it is advisable to look into the various industrial polices. The official stances keep changing with every upcoming industrial policy. Understanding these policies become even more important to understand the finer aspects of the reform process which the country will commence by the early 1990s. Here, a brief review of India's industrial policies are being dicussed to serve the purpose.

Industrial Policy Resolution, 1948

Announced on 8 April, 1948 this was not only the first industrial policy statement of India, but also decided the model of the economic system (i.e., the mixed economy), too. Thus, it was the *first* economic policy of the country. The major highlights of the policy are given below:

(i) India will be a mixed economy.[1]

(ii) Some of the important industries were put under the ***Central List*** such as coal, power, railways, civil aviation, arms and ammunition, defence, etc.

(iii) Some other industries (usually of medium category) were put under a ***State List*** such as paper, medicines, textiles, cycles, rickshaws, two-wheelers, etc.

(iv) Rest of the industries (not covered by either the central or the state lists) were

---

1. Here this should be noted that India will be a planned economy, was well-decided before this industrial policy which articulated for an ***active role*** of the state in the economy. The main objective of planning pointed out at this time was ***poverty alleviation*** by a judicious exploitation of the resources of the country. Only a 'mixed economy' did fit such a wish (***Conference of State Industry Ministers, 1938***).

left open for private sector investment—with many of them having the provision of compulsory licencing.

(v) There was a 10 year period for review of the policy.

Industrial Policy Resolution, 1956

The government was encouraged by the impact of the industrial policy of 1948 and it was only after eight years that the new and more crystallised policies were announced for the Indian industries. The new industrial policy of 1956 had the following major provisions.

1. Reservation of Industries

A clear-cut classification of industries (also known as the **Reservation of Industries**) were affected with three schedules:

(i) Schedule A

This schedule had 17 industrial areas in which the Centre was given complete monopoly. The industries set up under this provision were known as the Central Public Sector Undertakings (CPSUs) later getting popularity as 'PSUs'. Though the number of industries were only 17, the number of PSUs set up by the Government of India went to 254 by 1991. These included those industrial units too which were taken over by the government between 1960 to 1980 under the *nationalisation* drives.[2] These industries belonged to Schedules B and C (other than Schedule A).

(ii) Schedule B

There were 12 industrial areas put under this schedule in which the state governments were supposed to take up the initiatives with a more expansive follow up by the private sector. This schedule also carried the provisions of compulsory licencing. It should be noted here that neither the states nor the private sector had monopolies in these industries unlike Schedule A, which provided monopoly to the Centre.[3]

(iii) Schedule C

All industrial areas left out of Schedules A and B were put under this in which the private enterprises had the provisions to set up industries. Many of them had the provisions of licencing and have *necessarily* to fit into the framework of the social and economic policy of the state and were subject to control and regulation in terms of the Industries Development and Regulation (IDR) Act and other relevant legislations.[4]

The above classification of industries had an in-built bias in favour of government-owned companies (i.e., the CPSUs) which went according to the ideas of the planning process, too. Thus, expansion of the public sector became almost a directive principle of economic policy and the PSUs did expand in the coming times.[5]

It was this industrial policy in which the then PM Pandit Jawaharlal Nehru had termed the PSUs the *'temples of modern India'*, symbolically pointing to their importance.[6] There was a time soon after Independence when the PSUs were regarded as the principal instrument for raising

---

2. The nationalisation of industrial units allowed the government to enter the unreserved areas, which consequently increased its industrial presence. Though the nationalisation was provided a highly rational official reason of **greater public benefit,** the private sector always doubted it and took it as an insecurity and major unseen future hurdle in the expansion of private industries in the country.

3. The Central government had always the option to set up an industry in any of these 12 industrial areas. This happened in the coming years via two methods—first, through *nationalisation* and second, through the *joint sector.*

4. Industrial Policy Resolution, 1956 (30 October).

5. V. M. Dandekar, *Forty Years After Independence* in Bimal Jalan edited *Indian Economy: Problems and Prospects,* Penguin Books, New Delhi, 2004, p. 63.

6. This statement we get in the **Second Five Year Plan (1956–61),** too.

savings and growth in the economy.[7] The rapid expansion of PSUs accounted for more than half of the GDP of the economy by 1988–89.[8]

2. Provision of Licencing

One of the most important developments of independent India, the provision of compulsory licencing for industries, was cemented in this policy. All the schedule B industries and a number of schedule C industries came under this proivision. This provision established the so-called *'Licence-Quota-Permit'* regime (*raj*) in the economy.[9]

3. Expansion of the Public Sector

Expansion of the public sector was pledged for the accelerated industrialisation and growth in the economy—glorification of government companies did start with this policy. The emphasis was on heavy industries.

4. Regional Disparity

To tackle the widening **regional disparity,** the policy committed to set up the upcoming PSUs in the comparatively backward and underdeveloped regions/areas in the economy.[10]

5. Emphasis on Small Industries

There was emphasis on small industries as well as the khadi and village industries.

7. Bimal Jalan, *India's Economic Policy* (New Delhi: Penguin Books, 1992), p. 23.
8. V.M., Dandekar, **'Forty years After Independence'**, p. 64.
9. These industries which were set up after procuring *'licences'* from the government had fixed upper limits of their production known as *'quota'* and they needed to procure timely 'permit' (i.e., permission) for the supply of, raw materials—that is why such a name was given to the whole system.
10. Such a commitment went completely against the *'theory of industrial location'*.

6. Agricultural Sector

The agricultural sector was pledged as a priority.

Importance

This is considered as the most important industrial policy of India by the experts as it decided not only the industrial expansion but structured the very nature and scope of the economy till 1991 with minor modifications. All the industrial policies were nothing but minor modifications in it except the new industrial policy of 1991 which affected deeper and structural changes in it with which India started a wider process of economic reforms.

Industrial Policy Statement, 1969

This was basically a licencing policy which aimed at solving the shortcomings of the licencing policy started by the Industrial Policy of 1956. The experts and industrialists (new comers) complained that the industrial licencing policy was serving just the opposite purpose for which it was mooted. Inspired by the socialistic ideals and nationalistic feelings the licencing policy had the following reasons:

(i) exploitation of resources for the development of all;
(ii) priority of resource exploitation for the industries;
(iii) price-control of the goods produced by the licenced industries;
(iv) checking concentration of economic power;
(v) channelising investment into desired direction (according to the planning process).

In practice, the licencing policy was not serving the above-given purpose properly. A powerful industrial house was always able to procure fresh licences at the cost of a new budding entrepreneur. The price regulation policy via licencing was aimed at helping the public by providing cheaper goods, but it indirectly served the private licenced industries ultimately (as central subsidies were given to the private companies from where it was to benefit the poor in the form of cheaper goods). Similarly, the older and well-established industrial houses were capable of creating hurdles for the newer ones with the help of different kinds of trade practices forcing the latter to agree for sell-outs and takeovers. A number of committees were set up by the government to look into the matter and suggest remedies.[11] The committees on industrial licencing policy review not only pointed out several shortcomings of the policy, but also accepted the useful role of industrial licencing.[12] Finally, it was in 1969 that the new industrial licencing policy was announced which affected the following major changes in the area:

(i) The Monopolistic and Restrictive Trade Practices (MRTP) Act was passed. The Act intended to regulate the trading and commercial practices of the firms and checking monopoly and concentration of economic power.

(ii) The firms with assets of Rs. 25 crore or more were put under obligation of taking permission from the Government of India before any expansion, greenfield venture and takeover of other firms (as per the MRTP Act). Such firms came to be known as the *'MRTP Companies'*. The upper limit (known as the *'MRTP limit'*) for such companies was revised

upward to Rs. 50 crore in 1980 and Rs. 100 crore in 1985.[13]

(iii) For the redressal of the prohibited and restricted practices of trade, the government did set up an *MRTP Commission*.

Industrial Policy Statement, 1973

The Industrial Policy Statement of 1973 introduced some new thinking into the economy with major ones being as follows:

(i) A new classificatory term i.e., *core industries* was created. The industries which were of fundamental importance for the development of industries were put in this category such as iron and steel, cement, coal, crude oil, oil refining and electricity. In the future, these industries came to be known as *basic industries, infrastructure industries* in the country.

(ii) Out of the six core industries defined by the policy, the private sector may apply for licences for the industries which were not a part of schedule A of the Industrial Policy, 1956.[14] The private firms eligible to apply for such licences were supposed to have their total assets at Rs. 20 crore or more.

(iii) Some industries were put under the *reserved list* in which only the small or medium industries could be set up.[15]

---

11. There were four specific committees set up on this issue, namely *Swaminathan Committee (1964), Mahalanobis Committee (1964), R.K. Hazari Committee (1967)* and *S. Dutt Committee (1969)*. The Administrative Reform Commission (1969) also pointed out the short comings of the industrial licencing policy perpetuated since 1956.

12. *Dutt Committee* (New Delhi: Government of India, 1969).

13. The upward revision was logical as it was hindering the organic growth of such companies—neither the capacity addition was possible nor an investment for technological upgrading.

14. Out of the six core industries only the cement and iron & steel industries were open for private investment with the rest fully *reserved* for the central public sector investment.

15. This is considered a follow up to such suggestions forwarded by the *Industrial Licensing Policy Inquiry Committee* (S. Dutt, Chairman) (New Delhi: Government of India, 1969).

(iv) The concept of *'joint sector'* was developed which allowed partnership among the Centre, state and the private sector while setting up some industries. The governments had the discretionary power to exit such ventures in future. Here, the government wanted to promote the private sector with state support.

(v) The Government of India had been facing the foreign exchange crunch during that time. To regulate foreign exchange the Foreign Exchange Regulation Act (FERA) was passed in 1973.[16] Experts have called it a *'draconian'* Act which hampered the growth and modernisation of Indian industries.

(vi) A limited permission to foreign investment was given, with the multinational corporations (MNCs) being allowed to set up subsidiaries in the country.[17]

Industrial Policy Statement, 1977

The Industrial Policy Statement of 1977 was chalked out by a different political set up from the past with a different political fervour—the dominant voice in the government was having an anti-Indira stance with an inclination towards the Gandhian-socialistic views towards the economy. We see such elements in this policy statement:

(i) Foreign investment in the *unnecessary areas* were prohibited (opposite to the IPS of 1973 which promoted foreign investment via technology transfer in the areas of lack of capital or technology). In practice, there was a complete 'no' to foreign investment.[18]

(ii) Emphasis on village industries with a redefinition of the small and cottage industries.

(iii) Decentralised industrialisation was given attention with the objective of linking the masses to the process of industrialisation. The District Industries Centres (DICs) were set to promote the expansion of small and cottage industries at a mass scale.

(iv) Democratic decentralisation got emphasised and the khadi and village industries were restructured.

(v) Serious attention was given on the level of production and the prices of essential commodities of everyday use.

Industrial Policy Resolution, 1980

The year 1980 saw the return of the same political party at the Centre. The new government revised the Industrial Policy of 1977 with few exceptions in the Industrial Policy Resolution, 1980. The major initiatives of the policy were as given below:

(i) Foreign investment via the technology transfer route was allowed again (similar to the provisions of the IPS, 1973).

(ii) The 'MRTP Limit' was revised upward to Rs. 50 crore to promote setting of bigger companies.

16. The FERA got executed on 1 January, 1974. The private sector in the country always complained against this act and doubted its official intentions.

17. This limited permission was restricted to the areas where there was a need of foreign capital. Such MNCs entered the Indian economy with the help of a partner from India—the partner being the major one with 74 per cent shares in the subsidiaries set up for by the MNCs. The MNCs invested via *technology transfer route.* Basically, this was an attempt to make up for the loss being incurred by the FERA. This was the period when most of the MNCs had the chances to enter India. Once economic reforms started by 1991, many of them increased their holdings in the Indian subsidiaries with the Indian partner getting minority shares or a total exit.

18. The permission of working was withdrawn in the case of the already functioning soft drink MNC the *Coca Cola*. The ongoing process of entry to the computer giant *IBM* and automobile major *Chrysller* was soon called off. These instances played a highly negative role when India invited FDI in the post-1991 reform era.

(iii) The DICs were continued with.

(iv) Industrial licencing was simplified.

(v) Overall liberal attitude followed towards the expansion of private industries.

Industrial Policy Resolution, 1985 & 1986

The industrial policy resolutions announced by the governments in 1985 and 1986 were very much similar in nature and the latter tried to promote the initiative of the former. The main highlights of the policies are:

(i) Foreign investment was further simplified with more industrial areas being open for their entries. The dominant method of foreign investment remained as in the past, i.e., **technology transfer,** but now the equity holding of the MNCs in the Indian subsidiaries could be upto 49 per cent with the Indian partner holding the rest of the 51 per cent shares.

(ii) The *'MRTP Limit'* was revised upward to Rs. 100 crore—promoting the idea of bigger companies.

(iii) The provision of industrial licencing was simplified. Compulsory licencing now remained for 64 industries only.[19]

(iv) High level attention on the sunrise industries such as telecommunication, computerisation and electronics.

(v) Modernisation and the profitability aspects of public sector undertakings were emphasised.

(vi) Industries based on imported raw materials got a boost.[20]

(vii) Under the overall regime of FERA, some relaxations concerning the use of foreign exchange was permitted so that essential technology could be assimilated into Indian industries and international standard could be achieved.

(viii) The agriculture sector was attended with a new scientific approach with many *technology missions* being launched by the government.

These industrial policies were mooted out by the government when the developed world was pushing for the formation of the WTO and a new world economic order looked like a reality. Once the world had become one market, only bigger industrial firms could have managed to cater to such a big market. Side by side sorting out the historical hurdles to industrial expansion perpetuated by the past industrial policies, these new industrial policy resolutions were basically a preparation for the *globalised* future world.

These industrial provisions were attempted at liberalising the economy without any slogan of 'economic reforms'. The government of the time had the mood and willingness of going for the kind of economic reforms which India pursued post-1991 but it lacked the required political support.[21]

The industrial policies conjoined with the overall micro-economic policy followed by the government had one major loophole that it was

---

19. A total number of 95 industries had the compulsions of licencing till then. These industries belonged to Schedules B and C of the Industrial Policy Resolution, 1956.

20. This was similar to the policy being followed by Gorbachev in the USSR with the similar fiscal results—a severe balance of payment (BoP) crisis by end 1980s and the early 1990s (J. Barkley Rosser Jin and Marina V. Rosser, *Comparative Economics in A Transforming World,* (New Delhi: PHI & MIT Press, 2004), pp. 469–75)).

21. The *Seventh Five Year Plan (1985–90)* as well as the *Sixth Five Year Plan (1980–85)* had already suggested the government to re-define the role of the state in the economy and permit the private sector into those areas of industries where the presence of the government was non-essential, etc. But such a radical approach might not be digested by the country as it was like 'rolling back' the state. This is why the government of the time looks not going for full-scale economic reforms or vocal moves of liberalisation.

more dependent on foreign capital with a big part being costlier ones. Once the economy could not meet industrial performance, it became tough for India to service the external borrowings—the external events (the Gulf war, 1990–91) vitiated the situation, too. Finally, by the end of 1980s India was in the grip of a severe balance of payment crisis with higher rate of inflation (over 13 per cent) and higher fiscal deficit (over 8 per cent).[22] The deep crisis put the economy in a financial crunch, which made India opt for a new way of economic management in the coming times.

NEW INDUSTRIAL POLICY, 1991

It were the industrial policies of past which had shaped the nature and structure of the Indian economy. The need of the hour was to change the nature and structure of the economy by early 1990s. The Government of India decided to change the very nature of the industrial policy which will automatically lead to change in the nature and scope of the economy. And here came the New Industrial Policy of 1991.

With this policy the government kickstarted the very process of reform in the economy, that is why the policy is taken *more as a process than a policy*.

Background: India was faced with severe balance of payment crisis by June 1991. Basically, in early 1990s, there were inter-connected set of events, which were growing unfavourable for the Indian economy:

(i) Due to the Gulf War (1990–91), the higher oil prices were fastly[23] depleting India's foreign reserves.

(ii) Sharp decline in the private remittances from the overseas Indian workers in the wake of the Gulf War[24], specially from the Gulf region.

(iii) Inflation peaking at nearly 17 per cent.[25]

(iv) The gross fiscal deficit of the Central Government reaching 8.4 per cent of the GDP.[26]

(v) By the month of June 1991, India's foreign exchange had declined to just *two weeks* of import coverage.[27]

India's near miss with a serious balance of payments crisis was the proximate cause that started India's market liberalisation measures in 1991 followed by a gradualist approach.[28] As the reforms were induced by the crisis of the BoP, the initial phase focussed on macroeconomic stabilisation while the reforms of industrial policy, trade and exchange rate policies, foreign investment policy, financial and tax reforms as well as public sector reforms did also follow soon.

The financial support India recieved from the IMF to fight out the BoP crisis of 1990–91 were having a tag of conditions to be fulfilled by India. These IMF conditionalities required the Indian economy to go for a structural re-adjustment. As the nature and scope of the economy were moulded by the various industrial policies India did follow till date, any desired change in the economic structure had to be induced with the help of another industrial policy. The new

---

22. Vijay Joshi and I.M.D. Little, *India's Economic Reforms, 1991–2001,* (Oxford: Clarendon Press, 1996), p. 17.

23. Ministry of Finance, Economic Survey 1990–91 (New Delhi: Government of India, 1991); Ministry of Finance, Economic Survey 1991–92 (New Delhi: Government of India, 1992).

24. Jeffrey D. Sachs, Ashutosh Varsheny and Nirupam Bajpai, *India in the Era of Economic Reform* (New Delhi: Oxford University Press, 1999), p. 1.

25. Department of Economic Affairs, **'Economic Reforms: Two Years After and the Task Ahead'**, Discussion Paper (New Delhi: Government of India, 1993), p. 6.

26. Ibid.

27. Bimal Jalan, *India's Economic Crisis: The Way Ahead,* (New Delhi: Oxford University Press, 1991), pp. 2–12.

28. Sach, Varseny and Bajpai, *India in the Era of Economic Reforms,* p. 2.

industrial policy, announced by the government on 23 July, 1991 had initiated a bigger process of economic reforms in the country, seriously motivated towards the structural readjustment naturally obliged to 'fulfill' IMF conditionalities.[29] The major highlights of the policy are as follows:

1. De-reservation of the Industries

The industries which were reserved for the Central Government by the IPR, 1956, were cut down to only eight. In coming years many other industries were also opened for private sector investment. At present there are only two industries which are fully or partially reserved for the Central Government:

(i) Atomic energy and nuclear research and other related activities, i.e., mining, use management, fuel fabrication, export-import, waste management, etc., of radioactive minerals (none of the nuclear powers in the world have allowed entry of private sector players in these activities, thus no such attempts look logical in India, too).

(ii) Railways (many of the functions related to the railways have been allowed private entry, but still the private sector cannot enter the sector as a full-fledged railway service provider).

2. De-licencing of the Industries

The number of industries put under the compulsory provision of licencing (belonging to Schedules B and C as per the IPR, 1956) were cut down to only 18. Reforms regarding the area were further followed and presently there are only *five industries*[30] which carry the burden of compulsory licencing:

(i) Aero space and defence related electronics
(ii) Gun powder, industrial explosives and detonating fuse
(iii) Dangerous chemicals
(iv) Tobacco, cigarette and related products
(v) Alcoholic drinks

3. Abolition of the MRTP Limit

The MRTP limit was Rs. 100 crore so that the mergers, acquisitions and takeovers of the industries could become possible. In 2002, a competition Act was passed which has replaced the MRTP Act. In place of the MRTP commission, the Competition Commission has started functioning (though there are still some hitches regarding the compositional form of the latter and its real functions and jurisdictions).

4. Promotion to Foreign Investment

Functioning as a typical closed economy, the Indian economy had never shown any good faith towards foreign capital. The new industrial

---

29. Rakesh Mohan, 'Industrial Policy and Control's, in Bimal Jalan (ed.), *The Indian Economy: Problems and Prospects* (New Delhi: Penguin Books, 1992), pp. 92–123.

30. In 1985–86 there were just 64 industries under the compulsory licencing provision. By the fiscal 2015–16 the number remained five Publications Division, **India 2016** (New Delhi: Government of India, 2016)). Though the numbers are still five, all these five industries have many internal areas which today carry no obligation of licencing. As for example, the electronic industry was under this provision and entrepreneurs needed licences to produce radio, tv, tape-recorder, etc., what to ask of mobile phones, computers, DVDs and i-pods. Now only those electronic goods carry licencing provision which are related to either the aero-space or the defence sectors—thus we see a great number of electronic industries freed from the licencing provision the item 'electronics' still remains under it. Similarly while 'drug & pharma' still belong to the licenced industries, dozens of drugs and pharmaceuticals have been made free of it. The six industries have gone for high-level internal de-licencing since the reforms started.

policy was a pathbreaking step in this regard. Not only the draconian FERA was committed to be diluted, but the government went to encourage foreign investment (FI) in both its forms—direct and indirect. The direct form of FI was called as the foreign direct investment (FDI) under which the MNCs were allowed to set up their firms in India in the different sectors varying from 26 per cent to 100 per cent ownership with them—*Enron* and *Coke* being the flag-bearers. The FDI started in 1991 itself. The indirect form of foreign investment (i.e., in the assets owned by the Indian firms in equity capital) was called the *portfolio investment scheme* (PIS) in the country, which formally commenced in 1994.[31] Under the PIS the *foreign institutional investors* (FIIs) having good track record are allowed to invest in the Indian security/stock market. The FIIs need to register themselves as a stock broker with SEBI. It means India has not allowed *individual foreign investment* in the security market still, only *institutional investment* has been allowed till now.[32]

5. FERA Replaced by FEMA

The government committed in 1991 itself to replace the draconian FERA with a highly liberal FEMA, which same into effected in the year 2000–01 with a sun-set clause of two years.[33]

6. Location of Industries

Related provisions were simplified by the policy which was highly cumbersome and had time-consuming process. Now, the industries were classified into 'polluting' and 'non-polluting' categories and a highly simple provision deciding their location was announced:

(i) Non-polluting industries might be set up anywhere.

(ii) Polluting industries to be set up at least 25 kms away from the million cities.

7. Compulsion of Phased Production Abolished

With the compulsion of phased production abolished, now the private firms could go for producing as many goods and models simultaneously.[34] Now the capacity and capital of industries could be utilised to their optimum level.

---

31. Ministry of Finance, *Economic Survey, 1994–95,* (New Delhi: Government of India, 1995).

32. It becomes very complex and tough to regulate the individual foreign investment in the share market though it is an easier way of attracting foreign exchange. It should be noted that the South East Asian economies which faced financial crisis in 1996–97 all had allowed individual foreign investment in their share market. As the Indian security market was learning the art of regulation in its nascent phase, the government decided not to allow such foreign investment. The logic was vindicated after the South East Asian currency crisis when India had almost no shocks (Ministry of Finance, Economic Survey 1996–97 (New Delhi: Government of India, 1997).

33. The delayed action by the government in the foreign exchange liberalisation was due to the delayed comfort the economy felt regarding the availability of foreign exchange.

34. This was another hurdle which the private sector industries have been complaining about. As the industrial products were completely new to the Indian market and its consumers alike, the government followed this policy with the logic to provide enough time so that the products become domesticised i.e.,development of awareness about the product and its servicing, maintenance, etc. As for example, the MNC subsidiary Phillips India was allowed to produce a highly simple radio *Commandar* and *Jawan* models for comparatively longer periods of time then they were allowed to come up with the smaller fashionable radio sets or two-in-ones and three-in-ones. Such provisions hampered their full capacity utilisation as well as achieving the economy of scale had also been tougher. The new industrial policy of 1991 did away with such impediments. By that time, the Indian consumer as well as the market was fully aware of the modern industrial goods.

8. Compulsion to Convert Loans into Shares Abolished

The policy of nationalisation started by the Government of India in the late 1960s was based on the sound logic of *greater public benefit* and had its origin in the idea of *welfare state*—it was criticised by the victims and the experts alike. In the early 1970s, the Government of India came with a new idea of it. The major banks of the country were now fully nationalised (14 in number by that time), which had to mobilise resources for the purpose of planned development of India. The private companies who had borrowed capital from these banks (when the banks were privately owned) now wanted their loans to be paid back. The government came with a novel provision for the companies who were unable to repay their loans (most of them were like it)—they could opt to convert their loan amounts into equity shares and hand them over to the banks. The private companies which opted this route (this was a compulsory option) ultimately became a government-owned company as the banks were owned by the Government of India—this was an *indirect* route to nationalise private firms. Such a compulsion which hampered the growth and development of the Indian industries was withdrawn by the government in 1991.[35]

The picture presented by the New Industrial Policy of 1991 was taken by many experts, the opposition in the Parliament and even the public figures as well as the business and industry of the country as a *'rolling back'* of the state. The glorious role given to the state by the Nehruvian economy seemed completely toppled down. Any one idea the new policy challenged was an emphatic good bye to the 'control regime' perpetuated till now by the government. There was a coalition of interests of politicians, bureaucrats, multinationals as well as the domestic industrial and business houses whose interests were sheltered and by the control regime.[36] Thus, a memorandum to the government requesting not to dismantle the control regime by the major industrial houses of India as well as arrival of the *'Swadeshi Jagaran Manch'* were not illogical. But the governments continued with the reform programme with politically permissible pace and a time came when the same industrial houses requested the government (2002) to expedite the process of reform. Now the Indian industry and business class has been able to understand the economics of 'openness' and a different kind of the mixed economy. But the process of reforms have still to go miles before its real benefits start reaching the masses and development together with reform could be made a mass movement.

This is why experts have suggested that only assuming that reforms will benefit the masses will not be enough to make it happen politically, but the governments, the administrative agencies and the economists all need to link it positively to *mass welfare*—it might require to create a popular climate and form the political coalitions in favour of the argument that privatisation and accordingly restructured labour laws are basically aimed at creating jobs, better job prospects, alleviating poverty, enriching education and

---

35. Combined with nationalisation, this *indirect route* to nationalisation failed to provide the confidence among the entrepreneurs that the industrial units they are intending to set up will be owned by them. This discouraged entrepreneurship in India while taking risk. The abolition of this compulsion was an indirect indication by the government of no more direct or indirect nationalisation in future. This has served the purpose, there is no doubt in it.

36. This nexus of the interests of the vested groups to the control regime of the economy has been beautifully elaborated by Rakesh Mohan in **'Industrial Policy and Controls'** pp. 92–123. He also points out that the control system perpetuating the academic and intellectual ideological leanings negated the very need for re-examination of the system. The 'planners' and the 'bureaucrats' were able to preserve their powers via the control regime did everything to maintain the status quo, Rakesh Mohan further adds.

providing healthcare to the masses.[37] In the coming times, the government went from one to another generations of the reforms, setting new targets and every time trying to make reforms socio-politically possible.

Reforms with the human face was one such attempt of the United Progressive Alliance in 2003 when it formed the government at the Centre. It was believed that the 'India Shining' slogan of the outgoing government (i.e., the NDA) was correct, but remained localised in its effects to the urban middle class only.[38] The new government seemed taking lessons from the past and tried to make India shine for the rural masses, too. Its one programme, the *Bharat Nirman* (a rural infrastructure focused programme), could be seen as a political attempt to make it happen.[39]

Only the coming times will tell as to what extent the government has been able to educate the masses (better say the voters who vote!) the needful logic of the reforms.

37. First of the series of such suggestions came from Sach, Varshney and Bajpai, *India in the Era of Economic Reforms,* p. 24).

38. It should be noted that *'reform with the human face'* was not a new slogan or call given by the UPA Government but this was the same slogan with which the reform programme was launched by the Rao-Manmohan Government in 1991—it has only been 're-called back' by the new government with a new committment to live it up.

39. Point should be noted that **Bharat Niraman** has been the only time-bound programme of infrastructure building in rural areas which is supposed to be completed within four years (the time left out of the total term of the Government when the programme was launched). The UPA naturally, tries to make it a political statement and a point for the next General Elections—development becoming an issue of real politics.

DISINVESTMENT

Disinvestment is a process of selling government equities in public sector enterprises. Disinvestment in India is seen connected to three major inter-related areas, namely—

(i) A tool of public sector reforms[40]

(ii) A part of the economic reforms started in mid-1991. It has to be done as a complementary part of the *de-reservation of industries*.[41]

(iii) Initially motivated by the need to raise resources for budgetary allocations.[42]

The approach towards public sector reforms in India has been much more cautious than that

40. Publication Division, **India 1991** (New Delhi: Government of India, 1992).

41. The de-reservation of industries had allowed the private sector to enter the areas hitherto reserved for the Central Government. It means in the coming times in the unreserved areas the PSUs were going to face the international class competitiveness posed by the new private companies. To face up the challenges the existing PSUs needed new kind of technological, managerial and marketing strategies (similar to the private companies). For all such preparations there was a requirement of huge capital. The government thought to partly fund the required capital out of the proceeds of disinvestment of the PSUs. In this way disinvestment should be viewed in India as a way of increasing investment in the divested PSUs (which we see taking place in the cases of BALCO, VSNL, etc.).

42. Right since 1991 when disinvestment began, governments have been using the disinvestment proceeds to manage fiscal deficits in the budget at least up to 2000–01. From 2000–01 to 2002–03 some of the proceeds went for some social sector reforms or for labour security. After 2003 India established National Investment Fund to which the proceeds of disinvestment automatically flow and is not regarded as a *capital receipt* of the Union Government. This idea of Indian experiment with disinvestment was articulated by Sach, Varshney and Bajpai, *India in the Era of Economic Reforms*, pp. 62–63.

of the other developing countries. India did not follow the radical solution to it—under which outright privatisation of commercially viable PSUs is done and the unviable ones are completely closed.[43] There was an emphasis on increasing functional autonomy of public sector organisations to improve their efficiency in the 1980s in India as part of the public sector reforms. Once the process of economic reforms started in the early 1990s, disinvestment became a part of the public sector reforms. The C. Rangarajan Commission on Disinvestment of the Public sector Enterprises (1991) went on to suggest the government on the issue in a highly commendable and systematic way, taking empirical notes from the experiences of disinvestment around the world. The government started the process of disinvestment in 1991 itself. In 1997 the goverment did set up a Disinvestment Commission to advice upon the various aspects of the disinvestment process. The financial year 1999–2000 saw a serious attempt by the government to make disinvestment a political process to expedite the process of disinvestment in the country—first a Disinvestment Department and later a full-fledged Ministry of Disinvestment was set up.[44] The new government (UPA) dismantled the Ministry of Disinvestment and today only the Department of Disinvestment is taking care of the matter, working under the Ministry of Finance.

Types of Disinvestment

Since the process of disinvestment was started in India (1991), its consisted of *two official types*. A brief discussion on them is given below:

1. Token Disinvestment

Disinvestment started in India with a high political caution—in a symbolic way known as the *'token' disinvestment* (presently being called as 'minority state sale'). The general policy was to sell the shares of the PSUs maximum upto the 49 per cent (i.e., maintaining government ownership of the companies). But in practice, shares were sold to the tune of 5–10 per cent only. This phase of disinvestment though brought some extra funds to the government (which were used to fill up the fiscal deficit considering the proceeds as the 'capital receipts') it could not initiate any new element to the PSUs, which could enhance their efficiency. It remained the major criticism of this type of disinvestment, and experts around the world started suggesting the government to go for it in the way that the ownership could be transferred from the government to the private sector. The other hot issue raised by the experts was related to the question of using the *proceeds* of disinvestment.

2. Strategic Disinvestment

In order to make disinvestment a process by which efficiency of the PSUs could be enhanced and the government could de-burden itself of the activities in which the private sector has developed better efficiency (so that the government could concentrate on the areas which have no attraction for the private sector such as social sector support for the poor masses), the government initiated the process of strategic disinvestment. The government

43. As was done by **Margaret Thatcher** in the UK in the mid-1980s. Her brand of privatisation was driven by the conviction that government control makes PSUs inherently less efficient and privatisation therefore improves its economic efficiency and is good for the consumers. However, this idea has been rejected around the world on the empirical bases. *A PSUs could also have comparable economic efficiency even being under full government control.* This was followed by Mrs. Thatcher (1979–90) forcefully in Great Britain conjoined with the supply-side economics as was done by Ronald Reagan (1981–89) in the United States as discussed by P.A. Samuelson and W.D. Nordhaus, *Economics* (New Delhi; Tata McGraw Hill, 2005), p. 703.

44. A highly experienced person from the media world, Arun Shourie remained the Minister for the whole term of the NDA government. Some highly accelerated and successful disinvestments were done during this period but not without controversies.

classifying the PSUs into *'strategic'* and *'non strategic'* announced in March 1999 that it will generally reduce its stake (share holding) in the *'non-strategic'* public sector enterprises (PSEs) to 26 per cent or below if necessary and in the *'strategic'* PSEs (i.e., arms and ammunition; atomic energy and related activities; and railways) it will retain its majority holding.[45] There was a major shift in the disinvestment policy from selling small lots of share in the profit-making PSUs (i.e., token disinvestment) to the strategic sale with change in management control both in profit and loss-making enterprises. The essence of the strategic disinvestment was—

(i) The minimum shares to be divested will be 51 per cent, and

(ii) the wholesale sale of shares will be done to a *'strategic partner'* having international class experience and expertise in the sector.

This form of disinvestment commenced with the Modern Food Industries Ltd. (MFIL). The second PSUs was the BALCO which invited every kind of criticism from the opposition political parties, the Government of Chattisgarh and experts, alike. The other PSUs were CMC Ltd, HTL, IBPL, VSNL, ITDC (13 hotels), Hotel Corporation of India Ltd. (3 hotels), Paradeep Phosphate Ltd (PPL), HZL, IPCL, MUL and Lagan Jute Manufacturing Company Ltd. (LJMC)—a total number of 13 public sector enterprises, were part of the *'strategic sale'* or *'strategic disinvestment'* of the PSEs.[46] The new government at the Centre did put this policy of strategic disinvestment on the hold practically and came up with a new policy in place.

Current Disinvestment Policy

India's disinvestment policy[47] has evolved over time since it commenced in 1991. It has two major features— 'ideology' behind the policy and the 'policy' itself. The *ideology* behind the policy is:

(i) Public ownership of PSUs to be promoted as they are wealth of nation;

(ii) Government to hold minimum 51 per cent shares in case of 'minority stake sale'; and

(iii) Upto 50 per cent or more shares might be sold off under 'strategic disinvestment'.

The current *policy* of disinvestment followed by the government is as given below:

(i) Minority stake sale (the policy of November 2009 continues):

- Listed PSUs to be taken first to comply to minimum 25 per cent norm;

- New PSUs to be listed which have earned net profit in three preceding consecutive years;

- 'Follow-on' public offers on case by case basis once capital investment needed; and

- DIPAM (Department of Investment and Public Asset Management) to identify PSUs and suggest disinvestment in consultation with respective ministries.

(ii) Strategic Disinvestment i.e., selling 50 per cent or more shares of the PSUs (announced in February 2016):

- To be done through consultation among Ministries/Departments and NITI Aayog;

45. *Concept Classification of the PSEs,* Government of India, 1999.

46. Publications Division, *India 2003* (New Delhi: Government of India, 2004).

47. **Ministry of Finance**, Department of Investment and Public Asset Management, Government of India, N. Delhi, March 2017.

- NITI Aayog to identify PSUs and advice on its different aspects; and

- CGD (Core Group of Secretaries on Disinvestment) to consider the recommendations of NITI Aayog to facilitate a decision by the CCEA (Cabinet Committee on Economic Affairs) and to supervise/monitor the implementation process.

The disinvestment policy is today seen as a part of the Government's *comprehensive management of its investment in the PSUs.* Under this, the Government considers its investment in PSUs as an important asset for accelerating economic growth and is committed to their efficient use to achieve optimum return through the following measures:

- Leveraging of assets, capital and financial restructuring, etc.

- Raising fresh investments by improving investors' confidence;

- Efficient management through rationalization of decision making process.

Proceeds of Disinvestment: Debate Concerning the Use

In the very next year of disinvestment, there started a debate in the country concerning the suitable use of the proceeds of disinvestment (i.e., accruing to the government out of the sale of the shares in the PSUs). The debate has by now evolved to a certain stage coming off basically in three phases:

Phase I: This phase could be considered from 1991–2000 in which whatever money the governments received out of disinvestment were used for fulfilling the budgetary requirements (better say bridging the gap of fiscal deficit).[48]

Phase II: This phase which has a very short span (2000–03) saw two new developments. *First,* the government started a practice of using the proceeds not only for fulfilling the need of fiscal deficit but used the money for some other good purposes, such as—re-investment in the PSEs, pre-payment of public debt and on the social sector. *Second,* by the early 2000–01 a broad concensus emerged on the issue of the proposal by the then Finance Minister.[49] The proposal regarding the use of the proceeds of disinvestment was as given below:

Some portions of the disinvestment proceeds should be used:

(i) in the divested PSU itself for upgrading purposes

(ii) in the turn-around of the other PSUs

(iii) in the public debt repayment/pre-payment

(iv) in the social infrastructure (education, healthcare, etc.)

(v) in the rehabilitation of the labour-force (of the divested PSUs) and

(vi) in fulfilling the budgetary requirements.

Phase III: Two major developments of this phase are as given below:

1. **National Investment Fund:** In January 2005, the Government of India decided to constitute a 'National Investment Fund' (NIF)[50] which has the following *salient features:*

   (a) The proceeds from disinvestment will be channelised into the NIF,

---

48. Ministry of Finance, Various issue of the *Economic Survey* (New Delhi: Government of India).

49. It was proposed by Yashwant Sinha and thus got popularity as the *'Yashwant Formula'* of using disinvestment proceeds. Being his personal proposal, the Government of the time was not officially bound to it. However, the idea got support inside and outside of the Parliament and looked having an impact on the government's thinking about the issue.

50. Ministry of Finance, Disinvestment Policy Announcement, Department of Disinvestment (New Delhi: Government of India, 2005).

which is to be maintained outside the Consolidated Fund of India.

(b) The corpus of the National Investment Fund will be of a permanent nature.

(c) The Fund will be professionally managed, to provide sustainable returns without depleting the corpus, by selected Public Sector Mutual Funds *(they are, UTI Asset Management Company Ltd.; SBI Funds Management Company Pvt. Ltd.; LIC Mutual Fund Asset Management Company Ltd.)*.

(d) 75 per cent of the annual income of the Fund will be used to finance selected social sector schemes, which promote education, health and employment. The residual 25 per cent of the annual income of the Fund will be used to meet the capital investment requirements of profitable and revivable PSUs that yield adequate returns, in order to enlarge their capital base to finance expansion/diversification.

The income from the NIF investments was utilised on selected social sector schemes, namely the Jawaharlal Nehru National Urban Renewal Mission (JNNURM), Accelerated Irrigation Benefits Programme (AIBP), Rajiv Gandhi Gramin Vidyutikaran Yojana (RGGVY), Accelerated Power Development and Reform Programme, Indira Awas Yojana and National Rural Employment Guarantee Scheme (NREGS).

2. **Restructuring of NIF:** In November 2009, the governement approved a change in the policy on utilisation of disinvestment proceeds. In view of the difficult situation caused by the global slowdown of 2008–09 and a severe drought in 2009–10, a *one-time exemption* was accorded to disinvestment proceeds being deposited into NIF—to be operational for the fiscals 2009–12, which was furhter extended to 2012–13, in view of the persistent difficult condition of the economy. All disinvestment proceeds *(in place of the income accruing out of the investment of the NIF corpus)* obtained during the three year period were to be used for selected social sector schemes.

Current Policy: In January 2013, the government approved **restructuring** of the NIF and decided that the disinvestment proceeds with effect from the fiscal year 2013–14 will be credited to the existing *'Public Account'* under the head NIF and they would remain there until withdrawn/invested for the approved purpose. It was decided that the NIF would be utilised for the following purposes:

(a) Subscribing to the shares being issued by the CPSE including PSBs and public sector insurance companies, on *rights basis* so as to ensure 51 per cent government ownership in them.

(b) *Preferential allotment* of shares of the CPSE to promoters, so that government shareholding does not go down below 51 per cent in all cases where the CPSE is going to raise fresh equity to meet its Capex [51] programme.

---

51. The Prime Minister's Office has been monitoring the CAPEX (Capital Expenditure) programme and investment plans of selected Central Public Sector Enterprises (CPSEs) since 2012-13. The purpose of this exercise was to enhance investment in the economy, utilizing the substantial cash surpluses that are available with some of the CPSEs to drive economic growth.

(c) *Recapitalisation* of public sector banks and public sector insurance companies.

(d) Investment by the government in RRBs, IIFCL, NABARD, Exim Bank;

(e) Equity infusion in various metro projects;

(f) Investment in Bhartiya Nabhikiya Vidyut Nigam Limited and Uranium Corporation of India Ltd.;

(g) Investment in Indian Railways towards capital expenditure.

The allocations out of the NIF will be decided in the government **budget**. This way, the policy regarding use of the disinvestment proceeds has become flexible enough to adjust to the current socio-economic needs.

MSME SECTOR

As per the SMSE Act, 2006 the MSME are classified in two classes—*manufacturing* and *service* enterprises—and they are defined in terms of investment in plant & machinery[52]. The Micro, Small and Medium Enterprises (MSMEs) play a very vital role in the economy—**3.6** crore such units employ **8.05** crore people and contribute **37.5** per cent to the country's GDP. The sector has huge potential for helping address structural problems like, unemployment, regional imbalances, unequal distribution of national income and wealth. Due to comparatively low capital costs and their forward-backward linkages with other sectors, they are headed to play a crucial role in the success of the Make in India initiative.

---

52. As per the **SMSE Act, 2006**, the classification is – for *Micro* enterprises investment up to Rs. 25 lakh in manufacturing & Rs. 10 lakh in services; for *Small* enterprises between Rs. 25 lakh to Rs. 5 crore in manufacturing & between Rs. 10 lakh to Rs. 2 crore in services; and for *Medium* enterprises between Rs. 5 to Rs. 10 crore in manufacturing & Rs. 2 to Rs. 5 crore in services.

Realising the importance of the sector, over the time, the government has undertaken a number of schemes for the establishment of new enterprises and development of existing ones like:

(i) PMEGP (Prime Minister's Employment Generation Programme),

(ii) CGTMSE (Credit Guarantee Trust Fund for Micro and Small Enterprises)

(iii) CLCSS (Credit Linked Capital Subsidy Scheme) for Technology Upgradation,

(iv) SFURTI (Scheme of Fund for Regeneration of Traditional Industries), and

(v) MSECDP (Micro and Small Enterprises-Cluster Development Programme)

Some of the ***recent initiatives*** (*Economic Survey 2015–16*) undertaken by the government for the promotion and development of the MSMEs, have been as given below:

(i) *UAM (Udyog Aadhar Memorandum):* The UAM scheme, notified in September 2015, to promote ease of doing business. Under it, entrepreneurs just need to file an *online* entrepreneurs' memorandum to get a unique Udyog Aadhaar Number (UAN)—a significant improvement over the earlier complex and cumbersome procedure.

(ii) *Employment Exchange for Industries:* To facilitate *match making* between prospective job seekers and employers an employment exchange for industries was set up in June 2015 (in line with Digital India).

(iii) *Framework for Revival and Rehabilitation of MSMEs:* Under this (May 2015), banks need to constitute a Committee for Distressed MSMEs to prepare a Corrective Action Plan (CAP) for them.

(iv) *ASPIRE (Promoting Innovation and Rural Entrepreneurs):* Launched in March

2015 with the objective of setting up a *network* of technology and incubation centres to accelerate entrepreneurship and promote start-ups for innovation and entrepreneurship in rural and agriculture-based industry.

SECTORAL CONCERNS

Due to several global and domestic reasons two industrial sectors, namely – steel and aluminium – are presently faced with certain challenges. Though, the government has taken several timely steps[53], they are still faced with huge challenges –

Steel Industry

Due to global and domestic factors Indian steel industry has been faced with **certain problems** in recent times. India is the *fourth* largest producer of crude steel in the world (with a total production of 86.5 MT with installed capacity of around 110 MT today) – having 5 per cent share in the global production. Global demand of steel has been near-stagnant (particularly China) – forcing global prices to fall up to 45 per cent in 2015 (in India prices fall has been up to 35 per cent). This has made major global steel producers to 'push' steel products into Indian market, thus raising two major concerns:

(i) A surge in steel imports, and

(ii) Interest of domestic steel industry hit hard.

The Indian steel industry due to higher borrowings, higher raw material costs with lower productivity is at a comparative disadvantage. The GoI took the following **measures** to curb the surging steel imports and make domestic production sustainable:

53. Ministry of Finance, *Economic Survey 2015–16*, Vol. 2, (New Delhi: Government of India, 2016), pp. 127–29.

(i) Custom duty increased by up to 2.5 per cent on certain primary iron and steel products.

(ii) Anti-dumping imposed on industrial grade steel imports from China, Malaysia and S. Korea (ranging from US\$180 to \$316 per tonne). Similar measures were taken by 40 other countries in the world.

(iii) Provisional safeguard custom duty of 20 per cent imposed on hot-rolled flat products of non-alloy and other alloy steel in coils.

(iv) Minimum import price imposed on a number of steel product for a six month period.

(v) Reduced export duty on iron ore to 10 per cent for select steel (from 30 per cent).

As per the government, any further custom increase will impact the downstream industries as steel is used as an *input* in different industries. This makes it clear that the Indian steel industry needs to get more competitive via cutting its borrowings and raw material costs together with enhancing productivity.

Aluminium Industry

Though India has been a major player in the global aluminium industry, in past few years it has been facing **certain challenges** due to global reasons. India is second largest producer (after China) and third largest consumer (after China) of aluminium in the world. Today, India produces *around* 4 MT (China- 21.5 MT) and consumes 3.8 MT (China- 22 MT, USA- 5.5 MT). The **challenges** Indian aluminium industry is faced with, may be summed-up as given below:

(i) World aluminium prices have dropped by 41 per cent between 2011 and 2015. During this period in India, imports as a proportion of total demand (sales plus imports) have increased substantially from around 40 per cent to 57 per cent.

(ii) Huge capacity has been created in China and world growth has slowed down.

(iii) The cost of production for India is presently higher than international prices. India's cost of production of aluminium has been increasing gradually while world costs remained static.

(iv) The Indian capacity has increased substantially in 2014–15 and 2015–16 but its utilization has not improved—utilisation was nearly 100 per cent up to 2013-14 and has declined to 50 per cent by late 2015. This has happened due to fall in global prices.

(v) The Indian aluminium industry will continue to face difficulty unless world prices increase, because in the short run it is virtually impossible to reduce the cost of production.

Global aluminium prices, like other metal prices, are *cyclical* and it is difficult to forecast when they will begin to move upwards. But the trend is expected to change when world industrial growth improves. India is avoiding custom duty to reduce import of aluminium because it may erode the competitiveness of downstream sectors like power, transport and construction.

Apparel and Footwear Sectors

Since the industrial revolution, no country has become a major economy without becoming an industrial power. In case of India, industrial expansion had been not only stunted but largely capital-intensive (job creation being not compatible to investments). Sitting on the cusp of demographic dividend, India needs to generate jobs that are formal, productive and compatible to investment. Besides, the economy has to search for alternatives for promoting growth, exports

and broader social transformation. In this case two sectors—apparel and leather & footwear, presently, look eminently suitable candidates[54].

Growth and exports

Almost every high growth economies in post-war history in East Asia has been associated with rapid expansion in clothing and footwear exports in the early stages. In the successful East Asian economies where GDP growth booms averaged between 7-10 per cent, growth in the exports of these two sectors was exceptional—the average annual growth of apparel exports was over 20 per cent, with some close to 50 per cent; and that of leather and footwear averaged more than 25 per cent. In its take-off phase of growth, India has underperformed relative to the East Asian competitors. The Indian underperformance, has been particularly marked in the leather sector.

Social transformation through women empowerment

These industries create high number of jobs, especially for women—apparel sector is the most labour-intensive followed by footwear. Apparels are 80-fold more labour-intensive than auto industry and 240-fold more jobs creating than steel industry—the comparable numbers for leather goods are 33-fold and 100-fold, respectively. As per the World Bank's employment elasticities, it is estimated that rapid export growth in these sectors could generate about 5 lakh additional direct jobs every year. Enhanced opportunity for women implies that these sectors could be 'vehicles for social transformation'—in Bangladesh, female education, total fertility rates, and women's labour force participation moved positively due to the expansion of the apparel sector.

54. **Economics Survey 2016-17**, Vol. 1, Ministry of Finance, Government of India, N. Delhi, pp. 128-138.

A historic opportunity

India has an opportunity to promote the exports from these sectors as Chinese market shares are either stabilising or falling. The space vacated by China is fast being taken over by Bangladesh and Vietnam in case of apparels; Vietnam and Indonesia in case of leather and footwear. At present, Indian apparel and leather firms are relocating to Bangladesh, Vietnam, Myanmar, and even Ethiopia. The window of opportunity is narrowing and India needs to act fast if it is to regain competitiveness and market share in these sectors.

Challenges

These sectors face a set of *common* challenges—logistics, labour regulations, the policies related to tax and tariff, and disadvantages emanating from the international trading environment compared to the competitors. In addition, the leather and footwear sector faces the *specific* challenge relating to policies that prevent converting its comparative advantage—abundance of cattle—into export opportunities. India still has potential comparative advantage in terms of cheaper and abundant *labour*, but these are nullified by other factors. A brief idea about the challenges are as given below:

(i) *Logistics:* On logistics, India is handicapped relative to competitors in a number of ways. The costs and time involved in getting goods from factory to destination are higher.

(ii) *Labour regulations:* Labour cost is one advantage to India but it is also not working in its favour. The problems are well-known—

  • regulations on minimum overtime pay (the Minimum Wages Act 1948 mandates payment of overtime wages at twice the rate of ordinary rates);

  • lack of flexibility in part-time work;

  • onerous mandatory contributions (employees funds) that become *de facto* taxes for low-paid workers in small firms that results in a 45 per cent lower disposable salary {due to their contributions to the Employee Provident Fund Organisation (EPFO), Employee Pension Scheme (EPS), Labour Welfare Fund (LWF), Employees' Deposit Linked Insurance Scheme (EDLI), and Employee State Insurance (ESI) etc.}.

  • apparel and leather firms in India are smaller compared to firms in say China, Bangladesh and Vietnam (an estimated 78 per cent of firms in India employ less than 50 workers with 10 per cent employing more than 500. In China, the comparable numbers are about 15 per cent and 28 per cent respectively).

(iii) *Tax and Tariff Policies:* Tax and tariff policies create distortions impeding India's export competitiveness. In the case of apparels, there are two sets of policies both of which impede competitiveness in man-made fibres and favour instead cotton-based exports. This is serious because internationally, world demand is shifting strongly towards man-made fibres. Similarly, while world's exports are shifting from leather to non-leather footwear, India imposes higher tax on the latter.

(iv) *Discrimination in export markets:* India's competitor exporting nations for apparels and leather and footwear enjoy better market access by way of zero or at least lower tariffs in the two major importing markets, namely, the USA and EU (European Union):

- Bangladesh's exports enter the EU mostly duty free (former being a Less Developed Country), while Indian exports of apparels face average tariffs of 9.1 per cent.
- Vietnam could also attract zero tariffs once the EU–Vietnam FTA (Free Trade Agreement) comes into effect.
- In the US, India faces tariff of 11.4 percent. Ethiopia, which is an emerging new competitor in apparels and leather, enjoys duty free access in US, EU and Canada.
- Indian leather exports also face high tariffs in partner country markets in exports of leather goods and non-leather footwear, with considerable added disadvantage in Japan.

(v) *Specific challenge in leather & footwear sectors:* The sectors use raw hides and skins of a number of animals like cattle, buffalo, goat, sheep and other smaller animals. Amongst these, leather made from cattle hides has greater global demand (owing to its strength, durability and superior quality)—cattle-based global exports dominate buffalo-based exports by a factor of 8 to 9. However, despite having a large cattle population, India's share of global cattle population and exports of cattle hides is low and declining. This trend can be attributed to the limited availability of cattle for slaughter in India, thereby leading to loss of a potential comparative advantage due to underutilization of the abundantly available natural resource.

Several measures of the package approved by the Government for textiles and apparels in *June 2016* are aimed at addressing the challenges described above. Similar provisions are needed for the leather exporters. Immediate actions are needed in the areas of reforming—labour laws, tax rationalisation (GST will be helpful), employees contributions to security schemes and articulating new FTAs, etc.

FDI POLICY MEASURES

Foreign direct investment (FDI) is an important driver of economic growth which helps in—sustaining high growth rate, increasing productivity, a major source of non-debt financial resources, and employment generation. A favourable policy regime and sound business environment facilitate FDI flows.

The government has taken various reforms to liberalizing and simplifying the FDI policy to provide *ease of doing business* climate in the country that will also lead to larger FDI inflows. A number of sectors have been liberalized, including defence, construction, broadcasting, civil aviation, plantation, trading, private sector banking, satellite establishment and operation and credit information companies. By early 2017, the government had taken the following policy steps to promote FDI in the economy:

(i) Up to 49 per cent FDI permitted in *insurance* and *pension funds* (26 per cent under automatic route) and defence sector.

(ii) 100 per cent FDI permitted in manufacturing of *medical devices*; the *white label ATM* and *railway* infrastructure.

(iii) 100 per cent FDI allowed in marketing of food products produced and manufactured in India *(Union Budget 2016–17)*.

(iv) To undertake important banking sector reforms and public listing of general insurance companies undertake significant changes in FDI policy *(Union Budget 2016–17)*.

(v) Reforms in FDI policy in the areas of Insurance and Pension, Asset

Reconstruction Companies, Stock Exchanges (*Union Budget 2016–17*).

(vi) A new policy for management of the PSUs, including strategic disinvestment—this is supposed to have liberal provisions for the FDI (*Union Budget 2016–17*).

As per the *Economic Survey 2016-17*, boosted by the government initiatives, during first half of 2016-17, FDI inflows improved to US\$ 21.7 billion (from US\$ 16.6 billion for the same period of the previous year) showing a growth of 30.7 per cent.

Meanwhile, the **Union Budget 2017-18** has announced to abolish the FIPB (Foreign Investment Promotion Board) and promised to further liberalise the FDI policy. More than 90 per cent of the FDI inflows coming under *automatic route* together with their *online processing*, the inter-ministerial nodal body (i.e. FIPB) approving FDI has lost much of its relevance. The few areas in which FDI needs a government approval (such as defence, telecom, insurance, banking, retail trade, etc.), in future, the approval will be given by either the concerned ministries or the regulatory bodies.

EASE OF DOING BUSINESS

Doing Business report, an annual publication (since 2004) of the World Bank Group ranks the countries of the world on the basis of their 'regulations that enhance business activity and those that constrain it'. Popularly known as the *'ease of doing business report'*, it measures regulations affecting **11 areas** of the life of a business[55]:

1. Starting a business,
2. Dealing with construction permits,
3. Getting electricity,
4. Registering property,
5. Getting credit,
6. Protecting minority investors,
7. Paying taxes,
8. Trading across borders,
9. Enforcing contracts,
10. Resolving insolvency, and
11. Labour market regulation.

Doing Business 2017 report (released in October 2016) recognizes India's achievements in implementing reforms in four of its ten indicators—Trading Across Borders, Getting Electricity, Enforcing Contracts and Paying Taxes. India's rank has improved to rank 130th in this report (from 142nd of 2015 report) among the 190 countries included in the report. Basically, the report acknowledges only those reforms which have been implemented in Mumbai and Delhi by June 1 each year. This way, several major reform initiatives of India (after 1st June 2016) were not accounted for in this year's report and will enhance India's rank in the next report. This year's report did not include the 'labour market regulaton'.

Reforms for next year's ranking: The Government is committed to its goal of achieving *among top 50 rank in the next report* (2018) and the Government has implemented a host of reforms to make it easier for businesses to *start, operate* and *exit*. Following actions are on anvil in this regard:

(i) Implementing the Insolvency and Bankruptcy Code.

(ii) Implementing GST nationwide by July 1, 2017.

(iii) Implementing a single form for company incorporation, name availability and director's identification number and making it mandatory.

(iv) Merging registries to build a unified online data base of security interests over movable assets.

---

55. **Doing Business 2017**, World Bank, Washington DC, 2017 and **Ministry of Commerce and Industry**, Government of India, N. Delhi, Press Release, October 28, 2016.

(v) Further streamlining processes related to customs clearances aimed at faster and cheaper processing.

(vi) Introduction of paperless court procedures and systems including e-filing, e-payment, e-summons.

(vii) Make the colour coded maps of Airports Authority of India, Delhi Urban Arts Commission, Delhi Metro Rail Corporation, Archaeological Survey of India GIS enabled and integrate them with the Single Window System of Municipal Corporation of Delhi.

(viii) Allow online filing of application, scheduling of appointment and payment of fees for registering properties.

(ix) Digitize all encumbrances and record of rights of lands for last 30 years and make them available online.

(x) Integrate land records with sale deeds at Sub-Registrar offices.

As per the ***Economic Survey 2016-17***, the Government is working on several fronts to enhance of the 'ease of doing business' in the country by— improving investment environment; resolving the 'twin balance-sheet' problem; initiating labour law reforms; digitising procedures of businesses and commercial courts; improving governance and checking the menace of black money; being the major ones.

MAKE IN INDIA

Make in India was launched in September 2014 by the GoI to encourage multinational as well as domestic companies to manufacture their products in India. The initiative is set to boost entrepreneurship, not only in manufacturing but in relevant infrastructure and *service sectors* as well.

Major features of the initiative[56] are as given below:

Vision: attracting both capital and technological investment in India enabling it to become the top global FDI, surpassing even China and the United States.

Objective: To focus on job creation and skill enhancement in 25 key sectors of the economy, including automobiles, aviation, biotechnology, defence manufacturing, electrical machinery, food processing, oil & gas, and pharmaceuticals, among others.

Logo: is inspired from Ashoka Chakra – is a striding lion made of cogs, symbolising manufacturing, strength and national pride.

The initiative also aims at imposing *high quality standards* and the dimensions of *sustainability*. Key policies to be followed are: ease of doing business, getting away with archaic laws, 100 Smart Cities, disinvestment of the PSUs, skills and jobs for the youth, etc. Major *challenges* to the initiatives include – creating a healthy business environment, removal of unfavourable factors, more focus on Indian's MSMEs, lack of world class research and development (R&D), and comparisons with China's 'Made in China' campaign.

Some experts have also highlighted few concerns related to the Make in India campaign. It will be advisable to take care of the concerns:

(i) allegations of siphoning of funds,

(ii) higher pricing,

(iii) more profits to MNCs for setting up plants in India,

(iv) land-grabbing, and

(v) re-entry of black money.

56. Government of India launch of the initiative, **Make in India**, N. Delhi, 25 September, 2014.

The initiative is based on *four pillars* – new processes; new infrastructure; new sectors; and new mindset. The **major steps**[57] taken by the government in this regard are as summed-up below:

(i) An interactive portal for dissemination of information and interaction with investors has been created with the objective of generating awareness about the investment opportunities and prospects of the country, to promote India as a preferred investment destination in markets overseas and to increase Indian share of global FDI.

(ii) *Invest India* set up as the national investment promotion and facilitation *agency*.

(iii) With the objective of promoting investment in the country, a full-fledged Investment Facilitation Cell has been set-up under the Make in India initiative, primarily to support all investment queries as well as to *handhold and liaise* with various agencies on behalf of potential investors.

(iv) As envisaged by the *National Manufacturing Policy 2011*, Make in India seeks to enable the sector to contribute 25 per cent to the GDP and create 100 million additional jobs by 2022.

(v) A number of steps to enhance the skills of workers/the unemployed in India in order to improve their employability.

(vi) In order to tap the creative potential and boost entrepreneurship in India, the *Start-up India* and *Stand-up India* campaign has been announced.

(vii) An innovation promotion platform called *AIM* (Atal Innovation Mission) and a techno-financial, incubation and facilitation programme called *SETU* (Self-Employment and Talent Utilization) are being implemented to encourage innovation and start-ups in India.

(viii) For supporting the financial needs of the *small* and *medium* enterprise sector and promote start-ups and entrepreneurship, various steps taken through Make in India –

(a) The *India Aspiration Fund* has also been set up under the SIDBI for *venture capital financing* to the MSME sector.

(b) SIDBI Make in India Loan for Small Enterprises *(SMILE)* launched to offer quasi-equity and term-based short-term loans to Indian SMEs on liberal terms.

(c) A Micro Units Development Refinance Agency *(MUDRA)* Bank set up to provide development and refinance to commercial banks/NBFCs/cooperative banks for loans given to *micro-units*. MUDRA follow a 'credit-plus approach' by also providing several other services such as – financial literacy and addressing skill gaps, information gaps, etc.

START-UP INDIA

The Start-up India scheme was launched by the GoI in January 2016 with a slogan, *Start-up India* and *Stand-up India*. The mission/scheme aims to build a strong ecosystem for nurturing innovation, driving sustainable economic growth and generating large-scale employment opportunities. Apart from the technology sector the start-up movement will extend to a wide array of other sectors including agriculture, manufacturing, healthcare and education.; and from existing tier 1 cities will extend to tier 2 and tier 3 cities including

---

57. Ministry of Finance, **Economic Survey 2015-16**, p. 135.

semi-urban and rural areas. The proposed *action plan (Economic Survey 2015–16)* for the firms is as given below:

- Creating a compliance regime based on self-certification to reduce the regulatory burden and keep compliance cost low.

- Setting up *Start-up India hub* to create a single point of contact for the entire Start-up ecosystem and enable knowledge exchange and access to funding.

- Rolling out of *mobile app* and *portal* to serve as the single platform for start-ups to interact with government and regulatory institutions and various stakeholders.

- Relaxed norms of public procurement.

- Legal support and fast-tracking of *patent* examination at lower costs to promote awareness of IPR (Intellectual Property Rights).

- Faster and easier exit norms.

- Providing funding support through a *fund of funds* with a corpus of Rs. 10,000 crore.

- Credit Guarantee Fund to catalyse entrepreneurship.

- Tax exemption on capital gains

- Income Tax exemption for three years

- Launch of AIM (Atal Innovation Mission) with the SETU (Self-Employment and Talent Utilisation) programme to serve as a platform for promotion of world-class innovation hubs, start-up businesses and other self-employment activities, particularly in technology-driven areas.

- Building *innovation centres* at national institutes to propel successful innovation through augmentation of incubation and R&D efforts.

- Setting up of 7 new research parks (modelled on the research park at IIT Madras).

- Promoting start-ups in the *biotechnology* sector.

- Launching of innovation-focused programmes for students to foster a *culture of innovation* in the field of science and technology

Start-up India will turn Indian youths from *job seekers into job creators*. It will encourage entrepreneurship, innovation and creation of revolutionary new products in India, that will be used by people around the world. The initiative aspires to give India *wings to fly above the sky*.

INDIAN INFRASTRUCTURE

An Introduction

Infrastructure is the 'lifeline' of an economy as protein is the lifeline of the human body. Whichever sector be the prime moving force of an economy, i.e., primary, secondary or tertiary, suitable level of infrastructure presence is a pre-requisite for growth and development. This is why the Government in India has always given priority to the developmental aspects of the sector. But the level of preparedness and performance had been always less than required by the economy. Which sector are called the infrastructure? *Basically, the goods and services usually requiring higher investment, considered essential for the proper functioning of an economy is called the infrastructure of an economy.*[58] Such sector might be as many as required by a particular economy such as power, transportation, communication, water supply, sewerage, housing, urban amenities, etc.

There are three sectors which are considered as the infrastructure universally around the world namely power, transportation and communication. Since, infrastructure benefits the whole economy,

58. **Oxford Dictionary of Business**, (New Delhi: Oxford University Press, 2004).

it has been often argued by the economists that the sector should be funded by the government by means of taxation, partly not wholly.

Indian infrastructure sector is clearly overstrained and has suffered from underinvestment in the post-reforms period.[59] Infrastructure bottlenecks are always constraint in achieving a higher growth for the economy. India needs massive investment, both from the public and private sectors, to overcome infrastructure bottlenecks. Investments by the public and private sectors are not alternatives, but complimentary to each other as the required investment is very high. Public investment in the sector depends upon the ability to raise resources (capital) in the public sector and this in turn depends upon the ability to collect the user charges from the consumers. To make this happen following *three* factors are extremely important:

(i) Reform of the power sector,

(ii) Introduction of road user charges (either directly via tolls or indirectly via a cess on petrol diesel), and

(iii) Rationalisation of railway fares.

Experts[60] have suggested for expanding public investment in the sector supplemented duly by a vigorous effort of attracting private investment (domestic as well as foreign). Creating the conducive environment to attract private investment in infrastructure should include:

(i) Simplification and transparency in the clearance procedures;

(ii) Unbundling an infrastructure project so that the private sector may go for only those unbundled segment of the project whose they are able to bear; and

(iii) Providing credible and independent regulatory framework so that the private players get fair treatment.

Official Ideology

Putting in place the quality and efficient infrastructure services is essential to realise the full potential of the growth impulses surging through the Indian economy. There is now a widespread consensus[61] (now clearly accepted by the Planning Commission) that exclusive dependence on the government for the provision of all infrastructure services introduces difficulties concerning adequate scale of investment, technical efficiency, proper enforcement of user charges, and competitive market structure. At the same time, complete reliance on private production, particularly without appropriate regulation, is also not likely to produce optimal outcomes.[62] India, while stepping up public investment in infrastructure, has been actively engaged in finding the appropriate policy framework, which gives the private sector adequate confidence and incentives to invest on a massive scale, but simultaneously preserves adequate checks and balances through transparency, competition and regulation.

The Eleventh Plan[63] emphasised the need for removing infrastructure bottlenecks for sustained growth—proposed an investment of US$500 billion in infrastructure sectors through a mix of public and private sectors to reduce deficits in identified infrastructure sectors. As a percentage of the gross domestic product (GDP), investment in infrastructure was expected to increase to around 9 per cent. For the first time the contribution of the private sector in total investment in

59. *India Infrastructure Report 1994.* (New Delhi: Government of India, 1994).

60. One of such major suggestion was forwarded by Sachs, Varsheny and Bajpai, *India in the Era of Economic Reforms,* p. 79.

61. Ministry of Finance, *Economic Survey,* 2006–07, (New Delhi: Government of India, 2007).

62. *India Infrastructure Report 2007* (New Delhi: Government of India, 2011).

63. Planning Commission, *Mid Term Appraisal of the 11th Pan* (New Delhi: Government of India, 2011).

infrastructure was targeted to exceed 30 per cent. Total investment in infrastructure during the Eleventh Plan is estimated to increase to more than 8 per cent of the GDP in the terminal year of the Plan, which was higher by 2.47 percentage points as compared to the Tenth Plan. The private sector is expected to be contributing nearly 36 per cent of this investment.

An analysis[64] of the creation of infrastructure in physical terms indicates that while the achievements in some sectors have been remarkable during the Eleventh Plan as compared to the previous Five Year Plans, there have been slippages in some sectors. The success in garnering private-sector investment in infrastructure through the public-private partnership (PPP) route during the Plan has *laid solid foundation* for a substantial step up in private-sector funding in coming years. PPPs are expected to augment resource availability as well as improve the efficiency of infrastructure service delivery.

The Planning Commission[65], in its aproach paper has projected an investment of over Rs. 45 lakh crore (for about US $1 trilion) during the **Twelfth Plan (2012–17).** It is projected that at least 50 per cent of this investment will come from the private sector as against the 36 per cent anticipated in the Eleventh Plan and public sector investment will need to increase to over Rs. 22.5 lakh crore as against an expenditure of Rs. 13.1 lakh crore during the Eleventh Plan. Financing infrastructure will, therefore, be a big challenge in the coming years and will equire some innovative ideas and new models of financing.

---

64. *Planning Commission,* while announcing the *Approach for the 12th Plan.*

65. Planning Commission, *Approach to the 12th Plan* (New Delhi: Government of India,).

UDAY SCHEME

Without improving the performance of the electricity distribution companies (DISCOMs) of the state governments efforts towards 100 per cent village electrification, 24x7 power supply and clean energy cannot bear fruit. Power outages also adversely affect national priorities like 'Make in India' and 'Digital India'. In addition, default on bank loans by financially stressed DISCOMs has the potential of seriously impacting the banking sector and the economy at large.

For financial and operational turnaround of DISCOMs and to ensure a sustainable permanent solution to the problem, the *UDAY* (Ujwal DISCOM Assurance Yojana) was launched by the GoI, in November 2015. The scheme also aims to reduce interest burden of the DISCOMs, cost of power and their AT&C (Aggregate Transmission & Technical) losses.

Due to legacy issues, DISCOMs are trapped in a vicious cycle with operational losses being funded by debt. Outstanding debt of DISCOMs were Rs. 4.3 lakh crore by 2014-15, with interest rates upto 14–15 per cent and AT&C losses as high as 22 per cent. The scheme assures the rise of vibrant and efficient DISCOMs through a permanent resolution of past as well as potential future issues of the sector. It empowers DISCOMs with the opportunity to break even in the next 2-3 years. This is to take place through *four* initiatives:

(i) Improving operational efficiencies;

(ii) Reduction of cost of power;

(iii) Reduction in interest cost; and

(iv) Enforcing financial discipline.

Operational efficiency to be improved via steps such as – compulsory smart metering, upgradation of transformers, meters, etc., *energy efficiency* via steps like efficient LED bulbs, agricultural pumps, fans & air-conditioners etc.—to reduce the average AT&C loss from around 22 per cent to 15 per cent and eliminate the gap between ARR (Average Revenue Realised) and ACS (Average Cost of Supply) by 2018-19.

Reduction in cost of power would be achieved through measures such as increased supply of cheaper domestic coal, coal linkage rationalisation, liberal coal swaps from inefficient to efficient plants, coal price rationalisation based on GCV (Gross Calorific Value), supply of washed and crushed coal, and faster completion of transmission lines. NTPC alone is expected to save Rs. 0.35 unit through higher supply of domestic coal and rationalization and swapping of coal which will be passed on to DISCOMs.

The ***salient features*** of the scheme are as given below[66]:

- States shall take over 75 per cent of the DISCOM debt—50 per cent in 2015–16 and 25 per cent in 2016–17. This will reduce the interest cost to 8–9 per cent, from as high as 14–15 per cent.

- GoI will not include the debt taken over by the states in the calculation of fiscal deficit of the States in the financial years 2015–16 and 2016–17.

- States will issue non-SLR including SDL (State Development Loan) bonds in the market or directly to the respective banks and Financial Institutions (FIs).

- DISCOM debt not taken over by the State shall be converted by the Banks and FIs into loans or bonds with interest rate not more than the bank's base rate plus 0.1 per cent. Alternately, this debt may be fully or partly issued by the DISCOM as State guaranteed DISCOM bonds at the prevailing market rates which shall be equal to or less than bank base rate plus 0.1 per cent.

- States to take over the future losses of DISCOMs in a graded manner.

- States accepting UDAY and performing as per *operational milestones* will be given additional / priority funding through Deendayal Upadhyaya Gram Jyoti Yojana (DDUGJY),Integrated Power Development Scheme (IPDS), Power Sector Development Fund (PSDF) or other such schemes of Ministry of Power and Ministry of New and Renewable Energy. States not meeting operational milestones will be liable to forfeit their claim on IPDS and DDUGJY grants.

- Such States shall also be supported with additional coal at notified prices and, in case of availability through higher capacity utilisation, low cost power from NTPC and other Central PSUs.

- UDAY is *optional* for all States. However, States are encouraged to take the benefit at the earliest as benefits are dependent on the performance. [By March 2017, most of the states/UTs had joined the scheme.]

Basically, financial liabilities of DISCOMs are the contingent liabilities of the respective States and need to be recognized as such. Debt of DISCOMs is *de facto* borrowing of States which is not counted in *de jure* borrowing. However, credit rating agencies and multilateral agencies are conscious of this de facto debt in their appraisals. The 14th Finance Commission also had similar observations. Similarly, the new scheme, DDUGY (Deendayal Upadhyaya Gram Jyoti Yojana), was launched to promote rural electrification. The budgetary support for continuation of the RGGVY (Rajiv Gandhi Grameen Vidyutikaran) in 12th and 13th Plans, has also been carried forward to the new scheme.

---

66. Ministry of Finance, **Economic Survey 2015–16**, pp. 137–138.

UDAY accelerates the process of reform across the entire power sector and will ensure that power is accessible, affordable and available for all. UDAY truly heralds the *uday* (rise), of a 'Power'ful India.

National LED Programme: The Government of India, in January 2015, launched the 100 cities National LED Programmes with the aim of promoting use of the most efficient lighting technology at affordable rates. This programme has two components: *(i) DELP (Domestic Efficient Lighting Programme)* aims to replace incandescent bulbs (77 crore) with LED bulbs (by providing LED bulbs to domestic consumers). *(ii) SLNP (Street Lighting National Programme)* aims to replace conventional streetlights (3.5 crore) with smart and energy-efficient LED streetlights by March 2019.

The programme is supposed to bring in *multiple benefits* to the economy:

(i) Demand reduction in electricity by around 21,500 MW with a monetary savings of Rs. 45,500 crore to domestic consumers and urban local bodies.

(ii) To help in mitigating climate change by cutting CO_2 emission by 85 million tonnes annually. India has committed to reduce its emission intensity per unit GDP by 33-35 per cent below 2005 levels by 2030 (under its Intended Nationally Determined Contribution-INDC).

(iii) To encourage and support domestic manufacturing of LED bulbs, making it consistent with the 'Make in India' policy.

Besides, the government also approved the establishment of a National Smart Grid Mission (NSGM) in the power sector to plan and monitor implementation of policies and programmes related to smart grid activities in India.

AT&C Losses: Due to lack of adequate investment on 'transmission and distribution' (T&D) works, the T&D losses have been consistently on the higher side, and reached to the level of 32.86 Per cent in the year 2000-01. The reduction of these losses was essential to bring economic viability to the state utilities (SEBs). As the T&D loss was not able to capture all the losses in the network, concept of *Aggregate Technical and Commercial (AT&C)* loss was introduced. AT&C loss captures technical as well as commercial losses in the network and is a true indicator of total losses in the system.

High technical losses in the system are primarily *due to* inadequate investments over the years for system improvement works, which has resulted in unplanned extensions of the distribution lines, overloading of the system elements like transformers and conductors, and lack of adequate reactive power support.

The commercial losses are mainly due to:

(i) low metering efficiency

(ii) theft, and

(iii) pilferages

This may be eliminated by improving metering efficiency, proper energy accounting & auditing and improved billing & collection efficiency. Fixing of accountability of the personnel/feeder managers may help considerably in reduction of AT&C loss.

In December 2014, the GoI launched a new programme – IPDS (Integrated Power Development Scheme) – a centrally sponsored scheme (CSS) with a Central *grant* between 60 to 85 per cent. Its *core aim* is to attain 24x7 power supply in the country – to be achieved by strengthening sub-transmission network, metering, IT application, Customer Care Services, provisioning of solar panels, reduction in the AT&C of the state DISCOMs. This scheme subsumed the existing scheme, R-APDRP (Restructured Accelerated Power Development and Reforms Programme) of 2008.

RAILWAYS

Indian Railways (IR) is faced with a number of challenges. For speedy capacity creation, IR recognizes the importance of enhancing project execution capabilities. Considering the enormity of the resources required for plan investment in rail infrastructure, and given the limitation of public resources, efforts are on by IR to generate sufficient *internal surplus*, and tap innovative methods of financing, to meet these needs.

The focus is on prioritising investments in important areas like dedicated freight corridors, high speed rail, high capacity rolling stock, last mile rail linkages and port connectivity, and attracting private and FDI investments to supplement available resources. Major *initiatives* taken by the GoI are as given below:

- Various measures to improve passenger amenities, infrastructure and services, and initiatives under Make in India, freight initiative, resource mobilisation initiative and green initiatives, etc. High-speed communication network put in place with the help of 48,818 route kilometres. Integral Coach Factory, Chennai, has developed a first-of-its-kind stainless steel three-phase energy-efficient AC-AC transmission 1600 HP DEMU train set.
- Mobile application for freight operations – *Parichaalan* – has been introduced.
- IR is installing solar panels on rooftops of coaches for the train lighting system. Solar plants of 50 MW to come up on the rooftops of IR buildings.
- Diamond Quadrilateral network of High Speed Rail connecting major metros (Delhi, Mumbai, Kolkata and Chennai) to come up.

High Speed Train Project: The feasibility report of the Japan International Cooperation Agency (JICA) was approved by the GoI in December 2015. A new special purpose vehicle with 50 per cent equity participation from the Ministry of Railways and 50 per cent from the state governments of Maharashtra and Gujarat will be set up to implement the project. *Major features* of the project are as given below:

- Project completion cost is approximately Rs. 97,636 crore (including price escalation, interest during construction and import duties) – average per km cost of construction works out to be Rs. 140 crore. To be completed in 7 years.
- Japan's ODA (official development assistance) will be Rs. 79, 165 crore (81 per cent of project cost) for 50 years with 0.1 per cent interest and a 15-year moratorium.
- Total length of the proposed corridor will be 508 km between the Bandra Kurla complex in Mumbai and Sabarmati/Ahmedabad in Gujarat – to cover 12 stations with a maximum design speed of 350 kmph (with a 320 kmph operating speed).
- Sixty-four per cent of the corridor will be constructed on embankment, 25 per cent via duct and 6 per cent tunnel, with a standard gauge.
- To have 10-car trains (750 seats) in the beginning and 16-car trains (1200 seats) in the future. Thirty-five trains per day each way will operate by 2023, and will go up to 105 trains per day each way in 2053.
- It will have approximately 36,000 daily users per day (both ways) in 2023, which will go up to 186,000 per day (both ways) or 68 million per annum by 2053.

ROADS

With about 52.32 lakh km of road network comprising National Highways, State Highways and other roads, India has the *second* largest road network in the world. The NH in the country cover a total length of 1,00,475 km and carry about 40 per cent of the road traffic.

Financing of the NHDP: A part of the **fuel cess** imposed on petrol and diesel is allocated to the NHAI for funding the implementation of the NHDP. The NHAI leverages the cess flow to borrow additional funds from the debt market. Till date, such borrowings have been limited to funds raised through 54 EC (capital gains tax exemption) bonds and the short-term overdraft facility. Government has also taken loans for financing projects under the NHDP from the World Bank (US$ 1,965 million), Asian Development Bank (US$ 1,605 million) and Japan Bank for International Cooperation (32,060 million yen) which are passed on to the NHAI partly in the form of grants and partly as loan. The NHAI has also availed a direct loan of US$ 180 million from the ADB for the Surat-Manor Expressway Project.

Special Accelerated Road Development Programme for North-East region (SARDP-NE) aims at improving road connectivity to state capitals, district headquarters, and remote places of the north-east region. Development of roads in Left Wing Extremism *(LWE)*-affected areas in the states of Andhra Pradesh, Bihar, Chhattisgarh, Jharkhand, Madhya Pradesh, Maharashtra, Odisha, and Uttar Pradesh is continuing; Prime Minister's Reconstruction Plan *(PMRP)* for Jammu and Kashmir, launched in November 2004.

By **early 2017**, few new initiatives were taken by the GoI – *Bharatmala* programme to connect non-major ports; *Backward Areas, Religious, Tourist Places Connectivity* programme; *Setubhratam Pariyojana* to construct about 1500 major bridges; and the *District Head Quarter Connectivity Scheme* for development of about 9000 km newly declared NHs.

Pradhan Mantri Gram Sadak Yojna (PMGSY): Launched to provide single all-weather road connectivity to eligible unconnected habitations having population of 500 persons and above in plain areas and 250 persons and above in hill states, tribal (Schedule V) areas, desert (as identified in the Desert Development Programme) areas, and LWE-affected districts as identified by the Ministry of Home Affairs. Rural roads has also been identified as one of the *six components* of Bharat Nirman which has the goal of providing all-weather road connectivity to all villages with a population of 1,000 (500 in the case of hilly or tribal areas).

By the terminal year of the *12th Plan* (i.e., March 2017), there is a target of developing National Highways network upto a *minimum two-lane standard*. As private investment in the infrastructure have been slowing down due to 'twin balance sheet' problem, the Government has decided to enhance public investment in the sector—**Union Budget 2017-18** has allocated a fund of Rs. 64,900 crores for the road sector (around 13 per cent higher than the previous year).

CIVIL AVIATION

Airport infrastructure development continues to be a matter of concern. Upgradation of many airports, including construction of new terminals, upgradation in 18 non-metro airports, for improving air navigation services the Airport Authority of India (AAI) installing the new ATS automation system. In order to address issues concerning viability of the civil aviation sector, particularly the airline industry, a Working Group was constituted on 12, December 2011 under the chairmanship of the Secretary civil aviation. Their major recommendations were:

(i) state governments should rationalise the value added tax (VAT) on aviation turbine fuel (ATF),

(ii) foreign airlines be permitted to invest in domestic airlines undertakings,

(iii) direct import of ATF by airlines for their own consumption be allowed,

(iv) airlines should be asked to prepare their turnaround plans,

(v) fare structure should be reviewed by airlines to cover the cost of their operations.

(vi) an economic regulatory framework suggested with regard to excessive/predatory pricing by 31, May 2012.

MARITIME AGENDA 2010-20

The **objective** of the Maritime Agenda 2010–20 is not only creating more capacity but setting up ports on a par with the best international ports in terms of performance:

(i) A target of 3,130 MT port capacity has been set for the year 2020. More than 50 per cent of this capacity is to be created in the non-major ports as the traffic handled by these ports is expected to increase to 1,280 MT.

(ii) This enlarged scale of operation is expected to reduce transaction costs considerably and make Indian ports *globally competitive.*

(iii) Proposed investment in major and non-major ports by 2020 is expected to be around Rs. 2,96,000 crore.

(iv) Most of the investment to come from the private sector including FDI (up to 100 per cent under the automatic route is permitted for construction and maintenance of ports), around 96 per cent, private sector to fund most of the projects through PPP or on 'build operate transfer' (BOT) or 'build operate own transfer' (BOOT) basis.

(v) Private-sector participation will not only increase investment in the ports infrastructure, it is expected to improve operations of the ports through the induction of the latest technology and better management practices.

(vi) Public funds will be mainly deployed for common use infrastructure facilities like deepening of port channels, rail and road connectivity from ports to hinterland, etc.

SMART CITIES

The GoI has launched the Smart Cities Mission with the collaboration of states and UTs for urban development. The *purpose* of the mission is – to drive economic growth and improve the quality of life of people by enabling local area development and harnessing technology, especially technology that leads to smart outcomes.

The Mission targets *promoting* cities that provide core infrastructure and give a decent quality of life to its citizens, a clean and sustainable environment and application of 'smart' solutions. The focus is on sustainable and inclusive development and the idea is to look at compact areas and create a replicable model which will act like a lighthouse to other aspiring cities. The smart city includes the following *core* infrastructure development:

- adequate water supply;
- assured electricity supply;
- sanitation, including solid waste management;
- efficient urban mobility and public transport;
- affordable housing, especially for the poor;
- robust IT connectivity and digitalization;
- good governance, especially e-Governance and citizen participation;
- sustainable environment;

- safety and security of citizens, particularly women, children and the elderly; and
- health and education.

Strategy: The strategic components of area-based development in the mission are:
- city improvement (retrofitting);
- city renewal (redevelopment);
- city extension (greenfield development); and
- a pan-city initiative in which smart solutions are applied.

Retrofitting will introduce planning in an existing built-up area to achieve smart city objectives, along with other objectives, to make the existing area more efficient and liveable. In retrofitting, an area consisting of more than 500 acres will be identified by the city in consultation with citizens. Redevelopment will effect a replacement of the existing built-up environment and enable co-creation of a new layout with enhanced infrastructure using mixed land use and increased density. Redevelopment envisages an area of more than 50 acres, identified by urban local bodies (ULBs) in consultation with citizens.

Greenfield development will introduce most of the smart solutions in a previously vacant area (more than 250 acres) using innovative planning, plan financing and plan implementation tools (e.g. land pooling/ land reconstitution) with provision for affordable housing, especially for the poor. Greenfield development is required around cities in order to address the needs of the expanding population.

Finance: The Mission will cover 100 cities which have been distributed among the states and UTs on the basis of equitable criteria. The distribution of smart cities will be reviewed after two years of the implementation of the mission.

The Smart City Mission will be operated as a Centrally Sponsored Scheme (CSS) and the central government proposes to give it financial support to the extent of Rs. 48,000 crore over five years, i.e. on an average Rs. 100 crore per city per year. An equal amount, on a matching basis, will have to be contributed by the state/ULB; therefore, nearly one lakh crore of government/ULB funds will be available for smart cities development. In the first phase of implementation, *twenty* cities have been shortlisted to roll out the programme.

The migration from the rural areas to the cities is increasing with a higher pace. A *neo middle class* is emerging which has aspirations of better living standards. With all these challenges to the successful implementation of the mission, the centre of attention is the citizen. In other words, a smart city will work towards ensuring the best for all people, regardless of social status, age, income levels and gender, only when *citizens will actively participate* in governance and reforms. Smart Cities Mission requires involvement of *smart people* in the process of making decisions on deploying smart solutions, implementing reforms, doing more with less, maintaining oversight during implementation and designing post-project structures in order to make the smart city developments sustainable.

Other Urban Infrastructure: With increasing urbanization, opportunities as well as challenges related to urban infrastructure are also increasing. In this context, up to early 2016, the government has taken various ***new initiatives*** to improve urban infrastructure:

SBM (Swachh Bharat Mission) aims at making India *free from open defecation* and at achieving 100 per cent scientific management of municipal solid waste in 4041 statutory towns/cities in the country. The targets set for the mission which have to be achieved by 2 October 2019.

HRIDAY (National Heritage City Development and Augmentation Yojana) aims at preserving and revitalizing the soul and unique character of *heritage cities* in India. In the first phase, it contains 12 cities – Ajmer, Amaravati, Amritsar, Badami,

Dwarka, Mathura, Puri, Varanasi, Velankanni, Kanchipuram, Gaya and Warangal.

AMRUT (Atal Mission for Rejuvenation and Urban Transformation) aims at improving basic urban infrastructure in 500 cities/towns which will be known as *mission cities/towns*. This a Centrally Sponsored Scheme (CSS) funded by GoI, States and the local bodies.

A number of other initiatives in the existing scheme of the policy framework have also been taken – public transport through Bus Rapid Transit Systems (BRTS) approved for 11 cities under the JNNURM (Jawaharlal Nehru National Urban Renewal Mission); Buses and Metro Rail Projects to be equipped with ITS (Intelligent Transport System).

PRIVATE SECTOR AND URBANISATION

Proper urban planning becomes an important issue for India as it is urbanising fast. Given the Government push to the Smart City scheme, it will be needful to tap the potential of every possible candidate in this regard. One of such candidate is the private sector. There are few examples where we find the sector able to develop praiseworthy townships—in certain areas beating the public sector also—though they have their own limitations, too. Two such cases have been cited by the **Economic Survey 2016-17** (quoting case studies)[67] in this regard—of two different time periods:

1. **Gurgaon:** It was in 2001 when Haryana government removed restrictions on the land acquisition process and empowered the HUDA (Haryana Urban Development Authority) and allowed private builders to develop township on the erstwhile

agricultural land—and here started the development of today's Gurgaon. Today the city is under the control of HUDA, Municipal Corporation of Gurgaon (created in 2008) and the private builders. In Gurgaon, the private sector has stepped in to address many of the failings of the public sector, with mixed success:

*   Corrected the failure of the public sector by creating private sewage, water, electricity, security and fire prevention.
*   Rapid Metro in Gurgaon was built by DLF and Infrastructure Leasing & Financial Services Limited (IL&FS), with HUDA providing the requisite land.
*   Roads are of good quality.
*   Shortfall in transport facilities is covered by the private modes of transport.

Precisely speaking, private players have addressed most challenges but they have been unable to provide services beyond their own property line as cooperation lacks amongst them and the authorities. The public authorities have had limited success in providing the city with large scale infrastructure. The failures of the city are also well known:

*   It suffered from lack of cohesive urban plan and its explosive growth has outpaced the planning efforts (like in any other Indian cities).
*   Multiple layers of local and higher authorities, having greater power to extract rents, have increased the transaction costs for the private builders. Different private builders have to seek different political patronage as otherwise none would manage to function.

---

67. **Economic Survey 2016-17** (Vol. 1, p. 313) cites the studies of S. Rajagopalan & A. Tabarrok, *Lessons from Gurgaon, India's Private City*, in D. Anderson & S. Moroni (Ed.), Cities and Private Planning, Cheltenham, UK: Edward Elgar, 2014.

- Competition among private suppliers has produced two failures:

(i) Prices of water, electricity, sewage, and so forth are close to marginal cost but average cost is far too high (because of the failure to exploit economies of scale).

(ii) Competitive suppliers have produced negative externalities such as excess pollution with diesel fumes, over used common resources by dumping sewage waste and, groundwater dissipation leading to unsustainable level of water table. A vibrant civil society could have been able to put checks on such issues (but city being quite young this is almost absent by now).

2. **Jamshedpur:** This is a private township and one of the best-governed cities in India. Jamshedpur Utilities and Services Company Ltd. (JUSCO), a wholly-owned subsidiary of Tata Steel, is responsible for provisioning of the basic services here. The township is widely regarded as having some of the best urban infrastructure in the country and JUSCO is considered a *model provider*. It has a grown up civil society which checks negative externalities of the urban expansion. The township was rated the second best in the country by *ORG Marg Nielsen* (the worldwide market research firm) on its "quality-of-life index" in 2008, and in 2010 the city was ranked 7th of 441 cities and towns in India on "sanitation" and "cleanliness" by the Ministry of Urban Development.

India needs to take few important lessons from the experience the above-cited examples—so that the privately developed townships are ideal ones:

(i) Private sector can develop quite a competitive urban centres.

(ii) Private sector will have to bear the burden of higher transaction costs, if the city is managed by multiple authorities. Such costs would also be higher if initial cohesive development plan for the city is not put in place. Post-growth infrastructure development costs are much higher and at times prohibitive.

(iii) The active role of *civil society* can prevent excessive exploitation of resources and reduce the impact of negative externalities associated with rapid urbanisation. We see this being present in the latter but absent in the former.

PPP MODELS

Managing adequate amount of fund for infrastructure development has been always a challenge for India. In reform era, the government evolved the idea of public private partnership (PPP) for the sector aimed at attracting investments from the private sector (domestic as well as foreign). We see an encouraging contributions coming from the private sector in this regard also. But by 2013-14, the PPPs started getting unattractive for the private sector—primarily caused by the in-built flaws in the PPP models together with regulatory reasons—although external reasons have been also there (slowdown in the country's economy due to recession among the western economies).

Various volumes of the *Economic Survey* together with the *Kelkar Committee* on the PPP have discussed about the various flaws in the existing model of the PPP, primarily used for the development of road projects in the country. In this backdrop, a better PPP model was announced by the Government by early 2016—the *Hybrid*

Annuity Model (HAM). A brief review of the major PPP models (few of them are non-PPP models, too) are given below:

(i) *BOT-TOLL:* The 'Build-Operate-Transfer-Toll' was one of the earliest models of PPP. Other than sharing the project cost (with the Government) the private bidder was to build, maintain, operate the road and collect toll on the vehicular traffic. The bid was given to the private company offering to share maximum toll revenue to the government. The private party used to cover "all risks" related to—land acquisition, construction (damage), inflation, cost over-runs caused by delays and commercial. The government was responsible for only regulatory clearances.

Due to inherent drawbacks, this model proved to be unsustainable for the private bidder—undue delay in land acquisition due to litigation, cost over-runs and uncertainties in traffic movement (commercial risk)—made the road projects economically unviable.

(ii) *BOT-ANNUITY:* This was an improvement over the BOT-TOLL model aimed at reversing the declining interest of the private companies towards road projects by manly reducing the risk for the private players. Other than sharing the project cost the private player was to build, maintain and operate the road projects without any responsibility of collecting toll on the traffic. The private players were offered a fixed amount of money annually (called 'annuity') as compensation—the party bidding for the minimum 'annuity' used to get the project. Toll collection was the responsibility of the Government.

This was different from the previous model (BOT-TOLL) in one sense—private players were not having any commercial risk (traffic)—but they remained very much exposed to other risks (land acquisition delays, inflation, cost over-runs, construction). Even this model, over the time proved to be unviable for the private sector due to the leftover risks they were exposed to.

(iii) *EPC MODEL:* The PPP model which was seen to be a better way out to promote the infra projects were visibly failing by the year 2010 and Government was unable to attract the private players towards the road sector. It was in this backdrop that the Engineering-Procurement-Construction (EPC) Model was announced. In this model, project cost was fully covered by the Government (it means, it was not a PPP model and was like normal contracts given to the bidders) together with majority of the risks—land acquisition, cost over-runs due to delay, inflation and commercial.

The private developers were supposed to design, construct and hand over the road projects to the government—maintenance, operation and toll collection being the government's responsibilities. Contract was given to the private player who offered to construct roads at the lowest cost/price guaranteeing the desired quality levels. It means, the private player in this model was only exposed to the construction-related risks which is a normal risk involved in any contract given by the government to the private party.

EPC Model could have been a temporary way out to develop road projects as it was fully funded by the government—reform era had aimed to attract investment from the private players by evolving a 'business model' for the road sector—need was to develop a new PPP model. In this backdrop we see the government coming up with a new PPP model for the road projects—the Hybrid Annuity Model.

(iv) *HAM:* Hybrid Annuity Model (HAM) is a mix of EPC and BOT-ANNUITY models. In this model the project cost is shared by the government and the private player in ratio of 40:60, respectively. The private player is responsible to construct and hand over the roads to the government which will collect toll (if wishes)—maintenance remaining the responsibility of the private player till the annuity period. Private player is paid a fixed sum of economic compensation (called 'annuity', similar to the BOT-ANNUITY model of past) by the government for a fixed tenure (normally 15 years, though it is flexible). The private player which demands lowest annuity (in bidding) gets the contract.

In this model, most of the major risks are covered by the government—land acquisition, clearances, operation, toll collection and commercial while the risks related to inflation and cost over-runs are shared in ration of the project cost sharing. But the private sector is still exposed to the construction and maintenance risks (delays from the government side in clearances and land acquisition have chances to enhance the degree of risks private players are exposed to). But overall, this is the best PPP model for the time devoid of most of the flaws of past. By early 2017, private sector had shown good response to this model.

(v) *Swiss Challenge Model:* Government of India, for the first time, announced the use of this model for redevelopment of railway stations in the country (by late 2015). This is a very flexible method of giving contracts (i.e., public procurement) which can be used in PPP as well as non-PPP projects.

In this, one bidder is asked by the government to submit the proposal for the project which is put in public domain. Afterwards, several other bidders submit their proposals aimed at improving and beating the original (first) bidder—finally an improved bid is selected (called counter proposal). If the original bidder is not able to match the counter proposal, the project is awarded to the counter bidder. Government has made it an online method.

Though, the Government of India used this model for the first time, this has already been used by several states by now—Karnataka, Andhra Pradesh, Rajasthan, Madhya Pradesh, Bihar, Punjab and Gujarat—for roads and housing projects. In 2009, the Supreme Court approved the method for award of contracts.

(vi) *PPP Model for other sectors:* Though, the idea of PPP model was originally evolved for the infrastructure sector, in recent times, there have been proposals for its uses in other areas, too—such as education, healthcare and even agriculture. The model is getting popular support from the urban local bodies in the country and it is believed that in the *Smart Cities* scheme it could play a very lucrative role. Recently, the **Economic Survey 2016-17** suggested[68] the government to create a

---

68. Basically, the **Economic Survey 2016-17** (Vol. 1, pp. 156 & 170) has supported the advice of the *Committee on Incentivising Pulses Production Through Minimum Support Price (MSP) and Related Policies* headed by Arvind Subramanian, Chief Economic Adviser (report submitted in September, 2016)—the expert committee was set up by the government on account of the price volatility of pulses seen during 2015-16.

new institution as a PPP to compete with and complement existing institutions to procure stock and dispose pulses.

(vii) *PPPP Model:* Experts have suggested public private people partnership (PPPP) model, too for certain sector in the country. Though such a model has been in use since 2000-01 itself by in agriculture sector to promote participatory irrigation development—in the Command Area Development Programme of 1974 (renamed as Command Area Development and Watershed Management Programme in 2004)—in which individual financial contributions come from the farmers (around 15 per cent of the total cost) to develop field channels and drains.

It is believed that in the area of developing, maintaining and protecting local public assets this model could be highly effective. In future, the local bodies—urban as well as rural—may be using this model to develop social and economic infrastructure.

CONCERNS OF PETROLEUM SECTOR

In the absence of a global gas market for benchmarking domestic gas prices in India, various formulae have been suggested. Since October 2014 a formula based on producer and consumer markets is being used to arrive at domestic gas prices in India. It was expected that the formula would balance the interest of producers and consumers in the country.

However, market-determined arm's length pricing for domestic gas, with an effective regulator, to provide adequate incentive for investment and also ensure competiveness and transparency remains the *first-best solution* that merits consideration. It would reflect the appropriate gas price in relation to alternative fuels. In the medium-term, being a large consumer, India may be able to be a *price setter* for gas prices in the region. Possible steps to address the concerns of the sector are as given below (*Economic Survey 2015–16*):

- Petroleum products and natural gas should be included under the Goods and Services Tax (GST), or at least its exclusion should not be indicated in the Constitution Amendment Bill.

- The cess collections could be used to support construction of a network of gas pipelines, which is of crucial importance for providing clean energy to deprived regions of the country. The progress is somewhat constrained at present by having been linked to revival of fertilizer units and development of small industries in areas along the gas highway projects. Alternatively, in order to promote the gas pipeline network, Viability Gap Funding (VGF) may be provided for promoting pipeline assets creation and development of efficient markets.

- Impetus is required for construction of not only cross-country pipelines but also city gas distribution. The present system of bidding by the Petroleum and Natural Gas Regulatory Board (PNGRB) is lopsided and long-drawn-out and needs to be reformed since it has constrained development of the gas network.

- Expansion of the PNG/CNG (Compressed Natural Gas) network could help provide gas connections to rural areas.

- Rationalization of LPG subsidy is essential. It may be useful to cap subsidy to 10 LPG cylinders for each household (that being the maximum used for usual domestic cooking) while aligning taxes and duties on domestic and commercial LPG users.

- Import of liquefied Natural Gas (LNG) for use in the power industry is exempt from customs duty while LNG for all other uses attracts 5 per cent customs duties. There should be no exemptions for any sector.

- In order to develop a cost-effective and revenue-neutral mechanism for *swapping of gas* across producing and consuming states for the *national gas grid*, it is important to make special tax provision for sale of natural gas under the Central Sales Tax Act 1956. Natural gas and LNG may be treated as *declared goods* to bring about tax parity with crude oil and make prices uniform across states.

Meanwhile, India has entered into exploring the **unconventional** resources of energy such as the *CBM (Coal Bed Methane)* and *Shale Oil & Gas.* The estimated CBM resources are about 92 TCF (trillion cubic feet) of which only 9.9 TCF has so far been confirmed – current production is about 1 million cubic metre per day. In the *Shale Oil & Gas* areas, presently, the assessment process is going on in 50 blocks. Commercial production is yet to begin.

RENEWABLE ENERGY

India's renewable energy potential has been assessed (in the medium-term) at 8, 96,602 MW, which includes the potential from *solar* (7,48,990 MW), *wind* (1, 00,000 MW), *small hydro* (20,000 MW) and *biomass* (26,800 MW) power.

Apart from grid power requirement, renewable energy sources are also being used for distributed generation, lighting, pumping and motive power requirement in remote and inaccessible areas. India is graduating from Mega watts to Gig watts in the generation of clean renewable energy. The target from various renewable energy sources has been increased by the GoI to **175 GW** by the year **2022** – solar and wind to contribute 100 GW and 60 GW, respectively. The **major steps** taken by the government to boost the sector in recent times are as given below *(by early 2017):*

(i) *Solar Rooftop:* Grid-connected rooftops systems to come up by 2019-20 under the National Solar Mission (NSM).

(ii) *Solar Parks:* 25 solar parks and ultra mega solar power projects with an aggregate capacity of 20,000 MW to be set up in the next five years (from 2015-16 to 2019-20).

(iii) *Solar Projects under the NSM:* In February 2015, the government announced to set up 15,000 MW of grid-connected solar PV power projects under the NSM by 2018-19.

(iv) *Solar Pumps:* Target of installing of one lakh solar pumps for irrigation and drinking water by 2016.

(v) *Solar Cities:* Approval granted for 56 solar city projects under the Development of Solar Cities Programme.

- *The Surya Mitra*: This scheme was launched in May 2015 for creating 50,000 trained personnel within a period of five years (2015-16 to 2019-20).

In addition to the above, major policy initiatives taken by the government up to March 2016 include:

(i) National Offshore Wind Energy Policy 2015 to exploit the vast 7600 km coastline for development of offshore wind energy in the Indian Exclusive Economic Zone (EEZ),

(ii) Inclusion of renewable energy in the *priority sector* and bank loans up to Rs. 15 crore limit to borrowers categories for purposes like solar-based power generators, biomass- based power generators, windmills, micro-hydel plants and for nonconventional energy-based public utilities like street lighting systems, and remote village electrification. For individual households this is up to Rs. 10 lakh per borrower.

(iii) Investments in renewable energy are on *automatic route*, i.e. automatic approval for up to **74** per cent *foreign equity participation* in a JV and **100** per cent foreign investment as equity is permissible with the approval of the Foreign Investment Promotion Board (FIPB).

(iv) Approval to the amendments in the National Tariff Policy 2005, for promotion of renewable power.

CHALLANGES AND REMEDIES

Infrastructural concerns have been always there in case of India. The GoI designed a format of PPP to boost the sector. But due to several global and domestic factors, it got almost derailed by late 2013–14. Of late, the infrastructure projects were hit by variety of hurdles:

(i) Delays in project approval – causing high cost over-runs,

(ii) Delays in land acquisition,

(iii) Scarcity of fund due to longer gestation periods,

(iv) Drawbacks in the existing PPP format,

(v) A situation of policy paralysis form 2010-11 to 2013–14,

(vi) Slowdown in growth of the economy (due to global and domestic slackness), and

(vii) Twin Balance Sheet problem.

The major concerns of the infrastructure sector have been outlined by several government documents – which are briefly summed-up as given below[69]:

(i) The *Twelfth Plan* lays special emphasis on development of the infrastructure sector including:

(a) Energy, as the availability of quality infrastructure is important not only for sustaining high growth, but also ensuring that the growth is inclusive.

(b) The total investment in the infrastructure sector during the Plan, estimated at Rs. 56.3 lakh crore (approx. US$1 trillion), will be nearly double the amount committed during the Eleventh Plan.

(c) This step up in investment will be feasible primarily because of enlarged private-sector participation that is envisaged.

(ii) Unbundling of infrastructure projects, *public private partnerships* (PPP), and more transparent regulatory mechanisms have induced private investors to increase their participation in infrastructure sectors:

(a) Their share in infrastructure investment increased from 22 per cent in the Tenth Plan to 38 per cent in the Eleventh Plan and was expected to be about 48 per cent during the Twelfth Plan.

(b) Yet, more than half of the resources required for infrastructure would need to come from the public sector, from the government, and the parastatals.

---

69. Planning Commission, **12th Plan (2012-17),** (New Delhi: Government of India, 2012); Ministry of Finance, *Economic Survey 2015–16* & *Economic Survey 2016–17.*

(c) This would require not only the creation of the fiscal space but also use of a *rational pricing policy*.

(d) Scaling up private-sector participation on a sustainable basis will require *redefining the contours of their participation* for the development of infrastructure sector in a transparent and objective manner with a comprehensive regulatory mechanism in place.

(e) From a *macroeconomic perspective*, a high level of investment in the infrastructure sector is essential for the overall revival of investment climate which may finally lead to sustainable growth in an economy.

(f) However, in the current macroeconomic environment, to achieve this objective, there is need to address sector-specific issues over the medium-to-long-term horizon in India.

(iii) There is an **overall shortage of power** in the country both in terms of energy deficit and peak shortage:

(a) At present, overall energy deficit is about 8.6 per cent and peak shortage of power is about 9.0 per cent.

(b) The Eleventh Plan added 55,000 MW of generation capacity which was more than twice the capacity added in the Tenth Plan.

(c) The Twelfth Plan aims to add another 88, 000 MW.

(d) Delivery of this additional capacity would critically depend on resolving *fuel* availability problems, especially when *about half* the generated capacity is expected to come from the private sector.

(e) The private developers may not be able to finance the projects if *coal linkages* are not resolved and there are delays in finalisation of fuel supply agreements (FSAs).

(f) While some decisions have been taken for restructuring Discoms' finances, these may need to be monitored and implemented in spirit.

(iv) Although India has large **coal** reserves, demand for coal is substantially outpacing its domestic availability, with Coal India Ltd. not being able to meet its coal production targets in the Eleventh Plan:

(a) Domestic coal supplies are therefore *not assured* for coal-based power projects planned during the Twelfth Plan. Thus, it is essential to ensure that domestic production of coal increases from 540 million tonnes in 2011-12 to the target of 795 million tonnes at the end of the 12th Plan.

(b) This increase of 255 million tonnes assumes an increase of 64 million tonnes of captive capacity with the rest being met by Coal India Limited.

(c) However, even with this increase, there will be a need to import 185 million tonnes of coal in 2016–17, which may further add to the financing cost of power projects.

(d) More effort must be made for improving competition and efficiency in the coal sector, which may entail structural reforms.

(e) Problems like delays in obtaining environmental clearances, land acquisitions, and rehabilitation need to be suitably addressed in fast-track mode to achieve the Twelfth Plan targets for coal production, while maintaining a balance between growth needs and *environmental concerns*.

(v) Progress of *road* projects has also suffered on account of similar factors:

(a) The creation of a High-Level Cabinet Committee on Investment to quicken the pace of decision making in critical infrastructure projects by the government is expected to resolve any issues involving inter-ministerial coordination.

(b) Of late, financing of *road* projects has also run into difficulty as leveraged companies implementing road projects are unable to raise more debt in the absence of fresh equity. In current market conditions, these firms are unable to raise *new equity*.

(c) Exit route needs to be eased so that promoters can sell equity positions after construction, passing on all benefits and responsibilities to entities that step in.

(d) Promoters can then use the equity thus released for new projects.

(e) Steps are also needed to up-scale projects in PPP mode for achieving the targets envisaged for the development of roads in the Twelfth Plan.

(vi) The process of extending *transparent policies* and mechanisms for allocation of scarce natural resources to private companies for commercial purposes has also been initiated:

(a) The Mines & Mineral (Development and Regulation) Bill 2011 aims at providing a simple and transparent mechanism for grant of mining lease or prospecting licence through competitive bidding in areas of known mineralisation and on first-in-time basis in areas where mineralisation is not known.

(b) *However*, in order to meet the objective of revenue maximisation in an open, transparent and competitive manner, this should be preceded by detailed geological mapping of the mineral wealth of the country.

(c) Further, any policy prescription regarding the use of natural resources must ensure that the process of selection is fair, reasonable, non-discriminatory, transparent, and aimed at promoting healthy competition and equitable treatment.

(vii) Owing to a number of external and internal factors, viability of *airline* operations in India has come under stress.

(a) A high operating cost environment owing to high and rising cost of aviation turbine fuel (ATF) coupled with rupee depreciation is making operations unviable for carriers in India.

(b) The Expert Report of Nathan Economic Consulting India Private Ltd. (Nathan India) which went into the question of pricing and the tax regime governing ATF concluded that ATF prices in India are significantly higher (at least 40 per cent) than in competing hubs in the region such as Singapore, Hong Kong and Dubai.

(c) Therefore, there is need to rationalise the tax regime particularly value added tax on ATF which is in the range of 20–30 per cent in most of the states.

(d) The Ministry of Civil Aviation is of the view that ATF should be included under the declared goods category under the relevant provision of the Central Sales Tax Act so that a uniform levy of 5 per cent is achieved.

(e) Equally important is the need for a transparent pricing regime for ATF in India. A high tax regime for aviation in general, and ATF in particular, will reduce the wider economic benefits available from aviation, resulting in a negative impact on economic growth and overall government revenue bases.

(viii) The **Railways** is another urgent priority for the Twelfth Plan:

(a) Capacity in railways has lagged far behind what is needed, especially given the requirement of shifting from road transport to rail in the interests of improving energy efficiency and reducing carbon footprints in development.

(b) The funding pattern of the Twelfth Plan clearly shows that the modernisation of Indian Railways cannot be achieved by simply relying on GBS (Gross Budgetary Support) as about 62 per cent of the resources would have to be generated through non-GBS sources and nearly 20 per cent through private-sector investment.

(c) There is a need to draw up clear strategies to generate resources by identifying segments where Indian Railways can adopt a low-cost policy by playing on volumes and taking advantage of economies of scale and segments where it can adopt a differentiation approach by providing high-quality services and command premium prices.

(ix) The Twelfth Plan document, a GDP growth rate of about 8 per cent requires a growth rate of about 6 per cent in total **energy use** from all sources:

(a) Unfortunately, the capacity of the economy to expand domestic energy supplies to meet this demand is severely limited.

(b) The country is not well-endowed with energy resources, except coal, and the existence of policy distortions makes management of demand and supply more difficult.

(c) Accordingly, the short-run action needed to remove impediments to implementation of projects in infrastructure, especially in the area of energy, includes ensuring fuel supply to power stations, financial restructuring of Discoms, and clarity in terms of the NELP.

(d) At the same time, the long-term strategy should focus on issues like coal production, petroleum price distortion, natural gas pricing, and effective management of the urbanisation process.

CURRENT SCENARIO

As per the *Economic Survey 2016-17*, investment promotion to industry in general and infrastructure in particular has turned out to be the biggest challenge of the current times[70]. Since no clear progress is yet visible in tackling the TBS (twin balance sheet) problem, *private investment* is unlikely to recover significantly from the levels of the fiscal 2016-17. Some of this weakness could

---

70. **Economic Survey 2016-17**, Government of India, Ministry of Finance, N. Delhi, Vol. 1, pp. 20-22.

be offset through higher *public investment*, but that would depend on the fiscal challenges of 2017-18 (government has to balance the short-term requirements of the economy recovering from demonetisation against the medium-term necessity of adhering to fiscal discipline.(p.20)

The *Survey* further adds that till 2016-17, the financing strategy of India has worked to allow India grow rapidly. But this strategy may now be reaching its limits. After eight years of buying time (since the recession among the western economies, led by the US sub-prime crisis), there is still no sign that the affected companies are regaining their health, or even that the bad debt problem is being contained. Opposite to it, the stress on corporate sector and banks is continuing to intensify, and this in turn is taking a measurable toll on investment and credit. Moreover, efforts to offset these trends by providing macroeconomic stimulus are not proving sufficient—the increase in public investment has been more than offset by the fall in private investment, while until demonetisation monetary easing had not been transmitted to bank borrowers (as banks had been widening their margins instead). In these circumstances, it has become increasingly clear that the underlying debt problem will finally need to be addressed[71], lest it derails India's growth trajectory.

Meanwhile, the government has announced various measures in the *Union Budget 2017-18* which are expected to boost the demand and investment sentiments in the economy—tax breaks, higher public investment, higher allocations to agriculture and infrastructure sectors, commitment to implement the GST and disciplined fiscal compliance. Though commodity prices in the international market, high chance of interest rate revision by the US central bank together with an expected inflation pressure (by the mid-2017-18) are the areas of concerns in this regard.

---

71. **Economic Survey 2016-17**, Government of India, Ministry of Finance, N. Delhi, Vol. 1, pp.90-94.

10

SERVICES SECTOR

India's dynamic services sector has grown rapidly in the last decade with almost 72.4 per cent of the growth in India's GDP in 2014–15 coming from this sector. Unlike other developing economies, the Indian growth story has been led by services-sector growth which is now in double digits.*

- ❑ Introduction
- ❑ Global Scenario
- ❑ Services Performance
- ❑ Research & Development (R & D) Services
- ❑ Manufacturing vs. Services
- ❑ Global Negotiations

- ❑ Restrictions and Regulations
- ❑ The Need for Reforms
- ❑ Outlining Future

* Ministry of Finance, Economic Survey 2014–15, Vol. 2 (New Delhi: Government of India, 2015), p. 106.

INTRODUCTION

India's services sector has not only outperformed other sectors of the Indian economy, but has also played an important role in India's integration with world trade and capital markets. India's liberalisation of services has been a challenging process in several sub-sectors, but clearly those services where integration through trade and FDI has gone further are also the ones that have exhibited more rapid growth along with positive spillovers on the rest of the economy.

There is, however, a concern[1] about the *sustainability* of a services-led growth process which largely stems from exports of skill-based services. The prevailing view is that for services growth to be sustained, the sector cannot remain dependent on external demand. It must also be driven by internal demand. More broad-based growth within the services is also required to ensure balanced, equitable and employment-oriented growth, with backward and forward linkages to the rest of the economy. In this regard further infrastructural and regulatory reforms and FDI liberalisation in services can help diversify the sources of growth withing India's services sector and provide the required momentum.

In recent years, there has been a debate in the country regarding the selection of the sector which can lead the growth process in the country. This debate originated from the fact that the services sector contributed over 62 per cent in the GDP during the decade 2001–12. But the debate has been somewhat solved by the newly published *Economic Survey 2014–15* in favour of the *manufacturing sector*. The Survey has gone to quote several empirical studies of recent times linking both services and manufacturing sectors to a great many real issues—potential to create employment, need of skilled and unskilled labour force, formality anf informality of the sector, etc. For this, the idea of 'Make in India' has acclaimed timely action from the government. Again, the importance of expanding the Railways and enhancing public investment in it have also been pointed out.[2] These findings are also in line with several other studies of the recent times.[3]

GLOBAL SCENARIO

The services sector has emerged as the most dynamic sector of the world economy, contributing almost *one-third* of world gross value added, half of world employment, one-fifth of global trade and more than half of the world FDI flows. A brief idea of the current trends[4] in the sector follows below:

World Services GVA

The global services performance are as given below:

- In 2015, in the US$ 69 trillion world gross value added (GVA), the share of services (at current prices), and growth rate (at constant prices), improved marginally to 63 per cent and 2.3 per cent respectively over 2014.

- In the last 14 years, the share of the services sector in world GVA has declined by 2.9 percentage points (pp). Among the world's top 15 countries in terms of gross domestic product (GDP), the US ranks *first*, in both services GVA and overall GDP, China being *second* and Japan *third*.

1. Rupa Chanda, in Kaushik Basu and Annemie Maertens (eds) 'Services-led Growth' *The New Oxford Companion to Economics in India*, Vol. II (New Delhi: Oxford University Press, 2012), pp. 624–32.

2. For a detailed description See Ministry of Finance, *Economic Survey 2014–15*, Vol. 1. Though, the theme of the analysis has been included in this book itself, in the Chapter-9 'Industry and Infrastructure'.

3. *India Development Report 2012–13* (New Delhi: Oxford University Press, 2013), pp. 116–31.

4. *Economic Survey 2016-17* & *2015-16*; Ministry of Commerce & Industry, GoI, N. Delhi.

- India ranked *ninth* in terms of overall GDP and *tenth* in terms of services GVA in 2015, climbing one rung in both rankings.
- Among these top 15 nations, in the period 2001-14, the maximum increase in services share to GVA was recorded by Spain (9.3 pp), followed by *India (7.6 pp)* and China (6.6 pp).
- Services sector has not recovered from the impact of the 2008 financial crisis (Brazil being exception).
- In India, the growth rate in the sector was estimated to be **8.8** per cent in 2016-17 with a slight deceleration in 2016–17 (for China it was at **8.0** per cent).

World Services Employment

The global employment scenario in the services sector shows a mixed picture.

- As per the *World Bank*, the share of services in global employment has increased to 53 per cent in 2016 (from 35.9 per cent of 2001).
- Among the top 15 services producing countries, the share of services in employment is high, contributing more than *two-thirds* of total employment in 2015 in most of them (except India and China). India has the *lowest share* of 27.4 per cent.
- Of the 15 countries, in the last 14-year period (2001–15), China had the highest increase in the *share of services employment* (33.8 pp), followed by Brazil (17.0 pp) and Spain (14.3 pp). For India, the increase was by only 4.5 pp.

As per the *ILO Report* on "*Global Employment and Social Outlook: Trends 2016*", job in the coming years will be mainly in the services sector though with lower rate.

SERVICES PERFORMANCE

Service sector was having a robust performance in India for the last decade and by 2014-15 its contribution in the GDP had reached the record level of 72.4 per cent. But in the last few years it has not been able to grow as good mainly due to unfavourable international environment. The present performance scenario for the sector is briefly highlighted below[5]:

- In 2016-17 the sector is estimated to have a growth rate of **8.8** per cent (almost same as 2015-16), as per the 1st advance estimates of the CSO, released *January 2017*.
- India's commercial services exports increased from US$ 51.9 billion in 2005 to US$ 155.3 billion in 2015 (WTO).
- The share of India's *commercial services* to global services exports increased to **3.3** per cent in 2015 from 3.1 per cent in 2014 despite negative growth of 0.2 per cent in 2015 as compared to 5.0 per cent growth in 2014. This was due to the relatively greater fall in world services exports by 6.1 per cent in 2015 (WTO).
- As per RBI's BoP data, India's services exports declined by 2.4 per cent in 2015-16 as a result of slowdown in global output and trade. However, in H1 of 2016-17, services exports increased by 4.0 per cent compared to 0.3 per cent growth in the same period of previous year.
- Growth of net services, which has been a major source of financing India's trade deficit in recent years, was (-) 9.0 per cent in 2015-16 and (-) 10.0 per cent in H1 of 2016-17 due to relatively higher growth in imports of services.

5. **Economic Survey 2016-17**, Government of India, ministry of Finance, N. Delhi, Vol. 1, pp.159-160.

- Growth of *software* exports which accounted for **48.1** per cent share in services exports was 1.4 per cent in 2015-16 and 0.1 per cent in H1 of 2016-17.

- India's *tourism* sector witnessed a growth of 4.5 per cent in terms of foreign tourist arrivals (FTAs) with 8.2 million arrivals in 2015, and a growth of 4.1 per cent in foreign exchange earnings (FEEs) of US$ 21.1 billion. In 2016 (January-December), FTAs were 8.9 million with growth of 10.7 per cent and FEE (US$ terms) were at US$ 23.1 billion with a growth of 9.8 per cent.

Regional Outlook

A regional differentiation is found in India regarding the sector –

- Out of the 33 states and union territories(UT) for which data was available, the services sector was the dominant sector contributing more than half of the gross state domestic products (GSDP) in 21 states and UTs and more than 40 per cent in all states except Sikkim and Arunachal Pradesh. The major services in most of the states are trade, hotels and restaurants, followed by real estate, ownership of dwellings and business services.

- Out of the 23 states and UTs for which data is available for 2014–15, Delhi is at the top in services GSDP with a share of 87.5 per cent followed by Maharashtra at 63.8 per cent, with growth rates of 8.2 per cent and 5.7 per cent respectively.

- Puducherry had the highest services growth at 16.3 per cent followed by Meghalaya at 13.2 per cent, owing to increase in growth rate of high weighted sectors like trade, hotels and restaurants and real estate and business services in the

case of the former and other services in the case of the latter.

- Jammu and Kashmir had the lowest services growth at 2.0 per cent, mainly due to low and negative growth in most of the sectors except public administration. Bihar's services sector growth was among the fastest with a consistent double-digit growth in the last seven years due to high growth in the high weighted sectors like trade, hotels and restaurants, and real estate and business services besides transport by other means.

Consultancy Services

Consultancy services are emerging as one of the fastest growing service segments in India, overlapping. A large number of consultancy firms and individual consultants are operating in India at various levels across the sectors.

Technical consulting constitutes about *two-thirds* of the total consulting market, while management consulting constitutes about one-third. Technical consulting in India, which mainly consists of engineering consulting, is much stronger than management consulting in terms of the number of players, consulting capabilities and size of consulting firms. The Indian management consulting market, on the other hand, is mainly captured by large size foreign multinational consulting firms. Though there are huge opportunities for the growth of the Indian consulting industry, there are some key inhibitors like low brand equity, inadequate international experience of Indian consultants working abroad, lack of local presence, lack of strategic tie-ups, low competency image, lack of market intelligence on consulting opportunities abroad and lack of a strong competency framework of consultants that improves quality in delivery of consulting assignments. The GoI has taken many *initiatives* to help the industry –

(i) Marketing Development Assistance and Market Access Initiative schemes;

(ii) Guidelines on broad policies and procedures for selection, contracting and monitoring of consultants; and

(iii) Initiatives aimed towards capacity development of domestic consultants and sensitisation of client organisations.

Recent initiatives taken by the GoI such as Make in India, development of smart cities, skill development, along with the focus on improving industrial policies and procedures, have opened up a plethora of opportunities for consultants.

The *key areas with enormous potential* for Indian consultancy firms are: building of urban & transport infrastructure, power generation, renewable energy, electricity transmission & distribution, roads & bridges, water supply & sewerage, IT & telecom, health care and manufacturing. *Emerging sectors* such as bio-technology, nano-technology and other advanced disciplines also offer tremendous opportunities to consultants. Consultancy services can also look forward to deriving revenues from newer services and newer geographies with Big Data, cloud, M2M and Internet of Things becoming a reality.

Internal Trade

It refers to the movement of goods and services across different geographical regions in the country. It includes *self-employed* and persons engaged in both wholesale and retail trade. Presently internal trade is governed by a diversity of controls, multiple organizations and a plethora of orders. This has resulted in a *fragmented market*, hindering the free flow of goods within the country, higher transportation costs and in general a lower level of efficiency and productivity. Unhindered flow of goods and services is an essential pre-requisite for building a common market that will promote growth, trade across regions and also enable specialization and higher levels of economic

efficiency. Major *highlights* of the sector are as follows:

- The trade and repair services sector grew by 10.7 per cent in 2014–15.

- A report by *KPMG-FICCI* – late 2015, put the overall size of the Indian retail sector at Rs. 40 trillion in 2014 and projected it to reach Rs. 70 trillion by 2020 with a compound annual growth rate (CAGR) of 9.6 per cent.

- The penetration of modern retail is expected to reach 18 per cent from the current 9.8 per cent in this period, driven by the increasing appeal of modern retail among shoppers as well as changes in shoppers' expectations and behaviour.

- It will be a key sector for skill of **58** million people by 2022 and accounting for 14 per cent of the incremental human resource and skill requirement from 2013 to 2022. With organized retail penetrating the smaller towns and cities, there would be a need for skilled manpower in this sector.

- As per the AT Kearney's *Global Retail Development Index (GRDI)* report, India's retail trade ranking has risen to 15 from 20 in 2014, mainly due to solid expansion in retail sales and strong prospects for future GDP growth. India's retail market is expected to grow to US$1.3 trillion by 2020, making India the world's fastest-growing major developing market.

- Real estate availability could be the biggest barrier to retail expansion in India since it has four times the population of the United States but just one-tenth of the mall space. This market still has a long way to go as online remains just **0.5** per cent of the total retail market, internet penetration is just **20** per cent of the population, and infrastructure needs to improve significantly.

- As per the ASSOCHAM-Deloitte report (April 2015), *E-commerce* market has grown steadily from US$ 4.4 billion in 2010 to US$ 13.6 billion in 2014. Online travel accounts for nearly 61 per cent of e-commerce business while e-tailing constitutes about 29 per cent. Some estimates indicate that companies will spend between US $1 billion and US $2 billion on e-commerce-related infrastructure over the next five years.

- No official data is available on the direct selling/multi-level marketing (MLM) sector. According to a KPMG-FICCI study (December 2015), the direct selling market in India has grown at a CAGR of 16 per cent over the last five years from Rs. 41 billion in 2009–10 to Rs. 75 billion in 2013–14. Total employment in this sector is around 5.8 million. There is at present no separate legislation for regulation of direct selling activities, hence they come directly under the purview of the *Prize Chits & Money Circulation Schemes (Banning) Act 1978*, administered by the Department of Financial Services. As it is a banning act, there is no provision for differentiating the genuine direct selling business from banned pyramid/money circulation schemes, and this has resulted in alleged harassment/ criminal action against the industry. An inter-ministerial committee was constituted on 12 November 2014 to examine the need for a separate legislation for this sector. Based on the decision taken in the last meeting, a draft guidelines is under examination.

RESEARCH & DEVELOPMENT (R & D) SERVICES

The Research & Development sector of India[6] grew by 20.8 per cent in 2012–13 and contributed 1.4 per cent of GDP (old method). As per the CSO's new method, there is no separate head for R&D. It is a part of the professional scientific & technical activities including R&D classification which grew at **3.1** per cent and **23.4** per cent respectively in 2014–15 and 2015–16 *(Ministry of Commerce & Industry, Feb. 2017)*.

India's R&D expenditure has been low – the STO (Science, Technology and Innovation) Policy, 2013 aims to raise it to **2** per cent of GDP with enhanced participation of the private sector.

Findings of the *Global Competitiveness Report 2016–17* are as given below –

(a) India's capacity for innovation has been lower than that of many countries like the USA, the UK, South Korea, and even South Africa.

(b) Even in quality of scientific research institutions, India scores lower than China and South Africa. This is also exhibited through its poor score on university–industry collaboration on R&D as compared to some other BRICS (Brazil, Russia, India, China and South Africa) nations like China and South Africa.

(c) In terms of *patents* granted per million population, India fares badly compared to other BRICS countries. In terms of

---

6. Ministry of Finance, *Economic Survey 2015–16,* pp. 167–68.

company spending on R&D also, India ranks below China. Only in terms of availability of scientists and engineers, does India score better or is equal to other BRICS countries.

The Government of India has taken many **initiatives** in recent times to promote the R&D sector in India –

(i) The weighted tax deduction of 200 per cent for R&D expenditure.

(ii) Establishment of the *AIM* (Atal Innovation Mission) in the NITI Aayog. This will be an innovation promotion platform involving academics, entrepreneurs, and researchers and draw upon national and international experiences to foster a culture of innovation, R&D and scientific research in India. The platform will also promote a network of world-class innovation hubs.

(iii) *SETU* (Self Employment and Talent Utilization) programme, aimed at setting up world class technology business incubators to promote **start-up** business in India coupled with Start-up-India, Make in India.

(iv) *IMPRINT* (Impacting Research Innovation and Technology), a Pan-IIT and IISc joint initiative to develop a roadmap for research to solve major engineering and technology challenges in ten technology domains relevant to India.

MANUFACTURING VS. SERVICES

All the focus being on the manufacturing exports in India has distracted attention from what might be a no less noteworthy development[7]. In past few years, it is India's exports of services that has changed in the most significant, and perhaps alarming, way. One can see the problem looking at market shares. India's share of world exports of services, after surging in the mid-2000s, has flattened out.

What makes this development puzzling is that in recent years the composition of Indian exports of services is more favourable than that of Indian exports of manufactured goods. More of the former goes to the United States, and more of the latter to Asia. Since Asia has slowed down more rapidly, India's exports of manufactures should have been more affected. Furthermore, in 2015, the rupee has depreciated strongly against the dollar which should have helped India's exports of services.

These developments have longer-term implications. Realising India's medium-term growth potential of 8-10 per cent will require rapid growth of exports. How rapid this should be is suggested by comparing India's export performance in services with China's performance in manufacturing at a comparable stage of the growth surge.

China's global market share in manufacturing exports beginning in 1991 and India's global market share beginning in 2003 were roughly similar. The magnitude of the challenge becomes evident when examining China's trajectory over the last fifteen years.

To achieve a similar trajectory, India's competitiveness will have to improve so that its services exports, currently about **3** per cent of world exports, capture nearly **15** per cent of world market share. That is a sizeable challenge, and recent trends suggest that a major effort at improving competitiveness will be necessary to meet it.

GLOBAL NEGOTIATIONS

India aims to position itself as a key player in world services trade. To promote services exports, the government has taken a number of

---

7. Ibid.

policy initiatives – SEIS (Service Exports from India Scheme) for increasing exports of notified services from India; organising GES (Global Exhibitions on Services); and SCs (Services Conclaves). Besides, some initiatives in sectors like tourism and shipping have also been taken in this regard. Given the potential of India's services exports, services-sector negotiations both at multilateral and bilateral and regional levels are of vital importance to India. Some of the recent negotiations[8] are as given below.

WTO Negotiations

Following important decisions were taken at the 10th session of the WTO Ministerial Conference held in Nairobi, Kenya (15–18 December 2015).

(i) Implementation of preferential treatment in favour of services and service suppliers of least developed countries (LDC) and increasing LDC participation in services trade;

(ii) To maintain the current practice of not imposing customs duties on electronic transmissions (e-Commerce) until the next Ministerial Conference to be held in 2017.

(iii) India, together with 20 other members have notified preferential treatment to LDCs in services trade. India has offered this in respect of:

(a) Market access

(b) Technical assistance and capacity building; and

(c) Waiver of visa fees for LDC applicants for business and employment.

In *February 2017*, India made a presentation a proposal to the WTO for a global pact to boost services trade. The proposal—Trade Facilitation in Services (TFS)—is mainly aimed at 'ensuring'—easier norms for movement of foreign skilled workers/professionals across borders for short-term work; portability of social security contributions; reasonable fees for immigration; cross-border insurance coverage; boosting medical tourism; and publication availability of relevant information for cross-border supply of services. *World Bank* data shows the growing share of services in the world economy, the sources said, adding, however, that global trade flows in services remain subject to numerous border and behind-the-border barriers *(Ministry of Commerce & Industry)*.

Bilateral Agreements

The bilateral agreements signed by India in recent times are:

(i) Comprehensive bilateral trade agreements signed, including trade in services, with the governments of Singapore, South Korea, Japan and Malaysia. An FTA in services and investment was signed with the Association of South East Asian Nations (ASEAN) effective since mid-2015.

(ii) India has joined the **RCEP** (Regional Comprehensive Economic Partnership) pluri- lateral negotiations. The proposed FTA includes the 10 ASEAN countries and its six FTA partners, viz. Australia, China, India, Japan, South Korea and New Zealand. The RCEP is the only mega-regional FTA of which India is a part.

(iii) India is also engaged in bilateral **FTA** negotiations including trade in services with Canada, Israel, Thailand, the EU, the EFTA (European Free Trade Association), Australia and New Zealand. Dialogue is under way with the US under the India-US Trade Policy Forum (TPF), with Australia under the India-Australia JMC (Joint Ministerial Commission),

---

8. Ibid.

with China under the India-China Working-Group on Services, and with Brazil under the India-Brazil Trade Monitoring Mechanism (TMM).

RESTRICTIONS AND REGULATIONS

One major issue in services is the domestic barriers and regulations. Domestic regulations, in strict WTO terms, include licensing requirements, licensing procedures, qualification requirements, qualification procedures, and technical standards but here other restrictions and barriers are also considered. While there are many domestic regulations in our major markets, which deny market access to us and therefore need to be negotiated at multilateral and bilateral levels, there are also many domestic regulations in India which hinder the growth of this sector.

Since domestic regulations perform the role of tariffs in regulating services, there is need to list the domestic regulations in India which need to be curbed to help growth of the sector and its exports, while retaining those which are necessary for regulating the sector at this stage. An indicative list of some important domestic regulations in India which need to be examined for suitable policy reforms[9] in the services sector is as follows:

Trade and Transport Services

Some constraints in these sectors include restrictions on inter-state movement of goods which could ease with the adoption of the model *Agriculture Produce and Marketing Committee (APMC) Act* by many states; the *Multimodal Transportation of Goods Act 1993* which needs revision to ease the existing restrictions on transportation and documentation

through different modes of transport, particularly restrictions in the *Customs Act*, which do not allow seamless movement of goods; and restrictions on free movement of cargo between *Inland Container Depots (ICDs), Container Freight Stations (CFSs)* and *Ports*.

Construction Development

In this sector, bottlenecks result from continuation of restrictions under the *Urban Land Ceiling and Regulation Act (ULCRA)* in some states namely Andhra Pradesh, Assam, Bihar, and West Bengal, which have not yet repealed it and the confusion in the process required for clearance of buildings even after the repeal of ULCRA by passing of the Urban Land(Ceiling and Regulations) Repeal Act 1999 by the other states.

There is also lack of clarity on the role of states as facilitators in the *land acquisition* policy resulting in increasing number of court litigations adding to risk profile of builders/projects thereby restricting lenders from extending finance to such builders/ projects.

There are also restrictions on floor area ratio (FAR) in many states; and other restrictions like the application of bye laws/regulations and its exemptions, e.g., increase in FAR which varies from project to project and is sometimes discriminatory. Obtaining environment clearance is another major hindrance.

Accountancy Services

While the accountancy professionals were hitherto allowed to operate either as a partnership firm or as a sole proprietorship firm or in their own name since the Indian regulations do not permit exceeding 20 professionals under one firm, the emergence of *Limited Liability Partnership (LLP)* structure is likely to address this impediment. However, the number of statutory audits of companies per partner is restricted to 20.

FDI is also not allowed in this sector and

9. H.A.C. Prasad and R. Sathish, Working Paper No. 1/2010-DEA on 'Policy of India's Services Sector, 2010' with updates from concerned Departments and Institutions, as quoted in, Ministry of Finance, (New Delhi: Government of India, *Economic Survey 2013-14*, p. 228).

foreign service providers are not allowed to undertake statutory audit of companies as per the provisions of the laws in India. There are also domestic regulations like prohibition on the use of individual *logos* for partnership and single proprietorship accounting firms. These regulations need to be relaxed and streamlined to facilitate tie-ups and penetrate foreign markets given the potential for exporting these services by the outsourcing mode.

Legal Services

In this sector, FDI is not permitted and international law firms are not authorised to advertise and open offices in India. Foreign service providers can neither be appointed as partners nor sign legal documents and represent clients. The *Bar Council* is opposed to entry of foreign lawyers/law firms in any manner. Indian advocates are not permitted to enter into profit-sharing arrangements with persons other than Indian advocates.

Education Services

These come under the *Concurrent List* with multiple controls and regulations by central and state governments and statutory bodies. Regulations of minimum of 25 acres of land to establish a medical college restricts the setting up of medical colleges in cities like Delhi. *Patient load factor* regulations related to establishment of new medical colleges also need to be in tune with present day equipment-intensive patient care and modern practices and procedures of medical education.

THE NEED FOR REFORMS

Indian services sector have the potential to garner higher economic benefits to the country. But there are many issues both general and sector specific including domestic regulations hinder the growth prospects of the services sector. If these issues are addressed deftly the sector could lead to

exponential gains for the economy. The need of policy reforms[10] in this regards are outlined in the following way:

General Issues

There are some general issues related to the policy framework which hamper the healthy growth and expansion of the services sector in the country. They are broadly related to the following areas:

Nodal agency and marketing: Despite having strong growth potential in various services sub-sectors, there is no single nodal department or agency for services. An inter-ministerial committee for services has been set up to look into this. But services activities cover issues beyond trade and a more proactive approach and proper institutional mechanism is needed to weed out *unwanted regulations* and tap the opportunities in the services sector in a coordinated way. There is also need for promotional activities for service exports like,

(i) setting up a portal for services,

(ii) showcasing India's competence also in non-software services in trade exhibitions, c) engaging dedicated brand ambassadors and experts.

Disinvestment: There is plenty of scope for disinvestment in services PSUs under both central and state governments. Speeding up disinvestment in some services-sector PSUs could not only provide revenue for the government but also speed up the growth of these services.

Credit related: The issues here include 'collateral free' soft loans to support the sector's cash needs and possibility of considering even export or business orders as collateral for credit-worthy service firms.

10. H.A.C. Prasad, R. Sathish, and Salam Shyamsunder Singh (2014), working paper 1/2014-DEA on 'Emerging Global Economic Situation: Opportunities and Policy Issues for Services Sector' and updates from some ministries and institutions, as quoted in, Ministry of Finance, *Economic Survey 2013–14* (New Delhi: Government of India, 2017), p. 190.

Tax and Trade Policy related: These include use of 'net' instead of 'gross' foreign exchange criteria for export benefit schemes, the issue of *retrospective* amendments of tax laws like,

(i) amendment to the definition of royalty to include payment of any rights via any medium for use of computer software,

(ii) tax administrative measures to tackle delay in refunds,

(iii) introducing VAT (value added tax) refund for foreign tourists, and

(iv) addressing the issue of bank guarantees based on past performance to avail of export promotion benef its in services.

Sectoral Issues

Area-specific policy hurdles to the services sector are also there. Together with the general issues, these area-sepcific bottlenecks do not allow the sector to realise its real potential. The major ones in this area are being outlined below.

Tourism and hospitality sector: As per the latest data of world tourism, India's tourism has not been competitive enough to attract tourist due to several reasons, such as,

(i) India's share in world tourist inflows was only **0.64** per cent in 2012 (rank **41**), while that of the USA was 6.47 per cent (rank 2) and China 5.57 per cent (rank 3).

(ii) India's share in world tourism expenditure is relatively higher at **1.65** per cent (rank 16) implying that foreign tourists spend relatively more in India.

(iii) Singapore, a small country, attracted 11.10 million tourists in 2012, while a large country like India attracted only 6.97 million foreign tourists during 2013.

Some suggested measures in this area, as per the *Economic Survey 2014–15,* are:

(i) creating world class tourism infrastructure even by PPP;

(ii) addressing multiple taxation issues;

(iii) skill and etiquettes training to cater to the needs of tourists;

(iv) special focus on cleanliness at tourist sites and safety of tourists;

(v) using the MGNREGA for creating permanent assets like tourism infrastructure and facilities;

(vi) organising mini India cultural shows on a daily basis at important tourist sites that will not only attract tourists but also generate employment for Indian artists; and

(vii) implementing urgently visa on arrival and E visa facilities at 9 airports to 180 countries barring 8 'prior reference' countries (this decision has already been taken).

Port services: Indian ports are not world-class ports and lack the necessary draft. As a result, 'third-generation ships' are not able to enter the harbour and goods have to be offloaded outside in smaller ships, adding to costs. If India can develop world-class airport infrastructure and metros, there is every reason to attend the concerns of the port services. Its immediate focus should be on—

(i) building world class ports providing world class services that will also help the trade sector by reducing costs and turnaround time in ports, and

(ii) reducing port charges which are considerably higher.

Shipping, shipbuilding and ship repairs: Indian ships in the carriage of India's overseas cargo has fallen sharply and Indian ships are ageing, too. Government-owned shipyards like Visakhapatnam are facing problems like declining orders. India's shipbuilding industry has the capacity and expertise but is functioning below capacity. Some of the suggested steps to boost the sector are:

    (i) need to replace our ageing ships with new ones,

  (ii) increasing shipping fleet (with prices falling on account of global slowdown),

 (iii) a special financing mechanism needs to be developed.

 (iv) utilising India's shipbuilding and repairs yards and enhancing their capacity (as India needs to replace many old ships and growing ship repairs business in the world).

Railways: The FDI policy of Railways sector restricts FDI in rail transport, except in mass rapid transit systems. FDI and privatisation in the railways could be the next big ticket reforms. A proposal has been initiated by Indian Railways, for making suitable changes in the existing FDI policy in order to allow FDI in railways, to foster creation of world class rail infrastructure. The proposal envisages—

    (i) allowing FDI in all areas of the rail sector except railway operations.

  (ii) even in railway operations, FDI is proposed in PPP projects, for suburban corridors, high speed train systems, and dedicated freight lines.

While privatisation of railways has been successful in some countries like Japan, it has failed in some others like the UK. So this proposal needs to be examined carefully and quickly to allow privatisation and inflows of FDI in areas where it is feasible.

OUTLINING FUTURE

With plenty of opportunities, the services sector is like an uncharted sea. As yet, its potential has not been tapped fully by India. A targeted policy of removing bottlenecks in major and potential services can result in large dividends in the form of higher services growth and services exports, which in turn can help in pulling up the economy to higher growth levels. The future actions in the sector can be outlined as given below[11]:

    (i) India's services sector, which showed resilient growth after the recovery of the global economy following the global financial crisis, has been showing subdued performance in recent times. Despite the slowdown, the prospects continue to be bright for many segments of the sector.

  (ii) In future, government's focus on the following are expected to provide impetus to logistics services—

    (a) infrastructure development,

    (b) favourable regulatory policies like liberalisation of FDI norms,

    (c) increasing number of multimodal logistics service providers,

    (d) growing trend of outsourcing logistics to third party service providers, and

    (e) entry of global players.

 (iii) Though ***shipping*** services are at a low key at present, with increased imports of POL (petroleum, oil and lubricants) for stocks build up to take advantage of low crude oil prices, containerisation of export and import cargo and modernisation of ports with private sector participation, recovery of the shipping and port services sector can be expected.

 (iv) The prospects for Indian ***aviation*** services have improved following—

---

11. Ministry of Finance, *Economic Survey 2015–16,* and *Economic Survey 2016-17.*

(a) the fall in prices of aviation fuel, which accounts for nearly 40 per cent of the operating expenses of airlines in India;

(b) liberalisation of FDI policies in civil aviation; and

(c) strong growth in passenger traffic – expected to continue in the near future.

(v) The outlook for the **retail** industry remains positive as India continues to remain an attractive long-term retail destination despite the various challenges faced by the sector. Following initiatives are expected to give a fillip to the sector—

(a) allocation of Rs. 1000 crore to technology and start-up sectors,

(b) promotion of cashless transactions via *RUPay* debit cards, and

(c) growth of e-commerce.

(vi) Government's focus on the **tourism** sector including easing visas by *eTV* and building tourism infrastructure could help in the recovery of the tourism sector.

(vii) Despite challenges in the global market, the Indian **IT industry** is expected to maintain double or near-double-digit growth as India offers depth and breadth across different segments of this industry, such as, IT services, BPM, ER&D, internet & mobility and software products.

(viii) In the **telecom** sector, the introduction of *4G* which could be a game changer and inclusion of *fibre optic* connectivity which will tremendously increase the reach and bandwidth along with greater use of mobiles in government's *social sector* programmes could give a further boost to this fast growing sector.

Several relevant and contemporary suggestions have been articulated by a Working Paper of the Ministry of Finance by late February 2016. Dealing with the sectors like tourism, shipping and port, IT and software the advices are deeper and effective[12].

As per the **Economic Survey 2016-17**, the growth prospects of the services sector has slowed in recent times caused by several external and domestic reasons. The *Nikkei/Markit Services PMI* (Purchase Manager's Index) for India was at a high of 57.5 in January of 2013 which fell down to 46.7 in **November 2016** from 54.5 in October 2016. However, it increased marginally to 46.8 in December 2016. The *Baltic Dry Index (BDI)* an indicator of both merchandise trade and shipping services, which showed some improvement up to 18 November 2016 (at 1030) declined to 910 on **13 January 2017.**

---

12. A working paper by H.A.C. Prasad and S.S. Singh: **'India's Services Sector: Performance, Some Issues and Suggestions'**, Department of Economic Affairs, Ministry of Finance (New Delhi: Government of India, 2016).

CHAPTER 11

INDIAN FINANCIAL MARKET

> *There is now ample empirical research to corroborate Schumpeter's conjecture that financial development facilitates real economic growth. The depth of the financial markets and availability of diverse products should therefore not be treated as mere adornment but as critical ingredients of inclusive growth.* *

* As the **Economic Survey 2011–12** refers to the Australian economist Joseph A. Schumpeter (1883–1950) to emphasise the importance of the financial market in an economy. See Ministry of Finance, **Economic Survey 2011–12** (New Delhi: Government of India, 2012), p. 40.

INTRODUCTION

The market of an economy where funds are transacted between the fund-surplus and fund-scarce individuals and groups is known as the financial market *(definition)*.[1] The basis of transaction is either *interest* or *dividend*. This market might have its organised (institutionalised) as well as non-organised (unregulated/non-institutionalised) segments in an economy.

Financial markets in every economy are having two separate segments today, one catering to the requirements of *short-term funds* and the other to the requirements of *long-term funds*.[2] The short-term financial market is known as the **money market,** while the long-term financial market is known as the **capital market.** The money market fulfils the requirements of funds for the period upto 364 days (*i.e., short term*) while the capital market does the same for the period above 364 days (*i.e., long term*).[3] A brief discussion on the Indian financial market is given below.

INDIAN MONEY MARKET

Money market is the short-term financial market of an economy. In this market, money is traded between individuals or groups (i.e., financial institutions, banks, government, companies, etc.), who are either *cash-surplus* or *cash-scarce*. Trading is done on a rate known as *discount rate* which is determined by the market and guided by the availability of and demand for the cash in the day-to-day trading.[4] The 'repo rate' of the time

(announced by the RBI) works as the guiding rate for the current 'discount rate'. Borrowings in this market may or may not be supported by collaterals. In the money market the *financial assets*, which have quick conversion quality into money and carry minimal transaction cost, are also traded.[5] Money market may be *defined* as a market where short-term lending and borrowing take place between the cash-surplus and cash-scarce sides.

The market operates in both 'organised' and 'unorganised' channels in India. Starting from the 'person-to-person' mode and converting into 'telephonic transaction', it has now gone *online* in the age of internet and information technology. The transactions might take place through the intermediaries (known as brokers) or directly between the trading sides.

Need for Money Market: Income generation (i.e., growth) is the most essential requiremnt of any economic system. In the modern industrial economies creation of productive assets is not an easy task, as it requires investible capital of long-term nature. Long-term capital can be raised either through bank loans, corporate bonds, debentures or shares (i.e., from the capital market). But once a productive asset has been created and production starts there comes the need of another kind of capital, to meet the day-to-day shortfalls of working capital. It means that only setting-up of firms does not guarantee production as these firms keep facing *fund mismatches* in the day-to-day production process. Such funds are required only for a short period (days, fortnights or few months) and are needed to meet shortfalls in working capital requirements. This requires creation of a different segment of the financial market which can cater to the short-term requirements of such funds for the eneterprises—known as the **money market** or the **working capital market.** The

---

1. Based on the discussion in P.A. Samuelson and W.D. Nordhaus, *Economics* (New Delhi: Tata McGrawHill, 2005), pp. 543–45.

2. Based on J.E. Stiglitz and C.E. Walsh, *Economics* (New York: W.W. Norton & Campany, 2006), pp. 612–14.

3. See Reserve Bank of India, *Report on Currency and Finance* (New Delhi: Government of India, multiple years).

4. In the capital market, money is traded on interest rate as well as on dividends. Long-term loans are raised on well-defined interest rates, while long-term capital is raised on dividends through the sale of shares.

---

5. Such financial assets are known as 'close substitutes for money '.

short-term period is defined as upto 364 days. The crucial role money market plays in an economy is proved by the fact that if only a few lakhs or crores of rupees of working capital is not met in time, it can push a firm or business enterprise to go for lock-out, which has been set-up with thousands of crores of capital. If lock-out happens, the firm might default in its payments, losing its age-old credit-worthiness, consequently creating a chain of negatives in the economic system. This is why it is essential for every economy to organise a strong and vibrant money market which has wider geographic presence (the reason why it is today internet-based).

Money Market in India: The organised form of money market in India is just close to three decades old. However, its presence has been there, but restricted to the government only.[6] It was the **Chakravarthy Committee** (1985) which, for the first time, underlined the need of an organised money market in the country[7] and the **Vahul Committee** (1987) laid the blue print for its development.[8] Today, money market in India is not an integrated unit and has two segments— *Unorganised Money Market* and *Organised Money Market*.

1. Unorganised Money Market

Before the government started the organised development of the money market in India,

---

6. The only instrument of the money market was the Treasury Bills, which were sold by tender at weekly auctions upto 1965. But later these bills were made available throughout the week at discount rates by the Reserve Bank of India.

7. Sukhomoy Chakravarthy, *Review of the Working of the Monetary System* (New Delhi: Reserve Bank of India, 1985).

8. M. Vaghul, *Working Group on Money Market* (New Delhi: Reserve Bank of India, 1987). The committee was set up in 1986, and came to be known as the Vaghul Committee.

its unorganised form had its presence since the ancient times—its remnant is still present in the country. Their activities are not regulated like the organised money market, but they are recognised by the government. In recent years, some of them have been included under the regulated organised market (for example, the NBFCs were put under the regulatory control of the RBI in 1997). The unorganised money market in India may be divided into three differing categories:

(i) **Unregulated Non-Bank Financial Intermediaries:** Unregulated Non-Banking Financial Intermediaries are functioning in the form of *chit funds, nidhis* (operate in South India, which lend to only their members) and loan companies. They charge very high interest rates (i.e., 36 to 48 per cent per annum), thus, are exploitative in nature and have selective reach in the economy.

(ii) **Indigenous Bankers:** Indigenous bankers receive deposits and lend money in the capacity of an individual or a private firms. There are, basically, four such bankers in the country functioning as non-homogenous groups:

(a) *Gujarati Shroffs*: They operate in Mumbai, Kolkata as well as in industrial, trading and port cities in the region.

(b) *Multani* or *Shikarpuri Shroffs*: They operate in Mumbai, Kolkata, Assam tea gardens and North Eastern India.

(c) *Marwari Kayas*: They operate mainly in Gujarat with a little bit of presence in Mumbai and Kolkata.

(d) *Chettiars*: They are active in Chennai and at the ports of southern India.

(iii) **Money Lenders:** They constitute the most localised form of money market in India and operate in the most exploitative way. They have their two forms:

(a) The professional money lenders who lend their own money as a profession to earn income through interest.

(b) The non-professional money lenders who might be businessmen and lend their money to earn interest income as a subsidiary business.

Today, India has **eight** organised instruments of the money market which are used by the prescribed firms in the country, but the unorganised money market also operates side by side—there are certain reasons[9] behind this:

(i) Indian money market is still under-developed.

(ii) Lack of penetration and presence of the instruments of the organised money market.

(iii) There are many needful customers in the money market who are current outside the purview of the organised money market.

(iv) Entry to the organised money market for its customers is still restrictive in nature—not allowing small businessmen.

2. Organised Money Market

Since the government started developing the organised money market in India (mid-1980s), we have seen the arrival of a total of **eight** instruments designed to be used by different categories of business and industrial firms. A brief description of these instruments follows:

(i) *Treasury Bills (TBs):* This instrument of the money market though present since Independence got organised only in 1986. They are used by the Central Government to fulfil its short-term liquidity requirement upto the period of 364 days. There developed **five types** of

the TBs in due course of time:

(a) 14-day (Intermediate TBs)

(b) 14-day (Auctionable TBs)

(c) 91-day TBs

(d) 182-day TBs

(e) 364-day TBs

Out of the above five variants of the TBs, at present only the **91-day TBs**, **182-day TBs** and the **364-day TBs** are issued by the government. The other two variants were discontinued in 2001.[10]

The TBs other than providing short-term cushion to the government, also function as short-term investment avenues for the banks and financial institutions, besides functioning as requirements of the CRR and SLR of the banking institutions.

(ii) *Certificate of Deposit (CD):* Organised in 1989, the CD is used by **banks** and issued to the depositors for a specified period ranging less than one year—they are negotiable and tradable in the money market. Since 1993 the RBI allowed the **financial institutions** to operate in it—IFCI, IDBI, IRBI (IIBI since 1997) and the Exim Bank—they can issue CDs for the maturity periods above one year and upto three years.

(iii) *Commercial Paper (CP):* Organised in 1990 it is used by the **corporate houses** in India (which should be a listed company with a working capital of not less than Rs. 5 crore). The CP issuing companies need to obtain a specified credit rating from an agency approved by the RBI (such as CRISIL, ICRA, etc).

---

9. Based on the suggestions of experts belonging to the Indian financial market.

10. Ministry of Finance, *Economic Survey 2001–02* (New Delhi: Government of India, 2002); Ministry of Finance, Economic Survey 2009–10 (New Delhi: Government of India, 2010).

(iv) *Commercial Bill (CB):* Organised in 1990, a CB is issued by the **All India Financial Institutions** (AIFIs), **Non-Banking Finance Companies** (NBFCs), **Scheduled Commercial Banks, Merchant Banks, Co-operative Banks** and the **Mutual Funds**. It replaced the old Bill Market available since 1952 in the country.

(v) *Call Money Market (CMM):* This is basically an **inter-bank** money market where funds are borrowed and lent, generally, for one day—that is why this is also known as **over-night borrowing market** (also called **money at call**). Fund can be borrowed/raised for a maximum period upto 14 days (called **short notice**). Borrowing in this market may take place against securities or without securities.[11] Rate of interest in this market 'glides' with the 'repo rate' of the time the principle remains very simple—longer the period, higher the interest rate. Depending upon the availability and demand of fund in this market the real call rate revolves nearby the current repo rate.

The scheduled commercial banks, co-operative banks operate in this market as both the borrowers and lenders while LIC, GIC, Mutual Funds, IDBI and NABARD are allowed to operate as only lenders in this market.

(vi) *Money Market Mutual Fund (MF):* Popular as Mutual Funds (MFs) this money market instrument was introduced/organised in 1992 to provide short-term investment opportunity to **individuals**. The initial guidelines for the MF have been liberalised many times. Since March 2000, MFs have been brought under the preview of SEBI, besides the RBI. At present, a whole lot of financial institutions and firms are allowed to set up MFs, viz., commercial banks, public and private financial institutions and private sector companies. At present 45 MFs are operating in the country—managing a corpus of over Rs. 4 lakh crore.

(vii) *Repos and Reverse Repos:* In the era of economic reforms there developed two new instruments of money market—**repo** and **reverse repo.** Considered the most dynamic instruments of the Indian money market they have emerged the most favoured route to raise short-term funds in India. 'Repo' is basically an acronym of the **rate of repurchase.** The RBI in a span of four years, introduced these instruments—**repo** in December 1992 and **reverse repo** in November 1996.

Repo allows the banks and other financial institutions to borrow money from the RBI for short-term (by selling government securities to the RBI). In **reverse repo,** the banks and financial institutions purchase government securities from the RBI (basically here the RBI is borrowing from the banks and the financial institutions). All government securities are dated and the interest for the repo or reverse repo transactions are announced by the RBI from time to time. The provision of repo and the reverse repo have been able to serve the liquidity evenness in the economy as the banks are able to get the required amount of funds out of it, and they can park surplus

---

11. The State Bank of India (operates in this market as lender as it is in a comfortable cash position) lends against government securities, while others lend against the 'deposit receipts' of the borrowing banks. The SBI functions as the 'lender of intermediate resort' (while the RBI functions as the 'lender of last resort').

idle funds through it. These instruments have emerged as important tools in the management of the monetary and credit policy in recent years.[12]

Accepting the recommendations of the **Urjit Patel Committee**, the RBI in April 2014 (while announcing the first *Bi-monthly Credit & Monetary Policy-2014–15*) announced to introduce **term repo** and **term reverse repo**. This is believed to bring in higher stability and better signalling of interest rates across different loan markets in the economy.

(viii) *Cash Management Bill (CMB):* The Government of India, in consultation with the RBI, decided to issue a new short-term instrument, known as Cash Management Bills, since August 2009 to meet the temporary cash flow mismatches of the government. The Cash Management Bills are *non-standard* and *discounted instruments* issued for maturities less than 91 days.

The CMBs have the *generic character of Treasury Bills* (issued at discount to the face value); are tradable and qualify for *ready forward facility;* investment in it is considered as an eligible investment in government securities by banks for SLR.

It should be noted here that the existing Treasury Bills serve the same purpose, but as they were put under the WMAs (Ways & Means Advances) provisions by the Government of India in 1997, they did not remain a discretionary route for the government in meeting its short-term requirements of funds at will (see 'Fiscal Consolidation in India', sub-topic in

Chapter 18 *Public Finance* for details). CBM does not come under the similar WMAs provisions.

MUTUAL FUNDS

Of all investment options, mutual funds are touted to be the best tool for wealth creation over the long term. They are of several types, and the risk varies with the kind of asset classes these funds invest in. As the name suggests, a mutual fund *is a fund that is created when a large number of investors put in their money, and is managed by professionally qualified persons with experience in investing in different asset classes—shares, bonds, money market instruments like call money, and other assets such as gold and property.* Their names usually give a good idea about what type of asset class a fund, also called a scheme, will invest in. For example, a **diversified equity fund** will invest in a large number of stocks, while a **gilt fund** will invest in government securities, while a **pharma fund** will mainly invest in stocks of companies from the pharmaceutical and related industries.

Mutual funds, first of all came in the money market (regulated by the RBI), but they have the freedom to operate in the capital market, too. This is why they have provision of dual regulator—the RBI and SEBI. Mutual funds are compulsorily registered with the Securities and Exchange Board of India (SEBI), which also acts as the **first wall of defence** for all investors in these funds. For those who do not understand how mutual funds operate but are willing to invest, the move by SEBI is seen as a big relief.

Each mutual fund is run by a group of qualified people who form a company, called an *asset management company (AMC)* and the operations of the AMC are under the guidance of another group of people, called *trustees*. Both, the people in the AMC as well as the trustees, have a *fiduciary responsibility,* because these are the people who are entrusted with the task of managing the hard-

---

12. Reserve Bank of India, **Report on Currency and Finance** (New Delhi: Government of India, 1999); Reserve Bank of India, Report on Currency and Finance (New Delhi: Government of India, 2000).

earned money of people who do not understand much about managing money.

A fund house or a distributor working for the fund house (which could be an individual, a company or even a bank) are qualified to sell mutual funds. The fund house allots the 'units' of the MF to the investor at a price that is fixed through a process approved by SEBI, which is based on the net asset value (NAV). In simple terms, NAV is the total value of investments in a scheme divided by the total number of units issued to investors in the same scheme. In most mutual fund schemes, NAVs are computed and published on a daily basis. However, when a fund house is launching a scheme for the first time, the units are sold at Rs. 10 each. There are **three types** of schemes offered by MFs:

(i) **Open-ended Schemes:** An open-ended fund is one which is usually available from an MF on an ongoing basis, that is, an investor can buy or sell as and when they intend to at a NAV-based price. As investors buy and sell units of a particular open-ended scheme, the number of units issued also changes every day and so changes the value of the scheme's portfolio. So, the NAV also changes on a daily basis. In India, fund houses can sell any number of units of a particular scheme, but at times fund houses restrict selling additional units of a scheme for some time.

(ii) **Closed-ended Schemes:** A close-ended fund usually issue units to investors only once, when they launch an offer, called *new fund offer (NFO)* in India. Thereafter, these units are listed on the stock exchanges where they are traded on a daily basis. As these units are listed, any investor can buy and sell these units through the exchange. As the name suggests, close-ended schemes are managed by fund houses for a limited number of years, and

at the end of the term either money is returned to the investors or the scheme is made open ended. However, there is a word of caution here that usually, units of close ended funds which are listed on the stock exchanges, trade at a high discount to their NAVs. But as the date for closure of the fund nears, the discount between the NAV and the trading price narrows, and vanishes on the day of closure of the scheme.

(iii) **Exchange-Traded Funds (ETFs):** ETFs are a mix of open-ended and close-ended schemes. ETFs, like close-ended schemes, are listed and traded on a stock exchange on a daily basis, but the price is usually very close to its NAV, or the underlying assets, like gold ETFs.

If investment have been done in a well-managed MF, the advantages outweigh disadvantages in the long term, which is 10 years or more. There is a very high probability for investors of making more money than by investing in other risk-free investments such as FDs, public provident fund etc. Advantages of investing in MFs include:

(a) diversification of portfolio,

(b) good investment management services,

(c) liquidity,

(d) strong government-backed regulatory help,

(e) professional service, and

(f) low cost for all the benefits.

An investor, by investing in a mutual fund scheme that has blue chip stocks in its portfolio, indirectly gets an exposure to these stocks. Compared to this, if the same investor wants to have each of these stocks in his portfolio, the cost of buying and managing the portfolio will be much higher.

Mutual funds invest the investors money in both the **loan** and **share** markets. Buyers of MF units are given choice/option as in which of the markets they wish their money to be invested by the fund managers of the MF. This way investors get the following choices:

(i) *Loan* (100 per cent of the funds will be invested in the loan market),

(ii) *Share* (100 per cent of the funds will be invested in the share market), and

(iii) *Balance* (60 per cent of the funds will be invested in the loan market while the rest 40 per cent in the share market—this provision keeps changing depending upon the health of the share market—clearly announced by the MFs).

DFHI

The Discount and Finance House of India Limited[13] (DFHI) was set up in April 1988 by the RBI jointly with the public sector banks and financial investment institutions (i.e., LIC, GIC and UTI). Its establishment was an outcome of the long-drawn need of the following two types:

(i) to bring an equilibirium of liquidity in the Indian banking system and

(ii) to impart liquidity to the instruments of the money market prevalent in the economy.

---

13. It was in 1979 that the Chore Committee for the first time recommended for a discount house to level the liquidity imbalances in the banking system. The government became active after the recommendations of the Working Group on the Money Market (i.e., the Vaghul Committee, 1987) and finally established DFHI in 1988. The Vaghul Committee suggested to set up a discount finance institution which could deal in short-term money market instruments so that liquidity could be provided to these instruments. The committee also recommended the house to operate on 'commercial basis', which was accepted by the government while setting up DFHI.

In 2004, the RBI transferred its total holding in the DFHI to the State Bank of India arm SBI Gilts Limited. Its new name is SBI DFHI. It functions as the biggest 'primary dealer' in the economy and functions on commercial basis. It deals in all kinds of instruments in the money market without any upper ceiling. Operating in 'two way' (as a lender and borrower) its objective is to provide needful liquidity and stability in the financial market of the country.

INDIAN CAPITAL MARKET

The long-term financial market of an economy is known as the 'capital market'. This market makes it possible to raise *long-term money* (capital), i.e., for a period of minimum 365 days and above. Ceation of productive assets is not possible without a string capital market—the market gained more importance once most of the economies in the world started industrialising. Across the world, banks emerged as the first and the foremost segment of the capital market. In coming times many other segments got added to it, viz., insurance industry, mutual funds, and finally the most attractive and vibrant, the security/stock market. Organised development of capital market together with putting in place the right regulatory framework for it, has always been a tough task for the economies. It is believed today that for strong growth prospects in an economy presence of a strong and vibrant capital market is essential.

Though the capital market of India is far stronger and better today in comparision to the periods just after Independence, the process of emergnece has not been easy and smooth. Once India opted 'industry' as its prime moving force, the first challenge was to raise long-term funds for industral establishments and their expansion. As banks in India were weak, small and geographically unevenly distributed they were not in a position to play the pivotal role they played in case of the industrialising Western economies. This is why the government decided to set up 'financial institutions' which could play the role of banks (till banks gain strength and presence) and carry on the responsibilities of 'project financing'.

Project Financing

After Independence, India went for intensive industrialisation to achieve rapid growth and development. To this end, the main responsibility was given to the Public Sector Undertakings (PSUs). For industrialisation we require capital, technology and labour, all being typically difficult to manage in the case of India. For capital requirement, the government decided to depend upon internal and external sources and the government decided to set up financial institutions (FIs). Though India was having banks, but due to low saving rate and lower deposits with them, the upcoming industries could not be financed through them. The main borrowers for industrial development were the PSUs. To support the capital requirement of the 'projects' of the public sector industries, the government came up with different types of financial institutions in the coming years. The industrial financing supported by these financial institutions was known as 'project financing' in India. Over the time, Indian capital market started to have the following segments:

1. Financial Institutions

The requirement of project financing made India to go for a number of FIs from time to time, which are generally classified into four categories:[14]

(i) All India Financial Institutions (AIFIs)

The all India FIs are IFCI (1948); ICICI (1955); IDBI (1964); SIDBI (1990) & IIBI (1997). All of them were public sector FIs except ICICI, which was a joint sector venture with initial capital

coming from the RBI, some foreign banks and FIs. The public sector FIs were funded by the Government of India.

By 1980s, all Indian banks acquired wider capital base and by early 1990s when the stock market became popular, it became easier for the corporate world to tap cheaper capital from these segments of the capital market.[15] The era of economic reforms had given the same option to the PSUs to tap new capital. As the AIFIs had more or less fixed rate of interest as compared to the banks which could mobilise cheaper deposits to lend cheaper—the AIFIs seemed to become irrelevant. The AIFIs witnessed a sharp decline in recent years.[16] At this juncture the government decided to convert them into **Development Banks**[17] (suggested by the Narasimhan Committee-I) to be known as the All India Development Banks (AIDBs). In 2000, the government allowed ICICI to go for a **reverse merger** (when an elder enterprise is merged with a younger one) with the ICICI Bank—the first AIDB emerged with no obligation of project financing—such entities in coming times will be known as the **universal banks**[18] (allowed to set up as many financial institutions they wish to, such as insurance, merchant banks, mutual funds, etc.). In a similar move, the IDBI was reverse merged with the IDBI Bank in 2002 and the second AIDB emerged. But it has still the obligation of carrying its project financing duties.

In 2002, the government, proposed to merge IFCI and IIBI with the nationalised bank PNB to

---

14. *Industrial Finance Corporation of India Act, 1948*, Government of India, New Delhi.

15. Ministry of Finance, *Economic Survey 2000-01*, (New Delhi: Government of India, 2010).

16. Ministry of Finance, *Economic Survey 2006-07*, (New Delhi: Government of India, 2007).

17. **Narasimhan Committee on the Financial System (CFS), 1991** suggested for the conversion of the AIFIs into Development Banks.

18. It was the **S. H. Khan Committee on Development Financial Institutions (DFIs), 1998** which forwarded the concept/idea of Universal Banking in India.

ctraete a big **Universal Bank.** It is believed that PNB was unwilling to go for this merger as these FIs were running at heavy losses. This move was part correct as per the recommendations of the Narasimhan Committe-II (to the extent merger is concerned, following its 3-Tier Banking Structure of India), but part against it (the committee has advised not to merge weak banks/FIs with either weak or strong banks/FIs).[19] Presently, the government is trying to make IFCI and IIBI to turn around their business and emerge as profitable entities—they are busy recovering their dues and improving their balance sheet.

Meanwhile, at present, there are only **four** financial institutions operating in the country as AIFIs **regulated** by the RBI, viz., the NABARD, SIDBI, Exim Bank and the NHB.

(ii) Specialised Financial Institutions (SFIs)[20]

Two new FIs were set up by the Central Government in the late 1980s to finance **risk** and **innovation** in the area of industrial expansion; this was India's trial in the area of **venture capital funding**.

(a) *IFCI Venture Capital Funds Ltd (IFCI Venture), 2000:* It was promoted as a Risk Capital Foundation (RCF) in 1975 by IFCI Ltd., a society to provide financial assistance to first generation professionals and technocrat entrepreneurs for setting up own ventures through soft loans, under the Risk Capital Scheme.

In 1988, RCF was converted into a company—Risk Capital and Technology Finance Corporation Ltd. (RCTC)—when it also introduced the Technology

Finance and Development Scheme (TFDS) for financing development and commercialisation of indigenous technology. Besides, under Risk Capital Scheme, RCTC started providing financial assistance to entrepreneurs by way of direct equity participation. Based on IFCI Venture's credentials and strengths, Unit Trust of India (UTI), entrusted RCTC with the management of a new venture capital fund named **Venture Capital Unit Scheme (VECAUS-III)** in 1991 with its funds coming from the UTI and IFCI. To reflect the shift in the company's activities, the name of RCTC was changed to IFCI Venture Capital Funds Ltd. (IFCI Venture) in February 2000.

In order to focus on Asset Management Activities, IFCI Venture discontinued Risk Capital and Technology Finance Schemes in 2000-01 and continued managing VECAUS-III. In 2007, as UTI had ceased to carry out its activities and its assets vested with **Specified Undertaking of the Unit Trust of India (SUUTI)**, the portfolio of VECAUS-III under management of IFCI Venture was transferred to SUUTI.

(b) *Tourism Finance Corporation of India Ltd (TFCI), 1989:* The Government of India had, on the recommendations of the National Committee on Tourism *(Yunus Committee)* set up under the aegis of the Planning Commission, decided in 1988, to promote a separate All India Financial Institution for providing financial assistance to tourism-related activities/projects. In accordance with the above decision, the IFCI Ltd. along with other all-India financial/investment institutions and some nationalised banks promoted a Public Limited Company

19. Ministry of Finance, *Economic Survey 2011–12* (New Delhi: Government of India, 2011), pp. 115–16.
20. The write-up is based on information available from **SEBI, RBI** and different announcements/published reports of the **Ministry of Finance,** since 1996 onwards.

under the name of "Tourism Finance Corporation of India Ltd. (TFCI)" to function as a Specialised All-India Development Financial Institution to cater to the financial needs of the tourism industry.

TFCI was incorporated as a Public Limited Company in 1989 and became operational with effect from 1989. TFCI was notified as a Public Financial Institution in January 1990. Its promoter, the IFCI, holds major share (41.6 per cent) in it, while the rest of the shares are with the 'public' (26 per cent), public sector banks, public insurance companies and public mutual fund (i.e., UTI Mutual Fund Ltd.).

(iii) Investment Instituions (IIs)

Three investment institutions also came up in the public sector, which are yet another kind of FIs, i.e., the LIC (1956), the UTI (1964) and the GIC (1971).

In the present time they are no more known as DIIs (Domestic Investment Institutions) or DFIs (Domestic Financial Institutions). LIC is now the public sector insurance company in the life segment, GIC was been converted into a public sector re-insurance company in 2000, while UTI was converted into a mutual fund company in 2002. Now these investment institutions (IIs) are no more like the past. LIC is now called an 'insurance company', part of the Indian Insurance Industry and is the lone public sector playing in the life insurance segment competing with the private life insurance companies. Similarly, the UTI is now part of the Indian Mutual Fund industry and the lone such firm in the public sector competing with other private sector mutual funds. Similarly, the earstwhile four public sector general insurance companies are part of India's general insurance industry and competing with private companies in the area (they were Holding Comapnies of the GIC—now these are owned by the GoI directly and GIC only looks after its 're-insurance' business). This is why we do not get the use of the term 'IIs' in recent times in any of the GoI official documents.

(iv) State Level Finance Institutions (SLFIs)

In the wake of states involvement in the industrial development, the central government allowed the states to set up their own financial institutions (after the states demanded so). In this process two kinds of FIs came up:

(a) *State Finance Corporations (SFCs):* First came up in Punjab (1955) with other states following its example. There are 18 SFCs working presently.

(b) *State Industrial Development Corporations (SIDCs):* A fully dedicated state public sector FI to the cause of industrial development in the concerned states. First such FIs were set up (1960) in Andhra Pradesh and Bihar.

Almost all of the SFCs and SIDCs are at present running in huge losses. They may be re-structured on the lines of the AIFIs, but there is lack of will from the states and private financiers who are not interested to go in for their takeovers as such.

2. Banking Industry

With the passage of time, the industry saw its nationalisation (1969 and 1980) and again opening up for private sector entry (1993–94) to emerge as the most dependable segement of Indian financial system—in a way its mainstay. Presently, the industry consists of commercial banks both in public and private sectors, Regional Rural Banks (RRBs) and co-operative banks—a total of 171 Scheduled Commercial Banks (SCBs) out of whch 113 are in the public sector (19 nationalised banks, 7 banks in SBI group, one IDBI Bank Ltd. and 86 RRBs); with the rest of the 58 banks owned by the private sector (domestic and foreign—FDI in banks is allowed upto 26 per cent).[21]

In the wake of the economic reforms the government has promised speedier expansion of the banking sector. But the entry of new private players in the banking sector has been slow, hapmering the growth and expansion of the sector. But in a *recent release* the RBI has committed to allow new banks to come up on regular basis— in **April 2014** the RBI allowed two new private sector banks to start their operations. [for a detailed discussion on the banking sector refer the *Chapter 12*].

3. Insurance Industry

After Independence, for the purpose of expanding the industry, one after another the life and non-life insurance businesses were nationalised by the government (in 1956 and 1970, respectively), and the public sector insurance companies did serve the better purpose in the areas of providing safety net and nation-building. In the wake of the process of economic refroms a restructuring of the sector was started and the industry was opened for entry of private players in 1999 and an independent regulator was set up—the IRDA (domestic and foreign—with an FDI cap of 49 per cent). Since then many private players have entered the industry. Presently, Indian insurance industry consists of one public sector life insurer (LIC) and four public sector general insurers; two specialised public sector insurers (AICIL and ECGC); one public sector re-insurer (GIC) and 37 private insurance companies (in collaboration with established foreign insurers from across the world).[22] The expansion and penetration insurance in the country have increased during the reform period, but not as per the expectations of the governments and the experts—several reasons

have been responsible for this (for a detailed discussion on the insurance industry refer *Chapter 13*).

4. Security Market

After the government's attempts to formally organise the security and stock market of India, the segment has seen accelerated expansion. Today, it is counted among the most vibrant share markets of the world and has challenged the monopoly of banks in the capital market of the country.[23] The security market of India is regulated by SEBI. India has developed a regulated 'forward market' also where hunderds of commodities and derivatives are traded on spot and non-spot basis—regulated by FMC which merged into SEBI by late 2015.

FINANCIAL REGULATION

India has a multiple regulatory architecture in the financial sector. The design has developed complexities over the time due to: the *number* of regulatory, quasi-regulatory, non-regulatory-but-still-regulating bodies; *overlapping ambiguous* operational design and their influence.[24] A brief overview of the financial regulatory framework is being give here.

Regulatory Agencies

India has product-wise regulators—Reserve Bank of India (RBI) regulates credit products, savings and remittances; the Securities and Exchange Board of India (SEBI) regulates investment products; the Insurance Regulatory and Development Authority (IRDA) regulates insurance products; and the Pension Fund Regulatory and Development Authority (PFRDA) regulates pension products. The Forward Markets

21. Publications Division, *India 2014*, (New Delhi: Government of India, 2015), p. 326.

22. Ibid, p. 329.

23. Ministry of Finance, *Economic Survey 2012–13* (New Delhi: Government of India, 2013), p. 116.

24. **Financial Sector Legislative Reforms Commission** report, March 2013, N. Delhi.

Commission (FMC) regulates commodity-based exchange-traded futures (which was merged with the SEBI by late 2015).

Certain entities, primarily engaged in one product (i.e., the insurance companies) also offer other products making it difficult for product-based regulation (this came to light in the PFRDA-IRDA controversy of early 2010s). Thus, most regulation turns out to be entity-based. Another example is of *cooperative banks*, which, except in terms of their ownership structure, are very much like other banks—they take deposits and give loans. Still, their regulation is largely left to the Registrar of Cooperatives.

Quasi-regulatory Agencies

Several other government bodies perform quasi-regulatory functions—National Bank for Agriculture and Rural Development (NABARD), Small Industries Development Bank of India (SIDBI), and National Housing Bank (NHB). NABARD supervises regional rural banks as well as state and district cooperative banks. NHB regulates housing finance companies, and SIDBI regulates the state finance corporations (SFCs).

Central Ministries

Certain ministries of the GoI also involved in policy making in the financial system. Ministry of Finance (MoF) is most prominently involved, through its representatives on the Boards of SEBI, IRDA and RBI. MoF and Ministry of Small Scale Industries have representatives on SIDBI Board, and Ministry of Urban Development is represented on the NHB Board. MoF representatives are also on Boards of public sector banks (PSBs) and Development Financial Institutions (DFIs). Forward Market Commission (FMC), which used to regulate the commodity exchanges and brokers, under the Ministry of Consumer Affairs, shifted to the Ministry of Finance in 2014 (merged with the SEBI, MoF by September, 2015).

State Governments

Through the Registrar of Cooperatives, who are under the departments of agriculture and cooperation, the state governments regulate the cooperative banking institutions in their respective states. The state government have also sometimes claimed a regulatory role in certain other cases. Though it never became an open battle, the Andhra Pradesh government's Ordinance directing operations of Micro Finance Institutions (MFIs)—many of them NBFCs registered with and regulated by RBI—falls into this space.

Such actions by state government have been matters of contention in the past as well, and some of them have gone to the courts, too (the judgement on the court cases to clarify the *RBI vs. State Government* issue are before the Supreme Court).

Special Statutes for Certain Financial Intermediaries

Some key financial services intermediaries like SBI and its Associate Banks, Public Sector Banks, LIC and GIC are governed by their own statutes. These statutes give a special status to these institutions vis-á-vis the other institutions performing the same functions. Earlier, IFCI, UTI and IDBI also operated under special statutes, but now there special statutes have been repealed.

Establishment of FSDC

Few years back, an important addition was made to the regulatory architecture—the Financial Sector Development Council (FSDC) was set up which replaced the High Level Committee on Capital Markets. The council is convened by Ministry of Finance and does not have statutory authority—it is structured as a *council of regulators*—Finance Minister as chairman. It has a permanent secretariat.

The council resolves inter-agency disputes; look after the regulation of financial conglomerates that fall under various regulators' purview; and performs wealth management functions dealing with multiple products.

The *FSLRC* (Financial Sector Legislative Reforms Commission), set up (headed by Justice B. N. Srikrishna) to **examine** the regulatory structure and the laws governing the financial sector, submitted its report by early 2013. In a broad sense, the commission has recommended for changeover from an 'area-based' division of regulators to a 'task-based' division. Major highlights of the recommendations are as follows:

(i) Developing a 'horizontal structure' whereby, the basic regulatory/monitoring functions to be done by a UIA (Unified Financial Agency)—in place of each agency (like SEBI, IRDA, etc.) looking after one financial type and area. It will eliminate *regulatory overlap* (due to which the ULIP controversy happened between the SEBI and IRDA).

(ii) Setting up a FRA (Financial Redressal Agency) to handle consumer complaints, regardless of area. It means, regulator not to oversee the consumer complaints.

(iii) FSAT (Financial Sector Appellate Tribunal) to be set up to hear the appeals of entire financial sector.

(iv) Advice to set up three other agencies which will oversee banking, besides the RBI.

The advices of the commission are under government's consideration with some of them in the process of getting adopted, too.

BANKING IN INDIA

> *Banks are perhaps the most important financial intermediary. In the nineteenth century, banks mainly lent money to firms to help finance their inventories – which were held as collateral–in the cases of defaulters banks seized them. Gradually, banks expanded their lending activities –to finance houses and commercial real estates – holding the buildings as collateral. Emergence of information technology has presented special problems to these traditional forms of finance–if the idea does not pan out, the firm may go bankrupt, but there is no collateral– there is little of value that the creditor can seize.* *

* See Joseph E. Stiglitz and Carl E. Walsh, *Economics*, 4th Edition (New York: W.W. Norton, 2006), p. 205.

INTRODUCTION

The sense in which we today use the term banking has its origin in the western world. It was introduced in India by the British rulers, way back in the 17th century. Since then, enough water has flown and today Indian banks are considered among the best banks in the developing world and its attempts to emerge among the best in the world is going on.

NBFCs

Bank is a financial institution engaged primarily in mobilising deposits and forwarding loans The deposits and loans are highly differentiated in nature. Banks are regulated by the Central bank of the country—in case of India, the RBI (Reserve Bank of India). The another category of financial institution—the **non-bank**— is almost similar in its functions but *main* difference (though, highly simplified) being that it does not allow its depositors to withdraw money from their accounts.

NBFCs (Non-Banking Financial Companies)[1] are fast emerging as an important segment of Indian financial system. It is an *heterogeneous group* of institutions (other than commercial and co-operative banks) performing financial intermediation in a variety of ways, like accepting deposits, making loans and advances, leasing, hire purchase, etc. They *can not* have certain activities as their principal business—agricultural, industrial and sale-purchase or construction of immovable property.

They raise funds from the public, directly or indirectly, and lend them to ultimate spenders. They advance loans to the various wholesale and retail traders, small-scale industries and self-employed persons. Thus, they have broadened and diversified the range of products and services offered by a financial sector. Gradually, they are being recognised as *complementary* to the banking sector due to their—

  (i) customer-oriented services;

 (ii) simplified procedures;

(iii) attractive rates of return on deposits; and

(iv) flexibility and timeliness in meeting the credit needs of specified sectors.

RBI, the regulator of the NBFCs, has gives a very wide definition of such companies (a kind of 'umbrella' definition)—"a financial institution formed as a company involved in receiving deposits or lending in any manner." Based on their liability structure, they have been classified into two broad categories:

  (i) deposit-taking NBFCs (NBFC-D), and

 (ii) non-deposit taking NBFCs (NBFC-ND).

It is *mandatory* for a NBFC to get itself registered with the RBI as a *deposit taking* company. For registration they need to be a *company* (incorporated under the Companies Act, 1956) and should have a minimum NOF (net owned fund)[2] Rs. 2 crore.

Presently, there are **11,781** NBFCs registered with the RBI, out of which 212 are NBFCs-D and 11,569 are NBFCs-ND. They account for **14.8** per cent of the assets and **0.3** per cent of the deposits of the SCBs (Schedule Commercial Banks), respectively.[3]

---

1.   **RBI** update, 11 March, 2016 and the **Business.gov.in**, Government of India, April 2016.

2.   The term 'NOF' means, owned funds (*paid-up capital* and *free reserves* minus *accumulated losses, deferred revenue expenditure* and *other intangible assets*) less, (i) investments in shares of subsidiaries/companies in the same group and all other NBFCs; and (ii) the book value of debentures, bonds, outstanding loans and advances, including hire-purchase and lease finance made to, and deposits with, subsidiaries/companies in the same group, in excess of 10 per cent of the owned funds.

3.   Ministry of Finance, *Economic Survey 2015–16*, Vol. 2, (New Delhi: Government of India, 2016), pp. 57–58.

To *obviate dual* regulation, certain category of the NBFCs which are regulated by other financial regulators are exempted from the regulatory control of the RBI:

(i) venture capital fund, merchant bank, stock broking firms (SEBI registers and regulates them);

(ii) insurance company (registered and regulated by the IRDA);

(iii) housing finance company (regulated by the National Housing Bank);

(iv) nidhi company (regulated by the Ministry of Corporate Affairs under the Companies Act, 1956);

(e) chit fund company (by respective state governments under Chit Funds Act, 1982).

[Detailed discussion on the *Nidhi, Chit, Chitty, Kuri* and *MNBCs* are in the following sections of this Chapter.]

Some of the ***important regulations*** relating to acceptance of deposits by the NBFCs are:

- allowed to accept and/or renew public deposits for a minimum period of 12 months and maximum period of 60 months.

- cannot accept demand deposits (i.e., the *saving* and *current* accounts).

- cannot offer interest rates higher than the ceiling rate prescribed by the RBI.

- cannot offer gifts, incentives or any other additional benefit to the depositors.

- should have minimum investment grade credit rating.

- their deposits are not insured.

- the repayment of deposits by NBFCs is not guaranteed by RBI.

- need to maintain Capital Adequacy Ratio (CAR) norm as prescribed by the RBI.

The NBFCs registered with the RBI have different **types** depending on their *main business*:-

(i) *Equipment leasing company*—leasing of equipments.

(ii) *Hire-purchase company*—hire-purchase.

(iii) *Loan company*— forwarding loans.

(iv) *Investment company*—buying and selling of securities.

These NBFCs have been reclassified into ***three*** categories:

(i) Asset Finance Company (AFC)

(ii) Investment Company (IC) and

(iii) Loan Company (LC).

Under this classification, an AFC is defined as a financial institution whose principal business is that of financing the physical assets, which support various productive and economic activities in the country. Such NBFCs are supposed to play a very vital role in financing infrastructure projects in 2016–17, as per the Government of India.

The **Union Budget 2016–17** has proposed to give additional options to NBFCs (including banks and financial institutions), for reversal of input tax credits with respect to non-taxable services. As a *prudential measure* (to prevent their defaulter), the RBI in mid-March 2016 made it compulsory for all deposit and non-deposit taking NBFCs to set aside 15 per cent of their aggregate capital in the debt instruments of the Central and state governments. This will function as CAR for them.

Debenture Redemption

The norm of the NBFCs, which raise capital through debentures, have became stricter after the new Company Act, 2013 came into effect (w.e.f. 1 April, 2014), which are given below:

(i) They need to create a **debenture redumption reserve** (DRR) account out of the profits, to be used only to redeem debentures. The corpus of DRR should be atleast 50 per cent of the amount raised through debentures.

(ii) The need to invest or deposit a sum not less than 15 per cent of the amount in the form of deposits in banks or government on corporate bounds. The amount canot be used for any purpose other than redeeming debentures.

The norms are aimed at minimising the risk of debenture buyers in an NBFC and check the mishaps like the 'Sahara OFCD' [for Sahara ODFC see Chapter 14].

RESERVE BANK OF INDIA

The Reserve Bank of India (RBI) was set up in 1935 (by the *RBI Act, 1934*) as a private bank with two extra functions—regulation and control of the banks in India and being the banker of the government. After nationalisation in 1949, it emerged as the central banking body of India and it did not remain a 'bank' in the technical sense. Since then, the governments have been handing over different functions[4] to the RBI, which stand today as given below:

(i) It is the issuing agency of the currency and coins other than rupee one currency and coin (which are issued by Ministry of Finance itself with the signature of the Finance Secretary on the note).

(ii) Distributing agent for currency and coins issued by the Government of India.

(iii) Banker of the government.

(iv) Bank of the banks/Bank of last resort.

(v) Announces the credit and monetary policy for the economy.

(vi) Stabilising and targeting (CPI–C) the rate of inflation.

(vii) Stabilising the exchange rate of rupee.

(viii) Keeper of the foreign currency reserves.

(ix) Agent of the Government of India in the IMF.

(x) Performing a variety of developmental and promotional functions under which it did set up institutions like IDBI, SIDBI, NABARD, NHB, etc.

CREDIT AND MONETARY POLICY

The policy by which the desired level of money flow and its demand is regulated is known as the credit and monetary policy. All over the world it is announced by the central banking body of the country—as the RBI announces it in India. In India there has been a tradition of announcing it twice in a financial year—before the starting of the *busy* and the *slack* seasons. But in the reform period, this tradition has been broken. Now the RBI keeps modifying this as per the requirement of the economy, though the practice of the two policy announcements a year still continues.

In India, a debate regarding autonomy to the RBI regarding announcement of the policy started when the Narasimham Committee-I recommended on these lines. As the Governor RBI it was Bimal Jalan who vocally supported the idea. No such move came from the governments officially, but it is believed that the RBI has been given almost working autonomy in this area. In most of the developed economies, the central bank functions with autonomous powers in this area (bifurcation of politics from the economics). Though we lack such kind of officially open autonomy for the RBI, we have learnt enough by now and are better off today.

RBI uses many instruments/tools to put in place the required kind of credit and monetary policy such as—CRR, SLR, Bank Rate, Repo & Reverse Rates, MSF Rate, OMOs, etc. on which it has regulatory controls.

---

4. Based on the ***RBI Nationalisation Act, 1949*** and further announcements of the, Ministry of Finance, Government of India.

CRR

The cash reserve ratio (CRR) is the ratio (fixed by the RBI) of the total deposits of a bank in India which is kept with the RBI in the form of cash. This was fixed to be in the range of 3 to 15 per cent.[5] A recent Amendment (2007) has removed the 3 per cent floor and provided a free hand to the RBI in fixing the CRR.

At present (March 2017) it is 4 per cent and a 1 per cent change in it today affects the economy with Rs. 96,000 crore[6]—an increase sucks this amount from the economy, while a decrease injects this amount into the economy.

Following the recommendations of the Narasimham Committee on the Financial System (1991) the government started two major changes concerning the CRR:

(i) Reducing the CRR was set as the medium-term objective and it was reduced gradually from its peak of 15 per cent in 1992 to 4.5 per cent by June 2003.[7]

After the RBI (Amendment) Act has been enacted in June 2006, the RBI can now prescribe CRR for scheduled banks without any floor or ceiling rate thereby removing the statutory minimum CRR limit of 3 per cent.[8]

(ii) Payment of interest by the RBI on the CRR money to the scheduled banks started in financial year 1999–2000 (in the wake of the banking slow down). Though the RBI discontinued interest payments from mid-2007.[9]

SLR

The statutory liquidity ratio (SLR) is the ratio (fixed by the RBI) of the total deposits of a bank which is to be maintained by the bank with itself in non-cash form prescribed by the government to be in the range of 25 to 40 per cent.[10]

The ratio was cut to 25 per cent (done in October 1997 after CFS suggestions).[11] It used to be as high as 38.5 per cent. The CFS has recommended the government not to use this money by handing G-Secs to the banks. In its place a *market-based interest* on it should be paid by the government, it was being advised. However, there has been no follow up in this regard by the governments. The Government of India has removed the 25 per cent floor for the SLR by an Amendment (2007) providing the RBI a free hand in fixing it—by **March 2017** it was 20.50 per cent.

Bank Rate

The interest rate which the RBI charges on its **long-term** lendings is known as the Bank Rate. The clients who borrow through this route are the Government of India, state governments, banks, financial institutions, co-operative banks, NBFCs, etc. The rate has direct impact on long-term lending activities of the concerned lending bodies operating in the Indian financial system. The rate was realigned[12] with the MSF (Marginal Standing Facility) by the RBI in February 2012. By **March 2017**, it was 6.75 per cent.

Repo Rate

The rate of interest the RBI charges from its clients on their *short-term* borrowing is the repo rate in

5. *RBI Act, 1934,* sub-section (1) of Section 42.

6. Reserve Bank of India, **Financial Stability Report**, Government of India, New Delhi, 2015.

7. Reserve Bank of India, *Economic Survey, 2006–07,* (New Delhi: Government of India, 2007).

8. *RBI (Amendment) Act, 2006*, (Mumbai: Government of India, 2007).

9. Reserve Bank of India, *Credit and Monetary Policy,* (Mumbai: Government of India, 2015).

10. *RBI Act, 1934* and *Banking Regulation Act, 1949* Section 24.

11. *Committee on Financial System* (CFS) headed by the then RBI Deputy Governor M. Narasimhan, 1991.

12. Through an RBI announcement on 15th February. 2012.

India.[13] Basically, this is an abbreviated form of the 'rate of repurchase' and in western economies it is known as the 'rate of discount'.[14]

In practice it is not called an interest rate but considered a discount on the dated government securities, which are deposited by institution to borrow for the short term. When they get their securities released from the RBI, the value of the securities is lost by the amount of the current repo rate. The Call Money Market of India (inter-bank market) operates at this rate and banks use this route for *overnight* borrowings. This rate has direct relation with the interest rates banks charge on the loans they offer (as it affects the operational cost of the banks). The rate was 6.25 per cent in **March 2017.**

In October 2013, RBI introduced *term repos* (of different tenors, such as, 7/14/28 days), to inject liquidity over a period that is longer than overnight. It has several purposes to serve— stronger money market, stability, and better costing and signalling of the loan products.

Reverse Repo Rate

It is the rate of interest the RBI pays to its clients who offer short-term loan to it. At present **(March 2017)** the rate is at 5.75 per cent.

It is reverse of the repo rate and this was started in November 1996 as part of liquidity Adjustment Facility (LAF) by the RBI. In practice, financial instituions operating in India park their surplus funds with the RBI for short-term period and earn money. It has a direct bearing on the interest rates charged by the banks and the financial institutions on their different forms of loans.

This tool was utilised by the RBI in the wake of over money supply with the Indian banks and lower loan disbursal to serve twin purposes of cutting down banks losses and the prevailing

interest rate.[15] It has emerged as a very important tool in direction of following cheap interest regime—the general policy of the RBI since reform process started.

Marginal Standing Facility (MSF)[16]

MSF is a new scheme announced by the RBI in its Monetary Policy, 2011–12 which came into effect from May, 2011. Under this scheme, banks can borrow overnight upto 1 per cent of their net demand and time liabilities (NDTL) from the RBI, at the interest rate 1 per cent (100 basis points) higher than the current repo rate. In an attempt to strengthen rupee and checking its falling exchange rate, the RBI increased the gap between 'repo' and MSF to 3 per cent (late July 2013).

The MSF rate has been floated as a *penal rate* and since mid-2015 RBI has maintained it 1 per cent higher than the prevailing repo rate. By end **March 2017** it was at 6.75 per cent, fully aligned with the Bank rate (i.e., equal to the Bank rate).

Other Tools

Other than the above-given instruments, RBI uses some other important , too to activate the right kind of the credit and monetary policy—

(i) *Call Money Market:* The call money market is an important segment of the money market where borrowing and lending of funds take place on over night basis. Participants in the call money market in India currently include scheduled commercial banks (SCBs)—excluding regional rural banks), cooperative banks

---

13. **RBI Act, 1934** and **Banking Regulation Act, 1949.**

14. Stiglitz and Walsh, *Economics*, pp. 629–30.

15. Ministry of Finance, *Economic Survey 2001–02,* (New Delhi: Government of India, 2002).

16. The write-up is based on the RBI's *Credit & Monetary Policy, 2011-12* (in which the scheme was introduced); and the *European Central Bank*, Frankfurt, Germany and *Federal Reserve System* (also known as the *Federal Reserve*, and informally as the *Fed*) Washington DC, USA

(other than land development banks), insurance. Prudential limits, in respect of both outstanding borrowing and lending transactions in the call money market for each of these entities, are specified by the RBI.

In recent times, several changes have been introduced by the RBI in this market. By **April 2016**, banks were allowed to borrow only 1 per cent of their NDTL (net demand and time liabilities, i.e., total deposit of the banks, in layman term) under overnight facility at repo rate. For the rest of 0.75 per cent of their NDTL, they may use the *term repos* of different tenors. In a sense, since late 2013, RBI has been discouraging banks to use repo route and switch over to term repos for their requirements of the short-term funds. Promoting stability and signalling better cost of loans are the main objectives of this changed stance.

(ii) *Open Market Operations (OMOs):* OMOs are conducted by the RBI via the sale/purchase of government securities (G-Sec) to/from the market with the *primary aim* of modulating rupee liquidity conditions in the market. OMOs are an effective quantitative policy tool in the armoury of the RBI, but are constrained by the stock of government securities available with it at a point in time. Other than the institutions, now individuals will also be able to participate in this market (as per the **Union Budget 2016–17**).

(iii) *Liquidity Adjustment Facility (LAF):* The LAF is the key element in the monetary policy operating framework of the RBI (introduced in June 2000). On daily basis, the RBI stands ready to lend to or borrow money from the banking system, as per the need of the time, at fixed interest rates (repo and reverse repo rates). Together with moderating the fund-mismatches of the banks, LAF operations help the RBI to effectively transmit *interest rate signals* to the market. The recent changes regarding a **cap** on the repo borrowing and provision of the **term repo** have changed the very dynamics of this facility after 2013.

(iv) *Market Stabilisation Scheme (MSS):* This instrument for monetary management was introduced in 2004. Surplus liquidity of a more enduring nature arising from large capital inflows is absorbed through sale of short-dated government securities and treasury bills. The mobilised cash is held in a separate government account with the Reserve Bank. The instrument thus has features of both, SLR and CRR.

BASE RATE

Base Rate is the interest rate below which Scheduled Commercial Banks (SCBs) will lend no loans to its customers—its means it is like prime lending rate (PLR) and the benchmark prime lending Rate (BPLR) of the past and is basically a floor rate of interest. It replaced[17] the existing idea of BPLR on 1 July, 2010.

The BPLR system (while the existing system was of PLR), introduced in 2003, fell short of its original objective of *bringing transparency* to lending rates. This was mainly because under this system, banks could lend below BPLR. This made a bargaining by the borrower with bank-ultimately one borrower getting cheaper loan than the other, and blurred the attempts of bringing in transparency in the lending business. For the same reason, it was also difficult to assess the transmission of *policy rates* (i.e., repo rate, reverse repo rate, bank rate) of the Reserve Bank to lending

---

17. **Reserve Bank of India, Announcement,** 5 April, 2010 (New Delhi: Government of India).

rates of banks. The Base Rate system is **aimed at** enhancing transparency in lending rates of banks and enabling better assessment of transmission of monetary policy.

After its deregulation by the RBI in 2010, banks fix their own base rates. Thus, in practice base rate shows differentiation—changing from bank to bank according to differentiation in the operational costs of the banks. Banks are not allowed to offer any loan below their base rates. By **March 2017**, the base rate of the banks were in the range of 9.25 to 9.65 per cent[18].

By the *fiscal 2015–16*, several new initiatives were taken by the RBI in the area of credit and monetary policy management—*major ones* are being given below:

(i) Transition to a *bi-monthly* monetary policy cycle.

(ii) Recognition of the *glide path for disinflation* (recommendation of *Urjit Patel Committee* report implemented). Under it, the **CPI (C)** is used by the RBI as the **"Headline Inflation"** for monetary management.

(iii) A *Monetary Policy Framework* has been put in place – an agreement in this regard was signed between the Government of India and the RBI late February 2015. Under the framework, the RBI is to *'target inflation'* at 4 per cent with a variations of 2 per cent. It means, the 'range of inflation' is to be between 2 to 6 per cent (of the CPI-C).

(iv) Besides the existing repo route, **term repos** have been introduced for three set of tenors—7, 14 and 28 days.

(v) RBI is progressively *reducing* banks' access to overnight liquidity (at the fixed repo rate), and encouraging the banks to *increase* their dependency on the term repos. By **March 2016**, banks were allowed to borrow only up to 1 per cent of their NDTL from the Call Money Market—0.25 per cent through *repo* and the rest of 0.75 per cent through *term repo*. This aims to improve the transmission of policy impulses across the interest rate spectrum and providing stability to the loan market.

(vi) As per the **Union Budget 2016-17**, individuals will also be allowed by the RBI to participate in the government security market (similar to the developed economies like the USA).

MCLR

From the financial year **2016-17** (i.e., from 1st April, 2016), banks in the country have shifted to a new methodology to compute their lending rate. The new methodology—**MCLR** (Marginal Cost of funds based Lending Rate)— which was articulated by the RBI in December 2015. The *main features* of the MCLR are—

• it will be a tenor linked internal benchmark, to be reset on annual basis.

• actual lending rates will be fixed by adding a spread to the MCLR.

• to be reviewed *every month* on a pre-announced date.

• existing borrowers will have the option to move to it.

• banks will continue to review and publish 'Base Rate' as hitherto.

As per the RBI, 'for monetary transmission to occur, lending rates have to be sensitive to the policy rate'. But this was not occurring by now. During 2015-16, the RBI reduced the policy rate (repo rate) by a total of **1.25** per cent. But in comparison, banks reduced the lending rate by maximum **0.6** per cent. By now, banks have

---

18. Reserve Bank of India **Bi-monthly Credit & Monetary Policy**, February 2017.

been using either of the following *three methods* to compute their Base Rate:

(a) average cost of funds,

(b) marginal cost of funds, or

(c) blended cost of funds (liabilities).

As per the RBI, the MCLR will bring in the *following* benefits:

- transmission of policy rate into the lending rates of banks to improve;

- computation of the interest rates by banks will get more transparent;

- cost of loan will be fairer to the borrowers as well as the banks.

- it will help the banks to become more competitive and enhance their long-run value.

The present MCLR of banks is 7.75–8.20 per cent (*March 2017*).

REVISED LMF

In August 2014, the RBI announced a revised Liquidity Management Framework (LMF) as a way to check volatility in the inter-bank call money markets, where banks lend to each other, and also allow the lenders to manage their liquidity needs better. Major features of the LMF is as given below:

- RBI started conducting 14-day *term repurchase* auctions four times a fortnight, up to an aggregate amount equal to 0.75 per cent of the system's deposit base or net demand and time liabilities (NDTL).

- Unlike earlier, RBI has announced a fixed schedule for these 14-day *term repo* operations, which are used by banks for their day-to-day liquidity requirements. One-fourth of the total amount of 0.75 per cent of NDTLs would be put up for auction in each of the four auctions, RBI said in a statement.

- No change in the amount that banks can access from the liquidity adjustment facility (LAF) window at fixed repo rate

of the time. Banks are currently allowed to borrow up to 0.25 per cent of their deposit base or NDTL from the LAF window.

- Additionally, RBI conducts overnight variable rate repo auctions based on an assessment of liquidity in the system and government cash balances available for auction for the day.

- The LMF is aimed at reducing volatility in the call rate. Better interest signalling and medium-term stability in the loan market are other objectives of it.

NATIONALISATION AND DEVELOPMENT OF BANKING IN INDIA

The development of banking industry in India has been intertwined with the story of its nationalisation. Once the Reserve Bank of India (RBI) was nationalised in 1949 and a central banking was in place, the government considered the nationalising of selected private banks in the country due to the following *major* reasons:

(i) As the banks were owned and managed by the private sector the services of the banking were having a narrow reach—the masses had no access to the banking service;

(ii) The government needed to direct the resources in such a way that greater public benefit could take place;

(iii) The planned development of the economy required a certain degree of government control on the capital generated by the economy. Nationalisation of banks in India took place in the following stages:

Emergence of the SBI

The Government of India, with the enactment of the *SBI Act, 1955* **partially nationalised** the three Imperial Banks (mainly operating in the three past Presidencies with their 466 branches) and named them the State Bank of India—the first public sector bank emerged in India. The RBI had purchased 92 per cent of the shares in this partial nationalisation.

Satisfied with the experiment, the government in a related move *partially nationalised* eight more private banks (with good regional presence) via the *SBI (Associates) Act, 1959* and named them as the Associates of the SBI—the RBI had acquired 92 per cent stake in them as well. After merging the State Bank of Bikaner and the State Bank of Jaipur as well, the RBI came up with the state Bank of Bikaner and Jaipur. Now the SBI Group has a total number of six banks—SBI being one and five of its associates.

Emergence of Nationalised Banks

After successful experimentation in the partial nationalisations the government decided to go for complete nationalisation. With the help of the *Banking Nationalisation Act, 1969,* the government nationalised a total number of 20 private banks:

(i) 14 banks with deposits were more than Rs. 50 crore of nationalised in July 1969, and

(ii) 6 banks with deposits were more than Rs. 200 crore of nationalised in April 1980.

After the merger of the loss-making New Bank of India with the Punjab National Bank (PNB) in September 1993, the total number of nationalised banks came down to 19. Today, there are 27 public sector banks in India out of which 19 are nationalised (though none of the so-called nationalised banks have 100 per cent ownership of the Government of India).

After the nationalisation of banks the government *stopped* opening of banks in the private sector though some foreign private banks were allowed to operate in the country to provide the external currency loans. After India ushered in the era of the economic reforms, the government started a comprehensive banking system reform in the fiscal 1992–93. Three related developments allowed the further expansion of banking industry in the country:

(i) In 1993 the SBI was allowed access to the capital market with permission given to sell its share to the tune of 33 per cent through *SBI (Amendment) Act, 1993.*

At present the Government of India has 59.73 per cent shares in the SBI. (*It was on 9 July, 2007 that the entire equity stake of the RBI was taken over by the Government of India. Thus, the RBI is no more the holding bank of the SBI and its Associates.*)

On 10 October, 2007 the government announced its proposal of selling the shares of the SBI and cutting down its stake in it to 53 per cent level so that the bank can go for capitalisation.

(ii) In 1994 the government allowed the nationalised banks to have access to the capital market with a ceiling of 33 per cent sale of shares through the *Banking Companies (Amendment) Act, 1994.*

Since then many nationalised banks have tapped the capital market for their capital enhancement—Indian Overseas Bank being the first in the row. Though such banks could be better called the public sector banks (as the Government of India holds more than 50 per cent stake in them) they are still known as the nationalised banks.

(iii) In 1994 itself the government allowed the opening of private banks in the country. The first private bank of the reform era was the UTI Bank. Since then a few dozens Indian and foreign private banks have been opened in the country.

Thus, since 1993–94 onwards, we see a reversal of the policies governing banks in the country. As a general principle, the public sector and the nationalised banks are to be converted into private sector entities. What would be the minimum government holding in them is still a matter of debate and yet to be decided.[19] The policy of bank consolidation is still being followed by the government, so that these banks could broaden their capital base and emerge as significant players in the global banking competition.[20] Every delay in it will hamper their interests, as per the experts.

REGIONAL RURAL BANKS (RRBs)

The Regional Rural Banks (RRBs) were first set up on 2 October, 1975 (only 5 in numbers) with the aim to take banking services to the doorsteps of the rural masses specially in the remote areas with no access to banking services with twin duties to fulfill

(i) to provide credit to the weaker sections of the society at concessional rate of interest who previously depended on private money lending, and

(ii) to mobilise rural savings and channelise them for supporting productive activities in the rural areas.

The GoI, the concerned state government and the sponsoring nationalised bank contribute the share capital of the RRBs in the proportion of 50 per cent, 15 per cent and 35 per cent, respectively. The area of operation of the RRB is limited to notified few districts in a state.

Following the suggestions of the *Kelkar Committee*, the government stopped opening new RRBs in 1987—by that time their total number stood at 196. Due to excessive leanings towards social banking and catering to the highly economically weaker sections, these banks started incurring huge losses by early 1980s. For restructuring and strengthening of the banks, the governments set up two committees—the *Bhandari Committee* (1994–95) and the *Basu Committee* (1995–96). Out of the total, 171 were running in losses in 1998–99 when the government took some serious decisions:

(i) The obligation of concessional loans abolished and the RRBs started charging commercial interest rates on its lendings.

(ii) The target clientele (rural masses, weaker sections) was set free now to lend to any body.

After the above-given policy changes, the RRBs started coming out of the red/losses. The CFS has recommended to get them merged with their managing nationalised or public sector banks and finally make them part of the would-be three-tier banking structure of India. At present there are 40 RRBs (after amalgamation) functioning in India even though the amalgamation and recapitalisation processes are going on (*India 2017*).

COPERATIVE BANKS

Banks in India can be broadly classified under two heads—commercial banks and co-operative banks. While commercial banks (nationalised banks, State Bank group, private sector banks, foreign banks and regional rural banks) account for an overwhelming share of the banking business, co-operative banks also play an important role. Initially *set up to* supplant indigenous sources of rural credit, particularly money lenders, today they mostly serve the needs of agriculture and allied activities, rural-based industries and to a lesser extent, trade and industry in urban centres.

---

19. As per the **Strategic Disinvestment Statement of 1999,** the government had decided to cut its holding in them to 26 percent. The policy was put on hold once the UPA Government came to power.

20. Y.V. Reddy, **Lectures on Economic and Financial Sector Reforms in India** (New Delhi: Oxford University Press, 2002), pp. 137–57.

Co-operative banks have a *three tier structure*—

(i) Primary Credit Societies-PCSs (agriculture or urban),

(ii) District Central Co-Operative Banks-DCCBs, and

(iii) State Co-Operative Banks-SCBc (at the apex level).

UCBs: Primary credit societies (PCSs) in urban areas that meet certain specified criteria can apply to RBI for a banking license to operate as urban co-operative banks (UCBs). They are registered and governed under the co-operative societies acts of the respective states and are covered by the Banking Regulation Act, 1949—thus are under dual regulatory control. The *managerial aspects* of these banks—registration, management, administration, recruitment, amalgamation, liquidation, etc. are controlled by the state governments, while the matters related to *banking* are regulated by RBI.

Traditionally, the area of operation of the UCBs is confined to metropolitan, urban or semi-urban centres and caters to the needs of small borrowers including MSMEs, retail traders, small entrepreneurs, professionals and the salaried class. However, there is no formal restriction as such and today UCBs can conduct business in the entire district in which they are registered, including rural areas. Well managed primary UCBs with deposits of over Rs. 50 crore are also allowed to operate in more than one state subject to certain norms.

As they are covered by the RBI Act, 1934 (2nd Schedule) they have certain rights and obligations—*rights* of obtaining refinance and loans from the RBI and *obligations* such as maintenance of cash reserves, submission of returns to the RBI etc. Presently, there are 29 UCBs.

DCCBs & SCBs: As their names suggest, they operate at the district and state levels. One district can have no more than one DCCB with a number of DCCBs reporting to the SCB. They were under supervision of the RBI—later on this function was delegated to the NABARD.

Problems of these banks

Co-operative banks play a very vital role in India's financial system they have been faced with certain long-drawn problems also—we may have brief look them:

- Regulation remains the biggest issue as they are under dual regulatory control—the UCBs come under the RBI and the Registrar of Co-operative Societies (RCS) of the respective states while the DCCBs and SCBs come under the NABARD, the RBI and the RCSs. Given the close links between politicians and co-operatives and the fact that the RCS functions under the state government, in practice this dual (or triple) custody of the co-operative banks has, in practice, led to poor supervision and control. Besides, most co-operative banks are lacking in skill and expertise.

- Recruitments are politicised as are appointments at most levels.

- Income recognition and prudential norms that were introduced for commercial banks in the early 1990s (under the process of banking reforms) are still to be this sector.

Co-operative banks have been in news mostly for fraudulent deals. Due to multiplicity of regulatory control of the federal nature it becomes really difficult to comply these banks to the prudential norms. Meanwhile, the Government of India decided (in the **Union Budget 2017-18**) to bring the co-operative banks into the ambit of the 'core banking' structure. Under the core banking solution (CBS), customers are able to avail banks' services across all of the branches rather the branch where the account is—making them customers of the bank rather than of a branch.

FINANCIAL SECTOR REFORMS

The process of economic reforms initiated in 1991 had redefined the role of government in the economy—in coming times the economy will be dependent on the greater private participation for its development.[21] Such a changed view to development required an overhauling in the investment structure of the economy. Now the private sector was going to demand high investible capital out of the financial system. Thus, an emergent need was felt to restructure the whole financial system of India.

The three decades after nationalisation had seen a phenomenal expansion in the geographical coverage and financial spread of the banking system in the country. As certain weaknesses were found to have developed in the system during the late eighties, it was felt that these had to be addressed to enable the financial system to play its role ushering in a more efficient and competitive economy.[22] Accordingly, a *high level* committee on Financial System (CFS) was set up on 14 August, 1991 to examine all aspects relating to *structure, organisation, function* and *procedures* of the financial system—based on its recommedations, a comprehensive reform of the banking system was introduced in the fiscal 1992–93.[23]

The CFS based its recommendations on certain *assumptions*[24] which are basic to the banking industry. And the suggestions of the committee became logical in light of this assumption, there is no second opinion about it. The assumption says that *"the resources of the banks come from the general public and are held by the banks in trust that they are to be deployed for maximum benefit of the depositors"*. This assumption automatically implied:

(i) That even the government had no business to endanger the solvency, health and efficiency of the nationalised banks under the pretext of using banks, resources for *economic planning, social banking, poverty alleviation,* etc.

(ii) Besides, the government had no right to get hold of the funds of the banks at low interest rates and use them for financing its consumption expenditure (i.e., revenue and fiscal deficits) and thus defraud the depositors.

The recommendations of the CFS (**Narasimham Committee I**) were *aimed* at:

(i) ensuring a degree of operational *flexibility;*

(ii) *internal autonomy* for public sector banks (PSBs) in their decision making process; and

(iii) greater degree of *professionalism* in banking operation.

Recommendation of CFS

The CFS recommondation[25] could be summed up under five sub-titles:

1. On Directed Investment

The RBI was advised not to use the CRR as a principal instrument of monetary and credit control, in place it should rely on open market

---

21. Repeated by the Government of India many times, i.e., the **New Industrial Policy 1991; the Union Budget 1992–93; Eighth Five Year Plan (1992–97) Draft Approach;** etc.

22. Announced by the government while setting up the M. Narasimham **Committee on Finacial System** on 14 August, 1991. See also Publication Division, India 2011 (New Delhi: Government of India, 2002).

23. The Narasimham Committee handed over its report in record time within 3 months after it was set up.

24. Reserve Bank of India, **Committee on Financial Systems,** 1991.

25. Ibid.

operations (OMOs) increasingly. Two proposals advised regarding the CRR:

(i) CRR should be progressively reduced from the present high level of 15 per cent to 3 to 5 per cent; and

(ii) RBI should pay interest on the CRR of banks above the basic minimum at a rate of interest equal to the level of banks, one year deposit.

Concerning the SLR it was advised to cut it to the minimum level (i.e., 25 per cent) from the present high level of 38.5 per cent in the next 5 years (it was cut down to 25 per cent in October 1997). The government was also suggested to progressively move towards market-based borrowing programme so that banks get economic benefits on their SLR investments.

These suggestions were directed to the goal of making more funds available to the banks, converting idle cash for use, and cutting down the interest rates banks charge on their loans.

2. On Directed Credit Programme

Under this sub-title the suggestions revolved around the compulsion of priority sector lending (PSL) by the banks:

(i) Directed credit programme should be phased out gradually. As per the committee, agriculture and small scale industries (SSIs) had already grown to a mature stage and they did not require any special support; two decades of interest subsidy were enough. Therefore, concessional rates of interest could be dispensed with.

(ii) Directed credit should not be a regular programme—it should be a case of extraordinary support to certain weak sections—besides, it should be temporary, not a permanent one.

(iii) Concept of PSL should be redefined to include only the weakest sections of the rural community such as marginal farmers, rural artisans, village and cottage industries, tiny sector, etc.

(iv) The "redefined PSL" should have 10 per cent fixed of the aggregate bank credit.

(v) The composition of the PSL should be reviewed after every 3 years.

3. On the Structure of Interest Rates

The major recommendations on the structure of interest rates are:

(i) Interest rates to be broadly determined by market forces;

(ii) All controls of interest rates on deposits and lending to be withdrawn;

(iii) Concessional rates of interest for PSL of small sizes to be phased out and subsidies on the IRDP loans to be withdrawn;

(iv) Bank rate to be the anchor rate and all other interest rates to be closely linked to it; and

(v) The RBI to be the sole authority to simplify the structure of interest rates.

4. On Structural Reorganisation of the Bank

For the structural reorganisation of banks some major suggestions were given:

(i) Substantial reduction in the number of the PSBs through mergers and acquisitions—to bring about greater efficiency in banking operations;

(ii) Dual control of RBI and Banking Division (of the Ministry of Finance) should go immediately and RBI to be made the primary agency for the regulation of the banking system;

(iii) The PSBs to be made free and autonomous;

(iv) The RBI to examine all the guidelines and directions issued to the banking system in the context of the independence and autonomy of the banks;

(v) Every PSB to go for a radical change in work technology and culture, so as to become competitive internally and to be at par with the wide range of innovations taking place abroad; and

(vi) Finally, the appointment of the Chief Executive of Bank (CMD) was suggested not to be on political considerations but on professionalism and integrity. An independent panel of experts was suggested which should recommend and finalise the suitable candidates for this post.

5. Asset Reconstruction Companies/Fund

To tackle the menace of the higher non-performing assets (NPAs) of banks and financial institutions, the committee suggested setting up of asset reconstruction companies/funds (taking clue from the US experience).

The committee directly blamed the Government of India and the Ministry of Finance for the sad state of affairs of the PSBs. These banks were used and abused by the GoI, the officials, the bank employees and the trade unions, the report adds. The recommendations were revolutionary in many respects and were opposed by the bank unions and the leftist political parties.

There were some other major suggestions of the committee which made it possible to get the following[26] things done by the government:

(i) opening of new private sector banks permitted in 1993;

(ii) prudential norms relating to income recognition, asset classification and provisioning by banks on the basis of objective criteria laid down by the RBI;

(iii) introduction of capital adequacy norms (i.e., CAR provisions) with international standard started;

(iv) simplification in the banking regulation (i.e., via board for financial supervision in 1994); etc.

BANKING SECTOR REFORMS

The government commenced a comprehensive reform process in the financial system in 1992–93 after the recommendations of the CFS in 1991. In December 1997 the government did set up another committtee on the banking sector reform under the chairmanship of M. Narasimham.[27] The objective of the committee is objectively clear by the *terms of reference* it was given while setting up:

"To review the progress of banking sector reforms to date and chart a programme of financial sector reforms necessary to strengthen India's financial system and make it internationally competitive"

The **Narasimham Committee-II** (popularly called by the Government of India) handed over its reports in April 1998, which included the following major suggestions:[28]

(i) Need for a stronger banking system for which mergers of the PSBs and the financial institutions (AIFIs) were suggested—stronger banks and the DFIs (development financial institutions, i.e., AIFIs) to be merged while weaker and unviable ones to be closed.

(ii) A 3-tier banking structure was suggested after mergers:

(a) *Tier-1* to have 2 to 3 banks of international orientation;

---

26. Based on Y.V. Reddy, *Lectures on Economic and Financial Sector Reforms in India, 2002*.

27. Ministry of Finance, *Economic Survey 1998–99,* (New Delhi: Government of India, 1999).

28. Based on the Report of the *Committee on Banking Sector Reforms,* April 1998 (Chairman: M. Narasimham).

(b) *Tier-2* to have 8 to 10 banks of national orientation; and

(c) *Tier-3* to have large number of local banks.

The first and second tiers were to take care of the banking needs of the corporate sector in the economy.

(iii) Higher norms of Capital-to-Risk—Weighted Adequacy Ratio (CRAR) suggested—increased to 10 per cent.

(iv) Budgetary recapitalisation of the PSBs is not viable and should be abandoned.

(v) Legal framework of loan recovery should be strengthened (the government passed the *SARFAESI (Act, 2002)*.

(vi) Net NPAs for all banks suggested to be cut down to below 5 per cent by 2000 and 3 per cent by 2002.

(vii) Rationalisation of branches and staffs of the PSBs suggested.

(viii) Licencing to new private banks (domestic as well as foreign) was suggested to continue with.

(ix) Banks' boards should be depoliticised under RBI supervision.

(x) Board for financial Regulation and Supervisions (BFRS) should be set up for the whole banking, financial and the NBFCs in India.[29]

DRI

The differential rate of interest (DRI) is a lending programme launched by the government in April 1972 which makes it obligatory upon all the public sector banks in India to lend 1 per cent of the total lending of the preceding year to *'the poorest among the poor'* at an interest rate of 4 per cent per annum.

Priority Sector Lending

All Indian banks have to follow the compulsory target of priority sector lending (PSL). The priority sector in India are at present the sectors—agriculture, small and medium enterprises (SMEs), road and water transport, retail trade, small business, small housing loans (not more than Rs. 10 lakhs), software industries, self help groups (SHGs), agro-processing, small and marginal farmers, artisans, distressed urban poor and indebted non-institutional debtors besides the SCs, STs and other weaker sections of society.[30] In 2007, the RBI included five minorities—Buddhists, Christians, Muslims, Parsis and Sikhs under the PSL. In its *new guidelines* of March 2015, the RBI added *'medium enterprise, sanitation and renewable energy'* under it.[31] The PSL target must be met by the banks operating in India in the following way:

(i) *Indian Banks* need to lend 40 per cent to the priority sector every year (public sector as well as private sector banks, both) of their total lending. There is a sub-target also—18 per cent of the total lending must go to agriculture and 10 per cent of the total lending or 25 per cent of the priority sector lending (whichever be higher) must be lent out to the weaker sections. Other areas of the priority sector to be covered in the left amount, i.e., 12 per cent of the total lending.

(ii) *Foreign Banks* (having less than 20 branches) have to fulfil only 32 per cent PSL target which has sub-targets for

---

29. An integrated system of regulation and supervision was suggested by the Committee so that soundness of the financial system could be ensured—the concept of a financial *super-regulator* gets vindicated, as opines Y. V. Reddy, in *Lecturers on Economic and Financial Sector Reforms in India,* 38.

30. See Publication Division, *India 2007* (New Delhi: Government of India, 2008) and **Economic Survey, 2006-07**.

31. RBI, **New Guidelines on the PSL,** 2 March, 2015.

the exports (12 per cent) and small and medium enterprises (10 per cent). It means they need to disburse other areas of the PSL from the remaining 10 per cent of their total lending (*lesser burden*).

The committee on financial System (CFS, 1991) had suggested to immediately cut it down to 10 per cent for all banks and completely phasing out of this policy for the betterment of the banking industry in particular and the economy in general. The committee also suggested to shuffle the sectors covered under PSL every three years. No follow up has been done from the government except cutting down PSL target for the foreign banks from 40 per cent to 32 per cent (remaining same for those which have less than 20 branches). Meanwhile, some new areas have been added to the PSL.

NON-PERFORMING ASSETS

Non-Performing Assets (NPAs) are the *bad loans* of the banks. The criteria to identify such assets have been changing over the time. In order to follow international best practices and to ensure greater transparency, the RBI shifted to the current policy in 2004. Under it, a loan is considered NPA if it has not been serviced for *one term* (i.e., 90 days). This is known as *'90 day' overdue norm*. For agriculture loans the period is tied with the period of the concerned crops—ranging from two crop seasons to one year overdue norm.[32]

NPAs were classified into three types:

(a) Sub-standard: remaining NPAs for less than or equal to 18 months;

(b) Doubtful: remaining NPAs for more than 18 months; and

(c) Loss assets: where the loss has been identified by the bank or internal/external

auditors or the RBI inspection, but the amount has not been written off.

Rising NPAs

After the RBI conducted an AQR (Asset Quality Review), which was completed in March 2016, the NPAs of the banks increased much higher[33]:

- It was **9.1** per cent of total loans by September 2016, double their year-ago level. Equally striking was the concentration of these bad loans. More than **80** per cent of the NPAs were in the PSBs (public sector banks), where the NPA ratio had reached almost **12** per cent.

- Meanwhile, on the corporate side around 40 per cent of the corporate debt was owed by companies which had an *interest coverage ratio* (ICR) less than 1 (it means that these companies did not earn enough to pay even the interest on their loans).

It means, India is suffering from a *twin balance sheet (TBS)* problem, where both the banking and corporate sectors were under stress. Not just a small amount of stress, but one of the highest degrees of stress in the world. At its current level, India's NPA ratio is higher than any other major emerging market (except Russia's 9.2 per cent), higher even than the peak levels seen in Korea (of 8.9 per cent) during the East Asian crisis of mid-1990s.

The main reasons for unprecedented increase in the NPAs of the banks have been as given below *(as per various volumes of the Economic Survey including that of 2016–17)*:

(i) Switchover to system-based identification of NPAs;

(ii) Current macro-economic situation in the country;

---

32. Reserve Bank of India, 'Master Circular - Income *Recognition, Asset Classification, Provisioning and Other Related Matters'*, July 2013.

33. **Economic Survey 2016-17**, Government of India, Ministry of Finance, N. Delhi, Vol. 1, pp. 83-84.

(iii) Increased interest rates in the recent past;

(iv) Lower economic growth; and

(v) Aggressive lending by banks in the past, especially during good times.

The RBI came out with a **new guidelines** to resolve the NPA issue by early 2014. The steps taken under it are :

(i) Banks have to start acting as soon as a sign of stress is noticed in a borrower's actions and not wait for it to become an NPA. Banks to carve out as special category of assets termed special mention accounts (SMAs) in which *early signs* of stress are visible.

(ii) Flexibility brought in project loans to infrastructure and core industry projects, both existing and new.

(iii) *Non-cooperative* borrowers in NPAs resolution will have to pay higher interest for any future borrowing. Banks will also be required to make higher provisions for further loans extended to borrowers who are considered to be 'non-cooperative'.

(iv) Towards strengthening recovery from *non-cooperative borrowers*, the norms for asset reconstruction companies (ARC) have been tightened, whereby the minimum investment in security receipts should be 15 per cent, as against the earlier norm of 5 per cent.

(v) Independent evaluation of large-value restructuring (above Rs. 500 crore) made mandatory.

(vi) If a borrower's interest or principal payments are overdue by more than 60 days, a *Joint Lenders' Forum* to be formed by the bankers for early resolution of stress.

(vii) The RBI has set up a central repository of information on large credits to collect, store and disseminate credit data to lenders. For this, banks need to furnish credit information on all their borrowers with an exposure of Rs.5 crore and above.

(viii) Incentives to banks to quickly and collectively agree to a resolution plan.

The *RBI guidelines* announced since early 2014 aimed at checking the NPAs from rising have not been effective due one or the other reason, as per the *Economic Survey 2016-17*, and the situation needs a deeper and multi-dimensional analyses.

Resolution of the NPAs

At one hand, while the RBI tried to check the NPAs from rising by announcing new guidelines for the banks, on the other hand, it has also taken several steps to 'resolve' the problem. By *February 2017* (since 2014-15), the RBI has implemented a number of schemes to facilitate resolution of the NPAs problem of the banks—briefly discussed below:

5/25 Refinancing: This scheme offered a larger window for revival of stressed assets in the infrastructure sectors and 8 core industries. Under this scheme lenders were allowed to extend the tenure of loans to 25 years with interest rates adjusted every 5 years, so tenure of the loans matches the long gestation period in the sectors. The scheme thus aimed to improve the credit profile and liquidity position of borrowers, while allowing banks to treat these loans as standard in their balance sheets, reducing provisioning costs against NPAs. However, with amortisation spread out over a longer period, this arrangement also meant that the companies faced a higher interest burden, which they found difficult to repay, forcing banks to extend additional loans (called 'evergreening'). This in turn has aggravated the initial problem.

ARCs (Asset Reconstruction Companies): ARCs were introduced to India under the SARFAESI

Act (2002), as specialists to resolve the burden of NPAs. But the ARCs (most are privately-owned) finding it difficult to resolve the NPAs they purchased, are today only willing to purchase such loans at low prices. As a result, banks have been unwilling to sell them loans on a large scale. Since (2014) the fee structure of the ARCs was modified (requiring ARCs to pay a greater proportion of the purchase price *up-front* in cash to the banks) purchases of NPAs by them have slowed down further—only about 5 per cent of total NPAs were sold during 2014-15 and 2015-16.

SDR (Strategic Debt Restructuring): In June 2015, RBI came up with the SDR scheme provide an opportunity to banks to convert debt of companies (whose stressed assets were restructured but which could not finally fulfil the conditions attached to such restructuring) to 51 per cent equity and sell them to the highest bidders—ownership change takes place in it. By end-December 2016, only 2 such sales had materialized, in part because many firms remained financially unviable, since only a small portion of their debt had been converted to equity.

AQR (Asset Quality Review): Resolution of the problem of bad assets requires sound recognition of such assets. Therefore, the RBI emphasized AQR, to verify that banks were assessing loans in line with RBI loan classification rules. Any deviations from such rules were to be rectified by March 2016.

S4A (Scheme for Sustainable Structuring of Stressed Assets): Introduced in June 2016, in it, an independent agency is hired by the banks which decides as how much of the stressed debt of a company is 'sustainable'. The rest ('unsustainable') is converted into equity and preference shares. Unlike the SDR arrangement, this involves no change in the ownership of the company.

PUBLIC SECTOR ASSET REHABILITATION AGENCY (PARA)

To resolve the twin problems of 'balance sheet syndrome' (of the banks as well as the corporate sector), the *Economic Survey 2016-17* has suggested the Government to set up a *public sector asset rehabilitation agency* (PARA)—charged with the largest and most complex cases of the 'syndrome'. Such initiatives were successfully able to handle the 'twin balance sheet' (TBS) problems in the countries hit by the South East Currency Crises of mid-1990s. As per the Survey, the Agency charged with working out the largest and most complex cases. Such an approach could eliminate most of the obstacles currently plaguing loan resolution.

- coordination problem as in this case, the debts would be centralised in one agency;
- it could be set up with proper incentives by giving it an explicit mandate to maximize recoveries within a defined time period; and
- it would separate the loan resolution process from concerns about bank capital.

The *Survey* has outlined seven reasons in support of its suggestion for setting up the PARA—which are as given below[34]:

(i) *It's not just about banks, it's a lot about companies.* So far, the NPAs issues revolved around the capital of the bank and how to fund them so that they start giving loans again. But more important issue is to find out a way to resolve the NPAs created by the corporate houses (as why they are stressed).

---

34. **Economic Survey 2016-17**, Government of India, Ministry of Finance, N. Delhi, Vol. 1, p. 85.

(ii) *It is an economic problem, not a morality play.* Diversion of funds (wilful defaults) have undoubtedly been one reason behind non-payment of the debts. But a large number of loan defaults have been caused by unexpected changes in the economic environment—timetables, exchange rates, and growth rate assumptions going wrong.

(iii) *The stressed debt is heavily concentrated in large companies.* This is an opportunity, because TBS could be overcome by solving a relatively small number of cases. But it presents an even bigger challenge, because large cases are inherently difficult to resolve.

(iv) *Many of these companies are unviable at current levels of debt requiring debt write-downs in many case.* Cash flows in the large stressed companies have been deteriorating over the past few years, to the point where debt reductions of more than 50 per cent will often be needed to restore viability. The only alternative would be to convert *debt to equity*, take over the companies, and then sell them at a loss.

(v) *Banks are finding it difficult to resolve these cases, despite a proliferation of schemes to help them.* Among other issues, they face severe coordination problems, since large debtors have many creditors, with different interests. If PSBs grant large debt reductions, this could attract the attention of the investigative agencies. But taking over large companies will be politically difficult, as well.

(vi) *Delay is costly.* Since banks can't resolve the big cases, they have simply refinanced the debtors—deteriorating the situation. But this is costly for the government, because it means the bad debts keep rising, increasing the ultimate recapitalization bill for the government and the associated political difficulties. Delay is also costly for the economy, because impaired banks are scaling back their credit, while stressed companies are cutting their investments.

(vii) *Progress may require a PARA.* The ARCs (Asset Reconstruction Companies) haven't proved any more successful than banks in resolving bad debts. But international experience shows that a professionally run central agency with government backing (not without its own difficulties) can provide the solution in this regard.

By late *February 2017*, Government hinted towards its interest to the idea of PARA. But before the idea takes shape several related issues are to be settled by the government, such as—its funding mechanism; selection of the companies for their balance sheet resolution; recovery mechanism of the banks' NPAs; etc. among others.

SARFAESI Act, 2002

GoI finally cracked down on the **wilful defaulters** by passing the *Securitisation and Reconstruction of Financial Assets and Enforcement of Security Interest (SARFAESI) Act, 2002*.

The Act gives far reaching powers to the banks/FIs concering NPAs:

1. Banks/FIs having 75 per cent of the dues owed by the borrower can collectively proceed on the following in the event of the account becoming NPA:

   (i) Issue notice of default to borrowers asking to clear dues within 60 days.

   (ii) On the borrower's failure to repay:

       (a) Take possession of security and/ or

       (b) take over the management of the borrowing concern and/or

(c) appoint a person to manage the concern.

(iii) If the case is already before the BIFR, the proceedings can be stalled if banks/FIs having 75 per cent share in the dues have taken any steps to recover the dues under the provisions of the ordinance.

2. The banks/FIs can also sell the security to a securitisation or Asset Reconstruction Company (ARC), established under the provisions of the Ordinance. [The ARC is sought to be set up on the lines similar to the USA, few years ago.]

WILFUL DEFAULTER

There are many people and entities who borrow money from lending institutions but fail to repay. However, not all of them are called wilful defaulters. As is embedded in the name, a wilful defaulter is one who does not repay a loan or liability, but apart from this there are other things that define a wilful defaulter. According to the RBI, a wilful defaulter is one who—

(i) is financially capable to repay and yet does not do so;

(ii) or one who diverts the funds for purposes other than what the fund was availed for;

(iii) or with whom funds are not available in the form of assets as funds have been siphoned off;

(iv) or who has sold or disposed the property that was used as a security to obtain the loan.

Diversion of fund includes activities such as using short-term working capital for long-term purposes, acquiring assets for which the loan was not meant for and transferring funds to other entities. *Siphoning of funds* means that funds were used for purposes that were not related to

the borrower and which could affect the financial health of the entity.

However, a lending institution cannot term an entity or an individual a wilful defaulter for a one-off case of default and needs to take into account the repayment track record. The default should be established to be intentional and the defaulter should be informed about the same. The defaulter should also be given a chance to clarify his stand on the issue. Also, the default amount needs to be at least Rs.25 lakh to be included in the category of wilful defaults.

If an entity's or individual's name figures in the list of wilful defaulters, the following restrictions get in action on them—

(i) Barred from participating in the capital market.

(ii) Barred from availing any further banking facilities and to access financial institutions for five years for the purpose of starting a new venture.

(iii) The lenders can initiate the process of recovery with full vigour and can even initiate criminal proceedings, if required.

(iv) The lending institutions may not allow any person related to the defaulting company to become a board member of any other company as well.

CAPITAL ADEQUACY RATIO

At first sight bank is a business or industry a segment of the service sector in any economy. But the failure of a bank may have far greater damaging impact on an economy than any other kind of business or commercial activity. Basically, modern economies are heavily dependent on banks today than in the past—banks are today called the backbone of economies. Healthy functioning of banks is today essential for the proper functioning of an economy. As credit creation (*i.e., loan disbursals*) of banks are highly risky business, the depositors' money depends on the banks' quality of lending. More importantly, the whole payment system, public as well as private, depends on banks. A bank's failure has the potential of creating chaos in an economy. This is why governments of the world pay special attention to the regulatory aspects of the banks. Every regulatory provision for banks tries to achieve a simple equation, i.e., *"how the banks should maximise their credit creation by minimising the risk and continue functioning permanently"*. In the banking business risks are always there and cannot be made 'zero'—as any loan forwarded to any individual or firm (irrespective of their credit-worthiness) has the risk of turning out to be a bad debt (*i.e., NPA in India*)—the probability of this being 50 per cent. But banks must function so that economies can function. Finally, the central banks of the world started devising tools to minimise the risks of banking at *one hand* and providing cushions (shock-absorbers) to the banks at the *other hand* so that banks do not go bust (i.e., shut down after becoming bankrupt). Providing cushion/shock-absorbers to banks has seen three major developments:[35]

(i) The provision of keeping a *cash ratio* of total deposits mobilised by the banks (known as the CRR in India);

(ii) the provision of maintaining some assets of the deposits mobilised by the banks with the banks themselves in *non-cash form* (known as the SLR in India); and

(iii) The provision of the capital adequacy ratio (CAR) norm.

---

35. Through various legislations, since the *RBI Nationalisation Act, 1949* and the *Banking Regulation Act, 1949* were enacted – and further *Amendments* to the Acts, Ministry of Finance, Government of India, New Delhi.

The capital adequacy ratio (CAR) norm has been the last provision to emerge in the area of regulating the banks in such a way that they can sustain the probable risks and uncertainties of lending. It was in 1988 that the central banking bodies of the developed economies agreed upon such a provision, the CAR—also known as the **Basel Accord**.[36] The accord was agreed upon at Basel, Switzerland at a meeting of the Bank for International Settlements (BIS).[37] It was at this time that the **Basel-I** norms of the capital adequacy ratio were agreed upon—a requirement was imposed upon the banks to maintain a certain amount of free capital (*i.e., ratio*) to their *assets*[38] (*i.e.*, loans and investments by the banks) as a cushion against probable losses in investments and loans. In 1988, this ratio capital was decided to be 8 per cent. It means that if the total investments and loans forwarded by a bank amounts to Rs. 100, the bank needs to maintain a *free capital*[39] of Rs. 8 at that particular time. *The*

---

36. Simon Cox (ed.), 'Economics', *The Economist*, 2007, p. 75.

37. The *BIS* is today a central bank for central bankers set up in 1930 in a round tower near Basel railway station in Switzerland as a private company owned by a number of central banks, one commercial bank (Citibank) and some private individuals. Today it functions as a meeting place for the bank regulators of many countries, a multilateral regulatory authority and a *clearing house* for many nations' *reserves* (i.e. foreign exchange). See Tim Hindle, 'Pocket Finance' *The Economist,* 2007, pp. 35–36.

38. Investments made and loans forwarded by banks are known as risky assets.

39. The capital of a bank was classified into Tier-I and Tier-II. While Tier-I comprises share capital and disclosed reserves, Tier-II includes revaluation reserves, hybrid capital and subordinated debt of a bank. As per the provision, Tier-II capital should not exceed the Tier I capital. The risk-weighting depends upon the type of assets—for example it is 100 per cent on private sector loans, while only 20 per cent for short-term loans.

capital adequacy ratio is the percentage of total capital to the total risk—weighted assets (see footnote 40).

CAR, a measure of a bank's capital, is expressed as a percentage of a bank's risk weighted credit exposures:

CAR= Total of the Tier 1 & Tier 2 capitals ÷ Risk Weighted Assets

Also known as 'Capital to Risk Weighted Assets Ratio (CRAR)' this ratio is used to protect depositors and promote the stability and efficiency of financial systems around the world. Two types of capital were measured as per the **Basel II** norms: *Tier 1* capital, which can absorb losses without a bank being required to cease trading, and *Tier 2* capital, which can absorb losses in the event of a winding-up and so provides a lesser degree of protection to depositors. The new norms (**Basel III**) has devised a third category of capital, i.e., *Tier 3* capital.

The RBI introduced the *capital-to-risk weighted assets ratio* (CRAR) system for the banks operating in India in 1992 in accordance with the standards of the BIS—as part of the financial sector reforms.[40] In the coming years the Basel norms were extended to term-lending institutions, primary dealers and non-banking financial companies (NBFCs), too. Meanwhile, the BIS came up with another set of CAR norms, popularly known as **Basel-II**. The RBI guidelines regarding the CAR norms in India have been as given below:

(i) **Basel-I** norm of the CAR was to be achieved by the Indian banks by March 1997.

(ii) The CAR norm was raised to 9 per cent with effect from March 31, 2000 (*Narasimham Committee-II had*

recommended to raise it to 10 per cent in 1998).[41]

(iii) Foreign banks as well as Indian banks with foreign presence to follow **Basel-II norms,** w.e.f. 31 March, 2008 while other scheduled commercial banks to follow it not later than 31 March, 2009. The Basel-II norm for the CAR is 12 per cent.[42]

Why to maintain CAR?

The basic question which comes to mind is as to why do the banks need to hold capital in the form of CAR norms? *Two reasons*[43] have been generally forwarded for the same:

(i) Bank capital helps to prevent bank failure, which arises in case the bank cannot satisfy its obligations to pay the depositors and other creditors. The low capital bank has a negative net worth after the loss in its business. In other words, it turns into insolvent capital, therefore, acts as a cushion to lessen the chance of the bank turning insolvent.

(ii) The amount of capital affects returns for the owners (equity holders) of the bank.

Basel Accords

The Basel Accords (i.e., Basel I, II and now III) are a set of agreements set by the Basel Committee on Bank Supervision (BCBS), which provides recommendations on banking regulations in regards to capital risk, market risk and operational risk. The purpose of the accords is to ensure that financial institutions have

---

40. The RBI is a member of the Board of the BIS. The financial sector reforms commenced in India in the fiscal 1992–93 after the report submitted by the Narasimham Committee on Financial system (CFS).

41. Ministry of Finance, **Committee on Banking Sector Reforms** (M Narasimhan Committee-II), (New Delhi: Government of India, April 1998).

42. Ministry of Finnace, **Economic Survey 2006–07**.

43. D. M. Nachane, Partha Ray and Saibal Ghosh, **India Development Report 2004–05** (New Delhi: Oxford University Press, 2005), p. 171.

enough capital on account to meet obligations and absorb unexpected losses. They are of paramount importance to the banking world and are presently implemented by over 100 countries across the world. The BIS Accords were the outcome of a long-drawn-out initiative to strive for greater international uniformity in prudential capital standards for banks' credit risk. The objectives of the accords could be summed up[44] as:

(i) to strengthen the international banking system;

(ii) to promote convergence of national capital standards; and

(iii) to iron out competitive inequalities among banks across countries of the world.

The Basel Capital Adequacy Risk-related Ratio Agreement of 1988 (**i.e., Basel I**) was not a legal document. It was designed to apply to internationally active banks of member countries of the Basel Committee on Banking Supervision (BCBS) of the BIS at Basel, Switzerland. But the details of its implementation were left to national discretion. This is why Basel I looked G10-centric.[45]

The first Basel Accord, known as **Basel I** focuses on the capital adequacy of financial institutions. The capital adequacy risk (the risk a financial institution faces due to an unexpected loss), categorises the assets of financial institution into five risk categories (0 per cent, 10 per cent, 20 per cent, 50 per cent, 100 per cent). Banks that operate internationally are required to have a risk weight of 8 per cent or less.

The second Basel Accord, known as **Basel II**, is to be fully implemented by 2015. It focuses on three main areas, including minimum capital requirements, supervisory review and market discipline, which are known as the *three pillars*. The focus of this accord is to strengthen international banking requirements as well as to supervise and enforce these requirements.

The third Basel Accord, known as **Basel III** is a comprehensive set of reform measures aimed to strengthen the regulation, supervision and risk management of the banking sector. These measures aim to[46]:

(i) improve the banking sector's ability to absorb shocks arising from financial and economic stress, whatever the source be;

(ii) improve risk management and governance; and

(iii) strengthen banks' transparency and disclosures.

The capital of the banks has been classified into *three tiers* as given below:

Tier 1 Capital: A term used to describe the capital adequacy of a bank—it can absorb losses without a bank being required to cease trading. This is the **core measure** of a bank's financial strength from a regulator's point of view (this is the *most reliable* form of capital). It consists of the types of financial capital considered the most reliable and liquid, primarily stockholders' equity and disclosed reserves of the bank—equity capital can't be redeemed at the option of the holder and disclosed reserves are the liquid assets available with the bank itself.

Tier 2 Capital: A term used to describe the capital adequacy of a bank—it can absorb losses in the event of a winding-up and so provides a

44. Ibid, p. 172.

45. G-10 comprises Belgium, Canada, France, Germany, Italy, Japan, The Netherlands, Sweden, UK and USA; later the group incorporated Luxembourg, Switzerland and recently Spain into its fold.

46. *Bank of International Settlemets,* Basel, Switzerland, 15 May, 2012.

lesser degree of protection to depositors. Tier II capital is secondary bank capital (the *second most reliable* forms of capital). This is related to Tier 1 Capital. This capital is a measure of a bank's financial strength from a regulator's point of view. It consists of accumulated after-tax surplus of retained earnings, revaluation reserves of fixed assets and long-term holdings of equity securities, general loan-loss reserves, hybrid (debt/equity) capital instruments, and subordinated debt and undisclosed reserves.

Tier 3 Capital: A term used to describe the capital adequacy of a bank—considered the *tertiary capital* of the banks which are used to meet/support market risk, commodities risk and foreign currency risk. It includes a variety of debt other than Tier 1 and Tier 2 capitals. Tier 3 capital debts may include a greater number of subordinated issues, undisclosed reserves and general loss reserves compared to Tier 2 capital. To qualify as Tier 3 capital, assets must be limited to 250 per cent of a bank's Tier 1 capital, be unsecured, subordinated[47] and have a minimum maturity of two years.

Disclosed Reserves are the total liquid cash and the SLR assets of the banks that may be used any time. This way they are part of its *core capital* (Tier 1). *Undisclosed Reserves* are the unpublished or hidden reserves of a financial institution that may not appear on publicly available documents such as a balance sheet, but are nonetheless real assets, which are accepted as such by most banking institutions, but cannot be used at will by the bank. That is why they are part of its *secondary capital* (Tier 2).

Basel III Provisions[48]

The new provisions have defined the capital of the banks in different way. They consider common equity and retained earnings as the predominant component of capital (as the past), but they restrict inclusion of items such as deferred tax assets, mortgage-servicing rights and investments in financial institutions to no more than 15 per cent of the common equity component. These rules aim to improve the *quantity* and *quality* of the capital.

While the key capital ratio has been raised to 7 per cent of risky assets, according to the new norms, Tier-I capital that includes common equity and perpetual preferred stock will be raised from 2 to 4.5 per cent starting in phases from January 2013 to be completed by January 2015. In addition, banks will have to set aside another 2.5 per cent as a *contingency* for future stress. Banks that fail to meet the buffer would be unable to pay dividends, though they will not be forced to raise cash.

The new norms are based on renewed focus of central bankers on 'macro-prudential stability'. The global financial crisis following the crisis in the US sub-prime market has prompted this change in approach. The previous set of guidelines, popularly known as *Basel II* focused on 'macro-prudential regulation'. In other words, global regulators are now focusing on financial stability of the system as a whole, rather than micro regulation of any individual bank.

Banks in the West, which are market leaders for the most part, face low growth, an erosion in capital due to sovereign debt exposures and stiffer regulation. They will have to reckon with a permanent decline in their returns on equity thanks to enhanced capital requirements under

---

47. Subordinated debt ranks below other debts with regard to claims on assets or earnings (also known as a 'junior debt'). In the case of default, such creditors get paid out until after the senior debtholders were paid in full. Thus, such capitals of banks are more risky than unsubordinated debt.

48. ***Reserve Bank of India,*** MoF, GoI, New Delhi, May 5, 2012.

the new norms. In contrast, Indian banks—and those in other emerging markets such as China and Brazil—are well-placed to maintain their returns on capital consequent to Basel III. Financial experts have opined that Basel III looks changing the economic landscape in which banking power shifts towards the emerging markets.

BASEL III COMPLIANCE OF THE PSBs & RRBs

The capital to risk weighted assets ratio (CRAR) of the scheduled commercial banks of India was 13.02 per cent by March 2014 (Basel-III) falling to 12.75 per cent by September 2014. The regulatory requirement for CRAR is **9** per cent for 2015. The decline in capital positions at aggregate level, however, was on account of deterioration in capital positions of PSBs. While the CRAR of the scheduled commercial banks (SCB) at 12.75 per cent as of September 2014 was satisfactory, going forward the banking sector, particularly PSBs will require substantial capital to meet regulatory requirements with respect to additional capital buffers.

In order to make the PSBs and RRBs compliant to the *Basel III* norms,[49] the government has been following a recapitalisation programme for them since 2011–12. A *High Level Committee* on the issue was also set up by the government which has suggested the idea of 'non-operating holding company' (HoldCo) under a special Act of Parliament (action is yet to come regarding this).

Meanwhile, the government has infused *three tranches* of capital into the banks (infused funds go to the RRBs, too through the PSBs under whom they fall) upto March 2015:

(i) Rs. 12,000 crore infused during 2012–13 in seven PSBs.

(ii) Rs. 12,517 crore infused in 2013–14 in 8 PSBs.

(iii) In 2014–15, the PSBs were recapitalised with Rs. 6,990 crore. This capital infusion was based on some new criteria— asset quality , efficiency and strength of the banks.

(iv) During 2015–16, the government released Rs. 19,950 crore to 13 PSBs *(Economic Survey 2015–16)*.

(v) For the year 2016-17, the government has announced a sum of Rs. 25,000 crore for the purpose of recapitalising the PSBs *(Union Budget 2016–17)*.

Given the deterioration in asset quality and gradual implementation of *Basel III norms*, PSBs will have to improve their capital positions to meet unforeseen losses in future. The estimated capital requirement (excluding internal generated profit) for the next four years up to 2018-19 is likely to be about *Rs. 1,80,000 crore*. Of this total requirement, the Government of India proposes to make Rs. 70,000 crore available out of budgetary allocations during 2016–17 and 2017–18.

Stock of Money

In every economy it is necessary for the central bank to know the stock (amount/level) of money available in the economy only then it can go for suitable kind of credit and monetary policy. Saying simply, credit and monetary policy of an economy is all about changing the level of the money flowing in the economic system. But it can be done only when we know the real flow of money. That's why it is necessary to first assess the level of money flowing in the economy.

Following the recommendations of the *Second Working Group on Money Supply (SWG)* in 1977,

---

49. **Basel III** norms prescribe a minimum regulatory capital of 10.5 per cent for banks by 1 January, 2019. This includes a minimum of 6 per cent *Tier I* capital, plus a minimum of 2 per cent *Tier II* capital, and a 2.5 per cent capital conservation buffer. For this buffer, banks are expected to set aside profits made during good times so that it can be drawn upon during periods of stress.

RBI has been publishing four *monetary aggregates* (component of money), viz., M^1, M^2, M^3 and M^4 (are basically short terms for Money-1, Money-2, Money-3 and Money-4) besides the Reserve Money. These components used to contain money of differing liquidities:

M^1 = Currency & coins with people + Demand deposits of Banks (Current & Saving Accounts) + Other deposits of the RBI.

M^2 = M^1+ Demand deposits of the post offices (i.e., saving schemes' money).

M^3 = M^1+ Time/Term deposits of the Banks (i.e., the money lying in the Recurring Deposits & the fixed Deposits).

M^4 = M^3+ total deposits of the post offices (both, Demand and Term/Time Deposits).

Now the RBI has started[50] publishing a set of new monetary aggregates following the recommendations of the *Working Group on Money Supply: Analytics and Methodology of Compilation* (Chairman, Dr. Y. V. Reddy) which submitted its report in June 1998. The Working Group recommended compilation of four monetary aggregates on the basis of the balance sheet of the banking sector in conformity with the norms of progressive liquidity: M^0 (monetary base), M^1 (narrow money), M^2 and M^3 (broad money). In addition to the monetary aggregates, the Working Group had recommended compilation of three liquidity aggregates namely, L^1, L^2 and L^3, which include select items of financial liabilities of non-depository financial corporations such as development financial institutions and non-banking financial companies accepting deposits from the public, apart from post office savings banks. The **New Monetary Aggregates** are as given below:

Reserve Money (M^0) = Currency in circulation + Bankers' Deposits with the RBI + 'Other'[51] deposits with the RBI.

Narrow Money (M^1) = Currency with the Public + Demand Deposits with the Banking System + 'Other' deposits with the RBI.

M^2 = M^1 + Savings Deposits of Post-office Savings Banks.

Broad Money (M^3) = M^1 + Time Deposits with the Banking System.

M^4 = M^3 + All deposits with Post Office Savings Banks (excluding National Savings Certificates).

While the Working Group did not recommend any change in the definition of reserve money and M^1, it proposed a new *intermediate monetary aggregate* to be referred to as NM^2 comprising currency and residents' short-term bank deposits with contractual maturity up to and including one year, which would stand in between narrow money (which includes only the non-interest-bearing monetary liabilities of the banking sector) and broad money (an all-encompassing measure that includes long-term time deposits). The new broad money aggregate (referred to as NM^3 for the purpose of clarity) in the Monetary Survey would comprise, in addition to NM^2, long-term deposits of residents as well as call/term borrowings from non-bank sources, which have emerged as an important source of resource mobilisation for banks. The critical *difference* between M^3 and NM^3 is the treatment of non-resident repatriable foreign currency liabilities of the banking system in the money supply compilation.

---

50. The working group was set up in December 1997 under the chairmanship of Y. V. Reddy (the then Deputy Governor, RBI) which submitted its report in June 1998.

51. 'Other' deposits with RBI comprise mainly: (i) deposits of quasi-government; other financial institutions including primary dealers, (ii) balances in the accounts of foreign Central Banks and Governments, and (iii) accounts of international agencies such as the International Monetary Fund.

There are **two basic changes** in the new monetary aggregates. *First,* since the post office bank is not a part of the banking sector, ***postal deposits*** are no longer treated as part of money supply, as was the case in the extant M^2 and M^4. *Second,* the residency criterion was adopted to a limited extent for compilation of monetary aggregates. The Working Group made a recommendation in favour of compilation of monetary aggregates on residency basis. Residency essentially relates to the country in which the holder has a centre of economic interest. Holdings of currency and deposits by the non-residents in the rest of the world sector, would be determined by their portfolio choice. However, these transactions form part of balance of payments (BoP). Such holdings of currency and deposits are not strictly related to the domestic demand for monetary assets. It is therefore argued that these transactions should be regarded as external liabilities to be netted from foreign currency assets of the banking system. However, in the context of developing countries such as India, which have a large number of expatriate workers who remit their savings in the form of deposits, it could be argued that these non-residents have a centre of economic interest in their country of origin. Although in a macro-economic accounting framework all non-resident deposits need to be separated from domestic deposits and treated as capital flows, the underlying economic reality may point otherwise. In the Indian context, it may not be appropriate to exclude all categories of non-resident deposits from domestic monetary aggregates as non-resident rupee deposits are essentially integrated into the domestic financial system. The new monetary aggregates, therefore, exclude only non-resident repatriable foreign currency fixed deposits from deposit liabilities and treat those as external liabilities. Accordingly, from among the various categories of non-resident deposits at present, only Foreign Currency Non-Resident Accounts (Banks) [FCNR(B)] deposits are classified as external liabilities and excluded from the domestic money stock. Since the bulk of the FCNR(B) deposits are held abroad by commercial banks, the monetary impact of changes in such deposits is captured through changes in net foreign exchange assets of the commercial banks. Thus, now the new monetary aggregates NM^2 and NM^3 as well as liquidity aggregates L^1, L^2, and L3 have been introduced, the components of which are elaborated as follows:

NM^1 = Currency with the Public + Demand Deposits with the Banking System + 'Other' Deposits with the RBI.

NM^2 = NM^1 + Short Term Time Deposits of Residents (including the contractual maturity of one year).

NM^3 = NM^2 + Long-term Time Deposits of Residents + Call/Term Funding from Financial Institutions.

L^1 = NM^3 + All Deposits with the Post Office Savings Banks (excluding National Savings Certificates)

L^2 = L^1 + Term deposits with Term Lending Institutions and Refinancing Institutions (FIs) + Term Borrowing by FIs + Certificates of Deposit issued by FIs

L^3 = L^2 + Public Deposits of Non-Banking Financial Companies.

Data on M^0 are published by the RBI on *weekly* basis, while those for M^1 and M^3 are available on *fortnightly* basis. Among liquidity aggregates, data on L^1 and L^2 are published *monthly,* while those for L^3 are disseminated *quarterly.* The working group advised for the quarterly publication of **Financial Sector Survey** to capture the dynamic linkages between banks and rest of the organised financial sector.

Liquidity of Money

As we move from M^1 to M^4 the liquidity (inertia, stability, spendability) of the money goes on decreasing and in the opposite direction, the liquidity increases.

Narrow Money

In banking terminology, M^1 is called narrow money as it is highly liquid and banks cannot run their lending programmes with this money.

Broad Money

The money component M^3 is called broad money in the banking terminology. With this money (which lies with banks for a known period) banks run their lending programmes.

Money Supply

In general discussion we usually use money supply to mean money circulation, money flow in the economy. But in banking and typical monetary management terminology the level and supply of M^3 is known as money supply. The growth rate of broad money (M^3), i.e., *money supply*, was not only lower than the indicative growth set by the Reserve Bank of India, but it also witnessed continuous and sequential deceleration in the last 7 quarters and moderated to 11.2 per cent by December 2012. Aggregate deposits with the banks were the major component of broad money counting for over 85 per cent remaining almost stable. The sources of broad money are net bank credit to the government and to the commercial sector. These two together accounted for nearly 100 per cent of the broad money in 2012–13, compared to 89 per cent in 2009–10.

High Power Money

The central banks of all the countries are empowered to issue the currency. The currency issued by the central bank is called 'high power money' because it is generally backed by supporting 'reserves' and its value is guaranteed by the government and it is the source of all other forms of money. The currency issued by the central bank is, in fact, is a liability of the central bank and the government. In general, therefore, this liability must be backed by an equal value of assets consisting mainly, gold and

foreign exchange reserves. In practice, however, most countries[#] have adopted a 'minimum reserve system'.

Under the *minimum reserve system* the central bank is required to keep a certain minimum 'reserve of gold and foreign securities and is empowered to **issue currency to any extent**. India adopted this system in October 1956. The RBI was required to hold a reserve worth of only Rs 515 crore consisting of foreign securities worth Rs 400 crore and gold worth Rs 115 crore. In 1957, however, the minimum reserves were further reduced to only gold reserve of Rs 115 crore and the rest in the form of rupee securities, mainly due to the scarcity of foreign exchange to meet essential import bill. A gold reserve of Rs. 115 crore against the currency of Rs. 17,00,000 crore in circulation today, makes only 0.7 per cent reserve which is of no consequence. This makes the Indian currency system a 'managed paper currency system'. In India, there are two sources of *high power money* supply:

(i) RBI; and

(ii) Government of India.

The RBI issues currency notes of rupees 2, 5, 10, 20, 50, 100, and 2000 denominations which RBI calls as the 'Reserve Money'. The RBI issues currency of one rupee notes and coins including coins of smaller denominations on behalf of the Government of India which accounts for around 2 per cent of the total high power money.

Minimum Reserve

The RBI is required to maintain a reserve equivalent of Rs. 200 crores in gold and foreign

---

\# In past, there were two other systems—first belongs Great Britain in which no reserve was maintained upto a certain limit of currency issued, called 'fiduciary system' and second known as the 'proportional reserve system' in which, generally, 40 per cent reserve was maintained, adopted by France and the USA in 1928 and by India during 1935-56, replaced in October 1956 by a 'minimum reserve system'.

currency with itself, of which Rs. 115 crores should be in gold. Against this reserve, the RBI is empowered to issue currency to any extent. This is being followed since 1957 and is known as the Minimum Reserve System (MRS).

Reserve Money

The gross amount of the following six segments of money at any point of time is known as Reserve Money (RM) for the economy or the government:

(i) RBI's net credit to the Government;

(ii) RBI's net credit to the Banks;

(iii) RBI's net credit to the commercial banks;

(iv) net forex reserve with the RBI;

(v) government's currency liabilities to the public;

(vi) net non-monetary liabilities of the RBI.

RM = 1 + 2 + 3 + 4 + 5 + 6

As per the *Economic Survey 2014–15*, the rate of growth of reserve money comprising currency in circulation and deposits with the RBI (bankers and others) decelerated from an average of 17.8 per cent in 2014–15 to 4.3 per cent in 2013–14. Almost the entire increase in the reserve money of Rs. 3.258 billion between the period consisted of increase in *currency in circulation*. As sources of reserve money, net RBI credit to the government and increase in net financial assets of the RBI contributed to the growth of *base money*.

Money Multiplier

At end March 2012, the *money multiplier* (ratio of M^3 to M^0) was 5.2, higher than end-March 2015, due to cumulative 125 basis point reduction in CRR. During 2012–13, the money multiplier generally stayed high reflecting again, the CRR cuts. As on **31 December, 2014**, the money multiplier was 5.5 compared with 5.2 on the corresponding date of the previous year *(Economic Survey 2014–15)*.

Credit Counselling

Advising borrowers to overcome their debt burden and improve money management skills is credit counselling. The first such well-known agency was created in the USA when credit granters created National Foundation for Credit Counselling (NFCC) in 1951.[52]

India's sovereign debt is usually rated by six major sovereign credit rating agencies (SCRAs) of the world which are :

(i) Fitch Ratings,

(ii) Moody's Investors Service,

(iii) Standard and Poor's (S&P),

(iv) Dominion Bond Rating Service (DBRS),

(v) Japanese Credit Rating Agency (JCRA), and

(vi) Rating and Investment Information Inc., Tokyo (R&I).

As on 15 *January, 2013* most of these rating agencies have put India under 'stable' category in foreign and local currencies barring Fitch and S&P which have put its foreign currency in 'negative' category. The government is taking a number of steps to improve its interaction with the major SCRAs so that they make informed decisions as the *Economic Survey 2012–13* says.

Credit Rating

To assess the credit worthiness (credit record, integrity, capability) of a prospective (would be) borrower to meet debt obligations is credit rating. Today it is done in the cases of individuals, companies and even countries. There are some world-renowned agencies such as the Moody's, S & P. The concept was first introduced by **John Moody** in the USA (1909). Usually equity share is not rated here. Primarily, ratings are an investor service.

52. Y. V. Reddy, the RBI Gonvernor, *The Economic Times,* N. Delhi, 11 September, 2006.

Credit rating was introduced in India is 1988 by the ICICI and UTI, jointly. The major credit rating agencies of India are:

(i) *CRISIL* (Credit Rating Information of India Ltd.) was jointly **promoted** by ICICI and UTI with share capital coming from SBI, LIC, United India Insurance Company Ltd. to rate debt instrument—**debenture**. In April 2005 its 51 per cent equity was acquired by the US credit rating agency S & P—a McGraw Hill Group of Companies.

(ii) *ICRA* (Investment Information and Credit Rating Agency of India Ltd.) was set up in 1991 by IFCI, LIC, SBI and select banks as well as financial institutions to rate debt instruments.

(iii) *CARE* (Credit Analyses and Research Ltd.) was set up in 1993 by IDBI, other financial institutions, nationalised banks and private sector finance companies to rate all types of debt instruments.

(iv) *ONICRA* (Onida Individual Credit Rating Agency of India Ltd.) was set up by ONIDA finance (a private sector finance company) in 1995 to rate credit-worthiness of non-corporate consumers and their debt instruments, i.e., credit cards, hire-purchase, housing finance, rental agreements and bank finance.

(v) *SMERA* (Small and Medium Enterprises Rating Agency) was set up in September 2005, to rate the overall strength of small and medium enterprises (SMEs)—the erstwhile SSIs. It is not a credit rating agency precisely, but its ratings are used for this purpose, too. A joint venture of SIDBI (the largest share-holder with 22 per cent stake), SBI, ICICI Bank, Dun & Bradstreet (an international credit information company), five public sector banks (PNB, BOB, BOI, Canara Bank, UBI with 28 per cent stake together) and CIBIL (Credit Information Bureau of India Ltd.).

A general credit rating service not linked to any debt issue is also availed by companies—already offered in India by rating agencies—CRISIL calls such ratings as **Credit Assessment.**[53] International rating agencies such as Moody's, S & P also undertake sovereign ratings, i.e., of countries—highly instrumental in external borrowings of the countries.

Individuals are also covered by credit appraisal which is on useful information for the consumer credit firms. To maintain a database on the credit records of individuals the credit Information Bureau of India Limited (CIBIL) was set up in May 2004 which makes credit informations available to banks and financial institutions about prospective individual borrowers[54]

NON-RESIDENT INDIAN DEPOSITS

Foreign Exchange Management (Deposit) Regulations, 2000 permits Non-Resident Indians (NRIs) to have deposit accounts with authorised dealers and with banks authorised by the Reserve Bank of India (RBI) which include:[55]

(i) Foreign Currency Non-Resident (Bank) Account [FCNR(B) Account]

(ii) Non-Resident External Account (NRE Account)

(iii) Non-Resident Ordinary Rupee Account (NRO Account)

FCNR(B) accounts can be opened by NRIs and Overseas Corporate Bodies (OCBs) with an authorised dealer. The accounts can be opened in

53. S. Sundararajan, *Book of Financial Terms,* (New Delhi: Tata McGraw Hill, 2004), p. 44.

54. As per the latest update by the *RBI,* 11 May, 2012.

55. As per the latest update by the *RBI,* 11 May, 2012.

the form of term deposits. Deposits of funds are allowed in Pound Sterling, US Dollar, Japanese Yen and Euro. Rate of interest applicable to these accounts are in accordance with the directives issued by RBI from time to time.

NRE accounts can be opened by NRIs and OCBs with authorised dealers and with banks authorised by RBI. These can be in the form of savings, current, recurring or fixed deposit accounts. Deposits are allowed in any permitted currency. Rate of interest applicable to these accounts are in accordance with the directives issued by RBI from time to time.

NRO accounts can be opened by any person resident outside India with an authorised dealer or an authorised bank for collecting their funds from local bonafide transactions in Indian Rupees. When a resident becomes an NRI, his existing Rupee accounts are designated as NRO. These accounts can be in the form of current, savings, recurring or fixed deposit accounts.

There were two more NRI deposit accounts in operation, viz., *Non-Resident (Non-Repatriable) Rupee Deposit Account* and *Non-Resident (Special) Rupee Account*—an amendment to Foreign Exchange Management (Deposit) Regulations, in 2002, discontinued the acceptance of deposits in these two accounts from April 2002 onwards.

Repatriation of funds in FCNR(B) and NRE accounts is permitted. Hence, deposits in these accounts are included in India's *external debt* outstanding. While the principal of NRO deposits is non-repatriable, current income and interest earning is repatriable. Account-holders of NRO accounts are permitted to annually remit an amount up to US$ 1 million out of the balances held in their accounts. Therefore, deposits in NRO accounts too are included in India's *external debt*.

Guidelines for Licensing of New Banks

The RBI on *February 22, 2013* released the Guidelines for *Licensing of New Banks in the*

Private Sector'. Key features of the guidelines are:

(i) *Eligible Promoters:* A private sector/public sector/NBFCs/entity/group eligible to set up a bank through a wholly-owned "Non-Operative Financial Holding Company (NOFHC)".

(ii) *'Fit and Proper' criteria:* A past record of sound credentials, integrity and sound financial background with a successful track record of 10 years will be required.

(iii) *Corporate structure of the NOFHC:* The NOFHC to be wholly owned by the promoter/promoter group which shall hold the bank as well as all the other financial services entities of the group.

(iv) *Minimum voting equity capital requirements for banks and shareholding by NOFHC:* The initial minimum *paid-up voting equity capital*[56] for a bank shall be Rs. 5 billion. The NOFHC shall initially hold a minimum of 40 per cent of the paid-up voting equity capital of the bank which shall be locked in for a period of *five years* and which shall be brought down to 15 per cent within '12 years. Bank's shares to be listed on the stock exchanges within *three years* of the business commencement.

(v) *Regulatory framework:* The bank to be regulated by the relevant Acts/Statutes/Directives, issued by the RBI and other regulators. The NOFHC shall be *registered as* an NBFC with the RBI and will be governed by a separate set of directions issued by the RBI.

---

56. The part of 'Authorised Capital' (the limit upto which a company can issue shares) which has been actually 'paid' by the shareholders is known as the 'Paid-up Capital' of a company. [For detailed analysis of different kind of 'Capitals' of a company refer the *Chapter 14: Security Market in India.*

(vi) *Foreign shareholding in the bank:* Foreign shareholding upto 49 per cent for the first 5 years after which it will be as per the extant policy.

(vii) *Corporate governance of NOFHC:* At least 50 per cent of the Directors of the NOFHC should be independent directors. The corporate structure should not impede effective supervision of the bank and the NOFHC by RBI.

(viii) *Prudential norms for the NOFHC:* The *prudential norms* will be applied to NOFHC on similar lines as that of the bank.

(ix) *Exposure norms:* The Bank/NOFHC allowed no *exposure* to the Promoter Group—the bank shall not invest in the equity/debt capital instruments of any financial entities held by the NOFHC.

(x) *Business Plan for the bank:* The business plan should be realistic and viable and should address how the bank proposes to achieve *financial inclusion.*

(xi) *Additional conditions for NBFCs promoting/converting into a bank:* Existing NBFCs, if considered eligible, may be permitted to promote a new bank or convert themselves into banks.

(xii) *Other conditions for the bank:*

(a) To open at least 25 per cent of its branches in un-banked rural centres (with population of upto 9,999 as per the latest census).

(b) To comply with the *priority sector lending* targets applicable to the existing domestic banks.

(c) Banks promoted by groups having 40 per cent or more assets/income from non-financial business will require RBI's prior approval for raising paid-up voting equity capital beyond Rs. 10 billion.

(d) Any non-compliance of terms and conditions will attract penal measures including cancellation of licence of the bank.

Two new banks get licence: The RBI by early April, 2014 granted *'in-principle'* approval to two applicants, IDFC Limited and Bandhan Financial Services Private Limited, to set up banks—'in-principle' approval granted will be valid for 18 months during which the applicants have to comply with the requirements and fulfil other conditions. Both are leading non-banking finance companies, while IDFC deals in infrastructure finance, Bandhan is in microfinance business. A High Level Advisory Committee headed by former RBI Governor Bimal Jalan recommended these two applicants out of a list of 25 applications. The case of India post will be decided by the RBI in consultation with the Government of India. The RBI also announced to work on giving licences more regularly, that is virtually 'on-tap'. As per the RBI, those applicants who have been denied licences can apply for the 'differentiated licences' (once RBI invites applications for it)—some of them may be better off applying for a differentiated licence rather than for a full licence. The so-called differentiated banks will be specialised institutions such as the 'payment banks' suggested by an RBI panel (headed by **Nachiket Mor**) on financial inclusion, to widen the spread of *payment services* and *deposit products* to small businesses and low-income households.

LABELS OF ATM

The automated teller machine (ATM) enetered India by late 1980s and have evolved into three of its types by now—

    (i) *Bank's own ATMs:* These are owned and operated by the concerned bank and carry the bank's 'logo'. They are the costliest way to provide such service to bank's customers.

    (ii) *Brown Label ATMs (BLAs):* These are owned by third party (a non-banking firm). The concerned banks only handle part of the process that is 'cash handling' and 'back-end server' connectivity. They carry 'logo' of the bank which outsources their service.

    (iii) *White Label ATMs (WLAs):* These are 'owned' and 'operated' by a third party (a non-banking firm). They do not bear 'logo' of the banks they serve (that is why such a name). In place, they carry logo of the firm which own them. They serve customers of all banks and are interconnected with the entire ATM network in the country. The role of the concerned bank is only limited to provide account information and back-end money transfers to the third parties managing these ATM machines. These entities have a mandate to deploy 67 per cent of ATMs in rural locations (Tier III-VI) and 33 per cent in urban locations (Tier I and II cities). The Tata Communications Payment Solutions became the first such firm to get permission of the RBI (by mid-2013) to set up such ATMs – its brand name is 'Indicash'.

The main objectives of the Brown/White Label ATMs are cutting operation cost of running them and financial inclusion.

Non-Operative Financial Holding Company (NOFHC)[57]

The difference between an *operating company* and a *holding company* lies in the fundamental structures of the two, in their management and their interactions with one another. Business goals are often different, and both business types are after profits, but holding companies can still benefit from operating company losses under certain conditions.

The primary function of a ***holding company*** is to invest in other companies, commonly known as subsidiaries. Holding companies are usually not involved in day-to-day operations of the operating company, but lend initial or ongoing financial support via cash reserves or stock sales, and may assist in restructuring the operational model to ensure profits. Holding companies are normally structured as *corporations* (limited liability firms i.e., known as a **Ltd.** company in India) to protect assets and absorb financial losses.

Operating companies are owned by the holding company, but are responsible for all day-to-day operations of the company. When a holding company creates or purchases an operating company, they are sometimes allowed to conduct business as usual, especially, if they are profitable. Net profits after expenses are then handed over to the holding company.

Ownership of operating companies, even when purchased, revert to the holding company. Former owners who are kept on-board are often given control of the operating company in the form of executive management responsibility, but have no ownership rights. All major decisions that may

---

affect profitability or involve large expenditures must first be approved by the holding company.

Although operating company's *profitability* should make sense for the holding company, this is not always the case. Especially for larger holding companies with heavy tax burdens, owning one or more operating companies that lose money can benefit the parent company in the form of a business loss when tax time rolls around. This does not benefit the operating company, as it is responsible for operating income to run the business. If the losses become too great, operating companies can go out of business, but the holding company can still benefit because the operating company can help to balance overall profits and stock prices.

There are *three basic types* of holding companies:

(i) A *pure holding company* that is non-operating and exists solely to invest in and hold the voting shares of its subsidiaries. This type of holding company derives its income from the dividends earned from its ownership of the shares of its subsidiaries and from any gains realised from other investments.

(ii) A *general* or *operating holding company* that earns its income from selling goods and services in addition to the income derived from its ownership of subsidiaries.

(iii) A *pyramid holding company* that owns controlling interest in its subsidiaries with less invested capital than the two other categories.

NIDHI

Nidhi in the Indian context means 'treasure'. However, in the Indian financial sector it refers to any *mutual benefit society*[58] notified by the Central / Union Government as a Nidhi Company. They are created mainly for cultivating the habit of *thrift* and *savings* amongst its members. The companies doing Nidhi business, viz., borrowing from members and lending to members only, are known under different names such as *Nidhi, Permanent Fund, Benefit Funds, Mutual Benefit Funds* and *Mutual Benefit Company.*

Nidhis are more popular in **South India** and are highly localised single office institutions. They are mutual benefit societies, because their dealings are restricted only to the members; and membership is limited to individuals. The principal source of funds is the contribution from the members. The loans are given to the members at relatively reasonable rates for purposes, such as

---

58. **Mutual Benefit Society** (also known globally as 'benefit society' or 'mutual aid society') is an organisation, or voluntary association formed to provide mutual aid, benefit, or insurance for relief from common difficulties. Such organisations may be formally organised with charters and established customs, or may arise ad hoc to meet unique needs of a particular time and place. They may be organised around a shared ethnic background, religion, occupation, geographical region or other basis. Benefits may include money or assistance for sickness, retirement, education, birth of a baby, funeral and medical expenses, unemployment. Often benefit societies provide a social or educational framework for members and their families to support each other and contribute to the wider community.

A benefit society may have some common features – members having equivalent opportunity in the organisation; members having equivalent benefits; aid goes to needy (stronger helping the weaker); payment of benefits by collection of funds from the members; educating others about a group's interest; preserving cultural traditions; and mutual defence. Examples of benefit societies include trade unions, self-help groups, etc. It is believed that such societies predate human culture are found around the world.

house construction or repairs and are generally secured. The deposits mobilised by Nidhis are not much when compared to the organised banking sector.

Nidhis are companies registered under the Companies Act, 1956 and are regulated by the Ministry of Corporate Affairs (MCA). Even though Nidhis are regulated by the provisions of the Companies Act, 1956, they are exempted from certain provisions of the Act, as applicable to other companies, due to limiting their operations within members.

Nidhis are also included in the definition of **NBFCs,** which operate mainly in the *unorganised money market*. However, since 1997, NBFCs have been brought increasingly under the regulatory ambit of the RBI. Non-banking financial entities partially or wholly regulated by the RBI include:

(i) NBFCs comprising equipment leasing (EL), hire purchase finance (HP), loan (LC), investment (IC) [including primary dealers (PDs) and residuary non-banking companies (RNBCs);

(ii) Mutual benefit financial company (MBFC), i.e., *nidhi company*;

(iii) Mutual benefit company (MBC), i.e., potential nidhi company; i.e., a company which is working on the lines of a Nidhi company, but has not yet been so declared by the Central Government; has minimum net owned fund (NOF) of Rs.10 lakh, has applied to the RBI for certificate of registration and also to the Department of Company Affairs (DCA) for being notified as a Nidhi company and has not contravened directions / regulations of RBI/DCA.

(iv) Miscellaneous non-banking company (MNBC), i.e., *chit fund company*.

Since Nidhis come under one class of NBFCs, RBI is empowered to issue directions to them in matters relating to their deposit acceptance activities. However, in recognition of the fact that these Nidhis deal with their shareholder-members only, RBI has exempted the notified Nidhis from the core provisions of the RBI Act and other directions applicable to NBFCs. As on date *(February 2013)* RBI does not have any specified regulatory framework for Nidhis.

The Central Government in March 2000 constituted a committee to examine the various aspects of the functioning of Nidhi Companies. There was no government notification defining the word 'Nidhi'. Taking into consideration the manner of functioning of Nidhis and the recommendations of the *P. Sabanayagam Committee* in its report and also to prevent unscrupulous persons using the word 'Nidhi' in their name without being incorporated by the Department of Company Affairs (DCA) and yet doing Nidhi business, the committee suggested the following **definition** for Nidhis (a part of this definition is appearing in the new *Companies Bill 2012 (Section 406)*:

"Nidhi is a company formed with the exclusive object of cultivating the habit of thrift, savings and functioning for the mutual benefit of members by receiving deposits only from individuals enrolled as members and by lending only to individuals, also enrolled as members, and which functions as per Notification and Guidelines prescribed by the DCA. The word Nidhi shall not form part of the name of any company, firm or individual engaged in borrowing and lending money without incorporation by DCA and such contravention will attract penal action."

CHIT FUND

Recently, Chit Fund was in centre of news after the Kolkata-based *Saradha Chit Fund* scam came to light. Most of the media people were themselves not very clear about the 'finer' points related to the idea of 'chits' in India, but they kept on highlighting chits as they needed to report on the scam. Let us try understand what 'chits' are and some other similar concepts in India:

Chit funds (also known by their other names, such as, *Chitty, Kuri, Miscellaneous Non-Banking Company*) are essentially saving institutions. They are of various forms and lack any standardised form. Chit funds have regular members who make periodical subscriptions to the fund. The periodic collection is given to some member of the chit funds selected on the basis of previously agreed criterion. The beneficiary is selected usually on the basis of bids or by draw of lots or in some cases by auction or by tender. In any case, each member of the chit fund is assured of his turn before the second round starts and any member becomes entitled to get periodic collection again. Chit funds are the Indian versions of 'Rotating Savings and Credit Associations' found across the globe.

Chit fund business is regulated under the Central *Chit Funds Act, 1982* and the rules framed under this Act by the various state governments for this purpose. The Central Government has not framed any rules of operation for them. Thus, registration and regulation of chit funds are carried out by *state governments* under the rules framed by them. Functionally, chit funds are included in the definition of NBFCs by the RBI under the sub-head *miscellaneous non-banking company*(MNBC). But RBI has not laid out any separate regulatory framework for them.

Official Definition: As per the Chit Funds Act, 1982, chit means "a transaction whether called *chit, chit fund, chitty, kuri* or by *any other name* by or under which a person enters into an agreement with a specified number of persons that every one of them shall subscribe a certain sum of money (or a certain quantity of *grain* instead) by way of periodical installments over a definite period and that each such subscriber shall, in his turn, as determined by lot or by auction or by tender or in such other manner as may be specified in the chit agreement, be entitled to the prize amount".

A transaction is not a chit, if in such transaction :

(i) Some alone, but not all, of the subscribers get the prize amount without any liability to pay future subscriptions; or

(ii) All the subscribers get the chit amount by turns with a liability to pay future subscriptions.

SMALL & PAYMENT BANKS

By mid-July 2014, the RBI issued the *draft guidelines* for setting up small banks and payment banks. The guidelines said that both are 'niche' or 'differentiated' banks with the common objective of furthering *financial inclusion*. It is in pursuance of the announcement made in the *Union Budget 2014–15*. The details regarding the provisions to set up such banks and their operational criteria are as given below:

The ***guidelines*** to set up both the banks are same—

(i) The minimum capital requirement would be Rs 100 crore.

(ii) Promoter contribution would be at least 40 per cent for the first five years. Excess shareholding should be brought down to 40 per cent by the end of fifth year, to 30 per cent by the end of 10th year and to 26 per cent in 12 years from the date of commencement of business.

(iii) Foreign shareholding in these banks will be as per current FDI policy.

(iv) Voting rights to be line with the existing guideline for private banks.

(v) Entities other than promoters will not be permitted to have shareholding in excess of 10 per cent.

(vi) The bank should comply with the corporate governance guidelines, including 'fit and proper' criteria for Directors as issued by RBI.

(vii) Operations of the bank should be fully networked and technology driven from the beginning.

Small Banks

The purpose of the small banks will be to provide a whole suite of basic banking products such as *deposits* and supply of *credit*, but in a *limited area of operation*. The **objective** of the Small Banks to increase financial inclusion by provision of savings vehicles to under-served and unserved sections of the population, supply of credit to small farmers, micro and small industries, and other unorganised sector entities through high technology low-cost operations. Other features of the small banks are as follows:

(i) Resident individuals with 10 years of experience in banking and finance, companies and Societies will be eligible as promoters to set up small banks. NFBCs, microfinance institutions (MFIs), and Local Area Banks (LABs) can convert their operations into those of a small bank. Local focus and ability to serve smaller customers will be a key criterion in licensing such banks.

(ii) For the initial three years, prior approval will be required for branch expansion.

(iii) The area of operations would normally be restricted to contiguous districts in a homogenous cluster of states or union territories so that the Small Bank has a 'local feel' and culture. However, if necessary, it would be allowed to expand its area of operations beyon contiguous districts in one or more states with reasonable geographical proximity.

(iv) The bank shall primarily undertake *basic banking activities* of accepting deposits and lending to small farmers, small businesses, micro and small industries, and unorganised sector entities. It cannot

set up subsidiaries to undertake non-banking financial services activities. After the initial stabilisation period of five years, and after a review, the RBI may liberalise the scope of activities for small banks.

(v) The promoters' other financial and non-financial services activities, if any, should be distinctly ring-fenced and not co-mingled with banking business.

(vi) A robust risk management framework is required and the banks would be subject to all prudential norms and RBI regulations that apply to existing commercial banks, including maintenance of CRR and SLR.

(vii) In view of concentration of area of operations, the Small Bank would need a diversified portfolio of loans, spread over it area of operations.

(viii) The maximum loan size and investment limit exposure to single/group borrowers/issuers would be restricted to 15 per cent of capital funds.

(ix) Loans and advances of up to Rs 25 lakhs, primarily to micro enterprises, should constitute at least 50 per cent of the loan portfolio.

(x) For the first three years, 25 per cent of branches should be in unbanked rural areas.

Payments Banks

The **objective** of payments banks is to increase financial inclusion by providing small savings accounts, payment/remittance services to migrant labour, low income households, small businesses, other unorganised sector entities and other users by enabling high volume-low value transactions in deposits and payments/remittance services in a secured technology-driven environment.

• Those who can promote a payments banks can be a non-bank PPIs, NBFCs, corporate's, mobile telephone companies, super market chains, real sector cooperatives companies and public sector entities. Even banks can take equity in Payments Banks.

- Payments Banks can accept demand deposits (only current account and savings accounts). They would initially be restricted to holding a maximum balance of Rs 100,000 per customer. Based on performance, the RBI could enhance this limit.

- The banks can offer payments and remittance services, issuance of prepaid payment instruments, internet banking, functioning as business correspondent for other banks.

- Payments Banks cannot set up subsidiaries to undertake NBFC business.

- As in the case of small banks, other financial and non-financial services activities of the promoters should be ring-fenced.

- The Payments Banks would be required to use the word 'Payments' in its name to differentiate it from other banks.

- No credit lending is allowed for Payments Banks.

- The float funds can be parked only in less than one year G-Secs.

Meanwhile, the RBI has received 72 applications for small banks and 41 applications for payments banks. The applications are, at present, under consideration of the RBI. It is expected that soon some of them will get the nod for setting up these niche banks.

FINANCIAL INCLUSION

Financial inclusion is an important priority of the government. The objective is to ensure the excluded sections, i.e., weaker sections and low income groups, access to various financial services such as a basic savings bank account, need-based credit, remittance facility, insurance and pension. The government has recently launched an effective scheme to promote the cause of financial inclusion—the PMJDY.

Pradhan Mantri Jan-Dhan Yojana

To achieve the objective of financial inclusion by extending financial services to the large hitherto unserved population of the country and to unlock its growth potential, the Pradhan Mantri Jan-DhanYojana (PMJDY) was launched on 28 August 2014. The Yojana envisages—

(i) Universal access to banking facilities with at least one basic banking account for every household,

(ii) Financial literacy, access to credit and insurance.

(iii) The beneficiaries will receive a *RuPay* Debit Card having inbuilt accident insurance cover of Rs1 lakh.

(iv) In addition, there is a life insurance cover of Rs. 30,000 to those who opened their bank accounts for the first time between 15 August 2014 and 26 January 2015 and meet other eligibility conditions of the Yojana.

The Yojana has entered the *Guinness World Records* for opening most bank accounts during the week starting 23 August, 2014 as part of the financial campaign. As on 28 January 2015, 12.31 crore bank accounts have been opened, of which 7.36 crore are in rural areas and 4.95 crore inurban areas. Under the PMJDY, 67.5 per cent of the accounts as on January 28, 2015 are with zero balance.

ALM OF BANKS

Banks have been faced with *Asset-Liability Management (ALM)* problems in recent times due to their existing long-term loans forwarded to certain sectors, viz., infrastructure, core sector and real estate sector. Again, raising new funds for new projects in these sectors had become quite difficult for the banks. These sectors constitute the major portion of banks' non-performing assests.

Banks have been seeking permission for longer tenor amortisation of the loan with periodic *refinancing* of balance debt. Banks have been raising resources in a significant way, issuance of long-term bonds for funding loans to infrastructure sector has not picked up at all. Infrastructure and core industries projects are characterised by long gestation periods and large capital investments. The long maturities of such project loans consist of the initial construction period and the economic life of the asset/underlying concession period (usually 25–30 years).

In pursuance of the *Union Budget 2015–16,* the RBI announced 'eased' norms in *July 2015* for the banks to take care of the Asset–Liability Management issues of the banks, which are as follows:

(i) Banks allowed to raise fund through long-term bonds (with maturity period of not less than 7 years),

(ii) Such bonds exempted from the mandatory regulatory norms such as the CRR, SLR and PSL.

(iii) Such funds to be used to finance long-term projects in infrastructure, core sector and affordable housing. Affordable housing means loans eligible under the priority sector lending (PSL), and loans up to Rs.50 lakh to individuals for houses costing up to Rs.65 lakh located in the six metropolitan centres. For other areas, it covers loans of Rs.40 lakh for houses with values up to Rs.50 lakh.

(iv) Banks can extend long term loans with flexible structuring to absorb potential adverse contingencies, known as the *5/25 structure.* Under the 5/25 structure, bank may fix longer amortisation period (25 years) with periodic refinancing (every 5 years.

India is looking at investing US $1 trillion in infrastructure development by 2017, half of which is expected to come from the private sector. The instructions announced by the RBI are in pursuance of the *Union Budget 2015–16* announcement.

GOLD INVESTMENT SCHEMES

Two new gold investment schemes were launched by the Government of India by November 2015—the Sovereign Gold Bonds and Gold Monetisation Schemes. The schemes are aimed at twin objectives:

(i) Reducing the demand for physical gold; and

(ii) Shifting a part of the gold imported every year for investment purposes into financial savings.

Brief feature of the schemes are as given below:

Sovereign Gold Bonds

These are issued by RBI on behalf of the GoI in rupees and denominated in grams of gold and restricted for sale to the resident Indian entities only, both in demat and paper form. The minimum and maximum investment limits are two grams and 500 grams of gold per person per fiscal year, respectively. The rate of interest for the year 2015–16 was 2.75 per cent per annum, payable on a half yearly basis. The tenor of the Bond is for a period of 8 years with exit option from 5th year onwards. KYC norms are the same as that for gold. Exemption from capital gains tax is also available. Redemption is made in the rupee value equivalent to the price of gold at the time of maturity.

Gold Monetisation Scheme

In this scheme, BIS (Bureau of Indian Standards) certified CPTCs (Collection, Purity Testing Centres) collect the gold from the customer on behalf of the banks. The minimum quantity of gold (bullion or jewellery) which can be deposited is 30 grams and there is no limit for maximum deposit.

Gold Saving Account can be opened with any of the designated bank and denomination in grams of gold for short-term period of 1–3 years, a medium-term period of 5–7 years and a long-term period of 12–15 years. The CPTCs transfer the gold to the refiners. The banks will have a tripartite/bipartite legal agreement with refiners and CPTCs.

For the year 2015–16 interest rates was fixed as 2.25 per cent and 2.5 per cent for the medium- and long- term, respectively. Redemption is made in cash/gold for short term and in cash for medium and long term deposits.

The difference between the current borrowing cost for the government and the interest rate paid by the government under the medium/long term deposit will be credited to the Gold Reserve Fund.

MUDRA BANK

As per the Government of India, large industries provide employment to only 1.25 crore people in the country while the *micro units* employ around 12 crore people. There is a need to focus on these 5.75 crore self-employed people (owners of the micro units) who use funds of Rs. 11 lakh crore, with an average per unit debt of merely Rs. 17,000.

Capital is the key to the small entrepreneurs. These entrepreneurs depend heavily on the local money lenders for their fund requirements.

Looking at the importance of these enterprises, the Government of India launched (April 2015) the *Micro Units Development and Refinance Agency Bank (MUDRA Bank)* with the aim of *funding* these *unfunded* non-corporate enterprises. This was launched as the PMMY (Prime Minister Mudra Yojana). Important features of the MUDRA Bank are as given below:

- Under this banking model, the micro units can avail up to Rs. 10 lakh loan through refinance route (through the Public and private sector banks, NBFCs, MFIs, RRBs, District Banks, etc).

- The products designed under it are categorized into three buckets of finance named *Shishu* (loan up to Rs. 50,000), *Kishor* (Rs. 50,000 to Rs 5 lakh) and *Tarun* (Rs. 5 lakh to Rs. 10 lakh).

- Though the scheme covers the traders of fruits and vegetables, in general, it does not refinance the agriculture sector.

- There is no fixed interest rate in this scheme. As per the Government of India, presently, banks are charging the interest rates between Base Rate plus one per cent to 7 per cent per annum. Interest rates on the loans are supposed to vary according the risk involved in the enterprises seeking loans. There is no general subsidy offered on interest rates except if the loan is linked to some other government scheme.

> *Insurance is a kind of gambling in reverse—a major form of 'risk spreading'—one person's risk which would be large, is spread around to make it small for a large number of people—in this process it serves two purposes—provides social security net to people and helps in nation-building by making available investible capital.* *

* See Paul A. Samuelson and William D. Nordhaus, *Economics*, (New Delhi: Tata McGraw Hill, 2005), pp. 210–12. See LIBNA, 1956 and GIBNA, 1971 of the GoI.

DEFINITION

In economic terms, anything used to cut down the risk is known as *insurance*. But in familiar terms, insurance is provided by an insurance company which covers a person's life (called life segment) or covers loss of assets, property (called non-life or general segment). The insurance policies are purchased at fixed premiums.

INSURANCE INDUSTRY

Insurance has a deep-rooted history in India. It finds mention in the writings of Manu *(Manusmrithi)*, Yagnavalkya *(Dharmasastra)* and Kautilya *(Arthasastra)*. The writings talk in terms of **pooling of resources** that could be re-distributed in times of calamities such as fire, floods, epidemics and famine. This was probably a precursor to modern day insurance. Ancient Indian history has preserved the earliest traces of insurance in the form of marine trade loans and carriers' contracts. Insurance in India has evolved over time heavily drawing from other countries (England in particular).

LIC

The life insurance business/industry in the country was nationalised by the Government of India in 1956 and a fully government-owned company, the Life Insurance Corporation of India (LIC) was set up (at that time 245 Indian and foreign companies were playing in the life segment of insurance). Opening of private life insurance companies was prohibited at that time. The LIC was called an investment institution by the government.

The nationalisation was motivated by twin objectives—*first*, to spread the message of life insurance for greater social security and *secondly*, to mobilise people's savings (collected as premiums) for nation building. The LIC had been the biggest investor in the government's procces of planned development purchasing government securities (G-Secs.) and equities of the big asset Public Sector Undertakings (PSUs).

GIC

In 1971, the government nationalised the private sector companies (107 Indian and foreign companies) playing in the general insurance segment and a government company, the General Insurance Corporation of India (GIC) was formed in 1972. The GIC started operation on January 1, 1973 with its four holding companies:

  (i)   National Insurance Company Ltd.

  (ii) New India Assurance Company Ltd.

  (iii) Oriental Fire and Insurance Comany Ltd.

  (iv) United India Insurance Company Ltd.

In the era of economic reforms, two major changes took place in this area—

  (i)   In November 2000, the GIC was notified as the Indian Reinsurer[1] (to be known as GIC Re).

  (ii) In March 2002 the GIC was withdrawn from holding company status of the four public sector general insurance companies. Now these four companies are directly owned by the Government of India.[2]

AICIL

The public sector insurance company, Agriculture Insurance Company of India Limited (AICIL) was set up by the Government of India in December 2002 (commenced its business in April 2003). This is a *dedicated agri-insurance* company and

---

1. Publication Division, *India 2002,* (New Delhi: Government of India, 2003).

2. Ministry of Finance, *Economic Survey 2002–03,* (New Delhi: Government of India, 2003).

aims "to serve the needs of farmers better and to move towards a sustainable actuarial regime".

This company was responsible to look after the National Agriculture Insurance Scheme (NAIS) which was launched in 1999. Since *January 2016*, the company is looking after the newly launched PMFBY (Prime Minister Fasal Bima Yojana)[3] which subsumed the existing agri-insurance schemes—the NAIS and the Modified NAIS (of 2010). Till the AICIL was not set up, the agri-insurance responsibility of the government was being looked after by the General Insurance Corporation (GIC).

AICIL is jointly promoted by public sector insurance companies and development financial institutions—majority shares owned by the GIC (35 per cent) and NABARD (30 per cent) while the four public sector general insurance companies own 8.75 per cent each in it.

Public Sector Insurance Companies

At present, there are 6 public sector *insurance companies* in India. Out of it one deals in the life segment (LIC); four are involved in the non-life (general) insurance segment; and one is the dedicated agri-insurer. Other than these companies, there is one *re-insurance company*, the *GIC Re* (wholly owned by the GoI).

INSURANCE REFORMS

Under the process of economic reforms an Insurance Reforms Committee (IRC) was set up in April 1993 under the chairmanship of the ex-RBI Governor R. N. Malhotra. The committee handed over its report (January 1994) with the following major suggestions:[4]

(i) Decontrolling insurance sector, i.e., allowing Indian as well as foreign private sector insurance companies to enter the sector (the government did it in 1999 passing the *IRDA Act*).

(ii) Restructuring the LIC and the GIC and cutting down the government's holding in them to 50 per cent (no follow up still, but the private insurance companies demanding it anxiously. The NDA government had taken steps in this area, but the UPA government has no such plans.) Late 2012, the government started sale of the LIC shares but to public sector undertakings—seen as a welcome move.

(iii) Delinking GIC and its four subsidiaries (which was done in 2000).

(iv) Discarding the system of licensing of surveyors by the controller of Insurance.

(v) Restructuring the Tariff Advisory Committee.

(vi) Setting up a regulatory anthority for the insurance industry (the IRDA set up in 2000).

IRDA

The Insurance Regulatory and Development Authority (IRDA) was set up in 2000 (the Act was passed in 1999) with one chairman and five members (two as full time and three as part-time members) appointed and nominated by the government. The authority is responsible for the regulation, development and supervision of the Indian insurance industry.

As per the latest *Annual Report 2014–15* of the IRDA, presently, there are 52 insurance companies in India of which 24 are involved in life insurance business while other 28 companies are involved in non-life (general) segment. Insurance industry of India is presently regulated under the Insurance Laws (Amendment) Act, 2015. The Act increased the permissible limit of foreign direct

---

3. Ministry of Finance, **Union Budget 2016–17** (New Delhi: Government of India, 2016); and Ministry of Finance, **Economic Survey 2015-16** (New Delhi: Government of India, 2016).

4. R. N. Malhotra headed *Insurance Reforms Committee*, Government of India, N. Delhi, January 1994.

investment (FDI) from 26 to 49 per cent in the insurance business. The FDI up to 99 per cent is allowed under the automatic route while beyond it the approval of the FIPB (Foreign Investment Promotion Board) is required.

REINSURANCE

Insurance is a very risky business. While the insurance companies offer insurance to its clients, they themselves get exposed to very high financial risks. Re-insurance business emerged out of this reality. When an insurance company buys insurance cover for its insurance business, a new segment comes into being i.e., re-insurance.

Experts believe that in absence of re-insurance, insurance industry in a country will not grow to the level of the social requirement—as insurance companies will either not provide insurance cover in several areas or they will charge very high premiums on the policies they offer (to neutralise the risk). Keeping this thing in mind, the Government of India took initiative to convert the existing public sector general insurer, the GIC, into a re-insurance company (in 2000). Known as the *GIC Re*, it remained the only reinsurance company in the country till now. Over the time, this emerged as a major player in the global reinsurance industry. Reinsurance industry is regulated by the IRDA in the country.

Reinsurance industry has a very low penetration in India. Lack of competition has been cited as a major factor behind it—it has only one player by now. To promote competition and vibrancy the IRDA announced (late 2015) to open up the industry for the entry of foreign companies. In **March 2016**, the IRDA gave *initial approval* (known as R1, in regulatory parlance) to four foreign reinsurance companies. Among them, two belong to Germany (Munich Re, Hannover), one each to Switzerland (Swiss Re) and France (SCOR). *Munich Re* is the largest reinsurance player in the world while *Swiss Re* is the second

largest and Hannover comes third in global size. Two other foreign companies (US-based Reinsurance Group of America and UK-based XL Catlin) are waiting for the initial approval. These companies will start their operation once they get the *final approval* (known as R2).

DEPOSIT INSURANCE AND CREDIT GUARANTEE CORPORATION (DICGC)

DICGC was set up by merging the Deposit Insurance Corporation (1962) and the Credit Guarantee Corporation (1971) in 1978. While Deposit Insurance had been introduced in India out of concerns to protect depositors, ensure financial stability, instill confidence in the banking system and help mobilise deposits, the establishment of the Credit Guarantee Corporation was essentially in the realm of affirmative action to ensure that the credit needs of the hitherto neglected sectors and weaker sections were met. The essential concern was to persuade banks to make available credit to not so creditworthy clients. After the merger, the focus of the DICGC had shifted onto credit guarantees. This owed in part to the fact that most large banks were nationalised. With the financial sector reforms undertaken in the 1990s, credit guarantees have been gradually phased out and the focus of the Corporation is veering back to its core function of Deposit Insurance with the objective of averting panics, reducing systemic risk and ensuring financial stability.

EXPORT CREDIT GUARANTEE CORPORATION (ECGC)

The overseas projects undertaken by the Indian companies face many **political** and **commercial risks** in the importing countries. To provide adequate credit insurance cover to such firms, the government has set up the Export Credit Guarantee Corporation of India Ltd. (ECGC) under the Ministry of Commerce and Industry, for medium- and long-term exports. But owing to its own limitations, at times it is difficult for ECGC to cover pure commercial risks in issues like long repayment period, the large value of contracts, difficult economic and political conditions of the importing country, together with the fact that *reinsurance* cover is generally not available for such projects.[5] Many times such projects look necessary considering the economic and political relationship of India with the proposed importing country. It means that in the absence of credit insurance cover, the ability of Indian exporters to go for such export projects is hampered. It should be noted that in many developed economies such projects are covered and underwritten on government account[6].

NATIONAL EXPORT INSURANCE ACCOUNT (NEIA)

For facilitating the service of the ECGC (discussed above), the Government of India did set up the National Export Insurance Account (NEIA) in March 2006 to promote medium- and long-term export by providing credit insurance support in the cases where ECGC was not able to provide credit cover on its own because of purely commercial reasons:[7]

(i) The corpus given to the account was Rs. 66 crore, raised to Rs. 246 crore by 2007–08 and was enhanced to Rs. 2,000 crore in the Eleventh Plan (2007–12).

(ii) Resources of the NEIA will be the corpus, the premium income, interest income and recovery of all the claims paid.

(iii) As per the provision, an exposure equal to ten times corpus can be taken by the NEIA.

The NEIA can cover projects which fulfil the following criteria:[8]

(i) The project by itself should be commercially viable;

(ii) The project should be strategically important for India, with regard to economic and political relationship of India with the importing country; and

(iii) The exporter should be capable of executing the contract, as evident from his previous track record.

The use and benefits of the NEIA need to be publicised among its beneficiaries. Meanwhile, many export projects pertaining to Indonesia, Vietnam, Iran, Sudan, etc., are under way. The NEIA will facilitate potential project exporters to enter the international trade area, as it is expected[9] to be so. In the era of globalisation it has been praised as a welcome development by the experts and the trade people alike.

THE CHALLENGE AHEAD

Since the opening up of the insurance sector, the number of participants in the insurance industry has gone up from seven insurers (including the Life Insurance Corporation of India [LIC], four public-sector general insurers, one specialised insurer, and the General Insurance Corporation as the national re-insurer) in 2000 to 52 insurers as on 30 September 2012 operating in the life, non-life,

---

5. Due to its underwriting constraint, the ECGC is unable to cover such projects on its own.

6. As for example the USA, France, the UK and many other Euro-American economies underwrite such medium and long-term projects in the governments' account. The SEIA also covers only medium- and long-term export projects.

7. Announced while setting up the NEIA, Ministry of Commerce and Industry, Government of India, N. Delhi, 9 March, 2006.

---

8. Ibid.

9. S. Prabhakaran, Executive Director, ECGC, Mumbai in *Survey of Indian Industry 2007,* The Hindu, p. 84.

and re-insurance segments (including specialised insurers, namely the Export Credit Guarantee Corporation and Agricultural Insurance Company [AIC]). Four of the general insurance companies, viz., Star Health and Alliance Insurance Company, Apollo Munich Health Insurance Company, Max BUPA Health Insurance Company, and Religare Health Insurance Company function as standalone health insurance companies. Of the 23 insurance companies that have set up operations in the life segment post opening up of the sector, 21 are in joint ventures with foreign partners. Of the 21 private insurers who have commenced operations in the non-life segment, 18 are in collaboration with foreign partners.

After the state monopoly in the insurance sector was dismantled and private players' entry allowed, the IRDA has played a crucial role in the development and expansion of the sector, there is no doubt in it. But still the sector faces many challenges which, if only tackled well may one say that insurance is serving the interests of the insuring companies and the covered alike. As per the concerned experts, the major challenges Indian insurance is facing today may be seen as given below:

(i) As per various estimates, only 20 per cent of the insurable Indian population is life-insured; the share of India in global life insurance is just 0.66 per cent; and life insurance penetration is at present 2.53 per cent (2004) in the country.[10]

The message of life insurance needs to be publicised among the population, specially in the rural areas. Moreover, social security schemes should be expanded to cover the poor masses who lack the premium-paying capacity.

(ii) Experts suggest that health insurance could emerge among the most important factors of improving human development in the country if expanded in a focussed way and via an *action plan.* It is estimated that around 15 per cent of the Indian population is covered under some form of pre-payment on healthcare which includes employees and beneficiaries covered under ESIS, CGHS, Armed forces, Central Police organisations, Railways, employer self-funded schemes, the PSUs and pensions covered under health insurance.[11] As the *out of pocket expenditure* in India is as high as 70 per cent, it is believed that the health insurance sector in the country needs strong presence. As per the *NSSO (2015),* the coverage of the government-funded health insurance schemes are 13.1 per cent in rural areas and 12 per cent in urban areas *(Economic Survey 2015–16).*

(iii) After the general insurance industry was opened up (2000) for the private sector participation, the experience has been positive.[12] Its growth compares favourably with that of many other emerging markets and is in line with global benchmark of two to three times the growth in GDP.[13] As the economy is on a strong growth path and the capital expenditure planned across industries is estimated to be over Rs. 9,00,000 crore over the next four to five years, a better scope for the general insurance expansion is probable.[14] The growth in both commercial and personal lines of general insurance business reflects positive trends. Over 70 per cent of India's

10. S. Krishnamurthy, CEO & MD, SBI Life Insurance Co. Ltd. *Survey of Indian Industry 2007,* The Hindu, p. 91

11. Aloke Gupta, Health Insurance Consultant, *Survey of Indian Industry,* The Hindu, p. 94.

12. Sandeep Bakhshi, CEO & MD, ICICI Lombard General Insurance Company, Mumbai, *Survey of Indian Industry 2007,* The Hindu, p. 99.

13. Ibid.

14. Ibid.

population lives in rural areas and along with organised financial services, general insurance companies are also expanding into these sectors.

(iv) People in their lives experience financial difficulties that can affect the entire family negatively, this is more true about the poor masses in India.

This is why experts suggested for the provision of **micro insurance.** A relatively new concept, micro insurance is today provided to the beneficiaries of micro finance covering the finance amount, reducing the risk of the clients as well as the micro-finance institutions (MFIs).[15]

The concept of micro insurance has been developed by the private insurance company Aviva Life Insurance (in partnership with MFIs) which has forged alliances with banks like Canara Bank, P&SB, RRBs, 23 cooperatives, etc., to promote micro finance.

Micro insurance has evolved in the past two decades of research in micro finance and has seen growth in countries like Sri Lanka, Philippines in the last decade.[16] Here NGOs and people's organisations are allowed to register themselves as micro insurance companies which sell such insurance. As they cover the risk themselves, they are allowed to *reinsure* with one of the large global companies like Swiss Re or Munich Re. Same model is suggested for India but for this to happen drastic changes in the existing insurance rules are required.[17]

(v) Many of the experts believe that insurance industry should benefit the insurers, reinsurers as well as the insured. The *social purpose* of the insurance sector is never praiseworthy to be marginalised by the corporate interests (be domestic or foreign)—at least it does never taste good in India which needs a strong social safety net.[18]

(vi) Almost all of the private insurance companies in India have been demanding that the government-owned insurance companies (i.e., LIC and the four general insurance companies) should be converted into private sector companies. Their reasons are logical as in comparison with the government-owned insurance companies, private companies are always ready with highly attractive and lucrative insurance schemes, but they have not been able to attract the clients for them. Therefore, the private insurance companies have been fetching huge operational losses due to lack of the desired level of their expansion and the overhead expenditure.[19]

INSURANCE PENETRATION

The growth in the insurance sector is internationally *measured* based on the standard of insurance penetration. Insurance penetration is defined as the ratio of premium underwritten in a given year to the gross domestic product (GDP). Likewise, insurance density is another well recognised benchmark and is defined as the ratio of premium

15. Vivek Khanna, Director, Aviva India, *Survey of Indian Industry 2007,* The Hindu, p. 102.
16. Ibid.
17. It has been beautifully shown taking example of the Self-employed Women's Association (SEWA) by Renana Jhabvala and Ravi Kanbur in the Kaushik Basu

(ed.) *India's Emerging Economy,* (New Delhi: Oxford University Press, 2005), pp. 309–110.
18. Biplab Dasgupta, *Globalisation: India's Adjustment Experience,* (New Delhi: Sage Publications, 2005), pp. 221–31.
19. G. V. Rao, CMD, Oriental Insurance Co. Ltd., *Survey of Indian Industry 2007,* The Hindu, pp. 87–90.

underwritten in a given year to total population (measured in US dollars for convenience of comparison). The Indian insurance business has in the past remained under-developed with low levels of insurance penetration.

At present[20], *insurance penetration* in India is **3.3** per cent of the GDP (it was 2.71 per cent in 2001) while the *insurance density* is at US$55 (it was US$11.5 in 2001). Globally, insurance penetration and density were 6.1 per cent and US$ 662, respectively.

As per the area experts and the insurance regulator, there are several factors responsible for the low insurance penetration in the country— *major ones* of them are as given below:

(i) Complex and delayed claim settlement procedures;

(ii) Vague and incomprehensible rules and regulations of the insurance companies;

(iii) Lack of education and awareness among the masses;

(iv) Lower income levels of the population;

(v) Socio-cultural factors;

(vi) Lack of level playing field in the industry; and

(vii) Less vibrancy in the regulatory framework.

Recently enacted Insurance Laws (Amendment) Act, 2015 is supposed to have positive impact on regulatory framework as well as insurance penetration.

Policy Initiatives

Committed to expand and strengthen, the insurance industry in the country (following the recommendations of the Malhotra Committee Report, 1993), the Government of India has taken the following policy initiatives[21] in recent years:

(i) **Health Insurance:** The Insurance Regulatory Development Authority (IRDA) has been taking a number of proactive steps as part of the initiatives for the spread of health insurance. It had set up a National Health Insurance Working Group in 2003, which provided a platform for the various stakeholders in the health insurance industry to work together and suggest solutions on various relevant issues in the sector. The IRDA is also co-ordinating with and supporting insurance industry initiatives in standardising certain key terminology used in health insurance documents, for better comprehension and in the interest of policyholders. The *General Insurance Council,* comprising all non-life insurers, evolved a consensus on a uniform definition of 'pre-existing diseases' and its exclusion wording, which has earlier been an expression with many definitions, still more interpretations, and certainly a whole lot of grievances. Such standardisation, effective 1 June, 2008 will help the insured by minimising ambiguity and also by better comparability of health insurance products. Also, with effect from 1 October, 2011, portability in health insurance has been started in which an insured, if not happy with services or the product of the existing insurer, can change to another insurer whilst enjoying the benefits (especially that of pre-existing diseases) of her/his existing policy.

20. Ministry of Finance, **Economic Survey 2015–16**, Vol. 2, pp. 62-63. and IRDA, **Annual Report 2014-15**, (New Delhi: Government of India, 2015).

21. Ministry of Finance, *Economic Survey 2011–12,* (New Delhi: Government of India, 2012), pp. 128–29.

(ii) **Micro Insurance:** Micro insurance regulations issued by the IRDA have provided a fillip to propagating micro insurance as a conceptual issue. With the positive and facilitative approach adopted under the micro insurance regulations, it is expected that all insurance companies would come out with a progressive business approach and carry forward the spirit of regulations thereby extending insurance penetration to all segments of the society. Presently, there are 10,482 micro–insurance agents operating in the micro–insurance sector.

NEW REFORM INITIATIVES

With a view to removing archaic and redundant provisions in the insurance laws, empowering the Insurance Regulatory and Development Authority (IRDA) to enable more effective regulation, and enhancing the foreign equity investment cap in an Indian insurance company with the safeguard of Indian ownership and control, the government has implemented the Insurance Laws (Ammendment) Act, 2015.

The Act paved the way for **major reform** related amendments in the Insurance Act, 1938, the General Insurance Business (Nationalization) Act, 1972 and the Insurance Regulatory and Development Authority (IRDA) Act, 1999. It provides greater powers to the IRDAI by which the insurance regulatory framework is supposed to become more flexibile, effective and efficient. Major changes as per the Act are given below:

(i) *Promotion of Foreign Investment*: In an Indian Insurance Company increased from to 49 per cent (from 26 per cent) with the safeguard of Indian ownership and control.

Greater availability of capital for the capital intensive insurance sector would lead to greater distribution reach to under/un-served areas, more innovative product formulations to meet diverse insurance needs of citizens, efficient service delivery through improved distribution technology and enhanced customer service standards.

(ii) *Capital Requirement in Government Companies:* The public sector general insurance companies (four), presently required as per the General Insurance Business (Nationalisation) Act, 1972 to be 100 per cent government owned, are now allowed to raise capital. This will enable them to have additional capital for the purposes of business expansion in the rural/social sectors and enhanced competitiveness. The Government of India ownership to be mainatained minimum at 51 per cent.

(iii) *Consumer Welfare:* It will enable the interests of consumers to be better served through provisions like those enabling penalties on intermediaries/ insurance companies for misconduct and disallowing multi-level marketing of insurance products in order to curtail the practice of mis-selling—

(a) The amended Law has several provisions for levying higher penalties ranging from up to Rs. 1 crore to Rs. 25 crore for various violations including mis-selling and misrepresentation by agents/insurance companies.

(b) With a view to serve the interest of the policy holders better, the period during which a policy can be repudiated on any ground, including mis-statement of facts etc., will be confined to three years from the commencement of the policy and no policy would be called in question on any ground after three years.

(c) The amendments provide for an easier process for payment to the nominee of the policyholder, as the insurer would be discharged of its legal liabilities once the payment is made to the nominee.

(d) It is now obligatory in the law for insurance companies to underwrite third party motor vehicle insurance as per IRDAI regulations. Rural and social sector obligations for insurers are retained in the amended laws.

(iv) *Empowerment of IRDAI:* The Act will entrust responsibility of appointing insurance agents to insurers and provides for IRDAI to regulate their eligibility, qualifications and other aspects—

(a) It enables agents to work more broadly across companies in various business categories; with the safeguard that conflict of interest would not be allowed by IRDAI through suitable regulations.

(b) IRDAI is empowered to regulate key aspects of Insurance Company operations in areas like solvency, investments, expenses and commissions and to formulate regulations for payment of commission and control of management expenses.

(c) It empowers the Authority to regulate the functions, code of conduct, etc., of surveyors and loss assessors. It also expands the scope of insurance intermediaries to include insurance brokers, re-insurance brokers, insurance consultants, corporate agents, third party administrators, surveyors and loss assessors and such other entities, as may be notified by the Authority from time to time.

(d) Further, properties in India can now be insured with a foreign insurer with prior permission of IRDAI; which was earlier to be done with the approval of the Central Government.

(v) *Health Insurance:* The Act defines 'health insurance business' inclusive of travel and personal accident cover and discourages non-serious players by retaining capital requirements for health insurers at the level of Rs. 100 crore, thereby paving the way for promotion of health insurance as a separate vertical.

(vi) *Promoting Reinsurance Business in India:* It enables foreign reinsurers to set up *branches* in India and defines 're-insurance' to mean 'the insurance of part of one insurer's risk by another insurer who accepts the risk for a mutually acceptable premium', and thereby excludes the possibility of 100 per cent ceding of risk to a re-insurer, which could lead to companies acting as front companies for other insurers.

(vii) *Strengthening of Industry Councils:* The Life Insurance Council and General Insurance Council have now been made *self-regulating bodies* by empowering them to frame bye-laws for elections, meetings and levy and collect fees, etc., from its members. Inclusion of representatives of *self-help groups* and *insurance cooperative societies* in insurance councils has also been enabled to broad base the representation on these Councils.

(viii) *Robust Appellate Process:* Appeals against the orders of IRDAI are to be preferred to SAT as the amended law provides for any insurer or insurance intermediary aggrieved by any order made by IRDAI to prefer an appeal to the Securities Appellate Tribunal (SAT).

Thus, the amendments incorporate enhancements in the insurance laws in keeping with the evolving insurance sector scenario and regulatory practices across the *globe*. The amendments will enable the regulator to create an operational framework for greater innovation, competition and transparency, to meet the insurance needs of citizens in a more complete and subscriber-friendly manner. The amendments are expected to enable the sector to achieve its full growth potential and contribute towards the overall growth of the economy and job creation.

NEW INSURANCE SCHEMES

During the fiscal **2015–16**, the Government of India launched two new insurance schemes aimed at creating a universal social security system for all Indians, especially the poor and the underprivileged. Salient features of these schemes have been briefly discussed below:

PMSBY (Pradhan Mantri Suraksha Bima Yojana): It offers a renewable one-year accidental-death-cum-disability cover to all subscribing bank account holders in the age group of 18 to 70 years for a premium of Rs. 12 per annum per subscriber.

The risk coverage available will be rupees two lakh for accidental death and permanent total disability and rupees one lakh for permanent partial disability, for a one-year period stretching from 1 June to 31 May. By January 2016, gross enrolment by banks under the scheme was over 9.28 crore.

PMJJBY (Pradhan Mantri Jeevan Jyoti Bima Yojana): The scheme offers a renewable one-year term life cover of rupees two lakh to all subscribing bank account holders in the age group of 18 to 50 years. By January 2016, gross enrolment by banks under it was over 2.93 crore.

CHAPTER 14

SECURITY MARKET
IN INDIA

Had there been no security market—undoubtedly, the most facinating segment of the financial market—there won't have been the big MNCs and TNCs in the world. Once the world moves towards the process of globalisation, the potential of this market has increased exponentially—its capacity of resource mobilization is just anybody's guess!*

* As many documents of the WTO, World Bank and OECD have accepted many times.

DEFINITION

The segment of a financial market of an economy from long-term capital is raised via instruments such as shares, securities, bonds, debentures, mutual funds, and is known as the security market of that economy.

A security market has components such as a security regulator (SEBI in India), stock exchanges, different share indices, brokers, FIIs, jobbers, etc. There are different kinds of transactions which take place in a security market such as badla, reverse badla, future trading, insider trading (not allowed), private placement, etc.

PRIMARY AND SECONDARY MARKETS

Every security market has two complementary markets—primary and the secondary. The market in which the instruments of security market are traded (procured) directly between the capital-raiser and the instrument purchaser is known as the primary market. As for example, a share being directly purchased by anybody from the issuer which may be the company itself. The person is known as the primary shareholder. The market where the instruments of security market are traded among the primary instrument holders is known as the *secondary market*. Such transactions need an institutionalised floor for their trading which is made available by the stock exchanges.

STOCK EXCHANGE

A physically existing institutionalised set-up where instruments of security stock market (shares, bonds, debentures, securities, etc.) are traded. It serves the following major functions:

(i) Makes a floor available to the buyers and sellers of stocks and liquidity comes to the stocks. It is the single most important institution in the secondary market for securities.

(ii) Makes available the prices of trading as an important piece of information to the investors.

(iii) By following institutionalised rules and procedures, it ensures that the participants in the stock market live up to their commitments.

(iv) Passes updated informations to the enlisted companies about their present stockholders (so that they can pass on dividends etc., to them).

(v) By publishing its 'Index', it fulfils the purpose of projecting the moods of the stock market.

World's first stock exchange was established in Antwerp, Belgium (then part of the Netherlands) in 1631, the London Stock Exchange opened in 1773 and then Philadelphia Stock Exchange (the first in the New World) opened in 1790.[1] The first stock exchange in India, the Bombay Stock Exchange known as *The Native Share and Stock Brokers' Association* was set up in 1870 (under a tree!).[2]

Top five largest stock exchanges (on the basis of market capitalisation) of the world in their decreasing order are—the New York Stock Exchange, the NASDAQ, the Tokyo Stock Exchange, the London Stock Exchange and the Bombay Stock Exchange.[3]

Trading in the stock exchanges takes place via the mediators known as the *brokers,* the *jobbers,* the *market-maker* (discussed later in this chapter).

1. Marc Levinson, *Guide to Financial Markets* (London: The Economist, 2006), p. 152.
2. V. Raghunathan, *Stock Exchanges and Investments* (New Delhi: Tata McGraw Hill, 1994).
3. Marc Levinson, *Guide to Financial Markets,* pp. 153–54; Ministry of Finance, *Economic Survey 2005–06* (New Delhi: Government of India, 2006).

As per the latest information,[4] presently, there are a total number of 26 stock exchanges operating in India—7 at the national level and rest 19 at the regional level (one of it, Coimbatore Stock Exchange recently sought for withdrawal of recognition, the matter is sub-judice under SEBI). A brief account of the 'national level stock exchanges' is given below.

NSE

The National Stock Exchange of India Ltd. (NSE) was set up in 1992 and became operationalised in 1994. The sponsors of the exchange are financial institutions, including IDBI, LIC and GIC with IDBI as its promotor.

It has a 50 share index and a 500 share index known as S&P CNX-50 (Nifty Fifty) and S&P CNX-500, respectively.

OTCEI

Though the Over the Counter Exchange of India Ltd (OTCEI) was set up in 1989, it could commence trading only in 1992. India's first fully computerised stock exchange was promoted by the UTI, ICICI, SBI Cap among others, in order to overcome problems such as lack of transparency and delays in settlements prevalent in the older stock exchanges. Another important goal of the exchange was to allow stock market exposure to comparatively smaller companies (companies with paid-up capital from Rs. 30 lakh to Rs. 25 crore are enlisted here). Trading in this exchange takes place via market-makers and commission is fixed.

ISE

The Interconnected Stock Exchange of India (ISE) is basically a single floor of India's 15 regional stock exchanges (RSEs), set up in 1998. The RSEs were provided increased reach through this. It is a web-based exchange.

BSE

The Bombay Stock Exchange Ltd. (BSE), earlier a regional stock exchange, converted into a national one in 2002. The *biggest* in India, it accounts for almost 75 per cent of total stocks traded in India and is the *fifth* largest in the world (on the basis of market capitalisation).

There are at present four indices connected with the BSE:

(i) *Sensex:* The sensitive index (i.e., Sensex) is a 30 stocks index of the BSE which was enlarged to include 50 stocks in 2000 but soon was cut down to the original level. This index represents the Indian stock market.

(ii) *BSE-200:* This is a 200 stock share index of the BSE (including the 30 stocks of the Sensex) which has its Dollar version too—*the Dollex*.

(iii) *BSE-500:* In mid-1999, the BSE came up with a 500-stock index representing major industries and many sub-sectors of the economy with information technology getting a significant weightage.

(iv) *National Index:* An index of 100 stocks being quoted nationwide (Bombay, Delhi, Kolkata, etc.) was developed to give broader/wider representation of the stock market since the Sensex consists of only 30 stocks. The 30 stocks of the sensex are included in the National Index.

This index is computed by the Statistics Department of the BSE hence it is called the BSE National Index (BSENI).

Indo Next

A new stock exchange to promote liquidity to the stocks of the small enterprises (SMEs) was launched in 2005 jointly and medium the BSE and the FISE (Federation of Indian Stock Exchanges, representing 18 regional stock exchanges).

---

4.   MoF, GoI, dated 22 April, 2013.

It is better known as the *BSE Indo Next.* It was also an effort to rejuvenate the RSEs which were facing falling volumes of trading on their floors. Due to absence of trading at the RSEs, the stocks of the SME, has become illiquid.

The BSE will transfer all its B1 and B2 groups to this exchange. The RSEs also transfer their enlisted companies to the new exchange.

Now the RSEs will be able to use the BSE network online—the 'Webex'.

SME Exchanges: BSESME and Emerge [5]

SME exchange is a stock exchange dedicated for trading the shares of small and medium scale enterprises (SMEs) who, otherwise, find it difficult to get listed in the main exchanges. The concept originated from the difficulties faced by SMEs in gaining visibility or attracting sufficient trading volumes when listed along with other stocks in the main exchanges.

To be listed on the SME exchange, the post-issue paid-up capital of the company should not exceed Rs. 25 crores. This means that the SME exchange is not limited to the small and medium scale enterprises (which are defined under the 'Micro, Small And Medium Enterprises Development Act, 2006' as enterprises where the investment in plant and machinery does not exceed Rs. 10 crores). As of now, to get listed in the main boards like, National Stock Exchange, the minimum paid-up capital required is Rs. 10 cr and that of the BSE is Rs. 3 cr. Hence, those companies with paid-up capital between Rs. 10 cr to Rs. 25 cr have the option of migrating to the Main Board/or to the SME exchange. The companies listed on the SME exchange are allowed to migrate to the Main Board as and when they meet the listing requirements of the Main Board. There shall be compulsory migration of the SMEs from the SME exchange, in case the post-issue paid-up capital is likely to go beyond the Rs 25 crore limit.

World over, trading platforms/exchanges for the shares of SMEs are known by different names such as Alternate Investment Markets or Growth Enterprises Market, SME Board etc. Some of the known markets for SMEs are *AIM* (Alternate Investment Market) in UK, *TSX Ventures* in Canada, *GEM* (Growth Enterprise's Market) in Hong Kong, *MOTHERS* (Market of the High-Growth and Emerging Stocks) in Japan, *Catalist* in Singapore and *Chinext*, the latest initiative in China [see 'World Federation of Exchanges' for latest comparative idea].

Globally, most of these SME exchanges are still at an evolving stage considering the many hurdles they face —

(i) Declining prices of listed stocks and their illiquidity,

(ii) A gradual reduction in new listings and decline in profits of the exchanges etc., (for instance, *AIM* had three predecessors; *CATALIST* succeeded *SESDAQ* with new regulations and listing requirements).

(iii) In most jurisdictions, idea of a separate exchange for SMEs have become unviable and hence tend to be platforms of existing exchanges, perhaps cross-subsidised by the main board/exchange.

In India, similarly, after the two previous attempts—*OTCEI* (Over the Counter Exchange of India, 1989) and *Indonext*—the market regulator, SEBI, on May 18, 2010 permitted setting up of a dedicated stock exchange or a trading platform for SMEs. The existing bourses/stock exchanges in India, BSE and NSE went live on March 13, 2012 with a separate trading platform for small

---

5. This section is based on various sources—the, SEBI, NSE, BSE, 'World Federation of Exchanges', select issues of *The Economist* and news reportings of *The HT Live Mint, The Business Line* and *The Economic Times.*

and medium enterprises (SMEs). BSE has named its SME platform as **BSESME**, while NSE has named it as **Emerge**.

Unlike in India, many of these SME exchanges in various countries operate at a global level, due to smallness of the market, allowing for listing by both domestic as well as foreign companies. Though the names suggest that they are set up for SMEs, these exchanges hardly follow the definition of SMEs in their respective jurisdictions. Also, many of them follow a 'Sponsor-supervised' market model, where sponsors or nominated advisors decide if the listing applicant is suitable to be listed or not, i.e., generally no quantitative entry criteria like track record on profitability or minimum paid-up capital or net worth, etc., are specified to be listed in these exchanges. Instead, they are designed as 'buyers beware' markets for informed investors. SEBI has also designed the SME exchanges in a similar format with provisions for *'market making'* for the specified securities listed on the SME exchange.

As is the case globally, certain relaxations are also provided to the issuers whose securities are listed on the SME exchange in comparison to the listing requirements in the Main Board (such as in BSE and NSE, in the case of India), which include:

(i) Publication of financial results on 'half yearly basis', instead of 'quarterly basis', making it available on their websites rather than publishing it.

(ii) Option of sending a statement containing the salient features of all the documents instead of sending a full Annual Report.

(iii) No continuous requirement of minimum number of shareholders, though at the time of IPO there needs to be a minimum of 50 investors, etc.

(iv) The existing eligibility norms like track record on profits, net worth/net tangible

assets conditions, etc., have been fully relaxed for SMEs as is the case globally.

(v) However, no compromise has been made to corporate governance norms.

Common Facts about the National Stock Exchanges

Before the arrival of national level stock exchanges, India was not having any exchange of national status—better say there was no Indian stock market, but stock markets showing only regional pictures. Besides, the national stock exchanges did solve some major problems of stock market, we may also call their arrivals as part of the stock market reforms in India. The common features of these exchanges are:

(i) all are situated in Mumbai;

(ii) all do screen-based trading (SBT);

(iii) all have their trading terminals in the major cities of the country;

(iv) all are web-enabled;

(v) all are limited liability companies;

(vi) the brokers registered here have no say in either the ownership or the management of the exchanges;

(vii) all are counted among the best and the most technology-equipped stock exchanges in the world.[6]

Players in the Stock Exchanges

Broker

Broker is a registered member of a stock exchange who buys or sells shares/securities on his client's behalf and charges a commission on the gross value of the deal—such brokers are also known as *commission brokers*.

6. P. Chidambaram while presenting the *Union Budget 2006–07,* (New Delhi; Government of India, 2006).

Brokers who offer services such as investment advice, clients' portfolio planning, credit when a client is buying on margin other than their traditional commission job are known as *full service brokers*. In India such brokers are just coming up.

Jobber

A jobber is a broker's broker or one who specialises in specific securities catering to the need of other brokers—in India also known as '*Taravaniwallah*' (in the BSE).[7] A jobber is located at a particular trading post on the floor of the stock exchange and does buying and selling for small price differences, called the *spread*. He has no contact with the investing public.

In the London Stock Exchange he is called a *market-maker* while in the New York Stock Exchange he is called a *specialist*. The Bombay Stock Exchange has made it mandatory for every company with a share capital of over Rs. 3 crore to appoint jobbers or market-makers if it seeks enlistment. Such an arrangement enables investors to buy and sell shares on the stock exchange and thus liquidity increases.

Market-Maker

Functions as an intermediary in the market ready to buy and sell securities. He simultaneously quotes two-way rates—like a jobber basically with the only difference that he quotes two-way rates, for buying and selling at the same time.[8]

On the floor of India's OTCEI, only market-makers are allowed to play. In the money market of India, the Discount and Finance House of India (DFHI) is the chief market-maker.[9]

Since he quotes the selling price while buying a particular share, he makes market for that share, hence such a name.

The NASDAQ of the USA is a market-maker's stock exchange where they are connected by the web-enabled trading terminals.

SEBI

The regulator of Indian stock market, set up under the *Security and Exchange Board of India Act, 1992* (as a non-statutory body set on 12 April, 1988 through a government resolution in an effort to give the Indian stock market an organised structure) with its head office in Mumbai. Its initial paid-up capital was Rs. 50 crore provided by the promoters—the IDBI, the IFCI and the ICICI.

The Board of SEBI comprises nine members excluding the chairman—one member each from the Ministries of Finance and Law, one member from the RBI and two other members appointed by the central government. It has four full-time members (including the chairman).

Main functions/powers of the Board as per the *SEBI Act, 1992* are:

(i) Registering and stock exchanges, merchant banks, mutual funds, underwriters, registrars to the issues, brokers, sub-brokers, transfer agents and others.

(ii) Levying various fees and other charges (as 1 per cent of the issue amount of every company issuing shares are kept by it as a caution money in the concerned stock exchange where the company is enlisted).

(iii) Promoting investor education.

(iv) Inspection and audit of stock exchanges and various intermediaries.

(v) Performing other concerned functions as may be prescribed from time to time.

---

7. Surendra Sundararajan, *Book of Financial Terms* (New Delhi: Tata McGraw Hill, 2004), p. 117.

8. Tim Hindle, op. cit., p. 129.

9. Surender Sundararajan, *Book of Financial Terms*, p. 134.

COMMODITY TRADING

Commodity trading happens similar to 'stocks' (shares, securities, debentures, bonds) trading in the stock market. However, commodities are actual physical goods such as corn, silver, gold, crude oil, etc. Futures are contracts for commodities that are traded at a futures exchange like the Chicago Board of Trade (CBOT). Futures contracts have expanded beyond just commodities, now there are futures contracts on financial markets like foreign currencies, interest rates, etc.

Commodity futures serve a great purpose in any economy. As we see in the case of agricultural commodity—their prices play a key role in determining the fortune of the agriculture and food processing industry in India. These prices undergo a *large degree of fluctuation*. Reasons for price fluctuation are crop failure, bad weather, demand-supply imbalance, etc. This fluctuation, in turn, leads to a 'price risk'. This price risk is largely borne by the farmer and the industries where agricultural commodities are used as raw material. Commodity exchanges are associations that determine and enforce rule, and set procedures for trading of commodities. The main objective of the exchange is to protect the participants from adverse movement in prices by facilitating futures trading in commodities.

If the participants *hedge* themselves against this price risk, then they would be able to insulate themselves against the inherent price fluctuations associated with agricultural commodities. One of the methods of doing this would be by using commodity exchanges as a trading platform. Apart from hedging against price risk, a commodity exchange helps in production and procurement planning as one can buy in small lots. Further as the exchange consists of various informed industry participants, *price discovery* is more efficient and discounts the local and global factors.

Let us take a very simple example to understand how trading on commodity exchanges help industry participants. A farmer who is producing wheat can sell 'wheat futures' on a commodity exchange. This will help him lock in a sale price of a specified quantity of wheat at a future date. Hence the farmer would now be able to get an assured price for his produce in future and any decline in the price of wheat would not impact his earnings. On the other hand, a user industry (e.g., a flour mill) could purchase the wheat futures from the exchange. Hence the flour mill would now be able to fix its future purchase cost for a specified quantity of wheat. Therefore, any increase in the price of wheat in future would not impact its cost of production.

However, what needs to be kept in mind is that farmers do not largely operate in the futures market. This is partly due to operational difficulties and lack of knowledge. Though, they observe the price trends emerging from a futures market and then decide what commodity in what proportion to cultivate.

In case of user industries, commodity exchanges help them to plan their production and determine their cost of production. Commodity exchanges are an effective tool to hedge price risk. However, the government needs to improve infrastructure, put in place vigilant governing systems, etc., to encourage trading on these exchanges.

Big money started flowing into commodity futures with the advent of online multi-commodity exchange. The boom, which began when the stock market was sluggish, has surprisingly not waned even after the Sensex crossed 20,000 (by 2004–06). High stakes, long trading hours and comparatively little knowledge about the derivative products have underscored the role of a regulator. The Forward Markets Commission (FMC), which for decades was entrusted with the job to curb forward trades, now has the job to develop and regulate the commodity futures market.

FMC

The Forward Markets Commission is a statutory body set up under the *Forward Contracts (Regulation) Act, 1952.* It functions under the administrative control of the Department of Consumer Affairs, Ministry of Consumer Affairs, Food & Public Distribution. In 2014, the commission was transferred to the Ministry of Finance. Headquartered at Mumbai with one regional office at Kolkata, the commission comprises a Chairman, and two members. The commission provides **regulatory oversight** in order to ensure—

(i) Financial integrity (i.e., to prevent systematic risk of default by one major operator or group of operators);

(ii) Market integrity (i.e., to ensure that futures prices are truly aligned with the prospective demand and supply conditions), and

(iii) Protection and promotion of the interest of consumers/non-members.

After assessing the market situation and taking into account the recommendations made by the *Board of Directors of the Commodity Exchange*, the Commission approves the rules and regulations of the **Commodity Exchanges** in accordance with which trading is to be conducted. It accords permission for commencement of trading in different contracts, monitors market conditions continuously and takes remedial measures wherever necessary by imposing various regulatory measures. At present, 113 commodities are notified for future trading and there are 21 commodity exchanges in India including three *'national level'* exchanges (other being regional) recognised for conducting futures/forward trading. The three national exchanges are:

(i) Multi-commodity Exchange of India Ltd. (MCX), Mumbai. The FTIL, its main promoter, has been asked by the FMC to exit its ownership in it after the firm was found involved in financial irregularities mid-2013 (it has 24 per cent stake in MCX).

(ii) National Commodity and Derivatives Exchange Ltd. (NCDEX), Mumbai.

(iii) National Multi-commodity Exchange of India Ltd. (NMCE), Ahmedabad.

In US, which has the *largest* commodity futures market, there are separate regulators for equities and commodities. Single regulator exists in China, UK, Australia, Hong Kong and Singapore. Japan has a different model for its derivatives market, with multiple product type based regulators.

The Government of India merged the FMC with the SEBI in September 2015.

SPOT EXCHANGES

In India, Spot Exchanges refer to electronic trading platforms which facilitate purchase and sale of specified commodities, including agricultural commodities, metals and bullion by providing *spot delivery contracts* in these commodities.

This market segment functions like the equity segment in the main stock exchanges. Alternatively, this can be considered as a guaranteed direct marketing by sellers of the commodities. Spot Exchanges leverage on the latest technology available in the stock exchange framework for the trading of goods. This is an innovative Indian experiment in the trading of goods and is distinct from what is commonly known as 'commodity exchanges' which trade in *futures contracts* in commodities.

Spot exchange has been **defined** by the Warehousing Development and Regulatory Authority (Electronic Warehouse Receipts) Regulations, 2011 as "a body corporate incorporated under the Companies Act, 1956 and engaged in assisting, regulating or controlling the business of trading in electronic warehouse receipts." However, present day spot exchange deals not just with warehouse receipts—this is an electronic market where a farmer or a trader can *discover* the prices of commodities on a national level and can buy or sell goods *immediately* (i.e., on the 'spot') to anyone across the country. All contracts on the exchange are *compulsory delivery contracts*—it means that all outstanding positions at the end of the day are marked for delivery, which implies that seller has to give delivery and buyer has to take the delivery.

The facilities provided by the spot exchange, like a normal stock exchange, include clearing and settlement of trades. Trades are settled on guaranteed basis (i.e., in case of default by any person exchange arranges for the payment of money/good) and the exchange collects various margin payments, to ensure this. The exchange also offers various other services, such as, quality certification, warehousing, warehouse receipt financing, etc.

Spot Exchanges in India

At present, there are **four** spot exchanges operating in the country:

(i) The National Spot Exchange Ltd. (NSEL), set up in 2008, is a national level commodity spot exchange promoted by the Financial Technologies India Ltd (FTIL) and National Agricultural Cooperative Marketing Federation of India Limited (NAFED). After the FTIL was found involved in irregularities, the FMC (Forward Market Commission), by *end-March 2014* asked it to exit the spot exchange.

(ii) NCDEX Spot Exchange Ltd (established in October 2006 by NSE).

(iii) Reliance Spot Exchange Ltd. (R-Next).

(iv) Indian Bullion Spot Exchange Ltd. (an online over the counter spot exchange).

Advantages of Spot Exchanges

Spot exchange provides various advantages over the traditional way of trading in commodities:

(i) Efficient price determination as price is determined by a wider cross-section of people from across the country, unlike the traditional 'mandis' where price discovery for commodities used to happen only through local participation.

(ii) Ensures transparency in price discovery—anonymity ensures convergence of different price perceptions, as the buyer or seller merely expresses their desire to trade without even meeting directly.

(iii) Ensures participation in large numbers by farmers, traders and processors across the country and eliminate the possibility of cartelisation and other such unhealthy practices prevalent in the commodity markets.

(iv) It brings in some best practices in commodity trading like, system of grading for quality, creating network of warehouses with assaying facilities, facilitating trading in relatively smaller quantities, lower transaction cost, etc.

(v) Bank finance available against the goods in the warehouse on easier terms improves holding capacity and can actually incentivise farm production and hence reduce rural poverty.

(vi) Since the trades are guaranteed (by the exchange), counter party risk is avoided.

Raising Capital in the Primary Market

There are three ways in which a company raises capital in the primary market.

Public Issue

A public offer is open for all Indian citizens, the most broad-based method of raising capital and the most prestigious, too (the Reliance Industries Ltd. is the biggest company of India in this category).

Rights Issue

Raising capital from the existing shareholders of a company, it means it is a preferential kind of issue restricted to a certain category of the public only.

Private Placement

Raising capital by selling shares to a select group of investors, usually financial institutions (FIs) but may be to individuals also. This is done through a process of direct negotiations (completely opposite to the public issue). The advantage of this route is the substantial saving a share issuing company makes on marketing expenses (but the risk of shifting loyalties of the investors in this route is also the highest).

Recent times have seen such capital raising by many companies privately placing their shares to the foreign institional investors (FIIs) as a route to source foreign exchange in India, and that too quickly.

IMPORTANT TERMS OF STOCK MARKET

Scrip Share

A share given to the existing shareholders without any charge—also known as *bonus share*.

Sweat Share

A share given to the employees of the company without any charge.

Rolling Settlement

An important reform measure started in the Indian stock market in mid-2001 under which all commitments of sale and purchase result into payment/delivery at the end of the 'X' days later (where 'X' stands for 5 days. Some shares have X as one, two or three days, too). Today, all shares are covered under this provision.

Badla

When the buyers want postponement of the transaction—in Western world called *Contango*.

Undha Badla

When the sellers want postponement of the transaction—also known as the *reverse badla* or *backwardation*.

Futures

A trading allowed in shares where a future price is quoted for the shares and the payment and delivery takes place on the pre-determined dates.

Depositories

Started in 1996 under which stocks are converted into *'paperless form'* (dematerialisation of shares shortly known as the 'demat'). At present, two public sector depositaries (Mumbai) are functioning in India set up under the *Depositories Act, 1996*—

  (i) NSDL (National Securities Depositories Ltd.)
  (ii) CDSL (Central Depositories Services Ltd.)

Spread

The difference between the buying and selling prices of a share is called spread. Higher the liquidity of a share lower its spread and vice versa. Also known as Jobber's *Turn or Margin or Hair cut.*

Kerb Dealings

The transactions of stocks which take place outside the stock exchanges—unofficially and take place after the normal trading hours.

NSCC

The National Securities Clearing Corporation (NSCC), a public sector company set up in 1996 takes the *counter party risk* of all transactions done at the NSE just as an intermediary guarantees all trades.

Demutualisation

A process started (2002) by SEBI under which ownership, management and trading membership was to be segregated from each other. No broker was to be on the Board of Directors or an office-bearer in a stock exchange.

This has been done in the case of all stock exchanges except three regional stock exchanges (RSEs) in India.

Authorised Capital

The limits upto which shares can be issued by a company—also known as the *nominal* or *registered* capital. This is fixed in the Memorandum of Association (MoA) and the article of association (AoA) of a company as required by the *Companies Act (Law)*.

Paid-up Capital

The part of the authorised capital of a company that has actually been paid by shareholders. A difference may arise because all shares authorised might not be *issued* or issued shares are only partly paid-up.

Subscribed Capital

The amount actually paid by the shareholders or have been committed by them for contribution.

Issued Capital

The amount which is sought by a company to be raised by issuing shares which cannot exceed the authorised capital of the company.

Greenshoe Option

A provision under which a company issuing shares for the first time is allowed to sell some additional shares to the public—usually 15 per cent, is also known as *over-allotment provision*. It gets its name from the first company (Greenshoe Company, USA) which was allowed such an option.

Penny Stocks

The share which remains low-priced at a stock exchange for a comparatively longer period. Speculators may start hoarding them for hefty margins, this was seen in India in mid-2006. And since such stocks get hoarded, ultimately their market prices increase. The speculators earn profit after offloading (selling) these shares at high prices and others who purchase these shares ultimately might fetch huge losses because price rise of these stocks are unintentional or each intentional manipulation and nothing else.

ESOP

The Employee Stock Ownership plan (ESOP) enables a foreign company to offer its shares to employees overseas. It was allowed in India (February 2005) provided that the MNC has minimum 51 per cent holding in its Indian company. Earlier a permission from the RBI was required for such an option.

SBT

Screen Based Trading (SBT) is trading of stock based on the electronic medium, i.e., with the help of computer monitor, internet, etc. First such trading was introduced in New York in 1972 by the bond broker *Cantor Fitzgerald.* India introduced it in 1989 at the OTCEI. Now it is carried out at all exchanges.

OFCDs

Debentures are the debt instruments which may be issued by a listed or non-listed firm to raise funds in a security market. They are of many types, viz., *Redeemable, Non-redeemable, Partially Convertible* and *Fully Convertible.* In case of 'fully convertible debentures' an 'option' (that is why the name OFCDs, i.e., Optionally Fully Covertible Debentures) is given to the debenture-holders who may wish to convert their OFCDs into shares (after expiry of the period fixed by the debenture issuing firm—known as 'lock-in' period). But the 'rate', will be decided by the company (e.g., how many shares against how many debentures). For debenture-holders the 'option' to convert debenture into shares is profitable and/or safer once either of the following situations are correct:

(i) The firm is likely to make high profit (so the shareholder can earn higher dividend), or

(ii) Firm's share-price is likely to rise in the share market (profit can be made by selling shares).

But suppose the firm has weak balance sheet (going bankrupt), then it is better to keep hold on the debenture rather than converting them into shares, because when a company is liquidated (i.e., its assets sold off), the debenture holders get *primacy* over shareholders in payment. It means OFCD is a bit **tricky** thing and is the only suitable route to invest in the security market for the investors who have some knowledge and understanding of share prices, company performance, etc.

Recently, the OFCDs issued by **Sahara** (an NBFC under regulatory control of the RBI) were in news due to some irregularities – it was a simple case of certain loopholes in the regulation of OFCDs and some violations by Sahara:

(i) Actually, an OFCD issue process has to be completed within 10 working days (Sahara continued for over two years).

(ii) If the OFCD is being issued through the 'Private Placement' route only 50 individuals/ institutions can subscribe to it (Sahara issued it to over 23 million people and raised over Rs. 24,000 crores). Such a tricky instruments being issued to novice public was a clear case of financial irregularities.

(iii) Unlisted companies do not come under the regulatory control of SEBI. In place they are regulated by the Ministry of Corporate Affairs (both the Sahara firms which issued OFCDs are unlisted). But SEBI contended that it can regulate even an unlisted firm if it issues OFCD, as the SEBI Act, 1992 contains the term OFCDs. There was really some regulatory confusion. This is why the government added a 'clause' in the recently passed *Companies Act, 2012* which gives SEBI **undisputed jurisdiction** over any investment scheme involving more than 50 investors whether the company is listed or unlisted. Menawhile, Sahara has been ordered to return the total capital it raised through OFCDs with an interest of 15 per cent per annum.

Derivatives

Derivative is a product whose value is derived from the value of one or more basic variables, called bases (underlying asset, index or reference rate), in a contractual manner.

The underlying asset can be equity, forex, commodity or any other asset. For example, wheat farmers may wish to sell their harvest at a future date to eliminate the risk of a change in prices by that date. Such a transaction is an example of a derivative. The price of this derivative is driven by the spot price of wheat which is the 'underlying'.

In the Indian context the *Securities Contracts (Regulation) Act, 1956* [SC(R)A] **defines derivative** to include :

(i) A security derived from a debt instrument, share, loan whether secured or unsecured, risk instrument or contract for differences or any other form of security.

(ii) A contract, which derives its value from the prices, or index of prices, of underlying securities.

Derivatives are securities under the SC(R)A and hence the trading of derivatives is governed by the regulatory framework under the SC(R)A and are allowed to be traded on the floors of the stock exchanges.

Indian Depository Receipts (IDRs)

As per the **definition** given in the *Companies (Issue of Indian Depository Receipts) Rules, 2004,* IDR is an instrument in the form of a depository receipt created by the Indian depository in India against the underlying equity shares of the issuing company. In an IDR, foreign companies would issue shares, to an Indian depository [say the National Security Depository Limited (NSDL)], which would in turn issue depository receipts to investors in India. The actual shares underlying IDRs would be held by an Overseas Custodian, which shall authorise the Indian depository to issue of IDRs.

Just try to understand in a simple way. An IDR is a mechanism that allows investors in India to invest in listed foreign companies, including multinational companies, in Indian rupees. IDRs give the holder the opportunity to hold an interest in equity shares in an overseas company. IDRs are denominated in Indian Rupees and issued by a Domestic Depository in India. They can be listed on any Indian stock exchange. Anybody who can invest in an IPO (Initial Public Offer) is/are eligible to invest in IDRs. *In other words, what ADRs/GDRs are for investors abroad with respect to Indian companies, IDRs are for Indian investors with respect to foreign companies.*

But one question comes in mind. How does investing in IDRs differ from investing in shares of foreign company listed on foreign exchanges? Indian individuals can invest in shares of foreign companies listed on foreign exchanges only upto US$ 200,000 and the process is costly and cumbersome as the investor has to open a bank account and demat account outside of India and comply with Know Your Customer (KYC) norms of respective companies. It also involves foreign currency risks. IDR subscription and holding is just like any equity share trading on Indian exchanges and does not involve such hassels.

Stan Chart is the **first** and the **only** issuer of IDRs in Indian markets which came out with its IDR issue in May 2010 through which it had raised Rs. 2,500 crore on high demand from institutional investors and was listed on the Bombay Stock Exchange and National Stock Exchange. Ten StanChart IDRs represent one underlying equity of the UK-listed bank. StanChart IDRs were due to come up for redemption on 11 June, 2011.

SEBI came out with the new guidelines in June 2011which ruled that after the completion of one year from date of issuance of IDRs, redemption of the IDRs will be permitted only if the IDRs are infrequently traded on the stock exchange in India. SEBI rules make it clear that if the annual trading turnover in IDRs in the preceding six calendar months before redemption is less than 5 per cent, then only the company could go into for redemption of IDRs. The regulator had said that the company issuing IDRs would have to test the frequency of trading the instrument on the bourses on a half-yearly basis ending June and December every year.

Shares 'at Par' and 'at Premium'

An ordinary share in India, in general, is said to have a *par value (face value)* of Rs. 10, though some shares issued earlier still carry a par value of Rs. 100. Par value implies the value at which a share is originally recorded in the balance sheet as 'equity capital' (this is the same as 'ordinary share capital'). SEBI guidelines for *public issues* by new companies established by individual promoters and entrepreneurs, require all new companies to offer their shares to the public *at par,* i.e., at Rs. 10. However, a new company set up by existing companies (and of course existing companies themselves) with a track record of *at least five years* of consistent profitability are allowed to issue shares at a **premium.**

When a company issues shares at a premium, it is able to raise the required amount of capital from the public by issuing a fewer number of shares. For example, while a *new company* promoted by first time entrepreneurs intending to raise say, Rs. 1 crore, has to offer 10 lakh ordinary shares at Rs. 10 each (at par), an *existing company* may raise the same amount by offering only 2 lakh shares at Rs. 50 each (close to the market value of its shares). The latter is said to have issued its share at a '*subscription price*' of Rs. 50 (Rs. 10 in the case of the former company), at a premium of Rs. 40 (being the excess of subscription price over par value). In such a situation in India, the company's books of accounts will show Rs. 10 towards *share capital account* and Rs. 40 towards *share premium account.* It means that the higher the premium, the fewer will be the number of shares a company will have to service. For this very reason, following the policy of free pricing of issues in 1993, many companies came out with issues at prices so high that in many cases they were higher than their market prices, leading to under-subscription of such issues. The companies are, however, learning fast about the pitfalls of high pricing of shares and it is only a matter of time before the issue prices become more realistic.

In India, no company is allowed to issue shares at a *discount*, i.e., at a price below par. Again, in India, once a company has issued the shares, it cannot easily reduce its capital base, (i.e., *buy back* or *redeem*) its own shares.

This means that ordinary share capital is a more or less permanent source of capital, which normally a company is never under an obligation to return to the investors, because a shareholder who wishes to *disinvest* (i.e., get back the invested capital) can always do so by selling the shares to other buyers in the secondary market. Also, in India, a company receives no tax benefits for the dividends distributed. In other words, dividends are paid by the companies out of the earnings left after taxes and they get taxed once again at the hands of the investors.

FOREIGN FINANCIAL INVESTORS

Through the Portfolio Invesment Scheme (PIS), the foreign financial investors (FIIs) were allowed to invest in the Indian stock market—the FIIs having good track record register with SEBI as brokers. FIIs make investments in markets on the basis of their *perceptions* of expected returns from such markets. Their perceptions among other things are influenced by :

(i) the prevailing macro-economic environment;

(ii) the growth potential of the economy; and

(iii) the corporate performance in competing countries.

Increased FII inflows into the country during the year 2012 helped the Indian markets become one of the best performing in the world in 2012, recovering sharply from their dismal performance in 2011. At the end of December 2012, **1,759** FIIs were registered with SEBI with their net FII flows to India at US$ 31.01 billion.[10] These flows were largely driven by equity inflows (80 per cent of total flows) which remained buoyant, indicating FII confidence in the performance

---

10. As per the Ministry of Finance, *Economic Survey 2012–13*, p. 121.

of the Indian economy in general and Indian markets in particular. The economic and political developments in the *Euro zone area* and the *United States* had their impact on markets around the world including India. The resolution of the **fiscal cliff**[11] in the US had a positive impact on the market worldwide including in India. Further, reform measures recently initiated by the government have been well received by the markets.

New Rules for Foreign Investment

To promote the flow of foreign funds into the economy the RBI, on 24 *January, 2013,* further liberalised the provisions of investment in India's security market—

(i) FIIs and *long-term investors*[12] investment limit in Government Securities

(G-Secs) enhanced by US $5 billion (to US $ 25 billion).

(ii) Investment limit in corporate bonds by the above-given entities enhanced by $5 billion (to $50 billion).

(iii) The RBI also relaxed some investment rules by removing the maturity restrictions for first time foreign investors on dated G-Secs (earlier a three-year residual maturity was must for first time foreign investors). But such investments will not be allowed in short-term paper like Treasury Bills.

(iv) Foreign investors restricted from investing in the 'money market' instruments —certificates of deposits (CDs) and commercial paper (CPs).

(v) In the total corporate debt limit of $50 billion, a sub-limit of $25 billion each for infrastructure and other than infrastructure sector bonds has been fixed.

(vi) Rules requiring FIIs to hold infrastructure debt for at least one year has been abolished.

(vii) The qualified foreign investors (QFIs) would continue to be eligible to invest in *corporate debt securities* (without any lock-in or residual maturity clause) and *mutual fund debt schemes*, subject to a total overall ceiling of $1 billion (this limit of $1 billion shall continue to be over and above the revised limit of $50 billion for investment in corporate debt).

(viii) As a measure of further relaxation, it has been decided to dispense with the condition of one year lock-in period for the limit of $22 billion (comprising the limits of infrastructure bonds of $12 billion and $10 billion for non-resident investment in IDFs) within the overall limit of $25 billion for foreign investment in infrastructure corporate bond.

---

11. **'Fiscal cliff'** is a term used to describe the crisis that the US government faced at the end of 2012, when the terms of the Budget Control Act of 2011 were scheduled to go into effect – a combination of—i). expiring tax cuts and ii). across-the-board government spending cuts scheduled to become effective December 31, 2012. The idea behind the fiscal cliff was that if the federal government allowed *these two* events to proceed as planned, they would have a detrimental effect on an already shaky economy, perhaps sending it back into an official *recession* as it cut household incomes, increased unemployment rates and undermined consumer and investor confidence [As per the conservative estimates by some US experts, it would have meant a tax increase to the size of which the country had never seen in the last in 60 years].

Who first use the term is not clear – some believe that it was first used by Goldman Sachs economist, *Alec Phillips,* while some others credit Federal Reserve Chairman *Ben Bernanke,* still others credit *Safir Ahmed,* a reporter for the *St. Louis Post-Dispatch,* who in 1989 used the term while writing a story detailing the state's education funding. **Sources:** The contemporary news reportings and articles which appeared during the time in *The Economist, The Guardian, The New York Times* and *The Newsweek.*

12. 'Long-term investors' include SEBI-registered 'sovereign wealth funds' (SWFs), multilateral agencies, endowment funds, insurance funds, pension funds and foreign central banks.

(ix) The residual maturity period (at the time of first purchase) requirement for the entire limit of $22 billion for foreign investment in the infrastructure sector has been uniformly kept at 15 months. The five-year residual maturity requirement for investments by QFIs within the $3 billion limit has been modified to three years original maturity.

SEBI has classified the FIIs into three broad categories, and they are allowed to issues PNs in accordance with the provision announced by the SEBI:

Category I: The government entities/institutions investing in Indian security market on behalf of the Central Bank.

Category II: The financial institutions, mutual funds, etc., which duly regulated in the countries of their origin.

Category III: The financial institutions which do not fall either of the above-given categories.

ANGEL INVESTOR

A new term in India's financial market, introduced in the *Union Budget 2013–14* which announced that SEBI will soon prescribe the provisions by which the **angel investor** can be recognised as *Category I AIF*[13] *venture capital funds.*

Angel investor is an investor who provides financial backing to entrepreneurs for 'starting their business'. Angel investors are usually found among an entrepreneur's family and friends but they may be from outside also. The capital they

---

13. As per the *SEBI (Alternative Investment Funds) Regulations, 2012 (AIF Regulations)*, **Category I AIF** are: those AIFs with 'positive spillover effects' on the economy, for which certain incentives or concessions might be considered by SEBI or the Government of India or other regulators in India; and which shall include *Venture Capital Funds, SME Funds, Social Venture Funds, Infrastructure Funds* and such other *Alternative Investment Funds (AIFs)* as may be specified.

provide can be a one-time injection of seed money or ongoing support to carry the company through difficult times—in exchange they may like owning share in the business or provide capital as loan (in case of a loan they lend at more favourable terms than other lenders, as they are usually investing in the *person* rather than the viability of the business). Other than investible capital, these investors provide technical advices and also help the 'start-up' business with their lucrative contacts.

They are focused on helping the business succeed, rather than reaping a huge profit from their investment. Angel investors are essentially the *exact opposite* of a venture capitalist in their 'intention' (who has high profit prospects as their prime focus). But in one sense both—an *angel investor* and a *venture investor*—serve the same purpose for the entrepreneur (who is in dire need of investible capital).

QFIs SCHEME

In the Budget 2011–12, the government, for the first time, permitted qualified foreign investors (QFIs), who meet the know-your-customer (KYC) norms, to invest directly in Indian mutual funds. In January 2012, the government expanded this scheme to allow QFIs to directly invest in Indian equity markets. Taking the scheme forward, as announced in *Budget 2012–13*, QFIs have also been permitted to invest in corporate debt securities (CDSs) and MF debt schemes subject to a total overall ceiling of US $ 1 billion.

In *May 2012*, QFIs were allowed to open individual non-interest-bearing rupee bank accounts with authorised dealer banks in India for receiving funds and making payment for transactions in securities they are eligible to invest in. In *June 2012*, the definition of QFI was expanded to include residents of the member countries of the Gulf Cooperation Council (GCC) and European Commission (EC) as the GCC and

EC are members of the Financial Action Task Force (FATF).

The speedier moves in the area of promoting higher foreign investment (FIs) in India should be seen in the light of two broad perspectives, viz.,

(i) India's rising current account deficit (which crossed an all-time high of 6.7 per cent by *March 2013*) which is creating heavy drain of foreign exchange; and

(ii) The objective of attracting more FIs while the Western economies are under the spell of recession (cashing in the opprtunity).

RFPIs

In *March 2014*, the RBI simplified foreign portfolio investment norms by putting in place an easier registration process and operating framework with an aim to attract inflows. Frow now onwards, the portfolio investor registered in accordance with the SEBI guidelines shall be called Registered Foreign Portfolio Investor (RFPI)— the existing portfolio investor class, namely, Foreign Institutional Investor (FII) and Qualified Foreign Investor (QFI) registered with SEBI shall be subsumed under it. The new guidelines for RFPIs are as given below:

(i) They may purchase and sell shares and convertible debentures of Indian companies through a registered broker on recognised stock exchanges in India as well as purchase shares and convertible debentures, which are offered to public in terms of relevant SEBI guidelines.

(ii) Such investors can acquire shares or convertible debentures in any bid for, or acquisition of, securities in response to an offer for *disinvestment* of shares made by the central government or any state government.

(iii) These entities would be eligible to invest in *government securities* and corporate debt, subject to limits specified by the RBI and SEBI from time to time.

(iv) Such investors would be permitted to trade in all exchange-traded derivative contracts on the stock exchanges, subject to the position limits as specified by SEBI from time to time.

(v) RFPI may offer cash or foreign sovereign securities with AAA rating or corporate bonds or domestic government securities, as collateral to the recognised stock exchanges for their transactions in cash as well as derivative segment of the market.

All investments made by that FIIs/QFIs in accordance with the regulations prior to registration as RFPI shall continue to be valid and taken into account for computation of aggregate limit.

PARTICIPATORY NOTES (PNs)

A Participatory Note (PN or P-Note) in the Indian context, in essence, is a *derivative* instrument issued in foreign jurisdictions, by a SEBI registered FII, against Indian securities—the Indian security instrument may be equity, debt, derivatives or may even be an index. PNs are also known as *Overseas Derivative Instruments*, *Equity Linked Notes*, *Capped Return Notes,* and *Participating Return Notes*, etc.

The investor in PN does not own the underlying Indian security, which is held by the FII who issues the PN. Thus, the investors in PNs derive the economic benefits of investing in the security without actually holding it. They benefit from fluctuations in the price of the underlying security since the value of the PN is linked with the value of the underlying Indian security. The PN holder also does not enjoy any voting rights in relation to security/shares referenced by the PN.

Reasons for the popularity of PNs

The reasons why PNs became such a popular ruote for foreign investors to invest in the Indian security market may be understood through the following points:

(i) One of the primary reasons for the emergence of the PN (an 'off-shore derivative instrument', i.e., an ODI) is the restrictions on foreign investments. For example, a foreign investor intending to make portfolio investments in India was required to seek FII registration for which he is required to meet certain eligibility criteria. Lack of full *Capital Account Convertibility* further enhances the entry barriers from the perspective of a foreign investor. However, Since *January 2012*, the Indian government has taken a decision to give direct access to such prospective 'foreign individual investors' who were hitherto banned to invest in equity of Indian companies.

(ii) The off-shore derivative market allows investors to gain exposure to the local shares without incurring the time and costs involved in investing directly. In return, the foreign investor pays the PN issuer a certain basis *point(s)* of the value of PNs traded by him as *costs*. For instance, directly investing in the Indian securities markets as an FII, has significant cost and time implications for the foreign investor. Apart from seeking FII registration, he is required to establish a domestic broker relationship, a custodian bank relationship, deal in foreign exchange and bear exchange rate fluctuation risk, pay domestic taxes and/or filing tax return, obtain or maintain an investment identity, etc. These investors would rather look for derivatives alternatives to gain a cost-effective exposure to the relevant market.

(iii) Besides reducing transactions costs, PNs also provide customised tools to manage risk, lower financing costs and enhance portfolio yields. For instance, PNs can also be designed for longer maturities than are generally available for exchange-traded derivative.

(iv) PNs also offer an important *hedging tool* to a foreign investor already registered as an FII. For example, an FII may wish to obtain 'long' exposure to a particular Indian security. The FII can hedge the downside exposure to the listed security, already purchased by purchasing a 'cash settled put option'. Although the Indian exchanges offer options contract, these contracts have a maximum life period of three months, beyond which the FII shall have to rollover its positions, i.e., purchase a fresh option contract. Alternatively, it can avail of a PN which can be customised to cater to its hedging requirements.

(v) Potential investors who would like to take direct Indian exposure in future, may make initial investments through the PN route so as to get a flavour of future anticipated returns.

(vi) Further, trading in ODI/PNs gives an opportunity to offshore entities to have a commission based business model. This route provides ease to subscribers as it bypasses the direct route which may be resource heavy for them.

(vii) And *lastly*, it was a highly 'safe and lucrative route' to invest the 'unaccounted', 'even illegal' money into the Indian security market for huge profits (during the booming period). Experts even imagined that it may be allowing the 'black money' of India (stashed away from India through 'hawala' kind of illegal channels and deposited in the tax havens of the world in 'Swiss Bank' kind of financial institutions) to get invested back in the market. Again, 'terrorist organisations' might have been using this route, too.

PNs are *thus* issued, to provide access to a set of foreign investors who intend to reduce their overall costs and the time involved in making investments in India. In other words, the attraction of investing in PNs is primarily one of efficiency (from an infrastructure and time perspective) for which they are willing to forego certain benefits of directly holding the local securities (for example, title and voting rights), whilst also assuming other risks.

Regulation of PNs

PNs are market instruments that are created and traded overseas. Hence, Indian regulators cannot ban the issue of PNs. However, they can regulated, as SEBI does—when a PN is traded on an overseas exchange, the regulator in that jurisdiction would be the authority to regulate that trade. PNs have been used by FIIs, since FIIs were permitted to invest in the securities market (1994)—they were not specifically dealt with under the regulations until 2003. According to the *SEBI Regulation, 2004* (and further amended in 2008) with the *objective* of tightening regulations in this regard—

(i) PNs can be issued only to those entities which are regulated by the relevant regulatory authority in countries of their incorporation and are subject to compliance of 'know your client' (KYC) norms.

(ii) Down-stream issuance or transfer of the instruments can also be made only to a regulated entity.

(iii) Further, the FIIs who issue PNs against underlying Indian securities are required to *report* the issued and outstanding PNs to SEBI in a prescribed format.

(iv) In addition, SEBI can call for any information from FIIs concerning off-shore derivative instruments (ODIs) issued by it.

(v) In order to monitor the investment through these instruments, SEBI on 31 *October, 2001*, advised FIIs to submit information regarding issuance of derivative instruments by them, on a monthly basis. These reports require the communication of details such as name and constitution of the subscribers to PNs, their location, nature of Indian underlying securities, etc.

(vi) FIIs cannot issue PNs to non-resident Indians (NRIs) and those issuing PNs are required to give an undertaking to the effect.

(vii) SEBI has also mandated that QFIs (qualified foreign investors), the recently allowed foreign investor class, shall not issue PNs.

SEBI in consultation with the government had decided in *October 2007*, to place certain restrictions on the issue of PNs by FIIs and their sub-accounts. This decision was taken with a view to moderate the surge in foreign capital inflows into the country and to address the 'know-your-client' concerns for PN holders. However, it was found that such restrictions were ineffective. Therefore, SEBI in October 2008 reviewed its earlier decision and decided to remove these restrictions in the light of the above factors. Rather, more attention is given to effective disclosures. As per a SEBI decision of October 2013, the Category III FIIs are not allowed to issue PNs.

The Concerns related to PNs

Being derivative instruments and freely tradable, PNs can be easily transferred, creating multiple layers, thereby obfuscating the real beneficial owner. It is in this respect that concerns about the *identity of ultimate beneficial* owner and the source of funds arises.

For the reason that such instruments are issued outside of India, these transactions are outside the purview of SEBI's surveillance and it is the FII which acts as mini-exchange overseas. The actual transactions in the underlying securities are executed by the FIIs only at its discretion, as and when necessary and there is no one-to-one correspondence between transactions in the underlying instruments and issuance of PNs.

The ex-post reporting requirement enjoined upon the FII in respect of PNs on a monthly basis effectively keeps the transactions in PNs out of the real time market surveillance mechanism and beyond the enforceability jurisdiction of SEBI.

There are also concerns that some of the money coming into the market via PNs could be the *'unaccounted wealth'* camouflaged under the guise of FII investment. However, this has not been proved so far. SEBI has indeed been successful in taking action against the FIIs who were non-compliant and those who had misreported offshore derivatives [as happened when SEBI took actions against two FIIs—*Barclays* in December 2009 and *Societe Generale* in January 2010]

At present, PNs are issued by large financial sector conglomerates which not only have strong presence in the global investment banking arena but also have asset management arms which invest across a number of securities markets globally. These entities are originally incorporated in well-regulated and developed jurisdictions like the US, UK, etc. Further, these entities also possess the financial wherewithal to issue PNs, complemented by skilled personnel who are adept at risk management and financial engineering activities.

International Situation

PN like products are not necessarily used to invest in restricted markets, but also reported to be available in the open developed/advanced economies like Japan, Hong Kong, Singapore, Australia, the USA and UK. In response to market manipulation concerns, in December 1999, *Taiwan Securities and Futures Commission* had amended its FII regulations to require periodic disclosure by FIIs of all offshore derivative activities linked to local shares, but this requirement was subsequently removed in June 2000 (as the Ashok Lahiri Committee Report says). *China*'s *Securities Regulatory Commission* requires entities to file reports related to these products with minimal 'reporting requirements that emphasize only on the quota utilised by them'. *Other Asian countries* like Hong Kong, Singapore and Japan have reportedly 'no restrictions' or requirements on PNs. Malaysia, Indonesia and Philippines which are restricted markets though, are having no reporting requirements in this regard.

Hedge Fund

This term has come up from another term *hedging*, a process by which businesses insulate themselves from the risk of price changes.[14] Hedge funds are the lot of investible (free floating capital) capital which move very swiftly towards the more profitable sectors of an economy.

At present, such funds easily move from the stock market of one economy to the other—away from the low profit fetching to high profit fetching ones. As stock markets fall and rise such funds change markets accordingly. By nature they are temporary. The period for which they continue

---

14. P.A. Samuelson and W.D. Norhdaus, *Economics* (New Delhi: Tata McGraw Hill, 2007), p. 207.

flowing into an economy there is naturally a boom time. But when they quit for a more attractive economy, the same economy might not be able to manage the accelerated foreign currency outflow and there are chances of imminent foreign currency crisis. This has been in news for the last two years in India where stock market has been in boom, riding on the FIIs inflow via Participatory Notes (PNs).

SHORT SELLING

Sale of a share which is not owned. This is done by someone after borrowing shares from stockbrokers promising to replace them at a future date on the hope (speculation) that the price will fall by then. He fetches profit if price of the share really fell down by the future date of replacement and sustains a loss if the price increased. Recently, short selling has been allowed in India by SEBI.

Bear and Bull

A person who speculates share prices to fall in future and so sells his shares and earns profit is a *bear*. He earns profit out of a falling market. Basically, here he is short selling the shares.

Opposite to bear, bull is a person who speculates share prices to go up in future so either stops selling the select group of shares for that time to be reached (he is basically taking long position on those shares) or starts purchasing that select group of shares.

Thus, a bear increases the number of shares in a stock market activating a general fall in the index—a bearish market. Opposite to it, a bull creates a scarcity of shares in the stock market activating a general rise in the share prices and the index—a bullish market.

Brokers play as a bear for some stocks and as a bull for some other stocks. while a bear broker is a non-entity, a bull is remembered for long time to come—Harshad Mehta was known as the Great Bull.

Book Building

A provision allowed by SEBI to all Initial Public offers (IPOs) in which individual investors are reserved and allotted shares by the company. But the issuer has to disclose the price (at which shares have been allotted the size of the issue and the number of shares offered to the public).

IPO

Initial Public Offer (IPO) is an event of share issuing when a company comes up with its share/ securities issued for the first time.

Price Band

A process of public issue where the company gives a price range (known as price band) and it is left upon the share applicants to quote their prices on it—the highest bidders getting the shares. This is a variant of share issue at premium but considered a safer choice.

ECB Policy

A prospective borrower can access external commercial borrowings (ECBs) under two routes, namely the 'automatic route' and the 'approval route'. ECBs not covered under the automatic route are considered on case-by-case basis by the RBI under the approval route. The High Level Committee on ECB took a number of decisions in *September 2011* to expand the scope of ECBs which include:

(i) High networth individuals (HNIs) who fulfil the criteria prescribed by SEBI can invest in IDFs.

(ii) IFCs have been included as eligible issuers for FII investment in the corporate bonds long-term infra category.

(iii) ECB would be permitted for refinancing of rupee loans of infrastructure projects on the condition that at least 25 per cent of such ECBs shall be used for repayment of the said rupee loan and 75 per cent invested in new projects in the infrastructure sector (but only under the approval route).

(iv) Refinancing of buyer's/supplier's credit through ECBs for the purchase of capital goods by companies in the infrastructure sector was approved. This would also be permitted only under the approval route.

(v) ECBs for interest during construction (IDC) that accumulates on a loan during the project execution phase for companies in the infrastructure sector would be permitted. This would be subject to the condition that the IDC is capitalised and is part of the project cost.

(vi) Renminbi (RMB)—the Chinese currency —was approved as an *acceptable currency* for raising ECBs subject to/ limit of US $ 1 billion within the existing ECB ceiling (allowed only through the approval route).

(vii) The existing **ECB limits** under the automatic route were enhanced from US $ 500 million to US$ 750 million for eligible corporates. For borrowers in the *services sector,* the limit has been enhanced from US$ 100 million to US$ 200 million and for *NGOs* engaged in *micro-finance* activities from the existing US$ 5 million to US$ 10 million.

Till **February 2017**, the norms for ECB were further simplified and streamlined by the government—major steps taken in this regard were as given below:

(i) Enhancing the limit for refinancing rupee loans through ECB from 25 per cent to 40 per cent for Indian companies in the power sector;

(ii) Allowing ECB for capital expenditure on the maintenance and operation of toll systems for roads and highways so long as they are a part of the original project

subject to certain conditions, and also for low cost housing projects;

(iii) Reducing the withholding tax from 20 per cent to 5 per cent for a period of three years (July 2012–June 2015) on interest payments on ECBs;

(iv) Introducing a new ECB scheme of US $10 billion for companies in the manufacturing and infrastructure sectors;

(v) Permitting the Small Industries Development Bank (SIDBI) as an eligible borrower for accessing ECB for on-lending to the micro, small and medium enterprises (MSMEs); and

(vi) Permitting the National Housing Bank (NHB)/Housing Finance Companies to avail themselves of ECBs for financing prospective owners of low cost /affordable housing units.

(vii) In *December 2015*, the RBI announced a *new ECB framework* which was more attuned to the current economic and business environment—from regulatory perspective, now, the ECBs will have three main clear-cut categories—

(a) Medium-term foreign currency-denominated ECB;

(b) Long-term foreign currency-denominated ECB (with minimum average maturity of 10 years); and

(c) Indian rupee-denominated ECB.

The new lenders comprise overseas regulated financial institutions, sovereign wealth funds, pension funds, insurance companies, etc. and has an exhaustive list of permissible end-users with only a small negative list for long-term foreign currency-denominated ECB and INR-denominated ECB.

(viii) In order to facilitate rupee-denominated borrowing from overseas, the government decided *(December 2015)* to put in place a framework for issuance of rupee-denominated overseas bonds (such bonds have got a popular tag of the *masala bonds*).

These bonds will have minimum maturity of 5 years. These bonds can not be issued for real estate and capital markets sectors. Withholding tax of 5 per cent will be applicable on interest income from these bonds, but the capital gains arising in case of appreciation of the rupee will be exempted from tax.

RGESS

On 23 *November, 2012*, the government notified a new tax saving scheme called the Rajiv Gandhi Equity Savings Scheme (RGESS), ***exclusively for first-time retail investors*** in the securities market. This scheme provides 50 per cent deduction of the amount invested from taxable income for that year to new investors who invest up to Rs. 50,000 and whose annual income is below Rs. 10 lakh. The Rajiv Gandhi Equity Saving Scheme (RGESS) will give tax benefits to new investors whose annual income is up to Rs. 10 lakh for investments up to a maximum of Rs. 50,000. The investor will get 50 per cent deduction of the amount invested from taxable income for that year. Salient features of the scheme are as follows :

(i) The scheme is open to new retail investors identified on the basis of their permanent account numbers (PAN).

(ii) The tax deduction allowed will be over and above the Rs. 1 lakh limit permitted allowed under Section 80 C of the IncomeTax Act.

(iii) In addition to the 50 per cent tax deduction for investments, dividend income is also tax free.

(iv) Stocks listed under BSE 100 or CNX 100, or stocks of public-sector undertakings (PSUs) that are Navratnas, Maharatnas,

and Miniratnas will be eligible under the scheme. Follow-on public offers (FPOs) of these companies will also be eligible.

(v) IPOs of PSUs, which are scheduled to get listed in the relevant financial year and whose annual turnover is not less than Rs. 4,000 crore for each of the immediate past three years, will also be eligible.

(vi) Exchange-traded funds (ETFs) and MFs that have RGESS-eligible securities have also been brought under the RGESS.

(vii) To benefit small investors, investments are allowed in instalments in the year in which tax claims are made.

(viii) The total lock-in period for investments will be three years including an initial blanket lock-in of one year. After the first year, investors will be allowed to trade in the securities.

The broad provisions of the scheme and the income tax benefits under it have already been incorporated as a new *Section 80 CCG* of the Income Tax Act 1961, as amended by the Finance Act 2012. The operational guidelines were issued by SEBI on 6 *December, 2012*.

CREDIT DEFAULT SWAP (CDS)

CDS is in operation in India since October 2011 – launched in only corporate bonds. The eligible participants are commercial banks, primary dealers, NBFCs, insurance companies and mutual funds.

CDS is a credit derivative transaction in which two parties enter into an agreement, whereby one party (called as the 'protection buyer') pays the other party (called as the 'protection seller') periodic payments for the specified life of the agreement. The protection seller makes no payment unless a credit event relating to a pre-determined reference asset occurs. If such an event occurs, it triggers the Protection Seller's settlement obligation, which can be either cash or physical (India follows physical settlement). It means, *CDS is a credit derivative that can be used to transfer credit risk from the investor exposed to the risk* (called protection buyer) *to an investor willing to take risk* (called protection seller).

It operates like an insurance policy. In an insurance policy, the insurance firm pays the loss amount to the insured party. Similarly, the buyer of the CDS—the bank or institution that has invested in a corporate bond issue—seeks to mitigate the losses it may suffer on account of a default by the bond issuer. Credit default swaps allow one party to 'buy' protection from another party for losses that might be incurred as a result of default by a specified reference instrument (a bond issue in India). The 'buyer' of protection pays a premium to the seller, and the 'seller' of protection agrees to compensate the buyer for losses incurred upon the occurrence of any one of the several specified 'credit events'. *Thus CDS offers the buyer a chance to transfer the credit risk of financial assets to the seller without actually transferring ownership of the assets themselves.*

Let us try to understand it by an example. Suppose Punjab National Bank (PNB) invests in Rs. 150 crore bond issued by TISCO. If PNB wishes to *hedge* losses that may arise from a default of TISCO, then PNB may buy a credit default swap from a financial institute, suppose, Templeton. PNB will pay fixed periodic payments to Templeton, in exchange for default protection (just like premium of an insurance policy).

CDS can be *used for different purposes* in a financial system, viz.,

(i) Protection buyers can use it to hedge their credit exposure while protection sellers can use it to participate in credit markets, without actually owning assets.

(ii) The protection buyer can transfer credit risk on an entity without transferring the under lying instrument, reap regular benefit in terms of lower capital charge, seek reduction of specific concentrations in credit portfolio and go short on credit risk.

(iii) The protection seller will be able to diversify his portfolio, create exposure to a particular credit, have access to an asset which may not otherwise be available, and increase the yield on his portfolio.

(iv) Banks can use it to transfer risk to other risk takers, create capital for more lending.

(v) Distribute risk widely throughout the system and prevent concentrations of risk.

Some analysts have serious **apprehensions** about CDS. *George Akerlof,* Nobel prize-winning economist, in 1993, predicted that the next meltdown will be caused by CDS. In 2003 investment legend *Warren Buffet* called them as 'weapons of mass destruction'. The former US Federal Reserve Chairman *Alan Greenspan*, who betted big on CDS said after the 'sub prime' crisis that 'CDS are dangerous'. A leading US weekly the *Newsweek* described CDS, 'the monster that ate Wall Street'. Many Indian experts had the opinion that 'CDS will not stabilise the economy rather could lead to destabilisation'.

CDS contract are dangerous because they can be manipulated for mischief. It's all about the insurable interest which is never there as it is used for *speculation*. A derivative that amounts to an insurance contract with no insurable interest is bad. But do the speculators have insurable interest? No they don't have any. The US 'sub prime' crisis was a fallout of such CDS contracts—one defaulting and another claiming the 'protection' finally resulting into the defaulter of the insuring company—overnight the biggest US insurance giant, AIG went bankrupt. So happened with many US banks also.

The most damaging aspect of CDS is that the credit risk of one country/region gets exported to another country/region very smoothly and silently. Thus There is a serious chance of 'contagion effect' suppose there are defaulters there, the thing which happened during the US 'sub prime' crisis.

SECURITISATION

This is the process of issuing 'marketable securities' backed by a pool of existing assets such as auto or home loans. After an asset is converted into a marketable security, it is sold to an investor who then receives interest and principal out of the cash flow generated from servicing of the loan. Financial institutions such as NBFCs and microfinance companies convert their loans into marketable securities and sell them to investors. This helps them get liquid cash out of assets that otherwise would be stuck on their balance sheets.

Global experience shows that if the value of the underlying asset falls then securitised assets lose value as it had happened during the US 'sub-prime crisis'—home loans against which securitised assets were sold to insurance companies and banks lost value, which in turn resulted in a crisis. To prevent such crises, the RBI has taken some precautionary steps in this regard. It has asked companies to hold securities for a certain minimum period:

(i) While NBFCs need to keep assets for six months, a minimum retention requirement of 5–10 per cent to ensure that they have a continuing stake in the performance of securitised assets.

(ii) Micro Finance Institutions (MFIs) need to hold them for three months.

Since it was allowed in India by the RBI, it has been in news – whether the 'securitisations trusts' will need to pay tax on it. Meanwhile, the *Government in 2015* cleared the air on the issue. There should not be any additional income-tax if the income distributed by the trust is received by a person who is exempted from tax. This is expected to bring back mutual funds into the securitisation market.

CORPORATE BOND IN INDIA

Economic vibrancy coupled with sophisticated state–of–the–art financial infrastructure has contributed to rapid growth in the equity market in India. In terms of market features and depth, the Indian equity market ranks among the best in the world. In parallel, the government securities market has also evolved over the years and expanded, given the increasing borrowing requirements of the government. In contrast, the corporate bond market has languished both in terms of market participation and structure. NBCs are the main issuers and very small amounts of finance are raised by companies directly. The *Economic Survey 2010–11*, cites many reasons for the less-developed bond market in India—

(i) Predominance of banks loans;

(ii) FII's participation is limited;

(iii) Pensions and insurance companies and household are limited participants because of lack of investor confidence; and

(iv) Crowding out by government bonds.

The *Economic Survey 2011–12* concluded[15] that there is now ample empirical research to corroborate Schumpeter's conjecture that financial development facilitates real economic growth. The depth of the financial markets and availability of diverse products should, therefore, not be treated as mere adornment, but as critical ingredients of inclusive growth.

Banks in India accounted for 14.4 per cent of the financing of large firms in 2000–01, which rose further to 17.8 per cent in 2010–11. The *bond market*, on the other hand, has been miniscule in comparison. The thinness of the bond market has been somewhat compensated by foreign borrowing done by Indians, which rose sharply over the last decade. Further, India is characterised by a disproportionate amount of secured borrowing. The small size of unsecured borrowing may, at first sight, not seem to be a matter of concern, but it could be a reflection of the weakness of contract enforcement and lack of adequate information. If contracts were quickly enforced and lenders had information on borrowers, they would be more willing to give unsecured loans. This would give a nimbleness to the financial markets which they presently lack.

There are *many reasons* why bond markets are important for an emerging economy. Prominent

15. Ministry of Finance, Economic Survey 2011–12 (New Delhi: Government of India, 2012), 34; quotes many contemporary references to bring the point home –
a). R. Rajan, and L. Zingales, 'Financial Dependence and Growth,' *American Economic Review*, vol. 88, 1998;
b). S. Banerji, K. Gangopadhyay, I. Patnaik, and A, Shah, 'New Thinking on Corporate Debt in India', mimeo.;
c). C. K. G. Nair, 2012; 'Financial Sector Reforms: Refining the Architecture,' in R. Malhotra (ed.), *A Critical Decade: Policies for India's Development,* (New Delhi: Oxford University Press, 2012) d). T. A. Bhavani, and N. R. Bhanumurthy, *Financial Access in Post-Reform India*;
e). P. Bolton, and X. Freixas, 'How can Emerging Market Economies Benefit from a Corporate Bond Market?', in E. Borzenstein, K. Cowan, B. Eichengreen, and U. Panizza (eds), *Bond Markets in Latin America*, (Massachusetts: MIT Press, 2008).

among these is the fact that they lead to more efficient entrepreneurship and greater value creation. When an entrepreneur takes a loan or issues bonds, all additional profit over and above the pre-fixed repayment amount accrues to the entrepreneur. So he or she is better incentivised to take sharper decisions. By having a weak bond market, we may be foregoing this efficiency. And further, this efficiency gap may well mean that there is less lending and hence less investment and entrepreneurship in the economy than is feasible. Further, as India tries to garner 500 billion dollars from the private sector in the Twelfth Plan for investment in the infrastructure sector, having an active bond market would be a valuable avenue for raising money.

There can be many reasons why, despite these advantages, the bond market has not developed adequately. One reason has to do with what economists call 'multiple equilibria'. Consider a situation where the bond market is small. If someone buys bonds and later wish to sell these off, he anticipates difficulty. Since the bond market is not active, he may not easily be able to sell the bonds and thus he will hold simply because he cannot find a buyer. Hence, this may lead to discourage someone from buying the bonds in the first place. If everybody reasons like this, the bond market remains thin. Hence, the need is for a push that nudges the market to another equilibrium, where people readily buy bonds because they know that they can easily sell these off and this becomes a self-fulfilling prophesy and sustains the large bond market.

There is effort currently on to try to boost India's debt and bond markets, and success in this can give another fillip to growth. With the intervention of the *Patil Committee (2005)* recommendations, the corporate bond market is slowly evolving. With bank finance drying up for long term infrastructure projects, in view of asset liability problems faced by the banking system, the need for further development of a deep and vibrant corporate bond market can hardly be overemphasised. Recent initiatives for further development of corporate bond markets, taken in the year *2012–13* are as given below :

(i) Banks allowed to take limited membership in SEBI-approved stock exchanges for the purpose of undertaking proprietary transactions in the corporate bond markets.

(ii) To enhance liquidity in the corporate bond markets, the IRDA has permitted insurance companies to participate in the repo market. The IRDA has also permitted insurance companies to become users of *'credit default swap'* (CDS).

(iii) The minimum **haircut**[16] (i.e., the difference between prices at which a market maker can buy and sell a security) requirement in corporate debt repo have been reduced from the existing 10 per cent; 12 per cent; 15 per cent to 7.5 per cent; 8.5 per cent; 10 per cent for AAA/AA+/AA-rated corporate bonds.

(iv) MFs have been permitted to participate in CDS in corporate debt securities, as users.

(v) Revised guidelines on CDS for corporate bonds by the RBI provide that in addition to listed corporate bonds, CDS shall also be permitted on *unlisted* but rated corporate bonds even for issues other than infrastructure companies.

(vi) Users shall be allowed to **unwind**[17] their CDS-bought position with the original protection seller at a mutually agreeable or FIMMDA (Fixed Income Money Market and Derivatives Association of India) price. If no agreement is reached, then unwinding has to be done with the original protection seller at FIMMDA price.

(vii) CDS shall be permitted on securities with original maturity up to *one year* like CPs, certificates of deposit, and non-convertible debentures with original maturity less than one year.

Till **March 2017**, the RBI has taken a number of measures to strengthen the corporate bond market in India. It accepted many of the recommendations of the *Khan Committee* (August 2016) to boost investor participation and market liquidity in the corporate bond market. The new measures as announced by the RBI include:

(i) Commercial banks are permitted to issue rupee-denominated bonds overseas *(masala bonds)* for their capital requirements and for financing infrastructure and affordable housing.

(ii) Brokers registered with the Securities and Exchange Board of India (SEBI) and authorized as market makers in corporate

---

16. **Haircut** is the difference between prices at which a *market maker* can buy and sell a security. The term comes from the fact that market makers can trade at such a *thin spread*. It also means that the percentage by which an asset's market value is reduced for the purpose of calculating capital requirement, margin and collateral. When they are used as collateral, securities will generally be devalued since a cushion is required by the lending parties in case the market value falls.

17. **Unwind** is used to close out a position that has offsetting investments or the correction of an error. Unwinds occur when, for example, a broker mistakenly sells part of a position when an investor wanted to add to it. The broker would have to unwind the transaction by selling the erroneously purchased stock and buying the proper stock. One type of investing that features unwind trading is *arbitrage investing (as happens in the CDS)*. If, for the sake of illustration, an investor takes a long position in stocks, while at the same time selling puts on the same issue, he will need to unwind those trades at some point. Of course, this entails covering the options and selling the underlying stock. A similar process would be followed by a broker attempting to correct a buying or selling error.

bond market permitted to undertake repo/reverse repo contracts in corporate debt securities. This move will make corporate bonds *fungible* and thus boost turnover in the secondary market.

(iii) Banks allowed to increase the partial credit enhancement they provide for corporate bonds to 50 per cent from 20 per cent. This move will help lower-rated corporates to access the bond market.

(iv) Permitting primary dealers to act as *market makers* for government bonds, to give further boost to government securities by making them more accessible to retail investors.

(v) To ease access to the foreign exchange market for hedging in 'over the counter' (OTC) and exchange-traded currency derivatives, the entities exposed to exchange rate risk allowed to undertake hedge transactions with simplified procedures, up to a limit of US$30 million at any given time.

INFLATION-INDEXED BONDS

To protect the returns of investors from the vagaries of inflation, the Reserve Bank of India plans to introduce inflation-indexed bonds (IIBs)—it was proposed by the *Union Budget 2013–14*. The government hopes this will help increase *financial savings instead of buying gold*. In the recent years, the rate of return on debt investments has often been below inflation, which effectively means that inflation was eroding savings. Inflation indexed bonds provide returns that are always in excess of inflation, ensuring that price rise does not erode the value of savings.

In 2013–14, RBI launched two such bonds —the first one in June 2013 linked with the WPI which had a very weak retail response and second one in *December 2013* linked with CPI. The latter one is called as **Inflation Indexed National**

Savings Securities-Cumulative (IINSS-C) with a 10 years tenure. These are internationally known as *inflation-linked securities* or simply *linkers*. Interest rate on these securities would be linked to final combined consumer price index [CPI (Base: 2010=100)]. Interest rate would comprise two parts: fixed rate (1.5 per cent) and inflation rate, based on three-month lag to CPI—thus, if a bond is being valued in December, the reference rate will be CPI of September. The new offering should attract higher attention from savers, especially due to its link to CPI instead of wholesale price index (WPI), which is a less accurate gauge of inflation. CPI is considered a more accurate gauge of the impact of inflation on consumers because it takes into account increases in the cost of education, food, transportation, housing and medical care; in WPI, the emphasis is on measuring the prices of traded goods and services.

It was in 1997 that the IIBs were issued for the first time in India—named as the *Capital Indexed Bonds (CIBs)*. But there remains a difference between these two bonds. While the CIBs provided inflation protection only to principal the new product IIBs provides inflation protection to both the components—principal and interest payments.

GOLD EXCHANGE TRADED FUNDS

Gold Exchange Traded Funds (ETFs) are *open-ended mutual fund schemes* that closely track the price of physical gold. Each unit represents *one gram* of gold having 0.995 purity, and the ETF is listed on stock exchanges. The net asset value of each unit is calculated based on the prices of physical gold prevailing on that day and .is designed to provide returns that would closely track the returns from physical gold.

e-Gold

e-Gold is another purchase option, involving investments in units traded on the National

Stock Exchange (NSEL). Here, the investor is required to have a demat account with an affiliate of NSEL. e-Gold's brokerage and transaction charges are lower than *gold ETFs* as there are no fund management charges. One can take delivery of gold or sell it in the exchange.

But there is also a *negative point* here from the tax angle—under e-Gold, one has to hold the yellow metal for 36 months to enjoy *long-term capital gain* benefits, and this is taxed at 20 per cent. For ETFs (Exchange Traded Funds) and gold funds, the holding period to be classified as long-term is only one year. After a year, ETF and gold funds will suffer 10 per cent tax without indexation and 20 per cent after indexation. For a small investor, gold ETF would appear to be the best option, as it meets his needs without difficulties in terms of creating a separate demat account, tax implications and wealth tax.

CPSE ETF

The Central Public Sector Enterprises Exchange Traded Fund (CPSE ETF) comprising the shares of 10 blue chip PSUs was listed on the BSE and NSE platforms on 41 April, 2014. The Government of India expected to raise a corpus of Rs. 3,000 crore through the fund while it got over-subscribed to the tune of Rs. 4,300 crores.

This scheme is conceived by the Government of India as a means to *disinvest* a part of its holding in Public Sector Units (PSUs) and would be managed by **Goldman Sachs Asset Management (India) Pvt. Ltd.**, a *mutual fund company* that specialises in managing exchange traded funds.

ETF is a security that tracks an index, a commodity or a basket of assets such as an index fund, but trades like a stock on an exchange – the CPSE ETF tracks the CPSE Index (of 10 PSUs included in the ETF). CPSE Index has been constructed by including companies that meet the following criteria:

(i) Owned 55 per cent or more by the GoI and listed on the NSE;

(ii) Large PSUs (those having more than Rs.1,000 crores as average free float market capitalisation for six months period ending June 2013); and

(iii) With a consistent dividend payment record (at least 4 per cent for 7 years immediately prior to or 7 out of 8/9 years immediately prior to June 2013).

The ten blue-chip PSUs which meet the above criteria and their weightages are: ONGC (26.72 per cent); GAIL (India) (18.48 per cent); Coal India (17.75 per cent); REC (7.16 per cent); Oil India (7.04 per cent); IOC (6.82 per cent); Power Finance Corp. (6.49 per cent); Container Corp. (6.40 per cent); Bharat Electronics (2 per cent) and Engineers India Ltd. (1.13 per cent).

CPSE ETF will invest the corpus in the above-given companies as per the given weightage. Hence, subject to the tracking error and expenses, CPSE ETF's returns will closely correspond to the CPSE Index returns.

Meanwhile, the Government has announced (**Union Budget 2017-18**) to launch a new ETF with diversified CPSE stocks and other Government holdings in the fiscal 2017-18.

PENSION SECTOR REFORMS

Pension has been the integral part of government jobs in India. Pension serves two important socio-economic objectives—

(i) It facilitates the flow of long-term savings for development, i.e., *nation-building*; and

(ii) Also helps establish a credible and sustainable *social security system* in the country.

The New Pension System (NPS) was introduced for the new recruits who join government service on or after **1 January, 2004**. Although the NPS is perhaps one of the cheapest financial products available in the country, in order to make it affordable for the economically disadvantaged, the government in September 2010 introduced a lower cost version, known as *Swavalamban Scheme*, which enables groups of people to join the NPS at a substantially reduced cost. As per existing scheme under NPS, Swavalamban could be availed either in 'unorganised sector' or in *'NPS Lite'*. NPS Lite is a model specifically designed to bring NPS within easy reach of the economically disadvantaged sections of the society —it is extremely affordable and viable due to its optimised functionalities, available at reduced charges. Under the Swavalamban scheme, the government provides subsidy to each NPS account holder and the scheme has been extended until 2016–17.

A customised version of the core NPS model, known as the *NPS Corporate Sector Model* was introduced from December 2011 to enable 'organised-sector' entities to move their existing and prospective employees to the NPS under its Corporate Model. All pubic sector banks have been asked to provide a link on their website to enable individual subscribers to open online NPS accounts.

As per the *Economic Survey 2012–13*, the pension reforms in India have generated widespread interest internationally but before universal inclusion of poorer sections of Indian society into the pension network is a reality, the economy needs to solve the following *major challenges* :

(i) Lower levels of financial literacy, particularly among workers in the unorganised sector;

(ii) Non-availability of even moderate surplus;

(iii) Lukewarm response so far from most of the state/UT governments to a co-contributory Swavalamban Scheme; and

(iv) Lack of awareness, on the supply side, about the NPS and of access points for people to open their accounts individually have been major inhibiting factors.

During **2015–16**, the government launched a new pension scheme, the *APY (Atal Pension Yojana)*. The scheme provides a defined pension, depending on the contribution and its period. The subscribers to it will receive a minimum pension of Rs. 1,000, 2,000, 3,000, 4,000 or 5,000 per month, from the age of 60 years, depending on their contributions, which are themselves based on the age of joining the scheme.

The scheme is open to all bank account holders. The central government co-contributes 50 per cent of the total contribution subject to a maximum of Rs. 1,000 per annum, to each eligible subscriber's account, for a period of five years (from 2015–16 to 2019–20), who joined the APY between 1 June 2015 and 31 March 2016 and who is not a member of any statutory social security scheme and is not an income tax payer.

Financial Stability Development Council (FSDC)

An apex level body, the FSDC, was set up by the GoI in December 2010. It was in line with the G-20 initiative which came in wake of the financial crises among the western economies triggered by the 2007–08 'sub-prime' crisis of the USA. The Council has the following *objectives:*

(i) To strengthen and institutionalise the mechanism for maintaining financial stability,

(ii) To enhance inter-regulatory coordination, and

(iii) To promote financial-sector development.

The council is *chaired* by the Finance Minister and has *heads* of financial-sector regulatory authorities, the Finance Secretary and/or Secretary of the Department of Economic Affairs, Secretary of the Department of Financial Services, and the

Chief Economic Adviser as members. Without prejudice to the autonomy of regulators, the Council *monitors*—

(i) macro-prudential supervision of the economy, including functioning of large financial conglomerates,

(ii) inter-regulatory coordination and financial-sector development issues, and

(iii) *financial literacy* and *financial inclusion*.

Financial Sector Assessment Programme (FSAP)

The *IMF Board* decided in September 2010, to include 25 *systemically* important economies, including India, under the Financial Stability Assessment Programme (FSAP) for members with systemically important financial sectors. The joint IMF-World Bank Financial Stability Assessment Programme (FSAP) was conducted for India in *January 2013* which assessed Indian financial system in relation to the highest international standards. The **assessment** recognises that the Indian financial system remained *largely stable* on account of a sound regulatory and supervisory regime. However, the assessment identifies *some gaps* in[18]—

(i) International and domestic supervisory information sharing and co-operation;

(ii) Consolidated supervision of financial conglomerates; and

(iii) Some limits on the *de jure* independence of the regulators (RBI and IRDA).

Despite having reservations on few issues, overall the Indian authorities expect the FSAP exercise to play a *significant role* in shaping India's post-crisis initiatives to strengthen the regulatory and supervisory architecture based on the evolving international consensus as well as careful examination of their relevance in the India-specific context. As a member of the FSB[19], BCBS*[20] and IMF[21], India is actively participating in post-

---

18. RBI, 16th January, 2013

---

19. The **FSB** was established in April 2009 as the successor to the Financial Stability Forum (FSF). The FSF was founded in 1999 by the G–7 for enhancing cooperation among the various national and international supervisory bodies and international financial institutions so as to promote stability in the international financial system. In November 2008, the leaders of the G–20 countries called for a larger membership of the FSF. As announced in the G–20 Leaders Summit of *April 2009*, the expanded FSF was re-established as the *Financial Stability Board (FSB)* with a broadened mandate to promote financial stability. The FSB is chaired by *Mark Carney*, Governor of the Bank of Canada. Its secretariat is located in Basel, Switzerland, and hosted by the Bank for International Settlements.

Its *objective* is to coordinate at the international level the work of national financial authorities and international standard setting bodies and to develop and promote the implementation of effective regulatory, supervisory and other financial sector policies. [*Source*: Financial Stability Board Secretariat, Bank for International Settlements, Basel , Switzerland].

20. The **BCBS** (Basel Committee on Banking Supervision) provides a forum for regular cooperation on banking supervisory matters. The Committee's members, today, come from 27 nations including India. The present Chairman of the Committee is *Stefan Ingves*, Governor of Sveriges Riksbank. It is located at the Bank for International Settlements (BIS) in Basel, Switzerland.

Its *objective* is to enhance understanding of key supervisory issues and improve the quality of banking supervision worldwide. It seeks to do so by exchanging information on national supervisory issues, approaches and techniques, with a view to promoting common understanding. At times, the Committee uses this common understanding to develop guidelines and supervisory standards in areas where they are considered desirable. In this regard, the Committee is *best known* for its international standards on *Capital Adequacy (i.e Basel I, Basel II and Basel III, by now)*; the *Core Principles for Effective Banking Supervision*; and the *Concordat* on cross-border banking supervision.

The *Committee* encourages contacts and cooperation among its members and other banking supervisory authorities. It circulates to supervisors throughout the world both published and unpublished papers providing guidance on banking supervisory matters. Contacts have been further strengthened by an *International Conference of Banking Supervisors (ICBS)* which takes place every two years. [*Source*: BIS, Basel, Switzerlad].

21. See **Chapter 16** for detailed discussion on the **IMF** (International Monetary Fund).

crisis reforms of the international regulatory and supervisory framework under the aegis of the **G20**. India remains committed to adoption of international standards and best practices, in a phased manner and calibrated to local conditions, wherever necessary, as it is a country characterised by complex and diverse socio-political and economic conditions.

Financial Action Task Force (FATF)

The FATF is an inter-governmental policy making body that has a ministerial mandate to establish international standards for combating *money laundering* and *terrorist financing*. *India joined the FATF as its 34th member in June 2010. At present, the FATF has 36 members comprising 34 countries and two organisations (European Union and Gulf Cooperation Council).*

REAL ESTATE & INFRASTRUCTURE INVESTMENT TRUSTS

The SEBI firmed up regulations that will govern Real Estate Investment Trusts (REITs), and the Infrastructure Investment Trusts (InvITs).[22] The long-pending proposal of 2008, the trusts have the **objective** of enabling the cash-strapped real estate and infrastruture developers to have easy access to funds. They create a new investment avenue for institutions and high net worth individuals, and eventually ordinary investors.

REITs

Major provisions announced by the SEBI for the REITs are as given below:

(i) To be close-ended real estate investment schemes that will invest in property with the aim of providing returns to unit holders.

(ii) The returns will be derived mainly from rental income or capital gains from real estate.

(iii) Allowed to invest in commercial real estate assets, either directly or through special purpose vehicles (SPVs). In SPVs, a REIT must have a controlling interest of at least 50 per cent of the share capital and will have to hold at least 80 per cent of their assets directly in properties.

(iv) To raise funds only through an initial offering and units of REITs have to be mandatorily listed on a stock exchange, similar to initial public offering (IPO) and listing for equity shares.

(v) Required to have assets worth at least Rs.500 crore at the time of an initial offer and the minimum issue size has to be Rs.250 crore. The minimum subscription size for units of a REIT on offer will be Rs.2 lakh and at least 25 per cent of the units have to be offered to the public.

(vi) Will be able to raise money through follow-on offers, rights issues or qualified institutional placements and the trading lot for such units will be Rs.1 lakh.

According to the norms, although a REIT may raise funds from any type of investors, resident or foreign, initially only wealthy individuals and institutions will be allowed to subscribe to REIT unit offers. The market regulator said a REIT may have up to three sponsors, with each holding at least 5 per cent and collectively holding at least 25 per cent for a period of at least three years from the date of listing. Subsequently, the sponsors' combined holding has to be at least 15 per cent throughout the life of the REIT.

Similar to the practice in the US, Australia, Singapore and other nations where REITs are common, Sebi has decided to allow these trusts to invest primarily in completed revenue-generating properties. To ensure that REITs generate continuous returns, Sebi said at least 80 per cent of the REIT's assets has to be invested in completed and revenue generating properties. And only up to 20 per cent of assets can be invested in properties that are being developed, mortgage-backed securities, debt of companies in the real estate sector, equity shares of listed companies that derive at least 75 per cent of their income from real estate, government securities, or money market instruments. No REIT can invest more than 10 per cent in properties that are under construction.

InvITs

SEBI also announced the launch of **InvITs** which are *somewhat similar* to REITs. However, an initial offer will not be mandatory for InvITs though listing will be mandatory for both publicly and privately placed InvITs. *Major provisions* are as given below:

(i) It can invest in infrastructure projects, either directly or through an SPV (Specila Purpose vehicle). In case of public-private-partnership (PPP) projects, such investments will be only through an SPV.

(ii) While listing, the collective holding of sponsors of an InvIT has to be at least 25 per cent for at least three years.

(iii) Required to have a holding worth at least Rs.500 crore in the underlying assets, and the initial offer size of the InvIT has to be at least Rs.250 crore.

(iv) Any InvIT, which looks to invest at least 80 per cent of its assets in completed and revenue generating infrastructure assets, has to raise funds only through a public issue of units, with a minimum 25 per cent public float and at least 20 investors.

(v) The minimum subscription size and trading lot of such a listed InvIT has to be Rs.10 lakh and Rs.5 lakh, respectively. A publicly offered InvIT may invest the remaining 20 per cent in under-construction infrastructure projects and other permissible investments.

An InvIT that proposes to invest more than 10 per cent of its assets in under-construction infrastructure projects can raise funds only through private placement from qualified institutional buyers with a minimum investment and trading lot of Rs.1 crore and from at least five investors, where single holding cannot be more than 25 per cent.

Recent developments: To promote the real estate and infrastructure trusts, a friendlier tax regime was put in place by the GoI through two successive *Union Budgets,* 2014–15 and 2015–16. However, the idea of the trusts could not get much momentum. Basically, due to subdued market conditions in the sectors attracting investors— new (greenfield) project or a trust—has remained difficult by now. Majority of the existing projects in the sectors are running into losses with weak balance sheets of their developers, unable to even service their bank loans.

To push the cause of the trusts, by **mid-March, 2016,** the security market regulator, SEBI, permitted the foreign portfolio investment (FPI) in the trusts. How much interest the FPIs will show in the trusts it will be known only in future, meanwhile, experts believe that real momentum in the sectors can be only expected once the macro-economic conditions improve in the economy.

OUTLOOK FOR 2017-18

In **February 2017**, the SEBI laid out a roadmap of reforms for the year 2017-18 in various segments including primary market, commodities and foreign investors among others:

• To reduce the listing time gap by bringing down the public issue timeline from the existing requirement of T+6. In other words, shares of a company are currently listed within six days from the day of the issue closure.

- To allow institutional participation in the commodity derivatives markets in a phased manner. Further, it will work towards integration between the commodity spot market and the derivatives segment.

- To initiate consultation with various stakeholders and also design a system of risk-based supervision for commodity brokers.

- To set up a *cyber security lab* for the securities market together with a facility for online registration of intermediaries.

- To allow listing and trading of securitisation receipts issued by Assets Reconstruction Companies.

- To introduce a common application form for registration, opening of a bank and *demat* account, and issue of PAN for Foreign Portfolio Investors.

- In what could be a major reform for institutions like exchanges, depositories and clearing corporations, the regulator plans to review the regulations pertaining to such Market Infrastructure Institutions.

To begin with, the board of the regulator approved the proposal for comprehensive review of *Securities Contracts (Regulation) (Stock Exchanges and Clearing Corporations) Regulations, 2012* and *SEBI (Depositories and Participants) Regulations, 1996* by releasing a consultation paper and seeking public comments.

Meanwhile, the **Union Budget 2017-18** has announced to set up an ***expert committee*** to study and promote creation of an operational and legal framework to integrate *spot market* and *derivatives market* in the agricultural sector, for commodities trading—e-NAM to be an integral part of the framework

EXTERNAL SECTOR IN INDIA

No country in today's globalised world can be fully insulated from what happens in the global economy and India is no exception to the rule. As the country is increasingly integrated into the world, it cannot remain impervious to developments abroad. The unfolding of the Euro zone crisis and uncertainty surrounding the global economy have impacted the Indian economy causing drop in growth, higher current account deficit and declining capital inflows.*

* As many documents of the WTO, World Bank and OECD have accepted many times.

DEFINITION

All economic activities of an economy which take place in foreign currency fall in the external sector such as export, import, foreign investment, external debt, current account, capital account, balance of payment, etc. (*definition*).[1]

FOREX RESERVES

The total foreign currencies (of different countries) an economy possesses at a point of time is its 'foreign currency assets/reserves'.[2] The Forex Reserves (short for 'foreign exchange reserves') of an economy is its 'foreign currency assets' added with its *gold reserves, SDRs* (Special Drawing Rights) and *Reserve Tranche* in the IMF.[3] In a sense, the Forex reserves is the upper limit upto which an economy can manage foreign currency in normal times if need be.

By **December 2016**, India's forex reserves were ate comfortable levels of US$ 360 billion—with a rise of US$ 10 billion since January 2016. This included the gold reserves of US$ 21 billion and SDRs of US$ 5.6 billion (inclusive of reserve tranche of US$ 1.3 billion), as per the *Economic Survey 2016-17*.

Optimum Forex – the Riddle

In recent times, there has been a debate over India's optimum level of the forex reserves. The RBI is aware of the downside risks to the exchange rate, as is reflected by its action of buying the US dollar. Officially, the RBI *targets neither* a particular exchange rate nor foreign exchange reserves, and maintains such interventions by it to just *reduce volatility* in the forex market. But in the

process of supporting weakening rupee, RBI needs to buy dollar, ultimately, leading to higher forex buid-ups. The Chief Economic Advisor of the Finance Ministry, however, clearly stated the kind of reserve accretion the government is looking at. Citing the example of China, the *Economic Survey 2014–15* said India could target foreign exchange reserves of US$750 billion to $1 trillion.

Today, China has *de facto* become one of the lenders of last resort to governments experiencing financial troubles. China, in its own heterodox and multiple ways, is assuming the roles of both an IMF and World Bank as a result of its reserves. The question for India, as a rising economic and political power, is whether it, too, should consider a substantial addition to its reserves.

While forex reserves act as insurance when the rupee tends to be volatile against the dollar, there are costs attached to it. When RBI purchases dollars in the spot, it leads to infusion of rupee into the system which leaves *inflationary* effect on the economy. Since the RBI does not want such actions to create inflationary pressure, so, it converts spot purchases into forwards. This way, it is a direct cost because of the forward premiums. If RBI opts for open market operations (OMOs) to mop up excess liquidity, that also involves costs.

RBI invests these dollars in instruments such as US treasuries, which offer *negligible* returns, owing to lower yields. But experts say these are unavoidable costs. The returns from rupee assets are much lower compared to returns from dollar assets. But RBI is not into investment management, it is there to maintain stability in the system.

In August 2014, RBI chief Raghuram Rajan agreed foreign exchange reserves came at a cost. India earns next to nothing for the foreign reserves it holds—actually, this way India finances another country when it has a significant financing needs. It is very difficult to state the level of reserves considered adequate by RBI. Though there are

1. Based on J.E. Stiglitz and C.E. Walsh, *Economics*, (New York: W.W. Norton & Company, 2006), pp. 757-58.
2. Based on P.A. Samuelson and W.D. Nordhaus, *Economics,* (New Delhi: Tata McGraw Hill, 2005), p. 604.
3. Ibid., pp. 605–07.

costs involved, the costs to benefit cannot be quantified by any model. Globally, there has been no study on the adequacy of reserves. In such an environment, RBI will have to go by experiences.

EXTERNAL DEBT

After the BoP crisis of 1991, India's prudent external debt policies and management with a focus on sustainability, solvency and liquidity have helped contain the increase in size of external debt to a moderate level and it is compositionally better with a longer term maturity profile.

By **September 2016**, India's external debt at US$ 484.3 billion, recording a decline of US$ 0.8 billion over the level at end-March 2016—mainly due to reduction in commercial borrowings (i.e., ECBs) and short-term debt, as per the *Economic Survey 2016-17*. Main features about is composition were as given below:

- *Share* of Government (Sovereign) debt was at 20.1 per cent (rest 79.9 per cent being non-Government debt).
- US dollar *denominated* debt accounted for 55.6 per cent; followed by Indian rupee (30.1 per cent); SDR (5.8 per cent); Japanese Yen (4.8 per cent); Pound Sterling (0.7 per cent); Euro (2.4 per cent) and others (0.6 per cent).
- The *maturity pattern* indicated dominance of long-term borrowings—long-term debt accounted for 83.2 per cent (rest 16.8 per cent being short-term i.e., of upto one year maturity period).
- *Short-term* debt (considered risky due to smaller maturity period) fell down by 16.8 per cent during March-September 2016.
- *Concessional debt* accounted for 9.4 per cent (same as June 2016)—rest (91.6 per cent being commercial debt).

- Forex reserves provided a *cover* of 76.8 per cent to the debt.

Cross-country comparison of external debt, (as per the *World Bank's International Debt Statistics 2017*), indicates that India continues to be among the less vulnerable countries and its key debt indicators compare well with other indebted countries of the developing world.

The prudential external debt management policy of India, over the reform period has led it to keep its external debt within safe and comfortable limits. The Government of India continues to emphasise monitoring of long- and short- term debt, raising sovereign loans on concessional terms with long-term maturities, regulating ECBs (external commercial borrowings) through end-use policy and rationalising interest rates on the NRI deposits.

FIXED CURRENCY REGIME[4]

A method of regulating exchange rates of world currencies brought by the IMF. In this system exchange rate of a particular currency was fixed by the IMF keeping the currency in front of a basket of important world currencies (they were UK£, US $, Japanese ¥, German Mark DM and the French Franc FFr). Different economies were supposed to maintain that particular exchange rate in future. Exchange rates of currencies were modified by the IMF from time to time.

FLOATING CURRENCY REGIME[5]

A method of regulating exchange rates of world currencies based on the market mechanism (i.e., demand and supply). In the follow up to the fixed currency system of exchange rate determination, it was the UK which blamed the system for its

---

4.   Ibid., pp. 610–11.

5.   Ibid., pp. 611–15.

payment crisis of late 1960s. Looking at the major loopholes in this system, the UK government decided to switch over to the floating currency regime in 1973— the same year the IMF allowed an option to its member countries to go for either of the currency systems.

In the floating exchange rate system, a domestic currency is left free to float against a number of foreign currencies in its foreign exchange market and determine its own value. Such exchange rates, are also called as *market driven* or *based* exchange rates, which are regulated by factors such as the demand and supply of the domestic and the foreign currencies in the concerned economy.

MANAGED EXCHANGE RATES

A managed-exchange-rate system is a hybrid or mixture of the fixed and flexible exchange rate systems in which the government of the economy attempts to affect the exchange rate *directly* by buying or selling foreign currencies or *indirectly*, through monetary policy[6] (i.e., by lowering or raising interest rates on foreign currency bank accounts, affecting foreign investment, etc.).

Today, most of the economies have shifted to this system of exchange rate determination. Almost all countries tend to intervene when the markets become *disorderly* or the *fundamentals* of economics are challenged by the exchange rate of the time. Some of the major examples of the managed exchange-rate system have been given below:[7]

(i) Some countries allow to *free float* their currencies and allow the market forces to determine their exchange rate with rare government intervention. This is the idea from which the *floating currency regime*

basically emerged. The USA and the EU are the major examples in this category.

(ii) Some economies have *managed but flexible* exchange rates, under which the governments buy or sell its currency to reduce day-to-day volatility of currency fluctuations and sometimes go for systematic intervention for desired objectives. Canada and Japan fall in this category, besides many developing countries. India too falls under this category which follows the *dual currency regime* since 1992–93 financial year.[8]

(iii) Some economies, particularly small ones, peg their currencies to a major currency or to a *basket* of currency in a fixed exchange rate—known as the *pegging of currencies.* At times, the peg is allowed to glide smoothly upward or downward—a system which is known as *gliding* or *crawling peg.* Some economies have a *hard fix* of a *currency board.* A *currency board* is working well in Hong Kong while the same failed in Argentina in 2002.

FOREIGN EXCHANGE MARKET

The market where different currencies can be bought and sold is called the foreign exchange market.[9] Out of the trades in different currencies, the exchange rate of the currency is determined by the economy.[10] This is an institutional framework for the exchange of one national currency for another.[11] This is particularly correct either in the case of a free float exchange (i.e., floating currency) regime or is a managed or hybrid exchange rate

---

6. Ibid., p. 615.

7. The discussion is based primarily on Samuelson and Nordhaus, *Economics,* 613–15 and D. Salvatore, *International Economics* (New Jersey: John Wiley & Sons, 2004) pp. 717–22.

8. Ministry of Finance, *LERMS, Union Budget 1992–93,* (New Delhi: Government of India, 1992).

9. Stiglitz and Walsh, *Economics,* p. 757.

10. Samuelson and Nordhaus, *Economics,* p. 604

11. D. Salvatore, *International Economics,* p. 7.

system. It is altogether not allowed either in a *fixed currency system* or a *hard fix* (in a hard fix this happens once the currency to which the hard fix has been done itself starts fluctuating).

EXCHANGE RATE IN INDIA

Indian currency, the 'rupee', was historically linked with the British Pound Sterling till 1948 which was fixed as far back as 1928. Once the IMF came up, India shifted to the fixed currency system committed to maintain rupee's external value (i.e., exchange rate) in terms of gold or the US ($ Dollar). In 1948, Rs. 3.30 was fixed equivalent to US $ 1.

In September 1975, India delinked rupee from the British Pound and the RBI started determining rupee's exchange rate with respect to the exchange rate movements of the basket of world currencies (£, $, ¥, DM, Fr.). This was an arrangement between the fixed and the floating currency regimes.

In 1992–93 financial year, India moved to the floating currency regime with its own method which is known as the 'dual exchange rate'.[12] There are two exchange rates for rupee, one is the 'official rate' and the other is the 'market rate'. Here the point should be noted that it is the everyday's changing market-based exchange rate of rupee which affects the official exchange rate and not the other way round. But the RBI may intervene in the forex market via the demand and supply of rupee or the foreign currencies. Another point which should be kept in mind is that none of the economies have till date followed an ideal free-floating exchange rate. They require some mechanism to intervene in the foreign exchange market because this is a highly speculative market.

TRADE BALANCE

The monetary difference of the total export and import of an economy in one financial year is called trade balance. It might be positive or negative, known to be either favourable or unfavourable, respectively to the economy.

TRADE POLICY

Broadly speaking, the economic policy which regulates the export-import activities of any economy is known as the trade policy. It is also called the foreign trade policy or the Exim Policy. This policy needs regular modifications depending upon the economic policies of the economies of the world or the trading partners.[13]

DEPRECIATION

This term is used to mean two different things. In foreign exchange market, it is a situation when domestic currency loses its value in front of a foreign currency if it is market-driven. It means depreciation in a currency can only take place if the economy follows the floating exchange rate system.

In domestic economy, depreciation means an asset losing its value due to either its use, wear and tear or due to other economic reasons. Depreciation here means *wear and tear*. This is also known as *capital consumption.* Every economy has an official annual rates for different assets at which fixed assets are considered depreciating.

DEVALUATION

In the foreign exchange market when exchange rate of a domestic currency is cut down by its government against any foreign currency, it is called devaluation. It means official depreciation is devaluation.

---

12. Ministry of Finance, *LERMS.*

13. D. Salvatore, *International Economics,* pp. 235–36.

REVALUATION

A term used in foreign exchange market which means a government increasing the exchange rate of its currency against any foreign currency. It is official appreciation.

APPRECIATION

In foreign exchange market, if a free floating domestic currency increases its value against the value of a foreign currency, it is appreciation. In domestic economy, if a fixed asset has seen increase in its value it is also known as appreciation. Appreciation rates for different assets are not fixed by any government as they depend upon many factors which are unseen.

CURRENT ACCOUNT

It has two meanings—one is related to the banking sector and the other to the external sector:

(i) In the banking industry, a business firms bank account is known as current account. The account is in the name of a firm run by authorised person or persons in which no interest is paid by the bank on the deposits. Every withdrawal from the account takes place by cheques with limitations on the number of deposits and withdrawals in a single day. The *overdraft* facility or the *cash-cum-credit* (c/c Account) facility to business firms is offered by the banks on this account only.

(ii) In the external sector, it refers to the account maintained by every government of the world in which every kind of current transactions is shown—basically this account is maintained by the central banking body of the economy on behalf of the government. Current transactions of an economy in foreign currency all over the world are—export, import,

interest payments, private remittances and transfers.

All transactions are shown as either inflow or outflow (credit or debit). At the end of the year, the current account might be positive or negative. The positive one is known as a surplus current account, and the negative one is known as a deficit current account. India had surplus current accounts for three consecutive years (2000–03)—the only such period in Indian economic history.

Current account deficit is shown either numerically by showing the total monetary amount of the deficit, or in percentage of the GDP of the economy for the concerned year. Both the data are used in analysis as per the specific requirement. As per a RBI release of April 2014, presently the sustainable level of current account deficit for India is 2.5 per cent of the GDP.

CAPITAL ACCOUNT

Every government of the world maintains a capital account, which shows the capital kind of transactions of the economy with outside economies. Every transaction in foreign currency (inflow or outflow) considered as capital is shown in this account—external lending and borrowing, foreign currency deposits of banks, external bonds issued by the Government of India, FDI, PIS and security market investment of the QFIs (Rupee is fully convertible in this case).

There is no deficit or surplus in this account like the current account .

BALANCE OF PAYMENT (BoP)

The outcome of the total transactions of an economy with the outside world in one year is known as the balance of payment (BoP) of the economy.[14] Basically, it is the net outcome of

---

14. Samuelson and Nordhaus, *Economics,* p. 601.

the current and capital accounts of an economy. It might be favourable or unfavourable for the economy. However, negativity of the BoP does not mean it is unfavourable. A negative BoP is unfavourable for an economy if only the economy lacks the means to fill the gap of negativity.

The BoP of an economy is calculated on the principles of accountancy (*double-entry book-keeping*)[15] and looks like the balance sheet of a company—every entry shown either as credit (inflow) or debit (outflow). If there is a positive outcome at the end of the year, the money is automatically transferred to the foreign exchange reserves of the economy. And if there is any negative outcome, the same foreign exchange is drawn from the country's forex reserves. If the forex reserves are not capable of fulfilling the negativity created by the BoP, it is known as a BoP crisis and the economy tries different means to solve the crisis in which going for forex help from the IMF is the last resort.

CONVERTIBILITY

An economy might allow its currency full or partial convertibility in the current and the capital accounts. If domestic currency is allowed to convert into foreign currency for all current account purposes, it is a case of full current account convertibility. Similarly, in cases of capital outflow, if the domestic currency is allowed to convert into foreign currency, it is a case of full capital account convertibility. If the situation is of partial convertibility, then the portion allowed by the government can be converted into foreign currency for current and capital purposes. It

---

15. It means that each external transaction is recorded/entered twice—once as a credit and once as a debit of an equal amount. This is because every transaction has two sides—we sell something and we receive payment for it, similarly we buy something and we have to pay for it (See Salvatore, *International Economics,* p. 432).

should always be kept in mind that the issue of currency convertibility is concerned with foreign currency *outflow* only.

Convertibility in India

India's foreign exchange earning capacity was always poor and hence it had all possible provisions to check the foreign exchange outflow, be it for current purposes or capital purposes (remember the draconian FERA). But the process of economic reforms has changed the situation to unidentifiable levels.

Current Account

Current account is today fully convertible (operationalised on 19 August, 1994). It means that the full amount of the foreign exchange required by someone for current purposes will be made available to him at official exchange rate and there could be an unprohibited outflow of foreign exchange (earlier it was partially convertible). India was obliged to do so as per Article VIII of the IMF which prohibits any exchange restrictions on current international transactions (keep in mind that India was under pre-conditions of the IMF since 1991).

Capital Account

After the recomendations of the S.S. Tarapore Committee (1997) on Capital Account Convertibility, India has been moving in the direction of allowing full convertibility in this account, but with required precautions. India is still a country of partial convertibility (40:60) in the capital account, but inside this overall policy, enough reforms have been made and to certain levels of foreign exchange requirements, it is an economy allowing full capital account convertibility—

(i) Indian corporate are allowed full convertibility in the automatic route upto $ 500 million overseas ventures (investment by Ltd. companies in foreign countries allowed) per annum.

(ii) Indian corporate are allowed to prepay their external commercial borrowings (ECBs) via automatic route if the loan is above $ 500 million per annum.

(iii) Individuals are allowed to invest in foreign assets, shares, etc., upto the level of $ 2,50,000 per annum.

(iv) Unlimited amount of gold is allowed to be imported (this is equal to allowing full convertibility in capital account via current account route, but not feasible for everybody) which is not allowed now.

The Second Committee on the Capital Account Convertibility (CAC)—again chaired by S.S. Tarapore—handed over its report in September 2006 on which the RBI/the government is having consultations.

LERMS

India announced the Liberalised Exchange Rate Mechanism System (LERMS) in the Union Budget 1992–93 and in March 1993 it was operationalised. India delinked its currency from the fixed currency system and moved into the era of floating exchange-rate system under it.

Indian form of exchange rate is known as the 'dual exchange rate', one exchange rate of rupee is official and the other is market-driven.[16] The market-driven exchange rate shows the actual tendencies of the foreign currency demand and supply in the economy vis-á-vis the domestic currency. It is the market-driven exchange rate which affects the official rate and not the other way round.

---

16. Ministry of Finance, **LERMS, Union Budget 1992-93**, GoI, MoF, N. Delhi.

NEER

The Nominal Effective Exchange Rate (NEER) of the rupee is a weighted average of exchange rates before the currencies of India's major trading partners.

REER

When the weight of inflation is adjusted with the NEER, we get the Real Effective Exchange Rate (REER) of the rupee. Since inflation has been on the higher side in recent months, the REER of the rupee has been more against it than the NEER.

EFF

The Extended fund Facility (EFF) is a service provided by the IMF to its member countries which authorises them to raise any amount of foreign exchange from it to fulfil their BoP crisis, but on the conditions of structural reforms in the economy put by the body. It is the first agreement of its kind. India had signed this agreement with the IMF in the financial year 1981–82.

IMF CONDITIONS ON INDIA

The BoP crisis of the early 1990s made India borrow from the IMF which came on some conditions. The medium term loan to India was given for the restructuring of the economy on the following conditions:

(i) Devaluation of rupee by 22 per cent (done in two consecutive fortnights—rupee fell from '21 to '27 against every US Dollar).

(ii) Drastic custom cut to a peak duty of 30 per cent from the erstwhile level of 130 per cent for all goods.

(iii) Excise duty to be increased by 20 per cent to neutralise the loss of revenue due to custom cut.

(iv) Government expenditure to be cut by 10 per cent per annum (the burden of salaries, pensions, subsidies, etc.).

The above-given conditions to which India was obliged were vehemently opposed by the Indian corporate sector, opposition in the Parliament and majority of Indians. But by the end of 1999–2000, when India saw every logic in strengthening its BoP position there was no ideological opposition to the idea. It should always be kept in mind that the nature of structural reforms India went through were guided and decided by these pre-conditions of the IMF.

This is how the direction of structural reforms of an economy are regulated by the IMF in the process of strengthening the BoP position of the crisis-driven economy. The purpose has been served in the Indian case. India has not only fulfilled these conditions but it has also moved ahead.

HARD CURRENCY

It is the international currency in which the highest faith is shown and is needed by every economy. The strongest currency of the world is one which has a high level of liquidity. Basically, the economy with the highest as well as highly diversified exports that are compulsive imports for other countries (as of high-level technology, defence products, life saving medicines and petroleum products) will also create high demand for its currency in the world and become the hard currency. It is always scarce.

Upto the second world war, the best hard currency was the Pound Sterling (£) of the UK, but soon it was replaced by the US Dollar. Some of the best hard currencies of the world today are the US Dollar, the Euro(€), Japanese Yen (¥) and the UK Sterling Pound (£). Meanwhile, by late 2015, the IMF allowed the SDR to be denominated in the chinese 'Yaan'–paving the way for a new hard currency to be implemented in 2016.

SOFT CURRENCY

A term used in the foreign exchange market which denotes the currency that is easily available in any economy in its forex market. For example, rupee is a soft currency in the Indian forex market. It is basically the opposite term for the hard currency.

HOT CURRENCY

Hot currency is a term of the forex market and is a temporary name for any hard currency. Due to certain reasons, if a hard currency is exiting an economy at a fast pace for the time, the *hard* currency is known to be *hot*. As in the case of the SE Asian crisis, the US dollar had become hot.

HEATED CURRENCY

A term used in the forex market to denote the domestic currency which is under enough pressure (heat) of depreciation due to a hard currency's high tendency of exiting the economy (since it has become hot). It is also known as *currency under heat* or *under hammering*.

CHEAP CURRENCY

A term first used by the economist J. M. Keynes (1930s). If a government starts re-purchasing its bonds before their maturities (at full-maturity prices) the money which flows into the economy is known as the cheap currency, also called cheap money.

In the banking industry, it means a period of comparatively lower/softer interest rates regime.

DEAR CURRENCY

This term was popularised by economists in early 1930s to show the opposite of the cheap currency. when a goverment issues bonds, the money which flows from the public to the government or the money in the economy in general is called dear currency, also called as *dear money*.

In the banking industry, it means a period of comparatively higher/costlier interest rates regime.

SPECIAL ECONOMIC ZONE

The special economic zone (SEZ) policy was announced by the government in 2000 which was concretised through the SEZ Act, 2005. It mainly aims to develop 'export hubs' in the country to promote growth and development. As an idea it was not new—India had set up *Asia's first* 'export processing zone' (EPZ) in Kandla in 1965 itself. Later on the idea got another encouragement through the 'export oriented units' (EOUs). After the SEZ policy was formalised through an Act, the EOUs and EPZs are open to conversion to SEZ. The SEZs can be set up by either the GoI, States or even private sector—in all three sectors of the economy—agriculture, industry and services. As per the Ministry of Commerce and Industry, the principal objectives behind creating SEZs in the country include:

(i) generation of additional economic activity;

(ii) promotion of exports of goods and services;

(iii) promotion of investment from domestic and foreign sources;

(iv) creation of employment opportunities; and

(v) development of infrastructure facilities .

Recent steps (till *March 2017*) taken by the Government to strengthen SEZs in the country are as given below[17]:

- Minimum Land Area requirement for setting up of new SEZs has been reduced to 50 per cent for multi-product and sector-specific SEZs.

- Sectoral broad-banding has been introduced to encompass similar and related areas under the same sector.

- A new sector 'agro-based food processing' sector has been introduced to encourage agro-based industries in SEZs (food processing getting government's nod by late 2016 for 100 per cent FDI by is expected to give a big push to it).

- Dual use of facilities like Social & Commercial infrastructure by SEZs and non-SEZs entities has been allowed in order to make SEZ operations more viable.

- Online processing of various activities relating to SEZ for improving 'ease of doing business'.

- 'SEZ India' mobile app launched to help the SEZs to track their transactions on SEZ Online System (launched in *January 2017*).

By *March 2017*, the Government had approved 405 proposals for setting up SEZs (in addition to 7 SEZs of the GoI and 11 of States/private sector which were set-up prior to the enactment of the SEZs Act, 2005)—out of which 206 SEZs are operational. Today, the SEZs are invested with Rs. 4.06 lakh crore and have created 16.88 lakh employment. They have 23 per cent share in India's total exports.

In recent times, the SEZs have lost their original synergy due to global economic slowdown which followed the great recession among the developed economies. meanwhile, the Government has been taking various steps to encourage them.

GAAR

The GAAR (General Anti-Avoidance Rules), originally proposed in the *Direct Taxes Code 2010*, are targeted at arrangements or transactions made

---

17. **Ministry of Commerce and Industry**, Government of India, N. Delhi, March 2017.

specifically to avoid taxes. The government had decided to advance the introduction of GAAR and implement it from the financial year 2013–14 itself. More than 30 countries have introduced GAAR provisions in their respective tax codes to check such tax evasion.

The *objective* of the GAAR provisions is to codify the doctrine of *'substance over form'* where the real intention of the parties and purpose of an arrangement is taken into account for determining the tax consequences, irrespective of the legal structure of the concerned transaction or arrangement. It essentially comes into effect where an arrangement is entered into with the main purpose or one of the main purposes of obtaining a *tax benefit* and which also satisfies at least one of the following *four tests*:

(i) The arrangement creates rights and obligations that are not at arm's length,

(ii) it results in misuse or abuse of provisions of tax laws,

(iii) lacks commercial substance or is deemed to lack commercial substance, or

(iv) it is not carried out in a bona fide manner.

Thus, if the tax officer believes that the main purpose or one of the main purposes of an arrangement is to obtain a tax benefit and even if one of the above *four tests* are satisfied, the tax officer has powers to declare it as an impermissible avoidance arrangement and re-characterise the entire transaction in a manner that is more conducive to maximising tax revenues. There are many troubling aspects of this provision that will make doing business in India even more *challenging*, than what it already is from a tax perspective—

(i) It is presumed that obtaining tax benefit is the main purpose of the arrangement unless otherwise proved by the taxpayer. This is an onerous burden that under a fair rule of law should be discharged by the revenue collector and not the taxpayer. In fact, the *Parliamentary Standing Committee on DTC* has specifically recommended that the onus of proving the existence of a tax-avoidance motive and a transaction lacking commercial substance, should rest with the revenue invoking GAAR and not shifted to the taxpayer. This is essentially to ensure that the revenue authorities exercise proper discretion, proper application of mind and gather enough credible data and evidence before attempting to invoke far-reaching provisions such as GAAR.

(ii) An arrangement will be deemed to lack commercial substance under GAAR if it involves the location of an asset or of a transaction or of the place of residence of any party that would not have been so located for any substantial commercial purpose other than obtaining tax benefit. This again is an amazingly wide provision that provides a great weapon in the armoury of the tax authorities to challenge almost every inbound or outbound transaction with respect to India, made through any of the favourable tax treaties that India has entered into. The governments intention becomes clear visibly by one of the finance ministry replies to the *Standing Committee on DTC*, where it has made it clear that the GAAR provisions will check *treaty shopping* by the taxpayer for avoidance of payment of tax in India.

(iii) GAAR allows tax authorities to call a business arrangement or a transaction 'impermissible avoidance arrangement' if they feel it has been primarily entered into to avoid taxes. Once an arrangement is ruled 'impermissible' then the tax authorities can deny tax benefits. Most aggressive tax avoidance arrangements would be under the risk of being termed impermissible. It has a provision according to which the onus to prove that an arrangement is 'impermissible' will lie with the tax department. The GAAR panel, the final body that will decide on the applicability of the law, will include an independent member. The rule can apply on domestic as well as overseas transactions.

(iv) GAAR is a very broadbased provision and can easily be applied to most tax-saving arrangements. Many experts feel that the provision would give unbridled powers to tax officers, allowing them to question any taxsaving deal. Foreign institutional investors are worried that their investments routed through Mauritius could be denied tax benefits enjoyed by them under the Indo-Mauritius Tax Treaty. The proposal *(announced on 8 May, 2012)* had spooked stock market as FII inflows dropped on concerns, and the rupee hit a low of Rs. 53.47 to the Dollar.

As per the decision taken last year, the Government in **February 2017** announced to enforce the GAAR from the financial year 2017-18. All consultations with the stakeholders have been completed and the regulatory framework for it is expected to be announced by late March 2017.

RISKS IN FOREIGN CURRENCY BORROWINGS

Corporate borrowers in India and other emerging economies are keen to borrow in foreign currency to benefit from lower interest and longer terms of credit. Such borrowings however, are not always helpful, especially in times of high currency volatility. During good times, domestic borrowers could enjoy triple benefits of

(i) lower interest rates,

(ii) longer maturity, and

(iii) capital gains

due to domestic currency appreciation. This would happen when the local currency is appreciating due to surge in capital flows and the debt service liability is falling in domestic currency terms. The opposite would happen when the domestic currency is depreciating due to reversal of capital flows during crisis situations, *as happened during the 2008 global crisis*.

A sharp depreciation in local currency would mean corresponding *increase in debt service liability*, as more domestic currency would be required to buy the same amount of foreign exchange for debt service payments. This would lead to *erosion in profit* margin and have 'mark-to-market' implications for the corporate. There would also be 'debt overhang' problem, as the volume of debt would rise in local currency terms. Together, these factors could create corporate distress, especially because the rupee tends to depreciate precisely when the Indian economy is also under stress, and corporate revenues and margins are under pressure.

In this context, it is felt that one of the factors contributing to faster recovery of the Indian economy after the 2008 global crisis was the low level of corporate external debt. As a result, the significant decline in the value of rupee did not have a major fallout for the corporate balance-sheets. Foreign currency borrowings, therefore, have to be contracted carefully, especially when no 'natural hedge' is available. Such natural hedge would happen when a foreign currency borrower also has an export market for its products. As a result, export receivables would offset, at least to some extent, the currency risk inherent in debt service payments. This happens because fall in the value of the rupee that leads to higher debt service payments is partly compensated by the increase in the value of rupee receivables through exports.

When export receivables and the currency of borrowings is different, the *prudent approach* is for corporations to enter *currency swaps* to re-denominate asset and liability in the same currency to create natural hedge. Unfortunately, too many Indian corporations with little foreign currency earnings leave foreign currency borrowings unhedged, so as to profit from low international interest rates. This is a dangerous gamble for reasons described above and should be avoided.

GLOBAL FDI

As per the *Global Investment Trends Monitor* (UNCTAD, February 1, 2017), the FDI flows in the year 2016 have weakened with wide regional variations:

- Global FDI flows fell 13 per cent in 2016, reaching an estimated US$1.52 trillion, as global growth and trade global remained weak. This decline was not equally shared across regions, reflecting the heterogeneous impact of the current economic environment on countries worldwide.

- A dip was there in FDI flows to developed economies (- 9 per cent to an estimated US$872 billion). FDI flows to Europe fell 29 per cent to an estimated US$385 billion, with a number of countries experiencing strong volatility in their inflows. This decline was tempered by modest growth in flows to North America (6 per cent) and a sizeable increase in investment in other developed economies, principally Australia and Japan.

- Flows to **India** fell by 5 per cent to an estimated US$42 billion, but nevertheless ranked among the *top ten largest* FDI recipients.

- FDI flows to **China** remained robust rising by 2.3 per cent to a new record of about US$139 billion.

- FDI to **Pakistan** also rose significantly (82 per cent to an estimated US$1.6 billion) as a result of rising Chinese investment in infrastructure.

- There was a rebound in flows to the Republic of Korea, at US$9.4 billion, up from their relatively low level of US$4 billion in 2015.

INDIA'S EXTERAL SCENARIO

After the global meltdown of 2007-08, the performance of India's external sector has been a kind of mixed bag—certain areas giving relief while certain other remain a matter of concern. The major indicators of the sector have been as discussed below[18]—

Foreign Trade: Global economic environment have been unfavourable for most of the world economies due to several global events—the Global Financial Crisis, Eurozone crisis, Brexit, etc. Though India has been able to manage one of the highest growth rate in the world it has its own quota of negatives. As per the *Economic Survey 2016-17*, meanwhile, some green shoots been seen on India's the trade front during 2016-17 (April-December):

Exports did show symptoms of recovery during 2016-17:

- During 2014-15 and 2015-16 India's exports had *declined* by 1.3 per cent and 15.5 per cent, respectively. The trend of negative growth was *reversed* somewhat during 2016-17 with exports registering a growth of 0.7 per cent (US$ 198.8 billion). A large number of export sectors have moved to positive zone during this period.

- India's exports to Europe, Africa, America, Asia and CIS and Baltics declined in 2015-16. However, India's exports to Europe, America and Asia increased by 2.6 per cent, 2.4 per cent and 1.1 per cent respectively.

---

18. **Economic Survey 2016-17**, Government of India, Ministry of Finance, N. Delhi, Vol. 1, pp. 151-153.

- Exports to Africa declined by 13.5 per cent.
- USA followed by UAE and Hong Kong were the top export destinations.

Imports did show mixed trend with decline being the chief feature:

- Value of imports declined from US$ 448 billion in 2014-15 to US$ 381 billion in 2015-16, mainly on account of *decline in crude oil prices* resulting in lower levels of POL (petroleum, oil and lubricants) imports. The trend continued in 2016-17 also with imports declining by 7.4 per cent to US$ 275.4 billion.
- Decline in imports was 10.8 per cent in POL; 35.9 per cent in gold and silver imports and 2 per cent in non-POL and non-gold & silver imports.
- Imports of capital goods declined by 8.8 per cent.
- Positive growth was registered in pearls and semi-precious stones (19.0 per cent) and Food and allied products (1.3 per cent).
- India's imports from Europe, Africa, America, Asia and CIS & Baltics regions declined in 2015-16. However, in 2016-17, imports from CIS & Baltics region increased by 10.3 per cent while other four regions witnessed decline.
- Top three import destinations of India were China followed by UAE and USA.

India's ***trade deficit*** has been declining since the last two years—while it declined by 13.8 per cent in 2015-16, it has fallen by 23.5 per cent during 2016-17 (falling to around US$ 100 billion). India's current account deficit (CAD) was very comfortable at **0.3** per cent by the first half of the fiscal 2016-17.

As of 2011, *India's openness*—measured as the ratio of trade in goods and services to GDP has far overtaken China's (a country famed for using trade as an engine of growth). India's "internal trade to GDP" is also comparable to that of other large countries and very different from the caricature of a barrier-riddled economy.

FDI: India had a net FDI (foreign direct investment) inflows of $ 21.3 billion during the first half of 2016-17 showing a whopping 29 per cent increase over the same period of the preceding year 2015-16. The inflows have shown accelerating growth—in the second half of 2016-17 it reached 3.2 per cent of GDP from 1.7 per cent of GDP of the same period of the preceding year.

FPI: Foreign portfolio investment (FPI) saw a net inflow of $ 8.2 billion in the first half of 2016-17 against an outflow of $ 3.5 billion in the same period of 2015-16. The net inflow to India during 2014 and 2015 were Rs. 2.56 lakh crore and Rs. 63,663 crore.

But the trend reversed in the following year— for the first time since the meltdown of 2008, net FPI turned *negative* during the year 2016— an outflow of Rs. 23,079 crore from the Indian markets. It was not special case with India but most of the EMEs (merging market economies) saw big outflows from their markets—as developed economies were giving higher returns.

Exchange rate: Indian rupee has depreciated during 2016-17 (April-December) which could be attributed largely to the strengthening of the US dollar globally following the US presidential election results and tightening of monetary policy there. However, it has performed better than the currencies of most of other emerging market economies (EMEs). On year-on-year basis, the rupee depreciated by 3.4 per cent against US dollar as compared to the depreciation of Mexican peso (14.4 per cent), South African Rand (8.6 per cent) and Chinese renminbi (6.3 per cent).

NEW STEPS TO PROMOTE TRADE

Several new initiatives were taken by the GoI, in recent times, to facilitate trade. These new steps (up to **March 2017**) were aimed at adopting internationally benchmarked best practices—major ones of them are as given below:

(i) *e-Filing & e-Payment:* Applications for various trade services can be filed online and application fees paid through electronic transfer. The number of mandatory documents required for exports and imports has also been cut down to just *three* each (which is comparable with international benchmarks).

(ii) *Single window for Customs:* Under this project, that importers and exporters electronically submit their *customs clearance* documents at a single point with customs. Permissions required from other regulatory agencies (such as animal quarantine, plant quarantine, drug controller and textile committee) could be obtained online without the having to separately approach these agencies.

   The single window is aimed at providing importers/exporters a single point interface for customs clearance, thereby reducing personal interface with governmental agencies, dwell time and cost of doing business.

(iii) *24x7 customs clearance:* The facility of '24x7 customs clearance' has been made available at 18 seaports and 17 air cargo complexes. This move is aimed at faster clearance of import and export, reducing dwell time and lowering the transaction cost.

(iv) *Paperless environment:* The government aims to move towards a paperless 24x7 working trade environment. A new facility has been created to upload documents in exporter/importer profile so that exporters are not required to submit documents repeatedly.

(v) *Simplification:* Attention has also been paid to simplifying various *'aayat niryat'* forms, bringing in clarity in different provisions, removing ambiguities and enhancing electronic governance. A mobile application also launched by the DGFT (Director General of Foreign Trade) in October 2016.

(vi) *Training/Outreach:* 'Niryat Bandhu Scheme', a training/outreach programme is aimed at Skill India—organised at MSME (micro, small and medium enterprises) clusters with the help of export promotion councils (EPCs) and other willing 'industry partners' and 'knowledge partners'. The DGFT in collaboration with the IIFT (Indian Institute of Foreign Trade) has launched 'Niryat Bandhu at Your Desktop', an online certificate programme in export-import business. Another training programme has been launched by the Department of Commerce (DoC) for exporters located in the major export clusters/cities. It focuses on training exporters to utilize free trade agreements (FTA).

(vii) *Participation of States/UTs:* In July 2015, a Council for Trade Development and Promotion (CTDP) was set up to ensure continuous dialogue with the governments of states/ union territories (UTs) on measures for providing an international trade-enabling environment and for making them active partners in boosting India's exports.

(viii) Once 90 per cent of the FDI inflows are now under 'automatic route' together with fully converted to 'online' procedure, the Government decided in the *Union*

Budget 2017-18 to phase out (abolish) the multi-ministerial body foreign investment promotion board (FIPB) in the year. In future, the FDI proposals not coming under the automatic route will be considered by either the concerned ministries or the regulatory body.

(ix) The *Union Budget 2017-18* promised *further liberalisation* of the FDI policy regarding which the announcements will be coming up in the year.

The Government of India has requested the state/UTs to develop their export strategy, appoint export commissioners, address infrastructure constraints restricting movement of goods, facilitate refund of value-added tax (VAT)/octroi/state-level cess, address other issues relating to various clearances and build capacity of new exporters in order to promote exports.

EXCHANGE RATE MONITORING

Indian currency has seen frequent exchange rate volatility in recent times. External variables have been changing more frequently than any time in past. This forces India to closely monitor the exchange rate dynamics of the world, its major trade partners and the emerging competitors in its export market. India needs to *rethink its exchange rate policy outlook* and go for a shift in it—this becomes even more clear by considering the following points[19]:

(i) International trading opportunities are becoming scarcer in the aftermath of three major events—global financial crisis, the eurozone crisis and the stock market meltdown of China (2015). The world 'export-GDP ratio' has declined since 2011. Going forward a sharp rise in the US dollar is expected with a corresponding decline in the currencies of India's competitors, notably China and Vietnam. Already, since July 2015, the yuan has depreciated about 11.6 per cent (form July 2015 to December 2016) against the dollar and as a consequence the rupee has appreciated by 6 per cent against the yuan. Given the situation there has been a continuous pressure of capital outflows on India.

(ii) To sustain high growth rate, India needs support of exports in the coming times. And this is only possible once rupee's exchange rate is able to maintains the competitive edge over its competitors in the export market. The rise of countries such as Vietnam, Bangladesh, and the Philippines is a new matter of concern which compete with India across a range of manufacturing and services.

(iii) India's present exchange rate management policy gives unusually high weight to UAE (due to high oil imports and a trans-shipment point for India's exports). But this trade has almost nothing to do with India's export competitiveness. The policy currently considers overall trade in place of the sectoral situations and their relations with the exchange rate. due to this India gives heavy weight to euro, even though it is really Asian countries which are India's main competitors (not Europe).

(iv) Ever since the developed countries came under the grip Great Recession, we have seen 'unconventional monetary policy' being pushed by most of them—with effective interest rates running in negatives, too. While the central banks in the west have been aiming to push up inflation and growth through it, RBI has been balancing them (till *March 2017*). Given the situation, it looks advisable

19. **Economic Survey 2016-17**, Government of India, Ministry of Finance, N. Delhi, Vol. 1, pp. 23-25.

for the RBI (through 'Monetary Policy Committee') to recalibrate its monetary policy outlook.

RTAs BY INDIA

In general, multilateral trade agreements are the first best solutions for deepening global trade and development as they are founded on the core principles of non-discrimination. Meanwhile, RTAs (Regional Trade Agreements) are efforts by nations aimed at deepening economic relations, usually with neighbouring countries, and tend to be *largely political* in nature. With the multilateral trade negotiations process under the WTO being a painfully slow one requiring broad-based consensus, RTAs have progressively assumed greater importance and a growing share in international trade.

While RTAs are broadly *compliant* with WTO mandates and remain broadly *supportive* of the WTO process, they remain **second-best** solutions that are discriminatory in nature against non-members and are inefficient as low cost producing non-members lose out to members. While bilateral RTAs have no equity considerations, mega-regional trading groups may not necessarily be equitable if membership is diverse and small countries may lose out either way—if they are part of it they may not have much say and if they are not, they may stand to lose.

India has always stood for an open, equitable, predictable, non-discriminatory and rule-based international trading system and views RTAs as building blocks in the overall objective of trade liberalization as well as complementing the multilateral trading system under the WTO.

By **March 2017**, India had signed 12 FTAs (Free Trade Agreements) and 6 PTAs (Preferential Trade Agreements) and all of these were in force. The *net impact* of the RTAs on export performance and trade outcome is a mixed bag and requires detailed analysis. India follows a gradual approach

of widening the process of negotiating the FTAs. Presently, negotiations on *24 FTAs* (including review) is under way:[20]

India-Thailand Comprehensive Economic Cooperation Agreement (CECA): Early Harvest Scheme has been implemented on 82 items. So far 29 rounds of India-Thailand Trade Negotiation Committee (ITTNC) meetings have been held. The 29th round was held in Bangkok in June 2015.

India- New Zealand FTA/CECA: Ten rounds of negotiation have been held so far. The 10th Round was held in Delhi by February 2015.

India--SACU (South Africa, Botswana, Lesotho, Swaziland and Namibia) PTA: Five rounds of negotiations have been held so far. The Ninth Joint Ministerial Commission (JMC) meeting was held at Durban in March 2015.

BIMSTEC (Bangladesh, India, Myanmar, Sri Lanka, Thailand, Bhutan and Nepal) FTA: Twenty meetings of the Trade Negotiating Committee (TNC) have taken place. The 20th meeting was held in September 2015 in Khon Kaen Province, Thailand.

India-Canada FTA: Nine rounds of negotiation on the India-Canada Comprehensive Economic Partnership Agreement (CEPA) have so far been held. The ninth round was held in Ottawa, Canada by March 2015.

India--Australia CECA: Nine rounds of negotiations have been held so far. The ninth round was held between by September 2015 in Delhi.

Regional Comprehensive Economic Partnership (RCEP) Agreement among ASEAN + Six FTA Partners (Australia, China, India, Japan, South Korea and New Zealand): Based on the Declaration of the Leaders during the ASEAN Summit in November 2012, negotiations for a

---

20. Ministry of Commerce & Industry, Government of India, N. Delhi, March 2017.

comprehensive economic partnership between the 10 ASEAN member states and its six FTA partners commenced in May 2013. Fourteen rounds of negotiations have so far been held.

NEW FOREIGN TRADE POLICY

The GoI announced the new Foreign Trade Policy 2015–20 on April 1, 2015. The new five year Foreign Trade Policy, 2015–20 provides a framework for increasing exports of goods and services as well as generation of employment and increasing value addition in the country, in keeping with the Make in India. The focus of the new policy is to support both the manufacturing and services sectors, with a special emphasis on improving the 'ease of doing business'. The special features of the FTP 2015–20 are as follows:

(i). Two new schemes have been intorduced, namely—

(a) Merchandise Exports from India Scheme (MEIS) for export of specified goods to specified markets.

(b) Services Exports from India Scheme (SEIS) for increasing exports of notified services, in place of a plethora of schemes earlier, with different conditions for eligibility and usage.

There would be no conditionality attached to any scrips issued under these schemes. Duty credit scrips issued under MEIS and SEIS and the goods imported against these scrips are fully transferable. For grant of rewards under MEIS, the countries have been categorized into 3 Groups, whereas the rates of rewards under MEIS range from 2 per cent to 5 per cent. Under SEIS the selected Services would be rewarded at the rates of 3 per cent and 5 per cent.

(ii) Measures have been adopted to nudge procurement of capital goods from indigenous manufacturers under the EPCG scheme by reducing specific export obligation to 75 per cent of the normal export obligation. This will promote the domestic capital goods manufacturing industry. Such flexibilities will help exporters to develop their productive capacities for both local and global consumption.

(iii) Measures have been taken to give a boost to exports of defense and hi-tech items. At the same time e-Commerce exports of handloom products, books/periodicals, leather footwear, toys and customized fashion garments through courier or foreign post office would also be able to get benefit of MEIS (for values upto INR 25,000). These measures would not only capitalize on India's strength in these areas and increase exports but also provide employment.

(iv) In order to give a boost to exports from SEZs, government has now decided to extend benefits of both the reward schemes (MEIS and SEIS) to units located in SEZs. It is hoped that this measure will give a new impetus to development and growth of SEZs in the country.

(v) Trade facilitation and enhancing the *ease of doing business* are the other major focus areas—

(a) One of the major objective of new FTP is to move towards paperless working in 24×7 environment.

(b) The government has reduced the number of mandatory documents required for exports and imports to three, which is comparable with international benchmarks.

(c) A facility has been created to upload documents in exporter/importer profile and the exporters will not be required to submit documents repeatedly.

(d) Attention has also been paid to simplify various *Aayat Niryat Forms*, bringing in clarity in different provisions, removing ambiguities and enhancing electronic governance.

(e) Approved Exporter System (AES) has been launched to enable manufacturers to self-certify their manufactured goods originating from India with a view to qualifying for preferential treatment under various forms of bilateral and regional trade agreements This will help these manufacturer exporters considerably in getting fast access to international markets.

(vi) A number of steps have been taken for encouraging manufacturing and exports under 100 per cent schemes. The steps include a fast track clearance facility for these units, permitting them to share infrastructure facilities, permitting inter unit transfer of goods and services, permitting them to set up warehouses near the port of export and to use duty free equipment for training purposes.

(vii) Considering the strategic significance of *small and medium scale enterprise* in the manufacturing sector and in employment generation, *MSME Clusters-108* have been identified for focused interventions to boost exports. Outreach activities will be organized in a structured way at these clusters with the help of EPCs and other willing *Industry Partners* and *Knowledge Partners*.

(viii) *Niryat Bandhu Scheme* has been galvanized and repositioned to achieve the objectives of Skill India.

The FTP Statement describes the market and product strategy and measures required for trade promotion, infrastructure development and overall enhancement of the trade ecosystem. It seeks to enable India to respond to the challenges of the external environment, keeping in step with a rapidly evolving international trading architecture and make trade a major contributor to the country's economic growth and development. The Government of India promised to have regular interactions with all stakeholders, including state governments to achieve the national objectives.

Need of Shift: The environment for global trade policy has probably undergone a *paradigm shift* in the aftermath of Brexit and the US elections. The Brexit was motivated by protectionist sentiments in the UK. Similar sentiments are being signalled by the new US government, too. This may lead to sharp appreciation in the US dollar—it has already appreciated 5.3 per cent during November-December 2016, settling at 3.1 per cent higher by January 2017 (against an index of partner currencies). During the most protectionist phase of the USA (mid to late 1980s) a sharp rise was seen in the dollar—caused by tighter monetary policy and relaxing fiscal policy.

A vacuum is being created in international trade leadership under the possible resurgence of protectionist pressures. In such a scenario needs to promote open markets and tap domestic growth. Similar moves are needed from the emerging market economies (EMEs), too. In this way, for India two specific opportunities[21] arise:

(i) India could get much benefits by promoting labour-intensive exports

---

21. **Economic Survey 2016-17**, Government of India, Ministry of Finance, N. Delhi, Vol. 1, pp. 25-26.

and negotiating free trade agreements with the UK and Europe. The potential gains for export and employment are substantial—additional export of US$ 3 billion (specially in the apparel and leather & footwear sectors) and additional employment of 1.5 lakhs.

(ii) The likely retreat of USA from regional initiatives such as the Trans-Pacific Partnership (TPP) in Asia and the Trans-Atlantic Trade and Investment Partnership (TTIP) with the EU, it is possible that the relevance of the WTO might increase. As a major stakeholder and given the geo-political shifts under way, India should proactively pursue to revive WTO and multilateralism.

TRANS-PACIFIC PARTNERSHIP

The **TPP** (Trans-Pacific Partnership) is a *new mega-regional* agreement. The 12 Pacific Rim nations (Australia, Brunei, Canada, Chile, Japan, Malaysia, Mexico, New Zealand, Peru, Singapore, the US and Vietnam) signed the TPP agreement on 5 October 2015. It is likely to set higher standards for goods and services trade and is considered a mega regional FTA which can be a *pioneer* in many ways and is likely to be a *game-changer* for the world economy and global trade.

The block accounts for around 40 per cent of global GDP and around 60 per cent of merchandise trade. In terms of economic size, it is larger than the existing NAFTA (North America Free Trade Area). The agreement is very comprehensive and not only encompasses the scope of tariff-eliminating mega regional trade pacts, but also aims at—

(i) setting higher global standards for international trade through lower benchmarks for non-tariff barriers;

(ii) more stringent labour and environment regulation;

(iii) higher IPRs (intellectual property rights) protection;

(iv) greater transparency in government procurement and limiting advantages to state-owned enterprises (SoEs);

(v) transparency in health care technology, competitiveness and supply chain.

(vi) it also includes new and emerging trade issues and cross-cutting concerns such as *internet* and *digital economy* and participation of state-owned enterprises (SoEs) in global trade and investment.

Experts have highlighted serious impact on the current global trade pattern once this agreement comes into force. India has its own share of concerns regarding it[22]. Meanwhile, by late *January 2017*, the USA (under its new President Mr. Donald Trump) pulled out from the ongoing negotiations of the TPP. Once the US (the biggest force behind it) has opted out from it, the pact looks losing its real steam. This may look a relief for India and other similar economies it may be temporary—as the new dispensation in the country has given clear signs of becoming protective regarding trade and globalisation (these issues were the benchmark of Trump's presidential election campaign).

TRANSATLANTIC TRADE AND INVESTMENT PARTNERSHIP

Considered a companion of the TPP (Trans-Pacific Partnership), the **TTIP** (Transatlantic Trade & Investment Partnership)[23] is a newly proposed trade agreement (a regional trade agreement of different kind which includes

22. We find a very detailed discussion on it in the **Economic Survey 2015-16**, Government of India, Ministry of Finance, N. Delhi (Vol. 2, pp. 76-78) which quoted several international studies in this regard.

23. Based on the several issues of **The Economist**, London, UK from 2013 to March 2017.

investment also) between the European Union and the United States. Planned to be finalised by 2014, the pact is still (by March 2017) under the negotiation process. This agreement touches three broad areas—market access; specific regulation and co-operation. The possible features and its impact are available in international media and other documents as given below:

- The major provisions included under this pact are—dilution in regulatory provisions to promote trade and investment, liberal banking regulation, liberal role and access given to the transnational companies, diluting sovereign powers of the nations.

- As per experts, it could liberalise *one third* of global trade and create millions of new jobs.

- As per the estimates of the European Commission, it will boost the EU's economy by €120 billion, the US economy by €90 billion and the rest of the world by €100 billion.

The agreement has been severely criticised and opposed by majority of the unions, charities, NGOs and environmentalists across Europe. Critics have highlighted several apprehensions also related to it such as—the number of net job gains as there are chances of job losses, and low economic gains accruing at the household level. The reports on the ongoing negotiations and its contents are not available in the public domain as only authorised persons can access them. Whatever comments, reactions or criticisms we find on it are on the multiple leaks which the world had by now through different sources.

As in case of the trans-pacific partnership (TPP), the new government in the USA—the most important force behind the pact—has dropped out (by late *January 2017*) of the TTIP, too. This way, the proposed pact looks becoming weaker before its finalisation. And finalising the partnership without USA is neither possible nor will it have much substance. In this case, the EU may be more open to new regional trade agreements with other nations—India may also explore one such pact with it.

DEGLOBALISATION AND INDIA

Global factors are yet to stabilise since the financial crisis hit the developed economies. Recovery among these economies are getting tough job—even unconventional monetary policies have been tried (pursuing for negative interest rate regime). Meanwhile, several of these economies have signalled 'protectionist' rhetoric—the Brexit. The new government in the USA has already taken various protectionist measures by now and many more are supposed to come in the coming times.

Besides, in past few years the world has seen increased debate on the drawbacks of the globalisation process. Among experts as well as several nations, a general feeling looked evolving against globalisation. The negotiations related to the WTO look almost stalled. At the end of the tunnel, by late 2016, the world witnessed rise in the 'protectionist sentiments' among important economies.

The above-given two events show as if the world (or at least the economies which matter most) has started to move slowly away from the much-celebrated idea of globalisation—*deglobalisation* taking over the world—shrinking scope for multilateral trade and economic interdependence. Again, this lack of willingness towards globalisation among different economies is not of the same degree nor universal to every economy—better say it looks selective.

India's prospects of export growth depends on its trading partners' carrying capacity of globalisation to it. Today, for India, three external developments are of significant consequence—

(i) In the *short-run*, global interest rates (as a result of the US elections and the implied change its fiscal and monetary policy) will impact on India's capital flows and exchange rates. Experts are already expecting high fiscal stimulus, more dependence on unconventional monetary policy, etc. to follow in the developed world.

(ii) The *medium-term* political outlook for globalisation and in particular for the world's 'political carrying capacity for globalisation' may have changed in the wake of recent developments. A strong US dollar and declining competitiveness might incline many countries to follow protectionist policies. This will result into declining global trade hitting India hard.

(iii) Developments in the US, especially the rise of the dollar, will have implications for China's currency and currency policy which will impact India and the world—if China is able to successfully re-balance its economy, the spillover effects will be positive; otherwise quite negative. China with its underlying vulnerabilities remains the country to watch for its potential to *unsettle* the global economy.

India's trade in goods and services both will be important in this case. India's services exports growth will test the world's 'globalisation carrying capacity' in services—depending on the restrictions in developed countries on two variables—*firstly*, the labour mobility and *secondly*, outsourcing.

It is possible that the world's carrying capacity will actually be *much greater* for India's services than it was for Chinese goods. After all, China's export expansion over the past two decades was imbalanced in several ways—

- the country exported far more than it imported;

- it exported manufactured goods to advanced countries, displacing production

there, but imported goods (raw materials) from developing countries; and

- when it did import from advanced economies, it often imported services rather than goods (though capital goods is a major exception).

As a result, China's development created relatively few export-oriented jobs in advanced countries, insufficient to compensate for the jobs lost in manufacturing—and where it did create jobs, these were in advanced services (such as finance), which were not possible for displaced manufacturing workers to obtain.

In contrast, India's expansion may well prove much more balanced:

- India has tended to run a current account deficit, rather than a surplus; and

- while its service exports might also displace workers in advanced countries, their skill set will make relocation to other service activities easier; indeed, they may well simply move on to complementary tasks, such as more advanced computer programming in the IT sector itself.

- on the other hand, since skilled labour in advanced economies will be exposed to Indian competition, their ability to mobilize political opinion might also be greater.[24]

Precisely speaking, the *political backlash* against globalisation in advanced countries, and China's difficulties in rebalancing its economy, could have major implications for India. And it will be advisable for India to close track of the changing global dynamics.

---

24. Based on the discussion given in the **Economic Survey 2016-17**, Government of India, Ministry of Finance, N. Delhi, Vol. 1, pp. 6-9.

16

INTERNATIONAL ECONOMIC ORGANISATIONS & INDIA

*If as T.S. Eliot said that humankind cannot bear too much reality, recent events suggest that the world cannot bear too much globalisation either.**

- ❏ International Monetary System
- ❏ Bretton Woods Development
- ❏ International Monetary Fund
- ❏ World Bank
- ❏ India's BIPA
- ❏ Asian Development Bank

- ❏ OECD
- ❏ World Trade Organization (WTO)
- ❏ Nairobi Negotiations & India
- ❏ BRICS Bank
- ❏ Asian Infrastructure Investment Bank

*Economic Survey 2016-17, Government of India, Ministry of Finance, N. Delhi, Vol. 1, p. 7.

INTERNATIONAL MONETARY SYSTEM

The international monetary system (IMS) refers to the customs, rules, instruments, facilities, and organisations facilitating international (external) payments. Sometimes the IMS is also referred to as an international monetary *order* or *regime*.[1] IMS can be classified according to the way in which exchange rates are determined (i.e., fixed currency regime, floating currency regime or managed exchange regime) and the form foreign reserves take (i.e., gold standard, a pure judiciary standard or a gold-exchange standard).

An IMS is considred good if it fulfils the following *two objectives*[2] in an impartial manner:

(i) maximises the flow of foreign trade and foreign investments, and

(ii) leads to an *equitable* distribution of the gains from trade among the nations of the world.

The evaluation of an IMS is done in terms of *adjustment, liquidity* and *confidence* which it manages to weild.

Adjustment

It refers to the process by which the balance-of-payment (BoP) crises of the nations of the world (or the member nations) are corrected. A good IMS tries to minimise the cost of BoP and time for adjustment for the nations.

Liquidity

It refers to the amount of foreign currency reserves available to settle the BoP crises of the nations. A good IMS maintains as much foreign reserves to mitigate such crises of the nations without any inflationary pressures on the nations.

1. D. Salvatore, *International Economics* (New Jersey: John Wiley & Sons 2005), pp. 737–38; Samuelson and Nordhaus, *Economics* (New Delhi: Tata McGraw-Hill, 2005) pp. 609–12.
2. D. Salvatore, International Economics, p. 738.

Confidence

It refers to the faith the nations of the world should show that the adjustment mechanism of the IMS is working adequately and that foreign reserves will retain their absolute and relative values. This confidence is based on the transparent knowledge information about the IMS.

BRETTON WOODS DEVELOPMENT

As the powerful nations of the world were hopeful of a new and more stable world order with the emergence of the UNO, on the contrary, they were also anxious for a more homogenous world financial order, after the Second World War. The representatives of the USA, the UK and 42 other (total 44 countries) nations met at Bretton Woods, New Hampshire, USA in July 1944 to decide a new international monetary system. The International Monetary Fund (IMF) and the World Bank (with its first group-institution IBRD) were set up together—popularly called as the *Bretton Woods' twins*[3]—both having their headquarters in Washington DC, USA.

3. For the new international monetary system, basically two plans were presented in the meeting—one by the US delegation led by *Harry D. White* (of the US Treasury) and the British delegation led by *John Meynard Keynes.* It was the US plan which was ultimately agreed upon.

J.M. Keynes had proposed a more impartial, practical and over-arching idea via his plan at Bretton Woods. His suggestions basically included three things:

(i) Proposal to set up an International Clearing Union (ICU), a central bank of all central banks, with its own currency (Keynes named this currency *'bancor'*)—to mitigate the balance of payment crises of member nations.

This bank was supposed to penalise (*no such provision in the IMF*) the countries holding trade surpluses (with a global tax of one per cent per month) on the ground that such countries were keeping world demand low by under-purchasing the products produced by other countries. The corpus collected via this tax was to be used to maintain an international buffer stock of primary goods (i.e., food articles)—to be used in the periods of food shortages among the member nations. (*In place, under the IMF provisions trade deficit countries are penalised*.)

(Contd...)

INTERNATIONAL MONETARY FUND

The International Monetary Fund (IMF) came up in 1944 whose Articles came into force on the 27 December, 1945 with the main functions as exchange rate regulation, purchasing short-term foreign currency liabilities of the member nations from around the world, allotting special drawing rights (SDRs) to the member nations and the most important one as the bailor to the member economies in the situation of any BoP crisis.

The *main functions*[4] of the IMF are as given below:

(i) to facilitate international monetary cooperation;

(ii) to promote exchange rate stability and orderly exchange arrangements;

(iii) to assist in the establishment of a multilateral system of payments and the elimination of foreign exchange restrictions; and

(iv) to assist member countries by temporarily providing financial resources to correct mal-adjustment in their balance of payments (BoPs).

(ii) For the reconstruction of war-devastated Europe, a *fund* was to be set up, on the basis of this plan for Relief and Reconstruction (in place of it the US-sponsored *Marshall Plan* took care of the needs of Europe).

(iii) There was a proposal of creating Commodity Buffer Stock to be operated by an International Trade Organization (ITO). This stock of primary goods was to be used to stabilise their prices in the international market.

The operation of this ITO making purchases when the world prices were low and selling when the prices became high. The buffer stock operations, however, were to be helpful to the poor countries, Keynes was primarily interested in stabilising the input prices of the rich countries. (*Though the charter of the ITO was drawn up and other formalities completed, it was never born because of US opposition.*) *For further readings see* D. Salvatore, *International Economics,* 742–43; B. Dasgupta, *Globalisation : India's Adjustment Experience* (New Delhi: Sage, 2005), p. 48.

4. *Basic Facts About the United Nations* (New York: United Nations, 2000), pp. 55–137.

The Board of Governors of the IMF consists of one Governor and one Alternate Governor from each member country. For India, Finance Minister is the Ex-officio Governor while the RBI Governor is the Alternate Governor on the Board.

The day-to-day management of the IMF is carried out by the Managing Director who is Chairman *(currently, Ms Christine Lagarde)* of the Board of Executive Directors. Board of Executive Directors consists of 24 directors appointed/elected by member countries/group of countries —is the executive body of the IMF. India is represented at the IMF by an Executive Director (*currently Arvind Virmani*), who also represents three other countries in India's constituency, viz., Bangladesh, Sri Lanka and Bhutan.

India's Quota & Ranking

IMF reviews members' quotas once in every five years—last done in December 2010—here, India consented for its quota increase. After this India's quota (together with its 3 constituency countries) has increased to **2.75** per cent (from 2.44 per cent) and it has become the **8th** (from 11th) largest quota holding country among the **24** constituencies. In absolute terms, India's quota has increased to SDR 13,114.4 million (from SDR 5,821.5 million) which is an increase of approximately US $ 11.5 billion or Rs. 56,000 crore). While 25 per cent of the quota is to be paid in *cash* (i.e., in 'Reserve' currency), the balance 75 per cent can be paid in *securities*.[5]

Once a member nation has signed the *EFF* (Extended Fund Facility) agreement with the IMF,

---

5. These securities are non-interest bearing note purchase agreements issued by the RBI which can be encashed by the IMF anytime as per its requirement. They do not entail any cash outgo unless the IMF calls upon India to encash a portion of these notes. The 'Reserve' (paid in 'cash') asset portion of the quots is counted as a part of country's 'Reserves'.

borrowing[6] can be done by the member nation—India signed this agreement in the fiscal 1981–82. ***India has been borrowing*** from the IMF due to critical balance of payment (BoP) situations—once between 1981–84 (SDR 3.9 billion) and next during 1991 (SDR 3.56 billion). All the loans taken from the IMF have been repaid. India is now a *contributor* to the IMF as it participates in the Financial Transactions Plan (FTP)[7] of the IMF since September 2002—at this time India was in strong balance of payment situation and in a comfortable forex reserves position.

Current US/EU Financial Crises: Challenges Regarding International Payments

The recent financial crises of the US and the EU nations have raised the questions of the challenges of international payments once again. At this crucial juncture, the world seems tossing the idea of a reserved currency for all international payments—as if the famous Keynesian idea of such a currency (Bancor) is going for a kind of revival. The **Bancor** was a supranational currency that John Maynard Keynes and E. F. Schumacher[8] conceptualised in the years 1940–42 which the United Kingdom proposed to introduce after the Second World War. The proposed currency was, viz., be used in international trade as a unit of account within a multilateral barter clearing system, the *International Clearing Union*, which would also have to be founded. The Bancor was to be backed by barter and its value expressed in weight of gold. However, this British proposal could not prevail against the interests of the United States, which at the Bretton Woods conference established the US Dollar as the world key currency. Milton Friedman[9], the famous US economist insisted that Keynes' theories were incorrect who believed that, 'inflation was highly destructive and that only monetary policy could control it and that monetary policy is a heavyweight instrument and cannot be used for short-term economic management.'

Since the outbreak of the financial crisis in 2008 ***Keynes's proposal*** has been revived—in a speech delivered in March 2009 entitled *Reform the International Monetary System*, Zhou Xiaochuan, the Governor of the People's Bank of China called Keynes's bancor approach **farsighted** and proposed the adoption of International Monetary Fund (IMF) special drawing rights (SDRs) as a global reserve currency as a response to the financial crisis of 2007–2010. He argued that a national currency was unsuitable as a global reserve currency because of the *Triffin dilemma*[10]—the difficulty faced by reserve currency issuers in trying to simultaneously achieve their domestic monetary policy goals and meet other countries' demand for reserve currency.[11] A similar analysis was articulated in the Report of the United Nation's *Experts on Reforms of the International*

---

6. Such facility from it is available once the member country has signed the agreement with the IMF called as the Extended Fund Facility (EFF). Popularly, this is known as the *'Conditionalities of the IMF'* under which India started its Economic Reform Programme in 1991-92 once it borrowed from the IMF in the wake of the BoP crisis of 1990–91.

7. FTP is the mechanism of the IMF through which it finances/repays its operations—member nations contribute money into it from their 'quota resources' on which they get 'interest'.

8. *E. F. Schumacher, Multilateral Clearing Economica,* New Series, Vol. 10, No. 38 (May, 1943), pp. 150-165.

---

9. *M. Friedman.,* (1968) *The American Economic Review,* Vol. 58, No. 1, pp. 1-17.

10. *Zhou Xiaochuan,* 'Reform the International Monetary System', BIS Review 2009, Bank of International Settlements, Basel, Switzerland, 28 November, 2011.

11. *Zhou Xiaochuan, Financial Times, 12th Dec. 2011.*

Monetary and Financial System[12] as well as in a recent IMF's study.[13]

WORLD BANK

The World Bank (WB) Group today consists of *five* closely associated institutions propitiating the role of development in the member nations in different areas. A brief account is as follows:[14]

IBRD

The International Bank for Reconstruction and Development is the oldest of the WB institutions which started functioning (1945) in the area of reconstruction of the war-ravaged regions (World War II) and later for the development of the middle-income and credit-worthy poorer economies of the world. Human development was the main focus of the developmental lending with a very low interest rate (1.55 per cent per annum)—the areas of focus being agriculture, irrigation, urban development, healthcare, family welfare, dairy development, etc. It commenced lending for India in 1949.

After the process of reforms started in the World Bank in 2010, India was alloted additional shares in IBRD (now holds 56,739 shares accounting to US $ 6,844.7 million). With this India emerged as the 7th largest shareholder (up from the 11th position) in IBRD with voting power of 2.91 per cent (up from 2.77 per cent).[15]

IDA

The International Development Agency (IDA) which is also known as the *soft window* of the WB was set up in 1960 with the basic aim of developing infrastructural support among the member nations, long-term lending for the development of economic services. Its loans, known as *credits* are extended mainly to economies with less than $895 per capita income. The credits are for a period of 35–40 years, *interest*-free, except for a small charge to cover administrative costs. Repayment begins after a 10-year grace period. There was no human angle to its lending. But now there remain no hard and fast differences between the purposes for the IBRD and IDA lending.

Every year developing nations make enough diplomatic attempts to carve out maximum loan disbursal for themselves. India had been the *biggest beneficiary* of the IDA support. The total support (IBRD + IDA) for India had been $ 91.81 billion till date.[16]

IFC

The International Finance Corporation (IFC) was set up in 1956 which is also known as the *private arm* of the WB. It lends money to private sector companies of its member nations. The interest rate charged is commercial but comparatively low. There are many attractive features of IFC's lending. It finances and provides advice for private-public ventures and projects in partnership with private investors and, through its advisory work, helps governments of the member nations to create conditions that stimulate the flow of both domestic and foreign private savings and investment.

It focuses on promoting economic development by encouraging the growth of productive enterprises and efficient capital markets in its member countries. It participates in an investment only when it can make a special

12. Recommendations by the Commission of Experts of the President of the General Assembly on reforms of the international monetary and financial system, UNO, 20th March, 2009.

13. *Reserve Accumulation and International Monetary Stability, IMF,* Washington DC, 13th April, 2010.

14. Based on *Basic Facts About the United Nations,* 52–55; Publication Division, *India 2004* (New Delhi: Government of India, 2007); Publication Division, *India 2013* (New Delhi: Government of India, 2014).

15. Publication Division, *India 2014* (New Delhi: Government of India, 2015), p. 322.

16. Publication Division, *India 2013*, p. 415.

contribution that complements the role of market investors (as a foreign financial investor (FFI). It also plays a catalytic role, stimulating and mobilising private investment in the developing world by demonstrating that investments there too can be profitable.

We have seen a great upsurge in the IFC investments in India which has undoubtedly strengthened the foreign investors' confidence in the Indian economy.

MIGA

The Multilateral Investment Guarantee Agency (MIGA), set up in 1988 encourages foreign investment in developing economies by offering insurance (guarantees) to foreign private investors against loss caused by *non-commercial (i.e., political) risks*, such as currency transfer, expropriation, war and civil disturbance. It also provides technical assistance to help countries disseminate information on investment opportunities.

ICSID

The International Centre for Settlement of Investment Disputes (ICSID), set up in 1966 is an investment dispute settlement body whose decisions are binding on the parties. It was established under the 1966 *Convention on the Settlement of Investment Disputes between States and Nationals of Other States.* Though recourse to the centre is voluntary, but once the parties have agreed to arbitration, they cannot withdraw their consent unilaterally. It settles the investment disputes arising between the investing foreign companies and the host countries where the investments have been done.

India is not its member (that is why the Enron issue was out of its preview). It is believed that being signatory to it encourages the foreign investment flows into an economy, but risks independent sovereign decisions, too.

INDIA'S BIPA

As part of the Economic Reforms Programme initiated in 1991, the foreign investment policy of the Government of India was liberalised and negotiations undertaken with a number of countries to enter into *Bilateral Investment Promotion & Protection Agreement (BIPA)* in order to **promote and protect on reciprocal basis investment of the investors**. Government of India have, so far, *(as by July 2012)* signed BIPAs with 82 countries out of which 72 BIPAs have already come into force and the remaining agreements are in the process of being enforced.[17] In addition, agreements have also been finalised and/or being negotiated with a number of other countries.

The **objective** of the BIPA is to promote and protect the interests of investors of either country in the territory of other country. Such agreements increase the comfort level of the investors by assuring a minimum standard of treatment in all matters and provides for justifiability of disputes with the host country *(it should be noted here that India is not a member of the World Bank group's body, the ICSID, serving the same purpose. BIPA is India's version. While the former is a multilateral body, the latter is a bilateral one).*

ASIAN DEVELOPMENT BANK

Set up in 1966 with 31 founding members (India being one of them), today (by *March 2017*) it has grown to encompass 67 members—of which 48 are from Asia and Pacific and 19 from outside. It has

---

17. Government of India, **Ministry of Commerce & Industry,** Government of India, N. Delhi, as on 5 April 5, 2016.

its headquarters situated at Manila, Philippines. The *purpose* of the Bank is to foster economic growth and co-operation in the region of Asia and the Far East and to contribute to economic development of the developing member countries, collectively and individually. The six *functions* of the Bank are as clubbed below:

(i) Promoting investment—public and private—and harmonious regional development with special regard to less developed member countries;

(ii) Coordinating development policies and plans (on request); promoting intra-regional trade; providing technical assistance in financing, execution and project proposals;

(iii) Co-operating with the UNO and other international institutions—public and private—and undertaking other activities and provide other services advancing its purpose.

India's subscription to the Bank's capital stock is 7.190 per cent with a voting power of 6.050 per cent (as per the *ADB Annual Report, 2016*).

India started borrowing from ADB's Ordinary Capital Resources (OCR) in 1986. The Bank's lending has been mainly in the energy, transport and communications, finance, industry and social infrastructure sectors.

The Bank has extended technical assistance to India in addition to loans from its OCR window. The technical assistance provided include support for institutional strengthening, effective project implementation and policy reforms as well as for project preparation.

India holds the position of Executive Director on the Board of Directors of the Bank—its constituency comprises India, Bangladesh, Bhutan, Lao PDR and Tajikistan. The Finance Minister is India's Governor on the Board of Governors of the Asian Development Bank and Secretary (EA) is the Alternate Governor.

OECD

The roots[18] of the Organisation for Economic Co-operation and Development (OECD), Paris, go back to the rubble of Europe after World War II. Determined to avoid the mistakes of their predecessors in the wake of World War I, European leaders realised that the best way to ensure lasting peace was to encourage co-operation and reconstruction, rather than punish the defeated.

The Organisation for European Economic Cooperation (OEEC) was established in 1947 to run the US-financed **Marshall Plan** for reconstruction of a continent ravaged by war. By making individual governments recognise the interdependence of their economies, it paved the way for a new era of cooperation that was to change the face of Europe. Encouraged by its success and the prospect of carrying its work forward on a global stage, Canada and the US joined OEEC members in signing the new OECD Convention on 14 December, 1960. The Organisation for Economic Co-operation and Development (OECD) was officially born on September 30, 1961, when the Convention entered into force.

Other countries joined in, starting with Japan in 1964. Today, **35** OECD member countries worldwide regularly turn to one another to identify problems, discuss and analyse them, and promote policies to solve them. The track record is striking. The US has seen its national wealth almost *triple* in the five decades since the OECD was created, calculated in terms of gross domestic product per head of population. Other OECD countries have seen similar, and in some cases even more spectacular, progress.

There are many countries that a few decades ago were still only minor players on the world stage—China, India and Brazil have emerged as

---

18. Publication Division, *India 2012* (New Delhi: Government of India, 2013), p. 418.

new economic giants. Most of the countries that formed part of the former Soviet bloc have either joined the OECD or adopted its standards and principles to achieve the common goals. Russia is negotiating to become a member of the OECD, and now the organisation has close relations with Brazil, China, India, Indonesia and South Africa through its 'enhanced engagement' programme. Together with them, the OECD brings around its table **40** countries that account for **80** per cent of world trade and investment, giving it a pivotal role in addressing the challenges facing the world economy.

India & OECD: India has got 'enhanced engagement' (since 2007) with the body 'accession' (membership) to it is distinct—though it has potential in future leading to it. The accession process to it is complex and longer as it involves a series of examinations to assess a country's ability to meet its OECD standards in a wide range of policy areas. Meanwhile, India's relationship with the OECD has developed steadily since 1998 (when it joined its Steel Committee)— since 2007 being its 'Key Partner'. By *early 2017*, India used to participate as an *Associate* or *Participant* in 21 OECD bodies and adheres to 9 OECD legal instruments, making it an important contributor to several areas of importance—from corporate governance to fiscal matters to nuclear energy. Furthermore, India plays an active role in OECD's regional activities in Asia together with co-operation on various international fora.

WORLD TRADE ORGANIZATION (WTO)

The World Trade Organization (WTO) came into being as a result of the evolution of the multilateral trading system starting with the establishment of the General Agreement on Tariffs and Trade (GATT) in 1947. The protracted Uruguay Round negotiations spanning the period 1986–1994, which resulted in the establishment of the WTO, substantially extended the reach of multilateral rules and disciplines related to trade in goods, and introduced multilateral rules applicable to trade in agriculture (Agreement on Agriculture), trade in services (General Agreement on Trade in Services—GATS) as well as Trade Related Intellectual Property Rights (TRIPS). A separate understanding on WTO dispute settlement mechanism (DSU) and trade policy review mechanism (TPRM) was also agreed upon.

The WTO provides a rule based, transparent and predictable multilateral trading system. The WTO rules envisage non-discrimination in the form of National Treatment and *Most Favoured Nation (MFN)* treatment to India's exports in the markets of other WTO Members. National Treatment ensures that India's products once imported into the territory of other WTO Members would not be discriminated vis-à-vis the domestic products in those countries. MFN treatment principle ensures that members do not discriminate among various WTO members. If a member country believes that the due benefits are not accruing to it because of trade measures by another WTO member, which are violative of WTO rules and disciplines, it may file a dispute under the Dispute Settlement Mechanism (DSM) of the WTO. There are also contingency provisions built into WTO rules, enabling member countries to take care of exigencies like balance of payment problems and situations like a surge in imports. In case of unfair trade practices causing injury to the domestic producers, there are provisions to impose Anti-Dumping or Countervailing duties as provided for in the Anti-Dumping Agreement and the Subsidies and Countervailing Measures Agreement.

Membership: The present membership[19] of the WTO is **164**. The last member to join was Afghanistan (March 2016) after a long negotiation process of eleven years. Other than its members,

---

19. As per the **WTO** website, March 2017.

at present, there are 22 observer governments including Afghanistan, Holy See (Vatican), Iran, Iraq, Libya, Uzbekistan, etc. As per the guidelines of the WTO, observers (except Holy See) must start accession negotiations within *five years* of becoming observers.

Ministerial Conferences: Ministerial Conferences are the highest decision-making body of the WTO which is to meet at least every two years. These conferences bring all members together which are countries or separate customs territories. During these conferences decisions on all matters can be taken. By now, there has been 10 such conferences of the body—the *10th Ministerial Conference* took place in *Nairobi*, Kenya in 15-19 December 2015.

Previous conferences: *Bali* (3-6 December 2013); *Geneva* (15-17 December 2011); *Geneva* (30 November–2 December 2009); *Hong Kong* (13–18 December 2005); *Cancun* (10-14 September 2003); *Doha* (9–13 November 2001); *Seattle* (30 November – 3 December, 1999); *Geneva* (18–20 May 1998) and *Singapore* (9–13 December 1996).

NAIROBI NEGOTIATIONS & INDIA

The WTO held its 10th Ministerial Conference in Nairobi, Kenya during 15–19 December 2015. This was the first such meeting to be hosted by an African nation. The outcomes of the Conference, referred to as the *Nairobi Package*, are as given below[20]:

(i) The Nairobi Declaration reflects divergence amongst the WTO membership on the relevance of reaffirming the *Doha Development Agenda (DDA)* as the basis of future negotiations. This was despite the fact that India, along with many other developing countries, from groups such as the G-33, LDCs, and the Africa

Group, wanted a reaffirmation of the mandate of the Doha Round. While reflecting that there are divergences, the Ministerial Declaration also notes the "strong commitment of all Members to advance negotiations on the remaining Doha issues". It records that WTO work would maintain development at its centre. It also reaffirms that provisions for special and differential treatment shall remain integral.

(ii) As the future of the Doha Round appeared in doubt, India sought and succeeded in obtaining a re-affirmative Ministerial Decision on *Public Stockholding for Food Security Purposes* honouring both the **Bali** Ministerial and General Council Decisions. The decision commits members to engage constructively in finding a ***permanent solution*** to this issue.

(iii) A large group of developing countries has long been seeking an SSM (Special Safeguard Mechanism) for *agricultural products*. In order to ensure that this issue remains on the agenda of future discussion in the WTO, India negotiated a Ministerial Decision which recognizes that developing countries will have the right to have recourse to an SSM as envisaged in the mandate. Members will continue to negotiate the mechanism in dedicated sessions of the Committee on Agriculture in Special Session.

(iv) It was also agreed to the elimination of *agricultural export subsidies* subject to the preservation of special and differential treatment for developing countries such as a longer phase-out period for transportation and marketing export subsidies for exporting agricultural products. Developed countries have committed to removing export subsidies

20. Ministry of Finance, **Economic Survey 2015–16** (New Delhi: Government of India, 2016), Vol. 2, pp. 73–75.

immediately, except for a few agricultural products, and developing countries will do so by 2018.

(v) Developing countries will keep the flexibility to cover *marketing and transport subsidies* for agriculture exports until the end of 2023, and the LDCs and net food-importing developing countries would have additional time to cut such export subsidies. The Ministerial Decision contains disciplines to ensure that other export policies are not used as a disguised form of subsidies. These disciplines include—

  (a) terms to limit the benefits of financing support to agriculture exporters;

  (b) rules on state enterprises engaging in agriculture trade; and

  (c) disciplines to ensure that food aid does not negatively affect domestic production.

(vi) One of the Decisions adopted extends the relevant provision to prevent *'ever-greening'* of patents in the pharmaceuticals sector. This decision would help in maintaining an affordable and accessible supply of *generic medicines*.

(vii) India supported outcomes on issues of interest to LDCs including enhanced preferential rules of origin for LDCs and preferential treatment for LDC services providers. India already offers duty-free, quota-free access scheme to all LDCs, which provides a comprehensive coverage with simple, transparent and liberal rules of origin. India has also recently (late 2015) made available substantial and commercially meaningful preferences in services to LDCs.

(viii) The issue of *fisheries* subsidies could not be resolved due to lack of consensus. Including India, several other countries (China, Egypt, South Africa, Korea and Saudi Arabia, etc) were opposed to disciplining rules on fisheries subsidies due to the lack of clarity.

(ix) On the issue of *Anti-dumping*, India strongly opposed a proposal that would give greater power to the WTO's Anti-Dumping Committee to review Members' practices. Due to lack of convergence, no outcome was achieved.

(x) A group of 53 WTO members, including both developed and developing countries, agreed on the timetable for implementing a deal to *eliminate tariffs* on 201 Information Technology products. This duty-free market will be available to all WTO members (even to India, which was not party to the agreement).

(xi) As regards the introduction of other **new issues** for discussion, the Declaration acknowledges the differences in views and states that any decision to launch negotiations multilaterally on such issues would need to be agreed by all Members. The rich (developed) countries wanted the introduction of new issues of their interests which included—*global value chain, e-commerce, competition laws, labour, environment* and *investments*.

BRICS BANK

Together with the process of globalisation world regional forces have also been asserting their power through different short of alignments— the *Fortaleza Declaration* of heads of state (late July 2014) from Brazil, Russia, India, China, and South Africa (the BRICS countries) is another such attempt—creation of a BRICS Bank i.e., New Development Bank (NDB). Major highlights about the bank are as given below:

(i) The bank will have initial subscribed capital of $50 billion—eqaully shared by the five nations.

(ii) The capital base is to be used for funding infrastructure and 'sustainable development' projects in the BRICS countries initially.

(iii) Other low and middle-income countries will be able get funding as time progresses.

(iv) A *Contingent Reserve Arrangement* (CRA) of $100 billion is to be also created to provide additional liquidity protection to member-nations during balance of payments problems.

(v) The CRA is being funded 41 per cent by China, 18 per cent each from Brazil, India, and Russia, and 5 per cent from South Africa.

(vi) CRA, according to the Declaration, is 'a framework for the provision of *currency swaps* in response to actual or potential short-term balance of payments pressures.'

More than the establishment of the NDB, the Fortaleza Declaration is remarkable for adoption of **one-nation one-vote** prescription for the proposed bank. The Bretton Woods institutions (the World Bank and the International Monetary Fund) have structures that are not equitable.

As per the experts, *two factors* have triggered the birth of the NDB:

(a) BRICS have *emerged as a big economic power*, and solidified their ties in terms of commerce with the emerging market economies and developing countries (EMDCs) and they are a force to reckon with in the global economy.

(b) Their *disenchantment* with the Bretton Woods institutions has been growing over the years.

Two statements of the *Fortaleza Declaration* make the situation more clear—

(i) "We are confronted with persistent political instability and conflict in various global hotspots and non-conventional emerging threats. On the other hand, international governance structures designed within a different power configuration show increasingly evident signs of losing legitimacy and effectiveness, as transitional and ad hoc arrangements become increasingly prevalent, often at the expense of multilateralism."

(ii) "We believe the BRICS are an important force for incremental change and reform of current institutions towards more representative and equitable governance, capable of generating more inclusive global growth and fostering a stable, peaceful and prosperous world."

The BRICS bank development comes at a time when reforms at the Bretton Woods institutions fail to fructify for one reason or the other and with the US and European nations still not reconciled to concede BRICS nations a greater voice in the governance structure of the Bretton-Woods institutions.

Whether the BRICS-sponsored NDB will be a fitting alternative to the Bretton Woods twin depends on a host of factors. Major ones of these factors, among others, are its ability—

(i) to put in place a conflict resolution mechanism,

(ii) to devise a robust credit appraisal mechanism, and

(iii) to put in place an effective supervisory regime.

The BRICS-sponsored development bank is not an isolated and unique initiative. Similar initiatives had sprung up in the past to blunt the might of Bretton-Woods twin. *Development Bank of Latin America* (created by *Andean* nations) in the

1960s, the Chiang Mai Initiative in early 2000s (of 10 ASEAN nations plus China, South Korea and Japan) to establish a network of bilateral *currency swap pacts* in the wake of Asian currency crisis, and the establishment of the *Bank of South* by Latin American countries in 2009 were the result of escalating dissatisfaction with the US-dominated IMF and World Bank.

ASIAN INFRASTRUCTURE INVESTMENT BANK

The AIIB (Asian Infrastructure Investment Bank) was first proposed by the Chinese President Xi Jinping in October 2013. A year later, at its official launch in Beijing, 21 Asian nations, including China, had signed up to be the foundation members. Currently another 21 nations—including Australia, the United Kingdom, New Zealand, Germany and France—have expressed a desire to join as well. An interesting applicant is Taiwan—which signed up just before the April 1, 2015 deadline—although issues around its membership name may complicate the deal. Russia also left it to the last minute to fire in its application. Chinese media reported that only 30 of the 42 member applications have been accepted. The Chinese foreign ministry has said that the full list of countries approved as founding members would be released by mid-April 2015.

The AIIB is aimed at providing finance to infrastructure projects in the Asia region, as a multilateral instituion. It is planned to operate broadly in the same manner as existing multilateral development banks (MDBs) such as the World Bank and the Asian Development Bank (ADB). While much of the debate is centred on whether the AIIB will complement or compete with existing organisations, it is intended to be more a commercial bank—with nations as shareholders, than a purely development aid institution. The AIIB will start with an authorised **capital base** of US$ 1 billion to be enhanced to **US $ 100 billion**.

Experts have termed it as a rival for the International Monetary Fund (IMF), the World Bank (WB) and the Asian Development Bank (ADB), which are regarded as dominated by developed countries like the United States.[21] The United Nations has addressed the launch of the AIIB as 'scaling up financing for sustainable development' and for the concern of Global Economic Governance.[22]

As per the experts and analysts, there are **several factors** which are behind such an initiative coming from China. Major ones are as given below:

(i) The Chinese government has been frustrated with what it regards as the slow pace of reforms and governance, and wants greater input in global established institutions like the IMF, World Bank and Asian Development Bank which it claims are dominated by American, European and Japanese interests.

(ii) The ADB, a Manila-based regional development bank designed to facilitate economic development in Asia, estimated in a report that developing Asian countries have an infrastructure demand of about US$ 8 trillion between 2010–2020—$2.5 trillion for roads and railroads, $4.1 trillion for power plants and transmission, $1.1 trillion for telecommunications, and $0.4 trillion for water and sanitation investments.[23]

(iii) Oxford Economics reported that by

---

21. The Guardian, 'Support for China-led development bank grows despite US opposition', UK edition, 13 March, 2015.

22. United Nations Financing for Development Office, 'Global Economic Governance', New York, 20 March, 2015.

23. *The Economist*, *'An Asian Infrastructure Bank: Only Connect'*, 4 October, 2013; Biswa N. Bhattacharyay, *Estimating Demand for Infrastructure in Energy, Transport, Telecommunications, Water and Sanitation in Asia and the Pacific: 2010-2020*, Asian Development Bank Institute, 9 September, 2010.

2025, the region will constitute 60 per cent of global infrastructure investment, with China's share alone is expected to increase from around 22 per cent to 36 per cent over the next decade.

(iv) Despite the significant economic growth enjoyed by countries such as China, India, and South Korea in recent decades, many countries among the developing Asian regions are still mired in poverty, suffering from a profound lack of access to modern-day necessities such as sanitation, a reliable power grid, and adequate transportation and communications networks.

(v) It is believed that the new bank could allow Chinese capital to finance these projects and allow it a greater role to play in the economic development of the region commensurate with its growing economic and political clout.

Stand of the USA and Japan: The United States, Japan and Canada remain firmly on the sidelines despite a number of their closest allies and partners recently breaking ranks. The US has argued that the AIIB doubles up on existing organisations, such as the World Bank and ADB, but doubts it will have adequate transparency and governance standards. However, it appears the US may be softening its stance. Japan has said it would not be bound by a deadline not ruling out the possibility of joining in. Though the US has been openly opposing this move some experts view that the US in place of opposing it should work with it. Experts have suggested that China is promoting a solution to the shortage of infrastructure capital in Asia and there is nothing wrong in supporting it.[24]

Size of the AIIB: The AIIB will be one of the largest development banks, but still a fair bit smaller than the European Development Bank,

World Bank and ADB. It will start off about the same size as the *BRICS Development Bank*, which was formed by Chinese initiation with Brazil, Russia, India and South Africa in 2014.

Based on the lending capital ratios of the World Bank and European Development Bank —the AIIB could extend loans for infrastructure spending at around 100 per cent to 175 per cent of its subscribed capital. This would mean having outstanding loans of up to $US175 billion. With Public Private Partnerships and increased subscriptions, considerably larger amounts could leveraged for projects in the future.

An edge to China: The Bank is supposed to give China an edge in the global economy, major ones are—

(i) The AIIB will be a better way for China to deploy its massive foreign exchange reserves which are currently earning next to nothing in US Treasury bonds. China believes that the commercial financing of infrastructure differentiates the AIIB from the likes of the ADB which places a greater emphasis on poverty reduction.

(ii) The AIIB also supports China's strategic interests in its hugely ambitious 'Silk Road Economic Belt' policy.

(iii) By exporting technology, transferring development know-how, and facilitating industrialisation using Chinese long-term finance to the under-developed economies, China will not only find a bigger market, promote prosperity of all nations along the 'Belt and Road', but also diversify its foreign asset portfolio.

(iv) It will make China emerge a much bigger global power player which is supposed to be keen to challenge America's long-established strategy of institutionalising power in a rules-based order. The case of the AIIB shows that China now seeks to

---

define this order for itself, with the battle for influence in Asia increasingly fought through rules and institutions.

(v) The so-called 'rules based order' was set up after the 2nd World War through policies such as the Bretton Woods agreement which established US dominated organisations such as the World Bank and IMF in which China plays a very small role.

Members of multilateral development banks, historically, enjoy benefit such as getting ahead of the queue for loans and enjoying a greater chance of success for national firms competing for project work. Put bluntly, without signing up it is highly likely that a large chunk of the billions of dollars worth of work on offer will simply be doled out to Chinese companies. Before conclusive remarks could be drawn, it will better to keep watching the future developments regarding the new bank.

CHAPTER 17

TAX STRUCTURE IN INDIA

> *Through taxes, government in reality decides how to draw the required resources from the nation's households and businesses for public purposes— the money raised so is the 'vehicle' by which real resources are transferred from private goods to public goods.* *

* See Paul A. Samuelson and William D. Nordhaus, **Economics**, The McGraw-Hill Company, New York, 2005, pp. 327–340. Also see Joseph E. Stiglitz and Carl E. Walsh, **Economics**, W. W. Norton, New Yok, 4th Edition, 2006, pp. 380–86.

TAX

Modern economics *defines* tax as a mode of income redistribution.[1] There might be other ways also to look at it—the usual meaning of tax people think is that a tax is imposed by the government to fulfil its important obligations on the expenditure front.[2] We may take an example to see how taxes redistribute income:

Suppose an economy has a flat rate of income tax 30 per cent. Just see the impact of this tax on the income disparity of two people A and B earning Rs. 50,000 and Rs. 80,000, respectively.

Indivi-dual	Nominal Income	Income Disparity before Tax	Income after Paying Tax	Income Disparity after Tax
A	Rs. 50,000	Rs. 30,000	Rs. 35,000	Rs. 21,000
B	Rs. 80,000		Rs. 56,000	

We see here through the above-given Table as how the income disparity between two individuals A and B decreases from Rs. 30,000 to Rs. 21,000 after paying taxes—this is the *first level* when incomes of these individuals have got re-distributed.

Now the money the government has got by tax collection, i.e., Rs. 39,000 (Rs. 15,000 + Rs. 24,000) will be spent on different sectors—infrastructure, education, health etc.—which will provide services to each and everybody alike. Here income is re-distributed at the *secondary* level. Consider a person who pays income tax, but does not take services of government schools for his children's education, nor goes to the government hospitals for medical services and compare him with a person who has no option other than

the government schools and the hospitals—the higher tax payer getting no government services and a lower tax payer getting all the services. Here income looks re-distributed from the consumption side.

Incidence of Tax

The point where tax looks as being imposed is known as the incidence of tax—the event of tax imposition.[3]

Impact of Tax

The point where tax makes its effect felt is known as the impact of tax—the after effect of tax imposition.[4]

Direct Tax

The tax which has incidence and impact both at the same point is the direct tax—the person who is hit, the same person bleeds.[5] As for example income tax, interest tax, etc.

Indirect Tax

The tax which has incidence and impact at the different points is the indirect tax—the person who is hit does not bleed[6] someone else's blood. As, for example, excise, sales tax, etc., are imposed on either the producers or the traders, but it is the general consumers who bear the burden of tax.

METHODS OF TAXATION

There are three methods of taxation prevalent in economies with their individual merits and demerits.

---

1. P.A. Samuelson and W.D. Nordhaus, *Economics,* (New Delhi: Tata McGraw Hill, 2005), p. 327.

2. For further reference, J.E. Stiglitz and C.E. Walsh, *Economics,* (New York: W.W. Norton & Company, 2006), pp. 378–79.

3. Samuelson and Nordhaus, *Economics,* pp. 75–77.

4. Ibid., pp. 75–77.

5. Ibid., p. 329.

6. Ibid., p. 329.

Progressive Taxation

This method has increasing rates of tax for increasing value or volume on which the tax is being imposed.[7] Indian income tax is a typical example of it. The idea here is less tax on the people who earn less and higher tax on the people who earn more—classifying income earners into different slabs. This method is believed to discourage more earnings by the individual to support low growth and development unintentionally. Being poor is rewarded while richness is punished. Tax payers also start evading tax by showing lower unreal income. But from different angles this tax is pro-poor and taxes people according to their affordability/sustainability. This is the most popular taxation method in the world and a populist one, too.

Regressive Taxation

This is just opposite to the progressive method having decreasing rates of tax for increasing value or volume on which the tax is being imposed.[8] There are not any permanent or specific sectors for such taxes. As a provision of promotion, some sectors might be imposed with regressive taxes. As for example, to promote the growth and development of small scale industries, India at one time had regressive excise duty on their productions—with increasing slabs of volume they produced, the burden of tax used to go on decreasing.

This method while appreciated for rewarding the higher producers or income-earners, is criticised for being more taxing on the poor and low-producers. This is not a popular mode of taxation and not as per the spirit of modern democracies.

Proportional Taxation

In such a taxation method, there is neither progression nor regression from the point of view rate of taxes point of view. Such taxes have fixed rates for every level of income or production, they are neutral from the poor or rich point view or from the point of view of the levels of production.[9] Usually, this is not used by the economies as an independent method of taxation. Generally, this mode is used as a complementary method with either progressive or regressive taxation. If not converted into proportional taxes, every progressive tax will go on increasing and similarly every regressive tax will decrease to zero, becoming completely a futile tax methods. That is why every tax, be it progressive or regressive in nature, must be converted into proportional taxes after a certain level.

A GOOD TAX SYSTEM

What are the characteristics of a good tax system? There has always been a debate among economists and policymakers on the issue of design of the tax system. Taxation in developing economies has been even more debated as the trade-off assessment generates enough controversy. Main debatable issues in the design of a tax system are whether progressive or regressive taxation, direct tax or indirect tax collections should be higher, whether revenue deficit is better, etc. The controversies set apart, there is a broad consensus on five *principles*[10] of a good tax system, among economists and the policymakers:

Fairness

Though fairness (i.e., the first criteria of a good tax

---

7. Samuelson and Nordhaus *Economics,* 329; Stiglitz and Walsh, *Economics,* p. 380.

8. Ibid.

9. Samuelson and Nordhaus, *Economics,* p. 329.

10. Stiglitz and Walsh, *Economics,* p. 382. A comprehensive analysis of good tax structure is also given in *Meade Committe Report,* Institute for Fiscal Studies (IFS), Washington DC, 1978.

system) is not always easy to define, economists suggest inclusion of two elements in the tax system to make it fair namely, *horizontal equity* and *vertical equity.* Individuals in identical or similar situations paying identical or similar taxes is known as *horizontal equity.* When 'better off' people pay more taxes it is known as *vertical equity.*

Efficiency

Efficiency of a tax system is its potential to affect or interfere the efficiency of the economy. A good tax system raises revenue with the least cost on the taxpayers and least interference on the allocation of resources in the economy. The tax system affects the economic decisions of individuals and groups by either encouraging or discouraging them to save, spend, invest, etc. Taxes can improve efficiency of the economy—taxes on pollution or on smoking give revenue to the government and serves broader social purposes, too. This is known as the *double dividend* of a tax.

Administrative Simplicity

This is the third criterion which includes factors like computation, filing, collection, etc. of the taxes that all should be as simple as possible. Simplicity checks tax evasion too. Tax reform in India has simplification of tax as its major plank— also recommended by the Chelliah Committee.

Flexibility

A good tax system has the scope of desirable modifications in it if there is any such need.

Transparency

How much tax taxpayers are actually paying and what are they getting against it in the form of the public services should be ascertainable, i.e., the transparency factor.

METHODS OF EXPENDITURE

Similar to the methods of taxation the modes of government expenditure are also of three types— Progressive, Regressive and Proportional.[11]

At first instance it seems that as a country achieves better levels of development, sectoral and the item-wise expenditure of the economy must have decreasing trends. But practical experience shows that the level of expenditure needs enhancement everyday and economy always needs more and more revenues to fulfil the rising expenditures. That is why for economies the best form of government expenditure is the progressive expenditure.

The best way of taxation is progressive and the best way of government expenditure is also progressive and they suit each other beautifully. Most of the economies around the world are having progressive taxation with progressive expenditure.

VALUE ADDED TAX

The value added tax (VAT) is a method of tax collection as well as name of a state level tax (*at present*) in India. A tax collected at every stage of value addition, i.e., either by production or distribution is known as value added tax.[12] The name itself suggests that this tax is collected on the value addition (i.e., production).

Production of goods or services is nothing but stages of value additions where production of goods is done by the industrialists or manufacturers. But these goods require value addition by different service providers/ producers (the agents, the wholesalers and the retailers) before they reach the

---

11. Based on the discussion on Government Expenditure in Samuelson and Nordhaus, *Economics.*

12. Ibid., p. 333

consumers. From production to the level of sale, there are many points where value is added in all goods. VAT method of tax collection is different from the non-VAT method in the sense that it is imposed and collected at different points of value addition chain, i.e., *multi-point tax collection*. That is why there is no chance of imposing tax upon tax which takes place in the non-VAT method—*single point tax* collection. This is why VAT does not have a 'cascading effect' on the prices of goods it does not increase inflation— and is therefore highly suitable for an economy like India where due to high level of poverty large number of people lack the market level purchasing capacity. It is a pro-poor tax system without being anti-rich because rich people do not suffer either.

Need of VAT in India

Over 160 nations in the world have implemented the VAT system of taxation regarding collecting their indirect taxes. There have been valid reasons why India should move towards the VAT method of tax collection. We may see some of the major reasons:[13]

(i) Due to single point tax collection, Indian indirect tax collection system was price-increasing (having *cascading effect* on the price) which was highly detrimental to the poor masses. Implementation of VAT will improve the purchasing capacity and so living standard of the poor people.[14]

(ii) India is having a federal political system where side by side the central government, states have also been given power to impose taxes and collect them. At the central level, there had been uniformity

of taxes for the economy. But there was no 'uniformity' at the state level taxes (i.e., state excise, sales tax, entertainment tax, etc.). This was detrimental to the development of a single market for Indian economy as a whole. India basically had many markets, but no Indian market as such. To bring in uniformity at the state-level taxes, VAT was a necessary step in India.

(iii) With the process of economic reforms, India moved towards the market economy. And for this, firstly India needed to have a single market. Without uniformity at the state level taxes (*uniform VAT*) this was not possible.

(iv) Indian federal design has resulted in economically weaker states and stronger centre. As VAT increases the total tax collection (experience of the world suggests so) it was fit to be implemented at the state level.

(v) India has been a country of high level tax evasion. By implementing VAT method of indirect tax collection, it becomes almost impossible to go for large scale tax evasion. To prove one's level of value addition, the purchase invoice/receipt is a must which ultimately makes it cross-check the level of production and sale in the economy.[15]

(vi) If some of the state level taxes (which are many) are converted into state VAT the complexity of taxation will also be minimised. And at the end, it is possible to merge some of the centre's indirect taxes with it, i.e., arrival of the *single VAT*.

Keeping all such things in mind, India started tax reform (*Chelliah Committee* and

13. Derived from the points forwarded by the *GoI* and the *Empowered Group of State Ministers*.

14. Raja C. Chelliah, Pawan K. Aggarwal, Mahesh C. Purohit and R. Kavita Rao, *Introduction to Value Added Tax* , in Amaresh Bagchi (ed.). *Readings in Public Finance* (New Delhi: Oxford University Press, 2005), pp. 277–78.

15. Ibid.

Kelkar Committee) and a certain level of sucess has been achieved in this area which can boost our motivation.

In the year 1996, the central government started collecting its excise duty on the VAT method and the tax was given a new name—the CENVAT.

The next proposal was to merge the states excise duty (imposed on intoxicants only) and their sales taxes into one tax—the state VAT or VAT. This could not take place due to states' lack of political will. Ultimately, only sales taxes of the states were changed to be named VAT and was started to be collected on the basis of the VAT method (some states did not join it and some joined later). The experience has been encouraging.

Experience of VAT

A total number of 20 states/UTs switched over to VAT (from their existing sales tax) in April 2005. Rest of the states went for it by 2008–09. Majority of the states/UTs saw revenue buoyancy due to VAT in the very first year of its implementation while few states availed the Central compensation facility for their revenue losses, that too for hardly one or two years. Experience of implementing VAT has been quite encouraging—by the financial year *2016–17*, the tax revenues of the states and UTs were estimated to grow with an annual rate of around 16 per cent.

This way, the view that the VAT will increase the tax collections of states has been validated. Similar impact of the proposed GST is believed to have on the indirect tax collections of the states as well as the Centre.

GOODS AND SERVICE TAX

After implementing the state VAT, the GoI wanted to go for the proposed GST (Goods and Services Tax). This is aimed at integrating the indirect taxes of Centre and states into a *single national tax*—popularly known as the *Single VAT* of India. By

creating a *single market* at the pan-India basis it will help the business and industry in a big way. The tax has potential to increase GDP up to 2 per cent (conservative estimates by some experts). All the benefits which the state VAT brought to the market and economy are the same in case of the GST, too. The *first proposal*[16] of the GST had suggested the following tax arrangements under it—

(i) To be collected on the VAT method (will have all the same features of the VAT).

(ii) To be imposed at *pan-India* level with uniformity in tax—better say a *single rate* of indirect tax—replacing the multiple central and state indirect taxes.

(iii) *Four* taxes of Centre (cenvat; service tax; stamp duty and central sales tax) and *nine* taxes (excise duty, sales tax/vat; entry tax; lease tax; works contract tax; luxury tax; turnover tax; octroi and cess) of the states to be merged into the GST.

(iv) To have a single rate of 20 per cent (12 per cent to flow to Centre and 8 per cent to the states).

Implementation Process

After studying the Kelkar Committee report, the Government in 2006 decided to introduce the new tax since the financial year 2010-11. Lack of consensus between the centre and states kept the process delayed—to sort out the contentious issues, one after another, two independent *expert committees* submitted[17] their advices to the Government. Finally, the Constitution (101st Amendment) Bill, 2016 was cleared by the Parliament by early August 2016—paving the

---

16. *Vijay Kelkar Task Force on the FRBM Act 2003*, Ministry of Finance, **Economic Survey 2004-05**, (New Delhi: Government of India, 2005), p. 40.

17. First it was from the **National Institute of Public Finance and Policy** (NIPFP) followed by the **Subramanian Committee**, during 2016-17.

way for its implementation. By late September 2016, the GST Council (GSTC) was created by the Government. The Council has been entrusted with the power to make recommendations to the Union and the States on various issues—rates, floor rates, exemption, etc.—related to GST.

By *February 2017*, the Council[18] had 10 rounds of meetings in which the major decisions taken were as given below:

(i) The central taxes to be subsumed in it are—central excise duty (cenvat); additional excise duty; service tax; additional customs duty (commonly known as countervailing duty; and special additional duty of customs (total 5 taxes).

(ii) The state taxes to be subsumed in it are—state vat; entertainment tax (other than the tax levied by the local bodies); central sales tax (levied by the centre and collected by the states); octroi and entry tax; purchase tax; luxury tax; and taxes on lottery, betting and gambling (total 8 taxes).

(iii) Concept of 'declared goods of special importance' dropped.

(iv) On inter-state transactions of goods and services an Integrated GST will be levied.

(v) Exception from GST on alcoholic liquor for human consumption, petroleum and petroleum products (on latter it will be imposed on a later date).

(vi) The threshold limit for exemption from levy of GST would be Rs. 20 lakhs for normal States and Rs. 10 lakhs for the Special Category States.

(vii) The threshold for availing the Composition scheme would be Rs. 50 lakhs—with the Service providers kept out of it.

(viii) States to get compensation for 5 years for loss of revenue due to implementation of GST (for this base year will be 2015-16 with growth rate of 14 per cent).

(ix) Minor changes in rules and regulations may be permitted with the approval of the Chairperson, if required (due to suggestions from the stakeholders or from the Law Department).

(x) All exemptions/incentives on indirect taxes will rest withdrawn with obligation to pay GST. If any of them continue it will be administered by way of a reimbursement mechanism.

(xi) Bands of rates (in per cent) of goods under GST shall be 5, 12, 18 and 28 and in addition there would be a category of exempt goods. Further, a cess would be levied on certain goods such as luxury cars, aerated drinks, pan masala and tobacco products, over and above the rate of 28 per cent (for payment of compensation to the States).

(xii) Keeping in mind the federal structure of India, there will be two components of GST—Central GST (CGST) and State GST (SGST)—both Centre and States levying GST across the value chain on every supply of goods and services. States will assess 90 per cent of assessees with annual turnover below Rs. 1.5 crore while remaining 10 per cent by the centre. For taxpayers with over Rs. 1.5 core turnover, the split is 50:50 between the centre and states.

The tax is decided to be "fully online" (no manual filing of tax) based on information technology (IT) put in place by the GST Network (a non-profit, non-government company registered by the centre and states). The network is to provide a standard and uniform interface to the taxpayers, shared infrastructure and services.

---

18. Based on the meetings of the **GST Council**, till February 2017.

Meanwhile, barring few reservations, the *Economic Survey 2016-17* has shown satisfaction[19] on the transformational tax GST—as per it, it will create a common Indian market (internal integration of India which will help in the external integration—i.e., globalisation), improve tax compliance, boost investment and growth, improve governance as well as it is a bold new experiment in the 'governance of cooperative federalism'. It has suggested to bring land and real estate into GST fold. The Government, in the *Union Budget 2017-18*, announced to implement the new tax from July 1, 2017.

ADDITIONAL EXCISE DUTY

There is a tax in India known as the Additional Excise Duty (AED) imposed and collected by the Centre. Basically, this is not a form of excise duty. At the same time, though the Centre collects it, the total corpus of collected tax is handed over to the states.

On the request of the states, the central government passed the Goods of Special Importance Act, 1957 which empowered the Centre to collect the AED on tobacco, textile and sugar in lieu of the states' sales tax on them so that these regionally produced goods (which are consumed nationally) have uniform and affordable prices across the country.

Once VAT is fully operational in the economy this responsibility will be handed over to the states (as proposed) to be integrated with their VAT with the condition that none of these commodities will be charged VAT exceeding 4 per cent.

CST REFORMS

The Central Sales Tax (CST), being an origin—based non-rebatable tax, it is generally agreed, is inconsistent with the concept of VAT. That is why it needs to be phased out; the CST reforms is a part of the tax reforms in India. The critical issue involved in phasing out of CST is that of compensating the states for revenue losses on account of such a phase out. Since phasing out of CST will entail a revenue loss, states have been insisting on a mechanism to compensate them on a permanent basis. The 4 per cent rate of the CST has to be phased out in stages with 1 per cent phase out in one financial year and the states duly compensated through tax devolution. Because of phasing out, it is now at 2 per cent. Menwhile, the tax has been subsumed in the proposd GST.

SERVICE TAX

The share of the services sector in the GDP of India has been going upward for the last decade. The introduction of service tax in 1994–95 by the Government of India has started paying the government on its tax revenue front. Introduced to redress the asymmentric and distortionary treatment of goods and services in the tax regime, the service tax has seen gradual expansion in the country.

Introduced on only three serviecs, by now, the applies on more than 100 services. The rate of service tax has been increased by the *Union Budget 2015–16* to 14 per cent inclusive of education cesses (it was 12.36 per cent inclusive of education cesses). The change has been done to facilitate a smooth transition to levy tax on services by both Centre and states, once India switches over to the GST by the next year. Other than imposing a 2 per cent Swachh Bharat Cess, the *Budget* has also put all services provided by the government entities under the service tax net (both to be notified in coming times).

It is one among the 5 central taxes which are being subsumed[20] in the upcoming indirect tax

---

19. **Economic Survey 2016-17**, Government of India, Ministry of Finance, N. Delhi, Vol. 1, pp. 3 & 78.

20. **Constitution (101st Amendment) Act, 2016** which clears the implementation of the new federal indirect tax GST subsuming 5 central and 8 state taxes.

GST—which is slated for enforcement from July 2017.

COMMODITIES TRANSACTION TAX

The *Union Budget 2013–14* has introduced (basically, *reintroduced*) the Commodities Transaction Tax (CTT), however, only for ***non-agricultural*** commodity futures at the rate of **0.01** per cent (which is equivalent to the rate of equity futures on which a *Securities Transaction Tax* is imposed in India). Alongwith this, transactions in commodity derivatives have been declared to be made *non-speculative*; and hence for traders in the commodity derivative segment, any losses arising from such transactions can be set off against income from any other source (similar provisions are also applicable for the securities market transactions).

Like all financial transaction taxes, CTT ***aims*** at discouraging excessive speculation, which is detrimental to the market and to bring parity between securities market and commodities market such that there is no tax/regulatory arbitrage. *Futures contracts* are financial instruments and provide for price risk management and price discovery of the underlying asset commodity / currency / stocks / interest. It is, therefore, essential that the policy framework governing them is uniform across all the contracts irrespective of the underlying assets to minimise the chances of regulatory arbitrage. The proposal of CTT also appears to have stemmed from the general policy of the government to widen the tax base.

Commodities Transaction Tax (CTT) is a tax similar to Securities Transaction Tax (STT), proposed to be levied in India, on transactions done on the domestic commodity derivatives exchanges. Globally, commodity derivatives are also considered as financial contracts. Hence CTT can also be considered as a type of 'financial transaction tax'.

The concept of CTT was ***first*** introduced in the *Union Budget 2008–09*. The government had then proposed to impose a commodities transaction tax (CTT) of 0.017 per cent (equivalent to the rate of equity futures at that point of time). However, it was withdrawn subsequently as the market was *nascent* then and any imposition of transaction tax might have adversely affected the growth of organised commodities derivatives markets in India. This has helped Indian commodity exchanges to grow to global standards [MCX is the world's ***No. 3*** commodity exchange; globally, MCX is ***No. 1*** in gold and silver, ***No. 2*** in natural gas and ***No. 3*** in crude oil].

SECURITIES TRANSACTION TAX

The Securities Transaction Tax (STT) is a type of 'financial transaction tax' levied in India on transactions done on the domestic stock exchanges. The rates of STT are prescribed by the central government through its budget from time to time. In tax parlance, this is categorised as a ***direct tax***. The tax came into effect from *1 October, 2004*. In India, STT is collected for the Government of India by the stock exchanges. With charging of STT, long-term capital gains tax was made ***zero*** and short-term capital gains tax was reduced to 10 per cent (subsequently, changed to 15 per cent since 2008).

The STT framework was subsequently reviewed by the central government in the year 2005, 2006, 2008, 2012 and ***2013***. The STT rates were revised upwards in the year 2005 and 2006 while it was reduced for certain segments in 2012 and 2013. The STT provisions were altered in the year 2008 such that for professional traders (brokers), STT came to be treated as an *expense* which can be deducted from the income instead of treating the same as an advance tax paid. [The 2004 STT provisions provided that the STT payments of professional traders, whose 'business income' arising from purchase and sale of securities could be set off against their total tax liability.]

As on date, STT is not applicable in case of *preference shares, government securities, bonds, debentures, currency derivatives, units of mutual fund other than equity oriented mutual fund,* and *gold exchange traded funds* and in **such cases**, tax treatment of short-term and long-term gains shall be as per normal provisions of law.

Transactions of the shares of listed companies on the floor of the stock exchange or otherwise, mandated under the regulatory framework of SEBI, such as *takeover, buyback, delisting offers*, etc., also does not come under STT framework. The *off-market* transactions of securities (which entails changes in ownership records at depositories) also does not attract STT.

CAPITAL GAINS TAX

This is a direct tax and applies on the sales of all 'assets' if a profit (gain) has been made by the owner of the asset—a tax on the 'gains' one gets by selling assets. The tax has been classified into two—

(i) *Short Term Capital Gain* (STCG): It applies 'if the Asset has been sold within 36 months of owning it'. In this case the 'rate' of this tax is similar to the normal income tax slab. But the period becomes '12 months' in cases of shares, mutual funds, units of the UTI and 'zero coupon bond'—in this case the 'rate' of this tax is **15** per cent.

(ii) *Long Term Capital Gain* (LTCG): It applies 'if the asset has been sold after 36 months of owning it'. In this case the 'rate' of this tax is **20** per cent. In cases of shares, mutual funds, units of the UTI and 'zero coupon bond' there is 'exemption' (zero tax) from this tax (provided that such transaction is subject to 'Securities Transaction Tax').

MINIMUM ALTERNATE TAX

The Minimum Alternate Tax (MAT) is a direct tax imposed on the 'zero tax' companies at the rate of 18.5 per cent on their book profit. This was first imposed in 1997–98.

Basically, income tax is paid as per the provisions of the Income Tax Act (IT Act), but companies calculate their profit (through profit and loss account) as per the provisions of the Companies Act. The IT Act allows several kinds of exemptions and other incentives from total income together with deductions on the gross income. Again, the rates of 'depreciation' under the Companies Act is higher than the IT Act. As a result of these exemptions, deductions and other incentives under IT Act together with higher depreciation under the Companies Act, companies show their taxable income either 'nil' or 'negative', and this way, the 'zero tax' companies emerge.

Practically, 'zero tax' companies, might be having high 'book profit' and distributing huge dividends (under the Companies Act) to their shareholders, too, but showing 'nil' or 'negative' taxable income (under the IT Act) they might not pay any income tax! To bring such companies under the income tax, *Section 115JB* was introduced in the IT Act in 1997–98 and MAT was imposed accordingly.

MAT is a way of making companies pay minimum amount of tax. It is applicable on all companies except those engaged in infrastructure and power sectors, free trade zones, charitable activities, venture and angel funds. Foreign companies with income sources in India also come under it. The *Union Budget 2015–16* has rationalised the MAT provisions for the FIIs (Foreign Financial Institutions)—now they do not need to pay MAT on their profits from capital gains on transactions in securities (which are liable lower tax rate).

We may take an example – suppose a company has 'book profit' of Rs. 10 lakh. And, after claiming the deductuions, exemptions and depreciation its 'gross taxable income' comes down to Rs. 6 lakh, its taxable income becoming Rs. 4 lakh. In this case, the applicable income tax would be Rs. 1.2 lakh (if rate of income tax is 30 per cent flat). But the comapny will pay a MAT of Rs. 1.85 lakh (at the rate of 18.5 per cent on its 'book profit' of Rs. 10 lakh). The concerned comapny needs to pay the tax which is higher—here, the tax to be paid will be Rs. 1.85 lakh.

At present the tax is collected as an advance tax. The tax can be carried forward and set off (adjusted) against regular tax payable during the subsequent 10-year period (known as MAT credit). There has been a strong demand to abolish this tax in the country. Meanwhile, the *Union Budget 2017-18* announced to start phasing out the exemptions available to the companies on it from April 2017. So that companies are able to use MAT credit, the carry forward period has been also increased to 15 years.

INVESTMENT ALLOWANCE

The GoI, in 2013–14, had announced an 'investment allowance' of 15 per cent to the companies investing Rs. 100 crore or more in plant and machineries. This was valid up to March 2016. This move was aimed at promoting investment in the industrial sector as part of the fiscal stimulus programme started in wake of the global recession.

Meanwhile, the government started a process of 'corporate tax rationalisation' linked to 'phasing out various incentives' availed by the companies *(calibration process)*. In its first phase, in 2016-17, two changes were implemented regarding the corporate tax liabilities of the companies:

(i) New manufacturing companies, incorporated on or after March 1, 2016,

will have an option to pay **25** per cent (plus surcharge and cess) corporate tax. To avail this, the companies will not have to claim profit-linked deductions, accelerated depreciation and *investment allowance.* For the other companies the rate of tax to remain 30 per cent (plus surcharge and cess).

(ii) **One** per cent cut in the corporate tax for the small companies. The companies which had turnover up to Rs. 5 crore till last year will now pay 29 per cent corporate tax (plus surcharge and cess). This is seen as an alternative to the existing investment allowance scheme.

TAX EXPENDITURE

There has been a divergence between the official tax rate and effective tax rate in India—defined as the ratio of total tax collected to the aggregate tax base. The divergence occurs mainly on account of tax exemptions. Tax expenditure is also known as *revenue forgone*. But such forgone taxes doe not necessarily mean that they have been waived off by the government. Better, it should be interpreted as incentives given by the government to promote certain sectors, in absence of which they may not have come up.

High tax expenditure can make the tax system unduly complex and bring in distortions in it. As a result of simplification in the tax system and improvements in tax administration in recent years have brought *tax expenditure down*—current situation[21] is as given below:

(i) 15 per cent for corporate tax (32 per cent of 2007-08).

(ii) 16 per cent for income tax (37 per cent in 2007-08).

---

21. Statement of Revenue Forgone, Budget documents & CSO, MInistry of Finance, **Economic Survey 2015–16**, p. 37.

(iii) 100 per cent for excise duty (70 per cent in 2007-08). It was at a high level of 162 per cent in 2009-10 on account of tax concessions announced by the GoI to control inflation.

(iv) 160 per cent for custom duty (92 per cent in 2007-08). It was at a high level of 235 per cent in 2009-10 due to concessions announced for custom duty in wake of controlling prices.

To realise full tax potential the governments needs to limit exemptions and their *grandfathering*[22] together with broadening the tax base. The level of tax expenditure is slated to fall steeply once the proposed GST is operationalised in the country. Under its process of rationalising the corporate tax (cutting it down from 30 to 25 per cent), the government is also aimed at calibrating (phasing out) the various tax exemptions/incentives which exists for the various industries. Its first phase has already commenced in 2016–17.

COLLECTION RATE

Collection rate is the ratio of total customs revenue and the total value of imports for a year. This is an indicator of overall incidence of customs including countervailing duties (CVD) and special additional duties (SAD) on imports. Several exemptions are offered by the GoI in customs duty on a variety of imports. This is the reason why India's customs collection does not increase as much as much its imports increase.

India's collection rates have been lower between 2009–2013 due to various exemptions announced by the GoI on the imports of petroleum, oil and lubricants (POL) and other commodities. These exemptions in the base custom duties were announced to check the rising commodities prices in the world market together with a general inflationary trend seen in India due to food inflation. At present the collection rate for India stands at 6.1 per cent[23].

14TH FINANCE COMMISSION

The 14th Finance Commission (FFC) was constituted on 2 *January, 2013* under the Chairmanship of Dr. Y. V. Reddy, former RBI Governor with Prof. Abhijit Sen, Ms. Sushma Nath, Dr. M. Govinda Rao and Dr. Sudipto Mundle as the other *four* members. The recommendations of the commission will apply on the period *2015–20* and its report has to be submitted by 31 October, 2014.

The broad *Terms of Reference* and the *matters* to be taken into consideration by the commission are:

(i) *Tax Devolution* & *Grant* related references

(a) the distribution between the union and states of the net *proceeds of taxes* which are to be, or may be, divided between them under *Chapter I, Part XII* of the Constitution and the allocation between the states of the respective shares of such proceeds;

(b) the principles which should govern the *grants-in-aid* of the revenues of the states out of the Consolidated Fund of India and the sums to be paid to the states which are in need of assistance by way of grants-in-aid of their revenues under *Article 275*

---

22. **Grandfather Clause** – a clause in a new law that exempts certain persons or businesses from abiding by it. For example, suppose a country passes a law stating that it is illegal to own a cat. A grandfather clause would allow persons who already own cats to continue to keep them, but would prevent people who do not own cats from buying them. Grandfather clauses are controversial, but they are common around the world. [*Source:* **Farlex Financial Dictionary**, Farlex Inc., N. York, USA, 2012; **Collins English Dictionary- Complete & Unabridged**, HaperCollins, N. York, USA, 2003.]

23. Department of Revenue Ministry of Finance, Government of India, New Delhi, March 2017.

of the Constitution for the purposes other than those specified in the provisos to *Clause (1)* of that article; and

(c) measures needed to augment the Consolidated Fund of a state to supplement the resources of the *panchayats* and *municipalities* in the state on the basis of the recommendations made by the finance commission of the state.

(ii) To review the state of finances, *deficit*, and *debt* levels of the union and states, and suggest measures for maintaining a stable and sustainable fiscal environment consistent with equitable growth including suggestions to amend the FRBMAs currently in force. The commission has been asked to consider and recommend incentives and disincentives for states for observing the obligations laid down in the FRBMAs.

(iii) In commission is required to consider—

(a) the *resources* of the Central government and the *demands* on the resources of the central government;

(b) the *resources* of the state governments and *demands* on such resources under different heads, including the impact of debt levels on resource availability in debt-stressed states;

(c) the objective of not only balancing the receipts and expenditure on revenue account of all the states and the union but also generating surpluses for capital investment;

(d) the *taxation efforts* of the central government and each state government and the potential for additional resource mobilisation;

(e) the level of *subsidies* required for sustainable and inclusive growth and equitable sharing of subsidies between the central and state governments;

(f) the *expenditure* on the non-salary component of maintenance and upkeep of capital assets and the non-wage-related maintenance expenditure on Plan schemes to be completed by March 31, 2015 and the norms on the basis of which specific amounts are recommended for the maintenance of capital assets and the manner of monitoring such expenditure;

(g) the need for *insulating the pricing* of public utility services like drinking water, irrigation, power, and public transport from policy fluctuations through statutory provisions;

(h) the need for making public-sector enterprises competitive and market oriented; listing and disinvestment; relinquishing of non-priority enterprises;

(i) the need to balance *management of ecology, environment, and climate change* consistent with sustainable economic development; and

(j) the impact of the proposed *goods and services tax* on the finances of the Centre and states and the mechanism for compensation in case of any revenue loss.

(iv) To review the present *public expenditure management* systems and recommend, including—

(a) budgeting and accounting standards and practices;

(b) the existing system of classification of receipts and expenditure;

(c) linking outlays to outputs and outcomes; and

(d) best practices within the country and internationally.

(vi) To review the present arrangements of financing of *Disaster Management* with reference to the funds constituted under the Disaster Management Act 2005 and make recommendations.

(vii) To indicate the basis on which it has arrived at its findings and make available the *state-wise estimates of receipts and expenditure.*

The commission is required to generally take the base of population figures as of 1971 in all cases where population is a factor for determination of devolution of taxes and duties and grants-in-aid. However, the commission may also take into account the demographic changes that have taken place subsequent up to 1971.

FFC RECOMMENDATIONS

The 14th Finance Commission (FFC) submitted its report by early 2015. It has advised for far-reaching changes for sharing of revenues between the Center and the States, on the one hand, and between the States, on the other. The advices apply on the period 2015–20 and are likely to have major implications for Center-State relations, for budgeting by, and the fiscal situation of, the Center and the states. 'Successful implementation of the advices will advance the cause of cooperative federalism that the new government has enthusiastically embraced', the *Economic Survey 2014–15* concluded. Some of the **major recommendations** are as follows:

(i) It has radically enhanced the share of the states in the central 'divisible pool' of taxes from the current **32** per cent to **42** per cent which is the biggest ever increase in vertical tax devolution. The last two Finance Commissions, viz., Twelfth (2005–10) and Thirteenth (2010–15)

had recommended a state share of 30.5 per cent (increase of 1 per cent) and 32 per cent (increase of 1.5 per cent), respectively in the central divisible pool.

(ii) It has also proposed a new horizontal formula for the distribution of the divisible pool among the states. There are changes both in the variables included/excluded as well as the weights assigned to them. Relative to the Thirteenth Finance Commission, the FFC has incorporated two new variables—

(a) 2011 population and forest cover; and

(b) Excluded the variable relating to fiscal discipline.

(iii) Implementing these recommendations will move the country toward greater *fiscal federalism,* conferring more fiscal autonomy on the states. For example, based on assumptions about nominal GDP growth and tax buoyancy and the policy measures that are contemplated for 2015–16, it is estimated that the additional revenue for the states could be as much as Rs. 2 lakh crores relative to 2014–15. Of this, a substantial portion represents the difference that is purely due to the change in the States' share in the divisible pool.

(iv) Preliminary estimates suggest that *all States stand to gain* from FFC transfers in absolute terms. However, to assess the distributional effects, the increases should be scaled by population, Net State Domestic Product (NSDP) at current market price, or by States' own tax revenue receipts. This will make the following effects on the ststes' revenue—

(a) The biggest gainers when scaled by any of these indicators tend to be the

Special Category States (SCS, mostly those in the North-East) and by orders of magnitude.

(b) The major gainers in per capita terms turn out to be Arunachal Pradesh, Mizoram and Sikkim for the SCS states and Kerala, Chhattisgarh and Madhya Pradesh for other states (GCS or General Category States). Clearly, this increase in taxes to the States is sustainable for the center, only if there is a reduction in the central (Plan) assistance to the states (CAS).

In other words, States will now have greater autonomy both on the revenue and expenditure fronts.

(v) It is also possible to tentatively estimate what the FFC recommendations would do to net spending capacity of the States, where net refers to the difference between the extra FFC transfers and the reduced CAS that will be required by the FFC recommendations. Broadly, the Special Category States will be the biggest gainers. In addition, there are nine States among the GCS which are expected to get more than 25 per cent of their own tax revenue.

(vi) A collateral benefit of moving from CAS to FFC transfers is that overall progressivity will improve; that is, on average, States with lower per capita NSDP will receive more than those with a higher per capita NSDP. This results from the fact that CAS transfers, which tended to be discretionary, were less progressive than Finance Commission transfers.

To be sure, there will be transitional costs entailed by the reduction in CAS transfers. But the scope for dislocation has been minimised because the extra FFC resources will flow broadly to the states that have the largest CAS-financed schemes.

The far-reaching recommendations of the FFC, along with the creation of the *NITI Aayog*, will further the government's vision of *cooperative* and *competitive* federalism. The necessary, indeed vital, encompassing of cities and other local bodies within the embrace of cooperative and competitive federalism is the next policy challenge, which is believed to be strengthened by the body NITI Aayog.

CONCEPTS RELATED TO FC

Tax Devolution

Advising a formula to distribute the Union tax proceeds between Union and the States is the most important task of a FC, as the share of states in the net proceeds of Union taxes is the *predominant channel* of resource transfer from the Centre to states.

Divisible Pool

It is that portion of gross tax revenue which is distributed between the Centre and the States. The divisible pool consists of all taxes, except surcharges and cess levied for specific purpose, net of collection charges.

Before the 80th Constitution Amendment (2000), the sharing of the Union tax revenues with the states was in accordance with the provisions of articles 270 and 272, as they stood then. This amendment altered the pattern of sharing of Union taxes in a fundamental way—dropping the Article 272 and substantially changing the Article 270. The new Article 270 provides for sharing of all the taxes and duties referred to in the Union List putting all in a 'divisible pool'. There are some exceptions to it. The taxes and duties referred in the Articles 268 and 269 of the Constitution, together with surcharges and cesses on taxes and duties (referred in the Article 271) and any cess levied for specific purposes—do not fall under this 'pool'.

The new arrangement of tax devolution came as a follow-up to the recommendations of the 10th FC (1995–2000) which the FC termed as the 'Alternative Method of Tax Devolution' (AMD). A concensus between Union and States was a advised by the FC for such an arragement to be effected. States were going to get extra 5 per cent share in the Union taxes in the AMD, thus, a serious demand came from them—ultimately, the AMD was accepted by the Centre. To make the AMD irreversible, the Goverment of India went for the 80th Amendment in the Constituion.

Grants-in-aid

Though, tax devolution (from the *Divisible Pool*) is the primary instrument to attend the issue of 'horizontal imbalances' of revenue accruing to the states, the grants-in-aid is a complimentary/secondary instrument regarding the same. As per the Article 275, the FC recommends the *principles* as well as the *quantum* of grants to those states which are in need of assistance – different sums may be fixed for different states (one of the pre-requisites for such grants is the assessment of the needs of the states). The 1st FC had laid down *five broad principles* for determining the eligibility of a state for grants:

(i) The Budget of a state as the starting point for examination of a need.

(ii) The efforts made by states to realize the potential.

(iii) The grants should help in equalizing the standards of basic services across states.

(iv) Any special burden or obligations of national concern, though within the state's sphere, should also be taken into account.

(v) Grants might be given to further any beneficent service of national interest to less advanced states.

The grants recommended by FC are predominantly in the nature of general purpose grants meeting the difference between the assessed expenditure on the *non-plan revenue* account of each state and the *projected revenue* including the share of a state in Central taxes. These are often referred to as 'gap filling grants'.

The scope of grants to states, over the yaer, was extended further to cover special problems. Following the 73rd and 74th Amendments to the Constitution, FCs were charged with the additional responsibility of recommending measures to augment the *Consolidated Fund of a State* to supplement the resources of local bodies. This has resulted in further expansion in the scope of FC grants. The 10th FC was the first Commission to recommend grants for *rural* and *urban local bodies*. This way, the scope of grants-in-aid has gone for considerable extension, over the time.

Fiscal Capacity

The *fiscal capacity* (also called 'income distance') criterion was first used by the 12th FC, measured by per capita GSDP as a proxy for the distance between states in *tax capacity*. When so proxied, the procedure implicitly applies a single average tax-to-GSDP ratio to determine fiscal capacity distance between states. The 13th FC changed the formula slightly and recommended the use of 'separate averages' for measuring tax capacity, one for general category states (GCS) and another for special category states (SCS).

Fiscal Discipline

This as a criterion for tax devolution was used by the 11th and 12th FCs to provide an *incentive* to states managing their finances prudently. The criterion was continued in the 13th FC also. The index of fiscal discipline is arrived at by comparing improvements in the ratio of own revenue receipts of a state to its total revenue expenditure relative to the corresponding average across all states in the country.

PC as Collaborator

While the 12th FC (2005–10) was being set up, the GoI decided to make the Planning Commission (PC) function as a 'collaborator' to the FC—one member of the PC was added as an 'additional member' on the panel of the FC (the FC includes four members including the Chairman)—as a link between the bodies. This arrangement was continued with in the 13th and 14 FCs. It is believed that this arrangement was greatly helpful in bringing in a better idea about the revenue imbalances of the states. While the government did set up the NITI Aayog, no announcement came in this regard – there might be some developments in this regard once the 15th FC (2020–25) is set up in future.

DIRECT TAX REFORMS

Several new measures have been taken by the Government related to the direct tax regime of the country. The *Direct Tax Code 2013* was fully complied with during 2016-17 which replaced the five decade old archaic direct tax law of India. The new tax law is aimed at equitable and effective tax regime, voluntary compliance and dispute reduction. The overarching vision has been of progressively taxing higher income, bringing greater clarity on applicability of tax provisions, broadening the tax base and improving tax administration.

Meanwhile, the *Union Budget 2017-18*, furthering the process of reforms, has announced the following new measures:

- Existing rate of taxation for individual assesses between income of Rs. 2.5 lakhs to 5 lakhs reduced to 5 per cent from the present rate of 10 per cent (estimated revenue loss of Rs. 15,000 crore).
- Surcharge of 10 per cent of tax payable on categories of individuals whose annual taxable income is between Rs. 50 lakhs and Rs. 1 crore (to make up the Rs. 15,000 crore loss estimated to take place as the 'slab' has been restructured).
- Simple one-page form to be filed as Income Tax Return for the category of individuals having taxable income upto Rs. 5 lakhs other than business income.
- Profit linked deduction available to the start-ups for 3 years out of 5 years is being changed to 3 years out of 7 years.
- Exemptions given on MAT (Minimum Alternate Tax) will be phased out starting from April 2017.
- Corporate tax which stands at 30 per cent has already been cut down to 25 per cent for those companies which do not avail any exemption. Those which have turnover less than Rs. 5 crore have to pay 29 per cent (the process of cutting it down to 25 per cent has not been pushed this year).
- Income tax rate for smaller companies with annual turnover of upto Rs. 50 crore is fixed at 25 per cent (from the effective rate of above 30 per cent)—benefiting 96 per cent of MSMEs. This measure has been taken to make them more viable and encourage to migrate to company format (formalisation). The Government is estimated to forgo a revenue of Rs. 7,200 crore due to it.

In the process of modifying *human behaviour*, the Budget specially appealed all citizens of the country to contribute to 'Nation Building' by making a small payment of 5 per cent tax if their income is falling in the lowest slab of Rs. 2.5 lakhs to 5 lakhs.

LEGITIMACY AND TAXATION

India commenced with a broad-based tax reforms programme in 1991 as an important part of the economic reforms process. Simplifying tax structure, cutting rate of taxes, enhancing tax compliance and broadening the tax base are the major contours of this reform programme. But even today, India has not fully translated its democratic vigour into commensurately strong fiscal capacity. The tax base of India is still not adequate. To build fiscal capacity it is essential to create legitimacy in the state. In this regard the latest *Economic Survey 2015-16* has presented a very timely and suitable piece of analysis. The document adds that to build fiscal capacity the government needs to put in place a better tax regime which is only possible once the government is able to enhance its legitimacy among the citizens. The suggestions[24] forwarded by the Survey in this regard are briefly being given here:

(i) The *spending priorities* of the government must include essential services which are consumed by all citizens. For that matter, action needs on public infrastructure, law and order, less pollution and congestion, etc.

(ii) *Reducing corruption* must be a high priority. Though this will be fiendishly (clever and imaginative) difficult. This is needed not just because of its economic costs but also because it undermines legitimacy of the state. The more citizens believe that public resources are not wasted, the greater they will be willing to pay taxes. Improving transparency through efficient auctioning of public assets will help create legitimacy, and over time strengthen fiscal capacity.

(iii) *Subsidies to the well-off* need to be scaled back. At present[25], it is estimated to be around Rs. 1 lakh

crore. Phasing down these bounties and targeting subsidies for the poor is important in strengthening legitimacy.

In the same way, the existing regime of tax exemptions redistributes income towards the richer private sector—it dilutes the legitimacy of the state in the eyes of the poor citizens. There is need of putting in place a reasonable taxation provision for the 'better off' section in the country regardless of where they get their income from— industry, services, real estate, or agriculture.

(iv) *Property taxation* needs to be developed. India lacks systematic data on property tax and whatever is there it is very sparse. This proves the low attention the country has given to this issue. As property taxes are 'progressive' they are desirable. It makes more sense because evading this tax is difficult as they are imposed on immovable (non-mobile) assets. With the help of today's technologies such properties can be easily identified.

Higher rates on properties (with values updated periodically) can be the foundation of local government's finances. This can provide local public goods and strengthen democratic accountability and more effective decentralisation. Higher property tax rates would also put sand in the wheels of property speculation. *Smart cities* require smart public finance and for India's urban future a sound property taxation regime will be vital.

One low hanging fruit is to avoid raising exemption threshold and allow natural growth in income to increase the number of the taxpayers. The Survey has suggested a simple method for it—*inaction*. The **Union Budget 2016–17** has already begun this process—exemption limit for individual income tax has been left unchanged together with a programme to link corporate

24. **Ministry of Finance**, Department of Revenue, Government of India, N. Delhi, April 2016.

25. Ministry of Finance, **Economic Survey 2015–16**, Vol. 1, pp. 105-117.

tax cut and phase out of the exemption regime existing for the companies.

INCOME AND CONSUMPTION ANOMALY

India's tax to GDP ratio is very low, and the proportion of direct tax to indirect tax is not optimal from the view point of social justice. The data released by the Government[26] indicate that India's direct tax collection is not commensurate with the income and consumption pattern of the people:

Corporate tax: As against 5.6 crore *informal sector* (unorganised sector) individual enterprises and firms doing small business, of which 1.81 crore filed tax returns. Out of the 13.94 lakh companies registered in India, 5.97 lakh filed tax returns for 2016-17 (Assessment Year) which show the following annual profit before tax pattern:

- 2.76 lakh companies have shown losses or zero income.
- 2.85 lakh companies had less than Rs. 1 crore profit.
- Profit of 28,667 companies was between Rs. 1 crore to Rs. 10 crore, and
- Only 7781 companies have profit of more than Rs. 10 crores.

Individual income tax: As against estimated 4.2 crore persons engaged in *organised sector* employment, the number of individuals filing return for salary income are only 1.74 crore. In 2015-16 (Assessment Year 2016-17), a total of 3.7 crore individuals filed income tax returns which did show the following annual income pattern:

- 99 lakh show annual income below the exemption limit of Rs. 2.5 lakh;
- 1.95 crore show income between Rs. 2.5 to Rs. 5 lakh;
- 52 lakh show income between Rs. 5 to Rs. 10 lakhs;
- Only 24 lakh people show income above Rs. 10 lakhs;
- 76 lakh people declared income above Rs. 5 lakh (56 lakh being salaried class); and
- Only 1.72 lakh people did show income more than Rs. 50 lakh.

The demonetisation process has given the government new data related to people's income—about 1.09 crore accounts saw average deposit between Rs. 2 to 80 lakh. Deposits of more than 80 lakh were made in 1.48 lakh accounts with average deposit size of Rs. 3.31 crores. This data mining will help the Government in increasing the tax net and tax revenue in future.

The above-given data can be contrasted with the fact that in the last five years, more than 1.25 crore cars have been sold, and number of Indian citizens who flew abroad, either for business or tourism, was 2 crore in the year 2015. From all these figures it can be concluded that India is largely a tax *non-compliant* society. The predominance of *cash* in the economy makes it possible for the people to evade their taxes. When too many people evade taxes, the burden of their share falls on those who are honest and compliant.

FUTURE OUTLOOK

Tax reform has been an integral part of the economic reform process in the country. Much reforms have been done by now, though the pace and method at times have not been so praiseworthy. As India's reforms have been gradual and incremental the laxity in tax reforms might be due to this also. In the backdrop of the developments by far, a five-pronged strategy has been suggested[27] by the latest *Economic Survey*:

26. Based on the **Union Budget 2017-18** and **Economic Survey 2016-17**.

27. **Economic Survey 2016-17**, Government of India, Ministry of Finance, N. Delhi, Vol. 1, p. 78.

(i) GST should be broad in coverage to include activities that are sources of black money creation—land and other immovable property;

(ii) Individual income tax rates and real estate stamp duties should be reduced;

(iii) The income tax should be widened gradually and which could progressively encompass all high incomes;

(iv) The timetable for reducing the corporate tax rate should be accelerated; and

(v) Tax administration should be improved by reducing discretionary powers of tax officials and improving accountability.

In the process of collecting taxes on newly disclosed and undisclosed wealth (in the aftermath of demonetisation) *tax harassment* must be avoided by officials at all rungs of hierarchy. The tax administration must *shift* to greater use of data, smarter evidence-based scrutiny and audit, greater reliance on *on-line assessments* with less physical interaction between tax payers and tax officials. Once GST is enforced much more data will be available on individual transactions—by using this data together with greater information sharing between the direct and indirect tax departments at the centre, along with coordination with the states, greater compliance can be achieved through 'non-punitive means'—in relation to indirect as well as direct tax collections. The promise of *digital age* can be used to improve the tax administration of the country in a big way.

PUBLIC FINANCE IN INDIA

The way the modern governments manage all money they get–the public money–is the subject matter of public finance. The policy stance taken in this regard is declared annually by the governments via their 'fiscal policy' popularly known as the Budget. *

* See Amaresh Bagchi (ed.), **Readings in Public Finance** (New Delhi: Oxford University Press, 2005). Also see Paul A. Samuelson and William D. Nordhaus, **Economics,** (New Delhi: The McGraw-Hill Company, 2005) 412-711. Also see Joseph E. Stiglitz and Carl E. Walsh, **Economics,** (New York: W. W. Norton, 2006) pp. 695–697.

INTRODUCTION

Public finance is a much wider title which includes all those matters which are connected with public money, i.e., the money a government gets, spends, borrows, lends, raises or prints. Public finance, i.e., finances of the government, now named as *public economics*, does not only discuss the issue that how much of the country's resources the government should acquire for its own use but also discusses the 'efficiency' with which the money should be used. Public finance gets reference in the ancient treatise **Arthashastra**[1] of Kautilya which covers 'treasury, sources of revenue, accounts and audit' in a very detailed way. However, the subject has gathered much significance in the post Second World War period once the governments' role in the economy started expanding[2] due to various reasons namely, the rise of public sector, the delivery of public goods, law and order, defence, etc. By the Second World War, the importance of the government's role in the economy was urgently felt and it was believed that all needs of the people cannot be met if the economy is left to the market (i.e., the private sector) in its entirety. For example, national defence, law enforcement and other major areas which must be cared for by the national government besides the supplies of **affordable or free** healthcare, education, social security measures, etc., could only be taken care of by the governments (*as they are not profit driven*). This is why there was an agreement among the experts and the policymakers to expand the government's role in the economy. This led to the ultimate rise of the public sector around the world.[3] Here we will be looking into the major concepts related to the area of public finance with special reference to India.

BUDGET

An annual financial statement of income and expenditure is generally used for a government, but it could be of a firm, company, corporation etc.[4] The 'word' has its origin in the British parliamentary exercise of preparing such statement way back in the mid-18th century from the French word *'Bugeut'* meaning a leather bag out of which the financial statement was brought out and presented in the parliament. Today, this word is used to mean the annual statement in all economies around the world.

The Constitution of India has a provision (Art. 112) for such a document called Annual Financial Statement to be presented in the Parliament before the commencement of every new fiscal year—popular as the Union Budget. Same provision is there for the states, too.

Data in the Budget

The Union Budget has **three sets**[5] of data for every concerned sector or sub-sector of the economy:

1. L. N. Rangarajan (ed.), **The Arthashastra**, Penguin Books, (New Delhi, 1992).

2. The size of government expenditure for the developed economies stood at almost 10 per cent of their GDPs at the begining of the 20th century—which could rise to 18 per cent only at the outbreak of the Second World War—went for a steep rise by 1980 to 40 per cent. The government expenditure was barely 9 per cent of the GDP in India at the time of Independence, nearly doubled in 1970s and reach 75 per cent in the 1980s—when questions were raised about their sustainability as revenue receipts failed to grow adequately resulting in rising budgetary deficits (see Amaresh Bagchi (ed.), **Readings in Public Finance,** Oxford University Press, (New Delhi: 2005) pp. 1–4.

3. It should be noted here that the world which had the form of the state economy (i.e., the Socialist countries at this time, majority of the economic activities were under government control. As the communist form of the state economy emerged by the late 1940s (i.e., Peoples Republic of China, 1949), it had 100 per cent state control over the economic activities.

4. *Collins Dictionary of Economics*, op. cit., & **Oxford Dictionary of Business,** op. cit.

5. Based on the budgetary documents of the Ministry of Finance, Government of India, New Delhi.

(i) Actual data of the preceding year (here preceding year means one year before the year in which the Budget is being presented. Suppose the Budget presented is for the year 2017–18, the Budget will give the final/actual data for the year 2015-16. After the data either we write 'A', means actual data/final data or write nothing (India writes nothing).

(ii) Provisional data of the current year (i.e., 2016–17) since the Budget for 2017–18 is presented at the end of the fiscal 2016–17, it provides Provisional Estimates for this year (shown as 'PE' in brackets with the data).

(iii) Budgetary estimates for the following year (here following year means one year after the year in which the Budget is being presented or the year for which the Budget is being presented, i.e., 2017–18). This is shown with the symbol 'BE' in brackets with the concerned data.).

One comes across certain other kinds of data, too in day-to-day government economic literature. There are three such data—

(i) Revised Estimate (RE)

Revised Estimate is basically a current estimation of either the budgetary estimates (BE) or the provisional estimates (PE). It shows the contemporary situation. It is an interim data.

(ii) Quick Estimate (QE)

Quick Estimate is a kind of revised estimate which shows the most latest situation and is useful in the process of going for future projections for some sector or sub-sector. It is an interim data.

(iii) Advance Estimate (AE)

Advance Estimate is a kind of quick estimate but done ahead (is advance) of the final stage when data should have been collected. It is an interim data.

Developmental and Non-developmental Expenditure

Total expenditure incurred by the government is classified into two segments—developmental and non-developmental. All expenditures of productive nature are developmental such as on the heads of new factories, dams, bridges, roads, railways, etc.—all *investments*.

The expenditures which are of consumptive kind and do not involve any production are non-developmental, i.e., paying salaries, pensions, interest payments, subsidies, defence expenses, etc.

This classification is not used in the Indian public finance management now (see *Plan and Non-Plan Expenditure,* in the next entry).[6]

Plan and Non-Plan Expenditure

Every expenditure incurred on the public exchequer is classified into two categories—the plan and the non-plan. All those expenditures which are done in India in the name of *planning* is the *plan expenditure* and rest of all are *non-plan expenditures*. Basically, all asset creating, and productive expenditures are planned and all consumptive, non-productive, non-asset building are non-plan expenditures and are developmental and non-developmental expenditures, respectively.

Since the financial year 1987–88, there was a terminology change in Indian public finance literature when developmental and non-developmental expenditures were replaced by the new terms plan and non-plan expenditures, respectively. (It was suggested by the Sukhomoy Chakravarti Committee.)[7]

Meanwhile, a high-power panel headed by Dr. C. Rangarajan (Chairman, Prime Minister's

6. MInistry of Finance, *Union Budget 1987–88* (New Delhi: Government of India, 1987).

7. *Review of the Working of the Monetary System,* headed by Sukhomoy Chaktravarthy, Reserve Bank of India, Government of India, New Delhi, 1985.

Economic Advisory Council), in *September 2011* suggested for redefining **Plan** and **Non Plan** expenditures as *Capital* and *Revenue* expenditures, as the former set of terms 'blur the classification' —this will facilitate linking expenditure to 'outcomes' and better public expenditure, the panels suggested. *Major* suggestions of the Panel are:

(i) *Plan* and *Non-Plan* distinction in the Budget is neither able to provide a satisfactory classification of 'developmental' and 'non-developmental' dimensions of government expenditure nor an appropriate budgetary framework. It has therefore become 'dysfunctional',

(ii) Suggests for *redefining the roles* of the Planning Commission (PC) and the Finance Ministry (FM). According to which the PC should be responsible for formulation of the five-year plan and the task of firming up the annual budgets should be entrusted to the FM.

(iii) The PC should dispense with the exercise of approving annual plans of states and it could hold a strategy or review meeting with representatives of the states.

(iv) Public expenditures should be split into *capital* and *revenue* expenditures.

(v) Public expenditure should have 'management approach' based on measurable 'outcomes', indicating that the reponsibility should be assigned to the FM.

Analysis of the Situation: While the need for looking beyond the budget is well accepted, there are many factors raising doubts on the 'efficacy' and 'relevance' of the five-year plans as the instrument. The division of expenditure between *Plan* and *non-Plan* is artificial and creates problems, such as :

(i) Plan expenditure tends to get priority especially when austerity and expenditure reduction has to be done periodically for fiscal consolidation. Non-Plan expenditure gets the *cut* even if it is vitally needed for economic development, an example is budget provision for maintenance of assets such as hospitals, schools and irrigation dams already created under Plan, but whose maintenance is treated as non-Plan.

(ii) Review and implementation of schemes is another area of direct responsibility for the Ministry of Finance and the Ministry of Statistics and Programme Implementation. The Finance Minister himself had, in the budget speech for 2005–06, promised to ensure that programmes and schemes were not allowed to continue indefinitely from one Plan period to another without an independent and in-depth evaluation. The Planning Commission, serving as the *focal point for Plan allocations*, dilutes the role of the Finance Ministry in this case.

(iii) 'Output' and 'Outcome Budgeting' was introduced by the Central Government from the Budget for 2005–06. Non-Plan expenditure remains out of its purview. This means, for example, the outcome of expenditure on running schools and hospitals will not be evaluated. This again is another fallout of the artificial division into Plan and non-Plan.

This classification used to adversely affect the whole budget process, formulation and implementation. Looking at this anomaly, the Government switched over from the 'plan' and 'non-plan' classification of expenditure to 'revenue' and 'capital' since the fiscal 2017-18 (as announced in the **Union Budget 2017-18**).

Revenue

Every form of money generation in the nature of income, earnings are revenue for a firm or a government which do not increase financial liabilities of the government, i.e., the tax incomes, non-tax incomes along with foreign grants.

Non-revenue

Every form of money generation which is not income or earnings for a firm or a government (i.e., money raised via borrowings) is considered a non-revenue source if they increase financial liablities.

Receipts

Every receiving or accrual of money to a government by revenue and non-revenue sources is a receipt. Their sum is called *total receipts*. It includes all incomes as well as non-income accruals of a government.

Revenue Receipts

Revenue receipts of a government are of two kinds—Tax Revenue Receipts and Non-tax Revenue Receipts—consisting of the following income receipts in India:

Tax Revenue Receipts

This includes all money earned by the government via the different taxes the government collects, i.e., all direct and indirect tax collections.

Non-tax Revenue Receipts

This includes all money earned by the government from sources other then taxes. In India they are:

(i) *Profits* and *dividends* which the government gets from its public sector undertakings (PSUs).

(ii) *Interests* recieved by the government out of all loans forwarded by it, be it inside the country (i.e., internal lending) or outside the country (i.e., external lending). It means this income might be in both domestic and foreign currencies.

(iii) *Fiscal services* also generate incomes for the government, i.e., currency printing, stamp printing, coinage and medals minting, etc.

(iv) *General Services* also earn money for the government as the power distribution, irrigation, banking, insurance, community services, etc.

(v) *Fees*, *Penalties* and *Fines* received by the government.

(vi) *Grants* which the governments receives— it is always external in the case of the Central Government and internal in the case of state governments.

Revenue Expenditure

All expenditures incurred by the government are either of *revenue kind* or *current kind* or *compulsive kind*. The basic identity of such expenditures is that they are of consumptive kind and do not involve creation of productive assets. They are either used in running of a productive process or running a government. A broad category of things that fall under such expenditures in India are:

(i) *Interest* payment by the government on the internal and external loans;

(ii) *Salaries, Pension* and *Provident Fund* paid by the government to government employees;

(iii) *Subsidies* forwarded to all sectors by the government;

(iv) *Defence* expenditures by the government;

(v) *Postal Deficits* of the government;

(vi) *Law and order* expenditures (i.e., police & paramilitary);

(vii) Expenditures *on social services* (includes all social sector expenditures as education, health care, social security, poverty alleviation, etc.) and *general services* (tax collection, etc.);

(viii) *Grants* given by the government to Indian states and foreign countries.

Revenue Deficit

If the balance of total revenue receipts and total revenue expenditures turns out to be negative it is known as revenue deficit, a new fiscal terminology used since the fiscal 1997–98 in India.[8]

This shows that the government's *Revenue Budget* (see the next topic) is running in losses and the government is earning less revenue and spending more revenues—incurring a deficit. Revenue expenditures are of immediate nature (this has to be done) and since they are consumptive/non-productive they are considered as a kind of expenditure which sums up to a heinous crime in the area of fiscal policy. Governments fulfil the gap/deficit with the money which could have been spent/intvested in productive areas.

A government might have its revenue expenditures less than its revenue receipts, i.e., having (*revenue surplus*) budget. Such fiscal policy is considered good where the government has been able to manage some money out of its revenue budget which could be spent for the creation of productive assets. Yes, another thing that should be kept in mind, as how the government has managed this surplus and whether the policies which made this happen are judicious enough or not. In the Second Plan, India emerged as a revenue-suplus state, but experts did not appreciate it as it had many bad impacts on the economy—higher tax rates culminated in tax evasion, corruption, creation of black money, etc.

8. Raja J. Chelliah, 'The Meaning and Significance of the Fiscal Deficit', in Amaresh Baghi (ed.), ***Readings in Public Finance,*** (New Delhi: Oxford University Press, 2005), pp. 387–88. Also see Ministry of Finance, ***Union Budget 1997–98,*** (New Delhi: Government of India, 1997).

Revenue deficit may be shown in the quantitative form (as how much the gross/total deficit is in currency terms) or in percentage terms of the GDP for that particular year (shown as percentage of GDP). Usually, it is shown as a percentage of the GDP for domestic as well as international analyses.

Effective Revenue Deficit

Effective revenue deficit (ERD) is a new term introduced in the *Union Budget 2011–12*. Conventionally, 'revenue deficit' (RD) is the difference between revenue receipts and revenue expenditures. Here, revenue expenditures includes all the grants which the Union Government gives to the state governments and the UTs—some of which ***create assets*** (though these assets are not owned by the Government of India but the concerned state governments and the UTs). According to the Finance Ministry (*Union Budget 2011–12*), such revenue expenditures contribute to the growth in the economy and therefore, *should not be treated as unproductive* in nature like other items in the revenue expenditures. And on this logic, a new methodology was introduced to capture the 'effective revenue deficit', which is the Revenue Deficit 'excluding' those revenue expenditures of the Government of India which were done in the form of **GoCA** (grants for creation of capital assets).

The GoCA includes the Government of India grants forwarded to the states & UTs for the implementation of the centrally sponsored programmes such as Pradhan Mantri Gram Sadak Yojana, Accelerated Irrigation Benefit Programme, Jawaharlal Nehru National Urban Renewal Mission, etc., these expenses though they are shown by the Government of India in its Revenue Expenditures they are involved with *asset creation* and cannot be considered completely 'unproductive' like other items put in the basket of the Revenue Expenditures—the reason why a new 'terminology' was created.

The term was innovated by the Government of the time to show some rationale in its high revenue deficit by bringing the logic that all of it were not like a typical revenue expenditure (which are consumptive in nature) and some of it were used to create 'capital assets' also (though they cannot be shown in the 'capital' heads of expenditures). Though, the new Government at centre does not give the same significance to the term, it has been releasing data related to it.

The **Union Budget 2017-18** has committed to reduce the *effective revenue deficit* to 0.7 per cent in 2017-18 and 0.2 per cent in 2018-19 (it was estimated to be 1.2 per cent for 2016-17). While the *revenue deficits* for 2017-18 and 2018-19 have been set at 1.9 per cent and 1.4 per cent by the budget.

Revenue Budget

The part of the Budget which deals with the income and expenditure of revenue by the government.

This presents the annual financial statement of the total revenue receipts and the total revenue expenditure—if the balance emerges to be positive it is a revenue surplus budget, and if it comes out to be negative, it is a revenue deficit budget.

Capital Budget

The part of the Budget which deals with the receipts and expenditures of the capital by the government. This shows the means by which the capital is managed and the areas where capital is spent.

Capital Receipts

All non-revenue reciepts of a government are known as capital receipts. Such receipts are for investment purposes and supposed to be spent on plan-development by a government. But the receipts might need their diversion to meet other needs to take care of the rising revenue expenditure of a government as the case had been with India. The capital receipts in India include the following capital kind of accruals to the government:

(i) Loan Recovery

This is one source of the capital receipts. The money the government had lent out in the past in India (states, UTs, PSUs, etc.) and abroad their capital comes back to the government when the borrowers repay them as capital receipts. The interests which come to the government on such loans are part of the revenue receipts.

(ii) Borrowings by the Government

This includes all long-term loans raised by the government inside the country (i.e., internal borrowings) and outside the country (i.e., external borrowings). Internal borrowings might include the borrowings from the RBI, Indian banks, financial institutions, etc. Similarly, external borrowings might include the loans from the World Bank, the IMF, foreign banks, foreign governments, foreign financial institutions, etc.

(iii) Other Receipts by the Government

This includes many long-term capital accruals to the government through the Provident Fund (PF), Postal Deposits, various small saving schemes (SSSs) and the government bonds sold to the public (as Indira Vikas Patra, Kisan Vikas Patra, Market Stabilisation Bond, etc.). Such receipts are nothing but a kind of loan on which the government needs to pay interests on their maturities. But they play a role in capital raising process by the government.

Capital Expenditure

All the areas which get capital from the government are part of the capital expenditure. It includes so many heads in India —

(i) Loan Disbursals by the Government

The loans forwarded by the government might be internal (i.e., to the states, UTs, PSUs, FIs, etc.) or external (i.e., to foreign countries, foreign banks, purchase of foreign bonds, loans to IMF and WB, etc.).

(ii) Loan Repayments by the Government

Again loan payments might be internal as well as external. This consists of only the *capital* part of the loan repayment as the element of interest on loans are shown as a part of the *revenue expenditure*.

(iii) Plan Expenditure of the Government

This consists of all the expenditures incurred by the government to finance the planned development of India as well as the central government financial supports to the states for their plan requirements.

(iv) Capital Expenditures on Defence by the Government

This consists of all kinds of *capital* expenses to maintain the defence forces, the equipment purchased for them as well as the modernisation expenditures. It should be kept in mind that *defence* is a non-plan expenditure which has capital as well as revenue expenditures in its maintenance. The revenue part of expenditure in the defence is counted in the revenue expenditures by the government.

(v) General Services

These also need huge capital expenditure by the government—the railways, postal department, water supply, education, rural extension, etc.

(vi) Other Liabilities of the Government

Basically, this includes all the repayment liabilities of the government on the items of the Other Receipts. The level of liabilities depends on the fact as to how much such receipts were made by the governments in the past. The amount of payment liabilities in the year also depends on the fact as to which years in the past the governments had other receipts and for what duration of maturity periods. As for example, the *PF liabilities* were not an item of such liabilities for almost first three decades after Independence. But once the government employees started retiring, it went on increasing. Future India (especially 1960s and 1970s) saw expansion of the PSUs and excessive employment generation in them (devoid of the logic of labour requirement). We see the PF liabilities expanding extensively throughout the 1990s—the governments had been under pressure to manage this segment either by cutting interest on PF or at present trying to make it a matter of market economy. Same thing happened with the element of *pension* and we have been able to devise a market mechanism for it once pension reforms took place and the arrival of a pension regulatory authority for the area.

Capital Deficit

There is no such term in public finance or in economics as such. But in practice one usually hears the use of the term capital crunch, scarcity of capital in day-to-day economic news items. Basically, the government in the news is facing the problem of managing as much funds, money, capital as is required by it for public expenditure. Such expenditure might be of revenue kind or capital kind. Such difficulties have always been with the developing economies due to their high level requirement of capital expenditures. Had there been a term to show this situation, it would naturally have been *Capital Deficit*.

Fiscal Deficit

When balance of the government's total receipts (i.e., revenue + capital reeipts) and total expenditures (i.e., revenue + capital expenditures) turns out to be negative, it shows the situation of fiscal deficit, a concept being used since the fiscal 1997–98 in India.[9]

The situation of fiscal deficit indicates that the government is spending beyond its means. To be more simple, we may say that the government is spending more than its income (though in practice all receipts of the government are not income. Basically, receipts are all forms of money accruing to the government, be it income or borrowings).

Fiscal deficit may be shown in the quantitative form (i.e., the total currency value of the deficit) or in the percentage form of the GDP for that particular year (percentage of GDP). In general, the percentage form is used for domestic or international (i.e., comparative economics) studies and analyses.

India has been a country of not only regular but higher fiscal deficits. Moreover, the composition of its fiscal deficit has been more prone to criticism (we will see this in the forthcoming sub-title ahead).

Primary Deficit

The fiscal deficit excluding the interest liabilities for a year is the primary deficit, a term India started using since the fiscal 1997–98.[10] It shows the fiscal deficit for the year in which the economy had not to fulfil any interest payments on the different loans and liabilities which it is obliged to—shown both in quantitative and percentage of GDP forms.

This is considered a very handy tool in the process of bringing in more transparency in the government's expenditure pattern. Any two years for example might be compared and so many things can be found out clearly such as, which year the government depended more on loans,

the reasons behind higher or lower fiscal deficits, whether the fiscal deficits have gone down due to falling interest liabilities or some other factors, etc.

Monetised Deficit

The part of the fiscal deficit which was provided by the RBI to the government in a particular year is Monetised Deficit, this is a new term adopted since 1997–98 in India.[11] This is shown in both the forms—in quantitative as well as a percentage of the GDP for that particular financial year.

It is an innovation in the fiscal management which brings in more transparency in the government's expenditure behaviour and also in its capabilities concerning its dependence on market borrowings by the RBI. Basically, every year both central and state governments in India had been depending heavily on market borrowings (internal) for its long-term capital requirements. Market borrowings of the government are done and managed by the RBI. Besides, the RBI is also the primary customer for government securities—yet another means of the government to raise long-term capital. This has been a major area of fiscal concern in India. After the process of **fiscal consolidation** was started by the government by the early 1990s, we see a visible improvement in this area. This term is itself arrived as the part of fiscal reforms in India (we will visit the issue of fiscal consolidation in India in the coming pages).

Deficit and Surplus Budget

When the budgetary proposals of a government for a particular year proposes higher expenditures than the receipts, it is known as a *deficit budget*. Opposite to this, if the budget proposes lesser expenditures than the receipts, then it is a *surplus*

9. Raja J. Chelliah, 'The meaning and significance of public deficit', p. 381 & p. 387. Also see Ministry of Finance, *Union Budget 1997–98.*

10. Ministry of Finance, *Union Budget 1997–98.*

11. Raja J. Chelliah, p. 389. Also see Ministry of Finance, *Union Budget 1997–98.*

budget.[12]

In practice, governments the world over usually do not present a surplus budget as it symbolises government's lower concerns towards development. But at times as a political weapon a government might come out with such a budget (for example the Uttaranchal Budget for 2006–07 was a surplus budget). How can a government propose for a surplus budget in a developing state when even developed countries still need development and are going for deficit budgets? The Union Budget in India had never been presented as a surplus budget.

DEFICIT FINANCING

The act/process of financing/supporting a deficit budget by a government is deficit financing. In this process, the government knows well in advance that its total expenditures are going to turn out to be more than its total receipts and enacts/follows such financial policies so that it can sustain the burden of the deficits proposed by it.

First used in the area of public finance in the early 1930s in USA,[13] today the term is being used by the corporate sector, too and such a financial management of a firm might be followed by it as part of its business strategy. Again, a sick firm might need to follow deficit financing route for many years to come as required by the firm to make it come out of the red (i.e., doing away with the losses).

Need of Deficit Financing

It was in the late 1920s that the idea and need of deficit financing was felt. It is when government needs to spend more money than it was expected to earn or generate in a particular period, to go for a desired level of growth and development. Had there been some means to go for more expenditure with less income and receipts, socio-political goals could have been realised as per the aspirations of the public policy. And once the growth had taken place, the extra money spent above the income would have been reimbursed or repaid. This was a good public/government wish which was fulfilled by the evolution of the idea of deficit financing.

It was by the early 1930s that the US first tried its hand at deficit financing soon to be followed by the whole Euro-American governments.[14] Through this route the developed world was able to come out of the menace of the Great Depression (1929).[15] The idea became popular around the world by the 1960s. India tried its hand at deficit financing in 1969 and since the 1970s it became a routine phenomenon, till it became wild and illogical, demanding immediate redressal. The fiscal deficits in India did not only peak to unsustainable levels but its composition was also not justified and not based on sound fundamentals of economics. Finally, India headed for a slow but confident process of fiscal reforms that is also

---

12. In the US economy if tax revenue falls short of government expenditures, the government has a *fiscal deficit,* and it means that the government needs to borrow in the capital market to cover the difference. Opposite to it, if the government runs a *fiscal surplus* (i.e., its tax revenues exceed its expenditure) then the government, like the household sector, will be a net saver and will represent a source of saving for the economy (see Stiglitz and Walsh, *Economics,* 549).

13. J. K. Galbraith, *A History of Economics,* (London: Penguin Books, 1987) p. 226. (*The whole Chapter XVII on J.M. Keynes (pp. 221–36) is interesting to refer on the topic.*)

14. For a detailed discussion on the topic one may refer to Joseph. E. Stiglitz, *Economics of the Public Sector,* (New York: W.W. Norton, 2000).

15. It should be noted here that although the governments had run deficits (i.e., budget deficit) even before the Keynesian idea of the deficit, the pre-Keynesian thinking was that in peacetime the budget should generally be *balanced* (i.e., neither deficit nor surplus), or even in surplus so that the government debt created by wartime deficits could be paid off. For further reference on the topic and its constraints, Stanley Fischer and William Easterly, *Economics of the Government Budget Constraints,* World Bank Research Observer, Vol. 5, No. 2, July 1990, pp. 127–42; also reproduced in Amaresh Bagchi (ed.), *Readings in Public Finance,* pp. 301–19.

known as the process of fiscal consolidation (to be discussed in the coming pages).

Means of Deficit Financing

Once deficit financing became an established part of public finance around the world, the means of going for it were also evolved by that time. These means, basically are the ways in which the government may utilise the amount of money created as the deficit to sustain its budget for developmental or political needs. These means are given below in order of their suggested and tried preferences.

(i) *External Aids*[16] are the best money as a means to fulfil a government's deficit requirements even if it is coming with soft interest. If they are coming without interest nothing could be better.

When India went to borrow from the IMF in the wake of the financial crisis of 1990–91, the body advised India to keep its fiscal deficit to the tune of 4.5 per cent of its GDP and noted it to be sustainable for the economy. What was the rationale behind this data? Basically, in those times with the foreign aids (soft loans either from the *WB* or from the *Aid India Forum*) India was able to manage its budget to the tune of 4.5 per cent of its GDP. In 2002, when India's fiscal deficit was around 6 per cent (5.7 per cent to be precise) the IMF validated it to be sustainable, the reasons were two—first, India was able to show a check on fiscal deficit and secondly, at the same time the forex reserves of the country were suitably higher to neutralise the negative impacts of the higher fiscal deficit than the suggested levels (4.5 per cent).

External Grants are even better elements in this case (which comes free—neither

interest nor any repayments) but it either did not come to India (since 1975, the year of the first Pokhran testings) or India did not accept it (as happened post-Tsunami, arguing grants/aids coming with a tag/condition). That is why here this segment has not been discussed as a means to manage deficit.

(ii) *External Borrowings*[17] are the next best way to manage fiscal deficit with the condition that the external loans are comparatively cheaper and long-term.

Though external loans are considered an erosion in the nation's sovereign decision making process, this has its own benefit and is considered better than the internal borrowings due to two reasons:

(a) External borrowing bring in foreign currency/hard currency which gives extra edge to the government spending as by this the government may fulfil its developmental requirements inside the country as well as from outside the country.

(b) It is prefered over the internal borrowings due to 'crowding out effect'. If the government itself goes on borrowing from the banks of the country, from where will others borrow for investment purposes?

(iii) *Internal Borrowings*[18] come as the third preferred route of fiscal deficit management. But going for it in a huge way hampers the investment prospects of the public and the corporate sector. It has the same impact on the expenditure pattern in the economy. Ultimately, economy heads for a double negative impact—lower investment (leading to lower production, lower GDPs and lower per capita income, etc.) and

---

16. Ibid.

17. Ibid.
18. Ibid.

lower demands (by the general public as well as by the corporate world) in the economy—the economy moves either for *stagnation* or for a *slowdown* (one can see them happening in India repeatedly throughout the 1960s, 1970s, 1980s). The situation improved after the mid-1990s.

(iv) *Printing Currency* is the last resort for the government in managing its deficit.[19] But it has the biggest handicap that with it the government cannot go for the expenditures which are to be made in the foreign currency. Even if the government is satisfied on this front, printing fresh currencies does have other damaging effects on the economy:

(a) It increases inflation proportionally. (India regularly went for it since the early 1970s and usually had to bear double digit inflations.)

(b) It brings in regular pressure and obligation on the government for upward revision in wages and salaries of government employees—ultimately increasing the government expenditures necessitating further printing of currency and further inflation—a vicious cycle into which economies entangle themselves.

Now, it remains a matter of choice and availability of the above-given means, and which means a government adopts and in what proportion, for fulfilling its deficit requirements.

Composition of Fiscal Deficit

The Keynesian idea of deficit financing, though he advocated it, had a catch in it also which was usually missed by third world economies or intentionally overlooked by them. The catch is related to the question as to why an economy wants to go for fiscal deficit. Thus, it becomes essential to go for an analysis of the composition[20] of the fiscal deficit of a government.

Out of the two broad expenditure obligations of a government—revenue expenditure and capital expenditure—the following combinations of expenditure composition are suggested:

(i) A fiscal deficit with a surplus revenue budget or a zero revenue expenditure is the best composition of fiscal deficit and the most suitable time for deficit financing.

(ii) The deficit requirements for lower revenue expenditures and higher capital expenditures are the next best situation for deficit financing, provided revenue deficit is eliminated soon.

(iii) The last could be the situation when major part of deficit financing is to fulfil revenue expenditures and a minor part to go for capital expenditures. The total money of the deficit might go to fulfil revenue expenditure, which could be the worst form of it.

Basically, there should be a judicious mix of plan and non-plan expenditure as well as revenue and capital expenditures in India. Lesser non-plan expenditure or higher plan-expenditure are better reasons behind deficit financing in India (though India has a typical feature of capital expenditure which makes this combination of deficit financing not a suggested form—discussed ahead).

Third world economies (including India) though went for higher and higher fiscal deficits and deficit financing, they either did not address or failed to address the composition of deficit favourable towards capital and non-revenue expenditures.

---

19. L.N. Rangarajan, *The Arthashastra*, pp. 259–62.

20. J. Cullis and P. Jones, *Public Finance and Public Choice* (New York: Oxford University Press, 1998).

FISCAL POLICY

The real meaning, significance and impact of fiscal policy emerged in the wake of the Great Depression and the Second World War. Fiscal policy has been **defined** as 'the policy of the government with regard to the level of government purchases, the level of transfers, and the tax structure'—probably the best and the most acclaimed definition among experts.[21] Later, the impact of fiscal policy on macro-economy was beautifully analysed.[22] As the policy has a deep impact on the overall performance of the economy, fiscal policy is also **defined** as the policy which handles public expenditure and tax to direct and stimulate the level of economic activity (numerically denoted by the Gross Domestic Product).[23] It was J. M. Keynes, the *first* economist who developed a theory linking fiscal policy and economic performance.[24]

Fiscal policy is also **defined** as 'changes in government expenditures and taxes that are designed to achieve macroeconomic policy goals'[25] (such as growth, employment, investment, etc.). Therefore, we say that 'fiscal policy denotes the use of taxes and government expenditures'.[26]

How the taxes and the government expenditures influence the overall economy, has been explained in a brief discussion here.[27] Let us first discuss the *taxes* and their impact on the economy:

  (i) Taxes have a direct bearing on people's income affecting their levels of disposable incomes, purchase of goods and services, consumption and ultimately their standard of living;

  (ii) Taxes directly affect the savings of individuals, families and firms which affect investment in the economy—as investment affects the output (GDP) thereby influencing the per capita income;

  (iii) Taxes affect the prices of goods and services as factor cost (production cost) is affected thereby affecting incentives and behaviour of economic activities, etc.

Government expenditures affect/influence the economy in two ways:

  (i) There are some expenditure on government purchases of goods and services, for example construction of roads, railways, ports, foodgrains, etc., in the goods category and salary payments to government employees in the services category; and

  (ii) There are some expenditure due to government's income support, to the poor, unemployed and old-age people (known as government *transfer payments*).

Deficit Financing in India

India was declared to be a planned economy right after Independence. As development responsibilities of the government were very high, there was a need of huge funds in rupee as well as in foreign currency forms. India faced continuous crises in managing the required fund to support its

21. The acclaimed definition first came up in the widely used work *Macroeconomics* by Dornbusch and Fisher which is now available as R.S. Dornbusch, S. Fisher and Richard Startz, **Microeconomics,** (New Delhi: Tata McGraw-Hill, 2002).

22. John Hicks, the British Nobel Laureate did show it referring changes in taxes and government expenditure using the framework of the famous IS-LM model (Ibid).

23. S. R. Maheshwari, *A Dictionary of Public Administration* (New Delhi: Orient Longman, 2002) p. 227.

24. In his acclaimed work *The General Theory of Employment, Interest and Money*, 1936.

25. Stiglitz and Walsh, **Economics,** p. 729.

26. Samuelson and Nordhaus, **Economics,** p. 412.

27. Based on the elaboration by Samuelson and Nordhaus, **Economics,** pp. 412–13.

Five Year Plans—neither foreign funds came nor internal resources could be mobilised in sufficient amount. (Due to lower tax collections, weaker banks that too privately owned, and negligible saving rate, etc.)[28]

By the late 1960s, the government headed for deficit financing and from the 1970s onwards, India started going for higher and higher fiscal deficits and became more and more dependent on increased deficit financing with every fresh year. We may classify dificit financing in India into three phases.

The First Phase (1947–1970)

This phase had no concept of deficit financing and the deficits were shown as Budgetary Deficits. Major aspects of this phase were—

(i) Trying to borrow from inside and outside the economy but unable to meet the target.

(ii) In the 1950s, a serious attempt was made to increase tax collections and check revenue expenditures to be ultimately able to emerge as a surplus revenue budget economy. But huge cost was paid in the form of tax evasion, rise in corruption, stagnating standard of life and a neglected social sector.

(iii) Taking recourse to heavy borrowings from the RBI and finally nationalisation of banks so that their money could be used by the government to support the plans. This not only increased the interest burden of the governments but also ruptured the whole financial system in coming years—banks did not remain commercial entities and became part of the government's political statement.

(iv) Establishing giant PSUs with higher revenue expenditures (salaries) which increased the revenue expenditures of the future governments when the pensions and the PFs needed to be serviced.

(v) Unable to go for the required level of investment even after taking recourse to all the above given means.

The Second Phase (1970–1991)

This is considered the period of deficit financing, follow up of unsound fundamentals of economics and finally culminating in severe financial crisis by the year 1990–91. Major highlights of this phase may be summed up as follows—

(i) This phase saw the nationalisation policy and simultaneous revival of an increased emphasis on expansion of the PSU (two points should be noted here specially—*first*, many of the South East Asian economies have, officially declared their acceptance of capitalism and privatisation. *Secondly*, China had declared that investment in the government-controlled companies are a loss of money at this time).

(ii) Upcoming PSUs increased the total expenditure of the government's revenue as well as capital.

(iii) Existing PSUs were taking their own due from the economy—the illogical employment creation excessively increased the burden of salaries, pensions and PF; many of them had started fetching huge losses by this time; as the public sector does not have profit as its primary goal; there was a lack of profit and loss analysis; as the PSUs had no connection between their need of labour force and the existing labour force. Ultimately, the responsibility of profit or loss did not remain the onus of the

---

28. For a detailed data-based discussion refer to Sudipto Mundle and M. Govinda Rao, *'Issues in Fiscal Policy'* in Bimal Jalan (ed.), *The Indian Economy: Problems and Prospects* (New Delhi: Penguin Books, 2004), pp. 258–85.

officers, thus making them centres of intentional losses and an institutionalised centre of corruption; etc.

(iv) The governments have failed on both the fronts—checking population rise and mass employment generation—the burden of different *subsidies* went on increasing making them unmanageable and highly illogical. Self-employment programmes could not pick up, or better said, it was politically suitable to go for piece-meal wage-employment programmes with different names.

(v) Planned development remained highly centralised and devoid of any place for local aspirations—frustrations of masses started showing up in the form extremist and radical organisations raising their heads creating a law and order problem and excessive expenditure on them. The outcome was a burdened police force and lagging judicial set up.

(vi) The plan expenditure which governments were going for were through investments in the PSUs which were not committed to profit motive, deficit financing for the PSUs was not based on sound economics. Majority of the plan expenditure in a sense turned out to be non-economic, i.e., non-plan expenditure at the end.

Due to the above-given reasons, it was tough to say whether it was sound to go for huge fiscal deficits in India.[29]

The Third Phase (1991 onwards)

This started with the initiation of the economic reforms process under the conditionalities put forth by the IMF (controlling fiscal deficit was one amongst them). As the economy moved from

government dominance to market dominance, things needed a restructuring and public finance also needed a touch of rationality.

INDIAN FISCAL SITUATION: A SUMMARY

In December 1985, the Government of India presented a discussion paper in the Parliament titled 'Long-Term Fiscal Policy'. It was for the *first time* in the fiscal history of India that we see a long-term perspective coming on the fiscal issue from the government. This also included the policy of government expenditure. The paper was bold enough to recognise the deterioration in India's fiscal position and accepted it among the most important challenges of the eighties—the paper set specific targets and policies to set the things right. This paper was followed by a country-wide debate on the issue and it was in 1987 that the government came ahead with *two* bold steps in the direction—

(i) a virtual freeze was announced on government expenditure, and

(ii) a ceiling on the budgetary deficit.

The above steps had a positive impact on the situation but it was temporary as since mid-1988 the situation again started deteriorating. The BoP crisis at the end of 1990 was generated partly by the alarmingly high *fiscal deficit*[30] and due to a high level of external borrowings. The IMF support to fight the crisis came in but with many macro-economic conditionalities, checking

---

29. This was the general feeling among experts, policymakers and the IMF, alike.

30. The proximate cause of the payment crisis in the mainstream perspective, was faulty macroeconomic policies, specially large fiscal deficits of the government during 1984–91, deficits that spilled over in country's current account of the balance of payment. (See Mihir Rakshit, 'The Micro-economic Adjustment Programme: A Critique', *Economic and Political Weekly* 26(34) (August), quoted by Mihir Rakshit, *'Some Microeconomics of India's Reform Experience'* in Kaushik Basu (ed.), *India's Emerging Economy: Performance and Prospects in the 1990s and Beyond* (New Delhi: Oxford University Press, 2004), p. 84.

the fiscal meance being a major one among them. With the process of economic reforms which started in 1991–92, the government also announced its commitment to reduce fiscal deficit to 3–4 per cent (of GDP) by the mid-1990s (from the level of about 8 per cent during 1987–90). This step was among the many measures which the government started with the objective of stabilising the economy. We may have a look at India's fiscal situation upto the 1990–91 in the following way:

(i) The fiscal deficits of the central government, after averaging below 4 per cent of the GDP till the 1970s started climbing up by being 5.77 per cent in 1980–81, 8.47 per cent in 1986–87 ending up at 7.85 per cent in 1990–91 after being above 7 per cent in the second half of the 1980s.[31]

(ii) The revenue (i.e., current) expenditure of the government (Centre and states combined) increased from 11.8 per cent of GDP to 23 per cent between 1960 and 1990. The revenue receipts of the government also went up on an average of 14.6 per cent in 1971–75 to 20 per cent in 1986–1990. But the gap between revenue receipts and expenditures remained negative—financed largely by domestic borrowings (as a result the interest payments on domestic debt increased from 0.5 to 2.5 per cent of the GDP during 1975–90.[32] The revenue deficit went on increasing after 1979–80 and reached the highest level of 3.26 per

cent of the GDP in 1990–91.[33]

(iii) The fiscal situation of the states was not good either. State governments which are primarily responsible for health, education and other social services had an aggregate revenue expenditure of 5 per cent of GDP on these accounts while their capital expenditure accounted for 2.5 per cent on social and other sectors.[34] The states' expenditure on the social sector went down while their interest payments had increased during the 1980s.[35]

As per the experts, the debt situation in the states would have been even worse, but for the fact that the states, unlike the Centre, did not have independent powers to borrow either from the RBI or the market because of the statutory overdraft regulatory scheme.[36] Thus, their deficits have been self-limiting—whenever the states tried to cut down their deficits the care of the social sector and capital expenditure suffered and development prospects in the states also suffered.

Now the question arises that why the government has not been able to check the menace of fiscal deficits even though there has been a consensus to do so? *There are reasons*[37] which can be cited for it:

(i) *Political factor:* The political lobbies and sectional politics as well as the subsidies

31. S. D. Tendulkar and T.A. Bavani, **Understanding Reforms** (New Delhi: Oxford University Press, 2007) p. 73.

32. Bimal Jalan, **India's Economic Policy** (New Delhi: Penguin Books, 1992) p. 48.

33. **Handbook of Statistics on the Economy 2002–03,** Reserve Bank of India, Table 221 (cited by Tendulkar and Bhavani, **Understanding Reforms**, p. 74).

34. Bimal Jalan, **India's Economic Policy,** p. 50

35. Reserve Bank of India, **The Report of Tenth Finance Commission** (New Delhi, Government of India, 1994) (as quoted in Bimal Jalan, India's Economic Policy, p. 50.

36. This scheme has changed now. After the implementation of the suggestions of the **12th Finance Commission** states are now allowed to go for market borrowings to take care of their plan expenditures once they have passed and enacted their Fiscal Responsibility Acts (FRAs) in consonance with the FRBM Act, 2003.

37. Based on the points raised by Bimal Jalan, p. 49.

are supposed to be one big factor for rising government expenditure. We see this on a higher scale if there is a probable mid-term election or closer to a general election.

(ii) ***Institutional factor:*** The administrative size combined with the processes of reporting, accounting, supervising and monitoring getting greater importance than the production and delivery of goods and services.[38]

(iii) ***Ethical factor:*** This is a more powerful factor as it easily generates wide public support for the government expenditure. There are many heads of such expenditures such as subsidies (food, power, fertilizer, irrigation, etc.) poverty alleviation programmes, employment generation programmes, education, health and social services. The logic for such expenditure comes from the idea that the government should function as protector of the poor and provider of jobs for them implying that such government expenditures benefit the poor.

It was in 2000 that the double menace of revenue and fiscal deficits got attention from the government at the Centre and some constitutional/statutory safeguards looked necessary. Consequently, the Fiscal Responsibility and Budget Management Bill, 2000 was proposed in the Parliament.

FRBM Act, 2003

The fiscal policy of an economy has been considered as the building block for enabling macro-environment by economists, policymakers and the IMF, alike. It does not only provide stability and predictability to the policy regime, but also

ensures that national resources are allocated in terms of their defined priorities through the tax transfer mechanism.

Unproductive government expenditures, tax distortions and high deficits are considered to have constrained the Indian economy from realising its full growth potential. At the begining of the fiscal reforms in 1991, the fiscal imbalance was identified as the ***root cause*** of the twin problems of inflation and the difficult balance of payments (BoPs) position.[39] Since then the ***medium-term fiscal policy stance*** of the government has been on the following lines:[40]

(i) reducing the deficits (revenue and fiscal);

(ii) prioritising expenditure and ensuring that these resulted in intended outcomes; and

(iii) augumenting resources by widening tax base and improving tax-compliance while maintaining moderate rates.

The fiscal consolidation which followed in 1991 failed to give the desired results as there was no defined mandate for it. Neither was there any statutory obligation to do so.[41] This is why the Fiscal Reforms and Budget Management Act (FRBMA) was enacted on 26 August, 2003 to provide the support of a strong institutional/statutory mechanism. Designed for the purpose of medium-term management of the fiscal deficit, the FRBMA came into effect on 5 July, 2004.

The FRBM Bill, 2000 was passed by the Parliament with all political parties voting in favour, and is considered a watershed in the area of fiscal reforms in the country. Main highlights of the FRBMA, 2003 are as given below:[42]

---

38. this factor seems getting redressal with the starting of *outcome* and *performance* budgeting 2004–05 onwards.

39. Ministry of Finance, *Economic Survey 2006–07,* (New Delhi: Government of India, 2007), p. 18.

40. Ibid.

41. Ibid.

42. Ministry of Finance, *Economic Survey 2003–04,* (New Delhi: Government of India, 2004).

(i) GoI to take measures to reduce fiscal and revenue deficit so as to eliminate revenue deficit by 31 March, 2008 (which was revised by the UPA Government to March 31, 2009) and thereafter build up adequate *revenue surplus.*

(ii) Rules to be made under the Act to specify *annual targets* for the reduction of fiscal deficit (FD) and revenue deficit (RD) contingent liabilities and total liabilities (*RD to be cut by 0.5 per cent per annum and FD by 0.3 per cent per annum*).

(iii) FD and RD may exceed the targets only on the grounds such as national security, calamity or on exceptional grounds.

(iv) GoI not to borrow from RBI except by Ways and Means Advances (WMAs).

(v) RBI not to subscribe to the primary issue of the GoI securities from 2006–07 (it means that these government bonds/papers will become market—based instrument to raise long-term funds by the government).

(vi) Steps to be taken to ensure greater transparency in fiscal operations.

(vii) Along with the Budget and Demands for Grants, the GoI to lay the following *three statements* before the Parliament in each financial year:

   (a) Fiscal Policy Strategy Statement (FPSS);

   (b) Medium Term Fiscal Policy Statement (MTFPS); and

   (c) Macroeconomic Framework Statement (MFS).

(viii) The Finance Minister to make *quarterly review* of trends in receipts and expenditure in relation to the Budget and place the review before the Parliament.

Recent changes: After the enactment of the FRMBA, the states also followed the suit passing

their FRAs (fiscal responsibility acts) in the forthcoming years. Both of the governments have shown better fiscal disciplines since then[43]. To the extent 'exact' follow-up to the FRBMA-linked targets are concerned, the performance has been mixed. The targets were exceeded many times due to fiscal escalations (either due to natural calamities or on exceptional ground), while many times they were better than the mandated targets, too. But this act brought the element of higher fiscal discipline among the governments, there is no doubt in it[44].

In the past few years a view has emerged as per which binding the government expenditures to a fixed number may be counterproductive to the economy at large. Due to a hard and fast discipline regarding fiscal targets, some highly desirable expenditures by the government may get blocked, for example—expenditures on infrastructure, welfare, etc. This is why we find a changed stance of the Government of India in the **Union Budget 2016–17** regarding the follow-up to the FRBMA. Terming it a *new school of thought* the Budget suggests two important changes in its fiscal road map:

   (i) It may be better to have a fiscal deficit *range* as the target in place of a fixed *number* as target. This would give necessary policy space to the government to deal with dynamic situations.

   (ii) A need is felt to align fiscal expansion or contraction with credit contraction or expansion respectively, in the economy.

In the opinion of the Budget, the government should remain committed to fiscal prudence and consolidation but a time has come when the working of the FRBMA needs a review—especially in the context of the uncertainty and

43. *Economic Survey 2013–14; 2014–15* and *2015–16*.

44. The acceptance to the recommendations of the **13th** and **14th Finance Commissions** by the Government of India in this regard have been highly effective.

volatility which have become the new norms of global economy[45]. In the backdrop of this changed stance, the the Government, in 2016 constituted a *Committee* to review the implementation of the FRBMA.

FRBM Review Committee

The five-member committee handed over its report by late January 2017. Though the report is yet to be put in the public domain, meanwhile, some important clues to its recommendations have been outlined by the *Union Budget 2017-18* as given below:

- It has done an elaborate exercise and has recommended that a sustainable debt path must be the *principal macro-economic anchor* of our fiscal policy.

- It has favoured *Debt to GDP* of 60 per cent for the General Government by 2023— consisting of 40 per cent for Central Government and 20 per cent for State Governments.

- Within the framework of debt to GDP ratio, it has derived and recommended *3 per cent* fiscal deficit for the next three years.

- It has also provided for *Escape Clauses*, for deviations upto 0.5 per cent of GDP, from the stipulated fiscal deficit target. Among the triggers for taking recourse to these *Escape Clauses*, it has included "far-reaching structural reforms in the economy with unanticipated fiscal implications" as one of the factors.

The budget has informed that the report will be carefully examined and appropriate decisions will be taken on its advices in due course.

LIMITING GOVERNMENT EXPENDITURE

Elected governments are composed of different interest groups and lobbies. At times, such governments might intend to use its economic policies in a highly populist way for greater political mileage without caring for the national exchequer. Such acts might force the governments to go in for excessive internal and external borrowing and printing of currency. Governments generally avoid to increase tax or impose new taxes for their revenue increase as such acts are politically unpopular. On the other hand, borrowings and printing of currency impose no immediate economic or political costs. A government in the election year usually spends money frugally by borrowings (from the RBI in India) because it is the coming government after the elections who is supposed to repay them. Government expenditures remain higher and expanding due to some economic reasons also—by doing so extra employment is generated and the output (GDP) of the economy is also boosted. If governments go for anti-expansionary fiscal and monetary policies with the objective of reducing its expenditures the employment as well as the GDP both will be hampered. This is considered a *bias* in the economic policies of the elected governments. But there has always been a consensus among the experts and policymakers that an external (i.e., outside the government) and some form of a statutory check must be over the government on its powers of money creation (i.e., by borrowings or printing). With the objective of removing the bias—to make fiscal policy less sensitive to electoral considerations, several countries had introduced some legal provisions on their governments before India enacted its FRBMA. We see mainly *three variants* of it around the world:

(i) It was *New Zealand* which *first* introduced such a legal binding on the government's powers of money creation. Here the central bank is legally bound

---

45. We find similar view being forwarded by the Ministry of Finance, *Economic Survey 2015–16*, Vol. 1 & Vol. 2 (New Delhi: Government of India, 2016).

to ensure that money creation by the government does not increase the rate of *inflation target*—it means that the central bank has the overriding powers on the government there in the area of extra money creation.[46]

(ii) The *second variant* is putting some firm legal or constitutional limit on the size of government deficits or the power of the government to borrow. *Germany* and *Chile* had such an arrangement—today Germany is bound to the fiscal limits prescribed by the Maastricht Treaty. In the late 1990s, an upper limit on the government's powers to create deficit was introduced.[47]

(iii) Some countries introduced the so-called *'Currency Board'* type of arrangement to serve the same purpose—this is the *third variant.* In this arrangement, money supply in the economy is directly linked to changes in the supply of foreign assets—neither the government nor the central bank has any independent powers to create money, as growth in money supply is not allowed to exceed growth in the foreign assets.[48]

It was in 1994 that India took the first step in this direction when the central government had a formal agreement with the RBI to limit its borrowing through *ad hoc* treasury bills to a predetermined amount (Rs. 6,000 crores in 1994–95).[49] However, it was a highly liberal arrangement with the government having the ultimate powers to revise the aforesaid predetermined amount by a fresh agreement with the RBI. The importance this beginning had was finally in the enactment of the FRBMA 2003—a historic achievement in the area of fiscal prudence in the country.

FISCAL CONSOLIDATION IN INDIA

The average combined fiscal deficits, of the Centre and states after 1975, had been above 10 per cent of the GDP till 2000–01. More than half of it had been due to huge revenue deficits. The governments were cautioned by the RBI, the Planning Commission as well as by the IMF and the WB about the unsustainability of the fiscal deficits. It was at the behest of the IMF that India started the politically and socially painful process of fiscal reforms, a step towards fiscal consolidation.[50] A number of steps were taken by the government at the Centre in this direction and there had been incessant attempts to do the same in the states' public finances too. Major highlights

---

46. Opposite to it, in the UK, the government has overriding powers on the central bank and there is absence of any legal checks on money creation powers of the government. Once the UK becomes part of the European Union it will come under such a check through the Maastricht Treaty. Before the enactment of the FRBMA, 2003. India was like the UK, however, the Constitution of India has a provision for imposing a statutory limit on the centre's borrowing powers under *Article 292*. But the Article is not mandatory and has not been invoked by any of the governments till date.

47. By the Congress passing the Balanced Budget Act, 1997 which promised to eliminate federal deficit spending by 2002 (see Nicholas Henry, *Public Administration and Public Policy* (New Delhi: Prentice-Hall, 2003), p. 217.

48. Argentina introduced this arrangement in the late 1990s.

49. Ministry of Finance, *Economic Survey 1994–95* (New Delhi: Government of India, 1995).

50. IMF imposed some macro-economic conditions on the economy while India borrowed from it for its BoP correction in 1990–91. One among the conditions was cutting down the government expenditure (i.e., salaries, pensions, interest and subsidies, etc.) by 10 per cent every year.

in this direction can be summed up as given below:

1. Policy initiatives towards cutting revenue deficits:

   (i) Cutting down expenditure—

   (a) Cutting down the burden of salaries, pensions and the PFs (down-sizing/right-sizing of the government, out of every 3 vacancies 1 to be filled up, interest cut on the PF, pension reforms-PFRDA, etc.);

   (b) Cutting down the subsidies (Administered Price Mechanism in petroleum, fertilizers, sugar, drugs to be rationalised, it was done with mixed successes);

   (c) Interest burden to be cut down (by going for lesser and lesser borrowings, pre-payment of external debts, debt swaps, promoting external lending, minimal dependence on costlier external borrowings, etc.);

   (d) Defence being one major item of the expenditure bilateral negotiations initiated with China and Pakistan (the historical. and psychological enemies against whom the Indian defence preparedness was directed to, as supposed) so that the defence force cut could be completed on the borders, etc.;

   (e) Budgetary supports to the loss-making PSUs to be an exception than a rule;

   (f) Expenditure reform started by the governments in different areas and departments;

   (g) General Services to be motivated towards profit with subsidised services to the needy only (railways, power, water, etc.);

   (h) Postal deficits to be checked by involving the post offices in other areas of profit;

   (i) Higher education declared as non-priority sector; fees of institutions of professional courses revised upward; etc.

   (ii) Increasing *revenue receipts*:

   (a) Tax reforms initiated (Cenvat, VAT, Service Tax, GST proposed, etc.);

   (b) The PSUs to be disinvested and even privatised (if a political concensus reached which alludes today);

   (c) Surplus forex reserves to be used in external lending and purchasing foreign high quality sovereign bonds, etc.

   (d) State governments allowed to go for market borrowing for their plan expenditure, etc.

2. The borrowing programme of the government:

   (i) The Ways and Means Advances (WMA) scheme commenced in 1997 under which the government commits to the RBI about the amount of money it will give as part of its market-borrowing programme, to bring transparency in public expenditure and to put political responsibility on the government.

   (ii) The RBI will not be the primary subscriber to government securities in the future—committed way back in 1997.

3. The fiscal responsibility on the governments:

   (i) The Fiscal Responsibility and Budget Management (FRBM) Act was passed in 2003 (voted by all political parties) which puts constitutional obligation on the government to commit so many things as fiscal responsibility comes in the public finance—fixing annual targets to cut revenue and fiscal deficits; the government not to borrow from the RBI except by the WMA; government to bring in greater transparency in fiscal operations; along with the Budget the government to lay statements regarding fiscal policy strategy in the House and Quarterly Review of trends of receipts and expenditures of the government.

(ii) A mechanism (to include state governments under the umbrella of fiscal responsibility) was advised (now implemented, too) by the 12th Finance Commission which allows the state governments to go for market borrowing (without central permission) for their need of plan development provided they pass their fiscal responsibility acts (FRAs) and commit to the fiscal responsibility regarding cutting their revenue and fiscal deficits. By March 2016, all states and UTs had implemented their FRAs.

India's fiscal consolidation process by now has had a mixed performance. By now, the FRBM Act has been amended twice (in 2004 and 2012), mainly to redefine the fiscal targets or shift the targets to future years. By early 2010, a new school of thinking emerged in the country as per which fixing hard and fast fiscal targets for the governments, at times, may be counterproductive to the economy. This why the GoI through the **Union Budget 2016-17** proposed to go for a *fixed range* for fiscal targets in place of a *fixed number*. The Government of India has accordingly announced to set up an expert committee to *review* the implementation of the FRBM Act.

ZERO-BASE BUDGETING

The idea of zero-base budgeting (ZBB) first came to the privately owned organisation of the USA by the 1960s. This basically belonged to a long list of guidelines for managerial excellence and success,

others being Management by Objectives (MBO), Matrix Management, Portfolio Management, etc to name a few.[51] It was the US financial expert **Peter Phyrr** who first proposed this idea for government budgeting and Jimmy Carter, Govornor of Georgia, USA was the first elected[52] executive to introduce ZBB to the public sector. When he presented the US Budget in 1979 *as the US President* it was the first use of the ZBB for any nation state. Since then many governments of the world have gone for such budgeting.

Zero-base budgeting is the allocation of resources to agencies based on periodic re-evaluation by those agencies of the need for all the programmes for which they are responsible, justifying the continuance or termination of each programme in the agency budget proposal—in other words, an agency reassesses what it is doing from top to bottom from a hypothetical *zero base.*[53]

There are three essential principles of ZBB. Some experts say it in a different way, there are three essential questions which must be answered objectively before going for any expenditure as per the techniques of ZBB:

(i) Should we spend?

(ii) How much should we spend?

(iii) Where should we spend?

There are *three* special features of this budgeting which distinguishes it from the traditional budgeting. These features, in brief, are as under:

51. George R. Terry and Stephen G. Franklin, *Principles of Management* (New Delhi: AITBS, 2002), pp. 9–10.

52. See Peter A. Phyrr, 'The zero Base Approach to Government Budgeting', *Public Administration Review, 37 (Jan./Feb., 1977)*, 7; and Thomas P. Lauth, 'Zero-Base Budgeting in Georgia State Government: Myth and Reality', *Public Administration Review*, 38 (Sept./Oct., 1978) pp. 420–30; (cited in Nicholar Henry, *Public Administration and Public Affairs* (New Delhi: Prentice-Hall, 2003), p. 217.

53. Nicholas Henry, *Public Administration and Public Affairs,* p. 218.

(i) The conventional aggregate approach is not applied in it, in which each department of the government prepares their own budget for many activities in the aggregate and composite form, making it difficult to scrutinise each and every activity. In place of it every department needs to justify its existence and continuance in the budget document by using the mathematical technique of econometrics, i.e., cost-benefit analysis. In a nutshell, every activity of each department is 'X-rayed' and once the justification is validated they are allocated the funds.

(ii) *Economy* in public expenditure is the *raison d'etre* of this budgeting. This is why the ZBB has provisions of close examination and scrutiny of each programme and public spending. Finally, the public spending is cut without affecting the current level of benefits of various public services accruing to the public.

(iii) *Prioritising* the competing needs is another special feature of ZBB. Before allocating funds to the different needs of the economy, an order of priority is prepared with utmost objectivity. As the resources/funds are always scarce, in the process of prioritised allocation, the item/items at the bottom might not get any funds.

Side by side its benefits, there are certain **limitations** too before the ZBB which prohibits its assumed success, according to experts. These limitations have made it subject to criticisms. The limitations are as given below:

(i) There are certain expenditures upon which the government/parliament does not have the power of scrutiny (as the 'Charged Expenditure' in India).

(ii) There are certains public services which defy the cost-benefit analysis—defence, law and order, foreign relations, etc.

(iii) Scrutiny is a subjective matter and so this might become prey to bias. Again, if the scrutinisers have a complete utilitarian view many long-term objectives of budgeting and public policy might get marginalised.

(iv) It has scope for emergence of the Ministry of Finance as the all-powerful institution dictating other ministries and departments.

(v) Bureaucracy does not praise it as it evaluates their decisions and performances in a highly objective way.

Despite the above-given strong limitation, the ZBB has a sound logic and should be considered a long-term budgetary reform process. The basic idea of this form of budgeting is to optimise the benefits of expenditure in every area of activity and in this sense it is exceptional. To the extent the corporate world is concerned, this has been a very successful financial management tool.

In India, it is believed to be in practice since 1997–99. We cannot say that India is a success in ZBB, but many of the profit-fetching PSUs have been able to use it successfully and optimise their profits.

CHARGED EXPENDITURE

It is the public expenditure which is beyond the voting power of the Parliament and is directly withdrawn from the Consolidated Fund of India.[54] For Example, the emoluments of the

---

54. In the Constitution of India it is deliberated in the *Article 112 (3), a - g*, where it is referred as *'expenditure charged'* on the consolidated fund of India—popular as the 'charged expenditure' (see Ministry of Law, Justice and Company Affairs, *The Constitution of India,* Government of India, New Delhi, 1999), pp. 38–39).

President, Speaker and Deputy Speaker of the Lok Sabha, Chairman and Deputy Chairman of the Rajya Sabha, Judges of the Supreme Court and the High Courts in India, etc.

TYPES OF BUDGETS

Golden Rule

The proposition that a government should borrow only to invest (i.e., plan expenditure in India) and not to finance current spending (i.e., revenue expenditure in India) is known as the golden rule of public finance. This rule is undoubtedly prudent but provided spending is honestly described as investment, investments are efficient and does not crowd out the important private sector investments.[55]

Balanced Budget

A budget is said to be a balanced budget when total public-sector spending equals total government income (revenue receipts) during the same period from taxes and charges for public services.[56] In other terms, a budget with zero revenue deficit is balanced budget. Such budget making is popularly known as *balanced budgeting*.

Gender Budgeting

A general budget by the government which allocates funds and reponsibilities on the basis of gender is gender budgeting. It is done in an economy where socio-economic disparities are chronic and clearly visible on a sex basis (as in India).

Gender budgeting started in India with the Union Budget 2006–07 which proposed an outlay of Rs. 28,737 crore dedicated to the cause of women and created gender budgeting cells in 32 ministries and departments.[57]

Outcome and Performance Budgets [58]

The concepts are part of result-oriented budgeting. While outcome budget is presented by different departments and divisions of a ministry or the government, the performance budget is presented by the Ministry of Finance on behalf of the government. Both go for 'quantitative' as well as 'qualitative' progress reports of the performance. The outcome budget is a micro level process while performance budget is a macro-level process in budgeting. There are many outcome budgets in any one performance budget.

The basic objective of such budgeting is to bring in transparency and thereby making the government more and more responsible to the House and the public. Naturally, they bring in prudence and optimisation elements in public spending (also see entry 'Outcome Budget' in Chapter 23).

CUT MOTION

In democratic political systems, there is a provision of Cut Motion in the House/Parliament (usually it is the opposition but floor might be crossed by members of the House belonging to the government due to presence of inner-party politics). In the US, the budget provisions presented by the government must be passed by the Congress. Only then they can be enacted. Unlike this, in the British parliamentary system though the budget of the government is voted by the House usually this is considered a political

55. See Samuelson and Nordhaus, *Economics*, 710; Stiglitz and Walsh, *Economics*, pp. 552–54.

56. Mathew Bishop, *Pocket Economist*, p. 104.

57. Ministry of Finance, *Union Budget 2006–07*, (New Delhi: Government of India, 2007).

58. Based on the notes released by the Ministry of Finance, Government of India, October 2006 while releasing the *Quarterly Review* of the Union Budget 2006–07.

document and passed unchanged. India has mixed provisions of voting on the budget after discussion in both the Houses. There are different constitutional provisions by which the Parliament starts discussion to reduce the demands, grants, etc. proposed by the government in the Budget[59]—

(i) **Token Cut:** This motion intends to *'reduce the demand by Rs. 100'*. Such a motion is moved in order to express a specific grievance which is within the sphere of the responsibility of the Government of India—the discussion remains confined to the particular grievance specified in the motion.

(ii) **Economy Cut:** This motion intends to *'reduce the demand by a specified amount'* representing the economy (in expenditure) that can be affected. Such specified amount may be either lump sum reduction in the demand or omission or reduction of an item in the demnd—the discussion remains confined to the matter in which the economy can be affected.

(iii) **Disapproval of Policy Cut:** This motion intends to *'reduce the demand to Re. 1'*. This represents *disapproval* of the policy underlying the demand—the discussion remains confined to the particular policy and is open to members to advocate an alternate policy.

(iv) **Guillotine** is the process in which the Speaker puts all the outstanding demands made by the Budget *directly to vote* in the House—ending further discussions (intended to cut short the discussion on the Budget). Through this, the Speaker may put the whole Budegt to vote (i.e., allowing 'no discussion' on the Budget by the House). In recent years, this route was taken time and again by the Government of India, to avoid the aggressive mood of the Opposition.

Though, this is a *short route* to get the Budget passed by the House (avoiding criticism by the opposition benchcs), it may turn out to be very dangerous —as the voting process may take the form of 'no confidence motion' and the government may be routed out of power. But, till date, *Guillotines* never resulted into routing a government out of power in India (as India follows the British Model of Parliamentary system).

TRILEMMAS

Putting the right kind of fiscal policy has always been the most challenging policy decision to be taken by the democratic governments around the world, there are some famous 'trilemmas' related to this aspect. Economics have by now many 'trilemmas' developed and articulated by economists from time to time and the process still continues. Let us see some highly popular and newsmaking ones:

(i) The **'financial stability trilemma'** put forward by Dirk Schoenmaker[60] (2008), explains the incompatibility within the Euro zone of :

• a stable financial system,

• an integrated financial system, and

• national financial stability policies.

(ii) By far the most high profile current trilemma of the Eurozone (by Edward Chancellor[61]) was believed to be the seeming irreconcilability between its **three wishes,** namely,

---

59. Rules of Procedure and Conduct of Business in Lok Sabha, Parliament Secretariat, New Dehli.

60. Dirk Schoenmaker, "A New Financial Stability Framework for Europe", *The Financial Regulator,* 0, 13 (3), 2009.

61. Edward Chancellor, "Germany's Eurozone Trilemma", *Financial Times,* 6 November, 2011.

- a single currency,

- minimal fiscal contribution to bail outs, and

- the ECB's commitment to low inflation.

(iii) Martin Wolf[62] spoke about the US Republican Party's **fiscal policy trilemma:**

- large budget deficits are ruinous;

- a continued eagerness to cut taxes; and

- an utter lack of interest in spending cuts on a large enough scale.

(iv) Then we have the **Earth Trilemma** (EEE), which posits that for:

- economic development (E),

- we need increased energy expenditure (E),

- but this raises the environmental issue (E).

(v) Above all these more recent trilemmas in economics, the prima donna of all of them is Mundell's **'impossible trinity'**. This old trilemma asserts that a country cannot maintain, simultaneously, all three policy goals of—

- free capital flows,

- a fixed exchange rate, and

- an independent monetary policy. The impossible trinity, has seen enough waters flowing down the time since it was articulated almost five decades ago which has a strong theoretical foundation in the *Mundell-Fleming Model* developed in the 1960s.

Dani Rodrik[63] argued that if a country wants more of globalisation, it must either give up some democracy or some national sovereignty. Niall Ferguson[64] highlighted the **trilemma** of a choice between commitment to globalisation, to social order and to a small state (meaning limited state intervention).

TREASURY COMPUTERISATION

Governments

A scheme for implementation of the mission mode project[65] 'Computerisation of State Treasuries' was put in place by the GoI in June 2010 under the *National e-Governance Plan (NeGP)*. The states and UTs are required to complete their projects in about three years beginning 2010–11. The funds are released against deliverables. The scheme will support states and UTs to fill the existing gaps in their treasury computerisation, upgradation, expansion and interface requirements, apart from supporting basic computerisation. The scheme covers installation of suitable hardware and application software systems in a networked environment on a wide area basis and building of interfaces for data sharing among various stakeholders.

The scheme for treasury computerisation is expected to make the budgeting process more efficient, improve cash flow management, promote real-time reconciliation of accounts, strengthen management information systems (MIS), improve accuracy and timeliness in accounts preparation,

---

62. Martin Wolf, "The Political Genius of Supply Side Economics", *Financial Times,* 2010.

63. Dani Rodrik, "The Inescapable Trilemma of the World Economy", 27 June, 2007, *(Erodrik.typepad.com/ dani_rodriks_weblog.*

64. *Niall Ferguson,* "Conservatism and the Crisis: A Transatlantic Trilemma", Centre for Policy Studies, Ruttenberg Lecture, 24 March, 2009.

65. Ministry of Finance, *Economic Survey 2011–12,* p. 69.

bring about transparency and efficiency in public delivery systems, help bring about better financial management along with improved quality of governance in states and UTs. The overall estimated cost of the scheme is Rs. 626 crore at Rs. 1 crore per district in existence on 1 April, 2011. Financial support is up to 75 per cent (90 per cent in case of northeastern states) of the individual project cost of admissible components limited to Rs. 75 lakh per district (Rs. 90 lakh per district for north-eastern states). Funds will be released as central assistance in three instalments of 40 per cent, 30 per cent, and 30 per cent each, subject to satisfactory receipt of utilisation certificates.

DIRECT BENEFIT TRANSFER[66]

In 2015, the new government in Centre introduced the game-changing potential of technology-enabled Direct Benefits Transfers (DBT), namely the *JAM (Jan Dhan-Aadhaar-Mobile) Number Trinity* solution. It offers possibilities for effectively targeting public resources to those who need them most, and including all those who have been deprived in multiple ways. Under it, the beneficiaries will get the money 'directly' into their bank or post-office accounts linked to their 12-digit biometric identity number (Aadhar) provided by the Unique Identification Authority of India (UIDAI). The idea was first initiated by the GoI in 2013 (UPA-II) on pilot basis with seven schemes in 20 district of the country.

Part of the technological platform—the *Digital India*—it is expected to provide, integration of various beneficiary' databases with Aadhaar and appropriate process re-engineering. It would result in:

• removal of fake and duplicate entities from beneficiary lists
• prevention of leakage and wastage
• substantial saving of effort, time and cost
• ensuring full traceability of flow of funds to the beneficiary.
• checking the element of corruption through transparency
• accountability of flow of funds
• expenditure rationalisation

Meanwhile, the *Aadhaar (Targeted Delivery of Financial and Other Subsidies, Benefits and Services) Bill, 2016* was passed by the Parliament and enforced by late 2016. This is a *transformative* piece of legislation which will benefit the poor and the vulnerable. The statutory backing to Aadhar will address the uncertainty surrounding the project after the Supreme Court restricted the use of the Aadhaar number until a Constitution Bench delivers its verdict on a number of cases challenging the mandatory use of Aadhaar in government schemes, and rules on the issue of privacy violation.

To ensure targeted disbursement of government subsidies and financial assistance to the actual beneficiaries, is a critical component of 'minimum government and maximum governance' of the Government of India. After the successful introduction of DBT in LPG, the government in 2016–17 introduced it on pilot basis for fertilizer in few districts. Similarly, the government has also started the *automation facilities* of the 5.35 lakh FPS (Fair Price Shops) which come under the PDS (Public Distribution System).

As per the **Union Budget 2017-18**, the country has made a strong beginning with regard to DBT with regard to LPG and kerosene consumers—Chandigarh and 8 districts of

---

66. Ministry of Finance, *Economic Survey 2015–16*, pp. 28, 123, 213; Publication Division, *India 2016* (New Delhi: Government of India, 2017) pp. 718.

Haryana have become kerosene free. Besides, 84 Government schemes have also been boarded on the DBT platform. The idea of DBT will also be key to India's transition to a **cashless economy**—as pointed by the *Economic Survey 2015-16* and vindicated in the *post-demonetisation* period.

The *Economic Survey 2015–16* suggested the DBT solution for farm loans and interest subvention schemes availed by the farmers. It further advised for replacing the existing system of MSP/procurement based PDS with DBT which will free the market of all controls on domestic movement and import. The present system distorts the concept of a market and needs to be discontinued to enhance productivity in agriculture, as per the Survey.

EXPENDITURE MANAGEMENT COMMISSION

By early September 2014, the GoI constituted an Expenditure Management Commission (EMC) through a Resolution. The EMC will look into various aspects of expenditure reforms to be undertaken by the government and other issues concerning Public Expenditure Management. The Commission has one full time, one part time and one ex-officio members other than Chairman of (Cabinet rank). Dr. Bimal Jalan is its first Chairman. The terms of reference of the Commission are as given below:

(i) Review the major areas of Central Government expenditure, and to suggest ways of creating fiscal space required to meet developmental expenditure needs, without compromising the commitment to fiscal discipline.

(ii) Review the institutional arrangement, including budgeting process and FRBM rules, for enforcing aggregate fiscal discipline and suggest improvements theirin;

(iii) Suggest measures to improve allocative effeciencies in the existing expenditure classification system, including focus on capital expenditure;

(iv) Design a framework to imrpove operational efficiency of expenditures through focus on utilization, targets and outcomes;

(v) Suggest an effective strategy for meeting reasonable proportion of expenditure on services through user charges;

(vi) Suggest measures to achieve reduction in financial costs through better Cash Management Ssystem;

(vii) Suggest greater use of IT tools for expenditure management;

(viii) Suggest improved financial reporting systems in terms of accounting, budgeting, etc., and

(ix) Consider any other relevant issue concerning Public Expenditure Management in Central Government and make suitable recommendations.

NEED OF PUBLIC INVESTMENT

We see the new government at the Centre initiating several reforms. Together with the experts, the Government of India also believe that this has revived the *investor sentiment*. But a real investment flow is yet to pick-up, especially from the private sector. The cause for such a situation has been identified as the "balance sheet syndrome with Indian characteristics". The *Economic Survey 2014–15* has analysed this situation in greater details.

In such a scenario, together with other measures, the most important action which has been suggested is "boosting the public investment". Merit of such an action has been emphasised by the *Mid Year Economic Analysis 2014–15,* too. The document says that reviving 'targeted public investment' will work as an cngine of growth in short-term and will lead to investment flows coming in from the private sector. It has not suggested public investment as a substitute for private investment but as a means to complement and kick start investment flows from the latter.

Role of Public Investment

Several recent studies, from India and abroad, have been quoted by the ***Economic Survey 2014–15*** to suggest an increase in the public investment—in a targeted way. Here, 'targeted' public investment means, government investment in the sector which can generate the largest 'spillover effects' to the economy. In present time, the Railways has that level of spillover potential. The Survey agrres with the famous observation of W. W. Rostow – 'the introduction of the railways has been historically the most powerful single initiator of take-offs'[67]. The rational for such a policy action has been emphasised by referring to the follwoing documents and studies:

(i) It has been found that there has been a 'link' between public and private investment in past which caused either rise or fall in the growth rate. The Central Statistics Office (CSO) data indicate that a 'boom' in private corporate investment in the high growth phase of 2004–08 was accompanied by an increase in public investment by about 1.5 per cent.

Similarly, a decline in public investment by more than 1 percentage point between 2008–13, is accompanied by a general decline in private corporate investment by more than 8 percentage points (except an increase during 2009–10 and 2010–11).

(ii) The *World Economic Outlook-2014* (an IMF report)[68] noted that increases in public infrastructure investment, if efficiently implemented, affects the economy in two ways:

(a) In the short run it boosts aggregate demand and crowds in (increases) private investment due to the complementary nature of infrastructure services.

(b) In the long run, a supply side effect also kicks in as the infrastructure built feeds into the productive capacity of the economy (infrastructure being the lifeline of an economy that bringing positive effects to all sectors).

The studies of the *IMF* confirm that increase in public investment can have positive effects on output. The medium-term public investment multiplier for developing economies is estimated to be between 0.5 and 0.9, however, the magnitudes depend on the efficiency of implementation.

(iii) In order of boosting public investment there are the *two challenges* in this regard are—

(a) Mobilisation of the financial resources to enhance public investment, and

(b) Implementation capacity.

To the extent implementation capacity is concerned, a sector with the maximum positive 'spillovers' together with proven capacity for investing quickly and efficiently, can serve the purpose. Two such sectors are: rural roads and railways. Enhancing road connectivity can have a huge positive spillover on

67. W. W. Rostow, *The Process of Economic Growth* (Oxford: Clarendon Press, 2nd edition, 1960), pp. 302-303, cited in B. R. Mitchell, 'The Coming of the Railway and United Kingdom Economic Growth), *The Journal of Economic History* 24(3), September 1964.

68. International Monetary Fund, ***World Economic Outlook-2014***, Is it Time for an Infrastructure Push? The Macroeconomic Effects of Public Investment, October 2014.

the economy—this has been shown by recent studies[69]—the examples in case are the National Highways Development Project and the PM Gram Sadak Yojana of early 2000s. These public investment moves encouraged rurl employment and earnings.

The *Survey* believes that the present government should encourage public investment in the hetherto neglected railways sector—it has the potential to have similar effects on the economy as the road sector could do in past. This has the potential to *crowd in* greater private investment and without jeopardising India's public debt dynamics.

(iv) Public investment has direct positive bearings on the growth prospects, as per the empirical studies. India's productivity surge around 1980 was due to boost in productivity led by enhanced public investments in the infrastructure sector (in contrast to the demand creating effects).[70] The study analyses the effects on overall growth using a framework[71] where government infrastructure services are an input into private production. The results of the study indicate that allowing for the appropriate lag (of around five years) between public infrastructure spending and growth, the former can explain around 1.5-2.9 percent of overall growth.

(v) A study[72] by the RBI reports the *long run* multiplier (of capital outlays on GDP) to be 2.4. The study also confirms that the effect of revenue expenditure on GDP, though high, fades out after the first year, suggesting gains from reprioritizing expenditures.

Thus, the Survey has emphasised a big role of enhancing public investment in the railways sector. It could be started as only public investment. But soon, the impetus given by the government will generate enough avenues and new possibilities that the sector will start attracting enough investment flows from the privates sector. Once such an effect is visible then there are several possible alternatives to promote investment—the PPP to dedicated private inevstments. Railways being a lead infrastructure sector it will bring in multi-dimensional positive spillovers in the economy. Linking people and places has great potential in creating great many numbers of openings in the economy.

FUTURE OUTLOOK

Today, Indian economy is much more exposed to the external dynamism than anytime in past—being unfavourable for the past many years. During this period, its domestic affairs were also not very favourable. For the *forthcoming year 2017-18*, the following outlook[73] may be predicted:

Real Gross Income

In this regard, it will be useful to examine the four following components of aggregate demand:

• *Exports:* Exports appear to be recovering

69. Sam Asher Paul Novosad, The Employment Effects of Road Construction in Rural India, Working Paper 2014, quoted by the Ministry of Finance, *Economic Survey 2014–15*.

70. D. Rodrik, and D. A. Subramanian, From 'Hindu Growth' to Productivity Surge: The Mystery of the Indian Growth Transition, *IMF Staff Papers*, 52(2), 2005.

71. Robert Barro, 'Government Spending in a Simple Model of Endogenous Growth", *Journal of Political Economy*, 98(5) 1990.

72. Reserve Bank of India, *Fiscal Multipliers in India*, Box II.16, *Annual Report 2011–12*, (New Delhi: Government of India, 2012).

73. The discussion is based on the **Economic Survey 2016-17**, Vol. 1, pp. 20-22 and the **Union Budget 2017-18** as well as other announcements of the Government of India.

on the back of increasing global economic activity. This looks continuing post-US elections which is expected to announce fiscal stimulus. The IMF's update *(World Economic Outlook, January 2017)* has projecting an increase in global growth from 3.1 per cent in 2016 to 3.4 per cent in 2017, with a corresponding increase in growth for advanced economies from 1.6 per cent to 1.9 per cent. As India's real export is highly elastic to global GDP, higher exports can contribute to 1 per cent growth in the year.

- **Consumption:** The outlook for private consumption is less clear. International oil prices are expected to be about 10-15 per cent higher in 2017 (compared to 2016), which would create a drag of about 0.5 percentage points. On the other hand, consumption is expected to receive a boost from two sources—*firstly,* catch-up after the demonetisation-induced reduction in the last two quarters of 2016-17; and *secondly,* due to cheaper borrowing costs (likely to be lower by 0.75 to 1 per cent). As a result, spending on housing and consumer durables and semi-durables could rise smartly. Predicting monsoon prospects for 2017 so early looks difficult thus clues regarding agricultural production are not certain—though the year 2016-17 is estimated to be a record year for foodgrain production.

- **Private Investment:** Since no clear progress is yet visible in tackling the *twin balance sheet* (TBS) problem, private investment is unlikely to recover significantly in the year.

- **Government:** Some of this weakness could be offset through higher public investment, but that would depend on the stance of fiscal for the year, which has to balance the short-term requirements of an economy recovering from demonetisation against the medium-term necessity of adhering to fiscal discipline—and the need to be seen as doing so.

Overall, the real GDP growth is expected to be between **6.75** to **7.5** per cent—the country to remain the fastest growing economy in the world. This prospect for the economy in 2017-18 is though exposed to three main downside risks—

(i) The extent to which the effects of *demonetisation* could linger into next year, especially if uncertainty remains on the policy response. Currency shortages also affect supplies of certain agricultural products, especially milk (where procurement has been low), sugar (where cane availability and drought in the southern states will restrict production), and potatoes and onions (where sowings have been low). Vigilance is essential to prevent other agricultural products becoming in 2017-18 what pulses were in 2015-16.

(ii) The geopolitics could take *oil prices* up further than forecast. The ability of shale oil production to respond quickly should contain the risks of a sharp increase, but even if prices rose merely to US $ 60-65 per barrel the Indian economy would nonetheless be affected by way of reduced consumption; less room for public investment; and lower corporate margins, further denting private investment. The scope for monetary easing might also narrow, if higher oil prices invited inflationary pressure.

(iii) There are risks from the possible eruption of *trade tensions* amongst the major countries, triggered by geo-politics or currency movements. This could reduce global growth and trigger capital flight from emerging markets including India.

The one significant *upside possibility* is a strong rebound in global demand and hence in India's exports. There are some nascent signs of that in the last two quarters of 2016. A strong export recovery would have broader spillover effects to investment.

Fiscal Outlook

The fiscal outlook for the central government for next year will be marked by three factors:

(i) The increase in the *tax to GDP ratio* of about 0.5 percentage points in each of the last two years, owing to the oil windfall will disappear. In fact, excise-related taxes will decline by about 0.1 percentage point of GDP, a swing of about 0.6 percentage points.

(ii) There will be a fiscal windfall both from the high *denomination* notes that are not returned to the RBI and from higher tax collections as a result of increased disclosure under the Pradhan Mantre Garib Kalyan Yojana (PMGKY). Both of these are likely to be one-off in nature, and in both cases the magnitudes are uncertain. The fiscal gains from it will take time to get fully realised.

(iii) It appears that the GST will probably be implemented later in the fiscal year (as per Government it will be implemented from *July 2017*). The transition to the GST is so complicated from an administrative and technology perspective that revenue collection will take some time to reach full potential. Combined with the government's commitment to compensating the states for any shortfall in their own GST collections (for next 5 years at a baseline of 14 per cent increase), the outlook must be cautious with respect to revenue collections. The fiscal gains from the GST will also take time to be fully realized.

The revenue outgo on account of the implementation of the 7th Pay Commission may dilute the fiscal gains discussed above.

Macroeconomic Policy Stance

Important macroeconomic policy requirements and needs will be as analysed below:

- The economy needs policy support to recover smoothly from demonetisation. If bank deposits grow—lending, and yields on G-Secs should be lower—and will provide a boost to the economy. Though, sharp rise in oil prices and those of agricultural products, would limit the scope for interest rate cuts from the RBI.

- The Government needs to continue its fiscal credibility and prudence by remaining committed to reducing fiscal deficit like past four years (it has been set at 3.2 per cent for the year by the *Union Budget 2017-18*). Fiscal deficit has been reduced by the Government from 4.5 per cent of 2013-14 to 4.1 percent, 3.9 per cent, and 3.5 per cent in the following three years.

- The use of the fiscal windfall (comprising the unreturned cash and additional receipts under the PMGKY) which is still uncertain, will be one key issue. Since the windfall to the public sector is both 'one off ' and a 'wealth gain' (not an income gain), it should be deployed to strengthening the government's balance sheet rather than being used for government consumption, especially in the form of programs (that create permanent entitlements). The best use of the windfall would be to create a "public sector asset reconstruction/rehabilitation company/agency" (i.e., advised as PARA) so that the *twin balance sheet* problem can be addressed—by three possible means:

(i) facilitating credit and investment revival;

(ii) compensating states for revenue shortfalls due to the GST; and

(iii) clearing debt.

Meanwhile, the Government by ***mid-February 2017*** indicated about its willingness to set up such an agency.

- On *reforms front*, structural reforms will be the most important boost to growth together with—strategic disinvestment, tax reform, subsidy rationalization and addressing the twin balance sheet problem. In the case of the twin balance sheet problem, past experiences suggest that creating a *rehabilitation agency* (PARA) will be the best way out of the situation.

- Given the difficulty of reforming *labour laws*, the thrust could be to move towards affording greater choice to workers which would foster competition amongst service providers. Choices would relate to:

(i) whether they want to make their own contribution to the Employees' Provident Fund Organisation (EPFO);

(ii) whether the employers' contribution should go to the EPFO or the National Pension Scheme; and

(iii) whether to contribute to the Employee State Insurance (ESI) or an alternative medical insurance program.

At the same time, there could be a gradual move to ensure that at least compliance with the central labour laws is made *paperless, presence-less,* and *cashless.*

On the *expenditure side*, the studies make clear that existing government programs suffer from poor targeting. One 'radical idea' to consider is the provision of a universal basic income (UBI). Another more modest proposal worth embracing is procedural—no new welfare programme should be launched without introspecting the improvement angle over the existing ones. Together with it, the government needs to evaluate and phase down existing programmes which are not serving their purposes. It will not only strengthen the cause of welfare targeting but bring in more legitimacy in the state.

CHAPTER 19

SUSTAINABILITY AND CLIMATE CHANGE: INDIA AND THE WORLD

*"... this is the only home we have and, as environmentalists are fond of saying, Mother Nature doesn't do bailouts ... so we better find a better way to grow."**

*Thomas L. Friedman, *Hot, Flat, & Crowded*, (London: Penguin Books, 2009), p. 23.

INTRODUCTION

Improving living standards for mankind has been the single minded goal of all nations and world bodies. After defining development in numerous ways for over two decades, there seems to be a consensus on 'Human Development'. While a large population on the earth is still to get the 'bare minimum' for development, humanity is at the crossroads where it is faced with the first of its kind challenge—the challenge of 'climate change'. The dilemma is that whatever we can do for our development, there has to be a repercussion on nature. An even bigger dilemma is in achieving a global consensus on how to check or restrict and finally reverse the process of climate change.

We may consider the year 2012, arguably, a high water mark in the field of environment and sustainable development initiatives. The global community met at the *UN Conference on Sustainable Development* that took place in **Rio** in June 2012, also marking the 20th anniversary of the first Earth Summit held in 1992. The conference reviewed the progress made, identified implementation gaps, and assessed new and emerging challenges, which resulted in a political outcome called the *'The Future We Want'*. In India, the Twelfth Five Year Plan was launched with a focus on sustainable growth. This along with sustainable development policies and programmes, which are being followed signalled to citizens at home and the world at large that India is committed to sustainable development with equal emphasis on its three dimensions—social, economic and environmental.

A survey of the global comparative opinion shows that people in India and indeed all countries, have a marked and rising concern about sustainable development and climate change (cited by the *Economic Survey 2014–15*). However, the challenges are also formidable, especially in the context of finding the matching resources of the required magnitude given the economic conditions. Climate science has rightly taken up an important position in the public debate. Even as the science of climate change grapples with uncertainties, the world is witnessing more extreme events. With rising extreme events, and rising citizen demand, the world has little option but to listen to the voice of evolving science and respond adequately with strategies and policies rooted in the principles of multilateralism with equitable and fair burden sharing.[1]

Since 2010 onwards, the world has witnessed increasing numbers of natural disasters and extreme weather conditions—frequently getting news headlines across the world. Policy-makers have been facing enormous pressure on availability of clean air, water and energy together with the problems of poverty and hunger, especially in the developing world. Though, the concerns of climate and environment have been there in India's policies, we see it increasing in the past half a decade. It was in *Economic Survey 2011–12* that a chapter 'Climate Change and Sustainable Development' appeared—the chapter has been retained by the upcoming volumes. This shows the inclusion of environmental concerns in India's policy-making.

The *year 2015* witnessed two landmark international events—the historic climate change agreement under the *UNFCCC in Paris* in December 2015 and the adoption of the *SDGs* (Sustainable Development Goals) in September 2015. The Paris Agreement aims at keeping the rise in global temperatures well below 2°C,which will set the world towards a low carbon, resilient and sustainable future, while the Sustainable Development Goals, which replace the MDGs (Millennium Development Goals), set the development agenda for the next fifteen years. On the domestic front too some important

---

1. Oliver Morton 'Megachange: The World in 2050', in Daniel Franklin and John Andrews, *The Economist* in London: 2012) pp. 92–110.

climate-related initiatives were taken, including the launching of the historic *International Solar Alliance* (an initiative taken by India) and the submission of the ambitious INDC (Intended Nationally Determined Contribution).

GLOBAL EMISSIONS

As per the WMO (World Meteorological Organization), 2016 was the *warmest* year, with temperature 1°C above the pre-industrial era. This was owing to *El Nino* and warming caused by greenhouse gases (GHGs). Anthropogenic emissions have been increasing at an unprecedented rate since the industrial revolution. According to an IEA (International Energy Agency) report 2015, concentration of CO_2 in 2014 was 40 per cent higher than in the mid-1800s. The energy sector is the largest contributor to GHG emissions and, within this, CO_2 emissions from combustion of fuels have the largest share. The global emissions profile[2] shows that emissions have been distributed very unequally among different countries:

(i) If historical CO_2 emissions from 1970 to 2014 are considered, India with 39.0 Gt is way behind the top three emitters—the USA (232 Gt), the EU (190.2 Gt) and China (176.2 Gt). USA's emissions, for example, were around six times India's.

(ii) Even if historical levels are discounted and only present levels considered, both in terms of absolute and per capita emissions, India is way behind the three major CO_2 emitters. Per capita emissions for USA, EU, China and India are—17 ton/capita, 7.5 ton/capita, 7 ton/capita and 2 ton/capita, respectively.

(iii) In terms of sectoral CO_2 emissions from fuel combustion, electricity and heat production was the largest contributor for China, India, the EU and the USA, more so for China and India, followed by the manufacturing industry for India and China and the transport sector for the US and the EU. These compositional patterns reflect the different priorities of these countries.

SUSTAINABLE DEVELOPMENT GOALS (SDGs)

The UN General Assembly in its 17th session in September 2015 announced a set of *17 SDGs* (Sustainable Development Goals) and 169 targets which will stimulate action over the next 15 years. This set of goals replaces the Millennium Development Goals (MDGs) which were coming to an end in 2015 and will try to work in the areas which could not be completed earlier.

The SDGs were adopted after one of the largest consultation exercises in UN history. The goals were proposed in the United Nations Conference on Sustainable Development *(Rio+20)* in June 2012. The SDGs will be effective between 2016–2030. *Major highlights* of the SDGs are as given below:

(i) poverty eradication;

(ii) combating inequalities;

(iii) promoting gender equality, women and girl empowerment;

(iv) improving health and education;

(v) making cities more sustainable;

(vi) combating climate change;

(vii) protecting oceans and forests;

(viii) integrating the socio-economic and environmental dimensions;

(ix) global partnership for sustainable development;

(x) enhancing capacities of stakeholders in better quality measurement;

2. PBL, **Trends in Global CO2 Emissions 2015 Report**, Netherlands Environmental Assessment Agency, as quoted by the **Economic Survey 2015–16**, Vol. 2 (New Delhi: Government of India, 2016), pp. 177–178.

(xi) compilation of data or information on sustainable development; and

(xii) effective follow-up and review architecture.

India's Performance: India had made significant progress on the MDGs and has already achieved the target of *gender parity* in primary school enrolment and halved the proportion of population who do not have access to clean drinking water and is on track on the poverty reduction target. But it is lagging on targets for achieving universal primary school enrolment, reducing child and infant mortality, and improving access to adequate sanitation.

In comparison to the MDGs, the SDGs have very comprehensive targets and finding indicators for each of the 169 targets will be a challenge. The financing and adequate monitoring mechanisms will pose other major challenges. Taking leads from its progress on the MDGs, India will have to prioritize its SDGs, as it will be difficult to target each goal.

PARIS AGREEMENT (COP 21)

The 21st Conference of Parties *(COP 21)* under the UNFCCC (United Nations Framework Convention on Climate Change) took place in Paris by December 2015. The Paris Agreement on post-2020 actions on climate change will succeed the *Kyoto Protocol*. Unlike the Kyoto Protocol, it provides a framework for all countries to take action against climate change. Placing emphasis on concepts like climate justice and sustainable lifestyles, the Paris Agreement for the *first time* brings together all nations for a common cause under the UNFCCC. One of the main focus of the agreement is to hold the increase in the global average temperature to well below 2°C above pre-industrial level and on driving efforts to limit it even further to 1.5°C.

The Agreement comprises of 29 articles and is supported by 139 decisions of the COP. It covers all the crucial areas identified as essential for a comprehensive and balanced agreement, including mitigation, adaptation, loss and damage, finance, technology development and transfer, capacity building and transparency of action and support.

A marked departure from the past is the Agreement's *bottom-up approach*, allowing each nation to submit its own national plan for reducing greenhouse gas emissions, rather than trying to repeat a top-down approach advocated by the Kyoto Protocol, giving each country an emission reduction target. *Salient features* of the Agreement[3]:

(i) It acknowledges the development imperatives of developing countries by recognising their right to development and their efforts to harmonize it with the environment, while protecting the interests of the most vulnerable.

(ii) It seeks to enhance the 'implementation of the Convention' while reflecting the principles of equity and CBDR-RC (Common but Differentiated Responsibilities and Respective Capabilities), in the light of different national circumstances.

(iii) Countries are required to communicate to the UNFCCC climate action plans known as nationally determined contributions (NDCs) every five years. Each Party's successive NDC will represent a progression beyond the Party's then current NDC thereby steadily increasing global effort and ambition in the long-term.

(iv) It is not mitigation-centric and includes other important elements such as adaptation, loss and damage, finance, technology development and transfer,

---

3. Ministry of Finance, **Economic Survey 2015-16**, Vol. 2, pp. 179–181.

capacity building and transparency of action and support.

(v) Developed countries are urged to scale up their level of financial support with a complete road map towards achieving the goal of jointly providing US$ 100 billion by 2020. At the same time, a new collective quantified goal based on US$ 100 billion floor will be set before 2025.

(vi) It mandates that developed countries provide financial resources to developing countries. Other Parties may also contribute, but on a purely voluntary basis.

(vii) Developed countries are urged to take the lead in mobilization of climate finance, while noting the significant role of public funds in the mobilization of finance which should represent a progression beyond their previous effort.

(viii) It includes a robust transparency framework for both action and support.

(ix) Starting in 2023, a global stock-take covering all elements will take place every five years to assess the collective progress towards achieving the purpose of the Agreement and its long-term goals.

(x) It establishes a compliance mechanism, overseen by a committee of experts that operates in a non-punitive way, and is facilitative in nature.

The Paris Agreement entered into force on 4th November 2016. The "22nd Session of the Conference of Parties" *(COP 22)* to UNFCCC was held from 7-19 November 2016 in Marrakesh, Morocco. The main thrust of COP 22 was on developing rules and action framework for operationalizing the Paris Agreement[4] and advance work on pre-2020 Actions. At COP 22, a deadline of 2018 for the rule book was agreed upon. Detailing exercise will include accounting of the NDCs, adaptation communication, building a transparency framework, global stock take every five years, etc.

The key decision adopted at COP 22 was *Marrakesh Action Proclamation for our Climate and Sustainable Development* which captured the "sense of urgency" to take action on climate change. It also emphasized the need to strengthen and support efforts to eradicate poverty, ensure food security and enhance resilience of agriculture. Mobilization of US $ 100 billion per year is a key element of the Proclamation.

GREEN FINANCE

In the past few years, the term 'green finance' has gained a lot of attention across the world. The idea gets its first mention in the UN document at the UN Conference on Sustainable Development (also known as *Rio+20*), 2012. Though it lacks an universal definition, green finance mostly refers to financial investments in projects and initiatives that encourage more sustainable economy.

There is no universal *definition* of green finance, though, it mostly refers to financial investments flowing towards sustainable development projects and initiatives that encourage the development of a more sustainable economy[5]. By now, several working definitions have come up—China's Green Credit Guidelines; the Climate Bonds Taxonomy of Green Bonds; the International Development Finance Club's (IDFC) approach to reporting on green investment; the World Bank/International Finance Corporation's (IFC) Sustainability Framework; and the UK Green Investment Bank Policies.

4. **Economic Survey 2016-17**, Government of India, Ministry of Finance, N. Delhi, Vol. 1, pp. 165-166.

5. *Green Finance Study Group*—as quoted by the Ministry of Finance, **Economic Survey 2015–16**, Vol. 2, pp. 182-83.

Current definitions in use reveals sizeable variance—clean energy; energy efficiency; green buildings; sustainable transport; water and waste management; greening the banking system, the bond market and institutional investment; as well as areas of controversy such as nuclear and large-scale hydro energy, bio-fuels and efficiency gains in conventional power.

The World Bank Group has set up an informal *Sustainable Banking Network* of banking regulators, led by developing countries, to promote sustainable lending practices. In 2015, green bonds issued by governments, banks, corporates and individual projects amounted to US$42 billion.

At the global level, more than 20 stock exchanges have issued guidelines on environmental disclosure, and many green indices and green ETFs (exchange-traded funds) have been developed. A growing number of institutions, including the Bank of England and Bank of China (Industrial and Commercial Bank of China), have begun to assess the financial impact of climate and environmental policy changes. Germany, the US and the UK have developed interest subsidy and guarantee programmes for green financing, and over a dozen government-backed green investment banks are operating globally. The G-20 has also recently set up a GFSG (green finance study group). The issue of mobilising *private finance* for transforming into a green global economy appeared at different global fora including the G20. Experts believe that for developing countries like India, private finance will not readily be forthcoming and public finance (both international and domestic) needs to be used to leverage private finance.

India and Green Development: Green finance is yet to pick up in India. Attaining the ambitious solar energy target, development of solar cities, setting up wind power projects, developing smart cities, providing infrastructure which is considered as a green activity and the sanitation drive under the 'Clean India' or 'Swach Bharath Abhiyan' are all activities needing green finance.

India created a corpus called the NCEF (National Clean Energy Fund) in 2010-11 out of the cess on coal produced/imported ('polluter pays' principle) for the purpose of financing and promoting clean energy initiatives and funding research in the area of clean energy. Some of the projects financed by this fund include innovative schemes like—

(i) a green energy corridor for boosting the transmission sector;

(ii) Jawaharlal Nehru National Solar Mission's (JNNSM) installation of solar photovoltaic (SPV) lights and small capacity lights, installation of SPV water pumping systems, SPV power plants, grid-connected rooftop SPV power plants; and

(iii) pilot project to assess wind power potential.

Six banks by **February 2017** had issued *green bonds* in India. Proceeds from these bonds are mostly used for funding renewable energy projects such as solar, wind and biomass projects and other infrastructure sectors, with infrastructure and energy efficiency being considered as green in their entirety. By early 2016, the SEBI (Securities and Exchange Board of India) approved the guidelines for green bonds. India needs to take care of ***certain issues***[6] involved with the mobilisation of green finance:

(i) For a developing country like India, poverty alleviation and development are of vital importance and resources should not be diverted from meeting these development needs. Green finance should not be limited only to investment in renewable energy, as, for a country

---

6. Ibid., Vol. 2, pp. 182–83.

like India, coal based power accounts for around 60 per cent of installed capacity. Emphasis should be on *greening coal technology*. In fact, green finance for development and transfer of green technology is important as most green technologies in developed countries are in the private domain and are subject to intellectual property rights (IPRs), making them cost prohibitive.

(ii) Green bonds are perceived as new and attach higher risk and their tenure is also shorter. There is a need to reduce risks to make them investment grade.

(iii) There is also a need for an internationally agreed upon definition of green financing as its absence could lead to over-accounting.

(iv) While environmental risk assessment is important, banks should not overestimate risks while providing green finance.

(v) Green finance should also consider unsustainable patterns of *consumption* as a parameter in deciding finance, particularly conspicuous consumption and unsustainable lifestyles in developed countries.

CLIMATE FINANCE

World is alive to the compulsion of combating climate change as unmitigated climate change risks pose irreversible costs. Complexity arises in the case of financing for addressing adaptation and mitigation of GHG emissions. Provision of finance is embedded in the convention and has also been mentioned in the *Paris Agreement* for addressing the adaptation and mitigation needs of developing countries. Tracking of climate finance is equally important. Lack of a clear **definition** of climate finance has led to controversies in recent estimates of climate finance.

The *Climate Finance in 2013-14 and the US$100 Billion Goal* report released (late 2015) by the OECD (Organisation for Economic Co-operation and Development) states that the mobilization of climate finance from developed to developing countries had reached US$62 billion in 2014. The report seems to include the full value of multilateral development bank (MDB) loans as well as official development assistance (ODA), some private finance, export credits, etc. as climate finance, leading to double counting. Also it includes the promises, pledges and multi-year commitments and not actual disbursements as climate finance. The decline in allocation of ODA to the least developed countries (LDC) in the past year, could perhaps be linked to higher allocation to 'climate-related objectives', implying that ODA is being diverted to 'climate-related activities'.

The Paris Agreement mandates that transparent and consistent information on support provided and mobilized through public interventions for developing country Parties be provided by developed countries. However, it is silent on the definition of climate finance. While the question of what counts as climate finance would be decided at a later stage by the Standing Committee on Finance under the UNFCCC, it is important that it should highlight certain basic elements like[7]—

(i) sources of funding, terms of funding and purpose of funding in addition to resources being committed/disbursed/new.

(ii) while defining climate finance, it is also important to define what cannot be counted towards climate finance.

(iii) aid money meant for development purpose should not be counted as climate finance. With reference to funds provided for multiple purposes, only the share

---

7. Ibid., pp. 185–86.

provided solely for climate change should be included under climate finance.

(iv) systems should be in place to check for double counting or treatment of ODA as climate finance.

There is an even greater gap in tracking adaptation finance and segregating it from development funds as a whole—as a result, very often the entire amount allocated to a project is erroneously treated as adaptation finance. Any climate finance tracking exercise needs to carefully account for these problems.

Global Climate Funds

Depending on the participating countries, global climate funds can either be multilateral or bilateral depending on. The funds may further be classified according to their area of focus, namely mitigation, adaptation or REDD (reducing emissions from deforestation and forest degradation). Currently, the Green Climate Fund (GCF) is the largest, with pledges amounting to US$10.2 billion. The second largest is the Clean Technology Fund (CTF) with pledges amounting to US$5.3 billion. With the capitalization of the GCF and the sunset clause of the CTF, there is ambiguity about the role of the CTF in the climate finance architecture post-2020.

GCF

It was established as an operating entity of the financial mechanism of the UNFCCC in 2011 and is expected to be a major channel for climate finance from developed to developing countries. It has so far been pledged US$10.2 billion by 38 governments. These include some developing countries with small contributions. The highest contribution of US$3 billion has been announced by the USA, followed by Japan (US$1.5 billion), the UK (US$1.2 billion), France (US$1.03 billion) and Germany (US$1.0 billion). The initial resource mobilization period extends from 2015 to 2018. At the 11th GCF board meeting (November 2015), the board approved commitment of US$168 million to eight specific projects, subject to certain conditions being met by the project proponents. The board aims to approve US$2.5 billion in commitments to additional projects in 2016.

GEF

The GEF (Global Environment Facility) was established as a *pilot programme* for environmental protection. The current project cycle is GEF-6 over the years 2014-18. In 1992, when the Biodiversity and Climate Change Conventions were adopted at *Rio de Janeiro*, the GEF was adopted as a financial mechanism for helping developing countries meet their financing needs for achieving their climate change goals. As of November 2015, the GEF has directly invested a total of US$14.5 billion in 3946 projects in 167 countries.

SUSTAINABLE DEVELOPMENT AND CLIMATE CHANGE IN THE INDIAN CONTEXT

In the past two decades, the key environmental challenges in India have been sharper. *The State of the Environment Report* by the MoEF clubs the issues under five key challenges faced by India—

(i) Climate Change,

(ii) Food Security,

(iii) Water Security,

(iv) Energy Security, and

(v) Managing Urbanisation.

Climate change is disturbing the natural ecosystems and is expected to have substantial adverse effects in India, mainly on agriculture (on which 58 per cent of the population still depends for livelihood), water storage in the Himalayan glaciers which are the source of major rivers and groundwater recharge, sea-level rise, and threats to a long coastline and habitations. Climate change will also cause increased frequency of extreme events such as floods, and droughts. These in turn will impact India's food security problems and water security. As per the *Second National Communication* submitted by India to the UNFCCC, it is projected that the annual mean surface air temperature rise by the end of the century ranges from **3.5°C to 4.3°C,** whereas the sea level along the Indian coast has been rising at the rate of about **1.3 mm/year** on an average. These climate change projections are likely to impact human health, agriculture, water resources, natural ecosystems and biodiversity.

Concerned of the threats imposed by climate change and pressures on natural resources, sustainability and environment are increasingly taking centrestage in the Indian policy domain. India has been part of 94 multilateral environmental agreements. India has also voluntarily agreed to reduce its emission intensity of its GDP by 20–25 per cent over 2005 levels by 2020, and emissions from the agriculture sector would not form part of the assessment of its emissions intensity. Indian economy is already moving along a lower carbon and sustainable path in terms of declining carbon intensity of its GDP which is expected to fall further through lower carbon strategies. It is estimated that India's per capita emission in 2031 will still be lower than the global per capita emission in 2005 (in 2031, India's per capita GHG emissions will be under 4 tonnes of carbon dioxide equivalent (CO_2 eq.) which is lower than the global per capita emissions of 4.22 tonnes of CO^2 eq. in 2005).

Together with the national efforts in different sectors, India also recognises that rural areas are equally prone to stress and pressures from natural resource exploitation. In this context, schemes for rural development and livelihood programmes are very relevant. A vast majority of the works under the Mahatma Gandhi National Rural Employment Guarantee Scheme (MGNREGS) are linked to land, soil, and water. There are also programmes for non- timber forest produce-based livelihood, promotion of organic and low-chemical agriculture, and increased soil health and fertility to sustain agriculture-based livelihoods. These schemes help mobilise and develop capacities of community institutions to utilise natural resources in a sustainable manner and their potential can be further developed.

Along with efforts to incorporate sustainability in the rural development process, India is increasingly making efforts to integrate the three pillars of sustainable development into its national policy space. In fact, environment protection is enshrined in our Constitution (Articles 48 A and 51A]). Various policy measures are being implemented across the domains of forestry, pollution control, water management, clean energy, and marine and coastal environment. Some of these are policies like Joint Forest Management, Green Rating for Integrated Habitat Assessment, Coastal Zone Regulation Zone, Eco Labelling and Energy Efficiency Labelling, Fuel Efficiency Standards etc. Over a period of time, a stable organisational structure has been developed for environment protection.

INDCs

The INDCs (Intended Nationally Determined Contributions) are plans by governments communicated to the UNFCCC regarding the steps they will take to address climate change domestically. As per the *COP 19* decision (Warsaw 2013), all Parties were requested to prepare their INDCs, without prejudice to the legal nature of the contributions towards achieving the objectives of the Convention and communicate well in advance of COP 21.

India's INDC: India submitted its INDC to the UNFCCC by early October 2015. It is comprehensive and covers all elements, i.e. adaptation, mitigation, finance, technology and capacity building. India's goal is to reduce the overall emission intensity and improve the energy efficiency of its economy over time. It also covers concerns to protect the vulnerable sectors and segments of its society. The *highlights* of India's INDC are as given below[8]:

(i) To put forward and further propagate a healthy and sustainable way of living based on traditions and values of conservation and moderation.

(ii) To adopt a climate friendly and cleaner path than the one hitherto followed by others at a corresponding level of economic development.

(iii) To reduce the emissions intensity of its GDP by 33 to 35 per cent of the 2005 level by 2030.

(iv) To achieve about 40 per cent cumulative electric power installed capacity from non-fossil fuel- based energy resources by 2030 with the help of transfer of technology and low cost international finance including from the Green Climate Fund (GCF).

(v) To create an additional carbon sink of 2.5 to 3 billion tonnes of CO_2 equivalent through additional forest and tree cover by 2030.

(vi) To better adapt to climate change by enhancing investments in development programmes in sectors vulnerable to climate change, particularly agriculture, water resources, the Himalayan region, coastal regions, health and disaster management.

(vii) To mobilize domestic and new and additional funds from developed countries for implementing these mitigation and adaptation actions in view of the resources required and the resource gap.

(viii) To build capacities, create a domestic framework and an international architecture for quick diffusion of cutting-edge climate technology in India and for joint collaborative R&D for such future technologies.

India's Challenges and Efforts: India houses 30 per cent of the global poor, 24 per cent of global population without access to electricity, and 92 million people without access to safe drinking water. Coupled with its vulnerability in terms of the impact of climate change, this entails that India faces formidable and complex challenges in terms of balancing the sustainable development agenda. Given the challenges it faces, it has prepared an ambitious plan in terms of clean energy, energy efficiency and lower emission intensity while addressing the critical issue of poverty and food security[9]—

(i) India's INDC sets ambitious renewable energy targets mainly in terms of solar and wind energy. With a potential of more than 100 GW, the target is to achieve 60 GW of wind power and 100 GW of solar power installed capacity by 2022. Given that in 2014 the world's entire installed solar power capacity was 181 GW, this target is extremely ambitious and clearly places India as a major potential renewable energy player *(World Resource Institute, October 2015)*.

(ii) India has also launched a historic *International Solar Alliance (ISA)* which is envisaged as a coalition of solar resource-rich countries to address their special energy needs and will provide a platform to collaborate on addressing the identified gaps through a common, agreed approach.

8. Ibid., pp. 183–84.

9. *Economic Survey 2016-17*, Vol. 1 and *Economic Survey 2015-16*, Vol. 2, Government of India, Ministry of Finance, N. Delhi.

(iii) Although there is lot of emphasis on boosting the renewable energy sector, the INDC clearly state that coal would continue to be the dominant source of power generation in the future. However, the INDC incorporates a lot of initiatives to improve the efficiency of coal-based power plants and to reduce their carbon footprint. *Clean coal technologies* would be critical to meeting the demand for power generation in the future.

(iv) In addition to mitigation-related activities, the INDC also incorporates adaptation-related activities. Out of the eight National Missions on Climate Change in India, five focus on *adaptation* in sectors like agriculture, water and forestry.

(v) Since June 2014, when international oil prices started declining, India has increased its excise duties from Rs. 15.5 per litre to Rs. 22.7 per litre as of *December 2016* for branded petrol and from Rs. 5.8 per litre to Rs. 19.7 per litre for branded diesel. The results of the climate change effort undertaken by the major G-20 countries and India are striking—the increase in petrol tax has been over 150 per cent in India. In contrast, the governments of most advanced countries have simply passed on the benefits to consumers, setting back the cause of curbing climate change. As a result, India now outperforms all the countries except those in Europe in terms of tax on petroleum and diesel.

(vi) Having decisively moved from a regime of carbon subsidies, it is now de facto imposing a *carbon tax* on petroleum products at about US$ 150 per ton, which is about 6 times greater than the level recommended by the 'Stern Review on Climate Change'.

(vii) India is faring relatively better to other countries at comparable stages of economic development in terms of the 'share of fossil fuel use in overall energy consumption'. India's reliance on fossil fuels remains well below China (the most relevant comparator) but also below the US, UK and Europe at comparable stages of development—this echoes India's commitment to never exceed the per capita emission of advanced countries.

Mobilising *finance* is critical to achieving the ambitious targets set by India. Preliminary estimates suggest that at least US$ 2.5 trillion (at 2014-15 prices) will be required for meeting India's climate change action under the INDC between now and 2030. While the maximum share of the country's current climate finance comes from *budgetary* sources, India is not relying solely on them and is experimenting with a careful mix of market mechanisms together with fiscal instruments and regulatory interventions. However, it needs to be emphasized that international finance is a critical enabler for the scaled up climate action plans.

INDIA AND CLIMATE CHANGE

India's concerns and actions towards climate change appear in its policies by early 1997 itself when it officially accepted the idea of sustainable development. Since then, several sectoral initiatives have been take by the country. By 2008, India had launched its eight national missions on climate change. Over the time, India has not only played a very dynamic role at the international fora but it has also taken appreciable domestic efforts in this direction[10]—

NAPCC: A major component of India's domestic actions against climate change is the National

---

10. Based on various documents of the Government of India including the *Economic Survey 2015–16* and *Economic Survey 2016-17*.

Action Plan on Climate Change (NAPCC). In March 2016, the PM's Council on Climate Change (PMCCC) directed the missions under the NAPCC to enhance their ambition in respect of adaptation, mitigation and capacity building and reprioritize them, besides recommending the setting up of some *new missions* in addition to the existing eight:

(i) Considering the adverse impacts that climate change could have on health, a new 'Mission on Climate Change and Health' is currently under formulation and a National Expert Group on Climate Change and Health has been constituted.

(ii) The proposed 'Waste-to-Energy Mission' will incentivize efforts towards harnessing energy from waste and is aimed at lowering India's dependence on coal, oil and gas for power production.

(iii) The 'National Mission on Coastal Areas' (NMCA) will prepare an integrated coastal resource management plan and map vulnerabilities along the entire (nearly 7000-km-long) shoreline.

(iv) The 'Wind Mission' seeks to increase the share of wind energy in the renewable energy mix of India. It is likely to be given an initial target of producing about 50,000–60,000 MW of power by the year 2022.

SAPCC

The State Action Plans on Climate Change (SAPCC) aim to create institutional capacities and implement sectoral activities to address climate change. These plans are focused on adaptation with mitigation as co-benefit in sectors such as water, agriculture, tourism, forestry, transport, habitat and energy. So far, 28 states and 5 union territories (UTs) have submitted their SAPCCs to the MoEF & CC (Ministry of Environment & Climate Change). Out of these, the SAPCCs of 32 states and UTs have been endorsed by the National Steering Committee on Climate Change (NSCCC) at the MoEF&CC.

NAFCC

A National Adaptation Fund for Climate Change (NAFCC) has been established with a budget provision of Rs. 1350 crore for the years 2015–16 and 2016–17. It is meant to assist in meeting the cost of national- and state-level adaptation measures in areas that are particularly vulnerable to the adverse effects of climate change.

The *overall aim* of the fund is to support concrete adaptation activities that reduce the adverse effects of climate change facing communities, sectors and states but are not covered under the ongoing schemes of state and central governments. The adaptation projects contribute towards reducing the risk of vulnerability at community and sector level.

Coal Cess and the National Clean Energy Fund

India is *one of the few countries* around the world to have a *carbon tax* in the form of a cess on coal. Not only has India imposed such a cess but it has also been progressively increasing it (form Rs. 50 per tonne of 2010 to Rs. 200 by 2015–16 and Rs. 400 by 2016-17). The NCEF (National Clean Energy Fund) which is supported by the cess on coal was created for the purposes of financing and promoting *clean energy initiatives*, funding research in the area of clean energy and for any other related activities.

Perform Achieve and Trade

The PAT (Perform Achieve and Trade) scheme under the National Mission on Enhanced Energy Efficiency was introduced as an instrument for reducing specific energy consumption in energy-intensive industries with a market-based mechanism that allowed the trading of *ESCerts* (energy saving certificates). The ESCerts, issued by the GoI, are traded through the power exchanges in the country.

Renewable Energy

For India, renewable energy has become a major focus area. The GoI has set an ambitious target of achieving 40 per cent cumulative electric capacity from non-fossil fuel-based energy resources by 2030. India is currently undertaking *the largest* renewable capacity expansion programme in the world.

Major highlights regarding it are as given below:

(i) Renewable energy capacity target has been increased to 175GW by the year 2022, out of which 100GW is to be from solar, 60 GW from wind, 10 GW from biomass and 5 GW from small hydro power projects.

(ii) The First *RE-INVEST* (Renewable Energy Global Investment Promotion Meet and Expo) were organized in February 2015 to provide a platform for the global investment community to connect with stakeholders in India.

The objective of the RE-INVEST series of conference expos is to showcase India's renewable energy potential and the government's efforts to develop and scale up the country's installed renewable energy capacity to meet the national energy requirement in a socially, economically and ecologically sustainable manner. A total of 273,000 MW green commitments, including 62,000 MW of renewable manufacturing, were received in the event.

(i) The *ISA (International Solar Agency)* was launched by India at COP 21 in Paris in December 2015. The ISA will provide a special platform for mutual cooperation among 121 solar-resource-rich countries lying fully or partially between the Tropic of Cancer and Tropic of Capricorn. The Secretariat of the ISA will be hosted by India.

(ii) Development of *Solar Cities Programme* is another ambitious scheme of India. Under it 56 solar cities projects have been approved.

(iii) *Solar Parks* (32 such parks approved by February), each with the capacity of 500 MW and above.

(iv) *Ultra Mega Solar Power Projects* to be developed in the next five years in various states.

(v) *National Offshore Wind Energy Policy 2015* is another major renewable energy policy initiative. It aims at helping offshore wind energy development, including setting up of offshore wind power projects and research and development activities in waters, in or adjacent to the country, up to the seaward distance of 200 nautical miles exclusive economic zone (EEZ) of the country from the base line.

(vi) *Accelerated Depreciation Benefits* scheme for wind power projects have been restored by the GoI in 2016 (which were withdrawn in July 2014). This will help in creating a robust manufacturing base for *wind turbines* in the country.

(vii) To provide adequate amount of investment, the Reserve Bank of India has included renewable energy in the *PSL* (priority sector lending) for scheduled commercial banks.

(viii) The new *National Tariff Policy* (January 2016) for electricity has a focus on the environmental aspect with major provisions such as *(Economic Survey 2016-17)*—

- 8 per cent of electricity consumption (excluding hydro power) shall come from solar energy by March 2022;

- New coal/lignite based thermal plants to establish/procure/purchase renewable capacity;
- Bundling of renewable power with power from plants whose Power Purchase Agreements have expired or completed their useful life;
- No inter-state transmission charges for solar and wind power;
- Procurement of 100 per cent power produced from 'waste-to energy' plants;
- Ancillary services to support grid operation for expansion of renewable energy, etc.

OUTLOOK FOR THE FUTURE

The year 2015 has been commendable regarding world's actions towards environmental protection and climate change. We see the world agree to a common framework on climate change and a set of SDGs in a single year was indeed a monumental achievement. In this regard, there will two important challenges[11] in front of the world—

(i) Mobilization of the funds needed for realizing the bold targets envisaged under both; and

(ii) Need of a clear action plan for implementation.

Budgetary sources of the countries (especially, in case of the developing countries) will not be sufficient enough for the successful implementation of the Paris Agreement, the SDGs and the ambitious targets set out in the INDCs. Looking at the size of funds which will be needed to realise these goals, the experts have advised to mobilise all channels in this regard—private finance, public finance—both national and international.

Epilogue

Hardly anything makes economic sense unless its continuance for a long time can be projected without running into absurdities. Growth and development can happen to a 'limited objective', but it cannot be stretched upto an 'unlimited extent'. How can the 'finite' earth support mankind's 'infinite' physical needs?—long before this was postulated by the 'Club of Rome' in 1972, exactly the same thing Gandhiji had said in late thirties itself, 'Earth provides enough to satisfy every man's need, but not for every man's greed'. Mankind needs to introspect not only about its present needs but the way those needs are being met.

Besides, we also need to 'differentiate' between our 'needs' and 'aspirations'. Our physical needs have a direct 'link' with the resources we have at our disposal to meet them. If mankind is to survive and prosper, we need to be aware of the repercussions of our activities on Mother nature.[12]

---

11. Ministry of Finance, *Economic Survey 2015–16*, Vol.2, p. 191.

12. These virtuous opinions can be seen in a number of contemporary thinkers and writers since 1970s:

E. F. Schumacher, *'The Economics of Permanence'*, *Resurgence*, 3(1), May/June 1970, reprinted in Robin Clarke, Editor, *'Notes for the Future: An Alternative History of the Past Decade' (London:* Thames & Hudson, 1975. Schumacher invoked Gandhi while advocating for the 'economics of permanence'.

Jeffery Sachs, *Common Wealth: Economics for a Crowded Earth* (London: Penguin Books, 2009, pp. 29–35, pp. 55–155.

Jeffery Sachs, *The End of Poverty*, Penguin Books, 2005, pp. 280-284.

Tim Harford, *'The Undercover Economist'*, Abacus, GB, London, 2006, pp. 90-104.

Thomas L. Friedman, *'The World is Flat'*, Penguin Books, GB, London, 2006, pp. 383-385, pp. 495-504

Ramachandra Guha, *' The Ecology of Affluence'* in *'The Ramachandra Guha Omnibus'*, Oxford University Press, N. Delhi, 2005, pp. 69-97.

HUMAN DEVELOPMENT IN INDIA

The basic purpose of development is to enlarge 'people's choices'. In principle, these choices can be infinite and can change over time. People often value achievements that do not show up at all, or not immediately, in income or growth figures—greater access to knowledge, better nutrition and health services, more secure livelihoods, security against crime and physical violence, satisfying leisure hours, political and cultural freedoms and sense of participation in community activities. The objective of development is to create an enabling environment for people to enjoy long, healthy and creative lives.*

* *Mahbub ul Haq (1934-1998), Founding Editor of the **Human Development Report**, UNDP, 1990.*

INTRODUCTION

Economic growth still remains the immediate focus of the world economies. But, income enhancement can only bring the desired development in the country once it is supported by a conscious public policy aimed at it. Again, the presence of 'good governance' in the policy framework can hardly be missed. After the increased acceptance to welfare economics, the standard of life of the masses has emerged as the most popular tool to measure developmental achievemnets of the economies—the idea is much similar to the concept[1] of 'human development' articulated by the UNDP. In recent times, the world has started accepting the role of people's *attitudinal* and *behavioural* dimensions, too in the gamut of devlopment promotion.[2] Further, we see an increased and consensual acceptance among the nations on the issue of delivering 'happiness' and 'life satisfaction' to the citizens.[3] It means, over the last few decades the whole idea about the 'ultimate' aim of the economies has gone for a kind of metamorphosis. Human development, increased social welfare and well-being of the people have been the ultimate objective of development planning in India. Increased social welfare of the people requires a more equitable distribution of development benefits along with better living environment. Development process, therefore, needs to continuously strive for broad-based improvement in the standard of living and quality of life of the people through an inclusive development strategy that focuses on both income and non-income dimensions. Making growth and development percolate to the '*marginalised and disadvantaged sections*' of society (i.e., the SCs, STs, OBCs, Minorities and Women) remains the offical policy of 'inclusive growth' for the country.[4]

The challenge is to formulate *inclusive* plans to bridge regional, social and economic disparities. The Approach Paper to the 12th Plan (2012–17) rightly stresses the need for more infrastructural investment with the aim of fostering a faster, sustainable and more inclusive growth. The GoI has been conscious about the development of the social sector which includes areas like, health, education, shelter, social welfare, social security, etc. Once the economy commenced the process of economic reforms we see an increased attention on the strengthening of social sector—enhancing the social infrastructre and situation.[5] But India is faced with a variety of interconnected and interdpendent issues and challenges in the areas, such as, inclusion, expansion, implementation, accountability, governance, decentralisation, etc.[6]

By 2020, India is projected to be the youngest nation in the world in terms of size—while this 'youth bulge' provides India great opportunities, it also 'poses challenges'—these young people need to be healthy, suitably educated and appropriately skilled to contribute optimally to the economy[7]. The proportion of economically active population (15-59 years) in India has increased from 57.7 per cent to 63.3 per cent during 1991 to 2013, as per Sample Registration System (SRS) data for 2013. If India has to reap the benefits of this *demographic dividend* in the years ahead, it is imperative that investments in social infrastructure are made

1. Amartya Sen, *Development as Freedom,* Oxford University Press, N. Delhi, 2000, pp. 3-11.
2. *World Development Report 2015: Mind, Society, and Behaviour*, world Bank, Washigton DC, 2015.
3. *World Happiness Report-2012 & 2013*, Sponsored by the UNO, N. York, 2013 & 2014.
4. *Eleventh Five Year Plan (2007–12)*, Planning Commission, GoI, N. Delhi.
5. Increased allocations of fund as well as enhanced performance is reported by the *Economic Surveys of 1991–92 to 2014–15*, MoF, GoI, N. Delhi.
6. Amartya Sen and Jean Dreze, *An Uncertain Glory: India and its Contradictions*, Allen Lane, Penguin Books, London, 2013, pp. vii-xiii.
7. *Economic Survey 2014–15*, MoF, GoI, N. Delhi, pp. 131–146.

in appropriate measure to achieve the desired educational and health outcomes.

India has to evolve a multi-pronged strategy with focus on bridging the gaps in access to social infrastructure through appropriate use of innovative technologies for enhancement of human potential for productive employment in various sectors and for improving the quality of life. Mobilising the civil society, media and other stakeholders of society in this regard will play a huge supportive role.

HDR 2015

As per the *HDR (Human Development Report) 2015*, India ranks **130** out of 188 countries. The UNDP report ranks the countries on its Human Development Index (HDI) on three parameters— life expectancy, educational attainment and per capita income. It is an alternative indicator of socio-economic development of the country. The report provides comparative data for the period *1980-2014*. *Major highlights* about India[8], as per the report are as given below:

- India has improved her ranking by *6 places* between 2009 and 2014. In comparison to other nations in the BRICS grouping, India has the lowest rank with Russia at 50, Brazil at 75, China at 90 and South Africa at 116.

- India's HDI value is 0.609 which is below the average of countries in the medium human development group (0.630) but marginally higher than the HDI average of South Asian countries (0.607).

- India's Gross National Income (GNI) per capita increased by about 338 per cent. Over the same period.

- Life Expectancy at Birth (LEB) increased by 14.1 years, an LEB that is lower than that of Brazil, China and Russia, but higher than that of South Africa. Bangladesh, with a lower GNI per capita than India, has a much higher LEB (71.6 years).

- Mean years of schooling increased by 3.5 years and expected years of schooling by 5.3 years. As compared to other BRICS nations, India reports the least mean years of schooling, This shows that the progress made in the education sector needs to be faster, with greater coverage and focus.

The **Gender Development Index (GDI)** published (for all 188 countries) along with the HDR 2015 has following figures for India:

- The HDI value for females in India is 0.525 in 2014, which remains unchanged in comparison to that in 2013 (i.e., HDR 2014). Except Pakistan, all the other four South Asian countries have reported higher HDI values for females in comparison to India.

- The mean years of schooling for girls in India at 3.6 years is substantially lower than the figure for males (7.2) and shows the extent of educational deprivation of girl children in India's cultural context.

As per the report, in case of India, the cultural and social factors prevent women from engaging in economically productive activities outside the household. Apart of these factors, the lack of education and skills restricts them from participating in economic activity, which leads to their further impoverishment and subjugation. Therefore, in the present cultural context, and with a large proportion of women in the growing population of India, it is necessary to address the gender inequality

---

8. **Human Development Report 2015**, UNDP, N. York, USA

GENDER ISSUES

India has gender discrimination embedded in its social fabric. It shows up in most spheres such as access to education, to social and economic opportunities. The reliance on a legal system to offer gender equality and justice, has not been built in a time dimension in the dispensation of justice. Further, dependence on schemes and programmes with inadequate coverage, outlays, inefficiencies and leakages in the delivery mechanism, the social, economic and legal condition of women shows inadequate improvement in terms of several indicators. We find gender discrimination in India at multiple levels—

(i) right from the womb with *sex determination* tests and abortion of the female foetuses,

(ii) discrimination in terms of nutrition offered to the girl child,

(iii) the length and type of schooling the girl child avails of vis-à-vis her male siblings,

(iv) inadequate or lack of access to higher education,

(v) discrimination in opportunities of employment and wages paid, and

(vi) unequal share in inheritance.

Society and the Government has relied on the legal route to address each of these discriminations, without matching changes in the social fabric or role model set by leaders in society from all spheres. The legal route suffers from several shortcomings, especially in terms of time taken for dispensation of justice. For each of the above discrimination, there is a law so all acts of discrimination are illegal, however, compliance requires a lot more to be done.

Privacy of Women

Women and girls in India carry disproportionate burden[9] of sanitation deficiencies in comparison to their male counterparts—which compromises with their fundamental right to privacy. This can take several forms—threat to life and safety while going out for open defecation, reduction in food and water intake practices to minimize the need to exit the home to use toilets, polluted water leading to women and children dying from childbirth-related infections, among others. Personal hygiene of women is for better health outcomes there is no doubt in it. But it is also needed to enjoy the freedom of having control on their bodies—the right to privacy. In absence, it may create 'gender-based sanitation insecurity'.

The Census 2011 reported a widespread lack of sanitation—more than half of the country's population defecated in the open. Recent data shows that about 60 per cent of rural households *(Ministry of Drinking Water and Sanitation-2017; up from 45 per cent NSS 2015)* and 89 per cent of urban households *(NSSO 2016)* have access to toilets—an improved situation over the Census. A 'rapid study' (by *WASH Institute* and *Sambodhi* in 2016), specially done for the *Economic Survey 2016-17* presents some new insight—

(i) Some worrisome trends were found for the majority of *households without toilets*— 76 per cent of women had to travel a considerable distance to use these facilities while 33 per cent of the women reported facing privacy concerns and assault while

---

9. ***Economic Survey 2016-17*** (MoF, GoI, N. Delhi, Vol. 1, pp. 27-30). The **Economic Survey**, for the last two years, featured very useful analyses on "women issues". While in *2014-15* it covered 'violence against women related coercive family planning methods', in *2015-16* it featured the importance of government interventions to ensure long-term wellbeing of women and child under the topic 'mother and child'. Continuing with the process, the *2016-17* issue has covered the issue of "women's privacy".

going out in the open. Due to these risks, the number of women who reduced consumption of food and water are 33 per cent and 28 per cent, respectively. While in short-term it creates problems like illness, disruptions, and deficiencies; in the long-term it compromises with overall health and cognitive development of infants and specially girls. Other studies have highlighted the concerns such as exposure to natural elements, snakebites, etc. also.

(ii) In *households with toilets*, women reported far greater use—showing greater need. Studies have found preference for households to defecate in the open because of a variety of factors (caste and soak pit latrines, especially). As per the 'rapid study', patterns of toilet usage are better for women than men (this was also confirmed by the NSSO Survey of 2016).

(iii) Women and girls use toilet more than their male counterparts—across rural and urban households. This *pattern of toilet usage* suggests a very important thing—women and girl-children could play a *key leadership role* in Swachh Bharat's objective of creating defecation free communities (by nudging men and boys of the household to change their own defecation behaviours).

(iv) Women did show *positive behavioural patterns* after getting access to sanitation services. Again, if these services are denied, they face considerable insecurity and nutritional risks.

For the reason cited above, ensuring safe and adequate sanitation—the objectives of Swachh Bharat—is becoming a serious policy issue—after all it is linked to the 'fundamental right to privacy'.

The Fallouts of Population Policy

The negative fallouts of pursuing a population policy that largely focuses on birth control also contributes to declining *child sex ratios*—if every family is to have fewer children, there is a greater anxiety that at least one of them should be *male*. In this instance, there may be a case for the government to undo as much as to do for example, by not setting targets expected levels of achievement (ELA), withdrawing incentives for female sterilisation and for mass camps. In addition, the *Economic Survey 2014–15* suggested the following actions to the government:

(i) Review the family planning program and re-orient it in such a way that it is aligned with reproductive health rights of women, and needs of India's population.

(ii) Increase budgets for quality services, static family planning clinics and quality monitoring and supervision.

(iii) Address youth needs, induct more counsellors for sexual health, more youth-friendly services, and adequate supply of spacing methods.

POVERTY ESTIMATES

Since India commenced the process of economic reforms, a major shift has taken place in the country's poliy-orientation towards poverty alleviation and employment generation—in place of *wage employment*, the focus has shifted to *self-employment* – so that 'gainful employment' could be created and poverty could be alleviated permanently[10].

---

10. *Economic Survey,* 1999–2000, Ministry of MoF, GoI, N. Delhi.

The Planning Commission used to estimate poverty using data from the large sample surveys on household consumer expenditure carried out by the National Sample Survey Office (NSSO) *every five years*. It **defines** poverty line on the basis of monthly per capita consumption expenditure (MPCE). The methodology for estimation of poverty followed by the Planning Commission has been based on the recommendations made by experts in the field from time to time—the recent estimates based on the recommendations of the Expert Group headed by *Prof. Suresh D. Tendulkar* which submitted its report in December 2009.

As per this methodology, poverty estimates (NSSO, 68th Round, 2011-12) for the period 2004-05 to 2011-12 are as given below:

(i) Total poverty declined from 37.2 to 21.9 per cent.

(ii) Rural poverty declined from 41.8 to 25.7 per cent.

(iii) Urban poverty declined from 25.7 to 13.7 per cent

Looking at the controversy and confusion related to per day monetary estimates of poverty line criteria, late 2015, the GoI did set up a task force under the vice-chairman of the NITI Aayog (Arvind Panagariya) to suggest a new method for poverty estimates. The report the task force is awaited *(March 2017)*.

PROMOTING INCLUSIVE GROWTH

The focus of the Indian development planning has been on formulation of programmes and policies aimed at bringing the 'marginalised and poor sections' of society into the mainstream. The government has been implementing many such programmes for social and financial inclusion. The disbursement of benefits needs a systematic channel which will provide for financial empowerment and make monitoring easier and the local bodies more accountable. The *Pradhan Mantri Jan Dhan Yojna (PMJDY)* launched in August 2014 and the *RuPay Card* (a payment solution), are important schemes in this regard. These two schemes are complementary and will enable achievement of multiple objectives such as financial inclusion, insurance penetration, and digitalisation.

We find an increased Government emphasis *(Economic Survey 2016-17)* on the socio-economic empowerment of the **minorities**. In this regard several new schemes have been launched in recent times—the 'Nai roshni' scheme for leadership development of minority women; *Padho Pardesh*, a scheme of interest subsidy on educational loans for overseas studies for the students belonging to the minority communities; for skill development and of the minorities, schemes like *Seekho Aur Kamao* (Learn & Earn), *USTTAD* (Upgrading Skill and Training in Traditional Arts/Crafts for Development) and *Nai Manzil*.

Accessible India Campaign

The number of persons with disabilities in India constituted 2.2 per cent of the population (Census 2011). It is imperative to promote, protect and ensure the full and equal enjoyment of all human rights and fundamental freedoms by all persons with disabilities, and to promote respect for their inherent dignity *(UN Convention on rights of Persons with Disabilities)*. In this direction, the Department of Empowerment of Persons with Disabilities (DEPwD) launched *Accessible India Campaign* (Sugamya Bharat Abhiyan) as a nation-wide Campaign for achieving "universal accessibility for Persons with Disabilities (PwDs)" with a focus on three verticals—Built Environment, Public Transportation and ICT (Information & Communication Technologies).

The Government has launched an *Inclusiveness and Accessibility Index* as part of this campaign. The index helps the industries and corporates to participate in the campaign by voluntarily evaluating their readiness for making the workplace accessible for PwDs. The index enables the organisations to introspect over their inclusive policies and organisational culture in aid of PwDs, employment of such workforce and adaptations to meet the needs of PwDs. Further, the *Rights of Persons with Disabilities Act, 2016* has been enacted by the Government aimed at securing and enhancing the rights and entitlements of PwDs (it includes the provision of increasing the reservation in government vacancies from 3 per cent to 4 per cent).

Strengthening the PRIs

The 73rd and 74th Constitutional Amendments marked a watershed in the history of decentralised governance, planning, and development in India as these made panchayat bodies the third tier of government with reasonable power and authority in addition to creating space for women and marginalised groups in the federal set-up. Decentralised democracy was also extended to Fifth Schedule areas through the provisions of another Panchayat (Extension to the Scheduled Areas) Act 1996 known as the Extension Act which not only made the gram sabha a strong body, but also put '*jal, jungle, and jamin*' (water, forest, and land) under its control.

These central acts, however, instead of clearly specifying the powers and functions of panchayats and municipalities, have left it to the discretion of state governments. Articles 243 G and 243 W of these acts decree that the legislature of a state may, by law, endow the panchayats/municipalities with such powers and authority as may be necessary to enable them to function as institutions of self-government. Such law may also contain provisions for devolution of powers and responsibilities upon panchayats/municipalities, subject to such conditions as may be specified therein, with respect to the preparation of plans and implementation of such schemes for economic development and social justice as may be entrusted to them. These may include inter alia *schemes* and *plans* in relation to socio-economic development and providing basic services as listed in the Eleventh and Twelfth Schedules of the Constitution.

Article 243 ZD of the 74th Amendment Act providing for constitution of district planning committees (DPC) by the state government in every district is a milestone in decentralised planning with people's participation. These committees are expected to consolidate the plans prepared by the panchayats and municipalities in the district and prepare a draft development plan for the district as a whole. DPCs have been set up in most of the states. Much of implementation of these panchayat acts, i.e., power-sharing with panchayat bodies, is left to the states. Over the years, the panchayat bodies have not been strengthened in terms of *functions, finances* and *functionaries (triple Fs)* with regard to preparation of plans and the listed subjects. The *Economic Survey 2014–15* suggests the following steps towards strengthening the PRIs:

(i) The panchayat bodies have the potential to become true vehicles for carrying out the government's slogan of "less government–more governance" if states show consensus.

(ii) In order to convert outlays of the local-centric programmes into outcomes, these institutions need greater *awareness, responsibility,* and *accountability*, which will also enable better connect of these programmes with the common man.

(iii) *Greater devolution* of powers to the panchayats and municipalities is need of the hour, in respect of the 'triple Fs' in a phased manner.

(iv) Majority of panchayat/municipality-centric programmes do have earmarked funds for awareness generation and capacity building. These funds across ministries need to be *pooled together* under the Panchayati Raj Ministry and

Ministry of Urban development to make infrastructure and capacity building of panchayats and municipalities a continuous and regular process.

These **steps** will create the following possibilities in the local bodies:

(a) Enable them to understand not only their role and rights but also their responsibilities and will make them accountable, bringing about qualitative improvement in governance at decentralised level.

(b) Transform them into *vibrant institutions* and enable them to perform their envisaged role in participatory planning, implementation, execution, monitoring, and supervision and also carry out social audit of all panchayat/municipality-centric programmes.

Government has given high priority to 'inclusion' factor—through the ideas of "inclusive growth" (as outlined by the 11th Plan, 2007-12) and the "third generation of economic reforms" (launched 2002, on the margins of the 10th Plan, 2002-07)—it is officially decided to use the PRIs as the *main tool*. In this way, it is essential for the governments (centre and states, both) to use the untapped potential of the PRIs as the vehicle of decentralising the fruits of growth and development to the 'grass-root' level. For this the PRIs need strengthening—newly created 'think tank', the NITI can play as an instrumental role in it (through its platform, the 'Governing Council')—in reaching a broad consensus among the governments regarding it.

DEMOGRAPHICS

The population of India has gone for some major changes in the recent decades. These changes have not only restructured the contours of Indian demographics but have brought new openings and challenges regarding it:

1. As per provisional results of *Census 2011*, the following facts regarding the Indian population dynamics are of high importance. The 2001–11 is the *first* decade in independent India wherein, the population momentum coupled with declining fertility has dampened the pace of net additions to population. Thus, the net addition in this decade is less than that of the pervious decade by 0.86 million. At present, a little more than *one out of every six* persons in the world is an Indian.

2. As per *Sample Registration System-2013* (SRS) data—

(a) There has been a gradual decline in the share of population in the age group 0-14 from 41.2 to 38.1 per cent during 1971 to 1981 and from 36.3 to 28.4 per cent during 1991 to 2013.

(b) On the other hand, the proportion of economically active population (15-59 years) or, India's 'demographic dividend', has increased from 53.4 to 56.3 per cent during 1971 to 1981 and from 57.7 to 63.3 per cent during 1991 to 2013.

(c) On account of better education, health facilities, and increase in life expectancy, the per centage of *elderly* (60+) has gone up from 5.3 to 5.7 per cent and 6.0 to 8.3 per cent respectively in the same two periods.

(d) The growth rate of the *labour force* will continue to be higher than that of the population until 2021.

3. According to an *Indian Labour Report* (Time Lease, 2007)—

(a) 300 million youth will enter the labour force by 2025, and 25 per cent of the world's workers in the next three years will be Indians.

(b) Population projections indicate that in 2020 the average age of India's population will be the lowest in the world—around 29 years compared to 37 years in China and the United States of America, 45 years in West Europe, and 48 years in Japan.

(c) Consequently, while the global economy is expected to witness a shortage of young population of around 56 million by 2020, India will be the only country with a youth surplus of 47 million *(Report on Education, Skill Development and Labour Force (2013–14) Volume III, Labour Bureau, 2014)*.

As per the *Economic Survey 2014–15*, the main issue to address then is not just providing employment but increasing the employability of the labour force in India. Employability is contingent upon knowledge and skills developed through quality education and training. Thus, any solution to the problem lies in a well-designed education and training regime that sets out to meet these objectives. The problem of low employability levels owing to poor quality of education is accentuated by the fact that fewer students opt for higher education in country. To garner the 'demographic dividend', the Survey suggested the following *policy initiatives* in this regard:

(i) A declining 0–14 population will impact both elementary (5–14 age group) and higher education (15–29 age group). Elementary education can be further subdivided into primary (5–9 age group) and middle/upper primary (10–14 age group). The first stage of impact will be felt in declining enrolment in primary schools. As stated earlier, total enrolment

in primary schools has fallen in 2013-14 while upper primary enrolment has grown. The dependency ratio for India is expected to fall from 54 per cent in 2010 to 49 per cent in 2020. In this scenario, given interstate disparities, states that are already facing this situation need to adopt specific policy measures in the field of education, wherein, instead of expanding the number of primary schools, focus should be on—

(a) Improving access to education considering the high dropout rates among senior students;

(b) Removing gender disparity especially in the higher age group and in rural areas;

(c) Improving quality of education, including pupil-teacher ratios and provision of amenities in schools, especially in view of the declining learning levels.

(ii) The *lag in demographic transition* between different states that necessitates state-specific policies to optimally garner the benefits of the demographic dividend. Owing to substantial fertility decline in the south during the last two decades, the south is ahead in the demographic transition compared to the north, thereby the window is already wide open in the south compared to the north. For instance, the projected average age of 29 years in 2020 has already been surpassed in some states like Kerala (33 years), Goa (32.3), Tamil Nadu (31.3), Himachal Pradesh (30.4), Punjab (29.9), Andhra Pradesh (29.3), and West Bengal (29.1). This lag in demographic transition among states in India could turn out to be a *great blessing* from the point of view of coping with the problem of declining population. India is better placed in this respect than most other countries. Thus, two set of policy initiatives emerge for the states—

(a) The states which are already well into the demographic window should actively pursue policies for employment generation to the already bulging labour force.

(b) The states just entering the window period have some time to plan and must pursue policies simultaneously in several areas like education, health (including reproductive health), gender issues, and employment generation from now on so that they can fully utilise the opportunity.

SOCIO-ECONOMIC AND CASTE CENSUS

The identification of the real beneficiaries is of paramount importance, for the success of any targeted approach. In line with this approach the *Dr. N. C. Saxena Committee* was constituted to advise on the 'methodology for a BPL census in rural areas'. Since June 2011, for the first time, a Socio-Economic and Caste Census (SECC) is being conducted through a comprehensive 'door-to-door' enumeration in both rural and urban India, authentic information is being made available on the socio-economic condition and educational status of various castes and sections through the SECC.

The exercise was completed by *late 2016* and presently, the errors are in the process of rectification—the reason the report of the census has not been put in the public domain yet. Once the census is fully ready, its findings are expected to be used in as guidelines in several areas such as— identifying the level of poverty, target population for the disbursal of subsidies, selection for eligibility for educational scholarships, old age pension,

re-orienting the existing reservation policy, better implementation (by correct identification the beneficiaries) of the MGNAREGS, National Food Security scheme, etc.

EDUCATIONAL SCENARIO

In the process of realising the demographic dividend, education and skill have to play the most vital role in the country. This is why the education sector remains a priority area for the governments. The present concerns regarding education is briefly highlighted as given below[11]:

Enrolment trends: Major findings of the *ASER 2014* have been highlighted below—

- There has been a decline in enrolment in the government schools in the rural areas which fell down from 72.9 per cent of 2007 to 63.1 per cent in 2014. This decline looks made up by an increase in the private schools during the same period which increased from 20.2 to 30.7 per cent. Concerns about the decline in enrolment in government schools need to be identified and addressed. Decline in enrolment in government schools and some shift to private schools might be largely related to the poor quality of education offered in government schools, since it is free or offered for a nominal fee.

- There is a sharp decline in the number of children in standard V who can read a textbook of standard II in both government and private schools.

- The decline in educational outcomes in private schools warrants equal attention since there is an increase in the share

---

11. Based on the *Annual Status of Education Report (ASER) 2014; Educational Statistics at a Glance 2014*, Ministry of HRD—as quoted by the **Economic Survey 2015-16** and **Economic Survey 2016-17**, Vol. 1, pp. 162-163.

of private providers of schooling and education across India.

As per the *Economic Survey 2016-17*, an important concern that is often raised in the context of school education is 'low learning outcomes'. This has been pointed out in several studies (including ASER, 2014). While there have been improvements in access and retention, the learning outcomes for a majority of children is still a cause of serious concern. Some of the underlying causes contributing to low quality of education in the primary sector are—

   (i) Teacher absenteeism, and

   (ii) Shortage of professionally qualified teachers.

Though the share of teacher component in total Sarva Shiksha Abhiyan (SSA) budget has been increasing over the years from 35 per cent in 2011-12 to 59 per cent in 2014-15, teacher absenteeism and the shortage of professionally qualified teachers remain an issue to be addressed. Biometric attendance of teachers—monitored by communities and parents together with putting the data in public domain—may prove useful in this regard. This should be backed by adequate teaching aids, recorded lectures, etc. to fill in for absentee teachers. learning outcomes should be part of the whole exercise. Attention should be given on the aspect of "quality teacher training".

Professional qualification & training: As per the latest report by the *U-DISE* (Unified-District Information System for Education) on *School Education in India 2014–15*, only 79 per cent of teachers are professionally qualified in the country. For the higher secondary level, the per centage of qualified teachers is around 69 per cent. There is need to increase the per centage of qualified teachers and also the training of both qualified and under-qualified teachers.

Gender parity: As per the Ministry of HRD's Educational Statistics, the Gender Parity Index (GPI) at various levels of school education has improved by 2014-15, except in the higher education in the case of total and Scheduled Caste (SC) students. In the case of Scheduled Tribe (ST) students, parity between girls and boys has not been achieved across all levels of school and higher education. There is need to bridge the gender disparity in higher education among total and SC students and, at all levels of education for ST students.

EMPLOYMENT SCENARIO

Employment issues have always been among the priorities of the GoI. As it is considered the best tool to alleviate poverty, the area gets even more importance. The latest employment scenario[12] and related concerns are as given below:

- The overall employment increased by 1.35 lakh—contributed by the IT/BPOs, textiles including apparels and metals sectors. However, the sectors such as gems & jewellery, handloom & power loom, leather, automobiles and transport saw decline in employment.

- Labour Force Participation Rate (LFPR) was estimated at 50.3 per cent— for females 23.7 per cent and males 75.0 per cent. The North Eastern and Southern States, in general, display high female LFPR as compared to low levels in Northern States.

- Unemployment rate for females (8.7 per cent) was higher than that of males (4.0 per cent) across rural and urban areas—with wide inter-state variations as seen in case of the LFPR.

- Employment growth has been sluggish. Further, States that show low

---

12. The latest and the *5th Annual Employment and Unemployment Survey (EUS)-2015-16*, Labour Bureau, Ministry of Labour & Employment—as quoted by the **Economic Survey 2016-17**, MoF, GoI, N. Delhi, pp. 161-162.

unemployment rates also generally rank high in the share of manufacturing. While States compete to seek investment offering incentives, linking incentives to the number of jobs created, sustained efforts need to be considered as a tool to increase employment.

- There is a clear shift in employment to secondary and tertiary sectors from the primary sector. The growth in employment by category reflects increase in both *casual labour* and *contract workers*. This has adverse implications on the level of wages, stability of employment, social security of employees owing to the 'temporary' nature of employment. It also indicates preference by employers away from regular/formal employment to circumvent labour laws.

- The multiplicity of labour laws and the difficulty in their compliance have been an impediment to the industrial development and employment generation.

Women's Unpaid Work

The conventional employment and unemployment surveys have not been able to capture the various types of *unpaid work* that women engage in both within and outside households in rural and urban areas in India. Globally, men's share in paid work is around 1.8 times that of women, while women have a share three times that of men in unpaid work. Therefore, paid work which is visible and accounted for by the System of National Accounts (SNA) is dominated by men, while unpaid work which is not accounted for is dominated by women and remains unrecognised and unaccounted for.

Valuing unpaid work is important since women's work gets subsumed under several types of activities. A TUS (Time Use Survey) was conducted in India in six select states on a pilot basis from July 1998 to June 1999. The results of the survey revealed the hidden contribution of women to the economy—

(i) Out of 168 hours in a week, males on an average spent about 42 hours in SNA-captured activities as compared to only about 19 hours by females. However, in the extended SNA activities, women spent 34.6 hours which included unpaid work at home and outside, as opposed to only about 3.6 hours by men.

(ii) The declining female participation rates in conventional surveys are largely explained by the high share of women in unpaid work. Based on the findings of the pilot TUS, the NCATUS (National Classification of Activities for Time Use Studies), which also provides a classification of unpaid activities that is crucial for capturing the various activities of women in the economy, has been developed.

Skill Gap

For improving the employability of the population 'skill development' is the best tool. This can be imparted through vocational education and training. However, there is a perception that vocational education and skill development are meant for people who have failed to join mainstream education. This perception is strengthened by the significantly lower wages paid to employees with vocational training vis-à-vis those with formal education.

As per the *NSDC* (National Skill Development Corporation), there is a severe quality gap and lack of availability of trainers in the vocational education and training sector. By 2017, this skill gap within the vocational training sector including both teachers and non-teachers will reach a figure of 211,000. The workforce requirement is projected to increase to 320,000 by 2022.

There is a need of government investment in bridging the skill gap in the vocational education and training sector to improve the employability of people. Across industries and their sub- sectors, there are substantial skill gaps that need to be filled up through appropriate skill development plans that leverage the private sector along with public initiatives. Some recent steps in this regard are as given below:

- With the setting up of the NSDC, progress is being made towards creating increased awareness about the skill gap and a thrust towards skill development in both the government and private sector employers as well as the Indian masses. The establishment of the *National Skill Qualification Framework (NSQF)* will also facilitate increased adoption of skill development programmes, with availability of pathways for progression between higher education and skill development.

- A multipronged policy approach to enable skill development including but not limited to initiatives such as setting up of Sector Skill Councils (SSCs), definition of Occupation Standards, drawing up of the NSQF and funding initiatives such as the Standard Training and Assessment Reward (STAR) scheme are likely to create a widespread positive impact on the skill ecosystem in India.

- The SSCs as autonomous industry-led bodies through the NSDC create National Occupational Standards (NOSs) and Qualification Packs (QP) for each job role in the sector, develop competency frameworks, conduct training of trainers, conduct skill gap studies and assess through independent agencies and certify trainees on the curriculum aligned to NOSs developed by them.

- Under the *PMKVY* (Pradhan Mantri Kaushal Vikas Yojana), which targets offering 24 lakh Indian youth meaningful, industry-relevant, skill-based training and a government certification on successful completion of training along with assessment to help them secure a job for a better future. The actual success of this initiative can be gauged by the number of trained personnel being employed, which also needs to be measured and periodically reported.

- The *DDU-GKY* (Deen Dayal Upadhyaya Grameen Kaushalya Yojana), a placement-linked skill development scheme for rural youth (who are poor), as a skilling component of the NRLM (National rural Livelihood Mission) has also been launched.

- *National Action Plan (NAP)* for skill and training has been launched with a view to increasing the scope of employability among differently-abled persons. Under it a network of skill training providers led by training partners from government and non-government sectors has to be established. It will also include vocational rehabilitation centres. The plan has a target of skilling 5 lakh differently-abled persons in next three years (up to 2017-18). Plans are also on the anvil to extend the NAP with an online skill-training platform with a target of 5 lakh every year.

- *National Policy on Skill Development and Entrepreneurship 2015* aims to ensure skilling on a large scale at a speed with high Standards and promote a culture of innovation based entrepreneurship to ensure sustainable livelihoods. Accordingly, a Policy Implementation Unit (PIU) will *identify* all the stakeholders involved and flag the actionable points to the responsible agency.

Given that India has one of the youngest populations in the world, there is immense potential for overseas employment opportunities for skilled persons from India. The process of mapping such opportunities through the NSDC is also in progress during 2016-17.

LABOUR REFORMS

We see a significant improvement in industrial harmony in India is evident from the fact that mandays lost on account of *strikes* and *lockout* have been steadily declining, from 17.6 million in 2009 to 1.79 million (Provisional) to December 2014. The multiplicity of labour laws and difficulty in complying with them has always been cited as an impediment to industrial development in India. This is why labour reforms has been made and active part of the ongoing economic reform process in the country. In a major initiative for *ensuring compliance* and promoting *ease of doing business*, the government has initiated a number of labour reform measures. Thus, amendments have been proposed to labour laws to align them with the demands of a changing labour market. Individually, states like Rajasthan have also introduced major reforms in three labour legislations—the Industrial Disputes Act, Factories Act, and Contract Labour Act. In the past few years, several new initiatives[13] have been taken by the GoI in this directions which may be *summed-up briefly* as given below:

1. The *Apprentice Act 1961* was amended in December 2014 to make it more responsive to industry and youth. The 'Apprentice Protsahan Yojana' was also launched to support MSMEs in the manufacturing sector in engaging apprentices. Government is also working affirmatively to bring a *single uniform law*

for the MSME sector to ensure operational efficiency and improve productivity while ensuring job creation on a large scale.

2. A unified labour portal scheme called *Shram Suvidha Portal* has been launched for timely redressal of grievances and for creating a conducive environment for industrial development. Its main features are—

   (i) Unique Labour Identification Number (LIN) allotted to around 0.7 million units facilitating online registration;

   (ii) Filing of selfcertified, simplified single online return instead of 16 separate returns by industry;

   (iii) Transparent labour inspection scheme via computerised system as per risk-based criteria and uploading of inspection reports within 72 hours by labour inspectors.

3. *Under Employees' State Insurance Corporation (ESIC)* **Project Panchdeep**: Digitisation of internal and external processes to ensure efficiency in operations, especially services to employers and insured persons. The portal enables employers to file monthly contributions, generate temporary identity cards and create monthly contribution challans online, issue of pehchan card for insured persons for fast and convenient delivery of services. Through the IP Portal, insured persons can check contributions paid/ payable by employers, family details, entitlement to various benefits, and status of claims. Integration of its services will promote ease of business and curb transaction costs.

4. *Under Employees Provident Fund (EPF)*: Digitisation of complete database of 42.3

---

13. **Ministry of Labour & Employment**, GoI, N. Delhi, March 2017 and **Economic Survey 2016-17**, MoF, GoI, N. Delhi, Vol. 1, pp. 162.

million EPF subscribers and allotment of universal account number (UAN) to each member, which facilitates portability of member accounts. UAN is being seeded with bank account, Aadhar Card and other KYC details to promote financial inclusion. Direct access to EPF accounts will enable members to access and consolidate previous accounts.

Online pensioners can view their account and disbursement details online. The statutory wage ceiling under the Employees Provident Fund and Miscellaneous Provisions (EPF&MP) Act was enhanced to Rs. 15,000 per month and a minimum pension of Rs.1,000 has been introduced for pensioners under the Employees' Pension Scheme-1995 from September 2014.

5. *For Unorganised Workers:* The Rashtriya Swasthya Bima Yojana (RSBY) is a scheme under the Unorganised Workers' Social Security Act 2008. It is a smart card-based cashless health insurance scheme, including maternity benefit, which provides a cover of Rs 30,000 per family per annum on a family floater basis to below poverty line (BPL) families in the unorganised sector. It is proposed to extend the RSBY to all **unorganised** workers in a phased manner.

6. *National Council for Vocational Training-Management Information System (NCVT-MIS)* portal has been developed for streamlining the functioning of Industrial Training Institutes (ITIs), Apprenticeship Scheme, and assessment/certification of all NCVT training courses.

7. *National Career Services Portal:* The Government is mandated to maintain a free employment service for its citizens. This is now being transformed with the launch of the National Career Service

(NCS) Portal in July 2015. The NCS is envisaged as a digital portal that will provide a nationwide *online platform* for job seekers and employers for job matching in a dynamic, efficient and responsive manner.

8. *Payment of Bonus (Amendment) Act 2015:* The Act passed in December 2015, has redefined the eligibility for bonus payment of the Payment of Bonus Act 1965 from Rs. 10,000 to Rs. 21,000 per month. This will not only enhance the bonus payment to the employees but make more eligible to the same.

Industrial development and employment generation have been hindered in India by multiplicity of labour laws and their compliance. Working in the direction to remedy this situation, the Government has proposed (by late **March 2017**) to group 39 central labour laws into 'four or five' Labour Codes in the coming days. There are several other new measures under consideration towards simplifying the labour regulation regime in the country.

CHILD LABOUR

India faces the problem of child labour. There is need of a multi-pronged strategy which can rehabilitate children withdrawn from work through specific schemes and universal elementary education. It needs supplemented with economic rehabilitation of their families also.

In 2015, the GoI launched the *National Child Labour Project (NCLP) Scheme* under which children rescued/withdrawn from work in the age group of 9-14 years are enrolled in NCLP special training centres, where they are provided bridge education, vocational training, midday meal, stipend, health care, etc., before being mainstreamed into formal education system. Children in the age group of 5-8 years are directly linked to the formal education system through close coordination with the Sarva Shiksha Abhiyaan (SSA).

Government has also proposed an amendment in the Child Labour (Prohibition & Regulation) Act, 1986 which aims at complete prohibition on employment of children below 14 years along with linking the age of prohibition with the age under the Right of Children to Free and Compulsory Education Act 2009. The amendment also includes the provisions for stricter punishment for employers.

HEALTH SCENARIO

The draft approach paper to the 12th Plan proposed the idea of universal healthcare in 2012, for the first time. The funding situation did not seem conducive enough this is why the government did not think to launch it—falling growth rate in wake of the western recession and many domestic factors. However, providing accessible, affordable and equitable quality health care, especially to the marginalised and vulnerable sections of the population is one of the key objectives of the Government. There are innumerable challenges to the delivery of efficient health services in India, given the paucity of resources and the plethora of requirements in the health sector. Population health is also significantly influenced by social and environmental determinants such as age at marriage, nutrition, pollution, access to potable water and hygienic sanitation facilities.

The Indian health sector has a *mix* of both public and private providers of health services. The private sector and the quality of care provided is variable, ranging from informal providers (quacks) to individually run nursing homes to large polyclinics and multiplex hospitals. The regulation for cost and quality of care is largely absent in most f the states. In the case of public sector, the health services are delivered through a network of health facilities including ASHA (a volunteer health worker) at the community level, Health Sub-Center (HSC), Primary Health Centres (PHCs), Community Health Centres (CHCs), District Hospitals, Government Medical College Hospitals and the state and central government assisted Employees' State Insurance (ESI) hospitals and dispensaries. Outreach and community level services are provided through coordination between ASHA, Anganwadi Workers (AWWs) and the Auxiliary Nurse Midwife (ANM) at the HSC.

The *Key Indicators of social consumption in India: Health-2015*, NSSO, 71st Round (January –June 2014) throws some interesting findings[14]—

- The private sector continues to play a significant role in the provision of outpatient and hospitalised care. However, it also points that there has been a nearly two-fold jump in the institutional deliveries since the last such survey.

- Further, over 60 per cent of all institutional deliveries are in the public sector and the *Out of Pocket expenditures* for childbirth in the public sector is about one-tenth that in the private sector. This is largely a result of sustained strengthening of health systems targeted towards maternal and child healthcare through programmes such as Janani Suraksha Yojana (JSY) and Janani Shishu Suraksha Karyakram (JSSK). This is also reflected in 50 per cent sharper decline in MMR in the country as compared to global average rate of decline from the baseline of MDG of 1990.

- The share of public providers in treatment of non-hospitalised patients is very low at 11.5 per cent at HSC, PHC including ASHAs and ANMs. This per centage is even lower for urban areas where the public provisioning of primary health

---

14. As the government documents have been quoted by the **Economic Survey 2015-16**, op. cit., Vol. 2, pp. 202-203.

care has been largely absent. This reflects confinement of primary care to selective primary care limited to Reproductive and Child Health (RCH) services. The National Urban Health Mission (NUHM) launched over a year back is trying to address the issue of inadequacy of public provisioning of primary health care in urban areas.

- India faces a challenge in the provision of affordable and accessible health care to the population. *Average medical expenditure* for treatment (excluding child birth) per hospitalised case if treated in private hospital was about four times than that of public hospital. On an average, Rs. 25,850 was spent for treatment per hospitalised case by people in the private facilities as against Rs. 6,120 in the public health facilities.

- The average total medical and other related non-medical expenditure per hospitalisation in rural and urban areas are Rs. 16,956 and Rs. 26,455 respectively.

- The average total medical expenditure for non- hospitalised treatment per ailing person in rural and urban areas is Rs. 509 and Rs. 639 respectively.

- The NSSO also reports that coverage by government-funded *insurance* schemes is 13.1 per cent of rural India and 12 per cent of urban population.

Health Indicators & Schemes: Health indicators have shown the trends of improvement in recent years mainly due to focussed steps taken by the governments. Some ***major highlights*** related to health indicators and health schemes, as per various government documents[15], are as given below:

- As per *Census 2011*, the share of children (0-6 years) accounts for 13.6 per cent of the total population in the country. An estimated 26 million children are born every year in India.

- According to the **NFHS** (National Family Health Survey), the immunisation coverage has improved substantially since *NFHS-1 (1992-93),* when only 36 per cent of children were fully vaccinated and 30 per cent had not been vaccinated at all. As per *NFHS-4 (2015-16),* the per centage of children fully immunised in the age group (12-23 months) is above 80 per cent in Sikkim and West Bengal. All the 12 states (from which the data are available) have more than 50 per cent children fully immunised. The per centage of children who are fully immunised is lower in urban areas compared to rural areas in majority of the States, indicating that although the private sector is more wide spread in urban areas, the availability of preventive health care is through the public health system, which needs strengthening in urban areas.

- High-risk patients like children and pregnant women do require special preventive healthcare services. Targeting coverage of all those children by 2020 who are either unvaccinated, or are partially vaccinated against seven vaccine-preventable diseases which include diphtheria, whooping cough, tetanus, polio, tuberculosis, measles and hepatitis

---

15. As the government documents have been quoted by the **Economic Survey 2015-16**, op. cit., Vol. 2, pp. 203-206.

B, *Mission Indradhanush* was launched in December 2014.

In addition, vaccination against Japanese Encephalitis and Haemophilus influenza type B will be provided in selected districts/states of the country. Pregnant women are also to be immunised against tetanus.

- India has one of the largest programmes of publicly financed ART (anti-retroviral therapy) drugs for HIV anywhere in the world. All drugs and diagnostics in all vector borne disease programmes, tuberculosis, leprosy, including rapid diagnostic kits and third generation anti-microbicidals are *free* and so are insecticide treated bed nets.

- Under the *Rashtriya Bal Swasthya Karyakram (RBSK),* support is being provided to States/UTs for child health screening and early intervention services through early detection and early management of common health conditions.

- *National Iron Plus Initiative* has been rolled out to address anaemia among children (6 months to 19 years) and women in reproductive age including pregnant and lactating women in both rural and urban areas throughout the country. Anaemia among pregnant women continues to be high (has been a chronic problem in the country).

- Several programmes and new policy initiatives have been taken by the Government to ensure holistic development of children and socio-economic empowerment and development of women to secure *gender equality* in all spheres of social life. The scope and coverage of the schemes for women and child development have been expanding persistently as reflected in the magnitude of gender budget which increased from 2.79 per cent to 4.46 per cent as a per centage of total budgets in the *Gender Budget Statement* during the period 2005-06 to 2015-16.

- Though there has been substantial improvement in *institutional births* particularly in public sector, expenditure towards private institutional births is on the rise, indicating the need to sustain and even expand the efforts of the public health system by increased investments.

- *Preventive health care* has always been a priority area because of its long-term societal benefits, Government has taken several steps in the direction of preventive health care to reduce the burden of diseases in India. Some of the important programmes aimed at investigation/screening and treatment cover Malaria; Kala-azar; Filaria; Dengue; Japanese Encephalitis and Chikungunya; detection and treatment of Tuberculosis, Leprosy, HIV/AIDs; and cataract surgery for blindness control.

- Considering the rising incidence of *Non-Communicable Diseases (NCDs),* the GoI has initiated an integrated National Programme for Prevention and Control of Cancers, Diabetes, Cardiovascular Diseases and Stroke (NPCDCS) jointly by the Ministry of Health and Family Welfare and Ministry of AYUSH (Ayurveda, Yoga, Unani, Siddha and Homeopathy) on pilot basis in six districts.

- Various initiatives under the National Health Mission (NHM), which subsume the National Rural Health Mission (NRHM) for rural areas and the NUHM for urban areas with a population of more than 30,000, have been taken up for providing *free health care* through a nationwide network of public health facilities like CHCs, PHCs and Sub-Centres (SCs).

- Dedicated *skilled health personnel* are a pre-requisite for efficient and effective delivery of health services. However, the availability of such personnel to meet various needs of the health sector is a huge challenge in India. The shortage of specialists, doctors, staff nurses, anaesthetists, and others, adversely affects the outreach of health services, especially in rural areas. As per an evaluation study of the NRHM (2011), there is a 95 per cent shortage of skilled health personnel in Jharkhand, around 80 per cent in Madhya Pradesh and 70 per cent in Uttar Pradesh. Assam reported only 11 per cent shortage, while Tamil Nadu did not report any shortage at all.

- *Rural Health Statistics 2015* reports that at the all-India level, CHCs are short of surgeons by 83 per cent of the total requirement. Only 27 per cent of the sanctioned posts have been filled. Adequate skilled personnel are necessary for strengthening the health sector's efficiency and delivery of services in rural areas.

Current situation: As per the *Economic Survey 2016-17*, despite the challenges faced by the government in providing affordable health services to the population, there have been some notable achievements in the health sector:

- Life expectancy has increased speedily and infant mortality and crude death rates have reduced sharply.
- Total fertility rate (TFR) has been steadily declining and was 2.3 (rural 2.5 & urban 1.8) by 2014.

- Infant Mortality Rate (IMR) has declined to 37 in 2015 from 44 in 2011. The challenge lies in addressing the huge gap between IMR in rural (41) and urban (25) areas.

- The Maternal Mortality Ratio (MMR) declined from 301 of 2001-03 to 167 in 2011-13 (per 100,000 live births). But wide regional disparities remains in it. Thus, India needs to focus on the states with MMR higher than the national average, by improving health and nutritional status of women.

- The high levels of *anaemia* prevalent among women in the age group 15-49 have a direct correlation with high levels of MMR. The National Health Mission has programmes to address the issue of anaemia through health and nutrition education to promote dietary diversification, inclusion of iron foliate rich food as well as food items that promote iron absorption.

Health policy of India aims at an integrated approach which will provide accessible, affordable and equitable quality health care to the marginalized and vulnerable sections. To reap benefits of the 'demographic dividend' India needs to work in the direction of providing 'good health and well-being for all'. India is signatory to the UN's sustainable development goals (SDGs) where the country commits to—*ensure healthy lives and promote well being for all at all ages.*

It is imperative for the governments to think in the direction of *universal healthcare*— the aim which was proposed by the 12th Plan (2012-17)—but the Government could not announced it formally due to lack of funding issue. The NITI Aayog has been working in this direction and it is expected that some actions may be in the pipeline.

UHC Index: The Universal Health Coverage (UHC) index[16] has been developed by the World Bank to measure the progress in the health sector in select countries. India ranks **143** among 190 countries in terms of per capita expenditure on health—for India it stands at $146 (at PPP). It has 157th position according to per capita government spending on health which is just about $44 (at PPP). India's performance on the indicator on treatment of diarrhoea needs improvement in terms of enhancing the coverage. The impoverishment indicator reflects the financial risk protection coverage, with a higher per centage reflecting better coverage.

Housing Amenities: Public health is closely linked to housing amenities such as access to safe drinking water, sanitation facilities and hygiene. Consumption of contaminated drinking water, improper disposal of human excreta, lack of personal and food hygiene and improper disposal of solid and liquid waste have been causes of many diseases in developing countries like India. The present situation[17] of the housing amenities are as given below:

- Around 70 per cent of India's population (650 million) lives in rural and slum areas. It increases the possibility of exposure of the population to water-borne and vector-borne diseases. This can also be attributed to the lack of basic sanitation facilities, unsafe water and unhygienic living conditions.

- Only 46.6 per cent of households in India have access to drinking water within their premises. A far lower, 43.5 per cent of households have access to tap water. Similarly, less than 50 per cent

households have latrine facilities within the household premises.

- The disparity across states in terms of access to household amenities like *tap water* and *latrine* facilities is sharp. While access and coverage of latrine facilities is as high as 95 per cent in Kerala, 91 per cent in Mizoram and 89 per cent in Manipur, less than 25 per cent of households have access to latrine facilities within the household premises in Bihar, Chhattisgarh, Jharkhand and Odisha.

- In some states over 75 per cent of households have no latrine facilities— in Bihar (77), Chhattisgarh (75), Jharkhand (78) and Odisha (78).

The *Swachh Bharat Abhiyan* aims at universal sanitation coverage and eliminate open defecation in India by 2 October 2019. It also aims to promote better hygiene amongst the population and improve cleanliness by initiating Solid and Liquid Waste Management (SLWM) projects in villages, towns and cities.

The progress in sanitation has witnessed a spurt since the launch of the Swachh Bharat Mission—sanitation coverage improved from 40.6 per cent to 48.8 per cent between October 2014 and *December 2015*, as per the latest NSSO data. The Swachh Bharat Mission will begin to show intended results if the constructed toilets are maintained after construction and also utilised by the beneficiaries.

In order to improve availability of drinking water in rural areas, the National Rural Drinking Water Programme (NRDWP) initiated a new project supported by the World Bank, the 'Rural Water Supply and Sanitation Project–Low Income States'. The project aims to provide safe, 24 x 7 piped drinking water supply to 7.8 million rural population in four low-income States—Assam, Bihar, Uttar Pradesh and Jharkhand—that have

---

16. **Economic Survey 2015-16**, op. cit., Vol. 2, p. 206.
17. As the government documents have been quoted by the **Economic Survey 2015-16**, op. cit., Vol. 2, pp. 207-209.

the *lowest* piped water supply and sanitation facilities.

SOCIAL SECTOR EXPENDITURE

India's expenditure on social sectors has not reflected a major increasing trend during the past few years (2008-2016), an increase in expenditure *per-se* may not always guarantee appropriate outcomes and achievements. The efficiency of expenditure incurred so far can be assessed by the performance of social sectors through various social indicators. An overall assessment of social sector expenditures in terms of achievements shows that wide gaps still exist in educational and health outcomes and there is need for substantial improvement and the need to remove inequalities in the country.

The latest data[18] regarding General Government (i.e., Centre plus States) expenditures of India on the "social sector" for the year 2016-17 (BE, i.e., Budget Estimates) were as given below:

(i) Total expenditure—28.4 per cent of the GDP (28.2 per cent in previous year).

(ii) Expenditure on social services— 7.0 per cent of GDP (6.9 per cent in the previous year).

(iii) Expenditure of education—2.9 per cent of GDP (same as in the previous year).

(iv) Expenditure on health—1.4 per cent of GDP (1.3 per cent in the previous year).

The year 2014-15, for which the latest actual figures are available, did show a significant decline from the revised estimates (RE) due to a large decrease in the actual social sector expenditure done by the states (from the revised estimates). This is matter of concern and adequate steps are needed in this direction to correct this anomaly.

POLICY SUGGESTIONS

Social infrastructure has positive externalities. It has a significant role in the economic development and welfare of a country. It is empirically proven and widely recognised that education and health impact the growth of an economy. Investing in *human capital* by way of education, skill development, training and provision of health care facilities enhances the productivity of the workforce and welfare of the population. In this regard, contemporary documents **suggest** the following actions[19] for the governments in the country:

(i) Action is needed in the direction of improving the quality of education provided in schools to arrest and reverse the decline in enrolment in government schools. Besides, it is essential to improve the educational outcomes in both public and private schools. An important contributor to improvement in the quality of education would be an increase in the per centage of *qualified teachers*.

(ii) India needs to overcome the development challenges through innovative models of *delivery of services*. It has a critical role to play in India's march towards double-digit growth.

(iii) Without improvement in social infrastructure development of a country is incomplete. To capitalise and leverage the advantages that India will have on the demographic front with a large segment in the productive age group, social infrastructure requires fresh impetus with focus on efficiency to improve the quality of human capital. To foster education

---

18. Latest data from the *Reserve Bank of India* quoted by the **Economic Survey 2016-17**, MoF, GoI, N. Delhi, Vol. 1, pp. 160-161.

19. The suggestions are based on the documents— **World Happiness Report-2015 (SDSN, UNO); World Development Report- 2015 & 2016 (World Bank); Economic Survey 2015-16 & 2016-17 (GoI); India Development Report-2015;** and the **NITI Aayog (GoI).**

and skill development of its diverse population, including the marginalised sections, women and the differently-abled, and to provide quality health and other social services, the Government has identified the potential of *technology platforms* which can significantly improve efficiency in the system.

(iv) Overhauling of the subsidy regime is needed with faster pace. It will not only rationalise the subsidies but bring in variety of *other benefits* in the service delivery system—inclusion of the needy population; exclusion of the fake accounts; prevention of corruption and leakages; traceability; authentication of delivery; transparency and accountability.

The idea of technology-enabled Direct Benefits Transfers (DBT), namely the JAM (Jan Dhan-Aadhaar-Mobile) number trinity solution, introduced by the GoI in this regard is believed to be a game-changing move.

(v) India needs to include the *behavioural dimensions* of the target population in its framework of policy-making to realise desired results in the area of promoting the cause of the social infrastructure. India has already included this aspect in its sanitation campaign (especially, in checking open defecation)—the same is needed in the other areas of importance, too.

(vi) There is a need of *integrating* the social sector initiatives of the Centre, states and the local bodies. The new 'think tank' NITI Aayog can play a suitable platform in this regard.

(vii) Strengthening of the *local bodies* (the PRIs) will not only boost the social sector but it will have an effect of externality in the form of an aware, awakened and participative citizenry. Through them, India can garner the support of civil society and the NGO.

(viii) There is need to orient the *private sector* (corporate world) towards this cause. Their inclusion in this area will not only bring in fund to this fund-scarce sector but enable the country to use their expertise in the promotion of the social infrastructure.

BURNING SOCIO-ECONOMIC ISSUES

1. BAD BANK

Introduction

The burden of bad debts, i.e., non-performing assets (NPAs) of banks, especially of the public sector banks (PSBs), has been increasing with every passing quarter for the last few years—caused by various reasons. By the end of March 2017, stressed assets of the banking system were over 12 per cent of their total loans. The PSBs that own almost 70 per cent of the banking assets, had a stress–loan ratio of almost 16 per cent. This is the main reason why for the past many quarters banks have been unwilling to process fresh loans. At the end of last quarter of the 2016-17, credit growth has become negative and the lowest in over two decades. To solve the crisis of the high NPAs, the Reserve Bank of India (RBI) has introduced multiple schemes over the last few years—Flexible Refinancing of Infrastructure (5/25 scheme), Asset Reconstruction Companies (ARC), Strategic Debt Restructuring (SDR), Asset Quality Review (AQR) and Sustainable Structuring of Stressed Assets (S4A). But these measures have not brought much relief to the banks. As conventional remedies seem to be failing to address the menace, a bit less conventional remedy is gaining ground, which suggests the Government to set up a *bad bank*.

The Concept

Theoretically, bad banks[1] work on simple concept, i.e., banks' loans are classified into two categories, good and bad. The bad loans of the banks are bought or taken over by the bad bank while the good loans are left with the bank itself. This way, bad loans do not contaminate the good assets of banks. As banks hit by the problem of bad loans become financially viable entities, they restart

---

1. The write-up is based on the **Economic Survey 2016-17**, documents of the RBI and other Government sources.

their lending process. While the concept of a bad bank is simple, the implementation can be quite complicated. A variety of organisational and financial options are there to design them. The RBI has signalled in favour of setting up such a bank, but it has also highlighted the concern of 'designing it properly'.

Models of Bad Bank

We find four different models of bad bank in the world depending on need of the hour, which are briefly described below:

(i) **On-balance-sheet guarantee:** In this model, the stressed banks get a loss-guarantee from government for a part of its portfolio (i.e., bad assets). This is a simple and less expensive format and can be implemented quickly. Though bad loans get government guarantee, they remain on the balance sheet of the bank. It means while the bank becomes confident about its bad assets, they are still not in position to start fresh lending. This model does not fit in India's needs of today.

(ii) **Internal restructuring unit:** This model is like creating a bad bank inside the stressed bank itself. Banks put their bad debts in a 'separate unit' inside their own financial structure and set up separate management team to handle the bad assets—the team is given clear incentives. This helps banks increase transparency (as figures related to bad loans become public) and boosts confidence among their shareholders. It however, fails to enable them restart fresh lending. This model also does not look suitable for India.

(iii) **Special-purpose entity:** This model is a bit different from the two described above. The bad loans of the banks are 'offloaded' from the balance-sheet of the banks and securitised into a kind of fund that is sold off to a diverse group of investors in financial system. In case of India these securitised bad loans can be run through sector-specific special purpose vehicles (SPVs). As the problem of the NPAs is concentrated in a few sectors (like infrastructure and metals), this model looks quite useful. As the process involves the 'market' (for the pricing of the securitised bad assets) the PSBs will attract less blame in this model. As the balance-sheet of banks become clean they can start fresh lending.

(iv) **Bad-bank spin-off:** This is the most familiar model tried across the world. In this format, stressed banks shift their bad loans to a separate banking body (i.e., the bad bank). This way the risk of bad loans is smoothly transferred from the stressed banks' balance-sheet to the bad bank making banks viable to start fresh lending. Though this format looks the most suitable one for India's situation, it needs certain arrangements to be put in place, such as setting up a separate body, putting desired kind of management skill in place, information systems and proper regulatory mechanism being the major ones. This is an expensive model, too. The idea of a public sector asset rehabilitation agency (PARA) suggested by the *Economic Survey 2016-17* falls in this category. However, the PARA is supposed to address another problem also—the stressed balance-sheet of some private sector corporate entities.

Conclusion

The situation of the bad loans in the banking system has reached such a level that it has started hitting the investment prospects in the economy,

and they need immediate attention from the Government, as per the *Economic Survey 2016-17*. If we go by the proposition of the survey, it looks suitable for the Government to think in the direction of setting up a separate body in the line of the PARA. Setting up a bad bank will only address the problem of banks' bad debt and may make them fit to restart lending. But this will not promote the cause of investment in the economy as some big corporates are unfit to borrow (on whom depends the investment prospects). It means India needs to leverage these corporate entities, too. In the aftermath of the presentation of the *Union Budget 2017-18*, the Government expressed its willingness in the direction of setting up such a body in the coming months. Meanwhile, business, industries and banks in India are waiting for the Government initiative in this regard.

2. DEMOGRAPHIC DIVIDEND

Introduction

India's turn to enjoy the opportunity of demographic dividend[2] has been repeatedly highlighted by the experts and international organisations alike. At the peak of discussion, it was covered thoroughly by the *Economic Survey 2012-13* devoting an exclusive chapter to it. As India's dependency ratio is declining fast, India will soon reach the peak of enjoying the demographic dividend—the highest economic contribution from the peak of working age (WA) population. It should be kept in mind that demography provides potential opportunity and is not destiny (as the *Economic Survey 2016-17* and *2015-16* remind). India needs to optimise the period to fill the great many economic gaps it has been fighting against since decades. Recent studies point out that India is in different situation today—from waiting to happening of the opportunity of the

2. The write-up is based on the analyses presented in the *Economic Survey 2016-17; 2015-16* and *2012-13*.

demographic dividend. And soon India will see the event receding, too—the opportunity must not be missed.

Turning point: Global demographics saw a turning point in 2016—for the first time since 1950, the combined WA population (age group 15–59 years) of the advanced countries declined. As per the projections of the UNO, for the next three decades China and Russia will see their WA declining by over 20 per cent. However, India seems to be in a demographic *sweet spot* with its WA population—projected to grow by a third over the same period. Economic research of the last two decades has suggested that the higher growth rates in East Asia were driven by demographic changes. Countries with large WA populations appear to benefit more (due to higher economic dynamism) as *younger populations:*

- are more entrepreneurial (adding to productivity growth);
- tend to save more, which may also lead to favourable competitiveness effects; and
- due to growth, they have a larger fiscal base, fewer dependents and government to support.

Theory suggests that the specific variable driving the demographic dividend is the ratio of the working age to non-working age (NWA) population.

India's Demographics

India's distinctiveness: The comparison of the WA/NWA ratio between 1970 and 2015 (based on the projections of the UNO) for India, Brazil, Korea and China illustrates three **distinct** features about Indian demographic profile—having implications for the growth outlook of India and its states:

(i) India's demographic cycle is about 10–30 years behind that of the other countries. This indicates that India has next few decades as opportunity to catch up to the per capita income levels of the three countries.

(ii) India's WA to NWA ratio is likely to peak at 1.7, a much lower level than Brazil and China, both of which sustained a ratio greater than 1.7 for at least 25 years.

(iii) India will remain close to its peak of WA and NWA ratio for a much longer period than other countries.

The 'distinctive' demographic pattern of India has a *cause* and *consequence* for it—

Cause: All these countries started the post-World War II era with roughly the same very high total fertility rates (TFRs). In China and Korea, TFR then declined rapidly to below-replacement levels (less than two children per female), causing the share of WA population to rise until the early 2000s, then to fall as ageing began to set in. In India, however, the decline in TFR has been much more gradual.

Consequence: India should not expect to see growth surges or growth decelerations of the magnitudes experienced by the East Asian countries due to demographic dividend—and might be able to sustain high levels of growth for a longer time.

Spatial differentiation: India has a large 'heterogeneity' among the states in their demographic profile and evolution—there is a clear divide between *peninsular India* (West Bengal, Kerala, Karnataka, Tamil Nadu and Andhra Pradesh) and the *hinterland states* (Madhya Pradesh, Rajasthan, Uttar Pradesh, and Bihar):

- The peninsular states exhibit a pattern that is closer to China and Korea, with sharp rises and declines in the WA population. The difference, of course, is that the WA ratio of most of the peninsular states will peak at levels lower than seen in East Asia (West Bengal comes closest to Korea's peak because of its very low TFR).

- In contrast, the hinterland states will remain relatively young and dynamic, with a rising WA population for some time.

This divide among the states is due to their differentiated TFRs. It means, demographically, there are *two Indias*, with different policy concerns.

(i) An India which is soon to begin ageing where the elderly and their needs will require greater attention; and

(ii) A young India where providing education, skills, and employment opportunities must be the focus.

Of course, heterogeneity within India offers the advantage of addressing some of these concerns via greater labour mobility, which would in effect reduce this demographic imbalance.

Growth impacts: India's special demographic pattern will have *two* important growth consequences:

(i) It seems that the peak of the demographic dividend is approaching fast for India—peaking early 2020s—with peninsular India peaking around 2020 while hinterland India by around 2040.

(ii) The distributional impacts of growth across India will be differentiated, too. The poorer states of today will have growth in their per capita GDP higher than the richer ones. It means, demographic dividend will bring an opportunity for income convergence across the states.

Outliers: The overall encouraging pattern masks some 'interesting outliers' which will have their own impacts on the regions and the population residing there.

- Bihar, Jammu and Kashmir, Haryana, and Maharashtra are *positive outliers* in that they can expect a greater demographic dividend over the coming years than would be suggested by their current level of income. This extra dividend will help Bihar converge, while already rich Haryana and Maharashtra will pull further away from the average level of income per capita in India.

- On the other hand, Kerala, Madhya Pradesh, Chhattisgarh, and West Bengal are *negative outliers*. Their future dividend is relatively low for their level of income.

This will make the poorer states fall back, unless offset by robust reforms and growth, while the relatively rich Kerala will probably converge to the average as its growth momentum declines rapidly.

Conclusion

The WA population of India is about to plateau. Thus, the boost in economic growth is likely to peak within the ***next five*** years. In comparison to the East Asian economies, India's WA ratio will fall much more gradually—the reason why India may be able to avoid sharp falls in growth (as seen in case of the former). In addition, the sharp demographic differences between peninsular and hinterland India will generate wide differences in the timing of the peak, as well as opportunities to attenuate demographic imbalances via greater labour mobility. India does not need to wait longer for the time of peaking of demographic dividend—better say the opportunity is "soon-to-recede". So that this once in a centuries opportunity is not missed, it is high time that requisite reforms, policies and compatible action are all put in place as soon as possible.

3. TWIN BALANCE SHEET CRISES

Introduction

The non-performing assets (NPAs) of banks, particularly the Public Sector Banks (PSBs), have been in news for being excessively high for the past several years. Several steps taken by the RBI to solve the crises have almost failed. Meanwhile, the debt-ridden big private sector companies came in news with their declining earnings. These corporate entities spread across infrastructure to steel to real estate have been causing the real problem of NPAs to the banks. It means the remedy does not lie in only de-stressing the banks but similar remedy is needed in case of the corporate sector, too.

The Problem

Though, India has today one of the fastest growth rates in the world, for the past few years, certain financial issues have been worsening. In the aftermath of the global financial crisis (GFC) of 2007, India has been trying to come to grips with the 'twin balance sheet' (TBS)[3] problem—

(i) High NPAs of the PSBs; and

(ii) Highly stressed balance sheet of the private corporate sector.

India has taken several steps by now to recover and control the bad loans of the banks. But they have not been very effective and banks are even today under high stress. On the other hand, India has been waiting for a recovery in the corporate sector for their balance sheet to come in good health but to no avail. Meanwhile, situation has been worsening over the time.

The stressed corporate sector has been forced to borrow more to continue their operations, as their earnings have been deteriorating. Since the GFC, till September 2016, the debts of the top 10 stressed corporate groups have multiplied five times, to more than Rs 7.5 lakh crore. These companies have been facing difficulty in even servicing their loans.

In the meanwhile, around 12 per cent of the total loans of the PSBs turned out to be NPAs. If some private sector estimates are to be believed,

the NPAs are considerably high (around 16 per cent).

The Solution

The TBS has started showing off its negative impacts on the economy—the private corporate sector has been forced to curb its investments while banks have been reducing their loan disbursals. To sustain growth, these trends need to be reversed. The only way to do so is by fixing the underlying balance sheet problems. The *Survey* suggests considering a different approach to address the issue of TBS—setting up a centralised 'public sector asset rehabilitation agency'—the PARA. As per it, the agency can take charge of the largest and most difficult cases, and make politically tough decisions to reduce debt.

So far, the official strategy has been to solve the TBS through a 'decentralised approach', under which banks have been put in charge of the 'restructuring' decisions. Several such schemes have been put in place by the RBI. Most of the time, this is indeed the best strategy. But in the current circumstances, effectiveness has proved elusive as banks have simply been overwhelmed by the size of the problem. The time might have come to try a 'centralised approach'—the PARA (a detailed discussion has been given in the new *'Economic Survey 2016-17'*). ***Some points*** are given below in support of the PARA.

Banks plus companies: Normally, public discussion of the bad loan problem has been centred on bank capital, as if the main obstacle to resolving TBS was finding the funds needed by the PSBs (we see Government recapitalising the banks since 2012-13 itself). Even if this capital is mobilised (might be up to three per cent of GDP), it will help only the banks to come out of red but not the stressed corporate entities (which are behind this crisis). A sustainable remedy for these corporates is also needed.

---

3. The write-up is based primarily on the **Economic Survey 2016-17**; articles and interviews of **Arvind Subramanian**, Chief Economic Advisor, Government of India and other **official releases**.

Economic rather moral problem: Whenever public discussion starts on the TBS problem it is linked to issue of crony capitalism, which looks correct also as many a time debt repayment problems have been caused by diversion of funds. But another dimension should also be kept in mind—the problem has been caused by "unexpected changes in the economic environment", such as, the tenures of loans, exchange rates and growth rate assumptions going badly wrong. Thus, the problem is not a moral one but economic. Repetitive narratives on crony capitalism may end into punishing some but it fails us to think in the direction of incentive-based remedies.

Concentrated debts: Stressed debts are heavily concentrated in large companies, which look as an opportunity because a relatively small number of cases need to be resolved. But large cases are inherently difficult to resolve and that will be the challenge.

Debt write downs: Many of these companies are unviable at current levels of debt, requiring debt writedowns. It is believed that about 50 per cent debt write-down may be needed to restore viability among them.

Banks' difficulty: Banks have faced difficulty to resolve NPA cases, despite RBI giving them multiple choices. Among other issues, they face severe coordination problems, since large debtors have many creditors, with different interests. If PSBs think of granting large debt reductions, this could attract the attention of investigative agencies. Debt restructuring by converting debt to equity or taking over the companies and then selling them in future to a prospective buyer—will be politically difficult, if they sell it at loss.

ARCs proving futile: The Asset Reconstruction Companies (ARCs) haven't proved any more successful than banks in resolving bad debts and are too small to handle large cases. The ARC–bank relationship can be inherently distorted; for example, ARCs keep earning management fees for handling bad debts, even if they don't work them out. The new bankruptcy law (legislated in 2016-17) is yet to start functioning—even after it is enforced, considerable time will be needed before it is ready to handle the large cases.

Delay is costly: Since banks can't resolve the big cases, they have simply refinanced the debtors, effectively "kicking the problems down the road". But this is costly for the government, because it means the bad debts keep rising, increasing the cost of recapitalisation for the government and the associated political difficulties.

Functioning of PARA

Possible variants are many though the broad outlines are simple. It would purchase specified loans (for example, those belonging to large, over-indebted infrastructure firms) from banks and then work them out, depending on professional assessments of the value-maximising strategy. Once the loans are off the books of the PSBs, the government would recapitalise them, thereby allowing them to use their resources (financial and human) in making new loans. Similarly, once the financial viability of the over-indebted enterprises is restored, they will be able to focus on their operations, rather than their finances. And they will become financially fit to borrow and go for fresh investments.

Moral hazards: Such a move looks facing moral dilemma. Of course, all this will come at a price, namely accepting and paying for the losses. But this cost is inevitable. Loans have already been made, losses already incurred and because the PSBs are the major creditors, the bulk of the burden will fall on the government (though shareholders in stressed enterprises will need to lose their equity as well). The issue for any resolution strategy (PARA or decentralised) is not whether the government should assume new liability. Rather, it is how to minimise a liability that has already been incurred by resolving the bad loan problem as effectively as possible. And that is precisely what the creation of PARA would aim to do.

Capital requirements: It would require large capital, which may be managed in the following way:

- First and the most important source of it would be the government (through issues of securities);
- Second source could be capital markets (if shares in the PSBs are sold or private sector buys stakes in the PARA);
- Third source of capital could be the RBI (the central bank may transfer some government securities it is holding to PSBs and PARA—this will decrease RBI's capital, the capital of the PSBs and PARA would increase. It would create no implications for monetary policy since no new money would be created).

Risks and difficulties: Creating the PARA is not without its own difficulties and risks; the country's history is not favourable to public sector endeavours. Yet, one must ask how long India should continue with the current decentralised approach, which has still not produced the desired results eight years after the GFC, even as East Asian countries were able to resolve their much larger TBS problems within two years. One reason, of course, was that the East Asian countries were under much more pressure that they were in crisis, whereas India has continued to grow rapidly. But an important reason was that it deployed a 'centralised strategy', which allowed debt problems to be worked out quickly using public asset rehabilitation companies. In sum, current efforts have not been successful in addressing the TBS problem. New solutions must be tried. Perhaps it is time for India to consider the PARA as one such solution.

The approach of PARA could eliminate most of the obstacles currently plaguing loan resolution:

- It could solve the coordination problem since debts would be centralised in one agency;
- It could be set up with proper incentives by giving it an explicit mandate to maximise recoveries within a defined time;
- It would separate the loan resolution process from concerns about bank capital.

Though the *Union Budget 2017-18* has just highlighted the concerns, it is in its aftermath that the Government has hinted to take steps in the direction of creating such a public vehicle to solve the twin crises India is faced with. Meanwhile, the Government looks busy studying the crises and working out a suitable solution.

4. UNIVERSAL HEALTHCARE

Introduction

It was the 12th Plan, the first official document, which advised in favour of the universal healthcare, estimating a total allocation of around 2.5 per cent of the GDP. The idea could not be implemented as the Government of the time could not commit itself to the required funds (estimated to allocate maximum 1.6 per cent of the GDP). At present, the total government expenditure (centre plus states) on healthcare is 1.4 per cent of the GDP (*Economic Survey 2016-17*). The healthcare related sufferings in the country have been always a matter of high concern—out of pocket expenditure being one of the highest in the world (at over 70 per cent since many decades). The idea has been a major issue of the public debate. During the last General Elections, the idea kept resonating across the promises of the political parties.

The Challenges

Committing to the cause of universal healthcare at the practical level has been a daunting task for the Government, given the scarcity of resources.

To implement such a policy, the Government needs to put in place a great many physical and non-physical support systems, such as number of hospitals, adequate number of personnel, medical colleges, nursing institutes, health insurance, public deliveries of vaccines and medicines; etc. naming the major ones. To implement such a policy mobilising the required financial resources has been the biggest challenge for the governments. Developing a *financial model* was the need of the hour.

Going for the Idea

After almost two years of consultations with various stakeholders, the Government of India, finally took the final call in the direction of 'universal healthcare' when the *National Health Policy 2017* was announced by mid-March 2017. The policy focusses "Preventive and Promotive Health Care and Universal access to good quality healthcare services". The major *highlights* of the policy[4] have been discussed below.

Primary aim: The primary aim of the policy is to inform, clarify, strengthen and prioritise the role of the Government in shaping health systems in all its dimensions— investment in health, organisation and financing of healthcare services, prevention of diseases and promotion of good health through cross sectoral action, access to technologies, developing human resources, encouraging medical pluralism, building the knowledge base required for better health, financial protection strategies and regulation and progressive assurance for health. The policy emphasises reorienting and strengthening the Public Health Institutions across the country, to provide universal access to free drugs, diagnostics and other essential healthcare.

Approach change: The policy denotes important change from very selective to comprehensive primary healthcare package which includes *geriatric healthcare, palliative care* and *rehabilitative care* services. The policy advocates allocating major proportion (up to two-thirds or more) of resources to primary care followed by secondary and tertiary care. The policy aspires to provide at the district level most of the secondary care which is currently provided at a medical college hospital.

Broad principle: The broad principle of the policy is centred on Professionalism, Integrity and Ethics, Equity, Affordability, Universality, Patient Cantered & Quality of Care, Accountability and Pluralism.

Affordability: It seeks to ensure improved access and affordability of quality secondary and tertiary care services through a combination of public hospitals and strategic purchasing in healthcare deficit areas from accredited non-governmental healthcare providers, achieve significant reduction in *out of pocket expenditure* due to healthcare costs, reinforce trust in public healthcare system and influence operation and growth of private healthcare industry as well as medical technologies in alignment with public health goals.

Pluralistic design: To leverage the pluralistic healthcare legacy, the policy recommends mainstreaming the different health systems. Towards mainstreaming the potential of AYUSH the policy envisages better access to AYUSH remedies through co-location in public facilities. Yoga would also be introduced much more widely in school and work places as part of promotion of good health.

Focus on pre-emptive care: The policy affirms commitment to pre-emptive care (aimed at pre-empting the occurrence of diseases) to achieve optimum levels of child and adolescent health. The policy envisages school health programmes as a major focus area as also health and hygiene being made a part of the school curriculum.

---

4. The write-up is based on the **Economic Survey 2016-17**, press release from the **Government of India** and other Government sources (till March 2017).

Funding: The policy proposes raising public health expenditure to 2.5 per cent of the GDP in a time bound manner. It aims at providing larger package of assured comprehensive primary healthcare through the HWCs (Health and Wellness Centres).

Private participation: The idea of universal healthcare is very realistic to the time as it has decided to enhance the participation of the private sector in a positive and proactive way in achieving the goals of the policy. It envisages private sector collaboration for strategic purchasing, capacity building, skill development programmes, awareness generation, developing sustainable networks for community to strengthen mental health services, and disaster management. The policy also advocates financial and non-incentives for encouraging the private sector participation.

Quantitative targets: The policy assigns specific quantitative targets aimed at reduction of disease prevalence/incidence, for health status and programme impact, health system performance and system strengthening. It seeks to strengthen the health, surveillance system and establish registries for diseases of public health importance, by 2020. It also seeks to align other policies for medical devices and equipment with public health goals.

Regulatory mechanism: The policy advocates extensive deployment of digital tools for improving the efficiency and outcome of the healthcare system and proposes establishment of National Digital Health Authority (NDHA) to regulate, develop and deploy digital health across the continuum of care.

Voluntary support: The policy supports voluntary service in rural and under-served areas on *pro-bono* (free of charge) basis by recognised healthcare professionals under a 'giving back to society' initiative.

Background: The Government of India adopted an elaborate procedure for formulation of the health policy. Its Draft was placed in public domain on 30th December 2014. After detailed consultations with stakeholders and State Governments, it was further fine-tuned. Finally, by late February 2016 it received the endorsement of the Central Council for Health & Family Welfare (the apex policy making body). Since the last health policy was announced in 2002, the country has seen much socio-economic and epidemiological changes. Besides, there are some burning current challenges as well as emerging ones. To address these issues in holistic and effective way, the Government needed to come out with a newly designed and contemporary kind of health policy—the outcome is the NHP 2017.

5. AFTEREFFECTS OF DEMONETISATION

Introduction

Early November 2016, the Government announced a historic measure, with profound implications for the economy—the largest denomination currency notes, Rs 500 and Rs 1000, were demonetised. Eighty-six per cent of the cash in circulation thus became invalid. According to the Government, this was aimed to serve four objectives[5]:

(i) Curbing corruption;

(ii) Counterfeiting of currencies;

(iii) Checking terrorism (as they use high denomination notes); and

(iv) Preventing accumulation of black money.

This action followed a series of earlier efforts to curb such illicit activities: the creation of the Special Investigative Team (SIT) in 2014, the

---

5. The write-up is primarily based on the Economic Survey 2016-17 and the primary sources of the Government of India released till March 2017.

Black Money and Imposition of Tax Act 2015, Benami Transactions Act 2016, the information exchange agreement with Switzerland, changes in the tax treaties with Mauritius, Cyprus and Singapore, and the Income Disclosure Scheme. This was not an unprecedented action as there were two previous instances of it—in 1946 and 1978, the latter[6] not having any significant effect on cash.

There have been reports of job losses, declines in farm incomes, and social disruption, especially in the informal, cash-intensive parts of the economy. However, a systematic analysis is not possible yet due to paucity of data. The benefits of demonetisation can be only felt in coming years—the move was more aimed at long-term goals than short-term. We may have a ***brief review*** about the impact of demonetisation on the economy and behavioural aspects in the following way.

Long-term benefits: It is too early to quantify the direction and magnitude of long-term changes. It will take *several years* to see the impact of demonetisation on illicit transactions, on black money, and on financial savings. But there are some signs pointing to change.

(a) *Digitalisation:* One intermediate objective of demonetisation is to create a *less-cash* or *cash-lite* economy. This will not only channelise more saving into the financial system but it will improve tax compliance also. Currently, India is far away from this objective: the *Watal Committee* has recently estimated that cash accounts for about 78 per cent of all consumer payments. According to *Pricewaterhouse Coopers (2015)* India has a very high predominance of consumer transactions carried out in cash relative to other countries (accounting for 68 per cent of total transactions by value and 98 per cent by volume).

People prefer cash transaction due to many reasons. It is convenient, accepted everywhere, its use is costless for ordinary people (though not of course for society at large), is anonymous, helps preserve privacy, which is not bad till it is not illicit or designed to evade tax. Digitalisation can broadly impact the three sections of society—*the poor*, who are largely outside the digital economy; the *less affluent*, who are becoming part of the digital economy having acquired Jan-Dhan accounts and RuPay cards; and the *affluent*, who are fully digitally integrated via credit cards.

(b) *Real estate:* This sector could have profound impact. In the past, much of the black money accumulated was ultimately used to evade taxes on property sales. A reduction in real estate prices is desirable as it will lead to affordable housing for the middle class, and facilitate labour mobility across India currently impeded by high and unaffordable rents.

Short-term impact: Demonetisation will impose short-term costs on the economy, which remain difficult to measure by now due to lack of the right data set. As the process has created a *large structural shock*, the underlying *behavioural parameters* of the past will be imperfect indicators of future behaviour and hence the outcomes. Although a framework of the short-term impact may be outlined:

(a) *Impact on Gross Domestic Product (GDP):* Economic activities have been affected adversely. Thus, national income will get hit also, but it will be only temporary. The GDP might be lower by 0.25 to 0.5

---

6. In 1970, a Committee headed by former Chief Justice K.N. Wanchoo, in its interim report, recommended demonetisation of the 10, 100, and higher denomination notes to combat the scourge of black money. These denominations accounted for 86.6 percent of the then money stock.

per cent (coming to around 7 per cent). The implementation of GST, follow-up to demonetisation and other structural reforms should put the growth to the 8–10 per cent range that India needs.

(b) *Redistribution of income:* It will redistribute resources also having following effects on the fiscal accounts of the Government:

- RBI/Government may receive some gains from the unreturned cash—wealth gains.

- Income taxes could go up as black money was deposited in bank accounts.

Against this there are three *negative effects*. *First,* costs of printing new notes; *secondly,* costs of sterilising the surge in liquidity into the banking system (via issuance of Market Stabilisation Scheme bonds); and *thirdly,* if nominal GDP growth declines, corporate and indirect tax revenues of the centre could decline but so far there is no clear evidence.

Tapping the Prospects

The Government needs to maximise the long-term benefits and minimise short-term costs of demonetisation. For this purpose, the following measures look beneficial:

(i) Remonetisation process should be faster.

(ii) Any windfall revenue arising from 'unreturned notes' should be used for *capital-type expenditures* and not revenue ones. As this income will be one-off, its use should be one-off.

(iii) Digitalisation must continue in medium term, though neither it is a panacea nor cash economy is bad. Balancing benefits and costs of both forms of payments will be sensible. The transition to digitalisation must be gradual and inclusive, too.

Digitalisation must be incentivised and the incentives favouring cash neutralised. The cost of incentivisation must be borne by the public sector (Government/RBI) and not the consumer or financial intermediaries.

(iv) Efforts to collect taxes on newly disclosed (and undisclosed) wealth should not lead to tax harassment by officials at all rungs of the hierarchy. A shift is needed to greater use of data, smarter evidence-based scrutiny, more reliance on online assessments with less interactions between tax payers and tax officials. Non-punitive means should be evolved to enhance tax compliance.

(v) So that demonetisation indeed proves a catalyst for long-run changes in *behaviour*, it will be required to complement demonetisation with other non-punitive, incentive-compatible measures that reduce the incentives for tax evasion. Demonetisation was a potentially powerful stick that now needs *carrots* as complements. A *five-pronged strategy* could be adopted:

(a) GST should include activities that are sources of black money creation—land and other immovable property;

(b) Individual income tax rates and real estate stamp duties could be reduced;

(c) Income tax net could be widened gradually and, consistent with constitutional arrangements progressively encompass all high incomes;

(d) The timetable for reducing the corporate tax rate could be accelerated; and

(e) To reduce discretion and improve accountability, tax administration needs improvement.

Conclusion

The actual cost of demonetisation will be known by the end of the fiscal 2016-17 only. While the short-term gains of it will be limited in nature, the success of this move will be mainly known by its long-term effects. However, to maximise the gains out of this, the Government needs to take several other timely and rational steps to complement it. Thus, the momentum generated should not get reduced so that economy can realise the gains from demonetisation.

6. ADDRESSING INEQUALITY

Introduction

Inequality has already been an important concern in India for the Government. In the wake of globalisation process, the debate has got even louder. Meanwhile, a few recent global reports (of early 2017) put India's inequality concern on top of the global debate. Several questions related to the issue became focus of the debate among the experts and policy makers—how inequality hurts, who gets maximum hurt, how to address the problem, etc[7].

Inequality Concerns

The latest *New World Wealth* (a Johannesburg-based company) report says India to be the second-most unequal country globally, with millionaires controlling 54 per cent of the nation's wealth. With a total individual wealth of US$5,600 billion, it's among the 10 richest countries in the world. Yet, average Indian is relatively poor. If we compare India with Japan (the most equal country in the world) situation looks even worse where millionaires control only 22 per cent of the

---

7. The write-up is based on several contemporary reports and Government releases such as—the **Economic Survey 2016-17, Union Budget 2017-18, World Economic Forum, Oxfam reports, Credit Suisse,** etc.

---

wealth. We may have a look at the latest data from the *Credit Suisse* related to India's inequality:

- The richest 1 per cent owns 53 per cent of the country's wealth.
- The richest 5 per cent own 68.6 per cent, while the top 10 per cent have 76.3 per cent.
- At the other end of the pyramid, the poorer half competes in just 4.1 per cent of the total wealth of the nation.
- India's richest 1 per cent owned just 36.8 per cent of the country's wealth in 2000, while the share of the top 10 per cent was 65.9 per cent. Since then they have steadily increased their share in the country's wealth—the share of the top 1 per cent now exceeds 50 per cent.
- India's situation looks worse than the United States where the richest 1 per cent owns 37.3 per cent of total wealth.
- While India's finest still have a long way to go before they match Russia, where the top 1 per cent owns a stupendous 70.3 per cent of the country's wealth.

As per the new India Human Development Survey (IHDS), which provides data on income inequality for the *first time*, India's score of income equality is lower than Russia, the United States, China and Brazil—is more egalitarian than only South Africa.

Inequality Needs to be Checked

Though inequality is found everywhere, its extremes hurt economies multi-dimensionally. As per *Oxfam*, sharp rise in inequality in India and the other countries around the world is damaging, and the governments of the countries need to make efforts to curb it. Rising inequality will have several negative consequences for the nations—slowing down poverty reduction, challenging sustainability of economic growth, compounding the inequalities between men and women, and drive inequalities in health, education and across the life chances.

The World Economic Forum's *Global Risks Report 2016* (third time in series) has found 'severe income disparity' to be one of the top global risks in the coming decade. A growing body of evidence has also demonstrated that economic inequality is associated with a range of health and social problems, such as mental illness and violent crimes. This is true across both rich and poor countries. Basically, inequality does not hurt only the poor ones but everyone.

Searching for the Remedies

But the question is whether inequality is inevitable? The answer is 'no'. It is the result of policy choices. Governments can reverse the situation of increase in inequality by taking some important steps, such as rejecting market fundamentalism, opposing the special interests of powerful elites, and changing the rules and systems that have led to this situation. Governments need to implement reforms that redistribute money and power, and level the playing field. There are two main areas where changes to policy could boost economic equality, namely taxation and social spending.

(i) *Progressive taxation:* Progressive taxation method has been proved to be quite effective in this regard. In this method of taxation corporations and the richest individuals pay more tax on their incomes to the state. The increased incomes from tax on income enables the governments to redistribute resources to the poorer people across the society. Similarly, a better indirect tax regime can enhance governments' income in a big way—as is being projected out of the proposed GST of India. The role of taxation in reducing inequality has been documented in OECD and developing countries in a very logical way by now. Thus, a required kind of taxation could play a big role in this direction.

As in the latest *Oxfam* report (early 2017), India performs relatively poorly on tax front. India's total tax collections are at 16.7 per cent of GDP while its potential is about 53 per cent. Its tax structure is not very progressive since direct taxes account for only a third of total taxes. By comparison, South Africa raises 27.4 per cent of GDP as taxes, 50 per cent of which are direct taxes. Though the Government of India has projected the share of direct taxes to improve to around 60 per cent of the total tax collections in the fiscal 2017-18.

(ii) *Social spending:* Governments' spending on public services can do miracles in reducing inequality. In India, such spending of the Governments is termed as the social sector spending which includes the fund allocations on education, nutrition, food, sanitation, general health care and social protection. *Oxfam* has provided evidences from more than 150 countries (rich and poor) spanning over three decades to show that overall investment in public services and social protection can tackle inequality. The group has for many years campaigned for free, universal public services across countries.

As per the latest report of *Oxfam*, India performs poorly on its social sector spending (centre and states put together). India spends about 3 per cent on education and 1.1 per cent (though this data has improved to 1.4 per cent by 2016–17) on healthcare of its GDP, respectively. In comparison, South Africa spends more than twice as much on education (6.1 per cent) and more than three times as much on health (3.7 per cent). Though South Africa is more unequal than India, the country performs much better in its commitment towards reducing inequality.

Conclusion

In recent years, the Government of India has become more sensitive to the issue of alarmingly high inequality in the country and looks committed to take suitable steps to check it also. Not only some effective right-based schemes have been launched in recent times but the Government has tried to address the issues related to proper identification of the beneficiaries and delivery also, with the help of Aadhar, Jan-Dhan Yojana and direct benefit transfer. Government is already on the path of reforming the tax regime. The recent move of demonetisation of high value currency notes also falls in this category, while the proposal of the universal basic income (UBI) coming from the *Economic Survey 2016-17* looks too innovative (by early March 2017, the Government has shown its willingness to go for it also). As ending extreme poverty is among the goals of the sustainable development goals (SDGs) it looks quite timely to move in the direction of checking inequality from rising first and reducing it afterwards.

7. UNIVERSAL BASIC INCOME

Introduction

In the last few years we have seen several experts suggesting for a universal basic income (UBI) for India. The idea got strengthened when the *Economic Survey 2016-17* proposed for the same—articulating very sound logic in its favour. By March 2017 the Government announced that such a scheme may be piloted by late-2017 and implemented to a limited scale by the year 2018-19. Although, before going for such a scheme[8] the Government of India (GoI) needs to settle several concerns involved with it.

An Effective Idea

We find the idea of UBI gaining ground among several countries across democracies and non-democracies—right from France to Finland to China (where a similar scheme, the *dibao*, is implemented). Such a scheme is generally proposed as a non-targeted one in which a fixed sum of cash is periodically transferred to all on individual basis. The idea is to ensure that every person in society has the means to live with a certain freedom and dignity, independent of capacity to earn or availability of employment. The idea really looks attractive as it has potential to reduce both poverty and inequality.

India already piloted such a scheme in Madhya Pradesh by 2010. *The Economic Survey 2016-17* proposed an amount of Rs 7,620 a year to be transferred into the bank accounts of the beneficiaries of the UBI. Though it is well short of what anyone might need to lead a life of leisure, it would cut absolute poverty from 22 per cent to less than 0.5 per cent. Theoretically, the UBI is proposed to be financed through recycling funds from around 950 welfare schemes (costing around 5 per cent of the GDP) presently run by the GoI aimed at offering subsidised food, water, fertilisers and many other things. A big part of Government's subsidies is enjoyed by the rich people in the country (as per the *Economic Survey 2015-17*) which can also be rejigged for this purpose.

Working Out the Scheme

There are several important issues to be settled before India launches such a scheme. A brief survey of the *major issues* involved with it is given below:

---

8. The write-up is based on primary sources such as the **Economic Survey 2016-17**, releases of the **Union** **Ministry of Finance**, the **NITI Aayog** and few issues of the journal **The Economist**, mainly.

Financial model: The first and foremost issue is mobilising adequate fund for it. If we go into the proposal of the *'Economic Survey 2016-17'*, the advice is to recycle the funds of the existing central sector and centrally sponsored schemes run by the GoI. But such schemes cannot be shut down to start UBI. This could be done in phased way only. Till then the GoI needs to mobilise additional funds for it through budgetary or non-budgetary sources. Given the projection that once the proposed GST is implemented from July 2017, the shortfall in the tax collections is estimated to remain around Rs 66,000 crore (due to curtailment of many cesses and surcharges), budgetary support does not look a very viable option.

Though certain other positive measures are also in the pipeline, such as increased tax compliance due to emphasis on less-cash, the proposed ceiling on cash transactions, linking Aadhar to PAN for filing income tax returns and linking Aadhar to transactions, etc., the implementation of the GST is supposed to increase tax collections (though in medium term) together with checking the evasion of direct and indirect taxes.

Selecting the beneficiaries: Clues from the name suggest it to be applying on all. But as per the Survey as well as the GoI expressions, the scheme is proposed to be launched partially. In this case, the target population may be taken from the lower strata of the below poverty line. The NITI Aayog CEO has proposed it for the bottom 20 per cent of the BPL population at the time of its launch. This could be linked to the general policy framework of social justice also. This will not only keep the financial requirements on lower side but also give some time to the government to recycle the funds from several welfare schemes it either runs or sponsors. A suggestion came from the GoI in favour of transferring the cash into the accounts of women head of the family (which will promote the *ideas* of inclusive growth and women empowerment also).

The amount of transfer: How much money should be transferred though is guided by the availability of resources, it should look sizeable to show an impact on the beneficiaries. As a proposal, the NITI Aayog CEO has proposed a sum of Rs 1,000 on monthly basis while the survey proposed (more as an example) a sum of Rs 7,620 monthly. Normally, it is believed that without transferring a sizeable amount of money (which may bring in comfort to the beneficiaries), the scheme may not remain effective. Though, to begin with even a lower sum of transfer also looks good.

Financial inclusion, inclusion and exclusion, regulation and assessment, etc. are the other involved issues related to it. The scheme looks under examination and study of the GoI in present time. Once it is announced only then these concerns will settle down.

The Benefits

The welfare schemes India has been implementing have been faced with certain common problems, misallocations of funds, wastage and seepage, inclusion and exclusion factors, ghost beneficiaries, corruption, the cost of operating them, etc. being the major ones. For this and other reasons, it has been argued to give serious consideration to the idea of the UBI. This will have several merits in it missing the current redistribution schemes, such as:

(i) It will be given from above minimising several maladies of existing schemes.

(ii) It is less likely to be prone to exclusion errors.

(iii) By directly transferring money to bank accounts, and bypassing multiple layers of bureaucracy, the scope for 'out of system' leakages (in case of the PDS running up to 45 per cent) will be quite lower.

Conclusion

There are considerable challenges of implementation, which will have to be debated and addressed properly before going for the UBI. But the challenges are not insurmountable; besides several possible ways are available to address them. As the support for the idea has come from a broad ideological spectrum, it looks as if the time for such a scheme has arrived in the country. We should think proactively in the direction.

8. LEGITIMACY IN STATE AND SOCIO-ECONOMIC TRANSFORMATION

Introduction

Democracies of the world have evolved much since they came into being. India joined the club late though it is among the most vibrant democratic economies of the world today with its own set of strengths and weaknesses. Socio-economic transformation of the country could be considered as the most prime aspiration of India. The same resonance we find throughout the period of freedom struggle, in the debates of the Constituent Assembly and the Constitution of India also. Numerous efforts have been made by the governments in this direction though the performances have not been up to the desired levels. There have been several minor reasons responsible for it, but the major reason has been the lack of financial resources to push it. The revenue that governments get by way of taxes is not a form of income only, but it is a measure of the fiscal potential of the nation, too. India has not been able to tap its actual fiscal potential by now. While its potential of tax collection is estimated to be

53 per cent of the GDP, it collects only about 17 per cent. It means a vast fiscal potential remains untapped. Given the resource crunch faced by the country, it is high time that the country moved in the direction of enhancing the fiscal capacity of the economy.

In case of India, 'income redistribution' (the recent proposal being UBI coming from the *Economic Survey 2016-17*) is suggested to be the single most important way out to promote socio-economic transformation today, provided the Government can mobilise adequate amount of fund for the process of redistribution. One very weak link to tapping fiscal capacity of the economy has been the lower legitimacy in the State.[9]

Global Experience

Higher legitimacy in state strengthens democracies in general. In case of tapping the fiscal capacity of the economy legitimacy in state has been found to be among the most important variables. In this regard, the history of developed countries suggests two important things:

(i) The foremost duty of the State is to supply 'essential services' such as, physical security, healthcare, education, infrastructure, etc.

(ii) Redistributive role of the State comes later on.

The above-described sequencing is not accidental. Unless the middle class in society perceives that it derives some benefits from the government/state, it will be unwilling to support (i.e., finance) the government moves of income redistribution. In other words, we can say that

9. The write-up is primarily based on the **Economic Survey 2016-17** and **2015-16** together with the **Union Budget 2017-18** and other releases of the Government of India.

a government needs to earn the legitimacy to redistribute income from the effectiveness of its public service deliveries.

If the Government tries to redistribute income without guaranteeing effective deliveries of the public services, the middle class starts 'exiting the state' (the famous idea of Albert Hirschman, 1978)—the middle class ultimately shies away from financing the schemes of income redistribution. One important sign of exit is fewer number of tax payers—abundantly evident in case of India. By reducing the pressure on the state, middle class exit will shrivel it, eroding its legitimacy further, leading to more exit in future. A state that is forced into inefficient redistribution, risks being trapped in a self-sustaining spiral of inefficient redistribution, reduced legitimacy, reduced resources, poor human capital investments, weak capacity and so on. The income and consumption anomaly has been specially highlighted by the *Union Budget 2017-18* where number of tax payers are miniscule to ratio of various income groups.

Suggestions for Today

It is suggested that the Government of the country should carry out their functions with utmost commitments to promote legitimacy in the State. Some of the *major steps* the state can take are as given below:

- The essential public services promised to the common citizens must reach them in an effective, transparent and non-partial way on a permanent basis.
- The visible instances of crony capitalism must be checked under which many of the times public assets are handed over to a select group of corporate houses that too at very cheaper prices by the governments.

- The issue of governance should not remain on paper only but it should show up to the citizens that the governments are committed to promote good governance.
- The menace of corruption must be rooted out with the help of transparency, greater devolution of power and involving the larger group of the stakeholders.
- People's participation should be enhanced by the governments in speedy way.

Conclusion

In the last few years, we have seen an increased emphasis by the Government on the above-suggested areas. Promoting the idea of 'minimum government and maximum governance' the government is not only promoting the governance factor but it is empowering the common masses, too. States have been included in the process of making the NITI Aayog the very 'vehicle of governance' (governance has been faltering more at the state level). The Government is using the different tools of information technology in every possible area to promote transparency, check corruption across the system and bringing speed in governance. Similarly, focus has shifted towards non-punitive measures of enhancing tax compliance and giving a push towards less-cash economy. Auction of public assets has become a fully online process, aimed at checking the problem of crony capitalism. Besides, the Government is committed to strengthening 'social trust' and 'co-operation' among the citizens and between the government and the masses to promote the level of happiness in citizens' lives. There is a declared shift in favour of modifying people's behaviour to achieve the desired objectives of socio-economic transformation in the country, too. Experts believe that the recent policy actions will surely improve the level of legitimacy in the State in the coming times.

9. FARM INDEBTEDNESS AND AGRIPOLICY

Introduction

Indebtedness among the farming community has always been a major concern for the Government. Once the number of suicides by farmers increased to the alarming levels, indebtedness among the community re-entered into the domain of the public debate. Today, considered as the biggest cause of suicides by farmers, the government policies related to farm sector need re-examination and the very framework of agri-policy needs restructuring.[10]

Farm Indebtedness

For farmers' suicides, bankruptcy and indebtedness have been cited as a major cause—around 37 per cent of all suicides by the farmers today. Usually, local money-lenders were portrayed as the villain in it. But as per the latest National Crime Records Bureau (NCRB), 2015 data, 80 per cent of the farmers who committed suicides in 2015 due to 'bankruptcy or debts' had borrowed money from institutional sources (banks and registered microfinance institutions). Besides, the country has seen a threefold increase in the famers' suicide due to bankruptcy and indebtedness (from 1163 of 2014 to 3097 in 2015). In 2015, a total of 8007 farmers committed suicides due to various reasons. It was for the *first time* that the NCRB categorised farmers' suicides due

---

10. The write-up is primarily based on the **Economic Survey 2016-17** and **2015-16** together with the latest **NCRB** report (2015), the latest **NSSO** report (2014) and other releases of the Government of India.

---

to debt or bankruptcy based on the source of loans. Similar findings come from the latest 'Situation Assessment Survey of Agricultural Households in India' report of the NSSO too. Nearly 52 per cent of agricultural households in India are indebted and levels of debt are as high as 93 per cent in Andhra Pradesh and 89 per cent in Telangana, as per the report.

The changed understanding about farm suicides make at least one thing clear that by allocating more funds to enhance farm loans is not enough.

Farm Income

The situation of farmers' income remains highly distressed in the country, as per the latest NSSO report (cited above). An agricultural household has been defined in by it as a household receiving value of produce of more than Rs 3,000 from agriculture with at least one member self-employed in farming. Interestingly, it shows that for 56 per cent of the marginal land owning families (with land less than 0.01 hectare) wage and salary employment, not agriculture, was their principal source of income. Another 23 per cent reported livestock as their principal source of income.

Average monthly income per agricultural household was estimated at Rs 6,426 while the net receipt from farm business (cultivation and farming of animals) accounted for 60 per cent of the average monthly income per agricultural household. Income from wages and salary accounted for nearly 32 per cent of the average monthly income.

About 44 per cent of the estimated agricultural households in the country had an employment guarantee scheme or MGNREGA job card. However, only 38 per cent in the lowest land class (less than 0.01 hectare) had job cards. Further, 12 per cent of all households and 13 per cent marginal land holding households did not have a ration card that entitles them to subsidised food.

Institutional and Non-Institutional Loans

There was a perception that except non-farm factors it was overall agrarian distress that forced farmers to suicides. Even if some suicides were caused by indebtedness, it was due to the high-handedness and exploitative behaviour of the local money-lenders on whom farmers largely depend for their loans. The official feeling was that once the spread of institutional lending gets healthier this problem will be addressed. But the latest data tell a completely different story—majority of farmers who committed suicides had taken loans from the institutional sources. It may be explained in the following way:

- Among the institutional sources, the micro-finance agencies have spread with much faster pace in recent years—the Government giving them liberal spread aimed at promoting financial inclusion in rural areas in general, and farming community in particular.

- Though micro-finance agencies are easily accessible, their interest rates are not less exploitative than the local money-lenders.

- Besides, the loan recovery method of these agencies lacks a 'human touch', which is not the case with money-lenders due to their feeling of belongingness to the same society or village.

- The case of banks is not much better other than some interest subsidies they give.

In the event of crop failures or for some other reasons, indebted farmers are available with no alternative of repaying their debt and even sustaining life. In absence of any other financial support system, such farmers are highly prone to committing suicides.

Possible Remedies

Given the current situation, allocation of higher funds for farm loans does not look serving the purpose (the *Union Budget 2017–18* allocating Rs. 9 Lakh Crore for it!). Such acts, on one hand have been increasing the financial burden on the exchequer, on the other hand they have not been able to protect the farmers from bankruptcy and indebtedness in the real sense either. In the changed scenario, to handle the crisis, the following steps look more suitable:

- Other than enhancing the penetration of formal/institutional lending (which increased fourfold in the last decade) there is a need of putting in place 'complementary income' support system for the farm community. Given the monsoonal and climate-related variability increasing, it looks even more apt.

- Majority of weak and marginal farmers fail to take benefit from the institutional sources of loans. This should be addressed on priority basis.

- Minimum support price operations should be able to include all of the weak farmers.

- To serve the purpose of creating additional sources of income to the farmers, the current scheme of 'skilling' and promoting agro-processing industries at the local level are needed. The scheme of 'smart cities' should be also linked to the farmers.

- Allied activities to agriculture such as dairy, poultry, fisheries, etc., should be promoted in a targeted way.

- Awareness regarding farm insurance must be enhanced among the farmers on high priority.

- The actions of the banks and micro-financing institutions should be monitored from all possible perspective at the local level.

- Once the proposed idea of 'UBI' is launched, small and marginal farmers should be necessarily included in the very first go (in case it is not launched universally, as the Government of India has indicated) taking clues form the latest findings of the NSSO reports.

- In general, the causes of 'agrarian distress/crises' should be re-examined and addressed with suitable policy actions on priority basis—a more holistic policy framework is need of the hour for the agriculture sector.

Conclusion

The latest reports remind us that little has changed for farmers in the past one decade (during which farmers' suicides have spread even in the traditional Green Revolution areas where farmers were believed to be richer and financially more secured). It clearly proves that the agriculture sector, which sustains half of the country, is still out of the real attention of Government policy, although in the last two years we see an increased focus from the Government of India on the farming sector.

10. DEGLOBALISATION—THE AFTEREFFECTS

Introduction

Countries moved on the path of globalisation under a highly legitimate global body, the World Trade Organisation (WTO) in 1995. The apprehensions of the developing nations soon diluted as they started reaping economic benefits out of it. Though the course of globalisation remained a bit chequered, it has proved to be better for the emerging economies to a large extent, the reason they are still the staunchest supporters of the process. But suddenly the world looks going

in the reverse gear and the process of reverse globalisation (deglobalisation)[11] looked certain by early 2017. This course will have differentiated effects on the developed and developing economies in short- and long-term. Meanwhile, the emerging market economies will have to face their own set of challenges due to it.

Changing Global Contours

The seeds of deglobalisation process can be found in the global financial crisis of 2007-08 and the failure of the developed economies to recover from it. Recovery from the Great Recession among these economies are getting tough. Even unconventional monetary policies have been tried (pursuing for negative interest rate regime) without much results. In the wake of this several of these economies have signalled 'protectionist' rhetoric. Right from the Brexit to the rise of protectionist US (in post-Trump period) are the major signals of reversal from the process of globalisation.

The other reason for reverse globalisation is rooted in the aftereffects of the globalisation since 1995. The experiences of globalisation have not been uniform and singular for the different member nations. Some have reaped high dividends while some other have gone into huge negative trade with their trading partners. Other than the contentious issues related to agriculture, public stockholding of food, drugs patenting and climate, in past one decade, the world has increasingly debated the 'negatives' of globalisation in a very vigorous way—increasing income inequality, adverse impact on environment and climate, etc. being the major ones. Due to this, negative sentiments have been growing among the developed economies towards the process of globalisation (interestingly, these were the apprehensions of the developing

---

11. The write-up is based on the **Economic Survey 2016-17**, various issues of **The Economist** and other media sources.

countries while the WTO was under the process of negotiation, between 1985 to 1994 and even after it!).

At the G20 Summit (Baden-Baden, Germany, mid-March 2017) loud voices against globalisation were heard. The US put its concerns regarding its huge trade deficits with key G20 members, such as Germany and China. Though the country denied its desire to get into trade wars but emphatically called for a farer trade with it. Not only this, on the margins of the Summit the US clearly expressed its desire towards re-negotiating not only with the NAFTA but the WTO, too. The rise of protectionist US has virtually failed not only the G20 Summit put it has put the course of globalisation in reverse gear. The course of globalisation looks completely uncertain.

The above-given events show as if the world (or at least the economies which matter most) has started to move slowly away from the much-celebrated idea of globalisation—*de-globalisation* taking over the world—shrinking scope for multilateral trade and economic inter-dependence. But all does not look lost—the lack of willingness towards globalisation among different economies is not of the same degree nor universal to every economy—better say it looks selective.

Impact of Regional Trade Agreements

The much-celebrated regional trade agreements look getting irrelevant given the rise of protectionist moves among the nations particularly among the developed economies. The most ambitious such agreement—Trans-Atlantic Partnership—has been derailed as the biggest force behind it, the USA, has backed out of it. How will it come without US is still not clear or whether it will die before coming into being is just anybody's guess today. Most of the regional trade agreements (for example, the NAFTA, SAFTA, etc.) involving USA and UK are in the process of transition.

Meanwhile, the situation regarding such agreements involving the developing nations are

different or better say just opposite. As the course of globalisation has been proving socio-economically correct for them to a large extent they are eager to promote inter-regional and multi-lateral trades. In case of India and the BRICS it is imperative to strengthen the course of globalisation. Particularly in case of India the course of socio-economic transformation depends heavily on the success of globalisation.

The Future of Multilateralism

Experts believe that the future course of multilateralism now will depend on the actions and steps of the emerging market economies. Another school of thinking feels history repeating itself—the world looks taking the same old course which caused the demise of the General Agreement on Trade and Tariff (GAAT) by the later part of 1970s. It is still not possible to give the verdict on the fate of globalisation but things look very weak in its favour.

India's Case

As per the views of the experts and the *Economic Survey 2016-17*, India necessarily needs a vibrant multilateral trading world to pursue its socio-economic aspirations of alleviating poverty, enhancing growth rate and joining the club of developed world. For that matter, the country needs to keep pushing in favour of a multilateral world. It needs to negotiate with the countries having higher appetite for globalisation on the priority basis—sketching out some more lucrative regional and preferential trade agreements. To scale up its growth to the level of 10 per cent, India needs an active support of exports.

If developed nations are apprehensive of trading with China, it does not mean they will have same concerns towards India, too. India might help the developed nations to grow with it. While China is busy re-balancing its economy and trade (finding it difficult, too), India must not miss the opportunity to clear its intentions and prioritise its actions in this regard. India cannot afford (so the emerging market economies) deglobalisation. Rather, it should support globalisation vigorously. There are high chances of finding viable partners in the developed world itself.

Conclusion

Everything is not lost about globalisation yet. There is no clarity yet about the benefits which the US or the UK will have out of being protectionist. May be after testing the waters of protectionism they get back to the course of globalisation. As the developed nations miscalculated the impact of WTO-promoted globalisation, chances are there that they may fail in calculating the positives and negatives of being protectionist, too. It means, the verdict on the course of globalisation is yet not out.

ECONOMIC CONCEPTS AND TERMINOLOGIES

(REFERENCE TO SELECTED TERMS RELATED TO ECONOMICS AND INDIAN ECONOMY)

Concepts are the constituents of thoughts—consequently, they are crucial to such psychological processes as categorization, inference, memory, learning, and decision-making. *

* See Eric Margolis and Stephen Laurence, 'Concepts', in the Edward N. Zalta **The Stanford Encyclopedia of Philosophy,** *Metaphysics Research Lab, Centre for the Study of Language and Information (CSLI), Stanford, USA, 2012.*

ABUSE OF DOMINANCE

A situation when a dominant firm/company (or a group of firms) is engaged in promoting its market position through 'anti-competitive' business practices, such as—predatory pricing, price squeezing, charging unreasonable prices, etc. Such practices hamper healthy competition in the economy and non-dominant firms face difficulties in their growth—they finally may shut down their operations. In recent times, it was in news globally—the US company *Microsoft* was facing litigation (under 'anti-trust' provision) for its Windows Operating System.

Though India used to regulate/restrict several such practices (under the MRTP Act, 1969), exact use of the term 'abuse of dominance' was not in practice. But the Competiton Act, 2002 (which replaced the MRTP Act) has clear use of it—it defines such situation in clear terms.

ACTIVITY RATE

The labour force of a country is known as the activity rate or *participation rate*. It is in per cent and always a proportion of the total population of the country—the economically active population. This rate varies from one country to another depending upon several factors such as school leaving age, retirement age, popularity of higher education, social customs, opportunities, etc.

ADRs

ADR stands for American Depository Receipt, which enables investors based in the USA to invest in stocks of non-US companies trading on a non US stock exchange. ADRs are denominated in dollars. Simply put, US brokers purchase shares of a foreign company, say Infosys (on behalf of their clients). ADRs are subsequently listed on US stock exchanges.

ADRs can be sponsored or unsponsored. Sponsored ADRs are those in which the company actively participates in the process. The ADRs were first offered in the US in the 1920s. A number of Indian companies have issued ADRs. Infosys Technologies was the *first* Indian company to use the ADR route.

The terms *ADR* and *ADS* are often used interchangeably. The individual shares representeted by an ADR are called American Depositary Shares (ADs). To the company issuing ADRs, it provides access to the American market. A company can, therefore, raise additional resources. To an American investor, it provides the opportunity to invest in stock of companies not listed in the US. Huge operational, custodial, and currency conversion issues can come into play if the ADR route is not used.

ADS CONVERSION OFFER

Conversion of local shares into American Depository Shares (ADS) of a company is called an ADS conversion offer. It is managed by investment bankers, mainly large investment banks familiar with Indian and global markets The offer allows local investors to convert their shares into ADS and then sell it in US markets. The proceeds of the sale in the US markets is distributed to Indian investors in rupees after deduction of expenses incurred in the process. The company does not issue any new shares. Existing shares are converted into ADS. The scheme obviously can only be offered by companies listed on the Indian and US markets which is the case for many large Indian corporates.

This allows companies to have new investors and creates visibility on the US stock exchanges. They also satisfy the local investor by offering an opportunity to sell their shares at a higher price than available locally on the Indian bourses.

ADVERSE SELECTION

One among the two kinds of the market failure often associated with insurance business which means doing business with the people one would have better avoided.

Adverse selection can be a problem when there is an asymmetry in information between the seller and the buyer of an insurance policy—as insurance will not be profitable when buyers have better information about their risk of claiming than does the seller of the insurance policy. In the ideal case, insurance premiums are set in accordance to the risk of a randomly selected person in the insured bracket (such as 40-year-old male smokers) of the population.

The other kind of market failure is *moral hazards* associated with the insurance sector.

AGRICULTURAL EXTENSION

Agricultural extension is a proper approach to motivate people to help themselves by applying agricultural research and development in their daily lives in farming, home making, and community living. It plays a vital role in community development. It is a two-way channel that brings scientific information to rural people and takes their problems to scientific institutes (for further research and development) for their solution.

In India, like many other developing countries, the role of agricultural extension is more than educational and it needs to deal with the human resource development of the agrarian population too, making it a comparatively tougher task than in the developed countries. The spread of information technology will serve a great purpose in this area.

AGRICULTURAL LABOURER

A person who works on another person's land for *wages* in money or kind or share is regarded as an agricultural labourer. He or she has no risk in the cultivation, but merely works on another person's land for wages. An agricultural labourer has no right of lease or contract on land on which he/she works.

ALPINE CONVERTIBLE BOND

An ACB (Alpine Convertible Bond) is a Foreign Currency Convertible Bond (FCCB) issued by an Indian company exclusively to the Swiss investors.

AMMORTISATION

Payment of a loan in installments by the borrower. It is usually done in an agreed period and every installment includes a part of the total loan plus the interest.

ANDEAN PACT

A regional pact to establish a common market link, started originally in 1969. At present it has peru, Equador, Columbia, Bolivia, and Venezuela. The pact had almost collapsed by the mid-1980s due to regional, economic, and political instabilities and was re-launched in 1990 (the original member Chile was dropped and the new member venezuela was added to it).

ANIMAL SPIRIT

'Confidence', considered as one of the essential ingredients of economic prosperity was called by J. M. Keynes as animal spirit. For Keynes, this is a 'naive optimism' by which an entrepreneur puts aside the fact of loss as a healthy man puts aside the expectation of death.

But from where does this animal spirit come has been a mystery—can it be created artificially from outside or whether it is an innate thing some are born with, etc.

ANTITRUST

A category of the government policy which deals with monopoly. Such laws intend to stop abuses of 'market power' by big companies and at times to prevent corporate mergers and acquisitions that would strengthen monopoly. The US has such laws and recently it was in news when Microsoft was its target.

APPRECIATION

It shows increase in value and is used in economics in the following two senses:

(i) It is an increase in the price of an asset over time, such as price rises in land, factory building, houses, offices, etc. It is also known as *capital appreciation.*

(ii) It is an increase in the value of currency against any foreign currency or currencies. It is market-based if the economy follows the floating-currency exchange-rate system.

ARBITRAGE

Earning profits out of the price differences of the same product in different markets at the same time. For example, buying and selling any product, financial securities (as bonds) or foreign currencies in different markets/economies. As globalisation is promoting liberalised cross-border movement of goods and services around the world, arbitrage is prevalent today. To avoid arbitrage the WTO member countries (i.e.) the official countries in the process of globalisation) are under compulsion to chalk out homogenous economic policies–and a level-playing field at the international level is emerging.

ARCs

Assets Reconstruction Companies (ARCs) acquire non-performing assets (NPAs) from banks or financial institutions along with the underlying securities mortgaged and/or hypothecated by the borrowers to the lenders. The ARCs then try and manage or resolve these NPAs acquired from banks. It can even infuse more funds in order to reconstruct the asset. If reconstruction is not possible and the borrower is unwilling to repay the loan, the ARCs *even sell* the secured assets.

While the basic principle of ARCs is the same everywhere—to acquire bad loans to resolve them—the essential difference is in the ownership of ARCs, public or private. After the Asian Crisis, countries like Indonesia, Korea, Malaysia, and Thailand have adopted government-owned and funded ARCs. The Philippines, on the other hand, has opted for private ARCs. India, too, has adopted the private sector model of asset resolution. Here, ARCs are set up as non-governmental vehicles mostly with support from the banking sector and other investors. Also, India has opted for multiple ARCs, which helps in better pricing of bad loans, as opposed to the single ARC model followed in many countries. The RBI has already allowed licenses to three ARCs and some banks are also planning to float ARCs.

ARCs acquire NPAs by way of 'true sale', i.e., once an NPA has been sold, the seller has no further interest in that asset. ARCs are a product of the Securitisation and Reconstruction of Financial Assets and Enforcement of Security Interest Act, 2002 (**SARFAESI Act**).

ASSET

Anything which has a 'money value' owned by an individual or a firm is an asset. It is of *three* types:

(i) *Tangible Asset:* All physical assets such as land, machinery, building, consumer durables (refrigerator, car, TV, Radio, etc.), etc. (*the assets which are in the material form*).

(ii) *Intangible Assets:* All non-physical/immaterial assets such as brand names, good-will, credit-worthiness, knowledge, know-how, etc.

(iii) *Financial Assets:* All financially valid valuables other than tangibles and intangibles such as currencies, bank deposits, bonds, securities, shares, etc.

ASSIGNED REVENUE

The term is used to refer to various tax/duty/cess/surcharge/levy etc., proceeds of which are (traditionally) collected by state government (on behalf of) local bodies (the PRIs), and subsequently adjusted with / assigned to the PRIs. Collection of such revenue is governed by relevant Acts of the local bodies.

Some examples of assigned revenue in India, include, entertainment tax, surcharge on stamp duty, local cess/surcharge on land revenue, lease amount of mines and minerals, sale proceeds of social forestry plantations, etc. State Finance Commissions recommend *devolution* of assigned revenue to local bodies on objective criteria, which may be specified by them in specific context.

AUTARKY

The idea of self-sufficiency and 'no' international trade by a country. None of the countries of the world has been able to produce all the goods and services required by its population at competitive prices, however, some tried to live it up at the cost of inefficiency and comparative poverty.

BACKWARDATION

A term of future trading which means a commodity is valued higher today (i.e., spots market) than in the futures (i.e., future market). When the situation is opposite, it is known as *contango*.

BACK-TO-BACK LOAN

A term of international banking, is an arrangement under which two firms (i.e., companies) in different economies (i.e., countries) borrow each other's currency and agree to repay (such loans) at a specified future date. Each company gets full amount of the loan on the repayment date in their domestic currency without any risk of losses due to exchange rate fluctuations. It has developed as a popular tool of minimising the exchange-rate exposure risk among the multi-national companies. This is also known as the *parallel loan.*

BAD BANK

A bank created specially to buy the *bad debts* (called 'non-performing assets' in India) of the existing banks to clear such loans of the latter. This way the banks with NPAs clear their 'balance sheet' and again start lending to the customers. The bad bank now tries to recover the bad debts it has bought through available legal means. Though such banks were set up in 20th century itself in the USA, it came in recent use once the US central banks' chief (Ben Bernanke) proposed the idea of using a government-run bad bank to clean up the 'sub-prime' loans of the private banks in the country (in wake of the sub-prime crisis of 2007).

It made news in India once the *Economic Survey 2016-17* suggested the Government of India to set up such a body— public sector asset rehabilitation agency (PARA)—to solve the 'twin balance sheet' (TBS) problem the country is faced with. At one hand the public sector banks are faced with high NPAs while on the other the corporate sector (who are the borrowers of these banks) of the country is also hit with negative balance sheet (unable to service or clear the loans due on them). The PARA is supposed to clear the balance sheets of both banks as well the corporate sector. The Survey has quoted the South East Asian economies where such agencies were used very effectively during the currency crises of 1996-97. By *March 2017*, it looked that the Government was prepared to set up such an agency (bank).

BAD DEBT

An accounting term to show the loans which are unlikely to be paid back by the borrower as the borrower has become insolvent/bankrupt. Banks might write off such bad debts against the profits of the trading as a business cost.

BADLA

An Indian term for 'contango' associated with the trading system in the stock market which is a postponement of either payments by the share buyer, or the person who needs to deliver the shares against the payment.

BALANCED BUDGET

The annual financial statement (i.e., the budget) of a government which has the total expenditures equal to the taxes and other receipts.

Most governments, in practice run unbalanced budgets, i.e., deficit budgets or surplus budgets—either the expenditures being higher or lower than the taxes and the other receipts, respectively. It is done to regulate the economic activities.

BALANCE OF PAYMENTS

A balance sheet of an economy showing its total external transactions with the world–calculated on the principles of accounting–is an annual concept.

BALLOON PAYMENT

When the final payment of a debt is more than the previous payments, it is balloon payment.

BASING POINT PRICE SYSTEM

A method of pricing in which a differential (i.e., varying) price is fixed for the same product for the customers of the different locations—nearer the customer, cheaper the product. This is done usually to neutralise the transportation cost of the bulky products such as cement, iron and steel, petroleum, etc.

BELLWETHER STOCK

A share which often reflects the state of the whole stock market. The technical analysts, associated with the stock market, usually keep a track-record of such shares and go on to forecast the future stock movements.

BFS

For the purpose of supervision and surveillance of the Indian financial system, a Board for Financial Supervision (BFS) was set up by the RBI in November 1994. The board supervises commercial banks, non-banking financial companies (NBFCs), financial institutions, primary dealers, and the clearing corporation of India (CCI).

BLACK-SCHOLES

A formula devised for the pricing of financial derivatives or options—made explosive growth possible in them by the early 1970s in the US.

Myron Scholes and Robert Merton were awarded Nobel Prize for Economics for their part in devising this formula—the co-inventor Fischer Black had died (1995) by then.

BOND

An instrument of raising long-term debt on which the bond-issuer pays a periodic interest (known as 'coupon'). In theory, bonds could be issued by governments as well as private companies.

Bonds generally have a maturity period, however, some bonds might not have any definite maturity period (which are known as *'Perpetual Bonds'*).

Bonds are supported/secured by collateral in the form of immovable property (i.e., fixed assets) while *debentures,* also used to raise long-term debt, are not supported by any collateral.

BOOK BUILDING

This is a public offer of equity shares of a company. In this process, bids are collected from the investors, in a certain price range fixed by the company. The issue price is fixed after the bid closing date depending on the number of bids received at various price levels. A company that is planning an initial public offer (IPO) appoints a merchant banker as a 'book runner'. The company issues a prospectus which does not mention the price, but gives other details about the company with regard to issue size, the business the company is in, promotes and future plans among other disclosures. A particular period is fixed as the bid period. The book runner builds an order book, that is, collates the bids from various investors, which shows the demand for the shares. Prospective investors can revise their bid at any time during the bid period. On closure of the book, the quantum of shares ordered and the perspective prices offered are known. The price discovery is a function of demand at various prices, and involves negotiations between those involved in the issue. The book runner and the company conclude the pricing and decide the allocation to each member.

BRACKET CREEP

Increasing incomes due to inflation (via increased dearness allowances, individual income goes for an increase) pushes individuals into higher tax *brackets* and leaves them worse off (as their real income has not increased and their disposable income i.e. income after tax payments, falls) – this phenomenon is known as the bracket creep.

BROAD BASED FUND

This is a fund established or incorporated *outside* India, which has at least 20 investors with no single individual investor holding more than 49 per cent of the shares or units of the fund. If the broad based fund has institutional investor (s), then it is not necessary for the fund to have 20 investors. Further, if the broad based fund has an institutional investor who holds more than 49 per cent of the shares or units in the fund, then the institutional investor must itself be a *broad based fund*.

In India, the entities, proposing to invest *on behalf of broad based funds*, are eligible to be registered as FIIs are: (i) Asset Management Companies, (ii) Investment Manager/Advisor, (iii) Institutional Portfolio Managers, (iv) Trustee of a Trust, and (v) Bank

BROWNFIELD LOCATION

A derelict industrial area that has been demolished to accommodate new industries. This is opposite to the *greenfield location* where a new industry is set up in a new area.

BUBBLE

The price rise of an asset unexplained by the fundamentals and still people interested in holding the assets. After the bursting of the bubble, assets cool down to their real prices.

BUDGET LINE

A line on the dual axis graph showing the alternate combinations of goods that can be purchased by a consumer with a given income at given prices.

BULLET REPAYMENT

'Bullet repayment' means a lump-sum payment for the *entire loan amount* paid at the time of maturity. Such arrangements may be put in place by the banking regulator (RBI in case of India) to fasten the process of recovery of the non-performings assets (NPAs) process of the banks. The distressed assests, in this way come back to bank, may be with a lower profit element to them.

Such an announcement was made by the RBI in 2014–15 allowing *bullet repayment* of loans extended against pledge of gold ornaments and jewellery for other than agricultural purposes.

BULLION

Precious metals such as gold, silver, and platinum that are traded in the form of *bars* and *coins* for investment purposes and are used for jewellery as base metals.

BUSINESS CYCLE

See the chapter with the same title.

BUSY AND SLACK SEASONS

The monetary authorities face the challenge of keeping the growth rate as high as possible, at the same time putting burden of adjustment on luxury and unproductive consumption. Monetary policy is an instrument in this respect. However, the right policies may not be palatable to the political and fiscal authorities, which is a serious problem for the economy.

From May beginning to end of September is the *slack season* and from October beginning to end-April is the *busy season* of the **Indian Economy**. During the slack season, crops are generally sown. Agriculture and related businesses are slack and loans taken during the previous busy season tend to be returned. Consequently, the growth rate of money is low or negative. Governments usually

borrow heavily during the slack season, since the demand for credit from the commercial sector is not very strong. Since there are no fresh crop arrivals in the market and the demand for crops is steady, the prices are expected to be generally upward in the slack season.

From October, the busy season commences and both agricultural and related industrial productions are high. Since crops arrive in the market during the busy season, prices generally are on the downward drift. It is the seasonal variation in the arrival of crops in the market, in the context of steady demand, that causes prices to fluctuate during the year.

The above pattern has been severely modified in recent years. The government borrows both during the slack and the busy seasons. Industry too is active in both the seasons. Because of greater storage and stocking facilities, the variations in the flows of agricultural products have been reduced. Money supply expands continuously and prices are generally up throughout.

BUYER'S MARKET

A short period of market situation in which there is excess supply of goods/services forcing price fall to the advantage of the buyers.

BUYOUTS

Private equity (PE) investors participate in two types of buyouts of firms (a PE-backed buyout simply means that the PE investor takes a controlling stake i.e. between 50–100 per cent in a company):

(i) *Management Buyout (MBO):* In such buyouts, the PE investor usually helps the existing management of the company to buy out the promoters of the company. In return, the PE investor takes a majority stake.

(ii) *Leveraged Buyout (LBO):* In such buyouts, a large portion of fund in acquiring the company is financed by debt—the normal ratio being 70 per cent debt and 30 per cent equity.

CAMELS

An acronym derived from the terms capital adequacy (C), asset quality (A), management (M), earnings (E), liquidity (L) and systems for control (S). The acronym is used as a technique for evaluating and rating the operations and performance of banks all over the world.

CAPITAL

Capital is one of the three main factors of production (*labour* and *natural resources* are the other two), classified into *physical capital* (i.e., factories, machines, office, etc.) and *human capital* (i.e., training, skill, etc.).

In a joint stock company, the capital has various specific terms showing different forms of the *share capital:*

(i) *Authorised Capital:* This is the amount of share capital fixed in the Memorandum of Association (MoA) and the article of association of a company as required by the Companies Act. This is also known as the *Nominal* or *Registered Capital.*

This is the limit (i.e., nominal value) upto which a company can issue shares. Companies often extend their authorised capital (via an amendment in the MoA) in advance of actual issue of new shares. This allows the timing of capital issue to be fixed in light of the company's need for new capital and the state of the capital market and allows share options to be exercised accordingly.

(ii) *Paid-up Capital:* The part of the authorised capital of a company that has

actually been paid up by the shareholders. A difference may arise because all shares authorised may not have been issued or the issued shares have been only partly paid-up by then.

(iii) *Subscribed Capital:* The capital that has actually been paid by the shareholders (as they might have committed more than this to contribute). It means, the subscribed capital is the actually realised paid-up capital (paid-up capital is subscribed capital plus credit/due on the shareholders).

(iv) *Issued Capital:* The amount of the capital which has been sought by a company to be raised by the issue of shares (it should be kept in mind that this cannot exceed the authorised capital).

(v) *Called-up Capital:* The amount of share capital the shareholders have been *called* to pay to date under the phased payment terms. It is usually equal to the 'paid-up capital' of the company except where some shareholders have failed to pay their due installments (known as *calls in arrears*).

CAPITAL ADEQUACY RATIO

A regulation on commercial banks, co-operative banks and the non-banking financial companies to maintain a certain amount of capital in relation to their assets (i.e., loans and investments) as a cushion (shock-absorber) against probable losses in their investments and loans.

A concept devised by the Bank for International Settlements (BIS), Basel, the provision was implemented in India in 1992 by the RBI (for more detailed discussion see the chapter on 'Banking').

CAPITAL CONSUMPTION

The capital that is consumed by an economy or a firm in the production process. Also known as *depreciation*.

CAPITAL-OUTPUT RATIO

A measure of how much additional capital is needed to produce each extra unit of the output. Put the other way round, it is the amount of extra output produced by each unit of added capital. The ratio indicates how efficient new investment contributes to the growth of an economy.

A capital-output ratio of 3:1 is better to the 4:1 as the former needs only three units extra capital to produce one extra output in comparison to the latter which needs four units for each extra unit output.

CARBON CREDIT

Amidst growing concern and increasing awareness on the need for pollution control, the concept of carbon credit came into vogue as part of an international agreement, known popularly as the Kyoto Protocol. Carbon credits are certificates issued to countries that reduce their emission of GHG (greenhouse gases) which leads to global warming. It is estimated that 60–70 per cent of the GHG emission is through fuel combustion in industries like cement, steel, textiles, and fertilisers. Some GHGs like hydro fluorocarbons, methane, and nitrous oxide are released as byproducts of certain industrial process which adversely affect the ozone layer, leading to global warming.

The concept of carbon credit trading seeks to encourage countries to reduce their GHG emissions, as it rewards those countries which meet their targets and provides financial incentives to the others to do so as quickly as possible. Surplus credits (collected by overshooting the emission reducing target) can be sold in the global market. One credit is equivalent to one tonne of CO_2 emission reduced. Carbon Credit (CC) is available for companies engaged in developing renewable energy projects that offset the use of fossil fields.

The trading of CC takes place on two stock exchanges, the Chicago Climate Exchange and the European Climate Exchange. CC trading can also take place in the open market as well. European countries and Japan are the major buyers of carbon credit. Under the Kyoto Protocol, global warming potential (GWP) was an *index* that allowed for the comparison of greenhouse gases with each other in the context of the relative potential to contribute to global warming. For trading purposes, one credit is considered equivalent to one tonne of CO_2 emission reduced.

CARRY TRADE

Borrowing in one currency and investing in another is termed as carry trade. In recent times (upto November 2007) trillions of dollars have been borrowed in low-cost 'yen' for deployment across money markets, stock markets, and even real estate markets across the globe and a part of the money flowed into India, too.

CASH COW

A profitable business or firm (may belong to either public or private sector) which gives regular cash flow to the owner (this happens either due to regular demand of the popular goods produced by the firm or the compulsions of the consumer to buy the products). As for example, the antiseptic lotion 'Dettol' is a cash cow for Reckitt and Colman in the private sector and LPG is a cash cow for the manufacturing and marketing government companies (provided there is no subsidy on LPG).

CAVEAT EMPTOR

A Latin phrase which means *'let the buyer beware'*. Simply put, it means that the supplier has no legal obligation to inform buyers about any defects in his goods or services; the onus is on the buyer to himself determine the level of satisfaction out of the products.

CETERIS PARIBUS

A Latin phrase which means *'other things being equal'*. The phrase is used by economists to cover their forecastings.

CHINESE WALL

The segregation of the different activities of a financial institution (such as, jobbing, stockbroking, fund management, etc.) in order to protect clients' interest.

CIRCUIT LIMIT

A limit of regular fall in share indices of Stock Exchanges around the world after which the exchange are closed for further trading. For example, circuit limit decided for the BSE (Bombay Stock Exchange) has been fixed at 10 per cent. The time there is a continuous fall in the BSE Sensex and it reaches 10 per cent, the exchange is closed to further trading.

Such a limit/provision prevents the share market from crashing down.

CLASSICAL ECONOMICS

A school of thought in economics based on the ideas of Smith, Ricardo, Mill, etc. The school dominated the economic thinking of the world until about 1870, when the *'marginalist revolution'* took place.

CLEAN COAL

Underground coal gasification and liquefaction which converts coal into liquid and gaseous fuel alternatives is a recognised 'clean coal' technology—handy in extraction of energy from coal seams which connot be mined through conventional methods.

COLLATERAL

Any item/asset which accompanies/subordinates/supplements a primary item is known as collateral. The term is used in banking industry while providing loans. This is also known as 'secondary/subordinate security'— which borrowers/guarantors provide in the form of an asset (like land, building, etc.) while seeking a loan. The principal/primary security is usually the borrower's personal guaranty, or the cash flow of a business.

Except for highly creditworthy customers (who can get loans against their signatures), lenders always demand a collateral if the primary security is not considered to be reliable or sufficient enough to recover the loan in case of a default— lenders have the legal right to seize the collateral.

CLOSED SHOP

The requirement that all employees of a given firm be members of a specified trade union. It is a method of restricting labour supply and maintaining high wages applied by a powerful trade union.

COLLECTIVE PRODUCTS

A product which can only be supplied to a group. Many goods and services provided by the governments fall in this category, such as, national defence, police administration, etc.

COMMITTED EXPENDITURE

The expenditure of the governments from which they can not deny (as they have already committed them to pay) are known as committed expenditure. The liabilities such as 'interest' (of the internal as well as external loans) and 'pension' (of the retired personnel of the governments) are examples of such expenditure.

By the year 2015-16, this expenditure for the Government of India was 41.5 per cent of the non-plan expenditure. Non-plan expenditure for the year was 73.8 per cent of the total expenditure (plan pluc non-plan). The GoI has decided to shift to the 'revenue' and 'capital' classification for its expenditure from *2017-18* (in place of the existing classification 'plan' and 'non-plan').

COMMODITIES TRANSACTION TAX

[See Chapter 17, *Tax Structure in India*]

COMMODITY MONEY

Products being used as the means of payment as in the traditional barter system. Such practices take place generally when the confidence in money has fallen down (as for example in the situations of high inflation and high depreciation).

COMMUNITISATION

A method of privatising public service delivery without going for the tendering process. It is done by transfering powers including financial powers to the user community who will take up the job of revenue collection along with an effective and more practical governance of the service delivery. This model is bereft of profit motive and so, more transparent.

Service delivery in communitised elementary schools and health service institutions has improved considerably and power tariff collection has risen by 100 per cent since the reform began in 2002 in Nagaland—Secretary, Union Ministry of Steel, Raghaw Sharan Pandey who did it in Nagaland as its Chief Secretary.

COMPARATIVE ADVANTAGE

It is about identifying activities that an individual, a firm or a country can do most efficiently, being together.

The idea, usually credited to David Ricardo, underpins the case of free trade. It suggests that countries can gain from trading with each other even if one among them is more efficient (i.e., it has an *absolute advantage*) in every kind of economic activity.

CONSOLS

This is the abbreviated form of *consolidated stock*. The government bonds which have no maturity and thus have an indefinite life are tradable on the floors of the stock exchanges.

CONSORTIUM

An *ad hoc* grouping of firms, governments, etc. brought together to undertake a particular project by pooling their resources and skills for major construction projects, loans, etc.

CONSUMER DURABLES

Consumer goods that are consumed over relatively long periods of time rather than immediately (opposite to the *consumer non-durables*) such as cars, houses, refrigerators, etc.

CONSUMER NON-DURABLES

Consumer goods which yield up all their satisfaction/utility at the time of consumption (opposite to the *consumer durables*), examples are cheese, pickles, jam, etc.

CONSPICUOUS CONSUMPTION

Consumption for the purpose of showing off ostentatiousness but not for the utility aspect –

for example, the use of diamond-studded sandals, watches, pens, etc.

CONTAGION

A situation or an effect of economic problems in one economy spreading to another also known as the *domino effect*.

CONTRARIAN

A person following an investment strategy (specially in share market) just opposite to the general investors in a given period. For example, when a share is generally being sold by the investors, a contrarion keeps on buying them—the logic is that due to selling pressure the price will fall below the intrinsic value of the share and there is a prospect of future profit out of the share.

CORE INVESTMENT COMPANIES (CICS)

A NBFC carrying on the business of acquisition of shares and securities which satisfied the conditions: it holds not less than 90 per cent of its total assets in this form; its investments in the equity shares in group companies constitutes not less than 60 per cent of its total assets; it does not trade in its investments in shares, debt or loans in group companies except through block sale for the purpose of dilution or disinvestment; and it does not carry on any other financial activity except investment in bank deposits, money market instruments, government securities, loans to and investments in group companies.

CORPORATE SUSTAINABILITY INDEX

The Bombay stock Exchange (BSE) has proposed to come out with a corporate sustainability index (CSI)—a possible new stock exchange which will be created for developing *trust marks* to denote a corporate's sustainability achievements. This will be the first such index in Asia.

CORRECTION

A term usually used in stock market which shows a reversals of share prices in reaction to an excessive rise or fall of the past.

COUNTERVAILING DUTY

Countervailing duty (CVD) is imposed by the importing nation on imports if the exporting nation is found to offer export subsidies to their exports. This measure aims at balancing the price of imports with the domestic products. This duty is imposed in such a way that imported item also remains competitive.

Similar duty, with the same aim, once imposed by the importing nation in case the exporting country is found to export at *below fair market price* (it means the exporting nation is dumping the item in the importing nation) is known as 'anti-dumping' duty.

Both of the duties are imposed after fulfilling the proper provisions of investigation conducted as per the specifications of the WTO.

CREATIVE DESTRUCTION

The process by which an innovative entrepreneur takes risks and introduces new technologies to stimulate economic activity, replacing old technologies is known as 'creative destruction'. As per *Schumpeter, Joseph A.* (1883–1950), creative destruction is the key to economic growth. But due to irregularity in such innovations, business cycle is followed by both collapse and crisis (J. A. Schumpeter, *Capitalism, Socialism and Democracy*, 1942).

CRONY CAPITALISM

An approach of doing business when the firms look after themselves by looking after their own people (i.e., families and friends). Used in negative sense.

CROSS SUBSIDY

The process of giving subsidy to one sub-area and fulfilling it through the profits from the other sub-area. As for example, in India kerosene oil is cross-subsidised against petrol and aviation fuel.

CROWDFUNDING

This is a method of mobilising finance/fund. Crowd-funding refers to the collective effort of individuals who pool money—mostly through the Internet—to support start-ups. There are two basic forms of crowdfunding— 'community' crowdfunding and 'financial return' crowdfunding. The *former* includes donation-based concepts (donators get no financial retuns in it) while in the *latter* contributors of funds get financial returns (from the project set up with the fund). In the financial model of crowdfunding, contributors might be given equity/share in the upcoming project.

CROWDING-OUT EFFECT

A concept of public finance which means an increase in the government expenditure which has an effect of reducing the private sector expenditure.

CSR

The concept of corporate social responsibility (CSR) is fast gaining popularity among the corporate sector of the world. As per the experts, the CSR is qualitatively different from the traditional concept of passive philanthropy by the corporate houses. Basically, the CSR acknowledges the *debt* that the corporates owe to the community within which they operate. It defines the corporates' partnership with social action groups (i.e., the NGOs) in providing financial and other resources to support development plans, especially among disadvantaged communities. There is stress on long-term sustainability of business and environment and the distribution of well-being.

DEBENTURE

An instrument of raising long-term loan by companies, having a maturity period bearing an interest (*coupon rate*). Theoretically they may be secured or unsecured by assets such as land and buildings of the issuing company (known as *collateral*).

Debenture holders are provided with a prior claim on the earnings (by interest) and assets of the company in the situation of liquidation of the company over the *preference* and *equity shareholders* of the company.

DEBT RECOVERY TRIBUNAL (DRT)

Banks and financial institutions have often faced a tough time in recovering loans, on which the borrowers have defaulted. To expedite the recovery process, the Committee on the Financial System, headed by *Mr. Narasimham* considered the setting up of special tribunals, with special adjudicator powers. This was felt to be necessary to carry through financial sector reforms. Since there is an immense overload on the Indian legal system at present, recovery of many unpaid debts, due to banks or financial institutions, are held up, indefinitely. This affects the balance sheets of the banks as the amounts involved are very large.

It was thought that an independent forum was needed to deal with debts of these types. Thus, in *1993* the *Recovery of Debts Due to Banks and Financial Institutions Act'* was passed. The Act, however, imposes a limitation and states that only those debts which are in excess of Rs. 10 lakhs (or upto Rs. 1 lakh, where the Central government specified certain types of debts) would come under its purview.

DECOUPLING THEORY

Decoupling theory holds that Asian economies, especially emerging ones, no longer depend on the United States economy for growth, leaving them *insulated* from a severe slowdown there, even recession—looked true for some time as Asian stocks rose while socks in the US fell - however, as fears of recession mounted in the US, stocks declined heavily. Looking this happen in late 2008 the decoupling theory regarding the Asian as well as the EU economies have now lost ground. But still the emerging economies are able to have higher growth rates and exports in comparision to the US – that is why the theory is still debated by the experts.

DEINDUSTRIALISATION

Sustained decrease in the share of the secondary sector in the total output (GDP) of an economy.

DEMAT ACCOUNT

It is a way of holding securities in electronic or dematerialised form. Demat form of shares can be traded online. As such, the transactions are concluded much faster, which prevents theft, misuse, forging of original shares certificates or other documents, and allows an investor to buy or sell shares in any quantity. Demat account allows for faster refund of money in case application is not accepted. Demat accounts are offered by banks, and the dematerialised stock is held by the depository (National Securities Depository Ltd.–[NSDL] or Central Securities Depository Ltd.–[CSDL]). The investor needs to fill up the requisite forms, submit the documents and pay the applicable charges in order to have the demat account opened.

DEMERGER

The breaking-up of a company into more separate companies. Such companies are usually formed through mergers.

DERIVATIVES

The financial assets that 'derive' their value from other assets, such as shares, debentures, bonds, securities, etc.

DIIs

Domestic Investment Institution (DIIs) are the financial institutions of Indian origin investing in India is different derivatives such as share, securities, corporate bounds, etc. They may be public/govt. owned or privately owned—mutual funds, pension funds and insurance (life) companies are the major ones in India.

DIRECT COST

The direct material and labour cost of a product–proportionally varies with the total output.

DIRECT INVESTMENT

The expenditure on physical assets (i.e., plant, machinery, etc.).

DIRTY FLOAT

A term of foreign exchange managment when a country manipulates its exchange rate under the floating currency system to take leverage in its external transactions.

DISCOUNT HOUSE

A financial institution specialising in buying and selling of short-term (i.e., less than one year) instruments of the money market.

DISGORGEMENT

Disgorgement is a common term in developed markets across the world, though for most market participants in India it is a new thing. Disgorgement means repayment of illegal gains by wrongdoers. Funds that were received through illegal or unethical business transactions are 'disgorged', or paid back, with interest to those affected by the action. It is for the first time in India that the capital markets regulator, SEBI has passed this order of disgorgement; internationally it is the civil courts that have this mandate along with the markets regulator.

Disgorgement is a 'remedial' civil action, rather than a 'punitive' civil action. In the US, individuals or companies that violate Securities and Exchange Commission regulations are typically required to pay both civil money penalties and disgorgement. Civil money penalties are punitive, while disgo-rgement is about paying back profits made from those actions that violated securities regulations.

Interestingly, disgorgement payments are not only demanded of those who violate securities regulations. In the US, anyone profiting from illegal or unethical activities may be required to disgorge their profits. The money disgorged from the violating parties is used to create a 'Fair Fund'— fund for the benefit of investors who were harmed by the violation.

DISSAVING

The situation of higher current consumption over current disposable income by the households—the difference is met by withdrawals from the past savings (*i.e., decrease in saving*).

DOMINO EFFECT

An economic situation in which one economic event causes a series of similar events to happen one after the other. For example, experts believe that the falling of share indices around the world in early-2008 was a domino effect of the sub-prime crisis faced by the US economy. A similar case is cited from the mid-1996 when all major stock markets crashed around the world due to the domino effect emanating from the South East Asian currency crisis.

DOW-JONES INDEX

The US share price index which monitors and records the share price movements of all compaines listed on the New York Stock Exchange (*with the exception of high-tech companies which are listed on the nasdaq stock exchange*). India has its equivalent in the BSE *Sensex*.

DUMPING

Exporting a good at a price lower than its price in the domestic market. To neutralise the effects of dumping the importing country may impose a *surcharge* on such imports which is known as the *anti-dumping duty*.

DUTCH DISEASE

When an increase in one form of net exports drives up a country's exchange rate, it is called the Dutch Disease. Such instances make other exports non-competitive in the world market and impairs the ability of domestic products to compete with imports.

The term originated from the supposed effect of natural gas discoveries on the Netherlands economy.

DUTY DRAWBACK SCHEME

The Duty Drawback Scheme (DDS) is provided by the Government of India as a part of export incentives to make exports competitive. Exporters get refund of the central excise (censat) and custom duties on the inputs they use in manufacturing the exportables. Those who are covered by the Duty Entitlement Passbook Scheme (DEPS) are not covered by it. The rates are announced from time to time.

DUTY ENTITLEMENT PASSBOOK SCHEME

The Duty Entitlement Passbook Scheme (DEPS) is an export incentive scheme of the GoI under which exporters get credit (pre-determined by the Direcor General of Foreign Trade) on the export value which they use in future imports thus neutralising all the taxes. No cash is given (unlike the Duty Drawback Scheme). It has been abolished by the GoI, w.e.f. October 1, 2011 after using it for 14 years – the WTO provisions do not allow member countries to carry such schemes.

E-BUSINESS

Using computers and the Internet to link both the *internal* operations (i.e., transactions and communications between the various departments/divisions of the business firm) and its *external* operations (i.e., all its dealings with the suppliers, customers, etc.).

E-COMMERCE

Method of buying and selling goods and services over the Internet – a kind of direct marketing i.e. without the help of any middle arrangement of sales.

ECONOMIES OF SCALE

The long-run reduction in average/unit cost that occurs as the scale of the firm's output increases. The opposite situation is known as *diseconomies of scale.*

ECONOMIES OF SCOPE

The long-run reduction in average/unit cost that occurs as the scope (diversification) of the firm's activities increase.

EDGEWORTH BOX

A concept for the purpose of analysing the possible relationships between two individuals or countries. It is done using indifference curve.

The concept was developed by Francis Ysidro Edgeworth (1845–1926) who is also credited for analytical tools of *indifference curves* and *contract curves.*

EFFECTIVE REVENUE DEFICIT

[See Chapter 18, *Public Finance in India*]

ENGEL'S LAW

The law which says that people generally spend a smaller part of their budget on food as their income rises. The idea was suggested by Ernst Engel, a Russian statistician in 1857.

ENVIRONMENTAL ACCOUNTING

The method of accounting which includes the ecological and environmental damages done by the economic activities in monetary terms. Integrated environment and economic (green) accounting attempts at accounting for both socioeconomic performance and its environmental effects and integrates environmental concerns into mainstream economic planning and policies. The *green GDP* of an economy is measured by the same method—experimented in Costa Rica, Mexico, Netherlands, Norway, and Papua New Guinea, among others. Indicative estimates suggest that conventionally measured GDP may exceed GDP adjusted for natural resources depletion and environmental degradation by a range between 1.5 per cent and 10 per cent.

ENVIRONMENTAL AUDIT

Assessment of the environmental impact of a firm/public body through its activities. This is done with an objective to reduce or eliminate the pollution aspect.

ENVIRONMENTAL TAXES

As against the Command and Control approach to managing environment, the Economic or Market Based Instruments (MBIs) approach sends economic signals to the polluters to modify their behaviour. The MBIs used for environmental taxes include pollution charges (emission/affluent & tax/pollution tax), marketable permits, deposit refund system, input taxes/product charges, differential tax rates, user administrative changes and subsidies for pollution abatement, which may be based on both price and quality. India has been already collecting taxes on *water* and *air* via the Water Act and the Air Act. Due to its experience India is among the chief participant in devising the MBIs in the world.

EQUITY LINKED SAVING SCHEME

Equity linked savings schemes (ELSS) are open-ended, diversified equity schemes offered by mutual funds. They offer tax benefits under the new section 80C introduced in the Finance Bill 2005–06.

Besides offering the tax benefits, the scheme invests in shares of frontline companies and offers long-term capital appreciation. This means unlike a guaranteed return by assured return schemes like Public Provident Fund or National Savings Certificate, the investor gets the benefit of the upside (if any) in the equity markets.

Unlike other mutual fund schemes, there is a three-year lock in period for investments made in these schemes. Investors planning to build wealth over the long-term and save on tax can use these schemes.

Returns in these schemes are linked to the fortunes of the stock market. Investors should assess their respective risk appetites before investing.

EQUITY SHARE

A security issued by a company to those who contributed capital in its formation shows ownership in the company. The other terms for it are 'stock' or 'common stock'.

Such shares might be issued via public issue, bonus shares, convertible debentures, etc. and may be traded on the stock exchanges.

Such shareholders have a claim on the earnings and assets of the company after all the claims have been paid for. This is why such shareholders are also known as the *residual owners*.

ESCROW ACCOUNT

In simple terms, an 'escrow account' is a *third party account*. It is a separate bank account to hold money which belongs to others and where the money parked will be released only under fulfilment of certain conditions of a contract. The term **escrow** is derived from the French term 'escroue' meaning a scrap of paper or roll of parchment, an indicator of the deed that was held by a third party till a transaction is completed.

An escrow account is an *arrangement for safeguarding* the 'seller' against its 'buyer' from the payment risk for the goods or services sold by the former to the latter. This is done by removing the control over cash flows from the hands of the buyer to an independent agent. The independent agent, i.e, the holder of the escrow account would ensure that the appropriation of cash flows is as per the agreed terms and conditions between the transacting parties. Escrow account has become the standard in various transactions and business deals. In India escrow account is widely used in public private partnership projects in infrastructure. RBI has also permitted Banks (Authorised Dealer Category I) to open escrow accounts on behalf of Non-Resident corporates for acquisition / transfer of shares / convertible shares of an Indian company.

ESOPs

Employee Stock Option Plans (ESOPs) is a provision under which a foreign company (i.e., MNC) offers shares to its employees overseas. Till February 2005 in the case of local firms, an MNC needed a permission from the RBI before allotting ESOPs, but since then, it does not need any permission provided the company has a minimum of 15 per cent holding in the Indian arm.

EXPLODING ARMS

A term associated with the mortgage business which became popular after the subprime crisis hit the US financial system in mid-2007. Exploding arms are mortgages with initial low, fixed interest rates which escalate to a high floating rate after a period of two to three years.

EXTERNALITIES

Factors that are not included in the gross income of the economy but have an effect on human welfare. They may be *positive* or *negative*–training personnel is an example of the former while pollution falls in the latter.

FCCB

Foreign Currency Convertible Bond, (FCCB) is an unsecured instrument to raise long-term loan in foreign currency by an Indian company which converts into shares of the company on a predetermined rate. It is counted as the part of

external debt. It is a safer route to raise foreign currency requirements of a company.

FEDERAL FUND RATE

The federal fund rate (also popular as *Fed Fund Rate* or *Fed Rate*) is the rate that interest banks charge each other on overnight loans in the USA. The rate is fixed by the US central bank Federal Reserve. This is equivalent to the *Repo rate* of India which is fixed by the RBI.

In wake of the sub-prime real estate crisis wrecking havoc on the US economy, the Fed Rate has been cut time and again to counter the possible future recession.

FIDUCIARY ISSUE

Issuance of currency by the government not matched by gold securities, also known as *fiat money*.

FINANCIAL CLOSURE

Financial closure is defined as a stage when all the conditions of a financing agreement are fulfilled prior to the initial availability of funds. It is attained when all the tie ups with banks or financial institutions for funds are made and all the conditions precedent to initial drawing of debt is satisfied.

In a Public Private Partnership (PPP) project, financial closure indicates the commencement of the *Concession Period*—the date on which financial closure is achieved is the appointed date which is deemed to be the date of commencement of concession period. In order to give a uniform interpretation to the term, the RBI has provided a definition for 'Greenfield' projects, financial closure is *"a legally binding commitment of equity holders and debt financiers to provide or mobilise funding for the project. Such funding must account for a significant part of the project cost which should not be less than 90 per cent of the total project cost securing the construction of the facility".*

FINANCIAL STABILITY BOARD (FSB)

The Financial Stability Forum (FSF) was established by the G7 finance ministers and central bank governors in 1999 to promote international financial stability through enhanced information exchange and international cooperation in financial market supervision and surveillance. It decided at its plenary meeting in London on March 2009 to broaden its membership by inviting the new members from the G20 countries, namely, Argentina, Brazil, China, India, Indonesia, Korea, Mexico, Russia, Saudi Arabia, South Africa, and Turkey. The FSF was relaunched as the Financial Stability Board (FSB) on April 2, 2009, in order to mark a change and convey that the FSF in future would play a more prominent role in this direction.

FISCAL DRAG

The restraining effect of the progressive taxation economies feel on their expansion—fall in the total demand in the economy due to people moving from lower to higher tax brackets and the government tax receipts go on increasing. To neutralise this negative impact, governments usually increase personal tax allowances.

FISCAL NEUTRALITY

A stance in policy making by governments when the net effect of taxation and public spending is neutral—neither encouraging nor discouraging the demand. As for example, a *balanced budget* is the same attempt of fiscal policy when the total tax revenue equals the total public expenditure.

FISHER EFFECT

A concept developed by *Irving Fisher* (1867–1947) which shows relationship between inflation and the interest rate, expressed by an equation popular as the *fisher equation,* i.e., the nominal interest rate on a loan is the sum of the real interest rate and the rate of inflation expected over the duration of the loan:

$$R = r + F;$$

where R = nominal interest rate, r = real interest rate and F = rate of annual inflation.

The concept suggests a direct relationship between inflation and nominal interest rates—changes in inflation rates leads to matching changes in nominal interest rates.

The Fisher effect can be seen each time one goes to the bank; the interest rate an investor has on a savings account is really the nominal interest rate. For example, if the nominal interest rate on a savings account is 4 per cent and the expected rate of inflation is 3 per cent, then money in the savings account is really growing at 1 per cent. The smaller the real interest rate the longer it will take for savings deposits to grow substantially when observed from a purchasing power perspective.

FLAG OF CONVENIENCE

Shipping rights in oceans and seas are governed by international treaties. Flag of convenience is a grant of a shipping 'flag' by a member of these treaties to a non-member nation establishing the legality of shipping to the latter (*usually used for illegal activities*).

FORCED SAVING

The enforced reduction of consumption in an economy. It may take place directly when the government increases taxes or indirectly as a consequence of higher inflation—a tool usually utilised by the developing countries to generate extra funds for investment. Also known as *involuntary saving*.

FOB

This is the abbreviation of 'free-on-board'—when in the balance of payment accounting, only the basic prices of exports and imports of goods (including loading costs) are counted. It does not count the 'cost-insurance-freigth' (CiF) charges incurred in transporting the goods from one to another country.

FORM OF A LIFE INSURANCE FIRM

A life insurance company can be a joint-stock or mutual entity. If joint-stock, it has to have some capital, to begin with. A mutual fund company need not have any. Prudential, the second largest life insurance company in the UK was a mutual fund company till a few years ago and had no capital. Standard Life, another big company, was a mutual company till a few months ago. If such big companies could function without any capital till recently, there is no reason why LIC cannot.

The policyholders are the owners of a mutual company and the entire profit goes to them. A significant proportion of the profit goes to shareholders in the case of joint-stock companies. The LIC, owned fully by the Government, is effectively a mutual fund company and it is not surprising, therefore, that pressure is being mounted to privatise it, so that a chosen few could not corner its huge profits.

FORWARD CONTRACT

A transaction contract of commodity on an agreed price which binds the seller and buyer both to pay and deliver the commodity on a future date. The price agreed upon is known as *forward* rate.

One must not confuse this with the term 'future contract' as in it, the term of the contract cannot be decided by the mutual needs of the parties involved (which is possible in a 'forward contract').

FORWARD TRADING

A trading system in certain shares (as allowed by the SEBI in India) in which buyers and sellers are allowed to postpone/defer payment and delivery respectively after paying some charges. If the buyer wants deferment, it is known as *badla* (an Indian term for *contango*) and if the seller goes for deferment of delivery of shares, it is known as *undha badla* (in India, elsewhere it is known as *backwardation*).

FRACTIONAL BANKING

A system of banking in which banks maintain a minimum reserve asset ratio in order to maintain adequate liquidity to meet the customer's cash demands in its everyday business (*the SLR in India is such a provision,*).

FREE GOODS

The goods which are in abundance (*as air and water*) and are not considered as scarce economic goods. As such goods have *zero supply price* and they will be used in large volumes resulting into rising environmental pollution (point should be noted that today air and water may not be considered as the typical free goods, at least the 'pure air' and 'pure water').

FREE TRADE

The international trade among an agreed-upon group of countries without any barriers (such as tariffs, quotas, forex controls, etc.), promoted with the objective of securing international specialisation and an edge in their foreign trade.

FREE PORT

A port that is designated as such is the one where imports are allowed without any duty, provided they are re-exported (i.e., *entrepot*). If the same is correct in the case of an area, it is known as the *free trade zone*.

FRINGE BENEFIT TAX

The Finance Act, 2005 introduced 30 per cent 'Income Tax on fringe benefit' on fringe benefits received by the employees from his employer.

It means any privilege, service, facility or amenity, directly or indirectly provided by an employer to his employees. It also includes such facilities provided to former employees. Any reimbursement made either directly or indirectly to the employer will also be considered as a fringe benefit. Travelling ticket provided by the employer to the employees and his family members would be a fringe benefit. Even an amount, which is a contribution by the employer to an approved superannuating fund would be called a fringe benefit.

It applies on *deemed* benefits, too such as entertainment, festival celebration, gifts, use of club facilities, provision of hospitality facilities, maintenance of any accommodation in the nature of a guest house, conference, employee welfare, use of health club, sports and similar facilities, sales promotion including publicity; conveyance tour and travel including foreign travel, hotel, boarding and lodging, repair, running and maintenance of motorcars, repair running and maintenance of aircrafts, consumption of fuel other than industrial fuel, use of telephone, scholarship to the children of the employees. The tax was abolished from 2009–10.

GALLUP POLL

A method of survey in which a representative sampling of public opinion or public awareness concerning a certain subject/issue is done and on this basis a conclusion is drawn.

The credit of developing this research methodology goes to *George H. Gallup* (1901–84), a US journalist and statistician who in 1935 did set up the *American Institute of Public Opinion*. Through his efforts the method developed between the period 1935–40. In the coming times, the poll technique was immensely used by business houses for their market research and the psephologists for election forecasting, around the world.

GAME THEORY

The analysis of situations involving two or more interacting decision makers (that may be individuals, competing firms, countries, etc.) who have conflicting objectives. It is a technique which uses logical deduction to explore the consequences of various strategies that might be adopted by game players having competing interests.

Game theory is a branch of *Applied Mathematics* that studies strategic interactions between agents–where the agents try maximising their pay off. It gives *formal modelling approach* to social situations in which decision makers interact with other agents. The theory generalises maximisation approaches developed to analyse markets such as supply and demand model.

The field dates back from the 1944 classic *Theory of Games and Economic Behaviour* by John von Neumann and Oskar Morgentern (Princeton University Press, N. Jersy, 1944 & 2004; 60th Anniversary Ed.). Neumann was a mathematician and Morgenstern an economist and this book was based on the former's prior research published in 1928 on the *Theory of Parlour Games* (in German).

The theory has found significant applications in many areas outside economics as usually construed, including formulations of nuclear strategies, ethics, political science, and evolutionary theory.

GDRs

While ADRs are denominated in dollars and traded on US National Stock Exchanges, GDRs can be denominated either in dollars or Euros and are commonly listed on European Stock Exchanges. Investors can cash in on the difference in price between local and foreign markets. Some time back ADRs and GDRs were *fungible* one way i.e. foreign investors could convert their ADRs/GDRs into underlying shares and sell them in the local market. However, they were not permitted to reconvert shares bought on the local exchange into ADRs/GDRs. In 2002, *two-way fungibility* was permitted. Under these rules reissuance of depository receipts is permitted to the extent to which they have been redeemed into underlying shares and sold in the domestic market.

GIFFEN GOOD

The good for which the demand increases as its price increases, rather than falls (opposite to the *general theory of demand*)—named after Robert Giffen (1837–1910). It applies to the large proportion of the goods belonging to the household budget (as flour, rice, pulses, salt, onion, potato, etc. in India)—an increase in their prices produces a large *negative income effect* completely overcoming the normal substitution effect with, people buying more of the goods.

GINI COEFFICIENT

An inequality indicator in an economy. The coefficient varies from 'zero' to 'one'. A 'zero' Gini coefficient indicates a situation of perfect equality (i.e., every household earning the same level of income) while a 'one' signifies a situation of absolute inequality (i.e., a single household earning the entire income in an economy).

GOLDEN HANDSHAKE

A payment (usually generous) made by a company to its employees for quitting the job prior to their service.

GOLDEN HANDCUFF

A royalty/bonus payment by a company to its staff (usually top ranking) to keep them with the company or to save them from poaching by the other companies.

GOLDEN HELLO

A large sum paid by a company to attract a new staff to its fold.

GOLDEN RULE

A fiscal policy stance which suggests that over the economic cycle, government should borrow only to 'invest' and not to finance the 'current expenditure'. The attempts towards 'balanced budgeting', 'zero-based budgeting' developed under influence of this rule.

GOODHART'S LAW

The idea of goodhart which suggests that attempts by a central bank (as RBI in India) to regulate the level of lending by banks imposing certain controls can be circumvented by the banks searching the alternatives out of the regulatory preview.

GO-GO FUND

The highly speculative mutual funds operating in the USA with the objective of earning high profits out of capital appreciation–adopt risky strategies for the purpose (investing in volatile unproven and small shares, etc.), also called the *performance funds*.

GREATER FOOL THEORY

A theory evolved by the technical analysts of stocks/shares according to which some even buy overvalued stocks with the conviction that they will find a *greater fool* who will buy them at higher prices. This is also popular as *castle-in-the-air theory*.

GREENFIELD INVESTMENT

An investment by a firm in a new manufacturing plant, workshop, office, etc.

GREENFIELD LOCATION

An area consisting of unused or agricultural land (*i.e., 'greenfield'*) developed to set up new industrial plants.

GREEN REVOLUTION & INSTITUTIONS

The support of institutions and the governments of the world did play a very vital role in the success of the Green Revolution all over the world.

The International Maize and wheat Improvement Centre (CIMMYT), Mexico and the International Rice Research Institute (IRRI), Manila were the two institutions in strong partnership with national programmes which developed the miracle varieties of rice and wheat that fuelled the green Revolution around the world.

The Consultative Group on International Agricultural Research (CGIAR), set up in 1971 (in Washington DC under the aegis of the World Bank) played a central role in Green Revolution, supporting the works of the CIMMYT and IRRI. Today, the 16 CGIAR support centres around the world generate new knowledge and farming technology for the agriculture sector. Its research products are "global public goods", freely available to all.

GREENSHOE OPTION

A term associated with the security/share market. This is a clause in the underwriting agreement of an initial public offer (IPO) by a company which allows to sell additional shares (usually 15 per cent) to the public if the demand for shares exceeds the expectation and the share trades above its offering price. It gets its name from the *Green Shoe* company which was the first company to be allowed such an option (in the USA, early 20th century). This is also known as *'over-allotment provision'*.

The company availing this option uses the proceeds (i.e. from the greenshoe option) to prevent any decline in market price of shares below the issue price in the post-listing period (in such cases the aforesaid company uses the money to purchase its own shares from the market—as demand increases, the market price of its shares picks up).

GRESHAM'S LAW

The economic idea that 'bad' money forces 'good' money out of circulation, named after Sir Thomas Gresham, an adviser to Queen Elizabeth I of England. This law does not apply to the economies where paper currencies are in circulation. The economies which circulate metallic coins (gold, silver, copper, etc.) of proportional intrinsic values face such situations when people start hoarding such coins.

GREENSPAN PUT

A financial market terminology named after the former chairman, of the US central bank, Federal Reserve, to mean the helpful way he responded to big declines in the stock market by delivering a cut in interest rates.

GREY MARKET

The 'unofficial' market of the newly issued shares before their formal listing and trading on the stock exchange.

GROWTH RECESSION

An expression coined by economists to describe an economy that is growing at such a slow pace that more jobs are being lost than are being added. The lack of job creation makes it 'feel' as if the economy is in a recession, even though the economy is still advancing. Many economists believe that between 2002 and 2003, the United States' economy was in a growth recession.

In fact, at several points over the past 25 years the US economy is said to have experienced a growth recession. That is, in spite of gains in real GDP, job growth was either non-existent or was being destroyed at a faster rate than new jobs were being added.

HEDGE FUNDS

These are basically mutual funds (MFs) which invest in various securities in order to contain or hedge risks. They are investment vehicles that take big bets on a wide range of assets and specialise in sophisticated techniques of investment. They are meant to perform well in falling as well as rising markets!

Run by former bankers or traditional investment managers by setting up their own funds, they make a lot of money by charging high fees typically 2 per cent management fees besides 20 per cent of the profits out of the investment. As they are unregulated in most of the economies (for example the USA, India, specially) and risky, they accept investments from wealthy and sophisticated investors. Hedge funds made news in recent times as some of them were caught out by betting the wrong way on the market movements. Some of them also made huge losses by buying the complex packages of debt that contain many of the US mortgage loans which turned sour.

In recent years, there have been several high-profile hedge fund collapses. The Long -Term capital Management (LTCM) of the US failing in 1998 had threatened the very stability of the US financial system—looking at the level in impact the regulators managed a bail out for it to prevent an imminent financial collapse. In 2006, the world saw the collapse of another hedge fund in the US, the *Amaranth* which lost $6.5 billion in a month in the natural gas market (The fund in place of a bail out was closed down by the regulators with the investors losing heavily.)

HERFINDAHL INDEX

This is a measure of the level of seller concentration in a market which takes into account the total number of firms and their relative share in the total market output. Also known as *Herfindahl-Hirschman Index.*

HIDDEN PRICE RISE

A quantitative or qualitative decrease in a product without changing the price.

HIDDEN TAX

Addition of an indirect tax into the price of a good or service without fully informing the consumer as, for example, the magnitude of the excise duty in tobacco and alcoholic products is so high that the taxes are added to the products directly.

HISTORIC COST

The original cost of purchasing an asset such as land, machine etc., which is shown in the balance sheet of a firm under this title with an adjustment for the replacement cost of the asset.

HOARDING

An act of unproductive retention of *money* or *goods*.

HOG CYCLES

The cycles of over and under production of goods. This takes place due to time lag in the production process–this happens in case of agricultural products specially.

IMPOSSIBLE TRINITY

This is a term to show the central bank's dilemma in targeting for stable exchange rate, interest rate and inflation while announcing the credit and monetary policy for the economy. As this task is not only challenging but also not possible, it is called as the 'impossible trinity'.

INDIA'S SOVEREIGN RATING

Presently, India is rated by six international credit rating agencies, namely Standard and Poor's (S&P), Moody's Investor Services, FITCH, Dominion Bond Rating Service (DBRS), the Japanese Credit Rating Agency (JCRA), and the Rating and Investment Information Inc., Tokyo(R&I). Information flow to these credit rating agencies has been streamlined.

INDIFFERENCE CURVE

A curve on the graph showing the alternative combinations of two products, each giving the same utility/satisfaction.

INDUCED INVESTMENT

The part of investment (increase or decrease) which takes place due to a change in the level of national income.

IIFCL

The India Infrastructure Finance company Ltd (IIFCL), a Government of India company set up in 2006 to promote public sector investments and public-private partnerships (PPPs) in all areas of infrastructure *except* the telecommunication.

INFERIOR PRODUCT

The good or service for which the income elasticity of demand is negative (i.e., as income rises, buyers go to purchase less of the product). For such products, a price cut results into lesser demands by the buyers.

INFLATION

For all types of inflation see the chapter with the same title.

INSIDER TRADING

A stock market terminology which means transactions of shares by the persons having access to confidential informations which are not yet public—such persons stand to gain financially out of this knowledge (the person might be an employee, director, etc. of the share issuing company or the merchant bank or the book runner to the issue, etc.). Such kind of trading in stocks is illegal all over the world.

INSOLVENCY

The situation when the liabilities of an individual or a firm to creditors exceeds its assets—inability to pay the liabilities from the assets. Also known as *bankruptcy*.

INVENTORY

The stocks of finished goods, goods under the production process and raw materials held by a firm.

INVISIBLE HAND

A term coined by Adam Smith (in his magnum opus *The Wealth of Nations, 1776*) to denote the way in which the market mechanism (i.e., the price system) coordinates the decisions of buyers and sellers without any outside conscious involvement. For him this maximises individual welfare.

IPO

An IPO or initial public offering refers to the issue of shares to the public by the promoters of a company for the first time. The shares may be made available to the investors at face value of the share or with a premium as per the perceived market value of the share by the promoters. The IPO can be in the form of a fixed price portion or book building portion. Some companies offer only demat form of shares, others offer both demat and physical shares.

The performance of an IPO depends on many factors such as the promoter's track record, experience in running the business, risk factors listed in the offer document, nature of industry, government policies associated with the industry performance of that sector in the previous years, and also any available forecasts for the industry for the near future.

I-S SCHEDULE

Here 'I-S' stands for 'investment saving'. This graphic schedule displays the combinations of levels of national income and interest rate where the equilibirium condition for the real economy (investment = savings) holds.

ISLAMIC BANKING

It is banking practiced as per the Islamic principle as prescribed in the *shariah* known as *Fiqh al-Muamalat* (Islamic rules on transaction). The Islamic law prohibits interest on both loans and deposits. Interest is also called *riba* in Islamic discourse. The argument against interest is that money is not a good and profit should be earned on goods and services only not on control of money itself. But Islam does not deny that capital, as a factor of production deserves to be rewarded. It, however, allows the owners of capital a share in a surplus which is *uncertain*.

It operates on the principle of sharing both profits and risks by the borrower as well as the lender. As such the depositor cannot earn a fixed return in the form of interest as happens in conventional banking. But the banks are permitted to offer incentives such as variable prizes or bonuses in cash or kind on these deposits. The depositor, who in the conventional banking system is averse to risk is a provider of capital here and equally shares the risks of the bank which lends his funds.

Investment finance is offered by these banks through *Musharka* where a bank participates as a joint venture partner in a project and shares the profits and losses. Investment finance is also offered through *Mudabha* where the banks contribute the finance and the client provides expertise, management, and labour, and the profits are shared in a prearranged proportion while the loss is borne by the bank.

Trade finance is also offered through a number of ways. One way is through *mare up*, where the bank buys an item for a client and the client agrees to repay the bank the amount along with an agreed profit later on. Banks also finance on lines similar to *leasing, hire purchase,* and *sell and buyback. Consumer lending* is without any interest, but the bank covers expenses by levying a service charge. Besides, these banks offer a host of fee-based products like money transfer, bill collections, and foreign exchange trading where the bank's won money is not involved.

Islamic banks have come into being since the early 1970s. There are nearly 30 Islamic banks all over the world from Africa to Europe to Asia and Australia and are regulated even within the conventional banking system. The whole banking system in Iran has moved over to the Islamic system since the early 1980s and even Pakistan is Islamising its banking system.

Many of the European and American Banks are now offering Islamic banking products not only in muslim countries, but also in developed markets such as the United Kingdom. The concept is also catching up in countries like Malaysia and Dubai.

As per the Islamic experts, with growing indebtedness of many governments and with bulk of the borrowing going to servicing of the past debt and payment of huge interests, it could be an alternative to conventional banking as practiced in the rest of the world. Wherever it is practiced, *studies* have shown that the rate of return is often comparable and sometimes even higher than the interest rate offered by conventional banks to depositors.

India has no such full-fledged bank, though few non-banking financial firms have been operating in Mumbai and Bangalore on Islamic principles. We find the traces of such financial operations by co-operatives even during pre-Independence era, too. In *2015-16*, an Expert Panel of the RBI recommended in favour of such banks. The panel suggested that commercial banks in India *may be* enabled to open specialized *interest-free* windows with simple products like demand deposits by— by putting participation securities on their liability side and deferred payment on the asset side. The RBI did not take any decision regarding it till late **May-2016**.

ISOCOST LINE

A line on the two-axis graph which shows the combination of factor inputs that can be purchased for the same money.

ISOCOST CURVE

A curve on the graph showing the varying combinations of factors of production (i.e., labour, capital etc.) that can be used to produce a given quantity of a product with a given technology.

J-CURVE EFFECT

The tendency for a country's balance of payments deficit to initially deteriorate following a devaluation of its currency before moving into surplus.

JOBBER

An individual active on the floors of the stock exchanges who buys or sells stocks on his own account. A jobber's profit is known as *jobber's spread*. They are also known as *Taravniwalla* on the Bombay Stock Exchange (BSE).

JUNK BOND

An informal term denoting the financial securities issued by a company/bidder as a means of borrowing to finance a takeover bid. Such securities generally include high-risk, high-interst loans, that is why the term 'junk' is used. It is also known as *mezzanine debt*.

KERB DEALINGS

All the transactions taking place outside the stock exchanges.

KHILJI EFFECT

The rulers of the Delhi sultanate didn't understand formal macroeconomics. But they knew one lesson very clearly—it was important to "signal the government's intent to keep expectations in check". Alauddin Khilji personally inspected markets and it worked—checking prices from rising. Such an effect on market is popular in India as the 'Khilji Effect'.

India saw these time-tested lessons followed by the GoI in 2014–15—Central Ministers publicly stated that matters are under control with sufficient quantity of 'onions' and 'potatoes'. The Government brought these two commodities under the purview of the Essential Commodities Act, too. This did show the 'strong intent' of the government to control prices.

Though, the routine statements claiming that 'prices will rise' often started the inflationary spiral (it was repeatedly done by the then Union Minister of Agriculture).

KLEPTOCRACY

A government which is corrupt and thieving— the politicians and bureaucrats in charge using the powers of the state to earn personal benefits/profits. Russia after the disintegration is condsiered to be a clear-cut example when Mafia-friendly government allotted valuable shares of the government companies when they were privatised.

KONDRATIEFF WAVE

A business cycle of 50 years, named after the Russian economist Nikolai Kondratieff (wrote so in his book *The Long Waves in Economic Life,* 1925).

He argued that capitalism was a stable system (the business cycle of 50 years implied it), in contrast to the Marxist view that it was self-destructive and unstable—he died in one of Stalin's prisons.

LAF

The abbreviated form of the Liquidity Adjustment Facility, is part of a financial policy provided to the banks by the RBI in India. The facility commenced in June 2000 under which the banks operating in India are allowed to park their funds

with the RBI for short-term periods (i.e., less than one year which is usually from one day to seven days, in practice), known as the *Reverse Reop.* On such deposits to the RBI, the banks get an interest rate of 6 per cent per annum at present.

LAFFER CURVE

A curve devised by the economist Arthur Laffer in 1974 which links average tax rates to total tax revenue. It suggests that higher tax rates initially increase revenue but after a point further increases in tax rates cause revenue to fall (for instance by discouraging people from working). But it is tough to know whether an economy is on the Laffer curve, as higher taxation breeds evasion of taxes too.

LIAR LOANS

A term associated with the financial world which created news after the US financial system was hit by the subprime crisis in mid-2007.

These are the loans wherein borrowers fraudulently mis-state their incomes often egged on by the lender or broker to the bank. Such frauds have been detected along the entire US mortgage financing chain by September 2007– websites freely advertised that for a nominal fee, they could produce sufficient proof of income by generating bank statements, pay slips, income tax returns, and provide references. Lenders in turn *lied* about the real terms and conditions of the loans to borrowers and lied about the quality of loans sold to investors. The whole gamut of these deeds make such mortgage loans the *'liar loans'.*

LIBOR

The London Interbank Offered Rate (LIBOR) is the interest rate on dollar and other foreign currency deposits at which larger banks are prepared to borrow and lend these currencies in the Euro-currency market. The rate reflects market conditions for international funds and are widely used by the banks as a basis for determining the interest rates charged on the US dollar and foreign currency loans to the business customers.

LIFE-CYCLE HYPOTHESIS

An idea which states that current consumption is not dependent solely on current disposable income of the consumers but is related to their anticipated lifetime income. This hypothesis has its high applied value in the real life economic management.

LIFE INSURANCE: SOME IMPORTANT TERMS

Endowment Policy

Insurance policies where a lump sum is payable either at the end of the policy term or if the insured dies during the policy tenure, are termed as endowment policies.

Beneficiary

A person or organisation legally entitled to receive benefits.

Term Life Insurance

In most cases, term life insurance refers to a product that provides death benefit protection for a specified period of time, say for 30 years. Benefits are doled out under this scheme only if the insured dies during the term.

Whole Life Insurance

It is a policy that provides insurance coverage for the entire life of the individual for a fixed premium throughout his life insurance, coupled with an investment component. Investments could be made in stocks or bonds that lead to accumulation of cash values. The augmented cash reserves are returned once one decides to surrender the policy.

Universal life insurance was created to provide more flexibility than whole life insurance by allowing the policy owner to shift money between the insurance and saving components of the policy.

Variable Universal Life Insurance Policy

A form of whole life insurance policy, this is a policy for those who weigh high risk threshold. It offers cash values that fluctuate based on the performance of the underlying mutual funds in the investment account. It is this investment of premiums in the equity market that carries with it an element of uncertainty.

Premium

This is the amount that the policy holder pays to the insurance company for the benefits provided under an insurance policy. The frequency of premium payments is opted by the individual. Typical premium modes include monthly, quarterly, semi-annual, and annual.

Annuity

An agreement sold by a life insurance company that provides fixed or variable payments to the policy holder, either immediately or at a future date.

Group Life Insurance

A life insurance policy issued to a group of people, usually through an employer.

Lapse

Defaulting on premium payments leads to the termination of an insurance policy. A lapse notice is sent in writing to the policy holder when the policy has lapsed.

Lump Sum

It refers to the proceeds of the policy that is paid to the beneficiary all at once rather than in installments. Typically, most life insurance policies make lump sum payment settlements.

LIQUIDATION

A process of 'winding up' a joint-stock company as a legal entity.

LIQUID ASSET

The monetary asset that can be used directly as payment.

LIQUIDITY

The extent to which an asset can be quickly and completely converted into currency and coins.

LIQUIDITY PREFERENCE

A term denoting a preference among the people for holding money instead of investing it.

LIQUIDITY TRAP

A situation when the interest rate is so low that people prefer to hold money rather than invest it.

In such situations investors do not go to increase investment even if the interest rates on loans are decreased. J. M. Keynes suggested for increased government expenditure or reduction in taxes to fight such a situation.

L-M SCHEDULE

Here 'L-M' stands for 'liquidity-money'. This is a schedule showing the combinations of levels of national income and interest rates where the equilibrium condition for the monetary economy, L = M, holds.

LOCAL AREA BANK

Announced in the Union Budget 1996–97 to ensure a focussed savings and credit mobilisation by defining the clear boundary of operation, the local Area Bank (LAB) operates to a narrow geographical area of three contiguous districts. The private sector is also allowed entry in the segment.

LOCOMOTIVE PRINICIPLE

The idea that in a situation of worldwide *recession* (see the chapter *Business Cycle*), increase in the total demand in one economy stimulates economic activities in the other economies via foreign trade.

LORENZ CURVE

A graph showing the degree of inequality in income and wealth in a given population or an economy. It is a rigorous way to measure income inequality. In this method (for example), personal incomes in an economy are arranged in increasing order; the cumulative share of total income is then plotted against the cumulative share of the population. The curve's slope is thus proportional to per capita income at each point of the population distribution. In the case of complete equality of income, the lorenz curve will be a straight line and with greater curvature the inequality rises proportionally–the *Gini Coefficient* measures this inequality.

LUMP OF LABOUR FALLACY

The fallacy in economics that there is a 'fixed amount of work' to be done i.e. a lump of labour—this may be shared in different ways to create fewer or more jobs in an economy. An economist, D.F. Schloss in 1891 called it the lump of labour fallacy because in reality, the amount of work to be done is not fixed.

MACRO AND MICRO ECONOMICS

In economics, two different ways of looking at the economy have been developed by economists i.e., macroeconomics and microeconomics.

Macroeconomics ('macro' in Greek language means 'large') looks at the behaviour of the economy *as a whole* such as the issues like inflation, rate of unemployment, economic growth, balance of trade, etc. It is the branch of economics which studies the economy in its *total* or *average* term.

Microeconomics (in Greek language 'micro' means 'small') looks on the behaviour of the *units* i.e. the individual, the households, the firms, a *specific* industry, which together make up the economy.

MARGINAL STANDING FACILITY (MSF)

Operationalised on the lines of the existing Liquidity Adjustment Facility (LAF – Repo) in May 2011 under which all Scheduled Commercial Banks can avail overnight funds, up to one per cent of their Net Demand and Time Liabilities (NDTL) outstanding at the end of the second preceding fortnight. The facility is availed at an interest which is 100 basis points above the LAF repo rate, or as decided by the Reserve Bank from time to time.

MARGINAL UTILITY

The increase in satisfaction/utility a consumer derives from the use/consumption of one *additional* unit of a product in a particular time period–it goes on decreasing, i.e., the *diminishing marginal utility.*

MARKET CAPITALISATION

A term of security market which shows the market value of a company's share—calculated by multiplying the current price of its share

to the total number of shares issued by the company.

MARKET MAKER

An intermediary (may be an individual or a firm) in the secondary market who buys and sells securities/shares simultaneously quoting two-way rates. For example, on the over the counter Stock Exchange of India (OTCEI) only 'market markers' are allowed to operate. The Discount and Finance House of India (SBI DFHI) is the chief market maker in the 'money market' of India.

A market maker plays a very vital role by providing sustainability to liquidity in the secondary market.

MASCs

The Multi-Application Smart Cards (MASCs) system to facilitate simplification of procedures and enhancing the efficiency of Government schemes has been suggested by a Planning Commission Working Group in the context of the Eleventh Five Year Plan. The *Smart Card* (i.e., MASCs) has been recognised to be useful in implementation of various Central government schemes like, PDS, Indira Awas Yojana and National Rural Employment Guarantee Scheme (NREGS).

Based on a web-enabled information system the Smart Cards will be based on unique ID, sharing ID, multi-application and access control. The whole system will consist of front, middle, and back end. The electronic card will be the 'front' end of the system which will be the point of delivery where the smart cards will be read and used. The office at 'middle' will be responsible for changing and updating the card periodically (i.e., monthly, quarterly, annually) depending on the type of information and requirement and transfer information from the front end to the back end and vice versa. The office at 'back' end will contain the computerised records, guidelines, accounts and management information systems. The complete digitisation of records will be required by this system.

MARSHALL PLAN

A programme of international aid named after General George Marshall (a US Secretary of State) under which North America contributed around 1 per cent of its GDP in total (between 1948–52) to western Europe to rebuild the economies ravaged in Second World War.

MENU COST

The cost a firm bears in changing the prices of its product—it includes retraining the sales staff, reprinting of the new price list, labelling of goods, and informing the customers about the price change. Higher menu costs discourage the firms going for frequent price changes.

MID-CAP FUNDS

Mutual funds launch sector-specific funds to attract investments. Similarly, they mobilise resources from investors with an objective of investing in mid-cap shares. The Fund Manager chooses the mid-cap shares that can become a part of the portfolio. His job is to outperform the benchmark like the CNX Midcap 200 indexes in terms of the returns. There are thousands of funds world over that focus on investing in medium or small-cap companies.

MFBS

In August 2007, the Reserve Bank of India released a Manual on Financial and Banking Statistics (MFBS), first of its kind, which works as a reference guide and provides a methodological framework for compilation of statistical indicators encompassing various sectors of the economy.

MID-CAP SHARES

There is no classical definition of mid-cap shares. The name 'mid-cap' originates from the term, *medium capitalised*. It is based on the market capitalisation of the stock. Market capitalisation is calculated by multiplying the current stock price with the number of shares outstanding or issued by the company. The definition of mid-cap shares can vary across markets and countries. In case of India, the National Stock Exchange defines the mid-cap universe as stocks whose average six months market capitalisation is between Rs. 75 crore and Rs. 750 crore. In the US, mid-cap shares are those stocks that have a market *capitalisation* of Rs. 9,000 crore to Rs. 45,000 crore. In India, these shares will be classified as *large cap shares*. Thus, classification of shares into large-caps, mid-cap and small-cap is made on the basis of the relative size of market in a country. The total market capitalisation of US markets is $15 trillion. In India, the market capitalisation of listed companies is around $600 billion.

The theory is that large-cap shares have lesser growth potential since the turnover and profits of large companies are already high in the context of that particular market. On the other hand, mid-cap shares are considered an attractive avenue for investing because their growth rate should be faster. It is analogous to investing in an emerging market, like India, as compared to a mature market. However, on the flip side, mid-cap shares are of small companies where revenue and profits could be more volatile than large companies. At the same time, the availability of shares for trading in the secondary market is also limited in comparison to large-cap shares.

The National Stock Exchange manages an index called CNX Midcap 200. The objective of such an index is to capture the movement in the mid-cap shares segment.

MERCHANT BANKING

A financial world business of providing various financial services other than lending such as public issue management, underwriting such issues, loan syndication management, mergers and acquisition related services, etc.

MEZZANINE FINANCING

Mezzanine financing is defined as a financial instrument which is a *mix* of 'debt and equity' finance. It is a debt capital that gives the lender the rights to convert to an ownership or equity interest in the company. It is listed as an asset on company's balance sheet. As it is treated as equity in a company's balance sheet, it allows the company to access other traditional sources of finance.

In the hierarchy of creditors, mezzanine finance is subordinate to *senior debt* but ranks higher than *equity*. The return on mezzanine finance is higher in relation to debt finance but lower than equity finance. It is also available quickly to the borrower with *little* or *no collateral*. The concept of mezzanine financing is just catching up in India. Mezzanine financing is used mainly for small and medium enterprises, infrastructure and real estate. *ICICI Venture's Mezzanine Fund* was the first fund in India to focus on mezzanine finance opportunities.

MIBID

The Mumbai Inter Bank Bid (MIBID) is the weighted average interest rate at which certain banks in Mumbai are ready to borrow from the call money market.

MIBOR

The Mumbai Inter Bank offer Rate (MIBOR) is the weighted average interest rate at which certain banks/institutions in Mumbai are ready to lend in the call money market.

Middle Class

We keep hearing and reading use the term 'middle class' frequently. But who are the middle classes? There are still no universally accepted criteria for defining the middle class. Simply put, they are neither rich nor poor. Even the income criterion has not been settled. According to the National Council of Applied Economic Research (NCAER), a family with an annual income between Rs. 3.4 lakh and Rs. 17 lakh (at the 2009-10 price levels) falls in the middle class category. According to NCAER, by 2015–16, India was a country of 53.3 million middle class households or about 267 million people.

Microcredit

Smaller credit/loan to small and needy borrowers who are outside the reach of commercial banks, for the purpose of undertaking productive activities.

Misery Index

An index of economic misery that is sum of the rates of inflation and unemployment for an economy–higher the value greater is the misery.

Monetary Neutrality

The idea that changes in money supply have no effect on real economic variables (such as output, real interest rates, unemployment etc.,) if money supply increases by 10 per cent, for example, the price will increase by the same level.

A core belief of Classical Economics, the idea was put forth by David Hume in the 18th century. Today this is not considered a valid idea.

MONEY ILLUSION

A phrase coined by J. M. Keynes to denote the misleading thinking among people that they are getting richer as a result of inflation when in reality the value of money decreases.

The phrase is used by some economists to argue that a small amount of inflation may not be a bad thing and could even be beneficial as it may help to 'grease the wheels' of the economy—a feeling of getting richer (let it be illusory itself!).

MORAL HAZARD

One among the two kinds of market failure often associated with the insurance sector. It means that the people with insurance cover may take greater risks than the uncovered ones as they know they are protected so the insurer may get more claims it bargained for. The other kind of market failure is the *adverse selections* also related to insurance business.

MOST FAVOURED NATION

As per the WTO agreements, member countries cannot *normally* discriminate between their trading partners. If any country grants one country a special favour such as a lower customs duty rate for one of their products the same would need to be extended to all other WTO members. This principle is known as Most Favoured Nation (MFN) treatment.

MFN is governs trade in *goods*. MFN is also a priority in the General Agreement on Trade in *Services* (GATS) and the Agreement on Trade-Related Aspects of *Intellectual Property* Rights (TRIPS). However, there are some *exceptions* under WTO regime which allow mwmber countries to—

(i) Set up a 'free trade agreemen't that applies only to *goods* traded within the group (discriminating against goods from outside).

(ii) Give developing countries special access to their markets.

(iii) Raise barriers against products that are considered to be traded unfairly from specific countries.

(iv) To discriminate, in limited circumstances, in services.

But the agreements only permit these exceptions under strict conditions. In general, MFN means that every time a country lowers a trade barrier or opens up a market, it has to do so for the same goods or services for all its trading partners whether developed or developing.

NARROW BANKING

Short-term lending in risk-free asset is narrow banking. A suggestion for such banking was given by the committee on Financial System (CFS) in 1991 for the weak banks of India.

NASH EQUILIBRIUM

A concept in game theory named after John Nash, a mathematician and Nobel prize winning economist, which occurs when each player is pursuing their best possible strategy in the full knowledge of the strategies of all the other players—once the equilibrium is reached, none of the players has any incentive to change their strategy.

NEO-CLASSICAL ECONOMICS

The school of economics based on the writings of Alfred Marshall (1842–1924) which replaced the classical economics by the 19th century, also known as the *'marginal revolution'*.

NET INCOME

This is related to a limited liability firm/company (i.e., Ltd.). It is derived by deducting the expenses of the company from its total revenue in a particular period (usually one year). If income tax and interest are not deducted, it is called *'operating profit'* (or 'loss', as the case may be). Net income is also called *earnings, net earnings* or *net profit*.

NET WORTH

Net worth for a company is its total assets minus total liabilities. This is an important determinant of the value of a company, considering it is composed primarily of all the money that has been invested since its inception, as well as the retained earnings for the duration of its operation. Net worth can be used to determine creditworthiness because it gives a snapshot of the company's investment history. This is also called as *owner's equity, shareholders' equity,* or *net assets.*

In case of an individual, net wroth is the value of a person's assets, including cash, minus all liabilities – the amount by which the individual's assets exceed their liabilities is considered the net worth of that person.

NEW PENSION SCHEME

Pension reforms in India have evolved primarily in response to the need of reform in the Government pension system. This had been designed to make a shift from defined-benefit to defined-contribution by putting a cap on Government's liability towards civil servants' pension. As a result of implementation of the New Pension System (NPS), all employees of the Central Government and Central autonomous bodies, with the exception of the armed forces, are now covered by this defined-contribution scheme with effect from January 1, 2004. Subsequently, all states and UTs State have notified and joined the NPS for their employees. The NPS to was opened to all citizens of India on May 1, 2009, on voluntary basis - the challenge is to spread the message of the NPS and old age income security to people in the unorganized sector across the country.

The pension fund managers manage three separate schemes, consisting of three asset classes, namely (i) equity, (ii) Government securities, and (iii) credit risk-bearing fixed income instruments, with the investment in equity subject to a cap of 50 per cent.

NINJA

A mortgage business terminology became common word after the US subprime crisis of mid-2007 which is an acronym for the borrowers with no income, no job or assets.

NOMINAL VALUE

The value of anything calculated at the current prices. It does not include the effect of inflation during the periods and gives misleading idea of value.

NON-WORKERS

The *Census of India* defines non-workers as the persons who did not 'work at all' during the reference period. They constitute—

(i) Students who did not participate in anyeconomic activity paid or unpaid,

(ii) Household duties who were attending to daily household chores like cooking, cleaning utensils, looking after children, fetching water, etc. and are not even helping in the unpaid work in the family farm or cultivation or milching,

(iii) Dependants such as infants or very elderly people not included as *worker*,

(iv) Pensioners drawing pension post-retirement, not engaged in any economic activity.

(v) Beggars, vagrants, prostitutes and persons having unidentified source of income and with unspecified sources of subsistence and not engaged in any economically productive work.

(vi) Others, which includes all Non-workers who may not come under the above categories such as rentiers, persons living on remittances, agricultural or non-agricultural royalty, convicts in jails or inmates of penal, mental or charitable institutions doing no paid or unpaid work and persons who are seeking/available for work.

[Also see entry *'Worker'*]

NORKA

Indians work abroad and *remit* much of their earnings back home. Kerala is a state where non-residents contribute significantly to the state's resources. Keeping this important revenue channel in mind, the Government of Kerala launched the department of Non-resident Keralites' Affairs (NORKA) in 1996 to redress the grievances of Non-Resident Keralites (NRKs). NORKA is the *first* of its kind formed by any Indian state.

It makes efforts to solve the grievances raised in petitions for remedial action on threats to the lives and property of those who are left at home, tracing of missing persons abroad, compensation from sponsors, harassment from sponsors, cheating by recruiting agents, educational facilities for children of NRKs, introduction of more flights, assistance to stranded Keralites, etc.

NORMAL GOODS

The goods whose demand increases as income of the people increases. It is just opposite of *inferior goods*.

NULL HYPOTHESIS

An idea that is put to the test. In econometrics, experts start with a null hypothesis (i.e., a particular variable equals a particular number), then crunch the data to verify it in accordance with the laws of *statistical significance*. The chosen null hypothesis is often just opposite to what the experimenter believes.

Statistical significance means that the probability of getting the result by chance is low. It is most commonly used measure is that there must be a 95 per cent chance that the result is right and only 1-in-20 chance of the result occurring randomly.

NUMERAIRE

A monetary unit which is used as the basis for denominating international exchanges in a product and financial settlements on a common basis. For example, the US dollar being used as the numeraire of international oil trade, the Special Drawing Rights (SDRs) as the numeraire of the IMF transactions, etc.

NVS

Non voting Shares (NVS) are the equity shares not having right to vote at the general meetings of the company. But these shares get higher dividend than the shares having voting rights. A company in India may issue such shares maximum to the 25 per cent of the total issued share capital and such shares cannot get more than 20 per cent higher dividend than the shares with voting rights.

OIL BONDS

Oil bonds are special bonds issued by the GoI to the oil marketing public sector companies to cover-up their losses in marketing. In case of global price rise in crude oil the companies needed to increase prices of their products. But to avoid inflationary effects on the economy, the oil marketing companies were not allowed to do so—ultimately leading them to fetch huge losses. So that these companies are able to arrange funds (to fill up their losses), the government used to issue oil bonds. These bonds, backed by sovereign power, are marketable in the financial system of India. After the domestic prices of petrol, diesel, lubricants and aviation turbine fuel (ATF) have been linked to the international crude prices need of issuing such bonds have not been felt. The declining global crude oil prices of recent times have also helped the GoI to avoid such instances.

OKUN'S LAW

Based on the empirical research of *Arthur Okun* (1928–80), the law describes the relationship between unemployment and growth rate in an economy. As per it, if GDP grows at 3 per cent p.a., the unemployment rate would not change. In the case of faster growth rates, every extra above the 3 per cent will have a decrease in the unemployment rate by its half (i.e., a 4 per cent growth rate will decrease unemployment by 0.5 per cent–half of 1 which is the extra above 3 per cent). Similarly, a growth rate below 3 per cent will have the same but opposite impact on unemployment (i.e., increases it).

Though the law was perfectly correct for the period of the US economy Okun studied, it may not be valid today in either US or anywhere else. But in general, the law is still used by experts and policy makers as a rule of thumb to estimate the relationship between growth rate and job creation.

OPEN MARKET OPERATION

An instrument/tool of monetary policy under which sale/purchase of government Treasury Bills and bonds takes place as a means of controlling money supply.

OPPORTUNITY COST

A measure of the economic cost of using scarce resources to produce one particular good or service in terms of the alternative thereby foregone, also known as the *economic cost*.

OVER THE COUNTER

The financial papers/securities which can be bought or sold through a private dealer or bank rather than on a financial exchange. The term has its use in the non-financial world too—purchasing medicines from a medical store without the doctor's prescription is an over-the-counter deal in drugs.

PARALLEL IMPORTING

A type of arbitrage where an independent importer buys product of a particular supplier at low price in one country and resells it in direct competition with the supplier's distributors in another country where prices are higher.

It promotes free trade and competition by breaking down barriers to international trade and undermines price discrimination between markets covered by the suppliers.

PARETO PRINCIPLE

The maximisation of the economic welfare of the community. Named after the Italian economist Vilfredo Pareto (1843–1923), this points to a situation in which nobody can be made better off without making somebody else worse off.

By an efficient use of resources an economy is able to do so i.e., without making somebody else worse off, somebody might be made better off. In reality, change often produces losers as well as winners. Pareto optimality does not help judge whether this sort of change is economically good or bad.

PARKINSON'S LAW

A proposition by C. Northcote Parkinson which suggests that work expands according to the time available in which it is done.

PENNY STOCKS

Very low-priced shares of small companies which have low market capitalisation. The term made news in mid-2006 when some of the 'penny stocks' did show a high rise in their trading prices in India at the BSE as well as the NSE.

PHILLIPS CURVE

A graphic curve depicting an empirical observation of the relationship between the level of unemployment and the rate of change of money wages and, by inference, the rate of change of prices.

It was in 1958 that an economist from New Zealand, A. W. H. Phillips (1914–75) proposed that there was a trade-off between inflation and unemployment–the lower the unemployment rate, the higher the inflation rate–governments simply need to choose the right balance between the two evils.

PIGGYBACK LOAN

A term associated with mortgage business got popular in the wake of the US subprime crisis mid-2007. Piggyback loan is a second mortgage enabling a borrower to buy a house with little or no equity.

PIGOU EFFECT

Named after Arthur Cecil Pigou (1877–1959), a sort of wealth effect resulting from deflation/disinflation (i.e., price fall) – a fall in price level increases the real value of people's money, making them wealthier inducing increased spending by them; higher demand creation leads to higher employment.

PREFERENCE SHARES

The shares which bear a stated dividend and carry a priority over equity shares (in matters of dividend and assets) are also known as hybrid securities (since they have the qualities of equity shares as well as bond). Such shares in India cannot have a life over 10 years.

PRICE-EARNING RATIO

A concept used in the share market to equate various stocks–is a ratio found/calculated by dividing market price of a share by the earning per share.

PRIMARY AND SECONDARY MARKET

Primary market refers to buying of shares in an initial public offering. The shares are bought by applying through a share application form. Secondary market refers to transactions where one investor buys shares from another investor at the prevailing market price or at an agreed price. The shares are bought and sold in the secondary market on the stock exchanges. The investors may buy and sell securities on the stock exchanges through stock brokers.

PRIMARY DEALER

Primary dealer (PD) is an intermediary participating in the *primary* auctions of the government securities (i.e., G-See or the Gilt-edge securities or the Gilt) and the Treasury Bills (TBs); through a PD these instruments reach the secondary market.

Primary dealers are allowed participation in the call money market and notice money market. They get liquidity support from RBI via repos or refinance (against the G-Secs.).

PRISONER'S DILEMMA

A popular example in *game theory* which concludes why co-operation is difficult to achieve even if it is mutually beneficial, ultimately making things worse for the parties involved. It is shown giving an example of two prisoners arrested for the same offence held in different cells. Each prisoner has two options, i.e., confess, or say nothing. In this situation there are *three* possible outcomes:

(i) One could confess and agree to testify against the other as a state witness, receiving a light sentence while his fellow prisoner receives a heavy sentence.

(ii) They can both say nothing and may turn out to be lucky getting light sentences or even be let off due to lack of firm evidence.

(iii) They may both confess and get lighter individual sentences than one would have received had he said nothing and the other had testified against him.

The second outcome looks the best for both the prisoners. However, the risk that the other might confess and turn state witness is likely to encourage both to confess, landing both with sentences that they might have avoided had they been able to co-operate by remaining silent.

In reality, firms behave like these prisoners, not setting prices as high as they could do if they only trusted the other firms not to undercut them. Ultimately, the firms are worse off i.e. all firms suffer.

POPULATION TRAP

A situation of population growth rate greater than the achievable economic growth rate. This makes it difficult to alleviate poverty;–government is suggested to implement population control measures.

POVERTY TRAP

A situation where an unemployed getting unemployment allowance is not encouraged to seek work/employment because his/her after-tax earnings as employed is less than the benefits as unemployed, also known as the *unemployment trap.*

PREDATORY PRICING

The pricing policy of a firm with the express purpose of harming rivals or exploiting the consumer. By price-cutting, firstly the rivals are ousted from the market and later the consumers are exploited as monopolistic suppliers by the firm.

PPP

Purchasing power parity (PPP) is a method of calculating the correct/real value of a currency which may be different from the market exchange rate of the currency. Using this method economies may be studied comparatively in a common currency. This is a very popular method handy for the IMF and WB (introduced by them in 1990) in studying the living standards of people in different economies. The PPP gives a different exchange rate for a currency which may be made the basis for measuring the national income of the economies. It is on this basis that the value of gross national product (GNP) of India becomes the fourth largest in the world (after the US, Japan, and China) though on the basis of market exchange rate of rupee, it stands at the *thirteenth rank.*

The concept of the PPP was developed by the great European conservative economist, Gustav Cassel (1866–1944), belonging to Sweden. This concept works on the assumption that markets work on the *law of one price,* i.e., identical goods and services (*in quantity* as well as *quality*) must have the same price in different markets when measured in a common currency. If this is not the case it means that the purchasing power of the two currencies is different.

Let us look at an example. Suppose that sugar is selling $1 in US and Rs. 20 in India a kilo then the PPP-based exchange rate of rupee will be $1 = Rs. 20. This is the way how *The Economist* of London has prepared its 'Big Mac Index' (comparing the

Mc Donald's Big Mac burger prices in different economies).

In theory, the value of currencies in terms of their market exchange rate should converge with their value in terms of the PPP in the long run. But that might not happen due to many factors like the fluctuations in inflation; level of money supply; follow-up to the exchange rate regimes (fixed, floating, etc.), and other.

For the calculation of the PPP, a comparable basket of goods and services is selected (a very difficult task) of the identical qualities and quantities. The other difficulty in computing PPP arises out of the flaw in the 'one price theory' i.e., due to transportation cost, local taxes, level of production, etc. The prices of goods and services cannot be the same in different markets (This is correct in theory only, not possible in practice.)

PURCHASE TAX

A tax collected by states in India on goods. This is imposed on the *purchases* done by traders/manufacturers—basically collected by the seller and given to the concerned states). This is deducted once the traders/manufacturers pay value added tax (VAT) to the states—as VAT is paid on the differential value of the traded/manufactured goods. This tax is among the 8 taxes to be merged into the upcoming indirect tax, the GST.

QIP

Qualified Institutional Placement (QIP) is a policy associated with the Indian stock market for raising capital by issuing equity shares. The companies listed on the BSE and the NSE are allowed (since May 2006) to raise capital by issuing equity shares, or any securities other than warrants, which are convertible into or exchangeable with equity shares. The attractive part of the new QIP is that the issuing company

does not have to undergo elaborate procedural requirements to raise this capital. These securities have to be issued to Qualified Institutional Buyers on a discretionary basis, with just a 10 per cent reservation for mutual funds.

Q THEORY

As investment theory for firms proposed by the Nobel prize winning (1981) economist James Tobin (1918–2002). He theorised that firms would continue to invest as long as the value of their shares exceeded the replacement cost of their assets–the ratio of the market value of a firm to the net replacement cost of the firm's assets is known as 'Tobin Q'. If Q is greater than 1, then it should expand the firm by investment as the profit it should expect to make from its assets (reflected by share price) exceeds the cost of the assets.

If Q is less than 1, the firm would be better off by selling its assets which are worth more than shareholders currently expect the firm to earn in profit by retaining them.

RANDOM WALK

When it is impossible to predict the next step. As per the Efficient Market Theory the prices of financial assets (such as shares) follow a random walk–there is no way of knowing the next change in the price. The reason this theory provides is that in an efficient market, all the information that would allow an investor to predict the next price move is already *reflected in the current price*. Such belief has led some economists to conclude that investors cannot outperform the market consistently.

As opposed to this, some economists argue that asset prices are predictable and that markets are not efficient–they follow a *non-random walk* perspective.

REDLINING

The act of not lending to people in certain poor or troubled neighbourhoods shown on the map with a 'red line'. Even if their credit-worthiness has been judged on the basis of other criteria, they are not considered as borrowers by the banks, simply because they live in that area.

RENT

It has two different meanings in economics:

(i) The first is layman i.e. the income accruing from hiring land or other durable goods.

(ii) The second (also known as *economic rent*) is a measure of *market power* i.e. the difference between what a factor of production is paid and how much it would need to be paid to remain in its current use.

For example, a cricket player may be paid Rs. 40,000 a week to play for his team when he would be willing to turn out for only Rs. 10,000, so his economic rent will be Rs. 30,000 a week.

RENT-SEEKING

Spending time and money not on the production of real goods and services, but rather on trying to get the government to change the rules so as to make one's business more profitable.

It is like cutting a bigger slice of the cake rather than making the cake bigger trying to make more money without producing more for customers. The term was coined by the economist Gordon Tullock.

RENT-SEEKING BEHAVIOUR

The behaviour which improves the welfare of someone at the expense of someone else. A protection racket is the most extreme example of it, in which one group (i.e., the protected one) betters itself without creating welfare-enhancing output at all.

REPLACEMENT COST

The cost of replacing an asset (such as machinery, etc.). Opposite to *historic cost* (i.e., the original cost of acquiring an asset), replacement cost adjusts the effects of inflation.

RESIDUAL RISK

What is left after one takes out all the other shared risk exposures to an asset, also known as *alpha* (a).

When one buys an asset one is exposed to a number of risks, many of them not unique to the asset but reflect broader possibilities (such as the future behaviour of stock market, interest rate, inflation or even government policies, etc.). Exposure to this risk can be reduced by diversification.

RETAIL BANKING

A way of doing banking business where the banks emphasise the individual-based lending rather than corporate lending–also known as *high street banking*. Such banking focusses on consumer loans, personal loans, hire-purchase, etc., considered more cumbersome and risky.

RETROCESSION

The term has got *three* different meanings in which it is used—

(i) The purchase of 'reinsurance' by a 'reinsurance company' (as in the case of India, the GIC going for 'reinsurance' on the 'reinsurance' it has provided to other 'insurance companies' operating in India). This limits the risk that a reinsurance company may face, since it has purchased insurance against an 'event' that might affect a company that it had underwritten (reinsured). If a reinsurance company *continues* to purchase insurance it might 'unknowingly' buy back its own risk, which is known as 'spiraling'.

(ii) The 'voluntary' act of returning ceded property by one to another which may be a result of 'request' to have property returned. But, by definition, it is not the result of a 'forced' transaction. Returning of Hong Kong to China by the UK in 1997 is the best such example of the recent times.

(iii) The act of 'differentiating' and 'diversifying' assets by consolidating and then dividing them amongst a number of stakeholders – by doing so the risk involved is 'retroceded' (i.e., cut down or minimised). This is, usually, done by the 'hedge funds' in their day-to-day portfolio management.

REVERSE TAKEOVER

The term is used to mean two different kinds of takeovers:

(i) Takeover of a public company by a private one, and

(ii) Takeover of a bigger company by a smaller one.

RESIDUAL UNEMPLOYMENT

Unemployment of those who remained unemployed even in the times of full employment (as for example employing a severely handicapped person may far outweigh the productivity obtained from him).

REVERSE MORTGAGE

A scheme for senior citizens in India announced in the Union Budget 2007–08. Under this scheme, the senior citizens go to mortgage their house owned by them in reverse to a bank and the bank pays them the agreed money either in installments or lumpsum. Guidelines for reverse mortgage announced by the National Housing Bank (NHB) in May 2007 has a provision of maximum period of 15 years for such mortgage. Once the period of mortgage is complete either the house should be vacated or the bank will sell the house at the market price and the loan of the bank will be settled. If the value of the house is more than the loan, the difference is paid to the senior citizens or their heirs. If the heir wants to possess the house, he/she needs to pay the loan.

REVERSE YIELD GAP

An excess of returns on gilt-edged (government) securities above those on equities. This occurs during periods of high inflation because equities provide capital gains to compensate inflation while the gilt-edged securities do not.

REVEALED PREFERENCE

The notion that what one wants is revealed by what one does, not by what one says—actions speak louder than words.

RICARDIAN EQUIVALENCE

An idea which (generated too much controversies) originally suggested by David Ricardo (1772–1823) and more recently by Barro, that government deficits do not affect the overall level of demand in an economy.

This is because tax-payers know that any deficit has to be paid later, and so they increase their savings in anticipation of a higher tax bill in future; thus government attempts to stimulate an economy by increasing public spending or cutting taxes, will be rendered impotent by private sector reaction.

The equivalence can be seen as part of a thread of economic thinking which holds that only decisions about real variables (e.g., consumption and production) matter, and that decisions about financing will, in a perfectly functioning market, never have an effect.

RISK SEEKING

An act whereby investors prefer an investment with an uncertain outcome to one with the same expected returns and certainty that it will deliver them – the act which cannot get enough risk.

RULE OF THUMB

A rough-and-ready decision-making aid that provides an acceptably accurate approximate solution to a problem. Where refined decision-making processes are expensive (in terms of information gathering and processing them), such a method looks justified.

ROUNDING ERROR

The error which comes up due to rounding off the figures in decimals, for example, considering 3.6 as 4 and 3.4 as 3. Such rounding off the data is never going to be mathematically correct.

SALARY

The payment made to employees of an organisation, firm, etc., for the use of labour as a factor of production. It differs from *wage* in the following two ways:

(i) It is not paid on hourly basis (or for the actual number of hours worked by the employee) as wages are paid, and

(ii) It is usually paid on monthly basis whereas wages are paid on daily or weekly basis.

SATISFYING THEORY

A theory which suggests that firms do not want only 'satisfactory' profits but maximum profits as well as other objectives such as sales increase, size increase, etc. might be having equal or greater importance than profits.

SAY'S LAW

Named after the French economist Jean Baptise say (1767–1832), the law proposes that aggregate supply creates its own aggregate demand.

The logic of the law goes like this—the very act of production generates an income (in the form of wages, salaries, profits, etc.) exactly equal to the output which if spent is just sufficient to purchase the whole output produced. Ultimately, it gives an important clue, i.e., in order to reach full-employment level all that is needed is to increase the aggregate supply.

The key assumption behind the law is that the economic system is 'supply-led' and that all income is spent. But in practice, some income 'leaks' into saving, taxation, etc., and there is no auto-guarantee that all income is 'injected' back as spending. This is why others suggest for a 'demand-led' idea of the economic system under which demand creation is attended vigorously.

SECOND-BEST THEORY

The idea was put forward by Richard Lipsey and Kelvin Lancaster (1924–99) in 1956 which suggests a way out of the situation when all the assumptions of an economic model are not met. As per the theory, the second-best situation is meeting as many of the assumptions as possible (but it might not give the optimum or the desired results).

SECURITIES TRANSACTION TAX

[See Chapter 17, *Tax Structure in India*]

SEIGNORAGE

A method of generating resource by a government through printing of fresh notes/currency notes. Money printing at higher rate to pay the government expenditures leads to inflation that enables the government to secure extra resources though that is called 'inflation tax' also.

SEQUESTRATION

The process under which a third party (*the sequestrator*) holds a part of the disputed assets till the dispute is settled.

SHADOW BANKING

When financial intitutions create credit (forward loan) like a bank but are not under the banking reguatory framework of the country, they are supposed to be involved in shadow banking. Hedge funds are one such example. It also includes unregulated activities of regulated entities. Credit default swaps (CDS) are the examples of it—regulated entities (like banks) provide loan protection in it to other lenders against default risks by the borrowers.

As such institutions do not accept traditional bank deposits they easily escape the regulatory design of a country. Such acts are financially risky to the economy, as in it 'capital requirements' (of CRR, SLR, etc.) are bypassed by the institutions. This is why in cases of default there remains no standby capital/asset to counter it. After the 'sub-prime' crisis in USA (2007-08), shadow banking came under increasing scrutiny and regulation across the world.

SHARPE RATIO

The idea of William Forsyth Sharpe (Nobel Economist) which checks whether the rewards from an investment justify the risk. For this Sharpe uses past data of rewards and calculates it using standard deviation. This is why the ratio says nothing about the future performance of the investment.

SHORT SELLING

Selling shares without possessing them. After the prices fell to a certain extent the short-seller covers his position by cheaper shares booking the difference in price as profits. It is also known as *bear operation*. Short-sellers, however, could get caught on the wrong foot if the market reverses the downtrend.

SHUTDOWN PRICE

That lower level of the prices for the product of a firm at which the firm decides to close (*shut*) down – as it has become impossible to recover even the short-run variable cost at the price. Many such instances we get in the Euro-American economies during the period of the Great Depression (1929).

SKIMMING PRICE

A pricing method of charging high profits— adopted by a firm when consumers are not price-sensitive and demand is price-inelastic.

SMURFING

Smurfing (also called structuring) is a method in which small sizes of money is kept in several number of bank accounts to hide the real identity of the real owner. This has been a very commonly used method of money-laundering. During the reform period, as more prudential norms of banking regulation evolved, such acts declined in India. 'Smurfer' (or 'money mule') is a person who does this.

SOCIAL COSTS

The costs borne by the society at large resulting from the economic activities by the firms—pollution being a prominent example.

SOLVENCY MARGIN

The term made news in the 1970s concerning a life insurance company. The only requirement, till then, by a life insurance company was that the value of its assets should not be less than the value of its liabilities. The regulators in many countries felt that the value of assets should exceed the value of liabilities by a certain margin. This margin which came to be known as *solvency margin* became a useful device to force shareholder of a life insurance company either to keep in reserve a certain portion of the profit or to bring in additional capital if there is not sufficient profit to meet unforeseen contigencies. The European Union developed an empirical formula taking recourse to the past experience to determine the quantum of margin required. The IRDA has stipulated that the excess of assets (including capital) over liabilities should not be less than 150 per cent of the solvency margin arrived at by the EU formula.

SOVEREIGN RISK

The risk of a government defaulting on its debt or a loan guaranteed by it (all international loans by the private companies are basically guaranteed by the government of an economy).

SPOT PRICE

The price quoted for anything in a transaction where the payment and delivery is to be done now.

SPREAD

A frequently used term of financial market which is the difference between two items, for example, the spread (i.e., the difference) an underwriter pays for an issue of bonds from a company and the price it charges from the public. Similarly, the returns on two different bonds if they are different; the difference is known as the spread.

STANDARD DEVIATION

It is a statistical technique to measure how far a variable moves over time away from its mean (average) value.

STEALTH TAX

A popular name given to an obscure tax increase as for example stamp duty, property tax etc. Which get implemented months later by the time they usually fade out from the public memory.

STOCHASTIC PROCESS

It is a process that shows random behaviour. As for example, *Brownian* motion which is often used to describe changes in share prices by the experts in an efficient market (random walk), is such a process.

SUB-PRIME CRISIS

The word 'sub-prime' refers to borrowers who do not have sound track record of repayment of loans (*it means such borrowers are not 'prime' thus they could be called as 'less than prime' i.e. 'sub-*

prime'). The 'sub-prime crisis' which has been echoing time and again recently has its origin in the United States housing market by Late 2007—being considered as the major financial crisis of the new millenium.

Basically, the period 2000-07 had seen a gradual softening of international interest rates, relatively easier liquidity conditions across the world motivating the investor (i.e., banks, financial institutions, etc.) to expand their presence in the sub-prime market, too. The risks inherent in sub-prime loans were sliced into different components and packed into a host of securities, referred to as asset-backed securities and *collaterised debt obligations* (CDOs). Credit rating agencies have assigned risk ranks (e.g., AAA, BBB, etc.) to them to facilitate their marketability. Because of the complex nature of these new products, intermediaries (such as hedge funds, pension funds, banks, etc.) who held them in their portfolio or through special purpose vehicle (SPVs), were not fully aware of the risks involved. When interest rates rose leading to defaults in the housing sector, the value of the underlying loans declined along with the price of these products. As a result institutions were saddled with illiquid and value-eroded instruments, leading to liquidity crunch. This crisis of the capital market subsequently spread to money market as well.

The policy response in the US and the Euro area has been to address the issue of enhancing liquidity as well as to restore the faith in the financial system. The sub-prime crisis has also impacted the emerging economies, depending on their exposure to the sub-prime and related assets.

India remained relatively insulated from this crisis. The banks and financial institutions in India do not have marked exposure to the sub-prime and related assets in matured markets. Further, India's gradual approach to the financial sector reforms process, with the building of appropriate safeguards to ensure stability, has played a positive role in keeping India immune from such shocks.

SUBSIDY BIDDING

It is competitive bidding for subsidies, where companies bid against one another to serve an area at the lowest price—the lure is the subsidy and other benefits. This system is a way of administrating subsidies without leaving any room for some competitors or technologies gaining an edge over others. But competitive bidding has anticompetitive effects, since it gives a special advantage to one company. Regulators should adopt a consumer choice system, under which any subsidy for each high cost customer it served. If the customer moved to a competing carrier, the subsidy would move, too.

SUBSTITUTION EFFECT

The replacement of one product for another resulting from a change in their relative prices.

SUNK COSTS

The costs in commercial activities that have been incurred and cannot be reversed. The cost on advertisement, research and development, etc. are examples of such costs. Sunk costs are a big deterrant to new entrants in the commercial world as after the venture has failed these costs cannot be recovered—there is no two-way process here.

SWAP

The act of exchanging one by another. It could be of many economic items:

Currency Swap

The simultanous buying and selling of foreign currencies could be *spot* or *forward/future* currency swaps. This is used by MNCs to minimise the risk of losses arising from exchange rate changes.

Debt swap

Exchanging one debt by another for a fresh term of repayment schedule at the same or usually lower interest rates.

Interest Rate Swap

Exchanging one debt of a particular interest rate for another at lower interest rate.

Product Swap

Exchanging one product for the other as wheat for milk (similar to barter).

SWFs

Sovereign wealth funds (SWFs) are the foreign currency funds held by the governments of the world, specially in Asia and West Asia. After the process of globalisation, freer capital movements to the developing economies had brought enough foreign currencies to some economies. Earlier, such funds used to originate in Singapore and Norway but now we see china, Russia, and the Middle East emerging as the new SWFs economies.

Such funds, estimated to be sitting on a total of $25 trillion, are eagerly looking to diversify into higher yielding riskier assets. Any fast growing economy with open and liberal attitudes to foreign investments with opportunities for investment may face up the inflow of such funds. India is one fit candidate today.

Such funds need to be studied and alloowed entry cautiously as they bring in non-market and extraneous factors with them too, having potential diplomatic, strategic and sovereign dangers to the host economies. In November 2007, the National Security Advisor of India voiced apprehension about such funds.

SWISS FORMULA

Tariff cut formulae are either linear or non-linear. A Swiss formula is a non-linear formula. In a linear formula, tariffs are reduced by the same percentage irrespective of how high the initial tariff is. As opposed to a linear formula, in a non-linear formula, tariff cuts are directly or inversely proportional to the initial tariff rate.

In the Swiss formula, tariff cuts are proportionally higher for tariffs which are initially higher. For instance, a country which has an initial tariff of 30 per cent on a product will have to undertake proportionally higher cuts than a country which has an initial tariff of 20 per cent on the same product.

In the on-going multilateral trade negotiations at the World Trade Organisation (WTO), it has been decided by all participating countries to use the Swiss formula for reducing import tariffs on industrial goods. After a long-standing debate on the number of reduction coefficients to be used in the formula, a unanimous decision was recently taken that there would be two sets of coefficients—one for the developed countries and another for developing countries. A decision on the value of the coefficient is yet to be taken.

India's average tariffs are much higher than those existing in the developed countries. If a linear formula for tariff reduction was used, then its reduction burden would have been proportional to that of developed countries. However, using a Swiss formula could lead India to taking on a greater reduction commitment than its developed counterparts with lower initial tariffs.

SYSTEMIC RISK

The risk of damage to the health of the whole financial system. In modern financial world, the collapse of one bank could bring down the whole financial system.

TAKEOVER

The process of one firm acquiring the other, also known as *acquisition*. As opposed to the merger which is an outcome of 'mutual agreement', takeovers are 'hostile' moves.

Takeovers may be classified into three broad categories:

(i) *Horizontal takeovers* involve firms which are direct competitors in the same market;

(ii) *Vertical takeovers* involve the firms having supplier-customer relationship; and

(iii) *Conglomerate takeovers* involve the firms operating in unrelated markets but intend diversification.

TAKEOVER BID

An attempt of acquiring the majority share in a firm by another firm. There are various *terms* to show the *'tactics'* applied in such bids either by the bidder or the bidded firms:

Black Knight

The launch of an unwelcome takeover bid (as the Mittal's for the Arcelor in recent past).

Golden Parachute

A generous severance term written into the employment contracts of the directors (of a firm) which makes it expensive to sack them if the firm is taken over.

Green Mail

A situation of takeover bid when the bought-up shares by a potential bidder is actually being bought by the directors of the firm itself.

Leveraged Bid

A takeover bid being financed primarily by the loan.

Pac-man Defence

A situation when the firm being bidded for takeover, bids for the bidder firm itself—also known as *reverse takeover bid*.

Poison Pill

A tactic used by the firm being bidded of merging with some other firm in order to make itself less attractive (financially or structurally) to the potential bidder.

Porcupine

Any agreements between the firm being bidded and its suppliers, creditors, etc., which are so complex that after the takeover the bidder firm feels diffculties integrating it.

Shark Repellants

The measures specially designed to discourage takeover bidders (e.g., altering the firm's articles of association to increase the proportion of shareholder votes needed to approve the bid above the usual 50 per cent level, etc.).

White Knight

The intervention of a third firm in a takeover bid which either merges with or takes over the victim firm to rescue it from the unwelcome bidder.

TAX INVERSION

This is a situation of tax structure. This takes place when a firm bases its headquarters in a low tax country while keeps its material operations in the high tax countries (generally their country of origin). This way, firms cut their tax payment liabilities. This is legal and is a method of tax avoidance. Multinational corporations (MNCs) keep doing this—several MNCs of the US-origin shifted their headquarters to the UK, during 1970s and 1980s. The countries in the world which have very low tax regime for corporations have emerged as a very attractive loactions for the headquarters of big corporations. Bermuda, Virgin Islands, etc. are such countries (popularly known as the 'tax havens').

TECHNOLOGICAL UNEMPLOYMENT

Unemployment which results from the automation of the production activities (*i.e., machines replacing men*).

THIRD-PARTY INSURANCE

Motor third-party insurance or third-party insurance is a statutory requirement under the Motor vehicle Act in India–also known as *'act only'* cover. A person purchasing a motor vehicle has to go for this compulsory insurance which benefits the third person (i.e. neither the vehicle owner nor the insurance company)–the person who becomes victim of an accident by the vehicle.

Till December 31, 2005, the premium for the insurance was fixed by the Tariff Advisory Committee (an arm of the IRDA) but since then it has been done away with. However, IRDA still continues to fix the premium for the mandatory third-party insurance, though the insurance companies have the freedom to decide on prices for comprehensive cover.

The amount of compensation is largely decided by the earning capacity of the accident victim.

THIRD WAY

An economic philosophy (better say rhetoric) which propagates it is neither capitalism nor socialism but a third (pragmatic) way.

The idea was popularised in the late 20th century by some political leaders having leftist leanings, including bill clinton and Tony Blair. Though it has been hard to pin down it was earlier used to describe the economic model of Sweden.

TIGHT MONEY

When money has become difficult to mobilise, the term is used to show the 'dear money' when the rates of interest run comparatively on the higher side.

TILL MONEY

The notes and coins the commercial banks keep to meet everyday cash requirements of their customers (this is counted as part of their CRR).

TOBIN TAX

A prosposal of imposing small tax on all foreign exchange transactions with the obejctive to discourage destabilising speculation and volatility in the foreign exchange markets.

Proposed by the Nobel prize-winning economist James Tobin (1918–2002), the tax has never been implemented anywhere in the world so far.

TOTAL PRODUCT

The main/core product supported by many peripheral products/services, as for example a car, coming with loan facility, warranties, insurance, and after sale service, etc.

TRADE CREATION

The increase in international trade that results from the elimination or reduction of trade barriers (such as quota, customs, etc.).

TRAGEDY OF THE COMMONS

Refers to the dangers of over-exploitation of resources due to lack of property rights over them ('commons' are the resources neither owned privately nor by the state but are open for free use by all). A rationing or imposing of levy on such resources as a check.

The concept was proposed by a 19th century amateur mathematician william Forster Lloyd.

TRANSFER PAYMENTS

The expenditure by the government for which it receives no goods or services. For example, the expenditures on tax collection, social sector, unemployment allowance, etc.

As such expenditures are not done against any products they are not counted in the national income of the economy.

TRANSFER EARNINGS

The return that an asset must earn to prevent its transfer to the next best alternative use. Any earning above the transfer earnings is known as its *'economic rent'*.

TRANSFER PRICE

A term of international economics via which an MNC charges lesser prices for its exportables to its arm in another economy where tax rates are high, for increasing income. The East India Company did it heavily in pre-independent India.

ULIPS & MFS

Unit Linked Insurance Policies (ULIPs) offer insurance plus investment objectives to those who want a higher amount of insurance cover at a marginally higher cost. However, unlike mutual funds, which may be a short-term investment play, ULIPs meet long-term investment objectives. Essentially, ULIPs must be treated as long-term (15-plus years) investment vehicles.

Returns are varied across the risk class. One can categorise risks into three classes for both MF and ULIP schemes—high, medium, and low risks. High-risk policies have a higher exposure to equities and low-risk policies might have low or no exposure to equities. For MFs, high-risk comparable products are diversified equity funds, medium-risks are balanced funds, and low risks are debt instruments.

UNDERWRITING

The process of acceptance by a financial institution of the financial risks of a transaction for a fee. For example, merchant banks underwrite new share issues, guaranteeing to buy up the shares not sold in a public offer (i.e., in the situations of under-subscription).

UNSECURED LOAN

The loan which is forwarded by bank only against the creditworthiness of borrower is known as 'unsecured' loan. Such loans are also known as—*signature loans* and *personal loans*. If the loan is supported by some form of collateral (of secondary type, such as land, building, etc.), then it is 'secured' loan.

Basically, loans are provided by banks against two kinds of securities—the creditwothiness of the borrower (known as the 'primary security') and collateral (known as the 'secondary security').

USURY

Charging an exorbitant rate of interest or even charging interest. Decried by many ancient philosophers and many religions, today most modern economies have some law regulating the upper limit of the interest rates and they consider interest as a reward to the lender for the lending risk.

VGF

The Viability Gap Funding (VGF) is a fund assistance facility provided by the GoI to the private players in the infrastructure projects being developed under public private partnership (PPP). The fund is given by the GoI as one time 'grant' and it could be maximum 20 per cent of the project cost (in special cases an additional 20 per cent might be approved by the ststes/ministries/authorities).

The facility which was operationalised in September 2006, was aimed at attracting private investment towards this socio-economically desirable sector. Several infra projects were economically 'non-viable' which used to discourage private players away from such projects—this facility encourage them to take part.

VEBLEN EFFECT

Named after the American economist Thorstein Bunde Veblen (1857–1929), this is a theory of consumption which suggests that consumers may have an 'upward-sloping demand curve' as opposed to a 'downward-sloping demand curve' because they practice conspicuous consumption (*a downward - sloping demand curve means that the quantity demanded varies inversely to the price i.e. demand falls with price rise*). The concept suggests that quantity demanded of a particular good varies directly with a change in price (*i.e., as price increases, demand increases*).

VELOCITY OF CIRCULATION

A measure of the average number of times each unit of money is used, to purchase the final goods and services produced in an economy in a year.

VENTURE CAPITAL

Generally, a private equity capital which lends capital to the entrepreneurs who are innovative and cannot get the required fund from the conventional set-up of the lending mechanism.

In India, it was the Government of India which did set up the first such fund in 1998–the IVCF.

VULTURE FUNDS

Vulture funds are privately owned financial firms which buy up sovereign debt issued by poor countries at a fraction of its value, then file lawsuits (sue) against the countries in courts, usually in London, New York, or paris, for their full face value plus interest.

A paper prepared for IMF/WB (October 18, 2007) showed that there are now $1.8b lawsuits against poor countries where people typically live below $1 a day; 24 countries that have received debt cancellation under Heavily Indebted Poor Countries (HIPCs)initiative, 11 have been targeted by such creditors (i.e., the VFs) and they has been awarded just under $1b.–money which have gone for schools and hospitals; they are neutralising the good deeds of WB/IMF. As per the IMF, the litigating creditors were concentrated in the US, UK as well as the British Virgin Islands (BVI)—the UK protectorate tax haven. Bush is being pressed by a motion signed by 110 MPs to change the law which allows them to file cases in US courts—VFs contradict US foreign policy.

VOSTRO ACCOUNT

Vostro is an account that one party holds for another. With a view to give more operational leeway, the RBI decided to dispense with the requirement of prior approval of the RBI for opening and maintaining each rupee **vostro account** in India of non-resident exchange houses in connection with the rupee drawing arrangements (RDAs) that banks enter into with them. The approved dealer banks could now take its permission the first time they entered into such an arrangement with non-resident exchange houses from the Gulf countries, Hong Kong, Singapore and Malaysia. Subsequently, they may enter into RDAs, and inform the RBI immediately.

WALRAS' LAW

As per this law, 'the total value of goods demanded in an economy is always idntically equal to the total value of goods supplied'. For this to happen the economy should be in equilibirium. It also means that if there is an excess supply of certain things in one market there must be excess demand for it in an another market. Here 'another market' does not mean the market of an another economy—it is taken as, apple's market, grape's market (as 'seperate' markets). This could be only correct in a barter eoconomy (it does not work in an economy with currency as its mode of exchnage).

The idea was part of the 'general equilibirium theory' developed by the French mathematical economist *Marie-Esprit-Leon Walras* (1834-1910), after whom it is named.

WASTING ASSET

The natural resource which has a finite but indeterminate life span depending upon the rate of depletion (such as coal, oil, etc.).

WEIGHTLESS ECONOMY

The situation of an economy when the output is increasingly produced from intellectual capital rather than physical materials—a shift in production from iron and steel, heavy machines, etc. to microprocessors, fibre optics and transistors, etc. This is the weightless economy, i.e., the *new economy* which arrived in the US (specially) by the end of the 20th century.

WELFARE ECONOMICS

The branch of economics which is concerned with the way economic activity ought to be organised so as to maximise economic welfare. The idea applies to the welfare of individuals as well as countries.

This is normative economics, i.e., it is based on value judgements. It is also called *'economics with a heart'*. This focuses on questions about *equity* as well as *efficiency*.

It employs value judgements about what *ought* to be produced, how production *should* be organised, the way income and wealth *ought* to be distributed, both in present times and in future. As different individuals in different communities have unique set of value judgements (guided by their attitutdes, religion, philosophy, and politics) it has been difficult for the economists to reach a consensual idea upon which they could advise the governments in policy making, known as the *welfare criteria*. Economists and philosophers have been suggesting their brands of the *welfare criteria* since long–Vilfredo Pareto, Nicholas Kaldor, John Hicks, Scitovsky, Amartya Sen, as the few famous ones.

WILDCAT STRIKE

A strike called on by a group of employees without the support of their organised trade union.

WILLIAMSON TRADE-OFF MODEL

A model for evaluating the possible benefits and detriments of a proposed merger that could be used in the application of a discretionary competition policy. The model was developed by Oliver Williamson.

WINNER'S CURSE

The possibility that the winning bidder in an auction will pay too much for an asset since the highest bidder places a higher value on the asset than all other bidders.

WITHHOLDING TAX

A tax imposed on the income on a foreign portfolio (investments). This tax is imposed to discourage foreign investments, to encourage domestic investment, and to raise money for the government.

WORKER (CENSUS DEFINITION)

The *first* definition of 'worker' by *Census* was given in 1872. Over time the term 'work' and 'worker' as defined by **Census of India** have undergone several amendments to suit the changing dimensions of work. 'Work' is defined as participation in any *economically productive activity* with or without compensation, wages or profit. Such participation may be physical and/or mental in nature. Work involves not only actual work but also includes –

(i) Effective supervision and direction of work;

(ii) Part time help or unpaid work on farm, family enterprise or in any other economic activity; and

(iii) Cultivation or milk production even solely for domestic consumption.

Accordingly, as per Census of India, all persons engaged in 'work' defined as participation in any economically productive activity with or without compensation, wages or profit are workers. The Reference period for determining a person as worker and non-worker is one year preceding the date of enumeration.

The Census *classifies* 'Workers' into two groups namely, *Main Workers* (those workers who had worked for the major part of the reference period, i.e., 6 months or more) and *Marginal Workers* (those workers who had not worked for the major part of the reference period i.e. less than 6 months). The *Main* workers are classified on the basis of Industrial category of workers into the following four categories: (i) Cultivators; (ii) Agricultural Labourers; (iii) Household Industry Workers; and (iv) Other Workers.

[See entry *'Non-Worker'* also.]

WORKER POPULATION RATIO

The employment-to-population ratio is defined as the proportion of an economy's working-age population that is employed. As an indicator, the employment-to-population ratio provides information on the ability of an economy to create jobs. Worker population ratio (WPR) is defined as the number of persons employed per thousand persons [WPR= No. of employed persons X 1000/ Total population]. Worker Population Ratio is an indicator used for analyzing the employment situation in the country. This is also useful in knowing the proportion of population that is actively contributing to the production of goods and services in the economy.

WORKFARE

Government programmes which make the receipt of unemployment-related benefits (as unemployment allowance) conditional upon participation in some local work scheme.

X-INEFFICIENCY

A graphic representation of the 'gap' a firm shows in its actual and minimum costs of supplying its products. As per the traditional theory of supply, firms always operate on minimum attainable costs. As opposed to this, x-inefficiency suggests that firms typically operate at higher costs than their minimum attainable costs. This takes place due to many *inefficiencies* (such as organising the works, lack of co-ordination, lack of motivation, bureaucratic rigidities, etc.). Large corporates usually face this problem as they lack effective competition which could 'keep them on their toes'.

YIELD GAP

A method of comparing the performance of bonds and shares in an economy. It is defined as the average returns on shares minus the average returns on bonds.

ZERO-COUPON BOND

A bond bearing zero coupon rate (i.e. no interest) sold at a price lower than its face value. Investors book profit when they sell it (at its face value). Such bonds are popularly used by the governments to raise long-term funds. In a situation of rate cut by the RBI, zero-coupon bonds gain value-it means, they sell at hipher prices. When there is an increase in rate, the opposite happens.

ZERO-SUM GAME

A situation in the *game theory* when the gains made by winners in an economic transaction is equal to the losses suffered by the losers. This is considered a special case in game theory. Most economic transactions are in some sense *positive-sum games.* But in popular discussion of economic issues, there are often examples of mistaken zero-sum mentality, such as profit comes at the expense of wages, 'higher productivity means fewer jobs', and 'imports mean fewer jobs here.'

ZERO TILLING

A relatively new farm production process, is a one-time operation in which a small drill places the seed and the fertiliser in a small furrow, saving the farmer a lot of time and other resources. At first utilised in Haryana in 1999–2000, by now it has spread to the other wheat growing states like, Punjab, Uttar Pradesh, Uttarakhand, and Bihar particularly. The technique gives comparatively higher yield (by over 5 per cent) than the conventional wheat farming.

SELECTED MCQs

(ECONOMIC AND SOCIAL DEVELOPMENT)

A thing may look specious in theory, and yet be ruinous in practice; a thing may look evil in theory, and yet be in practice excellent. *

* *Edmund Burke (1729–1797)*

SET- 1

1. Select the correct statements about the *'hybrid annuity model'* (HAM) which the government has launched recently to promote the road projects in the country—use the codes given below:

   1. It is an improvement over the existing 'engineering-procurement-construction' model of the PPP.

   2. Investment participation in this model is between the GoI and the private firm in the ratio of 40:60.

   3. Toll is to be collected by the government while the private participator gets a fixed amount of annuity for a defined period of time.

   4. Risks related to clearance, compensation, commercial and traffic are to be borne by the government.

   Code:
   (a) 1 and 2
   (b) 1, 2 and 4
   (c) 2, 3 and 4
   (d) 1, 2, 3 and 4

2. Select the correct statements related to the new System of National Accounts to which India shifted recently—using the code given below:

   1. Now, India accounts its national income at 'market price'.

   2. Growth rate of the economy is now measured by 'GDP at constant market price'.

   3. 'Product taxes' added to the 'gross value added' is the 'market price'.

   4. 'Product taxes' are ultimately paid by the consumers of goods and services.

   Code:
   (a) 1 and 2
   (b) 1, 2 and 4
   (c) 2, 3 and 4
   (d) 1, 2, 3 and 4

3. What is correct about the term 'customs value'?

   (a) The value of imported goods as appraised by the customs department and used as the basis for assessing the amount of import duty and other taxes.

   (b) A term to specify the real value of import by deducting any dumping duty imposed by the trading partner.

   (c) The real value of custom duty imposed on the imported item by the custom department.

   (d) None of the above.

4. Consider the following statements about 'terms of trade' of a country.

   1. It is the contractual conditions of sale between a buyer and a seller.

   2. It is the quantity of foreign goods and services that a country can purchase from the proceeds of the sale of its goods and services of a given quantity.

   3. It is a measure of a country's trading clout and is expressed as the ratio of an index of export prices to an index of import prices.

   Select the correct statements using the code given below:
   (a) Only 1
   (b) 2 and 3
   (c) 1 and 3
   (d) 1, 2 and 3

5. Consider the following statement—

   "Most of the world's poor people earn their living from agriculture, so if we knew the economics of agriculture, we would know much of economics of being poor".

   Which of the following document has used the above-given saying of the Economics Nobel Laureate Theodore Schultz?

   (a) Food and Agriculture Organisation Report- 2017 (UNO)

   (b) Economic Survey 2015-16 (GoI)

   (c) Union Budget 2017-18 (GoI)

   (d) World Development Report-2016 (World Bank)

6. Consider the following statements regarding the 'Taylor Rule'.

   1. A rule that suggests appropriate adjustments to interest rates, based on various economic factors such as inflation and employment rate.

   2. The rule indicates that if inflation or employment rates are higher than desired, interest rates should be increased in response to these conditions, and the opposite action should be taken under the opposite conditions.

   Select the incorrect statement/statements using the code given below:

   (a) Only 1

   (b) Only 2

   (c) Both 1 and 2

   (d) None of the above

7. Consider the following statements about the 'Laffer Curve'.

   1. This is a curve which supposes that for a given economy there is an optimal income tax level to maximise tax revenues.

   2. If the income tax level is set below this level, raising taxes will increase tax revenue.

   3. If the income tax level is set above this level, then lowering taxes will increase tax revenue.

   Select the incorrect statements using the code given below:

   (a) 1 and 2

   (b) 2 and 3

   (c) 1 and 3

   (d) 1, 2 and 3

8. Consider the following statements about the 'insurance repository system', recently introduced in India

   1. Insurance policies will be held in electronic form.

   2. This will provide speed as well as accuracy in revisions and changes in the policies.

   3. IRDA has given licences to five firms to function as insurance repositories.

   4. Repositories are expected to cut down the management cost of each insurance policy to almost one-fifth of the present cost.

   Select the correct statements using the code given below:

   (a) 1, 2 and 3

   (b) 2, 3 and 4

   (c) 1, 3 and 4

   (d) 1, 2, 3 and 4

9. Consider the following statements about the idea of 'inclusive growth'.

   1. The idea of 'inclusive growth' entered into the domain of planning with the Eleventh Plan.

   2. This is not only about economics but also about 'social' inclusion.

3. The main idea behind inclusive growth is to include SCs, STs, OBCs, minorities and women in the country's development process.

4. The 3rd Generation of Economic Reforms runs parallel to the idea of inclusive growth.

Select the correct statements using the code given below:

(a) 1, 2 and 3

(b) 2, 3 and 4

(c) 1, 3 and 4

(d) 1, 2 , 3 and 4

10. 'Bad bank' was recently in news—select the statements correct about it, using the code given below:

1. It is a bank which buys the bad loans of the banks

2. Government of India is presently consider to set up such a bank.

3. It will help India come out of the twin balance sheet problem.

Code:

(a) 1 and 2

(b) 2 and 3

(c) 1 and 3

(d) 1, 2 and 3

11. Consider the following statements about the *Results-Framework Document (RFD).*

1. 'RFD' provides a summary of the most important results that an organisation expects to achieve during the financial year.

2. It moves the focus of the organisation 'from process-orientation' to 'result-orientation'.

3. It provides an 'objective' and fair basis to 'evaluate' organisation's overall performance at the year end.

Select the correct statement/statements using the code given below:

(a) 1 and 2

(b) 2 and 3

(c) 1, 2 and 3

(d) None of the above

12. Consider the following statements about 'effective revenue deficit':

1. "Effective revenue deficit is a Western idea of public finance management, which India used it for the first time in the Union Budget 2011–12.

2. It is a modified kind of revenue deficit which excludes that part of revenue deficit by which assets have been created.

Select the correct statements using the code given below:

(a) Only 1

(b) Only 2

(c) 1 and 2

(d) Neither 1 nor 2

13. Consider the following statements about 'farm subsidies' in India.

1. The input subsidies in India such as on fertilizers fall under indirect farm subsidies.

2. Reduction in power and irrigation bills offered to farmers fall under direct farm subsidies.

3. The agricultural provisions of the WTO though allow direct farm subsidies, prohibits indirect subsidies.

4. All subsidies forwarded by the governments in India fall under the indirect category.

Select the correct statements using the code given below:

(a) 1 and 2

(b) 2 and 3

(c) 3 and 4

(d) 1 and 4

14. Consider the following statements related to the Bilateral Investment Promotion and Protection Agreement (BIPA).

1. The agreement is part of the World Bank's International Centre for Settlement of Investment Disputes (ICSID).

2. This promotes and protects the Indian investors investing abroad.

3. Promoting and protecting foreign investment in India is one of its objectives.

4. The Agreement functions in collaboration with the International Monetary Fund.

Select the correct statements using the code given below:

(a) 1 and 2

(b) 2 and 3

(c) 3 and 4

(d) 1 and 4

15. Consider the following statements about NSEL which was recently in news.

1. This is an NSE (National Stock Exchange) promoted commodity 'spot trading' platform.

2. 'NCDEX Spot' and 'R-Next' are the other such platforms.

3. Commodity exchanges in India are regulated by the Ministry of Consumer Affairs under the Forward Contract Regulation Act, 1989.

4. 'Spot contracts' has to be completed within 11 days, as per the Act.

Select the incorrect statements using the code given below:

(a) 1 and 2

(b) 2 and 3

(c) 2 and 4

(d) 1 and 3

16. Participatory Notes (P-Notes) were in news recently. Consider the following statements about P-Notes:

1. SEBI has classified three possible Categories of P-Notes issuing FIIs in the country.

2. Category-I are the offshore government entities/institutions investing solely on behalf of a country's central bank.

3. Category-II are regulated entities as Mutual Funds, supervised by their regulatory bodies in their countries of origin.

4. Category-III entities neither fall in Category-I or Category-II, which have been recently asked by the SEBI not to issue P-Notes.

Select the correct statements using the code given below:

(a) 1, 2 and 3

(b) 2, 3 and 4

(c) 1, 3 and 4

(d) 1, 2 , 3 and 4

17. Consider the statements about tenets of the 'three arrows' of the *Abenomics* which was recently in news.

1. A massive fiscal stimulus activated by quantitative easing targeted at increasing the rate of inflation.

2. Boost to investment in public works and infrastructure to promote jobs and R&D.

3. Structural reforms to boost country's global competitiveness.

4. It follows ideas started by J. M. Keynes, whose most famous contemporary admirer is the Nobel Economist Paul Krugman.

Select the correct statements using the code below.

(a) 1, 2 and 3

(b) 2, 3 and 4

(c) 1, 3 and 4

(d) 1, 2 , 3 and 4

18. Which of the following statements are correct about the Planning Commission members Som Pal, B. K. Chaturvedi and Abhijit Sen?

(a) They headed the Infrastructure Co-ordinating Monitoring Committees of the PC.

(b) They held the charge of being additional members to different Finance Commissions.

(c) They worked as head of the Committees working on inflation reforms in India in a World Bank assisted project.

(d) None of the above.

19. Consider the following statements about the Fourteenth Finance Commission.

1. The need for insulating the pricing of public utility services like drinking water, irrigation, power and public transport from policy fluctuations through statutory provisions.

2. The need for making the public sector enterprises competitive and market oriented; listing and disinvestment; and relinquishing of non-priority enterprises.

3. The need to balance management of ecology, environment and climate change consistent with sustainable economic development.

4. The impact of the proposed Goods and Services Tax on the finances of Centre and states and the mechanism for compensation in case of any revenue loss.

Which of the following does not belong to the 'terms of reference' given to the Fourteenth Finance Commission?

(a) 1, 2 and 3

(b) 2, 3 and 4

(c) 1, 3 and 4

(d) 1, 2 , 3 and 4

20. Consider the following statements about the recently set up Bharatiya Mahila Bank (BMB).

1. The bank will focus on lending predominantly to women and companies that focus on women's activities/products but there will be no restriction on deposits by men.

2. The bank is looking at providing assistance through credit to set up day-care centres and start organised catering services.

3. BNB will also tie up with NGOs, and train women in various vocations in order to penetrate deeper into rural areas.

4. Chhavi Rajawat, a Sarpanch from Rajasthan is one among the six Board members of the bank.

Select the correct statements using the code given below:

(a) 1, 2 and 3

(b) 2, 3 and 4

(c) 1, 3 and 4

(d) 1, 2 , 3 and 4

21. *Swiss Challenge* was recently in news. Select the correct statements related to it, using the code given below:

    1. It is a method of public procurement through awarding contracts.
    2. Bidders face challenge of improving upon the first bidder.
    3. The new method of awarding contacts is being first time used in India.
    4. This can be used for PPP and non-PPP projects.

    Code:
    (a) 1 and 2
    (b) 1, 3 and 4
    (c) 3 and 4
    (d) 1, 2, 3 and 4

22. Select the correct statements from the list given below, using the code:

    1. Infrastructure sector has the highest share in the non-performing assets of the public sector banks in the country, at the start of the year 2017-18.
    2. From 2001 till 2016-17, banks' lending to the infrastructure sector has grown annually around 40 per cent.

    Code:
    (a) Only 1
    (b) Only 2
    (c) 1 and 2
    (d) Neither 1 nor 2

23. Consider the following statements related to the current provision of using the disinvestment proceeds.

    1. The allocations out of the NIF will be decided by the Union Budget.
    2. Only the profits accruing out of the NIF can be used that too only on the social sector.

    3. During 2013–14, the government approved allocations from the NIF towards spending on recapitalisation of public sector banks.
    4. Fund of the NIF can be used for equity infusion in the Metro projects.

    Select the correct statements using the code given below:
    (a) 1, 2 and 3
    (b) 2, 3 and 4
    (c) 1, 3 and 4
    (d) 1, 2, 3 and 4

24. Consider the following statements related to the State Food Commissions provisioned in the National Food Security Act, 2013.

    1. The five-member commission must have two women and one member each from the SCs and STs.
    2. It may enquire into violations of entitlements either suo moto or on receipt of complaints and will hold powers of a civil court.
    3. It will prepare an annual report of the Act to be laid before the legislature.
    4. The commission will function as one of bodies of the two-tier grievance redressal structure as per the Act.

    Select the correct statements using the code given below:
    (a) 1, 2 and 3
    (b) 2, 3 and 4
    (c) 1, 3 and 4
    (d) 1, 2, 3 and 4

25. Consider the following statements related to the recommendations of the RBI-appointed committee to examine the

current 'monetary policy framework', which has handed over its report recently.

1. The apex bank should adopt the new CPI (consumer price index) as the measure of nominal anchor for policy communication.

2. Food and fuel account for more than 57 per cent of the CPI on which the direct influence of monetary policy is limited.

3. The panel suggests to adopt a longer-term target of 4 per cent for CPI inflation with a band of +/- 2 per cent.

4. The committee asked the central government to ensure that the fiscal deficit as a ratio of the GDP is brought down to 3.0 per cent by 2016–17.

Select the correct statements using the code given below:

Code:

(a) 1, 2 and 3

(b) 2, 3 and 4

(c) 1, 3 and 4

(d) 1, 2 ,3 and 4

Answer Key with Explanations _____

1. *(c)* Hybrid Annuity Model (HAM) is a PPP model to develop road projects while the 'engineering, procurement, construction' (EPC) was fully funded by the GoI. Private sector, in this model, has the responsibility to build the road and hand it over to the government. The selection takes place on the basis of bidding—the bidder which asks for lowest annuity gets the project. The new PPP model was announced by the GoI by late *January 2016*.

2. *(d)* India shifted to the new system in the financial year 2015–16. It is the standard practice across the world and was suggested by the IMF in 2008. Some examples of 'product taxes' are—cenvat, excise, sales tax, vat, service tax, etc. Though the product taxes are imposed on the producers they are ultimately borne by the consumers (it is an indirect tax).

3. *(a)* Customs value (or 'customs import value') is the value of imported goods as appraised/decided/calculated by the customs department of a country. This value is used as the basis for assessing the amount of import duty and other taxes. It may be computed in several ways, but the most-preferred method is transaction-value, which includes other costs incurred by the buyer, such as packaging costs, license fee or royalty, and any other expenses that accrue to the seller (in addition to the price paid by a buyer to a seller). It is the customs officer (and not the importer, exporter, or customs broker) who has the final say in assigning this value.

4. *(b)* This is not the contractual conditions of sale between a buyer and a seller, but the quantity of foreign goods and services (i.e., its total imports) that a country can purchase from the proceeds of the sale of its goods and services (i.e., its total exports) of a given quantity. It is a measure of a country's trading clout and is expressed as the ratio of an index of export prices to an index of import prices. Terms of trade of a country improves when the prices of its exports rise in comparison with the prices of its imports and vice versa.

5. *(b)* To highlight the importance of the agriculture sector in case of India, the Survey first quotes Mahatma Gandhi (India lives in villages) and then Theodore Schultz. In *2016–17*, we see a major shift

in the government's budgetary allocation in favour of the agriculture sector.

6. *(d)* Both the statements are correct about the Rule. The US Federal Reserve Board seems to take this rule under consideration (as many other central banks of the world) but does not always follow its suggestions when adjusting the interest rate. This rule was developed by John Taylor, a 20th century economist.

7. *(d)* All of the statements are correct about the Curve. Although the theory claims that there is a single maximum point of tax rate and moves in either of the directions from this point makes revenues fall, in reality this is only an approximation. This is a 'graphical representation' of a conceptual relationship between *marginal tax rates* and *total tax collections*. Named after the US economics professor Arthur Laffer who proposed that lower tax rates encourage additional output (supply) and thus increase aggregate income. Laffer curve is used by the supporters of 'supply side economics' to back their claim that low income tax policies spur non-inflationary growth by encouraging new investment.

8. *(d)* The present management cost of each insurance policy is Rs. 120, which will come down to Rs. 25 once repositories start functioning. The IRDA has licensed five firms to function as repositories (Karvy Insurance Repositories, NSDL Database Management Ltd, Central Insurance Repositories Ltd., SHCIL Projects Ltd. and CAMS Repositories Services Ltd. Out of the total 52 insurance firms in the country only 20 per cent are ready with the sufficient infrastructure for repositories—GoI may make it mandatory by the 2014–15 fiscal.

9. *(d)* The 3rd generations of economic reforms articulated the idea of 'decentralised' development planning—parallel to the idea of inclusive growth. The concept got reference while the government decided to go for the 2nd and 3rd generation of economic reforms (in the year 2000–01)—the benefits of reforms were found to be non-inclusive in nature.

10. *(d)* The *Economic Survey 2016–17* advised the government to set up such a body which it called 'public sector asset reconstruction agency (PARA)'. It will serve twin purposes—on one hand it will buy the 'non-performing assets' (i.e., bad debts) of the government banks while on the other it will help the corporate sector of the country to come out of the 'red' (their balance sheet in unsustainable)—this way helping India to come out of the 'twin balance sheet' (TBS) problem.

11. *(d)* All of the statements are correct about RFD—adopted by about 84 ministries and departments by 2014–15 since 2009–10 as part of the GoI *Performance Monitoring and Evaluation System (PMES)'* under which each ministries/departments is required to prepare an RFD. This is a step in the direction of improving 'performance' and 'efficiency'.

12. *(b)* The idea was for the first time used by the GoI in the Union Budget 2011–12, but it was not borrowed from the Western nations—this is an Indian idea.

13. *(d)* The agricultural provisions (i.e., the Agreement on Agriculture) of the WTO have put a ceiling on the amount of farm subsidies (both direct and indirect) of the member country—as they distort the free market prices of farm goods.

14. *(b)* The BIPA is a kind of India alternative of the ICSID (one of the World Bank group entity). But it has no links either with the ICISD or IMF. By now, India has signed such agreements with 82 countries.

15. *(c)* NSEL (National Spot Exchange Ltd.) is promoted by a private firm (which owns it by 99 per cent) Financial Technologies India Ltd. and NAFED (National Agricultural Cooperative Marketing Federation of India Ltd.) for 'spot trading' in commodities in India, operating since 2008. Other such bourses—the NCDEX Spot and R-Next, are promoted by the NSE and Reliance Capital, respectively. Since February 2012 'spot contracts' are being looked after by the Forward Market Commission (FMC)—regulated under the Forward Contract (Regulation) Act, 1952.

16. *(d)* All of the statements are correct about the P-Notes.

17. *(d)* Abenomics is the name given to a suite of measures introduced by the Japanese Prime Minister Shinzo Abe after his December 2012 re-election to the post he has held since 2007. Such measures by a government to boost growth is not possible in the case of the recession-hit economies of the Western world—the Japanese economy has an edge over them due to its low levels of inflation and fiscal deficit.

18. *(b)* In 2002 the GoI decided that from now onwards the Planning Commission (PC) will function more or less as a collaborator to the Finance Commission (FC)—the existing PC member Som Pal was made an Additional Member of the Twelfth Finance Commission. B. K. Chaturvedi was the Additional Member to the Thirteenth Finance Commission, Prof.

Abhijit Sen is the Additional Member to the Fourteenth Finance Commission (2015–20), headed by Y. V. Reddy, ex-RBI Governor. Such a suggestion was given by the Fourth Finance Commission headed by P. V. Rajamannar.

19. *(d)* All belong to the terms of reference given to the Fourteenth Finance Commission (2015–20).

20. *(d)* India's first women's bank, the Bharatiya Mahila Bank was inaugurated in Mumbai on November 19, 2013 at the iconic Air India building at Nariman Point in Mumbai.

21. *(b)* This method is being used by the GoI for the first time, though, it has been already used by the states (Andhra Pradesh, Bihar, Gujarat, MP, Punjab, etc.). By late *January 2016*, the Ministry of Railways used this method to award contracts for development of 400 railway stations in the country. Though, the government has been discouraged by the Vijay Kelkar Expert Committee (set up on 'Revisiting and Revitalising the PPP Model of Infrastructure Development'). The committee submitted its report in January 2016 itself.

22. *(c)* Both of the statements are correct.

23. *(c)* In January 2013, the government restructured the National Investment Fund (NIF) and decided that the disinvestment proceeds with effect from the fiscal year 2013–14 will be credited to the existing *Public Account* under the head NIF and they would remain there until withdrawn/invested for the approved purpose by an Union Budget. It was decided that the NIF would be utilised for subscribing to the shares of the CPSE, including public sector banks (their recapitalisation, too) and

insurance companies, to ensure 51 per cent government ownership in them; investment by the government in RRBs, IIFCL, NABARD, Exim Bank; equity infusion in various Metro projects; investment in Bhartiya Nabhikiya Vidyut Nigam Ltd. and Uranium Corporation of India Ltd.; investment in railways towards capital expenditure.

24. *(d)* The NFSA provisions for a two-tier grievance redressal structure—the State Food Commission (SFC) and District Grievance Redressal Officer (DGRO). The DGROs will be appointed by the state governments for each district to hear complaints and take necessary action according to norms to be prescribed by

the state governments. If a complainant (or the officer or authority against whom an order has been passed by the DGRO) is not satisfied, he or she may file an appeal before the SFC. The SFCs have been given power to impose penalties— if an order of the DGRO is not complied with, the concerned authority/officer can impose a fine of up to Rs. 5,000.

25. *(d)* All the statements are correct regarding the *Urjit Patel Committee* which handed over its report by late January 2014 to the RBI. The inflation-related advices of the panel has been accepted and implemented by the RBI, commencing with its 1st Bi-monthly Credit and Monetary Policy for 2014–15, announced in April 2014.

SET- 2

1. Consider the following statements:
   1. RBI takes recourse to open market operations (OMOs) to manage liquidity in the system.
   2. In OMOs, RBI generally sells G-Sec in open market, however, in rare cases it also buys back the same from the market.
   3. A 'debt switch' is a method in which the RBI buys back G-Secs of short-term maturity and replaces it with G-Secs with longer maturity periods.

   Which of the above statements are correct?
   (a) 1 and 2
   (b) 2 and 3
   (c) 1 and 3
   (d) 1, 2 and 3

2. Consider the following statements about Independent Evaluation Office (IEO).
   1. It is inspired from an IMF institution with the same name.

   2. Together with the Flagship Programmes it may evaluate any scheme run by the GoI.
   3. IEO may take the services of civil society and non-governmental research houses of India and abroad.
   4. Its reports will be directly put in the public domain.

   Which of the above statements are correct?
   (a) 1, 2 and 3
   (b) 2, 3 and 4
   (c) 1, 3 and 4
   (d) 1, 2, 3 and 4

3. Since 2016–17, a new methodology has been operationalised by the RBI, for the banks in India, to decide their lending rates—known as the *Marginal Cost of funds based Lending Rate* (**MCLR**). The new method *aims* for which of the following:select your answer using the code given below:

1. to improve transmission of policy rates into the lending rates of banks

2. to improve transparency in the methodology followed by banks for determining interest rates

3. to ensure availability of bank loans at interest rates which are fair to the borrowers as well as the banks

4. to help the banks to become more competitive and enhance their long run value

Code:

(a) 1 and 3

(b) 1, 2 and 4

(c) 1, 3 and 4

(d) 1, 2, 3 and 4

4. Consider the following statements regarding the Marginal Standing Facility (MSF):

1. MSF functions as the last resort for banks to borrow short-term funds.

2. MSF is on the line of the existing LAF and is part of it.

3. Being a penal rate, MSF is a costlier route than repo.

4. MSF is linked to the net demand and time liabilities of the banks.

Which of the above statements are correct?

(a) 1, 2 and 3

(b) 2, 3 and 4

(c) 1, 3 and 4

(d) 1, 2, 3 and 4

5. RBI recently announced revised norms for Priority Sector Lending in India. Consider the following statement in the light of the announcement.

1. Foreign banks' PSL target has been increased to 40 per cent at par with Indian banks irrespective of their number of branches.

2. Food and Agro-processing and overdrafts up to Rs. 50,000 in no-frill accounts have been included in it.

3. Off-grid solar and other renewable energy solutions together with vocational education are now under the PSL.

4. MSE loans up to Rs. 2 crore have also been added under the PSL lending of the banks.

Which of the above statements are correct?

(a) 1, 2 and 3

(b) 2, 3 and 4

(c) 1, 3 and 4

(d) 1, 2, 3 and 4

6. Which of the following segments of money is considered as the 'Other' deposits with the RBI?

1. Deposits of quasi-government bodies

2. Other financial institutions and primary dealers

3. Balance in the accounts of foreign central banks and governments

4. Accounts of international agencies

Select your answer using the code below:

(a) 1, 2 and 3

(b) 2, 3 and 4

(c) 1, 3 and 4

(d) 1, 2, 3 and 4

7. As per the New Monetary Aggregates of the RBI which of the following is not regarded as 'broad money'?

1. Bankers' deposits with the RBI

2. Demand & Time Deposits of the banks

3. Other Deposits with the RBI

4. Currency & coins with the public

5. Currency in circulation

6. Savings of Post Offices

Select your answer using the code below:

Code:

(a) 1, 2 and 4

(b) 3, 4 and 5

(c) 1, 5 and 6

(d) 2, 3 and 4

8. Which of the following segments of the money form India's 'Reserve Money'? Give your answer using the code given below:

1. Net forex reserves with the RBI

2. GoI currency liabilities to the public

3. RBI's net credit to Banks and the GoI

4. Non-monetary liabilities of the RBI

Select your answer using the code below:

(a) 1, 2 and 3

(b) 2, 3 and 4

(c) 1, 3 and 4

(d) 1, 2, 3 and 4

9. Consider the following statements regarding the Regional Rural Banks (RRBs) in India.

1. The share capital of the RRBs is sponsored by the GoI, RBI and the Scheduled Commercial Banks in the ratio of 50 percent, 35 percent and 15 percent.

2. Its main objective is to enlarge institutional credit for the rural and agriculture sector.

3. RRBs are being restructured by the GoI under the recommendations of the Vyas Committee.

4. Appointments to the RRB's are done by the sponsoring Scheduled Commercial Banks which falls outside the domain of the IBPS recruitment process.

Which of the above statements about RRBs are correct?

(a) 1 and 2

(b) 2 and 3

(c) 1 and 3

(d) 3 and 4

10. Which of the following statements is correct about the term 'bank run'?

(a) The net balance of money a bank has in its chest at the end of the day's business.

(b) A panic situation when deposit holders start withdrawing cash from the banks.

(c) The ratio of bank's total deposits and its total liabilities.

(d) The period in which a bank creates the highest credit in the market.

11. Consider the following statements.

1. Bond holders and depositors both suffer due to increased inflation.

2. RBI's profits out of its investments in the Treasury Bills fall due to increased inflation.

3. Bond holders' income increases with increased inflation in case of an inflation-indexed bond.

4. Cost of governments' market borrowings increases in deflationary situation.

Which of the above statements are correct?

(a) 1, 2 and 3

(b) 2, 3 and 4

(c) 1, 2 and 4

(d) 1, 2, 3 and 4

12. Consider the following statements regarding the operations of the various money market components in India:

1. Commercial Paper route of borrowing working capital is profitable once inflation has peaked.

2. Cost of operation for the banks in the Call Money Market falls in the wake of rising inflation.

3. Earnings from Money Market Mutual Funds.

4. Interest payments liabilities of the GoI on account of the Cash Management Bill increases in case of decreased inflation.

Select the correct statements using the code below.

(a) 1, 2 and 3
(b) 2, 3 and 4
(c) 1, 2 and 4
(d) 1, 2, 3 and 4

13. Consider the following statements.

1. Governments cost of loan repayment is minimum once the inflation is maximum.

2. Tax collections of governments increase with increased inflation.

3. Seignorage is a double-edged technique to increase governments' income.

Select the correct statements using the code below.

(a) 1 and 2
(b) 2 and 3
(c) 1 and 3
(d) 1, 2 and 3

14. Consider the following statements related to the functions of RBI.

1. The final decision regarding Credit & Monetary Policy is taken by the Union Ministry of Finance.

2. Open Market Operations by the RBI comes under its autonomous powers.

3. Ultimate power of issuing fresh currency notes in India remains with the RBI.

4. RBI has been given full autonomy in the area of regulating the All India Financial Institutions.

Which of the above statements are incorrect?

(a) 1, 2 and 3
(b) 2, 3 and 4
(c) 1, 3 and 4
(d) 1, 2, 3 and 4

15. Consider the following statements about 'market maker'.

1. Market maker is a kind of broker in India's security market who quotes two-way prices for the securities.

2. On the platform of the Over the Counter Stock Exchange of India Ltd. (OTCEI) only market makers are allowed to trade.

3. The Discount and Finance House of India (DFHI) is the chief market maker in India's Money Market.

4. Brokers have no compulsions of quoting two-way prices of securities though they may do so voluntarily.

Which of the above statements are correct?

(a) 1, 2 and 3
(b) 2, 3 and 4
(c) 1, 3 and 4
(d) 1, 2, 3 and 4

16. Consider the following statements regarding Commodity Future Trading in India.

1. It is the best tool of maintaining stable prices for the commodities.

2. Price discovery at Commodity Exchanges discounts the local and global factors in the process of price search.

3. This is highly suitable for the agricultural commodities in India where highest price fluctuations happen due to various natural and man-made reasons.

4. At times, GoI bans trading in certain agricultural commodities as in short-term it may lead to speculative price rises.

Which of the above statements are correct?

(a) 1, 2 and 3
(b) 2, 3 and 4
(c) 1, 3 and 4
(d) 1, 2, 3 and 4

17. Consider the following statements about the 'private placement' route to raise capital from the primary security market.

1. Shares are sold to a select group of investors through a process of direct negotiations.

2. This is completely opposite to the public issue route where no negotiation takes place with the investors.

3. Other than the foreign and domestic financial institutions, individuals too can participate in it.

Which of the above statements are correct?

(a) 1 and 2
(b) 2 and 3
(c) 1 and 3
(d) 1, 2 and 3

18. Consider the following statements related to a limited liability firm.

1. Nominal Capital of a company is the limit up to which a company can issue shares.

2. Registered Capital and Authorised Capital of a company are synonyms.

3. Paid-up Capital of a company can never be more than its Issued Capital.

4. Upper limit of Paid-up Capital of a company is its Authorised Capital.

Select the correct statements using the code below.

(a) 1, 2 and 3
(b) 2, 3 and 4
(c) 1, 3 and 4
(d) 1, 2, 3 and 4

19. Consider the following statements related to the Angel Investors.

1. Such investors are focused on helping the business succeed rather than reaping a huge profit from their investment.

2. Conceptually, in profit motive, they are exact opposite of a 'venture capitalist'.

3. They usually invest in 'person' rather than in the viability of the business.

4. In India, they are classified as a category of 'venture capital funds'.

Select the correct statements using the code below.

(a) 1, 2 and 3
(b) 2, 3 and 4
(c) 1, 3 and 4
(d) 1, 2, 3 and 4

20. Consider the following statements.

1. Indian Depository Receipts (IDRs) allow Indian investors to invest in foreign companies in rupees.

2. Global Depository Receipts (GDRs) make it possible for foreign investors

to invest in Indian companies in their currencies.

3. IDRs are issued in India by a Domestic Depository.

4. Though India has provisions for IDRs, foreign companies are yet to issue IDRs in India.

Select the correct statements using the code below.

(a) 1, 2 and 3

(b) 2, 3 and 4

(c) 1, 3 and 4

(d) 1, 2, 3 and 4

21. Consider the following statements about the recently set up Bharatiya Mahila Bank (BMB).

1. Its lending is restricted only to women; men are allowed to deposit money in BMB.

2. The bank is looking at providing assistance through credit to set up day care centres and start organised catering services.

3. The bank may tie up with NGOs in the process of promoting vocations among the rural women.

4. The savings interest rate for one lakh rupee and above is 5 per cent while interest for deposits of one year is 9 percent.

Which of the above statements are correct?

(a) 1, 2 and 3

(b) 2, 3 and 4

(c) 1, 3 and 4

(d) 1, 2 ,3 and 4

22. A new disinvestment policy was announced by the Government recently—select the correct statements related to it, using the code given below;

1. As per the new policy the PSUs can be now privatised.

2. Government of India can sell the shares of the PSUs upto 100 per cent, too.

3. PSUs will be used to attract more investment in the economy.

Code:

(a) Only 1

(b) 2 and 3

(c) Only 2

(d) 1, 2 and 3

23. Consider the following statements about 'capital consumption'.

1. A situation, when due to the losses of a company in consecutive years make it obliged to pay its current expenses using its capital base.

2. A situation when the listed firms under-report their losses so that they can take higher benefits of depreciation.

3. The process by which a company shows higher loss in its operation to withhold payments of dividends to its various share holders.

Which of the above statements are incorrect?

(a) 1 and 2

(b) 2 and 3

(c) 1 and 3

(d) 1, 2 and 3

24. Consider the following statements about the idea of 'micro-finance' in India.

1. Micro-finance is a small-scale financial intermediation, inclusive of savings, credit, insurance, business services and technical support provided to the needy borrower.

2. The thrust of the micro finance initiative is to channelize production and consumption credit in multiple doses based on the absorption capacity of the prospective borrower.

3. It has evolved through following different models at different times—a 'charity based model' to a 'thrift-based model' and finally to the 'trust and creditworthiness model'.

4. It was in Australia where the link between microfinance institutions and the formal financial institutions evolved.

Select the correct statements using the code below.

(a) 1, 2 and 3
(b) 2, 3 and 4
(c) 1, 3 and 4
(d) 1, 2, 3 and 4

25. In 2017–18, the Government has to launch a programme of 'human resource reforms for results' for which of the following?

(a) mason training in the rural areas
(b) panchayati raj institutions
(c) primary school education
(d) village and agro-industry

Answer Key with Explanations

1. *(c)* OMOs are an effective quantitative policy tool in the armoury of the RBI by which it modulates the liquidity in the system in the short-term. This is a two-way operation—through sell or buy of the G-Secs. The OMOs is constrained by the stock of the G-Secs available with the RBI—once it needs to siphon out money from the market.

2. *(d)* It was set up on February 22, 2014 under the Planning Commission, which

is headed by a Director General (Ajay Chhibber is its first DG). After the NITI Aayog was set up in January 2015, the IEO is there but without a DG – the body is supposed to be abolishe by 2017–18.

3. *(d)* All are the objectives of the new methodology. The MCLR will be a tenor linked internal benchmark and actual lending rates will be determined by adding the components of spread to the MCLR. Banks will review and publish their MCLR of different maturities *every month* on a pre-announced date. The periodicity of reset shall be one year or lower. Banks will continue to review and publish *Base Rate* as hitherto.

As per the RBI *(April 2016),* 'for monetary transmission to occur, lending rates have to be sensitive to the policy rate'. But this was not occurring by now. Banks, by now, have been using either of the following three methods to compute their Base Rate—(i) average cost of funds, (ii) marginal cost of funds, or (iii) blended cost of funds (liabilities).

4. *(c)* RBI announced this route in 2011–12 as a 'penal' route for banks to borrow once they have exhausted all borrowing option, i.e., the repo route. MSF rate is regulated by the RBI above the current repo rate. This route can be used by banks for only overnight borrowings and is linked to their net demand and time liabilities (NDTL).

5. *(b)* Only those foreign banks which have 20 or more branches in the country have been brought at par with domestic banks regarding PSL (in a phased manner over a maximum period of 5 years starting April 1, 2013 to March 31, 2018). The foreign banks with less than 20 branches have no sub-targets within the overall

priority sector lending target of 32 per cent. It is known that the RBI in August 2011 did set up a committee to re-examine the existing classification and suggest revised guidelines with regard to PSL and related issues (chaired by S. M. V. Nair). The committee submitted its report in February 2012.

6. *(d)* The stock of money in 'Other deposits' with the RBI is the liquidity which is available at its disposal for day-to-day uses and are not of any use for long-term purposes. Accounts in international agencies include agencies like IMF and other such bodies.

7. *(c)* In the new monetary aggregate M^3 is the 'broad money' (like the old one). Bankers' deposit is part of the 'reserve money'. Post Offices' saving deposits (excluding National Saving Certificates) are part of M^4. For 'other deposits' see the explanation of the Q. No. 8.

8. *(d)* Non-monetary liabilities of the RBI includes those liabilities which pile up due to its role as 'promoters' to the All India Financial Institutions.

9. *(b)* The share capital of the RRBs are jointly held by the GoI, the sponsoring scheduled commercial banks (SCBs) and the concerned state governments in the ratio of 50 percent, 35 percent and 15 percent. Since December 2012, appointments to the RRBs take place through the Institute of Banking Personnel Selection (IBPS). By now, the RRBs have been amalgamated into 64 only (originally there were 196 such banks set up to 1996 when GoI decided not to further them).

10. *(b)* This happens when there is a fear that the bank has insufficient funds with it—depositors lose confidence in the bank

and start withdrawing their deposits in the concerned bank. This term has been used in contemporary journalism recently in the wake of the high loss fetched by the United Bank of India. Similar situations were seen in the wake of the sub-prime crisis in the US economy—by now, over 300 banks have been closed down in the economy due to losses.

11. *(c)* This question is based on the situation where 'borrowers benefit out of inflation while lenders suffer' (i.e., inflation premium). Inflation-indexed bonds are neutral to the effects of inflation; if someone holds such bonds during inflationary pressures, the interest benefit on it does not see any erosion.

12. *(d)* This question is based on the idea of relationship between 'inflation' and 'real interest rate' which borrowers pay on their borrowings. Components of money market are tools of borrowing 'short-term' (i.e., working capital) money from the financial market—thus inflation affects them in similar ways.

13. *(d)* The idea is the same as 'inflation premium'. Seignorage is a technique by which government intends to increase its tax revenues by issuing fresh currency notes, which brings in extra cash to the government in two ways, one via printed currency and the other through increase in tax income.

14. *(b)* RBI avails no autonomy in its functioning—though the Narasimhan Committee-I in 1991 has suggested autonomy in areas of critical importance, similar to many Western economies. It is believed that it has been given a kind of working autonomy in the area of making and announcing the Credit & Monetary Policy (though there is no change in the official stand hitherto).

15. *(d)* Since market makers quote two-way prices for securities, they seem to 'make' market for the concerned securities. The OTCEI is modelled on the NASDAQ of the USA for listing of SMEs, which face lesser liquidity in their share transactions. The DFHI is a dedicated body for two transactions in the money market of India, operating since 1988.

16. *(d)* All the statements are correct. In case of India's agricultural commodities, such trading doesn't seem functioning well because other related institutional developments have not happened in time and farmers are not yet active players on the commodity exchanges of India (partly due to operational difficulties, smaller capital base and lack of knowledge). Once big farmers (contract/corporate farmers) emerge, it will start functioning in a better way for such commodities.

17. *(d)* Other routes of raising capital from the primary market are: (a) Public Issue and (b) Rights Issue.

18. *(d)* All the options are correct.

19. *(d)* Such investors are usually found among an entrepreneur's family and friends, but they may be from outside also providing financial backing to entrepreneurs for starting their business. The Union Budget 2013–14 promised a provision for them. As per *SEBI (Alternative Investment Funds) Regulations, 2012 (AIF Regulations)*, Category I AIF are those AIFs with 'positive spill over effects' on the economy, for which certain incentives or concessions might be considered by SEBI or the GoI or other regulators in India, which shall include *Venture Capital Funds, SME Funds, Social Venture Funds, Infrastructure Funds* and such other *Alternative Investment Funds(AIFs)* as may be specified.

20. *(a)* Standard Chartered Bank is the only company which has issued IDRs in India. In May 2010 it raised Rs. 2,500 crore through this route.

21. *(b)* It will predominantly deal with women clients, but there is no restriction on having male clients. Inaugurated in November 2013, the BMB focuses on Indian women across economic classes, with special attention to economically neglected, deprived, discriminated, under-banked, unbanked, rural and urban women to ensure inclusive and sustainable growth. The bank with a team of professionals with rich experience and expertise has designed and developed new products and services to suit the needs of women across different segments, including self help groups, women entrepreneurs, salaried women, HNIs and corporate—having six exclusive women members on its Board.

22. *(d)* As per the new policy announced by the Government in 2016–17, any amount of shares can be sold in the public sector undertakings (PSUs). Disinvestment is now seen as the part of 'comprehensive management of Government's investment in the PSUs'.

23. *(d)* Capital consumption is the other term for 'depreciation'. In the process of their uses fixed assets depreciate (go for wear and tear) at the rate decided by the government of the economy—the rates for the same assets may vary across economies.

In the new system of national income accounting it in written as CPC (Consumption of fixed capital)–in use since 2015–16 after the advice of the IMF.

24. *(d)* Microfinance (MF) is a small-scale financial intermediation, inclusive of savings, credit, insurance, business services and technical support provided to the needy borrower. The thrust of the MF initiative is to channelise production and consumption credit in multiple doses based on the absorption capacity of the prospective borrower. The presumption here is that the borrowers possess basic financial literacy and requisite capacity to operate their self-determined economic ventures profitably. The formal existence of MF was found in 1972. A *charity based model* (interest free loans where repayment was based on peer pressure) of MF was evolved in Ireland. Later on, in *Germany*, a *thrift-based model* was developed with establishment of saving funds. Bangladesh Grameen model is based on the principle of trust and creditworthiness of poor with both, obligatory and voluntary saving schemes. The Foundation for Development Cooperation (FDC) of Australia evolved a research project, The Banking with the Poor (BWTP) network to link microfinance institutions with formal financial institutions.

25. *(b)* This was announced in the Union Budget 2017–18. Under this programme the PRIs will be catered with the requisite skills so that they can implement the development programmes more effectively.

SET- 3

1. Consider the following statements about GIC Re.

   1. The public sector reinsurer provides reinsurance support to the life and non-life insurance companies in the country.

   2. It also manages Marine Hull Pool, Indian terrorism insurance pool and India motor third party insurance pool for commercial vehicles on behalf of Indian insurance industry.

   3. It has emerged as a preferred reinsurer in the Afro-Asian region.

   4. It is the third largest aviation reinsurer globally.

   Select the correct statements using the code below.

   Code:

   (a) 1, 2 and 3

   (b) 1, 3 and 4

   (c) 2, 3 and 4

   (d) 1, 2, 3 and 4

2. Which of the following is correct about 'coach mitra' recently in news—

   (a) A single window interface proposed by the Indian Railways to register all coach related complaints and needs.

   (b) An 'app' based service system to help rail passengers to avail entertainment and internet on the go.

   (c) A self-service window for buying rail and platform tickets.

   (d) None of the above.

3. Consider the following statements related to the Central Sales Tax (CST) and the VAT (Value Added Tax).

   1. CST is a destination-based tax of the Centre while VAT is an origin-based tax of the states.

   2. CST is inconsistent with VAT.

3. CST is a cascading-type tax not rebatable against the VAT.

Select the correct statement/statements using the code given below:
(a) Only 1
(b) 1 and 2
(c) Only 3
(d) 1, 2 and 3

4. Consider the given statements regarding subsidies.
   1. They are essential parts of public policy to the extent they are ad hoc arrangements.
   2. While everybody benefits from it, they are not paid by all.
   3. Capital part of subsidies is counted in the planned expenditure of the government.
   4. The FRBM Act has strict provisions regarding subdies.

Select the incorrect statements using the code given below:

Code:
(a) 1, 2 and 3
(b) 1, 3 and 4
(c) 2, 3 and 4
(d) 1, 2, 3 and 4

5. Which among the following is/are not counted as 'public expenditure'.
   1. Expenditure categorised as 'consumption'.
   2. Expenditure known as 'investment' and 'capital creation'
   3. Expenditure in 'running the government'.
   4. Expenditure in forwarding 'external grants'.

Select the correct answer using the code given below:
(a) 1, 2 and 3
(b) 1, 3 and 4
(c) 2, 3 and 4
(d) 1, 2, 3 and 4

6. If the RBI decides to adopt an 'expansionist' monetary policy, which of the following it would not do?
   1. Cut CRR and optimise SLR.
   2. Increase MSF Rate.
   3. Cut Bank Rate and increase Reverse Repo Rate

Select the answer using the code given below:
(a) 1 and 2
(b) Only 1
(c) 2 and 3
(d) Only 2

7. Which of the following 'redistributive' policies the government will not adopt if it wants to bridge economic inequality?
   1. Rationalising subsidies
   2. Progressive tax policies
   3. Regressive expenditure

Select the answer using the code given bolow.
(a) 1 and 2
(b) Only 2
(c) 2 and 3
(d) Only 3

8. Which of the following will be the outcome once an economy is under an inflationary pressure?
   1. Domestic currency heads for depreciation

2. Exports become less competitive with imports getting costlier

3. Cost of borrowing decreases

4. Bond-holders get benefitted

Select the answer using the code given below:

(a) 1 and 2

(b) Only 2

(c) 1 and 3

(d) Only 3

9. Consider the following statements related to the Regional Rural Banks (RRBs).

1. They were conceived as institutions that combine local feel and familiarity with the rural problems, which the cooperatives possess.

2. They were conceived on the line of a business organisation with the ability to mobilise deposits, like a commercial bank.

3. Originally they were intended to provide institutional credit to the weaker sections of the society called 'target groups'.

Select the incorrect statement/statements using the code given below:

(a) 1 and 2

(b) 2 and 3

(c) 1, 2 and 3

(d) None of these

10. Consider the following statements regarding the marginal standing facility rate of the RBI.

1. It is similar to the repo rate for the financial institutions.

2. It is on the lines of the liquidity adjustment facility and part of it.

3. Though it is a costlier route to fulfil overnight requirement of funds, it is not a penal rate.

4. Banks use this route once they exhaust all channels to raise short-term fund.

Select the incorrect statements using the code given below:

(a) 1, 2 and 3

(b) 1, 3 and 4

(c) 2, 3 and 4

(d) 1, 2, 3 and 4

11. Which one of the following statements is not true about Game Theory?

(a) It is a branch of economics that uses models to study interactions between countries, individuals and organisations.

(b) It was devised in 1944 by John Von Neumann and Oscar Morgenstern.

(c) It was often used in political or military context to explain conflicts between countries but has of late been used to map trends in the business world, ranging from how cartels sell prices to how companies can better their goods and services in new markets.

(d) Robert J. Aumann and Thomas C. Schelling were awarded Nobel Prize in Economics in 2005 for their work on this theory.

12. Select the correct statements about 'countervailing duty'—

(a) A tax imposed on import by the importing country to neutralise the benefit of export subsidies offered by the exporting country.

(b) Another name of the anti-dumping duty.

(c) It does not come under the preview of the WTO.

(d) It is opposite to custom duty.

13. Due to certain reasons, it becomes difficult for the Export Credit Gaurantee Corporation to cover pure commercial risks of the medium- and long-term exports originating from India. What are these reasons?

  1. Long repayment period
  2. Large value of contracts
  3. Difficult economic and political conditions in the importing countries
  4. Non-availability of reinsurance for such external projects

  Select the answer using the code give below:

  (a) 1, 2 and 3
  (b) 1, 3 and 4
  (c) 2, 3 and 4
  (d) 1, 2, 3 and 4

14. Consider the following statements about derivatives in India.

  1. A security derived from a debt instrument, share, secured or unsecured loan.
  2. A contract which derives its value from the prices or index of underlying assets.
  3. A security derived from exchange rates and interest rates.
  4. It may be derived from monsoon forcasting.

  Select the correct statements using the code given below:

  (a) 1, 2 and 3
  (b) 1, 3 and 4
  (c) 2, 3 and 4
  (d) 1, 2, 3 and 4

15. 'Net income' term was recently in news—which of the following is correct about it?

  (a) It is balance of a company's total income and its total expenditure.

  (b) The profit of a company after paying corporate tax.

  (c) The income earned by a company over their losses and interest payments.

  (d) The income of a company without deducting their losses.

16. Consider the following statements regarding 'angel investors'.

  1. Investors who provide financial backing to entrepreneurs for starting their business.
  2. They are investors with positive spillover effects.
  3. They may provide finance as loan or as share capital in the upcoming business.
  4. They usually invest in person rather than the economic viability of business.
  5. They are usually from the entrepreneur's family and friends, but may be from outside, too.
  6. Venture capital funds serve similar purpose to the extent arrangement of investible capital is concerned.

  Select the incorrect statements using the code given below:

  (a) 1, 2 and 5
  (b) 2, 3 and 4
  (c) 3, 5 and 6
  (d) None of the above

17. Consider the following items with respect to India's capital account.

  1. foreign currency deposits of the banks
  2. private remittances
  3. security market investments by the RFPIs and QFIs
  4. foreign direct investment
  5. external bonds issued by the GoI
  6. merchandise trade balance
  7. interest liabilities of the expernal loans

Which among the above items is associated with India's capital account?

(a) 1, 3, 4 and 5

(b) 2, 4, 6 and 7

(c) 1, 5, 6 and 7

(d) 1, 3, 6 and 7

18. Consider the following statement regarding the India Inclusive Innovation Fund.

1. The idea is to build innovative enterprise from the bottom of the pyramid (BOP).

2. The fund will provide risk capital to create solutions aimed at enhancing the quality of life at the BOP.

3. Will address the social impact objectives by kick-starting an ecosystem of capacity-building around BOP-focused entrepreneurship.

4. Will address economic return objectives by providing the capacities needed to deliver.

5. The fund will get mobilised from the government, public sector enterprises, corporate sector, venture funds, angel investment and investment firms.

Select the correct statements using the code given below:

(a) 1, 2, 4 and 5

(b) 2, 3, 4 and 5

(c) 1, 3, 4 and 5

(d) 1, 2, 3, 4 and 5

19. As per the circular of the RBI what is correct about the Core Investment Companies (CICs)?

(a) All those companies with a paid-up capital of over Rs. 1,000 crore, which invest primarily in the core industries.

(b) All those NBFCs which invest not less than 90 per cent of their total assets in the form of shares and securities for non-trading purposes.

(c) All the corporate houses with net-owned fund not less than Rs. 1,000 crore invested in the core sector for at least 10 years.

(d) All the Foreign Institutional Investors (FIIs) with a minimum of Rs. 1,000 crore paid-up capital base with at least 80 per cent of it invested in the core industries for long-term purposes.

20. An upsurge has been seen in the NPAs of the public sector banks, recently.

1. Lower economic growth in the country

2. Aggressive lending by banks in the past, especially during good times

3. Lack of right loan-recovery legal provisions

4. Banks shwitching over to a system-based identification of NPAs

Select the correct factors responsible for it using the code given below:

(a) 1, 2 and 3

(b) 2, 3 and 4

(c) 1, 2 and 4

(d) 1, 3 and 4

21. Which of the following are incorrect when the government starts repuchasing its bonds before their maturity periods?

1. Promotion of an 'expansionist' monetary policy

2. An attempt to increase the saving rate of the economy

3. A tool to check the rising inflation

4. Promotion to credit creation by the banks

Select the answer using the code given below:

(a) 1, 2 and 3

(b) 1, 3 and 4

(c) 2, 3 and 4

(d) 1, 2, 3 and 4

22. Consider the following statements about 'narrow banking'.

1. A banking business in which banks go for short-term risk-free lending.

2. A type of retail banking in which banks provide short-term 'open-ended' loans.

3. When banks prefer short-term 'closed-ended' lending to the corporate sector.

4. A banking business which adopts long-term collateralised loans to public.

Select the incorrect statements using the code given below:

(a) 1, 2 and 3

(b) 1, 3 and 4

(c) 2, 3 and 4

(d) 1, 2, 3 and 4

23. Consider the following statements about the 'ordinary shares' of a limited liability firm.

1. They undertake maximum entrepreneurial risk associated with a business venture.

2. These shares do not avail any voting right in the affairs of the company.

3. If a company is going for closure these shares get their claims after the bank loans have been settled and before the preference shares.

4. Company Law provides them no investment claims in the situations of closures.

Select the incorrect statements using the code given below:

(a) 1, 2 and 3

(b) 1, 3 and 4

(c) 2, 3 and 4

(d) 1, 2, 3 and 4

24. Consider the following statements about Grain Bank.

1. Run in tribal and non-tribal rural areas by the Ministry of Tribal Affairs and the Ministry of Consumer Affairs, Food and Public Distribution, respctively.

2. Foodgrains can be borrowed from it by mortgaging dwellings.

3. Established in the food scarce areas, it aims at providing safeguard to all against starvation during natural calamity and lean period.

4. Civil society bodies can also run it.

Select the incorrect statements using the code given below:

(a) 1, 2 and 3

(b) 1, 3 and 4

(c) 2, 3 and 4

(d) 1, 2, 3 and 4

25. NITI Aayog has suggested a new method, the *'price deficiency payment'*, for farmers which is consistent with India's agricultural obligations to the WTO. Select the correct statements regarding it, using the code given below:

1. It suggests to pay a bonus price above the minimum support price (MSP) announced for a crop which will be not more than the market price of the crop.

2. It looks into the prices in the mandis regulated by the Agriculture Produce

Market Committee (APMC) of the states.

3. Farmers to get a maximum payment of the difference between the MSP and market price of a crop.

4. The technology platform of direct benefit transfer (DBT) is to be used for the purpose.

Code:

(a) 1 and 2

(b) 1, 2 and 4

(c) 2, 3 and 4

(d) 1, 2, 3 and 4

Answer Key with Explanation

1. *(b)* It reinsures only 'non-life' segment of the insurance business and is the fifth largest aviation reinsurer in the world. Recently it has been selected as a Manager for Nat Cat Pool promoted by the Federation of Afro-Asian Insurers and Reinsurers (FAIR). GIC Re is financially strong and is rated 'A' (Excellent) by AM Best and 'AAA' by CARE. In 2016–17, the GoI allowed the foreign re-insurance to enter into India.

2. *(a)* This was one of the announcements of the **Union Budget 2017–18**, for railways. At present, for cleaning service of the rail coach a SMS based service (called 'clean my coach service') is operational.

3. *(d)* CST is levied under the provisions of the CST Act, 1956, on the sale of goods of the course of inter-state trade or commerce—levied by the Centre by virtue of Entry 92A of the Union List, but the same is assigned to the states within which the tax is leviable, by virtue of provisions of Article 269 of the Constitution of India. Thus, CST and VAT are inconsistent (similarly it

will be inconsistent with the proposed GST also). This is why after extensive consultations between the Centre and states, the roadmap for *phasing out* the CST by March 31, 2010 (i.e., before the date appointed for the introduction of the GST) has been finalised (the date has got automatically forwarded as the GST was not implemented by that date). Accordingly, the process of phasing out of CST commenced with reduction in CST from 4 per cent to 3 per cent, w.e.f. April 1, 2007, and further to 2 per cent w.e.f. June 1, 2008. Further cut in it is suspended due to delaying of the GST implementation. States have been getting compensation from the Centre for losses accruing due to the CST phase out.

4. *(d)* Basically, subsidies benefit some people while they are paid by the whole population of the economy. Subsidies have been advised by the economists provided they are used as short-term measures—if the ecomony uses them as a long-term measure, they make the population handicapped (those who get them). Subsidies are like putting someone on pain-killers in place of providing the real treatment for the pain! That is why it is always advised by economists that besides subsidies there should be an effective and time-bound long-term policy to impart market-linked purchasing capacity to the population getting subsidy benefit. All subsidies fall under the non-planned expenditure. The FRBM Act has no direct provisions regarding subsidies—it talks about the revenue and fiscal deficits only.

5. *(d)* Every expenditure by the government is part of the public expenditure, be they plan, non-plan, developmental, non-developmental, revenue or capital.

6. *(d)* Following the 'expansionist' policy means encouraging the circulation of money in the economy. Here, except the MSFR increase, all other measures are dedicated to increase liquidity in the system.

7. *(d)* Regressive expenditure will never serve the purpose. The government will need to tax the higher income bracket with higher rate of taxes and rationalise the subsidies so that they go to the needy only and in adequate amount. All these measures are already being operationalised by the GoI.

8. *(c)* Inflation is directly seen converting into proportionate depreciation in the domestic currency. In such situations, exports become cheaper for other countries (which make it more competitive in the world market), besides imports becoming costlier (as the domestic currency loses value in front of the external currency). Real cost of borrowing is calculated by deducting the current rate of inflation (which is higher) from the 'nominal rate of interest/borrowing' (that is the rate of interest banks announce on a certain category of loan). Bond-holders are basically lenders so they suffer—interest income sees dilution.

9. *(d)* The RRBs were modelled to have the local touch of the 'cooperatives' and the business touch of the Scheduled Commercial Banks (SCBs). Since April 1997 they have been allowed to break free from the ceilings interests they forward on deposits or charge on loans (these measures were taken to consolidate the loss-making RRBs). In September 2005 the GoI initiated a process of amalgamation of the banks in a phased manner—accordingly, the total number of RRBs has come down to 46 (from 196) by the end of 2013.

10. *(a)* This route is only for banks, on the lines of the LAF, but it is not its part. It is a penal rate that is why remains always higher than the repo rate. While putting this route in place the RBI has permitted banks to borrow maximum 1 per cent of their Net Demand and Time Liabilities, in coming times it was cut down, too. Similarly, it commenced with a rate of 1 per cent higher than the current repo rate, but over the time it went upto 3 per cent higher than the current repo (in the process of checking inflation, by end 2013).

11. *(a)* Game Theory is a branch of Applied Mathematics which uses models to study interactions between countries, individuals and organisations. It has been used by applied economists in different areas.

12. *(a)* Anti-dumping duty is imposed in similar case but not due to export subsidy given by the exporting country, rather when the country is exporting (dumping) something 'below fair market price'. In both of the taxes an investigation is provisioned by the WTO.

13. *(d)* Overseas projects undertaken by the Indian firms face many political and commercial risks in the importing countries—to provide adequate credit insurance cover to such firms, the government has set up the ECGC under the Ministry of Commerce and Industry, for medium- and long-term exports.

14. *(a)* The derivatives in India has not been allowed to derive their value from the weather forcastings (it is allowed in many developed economies, for example, the USA).

15. *(a)* It is derived by deducting the expenses of the company from its total revenue in

a particular period (usually one year). It is also called *earnings, net earnings* or *net profit*.

16. *(d)* All the statements are correct about angel investors—a term introduced in the Union Budget 2013–14. SEBI puts them in the Category I AIF (Alternative Investment Fund) with 'positive spillover effects'. The venture capital funds also come under this. A venture fund invests in business rather then the person (opposite to the angel investor).

17. *(a)* Private remittances, interest liabilities of foreign loans and trade balance are shown in the current account.

18. *(d)* The idea was proposed by the India Innovation Council for the fiscal 2011–12. This fund is based on the idea of inclusion in the promotion of entrepreneurship—it means it emphasises the social return model unlike the most popular model in the world of promoting the innovations on the items which are for the rich. The Union Budget 2014–15 (Interim) proposed a fund of Rs. 100 crore for this fund.

19. *(b)* CICs are basically the NBFCs carrying on the business of acquisition of shares and securities, which satisfies some conditions, i.e., it holds not less than 90 per cent of its total assets in this form; its investments in the equity shares in group companies constitutes not less than 60 per cent of its total assets; it does not trade in its investments in shares, debt or loans in group companies except through block sale for the purpose of dilution or disinvestment; and it does not carry on any other financial activity except investment in bank deposits, money market instruments, government

securities, loans and investments in group companies.

20. *(c)* Some other factors were also responsible for the increase in NPAs, i.e., increased interest rates in the recent past; current macro-economic situation in the country.

21. *(c)* The money which flows from the government into the system was called the 'cheap currency' by J. M. Keynes. By doing so, governments promote economic activities, which supports the business and trade.

22. *(c)* The term was coined in India by the Narasimhan Committee-II set up on the Banking Sector Reforms (report came in April 1998). This suggestion was given by the committee for the 'weak banks' at that time.

23. *(d)* These shares get voting rigths in their exact proportion as they cover the maximum risk—in a way it is a compensation. As these shares get dividend after all payments have been made by the company, similarly, if the company is being closed down they get their investment claims at the last—after settling the claims of employees, creditors, lenders, government, preference shares etc. Thus, both during life and death of a business, the 'ordinary share holders' are the last to receive their claims.

24. *(a)* Launched in 1996–97 by the Ministry of Tribal Affairs, the centrally sponsored scheme was transferred to the Ministry of Consumer Affairs, Food and Public Distribution in 2004–05. It lends foodgrains without any mortgage to the target population (marginalised people) only. The bank can be run by NGOs, self help group and gram sabha.

25. *(c)* This advice was given by a 'Task Force on Agriculture' of the NITI by late 2015. It suggested that farmers can be made a payment (say 50 per cent) of the difference between the market price and APMC regulated price for a crop, to encourage them produce more. This way, India will be able to promote more food crops as well as not violate the agricultural provisions of the WTO.

Set- 4

1. The 'Ducth disease' has been recently in news in case of the Indian economy. Consider the following statements about the disease.

   1. This is a situation of resource curse
   2. Country's domestic sector becomes uncompetitive
   3. Exchange rate gets bloated due to low inflow of foreign capital
   4. This may be caused by the foreign investments and high remittances

   Select the corrent statements using the code given below:
   (a) 1, 2 and 3
   (b) 2, 3 and 4
   (c) 1, 2 and 4
   (d) 1, 2, 3 and 4

2. Consider the following statements about the WTO-related groups.

   1. G-33 is the group of agricultural importing countries of the world.
   2. C-4 is the group of sub-Saharan countries lobbying for cotton trade reforms.
   3. Crains Group is the lobby of agricultural exporting countries.
   4. G-10 is the group of small countries most vulnerable to agricultural imports.

   Select the correct statements using the code given below:
   (a) 1, 2 and 3
   (b) 2, 3 and 4

   (c) 1, 3 and 4
   (d) 1, 2, 3 and 4

3. Consider the following statement related to the 'developmental' and 'non-developmental' expenditures in India.

   1. Plan expenditure was the leading development expenditure of the government in India.
   2. Maintenance expenses of the assets created by the plan expenditure of the previous years were also considered as developmental expenditures.
   3. Planning Commission mainly dealt with plan expenditures though, in practice, it provisions funds for the non-plan expenditures also.

   Select the incorrect statements using the code given below:
   (a) 1 and 2
   (b) 2 and 3
   (c) 1 and 3
   (d) 1, 2 and 3

4. Consider the following statements regarding depreciation.

   1. Fixed assets losing monetary value over time.
   2. Loss of value in a domestic currency in front of a foreign currency.
   3. Fall in the monetary value of the equipments of a plant due to their use.
   4. It does not happen in case of non-fixed assets.

Select the correct statements using the code given below:

Code:

(a) 1, 2 and 3
(b) 2, 3 and 4
(c) 1, 2 and 4
(d) 1, 2, 3 and 4

5. Deficit financing leads to inflation in general, but it can be checked if—

(a) Government expenditure leads to increase in the aggregate supply in ratio of the aggregate demand.
(b) Only aggregate demand is increased.
(c) All expenditures are used for the national debt payment only.
(d) Fresh currencies are printed to fulfil its deficit financial needs.

6. Consider the following options if all banks in an economy are nationalised and converted into a monopoly bank.

1. Deposits will decrease in the new bank
2. Deposits will increase in the new bank
3. There will be no effect on either saving rate or lending

Select the correct option/options using the code given below:

(a) Only 1
(b) 1 and 2
(c) Only 2
(d) 1 and 3

7. Consider the following statements about the Gross Domestic Capital Formation (GDCF):

(a) Expenditure dedicated to increase or maintain the capital stock in the economy.

(b) Expenditure incurred on physical assets only, even in the case of deficit financing.
(c) Production level overtaking the aggregate demand creating export surpluses.
(d) Addition to the stock of the economy after adjusting the effects of depreciation.

8. Which of the following factors responsible for a surplus in the current account of an economy?

1. Its exports are compulsory imports for other economies.
2. It imports low-technology items and exports high-technology items.
3. It has huge domestic market.
4. Its imports are non-compulsive in nature.

Select the answer using the code given below:

(a) 1, 2 and 3
(b) 2, 3 and 4
(c) 1, 3 and 4
(d) 1, 2 and 4

9. If RBI cuts down the cash reserve ratio it will have the following impact on the economy.

1. Banks will have higher leverage to liquidity
2. Economy may see increased investment
3. Supply of currency in the economy may broaden
4. Real interest rates may decline

Select the answer using the code given below:

(a) 1, 2 and 3
(b) 2, 3 and 4

(c) 1, 2 and 4

(d) 1, 2, 3 and 4

10. Which of the following items appear in a company's balance sheet?

1. Value of raw materials held by the company

2. Cash held in the banks in company's current account

3. Sales revenue of the company

4. The issued capital of the company

Select the answer using the code given below:

(a) 1, 2 and 3

(b) 2, 3 and 4

(c) 1, 2 and 4

(d) 1, 2, 3 and 4

11. The idea of 'currency convertibility' as it is used by the economies today originated in which of the following?

(a) Marshall Plan

(b) Washington Consensus

(c) IMF Plan

(d) None of these

12. Which of the following statement defines the term 'insurance penetration'?

(a) The number of insured per one hundred population in an economy

(b) Insured people per one thousand of the population of an economy

(c) Number of alive and insured per hundred population in an economy

(d) None of the above

13. The exchange rate of a currency in its forex market depends on

1. Its twin deficit

2. The currency regime economy follows for exchange determination

3. Inflation, printing of fresh currencies, levels of forex earnings

Select the answer using the code given below:

(a) 1 and 2

(b) 2 and 3

(c) 1 and 3

(d) 1, 2 and 3

14. Consider the following statements regarding the state of full convertibility of the rupee in the current account.

1. 100 per cent foreign currency is made available by the government at official rate of exchange for all visible and invisible imports.

2. Foreign investment in the Indian security market, though an issue of capital account, is considered as a matter of the current account for convertibility purpose.

3. In case of foreign grants, rupee is partially convertible in India.

4. Rupee is fully convertible if someone needs foreign currency to go for medical treatment abroad.

Select the incorrect statement/statements using the code given below:

(a) 1, 2 and 3

(b) 2, 3 and 4

(c) 1, 2 and 4

(d) 1, 3 and 4

15. The Reserve Bank of India calculates four components of money supply, viz., M^1, M^2, M^3 and M^4. Select the incorrect pair out of the the following.

(a) M^1 consists of the currency and coins with the public; demand deposits of the banks and other deposits with the RBI.

(b) M² consists of M¹ and demand deposits of the post offices.

(c) M³ includes the sum of M¹ and M².

(d) M⁴ includes the sum of M³ and demand as well as time deposits of post offices.

16. Consider the following statements in a situation when a currency goes for devaluation.

    1. Fall in the value of currency vis-á-vis a foreign currency

    2. Exports become less competitive

    3. Trading partners see fall in their export

    4. Imports become costlier

    Select the correct statements using the code given below:

    (a) 1, 2 and 3

    (b) 2, 3 and 4

    (c) 1, 2 and 4

    (d) 1, 3 and 4

17. Purchase tax was recently in news—select the correct statements about it, using the code given below:

    1. The state tax is subsumed in the upcoming GST.

    2. The tax is presently paid by traders and manufacturers on their purchases.

    3. The tax is deductable while paying VAT to the states.

    Code:

    (a) Only 1

    (b) 2 and 3

    (c) 1 and 2

    (d) 1, 2 and 3

18. A state of 'equilibirium' for a consumer means—

    (a) A state of saving rate equal to the growth rate of the economy for the consumer.

    (b) A state of zero saving for the consumer and full expenditure.

    (c) The consumer is unable to fulfil needs with the given income.

    (d) The consumer is able to fulfil needs with a given level of income.

19. Modern economics defines 'tax' as—

    (a) A mode of income redistribution

    (b) A method of effecting transfer pricing

    (c) A way to mobilise resources for government expenditures

    (d) A tool of meeting the social obligations of modern governments

20. Consider the following statements about 'Sensex'.

    1. Sensex is the representative share index of Indian stock market.

    2. Its rise means an overall rise in prices of shares of a group of companies registered with Bombay Stock Exchange.

    3. The shares which are kept in it are of the high net-worth companies.

    4. It is a previledge to be in this 30-shares index.

    Select the incorrect statement/statements using the code given below:

    (a) Only 1

    (b) 1 and 2

    (c) Only 2

    (d) None of these

21. 'Structural reform measures' was one of the two categories of measures announed by the government to be taken under the process of economic reforms in India. These measures deal with—

    1. Redefining the role of the state in the economy

2. Attempting higher participation of private capital—Indian and foreign

3. Increasing aggregate supply in the economy

4. Checking the excessive demand in the economy leading to inflation

Select the answer using the code given below:

(a) 1, 2 and 3

(b) 2, 3 and 4

(c) 1, 2 and 4

(d) 1, 3 and 4

22. Which of the following is correct about the term 'ex-factory price'?

(a) It is 'factory price' added with all indirect taxes of the Centre and the state.

(b) It is the 'ex-showroom price' after deducting the weight of indirect taxes from it.

(c) It is 'factor cost' added with weight of current rate of inflation.

(d) None of these above

23. Select the statement which correctly defines the concept of 'debt trap'.

(a) A situation of an economy which borrows to repay its past borrowings.

(b) A situation when an economy is borrowing higher than what it is repaying for its past borrowings.

(c) A situation when an economy is borrowing to repay even the interest of its past borrowings.

(d) A situation when the forex reserves growth rate of an economy starts lagging behind the growth rate of its external borrowings.

24. Which of the following policy steps a government usually takes to boost demand

and support the economy in deflationary situations?

1. Lowering interest rates together with cutting direct taxes

2. Emphasising savings and enhancing salaries

3. Increasing government expenditure

4. Going for tapering of fiscal stimulus

Select the answer using the code given below:

(a) 1 and 2

(b) 3 and 4

(c) 1 and 3

(d) 1 and 4

25. Recently, the government allowed formation of a new type of 'firm' (business entity) in India—LLP. Select the correct statements related to it, using the code given below:

1. it is a partnership firm.

2. liability of partners does not extend to their personal assets.

3. it can enter into contracts and hold property in its own name.

4. this will enable smaller firms higher access to credit.

Code:

(a) 1 and 2

(b) 1, 2 and 4

(c) 2, 3 and 4

(d) 1, 2, 3 and 4

Answer Key with Explanations

1. *(c)* This is a negative consequence of large increase in a country's income. This disease is primarily associated with a natural resource discovery, but it can result from any large increase in foreign

currency, including FDI, foreign aid or a substantial increase in natural resource prices.

Economists often describe resource-rich countries as suffering from the 'Dutch Disease' or 'resource curse'. The expression comes from the experience of the Netherlands half a century back (in 1960s when the country discovered huge natural gas in the North Sea), which brought in foreign revenue, but reduced the competitiveness of the domestic economy (i.e., exports) on account of a rising exchange rate (bloating of exchange rate). There are many other examples of this phenomenon including countries as different as United Kingdom, Australia and Nigeria.

2. *(b)* These are groupings/lobbies of member countries of the WTO which keep lobbying to serve their interests and create pressure for trade reforms on the platforms of the multilateral trade body. G-33 is also called the 'Friends of Special Product' in agriculture and is a coalition of the developing countries pressing for limited access to their market for agricultural products.

3. *(b)* From 2017–18, India will only have 'revenue' and 'capital' classification of expenditure (as per the **Union Budget 2017–18**).

4. *(d)* This is 'wear and tear' in a fixed/immovable asset due to their use. For different assets the rates of depreciation are announced by the countries—the rates may vary across countries. Depreciation is also used by countries as a toll of economic policy—for example, to boost the sales of heavy vehicles the Government of India has doubled the rate of depreciation of the vehicles (from 20 per cent to 40 per cent).

5. *(a)* The basic reason for price rises in the situatons of defect financing is that governemnts fail to equalise the total demand of the economy by the total supply.

6. *(a)* Monopoly will discourage the depositors from putting money in the bank. The saving rate of the economy together with the lending activities of the bank will also get hampered.

7. *(a)* It means the 'net' addition to the national stock. Future growth of the economy depends on the GDCF.

8. *(d)* Having a huge domestic market never supports current account positively; it may impact the account negatively if its consumers are demanding more of the items which are being imported by the economy. In case of India, the situation is: its imports are compulsive and most of its exports are non-complusive for its trade partners.

9. *(d)* The CRR provides more money in the hands of banks, which may be now lent out for investment and increase the supply of currency in the economy. As the supply of money increases to the banks, they may cut interest rates (cost of money remaining the same).

10. *(c)* The revenues a company gets out of its sale of the manufactured items are not shown in the balance sheet of a company.

11. *(d)* The idea of 'currency convertibility' originated at Bretton Woods, New Hampshire, USA where the twin international economic organisations, viz., the International Monetary Fund and World Bank came into being.

12. *(d)* 'Insurance penetration' is defined as the ratio of underwritten premium in a given year to the GDP of an economy.

13. (d) Exchange rate of a currency depends on so many variables as given in the question. If the economy follows the 'floating currency regime' for the exchange rate determination, the exchange rate is directly linked to all those factors which affects the availability of domestic and foreign currencies in the economy— higher the supply of foreign currency, higher the value domestic currency will have and vice versa.

14. (c) Foreign investments are of two types, viz., one is in the direct form and another in the indirect form (i.e., in security market), both are considered capital inflows. But in the case of convertibility the security investment part of the foreign investment is considered a matter of current account to make it liquid in which rupee is fully convertible (otherwise no foreign investor will come to invest in the share market). Going abroad is a matter of current account, thus rupee is fully convertible for this purpose.

15. (c) M^3 stands for the sum of M^1 and total deposits of the banks (i.e., demand and time deposits of banks). These components of money in India were defined by the 2nd Working Group on Money Stock set up by the RBI in 1972. The 3rd Working Group on the Money Stock submitted its report to the RBI in 1998—as per it the new components of money in India are— M^0, M^1, M^2 and M^3. Together with the new stock of money the Working Group has suggested liquidities formula for the stock, too, namely- L^0, L^1, L^2 and L^3.

16. (c) Though, devaluation in currencies are discouraged and negated with excessive pressure coming from the trading partners of the country, it ultimately makes goods of the country cheaper in the world market— the economy earns profit from exports. The increase in profit of export takes place due to increase in 'volume' of the exports (but in reality, exporters forego more goods to earn the same amount of foreign currency). As foreign currency becomes costlier the country sees decrease in its imports (provided its imports are non-compulsive in nature) due to import substitution.

17. (b) It is one among the eight state taxes which are to be merged into the new federal indirect tax, the GST.

18. (d) Though this ideal stage is reached only in hypothesis—with the changing times, consumers not only demand new goods and services, but new times come with the alternatives of it, too.

19. (a) Incomes of citizens get redistributed after tax—this happens at two levels: once after paying tax and once when the governments use this money to provide essential services to the population. The poorer population uses more of the government services than the richer. The option (c) is also correct but comes later in order.

20. (b) Being in this index does not bring any priviledge to a company. The shares put here are just for representation purpose of the industry.

21. (a) Government never did intend to check the demand—it basically went for the a set of reforms known as the 'macro-economic stabilation measures', which attempts to boost demand in the economy. The whole process of economic reforms in the economy is all about demand and supply management.

22. *(a)* 'Ex-factory Price' and 'Ex-showroom Price' are the same. Factory price is basically, the factor cost.

23. *(c)* Many of the highly indebted countires (HICs) in the sub-Saharan Africa fall under this category. India was very close to a similar situation in early 2000.

24. *(c)* Statement 2 will have contradictory/ neutralising effects on the economy as savings cut demand and salary enhancement increases demand. All these measures were taken by the government during 1996–99 in India when aggregate demand in the economy had fell down to a very low level and inflation was, at one time, just 0.5 per cent (the second fortnight of December, 1999). Tapering in the fiscal stimulus cuts demand in the economy as it syphons out liquidity from the market.

25. *(d)* All of the statements are correct. Such a business entity was allowed by the GoI through the Limited Liability Partnership (LLP) Act, 2008. By *May 2016*, over 36,000 such firms were operative in the country. This firm has certain legal qualities of the 'limited liability' firms with the ease of a 'proprietorship partnership' firms.

Set- 5

1. Which of the following is correct about the external concessional loans India get as Official Development Assistance—

   (a) only central government can used them
   (b) centre as well as the states, both can use such loans
   (c) such loans can be used by centre, states as well as the private sector
   (d) they can be used in only social sector

2. Consider the following statements about 'short-selling'.

   1. Short selling allows to sell those shares which will be owned in future.
   2. Short-selling is done by borrowing shares with a speculation that price of the share will fall in future.
   3. Short-sellers post losses if prices uptrend for the short-selled shares.

   Select the incorrect statements using the code given below:

   (a) Only 1
   (b) 1 and 2
   (c) Only 3
   (d) None of those

3. Select the correct statements related to the recently formed think tank, the NITI, using the code given below:

   1. it is to function as a vehicle of good governance.
   2. it has to develop a holistic and inclusive development model for the economy integrating the needs of Centre, states and the local bodies.
   3. the body, in a sense, subsumes the National Development Council in its Governing Council—this gives it more legitimacy.
   4. it has three specialised wings related to—research, conflict resolution and team India.

   Code:

   (a) 1 and 2
   (b) 1, 2 and 3
   (c) 2, 3 and 4
   (d) 1, 2, 3 and 4

4. Consider the following statements.

   1. The value of total goods demanded in an economy is always identically equal to the total value of goods supplied.

   2. Statement 1 is correct in the case of modern economies only, where use of currencies as the mode of exchange, but does not hold correct if it is a barter economy.

   Select the correct statement/statements using the code given below:

   (a) Only 1

   (b) Only 2

   (c) 1 and 2

   (d) None of the above

5. Consider the following statement which defines the 'wildcat strike'.

   1. A strike called by the labourers in between the work.

   2. The strike which is called without informing the management.

   3. The strike which is supported by an outside trade union.

   4. The strike not supported by the organised trade union of the firm.

   Select the incorrect statements using the code given below:

   (a) 1, 2 and 3

   (b) 2, 3 and 4

   (c) 1, 3 and 4

   (d) 1, 2, 3 and 4

6. Which among the following policy decision/decisions a government should take to promote foreign investments in the economy?

   1. Allowing full convertibility to its currency in current and capital accounts.

   2. Reducing or withdrawing the 'withholding tax'.

   3. Prohibitory laws for its nationals for overseas investments.

   Select your answer using the code given below:

   (a) 1 and 2

   (b) 2 and 3

   (c) 1 and 3

   (d) 1, 2 and 3

7. An economy is following the policies given below:

   1. Creating self-employment sources with high speed.

   2. Cutting its expenditures on the heads of salaries, subsidies and pension.

   3. Promoting public-private partnerships in the infrastructure sector.

   Select the correct outcome which the economy wants out of such a policy.

   (a) Promoting revenue expenditure at the cost of capital expenditures.

   (b) Cutting revenue ependitures to promote capital expenditure.

   (c) Promoting development expenditures without risking welfare.

   (d) Both (b) and (c)

8. Select the correct statement about 'zero-coupon bond' from the following:

   (a) A bond with zero coupon rate which is sold at a price lower than its face value and investors get face value price at maturity.

   (b) A bond with zero rate of interest but of the highest value of liquidity for which investors get other concessions like tax breaks.

   (c) A special category of bond used as 'express money' to finance immediate needs of the economy which carries zero interest but gives tax credits to investors in their income tax returns.

(d) A kind of bond which is generally issued by governments in the times of financial crises to the high income group citizens, which carries no interest but investors get tax concessions for investing in it.

9. Select the incorrect statement from the following statements regarding deficit financing which an economy might be following.

(a) 'Factory price' of a product at constant prices is always lower than its 'factor cost' at current prices.

(b) 'Ex-factory price' of a product at the current prices is always lower than its 'market cost' at the constant prices.

(c) 'Maximum retail price' of a product is always higher than its 'ex-showroom price' at current prices.

(d) 'Factor cost' and 'market cost' may be calculated both at constant and current prices.

10. Consider the following statements about 'indicative planning'.

1. Dominance of imperative policies in the planning process.

2. Inclusion of incentives-based and co-ordinating policies.

3. Suitable for planned development of the state and mixed economies.

4. This kind of planning commenced in India with the economic reforms.

Select the incorrect statements using the code given below:

(a) 1, 2 and 3

(b) 2, 3 and 4

(c) 1, 3 and 4

(d) 1, 2, 3 and 4

11. Select the correct statement from the following about 'vulture funds'—

(a) The privately-owned funds which lend out capital for hostile bids of takeovers around the world charging high returns in the form of interests.

(b) The privately owned financial firms which buy sovereign debts of highly indebted countries at fraction of their value and collecting full amount via legal intervention.

(c) The enormous amount of private funds which have accumulated in major tax-havens of the world attacking high rising economies in the form of the so-called 'hedge funds'.

(d) The privately-owned equity capital which covers a very high risk of repayment as they lend money to secretive groups in the world to fight against the nation states—considered playing a major role in promoting majority of terror outfits today.

12. Consider the following statements.

1. Hedging is similar to insurance.

2. In badla, a buyer wants postponement of deal—it is called contango in Western economies.

3. In undha badla, a seller wants postponement of deal—it is called backwardation in the Western economies

4. Scrip share is the other name for sweat share.

Select the correct statements using the code given below:

(a) 1, 2 and 3

(b) 2, 3 and 4

(c) 1, 3 and 4

(d) 1, 2, 3 and 4

13. Consider the following statements about the process of issuing shares through 'private placement'.

1. This is one among three routes through which a company raises capital in the primary market by issuing shares.

2. Companies directly negotiates with the investors which may be financial institutions as well as individuals.

3. This is completely opposite to the public issue route to issue shares.

Select the correct statements using the code given below:

(a) 1 and 2

(b) 2 and 3

(c) 1 and 3

(d) 1, 2 and 3

14. Consider the following statements.

1. Raising capital by public issue is the most broad-based method, though it is the most time taking, too.

2. Though private placement route to raise capital is the least time taking, it is the riskiest route, too.

Select the correct statement/statements using the code given below:

(a) Only 1

(b) Only 2

(c) 1 and 2

(d) Neither 1 nor 2

15. Consider the following statements.

1. 'Trade creation' has taken place in India via the provisions of the WTO.

2. Growth stories of the industrialised economies were the outcome of follow-up to 'creative destruction'.

3. 'Trade creation' may be led by 'creative destructions'.

Select the correct statements using the code given below:

(a) 1 and 2

(b) 2 and 3

(c) 1 and 3

(d) 1, 2 and 3

16. What is correct about the term 'transfer payments' which was in news recently?

(a) The payments which takes place indirectly from the high bracket direct taxpayers to the subsidy-based sectors which are consumed by someone else.

(b) The expenditure by government for which it receives no goods or services, such as tax collection, unemployment allowance etc.

(c) The minimum return an asset must earn to prevent its transfer to the next best alternative use.

(d) Tax is a mode of income redistribution through which payments get transferred from high to low income group directly and indirectly, both ways.

17. Consider the following statements about 'Venture Capital Fund'.

1. A dedicated corpus of capital to promote innovative enrepreneurship.

2. It may be public-owned or privately-owned.

3. The IVCF was India's first such fund set up under private ownership.

Select the correct statements using the code given below:

(a) 1 and 2

(b) 2 and 3

(c) 1 and 3

(d) 1, 2 and 3

18. In **2016–17**, the Centrally Sponsored Schemes (CSSs) were restructured by the GoI.

Select the correct statements related to the restructuring, using the code given below:

1. the decision of restructuring was taken by the Governing Council of the NITI Aayog.

2. this will avoid overlapping of expenditure and provide visibility and impact to the CSSs.

3. the CSSs have been classified into 'flagship' and 'extra-flagship' categories.

4. the existing number of the CSSs is 37.

Code:

(a) 1 and 2

(b) 1, 2 and 3

(c) 2, 3 and 4

(d) 1, 2, 3 and 4

19. Select the correct statement about the 'unemployment trap'.

(a) A situation in the economy when the rate of employment growth is less than the rate of increase in the unemployed population.

(b) A situation of frictional unemployment when there is a heavy rush of labour force from the primary to the secondary activities.

(c) A situation when existing job loss is higher than the new jobs created.

(d) A situation when unemployed population of an economy does not feel encouraged to become employed.

20. Consider the following statements.

1. The risk of a government defaulting on overseas loan is known as sovereign risk.

2. All kinds of overseas borrowings by private companies also carry the burden of sovereign risk.

3. A member nation may insure its sovereign risk with the World Bank arm known as Multi-Lateral Insurance Guarantee Agency.

Select the correct statement using the code given below:

Code:

(a) 1 and 2

(b) 2 and 3

(c) 1 and 3

(d) 1, 2 and 3

21. Which of the following is correct statement regarding the external loans India get from the European Investment Bank—

(a) these loans can be only used by the central government

(b) these loans can be used by public as well as private sector

(c) these loans are more concessional than the official development assistance (ODAs) which India gets from foreign countries.

(d) these loans are availed by only private sector companies of India

22. Consider the following statements.

1. Expenditures done on advertisement, research and development are known as 'essential costs'.

2. The costs which are borne on account of salaries, fringe benefits, pensions and provident funds are known as 'sunk cost'.

Select the incorrect statement/statements using the code given below:

(a) Only 1

(b) Only 2

(c) 1 and 2

(d) None of these

23. Consider the following statements.

1. 'Product swap' functions just opposite to the system of barter.

2. 'Currency swap' is a mode of hedging against exchange rate fluctuations.

3. 'Subsidy swap' is a method of cross-subsidising two products.

Select the correct statement/statements using the code given below:

(a) 1 and 2

(b) Only 2

(c) 2 and 3

(d) Only 3

24. Consider the following statements.

1. 'Market cost' is 'factory price' added with all the indirect taxes.

2. 'Market cost' and 'ex-factory price' are different things.

3. 'Maximum retail price' and 'market cost' are the same things.

Select the correct statement/statements using the code given below:

(a) Only 1

(b) 1 and 2

(c) Only 3

(d) 1 and 3

25. Select the correct statements regarding India's present composition of the external debt, using the code given below:

1. Concessional part is around 10 per cent.

2. Forex reserves provide around 77 per cent cover to it.

3. Long-term part of the debt is around 83 per cent.

Code:

(a) Only 1

(b) Only 3

(c) 2 and 3

(d) 1, 2 and 3

Answer Key with Explanations

1. *(b)* private sector can not avail its use. There is no sectoral compulsion though the areas are outlined before loan is availed.

2. *(d)* All are correct about the action of 'short selling'. Short-sellers basically speculate that prices of the short-selled shares will fall in future. Thus, they borrow those shares (it means they don't own it) and post profit. In case the prices increase in place of falling, the short-seller posts loss (as the borrowed shares are to be handed over to the original owner at a higher price now).

3. *(b)* Though, the National Development Council (NDC) is still there, it has not met since December 2012 (when it had its 57th meeting). It is believed that either the body will be abolished or considered subsumed into the Governing Council of the NITI Aayog. The three 'specialised wings of the NITI are related to—research, consultancy and team India. Basically, 'conflict resolution' is one its functions.

4. *(a)* This is known as the *'Walras's Law'* which is correct only in the case of a barter economy. This is so because the economies which have currency as a mode of exchange, currency supplies depend on so many factors and not on the level

of the goods and services produced in the economy. The best example is shown by the instances of inflation.

5. (a) This is a strike which is not supported by the organised trade union of the firm. At times, such strikes may be supported by a trade union from outside.

6. (a) The 3rd statement is neutral to the issue of attracting foreign investment and its promotion. Once the domestic currency becomes fully convertible in the capital account such prohibitory laws are not possible—that is why India is believed to not allowing such convertibility at the full scale—as the economy does not want foreign exchange taking flight from the economy (since it is itself trying to attract it).

7. (b) The Government of India also wants to do the same but its subsidy rationalising programmes have not taken place on expected lines.

8. (a) G-Secs are issued by the GoI through this route, too.

9. (b) Price of anything at current price has to be higher than its price at constant price as the former includes the weight of current inflation.

10. (c) Planning in India was already indicative, during reform period it became more so. Imperative policies are the symptom of 'target planning' popular among the State economies (in ex-USSR, China before they switched over to mixed economy). Planning of the mixed economies can only reach its goals once private sector is also included in the process—this requires provision of incentives and co-ordination by the government.

11. (b) These funds file lawsuits in London, New York, Paris and collect full face values plus interest of the national debts of the poor nations—many of the nations falling in the Heavily Indebted Poor Countries (HIPC). As per the IMF, these funds are concentrated in the US, UK as well as the British Virgin Islands (the UK protectorate tax haven). These countries have enough political pressure to ban these funds as their activities are against the soul of the foreign policies of the UK and US.

12. (a) 'Scrip shares' are given to the existing shareholders without any change and are also called 'bonus shares'. The shares given to employees (usually top officials) by a company without any charge is called 'sweat share'.

13. (d) In a 'public issue' the company does not negotiate directly with the public who want to purchase the shares.

14. (c) Public issue makes a company to broad-base its share-ownership, but this is a complex and time-consuming process. While private placement is the quickest method to raise capital from the security market, a company covers the risk of takeovers in it (due to shift in the share holders loyalties to a competing firm).

15. (d) The increase in international trade which results from the elimination or reduction of trade barriers (such as quota, customs, surcharge etc.), is 'trade creation'. Innovation is known as 'creative destruction' (the term was coined by the Australian economist J. Schumpeter).

16. (b) All loss-making activities done by the government in the head of social sector come under it—poverty alleviation, healthcare, education, social security etc.

17. (a) The IVCF was a public-owned Venture Capital Fund (VCF), set up in 1998. First such fund in India in which 'I' stands for IFCI (Industrial Finance Corporation of India, set up 1948), a

Government of India's wholly-owned Specialised Financial Instituion (SFIs).

18. *(a)* The 50 existing CSSs were restructured into 30 and classified as 'core' and 'optional' categories. Earlier they were restructured into 66 (from 137) for the 12th Plan period—among them 17 were announced as the 'flagship programmes' by the GoI. They were further restructured into 50 by the Union Budget 2015–16.As per the government, the schemes which are for *social protection* and *social inclusion* will be considered as the 'core of the core' of the CSSs.

19. *(d)* This is the another term for 'poverty trap'. Such situation arises in an economy where there are provisions of unemployment allowance—disposable income (income after paying direct taxes) becomes less than the allowance they get.

20. *(a)* World Bank arm, MIGA, provides insurance services, but to the companies which go for foreign direct investment; it covers non-commercial risk.

21. *(b)* These loans are less concessional than that of the ODAs—but more flexible as they can be used by centre, states as well as the private sector.

22. *(c)* The expenditure on the items discussed in Statement 1 are 'sink costs'. There is nothing like 'essential costs' in business economics.

23. *(b)* 'Product swap' is similar to barter while there is nothing like 'subsidy swap' in public finance management.

24. *(a)* 'Market Cost' and 'ex-factory price' are same things. 'Market cost' added with the traders margins and effect of the current inflation is 'maximum retail price' (MRP).

25. *(d)* As per the *Economic Survey 2016–17*, India's external debt was US $ 484.3 billion by end-September 2016, while its forex reserve was US $ 360 billion.

Set- 6

1. Select the items which India shows in its current account, using the code given below:
   1. inflows due to exports and outflows due to imports
   2. inflows and outflows due to income repatriation
   3. inflows and outflows due to foreign portfolio investment
   4. external lending and borrowings

   Code:
   (a) 1 and 2
   (b) 2 and 3
   (c) 3 and 4
   (d) 2 and 4

2. Select the statement which correctly defines the difference between 'factor cost' and 'factory price':
   (a) 'Factor cost' is the manufacturing price of any product, while the 'factory price' includes the burden of indirect taxes on the product, too.
   (b) While 'factory price' of a product includes the current rate of inflation, the 'factor cost' does not.
   (c) When the weight of the state taxes are added to the 'factor cost' it becomes 'factory price'.
   (d) None of the above

3. What is correct about the concept 'transfer earnings'?

(a) The return that an asset must earn to prevent its transfer to the next best alternative use.

(b) The private remittances' earnings of an economy with the help of the transferred part of income to it by its nationals living abroad.

(c) The earnings companies get on their exports by drawing back the full amount of indirect taxes on the exported items popularly known as 'duty drawback scheme'.

(d) The transfer of the earnings by one arm of a company from one economy to its other arm in another economy under the agreement of 'double taxation'.

4. Select the correct statement about the popular stock market term 'reverse yield gap' from the options given below:

(a) A situation when the returns of government securities is in excess over the equities.

(b) A situation when the capital gains compensate the negative impact of inflation on the equities' returns.

(c) The instance of comparatively higher inflation which depletes the returns earned by investors on the government bonds.

(d) The situation when due to low long-term capital gains tax, returns on the government securities become higher.

5. Consider the following statements.

1. 'Liquidity trap' is a situation when people prefer to hold money rather than investing it.

2. 'Liquidity preference' is the situation when people prefer to invest money rather than hold it.

3. 'Liquidity crunch' is a situation of short-supply of money in the Money Market.

4. 'Credit crunch' is a situation of short-supply of money in the loan market.

Select the correct statements using the code given below:

(a) 1, 2 and 3

(b) 2, 3 and 4

(c) 1, 2 and 4

(d) 1, 3 and 4

6. Consider the following statements. about the 'Lorenz curve'.

1. A straight line on it represents complete equality of income.

2. With greater curvature in it, inequality of income rises proportionally—this inequality is measured by the 'Gini Coefficient'.

Select the incorrect statement/statements using the code given below:

(a) Only 1

(b) Only 2

(c) Both 1 and 2

(d) Neither 1 nor 2

7. What does the term 'Ninja' mean which became a common word in the financial world after the US sub-prime crisis?

(a) A loan given on false claims of credit-worthiness by the banks.

(b) Borrower with no assets, no income or no job

(c) Highly competitive form of lending, compromising the financial fundamentals.

(d) A loan given to someone who is on the brink of bankruptcy.

8. Select the correct effect of fall in the rate of inflation—
    (a) Government's interest payment liabilities increases.
    (b) Interest income on saving bank accounts goes down.
    (c) Lending and bank business grows.
    (d) Bondholders' incomes decrease.

9. Consider the following statements about 'Pareto Optimality'.
    1. It deals with distribution in an economy at the optimum level of taxation prevailing in the economy.
    2. It suggests that in an economy somebody may be made better off by making somebody else worse off.
    3. The idea works as a guide to finance managers in deciding how to spend limited funds.

    Select the correct statements using the code given below:

    Code:
    (a) 1 and 2
    (b) 2 and 3
    (c) 1 and 3
    (d) 1, 2 and 3

10. Consider the following statements about the 'penny stocks'.
    1. The shares listed on a stock exchange which show high market capitalisation with relatively low volume of shares.
    2. The shares which are issued at a par value of rupee one.
    3. Their trading price shows high volatility.

    Select the incorrect statements using the code given below:
    (a) 1 and 2
    (b) 2 and 3
    (c) 1 and 3
    (d) 1, 2 and 3

11. Consider the following statements about a 'preference share' in India.
    1. These shares bear a stated dividend
    2. They get priority over equity shares
    3. Such shares can be issued for a period of less than 1 year.

    Select the correct statements using the code given below:
    (a) 1 and 2
    (b) 2 and 3
    (c) 1 and 3
    (d) 1, 2 and 3

12. Recently, India shifted to a new method for measuring its national income. The new method classifies taxes into 'product' and 'production'. Select the statements given below which are correct about these taxes. Use the code for your answer—
    1. both of the taxes are imposed on the producers.
    2. while product taxes are variable, the production taxes are fixed.
    3. land revenue, profession tax, stamps and registration fees are some of the examples of production taxes in India.
    4. sales tax, excise duty, service tax, export and import taxes are the examples of product taxes in India.

Code:

(a) 1 and 2

(b) 1, 2 and 3

(c) 2, 3 and 4

(d) 1, 2, 3 and 4

13. Select the correct statement regarding the process of 'disinflation'—

(a) prices fall towards the upper limit of the healthy range of the headline inflation

(b) price levels fall below the lower limit of the healthy range of inflation

(c) retail inflation index falls down to single digit

(d) it is similar to deflation

14. Which one of the following decisions follow the idea of 'prisoner's dilemma'?

1. Companies fixing prices of their products at the levels less than they could in the trust that other companies do not fix lower prices.

2. The dilemma, ultimately, hampers the companies which fixes the higher prices.

Select the answer using the code given below:

Code:

(a) Only 1

(b) Only 2

(c) 1 and 2

(d) Neither 1 nor 2

15. Which of the following defines an economy in the situation of a 'population trap'?

(a) When the population control policies of the economy almost fail and it goes for a situation of population boom.

(b) When the population of an economy starts increasing after achieving the stage of 'replacement level'.

(c) When the 'natural rate of increase' in an economy starts falling drastically below the 'replacement level'.

(d) None of the above

16. Select the correct situation which defines 'poverty trap'—

(a) When the population in an economy continues to remain poor even after increase in its 'nominal income'.

(b) When the rise in income of the poor people is equitably neutralised by inflation.

(c) When unemployment rate starts increasing together with the inflation.

(d) When unemployed population getting unemployment allowance does not feel encouraged to become employed.

17. Consider the following statements about 'predatory pricing'.

1. Fixing of exceptionally high prices by the companies for their goods

2. Such pricing policy has an express purpose of harming rivals or exploiting the consumer.

Select the correct statement/statements using the code given below:

Code:

(a) Only 1

(b) Only 2

(c) 1 and 2

(d) Neither 1 nor 2

18. Which of the following is correct about 'high street banking'?

(a) When banks emphasise retail lending.

(b) When banks emphasise corporate lending.

(c) When banks emphasise long-term but risk-free lending.

(d) When banks emphasise short-term, low interest and risk-free lending.

19. Consider the following statements.

1. The paid-up capital of a company is never more than its authorised capital

2. The issued capital of a company can be maximum upto its authorised capital

3. The subscribed capital of a company can never be higher than its issued capital

Select the correct statements using the code given below:

(a) 1 and 2

(b) 2 and 3

(c) 1 and 3

(d) 1, 2 and 3

20. Consider the following statements.

1. A situation when people think that they are getting richer during the times of inflation is known as 'money illusion'.

2. It is believed that lower levels of 'money illusion' are beneficial to 'grease the wheels' of the economy.

Select the correct statement/statements using the code given below:

Code:

(a) Only 1

(b) Only 2

(c) Both 1 and 2

(d) Neither 1 nor 2

21. 'Bad' money forces 'good' money out of circulation—proposes the Gresham's Law.

1. it analyses the circulation of 'black' money in the Indian economy—

usually getting deposited in the tax havens through hawala route.

2. the Chinese currency Yuan headed to replace the dominance of the US dollar in the world foreign exchange market.

In light of the law select the incorrect statement/statements given above using the code below.

(a) Only 1

(b) Only 2

(c) Both 1 and 2

(d) Neither 1 nor 2

22. What does a 'J-curve effect' mean in the area of foreign exchange management?

(a) A deficit in BoP is followed after devaluation before posting surplus.

(b) Though foreign exchange earnings of an economy in primary anticles are lower, they are consistent.

(c) All transactions outside a stock exchange get accounted once the stock exchange opens the next day follows a J-curve.

(d) None of the world economies are as expert at managing their foreign exchange as one preceding successful economy.

23. Consider the following statements about 'earth trilemma'.

1. For economic development world needs increased energy expenditure but thisraises the environmental issues

2. The 'EEE' trilemma is synonymous to it

3. Without limiting the levels of consumption, earth as a system, can not sustain

4. Three issues need attention to sustain the earth—low consumption, high saving and an attitude of conservation

Select the correct statements using the code given below:

(a) 1 and 2

(b) 3 and 4

(c) 1 and 4

(d) 1 and 3

24. Which of the following is correct about the 'impossible trinity'?

(a) A country can not maintain all three policy goals—stable financial market, global integration and stable exchange rate.

(b) A country can not maintain all three policy goals—free capital flows, a fixed exchange rate and an independent monetary policy.

(c) A country can not maintain all three policy goals—stable exchange rate, global integration and continuous economic growth.

(d) A country can not maintain all three policy goals—small fiscal deficits, social welfare and high economic growth.

25. Select the correct statements regarding the central sector and centrally sponsored schemes run by the Government of India, using the code given below:

1. presently, there are 950 such schemes

2. budgetary allocation on them are today around 5 per cent of country's GDP

3. in case the country goes for the 'universal basic income', it is advisable to prune them

Code:

(a) Only 1

(b) Only 2

(c) 1 and 3

(d) 1, 2 and 3

Answer Key with Explanations

1. *(a)* Foreign portfolio investments and loans are part of the capital account.

2. *(d)* 'Factor Cost' and 'Factory Price' mean same thing—the cost of all inputs which are needed to produce a product (such as raw material, labour, power, interest, rent, maintenance, etc).

3. *(a)* Any earning above the 'transfer earning' is known as its 'economic cost'.

4. *(b)* Such a situation arises during the periods of high inflation—because equities provide capital gains which compensate the negative impact of inflation on them while government securities do not get this advantage. This is why during higher inflation it is suggested to invest in equities rather than government bonds (provided the security market in healthy mode).

5. *(c)* 'Liquidity trap' and 'liquidity preference' are used synonymously. Liquidity crunch is short-supply of money in the money as well as capital market.

6. *(d)* The 'Lorenz Curve' is a graphical representation of wealth distribution (US economist Max Lorenz, 1905) in which a straight diagonal line represents perfect equality of wealth distribution—the Lorenz curve lies beneath it, showing the reality of wealth distribution. The difference between the straight line and the curved line is the amount of inequality of wealth distribution, a figure described by the Gini coefficient. The curve is used to show what percentage of a nation's residents possess what percentage of that nation's wealth.

'Gini Coefficient' (developed by the Italian Statistian and Sociologist, 1912) measures the inequality in income in an economy (also known as the Gini index or Gini ratio). This is a measure of statistical dispersion intended to represent the income distribution of a nation's residents. This measures the inequality among values of a frequency distribution (for example levels of income)—a Gini coefficient of zero expresses perfect equality, where all values are the same (for example, where everyone has the same income) while a Gini coefficient of one (i.e., 100 per cent) expresses maximal inequality among values (for example, where only one person has all the income). However, a value greater than one may occur if some persons represent negative contribution to the total (e.g., have negative income or wealth). For larger groups, values close to or above 1 are very unlikely in practice. This is commonly used as a measure of inequality of income or wealth.

7. *(b)* Banks require the borrower to show a stable income source or sufficient collateral, a 'ninja loan' ignores the verification process. A ninja loan is often found in the mortgage market. In such loans, generally, interest rate initially remain lower and is increased later. Such borrowers hope to pay their loan once their property appreciate. But in case if the property doesn't appreciate, many borrowers default repayments. This why such loans are very risky for lenders.

8. *(a)* Due to fall in inflation 'real cost of borrowing' increases which makes Government's loan payment costly. Other statements are written just their opposite.

9. *(b)* The concept is not connected to taxation. This idea of the Italian economist Vilfredo Pareto (1843–1923) suggests that 'nobody can be made better off without making someone else worse off'.

10. *(d)* They are low-priced shares of small companies with very low market capitalisation. They were in news recently as some of such shares did show high rise in their trading prices on the security bourses.

11. *(a)* Such shares may get dividend even if the company has gone in loss and they are issued for a period upto 10 yrs.

12. *(d)* All of the statements are correct. While the product taxes are imposed on the producers they are ultimately paid by the consumers of the goods and services—these taxes are linked to the production volumes of the producers (so they are variable). Production taxes are paid by producers are not linked to the volume of their productions that is why they are 'fixed cost' of production.

13. *(a)* For example, in case of India, retail price index falling towards 6 per cent (that is the upper limit of India's healthy range of inflation) from above 6 per cent levels (such as 7 or 8).

14. *(a)* This is a famous example in the 'game theory' which concludes that why co-operation is difficult to achieve even if it is mutually beneficial, ultimately making things worse for the parties involved.

15. *(d)* This is a situation of population growth rate (i.e., natural rate of increase) greater than the achievable growth rate in the economy.

16. *(d)* Such situations occur since the after tax income (i.e., disposable income) turns out to be less than the benefit of the unemployment allowance.

17. *(b)* Exceptionally low prices are fixed by the firms under such pricing policy which has the objective of harming and finally eliminating rivals from the market—when they have monopolistic presence in

the market they start exploiting the consumers.

18. *(a)* This is another term for 'retail lending'— in such lending, banks forward a large number of loans to individual borrowers rather than putting the same money to a few corporate (non-individual i.e. group) borrowers—though the former is more risky and cumbersone, too.

19. *(d)* The limit upto which shares can be issued by a company is upto its authorised capital (the capital which is written in its Article of Association).

20. *(c)* The phrase was coined by the economist J.M. Keynes.

21. *(c)* The Law proposed by Sir Thomas Gresham (an advisor to Queen Elizabeth—I of England) does not deal with 'black', 'white' or any weakening world currency, nor it is correct in the case of paper currencies. The law is correct once metallic currencies are in circulation which have proportional intrinsic value—such currencies are hoarded (as in the case of price rise).

22. *(a)* This theory states that a country's trade deficit will worsen initially after the depreciation/devaluation of its currency because higher prices on foreign imports will be greater than the reduced volume of imports. The effects of the change in the price of exports compared to imports will eventually induce an expansion of exports and a cut in imports—which, in turn, will improve the balance of payment situation.

23. *(a)* The 'EEE' trilemma is also known as the 'Earth Trilemma' which says that for economic development, mankind needs to increase energy consumption but this accelerates environmental degradation. In a sense, energy model needs re-thinking.

24. *(b)* This remains the prima donna of all 'trilemmas' articulated by the economists. This is also known as 'Mundell's Impossible Trinity' which has strong theoretical foundations in the Mundell-Fleming Model developed in 1960s.

25. *(d)* Several of the schemes are very old and fund allocation on them are also low. For example, one scheme (Livestock Health & Disease Control) is 96 years old! While suggesting the Government to think in the direction of the 'universal basic income' scheme, the *Economic Survey 2016-17* has suggested to wind up these schemes in phased manner.

MODEL ANSWERS*
TO SELECTED
QUESTIONS

*Reading maketh a full man; conference a ready man; and writing an exact man.***

* The answers given to some of the questions may be comprehensive. Readers are suggested to cut it short as per the requirement of the question. Questions in the civil services examination are generally asked in parts, i.e., budgetary measures, monetary measures, administrative measures etc.

** Francis Bacon (1561-1626), 'Of Studies' **Essays**, London, UK, 1625.

Q.1 "A hard and fast control on the government's fiscal freedom may be counterproductive to the economy". In light of this statement, discuss the changing idea about the FRBM Act in the country.

Ans. Aimed at fiscal consolidation, India passed the fiscal responsibility and budget management (FRBM) Act in 2003—soon states also passed their fiscal responsibility acts (FRAs) on the similar line. To the extent 'exact' follow-up to the FRBMA-linked targets are concerned, the performance has been mixed. The targets were exceeded many times due to fiscal escalations (either due to natural calamities or on exceptional ground), while many times they were better than the mandated figures. The implementation of the Act has also been postponed thrice by now. But this act brought the element of higher fiscal discipline among the governments, there is no doubt in it. In the past few years a view has emerged as per which binding the government expenditures to a fixed number may be counterproductive to the economy at large. Due to a hard and fast discipline regarding fiscal targets, some highly desirable expenditures by the government may get blocked, for example—expenditures on infrastructure, welfare, etc.

Accordingly, we saw the Government proposing (in 2016–17) two important changes in the FRBM mandate, namely—

(i) Provision of a 'range' as a target of fiscal deficit in place of a 'number'; and

(ii) Linking 'fiscal expansion or contraction' with the 'credit expansion or contraction'.

In this backdrop, an expert committee was set up by the Government which handed over its report to the Government by late *January 2017*. The report (which is still not in the public domain) will be carefully studied by the Government (as per the *Union Budget 2017–18*) and decisions will be taken later on.

Q.2 Write a short note on the new initiatives taken by the RBI in recent times aimed at streamlining the credit and monetary policy.

Ans. In the past two and half years, several new initiatives have been taken by the RBI aimed at strengthening the current regime of credit and monetary policy—major ones are as given below:

- now RBI announces the policy on *bi-monthly* basis.

- the *glide path for disinflation* policy adopted under which the CPI (C) is used by the RBI as the 'Headline Inflation' for monetary management.

- a *Monetary Policy Framework* has been put in place—under it, the RBI is to *'target inflation'* at 4 per cent with a variations of 2 per cent. It means, the 'range of inflation' is to be between 2 to 6 per cent (of the CPI-C).

- besides the existing repo route, *term repos* have been introduced for three set of tenures—7, 14 and 28 days.

- banks overnight access to liquidity is being progressively *reduced* and in place they are being encouraged to *increase* their dependency on the term repos. By *March 2016*, banks were allowed to borrow only up to 1 per cent of their NDTL from the Call Money Market—0.25 per cent through *repo* and the rest of 0.75 per cent through *term repo*. This aims to improve the transmission of policy impulses across the interest rate spectrum and providing stability to the loan market.

- As per the *Union Budget 2016–17*, individuals will also be allowed by the RBI to participate in the Government Security market (similar to the developed economies like the USA).

- the initiation of the *MCLR* (Marginal Cost of fund based Lending Rate) from the new financial year *2016–17*. This is aimed at quickening the transition of the interest rate signaling from the RBI to the loan market.

Q.3 Briefly discuss the Marginal Cost of funds based Lending Rate (MCLR) and its objectives, operationalised by the RBI since 2016–17.

Ans. As per the new guideline of the RBI, from financial year 2016–17, banks in the country switched over to a new method of computing their lending rate—called the *MCLR (Marginal Cost of funds based Lending Rate)*. The **major highlights** of the guideline are as under:

- The MCLR will be a tenor linked internal benchmark.
- Actual lending rates will be determined by adding the components of spread to the MCLR.
- Banks will review and publish their MCLR of different maturities *every month* on a pre-announced date.
- Existing borrowers will also have the option to move to at mutually acceptable terms.
- Banks will continue to review and publish Base Rate as hitherto.

Banks, by now, have been using either of the following *three methods* to compute their Base Rate:

    (a) average cost of funds,

    (b) marginal cost of funds, or

    (c) blended cost of funds (liabilities).

As per the RBI, 'for monetary transmission to occur, lending rates have to be sensitive to the policy rate'. But this was not occurring by now.

The MCLR is supposed to bring in the *following benefits*:

- to improve transmission of policy rates into the lending rates of banks;
- to improve transparency in the methodology followed by banks for determining interest rates;
- to ensure availability of bank loans at interest rates which are fair to the borrowers as well as the banks.
- to help the banks to become more competitive and enhance their long run value.

Q.4 "The idea of the NITI has given a completely new dimension to the process of development planning in the country." Comment.

Ans. The economic 'think tank' set up by the GoI in January 2015 has the potential and imagination to change the very process of development planning in the country. This can be understood by the following *major initiatives* which has been taken under it—

- For the *first* time, a central think tank has tried to integrate the strength and aspirations of the Centre, states and the local bodies towards 'shared national agenda' of development. Through this India will usher into a new era of 'decentralised planning'.

  In place of the old design of one size fits all ('top-down' approach), now India goes for flexible and decentralised model of development (based on 'bottom-up' approach).

- It is for the *first* time that India is trying to evolve a 'development model' which could include which could be integrative in nature, rooted in India's ethos and open to the new ideas of the world.

- Development planning of the Centre has got more 'legitimacy' due to inclusion of the states and UTs in the Governing Council of the NITI—it should be noted that the decisions of the NITI are to come out after due negotiations in the Council.

- The idea of 'Team India' is a timely innovation in it—a federal political system can neither realise its developmental desires nor utilise its strength of diversities without integrating the central and state governments.

- The idea of 'competitive and co-operative federalism' has already given a new impetus among the states of India to search for a better way and method of development promotion (as the *Economic Survey 2015–16* concluded on the basis of empirical proofs).

- Some of the new ideas, such as—*conflict resolution, sounding board, vision and scenario planning* will make development planning more 'result-oriented' and suited to the changing times.

- It has high potential to strengthen the cause of socio-political development in the country as the planning has now become a 'socio-economic' process (unlike only economic in the past).

Experts believe that the workings and achievements of the NITI will depend on the federal maturity shown by the governments in the country.

Q.5 "MUDRA Bank is aimed at the twin objectives of financial inclusion and growth promotion." In light of this statement, write a short note on the Bank.

Ans. As per the GoI, large industries provide employment to only 1.25 crore people in the country while the *micro units* employ around 12 crore people. There is a need to focus on these 5.75 crore self-employed people (owners of the micro units) who use funds of Rs. 11 lakh crore, with an average per unit debt of merely Rs. 17,000. Capital is the key to the small entrepreneurs. These entrepreneurs depend heavily on the 'local money lenders' for their fund requirements.

Looking at the importance of these enterprises, GoI launched (April 2015) the *Micro Units Development and Refinance Agency Bank (MUDRA Bank)* with the aim of *funding* these *unfunded* non-corporate enterprises. This was launched as the PMMY (Prime Minister Mudra Yojana). Important features of the MUDRA Bank are as given below:

- Under this banking model, the micro units can avail up to Rs. 10 lakh loan through refinance route (through the Public and private sector banks, NBFCs, MFIs, RRBs, District Banks, etc).

- The products designed under it are categorized into three buckets of finance named *Shishu* (loan up to Rs. 50,000), *Kishor* (Rs. 50,000 to R5 lakh) and *Tarun* (Rs. 5 lakh to Rs. 10 lakh).

- Though the scheme covers the traders of fruits and vegetables, in general, it does not refinance the agriculture sector.

- There is no fixed interest rate in this scheme. As per the GoI, presently, banks are charging the interest rates between Base Rate plus one per cent to 7 per cent per annum. Interest rates on the loans are supposed to vary according the risk involved in the enterprises seeking loans. There is no general subsidy offered on interest rates except if the loan is linked to some other government scheme.

This way, the Mudra is aimed at *twin objectives*—

(i) it will make funds available to a large number of small enterprise (financial inclusion) which by now were not getting any such support from the organised financial system of the country;

(ii) by provided the scarce funds it will enhance the income and growth prospects of such a large number of firms—helping around 12 crore people earning livelihood in them.

Q.6 Briefly discuss the 'Nairobi Package' of the WTO's 10th Ministerial Conference.

Ans. At the 10th Ministerial Conference of the WTO, held in Nairobi, Kenya by late December 2015, the following *major decisions* were reached which is popularly known as the Nairobi Package—

- Amidst divergent opinions, a "strong commitment of all Members to advance negotiations on the remaining Doha issues".

- India sought and succeeded in obtaining a decision on 'Public Stockholding for Food Security Purposes'. The decision commits members to engage constructively in finding a *permanent solution* to this issue.

- Developing countries to avail the SSM (Special Safeguard Mechanism) for *agricultural products* though members to continue negotiations on it.

- Elimination of *agricultural export subsidies* agreed upon—differential treatment for developing countries such as a longer phase-out period for transportation and marketing export subsidies for exporting agricultural products. Developed countries to remove export subsidies immediately, except for a few agricultural products, and developing countries will do so by 2018.

- Developing countries will keep the flexibility to cover *marketing and transport subsidies* for agriculture exports until the end of 2023.

- Provision to prevent *'ever-greening'* of patents in the pharmaceuticals sector extended—to help in an affordable and accessible supply of *generic medicines*.

- Preferential treatment for LDC services providers. India was already doing so.

- No decision on *fisheries* subsidies—including India, several other countries (China, Egypt, South Africa, Korea and Saudi Arabia, etc) were opposed to disciplining rules on fisheries subsidies due to the lack of clarity.

- Giving greater power to WTO related to *Anti-dumping* was opposed by the members (including India)—no decision came on it.

- Duty-free market (no customs) for IT products (201 items) decided. This will be available to all WTO members (even to India, which was not party to the agreement).

Consensus cannot be reached regarding introducing *new issues* (global value chain, e-commerce, competition laws, labour, environment and investments) in the negotiation—the move was supported by the developed countries. The Package acknowledges that such issues can not be introduced without all members agreeing on them.

Q.7 "For a remunerative farming India needs to first secure a healthy industrial expansion". Give your comments in light of the changed economic contours of India.

Ans. There has been a strong case in the country to make farming a remunerative profession. In past few years, we see increase in the number of farmers' suicide, too. Though, all such suicides can not be linked to the farm sector, but around 43 per cent have been directly or indirectly linked to it (NCRB, 2015). Experts have cited several reasons for the farm distress which may finally lead to suicides by the farmers. But one very important factor for it has been *declining* or *non-remunerative* farm practices in the country. Even for non-remunerative farming there are many reasons responsible but one major reason has been structural—the under-developed industrial sector. In recent years, we see a strong view emerging in favour of speedier industrial expansion for the purpose of making India's farm sector remunerative. We may understand it in the following way:

- Presently, agriculture provides employment to 48.9 per cent of the population while contributes just 17.4 per cent of the GDP (*Economic Survey 2015–16*). This shows the non-remunerative condition of the farm sector.

- As farmers did not get other employment opportunities, the increasing rural population just remained piling up on the farm sector itself. This has been happening since decades.

- Several farmers keep migrating from the rural to urban sectors in search of jobs. But this makes a negligible dent in the size of population dependent on the sector.

- Had the industrial sector (particularly, the manufacturing sector) expanded in a healthy way together with skill generation among the farm community, the livelihood dependency on the farm sector could have been checked and per capita income of the farmers enhanced like many other countries across the world.

- India has missed several decades in chalking out a time-bound policy framework which can systematically try to make farming a remunerative profession. The suitable steps in this regard are as given below:

- India needs to expand the job-creating (labour-intensive) manufacturing industries as the first step. We see India trying hard on this front with a variety of related policy initiatives—New Manufacturing Policy, Make in India, Start-up India, MUDRA Yojana, etc.

- Promoting agro-based industries will serve a great purpose in this regard. It will not only provide farmers additional income but also check the rural-urban migration which leads to expansion of slums, urban congestion, etc.

- A concerted effort is needed in the direction of making farmers get non-farm sector job. For this a two pronged strategy is needed—firstly, skilling the farm community and creating enough sources of employment. A special care is needed in this regard is that the new jobs should be created as locally as possible (so that the farm community does not need to travel to a typical urban settlement which has its own social hazards—a touch of socio-cultural planning is needed in this regard. The idea of 'smart cities' have potential to serve this purpose.

- Lately, land acquisition has emerged as a major roadblock in industrial expansion. A friendly land acquisition policy is needed which could be effective, non-partisan and speedier. A very timely step is coming from the government in this regard—'land leasing' policy' (NITI Aayog is supposed to come with the policy by *mid-2016*).

This why experts believe that the path to remunerative farming in India goes through industrial expansion.

Q. 8 'In the changed global scenario India needs modify its policy outlook in monitoring its exchange rate". Comment.

Ans. Indian currency has seen frequent exchange rate volatility in recent times—in accordance to the changing external variables. This forces India to closely monitor the exchange rate dynamics of the world, its major trade partners and the emerging competitors in its export market. India needs to *rethink its exchange rate policy outlook* and go for a shift in it—due to the following main reasons—

- A sharp rise in the US dollar is expected with a corresponding decline in the currencies of India's competitors, notably China and Vietnam. Already, the yuan has depreciated about 11.6 per cent (between July 2015–December 2016 period) against the dollar and as a consequence the rupee has appreciated by 6 per cent against the yuan. This put a continuous concern of capital outflows from India.

- High growth rate needs support of exports which is only possible once the rupee's exchange rate competitive. The rise of countries such as Vietnam, Bangladesh, and the Philippines is a new matter of concern which compete with India across a range of manufacturing and services.

- India's present exchange rate management policy gives unusually high weight to UAE (due to high oil imports and a trans-shipment point for India's exports). But this trade has almost nothing to do with India's export competitiveness. The policy currently considers overall trade in place of the sectoral situations and their relations with the exchange rate. Due to this India gives heavy weight to euro, even though it is really Asian countries which are India's main competitors (not Europe).

- Ever since the developed countries came under the grip Great Recession, we have seen 'unconventional monetary policy' being pushed by most of them—with effective interest rates running in negatives, too. While the central banks in the west have been aiming to push up inflation and growth through it, RBI has been balancing them (till *March 2017*). Given the situation, it looks advisable for the RBI (through 'Monetary Policy Committee') to recalibrate its monetary policy outlook.

Q. 9 "India's trade outlook needs a policy shift amidst the global paradigm shift in the aftermath of the Brexit and the US elections". Analyse.

Ans. The environment for global trade policy has probably undergone a *paradigm shift* in the aftermath of Brexit and the US elections *(Economic Survey 2016–17)*. The Brexit was motivated by protectionist sentiments in the UK. Similar sentiments are being signalled by the new US government, too. This may lead to sharp appreciation in the US dollar—it has already appreciated 5.3 per cent during November-December 2016, settling at 3.1 per cent higher by January 2017 (against an index of partner currencies). During the most protectionist phase of the USA (mid to late 1980s) a sharp rise was seen in the dollar—caused by tighter monetary policy and relaxing fiscal policy.

On the other hand, a vacuum is being created in international trade leadership under the possible resurgence of protectionist pressures. In such a scenario India needs to promote open markets and tap domestic growth. Similar moves are needed from the emerging market economies

(EMEs), too. In this way, for India two specific opportunities arise—

(i) India could get much benefits by promoting 'labour-intensive exports' and 'negotiating free trade agreements' with the UK and Europe. The potential gains for export and employment are substantial—additional export of US$ 3 billion (specially in the apparel and leather & footwear sectors) and additional employment of 1.5 lakhs.

(ii) The likely retreat of USA from regional initiatives such as the Trans-Pacific Partnership (TPP) in Asia and the Trans-Atlantic Trade and Investment Partnership (TTIP) with the EU, it is possible that the relevance of the WTO might increase. As a major stakeholder and given the geo-political shifts under way, India should proactively pursue to revive WTO and multilateralism.

In this backdrop, India needs to recalibrate its foreign trade policy outlook so that it is able to minimise the negative impact of the global changes and maximise gains in its favour.

Q.10 Briefly discuss the legitimacy of preferential trade agreements (PTAs) and free trade agreements (FTAs). Review the India's experience regarding them. Give your suggestions to make them favourable to India.

Ans. Multilateral trade agreements, in general, are the first best solutions for deepening global trade as they are founded on the core principles of non-discrimination. Meanwhile, RTAs (Regional Trade Agreements) are efforts by nations aimed at deepening economic relations, usually with neighbouring countries, and tend to be *largely political* in nature. With the multilateral trade negotiations process under the WTO being

a painfully slow one requiring broad-based consensus, RTAs have progressively assumed greater importance and a growing share in international trade. While RTAs are broadly *compliant* with WTO mandates and remain broadly *supportive* of the WTO process, they remain *second-best* solutions that are discriminatory in nature against non-members and are inefficient as low cost producing non-members lose out to members. While bilateral RTAs have no equity considerations, mega-regional trading groups may not necessarily be equitable if membership is diverse and small countries may lose out either way—if they are part of it they may not have much say and if they are not, they may stand to lose.

India has always stood for an open, equitable, predictable, non-discriminatory and rule-based international trading system and views RTAs as building blocks in the overall objective of trade liberalization as well as complementing the multilateral trading system under the WTO. By *mid-2016*, India had signed 10 FTAs (Free Trade Agreements) and 6 PTAs (Preferential Trade Agreements) and all of these were in force. As per the official sources *(Economic Survey 2015–16)*, India's experience with them have not been so clear—

- The *net impact* of the RTAs on export performance and trade outcome is a *mixed bag* and requires detailed analysis.

- The trade increases have been much greater with ASEAN then other FTAs and theyhave been greater in certain industries such as metals on the import side.

- FTAs have led to increased dynamism in apparels, especially in ASEAN markets.

- The governmental analysis suggest that Indian PTAs do increase trade without apparently leading to inefficient trade.

Suggestions:

(i) Today, when global trade is shrinking with extra production capacity, instances of trade violations are high. In such a situation, if India pursues with the FTAs, India must enhance its ability to respond with WTO-consistent measures such as anti-dumping and conventional dutics and safeguard measures.

(ii) The big question is whether India should continue negotiating FTAs. With which country to negotiate them is another question. A related and even bigger question is as how India should 'position' itself relative to the new mega-regional agreements (such as the recently agreed upon, the *trans-pacific partnership*).

(iii) The WTO process of promoting multi-lateral trade seems to have been overtaken by preferential trade agreements in the world. In this backdrop, India needs to make a strategic choice—to play the *same PTA game* as everyone else or be excluded from this process. It is never advisable to be excluded.

Q. 11 Briefly discuss the Government's stand on the advices of the FRBM Act review committee which submitted its report recently.

Ans. Government's follow-up of the FRBM Act has given mixed results—results being better as well as worse as per the mandate. Based on the past experience Government called for a review in the mandate of the act, keeping in mind two important concerns—

(i) The target of fiscal deficit should be taken as 'range' in place of 'number'—which can provide enough flexibility to the Government expenditure; and

(ii) 'Fiscal expansion or contraction' should be linked to 'credit expansion and contraction'.

Accordingly, a five-member committee (headed by the former Revenue Secretary, N. K. Singh) was set up by the Government which submitted its report by late January 2017. As per the Government, the report will be carefully examined and appropriate decisions will be taken on its advices in due course. Though the report of the committee is not in the public domain, some of its major parts were shared by the *Union Budget 2017–18*, which are as given below:

- It has done an elaborate exercise and has recommended that a sustainable debt path must be the *principal macro-economic anchor* of our fiscal policy.

- It has favoured *Debt to GDP* of 60 per cent for the General Government by 2023— consisting of 40 per cent for Central Government and 20 per cent for State Governments.

- Within the framework of debt to GDP ratio, it has derived and recommended *3 per cent* fiscal deficit for the next three years.

- It has also provided for *Escape Clauses*, for deviations upto 0.5 per cent of GDP, from the stipulated fiscal deficit target. Among the triggers for taking recourse to these *Escape Clauses*, the committee has included "far-reaching structural reforms in the economy with unanticipated fiscal implications" as one of the factors.

Meanwhile, the current budget has aimed to stick to the conventional wisdom of controlling fiscal targets, as prescribed by the existing FRBM Act.

Q.12. India has tried to give a new impetus to its trade in recent years—briefly highlight the major latest steps taken by the GoI in this regard.

Ans. By mid-2016, the GoI took several new initiatives to facilitate trade, mainly aimed at adopting internationally best practices—

- e-Filing & e-Payment started. Mandatory documents required for export-import has also been cut down to just *three* each (international benchmarks).

- single window and online facility for customs clearance put in place—24x7 facility. (to cut time and cost of doing business).

- aim to move towards 24x7 paperless environment of trade.

- simplification of *'aayat niryat'* forms, bringing in clarity in different provisions, removing ambiguities and enhancing electronic governance—a mobile application also launched by the DGFT (Director General of Foreign Trade) by late 2015.

- for training/outreach, the 'Niryat Bandhu Scheme' launched aimed at Skill India.

- a Council for Trade Development and Promotion (CTDP) launched in July 2015, aimed at ensuring participation of states/ union territories (UTs) to enhance trade-enabling environment and for making them active partners in boosting India's exports.

- the state/UTs to develop their export strategy, appoint export commissioners, address infrastructure constraints restricting movement of goods, facilitate refund of value- added tax (VAT)/octroi/state-level cess, address other issues relating to various clearances and build capacity of new exporters in order to promote exports.

India's economic diplomacy has gathered a new momentum in past few years. World economies together with the international and regional economic agencies are taking India as a major source of global growth. In wake of this India needs to scale up its external sector governance paradigm.

Q.13. **"The NBFCs are fast emerging as an important segment of Indian financial system and are complementing the banking sector". Give your comments in light of the regulatory framework for the NBFCs.**

Ans. NBFCs (Non-Banking Financial Companies) are fast emerging as an important segment of Indian financial system. It is an *heterogeneous group* of institutions (other than commercial and co-operative banks) performing financial intermediation in a variety of ways, like accepting deposits, making loans and advances, leasing, hire purchase, etc. They *can not* have certain activities as their principal business—agricultural, industrial and sale-purchase or construction of immovable property. They advance loans to the various wholesale and retail traders, small-scale industries and self-employed persons. In this way, they have broadened and diversified the range of products and services offered by the Indian financial sector. Gradually, they are being recognised as *complementary* to the banking sector due to their—

- customer-oriented services;
- simplified procedures;
- attractive rates of return on deposits; and
- flexibility and timeliness in meeting the credit needs of specified sectors.

RBI, the regulator of the NBFCs, has given a very wide definition of such companies (a kind of 'umbrella' definition)—"a financial institution formed as a company involved in receiving deposits or lending in any manner." They are classified into two broad categories:

(a) deposit-taking NBFCs (NBFC-D), and

(b) non-deposit taking NBFCs (NBFC-ND).

It is *mandatory* for a NBFC to get itself registered with the RBI as a *deposit taking* company. For registration they need to be a *company* (incorporated under the Companies Act, 1956) and should have a minimum NOF (net owned fund) Rs. 2 crore.

There are certain other category of the NBFCs which are regulated by other financial regulators— venture capital fund, merchant bank, stock broking firms (SEBI registers and regulates them); insurance company (registered and regulated by the IRDA); housing finance company (regulated by the National Housing Bank); nidhi company (regulated by the Ministry of Corporate Affairs under the Companies Act, 1956); and chit fund company (by respective state governments under Chit Funds Act, 1982).

The Government has proposed to facilitate the process of their strengthening as they are seen to be a big fund-provider to the infrastructure sector.

Q. 14 Briefly highlight the major reasons for recent upsurge in the NPAs of the public sector banks and also describe the steps taken by the RBI to check them.

Ans. An upsurge has been seen in the non-performing assets (NPAs) of the public sector banks in the past few years. As per the official sources (Economic Surveys), the main reasons for this unpsurge have been as given below—

(i) Switchover to system-based identification of NPAs;

(ii) Current macroeconomic situation in the country;

(iii) Increased interest rates in the recent past;

(iv) Lower economic growth; and

(v) Aggressive lending by banks in the past, especially during good times.

(vi) 'Twin balance sheet' problem hitting banks as well as the corporate sector.

The RBI has taken several initiatives to resolve the NPA issue by ealry 2017. The steps taken under it are:

(a) Banks have to start acting as soon as a sign of stress is noticed in a borrower's actions and not wait for it to become an NPA. Banks to carve out as special category of assets termed special mention accounts (SMAs) in which *early signs* of stress are visible.

(b) Flexibility brought in project loans to infrastructure and core industry projects, both existing and new.

(c) *Non-cooperative* borrowers in NPAs resolution will have to pay higher interest for any future borrowing. Banks will also be required to make higher provisions for further loans extended to borrowers who are considered to be 'non-cooperative'.

(d) Towards strengthening recovery from *non-cooperative borrowers*, the norms for asset reconstruction companies (ARC) have been tightened, whereby the minimum investment in security receipts should be 15 per cent, as against the earlier norm of 5 per cent.

(e) Independent evaluation of large-value restructuring (above Rs. 500 crore) made mandatory.

(f) If a borrower's interest or principal payments are overdue by more than 60 days, a *Joint Lenders' Forum* to be formed by the bankers for early resolution of stress.

(g) The RBI has set up a central repository of information on large credits to collect, store and disseminate credit data to lenders. For this, banks need to furnish credit information on all their borrowers with an exposure of Rs.5 crore and above.

(h) Incentives to banks to quickly and collectively agree to a resolution plan.

Meanwhile, the *Economic Survey 2016–17* has advised the Government to set up a public sector assets rehabilitation agency (naming PARA) to solve the 'twin balance sheet' problem which will also resolve the NPAs crisis of the public sector banks, too.

Q. 15 Write a note on the current policy regarding the use of disinvestment proceeds and also justify the same.

Ans. The current policy regarding the use of the disinvestment proceeds are of January 2013. The proceeds of disinvestment proceeds with effect from the fiscal year 2013–14 are credited to the existing *'Public Account'* under the head NIF and they remain there until withdrawn/invested for the approved purpose—to be decided by the Union Budgets. Currently, the proceeds are used for the following purposes:

(i) Subscribing to the shares being issued by the CPSE including PSBs and Public Sector Insurance Companies, on *rights basis* so as to ensure government ownership in them at 51 per cent.

(ii) *Recapitalization* of public sector banks and public sector insurance companies.

(iii) Investment by Government in RRBs, IIFCL, NABARD, Exim Bank;

(iv) Equity infusion in various Metro projects;

(v) Investment in Bhartiya Nabhikiya Vidyut Nigam Limited and Uranium Corporation of India Ltd.;

(vi) Investment in Indian Railways towards capital expenditure.

Till the *Union Budget 2017–18* was presented we find the GoI following the same policy to use the proceeds of disinvestment—using the funds for acquiring new assets (for capital expenditures). The policy looks suitable to the time as capital expenditures have been shrinking due to lower investment coming from the 'debt-stressed' and 'profit-hit' private sector. As the policy is to be decided by the Union Budget, it gives enough flexibility to the government.

Q. 16 Write a note on the official criteria regarding the term 'wilful defaulter' and also discuss the regulatory norms which apply on such individuals/entities.

Ans. There are many individuals/entities who borrow money from lending institutions but fail to repay. However, not all of them are called wilful defaulters. As per the provisions of the RBI, a wilful defaulter is one who does not repay a loan or liability, but apart from this there are other things that define a wilful defaulter—

(i) Who is financially capable to repay and yet does not do so;

(ii) Or one who diverts the funds for purposes other than what the fund was availed for;

(iii) Or with whom funds are not available in the form of assets as funds have been siphoned off;

(iv) Or who has sold or disposed the property that was used as a security to obtain the loan.

Diversion of fund includes activities such as using short-term working capital for long-term purposes, acquiring assets for which the loan was not meant for and transferring funds to other entities. *Siphoning of funds* means that funds were used for purposes that were not related to the borrower and which could affect the financial health of the entity.

If an entity's or individual's name figures in the *list of wilful defaulters*, the following restrictions get in action on them—

(a) Barred from participating in the capital market.

(b) Barred from availing any further banking facilities and to access financial institutions for five years for the purpose of starting a new venture.

(c) The lenders can initiate the process of recovery with full vigour and can even initiate criminal proceedings, if required.

(d) The lending institutions may not allow any person related to the defaulting company to become a board member of any other company as well.

Q. 17 Write a shot note on current situation of the capital adequacy of public sector banks and also discuss the government's attempts to make them compliant to the Basel III norms.

Ans. The capital to risk weighted assets ratio (CRAR) of the scheduled commercial banks of India was 12.5 per cent by March 2015 (Basel-III) falling to 11.3 per cent by September 2015. The regulatory requirement for CRAR is **9** per cent for 2016. The decline in capital positions at aggregate level, however, was on account of deterioration in capital positions of PSBs. While the CRAR of the scheduled commercial banks (SCB) at 11.3 per cent as of September 2015 was satisfactory, going forward the banking sector, particularly PSBs will require substantial capital to meet regulatory requirements with respect to additional capital buffers.

In order to make the PSBs and RRBs compliant to the *Basel III* norms, the government has been following a recapitalisation programme for them since 2011–12. A *High Level Committee* on the issue was also set up by the government which has suggested the idea of 'non-operating holding company' (HoldCo) under a special Act of Parliament (action is yet to come regarding this).

Meanwhile, the GoI has been recapitalising (since 2011–12) the PSBs to make them capital compliant. The recent capital infusions into the PSBs are as given below—

(i) In 2014-15, infused with Rs. 6,990 crore. This capital infusion was based on some new criteria— asset quality, efficiency and strength of the banks.

(ii) During 2015–16, the government released Rs. 19,950 crore to 13 PSBs (*Economic Survey 2015–16*).

(iii) For the year 2016–17, Rs. 25,000 crore has been purposed for the purpose (*Union Budget 2016–17*).

(iv) For the fiscal 2017–18, Rs. 10,000 crore has been provisioned (*Union Budget 2017–18*). The budget has committed additional allocation as may be required.

As per the *Union Budget 2017–18*, the Government continues with its focus on resolution of banks' stressed assets (NPAs). The legal framework has been strengthened to facilitate resolution, through the enactment of the Insolvency and Bankruptcy Code and the amendments to the SARFAESI and Debt Recovery Tribunal Acts. Post-budget, the Government hinted to set up an agency to look into the 'twin balance sheet' problem India is faced with. Banks' NPAs crisis is supposed to get solved (technically), once such an agency is set up by the Government.

Q. 18 Briefly discuss the concept 'Divisible Pool' regarding the devolution of resources by the Fianance Commission and also highlight the changes which occured in it in recent times.

Ans. The 'Divisible Pool' is that portion of gross tax revenue which is distributed between the Centre and the States. The divisible pool consists of all taxes, except surcharges and cess levied for specific purpose, net of collection charges.

Before the 80th Constitution Amendment (2000), the sharing of the Union tax revenues with the states was in accordance with the provisions of articles 270 and 272, as they stood then. This amendment altered the pattern of sharing of Union taxes in a fundamental way—dropping the Article 272 and substantially changing the Article 270. The new Article 270 provides for sharing of all the taxes and duties referred to in the Union List putting all in a 'divisible pool'. There are some exceptions to it—the taxes and duties referred in the Articles 268 and 269 of the Constitution, together with surcharges and cesses on taxes and duties (referred in the Article 271) and any cess levied for specific purposes—do not fall under this 'pool'.

The new arrangement of tax devolution came as a follow-up to the recommendations of the 10th FC (1995–2005) which the FC termed as the 'Alternative Method of Tax Devolution' (AMD). A concensus between Union and States was a advised by the FC for such an arragnement to be effected. States were going to get extra 5 per cent share in the Union taxes in the AMD, thus, a serious demand came from them—ultimately, the AMD was accepted by the Centre. To make the AMD irreversible, the GoI went for the 80th Amendment in the Constituion.

Q. 19 Write a short note on the revised liquidity management framework (LMF) put in place recently by the RBI. Also describe the rationale behind this revision.

Ans. In August 2014, the RBI announced a revised Liquidity Management Framework (LMF) Major features of the LMF is as given below:

- RBI started conducting 14-day *term repurchase* auctions four times a fortnight, up to an aggregate amount equal to 0.75% of the system's deposit base or net demand and time liabilities (NDTL).

- Unlike earlier, RBI has announced a fixed schedule for these 14-day *term repo* operations, which are used by banks for their day-to-day liquidity requirements. One-fourth of the total amount of 0.75 per cent of NDTLs would be put up for auction in each of the four auctions, RBI said in a statement.

- No change in the amount that banks can access from the liquidity adjustment facility (LAF) window at fixed repo rate of the time. Banks are currently allowed to borrow up to 0.25 per cent of their deposit base or NDTL from the LAF window.

- Additionally, RBI conducts overnight variable rate repo auctions based on an assessment of liquidity in the system and government cash balances available for auction for the day.

The revised policy framework has been put in place to check volatility in the inter-bank call money markets, where banks lend to each other, and also allow the lenders to manage their liquidity needs better. Better interest signalling and medium-term stability in the loan market are other objectives of it.

Q. 20 What are tax-havens and how are they promoting corruption in India?

Ans. 'Tax havens' are nation-states or dominions imposing low or no taxes on personal and corporate incomes, and as a consequence tend to attract wealthy individuals and corporates seeking to minimise their tax liabilities. Other than saving taxes these havens are also used as a safe hub for parking **'black money'** created in different countries. As per the data of the OECD, there are at present over 70 such destinations in the world—popular ones are British Virgin Islands, Cayman Islands, Cook Islands, Dubai, Isle of Maw, Liechtenstein, Marshall Islands, St. Kitts and Nevis, Switzerland, Marritius, US Virgin Islands etc.

The tax havens are promoting corruption in India in so many ways:

(i) They have emerged safe hubs for parking money earned in India.

(ii) As there are such parking centres, the black money individuals and corporates make in India, are easily hidden with no risk of getting caught.

(iii) Many Indian corporates have their operations in such places which they use for transfer pricing.

(iv) The parked funds get back to India in the form of 'hedge funds' destabilising the economy.

(v) As corruption is supposed to be very high in India, even politicians are believed to park their black money.

(vi) They accelerate hawala, bribery etc., in India.

Recently, we have seen some effective actions being taken by the victim nations to unearth their funds parked in these havens such as the USA, Germany and many of the OECD nations. The Government of India has also started such initiatives recently.

Q. 21 'Economic reforms with a human face'. Examine the rationale behind it and the possible outcomes.

Ans. The UPA Government announced its committment to economic reforms, with this sentence and the proverb got media attention. The political elite looks convinced today that the process of economic reform has not been able to take care of the masses, thus the future of the process will focus on it.

Economic reform with a human face is no empty rhetoric as it is based on stark realities and sound logic. As we know, in the era of reforms, the economy is moving towards a market economy in which demand/supply and price mechanism plays the main role. As vast sections of the population lacks the desired level of purchasing power, the process looks 'anti-poor' and consequeafly 'pro-rich'. Such reform processes might bring higher economic growth, but for equitable development, a conscious attempt for *inclusive growth* is essential.

The masses who lack the real level of purchasing capacity, should be supplied with subsidised goods and services till micro-level growth takes place. This is why the government is emphasising upon the *social sector* and enhancing its expenditure on the delivery of the so-called 'public goods' (education, water, healthcare, shelter etc.).

By 2016–17, we see a changed thinking in the government's fiscal policy. Now, the government stance is 'pro-corporate' as well as 'pro-poor' (quoting the Finance Minister himself). Today, the government believes in subsidising goods and services for welfare of the poor but it also intends to rationalise the subsidies with the Aadhar-seeded technology-based platform the direct benefit transfer (DBT). On the other hand, there is an effort by the government to create the best possible environment for the growth and expansion of business and industry in the country (by improving the 'ease of doing business'). Naturally, the government needs revenue to do welfare for the poor. This fiscal stance looks quite logical and timely.

Q. 22 Write a note on the present situation regarding current and capital account convertibility of rupee.

Ans. In the Union Budget 1992–93, the Liberalised Exchange Rate Mechanism Scheme (LERMS) was announced. Since then, India has always been moving ahead in the direction of greater rupee convertibility, which may be seen as given below:

(i) In August 1994, rupee became **fully convertible** in the current account.

(ii) In August 1994, the rupee became **partially convertible** in the capital account (60:40).

(iii) The current policy regarding the capital account convertibility in India stands as given below:

(a) Rupee got full convertibility on Indian corporate's proposal of foreign investment upto US$ 500 million—put in automatic route approval.

(b) Rupee became fully convertible in case of corporates intending to prepay their external commercial borrowings (ECBs) above US$ 500 million—automatic route.

(c) In May 2015, the government allowed individuals to invest abroad with an upper limit of US$ 2,50,000 per year.

As India is becoming self-dependent in earning foreign exchange, we may hope that in the near future, the government might be announcing rupee's full convertibility in the capital account. India's cautious moves towards full capital account convertibility has been appreciated by the IMF.

Q. 23 What is the term 'balance of payment'? Write a note on recent policies regarding BoP management in India.

Ans. Balance of Payment or BoP is the overall *statement* of a country's economic transactions with the rest of the world over a period, generally a year. The statement shows receivings from the world and the payments to the world basically shown in the current and the capital accounts. This statement is based on the principles of *accounting*—similar to the *balance sheet* of a company. It might turn out to be favourable or unfavourable. If it is unfavourable and the economy is incapable to pay it, this is known as a BoP crisis. In such situations, the IMF remains as the last source of rescue.

• India had to rely on emergency operations from abroad to cope up with periodic BoP crises in 1973, 1979, 1981, and 1991. But after the economic reform process started, the situation started to improve.

As India started 'opening up' after 1991, as the part of the external sector reforms, its BoP has become *favourable* with each succeeding year. *Major policies* in this direction could be summed up as given below:

(i) Steps in the direction of opening the economy for healthy levels of foreign investments (FIs)—FDI as well as the (FIIs).

(ii) Optimum levels of convertibility to rupee in the current and the capital accounts.

(iii) Accelerated disinvestment of the prospective PSUs, including 'strategic sale' to the foreign bidders, too.

(iv) Follow up of LERMS (Liberalised Exchange Rate Mechanism System) in 1992–93.

(v) Modifications in FERA–FEMA

(vi) Prudential management of the financial market with inputs of the required kind of reforms—money market, banking, insurance, stock markets etc.

(vii) Required kind of trade policy, etc.

Q.24 Critically examine the recently announced disinvestment policy for the public sector undertakings.

Ans. A new disinvestment policy was announced by the Government by February 2016—pusing in favour of the 'strategic disinvestment'. It will be better to call it a modification in the existing policy of 2009. As per the government, such policy implies "the sale of substantial portion of Government share holding of the PSUs of upto 50 per cent, or higher along with transfer of management control". Main features of this policy are—

(i) To be undertaken through a consultation process among different Ministries, Departments and the NITI Aayog.

(ii) NITI Aayog to identify PSUs and advice on the mode of sale, percentage of shares to be sold and method for valuation.

(iii) Core Group of Secretaries on Disinvestment (CGD) to consider the recommendations of NITI Aayog to facilitate a decision by the Cabinet Committee on Economic Affairs (CCEA) on strategic disinvestment and to supervise/monitor the process of implementation.

The changed stance of the government regarding disinvestment policy is a borrowing from the past experiences of disinvestment. Strategic mode of disinvestment was started by the GoI in 1999–00 itself which was put on hold by the next Government in 2004. The new government announced a new policy which aimed at GoI owing at least 51 per cent stake in the divested PSUs believing in the 'ideology' that *public has right* to own national assets. The new policy has not changed this ideology but has taken a more dynamic stance.

The new policy of disinvestment should be seen in the *backdrop* of the newly begun process of the "comprehensive management of government investment in the PSUs". Under it, the government has recognised its investment in the PSUs as an important asset and aims to optimise returns from it by its efficient use and attracting investment in the economy.

Q. 25 Write a note on the prospects and challenges to Indian agriculture in the WTO regime.

Ans. As the provision of the WTO came into effect, experts rightly visualised great prospects and at the same time some serious challenges for the Indian agriculture sector. As far as the extent of the prospects are concerned, immense export potential is visible in the following areas:

(i) Cotton textile, yarn, readymade garments, etc.

(ii) Agricultural products, cereals, fishery products and forest goods.

(iii) Processed foods, beverages, and soft drinks. A joint projection of the OECD and the GATT did put an increase in the world merchandise trade by US $745 billion upto 2005 once the WTO provisions get implemented. As per the projection, 99 per cent of this trade almost falls in the agriculture sector. As India has been an agrarian economy and enough prospects for agricultural expansion are possible, it can encash this opportunity (NCAER survey supported this in 1993–94).

We may see the possible major challenges in the WTO regime:

(i) *Food self-sufficiency:* As cheaper food-grains will have unrestricted flow into India, we might become almost dependent upon import supplies for our food requirement—our self-reliance is badly threatened.

(ii) *Price-stability:* The price stability aspect of agricultural products, specially the sensitive foodgrains, will be in great risk as fluctuations in the imports are natural (agriculture being highly prone to weather and climatic variations) hurting the poor people.

(iii) *Cropping pattern:* Cropping pattern of India might go in for a major shift in favour of profitable crops threatening the fragile ecosystem and the balance of biodiversity.

All the above given challenges could be dealt with the suitable type of timely agricultural and trade policies—but WTO provision does not give such kind of sovereign choices to its member countries. It means we need to go for flexibility in the provisions of the WTO.

(iv) *Weaker sections:* Weaker sections of the society will again miss the train of globalisation for their upliftment as the process of globalisation is not neutral to area, crop and the individual. We will need a more focussed distributive kind of economic policies to do it.

(v) *Commitments towards the WTO:* Our agricultural subsidy cannot cross the 10 per cent mark of the agricultural GDP, any year. Though this is still not alarming, the higher subsidies forwarded by the USA and the EU is diluting the competitiveness of Indian agricultural goods—the 'Blue Box' and the 'Green Box' subsidies need redefinition immediately.

Agricultural provisions of the WTO have always been a matter of great concern for the developing nations and the ministerial negotiations were stalled on several occasions due to them. In the last and the *10th Ministerial Conference* of the WTO (Nairobi, Kenya, December 2015), certain consensus emerged regarding the sector—agricultural subsidies to be rationalised by the developed nations; permanent solution for public stockholding of food crops; and subsidies to continue on fisheries *(Economic Survey 2015–16).*

Q.26 "India's income and consumption pattern show a huge anomaly". Analyse with suitable illustrations.

Ans. India's tax to GDP ratio is very low, and the proportion of direct tax to indirect tax is not optimal from the view point of social justice. The recent data released by the Government *(Union Budget 2017–18)* indicate that India's direct tax collection is not commensurate with the income and consumption pattern of the people—

• 'Corporate tax' filing pattern is very weak—out of 5.6 crore informal enterprises, only one third filed tax returns. Similarly, out of total registered company (13.94 lakh) around half filed tax returns—of which around 20 per cent did show zero income and only 7781 companies did show profit above Rs. 10 crores.

• In case of 'individual income tax', the situation is not better—out of 4.2 crore employees of the organised sector (formal sector), around 45 per cent filed income tax returns. Only 3.4 core Indians filed income tax returns out of which—around half had income below exemption limit; only 24 lakh people had income above Rs. 10 lakhs and only 1.72 lakh had income above Rs. 50 lakhs.

• The above-given data can be contrasted with the fact that in the last five years, more than 1.25 crore cars were sold in the country, and number of Indian citizens who flew abroad (either for business or tourism), was 2 crore in the year 2015.

From the figures cited above it can be concluded that India is largely a tax *non-compliant* society. The predominance of *cash* in the economy makes it possible for the people to evade their taxes. When too many people evade taxes, the burden of their share falls on those who are honest and compliant. The demonetisation process has given the government new data related to people's income and it is believed that the data mining will help the Government in increasing the tax net and tax revenue in future.

Q. 27 Discuss the challenges related to providing universal healthcare in India.

Ans. Health indicators of India have been always low due to many reasons and they still remain a matter of great concern for the GoI and UN bodies. Despite higher economic growth, India fares poorly when compared to countries like China and Sri Lanka in term of parameters like per capita expenditure on health, number of physician/hospital beds and IMR. In addition, within the country, the improvement has been quite uneven across regions/states, gender, rural/urban areas etc. The health system in India is a mix of the public and private sectors, with the NGO sector playing a small role. In providing universal healthcare, the country faces the following challenges:

Physical challenges are related to having adequate number of trained personnel, hospitals and other infrastructure. The Centre and state need active participation from the private sector and the NGOs.

Economic challenges are related to the mobilisation of funds to meet the physical challenges at one hand, while on the other, delivering the required medical services to the needy people.

Universal health insurance is under consideration with government supported premium payment.

As per the Universal Health Coverage Index (UCH Index) of the World Bank, India ranks 143 among 190 countries in terms of per capita government spending on health. India needs to spend around 2.5 per cent of its GDP to go for universal healthcare which stands at just 1.4 per cent *(Economic Survey 2016–17)*. To mobilise enough funds and manpower for the purpose, India should aim at channelising all possible resources at the governments, private sector and civil society.

Q. 28 Write a short note on India's policy steps regarding harnessing the 'demographic dividend'.

Ans. There has been a marked decline in the dependency ratio (ratio of dependent to working age population) in India. The ratio fell down from 0.8 in 1991 to 0.73 in 2001 and is expected to further decline sharply to 0.59 by 2014. This decline sharply contrasts with the demographic trend in the industrialised countries and also in China, where the ratio is rising. It is projected that the proportion of population in the working age group (i.e., 15–64 years) in India will increase from 62.9 per cent (2006) to 68.4 per cent in 2026.

Low dependency ratio and a high proportion of the working population gives India a comparative cost advantage, and a progressively lower dependency ratio will result in improving India's competitiveness in the global economy. The Government of India seems fully aware of this advantage and that is why the Eleventh Plan (2007–12) is implementing a *three-pronged strategy* to tap demographic dividend:

(i) Ensuring proper healthcare to all,

(ii) Emphasis on skill development (knowledge industry), and

(iii) Encouragement of labour intensive industries.

The proportion of economically active population (15–59 years) has increased to 57.7 per cent during 1991 to 2013 (latest National Sample Registration–2013). Projections suggest that the working age group population share will continue rising till about 2035-2040, meaning that India has another 25 years to exploit this dividend *(Economic Survey 2015–16)*. Demographic dividend is an 'opportunity not destiny'—India needs to plan to reap its benefits.

Q. 29 Write a short note on the relationship between stock market and the economy.

Ans. After the Government of India started initiatives in the direction of an organised stock market by late 1980s, too much water has flown since then in this sector. Indian stock market has been making waves throughout the last decade. Today, it is in the headlines due to two paradoxical reasons. Firstly, the pessimism ensuing from the subdued performance of the major stock indices for the last many weeks and secondly, the international opinions and surveys putting Indian stock market among the fastest growing markets of the world. It is right time to analyse the relationship of the stock market to the economy at large. Though experts lack a complete consensus on the issue, we may point out the broader contours of the relationship in the following way:

(i) The equity prices can affect the household income. By their rise, households feel richer as the value of their equity holdings rises, and this 'wealth effect' then spills over into higher consumption ultimately boosting both demand and investment in the economy. The opposite can induce slowdown and even recession as well as sluggish investment.

(ii) Equity prices have a direct impact on the business confidence in an economy.

(iii) A strong and vibrant stock market increases borrowing capacity by raising the value of assets to put as collateral into the banks and the financial institutions.

(iv) Equity price rises raise the market capitalisation of a listed company relative to the replacement cost of its current assets (a factor known as **Tobin's q**) which induces entrepreneurs to add capacity.

There are many real life examples from around the world which validate the point that a vibrant and rising stock index has been resulting into higher growth rates for the concerned economies between 1951–2016.

Q. 30 Write a short note on the sub-prime crisis and point out the lessons for India.

Ans. The sub-prime crisis is related to the US mortgage market which first surfaced in July 2007. Simply said, this is a financial crisis generating from the default of the borrowers. It means that it is like the non-performing assets (NPAs) crisis of banks in India. But the analyses of the situation and the mode of financing involved make it highly complex. Let us have a look on the whole matter in the following steps:

Step 1: Borrowers with poor or less than standard (that is why 'sub-prime') credit records were encouraged (to borrow by some of the world's leading banks and financial institutions).

Step 2: These 'sub-prime loans' were then sold to other investment banks by the original lending banks and institutions.

Step 3: The investment banks (who purchased the sub-prime loans from the original lenders) in turn converted them (the loan papers) into marketable, complex financial instruments to spread risks and manage liquidity (i.e., fund).

Step 4: When the sub-prime borrowers defaulted in their repayment of mortgaged loans, the financial crisis originated—today known as the 'sub-prime crisis' around the world.

Basically, in the name of financial innovation and cut-throat competition in the financial world, there is always a risk that banks start adopting/promoting highly risky, complex and questionable financial practices. Two long-term measures will help to prevent such crises to occur again:

(i) The financial instruments should be made transparent enough and easily communicated to the buyers, and

(ii) The buyers should have at least basic knowledge of how these instruments work and the risk involved.

We find some similar actions among the Indian banking industry, too—for example, the SBI offering the 'teaser loans' (a bit cheaper interest rate on home loans for the first 2 years) to attract customers. During this period, the some substandard borrowers too got loans (as per the *Economic Survey 2008–09*). But soon after the sub-prime crisis in the USA, the RBI got more vigilant to such banking norms. By March 2017, the banking regulatory norms have been tweaked by the RBI several times. Today, India's banking industry being regulated by highly prudential norms and is getting compliant to the *Basel III* norms to in a time-bound way.

Q. 31   What is Double Taxation? Write a current note on the situation of the Double Taxation policy followed by India.

Ans. The situation of double taxation occurs when an individual is required to pay **two** or **more** taxes for the *same income*, *asset,* or *financial transaction* in different countries—mainly due to overlapping tax laws and regulations of the countries where an individual operates his business. When an Indian businessman makes a profit or some other type of taxable gain in another country, he may be in a situation where he will be required to pay a tax on that income in India, as well as in the country in which the income was generated. To protect Indian tax payers from this unfair practice, the Indian government has entered into tax treaties, known as **Double Taxation Avoidance Agreement** (DTAA) with 65 countries, including U.S.A, Canada, U.K, Japan, Germany, Australia, Singapore, U.A.E, and Switzerland. DTAA ensures that India's trade and services with other countries, as well as the movement of capital are not adversely affected.

Such agreements are known as "Double Tax Avoidance Agreements" (DTAA) also termed as *"Tax Treaties"* (TTs). The statutory authority to enter into such agreements is vested in the Central Government by the provisions contained in *Section 90* of the Income Tax Act.

The Income Tax relief against double taxation is provided in two ways:

(i) **Unilateral Relief:** Under *Section 91,* the Indian government can relieve an individual from double taxation irrespective of whether there is a DTAA between India and the other country concerned. Unilateral relief may be offered to a tax payer if:

a. The person or company has been a resident of India in the previous year.

b. The same income must be accrued to and received by the tax payer outside India in the previous year.

c. The income should have been taxed in India and in another country with which there is no tax treaty.

d. The person or company has paid tax under the laws of the foreign country in question.

(ii) **Bilateral Relief:** Under *Section 90,* the Indian government offers protection against double taxation by entering into a DTAA with another country, based on mutually acceptable terms. Such relief may be offered under two methods:

(a) *Exemption method:* This ensures complete avoidance of tax overlapping.

(b) *Tax credit method:* This provides relief by giving the tax payer a deduction from the tax payable in India.

In this regard, India articulated the GAAR (General Anti-Avoidance Rule) in 2010 like several other countries to be enforced from April 2017 (as per the *Union Budget 2017–18*).

Q. 32 'India's economic policies are neo-liberal.' Examine.

Ans. The process of economic reforms started by India in 1991 was a follow-up to liberal policies influenced by current world ideas of neo-liberalism via the IMF (as it agreed with Washington Consensus, 1985). This is why critics of the reform process call Indian economic policies neo-liberal (it was also remarked by the *Supreme Court of India*, in one of its judgements in 2012).

Through reform, India started redefining the economic role of state in the economy—a predominant role was assigned to the 'private sector', but the state today has a different and bigger role. We may cite some examples to show why India's policies are still not neo-liberal:

(i) State still manages majority stakes in the PSUs and many 'very big PSUs' have been newly set up.

(ii) Higher degree of regulation gives more economic authority to the government.

(iii) Even after liberalisation, India is ranked very low in being a liberal economy what to ask of a neo-liberal economy.

(iv) Subsidies are still on the higher side.

(v) Government expenditure on education, healthcare, social security has increased hugely post-1991.

(vi) Even liberal policies of the government are under several official checks and controls.

(vii) Had India followed neo-liberal policies, it would also have faced some financial crisis after the US 'sub-prime' crisis.

By 2016–17, we find a new stance in the fiscal policy of the GoI *(Union Budgets 2015–16 and 2016–17)*—

(i) Now, the government believes in doing all needful welfare works with a more performance-oriented policy framework. Rationalising the subsidy regime is an important part of the policy (with the help of Aadhar-enabled technology platform, the DBT).

(ii) On the other hand, the government is trying to tweak all possible options to enhance the 'ease of doing business' in the economy—so that the business and industry are able to realise their full potential.

This new stance in the fiscal framework has been termed by the government as 'pro-poor and pro-corporate'. Basically, to do welfare, the government needs revenues—in this backdrop the changed stance looks quite suitable.

Q.33 Discuss the transformational reforms initiated by the Government in recent times.

Ans. We have seen a major change in the Government's stance towards the need of reforms—several steps of reforms have been taken which have been termed as transformational. These reforms are 'transformational' in this sense that they are aimed at transforming the very outlook to policy making and are taken in a long-term perspective. We may have a look on the major ones—

(a) Inflation targeting and setting up the Monetary Policy Committee by amending the RBI Act, 1934;

(b) Restarting of the 'strategic disinvestment' of the PSUs;

(c) Demonetisation of the high denomination currency notes (aimed at checking corruption, black money, tax evasion, fake currency and terrorism);

(d) Enactment of the new Benami Law (aimed at checking black money);

(e) Bankruptcy Law (aimed at promoting the 'ease of doing business'); and

(f) Enactment of the Aadhar Act (aimed at rationalising and weeding out corruption in the present subsidy regime); and

(g) Attempts in the direction influencing the 'behavioural pattern' of the citizens to promote the cause of socio-economic well being; etc.

The *Union Budget 2017–18* has clearly termed them transformational reforms. As these reforms are aimed at long-term gains, there might be some political backlash on them. But this is the way, economies grow up and get mature. Remark from the latest *Economic Survey 2016–17* looks quite correct in this case—economic reforms are not, or not just, about overcoming vested interests, they are increasingly about shared narratives and vision on problems and solutions.

Q. 34 Discuss the challenges faced by the public sector banks in the light of the emerging business opportunities in the banking sector.

Ans. Once India started banking sector reforms in the early 1990s, the banking industry saw multi-dimensional growth where new private banks were given licences, foreign banks allowed entry, universal banking became possible etc. The hitherto closed banking sector with almost complete state monopoly (via the public sector banks—PSBs) was faced with multiple challenges. Private sector banks started entering the sector with state-of-the-art technology, making it more difficult for the PSBs to complete. Another challenging task for PSBs in the near future will be related to their

human resource management. The market in the financial sector and especially in banking, is seeing growth driven by new products and services that include opportunities in:

(i) credit cards, consumer finance and wealth management on the *retail side,* and

(ii) fee-based income and investment banking on the *wholesale side.*

These require new skills in sales and marketing, credit and operations. Furthermore, given the demographic shifts resulting from changes in the age profile and household income, consumers will increasingly demand enhanced institutional capabilities and levels, of service from banks. The PSBs need to fundamentally strengthen institutional skill levels especially in sales and marketing, service operations, risk management, and overall organisational performance.

The following steps (suggested by the RBI and experts) may help PSBs in handling these challenges:

(i) use of technology to reduce the gap created by shortage of staff and improving overall manpower efficiency.

(ii) a pool of talent for occupying leadership positions may be built up by banks by training and preparing promising officers to assume future leadership roles.

In the coming times the PSBs will have to gear up to face the new challenges, such as—increasing digitalisation; streamlining the payment systems; developing state-of-the-art cyber security system; competing against the new entrant, payment banks and private 'wallet' firms. As the government is pushing consolidation of the PSBs, it is believed that these concerns will be attended in the coming times accordingly. *(Economic Survey 2016–17 and Union Budget 2017–18).*

Q.35 **Briefly discuss the factors due to which insurance penetration remains low in India, even after insurance reforms commencing over two and half decades ago.**

Ans. India commenced insurance reforms in early 1990s itself. Though, the growth of the industry has been good, its expansion and insurance inclusion in the country has not been appreciable. At present, *insurance penetration* in India is **3.3** per cent of the GDP (it was 2.71 per cent in 2001) while the *insurance density* is at US$55 (it was US$11.5 in 2001). Globally, insurance penetration and density were 6.1 per cent and US$662, respectively.

As per the area experts and the insurance regulator, there are several factors responsible for the low insurance penetration in the country—*major ones* of them are as given below:

(i) Complex and delayed claim settlement procedures;

(ii) Vague and incomprehensible rules and regulations of the insurance companies;

(iii) Lack of education and awareness among the masses;

(iv) Lower income levels of the population;

(v) Socio-cultural factors;

(vi) Lack of level playing field in the industry; and

(vii) Less vibrancy in the regulatory framework.

It is believed that there is high potential for the growth of insurance sector in the country, especially, in the rural areas. Recently implemented Insurance Amendment Act, 2015 is supposed to improve the sector.

Q.36. **"To build fiscal capacity, it is essential for India to create legitimacy in the state". Comment.**

Ans. Tax reform was an integral part of India's economic reform programme which commenced in 1991. The tax base of India is still not adequate. To build fiscal capacity the government needs to put in place a better tax regime which is only possible once the government is able to enhance its 'legitimacy' among the citizens—following steps are advisable in this regard (*Economic Survey 2015–16*):

• The *spending priorities* of the government must include essential services which are consumed by all citizens. For that matter, action needs on public infrastructure, law and order, less pollution and congestion, etc.

• *Reducing corruption* must be a high priority. This is needed not just because of its economic costs but also because it undermines legitimacy of the state. The more citizens believe that public resources are not wasted, the greater they will be willing to pay taxes. Improving transparency through efficient auctioning of public assets will help create legitimacy, and over time strengthen fiscal capacity.

• *Subsidies to the well-off* need to be scaled back. At present, it is estimated to be around Rs. 1 lakh crore. Phasing down these bounties and targeting subsidies for the poor important in strengthening legitimacy.

• *Property taxation* needs to be developed. As property taxes are 'progressive' they are desirable. It makes more sense because evading this tax is difficult as they are imposed on immovable (non-mobile) assets. This could be good source of funds for the local bodies. *Smart cities* require smart public finance and for India's urban future a sound property taxation regime will be vital.

Based on the experience of the developed countries, it has been advised to the Governments to enhance the level of legitimacy in the state/government to prevent the middle class (the main force behind India's growth story) from 'exiting' the formal economic framework. We see the at least the central government conscious about this concern but India needs to sensitise the state governments also in this regard. (*Economic Survey 2016–17 & 2015–16*).

Q.37. **"Hybrid Annuity Model of the PPP recently announced by the GoI for the road sector is a timely modification of the existing model." Give your comments with suitable illustrations.**

Ans. Promoting road projects in the country has emerged into a major problem. Since the sector was opened for the private investment, the government has launched several model to attract investment to the sector—these models had run into myriads of difficulties over the time. To promote the cause, the GoI announced a new model by late January 2016—the 'hybrid annuity model' (HAM). It is a timely improvisation of the existing model—major features of it are given below:

- Investment participation to be in the ratio of 40:60 by the GoI and the private sector.
- Private sector to construct and hand over the road projects to the GoI.
- Toll collection will be the responsibility of the GoI.
- GoI will pay a fixed amount of 'annuity' to the private player for the defined period of time as per the contract.
- Private player to be selected through 'competitive bidding'—the player asking for the lowest annuity to get the contract.

- GoI to cover all the risks related to regulatory clearance, land acquisition, compensation, commercial, traffic.

The HAM is a mix of the existing EPC and BOT-Annuity models. The present model was 'engineering, procurement and construction' (EPC) in which the risks related to clearance, land acquisition, commercial and traffic all were borne by the GoI together with the 100 per cent funding. Toll collection was the government responsibility (which the government may decide to not collect). The was given to the lowest bidder. In fact, this model was hardly different from a normal contract. In it, there was no scope of attracting private investment to the fund-scarce road sector, this is why a replacement was needed.

Before the EPC model, India was having the 'build-operate-transfer-annuity' (BOT-Annuity) model till 2010. The PPP model was based on 'annuity' payment to the private player by the GoI with the latter covering no commercial and traffic risks. Toll collection was the responsibility of the government. The contract was given to the player which asked for the lowest annual annuity.

Q.38. **"There is a perception that vocational education and skill development are meant for people who have failed to join mainstream education." In light of this statement discuss the situation of 'skill gap' in the economy and the recent steps taken by the government in this regard.**

Ans. 'Skill' is considered the best tool to improve employability of the population. This can be imparted through vocational education and training. However, there is a perception that vocational education and skill development are meant for people who have failed to join mainstream education. This perception is strengthened by the significantly lower wages paid to employees with vocational training vis-à-vis those with formal education.

There is a severe quality gap and lack of availability of trainers in the vocational education and training sector as per the NSDC (National Skill Development Corporation). By 2017, this skill gap within the vocational training sector including both teachers and non-teachers will reach a figure of 211,000. The workforce requirement is projected to increase to 320,000 by 2022. Some *recent steps* taken by the GoI, in this regard, are as given below:

- The NSDC has given a big thrust towards this. The establishment of the *National Skill Qualification Framework (NSQF)* is aimed at bridging skill gap in the higher education.

- The SSCs (Sector Skill Councils) as autonomous industry-led bodies through the NSDC create National Occupational Standards (NOSs) and Qualification Packs (QP) for each job role in the sector, develop competency frameworks, conduct training of trainers, conduct skill gap studies and assess through independent agencies and certify trainees on the curriculum aligned to NOSs developed by them.

- The *PMKVY* (Pradhan Mantri Kaushal Vikas Yojana), which targets offering 24 lakh Indian youth meaningful, industry-relevant, skill-based training and a government certification on successful completion of training along with assessment to help them secure a job for a better future.

- The *DDU-GKY* (Deen Dayal Upadhyaya Grameen Kaushalya Yojana), a placement-linked skill development scheme for rural youth (who are poor), as a skilling component of the NRLM (National

rural Livelihood Mission) has also been launched.

- *National Action Plan (NAP)* for skill and training has been launched with a view to increasing the scope of employability among differently-abled persons.

- *National Policy on Skill Development and Entrepreneurship 2015* aims to ensure skilling on a large scale at a speed with high Standards and promote a culture of innovation based entrepreneurship to ensure sustainable livelihoods.

India has one of the youngest populations in the world. Given this, there is immense potential for overseas employment opportunities for skilled persons from India. The process of mapping such opportunities through the NSDC is also in progress.

Q.39. **"Improving the performance of social sector will make India achieve three goals in one move—fiscal consolidation, better human capital formation and enhanced welfare". Comment on the statement and also give your advices to improve the situation of the social sector.**

Ans. The whole gamut of expenditures the governments do on the social welfare falls under the social sector. It has a significant role in the economic development and welfare of a country. It is empirically proven and widely recognized social sector expenditures impact the growth of an economy. Investing in *human capital* by way of education, skill development, training and provision of health care facilities enhances the productivity of the workforce and welfare of the population. In this regard, contemporary documents *suggest* the following actions for the governments in the country:

- Improving the quality of education provided in schools to arrest and reverse the decline in enrolment in government schools. An important contributor to improvement in the quality of education would be an increase in the percentage of *qualified teachers.*

- Overcoming the development challenges through innovative models of *delivery of services.* It has a critical role to play in India's march towards double-digit growth.

- Improving the quality of human capital will be necessary to capitalise and leverage the advantages of the demographic dividend—through better healthcare, education and skill.

- Overhauling of the subsidy regime is needed with faster pace. It will not only rationalise the subsidies but bring in variety of *other benefits* in the service delivery system—inclusion of the needy population; exclusion of the fake accounts; prevention of corruption and leakages; traceability; authentication of delivery; transparency and accountability. The idea of technology-enabled Direct Benefits Transfers (DBT), namely the JAM (Jan Dhan-Aadhaar-Mobile) number trinity solution, introduced by the GoI in this regard is believed to be a game-changing move.

- India needs to include the *behavioural dimensions* of the target population in its framework of policy-making to realise desired results in the area of promoting the cause of the social infrastructure.

- There is a need of *integrating* the social sector initiatives of the Centre, states and the local bodies. The new 'think tank' NITI Aayog can play a suitable platform in this regard.

- Strengthening of the *local bodies* (the PRIs) will not only boost the social sector

but it will have an effect of externality in the form of an aware, awakened and participative citizenry. Through them, India can garner the support of civil society and the NGO.

- There is need to motivate and orient the *private sector* (corporate world) towards this cause. Their inclusion in this area will not only bring in additional funds to this fund-scarce sector but enable the country to use their expertise in the promotion of the social infrastructure.

This way, improved performance of the social sector serves three purposes— fiscal consolidation (by rationalising subsidies), better human capital formation (by better education, healthcare, skill, etc.) and enhanced welfare (by being free delivery of services to the poor masses).

Q.40 "Sanitation has a direct link with the women's fundamental right to privacy". Examine.

Ans. Deficiencies in sanitation forces women and girls in India to carry higher burden which compromises with their fundamental right to privacy, too. Hygiene improves health in general but more than that it provides control on body and promotes women's right to privacy. In absence, it may create 'gender-based sanitation insecurity'. Lack of sanitation can take several forms— threat to life and safety while going out for open defecation, reduction in food and water intake practices to minimize the need to exit the home to use toilets, polluted water leading to women and children dying from childbirth-related infections, among others.

The Census 2011 reported a widespread lack of sanitation—more than half of the country's population defecated in the open. Recent data shows that about 60 per cent of rural households *(up from 45 per cent, NSS 2015)* and 89 per cent of urban households *(NSSO 2016)* have access to toilets—an improved situation over the Census. A 'rapid study' specially done for the *Economic Survey 2016–17* presents some worrisome trends among the 'households without toilets'—

- 76 per cent of women had to travel a considerable distance to use these facilities;

- 33 per cent of the women reported facing privacy concerns and assault while going out in the open. Due to these risks, the number of women who reduced consumption of food and water are 33 per cent and 28 per cent, respectively.

- While in short-term it creates problems like illness, disruptions, and deficiencies; in the long-term it compromises with overall health and cognitive development of infants and specially girls.

- Other studies have highlighted the concerns such as exposure to natural elements, snakebites, etc.

Given the scenario it is imperative to address the issue of sanitation on priority. This will not only improve health situations of all but in case of women and girls it will be a major push in the direction of securing them their fundamental right to privacy. Sanitation is a major factor leading to women's privacy.

Q.41. "Enhancing water productivity and irrigation efficiency can do miracle to the agricultural development in India". Comment in light of the idea of 'more crop per drop'.

Ans. India's agriculture lacks irrigation facilities—just around one third of it gets it. Meanwhile, additional irrigation capacity is developed agricultural productivity can be boosted in a miraculous way by enhancing the efficiency of the existing irrigation system. The conventional systems of irrigation, over the time, have become non-viable in many parts of India *(NITI Aayog, Task Force on Agriculture, 2015)* due to three reasons—

(i) increasing shortages of water,

(ii) wastage of water due to over-irrigation, and

(iii) salination of soil.

Economically and technically efficient irrigation technologies like—*drip* and *sprinkler* irrigation (micro irrigation)—can improve water use efficiency, reduce costs of production by reducing labour costs and power consumption *(Economic Survey 2015–16)*—

- *sprinkler irrigation* resulted in 35 to 40 per cent savings of irrigation water in the cultivation of groundnut and cotton in Gujarat, Karnataka and Andhra Pradesh.

- *drip irrigation* resulted in 40 to 65 per cent savings in water for horticulture crops and 30 to 47 per cent for vegetables.

Water productivity in India is very low. The overall irrigation efficiency of the major and medium irrigation projects in India is estimated at around 38 per cent. The efficiency of the *surface irrigation* system can be improved from about 35–40 per cent to around 60 per cent and that of *groundwater* from about 65–70 per cent to 75 per cent *(NITI Aayog, Task Force on Agriculture, 2015)*. Water productivity needs to be enhanced by the following methods –

- tapping, harvesting and recycling water,
- efficient on-farm water management practices,
- micro irrigation,
- use of waste water, and
- resource conservation technologies.

In order to promote judicious use of water ensuring 'more crop per drop' of water in agriculture for drought proofing, the GoI recently launched the PMKSY aiming at providing water to every field of agriculture. In this regard, India needs to go for enhanced irrigation efficiency and water productivity.

Q. 42. "The gradual approach to economic reforms has given its own dividends to India". Comment with suitable illustrations.

Ans. The economic reforms which commenced in the world by mid-1980s reached several other countries in the next decade, more so after the arrival of the WTO. Over the time, experts together with the World Bank and the International Monetary Fund has classified such countries into two categories—one which went for the 'gradualist' approach and the other which followed the 'stop-and-go' approach.

India's reform process has been termed as gradualist (also known as 'incremental'). We see the traits of occasional reversals in the reform policies of India. There has been a lack of consensus among the different coalitions as well as the Centre and the states. It reflects the compulsions of India's highly pluralist and participative democratic policy-making process.

Though such approach helped India avoid socio-political upheavals, it either delayed or did not allow it to realise the desired objectives of reforms. The first generation of reforms could not bring the expected results out of the reforms due to absence of some other kind of reforms which India goes for after almost one decade. This has created a mood of disillusionment among the general public towards the benefits of the reforms—failing governments to muster enough political support in favour of it. But the gradualist nature of reform has given India certain other benefits which are considered bigger than gaining only the economic fruits out of it—

- India being a welfare state, it does not seem nice to follow reforms for only wealth creation which is the essence of reforms.

- With a huge population of poor and marginalised people subsidised or free delivery of essential goods and services becomes necessity on the part of the government.

- In India kind of economy, market forces can not be believed to have remedy for every economic issue. This makes a strong case for the intervention from the government.

- India has been able to avoid several economic crises too by following such an approach—first the impact of South East Financial Crisis (1996–97) and second, the western recession (2007–08) led by the US sub-prime crisis.

- In a sense, the incremental approach to reform made India delay adopting highly 'neo-liberal' policies and turned out to be a blessing in disguise.

Excessive inclination towards gradualist reforms may hamper the growth prospects of the economy. This is why the new government at the centre looks committed to the cause of essential reforms in a speedy manner—at times, even taking high political risks, too.

Q.43 "Farm mechanisation is not only the need of the hour but it has potential of giving high dividends to a largely non-remunerative farm sector of India". Comment.

Ans. India needs to introduce better equipment for each farming operation in order to reduce drudgery, to improve efficiency by saving on time and labour, improve productivity, minimize wastage and reduce labour costs for each operation.

Situation of farm mechanization in India (as per various documents of the GoI):

- although India is one of the top countries in agricultural production, the current level of farm mechanization, which varies across states, averages below 50 per cent as against more than 90 per cent in developed countries *(Economic Survey 2015–16).*

- the farm mechanization growth rate is less than 5 per cent for the last two decades.

- tractor penetration is very low—38 per cent for large farmers (with more than 20 acres), 18 per cent for medium farmers (5–20 acres) and just around 1 per cent for marginal farmers.

- farm mechanization has resulted in generating employment to rural youth and artisans for the production, operation, and maintenance of machines.

- the economic benefit of adoption of improved implements is about Rs. 83,000 crore per annum, which is only a small fraction of the potential *(NITI Aayog, 2016).*

Agricultural mechanization in case of India is increasingly needed as:

(a) due to shortage of labour for agricultural operations (owing to rural-urban migration), shift from agriculture to services and rise in demand for labour in non-farm activities, there is need to use labour for agricultural operations judiciously.

(b) agriculture sector in India has a high proportion of *female workforce*, therefore, ergonomically designed tools and equipment for reducing drudgery, enhancing safety and comfort and also to suit the needs of women workers.

Two important and contemporary policy *suggestions* may be given in this regard *(Economic Survey 2015–16):*

(i) Due to increased fragmentation of landholdings and low rates of tractor penetration among small farmers, there is need for a market in *tractor rentals*, akin to cars and road construction equipment, driven by private participation.

(ii) Appropriate farm equipment which are durable, light weight and low cost, region, crop and operation specific using indigenous/adapted technologies need to be made available for small and marginal farmers to improve productivity.

Q.44. "Of late, India has also realised that influencing social norms will bring in multiple socio-economic dividends to the economy." Comment with the help of suitable current illustrations.

Ans. Mankind is basically a social and psychological byproduct. It means, our actions have high influence of socio-psychological factors. This has been validated by the recent studies, too. Lately, even the international agencies have also suggested the world governments to include the behavioural dimensions of their citizens into their policy framework.

Several factors related to our behaviour are directly and indirectly related to the prospects of growth and development. For example, 'social norms' are considered a major factor of maternal health in India—young women are accorded low status in joint households. Within-household nutritional differentials are stark. A recent study *(Economic Survey 2015–16)* shows that children of younger brothers in joint family households are significantly more likely to be born underweight than children of their older brother. This is attached in part to the lower status of younger daughter-in-laws in families.

Like several other countries in the world, India too has recognised the importance of influencing 'social norms' in a wide variety of sectors—

- persuading the rich to give up subsidies they do not need,
- motivating citizens to take care of old people,
- inculcating a tendency to do good to others and philanthropic actions,
- enhancing the level of trust among the citizens. For this the GoI took initiative to first trust its own citizens (self-attestation of documents, etc.),
- reducing social prejudices against girls,
- educating people about the health externalities of keeping public spaces clean, and
- appealing to go against open defecation. India's attempts in this regard has been appreciated by the World Bank, too *(WDR-2015)*.

The government has a progressive role to play in changing norms, and indeed governments all over the world have embarked on systematic ways of studying how to promote behavioural change.

Q.45 **"Institutional lending does not provide any safeguard to farmers' suicides caused by bankruptcy and indebtedness". Examine with illustration.**

Ans. Farmers' suicides have been a major concern for the country. Bankruptcy and indebtedness have been cited as a major causes for it—as per the latest data (NCRB-2015), accounting for around 37 per cent of all suicides by farmers. By surveys and studies, local money-lenders were usually portrayed as the villain.

But as per the latest data, 80 per cent of the farmers who committed suicides in 2015 due to 'bankruptcy or debts' had borrowed money from institutional sources (banks and registered microfinance institutions). Besides, the country has seen a threefold increase in the famers' suicide due to bankruptcy and indebtedness within only one year period (from 1163 of 2014 to 3097 in 2015). In 2015, a total of 8007 farmers committed suicides due to various reasons. It was for the first time that the NCRB categorised farmers' suicides due to debt or bankruptcy based on the source of loans.

It means, the believe that institutional lending is better than local money-lenders and can be more inclusive has proved to be partially wrong—such lending may be more inclusive but it may turn out to be equally bad (or even worse) for the farmers. As institutional lending lacks human touch its nature of hardship could be even higher in comparison to the local money-lenders.

Looking at the current scenario only the size of fund allocated by the government for agriculture credit does not look sufficient. India needs to strengthen other support systems such as—enhancing the farm income together with expanding the agriculture insurance in a speedy manner.

Note: The Model Answers have been prepared by consulting a restricted list of references only to make them relevant and useful for the competitive examinations conducted by the various government bodies. Following main references have been consulted: various volumes of *Economic Survey;* various volumes of *India* reference manual; last four volumes of the *India Development Report*. Ministerial sources, websites of *RBI*, the **Planning Commission** and *NITI Aayog*.

CHAPTER

25

ECONOMIC SURVEY
2016–17

INTRODUCTION

As the date for the presentation of the *Union Budget 2017–18* was advanced to February 1, 2017, the *Economic Survey 2016–17* also got released almost one month earlier. But the release the survey was with a caveat—only volume one was being released—the volume two to come later in the year as a standalone document. The survey came in the wake of a set of 'tumultuous' international developments—the Brexit, political changes in advanced economies and two radical domestic policy actions, namely—the GST and demonetisation.

The survey accepts the difficulty to either 'deify' or 'demonise' the recent government move of demonetisation, but it tries to respond to it in an exclusive chapter. The document adds—" ....history, however, offers little guide for assessment and prognostication, given the unprecedented nature of the act of demonetisation....what we can definitely say is that there have been short-term costs but there are also potential long-term benefits—appropriate action can help minimize the former while maximizing the latter". The survey is structurally divided into three sections, namely—The Perspective, The Proximate, and The Persistent—with a section called "Eight Interesting Facts About India", to entice the reader. A concise analyses is presented here on the Survey—put in *three broad sections*, namely—"Performance in 2016–17"; "Policies in Perspective" and "Outlook for 2017–18".

SECTION 1: PERFORMANCE IN 2016–17

The important growth and fiscal indicators as per the latest advance estimates (AE) of the CSO, we find the following signals for the year 2016–17—

Growth rate: Growth rate at 7.1 per cent—with a likelihood of downward revisions. The gross value added (GVA) growth rate at 'constant basic prices' is estimated at 7.0 per cent, which was 7.2 per cent for the previous year. Sectoral growth rate estimates—*Agriculture* to grow at 4.1 per cent; *industry* by 5.2 per cent and *services* by 9.2 per cent.

GFCF: Fixed investment (GFCF-gross fixed capital formation) to GDP ratio (at current prices) is estimated to be 26.6 per cent (was 29.3 per cent in 2015–16). Fixed investment (at constant prices) estimated to decline to (–) 0.2 per cent (from 3.9 per cent of 2015–16 (it has been declining since 2011–12).

Consumption: Government final consumption expenditure (GFCE) estimated to grow by 23.8 per cent—the major driver of GDP growth. Private consumption is also projected to grow at a reasonable pace—contraction expected due to declining imports of gold, silver and other bullion, acquisition of valuables by households. Steeper contraction in imports, compared to exports, during the first half of 2016–17 led to a sharp decline in trade deficit. Despite slowing services exports, the decline in merchandise trade deficit helped improve the position of net exports of goods and non-factor services in the national accounts.

Fiscal developments: Fiscal consolidation continues with an estimated *fiscal deficit* of 3.5 per cent in the year (down from 3.9 per cent of the previous year)—strengthened by increases in 'non-debt receipts' (consisting of net tax revenue, non-tax revenue and non-debt capital receipts—estimated to grow by 25.8 per cent (higher than the budget estimates of 16.4 per cent). Estimates of growth rates of 'receipts' are—21.5 per cent for gross tax revenue; 33.6 per cent for tax revenue (net to centre); 1 per cent for non-tax revenue and 57.1 per cent for non-debt capital. The growth in 'revenue expenditure' seems very high—due to three main reasons—

(i) Salary component increased by 23.2 per cent (close to the budget target);

(ii) Major subsidies grew by 5.0 per cent (budget target was about a decline of 5.9

per cent)—21.6 per cent growth seen in the food subsidy.

(iii) Increase of 39.5 per cent in the 'grants for creation of capital assets' (GoCA)—all grants given to the states and UTs are treated as revenue expenditure, but a part of these grants are used for creation of capital assets.

Central government's *liabilities* (composed of internal debt, other internal liabilities like provident funds, small savings, etc. and external debt) estimated to grow by around 10 per cent (almost same as last two years) though it was budgeted to have a growth of only 7.9 per cent.

INFLATION

The headline inflation (at CPI-C) remained under control for the *third* successive financial year—declined to 4.9 per cent in 2015–16 from 5.9 per cent in 2014–15 (was 4.8 per cent during April-December 2016). Inflation hardened during the first few months of 2016–17, mainly due to upward pressure on the prices of *pulses and vegetables*. It dipped to two-year low of 3.4 per cent in December 2016 as a result of lower prices (especially of food items).

The average inflation (at WPI) declined to (–) 2.5 per cent in 2015–16 from 2.0 per cent in 2014–15. The downward trend, however reversed during 2016–17 partly due to impact of rise in global *commodity prices* and partly owing to *adverse base effect*. The global commodity and energy prices have increased by 18 per cent and 23 per cent respectively in the first eleven months of 2016 (as per *IMF* price indices). The WPI inflation stood at 3.4 per cent in December 2016 and the average inflation was 2.9 per cent during April–December 2016.

Food inflation: Inflation has been repeatedly driven in the country by narrow group of food items. *Pulses* continued to be the major contributor of food inflation—prices of pulses, in particular tur

and urad, remained persistently high from mid-2015 to mid-2016 (due to shortfall in domestic and global supply)—improved later on the back of better crops. *Sugar* prices also firmed up on account of lower production and hardening of price in the international market. *Vegetable* prices, which flared during the lean summer season, also declined sharply as supply picked up during the post monsoon and winter season. The CPI food inflation (CFPI) has, as a result, dipped to a *two-year low* of 1.4 per cent in December 2016. The inflation for pulses and products dipped to negative 1.6 per cent in December 2016, with vegetables inflation in negative since September 2016.

Core inflation: This remains sticky. CPI based refined core inflation (exclusive of food & fuel group, petrol & diesel) has been averaging around 5 per cent. Inflation for Pan, tobacco & intoxicants, Clothing & footwear, Housing and Education groups continued to be above 5 per cent and the major contributors of the core inflation. Inflation for the 'Transport & communication' group has been rising in recent months partly reflecting rise in global crude oil prices and its pass-through to domestic petrol and diesel prices. Price of crude oil (Indian basket) has increased from $39.9 in April 2016 to $52.7 in December 2016. Likewise, comparatively higher gold price in the international market this financial year has contributed towards sticky core inflation.

Inflation outlook: In view of the deceleration in the wholesale and retail prices of key food items during the second half of 2016–17, the average inflation based on CPI is projected to remain below 5 per cent. For the financial year 2017–18, the recent uptick in global commodity prices, in particular crude oil prices, pose an upside risk. The food inflation is likely to be subdued—caused by higher Rabi sowing, projected increase in the production of pulses and key agri-products globally.

FINANCIAL SECTOR

MPC: The monetary policy committee (MPC) was set up by amending the RBI Act of 1934— formal 'inflation targeting' commenced with target being 4 per cent (for the next 5 years, till the next revision) with tolerance level of +/- 2 per cent. Banks switched over to the marginal cost of fund based lending rate (MCLR) from April 2016— this is aimed at better transmission of monetary policy signals from the RBI. Though lending rates didi not fall as much the rate was cut by the RBI.

Liquidity situation: RBI has been managing liquidity through its liquidity management framework (LMF). By late 2016, RBI pumped liquidity through open market operations (OMOs). Post the withdrawal of specified bank notes (SBNs), RBI has mopped the large surplus liquidity through variable reverse repo rate. Government also increased the limit on securities under market stabilisation scheme from Rs. 30,000 crore to Rs. 6 lakh crore. The weighted average call money rate (WACR), on an average had been around policy rate.

Government bills/securities: There was a sharp fall in the 91 days treasury-bill rate in April 2016 owing to 25 bps cut in repo rate. Ten years government security (G-sec) yield however continued to tread high in spite of the rate cut and in fact increased marginally after the rate cut being 6.63 per cent by December 2016.

Banking sector: Banks performance, particularly the PSBs (public sector banks), continued to be subdued—asset quality deteriorating further. The gross non-performing assets (GNPAs) to total advances ratio of scheduled commercial banks (SCBs) increased to 9.1 per cent from 7.8 per cent between March and September 2016. Profit after tax (PAT) contracted on year-on-year basis in the first half of 2016–17 due to higher growth in risk provisions, loan write-off and decline in net interest income.

Credit growth: Non-food credit (NFC) outstanding grew at sub 10 per cent for all the months except for September 2016. Credit growth to industrial sector remained persistently below 1 per cent (with contraction in August, October and November). Agriculture and personal loans (PL) remained the major contributor to growth in NFC.

Corporate bond market: RBI took measures to strengthen the corporate bond market (accepting many recommendations of the Khan Committee)—

(i) Banks permitted to issue rupee-denominated bonds overseas (*masala bonds*) for their capital requirements and for financing infrastructure and affordable housing;

(ii) Brokers registered with the SEBI and 'market makers' in corporate bond market permitted to undertake repo/reverse repo contracts in corporate debt securities—aimed at promoting secondary market transactions in these bonds;

(iii) Banks allowed to increase the partial credit enhancement they provide for corporate bonds to 50 per cent from 20 per cent—aimed at helping lower-rated corporates to access the bond market;

(iv) Permitting primary dealers to act as market makers for government bonds—aimed at increasing accessibility to retail investors; and

(v) Entities exposed to exchange rate risk allowed to transact up to US$ 30 million.

Stock performance: For the calendar year 2016, Sensex grew by 1.95 per cent and Nifty by 3.0 per cent (as compared to losses registered in 2015). The upward momentum peaked around September 2016 and lost steam thereafter, due to foreign capital outflows. Global and domestic factors had a sizable impact—some of the closely watched developments were the Brexit, the US Presidential elections as well as policy announcements by the US Federal Reserve and the RBI. In addition, other factors which weighed on market sentiment included the policy decisions taken by the OPEC regarding oil production and the appointment of the new governor of the RBI.

Foreign Portfolio Investments: Net foreign portfolio investments turned *negative* (for the first time since the meltdown of 2008)—an outflow of Rs. 23079 crore. The outflow was not a phenomenon associated with Indian markets alone as they pulled out of most EMEs (emerging market economies) in a big way due to higher returns in advanced economies.

EXTERNAL SECTOR

Exports: During 2014–15 and 2015–16 India's exports had *declined* by 1.3 per cent and 15.5 per cent, respectively. The trend of negative growth was *reversed* somewhat during 2016–17 with exports registering a growth of 0.7 per cent (US$ 198.8 billion). A large number of export sectors have moved to positive zone during this period:

Imports: Imports did show mixed trend with decline being the chief feature—value of imports declined from US$ 448 billion in 2014–15 to US$ 381 billion in 2015–16, mainly on account of *decline in crude oil prices* resulting in lower levels of POL (petroleum, oil and lubricants) imports. The trend continued in 2016–17 also with imports declining by 7.4 per cent to US$ 275.4 billion. Top three import destinations of India were China followed by UAE and USA.

Trade deficit: India's *trade deficit* has been declining since the last two years—by 13.8 per cent in 2015–16 and 23.5 per cent during 2016–17 (falling to around US$ 100 billion)—current account deficit (CAD) being comfortable at **0.3** per cent by the first half of the fiscal 2016–17.

FDI: FDI (foreign direct investment) inflows increased by 29 per cent ($ 21.3 billion) during the first half of 2016–17 relative to 2015–16. The inflows have shown accelerating growth—in the

second half of 2016–17 it reached 3.2 per cent of GDP from 1.7 per cent of GDP of the same period of the preceding year.

Exchange rate: Rupee depreciated during 2016–17 (April-December) caused largely by strengthening of the US dollar globally and tightening of monetary policy there. However, it has performed better than the currencies of most of other emerging market economies (EMEs). On year-on-year basis, the rupee depreciated by 3.4 per cent against US dollar as compared to the depreciation of Mexican peso (14.4 per cent), South African Rand (8.6 per cent) and Chinese renminbi (6.3 per cent).

Forex reserves: Forex reserves were at comfortable levels of US$ 360 billion (December 2016)—with a rise of US$ 10 billion since January 2016.

External debt: External debt was at US$ 484.3 billion (September 2016), recording a decline of US$ 0.8 billion over the level at end-March 2016—mainly due to reduction in commercial borrowings (i.e., ECBs) and short-term debt—having the following features. Cross-country comparison (as per the World Bank's International Debt Statistics 2017), indicates India to be among the less vulnerable indebted countries among the developing world.

AGRICULTURE

Agriculture and allied sectors estimated to grow by 4.1 per cent in 2016–17 with the kharif foodgrains production reaching 135.0 million tonnes (from 124.1 million tonnes in 2015–16). Area sown (upto 14th October, 2016) under all kharif crops taken together was 1075.7 lakh hectares (3.5 per cent higher compared to the corresponding period of 2015–16)—with *arhar* showing the highest increase of 40.24 per cent. The rabi crops' sowing was in progress—the area coverage under rabi crops (by 13th January 2017) was 2016–17 at 616.21 lakh hectares (5.9 per cent higher than the corresponding week of last year). The area coverage under *wheat* was 7.1 per cent higher; under *gram* 10.6 per cent higher than that in the corresponding week of last year.

Monsoon: Country as a whole received 97 per cent rainfall during south west monsoon (long period average)—with wide regional variations—95 per cent in northwest, 106 per cent in central, 89 per cent in northeast and 92 per cent in south. Out of the total 36 meteorological subdivisions, 4 subdivisions received excess rainfall, 23 subdivisions received normal rainfall and the remaining 9 subdivisions received deficient rainfall.

Agri prices: The price policy of Government for major agricultural commodities seeks to ensure remunerative prices to the farmers to encourage higher investment and production, and to safeguard the interest of consumers by making available supplies at reasonable prices. On account of the volatility of prices of pulses, a Committee on *Incentivising Pulses Production Through Minimum Support Price (MSP) and Related Policies* was set up (headed by Arvind Subramanian, Chief Economic Adviser). To increase productivity of pulses, a new extra early maturing, high yielding variety of Arhar *(Pusa Arhar-16)* has been developed to be made available for farmers in the next Kharif season. During 2016–17, MSPs were raised substantially mainly for pulses to incentivize farmers.

Foodgrain stocks & procurement: The food-grain management involves procurement of rice and wheat following the norms for buffer stocks. The stocks of food-grains (rice and wheat) was 43.5 million tonnes on 1st December, 2016 (compared to 50.5 million tonnes as on 1st December, 2015) against the buffer stock norm of 30.77 million tonnes as on 1st October 2015. Procurement of rice as on 6th January 2017 was 23.2 million tonnes during kharif marketing season 2016–17 whereas procurement of wheat was 22.9 million tonnes during rabi marketing season 2016–17.

As part of the price policy to protect consumers, the *Central Issue Prices* of rice and wheat have remained unchanged since 1st July 2002.

Agriculture credit: Credit is an important input to improve agricultural output and productivity. To improve agricultural credit flow, the credit target for 2016–17 was fixed at Rs. 9 lakh crore against Rs. 8.5 lakh crore for 2015–16. As against the target, the achievement for 2016–17 (upto September 2016), was 84 percent of the target, higher than the corresponding figure of 59 per cent upto September 2015.

INDUSTRY AND INFRASTUTURE

Growth rate of the industrial sector (comprising mining & quarrying, manufacturing, electricity and construction) is projected to decline to 5.2 per cent in 2016–17 (from 7.4 per cent in 2015–16). A modest growth of 0.4 per cent was seen during April-November 2016–17. This was the 'composite effect' of a strong growth in electricity generation and moderation in mining and manufacturing. In terms of 'use-based classification', basic goods, intermediate goods and consumer durable goods attained moderate growth. Conversely, the production of capital goods *declined steeply* and consumer nondurable goods sectors suffered a modest contraction during this period.

Infrastructure industries: The eight core infrastructure supportive industries (coal, crude oil, natural gas, refinery products, fertilizers, steel, cement and electricity) that have a total weight of nearly 38 per cent in the IIP registered a cumulative growth of 4.9 per cent during April-November, 2016–17 (compared to 2.5 per cent during April-November, 2015–16). The production of refinery products, fertilizers, steel, electricity and cement *increased* substantially while production of coal, crude oil and natural gas *fell* during the period. Most indicators of infrastructure related activities showed expansion—thermal power grew with 6.9 per cent while hydro and nuclear power generation contracted marginally.

Corporate sector: Corporate sector (as per RBI, January 2017) had a sales growth of 1.9 per cent (2nd quarter of 2016–17) as compared to near stagnant growth of 0.1 per cent in 1st quarter. The growth of operating profits decelerated to 5.5 per cent in 2nd quarter of 2016–17 from 9.6 per cent in the previous quarter. Growth in net profits registered a remarkable growth of 16.0 per cent in 2nd quarter of 2016–17, as compared to 11.2 per cent in 1st quarter.

SERVICES SECTOR

Services sector is estimated to grow by 8.8 per cent, almost the same as in 2015–16 with the following major features:

- As per *WTO* data, India's commercial services exports increased from US$ 51.9 billion in 2005 to US$ 155.3 billion in 2015. The share of India's commercial services to global services exports increased to 3.3 per cent in 2015 from 3.1 per cent in 2014 despite negative growth of 0.2 per cent in 2015 as compared to 5.0 per cent growth in 2014. This was due to the relatively greater fall in world services exports by 6.1 per cent in 2015.

- As per RBI's BoP data, India's services exports declined by 2.4 per cent in 2015–16 as a result of slowdown in global output and trade. However, in the 1st half of 2016–17, services exports increased by 4.0 per cent compared to 0.3 per cent growth in the same period of previous year. Growth of net services, which has been a major source of financing India's trade deficit in recent years, was (–) 9.0 per cent in 2015–16 and (–) 10.0 per cent in 1st half of 2016–17 due to relatively higher growth in imports of services. Growth of software exports which accounted for 48.1 per cent share in services exports was

1.4 per cent in 2015–16 and 0.1 per cent in the 1st half of 2016–17.

- Tourism sector witnessed a growth of 4.5 per cent in terms of foreign tourist arrivals (FTA) with 8.2 million arrivals in 2015, and a growth of 4.1 per cent in foreign exchange earnings (FEE) ·of US$ 21.1 billion. In 2016 (January-December), FTAs were 8.9 million with growth of 10.7 per cent and FEE (US$ terms) were at US$ 23.1 billion with a growth of 9.8 per cent.

- The *Nikkei/Markit Services PMI* for India was at a high of 57.5 in January of 2013. It fell to 46.7 in November 2016 from 54.5 in October 2016. However, it increased marginally to 46.8 in December 2016.

- The *Baltic dry index (BDI)*, an indicator of both merchandise trade and shipping services, which showed some improvement up to 18 November 2016 declined to around 910 on 13 January 2017.

HUMAN DEVELOPMENT

Expenditure on social services by Centre and States, as a proportion of GDP was 7.0 per cent during 2016–17 (BE), with education and health sectors accounting for 2.9 per cent and 1.4 per cent respectively (as per the RBI). The year 2014–15 in respect of which latest actual figures are available showed a significant decline following a large decrease in actual social sector expenditure of the states.

Employment: The results of the quarterly quick employment surveys in select labour intensive and export-oriented sectors by the Labour Bureau for the period December, 2015 over December, 2014 show that the overall employment increased by 135 thousand. The sectors that contributed to this increase include—IT/BPOs sector, textiles including apparels and metals. Employment, however, declined in gems &

jewellery sector, handloom/power-loom sector, leather, automobiles sectors and transport sector during the same period. Major features regarding employment were as given follows:

- The Labour Force Participation Rate (LFPR) at the all India level based on usual principal status approach was estimated at 50.3 per cent with the LFPR of females being lower than that for males. There are wide interstate variations in the female LFPR as well. The North Eastern and Southern States, in general, display high female LFPR as compared to low levels in Northern States. As per EUS (employment and unemployment surveys), 2015–16, the unemployment rate for females was higher than that of males across rural and urban areas.

- As per EUS Surveys, employment growth has been sluggish. Further, States that show low unemployment rates also generally rank high in the share of manufacturing. While States compete to seek investment offering incentives, linking incentives to the number of jobs created, sustained efforts need to be considered as a tool to increase employment.

- There is a clear shift in employment to secondary and tertiary sectors from the primary sector—the data between 2011–12 and 2015–16 show the following trend—

  (i) Employed persons in the primary sector fell from 52.9 per cent to 46.1 per cent.

  (ii) Employed persons in the secondary sector increased from 19.3 per cent to 21.8 per cent.

  (iii) Employed persons increased from 27.8 per cent to 32 per cent.

- The growth in employment by category reflects increase in both casual labour and contract workers. This has adverse implications on the level of wages, stability of employment, social security of employees owing to the 'temporary' nature of employment. It also indicates preference by employers away from regular/formal employment to circumvent labour laws.

The multiplicity of labour laws and the difficulty in their compliance have been an impediment to the industrial development and employment generation. At present, there are 39 Central labour laws which have been broadly proposed to be grouped into four or five Labour Codes on functional basis with the enactment of special laws for small manufacturing units. In a *major initiative* for bringing compliance in the system, catalysing the need of job creation and to ensure ease of doing business while ensuring safety, health and social security of every worker, the Government has put forth a set of labour reform measures.

Education: Low learning outcomes has been a major concern of school education in the country—also pointed out in several studies including ASER, 2014. While there have been improvements in access and retention, the learning outcomes for a majority of children is still a cause of serious concern.

Some of the underlying causes contributing to low quality of education in the primary sector are 'teacher absenteeism' and the 'shortage of professionally qualified teachers'. Though the share of teacher component in total Sarva Shiksha Abhiyan (SSA) budget has been increasing over the years from 35 per cent in 2011–12 to 59 per cent in 2014–15, teacher absenteeism and the shortage of professionally qualified teachers remain an issue to be addressed.

An option to address teacher absenteeism that can be explored is 'biometric attendance' of all teachers in primary. Apart from the biometric attendance being regularly monitored by local communities and parents, it should also be put in public domain. This should be backed by adequate teaching aids, recorded lectures, etc. to fill in for absentee teachers.

Health: India's health policy aims at an integrated approach to provide accessible, affordable and equitable quality health care to the marginalized and vulnerable sections. The aim of good health and well-being for all as envisaged in the Sustainable Development Goal (SDG) *Ensure healthy lives and promote well being for all at all ages* should be synchronized with India's domestic targets to reap the benefits of the 'demographic dividend'.

The high levels of anaemia prevalent among women in the age group 15–49 have a direct correlation with high levels of MMR (maternal mortality rate). In Haryana and West Bengal more than 60 per cent of women suffer from anaemia. Under the National Health Mission, Government of India has programmes to address the issue of anaemia through health and nutrition education to promote dietary diversification, inclusion of iron foliate rich food as well as food items that promote iron absorption.

Inclusive growth: It is the vision of the Government to have an inclusive society in which equal opportunities are provided for the growth and development of all sections of the population including the marginalised, vulnerable and weaker sections to lead productive, safe and dignified lives. Accordingly, programmes have been initiated by the government towards attaining the objective of inclusive society like the *Accessible India Campaign.*

The government has various schemes meant for the "economic and social empowerment" of people belonging to the *minority communities*— the *Nai Roshni* scheme for leadership development of minority women; *Padho Pardesh*, a scheme of interest subsidy on educational loans for overseas studies for the students belonging to the minority communities; for skill development and economic empowerment of minorities, schemes like *Seekho Aur Kamao* (Learn & Earn), *Upgrading Skill and Training in Traditional Arts/Crafts for Development* (USTTAD) and to provide education and skill training to the youth from minority communities the *Nai Manzil.*

CLIMATE CHANGE

International negotiations: The Paris Agreement of 2015 (among the 196 Parties to the UNFCCC) brings all ambitious efforts to combat climate change and unleash actions and investment towards a low carbon, resilient and sustainable future. It sets the path for the post-2020 actions based on the Nationally Determined Contributions (NDCs) of the Parties—coming into force on 4th November 2016.

Meanwhile, the COP 22, in Marrakech, Morocco (November 2016) had its main thrust on developing rules and action framework for operationalizing the Paris Agreement and advance work on pre-2020 Actions. At COP 22, Parties agreed to a deadline of 2018 for the rule book. Detailing exercise will include accounting of the NDCs, adaptation communication, building a transparency framework, global stock take every five years, etc. The key decision adopted at COP 22 were—

(i) The sense of urgency to take action on climate change;

(ii) The need to strengthen and support efforts to eradicate poverty, ensure food security and enhance resilience of agriculture; and

(iii) The pre-2020 action including mobilization of USD 100 billion per year.

India's green actions: India ratified the Paris Agreement on 2nd October 2016. India's comprehensive NDC target is to lower the emissions intensity of GDP by 33 to 35 per cent by 2030 from 2005 levels, to increase the share of non-fossil fuels based power generation capacity to 40 per cent of installed electric power capacity by 2030, and to create an additional (cumulative) carbon sink of 2.5–3 GtCO2e through additional forest and tree cover by 2030. Major initiatives by India in the direction are—

- At present, India's renewable energy sector is *undergoing transformation* with a target of 175 GW of renewable energy capacity to be reached by 2022. In order to achieve the target, several programmes/ schemes are being implemented by the government. As a result of various actions in the right direction, India attained *4th position* in global wind power installed capacity after China, USA and Germany. India achieved 46.3 GW grid-interactive power capacity; 7.5 GW of grid-connected power generation capacity in renewable energy; and small hydro power capacity of 4.3 GW by October 2016. In January 2016, Government amended the *National Tariff Policy* for electricity with a focus on the environmental aspect.

- With India's initiative, International Solar Alliance (ISA) was launched, which is envisaged as a coalition of solar resource-rich countries to address their special energy needs and will provide a platform to collaborate on addressing the identified gaps through a common, agreed approach. 24 countries have signed the Framework Agreement of ISA after it was opened for signature on November 15, 2016. ISA is expected to become inter-governmental treaty-based organization that will be registered under Article 102 of the UN charter after 15 countries ratify the Agreement. With legal framework in place, ISA will be a major international body *headquartered* in India.

- Government of India has established the *National Adaptation Fund for Climate Change* to assist States and Union Territories to undertake projects and actions for adaptation to climate change.

- India is also one of the few countries in the world to impose a *tax on coal*. This coal cess which has been renamed as 'Clean Environment Cess' in 2016–17 funds the National Clean Environment Fund (NCEF). The Clean Environment Cess has been doubled in the 2016–17 to Rs. 400 per tonne. The proceeds of the NCEF are being used to finance projects under Green Energy Corridor for boosting up the transmission sector, Namami Gange, Green India Mission, Jawaharlal Nehru National Solar Mission, installation of SPV lights and small capacity lights, installation of SPV water pumping systems, SPV Power Plants and Grid Connected Rooftop SPV Power Plants.

SECTION 2: POLICIES IN PERSPECTIVE

The survey starts by giving a glance of the *8 interesting facts* about India, at the outset itself, as given below:

1. *Indians on The Move:* New estimates based on railway passenger traffic data reveal annual work-related migration of about 9 million people, almost double what the 2011 Census suggests.

2. *Biases in Perception:* China's credit rating was upgraded from A+ to AA- in December 2010 while India's has remained unchanged at BBB(–). From 2009 to 2015, China's credit-to-GDP soared from about 142 per cent to 205 per cent and its growth decelerated. The contrast with India's indicators is striking—it shows India in better

position. This shows poor standards followed by the global popular rating agencies.

3. *New Evidence on Weak Targeting of Social Programs:* Welfare spending in India suffers from misallocation—the districts with the most poor are the ones that suffer from the greatest shortfall of funds in social programs. The districts accounting for the poorest 40 per cent receive only 29 per cent of the total funding.

4. *Political Democracy but Fiscal Democracy:* India has 7 taxpayers for every 100 voters which ranks it at 13th amongst 18 of the democratic G-20 countries.

5. *India's Distinctive Demographic Dividend:* India's share of working age to non-working age population will peak later and at a lower level than that for other countries but last longer. The peak of the growth boost due to the demographic dividend is fast approaching, with peninsular states peaking soon and the hinterland states peaking much later.

6. *India Trades More Than China and a Lot Within Itself:* As of 2011, India's openness - measured as the "ratio of trade in goods and services to GDP" has far overtaken China's (a country famed for using trade as an engine of growth). India's internal trade to GDP is also comparable to that of other large countries and very different from the caricature of a barrier-riddled economy.

7. *Divergence within India, Big Time:* Spatial dispersion in income is still rising in India in the last decade (2004–14), unlike the rest of the world and even China. That is, despite more porous borders within India than between countries internationally, the forces of "convergence" have been elusive.

8. *Property Tax Potential Unexploited:* Evidence from satellite data indicates that Bengaluru and Jaipur collect only between 5 per cent to 20 per cent of their potential property taxes.

Introduction: The Economic Survey for 2014–15 spoke about the "sweet spot" for the Indian economy that could launch India onto a trajectory of sustained growth of 8–10 percent. The Survey 2015–16 assessed that "for now, but not indefinitely, that sweet spot is still beckoningly there". While this year's Survey (2016–17) suggests that shifts in the underlying vision will be needed to overcome the major challenges ahead, thereby accelerating growth, expanding employment opportunities, and achieving social justice. In the aftermath of demonetisation, and because cyclical developments will make economic management harder, articulating and embracing those shifts will be critical to ensuring that that sweet spot does not disappear.

The Survey cites the historic economic policy developments of 2016-16 in the following terms—

(i) On the domestic side, a constitutional amendment paved the way for the long-awaited and transformational goods and services tax (GST) while demonetisation of the large currency notes signalled a regime shift to punitively raise the costs of illicit activities.

(ii) On the international front, Brexit and the US elections may herald a tectonic shift, forebodingly laden with darker possibilities for the global, and even the Indian, economy.

Demonetisation: It was a "radical" governance-cum-social engineering measure (two largest denomination currency notes, Rs 500 and Rs 1000—comprising 86 percent of all the cash in circulation—were demonetised on November 8, 2016). The *aim* of the action was fourfold:

(i) Curbing corruption,

(ii) Curbing counterfeiting,

(iii) Checking terrorist activities, and

(iv) Curbing accumulation of black money.

Before demonetisation several steps were taken to curb such illicit activities—the creation of the Special Investigation Team (SIT) in the 2014 budget; the Black Money Act, 2015; the Benami Transactions Act of 2016; the information exchange agreement with Switzerland and changes in the tax treaties with Mauritius and Cyprus; and the Income Disclosure Scheme.

Demonetisation was aimed at signalling a regime change, emphasizing the government's determination to penalize illicit activities and the associated wealth. In effect, the tax on illicit activities as well as on legal activities that were not disclosed to the tax authorities was sought to be permanently and punitively increased. The public debate on demonetisation has raised three questions—

(a) its broader aspect of management, as reflected in the design and implementation of the initiative;

(b) its economic impact in the short and long run; and

(c) its implications for the broader vision of the future conduct of economic policy.

GST move: GST bill being cleared is transformational in nature, as per the Survey. The proposed tax will create a common Indian market, improve tax compliance, boost investment and growth—and improve governance. Besides, the tax is also a bold new experiment in the governance of *cooperative federalism*. In addition, the government—

(i) Overhauled the bankruptcy laws so that the "exit" problem that pervades the Indian economy—with high negative consequences (as highlighted in the Survey 2015–16) can be addressed effectively and speedily;

(ii) Codified the institutional arrangements on monetary policy with the Reserve Bank of India (RBI), that inflation control will be less susceptible to the whims of individuals and the caprice of governments; and

(iii) Solidified the legal basis for *Aadhaar*, to realise the long-term gains from the JAM *trifecta* (Jan Dhan-Aadhaar-Mobile).

Other reforms: Beyond these headline reforms were other less-heralded but nonetheless important actions—

(i) The government enacted a package of measures to assist the clothing sector that by virtue of being export-oriented and labour-intensive could provide a boost to employment, especially female employment.

(ii) The National Payments Corporation of India (NPCI) successfully finalized the Unified Payments Interface (UPI) platform. By facilitating inter-operability it will unleash the power of mobile phones in achieving digitalization of payments and financial inclusion, and making the "M" an integral part of the government's flagship JAM initiative.

(iii) Further FDI reform measures were implemented, allowing India to become one of the world's largest recipients of foreign direct investment.

These measures cemented India's reputation as one of the few bright spots in an otherwise grim global economy. India is not only among the world's fastest growing major economies, underpinned by a stable macro-economy with declining inflation and improving fiscal and external balances. It was also one of the few economies enacting major 'structural reforms'. Yet there is a gap between this reality of macro-economic stability and rapid growth, on the one hand, and the perception of the ratings agencies on the other. Economic reforms are not, or not just, about overcoming vested interests, they are increasingly about shared narratives and vision on problems and solutions.

FUTURE OUTLOOK

Domestic front: But India need to do much more. Especially after 1991, India has progressively distanced itself from statism and made considerable strides in improving the management of the economy. Yet a broader stock-taking suggests that India has to traverse a considerable distance to realize its ambitions on growth, employment and social justice. Broader societal shifts are required in ideas and narratives to address *three* major challenges—

(i) *Inefficient redistribution:* These structural challenges have their proximate policy counterparts. India's has made extensive efforts at redistribution. The central government alone runs about 950 central sector and centrally sponsored schemes and sub-schemes which cost about 5 per cent of GDP. Clearly, there are rationales for many of them. But there may be intrinsic limitations in terms of the effectiveness of targeting. Through Aadhar, the government has made great progress in improving redistributive efficiency over the last few years (the pilots for Direct Benefit Transfers in fertilizer represent a very important new direction in this regard). At the same time, prices facing consumers in many sectors are yet to move closer toward market levels. Even on the GST, concerns about ensuring low tax rates for essentials, risks creating an unduly complicated structure with multiple and excessively high peak rates, thereby foregoing large services efficiency gains. The idea of *universal basic income (UBI)* may be tried by India, but with caution—it should not become another scheme with the similar demerits—trimming down the existing schemes will serve double purposes in this regard—making it fiscally sustainable and improving governance in redistribution.

(ii) *State capacity:* Delivery of essential services such as health and education, which are predominantly the preserve of state governments, remains impaired. Regulatory institutions are still finding their way. The deepest puzzle has been—while competitive federalism has been a powerful agent of change in relation to attracting investment and talent, it has been less evident in relation to essential service delivery. There have, of course, been important exceptions, such as the improvement of the public distribution system (PDS) in Chhattisgarh, the incentivization of agriculture in Madhya Pradesh, reforms in the power sector in Gujarat which improved delivery and cost recovery, the efficiency of social programs in Tamil Nadu, and the recent use of technology to help make Haryana *kerosene-free*. But on health and education there are insufficient instances of good models that can travel widely within India and that are seen as attractive political opportunities. Competitive populism needs a counterpart in competitive service delivery.

(iii) *Property rights:* We find an ambivalence about protecting property rights and embracing the private sector—political dynamic have been lacking for decades. This is manifested in—

- the difficulties in advancing "strategic disinvestment";

- the persistence of the "twin balance sheet" problem (over-indebtedness in the corporate and banking sectors which requires difficult decisions about burden-sharing and perhaps even forgiving some burden on the private sector);

- the legacy issues of "retroactive taxation", which remain mired in litigation even though the government has made clear its intentions for the future;

- "agriculture", where the protection of intellectual property rights, for example in seeds, remains a challenge;

- frequent recourse to 'stock limits and controls' on trade in agriculture, which draws upon the antiquated Essential Commodities Act, and creates uncertainty for farmers.

- reform in the 'civil aviation sector', which has been interventionist rather liberalizing;

- reforms in the 'fertilizer sector', where it is proving easier to rehabilitate unviable plants in the public sector rather than facilitate the exit the inefficient ones;

In each of the above-given examples, there may be valid reasons for the *status quo* but overall they indicate that the embrace of markets—even in the modest sense of avoiding intrusive intervention, protecting property rights, disposing of unviable public sector assets and exiting from areas of comparative non-advantage, and allowing economic agents to face market prices—remains a work-in-progress.

External front: Even as the domestic agenda remains far from complete, the international order is changing—posing new challenges. The impact of Brexit and the US elections, though still uncertain, risk unleashing *paradigmatic shifts* in the direction of 'isolationism' and 'nativism'. The post war consensus in favour of globalisation of goods, services and labour in particular, and market-based economic organization more broadly, is under threat across the advanced economies—in a sense a process of "de-globalisation" looks ensuing. For India that is a late "converger"—that is an economy whose standards of living are well below countries at the frontier—these events have immense consequences. Given that India's growth ambitions of 8–10 per cent require export growth of about 15–20 per cent, any serious 'retreat from openness' on the part of India's trading partners would jeopardize those ambitions.

To these structural domestic and external developments must be added the proximate macro-economic challenges. Since the decline in oil prices from their peak in June 2014 there has been a lift to incomes which combined with government actions imparted dynamism by increasing private consumption and facilitating public investment, shoring up an economy buffeted by the headwinds of weak external demand and poor agricultural production. In 2017–18, this source of short-term dynamism may be taken away as international oil prices are now on the rise. Moreover, private investment remains weak because of the 'twin balance sheet' (TBS) problem that has been the economy's festering wound for several years now. Re-establishing private investment and exports as the predominant and durable sources of growth is the proximate macro-economic challenge.

Precisely speaking, the steady progress on structural reforms made in the last few years needs to be rapidly built upon, and the unfinished agenda completed. Especially, after demonetisation and given the ever-present late-term challenges, anxieties about the vision underlying economic policy and about the forgoing of opportunities created by the sweet spot need to be decisively dispelled.

SECTION 3: OUTLOOK FOR 2017–18

As per the CSO, the economy is estimated to grow by 7.1 per cent in 2016–17, however, it is based on first 7 to 8 months of the year only. Thus, it unlikely to have captured the impact of the 'denomination' of currency—though difficult to precisely pinpoint on GDP, there are chances of downward revisions in coming estimates of the CSO. Inflation could also be lower than what comes out from the implicit GDP deflator underlying the CSO's first advance estimates. The outlook for the upcoming year 2017–18 is expected to be as given below:

- Growth would return to normal as the new currency notes in required quantities come back into circulation and as follow up actions to demonetisation are taken.

- Helping to maintain the momentum of growth will be factors like possible normal monsoon, an increase in the level of exports following the projected increase in global growth and above all various reform measures taken by the Government to strengthen the economy.

- Some possible challenges to growth exist—the prices of crude oil have started rising and are projected to increase further in the next year. Estimates suggest that oil prices could rise by as much as *one sixth* over the 2016–17 level, which could have some dampening impact on the growth.

- Fixed investment rate in the economy has consistently declined in the past few years, more so the private investment. Raising the growth rate of the economy will to a great extent depend on quickly reversing this downward trend in the investment.

- The last few years have also witnessed a slowdown in global trade and investment flows. Although, India has not been particularly affected by this slowdown, lower growth in foreign portfolio investment cannot be ruled out, partly on account of the fact that the interest rates in the United States have begun to increase.

- On balance, there is a strong likelihood that Indian economy may recover back to a growth of 6.75 per cent to 7.5 per cent in the year.

LATEST

Meanwhile, the CSO released the 'advance estimates' of growth for the 3rd quarter of the year, on *February 28, 2017*. The growth rate of the economy, in October–December quarter, has been estimated at 7.0 per cent (against the 7.4 per cent of the preceding quarter). Demonetisation had negative impact on growth but not as much as majority of the experts were projecting. In this way, the newly released data have "masked the impact of demonetisation" on growth prospects of the economy, about which even the Survey was apprehensive.

26

UNION BUDGET
2017–18

INTRODUCTION

This year's Union Budget was presented on February 1st, in place of the long tradition of presenting on the last day of the February. In the aftermath of the demonetisation drive, there were high expectations from the budget regarding tax relaxation and some stimulus being announced. It has got mixed reactions from the business, trade and the experts. Overall, the budget has avoided populist announcements and has stuck to the fundamentals of fiscal policy. Main highlights of the budget are as given below.

Performance of 2016–17: The budget document, at the outset, gives a precise overview about *economic performance* of the previous year, in the following way—

- In the last two and half years administration has moved from discretionary, favouritism based to system and transparency based.

- Inflation brought under control. CPI-based inflation declined from 6% in July 2016 to 3.4% in December, 2016.

- Economy has moved on a high growth path. India's Current Account Deficit declined from about 1% of GDP last year to 0.3% of GDP in the first half of 2016–17. FDI grew 36% in H1 2016–17 over H1 2015–16, despite 5% reduction in global FDI inflows. Foreign exchange reserves have reached 361 billion US Dollars as on 20th January, 2017.

- War against black money launched.

- Government continued on path of fiscal consolidation, without compromising on public investment.

- The Indian economy has been robust to mild shocks and IMF forecasts, India to be one of the fastest growing major economies in 2017.

Transformational reforms: It enumerates three reforms of last year and titles them as 'transformational' of the previous year have been enumerated as follows—

(i) Passage of the Constitution Amendment Bill for GST.

(ii) Demonetisation of high denomination bank notes.

(iii) Enactment of the Insolvency and Bankruptcy Code; amendment to the RBI Act for inflation targeting; enactment of the *Aadhar* bill for disbursement of financial subsidies and benefits.

Global uncertainties: This year budget was will be faced with certain challenges in the form 'global uncertainties', namely—

(i) Global economy faces considerable uncertainty, in the aftermath of major economic and political developments during the last year.

(ii) The US central bank' intention to increase policy rates in 2017, may lead to lower capital inflows and higher outflows from the emerging economies.

(iii) Uncertainty around commodity prices, especially that of crude oil, has implications for the fiscal situation of emerging economies together with India.

(iv) Signs of 'retreat from globalisation' (de-globalisation) of goods, services and people, as pressures for protectionism are building up.

New reforms: This year's budget announces *three* major reforms—

(i) Presentation of the budget advanced to 1st February to enable the Ministries to operationalise all activities from the commencement of the financial year.

(ii) Merger of Railways Budget with General Budget to bring Railways to the centre stage of Government's Fiscal Policy and

(iii) Removal of 'plan' and 'non-plan' classification of expenditure to facilitate a holistic view of allocations for sectors and ministries.

Demonetisation: It has the following main comments on the demonetisation drive which the government activated by year end—

- Bold and decisive measure to curb tax evasion and parallel economy.
- Government's resolve to *eliminate corruption, black money, counterfeit currency* and *terror funding*.
- Drop in economic activity, if any, to be temporary.
- Generate long-term benefits including reduced corruption, greater digitisation, increased flow of financial savings and greater formalisation of the economy.
- Pace of remonetisation has picked up and will soon reach comfortable levels.
- The surplus liquidity in the banking system will lower borrowing costs and increase the access to credit.
- Announcements made by the PM on 31st Dec, 2016 focusing on—housing for the poor; relief to farmers; credit support to MSMEs; encouragement to digital transactions; assistance to pregnant women and senior citizens; and priority to dalits, tribals, backward classes and women under the Mudra Yojana—address key concerns of our economy.

Roadmap and Priorities: The budget document outlines the following 'roadmap & priorities' for the upcoming year 2017–18—

Agenda for the year: "Transform, Energise and Clean India", i.e., TEC India, which seeks to—

(i) Transform the quality of governance and quality of life of our people;

(ii) Energise various sections of society, especially the youth and the vulnerable, and enable them to unleash their true potential; and

(iii) Clean the country from the evils of corruption, black money and non-transparent political funding.

Themes: Ten distinct themes to foster the above-cited broad agenda are—

1. **Farmers:** committed to double the income in 5 years;
2. **Rural Population:** providing employment & basic infrastructure;
3. **Youth:** energising them through education, skills and jobs;
4. **The Poor and the Underprivileged:** strengthening the systems of social security, health care and affordable housing;
5. **Infrastructure:** for efficiency, productivity and quality of life;
6. **Financial Sector**: growth & stability by stronger institutions;
7. **Digital Economy**: for speed, accountability and transparency;
8. **Public Service**: effective governance and efficient service delivery through people's participation;
9. **Prudent Fiscal Management**: to ensure optimal deployment of resources and preserve fiscal stability;
10. **Tax Administration**: honouring the honest.

FARMERS AND FARM SECTOR

- Target for agricultural credit in 2017–18 has been fixed at a record level of Rs. 10 lakh crores.

- Farmers will also benefit from 60 days' interest waiver announced on 31 Dec 2016.

- To ensure flow of credit to small farmers, Government to support NABARD for computerisation and integration of all 63,000 functional Primary Agriculture Credit Societies with the Core Banking System of District Central Cooperative Banks. This will be done in 3 years at an estimated cost of Rs. 1,900 crores.

- Coverage under Fasal Bima Yojana scheme will be increased from 30% of cropped area in 2016–17 to 40% in 2017–18 and 50% in 2018–19 for which a budget provision of Rs. 9000 crore has been made.

- New mini labs in *Krishi Vigyan Kendras* (KVKs) and ensure 100% coverage of all 648 KVKs in the country for soil sample testing.

- As announced by the Honourable Prime Minister, the Long Term Irrigation Fund already set up in NABARD to be augmented by 100% to take the total corpus of this Fund to Rs. 40,000 crores.

- Dedicated Micro Irrigation Fund in NABARD to achieve 'per drop more crop' with an initial corpus of Rs. 5,000 crores.

- Coverage of National Agricultural Market (e-NAM) to be expanded from 250 markets to 585 APMCs. Assistance up to Rs. 75 lakhs will be provided to every e-NAM.

- A model law on contract farming to be prepared and circulated among the States for adoption.

- Dairy Processing and Infrastructure Development Fund to be set up in NABARD with a corpus of Rs. 2000 crores and will be increased to Rs. 8000 crores over 3 years.

RURAL POPULATION

- Over Rs. 3 lakh crores spent in rural areas every year, for rural poor from Central Budget, State Budgets, Bank linkage for self-help groups, etc.

- Aim to bring one crore households out of poverty and to make 50,000 Gram Panchayats poverty free by 2019, the 150th birth anniversary of Gandhiji.

- Against target of 5 lakh farm ponds under MGNREGA, 10 lakh farm ponds would be completed by March 2017. During 2017–18, another 5 lakh farm ponds will be taken up.

- Women participation in MGNREGA has increased to 55% from less than 48%.

- MGNREGA allocation to be the highest ever at Rs. 48,000 crores in 2017–18.

- Pace of construction of PMGSY roads accelerated to 133 km roads per day in 2016–17, against an avg. of 73 km during 2011–2014.

- Government has taken up the task of connecting habitations with more than 100 persons in left wing extremism affected Blocks under PMGSY. All such habitations are expected to be covered by 2019 and the allocation for PMGSY, including the State's Share is Rs. 27,000 crores in 2017–18.

- Allocation for Pradhan Mantri Awaas Yojana – Gramin increased from Rs. 15,000 crores in BE 2016–17 to Rs. 23,000 crores in 2017–18 with a target to complete 1 crore houses by 2019 for the houseless and those living in *kutcha* houses.

- Well on our way to achieving 100% village electrification by 1st May 2018.

- Allocation for Prime Minister's Employment Generation Program and Credit Support Schemes has been increased three fold.

- Sanitation coverage in rural India has gone up from 42% in Oct 2014 to about 60%. Open Defecation Free villages are now being given priority for piped water supply.

- As part of a sub mission of the National Rural Drinking Water Programme. (NRDWP), it is proposed to provide safe drinking water to over 28,000 arsenic and fluoride affected habitations in the next four years.

- For imparting new skills to people in rural areas, mason training will be provided to 5 lakh persons by 2022.

- A programme of "human resource reforms for results" will be launched during 2017–18 for human resources development in Panchayati Raj Institutions.

- Total allocation for Rural, Agriculture and Allied sectors is Rs. 187223 crores.

YOUTH

- To introduce a system of measuring annual learning outcomes in our schools.

- Innovation Fund for Secondary Education proposed to encourage local innovation for ensuring universal access, gender parity and quality improvement to be introduced in 3479 educationally backward districts.

- Good quality higher education institutions to have greater administrative and academic autonomy.

- SWAYAM platform, leveraging IT, to be launched with at least 350 online courses. This would enable students to virtually attend courses taught by the best faculty.

- National Testing Agency to be set-up as an autonomous and self-sustained premier testing organisation to conduct all entrance examinations for higher education institutions.

- *Pradhan Mantri Kaushal Kendras* to be extended to more than 600 districts across the country. 100 India International Skills Centres will be established across the country.

- Skill Acquisition and Knowledge Awareness for Livelihood Promotion programme (SANKALP) to be launched at a cost of Rs. 4000 crores. SANKALP will provide market relevant training to 3.5 crore youth.

- Next phase of Skill Strengthening for Industrial Value Enhancement (STRIVE) will also be launched in 2017–18 at a cost of Rs. 2,200 crores.

- A scheme for creating employment in the leather and footwear industries along the lines in Textiles Sector to be launched.

- Incredible India 2.0 Campaign will be launched across the world to promote tourism and employment.

THE POOR AND THE UNDERPRIVILEGED

- *Mahila Shakti Kendra* will be set up with an allocation of Rs. 500 crores in 14 lakh ICDS *Anganwadi* Centres. This will provide one stop convergent support services for empowering rural women with opportunities for skill development, employment, digital literacy, health and nutrition.

- Under Maternity Benefit Scheme Rs. 6,000 each will be transferred directly to the bank accounts of pregnant women who undergo institutional delivery and vaccinate their children.

- Affordable housing to be given infrastructure status.
- National Housing Bank will refinance individual housing loans of about Rs. 20,000 crore in 2017–18.
- Government has prepared an action plan to eliminate Kala-Azar and Filariasis by 2017, Leprosy by 2018, Measles by 2020 and Tuberculosis by 2025 is also targeted.
- Action plan has been prepared to reduce IMR from 39 in 2014 to 28 by 2019 and MMR from 167 in 2011–13 to 100 by 2018–2020.
- To create additional 5,000 Post Graduate seats per annum to ensure adequate availability of specialist doctors to strengthen Secondary and Tertiary levels of health care.
- Two new All India Institutes of Medical Sciences to be set up in Jharkhand and Gujarat.
- To foster a conducive labour environment, legislative reforms will be undertaken to simplify, rationalise and amalgamate the existing labour laws into 4 Codes on (i) wages; (ii) industrial relations; (iii) social security and welfare; and (iv) safety and working conditions.
- Propose to amend the Drugs and Cosmetics Rules to ensure availability of drugs at reasonable prices and promote use of generic medicines.
- The allocation for Scheduled Castes has been increased by 35% compared to BE 2016–17. The allocation for Scheduled Tribes has been increased to Rs. 31,920 crores and for Minority Affairs to Rs. 4,195 crores.
- For senior citizens, *Aadhar* based Smart Cards containing their health details will be introduced.

INFRASTRUCTURE

- For transportation sector as a whole, including rail, roads, shipping, provision of Rs. 2,41,387 crores has been made in 2017–18.
- For 2017–18, the total capital and development expenditure of Railways has been pegged at Rs. 1,31,000 crores. This includes Rs. 55,000 crores provided by the Government.
- For passenger safety, a *Rashtriya Rail Sanraksha Kosh* will be created with a corpus of Rs. 1 lakh crores over a period of 5 years.
- Unmanned level crossings on Broad Gauge lines will be eliminated by 2020.
- In the next 3 years, the throughput is proposed to be enhanced by 10%. This will be done through modernisation and up-gradation of identified corridors.
- Railway lines of 3,500 kms will be commissioned in 2017–18. During 2017–18, at least 25 stations are expected to be awarded for station redevelopment.
- 500 stations will be made differently-abled friendly by providing lifts and escalators.
- It is proposed to feed about 7,000 stations with solar power in the medium term.
- SMS based *Clean My Coach Service* has been started.
- 'Coach Mitra', a single window interface, to register all coach related complaints and requirements to be launched.
- By 2019, all coaches of Indian Railways will be fitted with bio toilets. Tariffs of Railways would be fixed, taking into consideration costs, quality of service and competition from other forms of transport.
- A new Metro Rail Policy will be announced with focus on innovative models of

implementation and financing, as well as standardisation and indigenisation of hardware and software.

- A new Metro Rail Act will be enacted by rationalising the existing laws. This will facilitate greater private participation and investment in construction and operation.

- In the road sector, Budget allocation for highways increased from Rs. 57,976 crores in BE 2016–17 to Rs. 64,900 crores in 2017–18.

- 2,000 kms of coastal connectivity roads have been identified for construction and development.

- Total length of roads, including those under PMGSY, built from 2014-15 till the current year is about 1,40,000 kms which is significantly higher than previous three years.

- Select airports in Tier 2 cities will be taken up for operation and maintenance in the PPP mode.

- By the end of 2017–18, high speed broadband connectivity on optical fibre will be available in more than 1,50,000 *gram panchayats,* under BharatNet. A DigiGaon initiative will be launched to provide tele-medicine, education and skills through digital technology.

- Proposed to set up strategic crude oil reserves at 2 more locations, namely, Chandikhole in Odisha and Bikaner in Rajasthan. This will take our strategic reserve capacity to 15.33 MMT.

- Second phase of Solar Park development to be taken up for additional 20,000 MW capacity.

- For creating an eco-system to make India a global hub for electronics manufacturing a provision of Rs. 745 crores in 2017–18 in incentive schemes like M-SIPS and EDF.

- A new and restructured Central scheme with a focus on export infrastructure, namely, Trade Infrastructure for Export Scheme (TIES) will be launched in 2017–18.

FINANCIAL SECTOR

- Foreign Investment Promotion Board to be abolished in 2017–18 and further liberalisation of FDI policy is under consideration.

- An expert committee will be constituted to study and promote creation of an operational and legal framework to integrate spot market and derivatives market in the agricultural sector, for commodities trading. e- NAM to be an integral part of the framework.

- Bill relating to curtail the menace of illicit deposit schemes will be introduced. A bill relating to resolution of financial firms will be introduced in the current Budget Session of Parliament. This will contribute to stability and resilience of our financial system.

- A mechanism to streamline institutional arrangements for resolution of disputes in infrastructure related construction contracts, PPP and public utility contracts will be introduced as an amendment to the Arbitration and Conciliation Act 1996.

- A Computer Emergency Response Team for our Financial Sector (CERT-Fin) will be established.

- Government will put in place a revised mechanism and procedure to ensure time bound listing of identified CPSEs on stock exchanges. The shares of Railway PSEs like IRCTC, IRFC and IRCON will be listed in stock exchanges.

- Propose to create an integrated public sector 'oil major' which will be able to match the performance of international and domestic private sector oil and gas companies
- A new ETF with diversified CPSE stocks and other Government holdings will be launched in 2017–18.
- In line with the *'Indradhanush'* roadmap, Rs. 10,000 crores for recapitalisation of Banks provided in 2017–18.
- Lending target under *Pradhan Mantri Mudra Yojana* to be set at Rs. 2.44 lakh crores. Priority will be given to Dalits, Tribals, Backward Classes and Women.

DIGITAL ECONOMY

- 125 lakh people have adopted the BHIM app so far. The Government will launch two new schemes to promote the usage of BHIM; these are, Referral Bonus Scheme for individuals and a Cashback Scheme for merchants.
- Aadhar Pay, a merchant version of Aadhar Enabled Payment System, will be launched shortly.
- A Mission will be set up with a target of 2,500 crore digital transactions for 2017–18 through UPI, USSD, Aadhar Pay, IMPS and debit cards.
- A proposal to mandate all Government receipts through digital means, beyond a prescribed limit, is under consideration.
- Banks have targeted to introduce additional 10 lakh new POS terminals by March 2017. They will be encouraged to introduce 20 lakh Aadhar based POS by September 2017.
- Proposed to create a Payments Regulatory Board in the Reserve Bank of India

by replacing the existing Board for Regulation and Supervision of Payment and Settlement Systems.

PUBLIC SERVICE

- The Government e-market place which is now functional for procurement of goods and services.
- To utilise the Head Post Offices as front offices for rendering passport services.
- A Centralised Defence Travel System has been developed through which travel tickets can be booked online by our soldiers and officers.
- Web based interactive Pension Disbursement System for Defence Pensioners will be established.
- To rationalise the number of tribunals and merge tribunals wherever appropriate.
- Commemorate both *Champaran* and *Khordha* revolts appropriately.

PRUDENT FISCAL MANAGEMENT

- Stepped up allocation for Capital expenditure by 25.4% over the previous year.
- Total resources being transferred to the States and the Union Territories with Legislatures is Rs. 4.11 lakh crores, against Rs. 3.60 lakh crores in BE 2016–17.
- or the first time, a consolidated Outcome Budget, covering all Ministries and Departments, is being laid along with the other Budget documents.
- FRBM Committee has recommended 3% fiscal deficit for the next three years, keeping in mind the sustainable debt target and need for public investment, fiscal deficit for 2017–18 is targeted at 3.2% of GDP and Government remains

committed to achieve 3% in the following year.

- Net market borrowing of Government restricted to Rs. 3.48 lakh crores after buyback in 2017–18, much lower than Rs. 4.25 lakh crores of the previous year.

- Revenue Deficit of 2.3% in BE 2016–17 stands reduced to 2.1% in the Revised Estimates. The Revenue Deficit for next year is pegged at 1.9%, against 2% mandated by the FRBM Act.

PROMOTING AFFORDABLE HOUSING AND REAL ESTATE SECTOR

- Between 8th November and 30th December 2016, deposits between 2 lakh Rupees and 80 lakh Rupees were made in about 1.09 crore accounts with an average deposit size of Rs. 5.03 lakh. Deposits of more than 80 lakh were made in 1.48 lakh accounts with average deposit size of Rs. 3.31 crores.

- Under the scheme for profit-linked income tax deduction for promotion of affordable housing, carpet area instead of built up area of 30 and 60 Sq.mtr. will be counted.

- The 30 Sq.mtr. limit will apply only in case of municipal limits of 4 metropolitan cities while for the rest of the country including in the peripheral areas of metros, limit of 60 Sq.mtr. will apply.

- For builders for whom constructed buildings are stock-in-trade, tax on notional rental income will only apply after one year of the end of the year in which completion certificate is received.

- Reduction in the holding period for computing long term capital gains from transfer of immovable property from 3 years to 2 years. Also, the base year for

indexation is proposed to be shifted from April 1, 1981 to April 1, 2001 for all classes of assets including immovable property.

- For Joint Development Agreement signed for development of property, the liability to pay capital gain tax will arise in the year the project is completed.

- Exemption from capital gain tax for persons holding land on June 2, 2014, the date on which the State of Andhra Pradesh was reorganised, and whose land is being pooled for creation of capital city of Andhra Pradesh under the Government scheme.

MEASURES FOR STIMULATING GROWTH

- Concessional withholding rate of 5% charged on interest earned by foreign entities in external commercial borrowings or in bonds and Government securities is extended to June 30, 2020. This benefit is also extended to Rupee Denominated (Masala) Bonds

- For the purpose of carry forward of losses in respect of start-ups, the condition of continuous holding of 51% of voting rights has been relaxed subject to the condition that the holding of the original promoter/promoters continues. Also the profit (linked deduction) exemption available to the start-ups for 3 years out of 5 years is changed to 3 years out of 7 years.

- MAT credit is allowed to be carried forward up to a period of 15 years instead of 10 years at present.

- In order to make MSME companies more viable, income tax for companies with annual turnover upto Rs. 50 crore is reduced to 25%.

- Allowable provision for Non-Performing Asset of Banks increased from 7.5% to 8.5%. Interest taxable on actual receipt instead of accrual basis in respect of NPA accounts of all non-scheduled cooperative banks also to be treated at par with scheduled banks.

- Basic customs duty on LNG reduced from 5% to 2.5%.

PROMOTING DIGITAL ECONOMY

- Under scheme of presumptive income for small and medium tax payers whose turnover is upto 2 crores, the present, 8% of their turnover which is counted as presumptive income is reduced to 6% in respect of turnover which is by non-cash means.

- No transaction above Rs. 3 lakh would be permitted in cash subject to certain exceptions.

- Miniaturised POS card reader for m-POS (other than mobile phones or tablet computers), micro ATM standards version 1.5.1, Finger Print Readers/ Scanners and Iris Scanners and on their parts and components for manufacture of such devices to be exempt from BCD, Excise/CV duty and SAD.

TRANSPARENCY IN ELECTORAL FUNDING

- Need to cleanse the system of political funding in India.

- Maximum amount of cash donation, a political party can receive, will be Rs. 2000 from one person.

- Political parties will be entitled to receive donations by cheque or digital mode from their donors.

- Amendment to the Reserve Bank of India Act to enable the issuance of electoral bonds in accordance with a scheme that the Government of India would frame in this regard.

- Every political party would have to file its return within the time prescribed in accordance with the provision of the Income-tax Act.

- Existing exemption to the political parties from payment of income-tax would be available only subject to the fulfilment of these conditions.

EASE OF DOING BUSINESS

- Scope of domestic transfer pricing restricted to only if one of the entities involved in related party transaction enjoys specified profit-linked deduction.

- Threshold limit for audit of business entities who opt for presumptive income scheme increased from Rs. 1 crore to Rs. 2 crores. Similarly, the threshold for maintenance of books for individuals and HUF increased from turnover of Rs. 10 lakhs to Rs. 25 lakhs or income from Rs. 1.2 lakhs to Rs. 2.5 lakhs.

- Foreign Portfolio Investor (FPI) Category I & II exempted from indirect transfer provision. Indirect transfer provision shall not apply in case of redemption of shares or interests outside India as a result of or arising out of redemption or sale of investment in India which is chargeable to tax in India.

- Commission payable to individual insurance agents exempt from the requirement of TDS subject to their filing a self-declaration that their income is below taxable limit.

- Under scheme for presumptive taxation for professionals with receipt upto Rs. 50 lakhs per annum advance tax can be paid in one instalment instead of four.

- Time period for revising a tax return is being reduced to 12 months from completion of financial year, at par with the time period for filing of return. Also the time for completion of scrutiny assessments is being compressed further from 21 months to 18 months for Assessment Year 2018–19 and further to 12 months for Assessment Year 2019–20 and thereafter.

PERSONAL INCOME-TAX

- Existing rate of taxation for individual assesses between income of Rs. 2.5 lakhs to Rs. 5 lakhs reduced to 5% from the present rate of 10%.
- Surcharge of 10% of tax payable on categories of individuals whose annual taxable income is between Rs. 50 lakhs and Rs. 1 crore.
- Simple one-page form to be filed as Income Tax Return for the category of individuals having taxable income upto Rs. 5 lakhs other than business income.

- Appeal to all citizens of India to contribute to Nation Building by making a small payment of 5% tax if their income is falling in the lowest slab of Rs. 2.5 lakhs to Rs. 5 lakhs.

GOODS AND SERVICES TAX

- The GST Council has finalised its recommendations on almost all the issues based on consensus on the basis of 9 meetings held.
- Preparation of IT system for GST is also on schedule.
- The extensive reach-out efforts to trade and industry for GST will start from 1st April, 2017 to make them aware of the new taxation system.

RAPID (REVENUE, ACCOUNTABILITY, PROBITY INFORMATION AND DIGITISATION)

- Maximise efforts for e-assessment in the coming year.
- Enforcing greater accountability of officers of Tax Department for specific act of commission and omission.